THE MIDDLE AGES
David / Donaldson

THE SIXTEENTH CENTURY
Logan / Greenblatt

THE EARLY SEVENTEENTH CENTURY
Lewalski / Adams

THE RESTORATION AND THE EIGHTEENTH CENTURY
Lipking / Monk

THE ROMANTIC PERIOD
Abrams / Stillinger

THE VICTORIAN AGE
Christ / Ford

THE TWENTIETH CENTURY
Stallworthy / Daiches

The Norton Anthology of English Literature

SEVENTH EDITION

VOLUME 2A

THE ROMANTIC PERIOD

The Norton Anthology
of English Literature

SEVENTH EDITION
VOLUME 2A
THE ROMANTIC PERIOD

M. H. Abrams

Jack Stillinger

CENTER FOR ADVANCED STUDY PROFESSOR OF ENGLISH,
UNIVERSITY OF ILLINOIS

M. H. Abrams, *General Editor*

CLASS OF 1916 PROFESSOR OF ENGLISH EMERITUS,
CORNELL UNIVERSITY

Stephen Greenblatt, *Associate General Editor*

COGAN UNIVERSITY PROFESSOR OF THE HUMANITIES,
HARVARD UNIVERSITY

W • W • NORTON & COMPANY • *New York* • *London*

Preface to the Seventh Edition

The outpouring of English literature overflows all boundaries, including the capacious boundaries of *The Norton Anthology of English Literature*. But these pages manage to contain many of the most remarkable works written in English during centuries of restless creative effort. We have included epic poems and short lyrics; love songs and satires; tragedies and comedies written for performance on the commercial stage and private meditations meant to be perused in silence; prayers, popular ballads, prophecies, ecstatic visions, erotic fantasies, sermons, short stories, letters in verse and prose, critical essays, polemical tracts, several entire novels, and a great deal more. Such works generally form the core of courses that are designed to introduce students to the history of English literature, a history not only of gradual development, continuity, and dense internal echoes, but also of radical contingency, sudden change, and startling innovation.

One of the joys of literature in English is its spectacular abundance. Even from within the geographical confines of Great Britain and Ireland, where the majority of texts brought together in this collection originated, there are more than enough distinguished and exciting works to fill the pages of this anthology many times over. The abundance is all the greater if one takes, as the editors of these volumes do, a broad understanding of the term *literature*. The meaning of the term has in the course of several centuries shifted from the whole body of writing produced in a particular language to a subset of that writing consisting of works that claim special attention because of their formal beauty or expressive power. But any individual text's claim to attention is subject to constant debate and revision; established texts are jostled both by new arrivals and by previously neglected claimants; and the boundaries between the literary and whatever is thought to be "non-literary" are constantly challenged and redrawn. The heart of this collection consists of poems, plays, and prose fiction, but these categories are themselves products of ongoing historical transformations, and we have included many texts that call into question any conception of literature as denoting only a limited set of particular kinds of writing.

The designation "English" provides some obvious limits to the unwieldy, unstable, constantly shifting field of literature, but these limits are themselves in constant flux, due in part to the complexity of the territory evoked by the term (as explained in our appendix on "Geographical Nomenclature") and in part to the multinational, multicultural, and hugely expansive character of the language. As Geoffrey Nunberg's informative essay "The Persistence of English," commissioned for this Seventh Edition, makes clear, the variations in the forms of the spoken language that all go by the name of

English are so great as to call into question the very notion of a single tongue, and the complex history and diffusion of the language have helped ensure that its literature is enormous. In the momentous process that transformed England into Great Britain and eventually into the center of a huge empire, more and more writers from outside England, beginning with the strong Irish and Scottish presence in the eighteenth century and gradually fanning out into the colonies, were absorbed into "English literature." Moreover, English has constantly interacted with other languages and has been transformed by this interaction. The scope of the cross-currents may be gauged by our medieval section, which includes selections in Old Irish and Middle Welsh, along with works by Bede, Geoffrey of Monmouth, Wace, and Marie de France—all of them authors living in the British Isles writing in languages other than English. Their works are important in themselves and also provide cultural contexts for understanding aspects of what we have come to think of as "English literature." Certain literary texts—many of them included in these volumes—have achieved sufficient prominence to serve as widespread models for other writers and as objects of enduring admiration, and thus to constitute a loose-boundaried canon. But just as there have never been academies in English-speaking countries established to regulate the use of language, so too there have never been firm and settled guidelines for canonizing particular texts. English literature as a field arouses not a sense of order but what the poet Yeats calls "the emotion of multitude."

The term "English Literature" in our title designates two different things. First, it refers to all the literary productions of a particular part of the world: the great preponderance of the works we include were written by authors living in England, Scotland, Wales, and Ireland. Second, it refers to literary works in the English language, a language that has extended far beyond the boundaries of its point of origin. Following the lead of most college courses, we have separated off, for purposes of this anthology, English literature from American literature, but in the selections for the latter half of the twentieth century we have incorporated a substantial number of texts by authors from other countries.

The linguistic mobility and cultural intertwining reflected in these twentieth-century texts are not new. It is fitting that among the first works in this anthology is *Beowulf*, a powerful epic written in the Germanic language known as Old English about a singularly restless Scandinavian hero, an epic newly translated for this edition by the Irish poet Seamus Heaney. Heaney, who was awarded the Nobel Prize for Literature in 1995, is one of the contemporary masters of English literature, but it would be potentially misleading to call him an "English poet," for he was born in Northern Ireland and is not in fact English. It would be still more misleading to call him a "British poet," as if his having been born in a country that was part of the British Empire were the most salient fact about the language he speaks and writes or the culture by which he was shaped. What does matter is that the language in which Heaney writes is English, and this fact links him powerfully with the authors assembled in these volumes, a linguistic community that stubbornly refuses to fit comfortably within any firm geographical or ethnic or national boundaries. So too, to glance at authors and writings included in the anthology, in the sixteenth century William Tyndale, in exile in the Low Countries and inspired by German religious reformers, translated the New

Testament from Greek and thereby changed the course of the English language; in the seventeenth century Aphra Behn touched her readers with a story that moves from Africa, where its hero is born, to South America, where she may have witnessed some of the tragic events she describes; and early in the twentieth century Joseph Conrad, born in Ukraine of Polish parents, wrote in eloquent English a celebrated novella whose vision of European empire was trenchantly challenged at the century's end by the Nigerian-born writer in English, Chinua Achebe.

A vital literary culture is always on the move. The Seventh Edition of *The Norton Anthology of English Literature* has retained the body of works that have traditionally been taught as the principal glories of English literature, but many of our new selections reflect the fact that the *national* conception of literary history, the conception by which English Literature meant the literature of England or at most of Great Britain, has begun to give way to something else. Writers like William Butler Yeats (born in Dublin), Hugh MacDiarmid (born in Dumfriesshire, Scotland), Virginia Woolf (born in London), and Dylan Thomas (born in Swansea, Wales) are now being taught, and are here anthologized, alongside such writers as Nadine Gordimer (born in the Transvaal, South Africa), Alice Munro (born in Wingham, Ontario), Derek Walcott (born on Saint Lucia in the West Indies), Chinua Achebe (born in Ogidi, Nigeria), and Salman Rushdie (born in Bombay, India). English literature, like so many other collective enterprises in our century, has ceased to be principally the product of the identity of a single nation; it is a global phenomenon.

A central feature of *The Norton Anthology of English Literature,* established by its original editors, was a commitment to provide periodic revisions in order to take advantage of newly recovered or better-edited texts, reflect scholarly discoveries and the shifting interests of readers, and keep the anthology in touch with contemporary critical and intellectual concerns. To help us honor this commitment we have, as in past years, profited from a remarkable flow of voluntary corrections and suggestions proposed by students, as well as teachers, who view the anthology with a loyal but critical eye. Moreover, we have again solicited and received detailed information on the works actually assigned, proposals for deletions and additions, and suggestions for improving the editorial matter, from over two hundred reviewers from around the world, almost all of them teachers who use the books in a course. In its evolution, then, this anthology has been the product of an ongoing collaboration among its editors, teachers, and students.

The active participation of an engaged community of readers has been crucial as the editors grapple with the challenging task of retaining (and indeed strengthening) the selection of more traditional texts even while adding many texts that reflect the transformation and expansion of the field of English studies. The challenge is heightened by the wish to keep each volume manageable, in size and weight, so that students will actually carry the book to class. The final decisions on what to include were made by the editors, but we were immeasurably assisted, especially in borderline cases, by the practical experience and the detailed opinions of teachers and scholars.

In addition to the new translation of *Beowulf* and to the greatly augmented global approach to twentieth-century literature in English, several other features of this Seventh Edition merit special mention. We have greatly expanded the selection of writing by women in all of the historical periods. The extraordinary work of scholars in recent years has recovered dozens of significant authors who had been marginalized or neglected by a male-dominated literary tradition and has deepened our understanding of those women writers who had managed, against considerable odds, to claim a place in that tradition. The First Edition of the *Norton Anthology* was ahead of its time in including six women writers; this Seventh Edition includes sixty, of whom twenty-one are newly added and twenty are reselected or expanded. Poets and prose writers whose names were scarcely mentioned even in the specialized literary histories of earlier generations—Isabella Whitney, Aemilia Lanyer, Lady Mary Wroth, Elizabeth Cary, Margaret Cavendish, Mary Leapor, Anna Letitia Barbauld, Charlotte Smith, Letitia Elizabeth Landon, and many others—now appear in the company of their male contemporaries. There are in addition three complete long prose works by women: Aphra Behn's *Oroonoko,* Mary Shelley's *Frankenstein,* and Virginia Woolf's *A Room of One's Own.*

The novel is, of course, a stumbling block for an anthology. The length of many great novels defies their incorporation in any volume that hopes to include a broad spectrum of literature. At the same time it is difficult to excerpt representative passages from narratives whose power often depends upon amplitude or upon the slow development of character or upon the on-rushing urgency of the story. Therefore, better to represent the remarkable achievements of novelists, the publisher is making available, in inexpensive and well-edited Norton Anthology Editions, a range of novels, including Jane Austen's *Pride and Prejudice,* Charles Dickens's *Hard Times,* Charlotte Brontë's *Jane Eyre,* and Emily Brontë's *Wuthering Heights.*

A further innovation in the Seventh Edition is our inclusion of new and expanded clusters of texts that resonate with one another culturally and thematically. Using the "Victorian Issues" section long featured in *The Norton Anthology of English Literature* as our model, we devised for each period groupings that serve to suggest some ways in which the pervasive concepts, images, and key terms that haunt major literary works can often be found in other written traces of a culture. Hence, for example, the adventures of Edmund Spenser's wandering knights resonate with the excerpts from Elizabethan travel accounts brought together in "The Wider World": Frobisher's violent encounters with the Eskimos of Baffin Island, Drake's attempt to lay claim to California, Amadas and Barlowe's idealizing vision of the Indians as the inhabitants of the Golden Age, and Hariot's subtle attempt to analyze and manipulate native beliefs. Similarly, the millenarian expectations voiced in the texts grouped in "The French Revolution and the 'Spirit of the Age' " helped shape the major writings of poets from William Blake to Percy Bysshe Shelley, while the historical struggles reflected in texts by Jawaharlal Nehru and others in "The Rise and Fall of Empire" echo in the fiction of Chinua Achebe, V. S. Naipaul, and J. M. Coetzee. We supplement the clusters for each period with several more topical groupings of texts and copious illustrations on the *Norton Anthology* Web site.

Period-by-Period Revisions

The scope of the revisions we have undertaken, the most extensive in the long publishing history of *The Norton Anthology of English Literature,* can be conveyed more fully by a list of some of the principal additions.

The Middle Ages. Better to represent the complex multilingual situation of the period, the section has been reorganized and divided into three parts: Anglo-Saxon England, Anglo-Norman England, and Middle English Literature of the Fourteenth and Fifteenth Centuries. Nearly fifteen years in the making, Seamus Heaney's translation of *Beowulf* comes closer to conveying the full power of the Anglo-Saxon epic than any existing rendering and will be of major interest as well to students of modern poetry. The selection of Anglo-Saxon poems has also been augmented by *The Wife's Lament.* We have added a new section, Anglo-Norman England, which provides a key bridge between the Anglo-Saxon period and the time of Chaucer, highlighting a cluster of texts that trace the origins of Arthurian romance. This section includes selections from the chronicle account of the Norman conquest; legendary histories by Geoffrey of Monmouth, Wace, and Layamon; Marie de France's *Lanval* (a Breton lay about King Arthur's court, here in a new verse translation by Alfred David), along with two of her fables; a selection from the *Ancrene Riwle* (Rule for Anchoresses); and two Celtic narratives: the Irish *Exile of the Sons of Uisliu* and the Welsh *Lludd and Lleuelys.* To Chaucer's works we have added *The Man of Law's Epilogue* and *Troilus's Song*; we have added to the grouping of Late Middle English lyrics and strengthened the already considerable selection from the revelations of the visionary anchoress Julian of Norwich; and we have included for the first time a work by Robert Henryson, *The Cock and the Fox.*

The Sixteenth Century. Shakespeare's magnificent comedy of cross-dressing and cross-purposes, *Twelfth Night,* is for the first time included in the *Norton Anthology,* providing a powerful contrast with his bleakest tragedy, *King Lear.* The raucous *Tunning of Elinour Rumming* has been added to Skelton's poems and the somber *Stand whoso list* to Wyatt's, while Gascoigne is now represented by his poem *Woodmanship.* Additions in poetry and prose works have similarly been made to Roger Ascham, Henry Howard, Earl of Surrey, Sir Walter Ralegh, Fulke Greville, Samuel Daniel, Thomas Campion, and Thomas Nashe. Along with the grouping of travel texts described above, another new cluster, "Literature of the Sacred," brings together contrasting Bible translations; writings by William Tyndale and Richard Hooker; Anne Askew's account, smuggled from the Tower, of her interrogation and torture, along with the martyrologist John Foxe's account of her execution; selections from the Book of Common Prayer and the Book of Homilies; and an Elizabethan translation of John Calvin's influential account of predestination. In addition to Anne Askew, another Elizabethan woman writer, Isabella Whitney, makes her appearance in the *Norton Anthology,* along with a new selection of texts by Mary Herbert and a newly added speech and letters by Queen Elizabeth.

The Early Seventeenth Century. In response to widespread demand and to our own sense of the work's commanding importance, both in its own time and in the history of English literature, we have for the first time included the whole of Milton's *Paradise Lost.* Other substantial works that newly appear in this section include Ben Jonson's *Masque of Blackness* and Andrew Marvell's *Upon Appleton House*, extensive selections from Elizabeth Cary's *Tragedy of Mariam*, and poetry and prose by Aemilia Lanyer and Margaret Cavendish. Additions have been made to the works of John Donne, Jonson, Lady Mary Wroth, George Herbert, Henry Vaughan, Richard Crashaw, Robert Herrick, and John Suckling. The "Voices of the War" cluster, introduced in the last edition, now includes Anna Trapnel's narrative of her eventful voyage from London to Cornwall; and a new cluster, "The Science of Self and World," brings together meditative texts, poems, and essays by Francis Bacon, Martha Moulsworth, Robert Burton, Rachel Speght, Sir Thomas Browne, Izaak Walton, and Thomas Hobbes.

The Restoration and the Eighteenth Century. John Gay's *The Beggar's Opera*—familiar to modern audiences as the source of Bertolt Brecht's *Threepenny Opera*—makes its appearance in the *Norton Anthology*, along with William Hogarth's illustration of a scene from the play. Hogarth's "literary" graphic art is represented by his satiric *Marriage A-la-Mode.* Two new clusters of texts enable readers to engage more fully with key controversies in the period. "Debating Women: Arguments in Verse" presents the war between the sexes in spirited poems by Jonathan Swift, Lady Mary Wortley Montagu, Alexander Pope, Anne Finch, Anne Ingram, and Mary Leapor. The period's sexual politics is illuminated as well in added texts by Samuel Pepys, John Wilmot, Second Earl of Rochester, and Aphra Behn. "Slavery and Freedom" brings together the disquieting exchange on the enslavement of African peoples between Ignatius Sancho and Laurence Sterne, along with Olaudah Equiano's ground-breaking history of his own enslavement. The narrative gifts of Frances Burney, whose long career spans this period and the next, are newly presented by six texts, including her famous, harrowing account of her mastectomy.

The Romantic Period. The principal changes here center on the greatly increased representation of women writers in the period: Mary Robinson and Letitia Elizabeth Landon are included for the first time, and there are substantially increased selections by Anna Letitia Barbauld, Charlotte Smith, Joanna Baillie, Dorothy Wordsworth, and Felicia Hemans; to Mary Wollstonecraft's epochal *Vindication of the Rights of Women*, we have now added a selection from her *Letters Written in Sweden.* Conjoined with Mary Shelley's *Frankenstein*, presented here in its entirety, these texts restore women writers, once marginalized in literary histories of the period, to the significant place they in fact occupied. A new thematic cluster focusing on the period's cataclysmic event, the French Revolution, brings together texts in prose and verse by Richard Price, Edmund Burke, Mary Wollstonecraft, Thomas Paine, Elhanan Winchester, Joseph Priestley, William Black, Robert Southey, William Wordsworth, Samuel Taylor Coleridge, and Percy Bysshe Shelley. The selection of poems by the peasant poet John Clare has been expanded and is printed in a new text prepared for this edition. We have also added to Sir Walter Scott the introductory chapter of his *Heart of Midlothian*, and to William Wordsworth his long and moving lyrical ballad *The Thorn.*

The Victorian Age. The important novelist, short story writer, and biographer Elizabeth Gaskell makes her appearance in the *Norton Anthology*, along with two late-nineteenth-century poets, Michael Field and Mary Elizabeth Coleridge. Rudyard Kipling's powerful story *The Man Who Would Be King* is a significant new addition, as is the selection from Oscar Wilde's prison writings, *De Profundis*. Dickens's somber reflection *A Visit to Newgate* has been added. There are new texts in the selections of many authors as well, including John Henry Cardinal Newman, Elizabeth Barrett Browning, Alfred, Lord Tennyson, Elizabeth Gaskell, George Eliot, Dante Gabriel Rossetti, William Morris, and Gerard Manley Hopkins. Bernard Shaw's play *Mrs. Warren's Profession* has been moved to its chronological place in this section. New texts have also been added to the "Victorian Issues" clusters on evolution, industrialism, and the debate about gender.

The Twentieth Century. The principal addition here, in length and in symbolic significance, is Chinua Achebe's celebrated novel *Things Fall Apart*, presented in its entirety, and, with Joseph Conrad's *Heart of Darkness* and Virginia Woolf's *A Room of One's Own*, the third complete prose work in this section. But there are many other changes as well, in keeping with a thoroughgoing rethinking of this century's literary history. We begin with Thomas Hardy (now shown as fiction writer as well as poet) and Joseph Conrad, both liminal figures poised between two distinct cultural worlds. These are followed by groupings of texts that articulate some of the forces that helped pull these worlds asunder. A cluster on "The Rise and Fall of Empire" brings together John Ruskin, John Hobson, the Easter Proclamation of the Irish Republic, Richard Mulcahy, James Morris, Jawaharlal Nehru, and Chinua Achebe, and these texts of geo-political crisis in turn resonate with "Voices from World War I" and "Voices from World War II," both sections newly strengthened by prose texts. We have added selections to E. M. Forster, James Joyce, and T. S. Eliot, among others, and for the first time present the work of the West Indian writer Jean Rhys and the Irish poet Paul Muldoon. Samuel Beckett is now represented by the complete text of his masterful tragicomedy, *Endgame*. Above all, the explosion of writing in English in "postcolonial" countries around the world shapes our revision of this section, not only in our inclusion of Achebe but also in new texts by Derek Walcott, V. S. Naipaul, Anita Desai, Les Murray, J. M. Coetzee, Eavan Boland, Alice Munro, and Salman Rushdie. Seamus Heaney's works, to which another poem has been added, provide the occasion to look back again to the beginning of these volumes with Heaney's new translation of *Beowulf*. This translation is a reminder that the history of literature is not a straightforward sequence, that the most recent works can double back upon the distant past, and that the words set down by men and women who have crumbled into dust can speak to us with astonishing directness.

Editorial Procedures

The scope of revisions to the editorial apparatus in the Seventh Edition is the most extensive ever undertaken in *The Norton Anthology of English Literature*. As in past editions, period introductions, headnotes, and annotation are designed to give students the information needed, without imposing an interpretation. The aim of these editorial materials is to make the anthology self-sufficient, so that it can be read anywhere—in a coffeehouse, on a bus, or under a tree. In this edition, this apparatus has been thoroughly revised in response to new scholarship. The period introductions and many headnotes have been either entirely or substantially rewritten to be more helpful to students, and all the Selected Bibliographies have been thoroughly updated.

Several new features reflect the broadened scope of the selections in the anthology. The new essay, "The Persistence of English" by Geoffrey Nunberg, Stanford University and Xerox Palo Alto Research Center, explores the emergence and spread of English and its apparent present-day "triumph" as a world language. It provides a lively point of departure for the study of literature in English. The endpaper maps have been reconceived and redrawn. New timelines following each period introduction help students place their reading in historical and cultural context. So that students can explore literature as a visual medium, the anthology introduces visual materials from several periods—Hogarth's *Marriage A-la-Mode*, engravings by Blake, and Dante Gabriel Rossetti's illustrations for poems by Tennyson, Christina Rossetti, and Rossetti himself. These illustrations can be supplemented by the hundreds of images available on Norton Topics Online, the Web companion to the *Norton Anthology*.

Each volume of the anthology includes an appendix, "Poems in Process," which reproduces from manuscripts and printed texts the genesis and evolution of a number of poems whose final form is printed in that volume. Each volume contains a useful section on "Poetic Forms and Literary Terminology," much revised in the Seventh Edition, as well as brief appendices on the intricacies of English money, the baronage, and religions. A new appendix, "Geographic Nomenclature," has been added to clarify the shifting place-names applied to regions of the British Isles.

Students, no less than scholars, deserve the most accurate texts available; in keeping with this policy, we continue to introduce improved versions of the selections where available. In this edition, for example, in addition to Seamus Heaney's new verse translation of *Beowulf*, we introduce Alfred David's new verse translation of Marie de France's *Lanval*, the Norton/Oxford text of *Twelfth Night*; and Jack Stillinger's newly edited texts of the poems of John Clare. To ease a student's access, we have normalized spelling and capitalization in texts up to and including the Victorian period to follow the conventions of modern English; we leave unaltered, however, texts in which modernizing would change semantic or metrical qualities and those texts for which we use specially edited versions (identified in a headnote or footnote); these include Wollstonecraft's *Vindication*, William Wordsworth's *Ruined Cottage* and *Prelude*, Dorothy Wordsworth's *Journals*, the verse and prose of P. B. Shelley and Keats, and Mary Shelley's *Frankenstein*. In The Twentieth Century, we have restored original spelling and punctuation to selections retained from the previous edition in the belief that the authors' choices, when they pose no difficulties for student readers, should be respected.

We continue other editorial procedures that have proved useful in the past. After each work, we cite (when known) the date of composition on the left and the date of first publication on the right; in some instances, the latter is followed by the date of a revised edition for which the author was responsible. We have used square brackets to indicate titles supplied by the editors for the convenience of readers. Whenever a portion of a text has been omitted, we have indicated that omission with three asterisks. If the omitted portion is important for following the plot or argument, we have provided a brief summary within the text or in a footnote. We have extended our longstanding practice of providing marginal glossing of single words and short phrases from medieval and dialect poets (such as Robert Burns) to all the poets in the anthology. Finally, we have adopted a bolder typeface and redesigned the page, so as to make the text more readable.

The Course Guide to Accompany "The Norton Anthology of English Literature," by Katherine Eggert and Kelly Hurley, University of Colorado at Boulder, based on an earlier version by Alfred David, Indiana University, has been thoroughly revised and expanded; it contains detailed syllabi for a variety of approaches to the course, teaching notes on individual authors, periods, and works, study and essay questions, and suggested ways to integrate the printed texts with material on the Norton Web site. A copy of the *Guide* may be obtained on request from the publisher.

Two cardinal innovations, one print and one electronic, greatly increase the anthology's flexibility: The book is now available in both the traditional two-volume format, in both clothbound and paperback versions, and in a new six-volume paperback version comprised of volume 1A, *The Middle Ages*, volume 1B, *The Sixteenth Century / The Early Seventeenth Century*, volume 1C, *The Restoration and the Eighteenth Century*, volume 2A, *The Romantic Period*, volume 2B, *The Victorian Age*, and volume 2C, *The Twentieth Century*. By maintaining the same pagination as in the original two volumes, the six-volume format offers a more portable option for students in survey courses, while the individual volumes can be used in courses dealing with periods of English literature.

Extending beyond the printed page, the Norton Topics Online Web Site (*www.wwnorton.com/nael*) augments the anthology's already broad representation of the sweep of English literature, and greatly enlarges the representation of graphic materials that are relevant to literary studies. For students who wish to extend their exploration of literary and cultural contexts, the Web site offers a huge range of related texts, prepared by the anthology editors, and by Myron Tuman, University of Alabama, and Philip Schwyzer, University of California, Berkeley. An ongoing venture, the Web site currently offers twenty-one thematic clusters—three per period—of texts and visual images, cross-referenced to the anthology, together with overviews, study explorations, and annotated links to related sites. The site also includes an electronic archive of over 185 texts to supplement the anthology. In addition, the Audio Companion to *The Norton Anthology of English Literature* is available without charge upon request by teachers who adopt the anthology. It consists of two compact discs of readings by the authors of the works represented in the anthology, readings of poems in Old and Middle English and in English dialects, and performances of poems that were written to be set to music.

The editors are deeply grateful to the hundreds of teachers worldwide who have helped us to improve *The Norton Anthology of English Literature*. A list of the advisors who prepared in-depth reviews and of the instructors who replied to a detailed questionnaire follows on a separate page, under Acknowledgments. The editors would like to express appreciation for their assistance to Tiffany Beechy (Harvard University), Mitch Cohen (Wissenschaftskolleg zu Berlin), Sandie Byrne (Oxford University), Sarah Cole

(Columbia University), Dianne Ferriss (Cornell University), Robert Folkenflik (University of California, Irvine), Robert D. Fulk (Indiana University), Andrew Gurr (The University of Reading), Wendy Hyman (Harvard University), Elissa Linke (Wissenschaftskolleg zu Berlin), Joanna Lipking (Northwestern University), Linda O'Riordan (Wissenschaftskolleg zu Berlin), Ruth Perry (M.I.T.), Leah Price (Harvard University), Ramie Targoff (Yale University), and Douglas Trevor (Harvard University). The editors give special thanks to Paul Leopold, who drafted the appendix on Geographic Nomenclature and revised the appendix on Religions in England, and to Philip Schwyzer (University of California, Berkeley), whose wide-ranging contributions include preparing texts and study materials for the Web site, assisting with the revision of numerous headnotes, and updating appendices on the British baronage and British money. We also thank the many people at Norton who contributed to the Seventh Edition: Julia Reidhead, who served not only as the inhouse supervisor but also as an unfailingly wise and effective collaborator in every aspect of planning and accomplishing this Seventh Edition; Marian Johnson, developmental editor, who kept the project moving forward with a remarkable blend of focused energy, intelligence, and common sense; Candace Levy, Ann Tappert, Barry Katzen, David Hawkins, and Will Rigby, project and manuscript editors; Anna Karvellas and Kirsten Miller, Web site editors; Diane O'Connor, production manager; Kristin Sheerin, permissions manager; Toni Krass, designer; Neil Ryder Hoos, art researcher; and Christa Grenawalt, editorial assistant and map coordinator. All these friends provided the editors with indispensable help in meeting the challenge of representing the unparalleled range and variety of English literature.

M. H. Abrams
Stephen Greenblatt

Acknowledgments

Among our many critics, advisors, and friends, the following were of especial help toward the preparation of the Seventh Edition, either with advice or by providing critiques of particular periods of the anthology: Judith H. Anderson (Indiana University), Paula Backsheider (Auburn University), Elleke Boehmer (Leeds University), Rebecca Brackmann (University of Illinois), James Chandler (University of Chicago), Valentine Cunningham (Oxford University), Lennard Davis (SUNY Binghamton), Katherine Eggert (University of Colorado), P. J. C. Field (University of Wales), Vincent Gillespie (Oxford University), Roland Greene (University of Oregon), A. C. Hamilton (Queen's University), Emrys Jones (Oxford University), Laura King (Yale University), Noel Kinnamon (Mars Hill College), John Leonard (University of Western Ontario), William T. Liston (Ball State University), F. P. Lock (Queen's University), Lee Patterson (Yale University), Jahan Ramazani (University of Virginia), John Regan (Oxford University), John Rogers (Yale University), Herbert Tucker (University of Virginia), Mel Wiebe (Queen's University).

The editors would like to express appreciation and thanks to the hundreds of teachers who provided reviews: Porter Abbott (University of California, Santa Barbara), Robert Aguirre (University of California, Los Angeles), Alan Ainsworth (Houston Community College Central), Jesse T. Airaudi (Baylor University), Edward Alexander (University of Washington), Michael Alexander (University of St. Andrews), Gilbert Allen (Furman University), Jill Angelino (George Washington University), Linda M. Austin (Oklahoma State University), Sonja S. Baghy (State University of West Georgia), Vern D. Bailey (Carleton College), William Barker (Fitchburg State University), Carol Barret (Northridge Campus, Austin Community College), Mary Barron (University of North Florida), Jackson Barry (University of Maryland), Dean Bevan (Baker University), Carol Beran (St. Mary's College), James Biester (Loyola University, Chicago), Nancy B. Black (Brooklyn College), Alan Blackstock (Wharton Community Junior College), Alfred F. Boe (San Diego State University), Cheryl D. Bohde (McLennan Community College), Karin Boklund-Lagopouloou (Aristotle University of Thessaloniki), Scott Boltwood (Emory and Henry College), Troy Boone (University of California, Santa Cruz), James L. Boren (University of Oregon), Ellen Brinks (Princeton University), Douglas Bruster (University of Texas, San Antonio), John Bugge (Emory University), Maria Bullon-Fernandez (Seattle University), John J. Burke (University of Alabama), Deborah G. Burks (Ohio State University), James Byer (Western Carlonia University), Gregory Castle (Arizona State University), Paul William Child (Sam Houston State University), Joe R. Christopher (Tarleton State University), A. E. B. Coldiron (Towson State University), John Constable (University of Leeds), C. Abbott Conway (McGill University), Patrick Creevy (Mississippi State University), Thomas M. Curley (Bridgewater State College), Clifford Davidson (Western Michigan University), Craig R. Davis (Smith College), Frank Day (Clemson University), Marliss Desens (Texas Tech University), Jerome Donnelly (University of Central Florida), Terrance Doody (Rice University), Max Dorsinville (McGill University), David Duff (University of Aberdeen), Alexander Dunlop (Auburn University), Richard J. DuRocher (St. Olaf College), Dwight Eddins (University of Alabama), Caroline L. Eisner (George Washington University), Andrew Elfenbein (University of Minnesota), Doris Williams Elliott (University of Kansas), Nancy S. Ellis (Mississippi State University), Kevin Eubanks (University of Tennessee), Gareth Euridge (Denison University), Deanna Evans (Bemidji State University), Julia A. Fesmire (Middle Tennessee State University), Michael Field (Bemidji State University), Judith L. Fisher (Trinity University), Graham Forst (Capilano College), Marilyn Francus (West Virginia University), Susan S. Frisbie (Santa Clara University), Shearle Furnish (West Texas A&M University), Arthur Ganz (City College of CUNY; The New School), Stephanie Gauper (Western Michigan University), Donna A. Gessell (North Georgia College and State University), Reid Gilbert (Capilano College), Jonathan C. Glance (Mercer University), I. Gopnik (McGill University), William Gorski (Northwestern State University of Louisiana), Roy Gottfried (Vanderbilt University), Timothy Gray (University of California, Santa Barbara), Patsy Griffin (Georgia Southern University), M. J. Gross (Southwest Texas State University), Gillian Hanson (University of Houston), Linda Hatchel (McLennan Community College), James Heldman (Western Kentucky University), Stephen Hemenway (Hope College), Michael Hennessy (Southwest Texas State University), Peter C. Herman (San Diego State University), James Hirsh (Georgia State University), Diane Long Hoeveler (Marquette University), Jerrold E. Hogle (University of Arizona), Brian Holloway (College of West Virginia), David Honick (Bentley College), Catherine E. Howard (University of Houston), David Hudson (Augsburg College), Steve Hudson (Portland Community College), Clark Hulse (University of Illinois, Chicago), Jefferson Hunter (Smith College), Vernon Ingraham (University of Massachusetts, Dartmouth), Thomas Jemielity (University of Notre Dame), R. Jothiprakash (Wiley College), John M. Kandl (Walsh University), David Kay (University of Illinois, Urbana-Champaign), Richard Kelly (University of Tennessee), Elizabeth Keyser (Hollins College), Gail Kienitz (Wheaton College), Richard Knowles (University of Wisconsin, Madison), Deborah Knuth (Colgate University), Albert Koinm (Sam Houston State University), Jack Kolb (University of California, Los Angeles), Valerie Krishna (City College, CUNY), Richard Kroll (University of California, Irvine), Jameela Lares (University of Southern Mississippi), Beth Lau (California State University, Long Beach), James Livingston (Northern Michigan University), Christine Loflin (Grinnell College), W. J. Lohman Jr. (University of Tampa), Suzanne H. MacRae (University of Arkansas, Fayetteville), Julia Maia (West Valley College), Sarah R. Marino (Ohio Northern University), Louis Martin (Elizabethtown College), Irene Martyniuk (Fitchburg State College), Frank T. Mason (University of South Florida), Mary Massirer (Baylor University), J. C. C. Mays (University College, Dublin), James McCord (Union College), Brian McCrea (University of Florida), Claie McEachern (University of California, Los Angeles), Joseph McGowan (University of San Diego), Alexander Menocal (University of North Florida), John Mercer (Northeastern State University),

Teresa Michals (George Mason University), Michael Allen Mikolajezak (University of St. Thomas), Jonathan Middlebrook (San Francisco State University), Sal Miroglotta (John Carroll University), James H. Morey (Emory University), Maryclaire Moroney (John Carroll University), William E. Morris (University of South Florida), Charlotte C. Morse (Virginia Commonwealth University), Alan H. Nelson (University of California, Berkeley), Jeff Nelson (University of Alabama, Huntsville), Richard Newhauser (Trinity University), Ashton Nichols (Dickinson College), Noreen O'Connor (George Washington University), Peter Okun (Davis and Elkins College), Nora M. Olivares (San Antonio College), Harold Orel (University of Kansas), Sue Owen (University of Sheffield), Diane Parkin-Speer (Southwest Texas State University), C. Patton (Texas Tech University), Paulus Pimoma (Central Washington University), John F. Plummer (Vanderbilt University), Alan Powers (Bristol Community College), William Powers (Michigan Technological University), Nicholas Radel (Furman University), Martha Rainbolt (DePauw University), Robert L. Reid (Emory and Henry College), Luke Reinsina (Seattle Pacific University), Cedric D. Reverand II (University of Wyoming), Mary E. Robbins (Georgia State University), Mark Rollins (Ohio University, Athens), Charles Ross (Purdue University), Donelle R. Ruwe (Fitchburg State College), John Schell (University of Central Florida), Walter Scheps (SUNY Stony Brook), Michael Schoenfeldt (University of Michigan), Robert Scotto (Baruch College), Asha Sen (University of Wisconsin, Eau Claire), Lavina Shankar (Bates College), Michael Shea (Southern Connecticut State University), R. Allen Shoaf (University of Florida), Michael N. Stanton (University of Vermont), Massie C. Stinson Jr. (Longwood College), Andrea St. John (University of Miami), Donald R. Stoddard (Anne Arundel Community College), Joyce Ann Sutphen (Gustavas Adolphus College), Max K. Sutton (University of Kansas), Margaret Thomas (Wilberforce University), John M. Thompson (U.S. Naval Academy), Dinny Thorold (University of Westminster), James B. Twitchell (University of Florida), J. K. Van Dover (Lincoln University), Karen Van Eman (Wayne State University), Paul V. Voss (Georgia State University), Leon Waldoff (University of Illinois, Urbana-Champaign), Donald J. Weinstock (California State University, Long Beach), Susan Wells (Temple University), Winthrop Wetherbee (Cornell University), Thomas Willard (University of Arizona), J. D. Williams (Hunter College), Charles Workman (Stanford University), Margaret Enright Wye (Rockhurst College), R. O. Wyly (University of Southern Florida), James J. Yoch (University of Oklahoma), Marvin R. Zirker (Indiana University, Bloomington).

The Norton Anthology of English Literature

SEVENTH EDITION

VOLUME 2A

THE ROMANTIC PERIOD

The Romantic Period
1785–1830

1789–1815:   Revolutionary and Napoleonic period in France.—1789: The
             Revolution begins with the assembly of the States-General
             in May and the storming of the Bastille on July 14.—1793:
             King Louis XVI executed; England joins the alliance against
             France.—1793–94: The Reign of Terror under Robespierre.
             1804: Napoleon crowned emperor.—1815: Napoleon
             defeated at Waterloo
1807:   British slave trade outlawed (slavery abolished throughout
             the empire, including the West Indies, twenty-six years later)
1811–20:   The Regency—George, Prince of Wales, acts as regent for
             George III, who has been declared incurably insane
1820:   Accession of George IV

The British Romantic period is at least as complex and diverse as any other period in literary history. For many decades of the twentieth century, scholars singled out five poets—Wordsworth, Coleridge, Byron, Percy Shelley, and Keats, adding Blake belatedly to make a sixth—and constructed notions of a unified Romanticism on the basis of their works. But there were problems all along: even the two closest collaborators of the 1790s, Wordsworth and Coleridge, interacting on a daily basis, would fit no single definition; Byron despised both Coleridge's metaphysics and Wordsworth's theory and practice of poetry; Shelley and Keats were at opposite poles from each other stylistically and philosophically; Blake was not at all like any of the other five.

Nowadays, although the six poets are still the principal canonical figures by any measure of canonicity, we recognize a much greater range of activities and accomplishments, literary and otherwise. In 1798, the year of Wordsworth and Coleridge's first *Lyrical Ballads,* neither of the authors had much of a reputation; Wordsworth was not even included among the 1112 entries in David Rivers's *Literary Memoirs of Living Authors of Great Britain* of that year, and *Lyrical Ballads* was published anonymously because, as Coleridge told the publisher, "Wordsworth's name is nothing—to a large number of persons mine *stinks.*" Some of the best-regarded poets of the time were women—Anna Barbauld, Charlotte Smith, Mary Robinson—and Wordsworth and Coleridge (both of whom were junior colleagues of Robinson when she was poetry editor of the *Morning Post* in the late 1790s) looked up to them and learned some of their craft from them. The rest of the then-established figures were the later eighteenth-century poets who are printed at the end of volume 1 of this anthology—Gray, Collins, Crabbe, and Cowper

1

in particular. Only Byron, among the principal poets, was instantly famous; and Felicia Hemans and Letitia Landon ran him a close race as best-sellers. The Romantic period had a great many more participants than the six canonical poets and was interinvolved with a multitude of political, social, and economic changes.

REVOLUTION AND REACTION

Following a widespread practice of historians of English literature, we denote by the "Romantic period" the span between the year 1785, the midpoint of the decade in which Samuel Johnson died and Blake and Burns published their first poems, and 1830, by which time the major writers of the preceding century were either dead or no longer productive. This was a turbulent period, during which England experienced the ordeal of change from a primarily agricultural society, where wealth and power had been concentrated in the landholding aristocracy, to a modern industrial nation, in which the balance of economic power shifted to large-scale employers, who found themselves ranged against an immensely enlarging and increasingly restive working class. And this change occurred in a context of revolution—first the American and then the much more radical French—and of wars, of economic cycles of inflation and depression, and of the constant threat to the social structure from imported revolutionary ideologies to which the ruling classes responded by the repression of traditional liberties.

The early period of the French Revolution, marked by the Declaration of the Rights of Man and the storming of the Bastille to release imprisoned political offenders, evoked enthusiastic support from English liberals and radicals alike. Three important books epitomize the radical social thinking stimulated by the Revolution. Mary Wollstonecraft's *A Vindication of the Rights of Men* (1790) justified the French Revolution against Edmund Burke's attack in his *Reflections on the Revolution in France* (1790). Tom Paine's *Rights of Man* (1791–92) also advocated for England a democratic republic that was to be achieved, if lesser pressures failed, by popular revolution. More important as an influence on Wordsworth, Percy Shelley, and other poets was William Godwin's *Inquiry Concerning Political Justice* (1793), which foretold an inevitable but peaceful evolution of society to a final stage in which all property would be equally distributed and all government would wither away. But English sympathizers dropped off as the Revolution followed its increasingly grim and violent course: the accession to power by Jacobin extremists; the "September Massacres" of the imprisoned and helpless nobility in 1792, followed by the execution of the king and queen; the invasion by the French Republic of the Rhineland and Netherlands, and its offer of armed assistance to all countries desiring to overthrow their governments, which brought England into the war against France; the guillotining of thousands in the Reign of Terror under Robespierre; and, after the execution in their turn of the men who had directed the Terror, the emergence of Napoleon first as dictator and then as emperor of France. As Wordsworth wrote in *The Prelude* (11.206–09),

> become Oppressors in their turn,
> Frenchmen had changed a war of self-defence
> For one of Conquest, losing sight of all
> Which they had struggled for. . . .

For Wordsworth and other English observers of liberal inclinations, these events posed a dilemma that became familiar again after the 1920s, in a parallel era of wars, revolutions, and the struggle by competing social ideologies—liberals had no side they could wholeheartedly espouse. Napoleon, the child and champion of the French Revolution, had become an arch-aggressor, a despot, and the founder of a new dynasty; yet almost all those who opposed him did so for the wrong reasons, with the result that his final defeat at Waterloo in 1815 proved to be the triumph, not of progress and reform, but of reactionary despotisms throughout continental Europe.

In England this was a period of harsh, repressive measures. Public meetings were prohibited, habeas corpus was suspended for the first time in over a hundred years, and advocates of even moderate political change were charged with high treason in time of war. The outlook of the Napoleonic wars put an end to reform for nearly three decades.

Yet this was the very time when profound economic and social changes were creating a desperate need for corresponding changes in political arrangements, and new classes—manufacturing, rather than agricultural— were beginning to demand a voice in government proportionate to their wealth. The "Industrial Revolution"—the shift in manufacturing that resulted from the invention of power-driven machinery to replace hand labor—had begun in the mid-eighteenth century with improvements in machines for processing textiles, and was given immense impetus when James Watt perfected the steam engine in 1765. In the succeeding decades steam replaced wind and water as the primary source of power in one after another type of manufacturing, and after centuries of almost imperceptibly slow change, there began that ever-accelerating alteration in economic and social conditions which shows no signs of slowing down in the foreseeable future. A new laboring population massed in the sprawling mill towns that burgeoned in central and northern England. In rural communities the destruction of home industry was accompanied by a rapid growth of the process—lamented by Oliver Goldsmith in *The Deserted Village* as early as 1770—of enclosing open fields and communally worked farms into privately owned agricultural holdings. Enclosure was by and large necessary for the more efficient methods of agriculture and animal breeding required to supply a growing population (although some of the land thus acquired was turned into vast private estates); in any case, it created a new landless class that either migrated to the industrial towns or remained as farm laborers, subsisting on starvation wages eked out by an inadequate dole. The landscape of England began to take on its modern appearance—the hitherto open rural areas subdivided into a checkerboard of fields enclosed by hedges and stone walls, with the factories of the industrial and trading cities casting a pall of smoke over vast areas of jerry-built houses and slum tenements. Meanwhile, the population was becoming increasingly polarized into what Disraeli later called the "Two Nations"—the two classes of capital and labor, the large owner or trader and the possessionless wageworker, the rich and the poor.

No attempt was made to regulate this shift from the old economic world to the new, not only because of inertia and the power of vested interests but because even liberal reformers were dominated by the social philosophy of laissez-faire. This theory of "let alone" holds that the general welfare can be ensured only by the free operation of economic laws; the government should maintain a policy of strict noninterference and leave people to pursue their private interests. For the great majority of the laboring class the results of this policy were inadequate wages, long hours of work under harsh discipline in sordid conditions, and the large-scale employment of women and children for tasks that destroyed both the body and the spirit. Reports by investigating committees on the coal mines, where male and female children of ten or even five years of age were harnessed to heavy coal-sledges that they dragged by crawling on their hands and knees, read like scenes from Dante's *Inferno*. In 1815 the conclusion of the French war, when the enlargement of the working force by demobilized troops coincided with the fall in the wartime demand for goods, brought on the first modern industrial depression. Since the workers had no vote and were prevented by law from unionizing, their only recourses were petitions, protest meetings, agitation, and hunger riots, which only frightened the ruling class into more repressive measures. In addition the introduction of new machines resulted in further loss of jobs, and this provoked sporadic attempts by dispossessed workers to destroy the machines. After one such outbreak, the House of Lords—despite Lord Byron's eloquent protest—passed a bill (1812) making death the penalty for destroying the frames used for weaving in the stocking industry. In 1819 meetings of workers were organized to demand parliamentary reform. In August of that year, a huge but orderly assembly at St. Peter's Fields, Manchester, was charged by troops, who killed nine and severely injured hundreds more; this was the notorious "Peterloo Massacre," so named with ironic reference to the Battle of Waterloo. The event incited Percy Shelley to write his poems for the working class, *England in 1819*, *A Song: "Men of England,"* and *To Sidmouth and Castlereagh*.

Suffering was largely confined to the poor, however, for all this while the landed classes, the industrialists, and many of the merchants prospered. The British Empire expanded aggressively both westward and eastward, becoming the most powerful colonial presence in the world. The British East India Company ruled the entire Indian subcontinent at this time, and black slave labor in the West Indies generated great wealth for British plantation owners and their overseers. In London the Regency period (1811–20) was for the leisure class a time of lavish display and moral laxity. In the provinces the gentry in their country houses carried on their family and social concerns—reflected in the novels of Jane Austen—almost untouched by great national and international events.

As in earlier English history, women constituted a deprived class that cut across social classes, for they were widely regarded as inferior to men in intellect and in all but domestic talents. They were therefore provided limited schooling and no facilities for higher education, had only lowly vocations open to them, were subjected to a rigid code of sexual behavior, and possessed (especially after marriage) almost no legal rights. In spite of these disabilities, this was the first era in British literature in which women writers began to rival men in their numbers, their success in sales, their literary reputations—and as poets and social commentators as well as novelists; just in the category of poetry, some nine hundred women are listed in J. R. de J. Jackson's recent bibliography, *Romantic Poetry by Women*. Unlike the men, they had, as a class, much in the way of deprivation and prejudice to contend with. In the revolutionary period, women finally acquired a strong and eloquent champion. Mary Wollstonecraft, who had written an early defense of the French Revolution, *A Vindication of the Rights of Men* (1790), followed this two years later with *A Vindication of the Rights of Woman*, a founding classic of the women's movement. Wollstonecraft asserted that women possess equal intellectual capacity and talents as men and demanded for them a greater share of social, educational, and vocational privileges. The cause of women's rights, however, was not taken up by effective proponents until the Victorian era, and even partial achievement of its aims was delayed until well along in the twentieth century.

But the pressures for reform in the privileges of men, as distinct from women, could not be eliminated in the early nineteenth century, especially since political disabilities were not limited to laborers. Gradually the working-class reformers acquired the support of the middle classes and the liberal Whigs. Finally, at a time of acute economic distress, and after unprecedented agitation and disorders that threatened to break out into revolution, the first Reform Bill was passed in 1832, amid widespread rejoicing. It eliminated the rotten boroughs (depopulated areas whose seats in Commons were at the disposal of a nobleman), redistributed parliamentary representation to include the new industrial cities, and extended the vote. Although about half the middle class, almost all the working class, and all women remained still without a franchise, the principle of the peaceful adjustment of conflicting interests by parliamentary majority had been firmly established, and reform was to go on, by stages, until England acquired universal adult suffrage in 1928.

THE "SPIRIT OF THE AGE"

Writers in Wordsworth's lifetime did not think of themselves as "Romantic"; the word was not applied until half a century later, by English historians. Contemporary critics and reviewers treated them as independent individuals, or else grouped them (often invidiously, but with some basis in fact) into a number of separate schools: "the Lake School" of Wordsworth, Coleridge, and Robert Southey; "the Cockney School," a derogatory term for the Londoners Leigh Hunt, William Hazlitt, and associated writers, including Keats; and "the Satanic School" of Byron, Percy Shelley, and their followers.

Many of the writers, however, did feel that there was something distinctive about their time—not a shared doctrine or literary quality, but a pervasive intellectual and imaginative climate, which some of them called "the spirit of the age." They had the sense that (as Keats said in one of his sonnets) "Great spirits now on earth are sojourning," and that there was evidence of a release of energy, experimental boldness, and creative power that marks a literary renaissance. In his *Defence of Poetry* Shelley claimed that the literature of the age "has arisen as it were from a new birth," and that "an electric life burns" within the words of its best writers which is "less their spirit than the spirit of the age." Shelley explained this literary spirit as an accompaniment of political and social revolution, and other writers agreed. Francis Jeffrey, the foremost conservative reviewer of the day, connected "the revolution in our literature" with "the agitations of the French Revolution, and the discussions as well as the hopes and terrors to which it gave occasion." Hazlitt, who published a book of essays called *The Spirit of the Age*, described how in his early youth the French Revolution had seemed "the dawn of a new era, a new impulse had been given to men's minds." The new poetry of the school of Wordsworth, he maintained, "had its origin in the French Revolution. . . . It was a time of promise, a renewal of the world—and of letters."

The imagination of many Romantic writers was, indeed, preoccupied with the fact and idea of revolution. In the early period of the French Revolution all the leading English writers except Edmund Burke were in sympathy with it, and Robert Burns, William Blake, Wordsworth, Coleridge, Southey, and Mary Wollstonecraft were among its fervent adherents. Later, even after the first boundless expectations had been disappointed by the events in France, the younger writers, including Hazlitt, Hunt, Shelley, and Byron, felt that its example, when purged of its errors, still constituted humanity's best hope. The Revolution generated a pervasive feeling that this was an age of new beginnings when, by discarding traditional procedures and outworn customs, everything was possible, and not only in the political and social realm but in intellectual and literary enterprises as well. In his *Prelude* Wordsworth wrote the classic description of the spirit of the early 1790s, with "France standing on the top of golden hours, / And human nature seeming born again," so that "the whole Earth, / The beauty wore of promise." Something of this sense of limitless possibilities survived the shock of first disappointment at events in France and carried over to the year 1797, when Wordsworth and Coleridge, in excited daily communion, revolutionized, on grounds analogous to the politics of democracy, the theory and practice of poetry. The product of these discussions was the *Lyrical Ballads* of 1798.

POETIC THEORY AND POETIC PRACTICE

Wordsworth undertook to justify the new poetry by a critical manifesto, or statement of poetic principles, first as a short Advertisement in the original *Lyrical Ballads*, then in the form of an extended Preface to the second edition in 1800, which he enlarged still further in the third edition of 1802. In it he set himself in opposition to the literary *ancien régime*, those writers of the eighteenth century who, in his view, had imposed on poetry artificial conventions that distorted its free and natural expression. Many of Wordsworth's later critical writings were attempts to clarify, buttress, or qualify points made in his first declaration. Coleridge said that the Preface was "half a child of my own brain"; and although he soon developed doubts about some of Wordsworth's unguarded statements, and undertook to correct them in *Biographia Literaria* (1817), he did not question the rightness of Wordsworth's attempt to overturn the reigning tradition. In the course of the eighteenth century there had been increasing opposition to the tradition of Dryden, Pope, and Johnson; and especially in the 1740s and later there had emerged many of the critical concepts, as well as a number of the poetic subjects and forms, that were later exploited by Wordsworth and his contemporaries. Wordsworth's Preface nevertheless deserves its reputation as a turning point in English literature, for Wordsworth gathered up isolated ideas, organized them into a coherent theory based on explicit critical principles, and made them the rationale for his own achievements as a poet. We can conveniently use the concepts in this influential essay as points of departure for a survey of distinctive elements that are widespread in the theory and poetry of the Romantic period.

1. The Concept of Poetry and the Poet

Representative eighteenth-century theorists had regarded poetry as primarily an imitation of human life—in a frequent figure, "a mirror held up to nature"—that the poet artfully renders and puts into an order designed to instruct and give artistic pleasure to the reader. Wordsworth, on the other hand, repeatedly described all good poetry as, at the moment of composition, "the spontaneous overflow of powerful feelings." Reversing earlier theory, he thus located the source of a poem not in the outer world, but in the individual poet, and specified that the essential materials of a poem were not external people and events, but the inner feelings of the author, or external objects only after these have been transformed or irradiated by the author's feelings. Other Romantic theories, however diverse in other aspects, concurred by referring primarily to the mind, emotions, and imagination of the poet, instead of to the outer world as perceived by the senses, for the origin, content, and defining attributes of a poem. Many writers, such as Charlotte Smith, identified poetry (in metaphors parallel to Wordsworth's "overflow") as the "expression" or "utterance" or "exhibition" of emotion. Blake and Shelley described a poem as an embodiment of the poet's imaginative vision, which they opposed to the ordinary world of common experience. Coleridge, following German precedents, introduced into English criticism an organic theory, based on the model of the growth of a plant. That is, he conceived a great work of literature to be a self-originating and self-organizing process that begins with a seedlike idea in the poet's imagination, grows by assimilating both the poet's feelings and the diverse materials of sense-experience, and evolves into an organic whole in which the parts are integrally related to each other and to the whole.

In accord with the view that poetry expresses the poet's own feelings and temperament, the lyric poem written in the first person, earlier regarded as a minor kind, became a major Romantic form, and was often described as the most essentially poetic of all the genres. And in the Romantic lyric the "I" often is not a conventionally typical lyric speaker, such as the Petrarchan lover or Cavalier gallant of Elizabethan and seventeenth-century love poems, but has recognizable traits of the poet's own person and circumstances. In the poems of Wordsworth, Coleridge, Shelley, Keats, Smith, Letitia Landon, and others, the experiences and states of mind expressed by the lyric speaker often accord closely with the known facts of the poet's life and with the personal confessions in the poet's letters and journals. Even in his ostensibly fictional writings (narrative and dramatic), Byron usually invites his readers to identify the hero with the author, whether the hero is presented romantically (as in *Childe Harold*, *Manfred*, and the Oriental tales) or in an ironic perspective (as in *Don Juan*). An extreme instance of this tendency to self-reference is Wordsworth's *Prelude*, which is a poem of epic length and epic seriousness about the growth of the poet's own mind.

The Prelude exemplifies two other important tendencies in the period. Like Blake, Coleridge in his early poems, and later on Shelley, Wordsworth presents himself as what he calls "a chosen son," or "Bard." That is, he assumes the persona and voice of a poet-prophet, modeled on Milton and the prophets in the Bible, and puts himself forward as a spokesman for traditional Western civilization at a time of profound crisis—a time, as Wordsworth said in book 2 of *The Prelude*, "of dereliction and dismay" and the "melancholy waste of hopes o'erthrown." (*Son* and *spokesman* are appropriate here; almost always, the bardic poet-prophet was a distinctively male persona.) As bards, Wordsworth and the other visionary poets set out to revise the biblical promise of divine redemption by reconstituting the grounds of hope and pronouncing the coming of a time in which a renewed humanity will inhabit a renovated earth on which men and women will feel thoroughly at home. *The Prelude* also is an instance of a central literary form of English, as of European, Romanticism—a long work about the formation of the self, often centering on a crisis, and presented in the radical metaphor of an interior journey in quest of one's true identity and destined spiritual home. Other English examples of this form are Blake's *Milton*, the crucial episode of Asia's underground journey in Shelley's *Prometheus Unbound*, Keats's *Endymion* and *The Fall of Hyperion*, and, in Victorian poetry, Elizabeth Barrett Browning's *Aurora Leigh*. There are equivalent developments in contemporary prose: the self-revelation in the personal essays of Lamb, Hazlitt, and Leigh Hunt and the currency of spiritual autobiography, whether fictionalized (Thomas Carlyle's *Sartor Resartus*) or presented as fact (Coleridge's *Biographia Literaria*, Thomas De Quincey's *Confessions of an English Opium Eater* and *Autobiographic Sketches*).

2. Poetic Spontaneity and Freedom

Wordsworth defined good poetry not merely as the overflow but as "the *spontaneous* overflow" of feelings. In traditional aesthetic theory, poetry had been regarded as supremely an art—an art that in modern times is practiced by poets who have assimilated classical precedents, are aware of the "rules" governing the kind of poem they are writing, and (except for the felicities that, as Pope said, are "beyond the reach of art") deliberately employ tested means to achieve foreknown effects upon an audience. But to Wordsworth, although the composition of a poem originates from "emotion recollected in tranquillity" and may be preceded and followed by reflection, the immediate act of composition must be spontaneous—that is, arising from impulse, and free from all rules and the artful manipulation of means to foreseen ends. Other important Romantic critics also voiced declarations of artistic independence from inherited precepts. Keats listed as an "axiom" that "if poetry comes not as naturally as the leaves to a tree it had better not come at all." Blake insisted that he wrote from "Inspiration and Vision" and that his long "prophetic" poem *Milton* was given to him by an agency not himself and "produced without Labor or Study." Shelley also thought it "an error to assert that the finest passages of poetry are produced by labor and study," and suggested instead that they are the products of an unconscious creativity: "A great statue or picture grows under the power of the artist as a child in the mother's womb." "The definition of genius," Hazlitt remarked, "is that it acts unconsciously." The surviving manuscripts of the Romantic poets, however, as well as the testimony of observers, show that they worked and reworked their texts no less arduously—if perhaps more immediately under the impetus of first conception—than the poets of earlier ages. Coleridge, who believed that truth lies in a union of opposites, came closer to the facts of Romantic practice when he claimed that the act of composing poetry involves the psychological contraries "of passion and of will, of *spontaneous* impulse and of *voluntary* purpose."

The emphasis in this period on the free activity of the imagination is related to an insistence on the essential role of instinct, intuition, and the feelings of "the heart" to supplement the judgments of the purely logical faculty, "the head," whether in the province of artistic beauty, philosophical and religious truth, or moral goodness. "Deep thinking," Coleridge wrote, "is attainable only by a man of deep feeling, and all truth is a species of revelation"; hence, "a metaphysical solution that does not tell you something in the heart is grievously to be suspected as apocryphal."

3. Romantic "Nature Poetry"

In his Preface, Wordsworth wrote that "I have at all times endeavored to look steadily at my subject," and in a supplementary Essay he complained that from Dryden through Pope there is scarcely an image from external nature "from which it can be inferred that the eye of the poet had been steadily fixed on his object." A glance at the table of contents of any collection of Romantic poems will show the degree to which the natural scene has become a primary poetic subject, while Wordsworth, Shelley, and even more Coleridge and Keats, described natural phenomena with an accuracy of observation that had no earlier match in its ability to capture the sensuous nuance.

Because of the prominence of landscape in this period, "Romantic poetry" has to the popular mind become almost synonymous with "nature poetry." Neither Romantic theory nor practice, however, justifies the opinion that the aim of this poetry was description for its own sake. Wordsworth in fact insisted that the ability to observe and describe objects accurately, although a necessary, is not at all a sufficient condition for poetry, "as its exercise supposes all the higher qualities of the mind to be passive, and in a state of subjection to external objects." And while many of the great Romantic lyrics—Wordsworth's *Tintern Abbey* and *Ode: Intimations of Immortality*, Coleridge's *Frost at Midnight* and *Dejection*, Shelley's *Ode to the West Wind*, Keats's *Nightingale*—begin with an aspect or change of aspect in the natural scene, this serves only as stimulus to the most characteristic human activity, that of thinking. The longer Romantic "nature poems" are in fact usually meditative poems, in which the presented scene serves to raise an emotional problem or personal crisis whose development and resolution constitute the organizing principle of the poem. As Wordsworth said in his Prospectus to *The Recluse*, not nature but "the Mind of Man" is "my haunt, and the main region of my song."

In addition, Romantic poems habitually endow the landscape with human life, passion, and expressiveness. In part such descriptions represent the poetic equivalent of the metaphysical concept of nature, which had developed in deliberate revolt against the worldviews of the scientific philosophers of the seventeenth and eighteenth centuries, who represented the ultimate reality as a mechanical world consisting of physical particles in motion. What is needed in philosophy, Coleridge wrote, is "the substitution of life and intelligence . . . for the philosophy of mechanism, which, in everything that is most worthy of the human intellect, strikes *Death*." But for many Romantic poets it was a matter of immediate experience to respond to the outer universe as a living entity that participates in the feelings of the observer. James Thomson and other descriptive poets of the preceding century had depicted the created universe as giving direct access to God, and even as itself possessing the attributes of divinity. In *Tintern Abbey* and other poems Wordsworth exhibits toward the landscape attitudes and sentiments that human beings had earlier felt not only for God, but also for a father, a mother, or a beloved. Elsewhere, as in the great passage on crossing Simplon Pass (*The Prelude* 6.625ff.), Wordsworth also revives the ancient theological concept that God's creation constitutes a symbol system, a physical revelation parallel to the written Apocalypse, the Book of Revelation in the Bible—

> Characters of the great Apocalypse,
> The types and symbols of Eternity,
> Of first, and last, and midst, and without end.

This view that natural objects correspond to an inner or a spiritual world underlay a tendency, especially in Blake and Percy Shelley, to write a symbolist poetry in which a rose, a sunflower, a mountain, a cave, or a cloud is presented as an object imbued with a significance beyond itself. "I always seek in what I see," Shelley said, "the likeness of something beyond the present and tangible object." And by Blake mere nature, as perceived by the physical eye and unhumanized by the imagination, was spurned "as the dirt upon my feet, no part of me."

4. *The Glorification of the Ordinary and the Outcast*

In two lectures on Wordsworth, Hazlitt declared that the school of poetry founded by Wordsworth was the literary equivalent of the French Revolution, translating political changes into poetical experiments. "Kings and queens were dethroned from their rank and station in legitimate tragedy or epic poetry, as they were decapitated elsewhere. . . . The paradox [these poets] set out with was that all things are by nature equally fit subjects for poetry; or that if there is any preference to be given, those that are the meanest and most unpromising are the best."

Hazlitt had in mind Wordsworth's statement that the aim of *Lyrical Ballads* was "to choose incidents and situations from common life" and to use a "selection of language really spoken by men," for which the source and model is "humble and rustic life." As Hazlitt shrewdly saw, this was a social rather than a distinctively literary definition of the proper materials and language for poetry. Versifiers of the later decades of the eighteenth century had experimented with the simple treatment of simple subjects, and Robert Burns—like Wordsworth, a sympathizer with the French Revolution—had achieved great poetic success in the serious representation of humble life in a language really spoken by rustics; the women poets especially—Barbauld, Robinson, Baillie—assimilated to their poems the subject matter of everyday life. But

Wordsworth underwrote his poetic practice with a theory that inverted the traditional hierarchy of poetic genres, subjects, and style by elevating humble and rustic life and the plain style, which in earlier theory were appropriate only to the lowly pastoral, into the principal subject and medium for poetry in general. And in his own practice, as Hazlitt also noted, Wordsworth went even further and turned for the subjects of his serious poems not only to humble people but to the ignominious, the outcast, the delinquent—to "convicts, female vagrants, gypsies . . . idiot boys and mad mothers," as well as to "peasants, peddlers, and village barbers." Hence the outrage of Lord Byron, who alone among his major contemporaries insisted that Dryden and Pope had laid out the proper road for poetry, and who—in spite of his liberalism in politics—maintained his literary allegiance both to aristocratic proprieties and to traditional poetic decorum:

> "Peddlers," and "Boats," and "Wagons"! Oh! ye shades
> Of Pope and Dryden, are we come to this?

Hazlitt also insisted that, in his democratization of poetry, Wordsworth was "the most original poet now living." Certainly Wordsworth in *Lyrical Ballads* was, in this respect, more radical than any of his contemporaries. He enlarged greatly his readers' imaginative sympathies and brought into the province of serious literature a range of materials and interests which are still being explored by writers of the present day.

It should be noted, however, that Wordsworth's aim in *Lyrical Ballads* was not simply to represent the world as it is but, as he announced in his Preface, to throw over "situations from common life . . . a certain coloring of imagination, whereby ordinary things should be presented to the mind in an unusual aspect." As this passage indicates, Wordsworth's concern in his poetry was not only with "common life" but with "ordinary *things*"; no one can read his poems without noticing the extraordinary reverence with which he invests words that in earlier writers had been derogatory—words like "common," "ordinary," "everyday," "humble," whether applied to people or to objects in the visible scene. His aim throughout is to shatter the lethargy of custom so as to refresh our sense of wonder—indeed, of divinity—in the everyday, the commonplace, the trivial, and the lowly.

Samuel Johnson had said that "wonder is a pause of reason" and that "all wonder is the effect of novelty upon ignorance." But for many Romantic writers, to arouse in the sophisticated mind that sense of wonder presumed to be felt by the ignorant and the innocent was a primary power of imagination and a major function of poetry. Commenting on the special imaginative quality of Wordsworth's early poetry (*Biographia Literaria*, chapter 6), Coleridge remarked: "To combine the child's sense of wonder and novelty with the appearances, which every day for perhaps forty years had rendered familiar . . . this is the character and privilege of genius," and its prime service is to awaken in the reader "freshness of sensation" in the representation of "familiar objects." Poetry, said Shelley in his *Defense of Poetry*, "reproduces the common universe" but "purges from our inward sight the film of familiarity which obscures from us the wonder of our being," and "creates anew the universe, after it has been blunted by reiteration." And in Carlyle's *Sartor Resartus* (1833–34), the chief—indeed the only—effect of the conversion of the protagonist from despairing unbelief is that he is able to sustain a sense of the "Natural Supernaturalism" in ordinary experience and so over-come the "custom" which "blinds us to the miraculousness of daily-recurring miracles." The great power of the imagination, according to all these writers, is that it makes the old world new again.

5. The Supernatural and "Strangeness in Beauty"

In most of his poems Coleridge, like Wordsworth, dealt with the everyday things of this world, and in *Frost at Midnight* he showed how well he too could achieve the effect of wonder in the familiar. But Coleridge tells us (*Biographia Literaria*, chapter 14) that according to the division of labor in *Lyrical Ballads*, his special function was to achieve wonder by a frank vio-lation of natural laws and the ordinary course of events in poems of which "the incidents and agents were to be, in part at least, supernatural." And in *The Rime of the Ancient Mariner, Christabel*, and *Kubla Khan*, Coleridge opened up to poets in the modern world the realm of mystery and magic, in which materials from ancient folklore, superstition, and demonology are used to impress upon the reader the sense of occult powers and unknown modes of being. Such poems are usually set in the distant past or in faraway places, or both; the milieu of *Kubla Khan*, for example, exploits the exoticism both of the Middle Ages and of the Orient. Next to Coleridge, the greatest master of this Romantic mode—in which supernatural events have a deep psychological import—was John Keats. In *La Belle Dame sans Merci* and *The Eve of St. Agnes* he adapted the old forms of ballad and romance to modern sophisticated use and, like Coleridge, established a medieval setting for events that violate our sense of realism and the natural order. Hence the term *medieval revival*, frequently attached to the Romantic period, which comprehends also the ballad imitations and some of the verse tales and his-torical novels of Sir Walter Scott.

Another side of the tendency that Walter Pater later called "the addition of strangeness to beauty" was the Romantic interest in unusual modes of experience, of a kind that earlier writers had largely ignored as either too trivial or too aberrant for serious literary concern. Blake, Wordsworth, and Coleridge in their poetry explored visionary states of consciousness that are common among children but violate the standard categories of adult judg-ment. Coleridge was interested in mesmerism (what we now call hypnotism) and, like Blake and Shelley, studied the literature of the occult and the esoteric. Coleridge also shared with De Quincey a concern with dreams and nightmares; both authors exploited in their writings the altered conscious-ness and distorted perceptions they experienced under their addiction to opium. Byron made repeated use of the fascination with the forbidden and the appeal of the terrifying Satanic hero. And Keats was extraordinarily sen-sitive to the ambivalences of human experience—to the mingling, at their highest intensity, of pleasure and pain, to destructive aspects of sexuality, and to the erotic quality of the longing for death. These phenomena had already been explored by eighteenth-century writers of terror tales and Gothic fiction, and later in the nineteenth century all of them, sometimes exaggerated to perversity, became the special literary province of Charles Baudelaire, Algernon Charles Swinburne, and writers of the European "Decadence."

INDIVIDUALISM, INFINITE STRIVING,
AND NONCONFORMITY

Through the greater part of the eighteenth century, humans had for the most part been viewed as limited beings in a strictly ordered and essentially unchanging world. A variety of philosophical and religious systems in that century coincided in a distrust of radical innovation, a respect for the precedents established through the ages by the common sense of humanity, and the recommendation to set accessible goals and to avoid extremes, whether in politics, intellect, morality, or art. Many of the great literary works of the period joined in attacking what was called "pride," or aspirations beyond the limits natural to our species. "The bliss of man," Pope wrote in *An Essay on Man,* "(could pride that blessing find) / Is not to act or think beyond mankind":

> This kind, this due degree
> Of blindness, weakness, Heaven bestows on thee.
> Submit.

The Romantic period, the age of unfettered free enterprise, industrial expansion, and boundless revolutionary hope, was also an age of radical individualism in which both the philosophers and poets put an extraordinarily high estimate on human potentialities and powers. In German post-Kantian philosophy, which generated many of the characteristic ideas of European Romanticism, the human mind—what was called the "Subject" or "Ego"— took over various functions that had hitherto been the sole prerogative of Divinity. Most prominent was the rejection by philosophers of a central eighteenth-century concept of the mind as a mirrorlike recipient of a universe already created, and its replacement by a new concept of the mind as itself creating the universe it perceives. In a parallel fashion, the poets of the new period also described the mind as creating its own experience. According to Blake, the mind creates its proper milieu only if it totally rejects the material world; in Coleridge and Wordsworth, however, the mind creates in collaboration with something given to it from without. Mind, wrote Coleridge in 1801, is "not passive" but "made in God's Image, and that too in the sublimest sense—the Image of the *Creator.*" And Wordsworth declared in *The Prelude* (2.258–61) that the individual mind

> Doth, like an Agent of the one great Mind,
> Create, creator and receiver both,
> Working but in alliance with the works
> Which it beholds.

Many Romantic writers also agreed that the mind has access beyond sense to the transcendant and the infinite, through a special faculty they called either Reason or Imagination. In *The Prelude* (6.600ff.) Wordsworth describes a flash of imagination "that has revealed / The invisible world," and affirms:

> Our destiny, our being's heart and home,
> Is with infinitude, and only there;
> With hope it is, hope that can never die,

> Effort, and expectation, and desire,
> And something evermore about to be.

The desire beyond human limits that, to the moralists of the preceding age, had been an essential sin, or tragic error, now becomes a glory and a triumph: the human being refuses to submit to limitations and, though finite, persists in setting infinite, hence inaccessible, goals. Wordsworth characteristically goes on to declare that "under such banners militant, the soul / Seeks for no trophies, struggles for no spoils"; for him, the infinite striving ends in physical quietism and moral fortitude. But for other writers, especially in Germany, the proper human aim is ceaseless activity—a "Streben nach dem Unendlichen," a striving for the infinite. This view is epitomized by Goethe's Faust, who in his quest for the unattainable violates ordinary moral limits, yet wins salvation by his very insatiability, which never stoops to contentment with the possibilities offered by this finite world. Infinite longing—in Shelley's phrase, "the desire of the moth for a star"—was a recurrent theme also in the English literature of the day. "Less than everything," Blake announced, "cannot satisfy man." Shelley's *Alastor* and Keats's *Endymion* both represent the quest for an indefinable and inaccessible goal, and Byron's *Manfred* has for its hero a man whose "powers and will" reach beyond the limits of that human clay "which clogs the ethereal essence," so that "his aspirations / Have been beyond the dwellers of the earth."

In a parallel fashion, Romantic theorists of art rejected the neoclassic ideal of a limited intention, perfectly accomplished, in favor of "the glory of the imperfect," in which the very failures of artists attest the unlimited reach of their aims. And in their own work, Romantic writers deliberately put themselves in competition with the greatest of their predecessors and experimented boldly in poetic language, versification, and design. Especially in their longer poems they struck out in new directions, and in the space of a few decades produced an astonishing variety of forms constructed on novel principles of organization and style. Blake's symbolic lyrics and visionary "prophetic" poems; Coleridge's haunting ballad-narrative of sin and retribution, *The Rime of the Ancient Mariner;* Wordsworth's epiclike spiritual autobiography, *The Prelude;* Shelley's cosmic symbolic drama, *Prometheus Unbound;* Keats's sequence of odes on the irreconcilable conflict in basic human desires; Byron's satiric survey of all European civilization, *Don Juan*—one can say of each of them, as Shelley said of Byron's poem, that it was "something wholly new and relative to the age."

The great eighteenth-century writers had typically dealt with men and women as members of an organized, and usually an urban, society. Literary authors regarded themselves as integral parts of this society, addressed their works to it, and undertook to express its highest ideals and its collective traditional wisdom. Some Romantic writers, on the other hand, deliberately isolated themselves from society to give scope to their individual vision. Wordsworth titled his masterwork *The Recluse*, and he described himself as "musing in solitude" on its subject, "the individual Mind that keeps her own / Inviolate retirement." And in almost all Wordsworth's poems, long or short, the words *single, solitary, by oneself, alone* constitute a leitmotif; typically, his imagination is released by the sudden apparition of a single figure or object, stark against a natural background. Coleridge also, and still more strikingly Byron and Shelley, represented a solitary protagonist who is separated from society because he has rejected it, or because it has rejected him. These last three poets introduced what became a persistent theme in many Victorian and modern writers—the theme of exile, of the disinherited mind that cannot find a spiritual home in its native land and society or anywhere in the modern world. The solitary Romantic nonconformist was sometimes represented as also a great sinner. Male writers of that time were fascinated by the outlaws of myth, legend, or history—Cain, Satan, Faust, the Wandering Jew, or the great, flawed figure of Napoleon—on whom they modeled a number of their villains or their heroes. In Coleridge's *Ancient Mariner* (as in Wordsworth's *Guilt and Sorrow* and *Peter Bell*) the guilty outcast—"alone, alone, all, all alone"—is made to realize and expiate his sin against the community of living things so that he may reassume his place in the social order. But in Byron the violator of conventional laws and limits remains proudly unrepentant. His hero Manfred, a compound of guilt and superhuman greatness, cannot be defeated by death, successfully defying the demons who, in the tradition of Marlowe's *Dr. Faustus*, have come to drag his soul to hell: "I . . . was my own destroyer, and will be / My own hereafter.—Back, ye baffled fiends!" A more reputable Romantic hero, who turns up frequently in Byron and other writers and is made the protagonist of Shelley's great lyrical drama, is the Prometheus of Greek mythology. He shares with Satan the status of superlative nonconformity, since he sets himself in opposition to deity itself; unlike Satan, however, he is the champion rather than the enemy of the human race. Mary Shelley makes ironic use of this figure in her subtitle of 1818: *Frankenstein; or, The Modern Prometheus*—Victor Frankenstein is decidedly not the champion of humankind.

MILLENNIAL EXPECTATIONS

Nowhere is the Romantic combination of boundless aspiration and the reliance on the power of the individual mind and imagination more evident than in the literary treatment of the ultimate hope of humanity. The French Revolution had aroused in many sympathizers the millennial expectations that are profoundly rooted in Hebrew and Christian tradition. "Few persons but those who have lived in it," Robert Southey reminisced in 1824, "can conceive or comprehend what the memory of the French Revolution was, nor what a visionary world seemed to open upon those who were just entering it. Old things seemed passing away, and nothing was dreamt of but the regeneration of the human race." Southey's language—like that of Wordsworth, Coleridge, Hazlitt, and other writers when they described their early Revolutionary fervor—is biblical; and it reflects the extent to which, in England, the Revolution was championed by members of radical Protestant sects, who envisioned it on the model of biblical prophecy.

The Bible ends with the book of Apocalypse (literally, "Revelation"), prophesying a return of human beings to their lost Edenic felicity, first in the millennium ("a thousand years") of an earthly kingdom, then in the eternity of "a new heaven and a new earth"; this consummation of history is symbolized by a marriage between the New Jerusalem and Christ the Lamb. At the outbreak of the French Revolution, Joseph Priestley and other Unitarian leaders hailed that event as the stage preceding the millennium prophesied in Revelation. Coleridge and Wordsworth, in their early poems, also interpreted the Revolution as the violent preliminary to the new earth and heaven of apocalyptic prophecy. And Blake's *The French Revolution* (1791) and *America, a Prophecy* (1793) represented both these revolutions as apocalyptic portents of the last days of the fallen world.

When the later events in France dashed their faith in political revolution as a means to the millennium, a number of Romantic writers salvaged their apocalyptic hope by giving it a new interpretation. They transferred the agency of apocalypse from mass action to the individual mind—from a political to a spiritual revolution—and proposed that "the new earth and new heaven" of Revelation is available here, now, to all of us, if only we can make our visionary imagination triumph over our senses and sensebound understanding. Hence the extraordinary Romantic emphasis on a new way of *seeing* (which is regarded as the restoration of a lost earlier way of seeing) as the chief aim in life. Blake's "Prophetic Books," for example, all deal with some aspects of the Fall and Redemption, and represent apocalypse as the recovery of the imaginative vision of things as they really are, seen "through and not with the eye." "The Nature of my Work," Blake wrote, "is Visionary or Imaginative; it is an Endeavor to Restore what the Ancients called the Golden Age." This concept of the imaginative re-creation of the old earth continues to be expressed by Romantic poets in the original biblical metaphor of a marriage—although now it is not a marriage of the New Jerusalem with the Lamb but a conjunction of the inner faculties into spiritual unity, or else a marriage between the mind and the external world. Coleridge put this latter version succinctly in *Dejection: An Ode*; it is the inner condition of "Joy," at life's highest moments, "Which, wedding nature to us, gives in dower / A new earth and new heaven." Wordsworth announced as his "high argument" in the Prospectus to *The Recluse* (the same theme serves as underpattern for *The Prelude*) that "Paradise, and groves Elysian" are not "a history only of departed things"—

> For the discerning intellect of Man
> When wedded to this goodly universe
> In love and holy passion, shall find these
> A simple produce of the common day.

In Shelley's *Prometheus Unbound*, Prometheus represents archetypal humanity whose total change in moral being frees the imaginative capacity to envision, and to achieve, a regenerate world; the fourth act symbolizes this event in the mode of a marriage festival in which the whole cosmos participates.

Carlyle's *Sartor Resartus*, to mention one other example, is the history of an individual's violent spiritual crisis and conversion, which turns out to be the achievement of an individual apocalypse: "And I awoke to a new Heaven and a new Earth." But, as Carlyle goes on to indicate, this new earth is the old earth, seen by his protagonist as though miraculously re-created, because he has learned to substitute the "Imaginative" faculty for what Carlyle represents as the chief faculty of the eighteenth-century Enlightenment, the "Logical, Mensurative faculty," or "Understanding." Writing in 1830–31, at the close of the period historians have labeled "Romantic," Carlyle thus summed up the tendency of a generation of writers to retain the ancient faith in apocalypse, but to interpret it not as a change of the world, but as a change in our worldview.

OTHER FORMS: THE FAMILIAR ESSAY

This was also, along with its apocalyptic expectations, the period when literature for the first time became big business. Enlightenment-inspired educational reform and a rapid growth in population produced an explosion of potential readership. A new aesthetics of valuing art and literature "as such" emphasized reading for pleasure (as opposed to strictly moral and utilitarian ends); and people in general had more leisure in which to read, as well as more disposable income with which to purchase reading materials. Technological improvements in printing facilitated production and distribution, and commercial and public lending libraries were established. Hence the provision of more literature of all kinds to satisfy the needs of a greatly enlarged literate public.

At the close of the eighteenth century, reviews and magazines were written largely by hacks who acceded to the political bias and financial interests of the publisher and advertisers. The essays they included were weak imitations of the type established nearly a century earlier by single-essay periodicals such as the *Tatler* and the *Spectator*. In 1802, however, the *Edinburgh Review* inaugurated the modern type of periodical publication. It allowed considerable latitude to its writers, set its literary standards high, and was able to meet these standards by paying its contributors rates good enough to command the best talents of the day.

The success of this new enterprise stimulated the founding of rival reviews and magazines. (A "review," usually issued four times yearly, consisted primarily of essays on important books and discussions of contemporary issues; a "magazine" was a monthly publication that printed more miscellaneous materials, including a high proportion of original essays, poems, and stories.) In 1820 appeared the *London Magazine*, liberal in politics and contemporary in literary interests; in its short but notable career until 1829 it printed the work of a group of brilliant writers, including the three men who soon established themselves as the greatest essayists of the age—Lamb, Hazlitt, and De Quincey. These new periodicals not only elevated the essay in literary dignity and quality but revolutionized its form and substance. They competed strenuously for talent, paying well enough so that an author (at least one as prolific as Hazlitt) could earn a living as a freelance essayist. And writers were treated as serious practitioners who were competent, within broad limits, to write as they pleased.

Under these new conditions the "familiar essay"—a commentary on a nontechnical subject written in a relaxed and intimate manner—flourished, and in a fashion that to some degree paralleled the course of Romantic poetry. Each of the three major essayists was in fact closely associated with important poets and supported at least some of the new poetic developments in critical commentaries whose perceptiveness and discrimination render them durably valuable. Like the poets, these essayists were personal and subjective; their essays are often candidly autobiographical, reminiscent, self-analytic; and when the writers treated other matters than themselves, they tended to do so impressionistically, so that the material is seen reflected in the temperament of the essayist. The subject matter of the essays, like that of the poetry, exhibits an extension of range and sympathy far beyond the earlier limits of the leisure class and its fashionable concerns; the essays now dealt with clerks, chimney sweeps, poor relations, handball players, prize-fighters, and murderers. Most strikingly, the essayists resemble the poets in rebelling against eighteenth-century conventions by reviving prose forms long disused and developing new prose styles and structural principles. The result was a notable variety of achievements, ranging from Hazlitt's hard-hitting plain style and seemingly casual order of topics, through Lamb's delicately contrived rhetoric and meticulously controlled organization, to De Quincey's elaborate experiments in applying to prose the rhythms, harmonies, and thematic structure of musical compositions.

THE DRAMA

Although favorable to the essay, literary conditions in the early nineteenth century were unfavorable in the extreme to writing for the stage. By a licensing act that was not repealed until 1843, only the Drury Lane and Covent Garden theaters had the right to produce "legitimate"—that is to say, spoken—drama; the other theaters were restricted by law to entertainments in which there could be no dialogue except to music, and so put on mainly dancing, pantomime, and various types of musical plays. The two monopoly theaters were vast and ill-lighted, and their audiences were noisy and unruly; as a result, actors played in a grandiose and orotund style. To succeed under such conditions, plays had to be blatant and magniloquent, so that the drama of that period (fettered also by rigid moral and political censorship) tended to the extremes of either farce or melodrama. None of the plays written by the professional playwrights of the time is read nowadays; they survive mainly in the limbo of scholarly monographs on the history of the theater.

Nonetheless, attracted irresistibly by the example of their idolized Shakespeare, all the major Romantic poets, and many minor ones, tried their hand at poetic plays. Some of these were written as closet drama—Byron's *Manfred* and Shelley's *Prometheus Unbound,* for example, and most of Joanna Baillie's widely read *Plays on the Passions*—but others were expressly written for the stage. The poets, however, lacked experience with the hard necessities of the practical theater, and they were for the most part unable to throw off the artifice of an archaic style dominated by Elizabethan and Jacobean models.

Above all, the genius of an age that excelled in subjective or visionary literary forms was ill adapted to the theater, which is a peculiarly social genre representing a variety of credible characters. Even Byron, the only important poet of his generation to produce major work in a literary kind that requires a highly developed social sensibility—satire—did not succeed as a practical dramatist. His stage plays, while readable, mainly exhibit various aspects of the Byronic hero; they lack theatrical vigor and variety, and their thin-skinned author wisely refused to let them be put on before the merciless and demonstrative audiences of his day. Coleridge achieved a minor hit with his tragedy *Remorse*, which ran for twenty nights at the Drury Lane in 1813. The most capable Romantic dramatist was, surprisingly, Shelley. In *The Cenci* (1820) Shelley, with great tact and genuine theatrical acumen, converts a true story of the Italian Renaissance—of a monstrous father who violates his daughter and is in turn murdered by her—into a powerful version of his own central fable of the instinctive desire of evil to destroy, by degrading, the defiant individual, and of the moral triumph of the unconquerable single spirit, even in death. The play was not staged, however, until long after Shelley's death.

THE NOVEL

Two new types of fiction were prominent in the late eighteenth century. One was the "Gothic novel," which had been inaugurated in 1764 by Horace Walpole's *The Castle of Otranto: A Gothic Story*, and continued by Clara Reeve in *The Champion of Virtue: A Gothic Story* (1777). The term derives from the frequent setting of these tales in a gloomy castle of the Middle Ages, but it has been extended to a larger group of novels, set somewhere in the past, that exploit the possibilities of mystery and terror in sullen, craggy landscapes; decaying mansions with dank dungeons, secret passages, and stealthy ghosts; chilling supernatural phenomena; and often, sexual persecution of a beautiful maiden by an obsessed and haggard villain. These novels opened up to later fiction the dark, irrational side of human nature—the savage egoism, the perverse impulses, and the nightmarish terrors that lie beneath the controlled and ordered surface of the conscious mind. Some of the most powerful and influential writings in the mode were by women— they doubtless afforded a fictional release for the submerged desires and compensatory fantasies of that rigidly restricted and disadvantaged class. In *The Mysteries of Udolpho* (1794), and better still in *The Italian* (1797), Ann Radcliffe developed the figure of the mysterious and solitary *homme fatal*, torturing others because he is himself tortured by unspeakable guilt, who, though a villain, usurps the place of the hero in the reader's interest. Matthew Gregory Lewis in *The Monk* (1797), which he wrote at the age of twenty, has a similar protagonist and brings to the fore the elements of diabolism, sensuality, and sadistic perversion that were pungent but submerged components in Radcliffe's Gothic formula. Gothicism is apparent also in Romantic poetry: in Coleridge's medieval terror poem *Christabel*, in Byron's recurrent hero-villain, in the setting and descriptive passages of Keats's *Eve of St. Agnes*, and in Shelley's inclinations (fostered by his early love for Gothic tales and his own youthful trials in that form) toward the fantastic, the macabre, and the exploration of the unconscious mind and of such aberrations as incest.

The second fictional mode popular at the turn of the century was the novel of purpose, often written to propagate the new social and political theories current in the period of the French Revolution. The best examples combine didactic intention with elements of Gothic terror. William Godwin, the political philosopher, wrote *Caleb Williams* (1794) to illustrate the thesis that the lower classes are helplessly subject to the power and privilege of the ruling class, but he did so in the form of a chilling story about the relentless pursuit and persecution by a wealthy squire of his young secretary, who has come upon evidence that the squire has committed murder. Mary Shelley—Percy Shelley's wife and the daughter of Mary Wollstonecraft, author of *A Vindication of the Rights of Woman*—wrote a thematic novel of terror that not only is a literary classic but has become a popular myth. Her *Frankenstein* (1818) transforms a story about a fabricated monster into a powerful representation of the moral distortion imposed on an individual who, because he diverges from the norm, is rejected by society. Maria Edgeworth's *Castle Rackrent* (1800), admired by Walter Scott, initiated what he later developed—the British regional novel and the British historical novel—and Hannah More's *Coelebs in Search of a Wife* (1808), a hugely successful novel about marriage and religion, was influential in both Britain and the United States.

The Romantic period produced, in addition to Mary Shelley, two novelists whose renown is worldwide, Jane Austen and Sir Walter Scott. Jane Austen (1775–1817) is the only major author who seems to be untouched by the political, intellectual, and artistic revolutions of her age. Charlotte Brontë, speaking for the Romantic sensibility, complained that Jane Austen's novels lack warmth, enthusiasm, energy; "she ruffles her reader by nothing vehement, disturbs him by nothing profound. The passions are perfectly unknown to her." But Austen deliberately elected to work within the circumference of her own experience—the life of provincial English gentlefolk—and to maintain the decorum of the novel of manners, based on such literary antecedents as the comedy of manners of William Congreve and Richard Brinsley Sheridan and the novels of the earlier women authors Fanny Burney and Maria Edgeworth. Within these elected limits both of subject and form, Austen achieved a fully particularized setting within which to examine and criticize the values men and women live by in their everyday social lives.

Sense and Sensibility and *Northanger Abbey* gently ridicule two later eighteenth-century deviations from the humanistic norm: the cult of sensibility and the taste for Gothic terrors. Austen's other novels, published between 1813 and 1818—*Mansfield Park, Persuasion*, and best of all, *Pride and Prejudice* and *Emma*—all deal with the subject of getting married. This was in fact a central preoccupation and problem for the young leisure-class lady of that age, who had no career open to her outside of domesticity; Austen, however, chose the subject because it provided her with the best realistic opportunities for testing her heroines' practical sense and moral integrity, their degree of knowledge of the world and of themselves, and their capacity to demonstrate grace under social and financial pressure.

Sir Walter Scott (1771–1832) was contemporary with Jane Austen, and admired her greatly, but his work in fiction was at an extreme from hers. In 1814, with the anonymous *Waverley*, he turned from narrative verse (in which Byron had displaced him in popularity) to narrative prose and managed to write almost thirty long works of fiction in the eighteen years before he died. They are in the mode that he himself defined as romance, "the interest of which turns upon marvelous and uncommon incidents," in contrast to the novel such as Jane Austen wrote, in which "the events are accommodated to the ordinary train of human events, and the modern state of society." Scott's originality lay in opening up to fiction the rich and lively realm of history; he sometimes alters the order of events for novelistic purposes, yet he maintains fidelity to the spirit of the past and a meticulous accuracy in antiquarian detail. His series of Scottish novels, including *Guy Mannering, The Antiquary, Old Mortality, Rob Roy*, and (most enduringly) *The Heart of Midlothian*, are rooted in historical events from the seventeenth century up to his own time; *Ivanhoe* is set in thirteenth-century England; *Kenilworth* takes place in the age of Elizabeth; and *Quentin Durward*, the best of his Continental romances, has for its background the French court of the fifteenth century.

Like Byron, Scott wrote with dash and grandiosity in a kind of sustained improvisation; his plotting is often loose, his romantic lovers pallid, and his kings and chieftains large-scale puppets. But in his great scenes of action there are a scope and sweep not to be exceeded in fiction for several decades. And although, unlike his liberal Romantic contemporaries, Scott's political sympathies were aristocratic and feudal, his most vivid and convincing characters are members of the middle and lower classes. His tradesmen, servants, peasantry, social outcasts, and demented old women, speaking a rich Scottish vernacular (Scott's language, like Robert Burns's in verse, tended to become stilted and conventional when he wrote in standard English), make up a populous world in which each person is an individual, rooted in the circumstances of time, place, class, and occupation.

Scott had an immense international vogue, equaling that of Byron and Goethe, and became the acknowledged master of some of the greatest nineteenth-century novelists, including Balzac and Tolstoy. Jane Austen, on the other hand, during her lifetime was admired only by a limited group of English readers. Her novels have, however, demonstrated greater staying power. Scott's combination of casualness in design and prodigality in detail puts off many readers who have formed their sensibilities on the fiction of the present century. But even after the achievements of such masters in the form as Henry James, Jane Austen remains the sovereign of the intricate, spare, and ironic art of the novel of manners.

THE ROMANTIC PERIOD

TEXTS	CONTEXTS
1774 J. W. von Goethe, *The Sorrows of Young Werther*	
	1775 American War of Independence (1775–83)
1776 Adam Smith, *The Wealth of Nations*	
1778 Frances Burney, *Evelina*	
1779 Samuel Johnson, *Lives of the English Poets* (1779–81)	
	1780 Gordon Riots in London
1781 Immanuel Kant, *Critique of Pure Reason*. Jean-Jacques Rousseau, *Confessions*. J. C. Friedrich Schiller, *The Robbers*	
	1783 William Pitt becomes prime minister (serving until 1801 and again in 1804–06)
1784 Charlotte Smith, *Elegiac Sonnets*	1784 Death of Samuel Johnson
1785 William Cowper, *The Task*	
1786 William Beckford, *Vathek*. Robert Burns, *Poems, Chiefly in the Scottish Dialect*	
	1787 W. A. Mozart, *Don Giovanni*
1789 Jeremy Bentham, *Principles of Morals and Legislation*. William Blake, *Songs of Innocence*	1789 Fall of the Bastille (beginning of the French Revolution)
1790 Joanna Baillie, *Poems*. Blake, *The Marriage of Heaven and Hell*. Edmund Burke, *Reflections on the Revolution in France*	1790 Henry James Pye succeeds Thomas Warton as poet laureate. J. M. W. Turner first exhibits at the Royal Academy
1791 William Gilpin, *Observations on the River Wye*. Thomas Paine, *Rights of Man*. Ann Radcliffe, *The Romance of the Forest*	
1792 Mary Wollstonecraft, *A Vindication of the Rights of Woman*	1792 September Massacres in Paris. First gas lights in Britain
1793 William Godwin, *Political Justice*	1793 Execution of Louis XVI and Marie Antoinette. France declares war against Britain (and then Britain against France). The Reign of Terror
1794 Blake, *Songs of Experience*. Godwin, *Caleb Williams*. Radcliffe, *The Mysteries of Udolpho*	1794 The fall of Robespierre
1796 Matthew Gregory Lewis, *The Monk*	
1798 Joanna Baillie, *Plays on the Passions*, volume 1. Bentham, *Political Economy*. Thomas Malthus, *An Essay on the Principle of Population*. William Wordsworth and Samuel Taylor Coleridge, *Lyrical Ballads*	
1800 Maria Edgeworth, *Castle Rackrent*. Mary Robinson, *Lyrical Tales*	

TEXTS	CONTEXTS
	1802 Treaty of Amiens. *Edinburgh Review* founded. John Constable first exhibits at the Royal Academy
	1804 Napoleon crowned emperor
	1805 The French fleet defeated by the British at Trafalgar
1807 Wordsworth, *Poems in Two Volumes*	**1807** Abolition of the slave trade in Britain
1808 Goethe, *Faust,* part 1	**1808** Ludwig van Beethoven, *Symphonies* 5 and 6
	1811 The Prince of Wales becomes regent for George III, who is declared incurably insane
1812 Lord Byron, *Childe Harold's Pilgrimage,* cantos 1 and 2. Felicia Hemans, *The Domestic Affections*	**1812** War between Britain and the United States (1812–15)
1813 Jane Austen, *Price and Prejudice*	**1813** Robert Southey succeeds Pye as poet laureate
1814 Walter Scott, *Waverley.* Wordsworth, *The Excursion*	
	1815 Napoleon defeated at Waterloo
1816 Byron, *Childe Harold,* cantos 3 and 4. Coleridge, *Christabel, Kubla Khan.* Percy Shelley, *Alastor*	
1817 Byron, *Manfred.* Coleridge, *Biographia Literaria* and *Sibylline Leaves.* John Keats, *Poems*	**1817** *Blackwood's Edinburgh Magazine* founded. Death of Princess Charlotte
1818 Austen, *Northanger Abbey.* Keats, *Endymion.* Thomas Love Peacock, *Nightmare Abbey.* Mary Shelley, *Frankenstein*	
1819 Byron, *Don Juan,* cantos 1 and 2	**1819** "Peterloo Massacre" in Manchester
1820 John Clare, *Poems Descriptive of Rural Life.* Keats, *Lamia, Isabella, The Eve of St. Agnes, and Other Poems.* Percy Shelley, *Prometheus Unbound*	**1820** Death of George III; accession of George IV. *London Magazine* founded
1821 Thomas De Quincey, *Confessions of an English Opium-Eater.* Percy Shelley, *Adonais*	**1821** Deaths of Keats in Rome and Napoleon at St. Helena
	1822 Franz Schubert, *Unfinished Symphony.* Death of Percy Shelley in the Bay of Spezia, near Lerici, Italy
1824 Letitia Landon, *The Improvisatrice*	**1824** Death of Byron in Missolonghi
1827 Clare, *The Shepherd's Calendar*	
1828 Hemans, *Records of Woman*	
1830 Charles Lyell, *Principles of Geology* (1830–33). Alfred Tennyson, *Poems, Chiefly Lyrical*	**1830** Death of George IV; accession of William IV
	1832 First Reform Bill

ANNA LETITIA BARBAULD
1743–1825

Anna Barbauld, born Anna Letitia Aiken, received an unusual education from her father, a nonconformist minister and schoolmaster, that enabled her to read English before she was three and to master French and Italian, and then both Latin and Greek, while still a child. She made her literary debut with *Poems,* a work that went through five editions between 1773 and 1777 and immediately established her as a leading poet. In 1774 she married Rochemont Barbauld, a dissenting minister, and with him co-managed a school at Palgrave, in Suffolk. Thereafter, becoming increasingly famous and respected in literary circles as (according to the custom of the day) "Mrs. Barbauld," she divided her time between the teaching of younger pupils at Palgrave and a series of writings focused on education, politics, and literature. She published *Devotional Pieces* (1775), three volumes of *Lessons for Children* (1778–79), and *Hymns in Prose for Children* (1781), all of which were reprinted many times. William Hazlitt records a common experience in recalling that he read her works "before those of any other author, male or female, when I was learning to spell words of one syllable in her story-books for children."

She wrote political pamphlets in the 1790s, defending dissenters, democratic government, and popular education and opposing Britain's declaration of war against France; she attacked the slave trade in a verse *Epistle to William Wilberforce* (1791). In the next decade she turned to editing, producing the *Correspondence of Samuel Richardson* (six volumes, 1804), *The British Novelists* (fifty volumes, beginning in 1810), and a popular anthology of poetry and prose for young women called *The Female Speaker* (1811). Her work *The British Novelists* was the first attempt to establish a national canon in fiction paralleling the multivolume collections of British poets (such as the one associated with Samuel Johnson's prefaces) that had been appearing since the 1770s. Her introductory essay, *On the Origin and Progress of Novel-Writing,* is a pioneering statement concerning the educational value of novels.

Barbauld's last major work in poetry was *Eighteen Hundred and Eleven* (1812), a 334-line tirade against contemporary Britain lamenting the war with France (then in its seventeenth year), the poverty of leadership, the fallen economy, colonialism, and the failure of genius (at the conclusion, the Spirit of Genius emigrates to South America). The critical response was anguished and unanimously negative, even from the more liberal critics; and Barbauld seems not to have attempted another long work after this (she was, by this time, in her late sixties). She continued to write shorter pieces, such as the sprightly *Life,* on into the 1820s.

A Summer Evening's Meditation[1]

> 'Tis past! The sultry tyrant of the south
> Has spent his short-lived rage; more grateful hours
> Move silent on; the skies no more repel
> The dazzled sight, but with mild maiden beams
> 5   Of tempered lustre court the cherished eye
> To wander o'er their sphere; where, hung aloft,
> Dian's bright crescent, like a silver bow

---

1. The excursion-and-return structure of this poem anticipates the high flights (and returns) of later lyrics by Coleridge, Percy Shelley, and Keats, among others. But Barbauld's journey, beginning with "mild maiden beams" in line 4 and continuing with Diana's crescent (line 7), Venus's sweetest beam (lines 10 and 11), and "meekened Eve" (line 14), is specifically gendered throughout: it is clearly a woman who is launching "into the trackless deeps of space" (line 82).

New strung in heaven, lifts high its beamy horns
Impatient for the night, and seems to push
10   Her brother down the sky. Fair Venus shines
Even in the eye of day; with sweetest beam
Propitious shines, and shakes a trembling flood
Of softened radiance from her dewy locks.
The shadows spread apace; while meekened[2] Eve,
15   Her cheek yet warm with blushes, slow retires
Through the Hesperian gardens of the west,
And shuts the gates of day. 'Tis now the hour
When Contemplation from her sunless haunts,
The cool damp grotto, or the lonely depth
20   Of unpierced woods, where wrapt in solid shade
She mused away the gaudy hours of noon,
And fed on thoughts unripened by the sun,
Moves forward; and with radiant finger points
To yon blue concave swelled by breath divine,
25   Where, one by one, the living eyes of heaven
Awake, quick kindling o'er the face of ether
One boundless blaze; ten thousand trembling fires,
And dancing lustres, where the unsteady eye,
Restless and dazzled, wanders unconfined
30   O'er all this field of glories; spacious field,
And worthy of the Master: he, whose hand
With hieroglyphics elder than the Nile
Inscribed the mystic tablet, hung on high
To public gaze, and said, "Adore, O man!
35   The finger of thy God." From what pure wells
Of milky light, what soft o'erflowing urn,
Are all these lamps so fill'd? these friendly lamps,
For ever streaming o'er the azure deep
To point our path, and light us to our home.
40   How soft they slide along their lucid spheres!
And silent as the foot of Time, fulfill
Their destined courses: Nature's self is hushed,
And, but a scattered leaf, which rustles through
The thick-wove foliage, not a sound is heard
45   To break the midnight air; though the raised ear,
Intensely listening, drinks in every breath.
How deep the silence, yet how loud the praise!
But are they silent all? or is there not
A tongue in every star, that talks with man,
50   And woos him to be wise? nor woos in vain:
This dead of midnight is the noon of thought,
And Wisdom mounts her zenith with the stars.
At this still hour the self-collected soul
Turns inward, and beholds a stranger there
55   Of high descent, and more than mortal rank;
An embryo God; a spark of fire divine,
Which must burn on for ages, when the sun,—
Fair transitory creature of a day!—

2. Softened, made meek.

Has closed his golden eye, and wrapt in shades
60 Forgets his wonted journey through the east.

Ye citadels of light, and seats of Gods!
Perhaps my future home, from whence the soul,
Revolving periods past, may oft look back
With recollected tenderness on all
65 The various busy scenes she left below,
Its deep-laid projects and its strange events,
As on some fond and doting tale that soothed
Her infant hours—O be it lawful now
To tread the hallowed circle of your courts,
70 And with mute wonder and delighted awe
Approach your burning confines. Seized in thought,
On Fancy's wild and roving wing I sail,
From the green borders of the peopled Earth,
And the pale Moon, her duteous fair attendant;
75 From solitary Mars; from the vast orb
Of Jupiter, whose huge gigantic bulk
Dances in ether like the lightest leaf;
To the dim verge, the suburbs of the system,
Where cheerless Saturn 'midst his watery moons
80 Girt with a lucid zone, in gloomy pomp,
Sits like an exiled monarch: fearless thence
I launch into the trackless deeps of space,
Where, burning round, ten thousand suns appear,
Of elder beam, which ask no leave to shine
85 Of our terrestrial star, nor borrow light
From the proud regent of our scanty day;
Sons of the morning, first-born of creation,
And only less than Him who marks their track,
And guides their fiery wheels. Here must I stop,
90 Or is there aught beyond? What hand unseen
Impels me onward through the glowing orbs
Of habitable nature, far remote,
To the dread confines of eternal night,
To solitudes of vast unpeopled space,
95 The deserts of creation, wide and wild;
Where embryo systems and unkindled suns
Sleep in the womb of chaos? fancy droops,
And thought astonished stops her bold career.
But O thou mighty mind! whose powerful word
100 Said, thus let all things be, and thus they were,
Where shall I seek thy presence? how unblamed
Invoke thy dread perfection?
Have the broad eyelids of the morn beheld thee?
Or does the beamy shoulder of Orion
105 Support thy throne? O look with pity down
On erring, guilty man! not in thy names
Of terror clad; not with those thunders armed
That conscious Sinai felt, when fear appalled

The scattered tribes;[3]—thou hast a gentler voice,
110 That whispers comfort to the swelling heart,
Abashed, yet longing to behold her Maker.

But now my soul, unused to stretch her powers
In flight so daring, drops her weary wing,
And seeks again the known accustomed spot,
115 Drest up with sun, and shade, and lawns, and streams,
A mansion fair, and spacious for its guest,
And full replete with wonders. Let me here,
Content and grateful, wait the appointed time,
And ripen for the skies: the hour will come
120 When all these splendours bursting on my sight
Shall stand unveiled, and to my ravished sense
Unlock the glories of the world unknown.

1773

The Rights of Woman[1]

Yes, injured Woman! rise, assert thy right!
Woman! too long degraded, scorned, opprest;
O born to rule in partial Law's despite,
Resume thy native empire o'er the breast!

5   Go forth arrayed in panoply divine;
That angel pureness which admits no stain;
Go, bid proud Man his boasted rule resign,
And kiss the golden sceptre of thy reign.

Go, gird thyself with grace; collect thy store
10   Of bright artillery glancing from afar;
Soft melting tones thy thundering cannon's roar,
Blushes and fears thy magazine of war.

Thy rights are empire: urge no meaner claim,—
Felt, not defined, and if debated, lost;
15   Like sacred mysteries, which withheld from fame,
Shunning discussion, are revered the most.

Try all that wit and art suggest to bend
Of thy imperial foe the stubborn knee;
Make treacherous Man thy subject, not thy friend;
20   Thou mayst command, but never canst be free.

Awe the licentious, and restrain the rude;
Soften the sullen, clear the cloudy brow:

3. When God came down to deliver the Ten Commandments "there were thunders and lightnings . . . so that all the people . . . trembled" (Exodus 19.16).

1. A response—seemingly favorable until the last two stanzas—to Mary Wollstonecraft's *A Vindication of the Rights of Woman* (1792).

Be, more than princes' gifts, thy favours sued;—
She hazards all, who will the least allow.

25 But hope not, courted idol of mankind,
On this proud eminence secure to stay;
Subduing and subdued, thou soon shalt find
Thy coldness soften, and thy pride give way.

Then, then, abandon each ambitious thought,
30 Conquest or rule thy heart shall feebly move,
In Nature's school, by her soft maxims taught,
That separate rights are lost in mutual love.

ca. 1792–95   1825

To a Little Invisible Being
Who Is Expected Soon to Become Visible

Germ of new life, whose powers expanding slow
For many a moon their full perfection wait,—
Haste, precious pledge of happy love, to go
Auspicious borne through life's mysterious gate.

5 What powers lie folded in thy curious frame,—
Senses from objects locked, and mind from thought!
How little canst thou guess thy lofty claim
To grasp at all the worlds the Almighty wrought!

And see, the genial season's warmth to share,
10 Fresh younglings shoot, and opening roses glow!
Swarms of new life exulting fill the air,—
Haste, infant bud of being, haste to blow!°   *bloom*

For thee the nurse prepares her lulling songs,
The eager matrons count the lingering day;
15 But far the most thy anxious parent longs
On thy soft cheek a mother's kiss to lay.

She only asks to lay her burden down,
That her glad arms that burden may resume;
And nature's sharpest pangs her wishes crown,
20 That free thee living from thy living tomb.

She longs to fold to her maternal breast
Part of herself, yet to herself unknown;
To see and to salute the stranger guest,
Fed with her life through many a tedious moon.

25 Come, reap thy rich inheritance of love!
Bask in the fondness of a Mother's eye!

Nor wit nor eloquence her heart shall move
Like the first accents of thy feeble cry.

Haste, little captive, burst thy prison doors!
30   Launch on the living world, and spring to light!
Nature for thee displays her various stores,
Opens her thousand inlets of delight.

If charmed verse or muttered prayers had power,
With favouring spells to speed thee on thy way,
35   Anxious I'd bid my beads° each passing hour,   *offer a prayer*
Till thy wished smile thy mother's pangs o'erpay.° *more than compensate*

ca. 1795?   1825

Washing-Day

> . . . *and their voice,*
> *Turning again towards childish treble, pipes*
> *And whistles in its sound.*[1]

The Muses are turned gossips; they have lost
The buskined° step, and clear high-sounding phrase, *tragic, elevated*
Language of gods, Come then, domestic Muse,
In slipshod measure loosely prattling on
5   Of farm or orchard, pleasant curds and cream,
Or drowning flies, or shoe lost in the mire
By little whimpering boy, with rueful face;
Come, Muse; and sing the dreaded Washing-Day.
Ye who beneath the yoke of wedlock bend,
10 With bowed soul, full well ye ken the day
Which week, smooth sliding after week, brings on
Too soon;—for to that day nor peace belongs
Nor comfort;—ere the first gray streak of dawn,
The red-armed washers come and chase repose.
15 Nor pleasant smile, nor quaint device of mirth,
E'er visited that day: the very cat,
From the wet kitchen scared and reeking hearth,
Visits the parlour,—an unwonted guest.
The silent breakfast-meal is soon dispatched;
20 Uninterrupted, save by anxious looks
Cast at the lowering sky, if sky should lower.
From that last evil, O preserve us, heavens!
For should the skies pour down, adieu to all
Remains of quiet: then expect to hear
25 Of sad disasters,—dirt and gravel stains
Hard to efface, and loaded lines at once
Snapped short,—and linen-horse° by dog thrown down, *drying rack*
And all the petty miseries of life.

---

1. Loosely quoted from Shakespeare's *As You Like It* 2.7.160–62.

Saints have been calm while stretched upon the rack,
30 And Guatimozin[2] smiled on burning coals;
But never yet did housewife notable
Greet with a smile a rainy washing-day.
—But grant the welkin° fair, require not thou   *sky*
Who call'st thyself perchance the master there,
35 Or study swept or nicely dusted coat,
Or usual 'tendance;—ask not, indiscreet,
Thy stockings mended, though the yawning rents
Gape wide as Erebus;° nor hope to find   *the underworld*
Some snug recess impervious: shouldst thou try
40 The 'customed garden walks, shine eye shall rue
The budding fragrance of thy tender shrubs,
Myrtle or rose, all crushed beneath the weight
Of coarse checked apron,—with impatient hand
Twitched off when showers impend: or crossing lines
45 Shall mar thy musings, as the wet cold sheet
Flaps in thy face abrupt. Woe to the friend
Whose evil stars have urged him forth to claim
On such a day the hospitable rites!
Looks, blank at best, and stinted courtesy,
50 Shall he receive. Vainly he feeds his hopes
With dinner of roast chicken, savoury pie,
Or tart or pudding:—pudding he nor tart
That day shall eat; nor, though the husband try,
Mending what can't be helped, to kindle mirth
55 From cheer deficient, shall his consort's brow
Clear up propitious:—the unlucky guest
In silence dines, and early slinks away.
I well remember, when a child, the awe
This day struck into me; for then the maids,
60 I scarce knew why, looked cross, and drove me from them:
Nor soft caress could I obtain, nor hope
Usual indulgencies; jelly or creams,
Relic of costly suppers, and set by
For me, their petted one; or buttered toast,
65 When butter was forbid; or thrilling tale
Of ghost or witch, or murder—so I went
And sheltered me beside the parlour fire:
There my dear grandmother, eldest of forms,
Tended the little ones, and watched from harm,
70 Anxiously fond, though oft her spectacles
With elfin cunning hid, and oft the pins
Drawn from her ravelled stocking, might have soured
One less indulgent.—
At intervals my mother's voice was heard,
75 Urging dispatch: briskly the work went on,
All hands employed to wash, to rinse, to wring,

2. The last of the Aztec emperors (Cuanhtémoc, d. 1525), who was tortured and executed by the Spanish conquistadors.

To fold, and starch, and clap,° and iron, and plait.   *flatten*
Then would I sit me down, and ponder much
Why washings were. Sometimes through hollow bowl
80   Of pipe amused we blew, and sent aloft
The floating bubbles; little dreaming then
To see, Mongolfier,[3] thy silken ball
Ride buoyant through the clouds—so near approach
The sports of children and the toils of men.
85   Earth, air, and sky, and ocean, hath its bubbles,[4]
And verse is one of them—this most of all.

1797

Life

Animula, vagula, blandula.[1]

Life! I know not what thou art,
But know that thou and I must part;
And when, or how, or where we met,
I own to me's a secret yet.
5   But this I know, when thou art fled,
Where'er they lay these limbs, this head,
No clod so valueless shall be,
As all that then remains of me.
O whither, whither dost thou fly,
10   Where bend unseen thy trackless course,
And in this strange divorce,
Ah tell where I must seek this compound I?

To the vast ocean of empyreal flame,
From whence thy essence came,
15   Dost thou thy flight pursue, when freed
From matter's base encumbering weed?
Or dost thou, hid from sight,
Wait, like some spell-bound knight,
Through blank oblivious years th' appointed hour,
20   To break thy trance and reassume thy power?
Yet canst thou without thought or feeling be?
O say what art thou, when no more thou 'rt thee?

Life! we've been long together,
Through pleasant and through cloudy weather;
25   'Tis hard to part when friends are dear;
Perhaps 't will cost a sigh, a tear;
Then steal away, give little warning,

3. Brothers Joseph-Michel and Jacques-Étienne Mongolfier successfully launched the first hot-air balloon, at Annonay, France, in 1783.
4. Cf. *Macbeth* 1.3.77: "The earth hath bubbles, as the water has."

1. From Aelius Spartianus's *Life of Hadrian* 25— the first line of a poem supposedly composed by the emperor Hadrian on his deathbed: "Charming little soul, hastening away."

Choose thine own time;
Say not Good night, but in some brighter clime
30   Bid me Good morning.

1825

CHARLOTTE SMITH
1749–1806

The melancholy of Charlotte Smith's *Elegiac Sonnets* was no mere literary posture. Smith married at fourteen and bore a dozen children (three of whom died in infancy or childhood) before permanently separating from her husband because of his abusive temper, infidelities, and financial irresponsibility. She began writing to make money when her husband was imprisoned for debt in 1783. Her first book, which came out in 1784 with the bold title *Elegiac Sonnets, and Other Essays by Charlotte Smith of Bignor Park, in Sussex*, went through nine expanding editions in the following sixteen years.

Beginning in the later 1780s, Smith had considerable success as a novelist, rapidly producing *Emmeline* (four volumes, 1788), *Ethelinde* (five volumes, 1789), *Celestina* (four volumes, 1791), *Desmond* (three volumes, 1792), *The Old Manor House* (four volumes, 1793), and several others. She also wrote children's stories, sketches, and several long poems. *The Emigrants* (1793), an eight-hundred-line descriptive-reflective work on the plight of French exiles in England during the early years of the French Revolution, has been called by Smith's modern editor, Stuart Curran, "the finest piece of extended blank verse in English between Cowper's *The Task* (1785) and Wordsworth's unpublished initial version of *The Prelude* (1799)."

The sonnet as a form, after its great flourishing in the Renaissance in the hands of Sidney, Spenser, Shakespeare, Donne, and Milton, dropped out of fashion in the eighteenth century. It was, Samuel Johnson declared in his *Dictionary* (1755), "not very suitable to the English language, and has not been used by any man of eminence since Milton." Its revival toward the end of that century—by Coleridge in the 1790s; Wordsworth (who wrote some five hundred sonnets beginning in 1802); and in the next generation, Shelley and Keats—was largely the result of Smith's influence. Coleridge noted in the introduction to his privately printed "sheet of sonnets" in 1796 that "Charlotte Smith and [William Lisle] Bowles are they who first made the Sonnet popular among the present English"; but Bowles's *Fourteen Sonnets* of 1789, imitating those that Smith first published five years earlier (which by 1789 had reached a fifth edition), rode on a wave of popularity of the form that she had already established.

Wordsworth, who read her sonnets when he was a student at Cambridge, observed in 1833 that Smith "wrote . . . with true feeling for rural nature, at a time when nature was not much regarded by English Poets." Coleridge in his 1796 introductory essay on the sonnet, using Smith as a principal example, remarked that "those Sonnets appear to me the most exquisite, in which moral Sentiments, Affections, or Feelings, are deduced from, and associated with, the scenery of Nature." Subsequently, of course, the connecting of feelings and nature became a central theme and strategy in Romantic poetry. Under the influence of Smith, Coleridge himself quickly progressed from the sonnet to the conversation poem, beginning with *The Eolian Harp*, and in turn influenced Wordsworth and subsequent writers of odes and kindred types of descriptive-meditative verse. Thus Smith helped to originate one of the most distinctive genres of English literature, what has been called "the greater Romantic lyric."

FROM ELEGIAC SONNETS

Written at the Close of Spring

The garlands fade that Spring so lately wove,
   Each simple flower, which she had nursed in dew,
Anemonies, that spangled every grove,
   The primrose wan, and hare-bell mildly blue.
5 No more shall violets linger in the dell,
   Or purple orchis variegate the plain,
Till Spring again shall call forth every bell,
   And dress with humid hands her wreaths again.—
Ah! poor humanity! so frail, so fair,
10 Are the fond visions of thy early day,
Till tyrant passion, and corrosive care,
   Bid all thy fairy colors fade away!
Another May new buds and flowers shall bring;
Ah! why has happiness—no second Spring?

                           1784

To Sleep

Come, balmy Sleep! tired nature's soft resort!
   On these sad temples all thy poppies shed;
And bid gay dreams, from Morpheus' airy court,
   Float in light vision round my aching head!
5 Secure of all thy blessings, partial Power!
   On his hard bed the peasant throws him down;
And the poor sea boy, in the rudest hour,
   Enjoys thee more than he who wears a crown.[1]
Clasp'd in her faithful shepherd's guardian arms,
10 Well may the village girl sweet slumbers prove
And they, O gentle Sleep! still taste thy charms,
   Who wake to labor, liberty, and love.
But still thy opiate aid dost thou deny
To calm the anxious breast; to close the streaming eye.

                           1784

To Night

I love thee, mournful, sober-suited Night!
   When the faint moon, yet lingering in her wane,

---

1. As Smith herself noted, lines 7 and 8 allude to King Henry's apostrophe to sleep in 2 *Henry IV* 3.1.5–31 (cf. Keats's *Sonnet to Sleep*, p. 847).

And veil'd in clouds, with pale uncertain light
Hangs o'er the waters of the restless main.
5   In deep depression sunk, the enfeebled mind
Will to the deaf cold elements complain,
And tell the embosom'd grief, however vain,
To sullen surges and the viewless wind.
Though no repose on thy dark breast I find,
10   I still enjoy thee—cheerless as thou art;
For in thy quiet gloom the exhausted heart
Is calm, though wretched; hopeless, yet resign'd.
While to the winds and waves its sorrows given,
May reach—though lost on earth—the ear of Heaven!

1788

Written in the Church-Yard at Middleton in Sussex[1]

Press'd by the Moon, mute arbitress of tides,
While the loud equinox its power combines,
The sea no more its swelling surge confines,
But o'er the shrinking land sublimely rides.
5   The wild blast, rising from the Western cave,
Drives the huge billows from their heaving bed;
Tears from their grassy tombs the village dead,
And breaks the silent sabbath of the grave!
With shells and sea-weed mingled, on the shore
10   Lo! their bones whiten in the frequent wave;
But vain to them the winds and waters rave;
They hear the warring elements no more:
While I am doom'd—by life's long storm opprest,
To gaze with envy on their gloomy rest.

1789

On Being Cautioned against Walking on an Headland Overlooking the Sea, Because It Was Frequented by a Lunatic

Is there a solitary wretch who hies
To the tall cliff, with starting pace or slow,
And, measuring, views with wild and hollow eyes
Its distance from the waves that chide below;
5   Who, as the sea-born gale with frequent sighs
Chills his cold bed upon the mountain turf,
With hoarse, half-utter'd lamentation, lies

1. Middleton is a village on the margin of the sea, in Sussex, containing only two or three houses. There were formerly several acres of ground between its small church and the sea, which now, by its continual encroachments, approaches within a few feet of this half ruined and humble edifice. The wall, which once surrounded the churchyard, is entirely swept away, many of the graves broken up, and the remains of bodies interred washed into the sea: whence human bones are found among the sand and shingles on the shore [Smith's note].

Murmuring responses to the dashing surf?
In moody sadness, on the giddy brink,
10   I see him more with envy than with fear;
He has no *nice felicities* that shrink
From giant horrors; wildly wandering here,
He seems (uncursed with reason) not to know
The depth or the duration of his woe.

1797

The Sea View[1]

The upland shepherd, as reclined he lies
On the soft turf that clothes the mountain brow,
Marks the bright sea-line mingling with the skies;
Or from his course celestial, sinking slow,
5   The summer-sun in purple radiance low,
Blaze on the western waters; the wide scene
Magnificent, and tranquil, seems to spread
Even o'er the rustic's breast a joy serene,
When, like dark plague-spots by the Demons shed,
10   Charged deep with death, upon the waves, far seen,
Move the war-freighted ships; and fierce and red,
Flash their destructive fire.—The mangled dead
And dying victims then pollute the flood.
Ah! thus man spoils Heaven's glorious works with blood!

1797

1. Suggested by the recollection of having seen, some years since, on a beautiful evening of Summer, an engagement between two armed ships, from the high down called the Beacon Hill, near Brighthelmstone [Smith's note, referring to a location near Brighton].

WILLIAM BLAKE
1757–1827

What William Blake called his "Spiritual Life" was as varied, free, and dramatic as his "Corporeal Life" was simple, limited, and unadventurous. His father was a London haberdasher. His only formal education was in art: at the age of ten he entered a drawing school and later studied for a time at the school of the Royal Academy of Arts. At fourteen he entered an apprenticeship for seven years to a well-known engraver, James Basire, and began reading widely in his free time and trying his hand at poetry. At twenty-four he married Catherine Boucher, daughter of a market gardener. She was then illiterate, but Blake taught her to read and to help him in his engraving and printing. In the early and somewhat sentimentalized biographies, Catherine is represented as an ideal wife for an unorthodox and impecunious genius. Blake, however, must have been a trying domestic partner, and his vehement attacks on the torment caused by a possessive, jealous female will, which reached their height in 1793 and remained prominent in his writings for another decade, probably reflect a troubled period at home. The couple was childless.

The Blakes for a time enjoyed a moderate prosperity while Blake gave drawing lessons, illustrated books, and engraved designs made by other artists. When the demand for his work slackened, Blake in 1800 moved to a cottage at Felpham, on the Sussex seacoast, to take advantage of the patronage of the wealthy poetaster, biographer, and amateur of the arts William Hayley, who with the best of narrow intentions tried to transform Blake into a conventional artist and breadwinner. But the caged eagle soon rebelled. Hayley, Blake wrote, "is the Enemy of my Spiritual Life while he pretends to be the Friend of my Corporeal."

At Felpham in 1803 occurred an event that left a permanent mark on Blake's mind and art—an altercation with one John Schofield, a private in the Royal Dragoons. Blake ordered the soldier out of his garden and, when Schofield replied with threats and curses against Blake and his wife, pushed him the fifty yards to the inn where he was quartered. Schofield brought charges that Blake had uttered seditious statements about king and country. Since England was at war with France, sedition was a hanging offense. Blake was acquitted—an event, according to a newspaper account, "which so gratified the auditory that the court was . . . thrown into an uproar by their noisy exultations." Nevertheless Schofield, his fellow soldier Cock, and other participants in the trial haunted Blake's imagination and were enlarged to demonic characters who play a sinister role in *Jerusalem*. The event exacerbated Blake's sense that ominous forces were at work in the contemporary world and led him to complicate the symbolic and allusive style by which he veiled the radical religious, moral, and political opinions that he expressed in his poems.

After three years at Felpham, Blake moved back to London, determined to follow his "Divine Vision," though it meant a life of isolation, misunderstanding, and poverty. When his single bid for public recognition, a one-man show put on in 1809, proved a total failure, Blake passed into almost complete obscurity. Only when he was in his sixties did he finally attract a small but devoted group of young painters who served as an audience for his work and his talk. Blake's old age was serene and self-confident, largely free from the bursts of irascibility with which he had earlier responded to what he viewed as the shallowness and blindness of the English public. He died in his seventieth year.

Blake's first book of poems, *Poetical Sketches*, which he had printed when he was twenty-six years old, showed his dissatisfaction with the reigning poetic tradition and his restless quest for new forms and techniques. For lyric models he turned back to the Elizabethan and early seventeenth-century poets, to the Ossianic poems, and to Collins, Thomas Chatterton, and other eighteenth-century writers outside the tradition of Pope; he also experimented with partial rhymes and novel rhythms and employed bold figures of speech that at times approximate symbols. In 1788 he began to experiment with relief etching, a method that he called "illuminated printing" and used to produce most of his books of poems. Working directly on a copper plate with pens, brushes, and an acid-resistant medium, he wrote the text in reverse (so that it would print in the normal order) and also drew the illustration; he then etched the plate in acid to eat away the untreated copper and leave the design standing in relief. The pages printed from such plates were colored by hand in water colors and stitched together to make up a volume. This process was laborious and time-consuming, and Blake printed very few copies of his books; for example, of *Songs of Innocence and of Experience* only twenty-eight copies (some of them incomplete) are known to exist; of *The Book of Thel*, sixteen; of *The Marriage of Heaven and Hell*, nine; and of *Jerusalem*, five.

It must be remembered that to read a Blake poem in a printed text without the illustrations is to see only an abstraction from an integral and mutually enlightening combination of words and design. In this mode of relief etching, he published *Songs of Innocence* (1789), then added supplementary poems and printed *Songs of Inno-*

cence and of Experience in 1794. The two groups of poems represent the world as it is envisioned by what he calls "two contrary states of the human soul." In the best of the songs of experience, such as *The Tyger* and *London*, Blake achieved his mature lyric technique of compressed metaphor and symbol that explode into a multiplicity of references.

Gradually Blake's thinking about human history and his experience of life and suffering articulated themselves in the "Giant Forms" and their actions, which came to constitute a complete mythology. As Blake's mythical character Los said, speaking for all imaginative artists, "I must Create a System or be enslaved by another Man's." This coherent but constantly altering and enlarging system composed the subject matter first of Blake's "minor prophecies," completed by 1795, and then of the major prophetic books on which he continued working until about 1820: *The Four Zoas, Milton,* and *Jerusalem.*

In his sixties Blake gave up poetry to devote himself to pictorial art. In the course of his life he produced hundreds of paintings and engravings, many of them illustrations for the work of other poets, including a representation of Chaucer's Canterbury pilgrims, a superb set of designs for the Book of Job, and a series of illustrations of Dante, on which he was still hard at work when he died. At the time of his death Blake was little known as an artist and almost entirely unknown as a poet. In the mid-nineteenth century he acquired a group of admirers among the Pre-Raphaelites, who regarded him as a precursor. Since the mid-1920s, Blake has finally come into his own, both in poetry and in painting, as one of the most dedicated, intellectually challenging, and astonishingly original of artists. His marked influence ranges from William Butler Yeats, who edited Blake's writings and modeled his own system of mythology on Blake's, to Allen Ginsberg and other Beat and counterculture writers, beginning in the 1950s, who admired Blake's stress on a visionary poetry and his rebellious stance against the conventional life and pieties of his day.

The explication of Blake's cryptic prophetic books has been the preoccupation of many scholars. Blake wrote them in the persona, or "voice," of "the Bard! / Who Present, Past, & Future sees"—that is, as a British poet who follows Spenser, and especially Milton, in a lineage going back to the prophets of the Bible. "The Nature of my Work," he said, "is Visionary or Imaginative." What Blake meant by the key terms *vision* and *imagination,* however, is often misinterpreted by taking literally what he, speaking the traditional language of his great predecessors, intended in a figurative sense. "That which can be made Explicit to the Idiot," Blake declared, "is not worth my care." Blake was a born ironist who enjoyed mystifying his well-meaning but literal-minded friends and who took a defiant pleasure in shocking the dull and complacent "angels" of his day by being deliberately outrageous in representing his work and opinions.

Blake declared that "all he knew was in the Bible" and that "The Old & New Testaments are the Great Code of Art." This is an exaggeration of the truth that all his prophetic writings deal, in various formulations, with some aspects of the overall biblical plot of the creation and the Fall, the history of the generations of humanity in the fallen world, redemption, and the promise of a recovery of Eden and of a New Jerusalem. These events, however, Blake interprets in what he calls "the spiritual sense." For such a procedure he had considerable precedent, not in the neoplatonic and occult thinkers with whom some modern commentators align him, but in the "spiritual" interpreters of the Bible among the radical Protestant sects in seventeenth- and eighteenth-century England. In *The French Revolution, America: A Prophecy, Europe: A Prophecy,* and the trenchant prophetic satire *The Marriage of Heaven and Hell*—all of which Blake wrote in the early 1790s while he was an ardent supporter of the French Revolution—he, like Wordsworth, Coleridge, Southey, and a number of radical English theologians, represented the contemporary Revolution as the purifying violence that, according to biblical prophecy, portended the imminent redemption of humanity and the world. In Blake's later poems, Orc, the fiery spirit of violent revolution, gives way as a central personage to Los, the type of the visionary imagination in the fallen world. Even in his early writings, however, Blake had represented political and social revolution as correlative with a radical change within the mind and imagination of the individual, so that the replacement of Orc by Los does not indicate Blake's recantation of former beliefs, but a shift of emphasis from an apocalypse by revolution to an apocalypse by imagination.

BLAKE'S MATURE MYTH

Blake's first attempt to articulate his full myth of humanity's present, past, and future was *The Four Zoas*, begun in 1796 or 1797. A passage from the opening statement of its theme exemplifies the long verse line (what Blake called "the march of long resounding strong heroic verse") in which he wrote his Prophetic Books and will serve also to outline the visualizable imaginative form in which Blake's thought embodied itself:

> Four Mighty Ones are in every Man; a Perfect Unity
> Cannot Exist, but from the Universal Brotherhood of Eden,
> The Universal Man. To Whom be Glory Evermore, Amen. . . .
> Los was the fourth immortal starry one, & in the Earth
> Of a bright Universe Empery attended day & night
> Days & nights of revolving joy, Urthona was his name
> In Eden; in the Auricular Nerves of Human life
> Which is the Earth of Eden, he his Emanations propagated. . . .
>   Daughter of Beulah, Sing
> His fall into Division & his Resurrection to Unity.

Blake's mythical premise, or starting point, is not a transcendent God but the "Universal Man" who is himself God and who incorporates the cosmos as well. (Blake elsewhere describes this founding image as "the Human Form Divine" and names him "Albion.") The fall, in this myth, is not the fall of humanity away from God but a falling apart of primal people, a "fall into Division." In this event the original sin is what Blake calls "Selfhood," the attempt of an isolated part to be self-sufficient. The breakup of the all-inclusive Universal Man in Eden into exiled parts, it is evident, serves to identify the Fall with the creation—the creation not only of man and of nature as we ordinarily know them but also of a separate sky god who is alien from humanity. Universal Man divides first into the "Four Mighty Ones" who are the Zoas, or chief powers and component aspects of humanity, and these in turn divide sexually into male Spectres and female Emanations. (Thus in the quoted passage the Zoa known in the unfallen state of Eden as Urthona, the imaginative power, separates into the form of Los in the fallen world.) In addition to Eden there are three successively lower "states" of being in the fallen world, which Blake calls Beulah (a pastoral condition of easy and relaxed innocence, without clash of "contraries"), Generation (the realm of common human experience, suffering, and conflicting contraries), and Ulro (Blake's hell, the lowest state, or limit, of bleak rationality, tyranny, static negation, and isolated Selfhood). The fallen world moves through the cycles of its history, successively approaching and falling away from redemption, until, by the agency of the Redeemer (who is equated with the human imagination and is most potently operative in the prophetic poet), it will culminate in an apocalypse. In terms of his controlling image of the Universal Man, Blake describes this apocalypse as a return to the original, undivided condition, "his Resurrection to Unity."

What is confusing to many readers is that Blake alternates this representation of the Fall (as a fragmentation of the one Primal Man into separate parts) with a different kind of representation, in terms of two sharply opposed ways of seeing the universe. In this latter mode, the Fall is a catastrophic change from imaginative insight (which sees the cosmos as unified and humanized) to sight by the physical eye (which sees the cosmos as a multitude of isolated individuals in an inhuman and alien nature).

In terms of this distinction, the apocalypse toward which Blake as imaginative artist strives unceasingly will enable men and women once again to envision all beings as participant in the individual life that he calls "the Universal Brotherhood of Eden"— that is, a humanized world in which all individuals, in familial union, can feel at home.

Although Blake did not know it, he shared with a number of contemporary German philosophers the point of view—it has in our own time become the prevailing point of view—that our fall (that is, the malaise of modern culture) is essentially a mode of psychic disintegration and of resultant alienation from oneself, one's world, and one's fellow human beings, and that our hope of recovery lies in a process of reintegration. As a poet, however, Blake does not present this view in abstract conceptual terms, but embodies it in picturable agents acting out an epic plot.

The text for Blake's writings is that of *The Complete Poetry and Prose of William Blake*, edited by David V. Erdman and Harold Bloom (revised edition, Berkeley, 1982). Blake's erratic spelling and punctuation have been altered when the original form might mislead the reader. The editors are grateful for the expert advice of Joseph Viscomi and Robert Essick in editing the selections from Blake.

FROM POETICAL SKETCHES[1]

To Spring[2]

O thou, with dewy locks, who lookest down
Thro' the clear windows of the morning; turn
Thine angel eyes upon our western isle,
Which in full choir hails thy approach, O Spring!

5 The hills tell each other, and the list'ning
Vallies hear; all our longing eyes are turned
Up to thy bright pavillions: issue forth,
And let thy holy feet visit our clime.

Come o'er the eastern hills, and let our winds
10 Kiss thy perfumed garments; let us taste
Thy morn and evening breath; scatter thy pearls
Upon our love-sick land that mourns for thee.

O deck her forth with thy fair fingers; pour
Thy soft kisses on her bosom; and put
15 Thy golden crown upon her languish'd head,
Whose modest tresses were bound up for thee!

1783

1. *Poetical Sketches*, Blake's only volume of poems to be set in type, went to press in 1783 but was never put on sale. A preface written by an anonymous friend apologized for the poems on the grounds that they had been composed between the ages of twelve and twenty. Although, like the work of other youthful poets, they echo earlier writers (including Spenser, Shakespeare, and Milton),

many of them are radical experiments in metaphor, meter, and rhyme.
2. *Poetical Sketches* includes four poems, each in the form of an invocation to one of the four seasons. *To Spring* is thronged with echoes from the poetry of the Old Testament as well as from Milton.

To Autumn

O Autumn, laden with fruit, and stained
With the blood of the grape, pass not, but sit
Beneath my shady roof; there thou may'st rest,
And tune thy jolly voice to my fresh pipe;
5   And all the daughters of the year shall dance!
Sing now the lusty song of fruits and flowers.

"The narrow bud opens her beauties to
The sun, and love runs in her thrilling veins;
Blossoms hang round the brows of morning, and
10   Flourish down the bright cheek of modest eve,
Till clust'ring Summer breaks forth into singing,
And feather'd clouds strew flowers round her head.

"The spirits of the air live on the smells
Of fruit; and joy, with pinions light, roves round
15   The gardens, or sits singing in the trees."
Thus sang the jolly Autumn as he sat;
Then rose, girded himself, and o'er the bleak
Hills fled from our sight; but left his golden load.

1783

To the Evening Star

Thou fair-hair'd angel of the evening,
Now, while the sun rests on the mountains, light
Thy bright torch of love;[1] thy radiant crown
Put on, and smile upon our evening bed!
5   Smile on our loves; and, while thou drawest the
Blue curtains of the sky, scatter thy silver dew
On every flower that shuts its sweet eyes
In timely sleep. Let thy west wind sleep on
The lake; speak silence with thy glimmering eyes,
10   And wash the dusk with silver. Soon, full soon,
Dost thou withdraw; then the wolf rages wide,
And the lion glares thro' the dun forest:
The fleeces of our flocks are cover'd with
Thy sacred dew: protect them with thine influence.[2]

1783

1. The evening star is Venus, goddess of love.
2. In astrology, the technical term for the occult power of stars over humans.

All Religions Are One[1]

The Voice of one crying in the Wilderness[2]

The Argument. As the true method of knowledge is experiment the true faculty of knowing must be the faculty which experiences. This faculty I treat of.

PRINCIPLE 1st. That the Poetic Genius is the true Man, and that the body or outward form of Man is derived from the Poetic Genius. Likewise that the forms of all things are derived from their Genius, which by the Ancients was call'd an Angel & Spirit & Demon.

PRINCIPLE 2d. As all men are alike in outward form, So (and with the same infinite variety) all are alike in the Poetic Genius.

PRINCIPLE 3d. No man can think write or speak from his heart, but he must intend truth. Thus all sects of Philosophy are from the Poetic Genius, adapted to the weaknesses of every individual.

PRINCIPLE 4. As none by travelling over known lands can find out the unknown, So from already acquired knowledge Man could not acquire more. Therefore an universal Poetic Genius exists.

PRINCIPLE 5. The Religions of all Nations are derived from each Nation's different reception of the Poetic Genius, which is every where call'd the Spirit of Prophecy.

PRINCIPLE 6. The Jewish & Christian Testaments are An original derivation from the Poetic Genius. This is necessary from the confined nature of bodily sensation.

PRINCIPLE 7th. As all men are alike (tho' infinitely various), So all Religions & as all similars have one source.

The true Man is the source, he being the Poetic Genius.

1788

There Is No Natural Religion[1]

[a]

The Argument. Man has no notion of moral fitness but from Education. Naturally he is only a natural organ subject to Sense.

I. Man cannot naturally Percieve but through his natural or bodily organs.

II. Man by his reasoning power can only compare & judge of what he has already perciev'd.

---

1. This and the following two selections are early illuminated works, probably etched in 1788. They are directed both against 18th-century Deism or "natural religion" (which bases its religious tenets not on scriptural revelation, but on evidences of God in the natural or "organic" world) and against Christian orthodoxy, whose creed is based on a particular Scripture. In this selection Blake ironically accepts the Deistic view that all particular religions are variants of the one true religion but rejects the Deists' "Argument" that this religion is grounded on reasoning from sense-experience. He attributes the one religion instead to the innate possession by all people of "Poetic Genius"—that is, of a capacity for imaginative vision.

2. Applied in the Gospels (e.g., Matthew 3.3) to John the Baptist, regarded as fulfilling the prophecy in Isaiah 39.3. Blake applies the phrase to himself, as a later prophetic voice in an alien time.

1. In this selection Blake presents his version of English empiricism, which derives all mental content (including the evidences from which, in "natural religion," reason is held to prove the existence of God) from perceptions by the physical senses.

III. From a perception of only 3 senses or 3 elements none could deduce a fourth or fifth.

IV. None could have other than natural or organic thoughts if he had none but organic perceptions.

V. Man's desires are limited by his perceptions; none can desire what he has not perciev'd.

VI. The desires & perceptions of man, untaught by any thing but organs of sense, must be limited to objects of sense.

Conclusion. If it were not for the Poetic or Prophetic character the Philosophic & Experimental would soon be at the ratio of all things, & stand still unable to do other than repeat the same dull round over again.

1788

There Is No Natural Religion[1]

[b]

I. Man's perceptions are not bounded by organs of perception; he percieves more than sense (tho' ever so acute) can discover.

II. Reason, or the ratio[2] of all we have already known, is not the same that it shall be when we know more.

[III lacking]

IV. The bounded is loathed by its possessor. The same dull round even of a universe would soon become a mill with complicated wheels.

V. If the many become the same as the few when possess'd, More! More! is the cry of a mistaken soul. Less than All cannot satisfy Man.

VI. If any could desire what he is incapable of possessing, despair must be his eternal lot.

VII. The desire of Man being Infinite, the possession is Infinite & himself Infinite.

Application. He who sees the Infinite in all things sees God. He who sees the Ratio only sees himself only.

Therefore God becomes as we are, that we may be as he is.

1788

---

1. In this third document Blake presents his assertions (in opposition to those in the preceding tract) that knowledge is not limited to the physical senses, but is as unbounded as the infinite desires of humankind and its godlike capacity for infinite vision.

2. In Latin *ratio* signifies both "reason" and "calculation." Blake applies the term derogatorily to the 18th-century concept of reason as a calculating faculty whose operations are limited to sense-perceptions.

FROM SONGS OF INNOCENCE AND OF EXPERIENCE[1]

SHEWING THE TWO CONTRARY STATES OF THE HUMAN SOUL

FROM SONGS OF INNOCENCE

Introduction

Piping down the valleys wild
Piping songs of pleasant glee
On a cloud I saw a child,
And he laughing said to me,

5   "Pipe a song about a Lamb";
So I piped with merry chear;
"Piper pipe that song again"—
So I piped, he wept to hear.

"Drop thy pipe thy happy pipe
10   Sing thy songs of happy chear";
So I sung the same again
While he wept with joy to hear.

"Piper sit thee down and write
In a book that all may read"—
15   So he vanish'd from my sight.
And I pluck'd a hollow reed,

And I made a rural pen,
And I stain'd the water clear,
And I wrote my happy songs
20   Every child may joy to hear.

1789

The Ecchoing Green

The Sun does arise,
And make happy the skies.
The merry bells ring
To welcome the Spring.

1. *Songs of Innocence* was etched in 1789, and in 1794 was combined with additional poems under the title *Songs of Innocence and of Experience*; this collection was reprinted at various later times with varying arrangements of the poems. In his songs of innocence Blake assumes the stance that he is writing "happy songs / Every child may joy to hear," but they do not all depict an innocent and happy world; many of them incorporate injustice, evil, and suffering. These aspects of the fallen world, however, are represented as they appear to a "state" of the human soul that Blake calls "innocence" and that he expresses in a simple pastoral language, in the tradition of Isaac Watts's widely read *Divine Songs for Children* (1715). The vision of the same world, as it appears to the "contrary" state of the soul that Blake calls "experience," is an ugly and terrifying one of poverty, disease, prostitution, war, and social, institutional, and sexual repression, epitomized in the ghastly representation of modern London. Though each stands as an independent poem, a number of the songs of innocence have a matched counterpart, or "contrary," in the songs of experience. Thus *Infant Joy* is paired with *Infant Sorrow,* and the meek *Lamb* reveals its other aspect of divinity in the flaming, wrathful *Tyger.*

Title page for *Songs of Innocence*
(1789)

5   The sky-lark and thrush,
     The birds of the bush,
     Sing louder around,
     To the bells' chearful sound.
     While our sports shall be seen
10   On the Ecchoing Green.

     Old John with white hair
     Does laugh away care,
     Sitting under the oak,
     Among the old folk.
15   They laugh at our play,
     And soon they all say:
     "Such, such were the joys.
     When we all, girls & boys,
     In our youth-time were seen,
20   On the Ecchoing Green."

     Till the little ones weary
     No more can be merry
     The sun does descend,
     And our sports have an end:
25   Round the laps of their mothers,

Many sisters and brothers,
Like birds in their nest,
Are ready for rest;
And sport no more seen,
30 On the darkening Green.

1789

The Lamb

Little Lamb, who made thee?
Dost thou know who made thee?
Gave thee life & bid thee feed,
By the stream & o'er the mead;
5 Gave thee clothing of delight,
Softest clothing wooly bright;
Gave thee such a tender voice,
Making all the vales rejoice!
Little Lamb who made thee?
10 Dost thou know who made thee?

Little Lamb I'll tell thee,
Little Lamb I'll tell thee!
He is callèd by thy name,
For he calls himself a Lamb;
15 He is meek & he is mild,
He became a little child;
I a child & thou a lamb,
We are callèd by his name.
Little Lamb God bless thee.
20 Little Lamb God bless thee.

1789

The Little Black Boy

My mother bore me in the southern wild,
And I am black, but O! my soul is white;
White as an angel is the English child,
But I am black as if bereav'd of light.

5 My mother taught me underneath a tree,
And sitting down before the heat of day,
She took me on her lap and kissèd me,
And pointing to the east, began to say:

"Look on the rising sun: there God does live
10 And gives his light, and gives his heat away;
And flowers and trees and beasts and men receive
Comfort in morning, joy in the noon day.

"And we are put on earth a little space,
That we may learn to bear the beams of love,
15   And these black bodies and this sun-burnt face
Is but a cloud, and like a shady grove.

"For when our souls have learn'd the heat to bear,
The cloud will vanish; we shall hear his voice,
Saying: 'Come out from the grove, my love & care,
20   And round my golden tent like lambs rejoice.'"

Thus did my mother say, and kissèd me;
And thus I say to little English boy:
When I from black and he from white cloud free,
And round the tent of God like lambs we joy,

25   I'll shade him from the heat till he can bear
To lean in joy upon our father's knee.
And then I'll stand and stroke his silver hair,
And be like him, and he will then love me.

1789

The Chimney Sweeper

When my mother died I was very young,
And my father sold me while yet my tongue
Could scarcely cry " 'weep! 'weep! 'weep! 'weep!"[1]
So your chimneys I sweep & in soot I sleep.

5   There's little Tom Dacre, who cried when his head
That curl'd like a lamb's back, was shav'd, so I said,
"Hush, Tom! never mind it, for when your head's bare,
You know that the soot cannot spoil your white hair."

And so he was quiet, & that very night,
10   As Tom was a-sleeping he had such a sight!
That thousands of sweepers, Dick, Joe, Ned, & Jack,
Were all of them lock'd up in coffins of black;

And by came an Angel who had a bright key,
And he open'd the coffins & set them all free;
15   Then down a green plain, leaping, laughing they run,
And wash in a river and shine in the Sun.

Then naked & white, all their bags left behind,
They rise upon clouds, and sport in the wind.
And the Angel told Tom, if he'd be a good boy,
20   He'd have God for his father & never want joy.

---

1. The child's lisping attempt at the chimney sweeper's street cry, "Sweep! Sweep!"

And so Tom awoke; and we rose in the dark
And got with our bags & our brushes to work.
Tho' the morning was cold, Tom was happy & warm;
So if all do their duty, they need not fear harm.

1789

The Divine Image

To Mercy, Pity, Peace, and Love,
All pray in their distress,
And to these virtues of delight
Return their thankfulness.

5 For Mercy, Pity, Peace, and Love,
Is God, our father dear:
And Mercy, Pity, Peace, and Love,
Is Man, his child and care.

For Mercy has a human heart,
10 Pity, a human face,
And Love, the human form divine,
And Peace, the human dress.

Then every man of every clime,
That prays in his distress,
15 Prays to the human form divine,
Love, Mercy, Pity, Peace.

And all must love the human form,
In heathen, Turk, or Jew.
Where Mercy, Love, & Pity dwell,
20 There God is dwelling too.

1789

Holy Thursday[1]

'Twas on a Holy Thursday, their innocent faces clean,
The children walking two & two, in red & blue & green;
Grey headed beadles[2] walkd before with wands as white as snow,
Till into the high dome of Paul's they like Thames' waters flow.

5 O what a multitude they seemd, these flowers of London town!
Seated in companies they sit with radiance all their own.
The hum of multitudes was there, but multitudes of lambs,
Thousands of little boys & girls raising their innocent hands.

1. In the Anglican Church, the Thursday celebrating the ascension of Jesus (thirty-nine days after Easter). It was the custom on this day to march the poor (frequently orphaned) children from the charity schools of London to a service at St. Paul's Cathedral.
2. Lower church officers, one of whose duties is to keep order.

Now like a mighty wind they raise to heaven the voice of song,
10   Or like harmonious thunderings the seats of heaven among.
Beneath them sit the agèd men, wise guardians of the poor;
Then cherish pity, lest you drive an angel from your door.[3]

ca. 1784   1789

Nurse's Song

When the voices of children are heard on the green
And laughing is heard on the hill,
My heart is at rest within my breast
And everything else is still.

5   "Then come home my children, the sun is gone down
And the dews of night arise;
Come, come, leave off play, and let us away
Till the morning appears in the skies."

"No, no, let us play, for it is yet day
10   And we cannot go to sleep;
Besides, in the sky, the little birds fly
And the hills are all coverd with sheep."

"Well, well, go & play till the light fades away
And then go home to bed."
15   The little ones leaped & shouted & laugh'd
And all the hills ecchoèd.

ca. 1784   1789

Infant Joy

"I have no name,
I am but two days old."
What shall I call thee?
"I happy am,
5   Joy is my name."
Sweet joy befall thee!

Pretty joy!
Sweet joy but two days old,
Sweet joy I call thee;
10   Thou dost smile,
I sing the while—
Sweet joy befall thee.

                                                                 1789

---

3. Cf. Hebrews 13.2: "Be not forgetful to entertain strangers: for thereby some have entertained angels unawares."

FROM SONGS OF EXPERIENCE

Introduction

Hear the voice of the Bard!
Who Present, Past, & Future sees;
Whose ears have heard
The Holy Word
5   That walk'd among the ancient trees;[1]

Calling the lapsèd Soul[2]
And weeping in the evening dew,
That might controll[3]
The starry pole,
10 And fallen, fallen light renew!

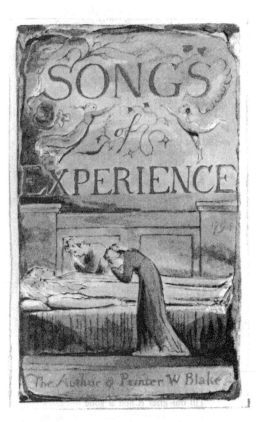

Separate title page for *Songs of Experience* (1794)

1. Genesis 3.8: "And [Adam and Eve] heard the voice of the Lord God walking in the garden in the cool of the day." The Bard, or poet-prophet, whose imagination is not bound by time, has heard the voice of the Lord in Eden.
2. The syntax leaves it ambiguous whether it is "the Bard" or "the Holy Word" who calls to the fallen ("lapsèd") soul and to the fallen earth to stop the natural cycle of light and darkness.
3. The likely syntax is that "Soul" is the subject of "might controll."

"O Earth, O Earth, return!
Arise from out the dewy grass;
Night is worn,
And the morn
15 Rises from the slumberous mass.

"Turn away no more;
Why wilt thou turn away?
The starry floor
The watry shore⁴
20 Is giv'n thee till the break of day."

                                          1794

Earth's Answer¹

Earth rais'd up her head,
From the darkness dread & drear.
Her light fled:
Stony dread!
5 And her locks cover'd with grey despair.

"Prison'd on watry shore
Starry Jealousy does keep my den,
Cold and hoar
Weeping o'er
10 I hear the Father of the ancient men.²

"Selfish father of men,
Cruel, jealous, selfish fear!
Can delight
Chain'd in night
15 The virgins of youth and morning bear?

"Does spring hide its joy
When buds and blossoms grow?
Does the sower
Sow by night,
20 Or the plowman in darkness plow?

"Break this heavy chain
That does freeze my bones around;
Selfish! vain!
Eternal bane!
25 That free Love with bondage bound."

                                          1794

4. In Blake's recurrent symbolism the starry sky
("floor") signifies rigid rational order, and the sea
signifies chaos.
1. The Earth's answer explains why she, the natural world, cannot by her unaided endeavors renew
the fallen light.

2. This is the character that Blake later named
"Urizen" in his prophetic works. He is the tyrant
who binds the mind to the natural world and also
imposes a moral bondage on sexual desire and
other modes of human energy.

The Clod & the Pebble

"Love seeketh not Itself to please,
Nor for itself hath any care;
But for another gives its ease,
And builds a Heaven in Hell's despair."

5   So sang a little Clod of Clay,
Trodden with the cattle's feet;
But a Pebble of the brook,
Warbled out these metres meet:

"Love seeketh only Self to please,
10   To bind another to its delight;
Joys in another's loss of ease,
And builds a Hell in Heaven's despite."

1794

Holy Thursday

Is this a holy thing to see,
In a rich and fruitful land,
Babes reduced to misery,
Fed with cold and usurous hand?

5   Is that trembling cry a song?
Can it be a song of joy?
And so many children poor?
It is a land of poverty!

And their sun does never shine,
10   And their fields are bleak & bare,
And their ways are fill'd with thorns;
It is eternal winter there.

For where-e'er the sun does shine,
And where-e'er the rain does fall,
15   Babe can never hunger there,
Nor poverty the mind appall.

1794

The Chimney Sweeper

A little black thing among the snow
Crying " 'weep, 'weep," in notes of woe!
"Where are thy father & mother? say?"
"They are both gone up to the church to pray.

5 "Because I was happy upon the heath,
And smil'd among the winter's snow;
They clothed me in the clothes of death,
And taught me to sing the notes of woe.

"And because I am happy, & dance & sing,
10 They think they have done me no injury,
And are gone to praise God & his Priest & King,
Who make up a heaven of our misery."

1790–92   1794

Nurse's Song

When the voices of children are heard on the green
And whisperings are in the dale,
The days of my youth rise fresh in my mind,
My face turns green and pale.

5 Then come home my children, the sun is gone down
And the dews of night arise;
Your spring & your day are wasted in play,
And your winter and night in disguise.

1794

The Sick Rose

O Rose, thou art sick.
The invisible worm
That flies in the night
In the howling storm

5 Has found out thy bed
Of crimson joy,
And his dark secret love
Does thy life destroy.

1794

The Fly

Little Fly
Thy summer's play
My thoughtless hand
Has brush'd away

5   Am not I
A fly like thee?
Or art not thou
A man like me?

For I dance
10   And drink & sing,
Till some blind hand
Shall brush my wing.

If thought is life
And strength & breath,

The Sick Rose

15   And the want
     Of thought is death;

     Then am I
     A happy fly,
     If I live,
20   Or if I die.

                                                    1794

The Tyger[1]

Tyger! Tyger! burning bright
In the forests of the night,
What immortal hand or eye
Could frame thy fearful symmetry?

5   In what distant deeps or skies
    Burnt the fire of thine eyes?
    On what wings dare he aspire?
    What the hand dare seize the fire?

    And what shoulder, & what art,
10 Could twist the sinews of thy heart?
    And when thy heart began to beat,
    What dread hand? & what dread feet?

    What the hammer? what the chain?
    In what furnace was thy brain?
15 What the anvil? what dread grasp
    Dare its deadly terrors clasp?

    When the stars threw down their spears[2]
    And water'd heaven with their tears,
    Did he smile his work to see?
20 Did he who made the Lamb make thee?

    Tyger! Tyger! burning bright
    In the forests of the night,
    What immortal hand or eye
    Dare frame thy fearful symmetry?

1790–92   1794

---

1. For the author's revisions while composing *The Tyger*, see "Poems in Process," in the appendices to this volume.

2. "Threw down" is ambiguous and may signify that the stars either "surrendered" or "hurled down" their spears.

The Tyger

My Pretty Rose Tree

A flower was offerd to me;
Such a flower as May never bore,
But I said, "I've a Pretty Rose-tree,"
And I passed the sweet flower o'er.

5   Then I went to my Pretty Rose-tree,
To tend her by day and by night.
But my Rose turnd away with jealousy,
And her thorns were my only delight.

1794

Ah Sun-flower

Ah Sun-flower! weary of time,
Who countest the steps of the Sun,
Seeking after that sweet golden clime
Where the traveller's journey is done;

5 Where the Youth pined away with desire,
And the pale Virgin shrouded in snow,
Arise from their graves and aspire,
Where my Sun-flower wishes to go.

1794

The Garden of Love

I went to the Garden of Love,
And saw what I never had seen:
A Chapel was built in the midst,
Where I used to play on the green.

5 And the gates of this Chapel were shut,
And "Thou shalt not" writ over the door;
So I turn'd to the Garden of Love,
That so many sweet flowers bore,

And I saw it was filled with graves,
10 And tomb-stones where flowers should be;
And Priests in black gowns were walking their rounds,
And binding with briars my joys & desires.

1794

London

I wander thro' each charter'd[1] street,
Near where the charter'd Thames does flow,
And mark in every face I meet
Marks of weakness, marks of woe.

5 In every cry of every Man,
In every Infant's cry of fear,
In every voice, in every ban,[2]
The mind-forg'd manacles I hear:

How the Chimney-sweeper's cry
10 Every blackning Church appalls,
And the hapless Soldier's sigh
Runs in blood down Palace walls.

But most thro' midnight streets I hear
How the youthful Harlot's curse

---

1. "Given liberty," but also, ironically, "preempted as private property, and rented out."
2. The various meanings of *ban* are relevant (political and legal prohibition, curse, public condemnation) as well as "banns" (marriage proclamation).

15 Blasts the new-born Infant's tear,[3]
And blights with plagues the Marriage hearse.[4]

1794

The Human Abstract[1]

Pity would be no more,
If we did not make somebody Poor;
And Mercy no more could be,
If all were as happy as we;

5 And mutual fear brings peace,
Till the selfish loves increase;
Then Cruelty knits a snare,
And spreads his baits with care.

He sits down with holy fears,
10 And waters the ground with tears;
Then Humility takes its root
Underneath his foot.

Soon spreads the dismal shade
Of Mystery over his head;
15 And the Catterpiller and Fly
Feed on the Mystery.

And it bears the fruit of Deceit,
Ruddy and sweet to eat;
And the Raven his nest has made
20 In its thickest shade.

The Gods of the earth and sea,
Sought thro' Nature to find this Tree,
But their search was all in vain:
There grows one in the Human Brain.

1790–92   1794

Infant Sorrow

My mother groand! my father wept.
Into the dangerous world I leapt,
Helpless, naked, piping loud;
Like a fiend hid in a cloud.

3. Most critics read this line as implying prenatal
blindness, resulting from a parent's venereal disease (the "plagues" of line 16) by earlier infection
from the harlot.
4. In the older sense: "converts the marriage bed
into a bier." Or possibly, because the current sense
of the word had also come into use in Blake's day,

"converts the marriage coach into a funeral
hearse."
1. The matched contrary to *The Divine Image* in
Songs of Innocence. The virtues of the earlier
poem, "Mercy, Pity, Peace, and Love," are now
represented as possible marks for exploitation, cruelty, conflict, and hypocritical humility.

5   Struggling in my father's hands,
    Striving against my swadling bands;
    Bound and weary I thought best
    To sulk upon my mother's breast.

                                                    1794

A Poison Tree

I was angry with my friend:
I told my wrath, my wrath did end.
I was angry with my foe:
I told it not, my wrath did grow.

5   And I waterd it in fears,
    Night & morning with my tears;
    And I sunnèd it with smiles,
    And with soft deceitful wiles.

    And it grew both day and night,
10 Till it bore an apple bright.
    And my foe beheld it shine,
    And he knew that it was mine,

    And into my garden stole,
    When the night had veild the pole;
15 In the morning glad I see
    My foe outstretchd beneath the tree.

                                                    1794

To Tirzah[1]

Whate'er is Born of Mortal Birth
Must be consumèd with the Earth
To rise from Generation free;
Then what have I to do with thee?[2]

5   The Sexes sprung from Shame & Pride,
    Blow'd° in the morn, in evening died;   blossomed
    But Mercy changd Death into Sleep;
    The Sexes rose to work & weep.

    Thou, Mother of my Mortal part,
10 With cruelty didst mould my Heart,

1. Tirzah was the capital of the northern kingdom of Israel and is conceived by Blake in opposition to Jerusalem, capital of the southern kingdom of Judah, whose tribes had been redeemed from captivity. In this poem, which was added to late versions of *Songs of Experience*, Tirzah is represented as the mother—in the realm of material nature and "Generation"—of the mortal body, with its restrictive senses.
2. Echoing the words of Christ to his mother at the marriage in Cana, John 2.4: "Woman, what have I to do with thee? mine hour is not yet come."

And with false self-deceiving tears
Didst bind my Nostrils, Eyes, & Ears.

Didst close my Tongue in senseless clay
And me to Mortal Life betray.
15 The Death of Jesus set me free;
Then what have I to do with thee?

ca. 1805

A Divine Image[1]

Cruelty has a Human Heart
And Jealousy a Human Face,
Terror, the Human Form Divine,
And Secrecy, the Human Dress.

5 The Human Dress is forgèd Iron,
The Human Form, a fiery Forge,
The Human Face, a Furnace seal'd,
The Human Heart, its hungry Gorge.°   maw, stomach

1790–91

The Book of Thel   Although Blake dated the etched poem 1789, its composition probably extended to 1791, so that he was working on it at the time he was writing the *Songs of Innocence* and some of the *Songs of Experience. The Book of Thel* treats the same two "states"; now, however, Blake employs the narrative instead of the lyrical mode and embodies aspects of the developing myth that was fully enacted in his later prophetic books. And like the major prophecies, this poem is written in the fourteener, a long line of seven stresses.

   The name *Thel* possibly derives from the Greek word for "wish" or "will" and may be intended to suggest the failure of desire, because of timidity, to fulfill itself. Thel is represented as a virgin dwelling in the Vales of Har, which seems equivalent to the sheltered state of pastoral peace and innocence in Blake's *Songs of Innocence*. Here, however, Thel feels useless and unfulfilled, and appeals for comfort, unavailingly, to various beings who are contented with their roles in Har. Finally, the Clay invites Thel to try the experiment of assuming embodied life. Part 4 (plate 6) expresses the brutal shock of the revelation to Thel of the world of sexual Generation and Experience—a revelation from which she flees in terror back to her sheltered, if unsatisfying, existence in Har.

   Some commentators propose that Thel is an unborn soul who rejects the ordeal of an embodied life in the material world. Others propose that Thel is a human virgin who shrinks from experiencing a life of adult sexuality. It is possible, however, to read Blake's little myth as comprehending both these areas of significance. The reader does not need to be an adept in Blake's mythology to recognize the broad symbolic

---

1. Blake omitted this poem from all but one copy of *Songs of Experience*, probably because *The Human Abstract* served as a more comprehensive and subtle contrary to *The Divine Image* in *Songs of Innocence*.

reach of this poem in ordinary human experience—the elemental failure of nerve to meet the challenge of life as it is, the timid incapacity to risk the conflict, physicality, pain, and loss without which there is no possibility either of growth or of creativity.

The Book of Thel

PLATE i[1]

Thel's Motto

Does the Eagle know what is in the pit?
Or wilt thou go ask the Mole?
Can Wisdom be put in a silver rod?
Or Love in a golden bowl?[2]

PLATE 1

1

The daughters of Mne[3] Seraphim led round their sunny flocks,
All but the youngest; she in paleness sought the secret air,

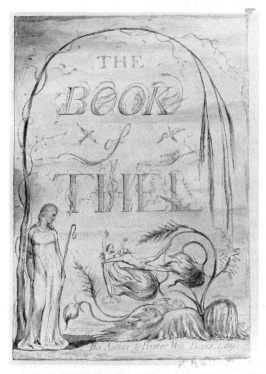

Title page for *The Book of Thel* (1789), plate ii. Copy N, ca. 1815

1. The plate numbers identify the page, each with its own pictorial design, as originally printed by Blake. These numbers are reproduced here because they are frequently used in references to Blake's writings.
2. Ecclesiastes 12.5–6 describes a time when "fears shall be in the way . . . and desire shall fail: because man goeth to his long home, and the mourners go about the streets: Or ever the silver cord be loosed, or the golden bowl be broken." Blake presumably changed the silver cord to a rod to make it, with the golden bowl, a sexual symbol.
3. There has been much speculation about this curious term. It may be an abbreviation for the name "Mnetha," the goddess of the Vales of Har in Blake's earlier poem *Tiriel*.

To fade away like morning beauty from her mortal day;
Down by the river of Adona[4] her soft voice is heard,
5   And thus her gentle lamentation falls like morning dew:

"O life of this our spring! why fades the lotus of the water?
Why fade these children of the spring? born but to smile & fall.
Ah! Thel is like a watry bow, and like a parting cloud,
Like a reflection in a glass, like shadows in the water,
10   Like dreams of infants, like a smile upon an infant's face,
Like the dove's voice, like transient day, like music in the air.
Ah! gentle may I lay me down, and gentle rest my head,
And gentle sleep the sleep of death, and gentle hear the voice
Of him that walketh in the garden in the evening time."[5]

15   The Lilly of the valley breathing in the humble grass
Answer'd the lovely maid and said: "I am a watry weed,
And I am very small, and love to dwell in lowly vales;
So weak, the gilded butterfly scarce perches on my head;
Yet I am visited from heaven, and he that smiles on all
20   Walks in the valley and each morn over me spreads his hand,
Saying: 'Rejoice, thou humble grass, thou new-born lilly flower,
Thou gentle maid of silent valleys and of modest brooks;
For thou shalt be clothed in light, and fed with morning manna,
Till summer's heat melts thee beside the fountains and the springs
25   To flourish in eternal vales.' Then why should Thel complain?

PLATE 2

Why should the mistress of the vales of Har utter a sigh?"

She ceasd & smild in tears, then sat down in her silver shrine.

Thel answerd: "O thou little virgin of the peaceful valley,
Giving to those that cannot crave, the voiceless, the o'ertired;
5   Thy breath doth nourish the innocent lamb, he smells thy milky
            garments,
He crops thy flowers, while thou sittest smiling in his face,
Wiping his mild and meekin° mouth from all contagious taints.   *humble*
Thy wine doth purify the golden honey; thy perfume,
Which thou dost scatter on every little blade of grass that springs,
10   Revives the milkèd cow, & tames the fire-breathing steed.
But Thel is like a faint cloud kindled at the rising sun:
I vanish from my pearly throne, and who shall find my place?"

"Queen of the vales," the Lilly answered, "ask the tender cloud,
And it shall tell thee why it glitters in the morning sky,
15   And why it scatters its bright beauty thro' the humid air.
Descend, O little cloud, & hover before the eyes of Thel."

4. Possibly suggesting an equation of the Vales of Har to Spenser's Garden of Adonis in *The Faerie Queene* 3.6, as well as to the paradisal garden in Genesis (in line 14).

5. Genesis 3.8: "And they heard the voice of the Lord God walking in the garden in the cool of the day."

The Cloud descended, and the Lilly bowd her modest head,
And went to mind her numerous charge among the verdant grass.

PLATE 3

2

"O little Cloud," the virgin said, "I charge thee tell to me,
Why thou complainest not when in one hour thou fade away:
Then we shall seek thee but not find; ah, Thel is like to Thee.
I pass away, yet I complain, and no one hears my voice."

5   The Cloud then shew'd his golden head & his bright form emerg'd,
Hovering and glittering on the air before the face of Thel.

"O virgin, know'st thou not our steeds drink of the golden springs
Where Luvah[6] doth renew his horses? Look'st thou on my youth,
And fearest thou because I vanish and am seen no more,
10 Nothing remains? O maid, I tell thee, when I pass away,
It is to tenfold life, to love, to peace, and raptures holy:
Unseen descending, weigh my light wings upon balmy flowers,
And court the fair eyed dew, to take me to her shining tent;
The weeping virgin trembling kneels before the risen sun,
15 Till we arise link'd in a golden band, and never part,
But walk united, bearing food to all our tender flowers."

"Dost thou O little Cloud? I fear that I am not like thee;
For I walk through the vales of Har and smell the sweetest flowers,
But I feed not the little flowers; I hear the warbling birds,
20 But I feed not the warbling birds; they fly and seek their food;
But Thel delights in these no more, because I fade away,
And all shall say, 'Without a use this shining woman liv'd,
Or did she only live to be at death the food of worms?' "

The Cloud reclind upon his airy throne and answer'd thus:

25 "Then if thou art the food of worms, O virgin of the skies,
How great thy use, how great thy blessing! Every thing that lives
Lives not alone, nor for itself; fear not, and I will call
The weak worm from its lowly bed, and thou shalt hear its voice.
Come forth, worm of the silent valley, to thy pensive queen."

30 The helpless worm arose, and sat upon the Lilly's leaf,
And the bright Cloud saild on, to find his partner in the vale.

PLATE 4

3

Then Thel astonish'd view'd the Worm upon its dewy bed.

---

6. The earliest mention in Blake's work of one of his "Giant Forms," the Zoas. Luvah is the mythical embodiment of the passional and sexual aspect of humankind. He is represented here, like the Greek Phoebus Apollo, as the driver of the chariot of the sun; he repairs to the Vales of Har simply to rest and water his horses. The cloud in this passage describes the cycle of water, from cloud to rain and (by the vaporizing action of the sun on water) back to the cloud.

"Art thou a Worm? Image of weakness, art thou but a Worm?
I see thee like an infant wrapped in the Lilly's leaf;
Ah, weep not, little voice, thou can'st not speak, but thou can'st weep.
5   Is this a Worm? I see thee lay helpless & naked, weeping,
And none to answer, none to cherish thee with mother's smiles."

The Clod of Clay heard the Worm's voice, & raisd her pitying head;
She bow'd over the weeping infant, and her life exhal'd
In milky fondness; then on Thel she fix'd her humble eyes.

10   "O beauty of the vales of Har! we live not for ourselves;
Thou seest me the meanest thing, and so I am indeed;
My bosom of itself is cold, and of itself is dark,

PLATE 5

But he that loves the lowly, pours his oil upon my head,
And kisses me, and binds his nuptial bands around my breast,
And says: 'Thou mother of my children, I have lovèd thee,
And I have given thee a crown that none can take away.'
5   But how this is, sweet maid, I know not, and I cannot know;
I ponder, and I cannot ponder; yet I live and love."

The daughter of beauty wip'd her pitying tears with her white veil,
And said: "Alas! I knew not this, and therefore did I weep.
That God would love a Worm, I knew, and punish the evil foot
10   That, wilful, bruis'd its helpless form; but that he cherish'd it
With milk and oil I never knew; and therefore did I weep,
And I complaind in the mild air, because I fade away,
And lay me down in thy cold bed, and leave my shining lot."

"Queen of the vales," the matron Clay answered, "I heard thy sighs,
15   And all thy moans flew o'er my roof, but I have call'd them down.
Wilt thou, O Queen, enter my house? 'tis given thee to enter
And to return; fear nothing, enter with thy virgin feet."

PLATE 6

4

The eternal gates' terrific porter lifted the northern bar:[7]
Thel enter'd in & saw the secrets of the land unknown.
She saw the couches of the dead, & where the fibrous roots
Of every heart on earth infixes deep its restless twists:
5   A land of sorrows & of tears where never smile was seen.

She wanderd in the land of clouds thro' valleys dark, listning
Dolours & lamentations; waiting oft beside a dewy grave,
She stood in silence, listning to the voices of the ground,
Till to her own grave plot she came, & there she sat down,
10   And heard this voice of sorrow breathed from the hollow pit:

---

7. Homer, in *Odyssey* 13, described the Cave of
the Naiades, of which the northern gate is for mortals and the southern gate for gods. The neopla-
tonist Porphyro had allegorized it as an account of
the descent of the soul into matter and then its
return.

"Why cannot the Ear be closed to its own destruction?
Or the glistning Eye to the poison of a smile?
Why are Eyelids stord with arrows ready drawn,
Where a thousand fighting men in ambush lie?
15 Or an Eye of gifts & graces, show'ring fruits & coinèd gold?
Why a Tongue impress'd with honey from every wind?
Why an Ear, a whirlpool fierce to draw creations in?
Why a Nostril wide inhaling terror, trembling, & affright?
Why a tender curb upon the youthful burning boy?
20 Why a little curtain of flesh on the bed of our desire?"[8]

The Virgin started from her seat, & with a shriek
Fled back unhinderd till she came into the vales of Har.

1789–91

Visions of the Daughters of Albion

This work, dated 1793 on the title page, is one of Blake's early illuminated books, and like his later and longer works is written in what Blake called "the long resounding strong heroic verse" of seven-foot lines. Unlike the timid heroine of *The Book of Thel*, the virgin Oothoon dares to break through into adult sexuality (symbolized by her plucking a marigold and placing it between her breasts) and sets out joyously to join her lover Theotormon, whose realm is the Atlantic Ocean. In her flight overseas she is waylaid and raped by Bromion in the figurative mode of a thunderstorm (1.16–17). The jealous Theotormon, condemning the victim as well as the rapist, binds the two "back to back" in a cave and sits weeping on the threshold. The rest of the work consists of monologues by the three characters, who remain fixed in these postures. Throughout this stage tableau the Daughters of Albion serve as the chorus who, in a recurrent refrain, echo the "woes" and "sighs" of Oothoon, but not her call to rebellion.

This simple drama is densely significant, for as Blake's compressed allusions indicate, the characters, events, and monologues have diverse areas of application. Blake's abrupt opening word, which he etched in very large letters, is *Enslav'd*, and the work as a whole embodies his view that contemporary men, and even more women, in a spiritual parallel to shackled black slaves, are in bondage to oppressive concepts and codes in all aspects of perception, thought, social institutions, and actions. As indicated by the refrain of the Daughters of Albion (that is, contemporary Englishwomen), Oothoon in one aspect represents the sexual disabilities and slavelike status of all women in a male-dominated society. But as "the soft soul of America" (1.3) she is also the revolutionary nation that had recently won political emancipation, yet continued to tolerate an agricultural system that involved black slavery and to acquiesce in the crass economic exploitation of her "soft American plains." At the same time, Oothoon is herself represented in the situation of a black female slave who has been branded, whipped, raped, and impregnated by her master.

Correlatively, the speeches of the boastful Bromion show him to be not only a sexual exploiter of women and a cruel and acquisitive slave owner but also a general proponent of the use of force to achieve mastery in wars, in an oppressive legal system, and in a religious morality based on the fear of hell (4.19–24). Theotormon is represented as even more contemptible. Broken and paralyzed by the prohibitions of a puritanical religion, he denies any possibility of achieving "joys" in this life, despairs of the power of intellect and imagination to improve the human condition and, ration-

---

8. This catalog of the life of Generation and Experience runs through the various senses to end with touch, the primary sexual sense.

alizing his own incapacity, bewails Oothoon's daring to think and act other than he does.

Oothoon's long and passionate oration that concludes the poem (plates 5–8) celebrates a free sexual life for both women and men. Blake, however, uses this open and unpossessive sexuality to typify the realization of all human potentialities and to represent an outgoing altruism, as opposed to an enclosed self-centeredness, "the self-love that envies all." To such a suspicious egotism, as her allusions indicate, Oothoon attributes the tyranny of uniform moral laws imposed on variable individuals, a rigidly institutional religion, the acquisitiveness that drives the system of commerce, and the property rights in another person that are established by the marriage contract.

Blake's poem reflects some prominent circumstances of the years of its composition, 1791–93. This was not only the time when the revolutionary spirit had moved from America to France and effected reverberations in England, but also the time of sporadic rebellions by black slaves in the Western Hemisphere and of widespread debate in England about the abolition of the slave trade. Blake himself, while composing the *Visions*, had illustrated the sadistic punishments inflicted on rebellious slaves in his engravings for J. G. Stedman's *A Narrative, of a Five Years' Expedition, against the Revolted Negroes of Surinam* (see David Erdman, *Blake: Prophet against Empire*, chapter 10). Blake's championing of women's liberation parallels some of the views expressed in the *Vindication of the Rights of Woman* published in 1792 by Mary Wollstonecraft, whom Blake knew and admired, and for whom he had illustrated a book the year before.

Visions of the Daughters of Albion

The Eye sees more than the Heart knows.

PLATE iii

The Argument

I loved Theotormon
And I was not ashamed
I trembled in my virgin fears
And I hid in Leutha's[1] vale!

5   I plucked Leutha's flower,
And I rose up from the vale;
But the terrible thunders tore
My virgin mantle in twain.

PLATE 1

Visions

ENSLAV'D, the Daughters of Albion weep: a trembling lamentation
Upon their mountains; in their valleys, sighs toward America.

For the soft soul of America, Oothoon[2] wandered in woe,
Along the vales of Leutha seeking flowers to comfort her;
5 And thus she spoke to the bright Marygold of Leutha's vale:

---

1. In some poems by Blake, Leutha is represented as a female figure who is beautiful and seductive, but treacherous.

2. The name is adapted by Blake from a character in James Macpherson's pretended translations, in the 1760s, from the ancient British bard Ossian.

Frontispiece, *Visions of the Daughters of Albion* (1793), plate i. Copy P, ca. 1815

"Art thou a flower! art thou a nymph! I see thee now a flower,
Now a nymph! I dare not pluck thee from thy dewy bed!"

The Golden nymph replied: "Pluck thou my flower Oothoon the mild.
Another flower shall spring, because the soul of sweet delight
10   Can never pass away." She ceas'd & closd her golden shrine.

Then Oothoon pluck'd the flower saying, "I pluck thee from thy bed,
Sweet flower, and put thee here to glow between my breasts,
And thus I turn my face to where my whole soul seeks."

Over the waves she went in wing'd exulting swift delight;
15   And over Theotormon's reign took her impetuous course.

Bromion rent her with his thunders. On his stormy bed
Lay the faint maid, and soon her woes appalld his thunders hoarse.

Bromion spoke: "Behold this harlot here on Bromion's bed,
And let the jealous dolphins sport around the lovely maid;
20   Thy soft American plains are mine, and mine thy north & south:
Stampt with my signet[3] are the swarthy children of the sun:
They are obedient, they resist not, they obey the scourge:
Their daughters worship terrors and obey the violent.

3. A small seal or stamp. The allusion is to the branding of black slaves by their owners.

PLATE 2

Now thou maist marry Bromion's harlot, and protect the child
Of Bromion's rage, that Oothoon shall put forth in nine moons' time."[4]

Then storms rent Theotormon's limbs; he rolld his waves around,
And folded his black jealous waters round the adulterate pair;
5 Bound back to back in Bromion's caves terror & meekness dwell.

At entrance Theotormon sits wearing the threshold hard
With secret tears; beneath him sound like waves on a desart shore
The voice of slaves beneath the sun, and children bought with money,
That shiver in religious caves beneath the burning fires
10 Of lust, that belch incessant from the summits of the earth.

Oothoon weeps not: she cannot weep! her tears are locked up;
But she can howl incessant, writhing her soft snowy limbs,
And calling Theotormon's Eagles to prey upon her flesh.[5]

"I call with holy voice! kings of the sounding air,
15 Rend away this defiled bosom that I may reflect
The image of Theotormon on my pure transparent breast."

The Eagles at her call descend & rend their bleeding prey;
Theotormon severely smiles; her soul reflects the smile,
As the clear spring mudded with feet of beasts grows pure & smiles.

20 The Daughters of Albion hear her woes, & eccho back her sighs.

"Why does my Theotormon sit weeping upon the threshold,
And Oothoon hovers by his side, perswading him in vain?
I cry, 'Arise O Theotormon, for the village dog
Barks at the breaking day, the nightingale has done lamenting,
25 The lark does rustle in the ripe corn, and the Eagle returns
From nightly prey, and lifts his golden beak to the pure east,
Shaking the dust from his immortal pinions to awake
The sun that sleeps too long. Arise my Theotormon, I am pure;
Because the night is gone that clos'd me in its deadly black.'
30 They told me that the night & day were all that I could see;
They told me that I had five senses to inclose me up,
And they inclos'd my infinite brain into a narrow circle,
And sunk my heart into the Abyss, a red round globe hot burning,
Till all from life I was obliterated and erased.
35 Instead of morn arises a bright shadow, like an eye
In the eastern cloud,[6] instead of night a sickly charnel house,
That Theotormon hears me not! to him the night and morn
Are both alike: a night of sighs, a morning of fresh tears;

4. Pregnancy enhanced the market value of a female slave in America.
5. The implied parallel is to Zeus's punishment of Prometheus for befriending the human race, by setting an eagle to devour his liver.
6. The contrast is between the physical sun perceived by the constricted ("inclos'd," line 32) sensible eye and "the breaking day" (line 24) of a new era perceived by Oothoon's liberated vision.

PLATE 3

And none but Bromion can hear my lamentations.

"With what sense is it that the chicken shuns the ravenous hawk?
With what sense does the tame pigeon measure out the expanse?
With what sense does the bee form cells? have not the mouse & frog
5   Eyes and ears and sense of touch? yet are their habitations
And their pursuits as different as their forms and as their joys.
Ask the wild ass why he refuses burdens, and the meek camel
Why he loves man; is it because of eye, ear, mouth, or skin,
Or breathing nostrils? No, for these the wolf and tyger have.
10 Ask the blind worm the secrets of the grave, and why her spires
Love to curl round the bones of death; and ask the rav'nous snake
Where she gets poison, & the wing'd eagle why he loves the sun,
And then tell me the thoughts of man, that have been hid of old.[7]

"Silent I hover all the night, and all day could be silent,
15 If Theotormon once would turn his loved eyes upon me.
How can I be defild when I reflect thy image pure?
Sweetest the fruit that the worm feeds on, & the soul prey'd on by woe,
The new wash'd lamb ting'd with the village smoke, & the bright swan
By the red earth of our immortal river:[8] I bathe my wings,
20 And I am white and pure to hover round Theotormon's breast."

Then Theotormon broke his silence, and he answered:

"Tell me what is the night or day to one o'erflowd with woe?
Tell me what is a thought? & of what substance is it made?
Tell me what is a joy? & in what gardens do joys grow?
25 And in what rivers swim the sorrows? and upon what mountains

PLATE 4

Wave shadows of discontent? and in what houses dwell the wretched
Drunken with woe, forgotten, and shut up from cold despair?

"Tell me where dwell the thoughts, forgotten till thou call them forth?
Tell me where dwell the joys of old! & where the ancient loves?
5   And when will they renew again & the night of oblivion past?
That I might traverse times & spaces far remote and bring
Comforts into a present sorrow and a night of pain.
Where goest thou, O thought? to what remote land is thy flight?
If thou returnest to the present moment of affliction
10 Wilt thou bring comforts on thy wings and dews and honey and balm,
Or poison from the desart wilds, from the eyes of the envier?"

Then Bromion said, and shook the cavern with his lamentation:

7. Oothoon implies that "thoughts" (powers of conceiving a liberated life in a better world) are as innate to human beings as instinctual patterns of behavior are to other species of living things.
8. "Red earth" is the etymological meaning of the Hebrew name "Adam" (cf. *The Marriage of Heaven and Hell* 2.13, p. 73). The "immortal river," accordingly, may refer to the "river" that "went out of Eden" (Genesis 2.10).

"Thou knowest that the ancient trees seen by thine eyes have fruit;
But knowest thou that trees and fruits flourish upon the earth
15   To gratify senses unknown? trees beasts and birds unknown:
Unknown, not unpercievd, spread in the infinite microscope,
In places yet unvisited by the voyager, and in worlds
Over another kind of seas, and in atmospheres unknown?
Ah! are there other wars, beside the wars of sword and fire?
20   And are there other sorrows, beside the sorrows of poverty?
And are there other joys, beside the joys of riches and ease?
And is there not one law for both the lion and the ox?⁹
And is there not eternal fire, and eternal chains?
To bind the phantoms of existence from eternal life?"

25   Then Oothoon waited silent all the day and all the night,

PLATE 5

But when the morn arose, her lamentation renewd.
The Daughters of Albion hear her woes, & eccho back her sighs.

"O Urizen!¹ Creator of men! mistaken Demon of heaven:
Thy joys are tears! thy labour vain, to form men to thine image.
5   How can one joy absorb another? are not different joys
Holy, eternal, infinite! and each joy is a Love.

"Does not the great mouth laugh at a gift? & the narrow eyelids mock
At the labour that is above payment? and wilt thou take the ape
For thy councellor? or the dog for a schoolmaster to thy children?
10   Does he who contemns poverty, and he who turns with
        abhorrence
From usury, feel the same passion, or are they moved alike?
How can the giver of gifts experience the delights of the merchant?
How the industrious citizen the pains of the husbandman?
How different far the fat fed hireling with hollow drum,
15   Who buys whole corn fields into wastes,² and sings upon the
        heath:
How different their eye and ear! how different the world to them!
With what sense does the parson claim the labour of the farmer?
What are his nets & gins° & traps? & how does he surround him   snares
With cold floods of abstraction, and with forests of solitude,
20   To build him castles and high spires, where kings & priests may dwell?
Till she who burns with youth, and knows no fixed lot, is bound
In spells of law to one she loaths; and must she drag the chain
Of life, in weary lust? must chilling murderous thoughts obscure
The clear heaven of her eternal spring? to bear the wintry rage
25   Of a harsh terror, driv'n to madness, bound to hold a rod
Over her shrinking shoulders all the day, & all the night
To turn the wheel of false desire, and longings that wake her womb

9. The last line of *The Marriage of Heaven and Hell* proclaims: "One Law for the Lion & Ox is Oppression."
1. This is the first occurrence of the name "Urizen" in Blake. Oothoon's liberated vision recognizes the error in the way God is conceived in conventional religion.
2. Probably a compressed allusion both to the wealthy landowner who converts fertile fields into a game preserve and to the recruiting officer ("with hollow drum") who strips the land of its agricultural laborers.

To the abhorred birth of cherubs in the human form
That live a pestilence & die a meteor & are no more;
30   Till the child dwell with one he hates, and do the deed he loaths,
And the impure scourge force his seed into its unripe birth
E'er yet his eyelids can behold the arrows of the day?[3]

"Does the whale worship at thy footsteps as the hungry dog?
Or does he scent the mountain prey, because his nostrils wide
35   Draw in the ocean? does his eye discern the flying cloud
As the raven's eye? or does he measure the expanse like the vulture?
Does the still spider view the cliffs where eagles hide their young?
Or does the fly rejoice because the harvest is brought in?
Does not the eagle scorn the earth & despise the treasures beneath?
40   But the mole knoweth what is there, & the worm shall tell it thee.
Does not the worm erect a pillar in the mouldering church yard,

PLATE 6

And a palace of eternity in the jaws of the hungry grave?
Over his porch these words are written: 'Take thy bliss O Man!
And sweet shall be thy taste & sweet thy infant joys renew!'

"Infancy, fearless, lustful, happy! nestling for delight
5   In laps of pleasure; Innocence! honest, open, seeking
The vigorous joys of morning light, open to virgin bliss,
Who taught thee modesty, subtil modesty? Child of night & sleep,
When thou awakest wilt thou dissemble all thy secret joys,
Or wert thou not awake when all this mystery was disclos'd?
10   Then com'st thou forth a modest virgin, knowing to dissemble,
With nets found under thy night pillow to catch virgin joy,
And brand it with the name of whore, & sell it in the night,
In silence, ev'n without a whisper, and in seeming sleep.[4]
Religious dreams and holy vespers light thy smoky fires;
15   Once were thy fires lighted by the eyes of honest morn.
And does my Theotormon seek this hypocrite modesty,
This knowing, artful, secret, fearful, cautious, trembling hypocrite?
Then is Oothoon a whore indeed! and all the virgin joys
Of life are harlots, and Theotormon is a sick man's dream,
20   And Oothoon is the crafty slave of selfish holiness.

"But Oothoon is not so; a virgin fill'd with virgin fancies
Open to joy and to delight where ever beauty appears.
If in the morning sun I find it, there my eyes are fix'd

PLATE 7

In happy copulation; if in evening mild, wearied with work,
Sit on a bank and draw the pleasures of this free born joy.

"The moment of desire! the moment of desire! The virgin
That pines for man shall awaken her womb to enormous joys

3. The reference is to the begetting of children, both in actual slavery and in the metaphoric slavery of a loveless marriage, from generation to generation.

4. Oothoon contrasts the natural, innocent sensuality of an infant to the socially acquired, hypocritical modesty of the adult virgin; the latter is Theotormon's concept of female virtue.

5   In the secret shadows of her chamber; the youth shut up from
The lustful joy shall forget to generate & create an amorous image
In the shadows of his curtains and in the folds of his silent pillow.
Are not these the places of religion? the rewards of continence?
The self enjoyings of self denial? Why dost seek religion?
10 Is it because acts are not lovely, that thou seekest solitude,
Where the horrible darkness is impressed with reflections of desire?

"Father of Jealousy,[5] be thou accursed from the earth!
Why hast thou taught my Theotormon this accursed thing?
Till beauty fades from off my shoulders, darken'd and cast out,
15 A solitary shadow wailing on the margin of non-entity.

"I cry, Love! Love! Love! happy happy Love! free as the mountain wind!
Can that be Love, that drinks another as a sponge drinks water?
That clouds with jealousy his nights, with weepings all the day,
To spin a web of age around him, grey and hoary! dark!
20 Till his eyes sicken at the fruit that hangs before his sight.
Such is self-love that envies all! a creeping skeleton
With lamplike eyes watching around the frozen marriage bed.

"But silken nets and traps of adamant[6] will Oothoon spread,
And catch for thee girls of mild silver, or of furious gold;
25 I'll lie beside thee on a bank & view their wanton play
In lovely copulation bliss on bliss with Theotormon:
Red as the rosy morning, lustful as the first born beam,
Oothoon shall view his dear delight, nor e'er with jealous cloud
Come in the heaven of generous love; nor selfish blightings bring.

30 "Does the sun walk in glorious raiment on the secret floor

PLATE 8

Where the cold miser spreads his gold? or does the bright cloud drop
On his stone threshold? does his eye behold the beam that brings
Expansion to the eye of pity? or will he bind himself
Beside the ox to thy hard furrow? does not that mild beam blot
5 The bat, the owl, the glowing tyger, and the king of night?
The sea fowl takes the wintry blast for a cov'ring to her limbs,
And the wild snake the pestilence to adorn him with gems & gold.
And trees & birds & beasts & men behold their eternal joy.
Arise you little glancing wings, and sing your infant joy!
10 Arise and drink your bliss, for every thing that lives is holy!"[7]

Thus every morning wails Oothoon, but Theotormon sits
Upon the margind ocean conversing with shadows dire.

The Daughters of Albion hear her woes, & eccho back her sighs.

1791–93   1793

5. I.e., Urizen (5.3), the false conceived God who
prohibits the satisfaction of human desires.
6. A legendary stone believed to be unbreakable.
(The name is derived from the Greek word for diamond.)
7. This last phrase is also the concluding line of
"A Song of Liberty," appended to *The Marriage of
Heaven and Hell*.

The Marriage of Heaven and Hell

This, the most immediately accessible of Blake's longer works, is a vigorous, deliberately outrageous, and at times comic onslaught against timidly conventional and self-righteous members of society as well as against stock opinions of orthodox Christian piety and morality. The seeming simplicity of Blake's satiric attitude, however, is deceptive.

Initially, Blake accepts the terminology of standard Christian morality ("what the religious call Good & Evil") but reverses its values. In this conventional use Evil, which is manifested by the class of beings called Devils and which consigns wrongdoers to the orthodox Hell, is everything associated with the body and its desires and consists essentially of energy, abundance, actions, and freedom. Conventional Good, which is manifested by Angels and guarantees its adherents a place in the orthodox Heaven, is associated with the Soul (regarded as entirely separate from the body) and consists of the contrary qualities of reason, restraint, passivity, and prohibition. Blandly adopting these conventional oppositions, Blake elects to assume the diabolic persona—what he calls "the voice of the Devil"—and to utter "Proverbs of Hell."

But this stance is only a first stage in Blake's complex irony, designed to startle the reader into recognizing the inadequacy of conventional moral categories. As he also says in the opening summary, "Without Contraries is no progression," and "Reason and Energy" are both "necessary to Human existence." It turns out that Blake subordinates his reversal of conventional values under a more inclusive point of view, according to which the real Good, as distinguished from the merely ironic Good, is not abandonment of all restraints but a "marriage," or union of the contraries, of desire and restraint, energy and reason, the promptings of Hell and the denials of Heaven—or as Blake calls these contraries in plate 16, "the Prolific" and "the Devouring." These two classes, he adds, "should be enemies," and "whoever tries to reconcile them seeks to destroy existence." Implicit in Blake's satire is the view that the good and abundant life consists in the sustained tension, without victory or suppression, of co-present oppositions.

Blake was stimulated to write this unique work in response to the writings of the visionary Swedish theologian Emanuel Swedenborg, whom he had at first admired but then had come to recognize as a conventional Angel in the disguise of a radical Devil. In plate 3 the writings of Swedenborg are described as the winding clothes Blake discards as he is resurrected from the tomb of his past self, as a poet-prophet who heralds the apocalyptic promise of his age. Blake wrote *The Marriage of Heaven and Hell* in the early 1790s, during the early years of the French Revolution, when he shared the expectations of a number of radical English writers, including the young poets Wordsworth, Coleridge, and Southey, that the revolution was the violent stage that, as the biblical prophets foresaw, immediately preceded the millennium. The double role of *The Marriage* as both satire and revolutionary prophecy is made explicit in *A Song of Liberty*, which Blake etched in 1792 and added as a coda.

The Marriage of Heaven and Hell

PLATE 2

The Argument

Rintrah[1] roars & shakes his fires in the burdend air;
Hungry clouds swag on the deep.

---

1. Rintrah plays the role of the angry Old Testament prophet Elijah as well as of John the Baptist, the voice "crying in the wilderness" (Matthew 3), preparing the way for Christ the Messiah. It has been plausibly suggested that stanzas 2–5 summarize the course of biblical history to the present

Once meek, and in a perilous path,
The just man kept his course along
5　The vale of death.
Roses are planted where thorns grow,
And on the barren heath
Sing the honey bees.

Then the perilous path was planted,
10　And a river, and a spring,
On every cliff and tomb;
And on the bleached bones
Red clay[2] brought forth;

Till the villain left the paths of ease,
15　To walk in perilous paths, and drive
The just man into barren climes.

Now the sneaking serpent walks
In mild humility,
And the just man rages in the wilds
20　Where lions roam.

Rintrah roars & shakes his fires in the burdend air;
Hungry clouds swag on the deep.

———————

PLATE 3

As a new heaven is begun, and it is now thirty-three years since its advent,
the Eternal Hell revives. And lo! Swedenborg[3] is the Angel sitting at the tomb;
his writings are the linen clothes folded up. Now is the dominion of Edom,
& the return of Adam into Paradise; see Isaiah xxxiv & XXXV Chap.[4]

Without Contraries is no progression. Attraction and Repulsion, Reason
and Energy, Love and Hate, are necessary to Human existence.

time. "Once" (line 3) refers to Old Testament history after the Fall; "Then" (line 9) is the time of
the birth of Christ. "Till" (line 14) identifies the
era when Christianity was perverted into an institutional religion. "Now" (line 17) is the time of the
wrathful portent of the French Revolution. In this
final era, the hypocritical serpent represents the
priest of the "angels" in the poem, while "the just
man" is embodied in Blake himself, a raging poet
and prophet in the guise of a devil. "Swag" (line 2):
sag, hang down.
2. In Hebrew, the literal meaning of "Adam," or
created man. The probable reference is to the birth
of the Redeemer, the new Adam.
3. Emanuel Swedenborg (1688–1772), Swedish
scientist and religious philosopher, had predicted,
on the basis of his visions, that the Last Judgment
and the coming of the Kingdom of Heaven would
occur in 1757. This was precisely the year of
Blake's birth. Now, in 1790, Blake is thirty-three,
the age at which Christ had been resurrected from
the tomb; correspondingly, Blake rises from the
tomb of his past life in his new role as imaginative
artist who will redeem his age. But, Blake ironically
comments, the works he will engrave in his resur-

rection will constitute the Eternal Hell, the contrary brought into simultaneous being by
Swedenborg's limited New Heaven.
4. Isaiah 34 prophesies "the day of the Lord's vengeance," a time of violent destruction and bloodshed; Isaiah 35 prophesies the redemption to
follow, in which "the desert shall . . . blossom as
the rose," "in the wilderness shall waters break out,
and streams in the desert," and "no lion shall be
there," but "an highway shall be there . . . and it
shall be called The way of holiness" (cf. "The Argument," lines 3–11, 20). Blake combines with these
chapters Isaiah 63, in which "Edom" is the place
from which comes the man whose garments are
red with the blood he has spilled; for as he says,
"the day of vengeance is in mine heart, and the year
of my redeemed is come." Blake interprets this last
phrase as predicting the time when Adam would
regain his lost Paradise.
With reference to affairs in 1790, Edom can be
taken to represent France, and the red man coming
from Edom (to England) to be the spirit of the
French Revolution, which Blake interprets as a
portent of apocalyptic redemption and the recovery
of Paradise.

From these contraries spring what the religious call Good & Evil. Good is the passive that obeys Reason. Evil is the active springing from Energy.
Good is Heaven. Evil is Hell.

PLATE 4

The Voice of the Devil

All Bibles or sacred codes have been the causes of the following Errors:
1. That Man has two real existing principles; Viz: a Body & a Soul.
2. That Energy, calld Evil, is alone from the Body, & that Reason, calld Good, is alone from the Soul.
3. That God will torment Man in Eternity for following his Energies.
But the following Contraries to these are True:
1. Man has no Body distinct from his Soul; for that calld Body is a portion of Soul discernd by the five Senses, the chief inlets of Soul in this age.
2. Energy is the only life, and is from the Body; and Reason is the bound or outward circumference of Energy.
3. Energy is Eternal Delight.

PLATE 5

Those who restrain desire, do so because theirs is weak enough to be restrained; and the restrainer or reason usurps its place & governs the unwilling.

And being restraind, it by degrees becomes passive, till it is only the shadow of desire.

The history of this is written in *Paradise Lost*,[5] & the Governor or Reason is call'd Messiah.

And the original Archangel, or possessor of the command of the heavenly host, is calld the Devil or Satan, and his children are call'd Sin & Death.[6]

But in the Book of Job, Milton's Messiah is call'd Satan.[7]

For this history has been adopted by both parties.

It indeed appear'd to Reason as if Desire was cast out; but the Devil's account is, that the Messi[PLATE 6]ah fell, & formed a heaven of what he stole from the Abyss.

This is shewn in the Gospel, where he prays to the Father to send the comforter or Desire that Reason may have Ideas to build on;[8] the Jehovah of the Bible being no other than he who dwells in flaming fire. Know that after Christ's death, he became Jehovah.

But in Milton, the Father is Destiny, the Son, a Ratio[9] of the five senses, & the Holy-ghost, Vacuum!

Note. The reason Milton wrote in fetters when he wrote of Angels & God,

---

5. What follows, to the end of this section, is Blake's "diabolical" reading of *Paradise Lost*.
6. Satan's giving birth to Sin and then incestuously begetting Death upon her is described in *Paradise Lost* 2.745ff.; the war in heaven, referred to three lines below, in which the Messiah defeated Satan and drove him out of heaven, is described in 6.824ff.
7. In the Book of Job, Satan plays the role of Job's moral accuser and physical tormentor.

8. Possibly John 14.16–17, where Christ says he "will pray the Father, and he shall give you another Comforter . . . Even the Spirit of truth."
9. The Latin *ratio* means both "reason" and "sum." Blake applies the term to the 18th-century view, following the empirical philosophy of John Locke, that the content of the mind, on which the faculty of reason operates, is limited to the sum of the experience acquired by the five senses.

and at liberty when of Devils & Hell, is because he was a true Poet and of the Devil's party without knowing it.

A Memorable Fancy[1]

As I was walking among the fires of hell, delighted with the enjoyments of Genius, which to Angels look like torment and insanity, I collected some of their Proverbs; thinking that as the sayings used in a nation mark its character, so the Proverbs of Hell shew the nature of Infernal wisdom better than any description of buildings or garments.

When I came home, on the abyss of the five senses, where a flat sided steep frowns over the present world, I saw a mighty Devil folded in black clouds, hovering on the sides of the rock; with cor[PLATE 7]roding fires he wrote the following sentence[2] now perceived by the minds of men, & read by them on earth:

> How do you know but ev'ry Bird that cuts the airy way,
> Is an immense world of delight, clos'd by your senses five?

Proverbs of Hell[3]

In seed time learn, in harvest teach, in winter enjoy.
Drive your cart and your plow over the bones of the dead.
The road of excess leads to the palace of wisdom.
Prudence is a rich ugly old maid courted by Incapacity.
5   He who desires but acts not, breeds pestilence.
The cut worm forgives the plow.
Dip him in the river who loves water.
A fool sees not the same tree that a wise man sees.
He whose face gives no light, shall never become a star.
10   Eternity is in love with the productions of time.
The busy bee has no time for sorrow.
The hours of folly are measur'd by the clock; but of wisdom, no clock can measure.
All wholsom food is caught without a net or a trap.
Bring out number, weight, & measure in a year of dearth.
15   No bird soars too high, if he soars with his own wings.
A dead body revenges not injuries.
The most sublime act is to set another before you.
If the fool would persist in his folly he would become wise.
Folly is the cloke of knavery.
20   Shame is Pride's cloke.

PLATE 8

Prisons are built with stones of Law, Brothels with bricks of Religion.
The pride of the peacock is the glory of God.

1. A parody of what Swedenborg called "memorable relations" of his literal-minded visions of the eternal world.
2. The "mighty Devil" is Blake, as he sees himself reflected in the shiny plate on which he is etching this very passage with "corroding fires," i.e., acid. See also the third from last sentence in plate 14.
3. A "diabolic" version of the Book of Proverbs in the Old Testament.

The lust of the goat is the bounty of God.
The wrath of the lion is the wisdom of God.
5   The nakedness of woman is the work of God.
Excess of sorrow laughs. Excess of joy weeps.
The roaring of lions, the howling of wolves, the raging of the stormy sea,
    and the destructive sword, are portions of eternity too great for the
    eye of man.
The fox condemns the trap, not himself.
Joys impregnate. Sorrows bring forth.
10   Let man wear the fell of the lion, woman the fleece of the sheep.
The bird a nest, the spider a web, man friendship.
The selfish smiling fool & the sullen frowning fool shall be both thought
    wise, that they may be a rod.
What is now proved was once only imagin'd.
The rat, the mouse, the fox, the rabbit watch the roots; the lion, the tyger,
    the horse, the elephant, watch the fruits.
15   The cistern contains; the fountain overflows.
One thought fills immensity.
Always be ready to speak your mind, and a base man will avoid you.
Every thing possible to be believ'd is an image of truth.
The eagle never lost so much time as when he submitted to learn of the
    crow.

PLATE 9

The fox provides for himself, but God provides for the lion.
Think in the morning, Act in the noon, Eat in the evening, Sleep in the
    night.
He who has sufferd you to impose on him knows you.
As the plow follows words, so God rewards prayers.
5   The tygers of wrath are wiser than the horses of instruction.
Expect poison from the standing water.
You never know what is enough unless you know what is more than
    enough.
Listen to the fool's reproach! it is a kingly title!
The eyes of fire, the nostrils of air, the mouth of water, the beard of earth.
10   The weak in courage is strong in cunning.
The apple tree never asks the beech how he shall grow, nor the lion the
    horse, how he shall take his prey.
The thankful reciever bears a plentiful harvest.
If others had not been foolish, we should be so.
The soul of sweet delight can never be defil'd.
15   When thou seest an Eagle, thou seest a portion of Genius; lift up thy head!
As the catterpiller chooses the fairest leaves to lay her eggs on, so the
    priest lays his curse on the fairest joys.
To create a little flower is the labour of ages.
Damn braces; Bless relaxes.
The best wine is the oldest, the best water the newest.
20   Prayers plow not! Praises reap not!
Joys laugh not! Sorrows weep not!

PLATE 10

The head Sublime, the heart Pathos, the genitals Beauty, the hands & feet
    Proportion.

As the air to a bird or the sea to a fish, so is contempt to the contemptible.
The crow wish'd every thing was black, the owl that every thing was white.
Exuberance is Beauty.
5 If the lion was advised by the fox, he would be cunning.
Improvement makes strait roads, but the crooked roads without
      Improvement are roads of Genius.
Sooner murder an infant in its cradle than nurse unacted desires.
Where man is not, nature is barren.
Truth can never be told so as to be understood, and not be believ'd.
10   Enough! or Too much.

PLATE 11

The ancient Poets animated all sensible objects with Gods or Geniuses, calling them by the names and adorning them with the properties of woods, rivers, mountains, lakes, cities, nations, and whatever their enlarged & numerous senses could perceive.

And particularly they studied the genius of each city & country, placing it under its mental deity.

Till a system was formed, which some took advantage of & enslav'd the vulgar by attempting to realize or abstract the mental deities from their objects; thus began Priesthood,

Choosing forms of worship from poetic tales.

And at length they pronounced that the Gods had ordered such things.

Thus men forgot that All deities reside in the human breast.

PLATE 12

A Memorable Fancy[4]

The Prophets Isaiah and Ezekiel dined with me, and I asked them how they dared so roundly to assert that God spake to them; and whether they did not think at the time that they would be misunderstood, & so be the cause of imposition.

Isaiah answer'd: "I saw no God, nor heard any, in a finite organical perception; but my senses discover'd the infinite in every thing, and as I was then perswaded, & remain confirm'd, that the voice of honest indignation is the voice of God, I cared not for consequences, but wrote."

Then I asked: "Does a firm perswasion that a thing is so, make it so?"

He replied: "All poets believe that it does, & in ages of imagination this firm perswasion removed mountains; but many are not capable of a firm perswasion of any thing."

Then Ezekiel said: "The philosophy of the East taught the first principles of human perception. Some nations held one principle for the origin & some another; we of Israel taught that the Poetic Genius (as you now call it) was the first principle and all the others merely derivative, which was the cause of our despising the Priests & Philosophers of other countries, and prophecying that all Gods [PL 13] would at last be proved to originate in ours & to be the tributaries of the Poetic Genius; it was this that our great poet, King David, desired so fervently & invokes so pathetically, saying by this he con-

4. Blake parodies Swedenborg's accounts, in his *Memorable Relations,* of his conversations with the inhabitants during his spiritual trips to heaven.

quers enemies & governs kingdoms; and we so loved our God, that we cursed in his name all the deities of surrounding nations, and asserted that they had rebelled; from these opinions the vulgar came to think that all nations would at last be subject to the Jews."

"This," said he, "like all firm perswasions, is come to pass, for all nations believe the Jews' code and worship the Jews' god, and what greater subjection can be?"

I heard this with some wonder, & must confess my own conviction. After dinner I ask'd Isaiah to favour the world with his lost works; he said none of equal value was lost. Ezekiel said the same of his.

I also asked Isaiah what made him go naked and barefoot three years? He answered, "the same that made our friend Diogenes,[5] the Grecian."

I then asked Ezekiel why he eat dung, & lay so long on his right & left side?[6] He answered, "the desire of raising other men into a perception of the infinite; this the North American tribes practise, & is he honest who resists his genius or conscience only for the sake of present ease or gratification?"

PLATE 14

The ancient tradition that the world will be consumed in fire at the end of six thousand years is true, as I have heard from Hell.

For the cherub with his flaming sword is hereby commanded to leave his guard at the tree of life;[7] and when he does, the whole creation will be consumed, and appear infinite and holy, whereas it now appears finite & corrupt.

This will come to pass by an improvement of sensual enjoyment.

But first the notion that man has a body distinct from his soul is to be expunged; this I shall do, by printing in the infernal method, by corrosives, which in Hell are salutary and medicinal, melting apparent surfaces away, and displaying the infinite which was hid.[8]

If the doors of perception were cleansed every thing would appear to man as it is, infinite.

For man has closed himself up, till he sees all things thro' narrow chinks of his cavern.

PLATE 15

A Memorable Fancy

I was in a Printing house in Hell & saw the method in which knowledge is transmitted from generation to generation.

In the first chamber was a Dragon-Man, clearing away the rubbish from a cave's mouth; within, a number of Dragons were hollowing the cave.

In the second chamber was a Viper folding round the rock & the cave, and others adorning it with gold, silver, and precious stones.

In the third chamber was an Eagle with wings and feathers of air; he

5. Greek Cynic (4th century), whose extreme repudiation of civilized customs gave rise to anecdotes that he had renounced clothing. In Isaiah 20.2–3, the prophet, at the command of the Lord, walked "naked and barefoot" for three years.
6. The Lord gave these instructions to the prophet Ezekiel (4.4–6).
7. In Genesis 3.24, when the Lord drove Adam and Eve from the Garden of Eden, he had placed Cherubim and a flaming sword at the eastern end "to keep the way of the tree of life."
8. See n. 2, p. 75.

caused the inside of the cave to be infinite; around were numbers of Eagle-like men, who built palaces in the immense cliffs.

In the fourth chamber were Lions of flaming fire, raging around & melting the metals into living fluids.

In the fifth chamber were Unnam'd forms, which cast the metals into the expanse.

There they were receiv'd by Men who occupied the sixth chamber, and took the forms of books & were arranged in libraries.[9]

PLATE 16

The Giants[1] who formed this world into its sensual existence, and now seem to live in it in chains, are in truth the causes of its life & the sources of all activity; but the chains are the cunning of weak and tame minds which have power to resist energy; according to the proverb, the weak in courage is strong in cunning.

Thus one portion of being is the Prolific, the other, the Devouring; to the Devourer it seems as if the producer was in his chains, but it is not so; he only takes portions of existence and fancies that the whole.

But the Prolific would cease to be Prolific unless the Devourer as a sea received the excess of his delights.

Some will say, "Is not God alone the Prolific?" I answer, "God only Acts & Is, in existing beings or Men."

These two classes of men are always upon earth, & they should be enemies; whoever tries [PLATE 17] to reconcile them seeks to destroy existence.

Religion is an endeavour to reconcile the two.

Note. Jesus Christ did not wish to unite but to separate them, as in the Parable of sheep and goats! & he says, "I came not to send Peace but a Sword."[2]

Messiah or Satan or Tempter was formerly thought to be one of the Ante-diluvians[3] who are our Energies.

A Memorable Fancy

An Angel came to me and said: "O pitiable foolish young man! O horrible! O dreadful state! consider the hot burning dungeon thou art preparing for thyself to all eternity, to which thou art going in such career."

I said: "Perhaps you will be willing to shew me my eternal lot, & we will contemplate together upon it and see whether your lot or mine is most desirable."

So he took me thro' a stable & thro' a church & down into the church vault at the end of which was a mill; thro' the mill we went, and came to a cave; down the winding cavern we groped our tedious way till a void boundless as a nether sky appeared beneath us, & we held by the roots of trees and hung over this immensity, but I said: "If you please, we will commit ourselves

9. In this "Memorable Fancy," Blake allegorizes his procedure in designing, etching, printing, and binding his works of imaginative genius.
1. In this section, human creative energies, called "the Prolific," in their relation to their indispen-

sable contrary, "the Devourer."
2. Matthew 10.34. The parable of the sheep and the goats is in Matthew 25.32–33.
3. Those who lived before Noah's Flood.

to this void, and see whether Providence is here also, if you will not I will."
But he answered: "Do not presume, O young man, but as we here remain,
behold thy lot which will soon appear when the darkness passes away."[4]

So I remaind with him sitting in the twisted [PLATE 18] root of an oak; he
was suspended in a fungus which hung with the head downward into the
deep.

By degrees we beheld the infinite Abyss, fiery as the smoke of a burning
city; beneath us at an immense distance was the sun, black but shining;
round it were fiery tracks on which revolv'd vast spiders, crawling after their
prey, which flew, or rather swum in the infinite deep, in the most terrific
shapes of animals sprung from corruption; & the air was full of them, &
seemed composed of them; these are Devils, and are called Powers of the
air. I now asked my companion which was my eternal lot? He said, "Between
the black & white spiders."

But now, from between the black & white spiders a cloud and fire burst
and rolled thro the deep, blackning all beneath, so that the nether deep grew
black as a sea & rolled with a terrible noise. Beneath us was nothing now to
be seen but a black tempest, till looking east between the clouds & the waves,
we saw a cataract of blood mixed with fire, and not many stones' throw from
us appeared and sunk again the scaly fold of a monstrous serpent. At last to
the east, distant about three degrees, appeared a fiery crest above the waves.
Slowly it reared like a ridge of golden rocks till we discovered two globes of
crimson fire, from which the sea fled away in clouds of smoke. And now we
saw it was the head of Leviathan; his forehead was divided into streaks of
green & purple like those on a tyger's forehead; soon we saw his mouth &
red gills hang just above the raging foam, tinging the black deep with beams
of blood, advancing toward [PLATE 19] us with all the fury of a spiritual
existence.

My friend the Angel climb'd up from his station into the mill. I remain'd
alone, & then this appearance was no more, but I found myself sitting on a
pleasant bank beside a river by moon light, hearing a harper who sung to the
harp, & his theme was: "The man who never alters his opinion is like standing
water, & breeds reptiles of the mind."

But I arose, and sought for the mill, & there I found my Angel, who surprised asked me how I escaped?

I answered: "All that we saw was owing to your metaphysics: for when you
ran away, I found myself on a bank by moonlight hearing a harper. But now
we have seen my eternal lot, shall I shew you yours? He laughd at my proposal; but I by force suddenly caught him in my arms, & flew westerly thro'
the night, til we were elevated above the earth's shadow; then I flung myself
with him directly into the body of the sun. Here I clothed myself in white,
& taking in my hand Swedenborg's volumes, sunk from the glorious clime,
and passed all the planets till we came to Saturn. Here I staid to rest & then
leap'd into the void between Saturn & the fixed stars.[5]

4. The "stable" is that where Jesus was born,
which, allegorically, leads to the "church" founded
in his name and to the "vault" where this institution effectually buried him. The "mill" in Blake is
a symbol of mechanical and analytic philosophy;
through this the pilgrims pass into the twisting
cave of rationalistic theology and descend to an
underworld that is an empty abyss. The point of
this Blakean equivalent of a carnival funhouse is
that only after you have thoroughly confused yourself by this tortuous approach, and only if you then
(as in the next two paragraphs) stare at this topsy-
turvy emptiness long enough, will the void gradually assume the semblance of the comic horrors of
the fantasied Hell of angelic orthodoxy.
5. In the Ptolemaic world picture Saturn was in
the outermost planetary sphere; beyond it was the
sphere of the fixed stars.

"Here," said I, "is your lot, in this space, if space it may be calld." Soon we saw the stable and the church, & I took him to the altar and open'd the Bible, and lo! it was a deep pit, into which I descended, driving the Angel before me. Soon we saw seven houses of brick;[6] one we enterd; in it were a [PLATE 20] number of monkeys, baboons, & all of that species, chaind by the middle, grinning and snatching at one another, but withheld by the short-ness of their chains. However, I saw that they sometimes grew numerous, and then the weak were caught by the strong, and with a grinning aspect, first coupled with & then devourd, by plucking off first one limb and then another till the body was left a helpless trunk. This, after grinning & kissing it with seeming fondness, they devourd too; and here & there I saw one savourily picking the flesh off of his own tail. As the stench terribly annoyd us both, we went into the mill, & I in my hand brought the skeleton of a body, which in the mill was Aristotle's Analytics.[7]

So the Angel said: "Thy phantasy has imposed upon me, & thou oughtest to be ashamed."

I answered: "We impose on one another, & it is but lost time to converse with you whose works are only Analytics."

Opposition is true Friendship.

PLATE 21

I have always found that Angels have the vanity to speak of themselves as the only wise; this they do with a confident insolence sprouting from system-atic reasoning.

Thus Swedenborg boasts that what he writes is new; tho' it is only the Contents or Index of already publish'd books.

A man carried a monkey about for a shew, & because he was a little wiser than the monkey, grew vain, and conceiv'd himself as much wiser than seven men. It is so with Swedenborg; he shews the folly of churches & exposes hypocrites, till he imagines that all are religious, & himself the single [PLATE 22] one on earth that ever broke a net.

Now hear a plain fact: Swedenborg has not written one new truth. Now hear another: he has written all the old falshoods.

And now hear the reason: He conversed with Angels who are all religious, & conversed not with Devils, who all hate religion, for he was incapable thro' his conceited notions.

Thus Swedenborg's writings are a recapitulation of all superficial opinions, and an analysis of the more sublime, but no further.

Have now another plain fact: Any man of mechanical talents may from the writings of Paracelsus or Jacob Behmen[8] produce ten thousand volumes of equal value with Swedenborg's, and from those of Dante or Shakespear, an infinite number.

But when he has done this, let him not say that he knows better than his master, for he only holds a candle in sunshine.

6. The "seven churches which are in Asia," to which John addresses the Book of Revelation 1.4. Blake now forces on the angel his own diabolic view of angelic biblical exegesis, theological spec-ulation and disputation, and Hell.
7. Aristotle's treatises on logic.
8. Jakob Boehme (1575–1624), a German shoe-maker who developed a theosophical system that has had persisting influence both on theological and on metaphysical speculation. Paracelsus (1493–1541), a Swiss physician and a pioneer in empirical medicine, was also a prominent theorist of the occult.

A Memorable Fancy

Once I saw a Devil in a flame of fire, who arose before an Angel that sat on a cloud, and the Devil utterd these words:

"The worship of God is, Honouring his gifts in other men, each according to his genius, and loving the [PLATE 23] greatest men best. Those who envy or calumniate great men hate God, for there is no other God."

The Angel hearing this became almost blue; but mastering himself, he grew yellow, & at last white, pink, & smiling, and then replied:

"Thou Idolater, is not God One? & is not he visible in Jesus Christ? and has not Jesus Christ given his sanction to the law of ten commandments, and are not all other men fools, sinners, & nothings?"

The Devil answer'd; "Bray a fool in a mortar with wheat, yet shall not his folly be beaten out of him.[9] If Jesus Christ is the greatest man, you ought to love him in the greatest degree. Now hear how he has given his sanction to the law of ten commandments: did he not mock at the sabbath, and so mock the sabbath's God?[1] murder those who were murderd because of him? turn away the law from the woman taken in adultery?[2] steal the labor of others to support him? bear false witness when he omitted making a defence before Pilate?[3] covet when he pray'd for his disciples, and when he bid them shake off the dust of their feet against such as refused to lodge them?[4] I tell you, no virtue can exist without breaking these ten commandments. Jesus was all virtue, and acted from im[PLATE 24]pulse, not from rules."

When he had so spoken, I beheld the Angel, who stretched out his arms embracing the flame of fire, & he was consumed and arose as Elijah.[5]

Note. This Angel, who is now become a Devil, is my particular friend; we often read the Bible together in its infernal or diabolical sense, which the world shall have if they behave well.

I have also The Bible of Hell,[6] which the world shall have whether they will or no.

One Law for the Lion & Ox is Oppression.

1790–93   1790–93

PLATE 25

A Song of Liberty[1]

1. The Eternal Female groand! it was heard over all the Earth.
2. Albion's coast is sick, silent; the American meadows faint!

9. Proverbs 27.22: "Though thou shouldst bray a fool in a mortar among wheat with a pestle, yet will not his foolishness depart from him." "Bray": pound into small pieces.
1. Mark 2.27: "The sabbath was made for man."
2. Cf. John 8.2–11.
3. Cf. Matthew 27.13–14.
4. Matthew 10.14: "Whosoever shall not receive you . . . when ye depart . . . shake off the dust of your feet."
5. In 2 Kings 2.11 the prophet Elijah "went up by a whirlwind into heaven," borne by "a chariot of fire."
6. I.e., the poems and designs that Blake is work-

ing on.
1. Blake etched this poem in 1792 and sometimes bound it as an appendix to *The Marriage of Heaven and Hell*. It recounts the birth, manifested in the contemporary events in France, of the flaming Spirit of Revolution (whom Blake later called Orc), and describes his conflict with the tyrannical sky god (whom Blake later called Urizen). The poem ends with the portent of the Spirit of Revolution shattering the ten commandments, or prohibitions against political, religious, and moral liberty, and bringing in a free and joyous new world. "Albion's" (line 2): England's.

3. Shadows of Prophecy shiver along by the lakes and the rivers and mutter across the ocean. France, rend down thy dungeon![2]

4. Golden Spain, burst the barriers of old Rome!

5. Cast thy keys, O Rome,[3] into the deep down falling, even to eternity down falling,

6. And weep.[4]

7. In her trembling hands she took the new born terror, howling.

8. On those infinite mountains of light now barr'd out by the Atlantic sea,[5] the new born fire stood before the starry king![6]

9. Flag'd with grey brow'd snows and thunderous visages, the jealous wings wav'd over the deep.

10. The speary hand burned aloft, unbuckled was the shield, forth went the hand of jealousy among the flaming hair, and [PLATE 26] hurl'd the new born wonder thro' the starry night.

11. The fire, the fire, is falling!

12. Look up! look up! O citizen of London, enlarge thy countenance! O Jew, leave counting gold! return to thy oil and wine. O African! black African! (Go, wingèd thought, widen his forehead.)

13. The fiery limbs, the flaming hair, shot like the sinking sun into the western sea.

14. Wak'd from his eternal sleep, the hoary element[7] roaring fled away:

15. Down rushd, beating his wings in vain, the jealous king; his grey brow'd councellors, thunderous warriors, curl'd veterans, among helms, and shields, and chariots, horses, elephants; banners, castles, slings and rocks,

16. Falling, rushing, ruining! buried in the ruins, on Urthona's[8] dens;

17. All night beneath the ruins; then, their sullen flames faded, emerge round the gloomy king,

18. With thunder and fire, leading his starry hosts thro' the waste wilderness [PLATE 27] he promulgates his ten commands, glancing his beamy eyelids over the deep in dark dismay,

19. Where the son of fire in his eastern cloud, while the morning plumes her golden breast,

20. Spurning the clouds written with curses, stamps the stony law[9] to dust, loosing the eternal horses from the dens of night, crying:

"Empire is no more! and now the lion & wolf shall cease."[1]

Chorus

Let the Priests of the Raven of dawn, no longer in deadly black, with hoarse note curse the sons of joy. Nor his accepted brethren, whom, tyrant, he calls

2. The political prison, the Bastille, was destroyed by the French revolutionaries in 1789.

3. The keys of Rome, a symbol of Papal power.

4. John 11.35: "Jesus wept."

5. The legendary continent of Atlantis, sunk beneath the sea, which Blake uses to represent the condition before the Fall.

6. Blake often uses the stars, in their fixed courses, as a symbol of the law-governed Newtonian universe.

7. The sea, which to Blake represents a devouring chaos, such as had swallowed Atlantis.

8. In the later Prophetic Books, Urthona is the unfallen form of Los, who in the fallen world represents the poetic imagination, the agent working for the regeneration of humanity.

9. I.e., the Ten Commandments (verse 18), which the "finger of God" had written on "tables [tablets] of stone" (Exodus 31.18).

1. Cf. Isaiah's prophecy, 65.17–25, of "new heavens and a new earth," when "The wolf and the lamb shall feed together, and the lion shall eat straw like the bullock."

free, lay the bound or build the roof. Nor pale religious letchery call that virginity, that wishes but acts not!

For every thing that lives is Holy.

1792   1792

FROM BLAKE'S NOTEBOOK[1]

Mock on, Mock on, Voltaire, Rousseau

Mock on, Mock on, Voltaire, Rousseau;[2]
Mock on, Mock on, 'tis all in vain.
You throw the sand against the wind,
And the wind blows it back again;

5   And every sand becomes a Gem
Reflected in the beams divine;
Blown back, they blind the mocking Eye,
But still in Israel's paths they shine.

The Atoms of Democritus
10   And Newton's Particles of light[3]
Are sands upon the Red sea shore,
Where Israel's tents do shine so bright.

Never pain to tell thy love

Never pain to tell thy love
Love that never told can be,
For the gentle wind does move
Silently, invisibly.

5   I told my love, I told my love,
I told her all my heart,
Trembling, cold, in ghastly fears—
Ah, she doth depart.

Soon as she was gone from me
10   A traveller came by
Silently, invisibly—
O, was no deny.

1. A commonplace book in which Blake drew sketches and jotted down verses and memoranda between the late 1780s and 1810. It is known as the Rossetti manuscript because it later came into the possession of the poet and painter Dante Gabriel Rossetti. These poems were first published in imperfect form in 1863, then transcribed from the manuscript by Geoffrey Keynes in 1935.

2. Blake regards both Voltaire and Rousseau as representing rationalism and Deism.
3. Newton in his *Opticks* hypothesized that light consisted of minute material particles. Democritus (460–362 B.C.E.) proposed that atoms were the ultimate components of the universe.

I askèd a thief

I askèd a thief to steal me a peach,
He turned up his eyes;
I ask'd a lithe lady to lie her down,
Holy & meek she cries.

5 As soon as I went
An angel came.
He wink'd at the thief
And smild at the dame—

And without one word said
10 Had a peach from the tree
And still as a maid
Enjoy'd the lady.

1796

And did those feet[1]

And did those feet in ancient time
Walk upon England's mountains green?
And was the holy Lamb of God
On England's pleasant pastures seen?

5 And did the Countenance Divine
Shine forth upon our clouded hills?
And was Jerusalem builded here,
Among those dark Satanic Mills?[2]

Bring me my Bow of burning gold,
10 Bring me my Arrows of desire,
Bring me my Spear; O clouds unfold!
Bring me my Chariot of fire!

I will not cease from Mental Fight,
Nor shall my Sword sleep in my hand,

1. These quatrains occur in the preface to Blake's prophetic poem *Milton*. There is an ancient belief, still current in parts of England, that Jesus came to England with Joseph of Arimathea. Blake adapts the legend to his own conception of a spiritual Israel, in which the significance of biblical events is as relevant to England as to Palestine. By a particularly Blakean irony, this poem of mental war in the service of apocalyptic desire is widely used as a hymn by those of us whom Blake called "angels."
2. There may be an allusion here to industrial England, but the mill is primarily Blake's symbol for a mechanistic and utilitarian worldview, according to which, as he said elsewhere, "the same dull round, even of a universe" becomes "a mill with complicated wheels."

15 Till we have built Jerusalem
In England's green & pleasant Land.

ca. 1804–10

ca. 1804–10

From A Vision of the Last Judgment[1]

For the Year 1810
Additions to Blake's Catalogue of Pictures &c

The Last Judgment [will be] when all those are Cast away who trouble Religion with Questions concerning Good & Evil or Eating of the Tree of those Knowledges or Reasonings which hinder the Vision of God turning all into a Consuming fire. When Imaginative Art & Science & all Intellectual Gifts, all the Gifts of the Holy Ghost, are lookd upon as of no use & only Contention remains to Man, then the Last Judgment begins, & its Vision is seen by the Imaginative Eye of Every one according to the situation he holds.

[PAGE 68] The Last Judgment is not Fable or Allegory but Vision. Fable or Allegory are a totally distinct & inferior kind of Poetry. Vision, or Imagination, is a Representation of what Eternally Exists, Really & Unchangeably. Fable or Allegory is Formd by the daughters of Memory. Imagination is Surrounded by the daughters of Inspiration, who in the aggregate are calld Jerusalem. [PAGE 69] Fable is Allegory, but what Critics call The Fable is Vision itself. [PAGE 68] The Hebrew Bible & the Gospel of Jesus are not Allegory, but Eternal Vision, or Imagination of All that Exists. Note here that Fable or Allegory is Seldom without some Vision. *Pilgrim's Progress* is full of it, the Greek Poets the same; but Allegory & Vision ought to be known as Two Distinct Things, & so calld for the Sake of Eternal Life. Plato has made Socrates say that Poets & Prophets do not know or Understand what they write or Utter; this is a most Pernicious Falshood. If they do not, pray is an inferior Kind to be calld Knowing? Plato confutes himself.[2]

The Last Judgment is one of these Stupendous Visions. I have represented it as I saw it. To different People it appears differently, as [PAGE 69] every thing else does; for tho on Earth things seem Permanent, they are less permanent than a Shadow, as we all know too well.

The Nature of Visionary Fancy, or Imagination, is very little Known, & the Eternal nature & permanence of its ever Existent Images is considered as less permanent than the things of Vegetative & Generative Nature; yet the Oak dies as well as the Lettuce, but Its Eternal Image & Individuality never dies, but renews by its seed. Just so the Imaginative Image returns by the seed of Contemplative Thought. The Writings of the Prophets illustrate these conceptions of the Visionary Fancy by their various sublime & Divine Images as seen in the Worlds of Vision. * * *

1. In this essay Blake describes and comments on his painting of the Last Judgment, now lost, which is said to have measured seven by five feet and to have included a thousand figures. The text has been transcribed and rearranged, as the sequence of the pages indicates, from the scattered fragments in Blake's Notebook. The opening and closing parts are reprinted here as Blake's fullest, although cryptic, statements of what he means by "vision." These sections deal with the relations of imaginative vision to allegory, Greek fable, and the biblical story; to uncurbed human passion and

intellectual power; to conventional and coercive virtue; to what is seen by the "corporeal" eye; to the arts; and to the Last Judgment and the apocalyptic redemption of humanity and of the created world—an apocalypse that is to be achieved through the triumph over the bodily eye by human imagination, as manifested in the creative artist.
2. In Plato's dialogue *Ion*, in which Socrates traps Ion into admitting that, because poets compose by inspiration, they do so without knowing what they are doing.

Let it here be Noted that the Greek Fables originated in Spiritual Mystery [PAGE 72] & Real Visions, Which are lost & clouded in Fable & Allegory, while the Hebrew Bible & the Greek Gospel are Genuine, Preservd by the Saviour's Mercy. The Nature of my Work is Visionary or Imaginative; it is an Endeavour to Restore what the Ancients calld the Golden Age.

[PAGE 69] This world of Imagination is the World of Eternity; it is the Divine bosom into which we shall all go after the death of the Vegetated body. This World of Imagination is Infinite & Eternal, whereas the world of Generation, or Vegetation, is Finite & Temporal. There Exist in that Eternal World the Permanent Realities of Every Thing which we see reflected in this Vegetable Glass of Nature.

All Things are comprehended in their Eternal Forms in the Divine [PAGE 70] body of the Saviour, the True Vine of Eternity, The Human Imagination, who appeard to Me as Coming to Judgment among his Saints & throwing off the Temporal that the Eternal might be Establishd. Around him were seen the Images of Existences according to a certain order suited to my Imaginative Eye. * * *

[PAGE 87] Men are admitted into Heaven not because they have curbed & governd their Passions, or have No Passions, but because they have Cultivated their Understandings. The Treasures of Heaven are not Negations of Passion, but Realities of Intellect from which All the Passions Emanate Uncurbed in their Eternal Glory. The Fool shall not enter into Heaven, let him be ever so Holy. Holiness is not The price of Enterance into Heaven. Those who are cast out Are All Those who, having no Passions of their own because No Intellect, Have spent their lives in Curbing & Governing other People's by the Various arts of Poverty & Cruelty of all kinds. Wo Wo Wo to you Hypocrites! Even Murder the Courts of Justice, more merciful than the Church, are compelld to allow, is not done in Passion but in Cool Blooded Design & Intention.

The Modern Church Crucifies Christ with the Head Downwards.

[PAGE 92] Many persons such as Paine & Voltaire,[3] with some of the Ancient Greeks, say: "We will not converse concerning Good & Evil; we will live in Paradise & Liberty." You may do so in Spirit, but not in the Mortal Body as you pretend, till after the last Judgment; for in Paradise they have no Corporeal & Mortal Body—that originated with the Fall & was calld Death & cannot be removed but by a Last Judgment; while we are in the world of Mortality we Must Suffer. The Whole Creation Groans to be deliverd; there will always be as many Hypocrites born as Honest Men & they will always have superior Power in Mortal Things. You cannot have Liberty in this World without what you call Moral Virtue, & you cannot have Moral Virtue without the Slavery of that half of the Human Race who hate what you call Moral Virtue.

*   *   *

Thinking as I do that the Creator of this World is a very Cruel Being, & being a Worshipper of Christ, I cannot help saying: "The Son, O how unlike

---

3. Blake represents Thomas Paine, author of *The Rights of Man* (1791), and Voltaire, the great author of the French Enlightenment, as proponents of the possibility of restoring an earthly paradise by political revolution. Such had been Blake's own view in the early 1790s (see, e.g., *The Marriage of Heaven and Hell*, p. 72).

uted to Seeking after. But I am contented whether I live by Painting or Engraving.

> I am Revd Sir Your very obedient servant,
>
> William Blake

To George Cumberland[3] (Apr. 12, 1827)

Dear Cumberland

I have been very near the Gates of Death & have returned very weak & an Old Man feeble & tottering, but not in Spirit & Life not in The Real Man The Imagination which Liveth for Ever. In that I am stronger & stronger as this Foolish Body decays. I thank you for the Pains you have taken with Poor Job.[4] I know too well that a great majority of Englishmen are fond of The Indefinite, which they Measure by Newton's Doctrine of the Fluxions of an Atom,[5] a Thing that does not Exist. These are Politicians & think that Republican Art[6] is Inimical to their Atom. For a Line or Lineament is not formed by Chance; a Line is a Line in its Minutest Subdivision[s]; Strait or Crooked, It is Itself, & Not Intermeasurable with or by any Thing Else. Such is Job, but since the French Revolution Englishmen are all Intermeasurable One by Another; Certainly a happy state of Agreement, to which I for One do not Agree. God keep me from the Divinity of Yes & No too, The Yea Nay Creeping Jesus, from supposing Up & Down to be the same Thing, as all Experimentalists must suppose.

You are desirous, I know, to dispose of some of my Works & to make [them] Pleasing. I am obliged to you & to all who do so. But having none remaining of all that I had Printed, I cannot Print more Except at a great loss, for at the time I printed those things I had a whole House to range in; now I am shut up in a Corner, therefore am forced to ask a Price for them that I scarce expect to get from a Stranger. I am now Printing a Set of the Songs of Innocence & Experience for a Friend at Ten Guineas, which I cannot do under Six Months consistent with my other Work, so that I have little hope of doing any more of such things. The Last Work I produced is a Poem Entitled "Jerusalem the Emanation of the Giant Albion," but find that to Print it will Cost my Time the amount of Twenty Guineas. One I have Finishd; it contains 100 Plates but it is not likely that I shall get a Customer for it.[7]

As you wish me to send you a list with the Prices of these things they are as follows:

	£	s	d
America	6.	6.	0
Europe	6.	6.	0
Visions &^c	5.	5.	0
Thel	3.	3.	0
Songs of Inn. & Exp.	10.	10.	0
Urizen	6.	6.	0

3. A businessman who was an old and loyal friend of Blake and a buyer of his illuminated books. Blake wrote this letter only four months before he died on Aug. 4, 1827.
4. Cumberland was trying to interest his friends in buying a set of Blake's engravings, *Illustrations of the Book of Job.*
5. Isaac Newton's *Method of Fluxions* (1704)

announced his discovery of the infinitesimal calculus. To Blake, Newton was the archrepresentative of materialist philosophy.
6. I.e., a free art, not subject to authoritarian control.
7. This single colored copy of Blake's *Jerusalem* survives in the Mellon Collection.

The Little Card[8] I will do as soon as Possible, but when you Consider that I have been reduced to a Skeleton, from which I am slowly recovering, you will I hope have Patience with me.

Flaxman[9] is Gone & we must All soon follow, every one to his Own Eternal House, Leaving the Delusive Goddess Nature & her Laws to get into Freedom from all Law of the Members into The Mind, in which every one is King & Priest in his own House. God Send it so on Earth as it is in Heaven.

I am, Dear Sir, Yours Affectionately

WILLIAM BLAKE

8. A small illustrated name card that Blake executed for Cumberland; it was his last engraving.

9. John Flaxman, a well-known sculptor of the time, had died the preceding December.

MARY ROBINSON
1758–1800

Among poets of the Romantic period, Mary Robinson, whom the *Dictionary of National Biography,* at the beginning of a long entry, describes as "actress, author, and mistress of George, Prince of Wales (afterwards George IV)," lived a more sensational life than either Byron or Shelley. Her father was a Bristol whaler, her mother a woman of "genteel background" who, after her husband deserted the family, ran a school for girls. At fifteen Mary was married to Thomas Robinson, an articled law clerk who seemed a good match but quickly proved a gambler and libertine; he was arrested for debt, and Mary and her infant daughter spent a year with him in debtors' prison, where, to pass the time, she began writing poetry. Her first pieces appeared in a two-volume *Poems* published under the patronage of the duchess of Devonshire in 1775.

In December 1776, accepting a long-standing invitation of David Garrick, the actor-manager of the Drury Lane theater, Robinson made her stage debut as Juliet, and for the next four years she was constantly before the public—in thirty or more leading roles, nine of them in plays by Shakespeare (she once acted Lady Macbeth on a night when she was advertised for Cordelia in *King Lear*). A remarkable beauty, she attracted many suitors and was painted by the leading portraitists of the day, including George Romney; Thomas Gainsborough; and Sir Joshua Reynolds, president of the Royal Academy. At a command performance of *The Winter's Tale* in December 1779, playing the role of Perdita, Robinson captivated the prince of Wales and, after negotiating financial compensation in the form of a £20,000 bond (because she would have to give up her acting career), became his mistress. When he abandoned her a year later, she was unsuccessful in suing for the £20,000 but subsequently was granted a pension of £500 per year through the efforts of the Whig parliamentarian and foreign minister Charles James Fox, another of her lovers. At twenty-five she formed an attachment with an army officer, Colonel Banastre Tarleton, that lasted for ten years but ended, again, in abandonment, with the additional complication that she was in increasingly poor health and, from a miscarriage (in some accounts) or rheumatic fever (in others), was paralyzed from the waist down. Even then she made a striking public figure, as four liveried servants, covering their arms with long white sleeves, bore her from the opera house to her waiting carriage.

She took up writing as a principal activity at the beginning of the 1790s, her final decade, when she was in her early thirties.

Scholars are just now sorting out her various productions in poetry, fiction, drama, and other forms. She published long poems and further collections of verse in 1777, 1791, 1793, 1796 (*Sappho and Phaon,* a series of Petrarchan sonnets), and 1800 (*Lyrical Tales,* a collection on the principles of Wordsworth and Coleridge's 1798 *Lyrical Ballads*), and numerous separate pieces under a dozen different pseudonyms in the magazines and newspapers, including the *Morning Post,* where she succeeded Robert Southey as poetry editor. She authored seven multivolume novels in the 1790s, beginning with *Vancenza; or, The Dangers of Credulity* (1792), whose first edition sold out in a single day. In drama, she wrote a farce that was never published and a five-act tragedy that was published but never performed. Other writings include pamphlets titled *Impartial Reflections on the Present Situation of the Queen of France* (1793) and *Thoughts on the Condition of Women, and on the Injustice of Mental Subordination* (1799). Her posthumous *Memoirs* (1801), an extremely lively autobiography in a period seemingly dominated by male self-construction, went through many editions in several languages.

Robinson is one of the accomplished writers of blank verse in the 1790s (as in *London's Summer Morning*) as well as one of the most irrepressibly musical in many different forms of rhyme. Outspokenly liberal in her politics and social views, good-humored, satirical, and sentimental by turns, she is one of the voices of what Stuart Curran calls "the new realism that will impel English poetry into the nineteenth century." Her *Lyrical Tales* appeared a month before the second edition of Wordsworth and Coleridge's *Lyrical Ballads*—from the same publisher and printer and in exactly the same format and typography (Wordsworth, in reaction, tried to change his own title to *Poems by W. Wordsworth*). Robinson's *The Poor Singing Dame* is modeled on the most popular of Wordsworth's 1798 ballads, *Goody Blake and Harry Gill.* Wordsworth in turn based one of his pieces (*The Seven Sisters; or, The Solitude of Binnorie*) on the elaborate metrical scheme of Robinson's *The Haunted Beach,* a poem that prompted Coleridge to exclaim to Southey, when he first saw it in the *Morning Post,* "the Metre—ay! that Woman has an Ear." Coleridge admired her "undoubted Genius," and Robinson returned the compliment in one of her last poems, *To the Poet Coleridge,* a shrewd reading of *Kubla Khan* sixteen years before it first got into print.

London's Summer Morning

Who has not wak'd to list the busy sounds
Of summer's morning, in the sultry smoke
Of noisy London? On the pavement hot
The sooty chimney-boy, with dingy face
5 And tatter'd covering, shrilly bawls his trade,
Rousing the sleepy housemaid. At the door
The milk-pail rattles, and the tinkling bell
Proclaims the dustman's office; while the street
Is lost in clouds impervious. Now begins
10 The din of hackney-coaches, waggons, carts;
While tinmen's shops, and noisy trunk-makers,
Knife-grinders, coopers, squeaking cork-cutters,
Fruit-barrows, and the hunger-giving cries
Of vegetable venders, fill the air.
15 Now ev'ry shop displays its varied trade,
And the fresh-sprinkled pavement cools the feet

Of early walkers. At the private door
The ruddy housemaid twirls the busy mop,
Annoying the smart 'prentice, or neat girl,
20 Tripping with band-box¹ lightly. Now the sun
Darts burning splendor on the glitt'ring pane,
Save where the canvas awning throws a shade
On the gay merchandise. Now, spruce and trim,
In shops (where beauty smiles with industry)
25 Sits the smart damsel; while the passenger
Peeps through the window, watching ev'ry charm.
Now pastry dainties catch the eye minute
Of humming insects, while the limy snare
Waits to enthral them. Now the lamp-lighter
30 Mounts the tall ladder, nimbly venturous,
To trim the half-fill'd lamp; while at his feet
The pot-boy² yells discordant! All along
The sultry pavement, the old-clothes-man cries
In tone monotonous, and side-long views
35 The area for his traffic: now the bag
Is slily open'd, and the half-worn suit
(Sometimes the pilfer'd treasure of the base
Domestic spoiler), for one half its worth,
Sinks in the green abyss. The porter now
40 Bears his huge load along the burning way;
And the poor poet wakes from busy dreams,
To paint the summer morning.

ca. 1795   1804

January, 1795

Pavement slipp'ry, people sneezing,
Lords in ermine, beggars freezing;
Titled gluttons dainties carving,
Genius in a garret starving.

5 Lofty mansions, warm and spacious;
Courtiers cringing and voracious;
Misers scarce the wretched heeding;
Gallant soldiers fighting, bleeding.

Wives who laugh at passive spouses;
10 Theatres, and meeting-houses;
Balls, where simp'ring misses languish;
Hospitals, and groans of anguish.

Arts and sciences bewailing;
Commerce drooping, credit failing;
15 Placemen° mocking subjects loyal;   *political appointees*
Separations, weddings royal.

---

1. Box for hats, gloves, etc.   2. Servant from a nearby pub.

Authors who can't earn a dinner;
Many a subtle rogue a winner;
Fugitives for shelter seeking;
20 Misers hoarding, tradesmen breaking.

Taste and talents quite deserted;
All the laws of truth perverted;
Arrogance o'er merit soaring;
Merit silently deploring.

25 Ladies gambling night and morning;
Fools the works of genius scorning;
Ancient dames for girls mistaken,
Youthful damsels quite forsaken.

Some in luxury delighting;
30 More in talking than in fighting;
Lovers old, and beaux decrepid;
Lordlings empty and insipid.

Poets, painters, and musicians;
Lawyers, doctors, politicians:
35 Pamphlets, newspapers, and odes,
Seeking fame by diff'rent roads.

Gallant souls with empty purses;
Gen'rals only fit for nurses;
School-boys, smit with martial spirit,
40 Taking place of vet'ran merit.

Honest men who can't get places,
Knaves who shew unblushing faces;
Ruin hasten'd, peace retarded;
Candor spurn'd, and art rewarded.

1795   1806

The Poor Singing Dame

Beneath an old wall, that went round an old castle,
    For many a year, with brown ivy o'erspread,
A neat little hovel, its lowly roof raising,
    Defied the wild winds that howl'd over its shed:
5 The turrets, that frown'd on the poor simple dwelling,
    Were rock'd to and fro, when the tempest would roar,
And the river, that down the rich valley was swelling,
    Flow'd swiftly beside the green step of its door.

The summer sun gilded the rushy roof slanting,
10   The bright dews bespangled its ivy-bound hedge,
And above, on the ramparts, the sweet birds were chanting,
    And wild buds thick dappled the clear river's edge.

When the castle's rich chambers were haunted and dreary,
 The poor little hovel was still and secure;
15 And no robber e'er enter'd, nor goblin nor fairy,
 For the splendors of pride had no charms to allure.

The Lord of the castle, a proud surly ruler,
 Oft heard the low dwelling with sweet music ring,
For the old Dame that liv'd in the little hut cheerly,
20 Would sit at her wheel, and would merrily sing:
When with revels the castle's great hall was resounding,
 The old Dame was sleeping, not dreaming of fear;
And when over the mountains the huntsmen were bounding
 She would open her lattice, their clamors to hear.

25 To the merry-ton'd horn she would dance on the threshold,
 And louder, and louder, repeat her old song:
And when winter its mantle of frost was displaying,
 She caroll'd, undaunted, the bare woods among:
She would gather dry fern, ever happy and singing,
30 With her cake of brown bread, and her jug of brown beer,
And would smile when she heard the great castle-bell ringing,
 Inviting the proud—to their prodigal cheer.

Thus she liv'd, ever patient and ever contented,
 Till envy the Lord of the castle possess'd,
35 For he hated that poverty should be so cheerful,
 While care could the fav'rites of fortune molest;
He sent his bold yeomen with threats to prevent her,
 And still would she carol her sweet roundelay;
At last, an old steward relentless he sent her—
40 Who bore her, all trembling, to prison away!

Three weeks did she languish, then died broken-hearted,
 Poor Dame! how the death-bell did mournfully sound!
And along the green path six young bachelors bore her,
 And laid her for ever beneath the cold ground!
45 And the primroses pale 'mid the long grass were growing,
 The bright dews of twilight bespangled her grave,
And morn heard the breezes of summer soft blowing
 To bid the fresh flow'rets in sympathy wave.

The Lord of the castle, from that fatal moment
50 When poor singing Mary was laid in her grave,
Each night was surrounded by screech-owls appalling,
 Which o'er the black turrets their pinions would wave!
On the ramparts that frown'd on the river, swift flowing,
 They hover'd, still hooting a terrible song,
55 When his windows would rattle, the winter blast blowing,
 They would shriek like a ghost, the dark alleys among!

Wherever he wander'd they follow'd him crying,
 At dawnlight, at eve, still they haunted his way!
When the moon shone across the wide common they hooted,

60   Nor quitted his path till the blazing of day.
    His bones began wasting, his flesh was decaying,
       And he hung his proud head, and he perish'd with shame;
    And the tomb of rich marble, no soft tear displaying,
       O'ershadows the grave of the Poor Singing Dame!

1799–1800   1800

The Haunted Beach

         Upon a lonely desart Beach,
            Where the white foam was scatter'd,
         A little shed uprear'd its head,
            Though lofty barks° were shatter'd.   *ships*
    5   The sea-weeds gath'ring near the door
            A somber path display'd;
         And, all around, the deaf'ning roar
         Re-echo'd on the chalky shore,
            By the green billows made.

    10   Above a jutting cliff was seen
            Where Sea Birds hover'd, craving;
         And all around the craggs were bound
            With weeds—for ever waving.
         And here and there, a cavern wide
    15   Its shad'wy jaws display'd;
         And near the sands, at ebb of tide,
         A shiver'd mast was seen to ride
            Where the green billows stray'd.

         And often, while the moaning wind
    20   Stole o'er the Summer Ocean,
         The moonlight scene was all serene,
            The waters scarce in motion;
         Then, while the smoothly slanting sand
            The tall cliff wrapp'd in shade,
    25   The Fisherman beheld a band
         Of Spectres gliding hand in hand—
            Where the green billows play'd.

         And pale their faces were as snow,
            And sullenly they wander'd;
    30   And to the skies with hollow eyes
            They look'd as though they ponder'd.
         And sometimes, from their hammock shroud,
            They dismal howlings made,
         And while the blast blew strong and loud
    35   The clear moon mark'd the ghastly crowd,
            Where the green billows play'd!

         And then above the haunted hut
            The Curlews screaming hover'd;

And the low door, with furious roar,
40   The frothy breakers cover'd.
For in the Fisherman's lone shed
    A murder'd man was laid,
With ten wide gashes in his head,
And deep was made his sandy bed
45   Where the green billows play'd.

A shipwreck'd Mariner was he,
    Doom'd from his home to sever;
Who swore to be through wind and sea
    Firm and undaunted ever!
50 And when the wave resistless roll'd,
    About his arm he made
A packet rich of Spanish gold,
And, like a British sailor bold,
    Plung'd where the billows play'd!

55 The Spectre band, his messmates brave,
    Sunk in the yawning ocean,
While to the mast he lash'd him fast,
    And brav'd the storm's commotion.
The winter moon upon the sand
60   A silv'ry carpet made,
And mark'd the Sailor reach the land,
And mark'd his murd'rer wash his hand
    Where the green billows play'd.

And since that hour the Fisherman
65   Has toil'd and toil'd in vain;
For all the night the moony light
    Gleams on the specter'd main!
And when the skies are veil'd in gloom,
    The Murd'rer's liquid way
70 Bounds o'er the deeply yawning tomb,
And flashing fires the sands illume,
    Where the green billows play!

Full thirty years his task has been
    Day after day more weary;
75 For Heav'n design'd his guilty mind
    Should dwell on prospects dreary.
Bound by a strong and mystic chain,
    He has not pow'r to stray;
But destin'd mis'ry to sustain,
80 He wastes, in Solitude and Pain,
    A loathsome life away.

1800

To the Poet Coleridge[1]

Rapt in the visionary theme!
   Spirit divine! with thee I'll wander,
Where the blue, wavy, lucid stream,
   'Mid forest glooms, shall slow meander!
5 With thee I'll trace the circling bounds
   Of thy new Paradise extended;
And listen to the varying sounds
   Of winds, and foamy torrents blended.

Now by the source which lab'ring heaves
10   The mystic fountain, bubbling, panting,
While gossamer° its net-work weaves,   *filmy cobweb*
   Adown the blue lawn slanting!
I'll mark thy *sunny dome*, and view
Thy *caves of ice*, thy fields of dew!
15 Thy ever-blooming mead, whose flow'r
Waves to the cold breath of the moonlight hour!
Or when the day-star, peering bright
On the grey wing of parting night;
While more than vegetating pow'r
20 Throbs grateful to the burning hour,
As summer's whisper'd sighs unfold
Her million, million buds of gold;
Then will I climb the breezy bounds,
   Of thy new Paradise extended,
25 And listen to the distant sounds
   Of winds, and foamy torrents blended!

Spirit divine! with thee I'll trace
Imagination's boundless space!
With thee, beneath thy *sunny dome*,
30   I'll listen to the minstrel's lay,
   Hymning the gradual close of day;
In *caves of ice* enchanted roam,
Where on the glitt'ring entrance plays
The moon's-beam with its silv'ry rays;
35   Or, when the glassy stream,
     That through the deep dell flows,
Flashes the noon's hot beam;
   The noon's hot beam, that midway shows
Thy flaming temple, studded o'er
40 With all Peruvia's° lustrous store!   *Peru's*
There will I trace the circling bounds
   Of thy new Paradise extended!
And listen to the awful sounds,
   Of winds, and foamy torrents blended!

45 And now I'll pause to catch the moan
   Of distant breezes, cavern-pent;

---

1. This poem is a tribute to, and running commentary on, Coleridge's *Kubla Khan*, which Robinson read in manuscript (Coleridge had drafted it in 1797 but did not publish it until 1816).

Now, ere the twilight tints are flown,
Purpling the landscape, far and wide,
On the dark promontory's side
50   I'll gather wild flow'rs, dew besprent,
And weave a crown for thee,
Genius of Heav'n-taught poesy!
While, op'ning to my wond'ring eyes,
Thou bidst a new creation rise,
55   I'll raptur'd trace the circling bounds
        Of thy rich Paradise extended,
And listen to the varying sounds
        Of winds, and foaming torrents blended.

And now, with lofty tones inviting,
60   Thy nymph, her dulcimer swift smiting,
Shall wake me in ecstatic measures!
Far, far remov'd from mortal pleasures!
        In cadence rich, in cadence strong,
Proving the wondrous witcheries of song!
65   I hear her voice! thy *sunny dome*,
Thy *caves of ice*, aloud repeat,
Vibrations, madd'ning sweet,
Calling the visionary wand'rer home.
She sings of thee, O favor'd child
70   Of *minstrelsy*, sublimely wild!
Of thee, whose soul can feel the tone
Which gives to airy dreams *a magic* all thy own!

Oct. 1800   1801

ROBERT BURNS
1759–1796

A favorite myth of later eighteenth-century primitivists was that there exist natural poets who warble their native woodnotes wild, independent of art or literary tradition. These artless poets were sought among peasants and proletarians, whose caste or rural habitation, it was thought, protected them from the artificialities of civilized life and culture. When Robert Burns published his first volume of *Poems* in 1786, he was at once hailed by the literati of Edinburgh as an instance of the natural genius, a "Heaven-taught plowman" whose poems were the spontaneous overflow of his native feelings. Burns rather enjoyed playing the role of the poet by instinct. But in fact he was a well-read (although largely self-educated) man whose quick intelligence and sensibility enabled him to make the most of limited opportunities. And although he broke clear of the contemporary conventions of decayed English neoclassicism, he did so not by instinct but as a deliberate craftsman who turned to two earlier traditions for his models. One of these was the oral tradition of Scottish folklore and folk song; the other was the highly developed literary tradition of poems written in the Scots dialect of English.

His father—William Burnes, as he spelled his name—was a God-fearing and hard-working farmer of Ayrshire, a county in southwestern Scotland, who, unable to make a go of it in a period of hard times and high rents, died in 1784 broken in body and spirit. Robert, with his brother Gilbert, was forced to do the toil of a man while still a boy and began to show signs of the heart trouble of which he was to die when only thirty-seven. Although his father had the Scottish esteem for education and saw to it that his sons attended school whenever they could, Burns's education in literature, theology, politics, and philosophy came mainly from his own reading. At the age of fifteen he fell in love, and was inspired by that event to write his first song. "Thus," he said, "with me began Love and Poesy." After he reached maturity, he cultivated assiduously both these propensities. He began a series of amorous affairs, fathering in 1785 the first of a number of illegitimate children; he also extended greatly the range and quantity of his attempts at poetry. So rapid was his development that by the time he published the Kilmarnock edition, at the age of twenty-seven, he had written all but a few of his greatest long poems.

The Kilmarnock volume (so named from the town in which it was published) is one of the most remarkable first volumes by any British poet, and it had a great and immediate success. Burns was acclaimed "Caledonia's Bard" and lionized by the intellectuals and gentlefolk when he visited Edinburgh soon after his book came out. The peasant-poet demonstrated that he could more than hold his own as a brilliant conversationalist and debater. But he was also wise enough to realize that once the novelty wore off, his eminence in this society would not endure. He had a fierce pride that was quick to resent any hint of contempt or condescension toward himself as a man of low degree. His sympathies were democratic, and he was an outspoken admirer of the republican revolutions in America and France. In religion, too, he was a radical, professing "the Religion of Sentiment and Reason" in opposition to the strict Calvinism in which he had been raised, and he offended many pious Presbyterians by his devastating satires against the rigid tenets and the moral authoritarianism of the Scottish kirk. Furthermore, his sexual irregularities were notorious, less because they were out of the common order at that time than because he flaunted them before the "unco guid"—as his biographer DeLancey Ferguson has said, "it was not so much that he was conspicuously sinful as that he sinned conspicuously." Most of Burns's friends in high station quickly fell away, and his later visits to Edinburgh did not repeat the social success of the first.

In 1788 Burns was given a commission as excise officer, or tax inspector, and he settled down with Jean Armour, a former lover, now his wife, at Ellisland, near Dumfries, combining his official duties with farming. This was the fourth farm on which Burns had worked; and when it, like the others, failed, he moved his family to the lively country town of Dumfries. Here he was fairly happy, despite recurrent illness and a chronic shortage of money. He performed his official duties efficiently and was respected by his fellow townspeople and esteemed by his superiors; he was a devoted family man and father; and he accumulated a circle of intimates to whom he could repair for conversation and conviviality. In 1787 James Johnson, an engraver, had enlisted Burns's aid in collecting Scottish folk songs for an anthology called *The Scots Musical Museum*. Burns soon became the real editor for several volumes of this work, devoting all of his free time to collecting, editing, restoring, and imitating traditional songs, and to writing verses of his own to traditional dance tunes. Almost all of his creative work during the last twelve years of his life went into the writing of songs for the *Musical Museum* and for George Thomson's *Select Collection of Original Scottish Airs*. This was for Burns a devoted labor of love and patriotism, done anonymously, for which he refused to accept any pay, although badly in need of money; and he continued the work when he was literally on his deathbed.

Burns's best poetry was written in Scots, a northern dialect of English spoken by rural people and (on other than formal occasions) by most eighteenth-century Scottish gentlefolk as well. When Burns attempted to write in standard English, the result—except in an occasional lyric such as the lucid and graceful *Afton Water*—

tended to be stilted and conventional, with the stock phrasing, sententiousness, and sentimentality of the genteel poetic tradition of his day. He is often considered a "pre-Romantic" who, anticipating Wordsworth, revived the lyric, exploited the literary forms and legends of folk culture, and wrote in the language really spoken by the common people. This reputation is based primarily on his songs. By far the major portion of the poems that Burns published under his own name are concerned with men and manners and are written in the literary forms that had been favored by earlier eighteenth-century poets; they include brilliant satire in a variety of modes, a number of fine verse epistles to friends and fellow poets, and one masterpiece of mock-heroic (or at any rate seriocomic) narrative, *Tam o' Shanter*. The claim could be supported that, next to Pope, Burns is the greatest eighteenth-century master of these literary types. Yet his writings in satire, epistle, and mock-heroic are very remote from Pope's in their heartiness and verve, no less than in their dialect and intricate stanza forms. The reason for the difference is that Burns turned for his models not to Horace and the English neoclassic tradition but to the native tradition that had been established in the golden age of Scottish poetry by Robert Henryson, William Dunbar, Gavin Douglas, and other Scottish Chaucerians of the fifteenth and sixteenth centuries. He knew this literature through his eighteenth-century Scottish predecessors, especially Allan Ramsay and Robert Fergusson, who had collected some of the old poems and written new ones based on the old models. Burns improved greatly on these predecessors, but he derived from them much that is characteristic in his literary forms, subjects, diction, and stanzas.

Burns's songs, however, are more widely known than his longer works and have in themselves been adequate to sustain his poetic reputation. He wrote over three hundred of them, in unequaled abundance and variety. In his songs he gives himself over wholeheartedly to the emotion of the moment, evoked by all the standard lyric subjects: love, drink, work, friendship, patriotism, and bawdry. His poetic character is hearty, generous, rollicking, tender, with a sympathy that encompasses humans of all types, from national heroes to tavern roarers. Burns is not only the national poet of Scotland but a song writer for all English-speaking people. Wherever in the world they may be on New Year's Eve, when, helped by drink and the reminder of their bondage to time, men and women indulge their instinct of a common humanity, they join hands and sing a song of Burns.

The texts printed here are based on *The Poems and Songs of Robert Burns,* ed. James Kinsley, 3 vols. (Oxford, 1968).

Green grow the rashes[1]

Chorus

Green grow the rashes,° O;   *rushes*
Green grow the rashes, O;
The sweetest hours that e'er I spend,
  Are spent among the lasses, O.

I

There's nought but care on ev'ry han',
  In ev'ry hour that passes, O:
What signifies the life o' man,
  An' 'twere na for the lasses, O.
          Green grow, &c.

---

1. Burns's revision of a song long current in a number of versions, most of them bawdy.

2

5 The warly° race may riches chase,   *worldly*
  An' riches still may fly them, O;
 An' tho' at last they catch them fast,
  Their hearts can ne'er enjoy them, O.
    Green grow, &c.

3

 But gie me a canny° hour at e'en,   *quiet*
10 My arms about my Dearie, O;
 An' warly cares, an' warly men,
  May a' gae tapsalteerie,° O!   *topsy-turvy*
    Green grow, &c.

4

 For you sae douse,° ye sneer at this,   *sober*
  Ye're nought but senseless asses, O:
15 The wisest Man[2] the warl' saw,
  He dearly lov'd the lasses, O.
    Green grow, &c.

5

 Auld Nature swears, the lovely Dears
  Her noblest work she classes, O:
 Her prentice han' she try'd on man,
20 An' then she made the lasses, O.
    Green grow, &c.

1784   1787

Holy Willie's Prayer[1]

And send the Godly in a pet to pray—
              Pope

Argument

Holy Willie was a rather oldish batchelor Elder in the parish of Mauchline, and much and justly famed for that polemical chattering which ends in tippling Orthodoxy, and for that Spiritualized Bawdry which refines to Liquorish Devotion.—In a Sessional process with a gentleman in Mauchline, a Mr. Gavin Hamilton, Holy Willie, and his priest, Father Auld, after full hearing in the Presbytry of Ayr, came off but second best; owing partly to the oratorical powers of Mr. Robt. Aiken, Mr. Hamilton's Counsel; but chiefly to Mr. Hamilton's being one of the most irreproachable and truly respectable

2. King Solomon.
1. This satire, in the form of a dramatic monologue, was inspired by one William Fisher, a self-righteous elder in the parish of Mauchline, and is directed against a basic Calvinist tenet of the old Scottish kirk. Holy Willie assumes that he is one of a small minority, God's "elect"—in other words that he has been predestined for grace, no matter what works he does in this vale of tears. The epigraph is from *The Rape of the Lock.*

characters in the country.—On losing his Process, the Muse overheard him
at his devotions as follows—

> O thou that in the heavens does dwell!
> Wha, as it pleases best thysel,
> Sends ane to heaven and ten to h-ll,
>   A' for thy glory!
> 5 And no for ony gude or ill
>   They've done before thee.
>
> I bless and praise thy matchless might,
> When thousands thou has left in night,
> That I am here before thy sight,
>   For gifts and grace,
> 10 A burning and a shining light
>   To a' this place.
>
> What was I, or my generation,
> That I should get such exaltation?
> 15 I, wha deserv'd most just damnation,
>   For broken laws
> Sax° thousand years ere my creation,   *six*
>   Thro' Adam's cause!
>
> When from my mother's womb I fell,
> 20 Thou might hae plunged me deep in hell,
> To gnash my gooms, and weep, and wail,
>   In burning lakes,
> Where damned devils roar and yell
>   Chain'd to their stakes.
>
> 25 Yet I am here, a chosen sample,
> To shew thy grace is great and ample:
> I'm here, a pillar o' thy temple
>   Strong as a rock,
> A guide, a ruler and example
> 30   To a' thy flock.
>
> O Lord thou kens what zeal I bear,
> When drinkers drink, and swearers swear,
> And singin' there, and dancin' here,
>   Wi' great an' sma';
> 35 For I am keepet by thy fear,
>   Free frae them a'.
>
> But yet—O Lord—confess I must—
> At times I'm fash'd° wi' fleshly lust;   *troubled*
> And sometimes too, in warldly trust
> 40   Vile Self gets in;
> But thou remembers we are dust,
>   Defil'd wi' sin.

O Lord—yestreen—thou kens—wi' Meg—
Thy pardon I sincerely beg!
45 O may't ne'er be a living plague,
        To my dishonor!
And I'll ne'er lift a lawless leg
        Again upon her.

Besides, I farther maun° avow,   *must*
50 Wi' Leezie's lass, three times—I trow°—   *believe*
But Lord, that Friday I was fou°   *drunk*
        When I cam near her;
Or else, thou kens, thy servant true
        Wad never steer° her.   *molest*

55 Maybe thou lets this fleshly thorn
Buffet thy servant e'en and morn,
Lest he o'er proud and high should turn,
        That he's sae gifted;
If sae, thy hand maun e'en be borne
60   Untill thou lift it.

Lord bless thy Chosen in this place,
For here thou has a chosen race:
But God, confound their stubborn face,
        And blast their name,
65 Wha bring thy rulers to disgrace
        And open shame.

Lord mind Gaun Hamilton's[2] deserts!
He drinks, and swears, and plays at cartes,°   *cards*
Yet has sae mony taking arts
70   Wi' Great and Sma',
Frae God's ain priest the people's hearts
        He steals awa.

And when we chasten'd him therefore,
Thou kens how he bred sic a splore,°   *disturbance*
75 And set the warld in a roar
        O' laughin at us:
Curse thou his basket and his store,
        Kail° and potatoes.   *broth*

Lord hear my earnest cry and prayer
80 Against that Presbytry of Ayr!
Thy strong right hand, Lord, make it bare
        Upon their heads!
Lord visit them, and dinna spare,
        For their misdeeds!

---

2. Burns's friend Gavin Hamilton, whom Holy Willie had brought up on moral charges before the Kirk Session of the Presbytery of Ayr. As Burns explains in the Argument, Hamilton was successfully defended by his counsel, Robert Aiken (referred to in line 85).

85 O Lord my God, that glib-tongu'd Aiken!
My very heart and flesh are quaking
To think how I sat, sweating, shaking,
     And piss'd wi' dread,
While Auld wi' hingin° lip gaed sneaking   *hanging*
90   And hid his head!

Lord, in thy day o'vengeance try him!
Lord visit him that did employ him!
And pass not in thy mercy by them,
     Nor hear their prayer;
95 But for thy people's sake destroy them,
     And dinna spare!

But Lord, remember me and mine
Wi' mercies temporal and divine!
That I for grace and gear° may shine,   *wealth*
100   Excell'd by nane!
And a' the glory shall be thine!
     Amen! Amen!

1789   1789

To a Mouse

On Turning Her up in Her Nest with the Plough, November, 1785[1]

Wee, sleeket,° cowran, tim'rous beastie,   *sleek*
O, what a panic's in thy breastie!
Thou need na start awa sae hasty,
     Wi' bickering brattle![2]
5 I wad be laith° to rin an' chase thee   *loath*
     Wi' murd'ring pattle!°   *plowstaff*

I'm truly sorry Man's dominion
Has broken Nature's social union,
An' justifies that ill opinion,
10   Which makes thee startle,
At me, thy poor, earth-born companion,
     An' fellow mortal!

I doubt na, whyles,° but thou may thieve;   *sometimes*
What then? poor beastie, thou maun° live!   *must*
15 A daimen-icker in a thrave[3]
     'S a sma' request:
I'll get a blessin wi' the lave,°   *remainder*
     An' never miss 't!

1. Burns's brother claimed that this poem was composed while the poet was actually holding the plow.

2. With headlong scamper.

3. An occasional ear in twenty-four sheaves.

Thy wee-bit housie, too, in ruin!
20 It's silly° wa's the win's are strewin!   *feeble*
An' naething, now, to big° a new ane,   *build*
    O' foggage° green!   *coarse grass*
An' bleak December's winds ensuin,
    Baith snell° an' keen!   *bitter*

25 Thou saw the fields laid bare an' waste,
An' weary Winter comin fast,
An' cozie here, beneath the blast,
    Thou thought to dwell,
Till crash! the cruel coulter° past   *cutter blade*
30   Out thro' thy cell.

That wee-bit heap o' leaves an' stibble°   *stubble*
Has cost thee monie a weary nibble!
Now thou 's turn'd out, for a' thy trouble,
    But° house or hald,⁴   *without*
35 To thole° the Winter's sleety dribble,   *endure*
    An' cranreuch° cauld!   *hoarfrost*

But Mousie, thou art no thy-lane,°   *not alone*
In proving foresight may be vain:
The best laid schemes o' Mice an' Men
40   Gang aft agley,⁵
An' lea'e us nought but grief an' pain,
    For promis'd joy!

Still, thou art blest, compar'd wi' me!
The present only toucheth thee:
45 But Och! I backward cast my e'e,
    On prospects drear!
An' forward tho' I canna see,
    I guess an' fear!

1785   1786

To a Louse

On Seeing One on a Lady's Bonnet at Church

Ha! whare ye gaun, ye crowlan° ferlie!°   *crawling / wonder*
Your impudence protects you sairly:°   *sorely*
I canna say but ye strunt° rarely,   *strut*
    Owre gawze and lace;
5 Tho' faith, I fear ye dine but sparely,
    On sic a place.

Ye ugly, creepan, blastet wonner,°   *wonder*
Detested, shunn'd, by saunt an' sinner,

---

4. Hold, holding (i.e., land).   5. Go oft awry.

How daur ye set your fit° upon her,   *foot*
10   Sae fine a Lady!
     Gae somewhere else and seek your dinner,
           On some poor body.

     Swith,° in some beggar's haffet° squattle;°   *swift / locks / sprawl*
     There ye may creep, and sprawl, and sprattle,°   *struggle*
15   Wi' ither kindred, jumping cattle,
           In shoals and nations;
     Whare horn nor bane[1] ne'er daur unsettle,
           Your thick plantations.

     Now haud you there, ye're out o' sight,
20   Below the fatt'rels,° snug and tight,   *ribbon ends*
     Na faith ye yet![2] ye'll no be right,
           Till ye've got on it,
     The vera tapmost, towrin height
           O' Miss's bonnet.

25   My sooth! right bauld ye set your nose out,
     As plump an' gray as onie grozet:°   *gooseberry*
     O for some rank, mercurial rozet,°   *rosin*
           Or fell,° red smeddum,°   *sharp / powder*
     I'd gie you sic a hearty dose o't,
30   Wad dress your droddum!°   *buttocks*

     I wad na been surpriz'd to spy
     You on an auld wife's flainen toy,°   *flannel cap*
     Or aiblins° some bit duddie° boy,   *perhaps / ragged*
           On 's wylecoat;°   *undershirt*
35   But Miss's fine Lunardi,[3] fye!
           How daur ye do 't?

     O Jenny dinna toss your head,
     An' set your beauties a' abread!°   *abroad*
     Ye little ken what cursed speed
40   The blastie's° makin!   *creature's*
     Thae° winks and finger-ends, I dread,   *those*
           Are notice takin!

     O wad some Pow'r the giftie gie us
     To see oursels as others see us!
45   It wad frae monie a blunder free us
           An' foolish notion:
     What airs in dress an' gait wad lea'e us,
           And ev'n Devotion![4]

1785   1786

1. I.e., fine-tooth comb made of horn or bone ("bane").
2. Confound you!
3. A balloon-shaped bonnet, named after Vin-cenzo Lunardi, who made a number of balloon flights in the mid-1780s.
4. I.e., even pretended piety.

Auld Lang Syne[1]

Should auld acquaintance be forgot
   And never brought to mind?
Should auld acquaintance be forgot,
   And auld lang syne!

Chorus

5 For auld lang syne, my jo,
    For auld lang syne,
We'll tak a cup o' kindness yet
   For auld lang syne.

And surely ye'll be° your pint stowp!°   *pay for / pint cup*
10 And surely I'll be mine!
And we'll tak a cup o' kindness yet,
   For auld lang syne.
     For auld, &c.

We twa hae run about the braes°   *slopes*
   And pou'd the gowans° fine;   *daisies*
15 But we've wander'd many a weary fitt,
   Sin auld lang syne.
     For auld, &c.

We twa hae paidl'd in the burn°   *stream*
   Frae morning sun till dine;°   *dinner, noon*
But seas between us braid° hae roar'd,   *broad*
20 Sin auld lang syne.
     For auld, &c.

And there's a hand, my trusty fiere!°   *friend*
   And gie's a hand o' thine!
And we'll tak a right gude-willie-waught,
   For auld lang syne.
     For auld, &c.

1788   1796

Afton Water[1]

Flow gently, sweet Afton, among thy green braes,°   *slopes*
Flow gently, I'll sing thee a song in thy praise;
My Mary's asleep by thy murmuring stream,
Flow gently, sweet Afton, disturb not her dream.

---

1. Long ago.   1. The Afton is a small river in Ayrshire.

⁵ Thou stock dove whose echo resounds thro' the glen,
Ye wild whistling blackbirds in yon thorny den,
Thou green crested lapwing thy screaming forbear,
I charge you disturb not my slumbering Fair.

How lofty, sweet Afton, thy neighbouring hills,
¹⁰ Far mark'd with the courses of clear winding rills;
There daily I wander as noon rises high,
My flocks and my Mary's sweet Cot° in my eye.   *cottage*

How pleasant thy banks and green vallies below,
Where wild in the woodlands the primroses blow;
¹⁵ There oft as mild ev'ning weeps over the lea,
The sweet scented birk° shades my Mary and me.   *birch*

Thy chrystal stream, Afton, how lovely it glides,
And winds by the cot where my Mary resides;
How wanton thy waters her snowy feet lave,
²⁰ As gathering sweet flowerets she stems thy clear wave.

Flow gently, sweet Afton, among thy green braes,
Flow gently, sweet River, the theme of my lays;
My Mary's asleep by thy murmuring stream,
Flow gently, sweet Afton, disturb not her dream.

1789   1792

Tam o' Shanter: A Tale[1]

> Of Brownyis and of Bogillis full is this buke.
> GAWIN DOUGLAS.

When chapman billies[2] leave the street,
And drouthy° neebors neebors meet,   *thirsty*
As market-days are wearing late,
An' folk begin to tak the gate;°   *road*
⁵ While we sit bousing at the nappy,°   *strong ale*
And getting fou° and unco° happy,   *drunk / very*
We think na on the lang Scots miles,
The mosses, waters, slaps,° and styles,   *gaps (in walls)*
That lie between us and our hame,

1. This poem, written to order for a book on Scottish antiquities, is based on a witch story told about Alloway Kirk, an old ruin near Burns's house in Ayr. As a mock-heroic rendering of folk material, *Tam o' Shanter* is comparable to *The Nun's Priest's Tale* of Chaucer. Burns recognized that the poem was his most sustained and finished artistic performance; it discovers "a spice of roguish waggery" but also shows "a force of genius and a finishing polish that I despair of ever excelling." The verve and seriocomic sympathy with which Burns manages this misadventure of a confirmed tippler won Wordsworth, a water drinker, to passionate advocacy against the moralists who objected to Burns's ribaldry: "Who, but some impenetrable dunce or narrow-minded puritan in works of art, ever read without delight the picture which he has drawn of the convivial exaltation of the rustic adventurer, Tam o' Shanter? . . . I pity him who cannot perceive that, in all this, though there was no moral purpose, there is a moral effect" (*Letter to a Friend of Burns*, 1816).
2. Peddler fellows.

10 Whare sits our sulky sullen dame,
   Gathering her brows like gathering storm,
   Nursing her wrath to keep it warm.

    This truth fand° honest Tam o' Shanter,   *found*
   As he frae Ayr ae night did canter,
15 (Auld Ayr, wham ne'er a town surpasses,
   For honest men and bonny lasses).

    O Tam! hadst thou but been sae wise,
   As ta'en thy ain wife Kate's advice!
   She tauld thee weel thou was a skellum,°   *good-for-nothing*
20 A blethering,° blustering, drunken blellum;°   *chattering / babbler*
   That frae November till October,
   Ae market-day thou was nae sober;
   That ilka° melder,³ wi' the miller,   *every*
   Thou sat as lang as thou had siller;°   *silver, money*
25 That every naig° was ca'd° a shoe on,   *nag / driven*
   The smith and thee gat roaring fou on;
   That at the Lord's house, even on Sunday,
   Thou drank wi' Kirkton Jean till Monday.
   She prophesied that late or soon,
30 Thou would be found deep drown'd in Doon;
   Or catch'd wi' warlocks° in the mirk,°   *wizards / night*
   By Alloway's auld haunted kirk.

    Ah, gentle dames! it gars° me greet°   *makes / weep*
   To think how mony counsels sweet,
35 How mony lengthen'd sage advices,
   The husband frae the wife despises!

    But to our tale: Ae market-night,
   Tam had got planted unco right;
   Fast by an ingle,° bleezing° finely,   *fireplace / blazing*
40 Wi' reaming swats,° that drank divinely;   *foaming new ale*
   And at his elbow, Souter° Johnny,   *Cobbler*
   His ancient, trusty, drouthy crony;
   Tam lo'ed him like a vera brither;
   They had been fou for weeks thegither.
45 The night drave on wi' sangs and clatter;
   And ay the ale was growing better:
   The landlady and Tam grew gracious,
   Wi' favours secret, sweet, and precious:
   The Souter tauld his queerest stories;
50 The landlord's laugh was ready chorus:
   The storm without might rair° and rustle,   *roar*
   Tam did na mind the storm a whistle.

    Care, mad to see a man sae happy,
   E'en drown'd himsel amang the nappy:

---

3. The amount of corn processed at a single grinding.

55   As bees flee hame wi' lades o' treasure,
     The minutes wing'd their way wi' pleasure:
     Kings may be blest, but Tam was glorious,
     O'er a' the ills o' life victorious!

     But pleasures are like poppies spread,
60   You seize the flower, its bloom is shed;
     Or like the snow falls in the river,
     A moment white—then melts for ever;
     Or like the borealis race,
     That flit ere you can point their place;
65   Or like the rainbow's lovely form
     Evanishing amid the storm.—
     Nae man can tether time or tide;
     The hour approaches Tam maun° ride;   *must*
     That hour, o' night's black arch the key-stane,
70   That dreary hour, he mounts his beast in;
     And sic a night he taks the road in,
     As ne'er poor sinner was abroad in.

     The wind blew as 'twad blawn its last;
     The rattling showers rose on the blast;
75   The speedy gleams the darkness swallow'd;
     Loud, deep, and lang, the thunder bellow'd:
     That night, a child might understand,
     The Deil had business on his hand.

     Weel mounted on his gray mare, Meg,
80   A better never lifted leg,
     Tam skelpit° on thro' dub° and mire,   *slapped / puddle*
     Despising wind, and rain, and fire;
     Whiles holding fast his gude blue bonnet;
     Whiles crooning o'er some auld Scots sonnet;
85   Whiles glowring° round wi' prudent cares,   *staring*
     Lest bogles° catch him unawares.   *hobgoblins*
     Kirk-Alloway was drawing nigh,
     Whare ghaists° and houlets° nightly cry.—   *ghosts / owls*

     By this time he was cross the ford,
90   Whare in the snaw, the chapman smoor'd;[4]
     And past the birks° and meikle stane,°   *birches / big stone*
     Whare drunken Charlie brak's neck-bane;
     And thro' the whins, and by the cairn,[5]
     Whare hunters fand the murder'd bairn;
95   And near the thorn, aboon the well,
     Where Mungo's mither hang'd hersel.—
     Before him Doon pours all his floods;
     The doubling storm roars thro' the woods;
     The lightnings flash from pole to pole;

4. The peddler smothered.
5. Stones heaped up as a memorial. "Whins": furze (an evergreen shrub).

100 Near and more near the thunders roll:
    When, glimmering thro' the groaning trees,
    Kirk-Alloway seemed in a bleeze;°   *blaze*
    Thro' ilka bore° the beams were glancing;   *hole*
    And loud resounded mirth and dancing.—

105   Inspiring bold John Barleycorn!
    What dangers thou canst make us scorn!
    Wi' tippeny,[6] we fear nae evil;
    Wi' usquabae,° we'll face the devil!—   *whisky*
    The swats sae ream'd in Tammie's noddle,
110 Fair play, he car'd na deils a boddle.[7]
    But Maggie stood right sair astonish'd,
    Till, by the heel and hand admonish'd,
    She ventured forward on the light;
    And, vow! Tam saw an unco° sight!   *strange*
115 Warlocks and witches in a dance;
    Nae cotillion brent° new frae France,   *brand*
    But hornpipes, jigs, strathspeys,[8] and reels,
    Put life and mettle in their heels.
    A winnock-bunker° in the east,   *window seat*
120 There sat auld Nick, in shape o' beast;
    A touzie tyke,° black, grim, and large,   *shaggy dog*
    To gie them music was his charge:
    He screw'd the pipes and gart° them skirl,°   *made / screech*
    Till roof and rafters a' did dirl.°—   *rattle*
125 Coffins stood round, like open presses,
    That shaw'd the dead in their last dresses;
    And by some devilish cantraip° slight   *charm, trick*
    Each in its cauld hand held a light.—
    By which heroic Tam was able
130 To note upon the haly° table,   *holy*
    A murderer's banes in gibbet airns;°   *irons*
    Twa span-lang,[9] wee, unchristened bairns;
    A thief, new-cutted frae a rape,°   *rope*
    Wi' his last gasp his gab° did gape;   *mouth*
135 Five tomahawks, wi' blude red-rusted;
    Five scymitars, wi' murder crusted;
    A garter, which a babe had strangled;
    A knife, a father's throat had mangled,
    Whom his ain son o' life bereft,
140 The grey hairs yet stack to the heft;
    Wi' mair o' horrible and awefu',
    Which even to name wad be unlawfu'.

    As Tammie glowr'd, amaz'd, and curious,
    The mirth and fun grew fast and furious:
145 The piper loud and louder blew;
    The dancers quick and quicker flew;

6. Twopenny (of drink).
7. I.e., he didn't care a farthing about devils (a "boddle" is a very small copper coin).
8. Slow Highland dance.
9. Two spans long (a span is the distance from outstretched thumb to little finger).

joined hands
old woman

They reel'd, they set, they cross'd, they cleekit,°   *joined hands*
Till ilka carlin° swat and reekit,   *old woman*
And coost her duddies to the wark,[1]
150   And linket° at it in her sark!°   *tripped lightly / shirt*

    Now, Tam, O Tam! had thae been queans,°   *girls*
A' plump and strapping in their teens,
Their sarks, instead o' creeshie flannen,°   *greasy flannel*
Been snaw-white seventeen hunder linnen![2]
155   Thir° breeks o' mine, my only pair,   *these*
That ance were plush, o' gude blue hair,
I wad hae gi'en them off my hurdies,°   *buttocks*
For ae blink o' the bonie burdies!°   *maidens*

    But wither'd beldams, auld and droll,
160   Rigwoodie° hags wad spean° a foal,   *bony / wean*
Lowping° and flinging on a crummock,°   *leaping / staff*
I wonder didna turn thy stomach.

    But Tam kend what was what fu' brawlie,°   *finely*
There was ae winsome wench and wawlie°   *strapping*
165   That night enlisted in the core,°   *corps*
(Lang after kend on Carrick shore;
For mony a beast to dead she shot,
And perish'd mony a bony boat,
And shook baith meikle corn and bear,°   *barley*
170   And kept the country-side in fear:)
Her cutty° sark, o' Paisley harn,°   *short / yarn*
That while a lassie she had worn,
In longitude tho' sorely scanty,
It was her best, and she was vauntie.°—   *proud*
175   Ah! little kend thy reverend grannie,
That sark she coft° for her wee Nannie,   *bought*
Wi' twa pund Scots ('twas a' her riches),
Wad ever grac'd a dance of witches!

    But here my Muse her wing maun cour;°   *lower*
180   Sic flights are far beyond her pow'r;
To sing how Nannie lap and flang,
(A souple jade she was, and strang),
And how Tam stood, like ane bewitch'd,
And thought his very een° enrich'd;   *eyes*
185   Even Satan glowr'd, and fidg'd fu' fain,[3]
And hotch'd° and blew wi' might and main: *jerked*
Till first ae caper, syne° anither,   *then*
Tam tint° his reason a' thegither,   *lost*
And roars out, 'Weel done, Cutty-sark!'
190   And in an instant all was dark:
And scarcely had he Maggie rallied,
When out the hellish legion sallied.

1. Cast off her clothes for the work.
2. Very fine linen, woven on a loom with seven- teen hundred strips.
3. Fidgeted with pleasure.

As bees bizz out wi' angry fyke,°   *fuss*
When plundering herds° assail their byke;°   *herdsmen / hive*
195 As open° pussie's mortal foes,   *begin to bark*
When, pop! she starts before their nose;
As eager runs the market-crowd,
When 'Catch the thief!' resounds aloud;
So Maggie runs the witches follow,
200 Wi' mony an eldritch° skreech and hollow.   *unearthly*

Ah, Tam! Ah, Tam! thou'll get thy fairin'!°   *deserts*
In hell they'll roast thee like a herrin!
In vain thy Kate awaits thy comin!
Kate soon will be a woefu' woman!
205 Now, do thy speedy utmost, Meg,
And win the key-stane of the brig;°   *bridge*
There at them thou thy tail may toss,
A running stream they dare na cross.
But ere the key-stane she could make,
210 The fient a tail she had to shake![4]
For Nannie, far before the rest,
Hard upon noble Maggie prest,
And flew at Tam wi' furious ettle;°   *intent*
But little wist she Maggie's mettle—
215 Ae spring brought off her master hale,°   *whole*
But left behind her ain gray tail:
The carlin claught° her by the rump,   *clutched*
And left poor Maggie scarce a stump.

Now, wha this tale o' truth shall read,
220 Ilk man and mother's son, take heed:
Whene'er to drink you are inclin'd,
Or cutty-sarks run in your mind,
Think, ye may buy the joys o'er dear,
Remember Tam o' Shanter's mare.

1790   1791

Robert Bruce's March to Bannockburn[1]

[SCOTS, WHA HAE]

Scots, wha hae wi' Wallace[2] bled,
Scots, wham Bruce has aften led,
Welcome to your gory bed,—
    Or to victorie.—

5 Now's the day, and now's the hour;
    See the front o' battle lour;

---

4. I.e., she had no tail left at all.
1. In this best-known of Burns's patriotic songs Robert Bruce is addressing his army before the great victory at Bannockburn (1314), at which the

English were driven from Scotland.
2. Sir William Wallace (ca. 1272–1305), the great Scottish warrior in the wars against the English.

See approach proud Edward's power,
   Chains and Slaverie.—

Wha will be a traitor-knave?
10 Wha can fill a coward's grave?
Wha sae base as be a Slave?
   —Let him turn and flie:—

Wha for Scotland's king and law,
Freedom's sword will strongly draw,
15 Free-man stand, or Free-man fa',
   Let him follow me.—

By Oppression's woes and pains!
By your Sons in servile chains!
We will drain our dearest veins,
20   But they *shall* be free!

Lay the proud Usurpers low!
Tyrants fall in every foe!
Liberty's in every blow!
   Let us Do—or Die!!!

1793   1794, 1815

A Red, Red Rose[1]

O my Luve's like a red, red rose,
   That's newly sprung in June;
O my Luve's like the melodie
   That's sweetly played in tune.

5 As fair art thou, my bonie lass,
   So deep in luve am I;
And I will love thee still, my Dear,
   Till a' the seas gang dry.

Till a' the seas gang dry, my Dear,
10   And the rocks melt wi' the sun:
O I will love thee still, my Dear,
   While the sands o' life shall run.

And fare thee weel, my only Luve!
   And fare thee weel, a while!
15 And I will come again, my Luve,
   Tho' it were ten thousand mile!

1794   1796

1. Like many of Burns's lyrics, this one incorporates elements from several current folk songs.

Song: For a' that and a' that

Is there, for honest Poverty
    That hangs his head, and a' that;
The coward-slave, we pass him by,
    We dare be poor for a' that!
5   For a' that, and a' that,
      Our toils obscure, and a' that,
    The rank is but the guinea's stamp,
    The Man's the gowd° for a' that.   *gold*

What though on hamely fare we dine,
10   Wear hodden grey,[1] and a' that.
Gie fools their silks, and knaves their wine,
    A Man's a Man for a' that.
For a' that, and a' that,
    Their tinsel show, and a' that;
15   The honest man, though e'er sae poor,
    Is king o' men for a' that.

Ye see yon birkie° ca'd a lord,   *brisk young fellow*
    Wha struts, and stares, and a' that,
Though hundreds worship at his word,
20   He's but a coof° for a' that.   *dolt*
For a' that, and a' that,
    His ribband, star and a' that,
The man of independant mind,
    He looks and laughs at a' that.

25 A prince can mak a belted knight,
    A marquis, duke, and a' that;
But an honest man's aboon° his might,   *above*
    Guid faith he mauna fa' that![2]
For a' that, and a' that,
30   Their dignities, and a' that,
The pith o' Sense, and pride o' Worth,
    Are higher rank than a' that.

Then let us pray that come it may,
    As come it will for a' that,
35 That Sense and Worth, o'er a' the earth
    Shall bear the gree,[3] and a' that.
For a' that, and a' that,
    It's coming yet for a' that,
That Man to Man the warld o'er,
40   Shall brothers be for a' that.

1795   1795

---

1. A coarse cloth of undyed wool.   3. Win the prize.
2. Must not claim that.

The French Revolution and the "Spirit of the Age"

In a letter to Byron in 1816, Percy Shelley called the French Revolution "the master theme of the epoch in which we live"; and in various letters and essays, he declared that, as the result of the repercussions of the Revolution, the literature of England "has arisen as it were from a new birth," and that "the electric life that burns" within the great poets of the time expresses "less their spirit than the spirit of the age." (See, for example, the concluding paragraph of Shelley's *Defence of Poetry,* page 802.) With these judgments, many of Shelley's contemporaries concurred. Writers during Shelley's lifetime were obsessed with the possibility of a drastic and inclusive change in the human condition; and the works of a number of major Romantic poets cannot be understood, historically, without awareness of the extent to which their distinctive themes, plot forms, imagery, and modes of imagining and feeling were shaped first by the boundless promise, then by the tragedy, of the great events in neighboring France. And for a number of young poets in the early years (1789–93) the enthusiasm for the Revolution had the impetus and intensity of a religious awakening, because they interpreted the events in France in accordance with the apocalyptic prophecies in the Hebrew and Christian Scriptures; that is, they viewed these events as fulfilling the promise, guaranteed by an infallible text, that a short period of retributive and cleansing violence would usher in an era of universal peace and felicity equivalent to a restored Paradise. Even after what they considered the failure of the revolutionary promise—signaled by the execution of the king and queen, the massacres during the Reign of Terror under Robespierre, and later the wars of imperial conquest under Napoleon—these poets did not surrender their hope for a radical transformation of the political and social world. Instead, they transferred the basis of that hope from violent political revolution to an inner revolution in the moral and imaginative nature of the human race.

ENGLISH CONTROVERSY ABOUT THE REVOLUTION

The French Revolution began with the storming of the Bastille and freeing of a handful of political prisoners by an angry mob of Parisians on July 14, 1789. A month later, the new French National Assembly passed the Declaration of the Rights of Man. Six weeks after that (in early October), citizens marched to the royal palace at Versailles, just south of the city, and arrested King Louis XVI and his queen, Marie Antoinette, confining them to the Tuileries palace in Paris. These happenings were quickly reported in the London newspapers. The British liberals applauded; the radicals were ecstatic; many ordinary people were confused by the events, which seemed to promise improvement of the common lot but at the cost of toppling long-standing traditions of royalty and aristocracy.

One reaction on the English side of the Channel was the so-called war of pamphlets, initiated by Richard Price's sermon *A Discourse on the Love of Our Country*, which he delivered on November 4, 1789, a month after the imprisonment of the king and queen. The controversy accelerated in the wake of Edmund Burke's response to Price a year later, *Reflections on the Revolution in France*, which itself drew more than fifty further responses, among which the two most famous are Mary Wollstonecraft's *A Vindication of the Rights of Men* and Thomas Paine's *Rights of Man*. The works of Burke and Wollstonecraft and part 1 of Paine's *Rights* appeared in a very short span, from November 1790 to March 1791.

All four of the writers in this section are concerned with the same questions: justification of hereditary rule, ownership of property, interpretation of the English constitution, and the "rights of men"—and women—in such things as (in Price's words) "liberty of conscience in religious matters," the "right to resist power when abused," the "right to chuse our own governors; to cashier them for misconduct; and to frame a government for ourselves." But the extracts have been chosen mainly to illustrate the *tones* of the debate: celebratory in Price, congratulating himself and his audience on having lived to see "Thirty Millions of people, indignant and resolute, spurning at slavery, and demanding liberty with an irresistible voice"; blatantly sensationalist in Burke, depicting the rude treatment of the king and especially the queen, in her nightgown ("almost naked"), "forced to abandon the sanctuary of the most splendid palace in the world, which they left swimming in blood, polluted by massacre, and strewed with scattered limbs and mutilated carcases"; forthrightly contemptuous in Wollstonecraft, who describes Burke's work as "many ingenious arguments in a very specious garb"; basically pointed and plain in Paine: "I am contending for the rights of the *living*, and against their being willed away, and controuled and contracted for, by the . . . assumed authority of the dead."

RICHARD PRICE

Richard Price (1723–1791) was a Unitarian minister in London and a writer on moral philosophy, population, and the national debt, among other topics. The full title of his sermon, which prompted Burke's *Reflections* and in turn the scores of responses to Burke, is *A Discourse on the Love of Our Country, Delivered on Nov. 4, 1789, at the Meeting-House in the Old Jewry, to the Society for Commemorating the Revolution in Great Britain*. The London Revolution Society had been founded a year earlier to mark the hundredth anniversary of the "bloodless" Glorious Revolution of 1688, which ended the short reign of King James II and produced the Declaration of Right, establishing a limited monarchy and guaranteeing the civil rights of privileged classes. The first two-thirds of the extracts given here commemorate that Revolution; in the final third, beginning "What an eventful period is this!" Price greets with religious fervor "two other Revolutions, both glorious," the American and the French. The *Discourse* went through six editions in its first year of publication.

From A Discourse on the Love of Our Country

We are met to thank God for that event in this country to which the name of THE REVOLUTION has been given; and which, for more than a century, it has been usual for the friends of freedom, and more especially Protestant Dissenters, under the title of the REVOLUTION SOCIETY, to celebrate with expressions of joy and exultation. * * * By a bloodless victory, the fetters which despotism had been long preparing for us were broken; the rights of the people were asserted, a tyrant expelled, and a Sovereign of our own choice appointed in his room. Security was given to our property, and our consciences were emancipated. The bounds of free enquiry were enlarged; the volume in which are the words of eternal life, was laid more open to our examination; and that *aera* of light and liberty was introduced among us, by which we have been made an example to other kingdoms, and became the instructors of the world. Had it not been for this deliverance, the probability is, that, instead of being thus distinguished, we should now have been a base people, groaning under the infamy and misery of popery and slavery. Let us, therefore, offer thanksgivings to God, the author of all our blessings. * * *

It is well known that King James was not far from gaining his purpose; and that probably he would have succeeded, had he been less in a hurry. But he was a fool as well as a bigot. He wanted courage as well as prudence; and, therefore, fled, and left us to settle quietly for ourselves that constitution of government which is now our boast. We have particular reason, as Protestant Dissenters, to rejoice on this occasion. It was at this time we were rescued from persecution, and obtained the liberty of worshipping God in the manner we think most acceptable to him. It was then our meeting houses were opened, our worship was taken under the protection of the law, and the principles of toleration gained a triumph. We have, therefore, on this occasion, peculiar reasons for thanksgiving.—But let us remember that we ought not to satisfy ourselves with thanksgivings. Our gratitude, if genuine, will be accompanied with endeavours to give stability to the deliverance our country has obtained, and to extend and improve the happiness with which the Revolution has blest us.—Let us, in particular, take care not to forget the principles of the Revolution. This Society has, very properly, in its Reports, held out these principles, as an instruction to the public. I will only take notice of the three following:

First: The right to liberty of conscience in religious matters.

Secondly: The right to resist power when abused. And,

Thirdly: The right to chuse our own governors; to cashier them for misconduct; and to frame a government for ourselves.

* * *

I would farther direct you to remember, that though the Revolution was a great work, it was by no means a perfect work; and that all was not then gained which was necessary to put the kingdom in the secure and complete possession of the blessings of liberty.—In particular, you should recollect, that the toleration then obtained was imperfect. It included only those who could declare their faith in the doctrinal articles of the church of England. It has, indeed, been since extended, but not sufficiently; for there still exist penal laws on account of religious opinions, which (were they carried into execution) would shut up many of our places of worship, and silence and imprison some of our ablest and best men.—The TEST LAWS are also still in force; and deprive of eligibility to civil and military offices, all who cannot conform to the established worship. It is with great pleasure I find that the body of Protestant Dissenters, though defeated in two late attempts to deliver their country from this disgrace to it, have determined to persevere. Should they at last succeed, they will have the satisfaction, not only of removing from themselves a proscription they do not deserve, but of contributing to lessen the number of public iniquities. For I cannot call by a gentler name, laws which convert an ordinance appointed by our Saviour to commemorate his death, into an instrument of oppressive policy, and a qualification of rakes and atheists for civil posts.—I have said, *should* they succeed—but perhaps I ought not to suggest a doubt about their success. And, indeed, when I consider that in Scotland the established church is defended by no such test—that in Ireland it has been abolished—that in a great neighbouring country it has been declared to be an indefeasible right of all citizens to be equally eligible to public offices—that in the same kingdom a professed Dissenter from the established church holds the first office in the state—that in the Emperor's dominions *Jews* have been lately admitted to the enjoyment of equal privileges with other citizens—and that in this very country, a Dissenter, though excluded from the power of *executing* the laws, yet is allowed to be employed in *making* them.—When, I say, I consider such facts as these, I am disposed to think it impossible that the enemies of the repeal of the Test Laws should not soon become ashamed, and give up their opposition.

But the most important instance of the imperfect state in which the Revolution left our constitution, is the *inequality of our representation*. I think, indeed, this defect in our constitution so gross and so palpable, as to make it excellent chiefly in form and theory. You should remember that a representation in the legislature of a kingdom is the *basis* of constitutional liberty in it, and of all legitimate government; and that without it a government is nothing but an usurpation. When the representation is fair and equal, and at the same time vested with such powers as our House of Commons possesses, a kingdom may be said to govern itself, and consequently to possess true liberty. When the representation is partial, a kingdom possesses liberty only partially; and if extremely partial, it only gives a *semblance* of liberty; but if not only extremely partial, but corruptly chosen, and under corrupt influence after being chosen, it becomes a *nuisance*, and produces the worst of all forms of government—a government by corruption, a government carried on and supported by spreading venality and profligacy through a kingdom. May heaven preserve this kingdom from a calamity so dreadful! It is the point of depravity to which abuses under such a government as ours naturally tend, and the last stage of national unhappiness. We are, at present, I hope, at a great distance from it. But it cannot be pretended that there are no advances towards it, or that there is no reason for apprehension and alarm.

* * *

What an eventful period is this! I am thankful that I have lived to it; and I could almost say, *Lord, now lettest thou thy servant depart in peace, for mine eyes have seen thy salvation* [Luke 2.29–30]. I have lived to see a diffusion of knowledge, which has undermined superstition and error—I have lived to see the rights of men better understood than ever; and nations panting for liberty, which seemed to have lost the idea of it.—I have lived to see THIRTY MILLIONS of people, indignant and resolute, spurning at slavery, and demanding liberty with an irresistible voice; their king led in triumph, and an arbitrary monarch surrendering himself to his subjects.—After sharing in the benefits of one Revolution, I have been spared to be a witness to two other Revolutions, both glorious.——And now, methinks, I see the ardour for liberty catching and spreading; a general amendment beginning in human affairs; the dominion of kings changed for the dominion of laws, and the dominion of priests giving way to the dominion of reason and conscience.

Be encouraged, all ye friends of freedom, and writers in its defence! The times are auspicious. Your labours have not been in vain. Behold kingdoms, admonished by you, starting from sleep, breaking their fetters, and claiming justice from their oppressors! Behold, the light you have struck out, after setting *America* free, reflected to *France,* and there kindled into a blaze that lays despotism in ashes, and warms and illuminates *Europe!*

Tremble all ye oppressors of the world! Take warning all ye supporters of slavish governments, and slavish hierarchies! Call no more (absurdly and wickedly) REFORMATION, innovation. You cannot now hold the world in darkness. Struggle no longer against increasing light and liberality. Restore to mankind their rights; and consent to the correction of abuses, before they and you are destroyed together.

1789

EDMUND BURKE

The great statesman and political theorist Edmund Burke (1729–1797) read Price's *Discourse* in January 1790 and immediately began drafting his *Reflections on the Revolution in France* as a reply in the form of a letter (as the lengthy subtitle describes it) "Intended to Have Been Sent to a Gentleman in Paris." The work was published at the beginning of November and was an instant best-seller: thirteen thousand copies were purchased in the first five weeks, and by the following September it had gone through eleven editions. Clearly, part of its appeal to contemporary readers lay in the highly wrought accounts of the mob's violent treatment of the French king and queen (who at the time Burke was writing were imprisoned in Paris and would be executed three years later, in January and October 1793). *Reflections* has become the classic, most eloquent statement of British conservatism favoring monarchy, aristocracy, property, hereditary succession, and the wisdom of the ages. Earlier in his career Burke had championed many liberal causes and sided with the Americans in their war for independence; opponents and allies alike were surprised at the strength of his conviction that the French Revolution was a disaster and the revolutionists "a swinish multitude."

From Reflections on the Revolution in France

* * * All circumstances taken together, the French revolution is the most astonishing that has hitherto happened in the world. The most wonderful things are brought about in many instances by means the most absurd and ridiculous; in the most ridiculous modes; and apparently, by the most contemptible instruments. Every thing seems out of nature in this strange chaos of levity and ferocity, and of all sorts of crimes jumbled together with all sorts of follies. In viewing this monstrous tragi-comic scene, the most opposite passions necessarily succeed, and sometimes mix with each other in the mind; alternate contempt and indignation; alternate laughter and tears; alternate scorn and horror.

*　*　*

You will observe, that from Magna Charta to the Declaration of Right,[1] it has been the uniform policy of our constitution to claim and assert our liberties, as an *entailed inheritance* derived to us from our forefathers, and to be transmitted to our posterity; as an estate specially belonging to the people of this kingdom without any reference whatever to any other more general or prior right. By this means our constitution preserves an unity in so great a diversity of its parts. We have an inheritable crown; an inheritable peerage; and an house of commons and a people inheriting privileges, franchises, and liberties, from a long line of ancestors.

This policy appears to me to be the result of profound reflection; or rather the happy effect of following nature, which is wisdom without reflection, and above it. A spirit of innovation is generally the result of a selfish temper and confined views. People will not look forward to posterity, who never look backward to their ancestors. Besides, the people of England well know, that the idea of inheritance furnishes a sure principle of conservation, and a sure principle of transmission; without at all excluding a principle of improvement. It leaves acquisition free; but it secures what it acquires. Whatever advantages are obtained by a state proceeding on these maxims, are locked fast as in a sort of family settlement; grasped as in a kind of mortmain[2] for ever. By a constitutional policy, working after the pattern of nature, we receive, we hold, we transmit our government and our privileges, in the same manner in which we enjoy and transmit our property and our lives. The institutions of policy, the goods of fortune, the gifts of Providence, are handed down, to us and from us, in the same course and order. Our political system is placed in a just correspondence and symmetry with the order of the world, and with the mode of existence decreed to a permanent body composed of transitory parts; wherein, by the disposition of a stupendous wisdom, moulding together the great mysterious incorporation of the human race, the whole, at one time, is never old,

1. The Magna Carta, the "great charter" of English personal and political liberty, dates from 1215. The Declaration of Right, another cornerstone of the English constitution, was a product of the Glorious Revolution of 1688.
2. A legal term (literally, "dead hand") for the perpetual holding of lands by an ecclesiastical or other corporation.

or middle-aged, or young, but in a condition of unchangeable constancy, moves on through the varied tenour of perpetual decay, fall, renovation, and progression. Thus, by preserving the method of nature in the conduct of the state, in what we improve we are never wholly new; in what we retain we are never wholly obsolete. By adhering in this manner and on those principles to our forefathers, we are guided not by the superstition of antiquarians, but by the spirit of philosophic analogy. In this choice of inheritance we have given to our frame of polity the image of a relation in blood; binding up the constitution of our country with our dearest domestic ties; adopting our fundamental laws into the bosom of our family affections; keeping inseparable, and cherishing with the warmth of all their combined and mutually reflected charities, our state, our hearths, our sepulchres, and our altars.

Through the same plan of a conformity to nature in our artificial institutions, and by calling in the aid of her unerring and powerful instincts, to fortify the fallible and feeble contrivances of our reason, we have derived several other, and those no small benefits, from considering our liberties in the light of an inheritance. Always acting as if in the presence of canonized forefathers, the spirit of freedom, leading in itself to misrule and excess, is tempered with an awful gravity. This idea of a liberal descent inspires us with a sense of habitual native dignity, which prevents that upstart insolence almost inevitably adhering to and disgracing those who are the first acquirers of any distinction. By this means our liberty becomes a noble freedom. It carries an imposing and majestic aspect. It has a pedigree and illustrating ancestors. It has its bearings and its ensigns armorial. It has its gallery of portraits; its monumental inscriptions; its records, evidences, and titles. We procure reverence to our civil institutions on the principle upon which nature teaches us to revere individual men; on account of their age; and on account of those from whom they are descended. All your sophisters cannot produce any thing better adapted to preserve a rational and manly freedom than the course that we have pursued, who have chosen our nature rather than our speculations, our breasts rather than our inventions, for the great conservatories and magazines of our rights and privileges.

*　　*　　*

Far am I from denying in theory; full as far is my heart from withholding in practice (if I were of power to give or to withhold) the *real* rights of men. In denying their false claims of right, I do not mean to injure those which are real, and are such as their pretended rights would totally destroy. If civil society be made for the advantage of man, all the advantages for which it is made become his right. It is an institution of beneficence; and law itself is only beneficence acting by a rule. Men have a right to live by that rule; they have a right to justice; as between their fellows, whether their fellows are in politic function or in ordinary occupation. They have a right to the fruits of their industry; and to the means of making their industry fruitful. They have a right to the acquisitions of their parents; to the nourishment and improvement of their offspring; to instruction in life, and to consolation in death. Whatever each man can separately do, without trespassing upon others, he has a right to do for himself; and he has a right to a fair portion of all which society, with all its combinations of skill and force, can do in his favor. In this partnership all men have equal rights; but not to equal things. He that has but five shillings in the partnership, has as good a right to it, as he that has five hundred pound has to his larger proportion. But he has not a right to an equal dividend in the product of the joint stock; and as to the share of power, authority, and direction which each individual ought to have in the management of the state, that I must deny to be amongst the direct original rights of man in civil society; for I have in my contemplation the civil social man, and no other. It is a thing to be settled by convention.

* * *

* * * History, who keeps a durable record of all our acts, and exercises her awful censure over the proceedings of all sorts of sovereigns, will not forget, either those events, or the aera of this liberal refinement in the intercourse of mankind. History will record, that on the morning of the 6th of October 1789, the king and queen of France, after a day of confusion, alarm, dismay, and slaughter, lay down, under the pledged security of public faith, to indulge nature in a few hours of respite, and troubled melancholy repose. From this sleep the queen was first startled by the voice of the centinel at her door, who cried out to her, to save herself by flight— that this was the last proof of fidelity he could give—that they were upon him, and he was dead. Instantly he was cut down. A band of cruel ruffians and assassins, reeking with his blood, rushed into the chamber of the queen, and pierced with an hundred strokes of bayonets and poniards the bed, from whence this persecuted woman had but just time to fly almost naked, and through ways unknown to the murderers had escaped to seek refuge at the feet of a king and husband, not secure of his own life for a moment.

This king, to say no more of him, and this queen, and their infant children (who once would have been the pride and hope of a great and generous people) were then forced to abandon the sanctuary of the most splendid palace in the world, which they left swimming in blood, polluted by massacre, and strewed with scattered limbs and mutilated carcases. Thence they were conducted into the capital of their kingdom. Two had been selected from the unprovoked, unresisted, promiscuous slaughter, which was made of the gentlemen of birth and family who composed the king's body guard. These two gentlemen, with all the parade of an execution of justice, were cruelly and publickly dragged to the block, and beheaded in the great court of the palace. Their heads were stuck upon spears, and led the procession; whilst the royal captives who followed in the train were slowly moved along, amidst the horrid yells, and shrilling screams, and frantic dances, and infamous contumelies, and all the unutterable abominations of the furies of hell, in the abused shape of the vilest of women. After they had been made to taste, drop by drop, more than the bitterness of death, in the slow torture of a journey of twelve miles, protracted to six hours, they were, under a guard, composed of those very soldiers who had thus conducted them through this famous triumph, lodged in one of the old palaces of Paris, now converted into a Bastile for kings.

*   *   *

I hear that the august person, who was the principal object of our preacher's triumph,[3] though he supported himself, felt much on that shameful occasion. As a man, it became him to feel for his wife and his children, and the faithful guards of his person, that were massacred in cold blood about him; as a prince, it became him to feel for the strange and frightful transformation of his civilized subjects, and to be more grieved for them, than solicitous for himself. It derogates little from his fortitude, while it adds infinitely to the honor of his humanity. I am very sorry to say it, very sorry indeed, that such personages are in a situation in which it is not unbecoming in us to praise the virtues of the great.

I hear, and I rejoice to hear, that the great lady, the other object of the triumph, has borne that day (one is interested that beings made for suffering should suffer well) and that she bears all the succeeding days, that she bears the imprisonment of her husband, and her own captivity, and the exile of her friends, and the insulting adulation of addresses, and the whole weight of her accumulated wrongs, with a serene patience, in a manner suited to her rank and race, and becoming the offspring of a sovereign distinguished for her piety and her courage;[4] that like her she has lofty sentiments; that she feels with the dignity of a Roman matron; that in the last extremity she will save herself from the last disgrace, and that if she must fall, she will fall by no ignoble hand.

It is now sixteen or seventeen years since I saw the queen of France, then the dauphiness,[5] at Versailles; and surely never lighted on this orb, which she hardly seemed to touch, a more delightful vision. I saw her just above the horizon, decorating and cheering the elevated sphere she just began to move in,—glittering like the morning-star, full of life, and splendor, and joy. Oh! what a revolution! and what an heart must I have, to contemplate without emotion that elevation and that fall! Little did I dream when she added titles of veneration to those of enthusiastic, distant, respectful love, that she should ever be obliged to carry the sharp antidote against disgrace concealed in that bosom; little did I dream that I should have lived to see such disasters fallen upon her in a nation of gallant men, in a nation of men of honor and of cavaliers. I thought ten thousand swords must have leaped from their scabbards to avenge even a look that threatened her with insult.—But the age of chivalry is gone.—That of sophisters, oeconomists, and calculators, has succeeded; and the glory of Europe is extinguished for ever. Never, never more, shall we behold that generous loyalty to rank and sex, that proud submission, that dignified obedience, that subordination of the heart, which kept alive, even in servitude itself, the spirit of an exalted freedom. The unbought grace of life, the cheap defence of nations, the nurse of manly sentiment and heroic enterprize is gone! It is gone, that sensibility of principle, that chastity of honor, which felt a stain like a wound, which inspired

---

3. A reference to Price's exclamation, in the final selection printed above from *A Discourse on the Love of Our Country*, that he has lived to see the French "king led in triumph . . . an arbitrary monarch surrendering himself to his subjects." "August person": King Louis XVI.
4. Marie Antoinette was the daughter of Maria Theresa, empress of Austria.
5. I.e., wife of the dauphin, who was heir to the throne of France.

courage whilst it mitigated ferocity, which ennobled whatever it touched, and under which vice itself lost half its evil, by losing all its grossness.

This mixed system of opinion and sentiment had its origin in the antient chivalry; and the principle, though varied in its appearance by the varying state of human affairs, subsisted and influenced through a long succession of generations, even to the time we live in. If it should ever be totally extinguished, the loss I fear will be great. It is this which has given its character to modern Europe. It is this which has distinguished it under all its forms of government, and distinguished it to its advantage, from the states of Asia, and possibly from those states which flourished in the most brilliant periods of the antique world. It was this, which, without confounding ranks, had produced a noble equality, and handed it down through all the gradations of social life. It was this opinion which mitigated kings into companions, and raised private men to be fellows with kings. Without force, or opposition, it subdued the fierceness of pride and power; it obliged sovereigns to submit to the soft collar of social esteem, compelled stern authority to submit to elegance, and gave a domination vanquisher of laws, to be subdued by manners.

But now all is to be changed. All the pleasing illusions, which made power gentle, and obedience liberal, which harmonized the different shades of life, and which, by a bland assimilation, incorporated into politics the sentiments which beautify and soften private society, are to be dissolved by this new conquering empire of light and reason. All the decent drapery of life is to be rudely torn off. All the superadded ideas, furnished from the wardrobe of a moral imagination, which the heart owns, and the understanding ratifies, as necessary to cover the defects of our naked shivering nature, and to raise it to dignity in our own estimation, are to be exploded as a ridiculous, absurd, and antiquated fashion.

On this scheme of things, a king is but a man; a queen is but a woman; a woman is but an animal; and an animal not of the highest order. All homage paid to the sex in general as such, and without distinct views, is to be regarded as romance and folly. Regicide, and parricide, and sacrilege, are but fictions of superstition, corrupting jurisprudence by destroying its simplicity. The murder of a king, or a queen, or a bishop, or a father, are only common homicide; and if the people are by any chance, or in any way gainers by it, a sort of homicide much the most pardonable, and into which we ought not to make too severe a scrutiny.

On the scheme of this barbarous philosophy, which is the offspring of cold hearts and muddy understandings, and which is as void of solid wisdom, as it is destitute of all taste and elegance, laws are to be supported only by their own terrors, and by the concern, which each individual may find in them, from his own private speculations, or can spare to them from his own private interests. In the groves of *their* academy, at the end of every visto, you see nothing but the gallows. Nothing is left which engages the affections on the part of the commonwealth. On the principles of this mechanic philosophy, our institutions can never be embodied, if I may use the expression, in persons; so as to create in us love, veneration, admiration, or attachment. But that sort of reason which banishes the affections is incapable of filling their place. These public affections, combined with manners, are required sometimes as supplements, sometimes as correctives, always as aids to law. The precept given by a wise man, as well as a great critic, for the construction of poems, is equally true as to states. *Non satis est pulchra esse poemata, dulcia sunto.*[6] There ought to be a system of manners in every nation which a well-formed mind would be disposed to relish. To make us love our country, our country ought to be lovely.

But power, of some kind or other, will survive the shock in which manners and opinions perish; and it will find other and worse means for its support. The usurpation which, in order to subvert antient institutions, has destroyed antient principles, will hold power by arts similar to those by which it has acquired it. When the old feudal and chivalrous spirit of *Fealty*,[7] which, by freeing kings from fear, freed both kings and subjects from the precautions of tyranny, shall be extinct in the minds of men, plots and assassinations will be anticipated by preventive murder and preventive confiscation, and that long roll of grim and bloody maxims, which form the political code of all power, not standing on its own honor, and the honor of those who are to obey it. Kings will be tyrants from policy when subjects are rebels from principle.

When antient opinions and rules of life are taken away, the loss cannot possibly be estimated. From that moment we have no compass to govern us; nor can we know distinctly to what port we steer. Europe undoubtedly, taken in a mass, was in a flourishing condition the day on which your Revolution was compleated. How much of that prosperous state was owing to the spirit of our old manners and opinions is not easy to say; but as such causes cannot be indifferent in their operation, we must presume, that, on the whole, their operation was beneficial.

We are but too apt to consider things in the state in which we find them, without sufficiently adverting to the causes by which they have been produced, and possibly may be upheld. Nothing is more certain, than that our manners, our civilization, and all the good things which are connected with manners, and with civilization, have, in this European world of ours, depended for ages upon two principles; and were indeed the result of both combined; I mean the spirit of a gentleman, and the spirit of religion. The nobility and the clergy, the one by profession, the other by patronage, kept learning in existence, even in the midst of arms and confusions, and whilst governments were rather in their causes than formed. Learning paid back what it received to nobility and to priesthood; and paid it with usury, by enlarging their ideas, and by furnishing their minds. Happy if they had all continued to know their indissoluble union, and their proper place! Happy if learning, not debauched by ambition, had been satisfied to continue the instructor, and not aspired to be the master! Along with its natural protectors and guardians, learning will be cast into the mire, and trodden down under the hoofs of a swinish multitude.

If, as I suspect, modern letters owe more than they are always willing to own to antient manners, so do other interests which we value full as much as they are worth. Even commerce, and trade, and manufacture, the gods of our oeconomical politicians, are themselves perhaps but creatures; are themselves but effects, which, as first causes, we choose to worship. They certainly

---

6. It is not enough for poems to have beauty; they must be sweet, tender, affecting (Latin; Horace's *Ars Poetica* 99).

7. Fidelity of a vassal or feudal tenant to his lord.

grew under the same shade in which learning flourished. They too may decay with their natural protecting principles. With you, for the present at least, they all threaten to disappear together. Where trade and manufactures are wanting to a people, and the spirit of nobility and religion remains, sentiment supplies, and not always ill supplies their place; but if commerce and the arts should be lost in an experiment to try how well a state may stand without these old fundamental principles, what sort of a thing must be a nation of gross, stupid, ferocious, and at the same time, poor and sordid barbarians, destitute of religion, honor, or manly pride, possessing nothing at present, and hoping for nothing hereafter?

I wish you may not be going fast, and by the shortest cut, to that horrible and disgustful situation. Already there appears a poverty of conception, a coarseness and vulgarity in all the proceedings of the assembly and of all their instructors. Their liberty is not liberal. Their science is presumptuous ignorance. Their humanity is savage and brutal.

*   *   *

1790

MARY WOLLSTONECRAFT

The first of the many published replies to Burke's *Reflections* was by Mary Wollstonecraft (1759–1797), who appears elsewhere in this anthology as author of *A Vindication of the Rights of Woman* (1792), the earliest substantial work in the history of the women's movement in Great Britain, and *Letters Written during a Short Residence in Sweden, Norway, and Denmark* (1796). Toward the end of 1790, when Burke's *Reflections* came out, she was working in London as a writer and translator for the radical publisher Joseph Johnson. Reading Burke, she was outraged at the weakness of his arguments and the exaggerated rhetoric with which he depicted the revolutionists as violators of royalty and womanhood. Always a rapid writer, she composed her reply, *A Vindication of the Rights of Men*, in a matter of days, and Johnson's printer set it in type as fast as the sheets of manuscript were turned in. It was published anonymously in November, less than a month after Burke's *Reflections* first appeared, and a second edition (this time with her name on the title page) was called for almost immediately.

From A Vindication of the Rights of Men

Advertisement

Mr. Burke's Reflections on the French Revolution first engaged my attention as the transient topic of the day; and reading it more for amusement than information, my indignation was roused by the sophistical arguments, that every moment crossed me, in the questionable shape of natural feelings and common sense.

Many pages of the following letter were the effusions of the moment; but, swelling imperceptibly to a considerable size, the idea was suggested of publishing a short vindication of *the Rights of Men*.

Not having leisure or patience to follow this desultory writer through all the devious tracks in which his fancy has started fresh game, I have confined my strictures, in a great measure, to the grand principles at which he has levelled many ingenious arguments in a very specious garb.

A Letter to the Right Honorable Edmund Burke

Sir,

It is not necessary, with courtly insincerity, to apologize to you for thus intruding on your precious time, nor to profess that I think it an honor to discuss an important subject with a man whose literary abilities have raised him to notice in the state. I have not yet learned to twist my periods, nor, in the equivocal idiom of politeness, to disguise my sentiments, and imply what I should be afraid to utter: if, therefore, in the course of this epistle, I chance to express contempt, and even indignation, with some emphasis, I beseech you to believe that it is not a flight of fancy; for truth, in morals, has ever appeared to me the essence of the sublime; and, in taste, simplicity the only criterion of the beautiful. But I war not with an individual when I contend for the *rights of men* and the liberty of reason. You see I do not condescend to cull my words to avoid the invidious phrase, nor shall I be prevented from giving a manly definition of it, by the flimsy ridicule which a lively fancy has interwoven with the present acceptation of the term. Reverencing the rights of humanity, I shall dare to assert them; not intimidated by the horse laugh that you have raised, or waiting till time has wiped away the compassionate tears which you have elaborately labored to excite.

From the many just sentiments interspersed through the letter before me, and from the whole tendency of it, I should believe you to be a good, though a vain man, if some circumstances in your conduct did not render the inflexibility of your integrity doubtful; and for this vanity a knowledge of human nature enables me to discover such extenuating circumstances, in the very texture of your mind, that I am ready to call it amiable, and separate the public from the private character.

* * *

Quitting now the flowers of rhetoric, let us, Sir, reason together; and, believe me, I should not have meddled with these troubled waters, in order to point out your inconsistencies, if your wit had not burnished up some rusty, baneful opinions, and swelled the shallow current of ridicule till it resembled the flow of reason, and presumed to be the test of truth.

I shall not attempt to follow you through "horse-way and foot-path;"[1] but, attacking the foundation of your opinions, I shall leave the superstructure to find a center of gravity on which it may lean till some strong blast puffs it into the air; or your teeming fancy, which the ripening judgment of sixty years has not tamed, produces another Chinese erection,[2] to stare, at every

1. *King Lear* 4.1.55.
2. Chinese pagodas were popular ornaments in late-eighteenth-century British landscaping.

turn, the plain country people in the face, who bluntly call such an airy edifice—a folly.

The birthright of man, to give you, Sir, a short definition of this disputed right, is such a degree of liberty, civil and religious, as is compatible with the liberty of every other individual with whom he is united in a social compact, and the continued existence of that compact.

Liberty, in this simple, unsophisticated sense, I acknowledge, is a fair idea that has never yet received a form in the various governments that have been established on our beauteous globe; the demon of property has ever been at hand to encroach on the sacred rights of men, and to fence round with awful pomp laws that war with justice. But that it results from the eternal foundation of right—from immutable truth—who will presume to deny, that pretends to rationality—if reason has led them to build their morality[3] and religion on an everlasting foundation—the attributes of God?

I glow with indignation when I attempt, methodically, to unravel your slavish paradoxes, in which I can find no fixed first principle to refute; I shall not, therefore, condescend to shew where you affirm in one page what you deny in another; and how frequently you draw conclusions without any previous premises:—it would be something like cowardice to fight with a man who had never exercised the weapons with which his opponent chose to combat, and irksome to refute sentence after sentence in which the latent spirit of tyranny appeared.

I perceive, from the whole tenor of your Reflections, that you have a mortal antipathy to reason; but, if there is any thing like argument, or first principles, in your wild declamation, behold the result:—that we are to reverence the rust of antiquity, and term the unnatural customs, which ignorance and mistaken self-interest have consolidated, the sage fruit of experience: nay, that, if we do discover some errors, our *feelings* should lead us to excuse, with blind love, or unprincipled filial affection, the venerable vestiges of ancient days. These are gothic[4] notions of beauty—the ivy is beautiful, but, when it insidiously destroys the trunk from which it receives support, who would not grub it up?

Further, that we ought cautiously to remain for ever in frozen inactivity, because a thaw, whilst it nourishes the soil, spreads a temporary inundation; and the fear of risking any personal present convenience should prevent a struggle for the most estimable advantages. This is sound reasoning, I grant, in the mouth of the rich and short-sighted.

Yes, Sir, the strong gained riches, the few have sacrificed the many to their vices; and, to be able to pamper their appetites, and supinely exist without exercising mind or body, they have ceased to be men.—Lost to the relish of true pleasure, such beings would, indeed, deserve compassion, if injustice was not softened by the tyrant's plea—necessity; if prescription was not raised as an immortal boundary against innovation. Their minds, in fact, instead of being cultivated, have been so warped by education, that it may require some ages to bring them back to nature, and enable them to see their true interest, with that degree of conviction which is necessary to influence their conduct.

3. As religion is included in my idea of morality, I should not have mentioned the term without specifying all the simple ideas which that comprehensive word generalizes; but as the charge of atheism has been very freely banded about in the letter I am considering, I wish to guard against misrepresentation [Wollstonecraft's note].

4. Barbarous.

The civilization which has taken place in Europe has been very partial, and, like every custom that an arbitrary point of honour has established, refines the manners at the expence of morals, by making sentiments and opinions current in conversation that have no root in the heart, or weight in the cooler resolves of the mind.—And what has stopped its progress?—hereditary property—hereditary honors. The man has been changed into an artificial monster by the station in which he was born, and the consequent homage that benumbed his faculties like the torpedo's[5] touch;—or a being, with a capacity of reasoning, would not have failed to discover, as his faculties unfolded, that true happiness arose from the friendship and intimacy which can only be enjoyed by equals; and that charity is not a condescending distribution of alms, but an intercourse of good offices and mutual benefits, founded on respect for justice and humanity.

* * *

It is necessary emphatically to repeat, that there are rights which men inherit at their birth, as rational creatures, who were raised above the brute creation by their improvable faculties; and that, in receiving these, not from their forefathers but, from God, prescription can never undermine natural rights.

A father may dissipate his property without his child having any right to complain;—but should he attempt to sell him for a slave, or fetter him with laws contrary to reason; nature, in enabling him to discern good from evil, teaches him to break the ignoble chain, and not to believe that bread becomes flesh, and wine blood, because his parents swallowed the Eucharist with this blind persuasion.

There is no end to this implicit submission to authority—some where it must stop, or we return to barbarism; and the capacity of improvement, which gives us a natural sceptre on earth, is a cheat, an ignis-fatuus, that leads us from inviting meadows into bogs and dung-hills. And if it be allowed that many of the precautions, with which any alteration was made, in our government, were prudent, it rather proves its weakness than substantiates an opinion of the soundness of the stamina, or the excellence of the constitution.

But on what principle Mr. Burke could defend American independence, I cannot conceive; for the whole tenor of his plausible arguments settles slavery on an everlasting foundation. Allowing his servile reverence for antiquity, and prudent attention to self-interest, to have the force which he insists on, the slave trade ought never to be abolished; and, because our ignorant forefathers, not understanding the native dignity of man, sanctioned a traffic that outrages every suggestion of reason and religion, we are to submit to the inhuman custom, and term an atrocious insult to humanity the love of our country, and a proper submission to the laws by which our property is secured.—Security of property! Behold, in a few words, the definition of English liberty. And to this selfish principle every nobler one is sacrificed.—The Briton takes place of the man, and the image of God is lost in the citizen! But it is not that enthusiastic flame which in Greece and Rome consumed every sordid passion: no, self is the focus; and the disparting rays rise not above our foggy atmosphere. But softly—it is only the property of the rich

---

5. Stingray, a fish with a whiplike, poisonous tail.

that is secure; the man who lives by the sweat of his brow has no asylum from oppression; the strong man may enter—when was the castle of the poor sacred? and the base informer steal him from the family that depend on his industry for subsistence.

* * *

But, among all your plausible arguments, and witty illustrations, your contempt for the poor always appears conspicuous, and rouses my indignation. The following paragraph in particular struck me, as breathing the most tyrannic spirit, and displaying the most factitious feelings. "Good order is the foundation of all good things. To be enabled to acquire, the people, without being servile, must be tractable and obedient. The magistrate must have his reverence, the laws their authority. The body of the people must not find the principles of natural subordination by art rooted out of their minds. They *must* respect that property of which they *cannot* partake. *They must labor to obtain what by labor can be obtained; and when they find, as they commonly do, the success disproportioned to the endeavor, they must be taught their consolation in the final proportions of eternal justice.* Of this consolation, whoever deprives them, deadens their industry, and strikes at the root of all acquisition as of all conservation. He that does this, is the cruel oppressor, the merciless enemy, of the poor and wretched; at the same time that, by his wicked speculations, he exposes the fruits of successful industry, and the accumulations of fortune, (ah! there's the rub)[6] to the plunder of the negligent, the disappointed, and the unprosperous."

This is contemptible hard-hearted sophistry, in the specious form of humility, and submission to the will of Heaven.—It is, Sir, *possible* to render the poor happier in this world, without depriving them of the consolation which you gratuitously grant them in the next. They have a right to more comfort than they at present enjoy; and more comfort might be afforded them, without encroaching on the pleasures of the rich: not now waiting to enquire whether the rich have any right to exclusive pleasures. What do I say?—encroaching! No; if an intercourse were established between them, it would impart the only true pleasure that can be snatched in this land of shadows, this hard school of moral discipline.

I know, indeed, that there is often something disgusting in the distresses of poverty, at which the imagination revolts, and starts back to exercise itself in the more attractive Arcadia of fiction. The rich man builds a house, art and taste give it the highest finish. His gardens are planted, and the trees grow to recreate the fancy of the planter, though the temperature of the climate may rather force him to avoid the dangerous damps they exhale, than seek the umbrageous retreat. Every thing on the estate is cherished but man; —yet, to contribute to the happiness of man, is the most sublime of all enjoyments. But if, instead of sweeping pleasure-grounds, obelisks, temples, and elegant cottages, as *objects* for the eye, the heart was allowed to beat true to nature, decent farms would be scattered over the estate, and plenty smile around. Instead of the poor being subject to the griping hand of an avaricious steward, they would be watched over with fatherly solicitude, by the man whose duty and pleasure it was to guard their happiness, and shield

6. *Hamlet* 3.1.67.

from rapacity the beings who, by the sweat of their brow, exalted him above his fellows.

I could almost imagine I see a man thus gathering blessings as he mounted the hill of life; or consolation, in those days when the spirits lag, and the tired heart finds no pleasure in them. It is not by squandering alms that the poor can be relieved, or improved—it is the fostering sun of kindness, the wisdom that finds them employments calculated to give them habits of virtue, that meliorates their condition. Love is only the fruit of love; condescension and authority may produce the obedience you applaud; but he has lost his heart of flesh who can see a fellow-creature humbled before him, and trembling at the frown of a being, whose heart is supplied by the same vital current, and whose pride ought to be checked by a consciousness of having the same infirmities.

✻　✻　✻

1790

THOMAS PAINE

Although he was born and lived his first thirty-seven years in England, Thomas Paine (1737–1809) enters the debate as a visitor from America, where by writing *Common Sense* (1776) and the sixteen *Crisis* pamphlets, beginning "These are the times that try men's souls" (1776–83), he had served as the most effective propagandist for American independence. His *Rights of Man: Being an Answer to Mr. Burke's Attack on the French Revolution*, published in March 1791 with a dedication "To George Washington, President of the United States of America," has the full weight of the American revolutionary experience behind it and is the strongest statement against hereditary monarchy of any of the works replying to Burke in this "war of pamphlets." Paine published a second part of *Rights of Man* the following year and, when charged with treason by the British, fled to France, where he was made a citizen and a member of the Convention. With the fall of the more moderate Girondists, he was imprisoned by the Jacobins for a year in 1793–94, during which he wrote his last famous work, *The Age of Reason* (1794).

From Rights of Man

Among the incivilities by which nations or individuals provoke and irritate each other, Mr. Burke's pamphlet on the French Revolution is an extraordinary instance. Neither the people of France, nor the National Assembly, were troubling themselves about the affairs of England, or the English Parliament; and why Mr. Burke should commence an unprovoked attack upon them, both in parliament and in public, is a conduct that cannot be pardoned on the score of manners, nor justified on that of policy.

There is scarcely an epithet of abuse to be found in the English language with which Mr. Burke has not loaded the French nation and the National

Assembly. Every thing which rancor, prejudice, ignorance or knowledge could suggest, are poured forth in the copious fury of near four hundred pages. In the strain and on the plan Mr. Burke was writing, he might have written on to as many thousands. When the tongue or the pen is let loose in a frenzy of passion, it is the man, and not the subject, that becomes exhausted.

Hitherto Mr. Burke has been mistaken and disappointed in the opinions he had formed of the affairs of France; but such is the ingenuity of his hope, or the malignancy of his despair, that it furnishes him with new pretences to go on. There was a time when it was impossible to make Mr. Burke believe there would be any revolution in France. His opinion then was, that the French had neither spirit to undertake it, nor fortitude to support it; and now that there is one, he seeks an escape by condemning it.

* * *

There never did, there never will, and there never can exist a parliament, or any description of men, or any generation of men, in any country, possessed of the right or the power of binding and controuling posterity to the *"end of time,"* or of commanding for ever how the world shall be governed, or who shall govern it; and therefore, all such clauses, acts or declarations, by which the makers of them attempt to do what they have neither the right nor the power to do, nor the power to execute, are in themselves null and void.—Every age and generation must be as free to act for itself, *in all cases*, as the ages and generations which preceded it. The vanity and presumption of governing beyond the grave, is the most ridiculous and insolent of all tyrannies. Man has no property in man; neither has any generation a property in the generations which are to follow. The parliament or the people of 1688, or of any other period, had no more right to dispose of the people of the present day, or to bind or to controul them *in any shape whatever*, than the parliament or the people of the present day have to dispose of, bind or controul those who are to live a hundred or a thousand years hence. Every generation is, and must be, competent to all the purposes which its occasions require. It is the living, and not the dead, that are to be accommodated. When man ceases to be, his power and his wants cease with him; and having no longer any participation in the concerns of this world, he has no longer any authority in directing who shall be its governors, or how its government shall be organized, or how administered.

I am not contending for nor against any form of government, nor for nor against any party here or elsewhere. That which a whole nation chooses to do, it has a right to do. Mr. Burke says, No. Where then *does* the right exist? I am contending for the rights of the *living*, and against their being willed away, and controuled and contracted for, by the manuscript assumed authority of the dead; and Mr. Burke is contending for the authority of the dead over the rights and freedom of the living.* * *

* * *

"We have seen," says Mr. Burke, "the French rebel against a mild and lawful Monarch, with more fury, outrage, and insult, than any people has been known to rise against the most illegal usurper, or the most sanguinary tyrant."—This is one among a thousand other instances, in which Mr. Burke shews that he is ignorant of the springs and principles of the French revolution.

It was not against Louis the XVIth, but against the despotic principles of the government, that the nation revolted. These principles had not their origin in him, but in the original establishment, many centuries back; and they were become too deeply rooted to be removed, and the augean stable[1] of parasites and plunderers too abominably filthy to be cleansed, by any thing short of a complete and universal revolution. When it becomes necessary to do a thing, the whole heart and soul should go into the measure, or not attempt it. That crisis was then arrived, and there remained no choice but to act with determined vigor, or not to act at all. The King was known to be the friend of the nation, and this circumstance was favorable to the enterprise. Perhaps no man bred up in the style of an absolute King, ever possessed a heart so little disposed to the exercise of that species of power as the present King of France. But the principles of the government itself still remained the same. The Monarch and the monarchy were distinct and separate things; and it was against the established despotism of the latter, and not against the person or principles of the former, that the revolt commenced, and the revolution has been carried.

Mr. Burke does not attend to the distinction between *men* and *principles;* and therefore, he does not see that a revolt may take place against the despotism of the latter, while there lies no charge of despotism against the former.

The natural moderation of Louis the XVIth contributed nothing to alter the hereditary despotism of the monarchy. All the tyrannies of former reigns, acted under that hereditary despotism, were still liable to be revived in the hands of a successor. It was not the respite of a reign that would satisfy France, enlightened as she was then become. A casual discontinuance of the *practice* of despotism, is not a discontinuance of its *principles;* the former depends on the virtue of the individual who is in immediate possession of power; the latter, on the virtue and fortitude of the nation. In the case of Charles I and James II of England, the revolt was against the personal despotism of the men;[2] whereas in France, it was against the hereditary despotism of the established government. But men who can consign over the rights of posterity for ever on the authority of a moldy parchment, like Mr. Burke, are not qualified to judge of this revolution. It takes in a field too vast for their views to explore, and proceeds with a mightiness of reason they cannot keep pace with.

But there are many points of view in which this revolution may be considered. When despotism has established itself for ages in a country, as in France, it is not in the person of the King only that it resides. It has the appearance of being so in show, and in nominal authority; but it is not so in practice, and in fact. It has its standard every where. Every office and depart-

---

1. King Augeas's stable, housing three thousand oxen and neglected for decades, was a classical symbol of filth and corruption. Hercules cleaned it by changing the course of a river.

2. Charles I was overthrown by the Civil War and executed in 1649. His son, James II, was dethroned in the Glorious Revolution of 1688.

ment has its despotism founded upon custom and usage. Every place has its Bastille,[3] and every Bastille its despot. The original hereditary despotism resident in the person of the King, divides and subdivides itself into a thousand shapes and forms, till at last the whole of it is acted by deputation. This was the case in France; and against this species of despotism, proceeding on through an endless labyrinth of office till the source of it is scarcely perceptible, there is no mode of redress. It strengthens itself by assuming the appearance of duty, and tyrannises under the pretence of obeying.

When a man reflects on the condition which France was in from the nature of her government, he will see other causes for revolt than those which immediately connect themselves with the person or character of Louis XVI. There were, if I may so express it, a thousand despotisms to be reformed in France, which had grown up under the hereditary despotism of the monarchy, and became so rooted as to be in a great measure independent of it. Between the monarchy, the parliament, and the church, there was a *rivalship* of despotism; besides the feudal despotism operating locally, and the ministerial despotism operating every where. But Mr. Burke, by considering the King as the only possible object of a revolt, speaks as if France was a village, in which every thing that passed must be known to its commanding officer, and no oppression could be acted but what he could immediately control. Mr. Burke might have been in the Bastille his whole life, as well under Louis XVI as Louis XIV and neither the one nor the other have known that such a man as Mr. Burke existed. The despotic principles of the government were the same in both reigns, though the dispositions of the men were as remote as tyranny and benevolence.

What Mr. Burke considers as a reproach to the French Revolution (that of bringing it forward under a reign more mild than the preceding ones), is one of its highest honors. The revolutions that have taken place in other European countries, have been excited by personal hatred. The rage was against the man, and he became the victim. But, in the instance of France, we see a revolution generated in the rational contemplation of the rights of man, and distinguishing from the beginning between persons and principles.

But Mr. Burke appears to have no idea of principles, when he is contemplating governments. "Ten years ago," says he, "I could have felicitated France on her having a government, without enquiring what the nature of that government was, or how it was administered." Is this the language of a rational man? Is it the language of a heart feeling as it ought to feel for the rights and happiness of the human race? On this ground, Mr. Burke must compliment every government in the world, while the victims who suffer under them, whether sold into slavery, or tortured out of existence, are wholly forgotten. It is power, and not principles, that Mr. Burke venerates; and under this abominable depravity, he is disqualified to judge between them.— Thus much for his opinion as to the occasions of the French Revolution.* * *

*   *   *

As to the tragic paintings by which Mr. Burke has outraged his own imagination, and seeks to work upon that of his readers, they are very well calculated for theatrical representation, where facts are manufactured for the

3. France's political prison (where the French Revolution began on July 14, 1789).

sake of show, and accommodated to produce, through the weakness of sympathy, a weeping effect. But Mr. Burke should recollect that he is writing History, and not *Plays*; and that his readers will expect truth, and not the spouting rant of high-toned exclamation.

When we see a man dramatically lamenting in a publication intended to be believed, that, *"The age of chivalry is gone!* that *The glory of Europe is extinguished for ever!* that *The unbought grace of life* (if any one knows what it is), *the cheap defence of nations, the nurse of manly sentiment and heroic enterprize, is gone!"* and all this because the Quixote age of chivalric nonsense is gone, What opinion can we form of his judgment, or what regard can we pay to his facts? In the rhapsody of his imagination, he has discovered a world of wind-mills, and his sorrows are, that there are no Quixotes to attack them. But if the age of aristocracy, like that of chivalry, should fall, and they had originally some connection, Mr. Burke, the trumpeter of the Order, may continue his parody to the end, and finish with exclaiming, *"Othello's occupation's gone!"*[4]

Notwithstanding Mr. Burke's horrid paintings, when the French Revolution is compared with that of other countries, the astonishment will be, that it is marked with so few sacrifices; but this astonishment will cease when we reflect that *principles*, and not *persons*, were the meditated objects of destruction. The mind of the nation was acted upon by a higher stimulus than what the consideration of persons could inspire, and sought a higher conquest than could be produced by the downfall of an enemy.* * *

1791

APOCALYPTIC EXPECTATIONS BY PREACHERS AND POETS

Looking back to his early radical years from his conservative middle age, Robert Southey declared:

> Few persons but those who have lived in it can conceive or comprehend what the memory of the French Revolution was, nor what a visionary world seemed to open upon those who were just entering it. Old things seemed passing away, and nothing was dreamt of but the regeneration of the human race. (*The Correspondence of Robert Southey with Caroline Bowles*, ed. Edward Dowden, 1881)

In the prologue to his highly successful play *The Road to Ruin* (1792), Thomas Holcroft used the occasion to predict that the French Revolution would "fertilize a world, and renovate old earth!" And in *The Prelude* (p. 346), Wordsworth remembered the early years of the Revolution as a time when all Europe

> was thrilled with joy,
> France standing on the top of golden hours,
> And human nature seeming born again.
> (6.340–42)

Human nature regenerated in a world made new: this was the theme of many enthusiasts in England during the first four or five years after the outbreak of the French

---

4. *Othello* 3.3.362 (Othello's feeling, when he thinks Desdemona has been unfaithful, that his life is over). "Quixote" as an adjective, referring to the hero of Cervantes's romance, means "impractically idealistic."

Revolution in 1789. The concepts are patently theological. They originate in the apocalyptic and millennial passages of the Hebrew and Christian Scriptures, and their use indicates that for a number of British idealists, the early enthusiasm for the Revolution had the fervor and conviction of a religious movement.

The term *apocalypse*, derived from the Greek word meaning "revelation," designates the disclosure, in the Bible, of God's providential design for the end of human history. In its developed form, an apocalypse is a prophetic vision, in elaborately symbolic form, of the imminent events that will abruptly end the existing order and replace it with a new and perfected condition both of humanity and of the world. The root elements of apocalypse are the concern of the Hebrew prophets with the catastrophic punishments to be visited upon an errant Israel and its enemies in "the latter end of the days," as well as with the expectation of a messiah, a deliverer from suffering in this disaster-ridden world. These elements were collected in the writings attributed to the prophet Isaiah, which foretell, after God has vented His wrath, the advent of a renovated world of ease, joy, and peace. "For, behold, I create new heavens and a new earth," in which "the wolf and the lamb shall feed together, and the lion shall eat straw like the bullock" (Isaiah 65.17–25). The Old Testament of the Bible also contains a full-fledged apocalypse, the Book of Daniel, which includes a symbolic vision of four beasts, signifying four successive monarchies; following the Fourth Monarchy, after a violent preliminary, "one like the Son of man came with the clouds of heaven" and was given by the "Ancient of days" "an everlasting dominion, which shall not pass away" (Isaiah 7.13–14).

Passages predicting an imminent apocalypse occur in the New Testament both in the Synoptic Gospels and in the Epistles of Paul. The New Testament concludes with the most spectacular, awesome, and intricately ordered of all apocalyptic prophecies, the Book of Revelation. A series of symbolic events—seven angels blow seven trumpet blasts and pour out seven vials of wrath—represent the conflict between the forces of Christ and of the Antichrist, culminating in a prodigious violence in which the stars fall like ripe figs (Revelation 6.13) and the harvest of the earth is cast "into the great winepress of the wrath of God . . . and blood came out of the winepress, even unto the horse bridles" (14.19–20). This fierce destruction, however, is a cleansing one, preparatory to the Second Coming of Christ to inaugurate the Kingdom of God on earth, which will last one thousand years—in Latin, a "millennium," from which are derived the terms *millennial* and *millenarian* to signify the belief in a blissful earthly condition at the end of history. After the millennium, the forces of evil will be loosed again and finally defeated, after which the original creation, its function in the divine plot accomplished, will pass away, to be replaced by a new creation and by a new Jerusalem that will reconstitute, for the deserving elect, the paradise that had been lost at the Fall: "And there shall be no more death . . . neither shall there be any more pain: for the former things are passed away" (Revelation 21.4).

Two distinctive images recur persistently in later writings that derive from biblical apocalypses. One is the image of a sacred marriage that signifies the consummation of history. In Isaiah (62.2–5), the final redemption is figured as a marriage between the people of Israel and their land; in Revelation (21.2, 9–10), it is figured as a marriage between Christ and the new, or purified, Jerusalem, "coming down from God out of heaven, prepared as a bride adorned for her husband." The second recurrent image represents the final condition of blessedness as a renovated heaven and earth: "For, behold," the Lord said to Isaiah, "I create new heavens and a new earth" (Isaiah 65.17 and 66.22). Thus also Revelation (21.1, 5): "And I saw a new heaven and a new earth: for the first heaven and the first earth were passed away."

The apocalyptic and millennial prophecies in the Bible are readily convertible into a program for violent political revolution, because they consist of an infallible text that ordains a necessary and total destruction of the forces of the evil and guarantees the outcome of this violence in an enduring condition of peace, plenty, and consummate happiness. In the civil wars in seventeenth-century England, for example, there were fervent apocalyptic expectations among radical parliamentary sects that were shared by Oliver Cromwell, as well as by John Milton, who voiced his conviction of an imminent millennium in the traditional figures of an apocalyptic marriage and a universal renovation: "Thy Kingdome is now at hand. . . . come forth out of thy Royall Chambers, O Prince of all the Kings of the earth . . . for now the voice of thy Bride calls thee, and all creatures sigh to be renewed" (1.707, *Animadversions,* in *Complete Prose Works*; see also 1.616).

The late eighteenth century was another age of apocalyptic expectation, when the promise of the American Revolution, followed by the greater and more radical hopes raised by the early years of the French Revolution, revived within some English Nonconforming sects the millenarian excitement of Milton and other seventeenth-century predecessors. The Unitarian Richard Price had in 1785 hailed the American Revolution as a crucial step in fulfilling the "old prophecies" of a reign of reason, virtue, and peace, when the wolf will "dwell with the lamb and the leopard with the kid." *Discourse on the Love of Our Country*—excerpted above as a major provocation of Burke's *Reflections on the Revolution in France*—although delivered less than three months after the fall of the Bastille—already envisioned the uprising in terms of biblical prophecy. Other preachers such as Joseph Fawcett (a model for the millenarian preachings by the Solitary in Wordsworth's *Excursion*), Elhanan Winchester (who delivered his apocalyptic discourses to the British Parliament), and Joseph Priestley (who was not only a great chemist but a founder of the Unitarian Society) all interpreted the convulsions in France as fulfilling the prophecies of the last days. They thus invested the promise of France with the explosive power of the great Western myth of apocalypse, expanding a local historical event into the perfervid expectation that all humanity, everywhere, was at the violent threshold of an earthly paradise.

This phenomenon is of special importance for literature because, during the formative period in the early 1790s, the first generation of Romantic poets shared this millenarian excitement and incorporated in their poems apocalyptic expectations—or at least apocalyptic imaginings—of the French Revolution as prelude to the abrupt culmination of history, in the emergence of a new humanity on a new paradisal earth. The poetic selections printed here are from some of the works, written in 1793 and 1794, in which Southey, Blake, Wordsworth, and Coleridge present their versions of the expected historical sequence that Coleridge, in the prose "Argument" prefixed to *Religious Musings* (1794), tersely summarized: "The French Revolution. Millennium. Universal Redemption. Conclusion." The selections end with a passage from *Queen Mab* (1813), in which the youthful Shelley recapitulates the millenarian hopes that had been expressed by his older contemporaries in the early stage of the revolution, two decades before.

ELHANAN WINCHESTER

Elhanan Winchester (1751–1797) was an American evangelist whose sermons at the Baptist Church of Philadelphia attracted large and enthusiastic audiences. In 1787, Winchester felt divinely called to go to London in order to preach his "universalist" doctrine that, at the end of time, all humans would be saved, including even the worst of sinners.

On February 3 and 24, 1793, Winchester delivered to the British Parliament two discourses, the substance of which were published that same year with the resounding title *The Three Woe-Trumpets, of which the first and second are already past and the third is now begun: under which the seven vials of the wrath of God are to be poured out upon the world*. The title page added that the discourses were a commentary on Revelation 11.14–18:

> 14. The second woe is past; and, behold, the third woe cometh quickly.
>
> 15. And the seventh angel sounded; and there were great voices in heaven, saying, The kingdoms of his world are become the kingdoms of our Lord, and of his Christ; and he shall reign for ever and ever.
>
> 16. And the four and twenty elders, which sat before God on their seats, fell upon their faces, and worshipped God,
>
> 17. Saying, We give thee thanks, O Lord God Almighty, which art, and wast, and art to come; because thou hast taken to thee thy great power, and hast reigned.
>
> 18. And the nations were angry, and thy wrath is come, and the time of the dead, that they should be judged, and that thou shouldest give reward unto thy servants the prophets, and to the saints, and them that fear thy name, small and great: and shouldest destroy them which destroy the earth.

Winchester elaborates his depiction of the divine wrath and of the coming kingdom by reference to other passages in Revelation and to other books in the Bible, considering them to be prophecies of the contemporary revolution in France and of events that are to follow. That Winchester's discourses were delivered to Parliament indicates the currency of the belief that the convulsions in France precede a millennial restoration, everywhere and to all peoples, of the felicity that had been lost at the fall of Adam and Eve. Winchester, who was a poet as well as a preacher, published that same year, 1793, *The Process and Empire of Christ: An Heroic Poem*, written in blank verse. Books 8–12 deal with the Second Coming, the millennium, and the "New Creation; or The Renovation of the Heavens and Earth after the Conflagration."

From The Three Woe-Trumpets

*   *   *

By the great earthquake, we are to understand a great political shaking of some nation, whereby the government shall be overthrown and broken in pieces, as really as any part of the earth was ever broken and destroyed by a natural earthquake. * * * And in this earthquake, which will be a sudden and surprizing Revolution, different from all others, there will be slain of names of men seven thousand; or, the whole number of the titles, or names of distinction will be destroyed; and all this will take place in a most sudden and unexpected manner.

Now look at the Revolution, and overturning of the government in France, and see if this prophecy is not exactly fulfilled, and therein a full proof given that *the second woe is past*, beyond all dispute; and this epoch is therefore interesting to all Christians in the highest degree.

*   *   *

I regard the late events in France, therefore, as Signs of the Times, and they mark the close of the preceding period with great exactness; and in this light their consequence is very great: they shew us whereabouts we are, and tend to confirm the authority of the Scriptures, and especially the book of the Revelation of St. John.

A new and very important period is now beginning to take place, under the sound of the Seventh Trumpet, which will continue to sound from this time, 'till after the personal appearance of JESUS, 'till all the seven vials of the wrath of God are poured out, and until *the kingdoms of this world are become the kingdoms of our Lord, and of his Christ.*

But great will be the woes and desolations that will come upon the world before this happy event will take place. And for this reason, the seventh trumpet is properly denominated *a woe trumpet,* for the woes that will take place while it is sounding, will be great beyond example, and terrible beyond description.

* * *

Under the seventh trumpet our glorious Savior will personally appear: I have already observed, that he will come between the time of the sixth and seventh vial; all these awful dispensations that are taking place are solemn preparations for that event; and therefore our Lord charges us when we hear of wars and rumors of wars, to see that we *be not troubled; for all these things must come to pass.** * * The coming of our Savior in glory, is such a joyful event in itself, and will be followed by so many glorious consequences, that it is almost impossible for a true christian to think of it without exultation. And this will actually take place under the sound of the seventh trumpet.

* * *

It is very easy to see that in a very short time all nations shall be brought to yield obedience to him; *and the kingdoms of this world shall become the kingdoms of our Lord and of his Christ, and he shall reign, eis tous aionas tan aionon*; which our translators have translated *forever and ever,* but which appears (in Chap. xx.2, 3, 4, 5, 6, 7) to be only *a thousand years,* and is six times limited to that period. So that here the words which are used imply *hidden duration,* or *ages of ages,* without specifying the exact length of the periods: But in Chap. xx the time is made known with great exactness. * * * There is nothing in this view of the kingdom of Christ, that has any tendency to give umbrage or dissatisfaction to the present monarchs, kings, rulers, or governors of the earth, for though all the kingdoms of the world shall become the Lord's, and his Christ's, yet this is no encouragement for any usurpers to rise and seize upon them, under a pretence of their being the Lord's people, and that they are going to take possession of the kingdoms for him; for Christ himself will come in person, to take the kingdoms of this world under his government, so that this part of my text will not be accomplished till after his appearing in glory, and the first resurrection has taken place.

* * *

I will now as a close of this discourse, just mention the blessings of the Millennium, or the personal kingdom of our Lord upon the earth. * * *

The kingdom or government of Christ shall be absolutely universal, and shall extend over the whole earth: All nations shall know his name, and shall serve and obey him. * * *

His government shall be *just, equitable, righteous,* friendly to mankind, especially to the poor and needy. * * *

Another blessing that shall take place under the Messiah's government, shall be universal and constant peace during the whole period of his reign. * * *

The earth shall be filled with plenty as well as peace, and neither war, famine, pestilence, nor the terrible fierceness of wild beasts shall annoy, hurt, destroy, or even terrify the inhabitants of the earth in those blessed days. * * *

In those blessed times there shall be no differences of sentiment: All shall be harmony and love: No contradiction in the public instructions: All ministers shall agree, in principle and practice, in faith and worship. * * *

* * * When this perfect unity takes place among believers, the conversion of the whole world shall commence, and all shall bow at the scepter of Jesus and become the willing subjects of his kingdom. * * *

1793

JOSEPH PRIESTLEY

Joseph Priestley (1733–1804) was a Unitarian minister, political theorist, and philosopher, as well as an eminent scientist who helped establish modern chemistry by discovering oxygen. In 1791 he wrote and published *Letters to the Right Honorable Edmund Burke,* a reply to Burke's *Reflections on the French Revolution,* in which he hailed the American and French Revolutions as inaugurating the state of universal peace and happiness that was "distinctly and repeatedly foretold in many prophecies, delivered more than two thousand years ago" (Birmingham, 1791, p. 150). Priestley's enthusiastic endorsement of the French Revolution led to the destruction of his house, library, and laboratory in Birmingham by rioters on the second anniversary of the fall of the Bastille, July 14, 1791.

Three years later, on February 28, 1794, Priestley published the sermon *The Present State of Europe Compared with Antient Prophecies,* in which he interpreted the events in France by detailed reference to apocalyptic and millennial passages in the Bible, especially the Book of Revelation. Soon after publishing this sermon, he emigrated to Pennsylvania, where he lived the last ten years of his life. In a sermon that he did not live to deliver, Priestley reaffirmed his millennial faith: "Let us then be ever *looking for,* as we are *hastening into,* the coming of this great day of God. . . ."

From The Present State of Europe Compared with Antient Prophecies:

A Sermon, Preached at the Gravel Pit Meeting in Hackney, February 28, 1794, Being the Day Appointed for a General Fast[1]

* * *

If we can learn any thing concerning what is before us, from the language of prophecy, great calamities, such as the world has never yet experienced, will precede that happy state of things, in which "the kingdoms of this world will become the kingdom of our Lord Jesus Christ;" and these calamities will chiefly affect those nations which have been the seat of the great antichristian power; or, as all Protestants, and I believe justly, suppose, have been subject to the see of Rome. And it appears to me highly probable, as I hinted in my last discourse on this occasion, that the present disturbances in Europe are the beginning of those very calamitous times.* * *

* * * It is enough for us to know the certainty of these great events, that our faith may not fail on the approach of the predicted calamity, confident that it will have the happiest issue in God's own time. For the same Being who foretold the evil which we shall see come to pass, has likewise foretold the good that is to follow it.

That the second coming of Christ will be coincident with the commencement of the millennium, or the future peaceable and happy state of the world (which, according to all the prophecies, will take place after the restoration of the Jews) is evident from what Peter said, in his address to the Jews, on the occasion of his healing the lame man at the gate of the temple, Acts iii.19. * * *

This great event of the late revolution in France appears to me, and many others, to be not improbably the accomplishment of the following part of the Revelation, chap. xi.3: "And the same hour there was a great earthquake, and the tenth part of the city fell, and in the earthquake were slain of men (or literally, *names of men*) seven thousand, and the remnant were affrighted, and gave glory to God."

An earthquake, as I have observed, may signify a great convulsion, and revolution, in states; and as the Papal dominions were divided into ten parts, one of which, and one of the principal of them, was France, it is properly called *a tenth part of the city*, or of the mystical *Babylon*. And if by *names of men*, we understand their *titles*, such as those of the nobility, and other hereditary distinctions, all of which are now abolished, the accomplishment of the prediction will appear to be wonderfully exact. * * *

* * * What could have been more unexpected than the events of any one of the last four years, at the beginning of it? What a total revolution in the ideas, and conduct of a whole nation! What a total subversion of principles, what reverses of fortune, and what a waste of life! In how bloody and eventful a war are we engaged, how inconsiderable in its beginning, how rapid and wide in its progress, and how dark with respect to its termina-

---

1. Fasts were proclaimed by the British government to obtain divine sanction for the war against France, which had begun in February 1793. Priest- ley's sermon, however, was not what the government had in mind.

tion! At first it resembled Elijah's cloud, appearing no bigger than a *man's hand* [1 Kings 18.44]; but now it covers, and darkens, the whole European hemisphere!

Now, whatever we may think, as politicians (and with us every man will have his own opinion, on a subject so interesting to us all) I would, in this place, admonish you not to overlook the hand of God in the great scene that is now opening upon us. Nothing can ever come to pass without his appointment, or permission; and then, whatever be the views of men, we cannot doubt, but that his are always wise, righteous, and good. Let us, therefore, exercise faith in him, believing that though "clouds and darkness are round about him, righteousness and judgment are for ever the habitation of his throne" [Psalm 97.2]. All those who appear in the theatre of public affairs, in the field, or the cabinet, both those whom we praise, and those whom we blame, are equally instruments in his hands, and execute all his pleasure. Let this reflection, then, in our cooler moments (and I hope we shall endeavour, in all the tumult of affairs, to make these as many as possible), lead us to look more to God, and less to man; and consequently, in all the troubles in which we may be involved, repose the most unshaken confidence in him, and thence "in patience possess our own souls" [Luke 21.19], especially when it is evident that it is wholly out of our power to alter the course of events. If we be careful so to live as to be at all times prepared to die, what have we to fear, even though, as the Psalmist says, the "earth be removed, and the mountains be carried into the midst of the sea?" [Psalm 46.2]. Whatever turn the course of things may take, it cannot then be to our disadvantage. What, then, should hinder our contemplating the great scene, that seems now to be opening upon us, awful as it is, with tranquillity, and even with satisfaction, from our firm persuasion, that its termination will be glorious and happy?

1794

WILLIAM BLAKE

The narrative poems that William Blake (1757–1827) wrote in the early 1790s show that he, like the radical preachers of the time, envisioned the French Revolution as the portent of apocalypse. He planned *The French Revolution* as an epic poem in seven books. Of these, only the first book survives, in a single set of page proofs set in type in 1791. It traces, largely without symbolism, the events of the revolution shortly before and just after the fall of the Bastille on July 14, 1789, and incorporates the prophecy of a millennial condition in which "men walk with their fathers in bliss." The next year, 1792, Blake wrote *A Song of Liberty* (p. 82), which represents Energy as a revolutionary "son of fire," moving from America to France and crying the advent of an Isaian peaceable kingdom: "Empire is no more! And now the lion & wolf shall cease."

In what are known as the "minor prophecies," whose composition ended in 1795, Blake reshaped the large-scaled but still historical agents of his *French Revolution* into what he called the "Giant Forms" of his mythical system. These works are represented here by *America: A Prophecy*, which Blake dated 1793. In this poem the tyrant King George becomes "Albion's Angel" and is presented as an advocate of Urizen, the misconceived sky god of rationality, prohibition, and oppression. The opponent of Urizen is "red Orc," who represents the spirit of energy, bursting out not only in political revolution but in rebellion against all forms of physical, religious, and sexual repression. The triumph of Orc will result in a universal human state of peace and exuberant joy.

From The French Revolution: A Poem in Seven Books[1]

        * * * Then the Abbe de S[i]eyes rais'd his feet
On the steps of the Louvre; like a voice of God following a storm, the
    Abbe follow'd
The pale fires of Aumont into the chamber, as a father that bows to his
    son;
Whose rich fields inheriting spread their old glory, so the voice of the
    people bowed
205 Before the ancient seat of the kingdom and mountains to be renewed.
"Hear, O Heavens of France, the voice of the people, arising from valley
    and hill,
O'erclouded with power. Hear the voice of vallies, the voice of meek cities,
Mourning oppressed on village and field, till the village and field is a
    waste.
For the husbandman weeps at blights of the fife, and blasting of trumpets
    consume
210 The souls of mild France; the pale mother nourishes her child to the
    deadly slaughter.
When the heavens were seal'd with a stone, and the terrible sun clos'd in
    an orb, and the moon
Rent from the nations, and each star appointed for watchers of night,
The millions of spirits immortal were bound in the ruins of sulphur
    heaven
To wander inslav'd; black, deprest in dark ignorance, kept in awe with the
    whip,
215 To worship terrors, bred from the blood of revenge and breath of desire,
In beastial forms; or more terrible men, till the dawn of our peaceful
    morning,
Till dawn, till morning, till the breaking of clouds, and swelling of winds,
    and the universal voice,
Till man raise his darken'd limbs out of the caves of night, his eyes and his
    heart
Expand: where is space? where O Sun is thy dwelling? where thy tent, O
    faint slumb'rous Moon?
220 Then the valleys of France shall cry to the soldier, 'Throw down thy sword
    and musket,

1. The speaker in this extract is the revolutionist and statesman Abbé Sieyès (1748–1836), who on July 6, 1789, addressed the French National Assembly to urge that the troops be withdrawn from Paris. The abbé's speech refers to the abolition of black slavery (lines 214–19) and to religious as well as political oppression (lines 223–26).

And run and embrace the meek peasant.' Her Nobles shall hear and shall weep, and put off

The red robe of terror, the crown of oppression, the shoes of contempt, and unbuckle

The girdle of war from the desolate earth; then the Priest in his thund'rous cloud

Shall weep, bending to earth embracing the valleys, and putting his hand to the plow

225 Shall say, 'No more I curse thee; but now I will bless thee: No more in deadly black

Devour thy labour; nor lift up a cloud in thy heavens, O laborious plow,

That the wild raging millions, that wander in forests, and howl in law blasted wastes,

Strength madden'd with slavery, honesty, bound in the dens of superstition,

May sing in the village, and shout in the harvest, and woo in pleasant gardens

230 Their once savage loves, now beaming with knowledge, with gentle awe adorned;

And the saw, and the hammer, the chisel, the pencil, the pen, and the instruments

Of heavenly song sound in the wilds once forbidden, to teach the laborious plowman

And shepherd deliver'd from clouds of war, from pestilence, from night-fear, from murder,

From falling, from stifling, from hunger, from cold, from slander, discontent and sloth;

235 That walk in beasts and birds of night, driven back by the sandy desert

Like pestilent fogs round cities of men: and the happy earth sing in its course,

The mild peaceable nations be opened to heav'n, and men walk with their fathers in bliss.'

Then hear the first voice of the morning: 'Depart, O clouds of night, and no more

Return; be withdrawn cloudy war, troops of warriors depart, nor around our peaceable city

240 Breathe fires, but ten miles from Paris, let all be peace, nor a soldier be seen!' "

1791

From America: A Prophecy[1]

PLATE 6

"The morning comes, the night decays, the watchmen leave their stations;
The grave is burst, the spices shed, the linen wrapped up;
The bones of death, the cov'ring clay, the sinews shrunk & dry'd,

---

1. This "minor prophecy" (i.e., a short poem of epiclike narrative) is dated 1793 but was drafted and revised over several years. It relates the American Revolution to current events in France. Blake identifies the speaker in plate 6 as "a voice" that "came forth"—presumably, the voice of prophetic vision. "Albion's Angel," who speaks in plate 7, is George III of England. The speaker in plate 8 is Orc, who appears to the terrified king in the serpent form of Satan, whom Blake regards as the original revolutionary against oppression by a tyrant God.

Reviving shake, inspiring move, breathing! awakening!
5 Spring like redeemed captives when their bonds & bars are burst.
Let the slave grinding at the mill run out into the field:
Let him look up into the heavens & laugh in the bright air;
Let the inchained soul shut up in darkness and in sighing,
Whose face has never seen a smile in thirty weary years,
10 Rise and look out; his chains are loose, his dungeon doors are open.
And let his wife and children return from the opressor's scourge.
They look behind at every step & believe it is a dream,
Singing, 'The Sun has left his blackness, & has found a fresher morning
And the fair Moon rejoices in the clear & cloudless night;
15 For Empire is no more, and now the Lion & Wolf shall cease.' "

PLATE 7

In thunders ends the voice. Then Albion's Angel wrathful burnt
Beside the Stone of Night; and like the Eternal Lion's howl
In famine & war, reply'd, "Art thou not Orc; who serpent-form'd
Stands at the gate of Enitharmon to devour her children?
5 Blasphemous Demon, Antichrist, hater of Dignities;
Lover of wild rebellion, and transgresser of God's Law,
Why dost thou come to Angels' eyes in this terrific form?"

PLATE 8

The terror answerd: "I am Orc, wreath'd round the accursed tree:
The times are ended; shadows pass, the morning 'gins to break;
The fiery joy, that Urizen perverted to ten commands,
What night he led the starry hosts thro' the wide wilderness:
5 That stony law I stamp to dust: and scatter religion abroad
To the four winds as a torn book, & none shall gather the leaves;
But they shall rot on desart sands, & consume in bottomless deeps,
To make the desarts blossom, & the deeps shrink to their fountains,
And to renew the fiery joy, and burst the stony roof,
10 That pale religious letchery, seeking Virginity,
May find it in a harlot, and in coarse-clad honesty
The undefil'd, tho' ravish'd in her cradle night and morn:
For every thing that lives is holy, life delights in life;
Because the soul of sweet delight can never be defil'd.
15 Fires inwrap the earthly globe, yet man is not consumed;
Amidst the lustful fires he walks: his feet become like brass,
His knees and thighs like silver, & his breast and head like gold."

1793

ROBERT SOUTHEY

Robert Southey (1774–1843), although in his time a prolific and distinguished author, is now remembered mainly for his close association with Coleridge and Wordsworth, for Byron's savage lampoons of him in *Don Juan* and *The Vision of*

Judgment, and for his story *The Three Bears*, a piece so often retold that it has acquired the status of an anonymous folktale. He attended Oxford; was for a short time a fervent supporter of the French Revolution; and developed with Coleridge (who became his brother-in-law) the abortive scheme to found Pantisocracy, a utopian community on the banks of the Susquehanna River in Pennsylvania. In 1803 he moved to Keswick in the Lake Country, within long walking distance of his friend Wordsworth. With advancing age, he settled into a Tory viewpoint more conservative than those of Wordsworth and Coleridge. All his life a learned and hardworking professional author, he wrote thousands of pages of epics and short poems, histories, essays, biographies, and reviews. He was awarded the poet laureateship in 1813.

In 1830 Southey confided to Caroline Bowles (whom he married nine years later, after the death of his first wife) that "forty years ago I could partake in the hopes of those who expected that political revolutions were to bring about a political millennium." During that radical period he wrote *Wat Tyler* (1794), a play about the English Peasants' Revolt in 1381, with obvious implications for his own time. He also wrote in 1793, but did not publish until 1796, *Joan of Arc: An Epic Poem*, which represents Joan as a martyr in the cause of liberation from tyranny. In the printed excerpt here from book 9 of the epic, the angel Theodore appears to Joan in a vision and reveals to her the paradisal state of the early world, the fall of humanity through its lust for power and wealth, and then (by a violent event that in manuscript Southey identified as the French Revolution) the future recovery of the blissful condition of the initial Paradise.

From Joan of Arc: An Epic Poem

"These are the Daemons that pervert the power
825   Of Love," said Theodore. "The time was once
When LOVE and HAPPINESS went hand in hand,
In that blest era of the infant world
Ere man had learnt to bow the knee to man.
Was there a youth whom warm affection fill'd,
830   He spake his honest heart; the earliest fruits
His toil produced, the sweetest flowers that deck'd
The sunny bank, he gather'd for the maid,
Nor she disdain'd the gift—for VICE not yet
Had burst the dungeons of her hell, and rear'd
835   Those artificial boundaries that divide
Man from his species. State of blessedness!
Till that ill-omen'd hour when Cain's stern son
Delved in the bowels of the earth for gold,
Accursed bane of virtue! of such force
840   As poets feign dwelt in the Gorgon's locks,
Which whoso saw, felt instant the life-blood
Cold curdle in his veins, the creeping flesh
Grew stiff with horror, and the heart forgot
To beat. Accursed hour! for man no more
845   To JUSTICE paid his homage, but forsook
Her altars, and bow'd down before the shrine
Of WEALTH and POWER, the Idols he had made.
Then HELL enlarg'd herself, her gates flew wide,
Her legion fiends rush'd forth. OPPRESSION came
850   Whose frown is desolation, and whose breath

Blasts like the Pestilence; and POVERTY,
A meager monster, who with withering touch
Makes barren all the better part of man,
MOTHER OF MISERIES; then the goodly earth
855 Which God had framed for happiness, became
One theatre of woe, and all that God
Had given to bless free men, these tyrant fiends
His bitterest curses made. Yet for the best
Hath he ordained all things, the ALL-WISE!
860 For by experience rous'd shall man at length
Dash down his Moloch-gods, Samson-like
And burst his fetters—only strong whilst strong
Believed; then in the bottomless abyss
OPPRESSION shall be chain'd, and POVERTY
865 Die, and with her, her Brood of Miseries;
And VIRTUE and EQUALITY preserve
The reign of LOVE, and Earth shall once again
Be Paradise, whilst WISDOM shall secure
The state of bliss which IGNORANCE betrayed."

870 "Oh age of happiness!" the Maid exclaim'd,
"Roll fast thy current, Time, till that blest age
Arrive! and happy thou my Theodore,
Permitted thus to see the sacred depths
Of wisdom!"

1796

WILLIAM WORDSWORTH

Descriptive Sketches is one of William Wordsworth's (1770–1850) first two books. It was published simultaneously with *An Evening Walk* by the radical publisher Joseph Johnson in January 1793. The poem describes Wordsworth's observations during a walking tour through the Alps with his Welsh friend Robert Jones in the summer of 1790, when the French were celebrating the first anniversary of the fall of the Bastille. (Wordsworth later represented the same tour in *The Prelude*, book 6; see p. 345.) The concluding section of *Descriptive Sketches,* written at the height of Wordsworth's republican enthusiasm, describes the promise of the French Revolution in terms that conjoin biblical millennialism with the Roman poet Virgil's fourth eclogue, which envisions the return of the primeval golden age. In the final text of *Descriptive Sketches* published in Wordsworth's lifetime, that of 1849–50, Wordsworth retracts his confidence in the millennial outcome of the French Revolution but does not renounce his millennial hope:

> Lo, from the flames a great and glorious birth;
> As if a new-made heaven were hailing a new earth!
> —All cannot be: the promise is too fair
> For creatures doomed to breathe terrestrial air:
> Yet not for this will sober reason frown

Upon that promise, nor the hope disown;
She knows that only from high aims ensue
Rich guerdons, and to them alone are due.

From Descriptive Sketches

—Tho' Liberty shall soon, indignant, raise
775 Red on his hills his beacon's comet blaze;
Bid from on high his lonely cannon sound,
And on ten thousand hearths his shout rebound;
His larum-bell from village-tow'r to tow'r
Swing on th' astounded ear its dull undying roar:
780 Yet, yet rejoice, tho' Pride's perverted ire
Rouze Hell's own aid, and wrap thy hills in fire.
Lo! from th' innocuous flames, a lovely birth!
With its own Virtues springs another earth;
Nature, as in her prime, her virgin reign
785 Begins, and Love and Truth compose her train;
With pulseless hand, and fix'd unwearied gaze,
Unbreathing Justice her still beam surveys:
No more, along thy vales and viny groves,
Whole hamlets disappearing as he moves,
790 With cheeks o'erspread by smiles of baleful glow,
On his pale horse shall fell Consumption go.
   Oh give, great God, to Freedom's waves to ride
Sublime o'er Conquest, Avarice, and Pride,
To break, the vales where Death with Famine scow'rs,
795 And dark Oppression builds her thick-ribb'd tow'rs;
Where Machination her fell soul resigns,
Fled panting to the center of her mines;
Where Persecution decks with ghastly smiles
Her bed, his mountains mad Ambition piles;
800 Where Discord stalks dilating, every hour,
And crouching fearful at the feet of Pow'r,
Like Lightnings eager for th' almighty word,
Look up for sign of havoc, Fire, and Sword;
—Give them, beneath their breast while Gladness springs,
805 To brood the nations o'er with Nile-like wings;
And grant that every sceptred child of clay,
Who cries, presumptuous, "here their tides shall stay,"
Swept in their anger from th' affrighted shore,
With all his creatures sink—to rise no more.

1793

The Excursion

The Excursion *The Excursion,* published in 1814, was Wordsworth's longest poem and was the subject of some noted negative reviews (Francis Jeffrey's in the *Edinburgh Review* began "This will never do"). It was, nonetheless, highly valued by John Keats and others and became one of the most influential works of its time. The passage printed here—from the late text of 1849–50 but virtually identical with that of the first edition—is spoken by the character called "the Solitary," who in the "Argument" to book 3 is described at first as "Roused by the French Revolution" but later oppressed by "Disappointment and Disgust." Wordsworth's account of the Solitary's early enthusiasm for the revolution reflects in part his own experience but is modeled also on Joseph Fawcett, a preacher and poet who had succeeded Richard Price, after Price's death in 1791, at the Dissenting Chapel in Old Jewry. During his residence in London in 1791, Wordsworth had attended Fawcett's sermons, which attracted a large and fashionable audience. The Solitary, in poems as well as sermons, projects the dazzling promise of the French Revolution in terms that like Wordsworth's autobiographical passage in *Descriptive Sketches*, fuse biblical prophecy with Virgil's prediction of a recurrence in the present of the golden age of humanity during the reign of the god Saturn.

From The Excursion

From *Book 3, Despondency*

*   *   *

"From that abstraction I was roused,—and how?
Even as a thoughtful shepherd by a flash
Of lightning startled in a gloomy cave
Of these wild hills. For, lo! the dread Bastille,
710   With all the chambers in its horrid towers,
Fell to the ground:—by violence overthrown
Of indignation; and with shouts that drowned
The crash it made in falling! From the wreck
A golden palace rose, or seemed to rise,
715   The appointed seat of equitable law
And mild paternal sway. The potent shock
I felt: the transformation I perceived,
As marvellously seized as in that moment
When, from the blind mist issuing, I beheld
720   Glory—beyond all glory ever seen,
Confusion infinite of heaven and earth,
Dazzling the soul. Meanwhile, prophetic harps
In every grove were ringing, 'War shall cease;
Did ye not hear that conquest is abjured?
725   Bring garlands, bring forth choicest flowers, to deck
The tree of Liberty.'—My heart rebounded;
My melancholy voice the chorus joined;
—'Be joyful all ye nations; in all lands,
Ye that are capable of joy be glad!
730   Henceforth, whate'er is wanting to yourselves
In others ye shall promptly find;—and all,
Enriched by mutual and reflected wealth,
Shall with one heart honour their common kind.'

"Thus was I reconverted to the world;
735   Society became my glittering bride,
And airy hopes my children.—From the depths

Of natural passion, seemingly escaped,
My soul diffused herself in wide embrace
Of institutions, and the forms of things;
740   As they exist, in mutable array,
Upon life's surface. What, though in my veins
There flowed no Gallic blood, nor had I breathed
The air of France, not less than Gallic zeal
Kindled and burned among the sapless twigs
745   Of my exhausted heart. If busy men
In sober conclave met, to weave a web
Of amity, whose living threads should stretch
Beyond the seas, and to the farthest pole,
There did I sit, assisting. If, with noise
750   And acclamation, crowds in open air
Expressed the tumult of their minds, my voice
There mingled, heard or not. The powers of song
I left not uninvoked; and, in still groves,
Where mild enthusiasts tuned a pensive lay
755   Of thanks and expectation, in accord
With their belief, I sang Saturnian rule
Returned,—a progeny of golden years
Permitted to descend, and bless mankind.
—With promises the Hebrew Scriptures teem:
760   I felt their invitation; and resumed
A long-suspended office in the House
Of public worship, where, the glowing phrase
Of ancient inspiration serving me,
I promised also,—with undaunted trust
765   Foretold, and added prayer to prophecy;
The admiration winning of the crowd;
The help desiring of the pure devout.

"Scorn and contempt forbid me to proceed!
But History, time's slavish scribe, will tell
770   How rapidly the zealots of the cause
Disbanded—or in hostile ranks appeared;
Some, tired of honest service; these, outdone,
Disgusted therefore, or appalled, by aims
Of fiercer zealots—so confusion reigned,
775   And the more faithful were compelled to exclaim,
As Brutus did to Virtue, 'Liberty,
I worshipped thee, and find thee but a Shade!'

"Such recantation had for me no charm,
Nor would I bend to it; who should have grieved
780   At aught, however fair, that bore the mien
Of a conclusion, or catastrophe.
Why then conceal, that, when the simply good
In timid selfishness withdrew, I sought
Other support, not scrupulous whence it came;
785   And, by what compromise it stood, not nice?
Enough if notions seemed to be high-pitched,

And qualities determined.—Among men
So charactered did I maintain a strife
Hopeless, and still more hopeless every hour;
790 But, in the process, I began to feel
That, if the emancipation of the world
Were missed, I should at least secure my own,
And be in part compensated. For rights,
Widely—inveterately usurped upon,
795 I spake with vehemence; and promptly seized
All that Abstraction furnished for my needs
Or purposes; nor scrupled to proclaim,
And propagate, by liberty of life,
Those new persuasions."

*　*　*

1814

SAMUEL TAYLOR COLERIDGE

Samuel Taylor Coleridge (1772–1834) was twenty-two when he drafted *Religious Musings: A Desultory Poem, Written on Christmas' Eve, in the Year of Our Lord, 1784.* It was first published in his *Poems* of 1796 and was his most ambitious poem up to that time. On it, Coleridge then said, "I build all my poetic pretensions." In the turbulence and excitement of the early period of the French Revolution, Coleridge felt the need to give public voice to his political, religious, and philosophical beliefs, and poetized such materials by assuming a visionary and oracular persona and adopting the elaborate rhetoric, allegorical tactics and contorted syntax of the late eighteenth-century "sublime ode." Soon, however, he rejected this mode (in which, he wrote in December 1794, "my Poetry . . . sweats beneath a heavy burthen of Ideas and Imagery! It has seldom Ease") for the relaxed style of heightened conversation represented at its best by *Frost at Midnight* (1798; see p. 457).

The passage of *Religious Musings* printed here, in the text and line numbering of 1796, covers the first three of the last four items listed in Coleridge's Argument for the poem: "The French Revolution. Millennium. Universal Redemption. Conclusion." Coleridge's notes stress his conviction that the contemporary events in France fulfil the prophecies in the Book of Revelation that a period of violence is the necessary prelude to an earthly millennium. Wordsworth judged the concluding section on "earth reparadis'd" to be the best in Coleridge's *Poems* of 1796—in considerable part, doubtless, because it matched his own prophetic vision in *Descriptive Sketches*, published the year before.

From Religious Musings

Argument

Introduction. Person of Christ. His Prayer on the Cross. The process of his Doctrines on the mind of the Individual. Character of the Elect. Superstition. Digression to the present War. Origin and Uses of Government and Property. The present State of Society. The French Revolution. Millennium. Universal Redemption. Conclusion.

         *   *   *

           O ye numberless,
   Whom foul Oppression's ruffian gluttony
   Drives from life's plenteous feast! O thou poor Wretch,
   Who nurs'd in darkness and made wild by want
300 Dost roam for prey, yea thy unnatural hand
   Liftest to deeds of blood! O pale-eyed Form,
   The victim of seduction, doom'd to know
   Polluted nights and days of blasphemy;
   Who in loath'd orgies with lewd wassailers
305 Must gaily laugh, while thy remember'd Home
   Gnaws like a viper at thy secret heart!
   O aged Women! ye who weekly catch
   The morsel tost by law-forc'd Charity,
   And die so slowly, that none call it murder!
310 O loathly-visag'd Suppliants! ye that oft
   Rack'd with disease, from the unopen'd gate
   Of the full Lazar-house, heart-broken crawl!
   O ye to scepter'd Glory's gore-drench'd field
   Forc'd or ensnar'd, who swept by Slaughter's scythe,
315 (Stern nurse of Vultures!) steam in putrid heaps!
   O thou poor Widow, who in dreams dost view
   Thy Husband's mangled corse, and from short doze
   Start'st with a shriek: or in thy half-thatch'd cot
   Wak'd by the wintry night-storm, wet and cold,
320 Cow'rest o'er thy screaming baby! Rest awhile,
   Children of Wretchedness! More groans must rise,
   More blood must steam, or ere your wrongs be full.
   Yet is the day of Retribution nigh:
   The Lamb of God hath open'd the fifth seal:[1]
325 And upward rush on swiftest wing of fire
   Th' innumerable multitude of Wrongs
   By man on man inflicted! Rest awhile,
   Children of Wretchedness! The hour is nigh:
   And lo! the Great, the Rich, the Mighty Men,
330 The Kings and the Chief Captains of the World,
   With all that fix'd on high like stars of Heaven
   Shot baleful influence, shall be cast to earth,
   Vile and down-trodden, as the untimely fruit

---

1. See the sixth chapter of the Revelation of St. John the Divine.—And I looked and beheld a pale horse; and his name that sat on him was Death, and Hell followed with him. And power was given unto them over the FOURTH part of the Earth to kill with sword, and with hunger, and with pestilence, and with the beasts of the Earth.—And when he had opened the fifth seal, I saw under the altar the souls of them that were slain for the word of God, and for the testimony which they held: and white robes were given unto every one of them; and it was said unto them, that they should rest yet for a little season, until their fellow servants also, and their brethren, that should be killed as they were should be fulfilled. And I beheld when he had opened the sixth seal, the stars of Heaven fell unto the Earth, even as a fig tree casteth her untimely figs when she is shaken of a mighty wind: And the Kings of the earth, and the great men, and the rich men, and the chief captains, &c. [Coleridge's note].

Shook from the fig-tree by a sudden storm.
335 Ev'n now the storm begins:[2] each gentle name,
Faith and meek Piety, with fearful joy
Tremble far-off—for lo! the Giant FRENZY
Uprooting empires with his whirlwind arm
Mocketh high Heaven; burst hideous from the cell
340 Where the old Hag, unconquerable, huge,
Creation's eyeless drudge, black RUIN, sits
Nursing th' impatient earthquake.

                                    O return!
Pure FAITH! meek PIETY! The abhorred Form[3]
Whose scarlet robe was stiff with earthly pomp,
345 Who drank iniquity in cups of gold,
Whose names were many and all blasphemous,
Hath met the horrible judgment! Whence that cry?
The mighty army of foul Spirits shriek'd
Disherited of earth! For She hath fallen
350 On whose black front was written MYSTERY;
She that reel'd heavily, whose wine was blood;
She that work'd whoredom with the DAEMON POWER
And from the dark embrace all evils things
Brought forth and nurtur'd: mitred ATHEISM!
355 And patient FOLLY who on bended knee
Gives back the steel that stabb'd him; and pale FEAR
Hunted by ghastlier terrors than surround
Moon-blasted Madness when he yells at midnight!
Return pure FAITH! return meek PIETY!
360 The kingdoms of the world are yours: each heart
Self-govern'd, the vast family of Love
Rais'd from the common earth by common toil
Enjoy the equal produce. Such delights
As float to earth, permitted visitants!
365 When on some solemn jubilee of Saints
The sapphire-blazing gates of Paradise
Are thrown wide open, and thence voyage forth
Detachments wild of seraph-warbled airs,
And odors snatch'd from beds of amaranth,
370 And they, that from the crystal river of life
Spring up on freshen'd wing, ambrosial gales!
The favor'd good man in his lonely walk
Perceives them, and his silent spirit drinks
Strange bliss which he shall recognize in heaven.
375 And such delights, such strange beatitude
Seize on my young anticipating heart
When that blest future rushes on my view!
For in his own and in his Father's might

2. The French Revolution [Coleridge's note].
3. And there came one of the seven Angels which had the seven vials and talked with me, saying unto me, come hither! I will shew unto thee the judgment of the great Whore, that sitteth upon many waters: with whom the Kings of the earth have committed fornication, &c. Revelation of St. John the Divine, chapter the seventeenth [Coleridge's note].

The SAVIOR comes! While as to solemn strains
380 The THOUSAND YEARS[4] lead up their mystic dance,
Old OCEAN claps his hands! The DESERT shouts!
And soft gales wafted from the haunts of Spring
Melt the primaeval North! The mighty Dead
Rise to new life, whoe'er from earliest time
385 With conscious zeal had urg'd Love's wond'rous plan,
Coadjutors of God. To MILTON'S trump
The odorous groves of earth reparadis'd
Unbosom their glad echoes: inly hush'd
Adoring NEWTON his serener eye
390 Raises to heaven: and he of mortal kind
Wisest, he[5] first who mark'd the ideal tribes
Down the fine fibers from the sentient brain
Roll subtly-surging. Pressing on his steps
Lo! Priestley[6] there, Patriot, and Saint, and Sage,
395 Whom that my fleshly eye hath never seen
A childish pang of impotent regret
Hath thrill'd my heart. Him from his native land
Statesmen blood-stain'd and Priests idolatrous
By dark lies mad'ning the blind multitude
400 Drove with vain hate: calm, pitying he retir'd,
And mus'd expectant on these promis'd years.

O Years! the blest preeminence of Saints!
Sweeping before the rapt prophetic Gaze
Bright as what glories of the jasper throne
405 Stream from the gorgeous and face-veiling plumes
Of Spirits adoring! Ye, blest Years! must end,
And all beyond is darkness!

*   *   *

1794

4. The Millennium:—in which I suppose, that Man will continue to enjoy the highest glory, of which his human nature is capable.—That all who in past ages have endeavored to ameliorate the state of man, will rise and enjoy the fruits and flowers, the imperceptible seeds of which they had sown in their former Life: and that the wicked will during the same period, be suffering the remedies adapted to their several bad habits. I suppose that this period will be followed by the passing away of this Earth, and by our entering the state of pure intellect; when all Creation shall rest from its labors [Coleridge's note, added in the 1797 edition].
5. David Hartley [Coleridge's note].
6. Sir Isaac Newton (line 390), Hartley (line 392), and Joseph Priestley were believers in apocalyptic prophecies, and all three had written interpretive commentaries on the Book of Revelation.

PERCY BYSSHE SHELLEY

Queen Mab, Percy Shelley's (1792–1822) first long work in verse, was written mainly in 1812, when the poet was twenty years old; it was printed and distributed privately (but never published by the author) in February 1813. It is an allegorical dream-vision in which the fairy queen Mab takes the mortal maiden Ianthe on an extra-terrestrial excursion to show her the past, present, and future states of the human world. The past is irrational, the woeful product of one human error after another. The ghastly present is corrupted by the institutions of king, priests, and statesmen. But the future, set forth in cantos 8 and 9, is one of human blessedness, when "A garden shall arise, in loveliness / Surpassing fabled Eden" (4.88–89). Shelley's is not a religious but a secular apocalypse, with the Spirit of Necessity replacing God's providence as the agent of redemption. Nonetheless, Shelley's anticipation of a "taint-less" humanity in a renovated world is for the most part imported from biblical mil-lennialism, especially in Isaiah and Revelation. In the selections printed here from cantos 8 and 9, Queen Mab is speaking to Ianthe.

From Queen Mab: A Philosophical Poem

From Canto 8

* * *

Then in her triumph spoke the Fairy Queen:
"I will not call the ghost of ages gone
To unfold the frightful secrets of its lore;
    The present now is past,
45 And those events that desolate the earth
Have faded from the memory of Time,
Who dares not give reality to that
Whose being I annul. To me is given
The wonders of the human world to keep,
50 Space, matter, time, and mind. Futurity
Exposes now its treasure; let the sight
Renew and strengthen all thy failing hope.
O human Spirit! spur thee to the goal
Where virtue fixes universal peace,
55 And midst the ebb and flow of human things,
Show somewhat stable, somewhat certain still,
A lighthouse o'er the wild of dreary waves.

"The habitable earth is full of bliss;
Those wastes of frozen billows that were hurled
60 By everlasting snow-storms round the poles,
Where matter dared not vegetate or live,
But ceaseless frost round the vast solitude
Bound its broad zone of stillness, are unloosed;
And fragrant zephyrs there from spicy isles
65 Ruffle the placid ocean-deep, that rolls
Its broad, bright surges to the sloping sand,
Whose roar is wakened into echoings sweet
To murmur through the heaven-breathing groves
And melodize with man's blest nature there.

70 "Those desarts of immeasurable sand,
Whose age-collected fervors scarce allowed

A bird to live, a blade of grass to spring,
Where the shrill chirp of the green lizard's love
Broke on the sultry silentness alone,
75   Now teem with countless rills and shady woods,
Corn-fields and pastures and white cottages;
And where the startled wilderness beheld
A savage conqueror stained in kindred blood,
A tygress sating with the flesh of lambs
80   The unnatural famine of her toothless cubs,
Whilst shouts and howlings through the desart rang,
Sloping and smooth the daisy-spangled lawn,
Offering sweet incense to the sun-rise, smiles
To see a babe before his mother's door,
85   Sharing his morning's meal
   With the green and golden basilisk[1]
       That comes to lick his feet.

"Those trackless deeps, where many a weary sail
Has seen above the illimitable plain,
90   Morning on night, and night on morning rise,
Whilst still no land to greet the wanderer spread
Its shadowy mountains on the sun-bright sea,
Where the loud roarings of the tempest-waves
So long have mingled with the gusty wind
95   In melancholy loneliness, and swept
The desart of those ocean solitudes,
But vocal to the sea-bird's harrowing shriek,
The bellowing monster, and the rushing storm,
Now to the sweet and many mingling sounds
100   Of kindliest human impulses respond.
Those lonely realms bright garden-isles begem,
With lightsome clouds and shining seas between,
And fertile vallies, resonant with bliss,
Whilst green woods overcanopy the wave,
105   Which like a toil-worn labourer leaps to shore,
To meet the kisses of the flowrets there.

"All things are recreated, and the flame
Of consentaneous love inspires all life:
The fertile bosom of the earth gives suck
110   To myriads, who still grow beneath her care,
Rewarding her with their pure perfectness:
The balmy breathings of the winds inhale
Her virtues, and diffuse them all abroad:
Health floats amid the gentle atmosphere,
115   Glows in the fruits, and mantles on the stream:
No storms deform the beaming brow of heaven,
Nor scatter in the freshness of its pride
The foliage of the ever verdant trees;
But fruits are ever ripe, flowers ever fair,

1. A legendary serpent whose breath and glance are death-dealing.

120 And autumn proudly bears her matron grace,
Kindling a flush on the fair cheek of spring,
Whose virgin bloom beneath the ruddy fruit
Reflects its tint, and blushes into love.

"The lion now forgets to thirst for blood:
125 There might you see him sporting in the sun
Beside the dreadless kid; his claws are sheathed,
His teeth are harmless, custom's force has made
His nature as the nature of a lamb.
Like passion's fruit, the nightshade's tempting bane
130 Poisons no more the pleasure it bestows:
All bitterness is past; the cup of joy
Unmingled mantles to the goblet's brim,
And courts the thirsty lips it fled before.

"But chief, ambiguous man, he that can know
135 More misery, and dream more joy than all;
Whose keen sensations thrill within his breast
To mingle with a loftier instinct there,
Lending their power to pleasure and to pain,
Yet raising, sharpening, and refining each;
140 Who stands amid the ever-varying world,
The burthen or the glory of the earth;
He chief perceives the change, his being notes
The gradual renovation, and defines
Each movement of its progress on his mind.

145 "Man, where the gloom of the long polar night
Lowers o'er the snow-clad rocks and frozen soil,
Where scarce the hardiest herb that braves the frost
Basks in the moonlight's ineffectual glow,
Shrank with the plants, and darkened with the night;
150 His chilled and narrow energies, his heart,
Insensible to courage, truth, or love,
His stunted stature and imbecile frame,
Marked him for some abortion of the earth,
Fit compeer of the bears that roamed around,
155 Whose habits and enjoyments were his own:
His life a feverish dream of stagnant woe,
Whose meagre wants, but scantily fulfilled,
Apprised him ever of the joyless length
Which his short being's wretchedness had reached;
160 His death a pang which famine, cold and toil,
Long on the mind, whilst yet the vital spark
Clung to the body stubbornly, had brought:
All was inflicted here that earth's revenge
Could wreak on the infringers of her law;
165 One curse alone was spared—the name of God.

"Nor where the tropics bound the realms of day
With a broad belt of mingling cloud and flame,

Where blue mists through the unmoving atmosphere
Scattered the seeds of pestilence, and fed
170 Unnatural vegetation, where the land
Teemed with all earthquake, tempest and disease,
Was man a nobler being; slavery
Had crushed him to his country's bloodstained dust;
Or he was bartered for the fame of power,
175 Which all internal impulses destroying,
Makes human will an article of trade;
Or he was changed with Christians for their gold,
And dragged to distant isles, where to the sound
Of the flesh-mangling scourge, he does the work
180 Of all-polluting luxury and wealth,
Which doubly visits on the tyrants' heads
The long-protracted fulness of their woe;
Or he was led to legal butchery,
To turn to worms beneath that burning sun,
185 Where kings first leagued against the rights of men,
And priests first traded with the name of God.

"Even where the milder zone afforded man
A seeming shelter, yet contagion there,
Blighting his being with unnumbered ills,
190 Spread like a quenchless fire; nor truth till late
Availed to arrest its progress, or create
That peace which first in bloodless victory waved
Her snowy standard o'er this favored clime:
There man was long the train-bearer of slaves,
195 The mimic of surrounding misery,
The jackal of ambition's lion-rage,
The bloodhound of religion's hungry zeal.

"Here now the human being stands adorning
This loveliest earth with taintless body and mind;
200 Blest from his birth with all bland impulses,
Which gently in his noble bosom wake
All kindly passions and all pure desires.
Him, still from hope to hope the bliss pursuing
Which from the exhaustless lore of human weal
205 Dawns on the virtuous mind, the thoughts that rise
In time-destroying infiniteness, gift
With self-enshrined eternity, that mocks
The unprevailing hoariness of age,
And man, once fleeting o'er the transient scene
210 Swift as an unremembered vision, stands
Immortal upon earth: no longer now
He slays the lamb that looks him in the face,
And horribly devours his mangled flesh,
Which still avenging nature's broken law,
215 Kindled all putrid humors in his frame,
All evil passions, and all vain belief,

Hatred, despair, and loathing in his mind,
The germs of misery, death, disease, and crime.
No longer now the winged habitants,
220 That in the woods their sweet lives sing away,
Flee from the form of man; but gather round,
And prune their sunny feathers on the hands
Which little children stretch in friendly sport
Towards these dreadless partners of their play.
225 All things are void of terror: man has lost
His terrible prerogative, and stands
An equal amidst equals: happiness
And science dawn though late upon the earth;
Peace cheers the mind, health renovates the frame;
230 Disease and pleasure cease to mingle here,
Reason and passion cease to combat there;
Whilst each unfettered o'er the earth extend
Their all-subduing energies, and wield
The sceptre of a vast dominion there;
235 Whilst every shape and mode of matter lends
Its force to the omnipotence of mind,
Which from its dark mine drags the gem of truth
To decorate its paradise of peace."

From *Canto 9*

"O happy Earth! reality of Heaven!
To which those restless souls that ceaselessly
Throng through the human universe, aspire;
Thou consummation of all mortal hope!
5 Thou glorious prize of blindly-working will!
Whose rays, diffused throughout all space and time,
Verge to one point and blend for ever there:
Of purest spirits thou pure dwelling-place!
Where care and sorrow, impotence and crime,
10 Languor, disease, and ignorance dare not come:
O happy Earth, reality of Heaven!"

*   *   *

1813

APOCALYPSE BY IMAGINATION

Reminiscing in 1815, Thomas Noon Talfourd—an eminent jurist who was also a poet and a playwright—attributed to the French Revolution a primary part in shaping the literature of what we now call the Romantic period. The revolution, which "shook society to its deepest foundations," also "completed the regeneration of our poetry":

At one moment, all was hope and joy and rapture; the corruption and iniquity of ages seemed to vanish like a dream; the unclouded heavens seemed once more to ring with the exulting chorus of peace on earth and good-will to men; and the

spirit of a mighty and puissant nation, long confined in the dungeons of superstition, seemed rising in native majesty to draw new inspiration from the rejoicing
heavens.

But "on a sudden," Talfourd says, "all was changed," in the release of barbaric passions that resulted in actions that far exceeded "the darkest imaginings of the past."
The effect of "this moral hurricane, this breaking up of the surface of society, this
rending of the general heart," was "to raise and darken the imagination" and so contributed "to form that great age of poetry which is now flourishing around us" ("An
Attempt to Estimate the Poetical Talent of the Present Age," 1815).

Talfourd clearly recognized the religious and millenarian nature of the high enthusiasm and unbounded hopes incited during the early revolutionary years. He saw also,
however, that an essential feature of the revolution as a cultural and literary influence
was, in the general estimate, the fact that it had failed. The greatest and most enduring
poetry of the age was written not in the mood of revolutionary exaltation but in the
mood of revolutionary disenchantment and despair, after the succession of disasters
that began with the massacres, the executions, and the Reign of Terror in 1793–94.
A number of major Romantic poets, however, did not break from the formative past
but set out to salvage the grounds for hope in the coming of a renewed and perfected
world. Romantic thinking and imagination, that is, remained apocalyptic in form, but
with a radical shift from violent political revolution to a revolution of consciousness
as the agency that will transform the world.

The continuity between the earlier and later Romantic hopes for transformation is
indicated by the persistence of the two central apocalyptic images: the sacred marriage
and the advent of a new heaven and new earth. Coleridge combined the two figures
in the fifth stanza *Dejection: An Ode* (1802), where an inner harmony that he calls
"Joy" is

> the spirit and the power,
> Which wedding Nature to us gives in dower
> A new Earth and new Heaven. . . .
> (lines 67–69; see p. 460)

In the "Prospectus" to his major poetic enterprises, Wordsworth announced that his
"high argument" is a marriage hymn—a "spousal verse"—that will effect a "creation"
equivalent to a restored Paradise; but as in Coleridge, the ground for the apocalyptic
hope has been shifted from political revolution to an inner spiritual revolution, and
the marriage between the Lamb and the New Jerusalem has been converted into a
marriage between the human mind and the nature from which it has been alienated:

> Paradise, and groves
> Elysian, Fortunate Fields . . .
> . . . the discerning intellect of Man,
> When wedded to this goodly universe
> In love and holy passion, shall find these
> A simple produce of the common day.
> (lines 47–71; see p. 302)

William Blake's confidence in a millennial result of political revolution was short-
lived, but his imagination remained stubbornly apocalyptic. In his major prophetic
poem *Jerusalem* (ca. 1809–20), the concluding chapter is prefaced with the voice of
the Bard arousing Albion (universal mankind) from his "sleep of death," so that he
may reunite with his separated female emanation Jerusalem. The poem closes with
"the Eternal Day" of universal resurrection in a restored Paradise, and this event is
illustrated by Blake's rendering of the apocalyptic marriage—an etching of Albion and
Jerusalem in an embrace of love. Some two decades later, Percy Shelley manifested

a parallel evolution in his thinking. He lost his faith in the millennial possibility of political revolution, but his long poems continued to embody his vision of a total renovation of humanity and its world. In his *Prometheus Unbound,* this world is one that reveals itself to the purged human imagination, and only after humanity has achieved a total revolution of its moral nature. Shelley continues to represent this imaginative achievement of a new heaven on earth in the form of an apocalyptic marriage, the reunion between Prometheus and Asia—an erotic as well as a spiritual reunion, with which, in the fourth act, the entire cosmos exuberantly participates (act 3.4 and act 4; see pp. 751 and 754).

The myth of apocalypse has remained deeply ingrained in Western culture and has continued into the twentieth century to provide a scenario, or interpretive frame, for a violent political revolution of which the expected result on human well-being will be sudden, absolute, and universal. In *New Year Letter* (1940), for example, the poet W. H. Auden drew a parallel between Wordsworth's early view of the French Revolution as an apocalyptic Second Coming ("Parousia")—he "Saw in the fall of the Bastille / The Parousia of liberty"—and the response of political idealists in his own generation to the Communist revolution in Russia that began in 1917. As in the Romantic period, so in the twentieth century, he comments ruefully,

> We hoped; we waited for the day
> The State would wither clean away,
> Expecting the Millennium
> That theory promised us would come,
> It didn't.

MARY WOLLSTONECRAFT
1759–1797

Mary Wollstonecraft's father inherited a substantial fortune and set himself up as a gentleman farmer. He was, however, both extravagant and incompetent, and as one farm after another failed, he became moody and violent and sought solace in heavy bouts of drinking and in tyrannizing over his submissive wife. Mary was the second of five children and the oldest daughter. She later told her husband, William Godwin, that she used to throw herself in front of her mother to protect her from her husband's blows, and that she sometimes slept outside the door of her parents' bedroom to intervene if her father should break out in a drunken rage. The solace of Mary's early life was her fervent attachment to Fanny Blood, an accomplished girl two years her senior; their friendship, which began when Mary was sixteen, endured and deepened until Fanny's death.

At the age of nineteen Mary Wollstonecraft left home to take a position as companion to a well-to-do widow living in Bath, where she for the first time had the opportunity to observe—and scorn—the social life of the upper classes at the most fashionable of English resort cities. Having left her job in 1780 to nurse her dying mother through a long and harrowing illness, Wollstonecraft next went to live with the Bloods, where her work helped to sustain the struggling family. Her sister Eliza meanwhile had married and, in 1784, after the birth of a daughter, suffered a nervous breakdown. Convinced that her sister's collapse was the result of her husband's cruelty and abuse, Wollstonecraft persuaded her to abandon husband and child and flee to London; because a divorce at that time was not commonly available, and a fugitive wife could be forced to return to her husband, the two women hid in secret quarters while awaiting the grant of a legal separation. The infant, automatically given into the father's custody, died before she was a year old.

The penniless women, together with Fanny Blood and Wollstonecraft's other sister, Everina, established a girls' school at Newington Green, near London. The project flourished at first, and at Newington, Wollstonecraft was befriended by the Reverend Richard Price, a leading radical author and reformer whose kindly guidance helped shape her social and political opinions. Blood, although already ill with tuberculosis, went to Lisbon to marry her longtime suitor, Hugh Skeys, and quickly became pregnant. Wollstonecraft rushed to Lisbon to attend her friend's childbirth, only to have Fanny die in her arms; the infant died soon afterward. The loss threw Wollstonecraft (already subject to bouts of depression) into black despair, which was heightened when she found that the school at Newington was in bad financial straits and had to be closed. Tormented by creditors, she rallied her energies to write her first book, *Thoughts on the Education of Daughters* (1786), a conventional and pious series of essays, and took up a position as governess for several daughters in the Anglo-Irish family of Viscount Kingsborough, a man of great wealth whose seat was in County Cork, Ireland.

The Kingsboroughs were well intentioned and did their best to introduce Wollstonecraft into the busy trivialities of their social life. But the ambiguity of her position as governess, halfway between a servant and member of the family, was galling. An antagonism developed between Wollstonecraft and Lady Kingsborough, in part because the children feared their mother and adored their governess. Wollstonecraft was dismissed. She returned to London, where Joseph Johnson in 1788 published her first novel, *Mary, a Fiction*, a partly autobiographical but conventionally sentimental novel written while she was in Ireland, as well as a book for children, *Original Stories from Real Life*. The latter, a considerable success, was translated into German and quickly achieved a second English edition illustrated with engravings by William Blake. Wollstonecraft was befriended and subsidized by Johnson, the major publisher in England of radical and reformist books, and she took a prominent place among the notable writers whom he regularly entertained at his rooms in St. Paul's Churchyard. She published translations from French and German (she had taught herself both languages) and began reviewing books for Johnson's newly founded journal, the *Analytical Review*. Though still in straitened circumstances, she helped support her two sisters and her improvident and importunate father, and was also generous with funds—and with advice—to one of her brothers and to the indigent family of Fanny Blood.

In 1790 Edmund Burke's *Reflections on the Revolution in France*—an eloquent and powerful attack on the French Revolution and its English sympathizers—quickly evoked Wollstonecraft's response, *A Vindication of the Rights of Men*. This was a formidable piece of argumentation; its most potent passages are those that represent the disabilities and sufferings of the English lower classes and impugn the motives and sentiments of Burke. This work, the first book-length reply to Burke, scored an immediate success, although it was soon submerged in the flood of other replies, most notably Tom Paine's classic *Rights of Man* (1791–92). In 1792 Wollstonecraft focused her defense of the underprivileged on her own sex and wrote, in six weeks of intense effort, *A Vindication of the Rights of Woman*.

Earlier writers both in France and England had proposed that, given an equivalence in education, women would equal men in achievement. Wollstonecraft was particularly indebted to Catharine Macaulay's *Letters on Education* (1790), of which she had written an enthusiastic review. But Wollstonecraft's *Vindication* was unprecedented in its firsthand observations of the disabilities and indignities suffered by women and in the articulateness and passion with which it exposed and decried this injustice. Wollstonecraft's views were conspicuously radical at a time when women had no political rights; were limited to a few lowly vocations as servants, nurses, governesses, and petty shopkeepers; and were legally nonpersons who lost their property to their husbands at marriage and were incapable of instituting an action in the courts of law. An impressive feature of her book, for all its vehemence, is the clear-sightedness and balance of her analysis of the social conditions of the time, as they affect men as well as women. She perceives that women constitute an oppressed class that cuts across the standard hierarchy of social classes; she shows that women, because they are denied political and domestic privileges, have been forced to seek their ends by means of coquetry and cunning; and she also recognizes that men, no less than women, inherit their roles, and that the wielding of irresponsible power corrupts the oppressor no less than it distorts the oppressed. Hence her surprising and telling comparisons between women on the one hand and men of the nobility and military on the other as classes whose values and behavior have been distorted because their social roles prevent them from becoming fully human. In writing this pioneering work, Wollstone-craft found the cause that she was to pursue the rest of her life.

In December 1792, Wollstonecraft went to Paris to observe the French Revolution at firsthand. The years that she lived in France, 1793–94, were those in which the early period of moderation was succeeded by extremism and violence. In Paris she joined a group of English, American, and European expatriates sympathetic to the Revolution and fell in love with Gilbert Imlay, a personable American who had briefly been an officer in the American Revolutionary Army and was the author of a widely read book on the Kentucky backwoods, where he had been an explorer. He played the role in Paris of an American frontiersman and child of nature, but was in fact an adventurer who had left America to avoid prosecution for debt and for freewheeling speculations in Kentucky land; he was also unscrupulous in his relations with women. The two became lovers, and Wollstonecraft bore a daughter, Fanny Imlay, in May 1794. Imlay, who was often absent on mysterious business deals, left mother and daughter for a visit to London that he kept protracting. After the publication of her book *An Historical and Moral View of the Origin and Progress of the French Revolution* (1795), Wollstonecraft followed Imlay to London, where, persuaded that he no longer loved her, she tried to commit suicide; the attempt, however, was discovered and prevented by Imlay. To get her out of the way, he persuaded her to take a trip as his business envoy to the Scandinavian countries. Although this was then a region of poor or impassible roads and primitive accommodations, the intrepid Wollstonecraft traveled there for four months, sometimes in the wilds, accompanied by the year-old Fanny and a French nurse.

Back in London, Wollstonecraft discovered that Imlay was living with a new mistress, a strolling actress. Finally convinced he was lost to her, she hurled herself from a bridge into the Thames but was rescued by a passerby. Imlay departed with his actress to Paris. Wollstonecraft, resourceful as always, used the letters she had written to Imlay to compose a book, *Letters Written during a Short Residence in Sweden, Norway, and Denmark* (1796), full of sharp observations of human character, the conditions of Scandinavian women, and the austere northern landscape.

In the same year Wollstonecraft renewed an earlier acquaintance with the philosopher William Godwin. His *Inquiry Concerning Political Justice* (1793), the most drastic proposal for restructuring the political and social order yet published in England, together with his novel of terror, *Caleb Williams* (1794), which embodies his social views, had made him the most famed radical writer of his time. The austerely rationalistic philosopher, then forty years of age, had an unexpected capacity for deep feeling, and what began as a flirtation soon ripened into affection and (as their letters show) passionate physical love. She wrote Godwin, with what was for the time remarkable outspokenness on the part of a woman: "Now by these presents [i.e., this doc-ument] let me assure you that you are not only in my heart, but my veins, this morning. I turn from you half abashed—yet you haunt me, and some look, word or touch thrills through my whole frame. . . . When the heart and reason accord there is no flying from voluptuous sensations, do what a woman can." Wollstonecraft was soon again with child, and Godwin (who had in his *Inquiry* attacked the institution of marriage as a base form of property rights in human beings) braved the ridicule of his radical friends and conservative enemies by marrying her.

They set up a household together, but Godwin also kept separate quarters in which to do his writing, and they further salvaged their principles by agreeing to live separate social lives. Wollstonecraft was happy for a brief six months. On August 30 she gave birth to a daughter, Mary Wollstonecraft Godwin, later the author of *Frankenstein* and wife of Percy Shelley. The delivery was not difficult, but resulted in massive blood poisoning. After ten days of agony, she lapsed into a coma and died. Her last whis-pered words were about her husband: "He is the kindest, best man in the world." Godwin wrote to a friend, announcing her death: "I firmly believe that there does not exist her equal in the world. I know from experience we were formed to make each other happy."

To distract himself in his grief Godwin published in 1798 *Memoirs of the Author of "A Vindication of the Rights of Woman"* in which he told, with the total candor on which he prided himself, of her affairs with Imlay and himself, her attempts at suicide, and her free thinking in matters of religion and sexual relationships; in four compan-ion volumes of her *Posthumous Works* he included her outspoken love letters to Imlay. The unintended result was to saddle Wollstonecraft with a scandalous reputation so enduring that through the Victorian era advocates of the equality of women circum-spectly avoided references to her *Vindication;* even John Stuart Mill, in his *Subjection of Women* (1869), neglected to mention the work. It was only in the twentieth cen-tury, and especially in the later decades, that Wollstonecraft's *Vindication* gained recognition as a classic in the literature not only of women's rights but of social analysis as well.

From A Vindication of the Rights of Woman[1]

Introduction

After considering the historic page, and viewing the living world with anxious solicitude, the most melancholy emotions of sorrowful indignation have depressed my spirits, and I have sighed when obliged to confess, that either nature has made a great difference between man and man, or that the civilization which has hitherto taken place in the world has been very partial. I have turned over various books written on the subject of educa-tion, and patiently observed the conduct of parents and the management of schools; but what has been the result?—a profound conviction that the neglected education of my fellow-creatures is the grand source of the mis-ery I deplore; and that women, in particular, are rendered weak and wretched by a variety of concurring causes, originating from one hasty conclusion. The conduct and manners of women, in fact, evidently prove

---

1. The text is from the second revised edition of 1792, as edited by Carol H. Poston for the Norton Critical Edition of *A Vindication* (1975). The edi- tors gratefully acknowledge Poston's permission to use the information in her annotations.

that their minds are not in a healthy state; for, like the flowers which are planted in too rich a soil, strength and usefulness are sacrificed to beauty; and the flaunting leaves, after having pleased a fastidious eye, fade, disregarded on the stalk, long before the season when they ought to have arrived at maturity.—One cause of this barren blooming I attribute to a false system of education, gathered from the books written on this subject by men who, considering females rather as women than human creatures, have been more anxious to make them alluring mistresses than affectionate wives and rational mothers; and the understanding of the sex has been so bubbled[2] by this specious homage, that the civilized women of the present century, with a few exceptions, are only anxious to inspire love, when they ought to cherish a nobler ambition, and by their abilities and virtues exact respect.

In a treatise, therefore, on female rights and manners, the works which have been particularly written for their improvement must not be overlooked; especially when it is asserted, in direct terms, that the minds of women are enfeebled by false refinement; that the books of instruction, written by men of genius, have had the same tendency as more frivolous productions; and that, in the true style of Mahometanism, they are treated as a kind of subordinate beings, and not as a part of the human species,[3] when improvable reason is allowed to be the dignified distinction which raises men above the brute creation, and puts a natural sceptre in a feeble hand.

Yet, because I am a woman, I would not lead my readers to suppose that I mean violently to agitate the contested question respecting the equality or inferiority of the sex; but as the subject lies in my way, and I cannot pass it over without subjecting the main tendency of my reasoning to misconstruction, I shall stop a moment to deliver, in a few words, my opinion.—In the government of the physical world it is observable that the female in point of strength is, in general, inferior to the male. This is the law of nature; and it does not appear to be suspended or abrogated in favor of woman. A degree of physical superiority cannot, therefore, be denied—and it is a noble prerogative! But not content with this natural pre-eminence, men endeavor to sink us still lower, merely to render us alluring objects for a moment; and women, intoxicated by the adoration which men, under the influence of their senses, pay them, do not seek to obtain a durable interest in their hearts, or to become the friends of the fellow creatures who find amusement in their society.

I am aware of an obvious inference:—from every quarter have I heard exclamations against masculine women; but where are they to be found? If by this appellation men mean to inveigh against their ardor in hunting, shooting, and gaming, I shall most cordially join in the cry; but if it be against the imitation of manly virtues, or, more properly speaking, the attainment of those talents and virtues, the exercise of which ennobles the human character, and which raise females in the scale of animal being, when they are comprehensively termed mankind;—all those who view them with a philosophic eye must, I should think, wish with me, that they may every day grow more and more masculine.

2. In an archaic sense, deluded, cheated.
3. It was a common but mistaken opinion among Europeans that the Koran, the sacred text of Islam, teaches that women have no souls.

This discussion naturally divides the subject. I shall first consider women in the grand light of human creatures, who, in common with men, are placed on this earth to unfold their faculties; and afterwards I shall more particularly point out their peculiar designation.

I wish also to steer clear of an error which many respectable writers have fallen into; for the instruction which has hitherto been addressed to women, has rather been applicable to *ladies*, if the little indirect advice, that is scattered through Sandford and Merton,[4] be excepted; but, addressing my sex in a firmer tone, I pay particular attention to those in the middle class, because they appear to be in the most natural state.[5] Perhaps the seeds of false refinement, immorality, and vanity, have ever been shed by the great. Weak, artificial beings, raised above the common wants and affections of their race, in a premature unnatural manner, undermine the very foundation of virtue, and spread corruption through the whole mass of society! As a class of mankind they have the strongest claim to pity; the education of the rich tends to render them vain and helpless, and the unfolding mind is not strengthened by the practice of those duties which dignify the human character.—They only live to amuse themselves, and by the same law which in nature invariably produces certain effects, they soon only afford barren amusement.

But as I purpose taking a separate view of the different ranks of society, and of the moral character of women, in each, this hint is, for the present, sufficient, and I have only alluded to the subject, because it appears to me to be the very essence of an introduction to give a cursory account of the contents of the work it introduces.

My own sex, I hope, will excuse me, if I treat them like rational creatures, instead of flattering their *fascinating* graces, and viewing them as if they were in a state of perpetual childhood, unable to stand alone. I earnestly wish to point out in what true dignity and human happiness consists—I wish to persuade women to endeavor to acquire strength, both of mind and body, and to convince them that the soft phrases, susceptibility of heart, delicacy of sentiment, and refinement of taste, are almost synonymous with epithets of weakness, and that those beings who are only the objects of pity and that kind of love, which has been termed its sister, will soon become objects of contempt.

Dismissing then those pretty feminine phrases, which the men condescendingly use to soften our slavish dependence, and despising that weak elegancy of mind, exquisite sensibility, and sweet docility of manners, supposed to be the sexual characteristics of the weaker vessel, I wish to shew that elegance is inferior to virtue, that the first object of laudable ambition is to obtain a character as a human being, regardless of the distinction of sex; and that secondary views should be brought to this simple touchstone.

This is a rough sketch of my plan; and should I express my conviction with the energetic emotions that I feel whenever I think of the subject, the dictates of experience and reflection will be felt by some of my readers. Animated by this important object, I shall disdain to cull[6] my phrases or

4. *The History of Sandford and Merton*, by Thomas Day, was a very popular story for children, published in three volumes (1786–89). In it a tutor, the Reverend Mr. Barlow, frequently cites the superiority in moral principles of Harry Sandford, the son of a poor farmer, over Tommy Merton, the

spoiled son of a rich family.
5. The middle class is viewed as more "natural" than the upper classes because it is uncorrupted by the artificialities of leisure-class life.
6. Be selective in.

polish my style;—I aim at being useful, and sincerity will render me unaffected; for, wishing rather to persuade by the force of my arguments, than dazzle by the elegance of my language, I shall not waste my time in rounding periods,[7] or in fabricating the turgid bombast of artificial feelings, which, coming from the head, never reach the heart. I shall be employed about things, not words!—and, anxious to render my sex more respectable members of society, I shall try to avoid that flowery diction which has slided from essays into novels, and from novels into familiar letters and conversation.

These pretty superlatives, dropping glibly from the tongue, vitiate the taste, and create a kind of sickly delicacy that turns away from simple unadorned truth; and a deluge of false sentiments and over-stretched feelings, stifling the natural emotions of the heart, render the domestic pleasures insipid, that ought to sweeten the exercise of those severe duties, which educate a rational and immortal being for a nobler field of action.

The education of women has, of late, been more attended to than formerly; yet they are still reckoned a frivolous sex, and ridiculed or pitied by the writers who endeavour by satire or instruction to improve them. It is acknowledged that they spend many of the first years of their lives in acquiring a smattering of accomplishments; meanwhile strength of body and mind are sacrificed to libertine notions of beauty, to the desire of establishing themselves,—the only way women can rise in the world,—by marriage. And this desire making mere animals of them, when they marry they act as such children may be expected to act:—they dress; they paint, and nickname God's creatures.[8]—Surely these weak beings are only fit for a seraglio![9]—Can they be expected to govern a family with judgment, or take care of the poor babes whom they bring into the world?

If then it can be fairly deduced from the present conduct of the sex, from the prevalent fondness for pleasure which takes place of ambition and those nobler passions that open and enlarge the soul; that the instruction which women have hitherto received has only tended, with the constitution of civil society, to render them insignificant objects of desire—mere propagators of fools!—if it can be proved that in aiming to accomplish them, without cultivating their understandings, they are taken out of their sphere of duties, and made ridiculous and useless when the short-lived bloom of beauty is over,[1] I presume that *rational* men will excuse me for endeavoring to persuade them to become more masculine and respectable.

Indeed the word masculine is only a bugbear: there is little reason to fear that women will acquire too much courage or fortitude; for their apparent inferiority with respect to bodily strength, must render them, in some degree, dependent on men in the various relations of life; but why should it be

---

7. I.e., in rounding out elaborate sentences. "Period": a formal sentence composed of balanced clauses.
8. Hamlet, charging Ophelia with the faults characteristic of women, says: "You jig, you amble, and you lisp, and / nickname God's creatures, and make your wantonness your ignorance" (*Hamlet* 3.1.143–45).
9. Harem, the women's quarters in a Muslim household.

1. A lively writer, I cannot recollect his name, asks what business women turned of forty have to do in the world? [Wollstonecraft's note]. Poston, in her edition of the *Vindication*, suggests that Wollstonecraft is recalling a passage in Fanny Burney's novel *Evelina* (1778), where the licentious Lord Merton exclaims: "I don't know what the devil a woman lives for after thirty; she is only in other folks' way."

increased by prejudices that give a sex to virtue, and confound simple truths with sensual reveries?

Women are, in fact, so much degraded by mistaken notions of female excellence, that I do not mean to add a paradox when I assert, that this artificial weakness produces a propensity to tyrannize, and gives birth to cunning, the natural opponent of strength, which leads them to play off those contemptible infantine airs that undermine esteem even whilst they excite desire. Let men become more chaste and modest, and if women do not grow wiser in the same ratio it will be clear that they have weaker understandings. It seems scarcely necessary to say, that I now speak of the sex in general. Many individuals have more sense than their male relatives; and, as nothing preponderates where there is a constant struggle for an equilibrium, without[2] it has naturally more gravity, some women govern their husbands without degrading themselves, because intellect will always govern.

Chap. 2. The Prevailing Opinion of a Sexual Character Discussed

To account for, and excuse the tyranny of man, many ingenious arguments have been brought forward to prove, that the two sexes, in the acquirement of virtue, ought to aim at attaining a very different character: or, to speak explicitly, women are not allowed to have sufficient strength of mind to acquire what really deserves the name of virtue. Yet it should seem, allowing them to have souls, that there is but one way appointed by Providence to lead *mankind* to either virtue or happiness.

If then women are not a swarm of ephemeron[3] triflers, why should they be kept in ignorance under the specious name of innocence? Men complain, and with reason, of the follies and caprices of our sex, when they do not keenly satirize our headstrong passions and groveling vices.—Behold, I should answer, the natural effect of ignorance! The mind will ever be unstable that has only prejudices to rest on, and the current will run with destructive fury when there are no barriers to break its force. Women are told from their infancy, and taught by the example of their mothers, that a little knowledge of human weakness, justly termed cunning, softness of temper, *outward* obedience, and a scrupulous attention to a puerile kind of propriety, will obtain for them the protection of man; and should they be beautiful, every thing else is needless, for, at least, twenty years of their lives.

Thus Milton describes our first frail mother; though when he tells us that women are formed for softness and sweet attractive grace,[4] I cannot comprehend his meaning, unless, in the true Mahometan strain, he meant to deprive us of souls, and insinuate that we were beings only designed by sweet attractive grace, and docile blind obedience, to gratify the senses of man when he can no longer soar on the wing of contemplation.

How grossly do they insult us who thus advise us only to render ourselves gentle, domestic brutes! For instance, the winning softness so warmly, and frequently, recommended, that governs by obeying. What childish expressions, and how insignificant is the being—can it be an immortal one? who

2. Unless.
3. A flying insect that lives only one day.
4. Milton asserts the authority of man over woman, on the grounds that "for contemplation he and valor formed, / For softness she and sweet attractive grace; / He for God only, she for God in him" (*Paradise Lost* 4.298ff.).

will condescend to govern by such sinister methods! "Certainly," says Lord Bacon, "man is of kin to the beasts by his body; and if he be not of kin to God by his spirit, he is a base and ignoble creature!"[5] Men, indeed, appear to me to act in a very unphilosophical manner when they try to secure the good conduct of women by attempting to keep them always in a state of childhood. Rousseau[6] was more consistent when he wished to stop the progress of reason in both sexes, for if men eat of the tree of knowledge, women will come in for a taste; but, from the imperfect cultivation which their understandings now receive, they only attain a knowledge of evil.

Children, I grant, should be innocent; but when the epithet is applied to men, or women, it is but a civil term for weakness. For if it be allowed that women were destined by Providence to acquire human virtues, and by the exercise of their understandings, that stability of character which is the firmest ground to rest our future hopes upon, they must be permitted to turn to the fountain of light, and not forced to shape their course by the twinkling of a mere satellite. Milton, I grant, was of a very different opinion; for he only bends to the indefeasible right of beauty, though it would be difficult to render two passages which I now mean to contrast, consistent. But into similar inconsistencies are great men often led by their senses.

> To whom thus Eve with *perfect beauty* adorn'd.
> My Author and Disposer, what thou bidst
> *Unargued* I obey; So God ordains;
> God is *thy law, thou mine*: to know no more
> Is Woman's *happiest* knowledge and her *praise*.[7]

These are exactly the arguments that I have used to children; but I have added, your reason is now gaining strength, and, till it arrives at some degree of maturity, you must look up to me for advice—then you ought to *think*, and only rely on God.

Yet in the following lines Milton seems to coincide with me; when he makes Adam thus expostulate with his Maker.

> Hast thou not made me here thy substitute,
> And these inferior far beneath me set?
> Among *unequals* what society
> Can sort, what harmony or true delight?
> Which must be mutual, in proportion due
> Giv'n and receiv'd; but in *disparity*
> The one intense, the other still remiss
> Cannot well suit with either, but soon prove
> Tedious alike: of *fellowship* I speak
> Such as I seek, fit to participate
> All rational delight[8]—

In treating, therefore, of the manners of women, let us, disregarding sensual arguments, trace what we should endeavor to make them in order to cooperate, if the expression be not too bold, with the supreme Being.

5. Francis Bacon's *Of Atheism* (1597).
6. Jean-Jacques Rousseau (1712–1778), who proposed limiting the role of rationality, as opposed to reliance on intuition and instinct. Rousseau's opinions about women and their appropriate education, as alluded to in this chapter, are expressed in his treatise *Émile* (1762), especially book 5, "Sophy, or Woman."
7. *Paradise Lost* 4.634–38 (Wollstonecraft's italics).
8. *Paradise Lost* 8.381–91 (Wollstonecraft's italics).

By individual education, I mean, for the sense of the word is not precisely defined, such an attention to a child as will slowly sharpen the senses, form the temper,[9] regulate the passions as they begin to ferment, and set the understanding to work before the body arrives at maturity; so that the man may only have to proceed, not to begin, the important task of learning to think and reason.

To prevent any misconstruction, I must add, that I do not believe that a private education can work the wonders which some sanguine writers have attributed to it. Men and women must be educated, in a great degree, by the opinions and manners of the society they live in. In every age there has been a stream of popular opinion that has carried all before it, and given a family character, as it were, to the century. It may then fairly be inferred, that, till society be differently constituted, much cannot be expected from education. It is, however, sufficient for my present purpose to assert, that, whatever effect circumstances have on the abilities, every being may become virtuous by the exercise of its own reason; for if but one being was created with vicious inclinations, that is positively bad, what can save us from atheism? or if we worship a God, is not that God a devil?

Consequently, the most perfect education, in my opinion, is such an exercise of the understanding as is best calculated to strengthen the body and form the heart. Or, in other words, to enable the individual to attain such habits of virtue as will render it independent. In fact, it is a farce to call any being virtuous whose virtues do not result from the exercise of its own reason. This was Rousseau's opinion respecting men: I extend it to women, and confidently assert that they have been drawn out of their sphere by false refinement, and not by an endeavour to acquire masculine qualities. Still the regal homage which they receive is so intoxicating, that till the manners of the times are changed, and formed on more reasonable principles, it may be impossible to convince them that the illegitimate power, which they obtain, by degrading themselves, is a curse, and that they must return to nature and equality, if they wish to secure the placid satisfaction that unsophisticated affections impart. But for this epoch we must wait—wait, perhaps, till kings and nobles, enlightened by reason, and, preferring the real dignity of man to childish state,[1] throw off their gaudy hereditary trappings: and if then women do not resign the arbitrary power of beauty—they will prove that they have *less* mind than man.

I may be accused of arrogance; still I must declare what I firmly believe, that all the writers who have written on the subject of female education and manners from Rousseau to Dr. Gregory,[2] have contributed to render women more artificial, weak characters, than they would otherwise have been; and, consequently, more useless members of society. I might have expressed this conviction in a lower key; but I am afraid it would have been the whine of affectation, and not the faithful expression of my feelings, of the clear result, which experience and reflection have led me to draw. When I come to that division of the subject, I shall advert to the passages that I more particularly disapprove of, in the works of the authors I have just alluded to; but it is first necessary to observe, that my objection extends to the whole purport of those

9. Temperament, character.
1. Pomp, costly display.
2. John Gregory, Scottish author of a widely read

book on the education of women, *A Father's Legacy to His Daughters* (1774).

books, which tend, in my opinion, to degrade one half of the human species, and render women pleasing at the expense of every solid virtue.

Though, to reason on Rousseau's ground, if man did attain a degree of perfection of mind when his body arrived at maturity, it might be proper, in order to make a man and his wife *one*, that she should rely entirely on his understanding; and the graceful ivy, clasping the oak that supported it, would form a whole in which strength and beauty would be equally conspicuous. But, alas! husbands, as well as their helpmates, are often only overgrown children; nay, thanks to early debauchery, scarcely men in their outward form—and if the blind lead the blind, one need not come from heaven to tell us the consequence.

Many are the causes that, in the present corrupt state of society, contribute to enslave women by cramping their understandings and sharpening their senses. One, perhaps, that silently does more mischief than all the rest, is their disregard of order.

To do every thing in an orderly manner, is a most important precept, which women, who, generally speaking, receive only a disorderly kind of education, seldom attend to with that degree of exactness that men, who from their infancy are broken into method, observe. This negligent kind of guess-work, for what other epithet can be used to point out the random exertions of a sort of instinctive common sense, never brought to the test of reason? prevents their generalizing matters of fact—so they do to-day, what they did yesterday, merely because they did it yesterday.

This contempt of the understanding in early life has more baneful consequences than is commonly supposed; for the little knowledge which women of strong minds attain, is, from various circumstances, of a more desultory kind than the knowledge of men, and it is acquired more by sheer observations on real life, than from comparing what has been individually observed with the results of experience generalized by speculation. Led by their dependent situation and domestic employments more into society, what they learn is rather by snatches; and as learning is with them, in general, only a secondary thing, they do not pursue any one branch with that persevering ardour necessary to give vigor to the faculties, and clearness to the judgment. In the present state of society, a little learning is required to support the character of a gentleman; and boys are obliged to submit to a few years of discipline. But in the education of women, the cultivation of the understanding is always subordinate to the acquirement of some corporeal accomplishment; even while enervated by confinement and false notions of modesty, the body is prevented from attaining that grace and beauty which relaxed half-formed limbs never exhibit. Besides, in youth their faculties are not brought forward by emulation; and having no serious scientific study, if they have natural sagacity it is turned too soon on life and manners. They dwell on effects, and modifications, without tracing them back to causes; and complicated rules to adjust behaviour are a weak substitute for simple principles.

As a proof that education gives this appearance of weakness to females, we may instance the example of military men, who are, like them, sent into the world before their minds have been stored with knowledge or fortified by principles. The consequences are similar; soldiers acquire a little superficial knowledge, snatched from the muddy current of conversation, and, from continually mixing with society, they gain, what is termed a knowledge of the world; and this acquaintance with manners and customs has frequently been confounded with a knowledge of the human heart. But can the crude fruit of casual observation, never brought to the test of judgment, formed by comparing speculation and experience, deserve such a distinction? Soldiers, as well as women, practice the minor virtues with punctilious politeness. Where is then the sexual difference, when the education has been the same? All the difference that I can discern, arises from the superior advantage of liberty, which enables the former to see more of life.

It is wandering from my present subject, perhaps, to make a political remark; but, as it was produced naturally by the train of my reflections, I shall not pass it silently over.

Standing armies can never consist of resolute, robust men; they may be well disciplined machines, but they will seldom contain men under the influence of strong passions, or with very vigorous faculties. And as for any depth of understanding, I will venture to affirm, that it is as rarely to be found in the army as amongst women; and the cause, I maintain, is the same. It may be further observed, that officers are also particularly attentive to their persons, fond of dancing, crowded rooms, adventures, and ridicule.[3] Like the *fair* sex, the business of their lives is gallantry.—They were taught to please, and they only live to please. Yet they do not lose their rank in the distinction of sexes, for they are still reckoned superior to women, though in what their superiority consists, beyond what I have just mentioned, it is difficult to discover.

The great misfortune is this, that they both acquire manners before morals, and a knowledge of life before they have, from reflection, any acquaintance with the grand ideal outline of human nature. The consequence is natural; satisfied with common nature, they become a prey to prejudices, and taking all their opinions on credit, they blindly submit to authority. So that, if they have any sense, it is a kind of instinctive glance, that catches proportions, and decides with respect to manners; but fails when arguments are to be pursued below the surface, or opinions analyzed.

May not the same remark be applied to women? Nay, the argument may be carried still further, for they are both thrown out of a useful station by the unnatural distinctions established in civilized life. Riches and hereditary honours have made cyphers of women to give consequence to the numerical figure; and idleness has produced a mixture of gallantry and despotism into society, which leads the very men who are the slaves of their mistresses to tyrannize over their sisters, wives, and daughters. This is only keeping them in rank and file, it is true. Strengthen the female mind by enlarging it, and there will be an end to blind obedience; but, as blind obedience is ever sought for by power, tyrants and sensualists are in the right when they endeavour to keep women in the dark, because the former only want slaves, and the latter a play-thing. The sensualist, indeed, has been the most dangerous of tyrants, and women have been duped by their lovers, as princes by their ministers, whilst dreaming that they reigned over them.

I now principally allude to Rousseau, for his character of Sophia[4] is, undoubtedly, a captivating one, though it appears to me grossly unnatural;

3. Why should women be censured with petulant acrimony, because they seem to have a passion for a scarlet coat? Has not education placed them more on a level with soldiers than any other class of men? [Wollstonecraft's note].

4. The title of book 5 of Rousseau's *Émile*.

however it is not the superstructure, but the foundation of her character, the principles on which her education was built, that I mean to attack; nay, warmly as I admire the genius of that able writer, whose opinions I shall often have occasion to cite, indignation always takes place of admiration, and the rigid frown of insulted virtue effaces the smile of complacency, which his eloquent periods are wont to raise, when I read his voluptuous reveries. Is this the man, who, in his ardor for virtue, would banish all the soft arts of peace, and almost carry us back to Spartan discipline? Is this the man who delights to paint the useful struggles of passion, the triumphs of good dispositions, and the heroic flights which carry the glowing soul out of itself?—How are these mighty sentiments lowered when he describes the pretty foot and enticing airs of his little favorite! But, for the present, I waive the subject, and, instead of severely reprehending the transient effusions of overweening sensibility, I shall only observe, that whoever has cast a benevolent eye on society, must often have been gratified by the sight of a humble mutual love, not dignified by sentiment, or strengthened by a union in intellectual pursuits. The domestic trifles of the day have afforded matters for cheerful converse, and innocent caresses have softened toils which did not require great exercise of mind or stretch of thought: yet, has not the sight of this moderate felicity excited more tenderness than respect? An emotion similar to what we feel when children are playing, or animals sporting,[5] whilst the contemplation of the noble struggles of suffering merit has raised admiration, and carried our thoughts to that world where sensation will give place to reason.

Women are, therefore, to be considered either as moral beings, or so weak that they must be entirely subjected to the superior faculties of men.

Let us examine this question. Rousseau declares that a woman should never, for a moment, feel herself independent, that she should be governed by fear to exercise her natural cunning, and made a coquetish slave in order to render her a more alluring object of desire, a *sweeter* companion to man, whenever he chooses to relax himself. He carries the arguments, which he pretends to draw from the indications of nature, still further, and insinuates that truth and fortitude, the corner stones of all human virtue, should be cultivated with certain restrictions, because, with respect to the female character, obedience is the grand lesson which ought to be impressed with unrelenting rigor.[6]

What nonsense! when will a great man arise with sufficient strength of mind to puff away the fumes which pride and sensuality have thus spread over the subject! If women are by nature inferior to men, their virtues must be the same in quality, if not in degree, or virtue is a relative idea; consequently, their conduct should be founded on the same principles, and have the same aim.

Connected with man as daughters, wives, and mothers, their moral char-

5. Similar feelings has Milton's pleasing picture of paradisiacal happiness ever raised in my mind; yet, instead of envying the lovely pair, I have, with conscious dignity, or Satanic pride, turned to hell for sublimer objects. In the same style, when viewing some noble monument of human art, I have traced the emanation of the Deity in the order I admired, till, descending from that giddy height, I have caught myself contemplating the grandest of all human sights;—for fancy quickly placed, in some solitary recess, an outcast of fortune, rising superior to passion and discontent [Wollstonecraft's note].

6. Rousseau had written in *Émile*: "What is most wanted in a woman is gentleness; formed to obey a creature so imperfect as man, a creature often vicious and always faulty, she should early learn to submit to injustice and to suffer the wrongs inflicted on her by her husband without complaint."

acter may be estimated by their manner of fulfilling those simple duties; but the end, the grand end of their exertions should be to unfold their own faculties and acquire the dignity of conscious virtue. They may try to render their road pleasant; but ought never to forget, in common with man, that life yields not the felicity which can satisfy an immortal soul. I do not mean to insinuate, that either sex should be so lost in abstract reflections or distant views, as to forget the affections and duties that lie before them, and are, in truth, the means appointed to produce the fruit of life; on the contrary, I would warmly recommend them, even while I assert, that they afford most satisfaction when they are considered in their true, sober light.

Probably the prevailing opinion, that woman was created for man, may have taken its rise from Moses's poetical story;[7] yet, as very few, it is presumed, who have bestowed any serious thought on the subject, ever supposed that Eve was, literally speaking, one of Adam's ribs, the deduction must be allowed to fall to the ground; or, only be so far admitted as it proves that man, from the remotest antiquity, found it convenient to exert his strength to subjugate his companion, and his invention to shew that she ought to have her neck bent under the yoke, because the whole creation was only created for his convenience or pleasure.

Let it not be concluded that I wish to invert the order of things; I have already granted, that, from the constitution of their bodies, men seem to be designed by Providence to attain a greater degree of virtue.[8] I speak collectively of the whole sex; but I see not the shadow of a reason to conclude that their virtues should differ in respect to their nature. In fact, how can they, if virtue has only one eternal standard? I must therefore, if I reason consequentially, as strenuously maintain that they have the same simple direction, as that there is a God.

It follows then that cunning should not be opposed to wisdom, little cares to great exertions, or insipid softness, varnished over with the name of gentleness, to that fortitude which grand views alone can inspire.

I shall be told that woman would then lose many of her peculiar graces, and the opinion of a well known poet might be quoted to refute my unqualified assertion. For Pope has said, in the name of the whole male sex,

> Yet ne'er so sure our passion to create,
> As when she touch'd the brink of all we hate.[9]

In what light this sally places men and women, I shall leave to the judicious to determine; meanwhile I shall content myself with observing, that I cannot discover why, unless they are mortal, females should always be degraded by being made subservient to love or lust.

To speak disrespectfully of love is, I know, high treason against sentiment and fine feelings; but I wish to speak the simple language of truth, and rather to address the head than the heart. To endeavor to reason love out of the world, would be to out-Quixote Cervantes,[1] and equally offend against common sense; but an endeavor to restrain this tumultuous passion, and prove

7. The story of the creation of Eve from the rib of Adam (Genesis 2.21–22). Traditionally, the first five books of the Old Testament were attributed to the authorship of Moses.
8. In the third paragraph of her Introduction, Wollstonecraft had said that men are, in general, physically stronger than women.
9. Alexander Pope's Moral Essays 2, Of the Characters of Women, lines 51–52.
1. I.e., to outdo the hero of Cervantes's Don Quixote (1605) in trying to accomplish the impossible.

that it should not be allowed to dethrone superior powers, or to usurp the sceptre which the understanding should ever coolly wield, appears less wild.

Youth is the season for love in both sexes; but in those days of thoughtless enjoyment provision should be made for the more important years of life, when reflection takes place of sensation. But Rousseau, and most of the male writers who have followed his steps, have warmly inculcated that the whole tendency of female education ought to be directed to one point:—to render them pleasing.

Let me reason with the supporters of this opinion who have any knowledge of human nature, do they imagine that marriage can eradicate the habitude of life? The woman who has only been taught to please will soon find that her charms are oblique sunbeams, and that they cannot have much effect on her husband's heart when they are seen every day, when the summer is passed and gone. Will she then have sufficient native energy to look into herself for comfort, and cultivate her dormant faculties? or, is it not more rational to expect that she will try to please other men; and, in the emotions raised by the expectation of new conquests, endeavor to forget the mortification her love or pride has received? When the husband ceases to be a lover—and the time will inevitably come, her desire of pleasing will then grow languid, or become a spring of bitterness; and love, perhaps, the most evanescent of all passions, gives place to jealousy or vanity.

I now speak of women who are restrained by principle or prejudice; such women, though they would shrink from an intrigue with real abhorrence, yet, nevertheless, wish to be convinced by the homage of gallantry that they are cruelly neglected by their husbands; or, days and weeks are spent in dreaming of the happiness enjoyed by congenial souls till their health is undermined and their spirits broken by discontent. How then can the great art of pleasing be such a necessary study? it is only useful to a mistress; the chaste wife, and serious mother, should only consider her power to please as the polish of her virtues, and the affection of her husband as one of the comforts that render her task less difficult and her life happier.—But, whether she be loved or neglected, her first wish should be to make herself respectable,[2] and not to rely for all her happiness on a being subject to like infirmities with herself.

The worthy Dr. Gregory fell into a similar error. I respect his heart; but entirely disapprove of his celebrated Legacy to his Daughters.

He advises them to cultivate a fondness for dress, because a fondness for dress, he asserts, is natural to them. I am unable to comprehend what either he or Rousseau mean, when they frequently use this indefinite term.[3] If they told us that in a pre-existent state the soul was fond of dress, and brought this inclination with it into a new body, I should listen to them with a half smile, as I often do when I hear a rant about innate elegance.—But if he only meant to say that the exercise of the faculties will produce this fondness—I deny it.—It is not natural; but arises, like false ambition in men, from a love of power.

Dr. Gregory goes much further; he actually recommends dissimulation, and advises an innocent girl to give the lie to her feelings, and not dance with spirit, when gaiety of heart would make her feel eloquent without mak-

---

2. I.e., morally worthy of respect. 3. I.e., "natural."

ing her gestures immodest. In the name of truth and common sense, why should not one woman acknowledge that she can take more exercise than another? or, in other words, that she has a sound constitution; and why, to damp innocent vivacity, is she darkly to be told that men will draw conclusions which she little thinks of?[4]—Let the libertine draw what inference he pleases; but, I hope, that no sensible mother will restrain the natural frankness of youth by instilling such indecent cautions. Out of the abundance of the heart the mouth speaketh;[5] and a wiser than Solomon hath said, that the heart should be made clean,[6] and not trivial ceremonies observed, which is not very difficult to fulfill with scrupulous exactness when vice reigns in the heart.

Women ought to endeavor to purify their heart; but can they do so when their uncultivated understandings make them entirely dependent on their senses for employment and amusement, when no noble pursuit sets them above the little vanities of the day, or enables them to curb the wild emotions that agitate a reed over which every passing breeze has power? To gain the affections of a virtuous man is affectation necessary? Nature has given woman a weaker frame than man; but, to ensure her husband's affections, must a wife, who by the exercise of her mind and body whilst she was discharging the duties of a daughter, wife, and mother, has allowed her constitution to retain its natural strength, and her nerves a healthy tone, is she, I say, to condescend to use art and feign a sickly delicacy in order to secure her husband's affection? Weakness may excite tenderness, and gratify the arrogant pride of man; but the lordly caresses of a protector will not gratify a noble mind that pants for, and deserves to be respected. Fondness is a poor substitute for friendship!

In a seraglio, I grant, that all these arts are necessary; the epicure must have his palate tickled, or he will sink into apathy; but have women so little ambition as to be satisfied with such a condition? Can they supinely dream life away in the lap of pleasure, or the languor of weariness, rather than assert their claim to pursue reasonable pleasures and render themselves conspicuous by practising the virtues which dignify mankind? Surely she has not an immortal soul who can loiter life away merely employed to adorn her person, that she may amuse the languid hours, and soften the cares of a fellow-creature who is willing to be enlivened by her smiles and tricks, when the serious business of life is over.

Besides, the woman who strengthens her body and exercises her mind will, by managing her family and practising various virtues, become the friend, and not the humble dependent of her husband; and if she, by possessing such substantial qualities, merit his regard, she will not find it necessary to conceal her affection, nor to pretend to an unnatural coldness of constitution to excite her husband's passions. In fact, if we revert to history, we shall find that the women who have distinguished themselves have neither been the most beautiful nor the most gentle of their sex.

Nature, or, to speak with strict propriety, God, has made all things right;

---

4. In *A Father's Legacy to His Daughters*, Gregory had advised a girl, when she dances, not "to forget the delicacy of [her] sex," lest she be "thought to discover a spirit she little dreams of."
5. Matthew 12.34.

6. Psalm 24 (attributed to David, the "wiser than Solomon"), 3–4: "Who shall ascend into the hill of the Lord? or who shall stand in his holy place? He that hath clean hands, and a pure heart."

but man has sought him out many inventions to mar the work. I now allude to that part of Dr. Gregory's treatise, where he advises a wife never to let her husband know the extent of her sensibility or affection. Voluptuous precaution, and as ineffectual as absurd.—Love, from its very nature, must be transitory. To seek for a secret that would render it constant, would be as wild a search as for the philosopher's stone, or the grand panacea:[7] and the discovery would be equally useless, or rather pernicious to mankind. The most holy band of society is friendship. It has been well said, by a shrewd satirist, "that rare as true love is, true friendship is still rarer."[8]

This is an obvious truth, and the cause not lying deep, will not elude a slight glance of inquiry.

Love, the common passion, in which chance and sensation take place of choice and reason, is, in some degree, felt by the mass of mankind; for it is not necessary to speak, at present, of the emotions that rise above or sink below love. This passion, naturally increased by suspense and difficulties, draws the mind out of its accustomed state, and exalts the affections; but the security of marriage, allowing the fever of love to subside, a healthy temperature is thought insipid, only by those who have not sufficient intellect to substitute the calm tenderness of friendship, the confidence of respect, instead of blind admiration, and the sensual emotions of fondness.

This is, must be, the course of nature.—Friendship or indifference inevitably succeeds love.—And this constitution seems perfectly to harmonize with the system of government which prevails in the moral world. Passions are spurs to action, and open the mind; but they sink into mere appetites, become a personal and momentary gratification, when the object is gained, and the satisfied mind rests in enjoyment. The man who had some virtue whilst he was struggling for a crown, often becomes a voluptuous tyrant when it graces his brow; and, when the lover is not lost in the husband, the dotard, a prey to childish caprices, and fond jealousies, neglects the serious duties of life, and the caresses which should excite confidence in his children are lavished on the overgrown child, his wife.

In order to fulfil the duties of life, and to be able to pursue with vigour the various employments which form the moral character, a master and mistress of a family ought not to continue to love each other with passion. I mean to say, that they ought not to indulge those emotions which disturb the order of society, and engross the thoughts that should be otherwise employed. The mind that has never been engrossed by one object wants vigor—if it can long be so, it is weak.

A mistaken education, a narrow, uncultivated mind, and many sexual prejudices, tend to make women more constant than men; but, for the present, I shall not touch on this branch of the subject. I will go still further, and advance, without dreaming of a paradox, that an unhappy marriage is often very advantageous to a family, and that the neglected wife is, in general, the best mother.[9] And this would almost always be the consequence if the female mind were more enlarged: for, it seems to be the common dispensation of

7. A medicine reputed to cure all diseases. "The philosopher's stone," in alchemy, had the power of transmuting base metals into gold.
8. Maxim 473 of La Rochefoucauld (1613–1680), the great French writer of epigrams.

9. Wollstonecraft's point is that a woman who is not preoccupied with her husband (and his attentions to her) has more time and attention for her children.

Providence, that what we gain in present enjoyment should be deducted from the treasure of life, experience; and that when we are gathering the flowers of the day and revelling in pleasure, the solid fruit of toil and wisdom should not be caught at the same time. The way lies before us, we must turn to the right or left; and he who will pass life away in bounding from one pleasure to another, must not complain if he acquire neither wisdom nor respectability of character.

Supposing, for a moment, that the soul is not immortal, and that man was only created for the present scene,—I think we should have reason to complain that love, infantine fondness, ever grew insipid and palled upon the sense. Let us eat, drink, and love for to-morrow we die, would be, in fact, the language of reason, the morality of life; and who but a fool would part with a reality for a fleeting shadow? But, if awed by observing the improbable[1] powers of the mind, we disdain to confine our wishes or thoughts to such a comparatively mean field of action; that only appears grand and important, as it is connected with a boundless prospect and sublime hopes, what necessity is there for falsehood in conduct, and why must the sacred majesty of truth be violated to detain a deceitful good that saps the very foundation of virtue? Why must the female mind be tainted by coquetish arts to gratify the sensualist, and prevent love from subsiding into friendship, or compassionate tenderness, when there are not qualities on which friendship can be built? Let the honest heart shew itself, and *reason* teach passion to submit to necessity; or, let the dignified pursuit of virtue and knowledge raise the mind above those emotions which rather imbitter than sweeten the cup of life, when they are not restrained within due bounds.

I do not mean to allude to the romantic passion, which is the concomitant of genius.—Who can clip its wing? But that grand passion not proportioned to the puny enjoyments of life, is only true to the sentiment, and feeds on itself. The passions which have been celebrated for their durability have always been unfortunate. They have acquired strength by absence and constitutional melancholy.—The fancy has hovered around a form of beauty dimly seen—but familiarity might have turned admiration into disgust; or, at least, into indifference, and allowed the imagination leisure to start fresh game. With perfect propriety, according to his view of things, does Rousseau make the mistress of his soul, Eloisa, love St. Preux, when life was fading before her;[2] but this is no proof of the immortality of the passion.

Of the same complexion is Dr. Gregory's advice respecting delicacy of sentiment,[3] which he advises a woman not to acquire, if she have determined to marry. This determination, however, perfectly consistent with his former advice, he calls *indelicate*, and earnestly persuades his daughters to conceal it, though it may govern their conduct;—as if it were indelicate to have the common appetites of human nature.

Noble morality! and consistent with the cautious prudence of a little soul that cannot extend its views beyond the present minute division of existence.

1. Poston points out that this may be a misprint in the second edition for "improvable," which occurs in the first edition.
2. In Rousseau's *Julie, ou la Nouvelle Héloise* (1761), Julie, after a life of fidelity to her husband, reveals on her deathbed that she has never lost her passion for St. Preux, her lover when she was young. Wollstonecraft accepts the common opinion that Julie represents Madame d'Houdetot, with whom Rousseau was in love when he wrote the novel.
3. I.e., too elevated and refined a notion of what to expect in a man.

If all the faculties of woman's mind are only to be cultivated as they respect her dependence on man; if, when a husband be obtained, she have arrived at her goal, and meanly proud rests satisfied with such a paltry crown, let her grovel contentedly, scarcely raised by her employments above the animal kingdom; but, if, struggling for the prize of her high calling, she look beyond the present scene, let her cultivate her understanding without stopping to consider what character the husband may have whom she is destined to marry. Let her only determine, without being too anxious about present happiness, to acquire the qualities that ennoble a rational being, and a rough inelegant husband may shock her taste without destroying her peace of mind. She will not model her soul to suit the frailties of her companion, but to bear with them: his character may be a trial, but not an impediment to virtue.

If Dr. Gregory confined his remark to romantic expectations of constant love and congenial feelings, he should have recollected that experience will banish what advice can never make us cease to wish for, when the imagination is kept alive at the expence of reason.

I own it frequently happens that women who have fostered a romantic unnatural delicacy of feeling, waste their[4] lives in *imagining* how happy they should have been with a husband who could love them with a fervid increasing affection every day, and all day. But they might as well pine married as single—and would not be a jot more unhappy with a bad husband than longing for a good one. That a proper education; or, to speak with more precision, a well stored mind, would enable a woman to support a single life with dignity, I grant; but that she should avoid cultivating her taste, lest her husband should occasionally shock it, is quitting a substance for a shadow. To say the truth, I do not know of what use is an improved taste, if the individual be not rendered more independent of the casualties of life; if new sources of enjoyment, only dependent on the solitary operations of the mind, are not opened. People of taste, married or single, without distinction, will ever be disgusted by various things that touch not less observing minds. On this conclusion the argument must not be allowed to hinge; but in the whole sum of enjoyment is taste to be denominated a blessing?

The question is, whether it procures most pain or pleasure? The answer will decide the propriety of Dr. Gregory's advice, and shew how absurd and tyrannic it is thus to lay down a system of slavery; or to attempt to educate moral beings by any other rules than those deduced from pure reason, which apply to the whole species.

Gentleness of manners, forbearance, and long-suffering, are such amiable Godlike qualities, that in sublime poetic strains the Deity has been invested with them; and, perhaps, no representation of his goodness so strongly fastens on the human affections as those that represent him abundant in mercy and willing to pardon. Gentleness, considered in this point of view, bears on its front all the characteristics of grandeur, combined with the winning graces of condescension; but what a different aspect it assumes when it is the submissive demeanour of dependence, the support of weakness that loves, because it wants protection; and is forbearing, because it must silently endure injuries; smiling under the lash at which it dare not snarl. Abject as

4. For example, the herd of Novelists [Wollstone-craft's note]. The author's reference is to women who have formed their expectations of love as it is misrepresented in the sentimental novels of their time.

this picture appears, it is the portrait of an accomplished woman, according to the received opinion of female excellence, separated by specious reasoners from human excellence. Or, they[5] kindly restore the rib, and make one moral being of a man and woman; not forgetting to give her all the "submissive charms."[6] How women are to exist in that state where there is to be neither marrying nor giving in marriage,[7] we are not told. For though moralists have agreed that the tenor of life seems to prove that *man* is prepared by various circumstances for a future state, they constantly concur in advising *woman* only to provide for the present. Gentleness, docility, and a spaniel-like affection are, on this ground, consistently recommended as the cardinal virtues of the sex; and, disregarding the arbitrary economy of nature, one writer has declared that it is masculine for a woman to be melancholy. She was created to be the toy of man, his rattle, and it must jingle in his ears whenever, dismissing reason, he chooses to be amused.

To recommend gentleness, indeed, on a broad basis is strictly philosophical. A frail being should labor to be gentle. But when forbearance confounds right and wrong, it ceases to be a virtue; and, however convenient it may be found in a companion—that companion will ever be considered as an inferior, and only inspire a vapid tenderness, which easily degenerates into contempt. Still, if advice could really make a being gentle, whose natural disposition admitted not of such a fine polish, something towards the advancement of order would be attained; but if, as might quickly be demonstrated, only affectation be produced by this indiscriminate counsel, which throws a stumbling-block in the way of gradual improvement, and true melioration of temper, the sex is not much benefited by sacrificing solid virtues to the attainment of superficial graces, though for a few years they may procure the individuals regal sway.

As a philosopher, I read with indignation the plausible epithets which men use to soften their insults; and, as a moralist, I ask what is meant by such heterogeneous associations, as fair defects, amiable weaknesses, &c.?[8] If there be but one criterion of morals, but one archetype of man, women appear to be suspended by destiny, according to the vulgar tale of Mahomet's coffin;[9] they have neither the unerring instinct of brutes, nor are allowed to fix the eye of reason on a perfect model. They were made to be loved, and must not aim at respect, lest they should be hunted out of society as masculine.

But to view the subject in another point of view. Do passive indolent women make the best wives? Confining our discussion to the present moment of existence, let us see how such weak creatures perform their part. Do the women who, by the attainment of a few superficial accomplishments, have strengthened the prevailing prejudice, merely contribute to the happiness of their husbands? Do they display their charms merely to amuse them?

5. *Vide* [see] Rousseau and Swedenborg [Wollstonecraft's note]. Rousseau's view was that a wife constituted an integral moral being only in concert with her husband. Emanuel Swedenborg (1688–1772), the Swedish theosophist, held that in the married state in heaven male and female are embodied in a single angelic form.
6. Milton says of Adam and Eve in *Paradise Lost* 4.497–99 that "he in delight / Both of her beauty and submissive charms / Smiled with superior love."
7. "For in the resurrection they neither marry, nor are given in marriage, but are as the angels of God in heaven" (Matthew 22.30).
8. In *Paradise Lost* 10.891–92 the fallen Adam refers to Eve as "this fair defect / Of Nature"; and in *Moral Essays* 2.43 Pope describes women as "Fine by defect, and delicately weak."
9. A legend has it that Mohammed's coffin hovers suspended in his tomb.

And have women, who have early imbibed notions of passive obedience, sufficient character to manage a family or educate children? So far from it, that, after surveying the history of woman, I cannot help, agreeing with the severest satirist, considering the sex as the weakest as well as the most oppressed half of the species. What does history disclose but marks of inferiority, and how few women have emancipated themselves from the galling yoke of sovereign man?—So few, that the exceptions remind me of an ingenious conjecture respecting Newton: that he was probably a being of a superior order, accidentally caged in a human body.[1] Following the same train of thinking, I have been led to imagine that the few extraordinary women who have rushed in eccentrical directions out of the orbit prescribed to their sex, were *male* spirits, confined by mistake in female frames. But if it be not philosophical to think of sex when the soul is mentioned, the inferiority must depend on the organs; or the heavenly fire, which is to ferment the clay, is not given in equal portions.

But avoiding, as I have hitherto done, any direct comparison of the two sexes collectively, or frankly acknowledging the inferiority of woman, according to the present appearance of things, I shall only insist that men have increased that inferiority till women are almost sunk below the standard of rational creatures. Let their faculties have room to unfold, and their virtues to gain strength, and then determine where the whole sex must stand in the intellectual scale. Yet let it be remembered, that for a small number of distinguished women I do not ask a place.

It is difficult for us purblind mortals to say to what height human discoveries and improvements may arrive when the gloom of despotism subsides, which makes us stumble at every step; but, when morality shall be settled on a more solid basis, then, without being gifted with a prophetic spirit, I will venture to predict that woman will be either the friend or slave of man. We shall not, as at present, doubt whether she is a moral agent, or the link which unites man with brutes.[2] But, should it then appear, that like the brutes they were principally created for the use of man, he will let them patiently bite the bridle, and not mock them with empty praise; or, should their rationality be proved, he will not impede their improvement merely to gratify his sensual appetites. He will not, with all the graces of rhetoric, advise them to submit implicitly their understanding to the guidance of man. He will not, when he treats of the education of women, assert that they ought never to have the free use of reason, nor would he recommend cunning and dissimulation to beings who are acquiring, in like manner as himself, the virtues of humanity.

Surely there can be but one rule of right, if morality has an eternal foundation, and whoever sacrifices virtue, strictly so called, to present convenience, or whose *duty* it is to act in such a manner, lives only for the passing day, and cannot be an accountable creature.

1. A possible reminiscence of Pope's *An Essay on Man* 2.31–34: "Superior beings [i.e., angels] . . . / Admired such wisdom in an earthly shape, / And showed a Newton as we show an ape."
2. Rousseau doubted that a woman, of herself, was a moral agent. There had been a long dispute about the question of woman being part of humankind. In the *Summa Theologica* (Question XVII, Art. 1) St. Thomas Aquinas concedes, with Aristotle, that the "production of woman comes from a defect in the active power, or from some material indisposition, or even from some external influence, such as that of a south wind, which is moist" (English Dominican translation of St. Thomas, edited by Anton C. Pegis, *The Basic Writings of Saint Thomas Aquinas* [New York, 1945], I, 880) [Poston's note].

The poet then should have dropped his sneer when he says,

> If weak women go astray,
> The stars are more in fault than they.[3]

For that they are bound by the adamantine chain of destiny is most certain, if it be proved that they are never to exercise their own reason, never to be independent, never to rise above opinion, or to feel the dignity of a rational will that only bows to God, and often forgets that the universe contains any being but itself and the model of perfection to which its ardent gaze is turned, to adore attributes that, softened into virtues, may be imitated in kind, though the degree overwhelms the enraptured mind.

If, I say, for I would not impress by declamation when Reason offers her sober light, if they be really capable of acting like rational creatures, let them not be treated like slaves; or, like the brutes who are dependent on the reason of man, when they associate with him; but cultivate their minds, give them the salutary, sublime curb of principle, and let them attain conscious dignity by feeling themselves only dependent on God. Teach them, in common with man, to submit to necessity, instead of giving, to render them more pleasing, a sex to morals.

Further, should experience prove that they cannot attain the same degree of strength of mind, perseverance, and fortitude, let their virtues be the same in kind, though they may vainly struggle for the same degree; and the superiority of man will be equally clear, if not clearer; and truth, as it is a simple principle, which admits of no modification, would be common to both. Nay, the order of society as it is at present regulated would not be inverted, for woman would then only have the rank that reason assigned her, and arts could not be practised to bring the balance even, much less to turn it.

These may be termed Utopian dreams.—Thanks to that Being who impressed them on my soul, and gave me sufficient strength of mind to dare to exert my own reason, till, becoming dependent only on him for the support of my virtue, I view, with indignation, the mistaken notions that enslave my sex.

I love man as my fellow; but his scepter, real or usurped, extends not to me, unless the reason of an individual demands my homage; and even then the submission is to reason, and not to man. In fact, the conduct of an accountable being must be regulated by the operations of its own reason; or on what foundation rests the throne of God?

It appears to me necessary to dwell on these obvious truths, because females have been insulated, as it were; and, while they have been stripped of the virtues that should clothe humanity, they have been decked with artificial graces that enable them to exercise a short-lived tyranny. Love, in their bosoms, taking place of every nobler passion, their sole ambition is to be fair, to raise emotion instead of inspiring respect; and this ignoble desire, like the servility in absolute monarchies, destroys all strength of character. Liberty is the mother of virtue, and if women be, by their very constitution, slaves, and not allowed to breathe the sharp invigorating air of freedom, they must ever languish like exotics, and be reckoned beautiful flaws in nature.

---

3. Matthew Prior, *Hans Carvel*, lines 11–12, alluding to *Julius Caesar* 1.2.141–42: "The fault, dear Brutus, is not in our stars, / But in ourselves."

As to the argument respecting the subjection in which the sex has ever been held, it retorts on man. The many have always been enthralled by the few; and monsters, who scarcely have shewn any discernment of human excellence, have tyrannized over thousands of their fellow-creatures. Why have men of superiour endowments submitted to such degradation? For, is it not universally acknowledged that kings, viewed collectively, have ever been inferior, in abilities and virtue, to the same number of men taken from the common mass of mankind—yet, have they not, and are they not still treated with a degree of reverence that is an insult to reason? China is not the only country where a living man has been made a God.[4] *Men* have submitted to superior strength to enjoy with impunity the pleasure of the moment—*women* have only done the same, and therefore till it is proved that the courtier, who servilely resigns the birthright of a man, is not a moral agent, it cannot be demonstrated that woman is essentially inferior to man because she has always been subjugated.

Brutal force has hitherto governed the world, and that the science of politics is in its infancy, is evident from philosophers scrupling to give the knowledge most useful to man that determinate distinction.

I shall not pursue this argument any further than to establish an obvious inference, that as sound politics diffuse liberty, mankind, including woman, will become more wise and virtuous.

From *Chap. 4. Observations on the State of Degradation to Which Woman Is Reduced by Various Causes*

＊　＊　＊

In the middle rank of life, to continue the comparison,[5] men, in their youth, are prepared for professions, and marriage is not considered as the grand feature in their lives; whilst women, on the contrary, have no other scheme to sharpen their faculties. It is not business, extensive plans, or any of the excursive flights of ambition, that engross their attention; no, their thoughts are not employed in rearing such noble structures. To rise in the world, and have the liberty of running from pleasure to pleasure, they must marry advantageously, and to this object their time is sacrificed, and their persons often legally prostituted. A man when he enters any profession has his eye steadily fixed on some future advantage (and the mind gains great strength by having all its efforts directed to one point), and, full of his business, pleasure is considered as mere relaxation; whilst women seek for pleasure as the main purpose of existence. In fact, from the education, which they receive from society, the love of pleasure may be said to govern them all; but does this prove that there is a sex in souls? It would be just as rational to declare that the courtiers in France, when a destructive system of despotism had formed their character, were not men, because liberty, virtue, and humanity, were sacrificed to pleasure and vanity.—Fatal passions, which have ever domineered over the *whole* race!

The same love of pleasure, fostered by the whole tendency of their edu-

4. The emperors of China were regarded as deities.
5. I.e., her comparison between the social condi-

tions of men and of women, which conduce to the degradation of women.

cation, gives a trifling turn to the conduct of women in most circumstances: for instance, they are ever anxious about secondary things; and on the watch for adventures, instead of being occupied by duties.

A man, when he undertakes a journey, has, in general, the end in view; a woman thinks more of the incidental occurrences, the strange things that may possibly occur on the road; the impression that she may make on her fellow-travellers; and, above all, she is anxiously intent on the care of the finery that she carries with her, which is more than ever a part of herself, when going to figure on a new scene; when, to use an apt French turn of expression, she is going to produce a sensation.—Can dignity of mind exist with such trivial cares?

In short, women, in general, as well as the rich of both sexes, have acquired all the follies and vices of civilization, and missed the useful fruit. It is not necessary for me always to premise, that I speak of the condition of the whole sex, leaving exceptions out of the question. Their senses are inflamed, and their understandings neglected, consequently they become the prey of their senses, delicately termed sensibility, and are blown about by every momentary gust of feeling. Civilized women are, therefore, so weakened by false refinement, that, respecting morals, their condition is much below what it would be were they left in a state nearer to nature. Ever restless and anxious, their over exercised sensibility not only renders them uncomfortable themselves, but troublesome, to use a soft phrase, to others. All their thoughts turn on things calculated to excite emotion; and feeling, when they should reason, their conduct is unstable, and their opinions are wavering—not the wavering produced by deliberation or progressive views, but by contradictory emotions. By fits and starts they are warm in many pursuits; yet this warmth, never concentrated into perseverance, soon exhausts itself; exhaled by its own heat, or meeting with some other fleeting passion, to which reason has never given any specific gravity, neutrality ensues. Miserable, indeed, must be that being whose cultivation of mind has only tended to inflame its passions! A distinction should be made between inflaming and strengthening them. The passions thus pampered, whilst the judgment is left unformed, what can be expected to ensue?—Undoubtedly, a mixture of madness and folly!

This observation should not be confined to the *fair* sex; however, at present, I only mean to apply it to them.

Novels, music, poetry, and gallantry, all tend to make women the creatures of sensation, and their character is thus formed in the mold of folly during the time they are acquiring accomplishments, the only improvement they are excited, by their station in society, to acquire. This overstretched sensibility naturally relaxes the other powers of the mind, and prevents intellect from attaining that sovereignty which it ought to attain to render a rational creature useful to others, and content with its own station: for the exercise of the understanding, as life advances, is the only method pointed out by nature to calm the passions.

Satiety has a very different effect, and I have often been forcibly struck by an emphatical description of damnation:—when the spirit is represented as continually hovering with abortive eagerness round the defiled body, unable to enjoy any thing without the organs of sense. Yet, to their senses, are women made slaves, because it is by their sensibility that they obtain present power.

And will moralists pretend to assert, that this is the condition in which one half of the human race should be encouraged to remain with listless inactivity and stupid acquiescence? Kind instructors! what were we created for? To remain, it may be said, innocent; they mean in a state of childhood.— We might as well never have been born, unless it were necessary that we should be created to enable man to acquire the noble privilege of reason, the power of discerning good from evil, whilst we lie down in the dust from whence we were taken, never to rise again.—

It would be an endless task to trace the variety of meannesses, cares, and sorrows, into which women are plunged by the prevailing opinion, that they were created rather to feel than reason, and that all the power they obtain, must be obtained by their charms and weakness:

Fine by defect, and amiably weak![6]

And, made by this amiable weakness entirely dependent, excepting what they gain by illicit sway, on man, not only for protection, but advice, is it surprising that, neglecting the duties that reason alone points out, and shrinking from trials calculated to strengthen their minds, they only exert themselves to give their defects a graceful covering, which may serve to heighten their charms in the eye of the voluptuary, though it sink them below the scale of moral excellence?

Fragile in every sense of the word, they are obliged to look up to man for every comfort. In the most trifling dangers they cling to their support, with parasitical tenacity, piteously demanding succour; and their *natural* protector extends his arm, or lifts up his voice, to guard the lovely trembler—from what? Perhaps the frown of an old cow, or the jump of a mouse; a rat, would be a serious danger. In the name of reason, and even common sense, what can save such beings from contempt; even though they be soft and fair?

These fears, when not affected, may produce some pretty attitudes; but they shew a degree of imbecility which degrades a rational creature in a way women are not aware of—for love and esteem are very distinct things.

I am fully persuaded that we should hear of none of these infantine airs, if girls were allowed to take sufficient exercise, and not confined in close rooms till their muscles are relaxed, and their powers of digestion destroyed. To carry the remark still further, if fear in girls, instead of being cherished, perhaps, created, were treated in the same manner as cowardice in boys, we should quickly see women with more dignified aspects. It is true, they could not then with equal propriety be termed the sweet flowers that smile in the walk of man; but they would be more respectable members of society, and discharge the important duties of life by the light of their own reason. "Educate women like men," says Rousseau, "and the more they resemble our sex the less power will they have over us."[7] This is the very point I aim at. I do not wish them to have power over men; but over themselves.

In the same strain have I heard men argue against instructing the poor;

6. Pope's actual words were "Fine by defect, and delicately weak" (*Moral Essays* 2.43).
7. In *Émile* Rousseau means this as a warning to women that if they are brought up to be like men, they will lose their sexual power over men.

for many are the forms that aristocracy assumes. "Teach them to read, and write," say they, "and you take them out of the station assigned them by nature." An eloquent Frenchman has answered them, I will borrow his sentiments. But they know not, when they make man a brute, that they may expect every instant to see him transformed into a ferocious beast.[8] Without knowledge there can be no morality!

Ignorance is a frail base for virtue! Yet, that it is the condition for which woman was organized, has been insisted upon by the writers who have most vehemently argued in favor of the superiority of man; a superiority not in degree, but essence; though, to soften the argument, they have labored to prove, with chivalrous generosity, that the sexes ought not to be compared; man was made to reason, woman to feel: and that together, flesh and spirit, they make the most perfect whole, by blending happily reason and sensibility into one character.

And what is sensibility? "Quickness of sensation; quickness of perception; delicacy." Thus is it defined by Dr. Johnson;[9] and the definition gives me no other idea than of the most exquisitely polished instinct. I discern not a trace of the image of God in either sensation or matter. Refined seventy times seven,[1] they are still material; intellect dwells not there; nor will fire ever make lead gold!

I come round to my old argument; if woman be allowed to have an immortal soul, she must have, as the employment of life, an understanding to improve. And when, to render the present state more complete, though every thing proves it to be but a fraction of a mighty sum, she is incited by present gratification to forget her grand destination, nature is counteracted, or she was born only to procreate and rot. Or, granting brutes, of every description, a soul, though not a reasonable one, the exercise of instinct and sensibility may be the step, which they are to take, in this life, towards the attainment of reason in the next; so that through all eternity they will lag behind man, who, why we cannot tell, had the power given him of attaining reason in his first mode of existence.

When I treat of the peculiar duties of women, as I should treat of the peculiar duties of a citizen or father, it will be found that I do not mean to insinuate that they should be taken out of their families, speaking of the majority. "He that hath wife and children," says Lord Bacon, "hath given hostages to fortune; for they are impediments to great enterprises, either of virtue or mischief. Certainly the best works, and of greatest merit for the public, have proceeded from the unmarried or childless men."[2] I say the same of women. But, the welfare of society is not built on extraordinary exertions; and were it more reasonably organized, there would be still less need of great abilities, or heroic virtues.

In the regulation of a family, in the education of children, understanding, in an unsophisticated sense, is particularly required: strength both of body and mind; yet the men who, by their writings, have most earnestly labored

---

8. Poston suggests that Wollstonecraft has in mind the comment by Mirabeau, the Revolutionary statesman, to the Abbé Siéyès, who had been rudely treated in the French Constituent Assembly in 1790: "My dear abbé, you have loosed the bull: do you expect he is not to make use of his horns?"
9. In his *Dictionary of the English Language*

(1747).
1. Jesus replies, when asked whether a brother's repeated sin should be forgiven "till seven times": "I say not unto thee, Until seven times: but, Until seventy times seven" (Matthew 18.22).
2. From Francis Bacon's essay *Of Marriage and the Single Life*.

to domesticate women, have endeavored, by arguments dictated by a gross appetite, which satiety had rendered fastidious, to weaken their bodies and cramp their minds. But, if even by these sinister methods they really *persuaded* women, by working on their feelings, to stay at home, and fulfil the duties of a mother and mistress of a family, I should cautiously oppose opinions that led women to right conduct, by prevailing on them to make the discharge of such important duties the main business of life, though reason were insulted. Yet, and I appeal to experience, if by neglecting the understanding they be as much, nay, more detached from these domestic employments, than they could be by the most serious intellectual pursuit, though it may be observed, that the mass of mankind will never vigorously pursue an intellectual object,[3] I may be allowed to infer that reason is absolutely necessary to enable a woman to perform any duty properly, and I must again repeat, that sensibility is not reason.

The comparison with the rich still occurs to me; for, when men neglect the duties of humanity, women will follow their example; a common stream hurries them both along with thoughtless celerity. Riches and honors prevent a man from enlarging his understanding, and enervate all his powers by reversing the order of nature, which has ever made true pleasure the reward of labor. Pleasure—enervating pleasure is, likewise, within women's reach without earning it. But, till hereditary possessions are spread abroad, how can we expect men to be proud of virtue? And, till they are, women will govern them by the most direct means, neglecting their dull domestic duties to catch the pleasure that sits lightly on the wing of time.

"The power of the woman," says some author, "is her sensibility";[4] and men, not aware of the consequence, do all they can to make this power swallow up every other. Those who constantly employ their sensibility will have most: for example; poets, painters, and composers.[5] Yet, when the sensibility is thus increased at the expence of reason, and even the imagination, why do philosophical men complain of their fickleness? The sexual attention of man particularly acts on female sensibility, and this sympathy has been exercised from their youth up. A husband cannot long pay those attentions with the passion necessary to excite lively emotions, and the heart, accustomed to lively emotions, turns to a new lover, or pines in secret, the prey of virtue or prudence. I mean when the heart has really been rendered susceptible, and the taste formed; for I am apt to conclude, from what I have seen in fashionable life, that vanity is oftener fostered than sensibility by the mode of education, and the intercourse between the sexes, which I have reprobated; and that coquetry more frequently proceeds from vanity than from that inconstancy, which overstrained sensibility naturally produces.

Another argument that has had great weight with me, must, I think, have some force with every considerate benevolent heart. Girls who have been thus weakly educated, are often cruelly left by their parents without any

---

3. The mass of mankind are rather the slaves of their appetites than of their passions [Wollstonecraft's note].

4. The sentiment is a commonplace, but Wollstonecraft may be referring to Edmund Burke's phrase: "The beauty of women is considerably owing to their weakness, or delicacy . . ." (Edmund Burke, *A Philosophical Enquiry into the Origin of Our Ideas of the Sublime and Beautiful* [London,

1759 (repr. The Scolar Press, 1970)], p. 219) [Poston's note].

5. Men of these descriptions pour it into their compositions, to amalgamate the gross materials; and, molding them with passion, give to the inert body a soul; but, in woman's imagination, love alone concentrates these ethereal beams [Wollstonecraft's note].

provision; and, of course, are dependent on, not only the reason, but the bounty of their brothers. These brothers are, to view the fairest side of the question, good sort of men, and give as a favor, what children of the same parents had an equal right to. In this equivocal humiliating situation, a docile female may remain some time, with a tolerable degree of comfort. But, when the brother marries, a probable circumstance, from being considered as the mistress of the family, she is viewed with averted looks as an intruder, an unnecessary burden on the benevolence of the master of the house, and his new partner.

Who can recount the misery, which many unfortunate beings, whose minds and bodies are equally weak, suffer in such situations—unable to work, and ashamed to beg? The wife, a cold-hearted, narrow-minded, woman, and this is not an unfair supposition; for the present mode of education does not tend to enlarge the heart any more than the understanding, is jealous of the little kindness which her husband shews to his relations; and her sensibility not rising to humanity, she is displeased at seeing the property of *her* children lavished on an helpless sister.

These are matters of fact, which have come under my eye again and again. The consequence is obvious, the wife has recourse to cunning to undermine the habitual affection, which she is afraid openly to oppose; and neither tears nor caresses are spared till the spy is worked out of her home, and thrown on the world, unprepared for its difficulties; or sent, as a great effort of generosity, or from some regard to propriety, with a small stipend, and an uncultivated mind, into joyless solitude.

These two women may be much upon a par, with respect to reason and humanity; and changing situations, might have acted just the same selfish part; but had they been differently educated, the case would also have been very different. The wife would not have had that sensibility, of which self is the centre, and reason might have taught her not to expect, and not even to be flattered by, the affection of her husband, if it led him to violate prior duties. She would wish not to love him merely because he loved her, but on account of his virtues; and the sister might have been able to struggle for herself instead of eating the bitter bread of dependence.

I am, indeed, persuaded that the heart, as well as the understanding, is opened by cultivation; and by, which may not appear so clear, strengthening the organs; I am not now talking of momentary flashes of sensibility, but of affections. And, perhaps, in the education of both sexes, the most difficult task is so to adjust instruction as not to narrow the understanding, whilst the heart is warmed by the generous juices of spring, just raised by the electric fermentation of the season; nor to dry up the feelings by employing the mind in investigations remote from life.

With respect to women, when they receive a careful education, they are either made fine ladies, brimful of sensibility, and teeming with capricious fancies; or mere notable women.[6] The latter are often friendly, honest creatures, and have a shrewd kind of good sense joined with worldly prudence, that often render them more useful members of society than the fine sentimental lady, though they possess neither greatness of mind nor taste. The intellectual world is shut against them; take them out of their family or

6. I.e., energetic in running a household.

neighborhood, and they stand still; the mind finding no employment, for literature affords a fund of amusement which they have never sought to relish, but frequently to despise. The sentiments and taste of more cultivated minds appear ridiculous, even in those whom chance and family connections have led them to love; but in mere acquaintance they think it all affectation.

A man of sense can only love such a woman on account of her sex, and respect her, because she is a trusty servant. He lets her, to preserve his own peace, scold the servants, and go to church in clothes made of the very best materials. A man of her own size of understanding would, probably, not agree so well with her; for he might wish to encroach on her prerogative, and manage some domestic concerns himself. Yet women, whose minds are not enlarged by cultivation, or the natural selfishness of sensibility expanded by reflection, are very unfit to manage a family; for, by an undue stretch of power, they are always tyrannizing to support a superiority that only rests on the arbitrary distinction of fortune. The evil is sometimes more serious, and domestics are deprived of innocent indulgences, and made to work beyond their strength, in order to enable the notable woman to keep a better table, and outshine her neighbours in finery and parade. If she attend to her children, it is, in general, to dress them in a costly manner—and, whether this attention arise from vanity or fondness, it is equally pernicious.

Besides, how many women of this description pass their days; or, at least, their evenings, discontentedly. Their husbands acknowledge that they are good managers, and chaste wives; but leave home to seek for more agreeable, may I be allowed to use a significant French word, *piquant*[7] society; and the patient drudge, who fulfils her task, like a blind horse in a mill, is defrauded of her just reward; for the wages due to her are the caresses of her husband; and women who have so few resources in themselves, do not very patiently bear this privation of a natural right.

A fine lady, on the contrary, has been taught to look down with contempt on the vulgar employments of life; though she has only been incited to acquire accomplishments that rise a degree above sense; for even corporeal accomplishments cannot be acquired with any degree of precision unless the understanding has been strengthened by exercise. Without a foundation of principles taste is superficial, grace must arise from something deeper than imitation. The imagination, however, is heated, and the feelings rendered fastidious, if not sophisticated; or, a counterpoise of judgment is not acquired, when the heart still remains artless, though it becomes too tender.

These women are often amiable; and their hearts are really more sensible to general benevolence, more alive to the sentiments that civilize life, than the square-elbowed family drudge; but, wanting a due proportion of reflection and self-government, they only inspire love; and are the mistresses of their husbands, whilst they have any hold on their affections; and the platonic friends of his male acquaintance. These are the fair defects in nature; the women who appear to be created not to enjoy the fellowship of man, but to save him from sinking into absolute brutality, by rubbing off the rough angles of his character; and by playful dalliance to give some dignity to the appetite that draws him to them.—Gracious Creator of the whole human race! hast thou created such a being as woman, who can trace thy wisdom

7. Stimulating.

in thy works, and feel that thou alone art by thy nature exalted above her,—for no better purpose?—Can she believe that she was only made to submit to man, her equal, a being, who, like her, was sent into the world to acquire virtue?—Can she consent to be occupied merely to please him; merely to adorn the earth, when her soul is capable of rising to thee?—And can she rest supinely dependent on man for reason, when she ought to mount with him the arduous steeps of knowledge?—

Yet, if love be the supreme good, let women be only educated to inspire it, and let every charm be polished to intoxicate the senses; but, if they be moral beings, let them have a chance to become intelligent; and let love to man be only a part of that glowing flame of universal love, which, after encircling humanity, mounts in grateful incense to God.

✳   ✳   ✳

1792

Letters Written in Sweden, Norway, and Denmark   In June 1795

Mary Wollstonecraft undertook an arduous and sometimes dangerous five-month trip through the Scandinavian countries, taking with her Fanny, her year-old infant, and Marguerite, a French maid she had brought from Paris to London. Wollstonecraft's American lover Gilbert Imlay—author, inaugurator of sometimes shady commercial deals, and inveterate philanderer—had conceived the scheme of sending her as his business emissary to the northern countries, thus leaving himself free to pursue an affair with another woman. Upon returning to London in September, Wollstonecraft prepared for publication the letters she had written to Imlay during her trip; they were issued the next year (1796) by her friend, the radical publisher Joseph Johnson. Contemporary readers were left to guess at the identity of the *you* to whom the letters were addressed and to speculate about the author's hints at a love relationship with the addressee and about the causes of her present unhappiness.

In the letters Wollstonecraft comments insightfully and incisively about the class divisions, manners, commerce, and conduct of the people she observed and especially about the care of children and the situation and disabilities of women. She is also a sensitive connoisseur, in the mode of that time, on natural scenery and moves easily from aesthetic contemplation to solitary meditations on life, death, and the possibility of an afterlife—meditations interspersed with sharply realistic observations of the world about her. And always, she manifests her own doughty, passionate, and impetuous temperament.

Carol Poston, who has edited both Wollstonecraft's *Vindication of the Rights of Woman* and her *Letters* from Scandinavia, justly describes the latter as "her most delightful work" and remarks that, in the unsystematic freedom that it permits, "it is possible that the epistolary journal is the perfect literary mode for Wollstonecraft's strengths as a writer and thinker."

From Letters Written during a Short Residence in Sweden, Norway, and Denmark

Advertisement

The writing travels, or memoirs, has ever been a pleasant employment; for vanity or sensibility always renders it interesting. In writing these desultory letters, I found I could not avoid being continually the first person—"the little hero of each tale." I tried to correct this fault, if it be one, for they were designed for publication; but in proportion as I arranged my thoughts, my letter, I found, became stiff and affected: I, therefore, determined to let my remarks and reflections flow unrestrained, as I perceived that I could not give a just description of what I saw, but by relating the effect different objects had produced on my mind and feelings, whilst the impression was still fresh.

A person has a right, I have sometimes thought, when amused by a witty or interesting egotist, to talk of himself when he can win on our attention by acquiring our affection. Whether I deserve to rank amongst this privileged number, my readers alone can judge—and I give them leave to shut the book, if they do not wish to become better acquainted with me.

My plan was simply to endeavor to give a just view of the present state of the countries I have passed through, as far as I could obtain information during so short a residence; avoiding those details which, without being very useful to travelers who follow the same route, appear very insipid to those who only accompany you in their chair.

Letter 1

Eleven days of weariness on board a vessel not intended for the accommodation of passengers have so exhausted my spirits, to say nothing of the other causes, with which you are already sufficiently acquainted, that it is with some difficulty I adhere to my determination of giving you my observations, as I travel through new scenes, whilst warmed with the impression they have made on me.

The captain, as I mentioned to you, promised to put me on shore at Arendall, or Gothenburg, in his way to Elsineur;[1] but contrary winds obliged us to pass both places during the night. In the morning, however, after we had lost sight of the entrance of the latter bay, the vessel was becalmed; and the captain, to oblige me, hanging out a signal for a pilot, bore down towards the shore.

My attention was particularly directed to the lighthouse; and you can scarcely imagine with what anxiety I watched two long hours for a boat to emancipate me—still no one appeared. Every cloud that flitted on the horizon was hailed as a liberator, till approaching nearer, like most of the prospects sketched by hope, it dissolved under the eye into disappointment.

Weary of expectation, I then began to converse with the captain on the subject; and, from the tenor of the information my questions drew forth, I soon concluded, that, if I waited for a boat, I had little chance of getting on shore at this place. Despotism, as is usually the case, I found had here cramped the industry of man. The pilots being paid by the king, and scantily, they will not run into any danger, or even quit their hovels, if they can possibly avoid it, only to fulfil what is termed their duty. How different is it on the English coast, where, in the most stormy weather, boats immediately hail you, brought out by the expectation of extraordinary profit.

Disliking to sail for Elsineur, and still more to lie at anchor, or cruise about

1. Helsingør, Denmark. "Arendall": in Norway [Wollstonecraft's note]. "Gothenburg": Göteborg, Sweden.

the coast for several days, I exerted all my rhetoric to prevail on the captain to let me have the ship's boat; and though I added the most forcible of arguments, I for a long time addressed him in vain.

It is a kind of rule at sea, not to send out a boat. The captain was a good-natured man; but men with common minds seldom break through general rules. Prudence is ever the resort of weakness; and they rarely go as far as they may in any undertaking, who are determined not to go beyond it on any account. If, however, I had some trouble with the captain, I did not lose much time with the sailors; for they, all alacrity, hoisted out the boat, the moment I obtained permission, and promised to row me to the lighthouse.

I did not once allow myself to doubt of obtaining a conveyance from thence round the rocks—and then away for Gothenburg—confinement is so unpleasant.

The day was fine; and I enjoyed the water till, approaching the little island, poor Marguerite, whose timidity always acts as a feeler before her adventuring spirit, began to wonder at our not seeing any inhabitants. I did not listen to her. But when, on landing, the same silence prevailed, I caught the alarm, which was not lessened by the sight of two old men, whom we forced out of their wretched hut. Scarcely human in their appearance, we with difficulty obtained an intelligible reply to our questions—the result of which was, that they had no boat, and were not allowed to quit their post, on any pretense. But, they informed us, that there was at the other side, eight or ten miles over, a pilot's dwelling; two guineas[2] tempted the sailors to risk the captain's displeasure, and once more embark to row me over.

The weather was pleasant, and the appearance of the shore so grand, that I should have enjoyed the two hours it took to reach it, but for the fatigue which was too visible in the countenances of the sailors who, instead of uttering a complaint, were, with the thoughtless hilarity peculiar to them, joking about the possibility of the captain's taking advantage of a slight westerly breeze, which was springing up, to sail without them. Yet, in spite of their good humor, I could not help growing uneasy when the shore, receding, as it were, as we advanced, seemed to promise no end to their toil. This anxiety increased when, turning into the most picturesque bay I ever saw, my eyes sought in vain for the vestige of a human habitation. Before I could determine what step to take in such a dilemma, for I could not bear to think of returning to the ship, the sight of a barge relieved me, and we hastened towards it for information. We were immediately directed to pass some jutting rocks when we should see a pilot's hut.

There was a solemn silence in this scene, which made itself be felt. The sunbeams that played on the ocean, scarcely ruffled by the lightest breeze, contrasted with the huge, dark rocks, that looked like the rude materials of creation forming the barrier of unwrought space, forcibly struck me; but I should not have been sorry if the cottage had not appeared equally tranquil. Approaching a retreat where strangers, especially women, so seldom appeared, I wondered that curiosity did not bring the beings who inhabited it to the windows or door. I did not immediately recollect that men who remain so near the brute creation, as only to exert themselves to find the food necessary to sustain life, have little or no imagination to call forth the

---

2. A British gold coin worth one pound and a shilling.

curiosity necessary to fructify the faint glimmerings of mind which entitles them to rank as lords of the creation.—Had they either, they could not contentedly remain rooted in the clods they so indolently cultivate.

Whilst the sailors went to seek for the sluggish inhabitants, these conclusions occurred to me; and, recollecting the extreme fondness which the Parisians ever testify for novelty, their very curiosity appeared to me a proof of the progress they had made in refinement. Yes; in the art of living—in the art of escaping from the cares which embarrass the first steps towards the attainment of the pleasures of social life.

The pilots informed the sailors that they were under the direction of a lieutenant retired from the service, who spoke English; adding, that they could do nothing without his orders; and even the offer of money could hardly conquer their laziness, and prevail on them to accompany us to his dwelling. They would not go with me alone which I wanted them to have done, because I wished to dismiss the sailors as soon as possible. Once more we rowed off, they following tardily, till, turning round another bold protuberance of the rocks, we saw a boat making towards us, and soon learnt that it was the lieutenant himself, coming with some earnestness to see who we were.

To save the sailors any further toil, I had my baggage instantly removed into his boat; for, as he could speak English, a previous parley was not necessary; though Marguerite's respect for me could hardly keep her from expressing the fear, strongly marked on her countenance, which my putting ourselves into the power of a strange man excited. He pointed out his cottage; and, drawing near to it, I was not sorry to see a female figure, though I had not, like Marguerite, been thinking of robberies, murders, or the other evil which instantly, as the sailors would have said, runs foul of a woman's imagination.

On entering, I was still better pleased to find a clean house, with some degree of rural elegance. The beds were of muslin, coarse it is true, but dazzlingly white; and the floor was strewed over with little sprigs of juniper (the custom, as I afterwards found, of the country), which formed a contrast with the curtains and produced an agreeable sensation of freshness, to soften the ardor of noon. Still nothing was so pleasing as the alacrity of hospitality— all that the house afforded was quickly spread on the whitest linen.— Remember I had just left the vessel, where, without being fastidious, I had continually been disgusted. Fish, milk, butter, and cheese, and I am sorry to add, brandy, the bane of this country, were spread on the board. After we had dined, hospitality made them, with some degree of mystery, bring us some excellent coffee. I did not then know that it was prohibited.[3]

The good man of the house apologized for coming in continually, but declared that he was so glad to speak English, he could not stay out. He need not have apologized; I was equally glad of his company. With the wife I could only exchange smiles; and she was employed observing the make of our clothes. My hands, I found, had first led her to discover that I was the lady. I had, of course, my quantum of reverences; for the politeness of the north seems to partake of the coldness of the climate, and the rigidity of its iron sinewed rocks. Amongst the peasantry, there is, however, so much of

---

3. The law then prohibited the import or consumption of coffee.

the simplicity of the golden age in this land of flint—so much overflowing of heart, and fellow-feeling, that only benevolence, and the honest sympathy of nature, diffused smiles over my countenance when they kept me standing, regardless of my fatigue, whilst they dropt courtesy after courtesy.

The situation of this house was beautiful, though chosen for convenience. The master being the officer who commanded all the pilots on the coast, and the person appointed to guard wrecks, it was necessary for him to fix on a spot that would overlook the whole bay. As he had seen some service, he wore, not without a pride I thought becoming, a badge to prove that he had merited well of his country. It was happy, I thought, that he had been paid in honor; for the stipend he received was little more than twelve pounds a year.—I do not trouble myself or you with the calculation of Swedish ducats. Thus, my friend, you perceive the necessity of *perquisites*.[4] This same narrow policy runs through every thing. I shall have occasion further to animadvert on it.

Though my host amused me with an account of himself, which gave me an idea of the manners of the people I was about to visit, I was eager to climb the rocks to view the country, and see whether the honest tars had regained their ship. With the help of the lieutenant's telescope I saw the vessel underway with a fair though gentle gale. The sea was calm, playful even as the most shallow stream, and on the vast bason[5] I did not see a dark speck to indicate the boat. My conductors were consequently arrived.

Straying further my eye was attracted by the sight of some heart's-ease[6] that peeped through the rocks. I caught at it as a good omen, and going to preserve it in a letter that had not conveyed balm to my heart, a cruel remembrance suffused my eyes; but it passed away like an April shower. If you are deep read in Shakspeare, you will recollect that this was the little western flower tinged by love's dart, which "maidens call love in idleness."[7] The gaiety of my babe was unmixed; regardless of omens or sentiments, she found a few wild strawberries more grateful than flowers or fancies.

The lieutenant informed me that this was a commodious bay. Of that I could not judge, though I felt its picturesque beauty. Rocks were piled on rocks, forming a suitable bulwark to the ocean. Come no further, they emphatically said, turning their dark sides to the waves to augment the idle roar. The view was sterile: still little patches of earth, of the most exquisite verdure, enameled with the sweetest wild flowers, seemed to promise the goats and a few straggling cows luxurious herbage. How silent and peaceful was the scene. I gazed around with rapture, and felt more of that spontaneous pleasure which gives credibility to our expectation of happiness, than I had for a long, long time before. I forgot the horrors I had witnessed in France,[8] which had cast a gloom over all nature, and suffering the enthusiasm of my character, too often, gracious God! damped by the tears of disappointed affection, to be lighted up afresh, care took wing while simple fellow feeling expanded my heart.

---

4. Payments in addition to salary. The suggestion is of income derived from bribes or smuggling.
5 I.e., basin.
6. A small wildflower, variously colored. Wollstonecraft goes on to make the first of many veiled allusions to her faithless lover Gilbert Imlay, to whom these letters are addressed.

7. Popular name for the pansy, whose juice Oberon put on the sleeping Titania's eyes to make her dote on the next person she saw (*A Midsummer Night's Dream* 2.1.165–72).
8. Wollstonecraft had lived in France at the time of the Reign of Terror under Robespierre (1793–94).

To prolong this enjoyment, I readily assented to the proposal of our host to pay a visit to a family, the master of which spoke English, who was the drollest dog in the country, he added, repeating some of his stories, with a hearty laugh.

I walked on, still delighted with the rude beauties of the scene; for the sublime often gave place imperceptibly to the beautiful, dilating the emotions which were painfully concentrated.

When we entered this abode, the largest I had yet seen, I was introduced to a numerous family; but the father, from whom I was led to expect so much entertainment, was absent. The lieutenant consequently was obliged to be the interpreter of our reciprocal compliments. The phrases were awkwardly transmitted, it is true; but looks and gestures were sufficient to make them intelligible and interesting. The girls were all vivacity, and respect for me could scarcely keep them from romping with my host, who, asking for a pinch of snuff, was presented with a box, out of which an artificial mouse, fastened to the bottom, sprung. Though this trick had doubtless been played time out of mind, yet the laughter it excited was not less genuine.

They were overflowing with civility; but to prevent their almost killing my babe with kindness, I was obliged to shorten my visit; and two or three of the girls accompanied us, bringing with them a part of whatever the house afforded to contribute towards rendering my supper more plentiful; and plentiful in fact it was, though I with difficulty did honor to some of the dishes, not relishing the quantity of sugar and spices put into every thing. At supper my host told me bluntly that I was a woman of observation, for I asked him *men's questions*.

The arrangements for my journey were quickly made; I could only have a car with post-horses, as I did not choose to wait till a carriage could be sent for to Gothenburg. The expense of my journey, about one or two and twenty English miles, I found would not amount to more than eleven or twelve shillings, paying, he assured me, generously. I gave him a guinea and a half. But it was with the greatest difficulty that I could make him take so much, indeed any thing for my lodging and fare. He declared that it was next to robbing me, explaining how much I ought to pay on the road. However, as I was positive, he took the guinea for himself; but, as a condition, insisted on accompanying me, to prevent my meeting with any trouble or imposition on the way.

I then retired to my apartment with regret. The night was so fine, that I would gladly have rambled about much longer; yet recollecting that I must rise very early, I reluctantly went to bed: but my senses had been so awake, and my imagination still continued so busy, that I sought for rest in vain. Rising before six, I scented the sweet morning air; I had long before heard the birds twittering to hail the dawning day, though it could scarcely have been allowed to have departed.

Nothing, in fact, can equal the beauty of the northern summer's evening and night; if night it may be called that only wants the glare of day, the full light, which frequently seems so impertinent; for I could write at midnight very well without a candle. I contemplated all nature at rest; the rocks, even grown darker in their appearance, looked as if they partook of the general repose, and reclined more heavily on their foundation.—What, I exclaimed, is this active principle which keeps me still awake?—Why fly my thoughts abroad when every thing around me appears at home? My child was sleeping with equal calmness—innocent and sweet as the closing flowers.—Some recollections, attached to the idea of home, mingled with reflections respecting the state of society I had been contemplating that evening, made a tear drop on the rosy cheek I had just kissed; and emotions that trembled on the brink of ectasy and agony gave a poignancy to my sensations, which made me feel more alive than usual.

What are these imperious sympathies? How frequently has melancholy and even misanthropy taken possession of me, when the world has disgusted me, and friends have proved unkind. I have then considered myself as a particle broken off from the grand mass of mankind;—I was alone, till some involuntary sympathetic emotion, like the attraction of adhesion,[9] made me feel that I was still a part of a mighty whole, from which I could not sever myself—not, perhaps, for the reflection has been carried very far, by snapping the thread of an existence which loses its charms in proportion as the cruel experience of life stops or poisons the current of the heart. Futurity, what hast thou not to give to those who know that there is such a thing as happiness! I speak not of philosophical contentment, though pain has afforded them the strongest conviction of it.

After our coffee and milk, for the mistress of the house had been roused long before us by her hospitality, my baggage was taken forward in a boat by my host, because the car could not safely have been brought to the house.

The road at first was very rocky and troublesome; but our driver was careful, and the horses accustomed to the frequent and sudden acclivities and descents; so that not apprehending any danger, I played with my girl, whom I would not leave to Marguerite's care, on account of her timidity.

Stopping at a little inn to bait[1] the horses, I saw the first countenance in Sweden that displeased me, though the man was better dressed than any one who had as yet fallen in my way. An altercation took place between him and my host, the purport of which I could not guess, excepting that I was the occasion of it, be it what it would. The sequel was his leaving the house angrily; and I was immediately informed that he was the custom-house officer. The professional had indeed effaced the national character, for living as he did with these frank hospitable people, still only the exciseman appeared,—the counterpart of some I had met with in England and France. I was unprovided with a passport, not having entered any great town. At Gothenburg I knew I could immediately obtain one, and only the trouble made me object to the searching my trunks. He blustered for money; but the lieutenant was determined to guard me, according to promise, from imposition.

To avoid being interrogated at the town-gate, and obliged to go in the rain to give an account of myself, merely a form, before we could get the refreshment we stood in need of, he requested us to descend, I might have said step, from our car, and walk into town.

I expected to have found a tolerable inn, but was ushered into a most comfortless one; and, because it was about five o'clock, three or four hours

---

9. The physical attraction between two different substances. 1. Feed.

after their dining hour, I could not prevail on them to give me any thing warm to eat.

The appearance of the accommodations obliged me to deliver one of my recommendatory letters, and the gentleman, to whom it was addressed, sent to look out for a lodging for me whilst I partook of his supper. As nothing passed at this supper to characterize the country, I shall here close my letter.

Your's truly.

Letter 4

The severity of the long Swedish winter tends to render the people sluggish; for, though this season has its peculiar pleasures, too much time is employed to guard against its inclemency. Still, as warm cloathing is absolutely necessary, the women spin, and the men weave, and by these exertions get a fence to keep out the cold. I have rarely passed a knot of cottages without seeing cloth laid out to bleach; and when I entered, always found the women spinning or knitting.

A mistaken tenderness, however, for their children, makes them, even in summer, load them with flannels; and, having a sort of natural antipathy to cold water, the squalid appearance of the poor babes, not to speak of the noxious smell which flannel and rugs retain, seems a reply to a question I had often asked—Why I did not see more children in the villages I passed through? Indeed the children appear to be nipt in the bud, having neither the graces nor charms of their age. And this, I am persuaded, is much more owing to the ignorance of the mothers than to the rudeness of the climate. Rendered feeble by the continual perspiration they are kept in, whilst every pore is absorbing unwholesome moisture, they give them, even at the breast, brandy, salt fish, and every other crude substance, which air and exercise enables the parent to digest.

The women of fortune here, as well as every where else, have nurses to suckle their children; and the total want of chastity in the lower class of women frequently renders them very unfit for the trust.[2]

You have sometimes remarked to me the difference of the manners of the country girls in England and in America; attributing the reserve of the former to the climate—to the absence of genial suns. But it must be their stars, not the zephyrs gently stealing on their senses, which here lead frail women astray.—Who can look at these rocks, and allow the voluptuousness[3] of nature to be an excuse for gratifying the desires it inspires? We must, therefore, find some other cause beside voluptuousness, I believe, to account for the conduct of the Swedish and American country girls; for I am led to conclude, from all the observations I have made, that there is always a mixture of sentiment and imagination in voluptuousness, to which neither of them have much pretension.

The country girls of Ireland and Wales equally feel the first impulse of nature, which, restrained in England by fear or delicacy, proves that society is there in a more advanced state. Besides, as the mind is cultivated, and

2. Because of the possibility of syphilis or other sexual disease.　　3. Erotic sensuality.

taste gains ground, the passions become stronger, and rest on something more stable than the casual sympathies of the moment. Health and idleness will always account for promiscuous amors; and in some degree I term every person idle, the exercise of whose mind does not bear some proportion to that of the body.

The Swedish ladies exercise neither sufficiently; of course, grow very fat at an early age; and when they have not this downy[4] appearance, a comfortable idea, you will say, in a cold climate, they are not remarkable for fine forms. They have, however, mostly fine complexions; but indolence makes the lily soon displace the rose. The quantity of coffee, spices, and other things of that kind, with want of care, almost universally spoil their teeth, which contrast but ill with their ruby lips.

The manners of Stockholm are refined, I hear, by the introduction of gallantry; but in the country, romping and coarse freedoms, with coarser allusions, keep the spirits awake. In the article of cleanliness, the women, of all descriptions, seem very deficient; and their dress shews that vanity is more inherent in women than taste.

The men appear to have paid still less court to the graces. They are a robust, healthy race, distinguished for their common sense and turn for humor, rather than for wit or sentiment. I include not, as you may suppose, in this general character, some of the nobility and officers, who having traveled, are polite and well informed.

I must own to you, that the lower class of people here amuse and interest me much more than the middling, with their apish good breeding and prejudices. The sympathy and frankness of heart conspicuous in the peasantry produces even a simple gracefulness of deportment, which has frequently struck me as very picturesque; I have often also been touched by their extreme desire to oblige me, when I could not explain my wants, and by their earnest manner of expressing that desire. There is such a charm in tenderness!—It is so delightful to love our fellow-creatures, and meet the honest affections as they break forth. Still, my good friend, I begin to think that I should not like to live continually in the country, with people whose minds have such a narrow range. My heart would frequently be interested; but my mind would languish for more companionable society.

The beauties of nature appear to me now even more alluring than in my youth, because my intercourse with the world has formed, without vitiating my taste. But, with respect to the inhabitants of the country, my fancy has probably, when disgusted with artificial manners, solaced itself by joining the advantages of cultivation with the interesting sincerity of innocence, forgetting the lassitude that ignorance will naturally produce. I like to see animals sporting, and sympathize in their pains and pleasures. Still I love sometimes to view the human face divine, and trace the soul, as well as the heart, in its varying lineaments.

A journey to the country, which I must shortly make, will enable me to extend my remarks.—Adieu!

---

4. Softly plump.

Letter 8

Tonsberg[5] was formerly the residence of one of the little sovereigns of Norway; and on an adjacent mountain the vestiges of a fort remain, which was battered down by the Swedes; the entrance of the bay lying close to it.

Here I have frequently strayed, sovereign of the waste, I seldom met any human creature; and sometimes, reclining on the mossy down, under the shelter of a rock, the prattling of the sea amongst the pebbles has lulled me to sleep—no fear of any rude satyr's approaching to interrupt my repose. Balmy were the slumbers, and soft the gales, that refreshed me, when I awoke to follow, with an eye vaguely curious, the white sails, as they turned the cliffs, or seemed to take shelter under the pines which covered the little islands that so gracefully rose to render the terrific ocean beautiful. The fishermen were calmly casting their nets; whilst the seagulls hovered over the unruffled deep. Every thing seemed to harmonize into tranquillity—even the mournful call of the bittern was in cadence with the tinkling bells on the necks of the cows, that, pacing slowly one after the other, along an inviting path in the vale below, were repairing to the cottages to be milked. With what ineffable pleasure have I not gazed—and gazed again, losing my breath through my eyes—my very soul diffused itself in the scene—and, seeming to become all senses, glided in the scarcely-agitated waves, melted in the freshening breeze, or, taking its flight with fairy wing, to the misty mountains which bounded the prospect, fancy tript over new lawns, more beautiful even than the lovely slopes on the winding shore before me.—I pause, again breathless, to trace, with renewed delight, sentiments which entranced me, when, turning my humid eyes from the expanse below to the vault above, my sight pierced the fleecy clouds that softened the azure brightness; and, imperceptibly recalling the reveries of childhood, I bowed before the awful throne of my Creator, whilst I rested on its footstool.

You have sometimes wondered, my dear friend, at the extreme affection of my nature—But such is the temperature of my soul—It is not the vivacity of youth, the hey-day of existence. For years have I endeavored to calm an impetuous tide—laboring to make my feelings take an orderly course.—It was striving against the stream.—I must love and admire with warmth, or I sink into sadness. Tokens of love which I have received have rapt me in elysium—purifying the heart they enchanted.—My bosom still glows.—Do not saucily ask, repeating Sterne's question, "Maria, is it still so warm?"[6] Sufficiently, O my God! has it been chilled by sorrow and unkindness—still nature will prevail—and if I blush at recollecting past enjoyment, it is the rosy hue of pleasure heightened by modesty; for the blush of modesty and shame are as distinct as the emotions by which they are produced.

I need scarcely inform you, after telling you of my walks, that my constitution has been renovated here; and that I have recovered my activity, even whilst attaining a little *embonpoint*.[7] My imprudence last winter, and some untoward accidents just at the time I was weaning my child, had reduced

5. Tönsberg, Norway.
6. In Laurence Sterne's novel *A Sentimental Journey* (1768), Parson Yorick, a man of acute sensibility, drenches his handkerchief with tears at hearing of young Maria's misfortunes. When Maria offers to wash the handkerchief in the stream, then dry it in her bosom, Yorick asks, "And is your heart still so warm, Maria?"
7. Plumpness (French).

me to a state of weakness which I never before experienced.[8] A slow fever preyed on me every night, during my residence in Sweden, and after I arrived at Tonsberg. By chance I found a fine rivulet filtered through the rocks, and confined in a bason for the cattle. It tasted to me like a chaly-beat;[9] at any rate it was pure; and the good effect of the various waters which invalids are sent to drink, depends, I believe, more on the air, exercise and change of scene, than on their medicinal qualities. I therefore determined to turn my morning walks towards it, and seek for health from the nymph of the fountain; partaking of the beverage offered to the tenants of the shade.

Chance likewise led me to discover a new pleasure, equally beneficial to my health. I wished to avail myself of my vicinity to the sea, and bathe; but it was not possible near the town; there was no convenience. The young woman whom I mentioned to you, proposed rowing me across the water, amongst the rocks; but as she was pregnant, I insisted on taking one of the oars, and learning to row. It was not difficult; and I do not know a pleasanter exercise. I soon became expert, and my train of thinking kept time, as it were, with the oars, or I suffered the boat to be carried along by the current, indulging a pleasing forgetfulness, or fallacious hopes.—How fallacious! yet, without hope, what is to sustain life, but the fear of annihilation—the only thing of which I have ever felt a dread—I cannot bear to think of being no more—of losing myself—though existence is often but a painful consciousness of misery; nay, it appears to me impossible that I should cease to exist, or that this active, restless spirit, equally alive to joy and sorrow, should only be organized dust—ready to fly abroad the moment the spring snaps, or the spark goes out, which kept it together. Surely something resides in this heart that is not perishable—and life is more than a dream.

Sometimes, to take up my oar, once more, when the sea was calm, I was amused by disturbing the innumerable young star fish which floated just below the surface: I had never observed them before; for they have not a hard shell, like those which I have seen on the seashore. They look like thickened water, with a white edge; and four purple circles, of different forms, were in the middle, over an incredible number of fibers, or white lines. Touching them, the cloudy substance would turn or close, first on one side, then on the other, very gracefully; but when I took one of them up in the ladle with which I heaved the water out of the boat, it appeared only a colorless jelly.

I did not see any of the seals, numbers of which followed our boat when we landed in Sweden; for though I like to sport in the water, I should have had no desire to join in their gambols.

Enough, you will say, of inanimate nature, and of brutes, to use the lordly phrase of man; let me hear something of the inhabitants.

The gentleman with whom I had business, is the mayor of Tonsberg; he speaks English intelligibly; and, having a sound understanding, I was sorry that his numerous occupations prevented my gaining as much information from him as I could have drawn forth, had we frequently conversed. The people of the town, as far as I had an opportunity of knowing their sentiments, are extremely well satisfied with his manner of discharging his office.

8. Wollstonecraft tells of these events in letters to Gilbert Imlay, January 1795, printed in *The Love Letters of Mary Wollstonecraft to Gilbert Imlay*, ed. Roger Ingpen (1908).
9. Mineral water containing salts of iron, taken as a tonic.

He has a degree of information and good sense which excites respect, whilst a cheerfulness, almost amounting to gaiety, enables him to reconcile differences, and keep his neighbors in good humor.—"I lost my horse," said a woman to me; "but ever since, when I want to send to the mill, or go out, the mayor lends me one.—He scolds if I do not come for it."

A criminal was branded, during my stay here, for the third offense; but the relief he received made him declare that the judge was one of the best men in the world.

I sent this wretch a trifle, at different times, to take with him into slavery. As it was more than he expected, he wished very much to see me; and this wish brought to my remembrance an anecdote I heard when I was in Lisbon.[1]

A wretch who had been imprisoned several years, during which period lamps had been put up, was at last condemned to a cruel death; yet, in his way to execution, he only wished for one night's respite, to see the city lighted.

Having dined in company at the mayor's, I was invited with his family to spend the day at one of the richest merchant's houses.—Though I could not speak Danish, I knew that I could see a great deal: yes; I am persuaded that I have formed a very just opinion of the character of the Norwegians, without being able to hold converse with them.

I had expected to meet some company; yet was a little disconcerted at being ushered into an apartment full of well-dressed people; and, glancing my eyes round, they rested on several very pretty faces. Rosy cheeks, sparkling eyes, and light brown or golden locks; for I never saw so much hair with a yellow cast; and, with their fine complexions, it looked very becoming.

These women seem a mixture of indolence and vivacity; they scarcely ever walk out, and were astonished that I should, for pleasure; yet they are immoderately fond of dancing. Unaffected in their manners, if they have no pretensions to elegance, simplicity often produces a gracefulness of deportment, when they are animated by a particular desire to please—which was the case at present. The solitariness of my situation, which they thought terrible, interested them very much in my favor. They gathered round me—sung to me—and one of the prettiest, to whom I gave my hand, with some degree of cordiality, to meet the glance of her eyes, kissed me very affectionately.

At dinner, which was conducted with great hospitality, though we remained at table too long, they sung several songs, and, amongst the rest, translations of some patriotic French ones.[2] As the evening advanced, they became playful, and we kept up a sort of conversation of gestures. As their minds were totally uncultivated, I did not lose much, perhaps gained, by not being able to understand them; for fancy probably filled up, more to their advantage, the void in the picture. Be that as it may, they excited my sympathy; and I was very much flattered when I was told, the next day, that they said it was a pleasure to look at me, I appeared so good-natured.

The men were generally captains of ships. Several spoke English very tolerably; but they were merely matter of fact men, confined to a very narrow circle of observation. I found it difficult to obtain from them any information

---

1. Wollstonecraft had gone to Lisbon in 1785, to nurse her dying friend Fanny Blood.

2. To indicate sympathy with the French Revolution.

respecting their own country, when the fumes of tobacco did not keep me at a distance.

I was invited to partake of some other feasts, and always had to complain of the quantity of provision, and the length of time taken to consume it; for it would not have been proper to have said devour, all went on so fair and softly. The servants wait as slowly as their mistresses carve.

The young women here, as well as in Sweden, have commonly bad teeth, which I attribute to the same causes. They are fond of finery, but do not pay the necessary attention to their persons, to render beauty less transient than a flower; and that interesting expression which sentiment and accomplishments give, seldom supplies its place.

The servants have likewise an inferior sort of food here; but their masters are not allowed to strike them with impunity. I might have added mistresses; for it was a complaint of this kind, brought before the mayor, which led me to a knowledge of the fact.

The wages are low, which is particularly unjust, because the price of clothes is much higher than provisions. A young woman, who is wet nurse to the mistress of the inn where I lodge, receives only twelve dollars[3] a year, and pays ten for the nursing of her own child; the father had run away to get clear of the expense. There was something in this most painful state of widowhood which excited my compassion, and led me to reflections on the instability of the most flattering plans of happiness, that were painful in the extreme, till I was ready to ask whether this world was not created to exhibit every possible combination of wretchedness. I asked these questions of a heart writhing with anguish, whilst I listened to a melancholy ditty sung by this poor girl. It was too early for thee to be abandoned, thought I, and I hastened out of the house, to take my solitary evening's walk—And here I am again, to talk of any thing, but the pangs arising from the discovery of estranged affection, and the lonely sadness of a deserted heart.

The father and mother, if the father can be ascertained, are obliged to maintain an illegitimate child at their joint expense; but, should the father disappear, go up the country or to sea, the mother must maintain it herself. However, accidents of this kind do not prevent their marrying; and then it is not unusual to take the child or children home; and they are brought up very amicably with the marriage progeny.

I took some pains to learn what books were written originally in their language; but for any certain information respecting the state of Danish literature, I must wait till I arrive at Copenhagen.

The sound of the language is soft, a great proportion of the words ending in vowels; and there is a simplicity in the turn of some of the phrases which have been translated to me, that pleased and interested me. In the country, the farmers use the *thou* and *thee*; and they do not acquire the polite plurals of the towns by meeting at market. The not having markets established in the large towns appears to me a great inconvenience. When the farmers have any thing to sell, they bring it to the neighboring town, and take it from house to house. I am surprised that the inhabitants do not feel how very incommodious this usage is to both parties, and redress it. They indeed perceive it; for when I have introduced the subject, they acknowledged that they were often in want of necessaries, there being no butchers, and they were

---

3. The local currency was the rixdollar, worth about one-fifth of a British pound sterling.

often obliged to buy what they did not want; yet it was the *custom*; and the changing of customs of a long standing requires more energy than they yet possess. I received a similar reply, when I attempted to persuade the women that they injured their children by keeping them too warm. The only way of parrying off my reasoning was, that they must do as other people did. In short, reason on any subject of change, and they stop you by saying that "the town would talk." A person of sense, with a large fortune, to insure respect, might be very useful here, by inducing them to treat their children, and manage their sick properly, and eat food dressed in a simpler manner: the example, for instance, of a count's lady.

Reflecting on these prejudices made me revert to the wisdom of those legislators who established institutions for the good of the body, under the pretext of serving heaven for the salvation of the soul. These might with strict propriety be termed pious frauds; and I admire the Peruvian pair[4] for asserting that they came from the sun, when their conduct proved that they meant to enlighten a benighted country, whose obedience, or even attention, could only be secured by awe.

Thus much for conquering the *inertia* of reason; but, when it is once in motion, fables, once held sacred, may be ridiculed; and sacred they were, when useful to mankind.—Prometheus alone stole fire to animate the first man; his posterity need not supernatural aid to preserve the species, though love is generally termed a flame; and it may not be necessary much longer to suppose men inspired by heaven to inculcate the duties which demand special grace, when reason convinces them that they are the happiest who are the most nobly employed.

In a few days I am to set out for the western part of Norway, and then shall return by land to Gothenburg. I cannot think of leaving this place without regret. I speak of the place before the inhabitants, though there is a tenderness in their artless kindness which attaches me to them; but it is an attachment that inspires a regret very different from that I felt at leaving Hull, in my way to Sweden. The domestic happiness, and good-humored gaiety, of the amiable family where I and my Frances were so hospitably received, would have been sufficient to insure the tenderest remembrance, without the recollection of the social evenings to stimulate it, when good-breeding gave dignity to sympathy, and wit, zest to reason.

Adieu!—I am just informed that my horse has been waiting this quarter of an hour. I now venture to ride out alone. The steeple serves as a landmark. I once or twice lost my way, walking alone, without being able to inquire after a path. I was therefore obliged to make to the steeple, or windmill, over hedge and ditch.

Your's truly.

Letter 19

Business having obliged me to go a few miles out of town this morning, I was surprised at meeting a crowd of people of every description; and inquiring the cause, of a servant who spoke French, I was informed that a man

---

4. Probably a reference to the Inca of Peru and his daughter Orazia in John Dryden and Robert Howard's drama *The Indian Queen* (1663). When the Aztec emperor Montezuma, as a reward for his military service, requests Orazia in marriage, the Inca, addressing him as "Thou glorious sun," says that Montezuma deserves to die for wanting to mix "such base blood" with his divine blood.

had been executed two hours before, and the body afterwards burnt. I could not help looking with horror around—the fields lost their verdure—and I turned with disgust from the well-dressed women, who were returning with their children from this sight. What a spectacle for humanity! The seeing such a flock of idle gazers, plunged me into a train of reflections, on the pernicious effects produced by false notions of justice. And I am persuaded that till capital punishments be entirely abolished, executions ought to have every appearance of horror given to them; instead of being, as they are now, a scene of amusement for the gaping crowd, where sympathy is quickly effaced by curiosity.

I have always been of opinion that the allowing actors to die, in the presence of the audience, has an immoral tendency; but trifling when compared with the ferocity acquired by viewing the reality as a show; for it seems to me, that in all countries the common people go to executions to see how the poor wretch plays his part, rather than to commiserate his fate, much less to think of the breach of morality which has brought him to such a deplorable end. Consequently executions, far from being useful examples to the survivors, have, I am persuaded, a quite contrary effect, by hardening the heart they ought to terrify. Besides, the fear of an ignominious death, I believe, never deterred any one from the commission of a crime; because, in committing it, the mind is roused to activity about present circumstances. It is a game at hazard,[5] at which all expect the turn of the die in their own favor; never reflecting on the chance of ruin, till it comes. In fact, from what I saw, in the fortresses of Norway, I am more and more convinced that the same energy of character, which renders a man a daring villain, would have rendered him useful to society, had that society been well organized. When a strong mind is not disciplined by cultivation, it is a sense of injustice that renders it unjust.

Executions, however, occur very rarely at Copenhagen; for timidity, rather than clemency, palsies all the operations of the present government. The malefactor, who died this morning, would not, probably, have been punished with death at any other period; but an incendiary excites universal execration; and as the greater part of the inhabitants are still distressed by the late conflagration,[6] an example was thought absolutely necessary; though, from what I can gather, the fire was accidental.

Not, but that I have very seriously been informed, that combustible materials were placed at proper distances, by the emissaries of Mr. Pitt;[7] and, to corroborate the fact, many people insist, that the flames burst out at once in different parts of the city; not allowing the wind to have any hand in it. So much for the plot. But the fabricators of plots in all countries build their conjectures on the "baseless fabric of a vision";[8] and, it seems even a sort of poetical justice, that whilst this minister is crushing at home, plots of his own conjuring up,[9] that on the continent, and in the north, he should, with as little foundation, be accused of wishing to set the world on fire.

I forgot to mention, to you, that I was informed, by a man of veracity, that two persons came to the stake to drink a glass of the criminal's blood, as an

5. A game played with dice, similar to craps.
6. Earlier in that year (1795) a great fire in Copenhagen had destroyed nearly a thousand houses and public buildings. "Incendiary": arsonist.
7. William Pitt, then prime minister of England.
8. Prospero in Shakespeare's *The Tempest*

4.1.151–54: "And like the baseless fabric of this vision, . . . shall dissolve."
9. Pitt was prosecuting what he claimed to be Jacobin plots against Great Britain, at a time of war with revolutionary France.

infallible remedy for the apoplexy. And when I animadverted in the company, where it was mentioned, on such a horrible violation of nature, a Danish lady reproved me very severely, asking how I knew that it was not a cure for the disease? adding, that every attempt was justifiable in search of health. I did not, you may imagine, enter into an argument with a person the slave of such a gross prejudice. And I allude to it not only as a trait of the ignorance of the people, but to censure the government, for not preventing scenes that throw an odium on the human race.

Empiricism[1] is not peculiar to Denmark; and I know no way of rooting it out, though it be a remnant of exploded witchcraft, till the acquiring a general knowledge of the component parts of the human frame, become a part of public education.

Since the fire, the inhabitants have been very assiduously employed in searching for property secreted during the confusion; and it is astonishing how many people, formerly termed reputable, had availed themselves of the common calamity to purloin what the flames spared. Others, expert at making a distinction without a difference, concealed what they found, not troubling themselves to enquire for the owners, though they scrupled to search for plunder any where, but amongst the ruins.

To be honester than the laws require, is by most people thought a work of supererogation;[2] and to slip through the grate of the law, has ever exercised the abilities of adventurers, who wish to get rich the shortest way. Knavery, without personal danger, is an art, brought to great perfection by the statesman and swindler; and meaner knaves are not tardy in following their footsteps.

It moves my gall to discover some of the commercial frauds practiced during the present war. In short, under whatever point of view I consider society, it appears, to me, that an adoration of property is the root of all evil. Here it does not render the people enterprising, as in America, but thrifty and cautious. I never, therefore, was in a capital where there was so little appearance of active industry; and as for gaiety, I looked in vain for the sprightly gait of the Norwegians, who in every respect appear to me to have got the start of them. This difference I attribute to their having more liberty: a liberty which they think their right by inheritance, whilst the Danes, when they boast of their negative happiness, always mention it as the boon of the prince royal, under the superintending wisdom of count Bernstorff. Vassallage[3] is nevertheless ceasing throughout the kingdom, and with it will pass away that sordid avarice which every modification of slavery is calculated to produce.

If the chief use of property be power, in the shape of the respect it procures, is it not among the inconsistencies of human nature most incomprehensible, that men should find a pleasure in hoarding up property which they steal from their necessities, even when they are convinced that it would be dangerous to display such an enviable superiority? Is not this the situation of serfs[4] in every country; yet a rapacity to accumulate money seems to become stronger in proportion as it is allowed to be useless.

Wealth does not appear to be sought for, amongst the Danes, to obtain

1. In the old sense: medical practices without a scientific basis.
2. More than is required.
3. Social system that holds servitors in legal bondage to their masters. Andreas Peter Bernstorff was an able administrator in the Danish foreign service.
4. Servitors who are owned by their masters.

the elegant luxuries of life; for a want of taste is very conspicuous at Copenhagen; so much so, that I am not surprised to hear that poor Matilda[5] offended the rigid Lutherans, by aiming to refine their pleasures. The elegance which she wished to introduce, was termed lasciviousness: yet I do not find that the absence of gallantry renders the wives more chaste, or the husbands more constant. Love here seems to corrupt the morals, without polishing the manners, by banishing confidence and truth, the charm as well as cement of domestic life. A gentleman, who has resided in this city some time, assures me that he could not find language to give me an idea of the gross debaucheries into which the lower order of people fall; and the promiscuous amors of the men of the middling class with their female servants, debases both beyond measure, weakening every species of family affection.

I have every where been struck by one characteristic difference in the conduct of the two sexes; women, in general, are seduced by their superiors, and men jilted by their inferiors; rank and manners awe the one, and cunning and wantonness subjugate the other; ambition creeping into the woman's passion, and tyranny giving force to the man's; for most men treat their mistresses as kings do their favorites: *ergo* is not man then the tyrant of the creation?

Still harping on the same subject, you will exclaim—How can I avoid it, when most of the struggles of an eventful life have been occasioned by the oppressed state of my sex:[6] we reason deeply, when we forcibly feel.

But to return to the straight road of observation. The sensuality so prevalent appears to me to arise rather from indolence of mind, and dull senses, than from an exuberance of life, which often fructifies the whole character when the vivacity of youthful spirits begins to subside into strength of mind.

I have before mentioned that the men are domestic tyrants, considering them as fathers, brothers, or husband; but there is a kind of interregnum between the reign of the father and husband, which is the only period of freedom and pleasure that the women enjoy. Young people, who are attached to each other, with the consent of their friends, exchange rings, and are permitted to enjoy a degree of liberty together, which I have never noticed in any other country. The days of courtship are therefore prolonged, till it be perfectly convenient to marry: the intimacy often becomes very tender: and if the lover obtain the privilege of a husband, it can only be termed half by stealth, because the family is wilfully blind. It happens very rarely that these honorary engagements are dissolved or disregarded, a stigma being attached to a breach of faith, which is thought more disgraceful, if not so criminal, as the violation of the marriage vow.

Do not forget that, in my general observations, I do not pretend to sketch a national character; but merely to note the present state of morals and manners, as I trace the progress of the world's improvement. Because, during my residence in different countries, my principal object has been to take such a dispassionate view of men as will lead me to form a just idea of the nature of man. And, to deal ingenuously with you, I believe I should have

5. Caroline Matilda, sister of the Hanoverian George III of Great Britain, was the young wife of Christian VII of Denmark. By the plotting of Crown Prince Frederick, who had become regent in 1784 when his father was judged mentally unfit to rule, she had been ordered imprisoned, but was rescued by an English ship and taken to Hanover, Germany, where she died in 1775 at the age of twenty-four.

6. Wollstonecraft had published A *Vindication of the Rights of Woman* three years earlier, in 1792.

been less severe in the remarks I have made on the vanity and depravity of the French,[7] had I travelled towards the north before I visited France.

The interesting picture frequently drawn of the virtues of a rising people has, I fear, been fallacious, excepting the accounts of the enthusiasm which various public struggles have produced. We talk of the depravity of the French, and lay a stress on the old age of the nation; yet where has more virtuous enthusiasm been displayed than during the two last years, by the common people of France and in their armies? I am obliged sometimes to recollect the numberless instances which I have either witnessed, or heard well authenticated, to balance the account of horrors, alas! but too true. I am, therefore, inclined to believe that the gross vices which I have always seen allied with simplicity of manners, are the concomitants of ignorance.

What, for example, has piety, under the heathen or christian system, been, but a blind faith in things contrary to the principles of reason? And could poor reason make considerable advances, when it was reckoned the highest degree of virtue to do violence to its dictates? Lutherans preaching reformation, have built a reputation for sanctity on the same foundation as the catholics; yet I do not perceive that a regular attendance on public worship, and their other observances, make them a whit more true in their affections, or honest in their private transactions. It seems, indeed, quite as easy to prevaricate[8] with religious injunctions as human laws, when the exercise of their reason does not lead people to acquire principles for themselves to be the criterion of all those they receive from others.

If travelling, as the completion of a liberal education, were to be adopted on rational grounds, the northern states ought to be visited before the more polished parts of Europe, to serve as the elements even of the knowledge of manners, only to be acquired by tracing the various shades in different countries. But, when visiting distant climes, a momentary social sympathy should not be allowed to influence the conclusions of the understanding; for hospitality too frequently leads travellers, especially those who travel in search of pleasure, to make a false estimate of the virtues of a nation; which, I am now convinced, bear an exact proportion to their scientific improvements.

Adieu.

1795   1796

7. See *Historical and Moral View of the French Revolution* [Wollstonecraft's note; she had published the book in 1794].
8. Evade or distort.

JOANNA BAILLIE
1762–1851

Joanna Baillie, who was born in Lanarkshire, Scotland, but lived in London and Hampstead from her early twenties until her death at the age of eighty-eight, is known primarily as a dramatist. Her first volume of *A Series of Plays: in Which It Is Attempted to Delineate the Stronger Passions of the Mind: Each Passion Being the Subject of a Tragedy and a Comedy*—now generally referred to as *Plays on the Passions*—appeared anonymously in 1798. It was an instant literary sensation, attracting as much speculation about its authorship as there was sixteen years later concerning Walter Scott's anonymous publication of *Waverley*. Two other volumes in the series followed in 1802 and 1812, winning acclaim for her as Britain's most distinguished woman playwright of the time—in some evaluations, the most distinguished regardless of gender. For Scott, she was "the best dramatic writer whom Britain has produced since the days of Shakespeare and Massinger"; Byron called her "our only dramatist since Otway and Southerne." She wrote and published, all told, twenty-eight plays—mostly as closet dramas (plays to be read rather than performed) but a number also for the stage—and exerted considerable sway on the serious drama of the first half of the nineteenth century.

Her preface to the original *Series of Plays*, a seventy-page "introductory discourse" advocating naturalness of language and subject matter, influenced both the Advertisement to Wordsworth and Coleridge's *Lyrical Ballads*, which appeared six months later, and Wordsworth's longer and more famous Preface two years later. "Those works," she wrote, "which most strongly characterize human nature in the middling and lower classes of society, where it is to be discovered by stronger and more unequivocal marks, will ever be the most popular"; the writer should forsake "the enchanted regions of simile, metaphor, allegory, and description" in favor of "the plain order of things in this every-day world." Baillie's prolonged focus on both the writer's and the reader's "sympathetick curiosity" in the essay probably also influenced William Hazlitt's concept of the sympathetic imagination and, through Hazlitt, Keats's notion of the self-effacing empathic "poetical Character."

Baillie's theories were better than her practice as a dramatist, and the modern reader is more likely to agree not with Scott and Byron but with Hazlitt's estimate of her plays: "With her the passions are, like the French republic, one and indivisible: they are not so in nature, or in Shakspeare." But Baillie's ideas about language and subject originated first of all in her poetry, with a volume of 1790 titled *Poems: Wherein It Is Attempted to Describe Certain Views of Nature and of Rustic Manners*, and she continues to be of interest as a poet today. The modern reader, admiring the homely but graceful blank verse of her *A Winter's Day*, can make connections with *The Prelude* (as in the descriptions of bird snaring, ice-skating, and the old discharged soldier), *The Excursion* (the character of the Wanderer), and *Michael* (Michael's thrift, Isabel's industrious spinning wheel)—works that were written a decade or more after Baillie's poem. Baillie also excelled as a songwriter both in standard English (as in *Up! quit thy bower*) and, like her contemporary Robert Burns, in the Scottish dialect (as in *Woo'd and married*).

A Winter's Day

The cock, warm roosting 'mid his feather'd mates,
Now lifts his beak and snuffs the morning air,
Stretches his neck and claps his heavy wings,
Gives three hoarse crows and, glad his task is done,
5   Low chuckling turns himself upon the roost,
Then nestles down again into his place.
The laboring hind,[1] who on his bed of straw
Beneath his home-made coverings, coarse but warm,

1. Hind does not perfectly express the condition of the person here intended, who is somewhat above a common laborer,—the tenant of a very small farm, which he cultivates with his own hands; a few cows, perhaps a horse, and some six or seven sheep being all the wealth he possessed. A class of men very common in the west of Scotland, ere political economy was thought of [Baillie's note].

Lock'd in the kindly arms of her who spun them,
10 Dreams of the gain that next year's crop should bring;
Or at some fair, disposing of his wool,
Or by some lucky and unlook'd-for bargain,
Fills his skin purse with store of tempting gold;
Now wakes from sleep at the unwelcome call,
15 And finds himself but just the same poor man
As when he went to rest.
He hears the blast against his window beat,
And wishes to himself he were a laird,°   landowner, lord
That he might lie a-bed. It may not be:
20 He rubs his eyes and stretches out his arms;
Heigh oh! heigh oh! he drawls with gaping mouth,
Then most unwillingly creeps from his lair,
And without looking-glass puts on his clothes.

With rueful face he blows the smother'd fire,
25 And lights his candle at the reddening coal;
First sees that all be right among his cattle,
Then hies him to the barn with heavy tread,
Printing his footsteps on the new-fall'n snow.
From out the heap'd-up mow he draws his sheaves,
30 Dislodging the poor red-breast from his shelter
Where all the live-long night he slept secure;
But now, affrighted, with uncertain flight,
Flutters round walls and roof to find some hole
Through which he may escape.
35 Then whirling o'er his head, the heavy flail
Descends with force upon the jumping sheaves,
While every rugged wall and neighboring cot°   cottage
The noise re-echoes of his sturdy strokes.

The family cares call next upon the wife
40 To quit her mean but comfortable bed.
And first she stirs the fire and fans the flame,
Then from her heap of sticks for winter stored
An armful brings; loud crackling as they burn,
Thick fly the red sparks upward to the roof,
45 While slowly mounts the smoke in wreathy clouds.
On goes the seething pot with morning cheer,
For which some little wistful folk await,
Who, peeping from the bed-clothes, spy well pleased
The cheery light that blazes on the wall,
50 And bawl for leave to rise.
Their busy mother knows not where to turn,
Her morning's work comes now so thick upon her.
One she must help to tie his little coat,
Unpin another's cap, or seek his shoe
55 Or hosen° lost, confusion soon o'er-master'd!   breeches
When all is o'er, out to the door they run
With new-comb'd sleeky hair and glistening faces,
Each with some little project in his head.

His new-soled shoes one on the ice must try;
60 To view his well-set trap another hies,
In hopes to find some poor unwary bird
(No worthless prize) entangled in his snare;
While one, less active, with round rosy cheeks,
Spreads out his purple fingers to the fire,
65 And peeps most wistfully into the pot.

But let us leave the warm and cheerful house
To view the bleak and dreary scene without,
And mark the dawning of a Winter day.
The morning vapor rests upon the heights,
70 Lurid and red, while growing gradual shades
Of pale and sickly light spread o'er the sky.
Then slowly from behind the southern hills
Enlarged and ruddy comes the rising sun,
Shooting athwart the hoary waste his beams
75 That gild the brow of every ridgy bank,
And deepen every valley with a shade.
The crusted window of each scatter'd cot,
The icicles that fringe the thatched roof,
The new-swept slide upon the frozen pool,
80 All keenly glance, new kindled with his rays;
And e'en the rugged face of scowling Winter
Looks somewhat gay. But only for a time
He shows his glory to the brightening earth,
Then hides his face behind a sullen cloud.

85 The birds now quit their holes and lurking sheds,
Most mute and melancholy, where through night,
All nestling close to keep each other warm,
In downy sleep they had forgot their hardships;
But not to chant and carol in the air,
90 Or lightly swing upon some waving bough,
And merrily return each other's notes;
No, silently they hop from bush to bush,
Can find no seeds to stop their craving want,
Then bend their flight to the low smoking cot,
95 Chirp on the roof, or at the window peck,
To tell their wants to those who lodge within.
The poor lank hare flies homeward to his den,
But little burthen'd with his nightly meal
Of wither'd coleworts² from the farmer's garden,
100 A wretched scanty portion, snatch'd in fear;
And fearful creatures, forced abroad by hunger,
Are now to every enemy a prey.

The husbandman lays by his heavy flail,
And to the house returns, where for him wait
105 His smoking breakfast and impatient children,

2. Kale or another cabbagelike vegetable.

Who, spoon in hand, and ready to begin,
Toward the door cast many an eager look
To see their dad come in.
Then round they sit, a cheerful company;
110 All quickly set to work, and with heap'd spoons
From ear to ear besmear their rosy cheeks.
The faithful dog stands by his master's side
Wagging his tail and looking in his face;
While humble puss pays court to all around,
115 And purrs and rubs them with her furry sides;
Nor goes this little flattery unrewarded.
But the laborious sit not long at table;
The grateful father lifts his eyes to heaven
To bless his God, whose ever bounteous hand
120 Him and his little ones doth daily feed,
Then rises satisfied to work again.

The varied rousing sounds of industry
Are heard through all the village.
The humming wheel, the thrifty housewife's tongue,
125 Who scolds to keep her maidens to their work,
The wool-card's grating, most unmusical!
Issue from every house.
But hark! the sportsman from the neighboring hedge
His thunder sends! loud bark the village curs;
130 Up from her cards or wheel the maiden starts
And hastens to the door; the housewife chides,
Yet runs herself to look, in spite of thrift,
And all the little town is in a stir.

Strutting before, the cock leads forth his train,
135 And, chuckling near the barn-door 'mid the straw,
Reminds the farmer of his morning's service.
His grateful master throws a liberal handful;
They flock about it, while the hungry sparrows,
Perch'd on the roof, look down with envious eye,
140 Then, aiming well, amidst the feeders light,
And seize upon the feast with greedy bill,
Till angry partlets° peck them off the field.   *hens*
But at a distance, on the leafless tree,
All woe-begone, the lonely blackbird sits;
145 The cold north wind ruffles his glossy feathers;
Full oft he looks, but dares not make approach,
Then turns his yellow beak to peck his side
And claps his wings close to his sharpen'd breast.
The wandering fowler from behind the hedge,
150 Fastens his eye upon him, points his gun,
And firing wantonly, as at a mark,
Of life bereaves him in the cheerful spot
That oft hath echo'd to his summer's song.

The mid-day hour is near; the pent-up kine cows
155 Are driven from their stalls to take the air.

How stupidly they stare! and feel how strange!
They open wide their smoking mouths to low,
But scarcely can their feeble sound be heard,
Then turn and lick themselves and, step by step,
160 Move, dull and heavy, to their stalls again.

In scatter'd groups the little idle boys,
With purple fingers molding in the snow
Their icy ammunition, pant for war;
And drawing up in opposite array,
165 Send forth a mighty shower of well-aim'd balls.
Each tiny hero tries his growing strength,
And burns to beat the foe-men off the field.
Or on the well-worn ice in eager throngs,
After short race, shoot rapidly along,
170 Trip up each other's heels, and on the surface
With studded shoes draw many a chalky line.
Untired and glowing with the healthful sport
They cease not till the sun hath run his course,
And threatening clouds, slow rising from the north,
175 Spread leaden darkness o'er the face of heaven;
Then by degrees they scatter to their homes,
Some with a broken head or bloody nose,
To claim their mother's pity, who, most skillful!
Cures all their troubles with a bit of bread.

180 The night comes on apace—
Chill blows the blast and drives the snow in wreaths;
Now every creature looks around for shelter,
And whether man or beast, all move alike
Towards their homes, and happy they who have
185 A house to screen them from the piercing cold!
Lo, o'er the frost a reverend form advances!
His hair white as the snow on which he treads,
His forehead mark'd with many a care-worn furrow,
Whose feeble body bending o'er a staff,
190 Shows still that once it was the seat of strength,
Though now it shakes like some old ruin'd tower.
Clothed indeed, but not disgraced with rags,
He still maintains that decent dignity
Which well becomes those who have served their country.
195 With tottering steps he gains the cottage door;
The wife within, who hears his hollow cough,
And pattering of his stick upon the threshold,
Sends out her little boy to see who's there.
The child looks up to mark the stranger's face,
200 And, seeing it enlighten'd with a smile,
Holds out his tiny hand to lead him in.
Round from her work the mother turns her head,
And views them, not ill pleased.
The stranger whines not with a piteous tale,

205 But only asks a little to relieve
      A poor old soldier's wants.
      The gentle matron brings the ready chair
      And bids him sit to rest his weary limbs,
      And warm himself before her blazing fire.
210 The children, full of curiosity,
      Flock round, and with their fingers in their mouths
      Stand staring at him, while the stranger, pleased,
      Takes up the youngest urchin on his knee.
      Proud of its seat, it wags its little feet,
215 And prates and laughs and plays with his white locks.
      But soon a change comes o'er the soldier's face;
      His thoughtful mind is turn'd on other days,
      When his own boys were wont to play around him,
      Who now lie distant from their native land
220 In honorable but untimely graves:
      He feels how helpless and forlorn he is,
      And big round tears course down his wither'd cheeks.
      His toilsome daily labor at an end,
      In comes the wearied master of the house,
225 And marks with satisfaction his old guest,
      In the chief seat, with all the children round him.
      His honest heart is fill'd with manly kindness,
      He bids him stay and share their homely meal,
      And take with them his quarters for the night.
230 The aged wanderer thankfully accepts,
      And by the simple hospitable board,
      Forgets the by-past hardships of the day.

      When all are satisfied, about the fire
      They draw their seats and form a cheerful ring.
235 The thrifty housewife turns her spinning-wheel;
      The husband, useful even in his hour
      Of ease and rest, a stocking knits, belike,
      Or plaits stored rushes, which with after skill
      Into a basket form'd may do good service,
240 With eggs or butter fill'd at fair or market.

      Some idle neighbors now come dropping in,
      Draw round their chairs and widen out the circle;
      And every one in his own native way
      Does what he can to cheer the social group.
245 Each tells some little story of himself,
      That constant subject upon which mankind,
      Whether in court or country, love to dwell.
      How at a fair he saved a simple clown°   peasant, rustic
      From being trick'd in buying of a cow;
250 Or laid a bet on his own horse's head
      Against his neighbor's bought at twice his cost,
      Which fail'd not to repay his better skill;
      Or on a harvest day bound in an hour

More sheaves of corn than any of his fellows,
255 Though e'er so stark,° could do in twice the time;   *strong, powerful*
Or won the bridal race with savory broose[3]
And first kiss of the bonny bride, though all
The fleetest youngsters of the parish strove
In rivalry against him.
260 But chiefly the good man, by his own fire,
Hath privilege of being listen'd to,
Nor dares a little prattling tongue presume,
Though but in play, to break upon his story.
The children sit and listen with the rest;
265 And should the youngest raise its lisping voice,
The careful mother, ever on the watch,
And ever pleased with what her husband says,
Gives it a gentle tap upon the fingers,
Or stops its ill-timed prattle with a kiss.
270 The soldier next, but not unask'd, begins
His tale of war and blood. They gaze upon him,
And almost weep to see the man so poor,
So bent and feeble, helpless and forlorn,
Who has undaunted stood the battle's brunt
275 While roaring cannons shook the quaking earth,
And bullets hiss'd round his defenseless head.
Thus passes quickly on the evening hour,
Till sober folks must needs retire to rest;
Then all break up, and, by their several paths,
280 Hie homeward, with the evening pastime cheer'd
Far more, belike, than those who issue forth
From city theatre's gay scenic show,
Or crowded ball-room's splendid moving maze.
But where the song and story, joke and gibe,
285 So lately circled, what a solemn change
In little time takes place!
The sound of psalms, by mingled voices raised
Of young and old, upon the night air borne,
Haply to some benighted traveler,
290 Or the late parted neighbors on their way,
A pleasing notice gives, that those whose sires
In former days on the bare mountain's side,
In deserts, heaths, and caverns, praise and prayer,
At peril of their lives, in their own form
295 Of covenanted worship offered up,
In peace and safety in their own quiet home
Are—(as in quaint and modest phrase is termed)
Engaged now in *evening exercise*.[4]

---

3. A race, from the bride's former home to the bridegroom's house, run by the young men attending a country wedding.
4. In the first edition of the *Winter Day*, nothing regarding family worship was mentioned: a great omission, for which I justly take shame to myself.

"The Evening exercise," as it was called, prevailed in every house over the simple country parts of the West of Scotland, and I have often heard the sound of it passing through the twilight air, in returning from a late walk [Baillie's note]. Lines 281–98 are a later addition to the poem.

But long accustom'd to observe the weather,
300 The farmer cannot lay him down in peace
Till he has look'd to mark what bodes the night.
He lifts the latch, and moves the heavy door,
Sees wreaths of snow heap'd up on every side,
And black and dismal all above his head.
305 Anon the northern blast begins to rise;
He hears its hollow growling from afar,
Which, gathering strength, rolls on with doubled might,
And raves and bellows o'er his head. The trees
Like pithless saplings bend. He shuts his door,
310 And, thankful for the roof that covers him,
Hies him to bed.

1790

Up! quit thy bower[1]

Up! quit thy bower, late wears the hour;
Long have the rooks caw'd round thy tower;
On flower and tree, loud hums the bee;
The wilding kid[2] sports merrily:
5 A day so bright, so fresh, so clear,
Shineth when good fortune's near.

Up! lady fair, and braid thy hair,
And rouse thee in the breezy air;
The lulling stream, that sooth'd thy dream,
10 Is dancing in the sunny beam:
And hours so sweet, so bright, so gay,
Will waft good fortune on its way.

Up! time will tell; the friar's bell
Its service sound hath chimed well;
15 The aged crone keeps house alone,
And reapers to the fields are gone:
The active day, so boon and bright,
May bring good fortune ere the night.

1812

Song: Woo'd and married and a'

The bride she is winsome and bonny,
    Her hair it is snooded[1] sae sleek,
And faithfu' and kind is her Johnny,
    Yet fast fa' the tears on her cheek.
5 New pearlins° are cause of her sorrow,   *lace trimmings*

---

1. This song opens act 1 of Baillie's *The Beacon:*
A Serious Musical Drama in Two Acts (1812).

2. Wild young goat.
1. Bound up with a ribbon.

New pearlins and plenishing° too,   *furnishings*
The bride that has a' to borrow,
Has e'en right mickle ado,
    Woo'd and married and a'!
10   Woo'd and married and a'!
Is na' she very weel aff
    To be woo'd and married at a'?

Her mither then hastily spak,
    "The lassie is glaikit° wi' pride;   *foolish*
15 In my pouch I had never a plack°   *farthing*
    On the day when I was a bride.
E'en tak' to your wheel, and be clever,
    And draw out your thread in the sun;
The gear° that is gifted,° it never   *goods, wealth / given*
20   Will last like the gear that is won.°   *earned*
    Woo'd and married and a'!
    Wi' havins° and toucher° sae sma',   *possessions / dowry*
I think ye are very weel aff,
    To be woo'd and married at a'!"

25 "Toot, toot!" quo' her gray-headed faither,
    "She's less o' a bride than a bairn;°   *child*
She's ta'en like a cout° frae the heather,   *colt*
    Wi' sense and discretion to learn.
Half husband, I trow, and half daddy,
30   As humor inconstantly leans,
The chiel° maun° be patient and steady,   *man / must*
    That yokes wi' a mate in her teens.
    A kerchief sae douce° and sae neat,   *sedate, respectable*
    O'er her locks that the winds used to blaw!
35 I'm baith like to laugh and to greet,°   *weep*
    When I think o' her married at a'!"

Then out spak' the wily bridegroom;
    Weel waled° were his wordies, I ween—   *chosen*
"I'm rich, though my coffer be toom,°   *empty*
40   Wi' the blinks o' your bonny blue een.°   *eyes*
I'm prouder o' thee by my side,
    Though thy ruffles or ribbons be few,
Than if Kate o' the Croft were my bride,
    Wi' purfles² and pearlins enow.
45   Dear and dearest of ony!
    Ye're woo'd and buikit³ and a'!"
And do ye think scorn o' your Johnny,
    And grieve to be married at a'?"

She turn'd, and she blush'd, and she smiled,
50   And she looket sae bashfully down;

2. Embroidered trimmings.
3. Booked, i.e., entered as betrothed in the official registry of the session clerk.

The pride o' her heart was beguiled,
  And she played wi' the sleeves o' her gown;
She twirled the tag o' her lace,
  And she nippet her boddice sae blue,
55 Syne° blinket sae sweet in his face,   *then*
  And aff like a maukin° she flew.   *hare*
      Woo'd and married and a'!
        Wi' Johnny to roose° her and a'!   *praise*
      She thinks hersel very weel aff,
60   To be woo'd and married at a'!

1822

WILLIAM WORDSWORTH
1770–1850

William Wordsworth was born in Cockermouth in West Cumberland, just on the northern fringe of the English Lake District. When his mother died, the eight-year-old boy was sent to school at Hawkshead, near Esthwaite Lake, in the heart of that thinly settled region that he and Coleridge were to transform into one of the poetic centers of England. William and his three brothers boarded in the cottage of Ann Tyson, who gave the boys simple comfort, ample affection, and freedom to roam the countryside at will. A vigorous, unruly, and sometimes moody boy, William spent his free days and occasionally "half the night" in the sports and rambles described in the first two books of *The Prelude*, "drinking in" (to use one of his favorite metaphors) the natural sights and sounds, and getting to know the cottagers, shepherds, and solitary wanderers who moved through his imagination into his later poetry. He also found time to read voraciously in the books owned by his young headmaster, William Taylor, who encouraged him in his inclination to poetry.

John Wordsworth, the poet's father, died suddenly when William was thirteen, leaving to his five children mainly the substantial sum owed him by Lord Lonsdale, whom he had served as attorney and as steward of the huge Lonsdale estate. That harsh and litigious nobleman managed to keep from paying the debt until he died in 1802. Wordsworth was nevertheless able to enter St. John's College, Cambridge, in 1787, where he found little in the limited curriculum of that time to appeal to him. He took his degree in 1791 without distinction.

During the summer vacation of his third year at Cambridge (1790), Wordsworth and his closest college friend, the Welshman Robert Jones, journeyed on foot through France and the Alps (described in *The Prelude* 6) at the time when the French were joyously celebrating the first anniversary of the fall of the Bastille. Upon completing his course at Cambridge, Wordsworth spent four months in London, set off on another walking tour with Robert Jones through Wales (the time of the memorable ascent of Mount Snowdon in *The Prelude* 14), and then went back alone to France to master the language and qualify as a traveling tutor.

During his year in France (November 1791 to December 1792) Wordsworth became a fervent "democrat" and proselyte of the French Revolution—which seemed to him, as to many other generous spirits, to promise a "glorious renovation"—and he fell in love with Annette Vallon, the impetuous and warm-hearted daughter of a French surgeon at Blois. It is clear that the two planned to marry, despite their differences in religion and political inclinations (Annette belonged to an old Catholic family whose sympathies were Royalist). But almost immediately after a daughter, Caroline, was born, lack of funds forced Wordsworth to return to England. The outbreak of war between England and France made it impossible for him to rejoin Annette until they had drifted so far apart in sympathies that a permanent union no longer seemed desirable. Wordsworth's agonies of guilt, his divided loyalties between England and France, his gradual disillusion with the course of the Revolution in France—according to his account in *The Prelude* 10 and 11—brought him to the verge of an emotional breakdown, when "sick, wearied out with contrarieties," he "yielded up moral questions in despair." His suffering, his near-collapse, and the successful effort, after his break with his past, to reestablish "a saving intercourse with my true self," are the experiences that underlie many of his greatest poems.

At this critical point a young friend, Raisley Calvert, died and left Wordsworth a sum of money just sufficient to enable him to live by his poetry. He settled in a rent-free house at Racedown, Dorsetshire, with his beloved sister, Dorothy, who now began her long career as confidante, inspirer, and secretary. At that same time Wordsworth met Samuel Taylor Coleridge; two years later he moved to Alfoxden House, Somersetshire, to be near Coleridge, who lived four miles away at Nether Stowey. Here he entered at the age of twenty-seven on the delayed springtime of his poetic career.

Even while he had been an undergraduate at Cambridge, Coleridge claimed that he had detected signs of genius in Wordsworth's rather conventional poem about his tour in the Alps, *Descriptive Sketches*, published in 1793. Now he hailed Wordsworth unreservedly as "the best poet of the age." The two men met almost daily, talked for hours about poetry, and composed prolifically. So close was their association that we find the same phrases occurring in poems by Wordsworth and Coleridge, as well as in the remarkable journals that Dorothy kept at the time; the two poets collaborated in some writings and freely traded thoughts and passages for others; and Coleridge even undertook to complete a few poems that Wordsworth had left unfinished.

The result of their joint efforts was a small volume, published anonymously in 1798, *Lyrical Ballads, with a Few Other Poems*. It opened with Coleridge's *Ancient Mariner*; included three other poems by Coleridge, a number of Wordsworth's verse anecdotes and psychological studies of humble people, and some lyrics in which Wordsworth celebrated impulses from a vernal wood; and closed with Wordsworth's great descriptive and meditative poem in blank verse (not a "lyrical ballad," but one of the "other poems" of the title), *Tintern Abbey*. In this last poem, Wordsworth inaugurated what some critics call his "myth of nature"; that is, his presentation of the "growth" of his mind to maturity, and the development of his emotional and moral life, as an interaction between his mind and the outer world. The volume of *Lyrical Ballads* clearly announces a new literary departure. William Hazlitt said that when he heard Coleridge read some of these newly written poems aloud, "the sense of a new style and a new spirit in poetry came over me," with something of the effect "that arises from the turning up of the fresh soil, or of the first welcome breath of spring." The professional reviewers were less enthusiastic. Nevertheless *Lyrical Ballads* sold out in two years, and Wordsworth published under his own name a new edition, dated 1800, to which he added a second volume of poems, many of them written in homesickness during a long, cold, and friendless winter that he and Dorothy had spent in Goslar, Germany, 1798–99. In his famous Preface to this edition, planned, like so many of the poems, in close consultation with Coleridge, Wordsworth enunciated the principles of the new criticism that served as rationale for the new poetry. Notable among the other works written in this prolific period is his austere and powerful tragic poem *The Ruined Cottage*.

Late in 1799 Wordsworth and Dorothy moved back permanently to their native lakes, settling at Grasmere in the little house later named Dove Cottage. Coleridge, following them, rented Greta Hall at Keswick, thirteen miles away. In 1802 Wordsworth finally came into his father's inheritance and, after an amicable settlement with Annette Vallon, married Mary Hutchinson, a Lake Country woman whom he had known since childhood. The course of his existence after that time was broken by various disasters: the drowning in 1805 of his favorite brother, John, a sea captain whose ship was wrecked in a storm; the death of two of his five children in 1812; a growing estrangement from Coleridge, culminating in a bitter quarrel (1810) from which they were not completely reconciled for almost two decades; and from the 1830s on, the physical and mental decline of his sister, Dorothy. The life of his middle age, however, was one of steadily increasing prosperity and reputation, as well as of political and religious conservatism. In 1813 an appointment as Stamp Distributor (that is, revenue collector) for Westmorland was concrete evidence of his recognition as a national poet. Gradually his residences, as he moved into more and more commodious quarters, became standard stops for tourists; he was awarded honorary degrees and, in 1843, was appointed poet laureate. He died in 1850 at the age of eighty; only then did his executors publish his masterpiece, *The Prelude,* the autobiographical poem that he had written in two parts in 1799, expanded to its full length in 1805, and then continued to revise almost to the last decade of his long life.

Most of Wordsworth's greatest poetry had been written by 1807, when he published *Poems in Two Volumes;* and after *The Excursion* (1814) and the first collected edition of his poems (1815), although he continued to write voluminously, there is an overall decline in his powers. The causes of the decline have been much debated; an important one seems to be inherent in the very nature of his most characteristic writing. Wordsworth is above all the poet of the remembrance of things past, or as he himself put it, of "emotion recollected in tranquillity." Some object or event in the present triggers a sudden renewal of feelings he had experienced in youth; the result is a poem exhibiting the sharp discrepancy between what Wordsworth called "two consciousnesses": himself as he is now and himself as he once was. But the memory of one's early emotional experience is not an inexhaustible resource for poetry, as Wordsworth himself recognized. He said in *The Prelude* 12, while describing the recurrence of "spots of time" from his memories of childhood:

> The days gone by
> Return upon me almost from the dawn
> Of life: the hiding places of Man's power
> Open; I would approach them, but they close.
> I see by glimpses now; when age comes on,
> May scarcely see at all.

The past that Wordsworth recollected was one of moments of intense experience, and of emotional turmoil which is ordered, in the calmer present, into a hard-won equilibrium. As time went on, however, he gained what, in the *Ode to Duty* (composed in 1804), he longed for, "a repose which ever is the same"—but at the expense of the agony and excitation which, under the calm surface, empowers his best and most characteristic poems.

Occasionally, in his middle and later life a jolting experience would revive the intensity of Wordsworth's remembered emotion, and also his earlier poetic strength. The moving sonnet *Surprised by Joy,* for example, was written in his forties at the abrupt realization that time was beginning to diminish his grief at the death some years earlier of his little daughter Catherine. And when Wordsworth was sixty-five years old, the sudden report of the death of James Hogg called up the memory of other and greater poets whom Wordsworth had loved and outlived; the result was his *Extempore Effusion,* written in a return to the simple quatrains of the early *Lyrical Ballads* and with a recovery of the elegiac voice that had uttered the dirges to Lucy, thirty-five years before.

FROM LYRICAL BALLADS

Simon Lee[1]

The Old Huntsman

WITH AN INCIDENT IN WHICH HE WAS CONCERNED

In the sweet shire of Cardigan,[2]
Not far from pleasant Ivor-hall,
An old man dwells, a little man,—
'Tis said he once was tall.
5   Full five-and-thirty years he lived
A running huntsman[3] merry;
And still the centre of his cheek
Is red as a ripe cherry.

No man like him the horn could sound,
10   And hill and valley rang with glee
When Echo bandied, round and round,
The halloo of Simon Lee.
In those proud days, he little cared
For husbandry or tillage;
15   To blither tasks did Simon rouse
The sleepers of the village.

He all the country could outrun,
Could leave both man and horse behind;
And often, ere the chase was done,
20   He reeled, and was stone-blind.°   *totally blind*
And still there's something in the world
At which his heart rejoices;
For when the chiming hounds are out,
He dearly loves their voices!

25   But, oh the heavy change![4]—bereft
Of health, strength, friends, and kindred, see!
Old Simon to the world is left
In liveried poverty.
His Master's dead,—and no one now
30   Dwells in the Hall of Ivor;
Men, dogs, and horses, all are dead;
He is the sole survivor.

1. This old man had been huntsman to the
Squires of Alfoxden. . . . I have, after an interval of
45 years, the image of the old man as fresh before
my eyes as if I had seen him yesterday. The expression when the hounds were out, "I dearly love their
voices," was word for word from his own lips
[Wordsworth's note, 1843]. Wordsworth and
Dorothy had lived at Alfoxden House, Somersetshire, in 1797–98.
2. Wordsworth relocates the incident from
Somersetshire to Cardiganshire in Wales.
3. Manager of the hunt and the person in charge
of the hounds.
4. Milton's *Lycidas*, line 37: "But O the heavy
change, now thou art gone."

And he is lean and he is sick;
His body, dwindled and awry,
35 Rests upon ankles swoln and thick;
His legs are thin and dry.
One prop he has, and only one,
His wife, an aged woman,
Lives with him, near the waterfall,
40 Upon the village Common.

Beside their moss-grown hut of clay,
Not twenty paces from the door,
A scrap of land they have, but they
Are poorest of the poor.
45 This scrap of land he from the heath
Enclosed when he was stronger;
But what to them avails the land
Which he can till no longer?

Oft, working by her Husband's side,
50 Ruth does what Simon cannot do;
For she, with scanty cause for pride,
Is stouter of the two.
And, though you with your utmost skill
From labour could not wean them,
55 'Tis very, very little—all
That they can do between them.

Few months of life has he in store
As he to you will tell,
For still, the more he works, the more
60 Do his weak ankles swell.
My gentle Reader, I perceive
How patiently you've waited,
And now I fear that you expect
Some tale will be related.

65 O Reader! had you in your mind
Such stores as silent thought can bring,
O gentle Reader! you would find
A tale in every thing.
What more I have to say is short,
70 And you must kindly take it:
It is no tale; but, should you think,
Perhaps a tale you'll make it.

One summer-day I chanced to see
This old Man doing all he could
75 To unearth the root of an old tree,
A stump of rotten wood.
The mattock tottered in his hand;
So vain was his endeavour,

That at the root of the old tree
80   He might have worked for ever.

"You're overtasked, good Simon Lee,
Give me your tool," to him I said;
And at the word right gladly he
Received my proffered aid.
85   I struck, and with a single blow
The tangled root I severed,
At which the poor old Man so long
And vainly had endeavoured.

The tears into his eyes were brought,
90   And thanks and praises seemed to run
So fast out of his heart, I thought
They never would have done.
—I've heard of hearts unkind, kind deeds
With coldness still returning;
95   Alas! the gratitude of men
Hath oftener left me mourning.

1798   1798

We Are Seven[1]

————A simple Child,
That lightly draws its breath,
And feels its life in every limb,
What should it know of death?

5   I met a little cottage Girl:
She was eight years old, she said;
Her hair was thick with many a curl
That clustered round her head.

She had a rustic, woodland air,
10   And she was wildly clad:
Her eyes were fair, and very fair;
—Her beauty made me glad.

"Sisters and brothers, little Maid,
How many may you be?"
15   "How many? Seven in all," she said,
And wondering looked at me.

"And where are they? I pray you tell."
She answered, "Seven are we;
And two of us at Conway[2] dwell,
20   And two are gone to sea.

1. Written at Alfoxden in the spring of 1798. . . . The little girl who is the heroine I met within the area of Goodrich Castle [in the Wye Valley north of Tintern Abbey] in the year 1793 [Wordsworth's note]. Wordsworth also tells us that he composed the last line of the last stanza first, and that Coleridge contributed the initial stanza.
2. A seaport town in north Wales.

"Two of us in the church-yard lie,
My sister and my brother;
And, in the church-yard cottage, I
Dwell near them with my mother."

25 "You say that two at Conway dwell,
And two are gone to sea,
Yet ye are seven! I pray you tell,
Sweet Maid, how this may be."

Then did the little Maid reply,
30 "Seven boys and girls are we;
Two of us in the church-yard lie,
Beneath the church-yard tree."

"You run about, my little Maid,
Your limbs they are alive;
35 If two are in the church-yard laid,
Then ye are only five."

"Their graves are green, they may be seen,"
The little Maid replied,
"Twelve steps or more from my mother's door,
40 And they are side by side.

"My stockings there I often knit,
My kerchief there I hem;
And there upon the ground I sit,
And sing a song to them.

45 "And often after sun-set, Sir,
When it is light and fair,
I take my little porringer,[3]
And eat my supper there.

"The first that died was sister Jane;
50 In bed she moaning lay,
Till God released her of her pain;
And then she went away.

"So in the church-yard she was laid;
And, when the grass was dry,
55 Together round her grave we played,
My brother John and I.

"And when the ground was white with snow,
And I could run and slide,
My brother John was forced to go,
60 And he lies by her side."

---

3. Bowl for porridge.

"How many are you, then," said I,
"If they two are in heaven?"
Quick was the little Maid's reply,
"O Master! we are seven."

65 "But they are dead; those two are dead!
Their spirits are in heaven!"
'Twas throwing words away; for still
The little Maid would have her will,
And said, "Nay, we are seven!"

1798   1798

Lines Written in Early Spring

I heard a thousand blended notes,
While in a grove I sate reclined,
In that sweet mood when pleasant thoughts
Bring sad thoughts to the mind.

5 To her fair works did Nature link
The human soul that through me ran;
And much it grieved my heart to think
What man has made of man.

Through primrose tufts, in that green bower,
10 The periwinkle[1] trailed its wreaths,
And 'tis my faith that every flower
Enjoys the air it breathes.

The birds around me hopped and played,
Their thoughts I cannot measure:—
15 But the least motion which they made,
It seemed a thrill of pleasure.

The budding twigs spread out their fan,
To catch the breezy air;
And I must think, do all I can,
20 That there was pleasure there.

If this belief from heaven be sent,
If such be Nature's holy plan,[2]
Have I not reason to lament
What man has made of man?

1798   1798

---

1. A trailing evergreen plant with small blue flowers (U.S. myrtle).
2. The version of these two lines in the *Lyrical* *Ballads* of 1798 reads: "If I these thoughts may not prevent, / If such be of my creed the plan."

Expostulation and Reply[1]

"Why, William, on that old grey stone,
Thus for the length of half a day,
Why, William, sit you thus alone,
And dream your time away?

5   "Where are your books?—that light bequeathed
To Beings else forlorn and blind!
Up! up! and drink the spirit breathed
From dead men to their kind.

"You look round on your Mother Earth,
10   As if she for no purpose bore you;
As if you were her first-born birth,
And none had lived before you!"

One morning thus, by Esthwaite lake,
When life was sweet, I knew not why,
15   To me my good friend Matthew spake,
And thus I made reply.

"The eye—it cannot choose but see;
We cannot bid the ear be still;
Our bodies feel, where'er they be,
20   Against or with our will.

"Nor less I deem that there are Powers
Which of themselves our minds impress;
That we can feed this mind of ours
In a wise passiveness.

25   "Think you, 'mid all this mighty sum
Of things for ever speaking,
That nothing of itself will come,
But we must still be seeking?

"—Then ask not wherefore, here, alone,
30   Conversing[2] as I may,
I sit upon this old grey stone,
And dream my time away."

Spring 1798   1798

---

1. This and the following companion poem have often been attacked—and defended—as Wordsworth's solemn deliverance on the comparative merits of nature and of books. But they are a dialogue between two friends who rally one another by the usual device of overstating parts of a whole truth. Wordsworth said that the pieces originated in a conversation "with a friend who was somewhat unreasonably attached to modern books of moral philosophy," and also that the lore of "a wise passiveness" made the poem a favorite among Quakers.

2. In the old sense of "communing" (with the "things for ever speaking").

The Tables Turned

An Evening Scene on the Same Subject

Up! up! my Friend, and quit your books;
Or surely you'll grow double:
Up! up! my Friend, and clear your looks;
Why all this toil and trouble?

5 The sun, above the mountain's head,
A freshening lustre mellow
Through all the long green fields has spread,
His first sweet evening yellow.

Books! 'tis a dull and endless strife:
10 Come, hear the woodland linnet,°   *small finch*
How sweet his music! on my life,
There's more of wisdom in it.

And hark! how blithe the throstle° sings!   *song thrush*
He, too, is no mean preacher:
15 Come forth into the light of things,
Let Nature be your Teacher.

She has a world of ready wealth,
Our minds and hearts to bless—
Spontaneous wisdom breathed by health,
20 Truth breathed by cheerfulness.

One impulse from a vernal wood
May teach you more of man,
Of moral evil and of good,
Than all the sages can.

25 Sweet is the lore which Nature brings;
Our meddling intellect
Mis-shapes the beauteous forms of things:—
We murder to dissect.

Enough of Science and of Art;
30 Close up those barren leaves;
Come forth, and bring with you a heart
That watches and receives.

1798   1798

The Thorn[1]

1

"There is a Thorn—it looks so old,
In truth, you'd find it hard to say
How it could ever have been young,
It looks so old and grey.
5 Not higher than a two years' child
It stands erect, this aged Thorn;
No leaves it has, no prickly points;
It is a mass of knotted joints,
A wretched thing forlorn.
10 It stands erect, and like a stone
With lichens is it overgrown.

2

"Like rock or stone, it is o'ergrown,
With lichens to the very top,
And hung with heavy tufts of moss,
15 A melancholy crop:
Up from the earth these mosses creep,
And this poor Thorn they clasp it round
So close, you'd say that they are bent
With plain and manifest intent
20 To drag it to the ground;
And all have joined in one endeavour
To bury this poor Thorn for ever.

3

"High on a mountain's highest ridge,
Where oft the stormy winter gale
25 Cuts like a scythe, while through the clouds
It sweeps from vale to vale;
Not five yards from the mountain path,
This Thorn you on your left espy;

1. Arose out of my observing, on the ridge of Quantock Hill [in Somersetshire], on a stormy day, a thorn which I had often past, in calm and bright weather, without noticing it. I said to myself, "Cannot I by some invention do as much to make this Thorn permanently an impressive object as the storm has made it to my eyes at this moment?" I began the poem accordingly, and composed it with great rapidity [Wordsworth's note, 1843]. In the prefatory Advertisement to the 1798 *Lyrical Ballads* Wordsworth wrote, "The poem of the Thorn . . . is not supposed to be spoken in the author's own person: the character of the loquacious narrator will sufficiently shew itself in the course of the story." In the editions of 1800–05 he elaborated in a separate note that reads, in part: "The character which I have here introduced speaking is sufficiently common. The Reader will perhaps have a general notion of it, if he has ever known a man, a Captain of a small trading vessel, for example, who, being past the middle age of life, had retired upon an annuity or small independent income to some village or country town of which he was not a native. . . . Such men, having little to do, become credulous and talkative from indolence; and from the same cause . . . they are prone to superstition. On which account it appeared to me proper to select a character like this to exhibit some of the general laws by which superstition acts upon the mind. Superstitious men are almost always men of slow faculties and deep feelings: their minds are not loose but adhesive; they have a reasonable share of imagination, by which word I mean the faculty which produces impressive effects out of simple elements. . . . It was my wish in this poem to show the manner in which such men cleave to the same ideas; and to follow the turns of passion . . . by which their conversation is swayed." "Thorn": hawthorn, a thorny shrub or small tree.

And to the left, three yards beyond,
30   You see a little muddy pond
Of water—never dry
Though but of compass small, and bare
To thirsty suns and parching air.

4

"And, close beside this aged Thorn,
35   There is a fresh and lovely sight,
A beauteous heap, a hill of moss,
Just half a foot in height.
All lovely colours there you see,
All colours that were ever seen;
40   And mossy network too is there,
As if by hand of lady fair
The work had woven been;
And cups, the darlings of the eye,
So deep is their vermilion dye.

5

45   "Ah me! what lovely tints are there
Of olive green and scarlet bright,
In spikes, in branches, and in stars,
Green, red, and pearly white!
This heap of earth o'ergrown with moss,
50   Which close beside the Thorn you see,
So fresh in all its beauteous dyes,
Is like an infant's grave in size,
As like as like can be:
But never, never any where,
55   An infant's grave was half so fair.

6

"Now would you see this aged Thorn,
This pond, and beauteous hill of moss,
You must take care and choose your time
The mountain when to cross.
60   For oft there sits between the heap
So like an infant's grave in size,
And that same pond of which I spoke,
A Woman in a scarlet cloak,
And to herself she cries,
65   'Oh misery! oh misery!
Oh woe is me! oh misery!'

7

"At all times of the day and night
This wretched Woman thither goes;
And she is known to every star,
70   And every wind that blows;
And there, beside the Thorn, she sits

When the blue daylight's in the skies,
And when the whirlwind's on the hill,
Or frosty air is keen and still,
75   And to herself she cries,
'Oh misery! oh misery!
Oh woe is me! oh misery!' "

8

"Now wherefore, thus, by day and night,
In rain, in tempest, and in snow,
80   Thus to the dreary mountain-top
Does this poor Woman go?
And why sits she beside the Thorn
When the blue daylight's in the sky
Or when the whirlwind's on the hill,
85   Or frosty air is keen and still,
And wherefore does she cry?—
O wherefore? wherefore? tell me why
Does she repeat that doleful cry?"

9

"I cannot tell; I wish I could;
90   For the true reason no one knows:
But would you gladly view the spot,
The spot to which she goes;
The hillock like an infant's grave,
The pond—and Thorn, so old and grey;
95   Pass by her door—'tis seldom shut—
And, if you see her in her hut—
Then to the spot away!
I never heard of such as dare
Approach the spot when she is there."

10

100   "But wherefore to the mountain-top
Can this unhappy Woman go,
Whatever star is in the skies,
Whatever wind may blow?"
"Full twenty years are past and gone
105   Since she (her name is Martha Ray)
Gave with a maiden's true good-will
Her company to Stephen Hill;
And she was blithe and gay,
While friends and kindred all approved
110   Of him whom tenderly she loved.

11

"And they had fixed the wedding day,
The morning that must wed them both;
But Stephen to another Maid
Had sworn another oath;

115 And, with this other Maid, to church
    Unthinking Stephen went—
    Poor Martha! on that woeful day
    A pang of pitiless dismay
    Into her soul was sent;
120 A fire was kindled in her breast,
    Which might not burn itself to rest.

                    12
    "They say, full six months after this,
    While yet the summer leaves were green,
    She to the mountain-top would go,
125 And there was often seen.
    What could she seek?—or wish to hide?
    Her state to any eye was plain;
    She was with child, and she was mad;
    Yet often was she sober sad
130 From her exceeding pain.
    O guilty Father—would that death
    Had saved him from that breach of faith!

                    13
    "Sad case for such a brain to hold
    Communion with a stirring child!
135 Sad case, as you may think, for one
    Who had a brain so wild!
    Last Christmas-eve we talked of this,
    And grey-haired Wilfred of the glen
    Held that the unborn infant wrought
140 About its mother's heart, and brought
    Her senses back again:
    And, when at last her time drew near,
    Her looks were calm, her senses clear.

                    14
    "More know I not, I wish I did,
145 And it should all be told to you;
    For what became of this poor child
    No mortal ever knew;
    Nay—if a child to her was born
    No earthly tongue could ever tell;
150 And if 'twas born alive or dead,
    Far less could this with proof be said;
    But some remember well,
    That Martha Ray about this time
    Would up the mountain often climb.

                    15
155 "And all that winter, when at night
    The wind blew from the mountain-peak,
    'Twas worth your while, though in the dark,

The churchyard path to seek:
For many a time and oft were heard
160 Cries coming from the mountain head:
Some plainly living voices were;
And others, I've heard many swear,
Were voices of the dead:
I cannot think, whate'er they say,
165 They had to do with Martha Ray.

16

"But that she goes to this old Thorn,
The Thorn which I described to you,
And there sits in a scarlet cloak,
I will be sworn is true.
170 For one day with my telescope,
To view the ocean wide and bright,
When to this country first I came,
Ere I had heard of Martha's name,
I climbed the mountain's height:—
175 A storm came on, and I could see
No object higher than my knee.

17

" 'Twas mist and rain, and storm and rain:
No screen, no fence could I discover;
And then the wind! in sooth, it was
180 A wind full ten times over.
I looked around, I thought I saw
A jutting crag,—and off I ran,
Head-foremost, through the driving rain,
The shelter of the crag to gain;
185 And, as I am a man,
Instead of jutting crag, I found
A Woman seated on the ground.

18

"I did not speak—I saw her face;
Her face!—it was enough for me;
190 I turned about and heard her cry,
'Oh misery! oh misery!'
And there she sits, until the moon
Through half the clear blue sky will go;
And, when the little breezes make
195 The waters of the pond to shake,
As all the country know,
She shudders, and you hear her cry,
'Oh misery! oh misery!' "

19

"But what's the Thorn? and what the pond?
200 And what the hill of moss to her?

And what the creeping breeze that comes
The little pond to stir?"
"I cannot tell; but some will say
She hanged her baby on the tree;
205 Some say she drowned it in the pond,
Which is a little step beyond:
But all and each agree,
The little Babe was buried there,
Beneath that hill of moss so fair.

20

210 "I've heard, the moss is spotted red
With drops of that poor infant's blood;
But kill a new-born infant thus,
I do not think she could!
Some say, if to the pond you go,
215 And fix on it a steady view,
The shadow of a babe you trace,
A baby and a baby's face,
And that it looks at you;
Whene'er you look on it, 'tis plain
220 The baby looks at you again.

21

"And some had sworn an oath that she
Should be to public justice brought;
And for the little infant's bones
With spades they would have sought.
225 But instantly the hill of moss
Before their eyes began to stir!
And, for full fifty yards around,
The grass—it shook upon the ground!
Yet all do still aver
230 The little Babe lies buried there,
Beneath that hill of moss so fair.

22

"I cannot tell how this may be,
But plain it is the Thorn is bound
With heavy tufts of moss that strive
235 To drag it to the ground;
And this I know, full many a time,
When she was on the mountain high,
By day, and in the silent night,
When all the stars shone clear and bright,
240 That I have heard her cry,
'Oh misery! oh misery!
Oh woe is me! oh misery!' "

Mar.–Apr. 1798   1798

Lines[1]

Composed a Few Miles above Tintern Abbey, on Revisiting the Banks of the Wye during a Tour, July 13, 1798

Five years have past; five summers, with the length
Of five long winters! and again I hear
These waters, rolling from their mountain-springs
With a soft inland murmur.—Once again
5 Do I behold these steep and lofty cliffs,
That on a wild secluded scene impress
Thoughts of more deep seclusion; and connect
The landscape with the quiet of the sky.
The day is come when I again repose
10 Here, under this dark sycamore, and view
These plots of cottage-ground, these orchard-tufts,
Which at this season, with their unripe fruits,
Are clad in one green hue, and lose themselves
'Mid groves and copses. Once again I see
15 These hedge-rows, hardly hedge-rows, little lines
Of sportive wood run wild: these pastoral farms,
Green to the very door; and wreaths of smoke
Sent up, in silence, from among the trees!
With some uncertain notice, as might seem
20 Of vagrant dwellers in the houseless woods,
Or of some Hermit's cave, where by his fire
The Hermit sits alone.

                   These beauteous forms,
Through a long absence, have not been to me
As is a landscape to a blind man's eye:
25 But oft, in lonely rooms, and 'mid the din
Of towns and cities, I have owed to them
In hours of weariness, sensations sweet,
Felt in the blood, and felt along the heart;
And passing even into my purer mind,
30 With tranquil restoration:—feelings too
Of unremembered pleasure: such, perhaps,
As have no slight or trivial influence
On that best portion of a good man's life,
His little, nameless, unremembered, acts
35 Of kindness and of love. Nor less, I trust,
To them I may have owed another gift,

---

1. No poem of mine was composed under circumstances more pleasant for me to remember than this. I began it upon leaving Tintern, after crossing the Wye, and concluded it just as I was entering Bristol in the evening, after a ramble of 4 or 5 days, with my sister. Not a line of it was altered, and not any part of it written down till I reached Bristol [Wordsworth's note]. The poem was printed as the last item in *Lyrical Ballads*.

Wordsworth had first visited the Wye valley and the ruins of Tintern Abbey, in Monmouthshire, while on a solitary walking tour in August 1793, when he was twenty-three years old. The puzzling difference between the present landscape and the remembered "picture of the mind" (line 61) gives rise to an intricately organized meditation, in which the poet reviews his past, evaluates the present, and (through his sister as intermediary) anticipates the future; he ends by rounding back quietly on the scene that had been his point of departure.

Of aspect more sublime; that blessed mood,
In which the burthen of the mystery,
In which the heavy and the weary weight
40 Of all this unintelligible world,
Is lightened:—that serene and blessed mood,
In which the affections gently lead us on,—
Until, the breath of this corporeal frame
And even the motion of our human blood
45 Almost suspended, we are laid asleep
In body, and become a living soul:
While with an eye made quiet by the power
Of harmony, and the deep power of joy,
We see into the life of things.

                                    If this
50 Be but a vain belief, yet, oh! how oft—
In darkness and amid the many shapes
Of joyless daylight; when the fretful stir
Unprofitable, and the fever of the world,
Have hung upon the beatings of my heart—
55 How oft, in spirit, have I turned to thee,
O sylvan Wye! thou wanderer thro' the woods,
How often has my spirit turned to thee!

   And now, with gleams of half-extinguished thought,
With many recognitions dim and faint,
60 And somewhat of a sad perplexity,
The picture of the mind revives again:
While here I stand, not only with the sense
Of present pleasure, but with pleasing thoughts
That in this moment there is life and food
65 For future years. And so I dare to hope,
Though changed, no doubt, from what I was when first
I came among these hills; when like a roe
I bounded o'er the mountains, by the sides
Of the deep rivers, and the lonely streams,
70 Wherever nature led: more like a man
Flying from something that he dreads, than one
Who sought the thing he loved. For nature then
(The coarser pleasures of my boyish days,
And their glad animal movements all gone by)
75 To me was all in all.—I cannot paint
What then I was. The sounding cataract
Haunted me like a passion: the tall rock,
The mountain, and the deep and gloomy wood,
Their colours and their forms, were then to me
80 An appetite; a feeling and a love,
That had no need of a remoter charm,
By thought supplied, nor any interest
Unborrowed from the eye.—That time is past,
And all its aching joys are now no more,

85 And all its dizzy raptures.[2] Not for this
    Faint° I, nor mourn nor murmur; other gifts   *lose heart*
    Have followed; for such loss, I would believe,
    Abundant recompense. For I have learned
    To look on nature, not as in the hour
90 Of thoughtless youth; but hearing oftentimes
    The still, sad music of humanity,
    Nor harsh nor grating, though of ample power
    To chasten and subdue. And I have felt
    A presence that disturbs me with the joy
95 Of elevated thoughts; a sense sublime
    Of something far more deeply interfused,
    Whose dwelling is the light of setting suns,
    And the round ocean and the living air,
    And the blue sky, and in the mind of man:
100 A motion and a spirit, that impels
    All thinking things, all objects of all thought,
    And rolls through all things. Therefore am I still
    A lover of the meadows and the woods,
    And mountains; and of all that we behold
105 From this green earth; of all the mighty world
    Of eye, and ear,—both what they half create,[3]
    And what perceive; well pleased to recognise
    In nature and the language of the sense,
    The anchor of my purest thoughts, the nurse,
110 The guide, the guardian of my heart, and soul
    Of all my moral being.

                                      Nor perchance,
    If I were not thus taught, should I the more
    Suffer my genial spirits[4] to decay:
    For thou art with me here upon the banks
115 Of this fair river; thou my dearest Friend,[5]
    My dear, dear Friend; and in thy voice I catch
    The language of my former heart, and read
    My former pleasures in the shooting lights
    Of thy wild eyes. Oh! yet a little while
120 May I behold in thee what I was once,
    My dear, dear Sister! and this prayer I make,
    Knowing that Nature never did betray
    The heart that loved her; 'tis her privilege,
    Through all the years of this our life, to lead
125 From joy to joy: for she can so inform
    The mind that is within us, so impress

2. Lines 66ff. contain Wordsworth's famed description of the three stages of his growing up, defined in terms of his evolving relations to the natural scene: the young boy's purely physical responsiveness (lines 73–74); the postadolescent's aching, dizzy, and equivocal passions—a love that is more like dread (lines 67–72, 75–85: this was his state of mind on the occasion of his first visit);

his present state (lines 85ff.), in which for the first time he adds thought to sense.
3. This view that the "creative sensibility" contributes to its own perceptions is often reiterated in *The Prelude*.
4. Creative powers. ("Genial" is here the adjectival form of the noun "genius.")
5. His sister, Dorothy.

With quietness and beauty, and so feed
With lofty thoughts, that neither evil tongues,
Rash judgments, nor the sneers of selfish men,
130 Nor greetings where no kindness is, nor all
The dreary intercourse of daily life,
Shall e'er prevail against us, or disturb
Our cheerful faith, that all which we behold
Is full of blessings. Therefore let the moon
135 Shine on thee in thy solitary walk;
And let the misty mountain-winds be free
To blow against thee: and, in after years,
When these wild ecstasies shall be matured
Into a sober pleasure; when thy mind
140 Shall be a mansion for all lovely forms,
Thy memory be as a dwelling-place
For all sweet sounds and harmonies; oh! then,
If solitude, or fear, or pain, or grief,
Should be thy portion, with what healing thoughts
145 Of tender joy wilt thou remember me,
And these my exhortations! Nor, perchance—
If I should be where I no more can hear
Thy voice, nor catch from thy wild eyes these gleams
Of past existence⁶—wilt thou then forget
150 That on the banks of this delightful stream
We stood together; and that I, so long
A worshipper of Nature, hither came
Unwearied in that service; rather say
With warmer love—oh! with far deeper zeal
155 Of holier love. Nor wilt thou then forget,
That after many wanderings, many years
Of absence, these steep woods and lofty cliffs,
And this green pastoral landscape, were to me
More dear, both for themselves and for thy sake!

July 1798   1798

Preface to *Lyrical Ballads* (1802)

To the first edition of *Lyrical Ballads*, published jointly with Coleridge in 1798, Wordsworth prefixed an "advertisement" asserting that the majority of the poems were "to be considered as experiments" to determine "how far the language of conversation in the middle and lower classes of society is adapted to the purposes of poetic pleasure." In the second, two-volume edition of 1800 Wordsworth, aided by frequent conversations with Coleridge, expanded the Advertisement into a preface that justified the new poetry not as experiments, but as exemplifying the principles of all good poetry. The Preface was enlarged for the third edition of *Lyrical Ballads*, published two years later; this last version of 1802 is the one that is reprinted here.

Although some of its individual ideas had antecedents in the later eighteenth century, the Preface as a whole deserves its reputation as a revolutionary manifesto about

6. I.e., reminders of his own "past existence" five years earlier (see lines 116–19).

the nature of poetry. Like many radical statements, however, it claims to go back to the implicit principles that governed the great poetry of the past but have been perverted in recent practice. Most discussions of the Preface, following the lead of Coleridge in his *Biographia Literaria*, have focused on Wordsworth's assertions about the valid language of poetry, on which he bases his attack on the "poetic diction" of eighteenth-century poets. As Coleridge pointed out, Wordsworth's argument about this issue is far from clear. It is apparent, however, that Wordsworth undertook to overthrow the basic theory, as well as the reigning practice, of neoclassic poetry. That is, his Preface implicitly denies the traditional assumption that the poetic genres constitute a hierarchy, from epic and tragedy at the top down through comedy, satire, pastoral, to the short lyric at the lowest reaches of the poetic scale; he also rejects the traditional principle of "decorum," according to which the subject matter (especially the social class of the protagonists) and the level of diction are contrived by the poet to conform to the status of the literary kind on the poetic scale.

When Wordsworth asserted in the Preface that he deliberately chose to represent "incidents and situations from common life," he translated his democratic sympathies into critical terms, justifying his use of peasants, children, outcasts, criminals, and idiot boys as serious subjects of poetic and even tragic concern. He also undertook to write in "a selection of language really used by men," on the grounds that there can be no "essential difference between the language of prose and metrical composition." In making this claim, Wordsworth subverted the neoclassic principle that, in many kinds of poem, the language must be elevated over standard speech by a special diction and by artful figures of speech, to match the language to the height and dignity of a particular genre. Wordsworth's own views about the valid language of poetry are based on the new premise that "all good poetry is the spontaneous overflow of powerful feelings"—spontaneous, that is, at the moment of composition, even though the process is influenced by prior thought and acquired poetic skill.

Wordsworth's assertions about the materials and diction of poetry have been greatly influential in expanding the range of serious literature to include the common people and ordinary things and events, as well as in justifying a poetry of sincerity rather than of artifice, expressed in the ordinary language of its time. But in the long view, other aspects of his Preface have been no less significant in establishing its importance, not only as a turning point in English criticism but also as a central document in modern culture. Wordsworth attributed to imaginative literature the primary role in keeping human beings emotionally alive and morally sensitive—that is, keeping them essentially human—in the modern era of a technological and increasingly urban society, with its mass media and mass culture that threaten, in his view, to blunt the mind's "discriminatory powers" and to "reduce it to a state of almost savage torpor."

From Preface to *Lyrical Ballads, with Pastoral and Other Poems* (1802)

[THE SUBJECT AND LANGUAGE OF POETRY]

The first volume of these poems has already been submitted to general perusal. It was published, as an experiment, which, I hoped, might be of some use to ascertain, how far, by fitting to metrical arrangement a selection of the real language of men in a state of vivid sensation, that sort of pleasure and that quantity of pleasure may be imparted, which a poet may rationally endeavour to impart.

I had formed no very inaccurate estimate of the probable effect of those poems: I flattered myself that they who should be pleased with them would read them with more than common pleasure: and, on the other hand, I was well aware, that by those who should dislike them they would be read with more than common dislike. The result has differed from my expectation in this only, that I have pleased a greater number than I ventured to hope I should please.

For the sake of variety, and from a consciousness of my own weakness, I was induced to request the assistance of a friend, who furnished me with the poems of the *Ancient Mariner*, the *Foster-Mother's Tale*, the *Nightingale*, and the poem entitled *Love*. I should not, however, have requested this assistance, had I not believed that the poems of my friend[1] would in a great measure have the same tendency as my own, and that, though there would be found a difference, there would be found no discordance in the colours of our style; as our opinions on the subject of poetry do almost entirely coincide.

Several of my friends are anxious for the success of these poems from a belief, that, if the views with which they were composed were indeed realized, a class of poetry would be produced, well adapted to interest mankind permanently, and not unimportant in the multiplicity, and in the quality of its moral relations: and on this account they have advised me to prefix a systematic defence of the theory upon which the poems were written. But I was unwilling to undertake the task, because I knew that on this occasion the reader would look coldly upon my arguments, since I might be suspected of having been principally influenced by the selfish and foolish hope of *reasoning* him into an approbation of these particular poems: and I was still more unwilling to undertake the task, because, adequately to display my opinions, and fully to enforce my arguments, would require a space wholly disproportionate to the nature of a preface. For to treat the subject with the clearness and coherence of which I believe it susceptible, it would be necessary to give a full account of the present state of the public taste in this country, and to determine how far this taste is healthy or depraved; which, again, could not be determined, without pointing out, in what manner language and the human mind act and re-act on each other, and without retracing the revolutions, not of literature alone, but likewise of society itself. I have therefore altogether declined to enter regularly upon this defence; yet I am sensible, that there would be some impropriety in abruptly obtruding upon the public, without a few words of introduction, poems so materially different from those upon which general approbation is at present bestowed.

It is supposed, that by the act of writing in verse an author makes a formal engagement that he will gratify certain known habits of association; that he not only thus apprizes the reader that certain classes of ideas and expressions will be found in his book, but that others will be carefully excluded. This exponent or symbol held forth by metrical language must in different eras of literature have excited very different expectations: for example, in the age of Catullus, Terence, and Lucretius and that of Statius or Claudian,[2] and in

---

1. The "friend" of course is Coleridge. When he read this *Preface* and the new poems included in the 1802 edition of *Lyrical Ballads*, Coleridge wrote to Robert Southey that although Wordsworth's Preface of 1800 had been "half a child of my own brain," he now suspects that "there is a radical difference in our theoretical opinions respecting poetry—this I shall endeavour to go to the bottom of." The results of this endeavor are Coleridge's discussions, fifteen years later, of Wordsworth's Preface in *Biographia Literaria*, chaps. 14 and 17.

2. Wordsworth's implied contrast is between the naturalness and simplicity of the first three Roman poets (who wrote in the last two centuries B.C.E.) and the elaborate artifice of the last two Roman poets (Statius wrote in the 1st and Claudian in the 4th century C.E.).

our own country, in the age of Shakespeare and Beaumont and Fletcher, and that of Donne and Cowley, or Dryden, or Pope. I will not take upon me to determine the exact import of the promise which by the act of writing in verse an author, in the present day, makes to his reader; but I am certain, it will appear to many persons that I have not fulfilled the terms of an engagement thus voluntarily contracted. They who have been accustomed to the gaudiness and inane phraseology of many modern writers, if they persist in reading this book to its conclusion, will, no doubt, frequently have to struggle with feelings of strangeness and awkwardness: they will look round for poetry, and will be induced to inquire by what species of courtesy these attempts can be permitted to assume that title. I hope therefore the reader will not censure me, if I attempt to state what I have proposed to myself to perform; and also (as far as the limits of a preface will permit) to explain some of the chief reasons which have determined me in the choice of my purpose: that at least he may be spared any unpleasant feeling of disappointment, and that I myself may be protected from the most dishonorable accusation which can be brought against an author, namely, that of an indolence which prevents him from endeavouring to ascertain what is his duty, or, when this duty is ascertained, prevents him from performing it.

The principal object, then, which I proposed to myself in these poems was to choose incidents and situations from common life, and to relate or describe them, throughout, as far as was possible, in a selection of language really used by men; and, at the same time, to throw over them a certain colouring of imagination, whereby ordinary things should be presented to the mind in an unusual way; and, further, and above all, to make these incidents and situations interesting by tracing in them, truly though not ostentatiously, the primary laws of our nature: chiefly, as far as regards the manner in which we associate ideas in a state of excitement.[3] Low and rustic life was generally chosen, because in that condition, the essential passions of the heart find a better soil in which they can attain their maturity, are less under restraint, and speak a plainer and more emphatic language; because in that condition of life our elementary feelings co-exist in a state of greater simplicity, and, consequently, may be more accurately contemplated, and more forcibly communicated; because the manners of rural life germinate from those elementary feelings; and, from the necessary character of rural occupations, are more easily comprehended; and are more durable; and lastly, because in that condition the passions of men are incorporated with the beautiful and permanent forms of nature. The language, too, of these men is adopted (purified indeed from what appear to be its real defects, from all lasting and rational causes of dislike or disgust) because such men hourly communicate with the best objects from which the best part of language is originally derived; and because, from their rank in society and the sameness and narrow circle of their intercourse, being less under the influence of social vanity they convey their feelings and notions in simple and unelaborated expressions. Accordingly, such a language, arising out of repeated experience and regular feelings, is a more permanent, and a far more philosophical language, than that which is frequently substituted for it by poets, who think that they are conferring honour upon themselves and their art, in proportion

---

3. Cf. Coleridge's account of their plan in *Biographia Literaria*, the beginning of chap. 14.

as they separate themselves from the sympathies of men, and indulge in arbitrary and capricious habits of expression, in order to furnish food for fickle tastes, and fickle appetites, of their own creation.[4]

I cannot, however, be insensible of the present outcry against the triviality and meanness both of thought and language, which some of my contemporaries have occasionally introduced into their metrical compositions; and I acknowledge, that this defect, where it exists, is more dishonorable to the writer's own character than false refinement or arbitrary innovation, though I should contend at the same time that it is far less pernicious in the sum of its consequences. From such verses the poems in these volumes will be found distinguished at least by one mark of difference, that each of them has a worthy *purpose*. Not that I mean to say, that I always began to write with a distinct purpose formally conceived; but I believe that my habits of meditation have so formed my feelings, as that my descriptions of such objects as strongly excite those feelings, will be found to carry along with them a *purpose*. If in this opinion I am mistaken, I can have little right to the name of a poet. For all good poetry is the spontaneous overflow of powerful feelings: but though this be true, poems to which any value can be attached, were never produced on any variety of subjects but by a man who, being possessed of more than usual organic sensibility, had also thought long and deeply. For our continued influxes of feeling are modified and directed by our thoughts, which are indeed the representatives of all our past feelings; and, as by contemplating the relation of these general representatives to each other we discover what is really important to men, so, by the repetition and continuance of this act, our feelings will be connected with important subjects, till at length, if we be originally possessed of much sensibility, such habits of mind will be produced, that, by obeying blindly and mechanically the impulses of those habits, we shall describe objects, and utter sentiments, of such a nature and in such connection with each other, that the understanding of the being to whom we address ourselves, if he be in a healthful state of association, must necessarily be in some degree enlightened, and his affections ameliorated.

I have said that each of these poems has a purpose. I have also informed my reader what this purpose will be found principally to be: namely, to illustrate the manner in which our feelings and ideas are associated in a state of excitement. But, speaking in language somewhat more appropriate, it is to follow the fluxes and refluxes of the mind when agitated by the great and simple affections of our nature. This object I have endeavored in these short essays to attain by various means; by tracing the maternal passion through many of its more subtile windings, as in the poems of the *Idiot Boy* and the *Mad Mother*; by accompanying the last struggles of a human being, at the approach of death, cleaving in solitude to life and society, as in the poem of the *Forsaken Indian*; by shewing, as in the stanzas entitled *We Are Seven*, the perplexity and obscurity which in childhood attend our notion of death, or rather our utter inability to admit that notion; or by displaying the strength of fraternal, or to speak more philosophically, of moral attachment when early associated with the great and beautiful objects of nature, as in *The Brothers*; or, as in the Incident of *Simon Lee*, by placing my reader in the

---

4. It is worth while here to observe that the affecting parts of Chaucer are almost always expressed in language pure and universally intelligible even to this day [Wordsworth's note].

way of receiving from ordinary moral sensations another and more salutary impression than we are accustomed to receive from them. It has also been part of my general purpose to attempt to sketch characters under the influence of less impassioned feelings, as in the *Two April Mornings, The Fountain, The Old Man Travelling, The Two Thieves,* &c., characters of which the elements are simple, belonging rather to nature than to manners, such as exist now, and will probably always exist, and which from their constitution may be distinctly and profitably contemplated. I will not abuse the indulgence of my reader by dwelling longer upon this subject; but it is proper that I should mention one other circumstance which distinguishes these poems from the popular poetry of the day; it is this, that the feeling therein developed gives importance to the action and situation, and not the action and situation to the feeling. My meaning will be rendered perfectly intelligible by referring my reader to the poems entitled *Poor Susan* and the *Childless Father,* particularly to the last stanza of the latter poem.

I will not suffer a sense of false modesty to prevent me from asserting, that I point my reader's attention to this mark of distinction, far less for the sake of these particular poems than from the general importance of the subject. The subject is indeed important! For the human mind is capable of being excited without the application of gross and violent stimulants; and he must have a very faint perception of its beauty and dignity who does not know this, and who does not further know, that one being is elevated above another, in proportion as he possesses this capability. It has therefore appeared to me, that to endeavour to produce or enlarge this capability is one of the best services in which, at any period, a writer can be engaged; but this service, excellent at all times, is especially so at the present day. For a multitude of causes, unknown to former times, are now acting with a combined force to blunt the discriminating powers of the mind, and, unfitting it for all voluntary exertion, to reduce it to a state of almost savage torpor. The most effective of these causes are the great national events which are daily taking place, and the increasing accumulation of men in cities, where the uniformity of their occupations produces a craving for extraordinary incident, which the rapid communication of intelligence hourly gratifies.[5] To this tendency of life and manners the literature and theatrical exhibitions of the country have conformed themselves. The invaluable works of our elder writers, I had almost said the works of Shakespeare and Milton, are driven into neglect by frantic novels, sickly and stupid German tragedies,[6] and deluges of idle and extravagant stories in verse.—When I think upon this degrading thirst after outrageous stimulation, I am almost ashamed to have spoken of the feeble effort with which I have endeavoured to counteract it; and, reflecting upon the magnitude of the general evil, I should be oppressed with no dishonorable melancholy, had I not a deep impression of certain inherent and indestructible qualities of the human mind, and likewise of certain powers in the great and permanent objects that act upon it which are equally inherent and indestructible; and did I not further add to this impression a belief, that the time is approaching when the evil will be sys-

5. This was the period of the wars against France, of industrial urbanization, and of the rapid proliferation in England of daily newspapers.
6. Wordsworth had in mind the "Gothic" terror novels by writers such as Ann Radcliffe and Mat-thew Gregory Lewis and the sentimental melodrama, then immensely popular in England, of August von Kotzebue and his German contemporaries.

tematically opposed, by men of greater powers, and with far more distinguished success.

Having dwelt thus long on the subjects and aim of these poems, I shall request the reader's permission to apprize him of a few circumstances relating to their *style*, in order, among other reasons, that I may not be censured for not having performed what I never attempted. The reader will find that personifications of abstract ideas rarely occur in these volumes; and, I hope, are utterly rejected as an ordinary device to elevate the style, and raise it above prose. I have proposed to myself to imitate, and, as far as is possible, to adopt the very language of men; and assuredly such personifications do not make any natural or regular part of that language. They are, indeed, a figure of speech occasionally prompted by passion, and I have made use of them as such; but I have endeavoured utterly to reject them as a mechanical device of style, or as a family language which writers in metre seem to lay claim to by prescription. I have wished to keep my reader in the company of flesh and blood, persuaded that by so doing I shall interest him. I am, however, well aware that others who pursue a different track may interest him likewise; I do not interfere with their claim, I only wish to prefer a different claim of my own. There will also be found in these volumes little of what is usually called poetic diction;[7] I have taken as much pains to avoid it as others ordinarily take to produce it; this I have done for the reason already alleged, to bring my language near to the language of men, and further, because the pleasure which I have proposed to myself to impart is of a kind very different from that which is supposed by many persons to be the proper object of poetry. I do not know how, without being culpably particular, I can give my reader a more exact notion of the style in which I wished these poems to be written than by informing him that I have at all times endeavoured to look steadily at my subject, consequently, I hope that there is in these poems little falsehood of description, and that my ideas are expressed in language fitted to their respective importance. Something I must have gained by this practice, as it is friendly to one property of all good poetry, namely, good sense; but it has necessarily cut me off from a large portion of phrases and figures of speech which from father to son have long been regarded as the common inheritance of poets. I have also thought it expedient to restrict myself still further, having abstained from the use of many expressions, in themselves proper and beautiful, but which have been foolishly repeated by bad poets, till such feelings of disgust are connected with them as it is scarcely possible by any art of association to overpower.

If in a poem there should be found a series of lines, or even a single line, in which the language, though naturally arranged and according to the strict laws of metre, does not differ from that of prose, there is a numerous class of critics, who, when they stumble upon these prosaisms as they call them, imagine that they have made a notable discovery, and exult over the poet as over a man ignorant of his own profession. Now these men would establish a canon of criticism which the reader will conclude he must utterly reject, if he wishes to be pleased with these volumes. And it would be a most easy task to prove to him, that not only the language of a large portion of every

---

7. In the sense of words, phrases, and figures of speech not commonly used in conversation or prose that are regarded as especially appropriate to poetry.

good poem, even of the most elevated character, must necessarily, except with reference to the metre, in no respect differ from that of good prose, but likewise that some of the most interesting parts of the best poems will be found to be strictly the language of prose, when prose is well written. The truth of this assertion might be demonstrated by innumerable passages from almost all the poetical writings, even of Milton himself. I have not space for much quotation; but, to illustrate the subject in a general manner, I will here adduce a short composition of Gray, who was at the head of those who by their reasonings have attempted to widen the space of separation betwixt prose and metrical composition, and was more than any other man curiously elaborate in the structure of his own poetic diction.[8]

> In vain to me the smiling mornings shine,
> And reddening Phoebus lifts his golden fire:
> The birds in vain their amorous descant join,
> Or cheerful fields resume their green attire:
> These ears, alas! for other notes repine;
> *A different object do these eyes require;*
> *My lonely anguish melts no heart but mine;*
> *And in my breast the imperfect joys expire;*
> Yet Morning smiles the busy race to cheer,
> And new-born pleasure brings to happier men;
> The fields to all their wonted tribute bear;
> To warm their little loves the birds complain.
> *I fruitless mourn to him that cannot hear*
> *And weep the more because I weep in vain.*

It will easily be perceived that the only part of this sonnet which is of any value is the lines printed in italics: it is equally obvious, that, except in the rhyme, and in the use of the single word "fruitless" for fruitlessly, which is so far a defect, the language of these lines does in no respect differ from that of prose.

By the foregoing quotation I have shewn that the language of prose may yet be well adapted to poetry; and I have previously asserted that a large portion of the language of every good poem can in no respect differ from that of good prose. I will go further. I do not doubt that it may be safely affirmed, that there neither is, nor can be, any essential difference between the language of prose and metrical composition. We are fond of tracing the resemblance between poetry and painting, and, accordingly, we call them sisters: but where shall we find bonds of connection sufficiently strict to typify the affinity betwixt metrical and prose composition? They both speak by and to the same organs; the bodies in which both of them are clothed may be said to be of the same substance, their affections are kindred and almost identical, not necessarily differing even in degree; poetry[9] sheds no

---

8. Thomas Gray had written, in a letter to Richard West, that "the language of the age is never the language of poetry." The poem that follows is Gray's *Sonnet on the Death of Richard West*.

9. I here use the word "poetry" (though against my own judgment) as opposed to the word "prose," and synonymous with metrical composition. But much confusion has been introduced into criticism by this contradistinction of poetry and prose, instead of the more philosophical one of poetry and matter of fact, or science. The only strict antithesis to prose is metre; nor is this, in truth, a *strict* antithesis; because lines and passages of metre so naturally occur in writing prose, that it would be scarcely possible to avoid them, even were it desirable [Wordsworth's note].

tears "such as Angels weep,"[1] but natural and human tears; she can boast of no celestial ichor[2] that distinguishes her vital juices from those of prose; the same human blood circulates through the veins of them both.

* * *

["What is a Poet?"]

Taking up the subject, then, upon general grounds, I ask what is meant by the word "poet"? What is a poet? To whom does he address himself? And what language is to be expected from him? He is a man speaking to men: a man, it is true, endued with more lively sensibility, more enthusiasm and tenderness, who has a greater knowledge of human nature, and a more comprehensive soul, than are supposed to be common among mankind; a man pleased with his own passions and volitions, and who rejoices more than other men in the spirit of life that is in him; delighting to contemplate similar volitions and passions as manifested in the goings-on of the universe, and habitually impelled to create them where he does not find them. To these qualities he has added a disposition to be affected more than other men by absent things as if they were present; an ability of conjuring up in himself passions, which are indeed far from being the same as those produced by real events, yet (especially in those parts of the general sympathy which are pleasing and delightful) do more nearly resemble the passions produced by real events, than any thing which, from the motions of their own minds merely, other men are accustomed to feel in themselves; whence, and from practice, he has acquired a greater readiness and power in expressing what he thinks and feels, and especially those thoughts and feelings which, by his own choice, or from the structure of his own mind, arise in him without immediate external excitement.

But, whatever portion of this faculty we may suppose even the greatest poet to possess, there cannot be a doubt but that the language which it will suggest to him, must, in liveliness and truth, fall far short of that which is uttered by men in real life, under the actual pressure of those passions, certain shadows of which the poet thus produces, or feels to be produced, in himself. However exalted a notion we would wish to cherish of the character of a poet, it is obvious, that, while he describes and imitates passions, his situation is altogether slavish and mechanical, compared with the freedom and power of real and substantial action and suffering. So that it will be the wish of the poet to bring his feelings near to those of the persons whose feelings he describes, nay, for short spaces of time perhaps, to let himself slip into an entire delusion, and even confound and identify his own feelings with theirs; modifying only the language which is thus suggested to him, by a consideration that he describes for a particular purpose, that of giving pleasure. Here, then, he will apply the principle on which I have so much insisted, namely, that of selection; on this he will depend for removing what would otherwise be painful or disgusting in the passion; he will feel that there is no necessity to trick out or to elevate nature: and, the more industriously he applies this principle, the deeper will be his faith that no

1. *Paradise Lost* 1.620.
2. In Greek mythology, the fluid in the veins of the gods.

words, which his fancy or imagination can suggest, will be to be compared with those which are the emanations of reality and truth.

But it may be said by those who do not object to the general spirit of these remarks, that, as it is impossible for the poet to produce upon all occasions language as exquisitely fitted for the passion as that which the real passion itself suggests, it is proper that he should consider himself as in the situation of a translator, who deems himself justified when he substitutes excellences of another kind for those which are unattainable by him; and endeavours occasionally to surpass his original, in order to make some amends for the general inferiority to which he feels that he must submit. But this would be to encourage idleness and unmanly despair. Further, it is the language of men who speak of what they do not understand; who talk of poetry as a matter of amusement and idle pleasure; who will converse with us as gravely about a *taste* for poetry, as they express it, as if it were a thing as indifferent as a taste for rope-dancing, or Frontiniac[3] or sherry. Aristotle, I have been told, hath said, that poetry is the most philosophic of all writing;[4] it is so: its object is truth, not individual and local, but general, and operative; not standing upon external testimony, but carried alive into the heart by passion; truth which is its own testimony, which gives strength and divinity to the tribunal to which it appeals, and receives them from the same tribunal. Poetry is the image of man and nature. The obstacles which stand in the way of the fidelity of the biographer and historian, and of their consequent utility, are incalculably greater than those which are to be encountered by the poet who has an adequate notion of the dignity of his art. The poet writes under one restriction only, namely, that of the necessity of giving immediate pleasure to a human being possessed of that information which may be expected from him, not as a lawyer, a physician, a mariner, an astronomer or a natural philosopher, but as a man. Except this one restriction, there is no object standing between the poet and the image of things; between this, and the biographer and historian there are a thousand.

Nor let this necessity of producing immediate pleasure be considered as a degradation of the poet's art. It is far otherwise. It is an acknowledgment of the beauty of the universe, an acknowledgment the more sincere because it is not formal, but indirect; it is a task light and easy to him who looks at the world in the spirit of love: further, it is a homage paid to the native and naked dignity of man, to the grand elementary principle of pleasure, by which he knows, and feels, and lives, and moves.[5] We have no sympathy but what is propagated by pleasure: I would not be misunderstood; but wherever we sympathize with pain it will be found that the sympathy is produced and carried on by subtle combinations with pleasure. We have no knowledge, that is, no general principles drawn from the contemplation of particular facts, but what has been built up by pleasure, and exists in us by pleasure alone. The man of science, the chemist and mathematician, whatever difficulties and disgusts they may have had to struggle with, know and feel this. However painful may be the objects with which the anatomist's knowledge is connected, he feels that his knowledge is pleasure; and where he has no

3. A sweet wine made from muscat grapes.
4. Aristotle in fact said that "poetry is more philosophic than history, since its statements are of the nature of universals, whereas those of history are

singulars" (*Poetics* 1451b).
5. A bold echo of the words of St. Paul, that in God "we live, and move, and have our being" (Acts 17.28).

pleasure he has no knowledge. What then does the poet? He considers man and the objects that surround him as acting and re-acting upon each other, so as to produce an infinite complexity of pain and pleasure; he considers man in his own nature and in his ordinary life as contemplating this with a certain quantity of immediate knowledge, with certain convictions, intuitions, and deductions which by habit become of the nature of intuitions; he considers him as looking upon this complex scene of ideas and sensations, and finding every where objects that immediately excite in him sympathies which, from the necessities of his nature, are accompanied by an overbalance of enjoyment.

To this knowledge which all men carry about with them, and to these sympathies in which without any other discipline than that of our daily life we are fitted to take delight, the poet principally directs his attention. He considers man and nature as essentially adapted to each other,[6] and the mind of man as naturally the mirror of the fairest and most interesting qualities of nature. And thus the poet, prompted by this feeling of pleasure which accompanies him through the whole course of his studies, converses with general nature with affections akin to those, which, through labour and length of time, the man of science has raised up in himself, by conversing with those particular parts of nature which are the objects of his studies. The knowledge both of the poet and the man of science is pleasure; but the knowledge of the one cleaves to us as a necessary part of our existence, our natural and unalienable inheritance; the other is a personal and individual acquisition, slow to come to us, and by no habitual and direct sympathy connecting us with our fellow-beings. The man of science seeks truth as a remote and unknown benefactor; he cherishes and loves it in his solitude: the poet, singing a song in which all human beings join with him, rejoices in the presence of truth as our visible friend and hourly companion. Poetry is the breath and finer spirit of all knowledge; it is the impassioned expression which is in the countenance of all science. Emphatically may it be said of the poet, as Shakespeare hath said of man, "that he looks before and after."[7] He is the rock of defence of human nature; an upholder and preserver, carrying everywhere with him relationship and love. In spite of difference of soil and climate, of language and manners, of laws and customs, in spite of things silently gone out of mind and things violently destroyed, the poet binds together by passion and knowledge the vast empire of human society, as it is spread over the whole earth, and over all time. The objects of the poet's thoughts are every where; though the eyes and senses of man are, it is true, his favorite guides, yet he will follow wheresoever he can find an atmosphere of sensation in which to move his wings. Poetry is the first and last of all knowledge—it is as immortal as the heart of man. If the labours of men of science should ever create any material revolution, direct or indirect, in our condition, and in the impressions which we habitually receive, the poet will sleep then no more than at present, but he will be ready to follow the steps of the man of science, not only in those general indirect effects, but he will be at his side, carrying sensation into the midst of the objects of the science itself. The remotest discoveries of the chemist, the botanist, or mineralogist,

---

6. On the mutual adaptation of man's mind and nature, see Wordsworth's Prospectus to The

Recluse, p. 302, lines 63–71.
7. *Hamlet* 4.4.37.

will be as proper objects of the poet's art as any upon which it can be employed, if the time should ever come when these things shall be familiar to us, and the relations under which they are contemplated by the followers of these respective sciences shall be manifestly and palpably material to us as enjoying and suffering beings.[8] If the time should ever come when what is now called science, thus familiarized to men, shall be ready to put on, as it were, a form of flesh and blood, the poet will lend his divine spirit to aid the transfiguration, and will welcome the being thus produced, as a dear and genuine inmate of the household of man.—It is not, then, to be supposed that any one, who holds that sublime notion of poetry which I have attempted to convey, will break in upon the sanctity and truth of his pictures by transitory and accidental ornaments, and endeavour to excite admiration of himself by arts, the necessity of which must manifestly depend upon the assumed meanness of his subject.

What I have thus far said applies to poetry in general; but especially to those parts of composition where the poet speaks through the mouth of his characters; and upon this point it appears to have such weight that I will conclude, there are few persons, of good sense, who would not allow that the dramatic parts of composition are defective, in proportion as they deviate from the real language of nature, and are coloured by a diction of the poet's own, either peculiar to him as an individual poet, or belonging simply to poets in general, to a body of men who, from the circumstance of their compositions being in metre, it is expected will employ a particular language.

It is not, then, in the dramatic parts of composition that we look for this distinction of language; but still it may be proper and necessary where the poet speaks to us in his own person and character. To this I answer by referring my reader to the description which I have before given of a poet. Among the qualities which I have enumerated as principally conducing to form a poet, is implied nothing differing in kind from other men, but only in degree. The sum of what I have there said is, that the poet is chiefly distinguished from other men by a greater promptness to think and feel without immediate external excitement, and a greater power in expressing such thoughts and feelings as are produced in him in that manner. But these passions and thoughts and feelings are the general passions and thoughts and feelings of men. And with what are they connected? Undoubtedly with our moral sentiments and animal sensations, and with the causes which excite these; with the operations of the elements and the appearances of the visible universe; with storm and sun-shine, with the revolutions of the seasons, with cold and heat, with loss of friends and kindred, with injuries and resentments, gratitude and hope, with fear and sorrow. These, and the like, are the sensations and objects which the poet describes, as they are the sensations of other men, and the objects which interest them. The poet thinks and feels in the spirit of the passions of men. How, then, can his language differ in any material degree from that of all other men who feel vividly and see clearly? It might be *proved* that it is impossible. But supposing that this were not the case, the poet might then be allowed to use a peculiar language, when expressing his feelings for his own gratification, or that of

8. Wordsworth is at least right in anticipating the poetry of the machine; he himself wrote an early instance, the sonnet *Steamboats, Viaducts, and Railways.*

men like himself. But poets do not write for poets alone, but for men. Unless therefore we are advocates for that admiration which depends upon ignorance, and that pleasure which arises from hearing what we do not understand, the poet must descend from this supposed height, and, in order to excite rational sympathy, he must express himself as other men express themselves. * * *

[“EMOTION RECOLLECTED IN TRANQUILLITY”]

I have said that poetry is the spontaneous overflow of powerful feelings: it takes its origin from emotion recollected in tranquillity: the emotion is contemplated till by a species of reaction the tranquillity gradually disappears, and an emotion, kindred to that which was before the subject of contemplation, is gradually produced, and does itself actually exist in the mind. In this mood successful composition generally begins, and in a mood similar to this it is carried on; but the emotion, of whatever kind and in whatever degree, from various causes is qualified by various pleasures, so that in describing any passions whatsoever, which are voluntarily described, the mind will upon the whole be in a state of enjoyment. Now, if nature be thus cautious in preserving in a state of enjoyment a being thus employed, the poet ought to profit by the lesson thus held forth to him, and ought especially to take care, that whatever passions he communicates to his reader, those passions, if his reader's mind be sound and vigorous, should always be accompanied with an overbalance of pleasure. Now the music of harmonious metrical language, the sense of difficulty overcome, and the blind association of pleasure which has been previously received from works of rhyme or metre of the same or similar construction, an indistinct perception perpetually renewed of language closely resembling that of real life, and yet, in the circumstance of metre, differing from it so widely, all these imperceptibly make up a complex feeling of delight, which is of the most important use in tempering the painful feeling which will always be found intermingled with powerful descriptions of the deeper passions. This effect is always produced in pathetic and impassioned poetry; while, in lighter compositions, the ease and gracefulness with which the poet manages his numbers are themselves confessedly a principal source of the gratification of the reader. I might perhaps include all which it is *necessary* to say upon this subject by affirming, what few persons will deny, that, of two descriptions, either of passions, manners, or characters, each of them equally well executed, the one in prose and the other in verse, the verse will be read a hundred times where the prose is read once.
* * *

I know that nothing would have so effectually contributed to further the end which I have in view, as to have shewn of what kind the pleasure is, and how the pleasure is produced, which is confessedly produced by metrical composition essentially different from that which I have here endeavoured to recommend: for the reader will say that he has been pleased by such composition; and what can I do more for him? The power of any art is limited; and he will suspect, that, if I propose to furnish him with new friends, it is only upon condition of his abandoning his old friends. Besides, as I have said, the reader is himself conscious of the pleasure which he has received from such composition, composition to which he has peculiarly attached the endearing name of poetry; and all men feel an habitual gratitude, and something of an honorable bigotry for the objects which have long continued to please them: we not only wish to be pleased, but to be pleased in that particular way in which we have been accustomed to be pleased. There is a host of arguments in these feelings; and I should be the less able to combat them successfully, as I am willing to allow, that, in order entirely to enjoy the poetry which I am recommending, it would be necessary to give up much of what is ordinarily enjoyed. But, would my limits have permitted me to point out how this pleasure is produced, I might have removed many obstacles, and assisted my reader in perceiving that the powers of language are not so limited as he may suppose; and that it is possible that poetry may give other enjoyments, of a purer, more lasting, and more exquisite nature. This part of my subject I have not altogether neglected; but it has been less my present aim to prove, that the interest excited by some other kinds of poetry is less vivid, and less worthy of the nobler powers of the mind, than to offer reasons for presuming, that, if the object which I have proposed to myself were adequately attained, a species of poetry would be produced, which is genuine poetry; in its nature well adapted to interest mankind permanently, and likewise important in the multiplicity and quality of its moral relations.

From what has been said, and from a perusal of the poems, the reader will be able clearly to perceive the object which I have proposed to myself: he will determine how far I have attained this object; and, what is a much more important question, whether it be worth attaining; and upon the decision of these two questions will rest my claim to the approbation of the public.

1800, 1802

Strange fits of passion have I known[1]

Strange fits of passion have I known:
And I will dare to tell,
But in the Lover's ear alone,
What once to me befel.

5 When she I loved looked every day
Fresh as a rose in June,
I to her cottage bent my way,
Beneath an evening moon.

Upon the moon I fixed my eye,
10 All over the wide lea;
With quickening pace my horse drew nigh
Those paths so dear to me.

---

1. This and the four following pieces are often grouped by editors as the "Lucy poems," even though *A slumber did my spirit seal* does not identify the "she" who is the subject of that poem. All but the last were written in 1799, while Words- worth and his sister were in Germany, and home- sick. There has been diligent speculation about the identity of Lucy, but it remains speculation. The one certainty is that she is not the girl of Words- worth's *Lucy Gray*.

And now we reached the orchard-plot;
And, as we climbed the hill,
15   The sinking moon to Lucy's cot
Came near, and nearer still.

In one of those sweet dreams I slept,
Kind Nature's gentlest boon!
And all the while my eyes I kept
20   On the descending moon.

My horse moved on; hoof after hoof
He raised, and never stopped:
When down behind the cottage roof,
At once, the bright moon dropped.

25   What fond and wayward thoughts will slide
Into a Lover's head!
"O mercy!" to myself I cried,
"If Lucy should be dead!"[2]

1799   1800

She dwelt among the untrodden ways[1]

She dwelt among the untrodden ways
    Beside the springs of Dove,[2]
A Maid whom there were none to praise
    And very few to love:

5   A violet by a mossy stone
    Half hidden from the eye!
—Fair as a star, when only one
    Is shining in the sky.

She lived unknown, and few could know
10   When Lucy ceased to be;
But she is in her grave, and, oh,
    The difference to me!

1799   1800

Three years she grew

Three years she grew in sun and shower,
Then Nature said, "A lovelier flower
On earth was never sown;

2. An additional stanza in an earlier manuscript version demonstrates how a poem can be improved by omission of a passage that is, in itself, excellent poetry: "I told her this: her laughter light / Is ringing in my ears; / And when I think upon that night / My eyes are dim with tears."

1. For the author's revisions while composing this poem, see "Poems in Process," in the appendices to this volume.
2. There are several rivers by this name in England, including one in the Lake District.

This Child I to myself will take;
5   She shall be mine, and I will make
A Lady of my own.[1]

"Myself will to my darling be
Both law and impulse: and with me
The Girl, in rock and plain,
10 In earth and heaven, in glade and bower,
Shall feel an overseeing power
To kindle or restrain.

"She shall be sportive as the fawn
That wild with glee across the lawn
15 Or up the mountain springs;
And hers shall be the breathing balm,
And hers the silence and the calm
Of mute insensate things.

"The floating clouds their state shall lend
20 To her; for her the willow bend;
Nor shall she fail to see
Even in the motions of the Storm
Grace that shall mould the Maiden's form
By silent sympathy.

25 "The stars of midnight shall be dear
To her; and she shall lean her ear
In many a secret place
Where rivulets dance their wayward round,
And beauty born of murmuring sound
30 Shall pass into her face.

"And vital feelings of delight
Shall rear her form to stately height,
Her virgin bosom swell;
Such thoughts to Lucy I will give
35 While she and I together live
Here in this happy dell."

Thus Nature spake—the work was done—
How soon my Lucy's race was run!
She died, and left to me
40 This heath, this calm, and quiet scene;
The memory of what has been,
And never more will be.

1799   1800

1. I.e., Lucy was three years old at the time when Nature made this promise; line 37 makes clear that Lucy had reached the maturity foretold in the sixth stanza when she died.

A slumber did my spirit seal

A slumber did my spirit seal;
   I had no human fears:
She seemed a thing that could not feel
   The touch of earthly years.

5 No motion has she now, no force;
   She neither hears nor sees;
Rolled round in earth's diurnal° course,   *daily*
   With rocks, and stones, and trees.

1799   1800

I travelled among unknown men

I travelled among unknown men,
   In lands beyond the sea;
Nor, England! did I know till then
   What love I bore to thee.

5 'Tis past, that melancholy dream!
   Nor will I quit thy shore
A second time; for still I seem
   To love thee more and more.

Among thy mountains did I feel
10   The joy of my desire;
And she I cherished turned her wheel
   Beside an English fire.

Thy mornings showed, thy nights concealed
   The bowers where Lucy played;
15 And thine too is the last green field
   That Lucy's eyes surveyed.

ca. 1801   1807

Lucy Gray[1]

Or, Solitude

Oft I had heard of Lucy Gray:
And, when I crossed the wild,

1. Written in 1799 while Wordsworth was in Germany, and founded on a true account of a young girl who drowned when she lost her way in a snowstorm. "The body however was found in the canal. The way in which the incident was treated and the spiritualizing of the character might furnish hints for contrasting the imaginative influences which I have endeavored to throw over common life with Crabbe's matter-of-fact style of treating subjects of the same kind" [Wordsworth's note]. Cf. Wordsworth's statement, in the Preface to *Lyrical Ballads*, of his undertaking to throw over ordinary things "a certain colouring of imagination" (p. 241).

I chanced to see at break of day
The solitary child.

5 No mate, no comrade Lucy knew;
She dwelt on a wide moor,
—The sweetest thing that ever grew
Beside a human door!

You yet may spy the fawn at play,
10 The hare upon the green;
But the sweet face of Lucy Gray
Will never more be seen.

"To-night will be a stormy night—
You to the town must go;
15 And take a lantern, Child, to light
Your mother through the snow."

"That, Father! will I gladly do:
'Tis scarcely afternoon—
The minster°-clock has just struck two,   *church*
20 And yonder is the moon!"

At this the Father raised his hook,
And snapped a faggot-band;[2]
He plied his work;—and Lucy took
The lantern in her hand.

25 Not blither is the mountain roe:
With many a wanton stroke
Her feet disperse the powdery snow,
That rises up like smoke.

The storm came on before its time:
30 She wandered up and down;
And many a hill did Lucy climb:
But never reached the town.

The wretched parents all that night
Went shouting far and wide;
35 But there was neither sound nor sight
To serve them for a guide.

At day-break on a hill they stood
That overlooked the moor;
And thence they saw the bridge of wood,
40 A furlong[3] from their door.

2. Cord binding a bundle of sticks to be used for   3. One eighth of a mile.
fuel.

They wept—and, turning homeward, cried,
"In heaven we all shall meet;"
—When in the snow the mother spied
The print of Lucy's feet.

45 Then downwards from the steep hill's edge
They tracked the footmarks small;
And through the broken hawthorn hedge,
And by the long stone-wall;

And then an open field they crossed:
50 The marks were still the same;
They tracked them on, nor ever lost;
And to the bridge they came.

They followed from the snowy bank
Those footmarks, one by one,
55 Into the middle of the plank;
And further there were none!

—Yet some maintain that to this day
She is a living child;
That you may see sweet Lucy Gray
60 Upon the lonesome wild.

O'er rough and smooth she trips along,
And never looks behind;
And sings a solitary song
That whistles in the wind.

1799   1800

The Two April Mornings[1]

We walked along, while bright and red
Uprose the morning sun;
And Matthew stopped, he looked, and said,
"The will of God be done!"

5 A village schoolmaster was he,
With hair of glittering grey;
As blithe a man as you could see
On a spring holiday.

And on that morning, through the grass,
10 And by the steaming rills,°   *small streams*
We travelled merrily, to pass
A day among the hills.

1. In this poem and another called *Matthew*, both written in 1799, the central figure is named after a onetime schoolmaster at Hawkshead School, which Wordsworth attended.

"Our work," said I, "was well begun,
Then, from thy breast what thought,
15 Beneath so beautiful a sun,
So sad a sigh has brought?"

A second time did Matthew stop;
And fixing still his eye
Upon the eastern mountain-top,
20 To me he made reply:

"Yon cloud with that long purple cleft
Brings fresh into my mind
A day like this which I have left
Full thirty years behind.

25 "And just above yon slope of corn
Such colours, and no other,
Were in the sky, that April morn,
Of this the very brother.

"With rod and line I sued the sport
30 Which that sweet season gave,
And, to the church-yard come, stopped short
Beside my daughter's grave.

"Nine summers had she scarcely seen,
The pride of all the vale;
35 And then she sang;—she would have been
A very nightingale.

"Six feet in earth my Emma lay;
And yet I loved her more,
For so it seemed, than till that day
40 I e'er had loved before.

"And, turning from her grave, I met,
Beside the churchyard yew,
A blooming Girl, whose hair was wet
With points of morning dew.

45 "A basket on her head she bare;
Her brow was smooth and white:
To see a child so very fair,
It was a pure delight!

"No fountain from its rocky cave
50 E'er tripped with foot so free;
She seemed as happy as a wave
That dances on the sea.

"There came from me a sigh of pain
Which I could ill confine;

55 I looked at her, and looked again:
And did not wish her mine!"

Matthew is in his grave, yet now,
Methinks, I see him stand,
As at that moment, with a bough
60 Of wilding² in his hand.

1799   1800

Nutting¹

——————It seems a day
(I speak of one from many singled out)
One of those heavenly days that cannot die;
When, in the eagerness of boyish hope,
5 I left our cottage-threshold, sallying forth
With a huge wallet o'er my shoulder slung,
A nutting-crook in hand; and turned my steps
Tow'rd some far-distant wood, a Figure quaint,
Tricked out in proud disguise of cast-off weeds°   clothes
10 Which for that service had been husbanded,
By exhortation of my frugal Dame²—
Motley accoutrement, of power to smile
At thorns, and brakes, and brambles,—and, in truth,
More ragged than need was! O'er pathless rocks,
15 Through beds of matted fern, and tangled thickets,
Forcing my way, I came to one dear nook
Unvisited, where not a broken bough
Drooped with its withered leaves, ungracious sign
Of devastation; but the hazels rose
20 Tall and erect, with tempting clusters hung,
A virgin scene!—A little while I stood,
Breathing with such suppression of the heart
As joy delights in; and, with wise restraint
Voluptuous, fearless of a rival, eyed
25 The banquet;—or beneath the trees I sate
Among the flowers, and with the flowers I played;
A temper known to those, who, after long
And weary expectation, have been blest
With sudden happiness beyond all hope.
30 Perhaps it was a bower beneath whose leaves
The violets of five seasons re-appear
And fade, unseen by any human eye;
Where fairy water-breaks³ do murmur on
For ever; and I saw the sparkling foam,

2. An uncultivated tree or plant, especially the wild apple tree.
1. Wordsworth said that these lines, written in Germany in 1798, were "intended as part of a poem on my own mind [*The Prelude*], but struck out as not being wanted there." He published them in the second edition of *Lyrical Ballads,* 1800.
2. Ann Tyson, with whom Wordsworth lodged while at Hawkshead grammar school.
3. Places where the flow of a stream is broken by rocks.

35 And—with my cheek on one of those green stones
    That, fleeced with moss, under the shady trees,
    Lay round me, scattered like a flock of sheep—
    I heard the murmur and the murmuring sound,
    In that sweet mood when pleasure loves to pay
40 Tribute to ease; and, of its joy secure,
    The heart luxuriates with indifferent things,
    Wasting its kindliness on stocks⁴ and stones,
    And on the vacant air. Then up I rose,
    And dragged to earth both branch and bough, with crash
45 And merciless ravage: and the shady nook
    Of hazels, and the green and mossy bower,
    Deformed and sullied, patiently gave up
    Their quiet being: and, unless I now
    Confound my present feelings with the past,
50 Ere from the mutilated bower I turned
    Exulting, rich beyond the wealth of kings,
    I felt a sense of pain when I beheld
    The silent trees, and saw the intruding sky.—
    Then, dearest Maiden,⁵ move along these shades
55 In gentleness of heart; with gentle hand
    Touch—for there is a spirit in the woods.

1798   1800

The Ruined Cottage¹

First Part

    'Twas summer and the sun was mounted high.
    Along the south the uplands feebly glared
    Through a pale steam, and all the northern downs
    In clearer air ascending shewed far off
5   Their surfaces with shadows dappled o'er
    Of deep embattled clouds: far as the sight
    Could reach those many shadows lay in spots
    Determined and unmoved, with steady beams
    Of clear and pleasant sunshine interposed;
10 Pleasant to him who on the soft cool moss
    Extends his careless limbs beside the root
    Of some huge oak whose aged branches make

---

4. Tree stumps. ("Stocks and stones" is a conventional expression for "inanimate things.")
5. In a manuscript passage originally intended to lead up to *Nutting,* the maiden is called Lucy.
1. Wordsworth wrote *The Ruined Cottage* in 1797–98, then revised it several times before he finally published an expanded version of the story as book 1 of *The Excursion,* in 1814. *The Ruined Cottage* was not published as an independent poem until 1949, when it appeared in the fifth volume of *The Poetical Works of William Wordsworth,* edited by Ernest de Selincourt and Helen Darbishire, who printed a version known as "MS. B." The text reprinted here is from "MS. D," dated

1799, as transcribed by James Butler in the Cornell Wordsworth volume, *"The Ruined Cottage" and "The Pedlar"* (1979).

This version is one of Wordsworth's earliest successes in verse narrative. The story presents the bleak facts of "a tale of silent suffering"—suffering that is undeserved, unrationalized, and irremissive. The event is "a common tale," and it poses the implicit question, What are we to make of human life, in which such things happen? The narrator confronts the fact of human suffering without reference to the creed of a beneficent power, whether in or out of nature.

A twilight of their own, a dewy shade
Where the wren warbles while the dreaming man,
15 Half-conscious of that soothing melody,
With side-long eye looks out upon the scene,
By those impending branches made more soft,
More soft and distant. Other lot was mine.
Across a bare wide Common I had toiled
20 With languid feet which by the slipp'ry ground
Were baffled still, and when I stretched myself
On the brown earth my limbs from very heat
Could find no rest nor my weak arm disperse
The insect host which gathered round my face
25 And joined their murmurs to the tedious noise
Of seeds of bursting gorse that crackled round.
I rose and turned towards a group of trees
Which midway in that level stood alone,
And thither come at length, beneath a shade
30 Of clustering elms that sprang from the same root
I found a ruined house, four naked walls
That stared upon each other. I looked round
And near the door I saw an aged Man,
Alone, and stretched upon the cottage bench;
35 An iron-pointed staff lay at his side.
With instantaneous joy I recognized
That pride of nature and of lowly life,
The venerable Armytage, a friend
As dear to me as is the setting sun.
40   Two days before
We had been fellow-travellers. I knew
That he was in this neighbourhood and now
Delighted found him here in the cool shade.
He lay, his pack of rustic merchandize
45 Pillowing his head—I guess he had no thought
Of his way-wandering life. His eyes were shut;
The shadows of the breezy elms above
Dappled his face. With thirsty heat oppress'd
At length I hailed him, glad to see his hat
50 Bedewed with water-drops, as if the brim
Had newly scoop'd a running stream. He rose
And pointing to a sun-flower bade me climb
The [   ]² wall where that same gaudy flower
Looked out upon the road. It was a plot
55 Of garden-ground, now wild, its matted weeds
Marked with the steps of those whom as they pass'd,
The goose-berry trees that shot in long lank slips,
Or currants hanging from their leafless stems
In scanty strings, had tempted to o'erleap
60 The broken wall. Within that cheerless spot,
Where two tall hedgerows of thick willow boughs

---

2. The brackets here and in later lines mark blank spaces left unfilled in the manuscript.

Joined in a damp cold nook, I found a well
Half-choked [with willow flowers and weeds.]³
I slaked my thirst and to the shady bench
65 Returned, and while I stood unbonneted
To catch the motion of the cooler air
The old Man said, "I see around me here
Things which you cannot see: we die, my Friend,
Nor we alone, but that which each man loved
70 And prized in his peculiar nook of earth
Dies with him or is changed, and very soon
Even of the good is no memorial left.
The Poets in their elegies and songs
Lamenting the departed call the groves,
75 They call upon the hills and streams to mourn,
And senseless rocks, nor idly; for they speak
In these their invocations with a voice
Obedient to the strong creative power
Of human passion. Sympathies there are
80 More tranquil, yet perhaps of kindred birth,
That steal upon the meditative mind
And grow with thought. Beside yon spring I stood
And eyed its waters till we seemed to feel
One sadness, they and I. For them a bond
85 Of brotherhood is broken: time has been
When every day the touch of human hand
Disturbed their stillness, and they ministered
To human comfort. When I stooped to drink,
A spider's web hung to the water's edge,
90 And on the wet and slimy foot-stone lay
The useless fragment of a wooden bowl;
It moved my very heart. The day has been
When I could never pass this road but she
Who lived within these walls, when I appeared,
95 A daughter's welcome gave me, and I loved her
As my own child. O Sir! the good die first,
And they whose hearts are dry as summer dust
Burn to the socket. Many a passenger
Has blessed poor Margaret for her gentle looks
100 When she upheld the cool refreshment drawn
From that forsaken spring, and no one came
But he was welcome, no one went away
But that it seemed she loved him. She is dead,
The worm is on her cheek, and this poor hut,
105 Stripp'd of its outward garb of household flowers,
Of rose and sweet-briar, offers to the wind
A cold bare wall whose earthy top is tricked
With weeds and the rank spear-grass. She is dead,
And nettles rot and adders sun themselves
110 Where we have sate together while she nurs'd

3. Wordsworth penciled the bracketed phrase into a gap left in the manuscript.

Her infant at her breast. The unshod Colt,
The wandring heifer and the Potter's ass,
Find shelter now within the chimney-wall
Where I have seen her evening hearth-stone blaze
115 And through the window spread upon the road
Its chearful light.—You will forgive me, Sir,
But often on this cottage do I muse
As on a picture, till my wiser mind
Sinks, yielding to the foolishness of grief.
120   She had a husband, an industrious man,
Sober and steady; I have heard her say
That he was up and busy at his loom
In summer ere the mower's scythe had swept
The dewy grass, and in the early spring
125 Ere the last star had vanished. They who pass'd
At evening, from behind the garden-fence
Might hear his busy spade, which he would ply
After his daily work till the day-light
Was gone and every leaf and flower were lost
130 In the dark hedges. So they pass'd their days
In peace and comfort, and two pretty babes
Were their best hope next to the God in Heaven.
—You may remember, now some ten years gone,
Two blighting seasons when the fields were left
135 With half a harvest.[4] It pleased heaven to add
A worse affliction in the plague of war:
A happy land was stricken to the heart;
'Twas a sad time of sorrow and distress:
A wanderer among the cottages,
140 I with my pack of winter raiment saw
The hardships of that season: many rich
Sunk down as in a dream among the poor,
And of the poor did many cease to be,
And their place knew them not. Meanwhile, abridg'd
145 Of daily comforts, gladly reconciled
To numerous self-denials, Margaret
Went struggling on through those calamitous years
With chearful hope: but ere the second autumn
A fever seized her husband. In disease
150 He lingered long, and when his strength returned
He found the little he had stored to meet
The hour of accident or crippling age
Was all consumed. As I have said, 'twas now
A time of trouble; shoals of artisans
155 Were from their daily labour turned away
To hang for bread on parish charity,
They and their wives and children—happier far
Could they have lived as do the little birds

---

4. As James Butler points out in his introduction, Wordsworth is purposely distancing his story in time. The "two blighting seasons" in fact occurred in 1794–95, only a few years before Wordsworth wrote The Ruined Cottage, when a bad harvest was followed by one of the worst winters on record. Much of the seed grain was destroyed in the ground, and the price of wheat nearly doubled.

That peck along the hedges or the kite
160 That makes her dwelling in the mountain rocks.
Ill fared it now with Robert, he who dwelt
In this poor cottage; at his door he stood
And whistled many a snatch of merry tunes
That had no mirth in them, or with his knife
165 Carved uncouth figures on the heads of sticks,
Then idly sought about through every nook
Of house or garden any casual task
Of use or ornament, and with a strange,
Amusing but uneasy novelty
170 He blended where he might the various tasks
Of summer, autumn, winter, and of spring.
But this endured not; his good-humour soon
Became a weight in which no pleasure was,
And poverty brought on a petted° mood   *ill-tempered*
175 And a sore temper: day by day he drooped,
And he would leave his home, and to the town
Without an errand would he turn his steps
Or wander here and there among the fields.
One while he would speak lightly of his babes
180 And with a cruel tongue: at other times
He played with them wild freaks of merriment:
And 'twas a piteous thing to see the looks
Of the poor innocent children. 'Every smile,'
Said Margaret to me here beneath these trees,
185 'Made my heart bleed,' " At this the old Man paus'd
And looking up to those enormous elms
He said, " 'Tis now the hour of deepest noon,
At this still season of repose and peace,
This hour when all things which are not at rest
190 Are chearful, while this multitude of flies
Fills all the air with happy melody,
Why should a tear be in an old man's eye?
Why should we thus with an untoward mind
And in the weakness of humanity
195 From natural wisdom turn our hearts away,
To natural comfort shut our eyes and ears,
And feeding on disquiet thus disturb
The calm of Nature with our restless thoughts?"

END OF THE FIRST PART

Second Part

He spake with somewhat of a solemn tone:
200 But when he ended there was in his face
Such easy chearfulness, a look so mild
That for a little time it stole away
All recollection, and that simple tale
Passed from my mind like a forgotten sound.
205 A while on trivial things we held discourse,
To me soon tasteless. In my own despite

I thought of that poor woman as of one
Whom I had known and loved. He had rehearsed
Her homely tale with such familiar power,
210 With such a[n active][5] countenance, an eye
So busy, that the things of which he spake
Seemed present, and, attention now relaxed,
There was a heartfelt chillness in my veins.
I rose, and turning from that breezy shade
215 Went out into the open air and stood
To drink the comfort of the warmer sun.
Long time I had not stayed ere, looking round
Upon that tranquil ruin, I returned
And begged of the old man that for my sake
220 He would resume his story. He replied,
"It were a wantonness and would demand
Severe reproof, if we were men whose hearts
Could hold vain dalliance with the misery
Even of the dead, contented thence to draw
225 A momentary pleasure never marked
By reason, barren of all future good.
But we have known that there is often found
In mournful thoughts, and always might be found,
A power to virtue friendly; were't not so,
230 I am a dreamer among men, indeed
An idle dreamer. 'Tis a common tale,
By moving accidents[6] uncharactered,
A tale of silent suffering, hardly clothed
In bodily form, and to the grosser sense
235 But ill adapted, scarcely palpable
To him who does not think. But at your bidding
I will proceed.
                           While thus it fared with them
To whom this cottage till that hapless year
Had been a blessed home, it was my chance
240 To travel in a country far remote,
And glad I was when, halting by yon gate
That leads from the green lane, again I saw
These lofty elm-trees. Long I did not rest:
With many pleasant thoughts I cheer'd my way
245 O'er the flat common. At the door arrived,
I knocked, and when I entered with the hope
Of usual greeting, Margaret looked at me
A little while, then turned her head away
Speechless, and sitting down upon a chair
250 Wept bitterly. I wist not what to do
Or how to speak to her. Poor wretch! at last
She rose from off her seat—and then, oh Sir!
I cannot tell how she pronounced my name:
With fervent love, and with a face of grief

5. Wordsworth penciled the bracketed phrase into a gap left in the manuscript.
6. Othello speaks "of most disastrous chances, / Of moving accidents by flood and field, / Of hair-breadth 'scapes" (*Othello* 1.3.133–35).

255   Unutterably helpless, and a look
      That seem'd to cling upon me, she enquir'd
      If I had seen her husband. As she spake
      A strange surprize and fear came to my heart,
      Nor had I power to answer ere she told
260   That he had disappeared—just two months gone.
      He left his house; two wretched days had passed,
      And on the third by the first break of light,
      Within her casement full in view she saw
      A purse of gold.[7] 'I trembled at the sight,'
265   Said Margaret, 'for I knew it was his hand
      That placed it there, and on that very day
      By one, a stranger, from my husband sent,
      The tidings came that he had joined a troop
      Of soldiers going to a distant land.
270   He left me thus—Poor Man! he had not heart
      To take a farewell of me, and he feared
      That I should follow with my babes, and sink
      Beneath the misery of a soldier's life.'
      This tale did Margaret tell with many tears:
275   And when she ended I had little power
      To give her comfort, and was glad to take
      Such words of hope from her own mouth as serv'd
      To cheer us both: but long we had not talked
      Ere we built up a pile of better thoughts,
280   And with a brighter eye she looked around
      As if she had been shedding tears of joy.
      We parted. It was then the early spring;
      I left her busy with her garden tools;
      And well remember, o'er that fence she looked,
285   And while I paced along the foot-way path
      Called out, and sent a blessing after me
      With tender chearfulness and with a voice
      That seemed the very sound of happy thoughts.
         I roved o'er many a hill and many a dale
290   With this my weary load, in heat and cold,
      Through many a wood, and many an open ground,
      In sunshine or in shade, in wet or fair,
      Now blithe, now drooping, as it might befal,
      My best companions now the driving winds
295   And now the 'trotting brooks'[8] and whispering trees
      And now the music of my own sad steps,
      With many a short-lived thought that pass'd between
      And disappeared. I came this way again
      Towards the wane of summer, when the wheat
300   Was yellow, and the soft and bladed grass
      Sprang up afresh and o'er the hay-field spread

---

7. The "bounty" that her husband had been paid for enlisting in the militia. The shortage of volunteers and England's sharply rising military needs had in some counties forced the bounty up from about £1 in 1757 to more than £16 in 1796 (J. R. Western, *English Militia in the Eighteenth Century*, 1965, p. 276).

8. From Robert Burns (*To William Simpson*, line 87).

Its tender green. When I had reached the door
I found that she was absent. In the shade
Where now we sit I waited her return.
305 Her cottage in its outward look appeared
As chearful as before; in any shew
Of neatness little changed, but that I thought
The honeysuckle crowded round the door
And from the wall hung down in heavier wreathes,
310 And knots of worthless stone-crop⁹ started out
Along the window's edge, and grew like weeds
Against the lower panes. I turned aside
And stroll'd into her garden.—It was chang'd:
The unprofitable bindweed spread his bells
315 From side to side and with unwieldy wreaths
Had dragg'd the rose from its sustaining wall
And bent it down to earth; the border-tufts—
Daisy and thrift and lowly camomile
And thyme—had straggled out into the paths
320 Which they were used to deck. Ere this an hour
Was wasted. Back I turned my restless steps,
And as I walked before the door it chanced
A stranger passed, and guessing whom I sought
He said that she was used to ramble far.
325 The sun was sinking in the west, and now
I sate with sad impatience. From within
Her solitary infant cried aloud.
The spot though fair seemed very desolate,
The longer I remained more desolate.
330 And, looking round, I saw the corner-stones,
Till then unmark'd, on either side the door
With dull red stains discoloured and stuck o'er
With tufts and hairs of wool, as if the sheep
That feed upon the commons thither came
335 Familiarly and found a couching-place
Even at her threshold.—The house-clock struck eight;
I turned and saw her distant a few steps.
Her face was pale and thin, her figure too
Was chang'd. As she unlocked the door she said,
340 'It grieves me you have waited here so long,
But in good truth I've wandered much of late
And sometimes, to my shame I speak, have need
Of my best prayers to bring me back again.'
While on the board she spread our evening meal
345 She told me she had lost her elder child,
That he for months had been a serving-boy
Apprenticed by the parish. 'I perceive
You look at me, and you have cause. Today
I have been travelling far, and many days
350 About the fields I wander, knowing this
Only, that what I seek I cannot find.
And so I waste my time: for I am changed;

9. A plant with yellow flowers that grows on walls and rocks.

And to myself,' said she, 'have done much wrong,
And to this helpless infant. I have slept
355 Weeping, and weeping I have waked; my tears
Have flow'd as if my body were not such
As others are, and I could never die.
But I am now in mind and in my heart
More easy, and I hope,' said she, 'that heaven
360 Will give me patience to endure the things
Which I behold at home.' It would have grieved
Your very heart to see her. Sir, I feel
The story linger in my heart. I fear
'Tis long and tedious, but my spirit clings
365 To that poor woman: so familiarly
Do I perceive her manner, and her look
And presence, and so deeply do I feel
Her goodness, that not seldom in my walks
A momentary trance comes over me;
370 And to myself I seem to muse on one
By sorrow laid asleep or borne away,
A human being destined to awake
To human life, or something very near
To human life, when he shall come again
375 For whom she suffered. Sir, it would have griev'd
Your very soul to see her: evermore
Her eye-lids droop'd, her eyes were downward cast;
And when she at her table gave me food
She did not look at me. Her voice was low,
380 Her body was subdued. In every act
Pertaining to her house-affairs appeared
The careless stillness which a thinking mind
Gives to an idle matter—still she sighed,
But yet no motion of the breast was seen,
385 No heaving of the heart. While by the fire
We sate together, sighs came on my ear;
I knew not how, and hardly whence they came.
I took my staff, and when I kissed her babe
The tears stood in her eyes. I left her then
390 With the best hope and comfort I could give;
She thanked me for my will, but for my hope
It seemed she did not thank me.
                                        I returned
And took my rounds along this road again
Ere on its sunny bank the primrose flower
395 Had chronicled the earliest day of spring.
I found her sad and drooping; she had learn'd
No tidings of her husband: if he lived
She knew not that he lived; if he were dead
She knew not he was dead. She seemed the same
400 In person [or]¹ appearance, but her house
Bespoke a sleepy hand of negligence;
The floor was neither dry nor neat, the hearth

1. The word *or* was erased here; later manuscripts read "and."

Was comfortless [   ],
The windows too were dim, and her few books,
405 Which, one upon the other, heretofore
Had been piled up against the corner-panes
In seemly order, now with straggling leaves
Lay scattered here and there, open or shut
As they had chanced to fall. Her infant babe
410 Had from its mother caught the trick of grief
And sighed among its playthings. Once again
I turned towards the garden-gate and saw
More plainly still that poverty and grief
Were now come nearer to her: the earth was hard,
415 With weeds defaced and knots of withered grass;
No ridges there appeared of clear black mould,
No winter greenness; of her herbs and flowers
It seemed the better part were gnawed away
Or trampled on the earth; a chain of straw
420 Which had been twisted round the tender stem
Of a young apple-tree lay at its root;
The bark was nibbled round by truant sheep.
Margaret stood near, her infant in her arms,
And seeing that my eye was on the tree
425 She said, 'I fear it will be dead and gone
Ere Robert come again.' Towards the house
Together we returned, and she inquired
If I had any hope. But for her Babe
And for her little friendless Boy, she said,
430 She had no wish to live, that she must die
Of sorrow. Yet I saw the idle loom
Still in its place. His Sunday garments hung
Upon the self-same nail, his very staff
Stood undisturbed behind the door. And when
435 I passed this way beaten by Autumn winds
She told me that her little babe was dead
And she was left alone. That very time,
I yet remember, through the miry lane
She walked with me a mile, when the bare trees
440 Trickled with foggy damps, and in such sort
That any heart had ached to hear her begg'd
That wheresoe'er I went I still would ask
For him whom she had lost. We parted then,
Our final parting, for from that time forth
445 Did many seasons pass ere I returned
Into this tract again.
                          Five tedious years
She lingered in unquiet widowhood,
A wife and widow. Needs must it have been
A sore heart-wasting. I have heard, my friend,
450 That in that broken arbour she would sit
The idle length of half a sabbath day—
There, where you see the toadstool's lazy head—
And when a dog passed by she still would quit

The shade and look abroad. On this old Bench
455 For hours she sate, and evermore her eye
Was busy in the distance, shaping things
Which made her heart beat quick. Seest thou that path?
(The green-sward now has broken its grey line)
There to and fro she paced through many a day
460 Of the warm summer, from a belt of flax
That girt her waist spinning the long-drawn thread
With backward steps.—Yet ever as there passed
A man whose garments shewed the Soldier's red,
Or crippled Mendicant in Sailor's garb,
465 The little child who sate to turn the wheel
Ceased from his toil, and she with faltering voice,
Expecting still to learn her husband's fate,
Made many a fond inquiry; and when they
Whose presence gave no comfort were gone by,
470 Her heart was still more sad. And by yon gate
Which bars the traveller's road she often stood
And when a stranger horseman came, the latch
Would lift, and in his face look wistfully,
Most happy if from aught discovered there
475 Of tender feeling she might dare repeat
The same sad question. Meanwhile her poor hut
Sunk to decay, for he was gone whose hand
At the first nippings of October frost
Closed up each chink and with fresh bands of straw
480 Chequered the green-grown thatch. And so she lived
Through the long winter, reckless and alone,
Till this reft house by frost, and thaw, and rain
Was sapped; and when she slept the nightly damps
Did chill her breast, and in the stormy day
485 Her tattered clothes were ruffled by the wind
Even at the side of her own fire. Yet still
She loved this wretched spot, nor would for worlds
Have parted hence; and still that length of road
And this rude bench one torturing hope endeared,
490 Fast rooted at her heart, and here, my friend,
In sickness she remained, and here she died,
Last human tenant of these ruined walls."
    The old Man ceased: he saw that I was mov'd;
From that low Bench, rising instinctively,
495 I turned aside in weakness, nor had power
To thank him for the tale which he had told.
I stood, and leaning o'er the garden-gate
Reviewed that Woman's suff'rings, and it seemed
To comfort me while with a brother's love
500 I blessed her in the impotence of grief.
At length [towards] the [Cottage I returned]²
Fondly, and traced with milder interest
That secret spirit of humanity

2. The words inside the brackets were added in MS. E.

Which, 'mid the calm oblivious tendencies
505   Of nature, 'mid her plants, her weeds, and flowers,
And silent overgrowings, still survived.
The old man, seeing this, resumed and said,
"My Friend, enough to sorrow have you given,
The purposes of wisdom ask no more;
510   Be wise and chearful, and no longer read
The forms of things with an unworthy eye.
She sleeps in the calm earth, and peace is here.
I well remember that those very plumes,
Those weeds, and the high spear-grass on that wall,
515   By mist and silent rain-drops silver'd o'er,
As once I passed did to my heart convey
So still an image of tranquillity,
So calm and still, and looked so beautiful
Amid the uneasy thoughts which filled my mind,
520   That what we feel of sorrow and despair
From ruin and from change, and all the grief
The passing shews of being leave behind,
Appeared an idle dream that could not live
Where meditation was. I turned away
525   And walked along my road in happiness."
    He ceased. By this the sun declining shot
A slant and mellow radiance which began
To fall upon us where beneath the trees
We sate on that low bench, and now we felt,
530   Admonished thus, the sweet hour coming on.
A linnet warbled from those lofty elms,
A thrush sang loud, and other melodies,
At distance heard, peopled the milder air.
The old man rose and hoisted up his load.
535   Together casting then a farewell look
Upon those silent walls, we left the shade
And ere the stars were visible attained
A rustic inn, our evening resting-place.

                     THE END

1797–ca.1799   1949

Michael[1]

A Pastoral Poem

If from the public way you turn your steps
Up the tumultuous brook of Green-head Ghyll,[2]

---

1. This poem is founded on the actual misfortunes of a family at Grasmere. For the account of the sheepfold, see Dorothy Wordsworth's *Grasmere Journals*, October 11, 1800 (p. 388). Wordsworth wrote to Thomas Poole, on April 9, 1801, that he had attempted to picture a mail "agitated by two of the most powerful affections of the human heart; the parental affection, and the love of property, *landed* property, including the feelings of

inheritance, home, and personal and family independence." The subtitle shows Wordsworth's shift of the term "pastoral" from aristocratic make-believe to the tragic suffering of people in what he called "humble and rustic life."
2. A ravine forming the bed of a stream. Green-head Ghyll is not far from Wordsworth's cottage at Grasmere. The other places named in the poem are also in that vicinity.

You will suppose that with an upright path
Your feet must struggle; in such bold ascent
5   The pastoral mountains front you, face to face.
But, courage! for around that boisterous brook
The mountains have all opened out themselves,
And made a hidden valley of their own.
No habitation can be seen; but they
10 Who journey thither find themselves alone
With a few sheep, with rocks and stones, and kites°   hawks
That overhead are sailing in the sky.
It is in truth an utter solitude;
Nor should I have made mention of this Dell
15 But for one object which you might pass by,
Might see and notice not. Beside the brook
Appears a straggling heap of unhewn stones!
And to that simple object appertains
A story—unenriched with strange events,
20 Yet not unfit, I deem, for the fireside,
Or for the summer shade. It was the first
Of those domestic tales that spake to me
Of Shepherds, dwellers in the valleys, men
Whom I already loved;—not verily
25 For their own sakes, but for the fields and hills
Where was their occupation and abode.
And hence this Tale, while I was yet a Boy
Careless of books, yet having felt the power
Of Nature, by the gentle agency
30 Of natural objects, led me on to feel
For passions that were not my own, and think
(At random and imperfectly indeed)
On man, the heart of man, and human life.
Therefore, although it be a history
35 Homely and rude, I will relate the same
For the delight of a few natural hearts;
And, with yet fonder feeling, for the sake
Of youthful Poets, who among these hills
Will be my second self when I am gone.

40   Upon the forest-side in Grasmere Vale
There dwelt a Shepherd, Michael was his name;
An old man, stout of heart, and strong of limb.
His bodily frame had been from youth to age
Of an unusual strength: his mind was keen,
45 Intense, and frugal, apt for all affairs,
And in his shepherd's calling he was prompt
And watchful more than ordinary men.
Hence had he learned the meaning of all winds,
Of blasts of every tone; and, oftentimes,
50 When others heeded not, he heard the South
Make subterraneous music, like the noise
Of bagpipers on distant Highland hills.
The Shepherd, at such warning, of his flock

Bethought him, and he to himself would say,
55 "The winds are now devising work for me!"
And, truly, at all times, the storm, that drives
The traveller to a shelter, summoned him
Up to the mountains: he had been alone
Amid the heart of many thousand mists,
60 That came to him, and left him, on the heights.
So lived he till his eightieth year was past.
And grossly that man errs, who should suppose
That the green valleys, and the streams and rocks,
Were things indifferent to the Shepherd's thoughts.
65 Fields, where with cheerful spirits he had breathed
The common air; hills, which with vigorous step
He had so often climbed; which had impressed
So many incidents upon his mind
Of hardship, skill or courage, joy or fear;
70 Which, like a book, preserved the memory
Of the dumb animals, whom he had saved,
Had fed or sheltered, linking to such acts
The certainty of honourable gain;
Those fields, those hills—what could they less? had laid
75 Strong hold on his affections, were to him
A pleasurable feeling of blind love,
The pleasure which there is in life itself.

His days had not been passed in singleness.
His Helpmate was a comely matron, old—
80 Though younger than himself full twenty years.
She was a woman of a stirring life,
Whose heart was in her house: two wheels she had
Of antique form; this large, for spinning wool;
That small, for flax; and if one wheel had rest,
85 It was because the other was at work.
The Pair had but one inmate in their house,
An only Child, who had been born to them
When Michael, telling o'er his years, began
To deem that he was old,—in shepherd's phrase,
90 With one foot in the grave. This only Son,
With two brave sheep-dogs tried in many a storm,
The one of an inestimable worth,
Made all their household. I may truly say,
That they were as a proverb in the vale
95 For endless industry. When day was gone,
And from their occupations out of doors
The Son and Father were come home, even then,
Their labour did not cease; unless when all
Turned to the cleanly supper-board, and there,
100 Each with a mess of pottage and skimmed milk,
Sat round the basket piled with oaten cakes,
And their plain home-made cheese. Yet when the meal
Was ended, Luke (for so the Son was named)

And his old Father both betook themselves
105 To such convenient work as might employ
Their hands by the fire-side; perhaps to card
Wool for the Housewife's spindle, or repair
Some injury done to sickle, flail, or scythe,
Or other implement of house or field.

110   Down from the ceiling, by the chimney's edge,
That in our ancient uncouth country style
With huge and black projection overbrowed
Large space beneath, as duly as the light
Of day grew dim the Housewife hung a lamp;
115 An aged utensil, which had performed
Service beyond all others of its kind.
Early at evening did it burn—and late,
Surviving comrade of uncounted hours,
Which, going by from year to year, had found,
120 And left the couple neither gay perhaps
Nor cheerful, yet with objects and with hopes,
Living a life of eager industry.
And now, when Luke had reached his eighteenth year,
There by the light of his old lamp they sate,
125 Father and Son, while far into the night
The Housewife plied her own peculiar work,
Making the cottage through the silent hours
Murmur as with the sound of summer flies.
This light was famous in its neighbourhood,
130 And was a public symbol of the life
That thrifty Pair had lived. For, as it chanced,
Their cottage on a plot of rising ground
Stood single, with large prospect, north and south,
High into Easedale, up to Dunmail-Raise,
135 And westward to the village near the lake;
And from this constant light, so regular
And so far seen, the House itself, by all
Who dwelt within the limits of the vale,
Both old and young, was named THE EVENING STAR.

140   Thus living on through such a length of years,
The Shepherd, if he loved himself, must needs
Have loved his Helpmate; but to Michael's heart
This son of his old age was yet more dear—
Less from instinctive tenderness, the same
145 Fond spirit that blindly works in the blood of all—
Than that a child, more than all other gifts
That earth can offer to declining man,
Brings hope with it, and forward-looking thoughts,
And stirrings of inquietude, when they
150 By tendency of nature needs must fail.
Exceeding was the love he bare to him,
His heart and his heart's joy! For oftentimes

Old Michael, while he was a babe in arms,
Had done him female service, not alone
155   For pastime and delight, as is the use
Of fathers, but with patient mind enforced
To acts of tenderness; and he had rocked
His cradle, as with a woman's gentle hand.

And, in a later time, ere yet the Boy
160   Had put on boy's attire, did Michael love,
Albeit of a stern unbending mind,
To have the Young-one in his sight, when he
Wrought in the field, or on his shepherd's stool
Sate with a fettered sheep before him stretched
165   Under the large old oak, that near his door
Stood single, and, from matchless depth of shade,
Chosen for the Shearer's covert from the sun,
Thence in our rustic dialect was called
The CLIPPING TREE, a name which yet it bears.
170   There, while they two were sitting in the shade,
With others round them, earnest all and blithe,
Would Michael exercise his heart with looks
Of fond correction and reproof bestowed
Upon the Child, if he disturbed the sheep
175   By catching at their legs, or with his shouts
Scared them, while they lay still beneath the shears.

And when by Heaven's good grace the boy grew up
A healthy Lad, and carried in his cheek
Two steady roses that were five years old;
180   Then Michael from a winter coppice[3] cut
With his own hand a sapling, which he hooped
With iron, making it throughout in all
Due requisites a perfect shepherd's staff,
And gave it to the Boy; wherewith equipt
185   He as a watchman oftentimes was placed
At gate or gap, to stem or turn the flock;
And, to his office prematurely called,
There stood the urchin, as you will divine,
Something between a hindrance and a help;
190   And for this cause not always, I believe,
Receiving from his Father hire of praise;
Though nought was left undone which staff, or voice,
Or looks, or threatening gestures, could perform.

But soon as Luke, full ten years old, could stand
195   Against the mountain blasts; and to the heights,
Not fearing toil, nor length of weary ways,
He with his Father daily went, and they
Were as companions, why should I relate
That objects which the Shepherd loved before

3. Grove of small trees.

200 Were dearer now? that from the Boy there came
Feelings and emanations—things which were
Light to the sun and music to the wind;
And that the old Man's heart seemed born again?

Thus in his Father's sight the Boy grew up:
205 And now, when he had reached his eighteenth year,
He was his comfort and his daily hope.

While in this sort the simple household lived
From day to day, to Michael's ear there came
Distressful tidings. Long before the time
210 Of which I speak, the Shepherd had been bound
In surety for his brother's son, a man
Of an industrious life, and ample means;
But unforeseen misfortunes suddenly
Had prest upon him; and old Michael now
215 Was summoned to discharge the forfeiture,
A grievous penalty, but little less
Than half his substance. This unlooked-for claim,
At the first hearing, for a moment took
More hope out of his life than he supposed
220 That any old man ever could have lost.
As soon as he had armed himself with strength
To look his trouble in the face, it seemed
The Shepherd's sole resource to sell at once
A portion of his patrimonial fields.
225 Such was his first resolve; he thought again,
And his heart failed him. "Isabel," said he,
Two evenings after he had heard the news,
"I have been toiling more than seventy years,
And in the open sunshine of God's love
230 Have we all lived; yet if these fields of ours
Should pass into a stranger's hand, I think
That I could not lie quiet in my grave.
Our lot is a hard lot; the sun himself
Has scarcely been more diligent than I;
235 And I have lived to be a fool at last
To my own family. An evil man
That was, and made an evil choice, if he
Were false to us; and if he were not false,
There are ten thousand to whom loss like this
240 Had been no sorrow. I forgive him;—but
'Twere better to be dumb than to talk thus.

"When I began, my purpose was to speak
Of remedies and of a cheerful hope.
Our Luke shall leave us, Isabel; the land
245 Shall not go from us, and it shall be free;
He shall possess it, free as is the wind
That passes over it. We have, thou know'st,
Another kinsman—he will be our friend

In this distress. He is a prosperous man,
250 Thriving in trade—and Luke to him shall go,
And with his kinsman's help and his own thrift
He quickly will repair this loss, and then
He may return to us. If here he stay,
What can be done? Where every one is poor,
What can be gained?"
255   At this the old Man paused,
And Isabel sat silent, for her mind
Was busy, looking back into past times.
There's Richard Bateman,[4] thought she to herself,
He was a parish-boy—at the church-door
260 They made a gathering for him, shillings, pence
And halfpennies, wherewith the neighbours bought
A basket, which they filled with pedlar's wares;
And, with this basket on his arm, the lad
Went up to London, found a master there,
265 Who, out of many, chose the trusty boy
To go and overlook his merchandise
Beyond the seas; where he grew wondrous rich,
And left estates and monies to the poor,
And, at his birth-place, built a chapel floored
270 With marble, which he sent from foreign lands.
These thoughts, and many others of like sort,
Passed quickly through the mind of Isabel,
And her face brightened. The old Man was glad,
And thus resumed:—"Well, Isabel! this scheme
275 These two days, has been meat and drink to me.
Far more than we have lost is left us yet.
—We have enough—I wish indeed that I
Were younger;—but this hope is a good hope.
Make ready Luke's best garments, of the best
280 Buy for him more, and let us send him forth
To-morrow, or the next day, or to-night:
—If he *could* go, the Boy should go to-night."

       Here Michael ceased, and to the fields went forth
With a light heart. The Housewife for five days
285 Was restless morn and night, and all day long
Wrought on with her best fingers to prepare
Things needful for the journey of her son.
But Isabel was glad when Sunday came
To stop her in her work: for, when she lay
290 By Michael's side, she through the last two nights
Heard him, how he was troubled in his sleep:
And when they rose at morning she could see
That all his hopes were gone. That day at noon
She said to Luke, while they two by themselves
295 Were sitting at the door, "Thou must not go:
We have no other Child but thee to lose,
None to remember—do not go away,

---

4. The story alluded to here is well known in the country. The chapel is called Ings Chapel and is on the
road leading from Kendal to Ambleside [Wordsworth's note].

For if thou leave thy Father he will die."
The Youth made answer with a jocund voice;
300 And Isabel, when she had told her fears,
Recovered heart. That evening her best fare
Did she bring forth, and all together sat
Like happy people round a Christmas fire.

With daylight Isabel resumed her work;
305 And all the ensuing week the house appeared
As cheerful as a grove in Spring: at length
The expected letter from their kinsman came,
With kind assurances that he would do
His utmost for the welfare of the Boy;
310 To which, requests were added, that forthwith
He might be sent to him. Ten times or more
The letter was read over; Isabel
Went forth to show it to the neighbours round;
Nor was there at that time on English land
315 A prouder heart than Luke's. When Isabel
Had to her house returned, the old Man said,
"He shall depart to-morrow." To this word
The Housewife answered, talking much of things
Which, if at such short notice he should go,
320 Would surely be forgotten. But at length
She gave consent, and Michael was at ease.

Near the tumultuous brook of Green-head Ghyll,
In that deep valley, Michael had designed
To build a Sheep-fold;[5] and, before he heard
325 The tidings of his melancholy loss,
For this same purpose he had gathered up
A heap of stones, which by the streamlet's edge
Lay thrown together, ready for the work.
With Luke that evening thitherward he walked:
330 And soon as they had reached the place he stopped,
And thus the old Man spake to him:—"My Son,
To-morrow thou wilt leave me: with full heart
I look upon thee, for thou art the same
That wert a promise to me ere thy birth,
335 And all thy life hast been my daily joy.
I will relate to thee some little part
Of our two histories; 'twill do thee good
When thou art from me, even if I should touch
On things thou canst not know of.——After thou
340 First cam'st into the world—as oft befals
To new-born infants—thou didst sleep away
Two days, and blessings from thy Father's tongue
Then fell upon thee. Day by day passed on,
And still I loved thee with increasing love.
345 Never to living ear came sweeter sounds

---

5. A sheepfold [pen for sheep] in these mountains is an unroofed building of stone walls, with different divisions [Wordsworth's note].

Than when I heard thee by our own fire-side
First uttering, without words, a natural tune;
While thou, a feeding babe, didst in thy joy
Sing at thy Mother's breast. Month followed month,
350 And in the open fields my life was passed
And on the mountains; else I think that thou
Hadst been brought up upon thy Father's knees.
But we were playmates, Luke: among these hills,
As well thou knowest, in us the old and young
355 Have played together, nor with me didst thou
Lack any pleasure which a boy can know."
Luke had a manly heart; but at these words
He sobbed aloud. The old Man grasped his hand,
And said, "Nay, do not take it so—I see
360 That these are things of which I need not speak.
—Even to the utmost I have been to thee
A kind and a good Father: and herein
I but repay a gift which I myself
Received at others' hands; for, though now old
365 Beyond the common life of man, I still
Remember them who loved me in my youth.
Both of them sleep together: here they lived,
As all their Forefathers had done; and when
At length their time was come, they were not loth
370 To give their bodies to the family mould.
I wished that thou should'st live the life they lived:
But, 'tis a long time to look back, my Son,
And see so little gain from threescore years.
These fields were burthened° when they came to me;   *mortgaged*
375 Till I was forty years of age, not more
Than half of my inheritance was mine.
I toiled and toiled; God blessed me in my work,
And till these three weeks past the land was free.
—It looks as if it never could endure
380 Another Master. Heaven forgive me, Luke,
If I judge ill for thee, but it seems good
That thou should'st go."
                          At this the old Man paused;
Then, pointing to the stones near which they stood,
Thus, after a short silence, he resumed:
385 "This was a work for us; and now, my Son,
It is a work for me. But, lay one stone—
Here, lay it for me, Luke, with thine own hands.
Nay, Boy, be of good hope;—we both may live
To see a better day. At eighty-four
390 I still am strong and hale;—do thou thy part;
I will do mine.—I will begin again
With many tasks that were resigned to thee:
Up to the heights, and in among the storms,
Will I without thee go again, and do
395 All works which I was wont to do alone,
Before I knew thy face.—Heaven bless thee, Boy!

Thy heart these two weeks has been beating fast
With many hopes; it should be so—yes—yes—
I knew that thou could'st never have a wish
400 To leave me, Luke: thou hast been bound to me
Only by links of love: when thou art gone,
What will be left to us!—But, I forget
My purposes. Lay now the corner-stone,
As I requested; and hereafter, Luke,
405 When thou art gone away, should evil men
Be thy companions, think of me, my Son,
And of this moment; hither turn thy thoughts,
And God will strengthen thee: amid all fear
And all temptation, Luke, I pray that thou
410 May'st bear in mind the life thy Fathers lived,
Who, being innocent, did for that cause
Bestir them in good deeds. Now, fare thee well—
When thou return'st, thou in this place wilt see
A work which is not here: a covenant
415 'Twill be between us; but, whatever fate
Befal thee, I shall love thee to the last,
And bear thy memory with me to the grave."

      The Shepherd ended here; and Luke stooped down,
And, as his Father had requested, laid
420 The first stone of the Sheep-fold. At the sight
The old Man's grief broke from him; to his heart
He pressed his Son, he kissèd him and wept;
And to the house together they returned.
—Hushed was that House in peace, or seeming peace,
425 Ere the night fell:—with morrow's dawn the Boy
Began his journey, and when he had reached
The public way, he put on a bold face;
And all the neighbours, as he passed their doors,
Came forth with wishes and with farewell prayers,
430 That followed him till he was out of sight.

      A good report did from their Kinsman come,
Of Luke and his well-doing: and the Boy
Wrote loving letters, full of wondrous news,
Which, as the Housewife phrased it, were throughout
435 "The prettiest letters that were ever seen."
Both parents read them with rejoicing hearts.
So, many months passed on: and once again
The Shepherd went about his daily work
With confident and cheerful thoughts; and now
440 Sometimes when he could find a leisure hour
He to that valley took his way, and there
Wrought at the Sheep-fold. Meantime Luke began
To slacken in his duty; and, at length,
He in the dissolute city gave himself
445 To evil courses: ignominy and shame

Fell on him, so that he was driven at last
To seek a hiding-place beyond the seas.

There is a comfort in the strength of love;
'Twill make a thing endurable, which else
450 Would overset the brain, or break the heart:
I have conversed with more than one who well
Remember the old Man, and what he was
Years after he had heard this heavy news.
His bodily frame had been from youth to age
455 Of an unusual strength. Among the rocks
He went, and still looked up to sun and cloud,
And listened to the wind; and, as before
Performed all kinds of labour for his sheep,
And for the land, his small inheritance.
460 And to that hollow dell from time to time
Did he repair, to build the Fold of which
His flock had need. 'Tis not forgotten yet
The pity which was then in every heart
For the old Man—and 'tis believed by all
465 That many and many a day he thither went,
And never lifted up a single stone.

There, by the Sheep-fold, sometimes was he seen
Sitting alone, or with his faithful Dog,
Then old, beside him, lying at his feet.
470 The length of full seven years, from time to time,
He at the building of this Sheep-fold wrought,
And left the work unfinished when he died.
Three years, or little more, did Isabel
Survive her Husband: at her death the estate
475 Was sold, and went into a stranger's hand.
The Cottage which was named the EVENING STAR
Is gone—the ploughshare has been through the ground
On which it stood; great changes have been wrought
In all the neighbourhood:—yet the oak is left
480 That grew beside their door; and the remains
Of the unfinished Sheep-fold may be seen
Beside the boisterous brook of Green-head Ghyll.

Oct. 11–Dec. 9, 1800   1800

Resolution and Independence[1]

I

There was a roaring in the wind all night;
The rain came heavily and fell in floods;

1. For the meeting with the old leech gatherer, see Dorothy Wordsworth's *Grasmere Journals*, October 3, 1800 (p. 387). Wordsworth himself tells us that "I was in the state of feeling described in the beginning of the poem, while crossing over Barton Fell from Mr. Clarkson's, at the foot of Ullswater, towards Askam. The image of the hare I then observed on the ridge of the Fell." He wrote the poem eighteen months after this event (see *Grasmere Journals*, May 4 and 7, 1802; pp. 393 and 394).

But now the sun is rising calm and bright;
The birds are singing in the distant woods;
5   Over his own sweet voice the Stock-dove broods;
The Jay makes answer as the Magpie chatters;
And all the air is filled with pleasant noise of waters.

2

All things that love the sun are out of doors;
The sky rejoices in the morning's birth;
10   The grass is bright with rain-drops;—on the moors
The hare is running races in her mirth;
And with her feet she from the plashy earth
Raises a mist; that, glittering in the sun,
Runs with her all the way, wherever she doth run.

3

15   I was a Traveller then upon the moor;
I saw the hare that raced about with joy;
I heard the woods and distant waters roar;
Or heard them not, as happy as a boy:
The pleasant season did my heart employ:
20   My old remembrances went from me wholly;
And all the ways of men, so vain and melancholy.

4

But, as it sometimes chanceth, from the might
Of joy in minds that can no further go,
As high as we have mounted in delight
25   In our dejection do we sink as low;
To me that morning did it happen so;
And fears and fancies thick upon me came;
Dim sadness—and blind thoughts, I knew not, nor could name.

5

I heard the sky-lark warbling in the sky;
30   And I bethought me of the playful hare:
Even such a happy Child of earth am I;
Even as these blissful creatures do I fare;
Far from the world I walk, and from all care;
But there may come another day to me—
35   Solitude, pain of heart, distress, and poverty.

6

My whole life I have lived in pleasant thought,
As if life's business were a summer mood;
As if all needful things would come unsought
To genial faith, still rich in genial good;
40   But how can He expect that others should
Build for him, sow for him, and at his call
Love him, who for himself will take no heed at all?

7

I thought of Chatterton,[2] the marvellous Boy,
The sleepless Soul that perished in his pride;
45 Of Him[3] who walked in glory and in joy
Following his plough, along the mountain-side:
By our own spirits are we deified:
We Poets in our youth begin in gladness;
But thereof come in the end despondency and madness.

8

50 Now, whether it were by peculiar grace,
A leading from above, a something given,
Yet it befel, that, in this lonely place,
When I with these untoward thoughts had striven,
Beside a pool bare to the eye of heaven
55 I saw a Man before me unawares:
The oldest man he seemed that ever wore grey hairs.

9

As a huge stone is sometimes seen to lie
Couched on the bald top of an eminence;
Wonder to all who do the same espy,
60 By what means it could thither come, and whence;
So that it seems a thing endued with sense:
Like a sea-beast crawled forth, that on a shelf
Of rock or sand reposeth, there to sun itself;

10

Such seemed this Man,[4] not all alive nor dead,
65 Nor all asleep—in his extreme old age:
His body was bent double, feet and head
Coming together in life's pilgrimage;
As if some dire constraint of pain, or rage
Of sickness felt by him in times long past,
70 A more than human weight upon his frame had cast.

11

Himself he propped, limbs, body, and pale face,
Upon a long grey staff of shaven wood:
And, still as I drew near with gentle pace,
Upon the margin of that moorish flood

2. Thomas Chatterton (1752–1770), a poet of great talent who, in his loneliness and dire poverty, poisoned himself at the age of seventeen and so became the prime Romantic symbol of neglected young genius.
3. Robert Burns, also considered at that time as a natural poet who died young and poor, without adequate recognition.
4. In Wordsworth's own analysis of this passage he says that the stone is endowed with something of life, the sea beast is stripped of some of its life to assimilate it to the stone, and the old man divested of enough life and motion to make "the two objects unite and coalesce in just comparison." He used the passage to demonstrate his theory of how the "conferring, the abstracting, and the modifying powers of the Imagination . . . are all brought into conjunction" (Preface to the *Poems* of 1815). Cf. Coleridge's brief definitions of the imagination in *Biographia Literaria*, chap. 13 (p. 477).

75 Motionless as a cloud the old Man stood,
   That heareth not the loud winds when they call;
   And moveth all together, if it move at all.

12

   At length, himself unsettling, he the pond
   Stirred with his staff, and fixedly did look
80 Upon the muddy water, which he conned,
   As if he had been reading in a book:
   And now a stranger's privilege I took;
   And, drawing to his side, to him did say,
   "This morning gives us promise of a glorious day."

13

85 A gentle answer did the old Man make,
   In courteous speech which forth he slowly drew:
   And him with further words I thus bespake,
   "What occupation do you there pursue?
   This is a lonesome place for one like you."
90 Ere he replied, a flash of mild surprise
   Broke from the sable orbs of his yet-vivid eyes.

14

   His words came feebly, from a feeble chest,
   But each in solemn order followed each,
   With something of a lofty utterance drest—
95 Choice word and measured phrase, above the reach
   Of ordinary men; a stately speech;
   Such as grave Livers⁵ do in Scotland use,
   Religious men, who give to God and man their dues.

15

   He told, that to these waters he had come
100 To gather leeches,⁶ being old and poor:
   Employment hazardous and wearisome!
   And he had many hardships to endure:
   From pond to pond he roamed, from moor to moor;
   Housing, with God's good help, by choice or chance;
105 And in this way he gained an honest maintenance.

16

   The old Man still stood talking by my side;
   But now his voice to me was like a stream
   Scarce heard; nor word from word could I divide;
   And the whole body of the Man did seem
110 Like one whom I had met with in a dream;

5. Those who live gravely.
6. Used to draw blood for curative purposes. A leech gatherer, bare legged in shallow water, stirred the water to attract them and, when they fastened themselves to his legs, picked them off.

Or like a man from some far region sent,
To give me human strength, by apt admonishment.

17

My former thoughts returned: the fear that kills;
And hope that is unwilling to be fed;
115 Cold, pain, and labour, and all fleshly ills;
And mighty Poets in their misery dead.
—Perplexed, and longing to be comforted,
My question eagerly did I renew,
"How is it that you live, and what is it you do?"

18

120 He with a smile did then his words repeat;
And said, that, gathering leeches, far and wide
He travelled; stirring thus about his feet
The waters of the pools where they abide.
"Once I could meet with them on every side;
125 But they have dwindled long by slow decay;
Yet still I persevere, and find them where I may."

19

While he was talking thus, the lonely place,
The old Man's shape, and speech—all troubled me:
In my mind's eye I seemed to see him pace
130 About the weary moors continually,
Wandering about alone and silently.
While I these thoughts within myself pursued,
He, having made a pause, the same discourse renewed.

20

And soon with this he other matter blended,
135 Cheerfully uttered, with demeanour kind,
But stately in the main; and when he ended,
I could have laughed myself to scorn to find
In that decrepit Man so firm a mind.
"God," said I, "be my help and stay⁷ secure;
140 I'll think of the Leech-gatherer on the lonely moor!"

May 3–July 4, 1802   1807

I wandered lonely as a cloud¹

I wandered lonely as a cloud
That floats on high o'er vales and hills,
When all at once I saw a crowd,
A host, of golden daffodils;

---

7. Support (a noun).
1. For the original experience, two years earlier,

see Dorothy Wordsworth's *Grasmere Journals*,
April 15, 1802 (p. 391).

5 Beside the lake, beneath the trees,
   Fluttering and dancing in the breeze.

   Continuous as the stars that shine
   And twinkle on the milky way,
   They stretched in never-ending line
10 Along the margin of a bay:
   Ten thousand saw I at a glance,
   Tossing their heads in sprightly dance.

   The waves beside them danced; but they
   Out-did the sparkling waves in glee:
15 A poet could not but be gay,
   In such a jocund company:
   I gazed—and gazed—but little thought
   What wealth the show to me had brought:

   For oft, when on my couch I lie
20 In vacant or in pensive mood,
   They flash upon that inward eye
   Which is the bliss of solitude;
   And then my heart with pleasure fills,
   And dances with the daffodils.

1804   1807

My heart leaps up

   My heart leaps up when I behold
        A rainbow in the sky:
   So was it when my life began;
   So is it now I am a man;
5 So be it when I shall grow old,
        Or let me die!
   The Child is father of the Man;
   And I could wish my days to be
   Bound each to each by natural piety.[1]

Mar. 26, 1802   1807

1. As distinguished from piety based on the Scriptures, in which God makes the rainbow the token of his covenant with Noah and all his descendants (Genesis 9.12–17). The religious sentiment that binds Wordsworth's mature self to that of his childhood is a continuing responsiveness to the miracle of ordinary things.

Ode: Intimations of Immortality   In 1843, Wordsworth said about this *Ode* to Isabella Fenwick:

This was composed during my residence at Town End, Grasmere; two years at least passed between the writing of the four first stanzas and the remaining part. To the attentive and competent reader the whole sufficiently explains itself; but there may be no harm in adverting here to particular feelings or *experiences* of my own mind on which the structure of the poem partly rests. Nothing was more difficult for me in childhood than to admit the notion of death as a state applicable to my own being. I have said elsewhere [in the opening stanza of *We Are Seven*]:

> —A simple child,
> That lightly draws its breath,
> And feels its life in every limb,
> What should it know of death!—

But it was not so much from [feelings] of animal vivacity that *my* difficulty came as from a sense of the indomitableness of the spirit within me. I used to brood over the stories of Enoch and Elijah [Genesis 5.22–24; 2 Kings 2.11], and almost to persuade myself that, whatever might become of others, I should be translated, in something of the same way, to heaven. With a feeling congenial to this, I was often unable to think of external things as having external existence, and I communed with all that I saw as something not apart from, but inherent in, my own immaterial nature. Many times while going to school have I grasped at a wall or tree to recall myself from this abyss of idealism to the reality. At that time I was afraid of such processes. In later periods of life I have deplored, as we have all reason to do, a subjugation of an opposite character, and have rejoiced over the remembrances, as is expressed in the lines—

> Obstinate questionings
> Of sense and outward things,
> Fallings from us, vanishings; etc.

To that dreamlike vividness and splendor which invest objects of sight in childhood, everyone, I believe, if he would look back, could bear testimony, and I need not dwell upon it here: but having in the Poem regarded it as presumptive evidence of a prior state of existence, I think it right to protest against a conclusion, which has given pain to some good and pious persons, that I meant to inculcate such a belief. It is far too shadowy a notion to be recommended to faith, as more than an element in our instincts of immortality. But let us bear in mind that, though the idea is not advanced in revelation, there is nothing there to contradict it, and the fall of Man presents an analogy in its favor. Accordingly, a pre-existent state has entered into the popular creeds of many nations; and, among all persons acquainted with classic literature, is known as an ingredient in Platonic philosophy. Archimedes said that he could move the world if he had a point whereon to rest his machine. Who has not felt the same aspirations as regards the world of his own mind? Having to wield some of its elements when I was impelled to write this Poem on the 'Immortality of the Soul,' I took hold of the notion of pre-existence as having sufficient foundation in humanity for authorizing me to make for my purpose the best use of it I could as a Poet.

Plato, to whom Wordsworth refers, held the doctrine that the soul is immortal and exists separately from the body both before birth and after death. But while the *Ode* proposes that the soul only gradually loses "the vision splendid" after birth, Plato maintained the contrary: that the knowledge of the eternal Ideas, which the soul had acquired by direct acquaintance, is totally lost at the instant of birth and must be gradually "recollected" by philosophical discipline in the course of this life (*Phaedo* 73–77). Wordsworth's metaphorical use of the concept of preexistence in his poem resembles more closely the view of some neoplatonists that the glory of the unborn soul is gradually quenched by its descent into the darkness of matter.

When he dictated this long note to Isabella Fenwick, at the age of seventy-two or seventy-three, Wordsworth was troubled by objections that his apparent claim for the preexistence of the soul violated the Christian belief that the soul, although it survives after death, does not exist before the birth of an individual. His claim in the note is that he used preexistence not as a doctrine but only as a postulate enabling him to deal "as a poet" with a general human experience: that the passing of youth involves the loss of a freshness and radiance investing everything one sees. Coleridge's *Dejection: An Ode*, which he wrote (in its earliest version) after he had heard the first four stanzas of Wordsworth's poem, employs a similar figurative technique for a comparable, though more devastating, experience of loss.

The original published text of this poem (in 1807) had as its title only "Ode," and then as epigraph *"Paulo maiora canamus"* ("Let us sing of somewhat higher things") from Virgil's *Eclogue 4*.

Ode

Intimations of Immortality from Recollections of Early Childhood

> The Child is Father of the Man;
> And I could wish my days to be
> Bound each to each by natural piety.[1]

1

There was a time when meadow, grove, and stream,
The earth, and every common sight,
    To me did seem
    Apparelled in celestial light,
5 The glory and the freshness of a dream.
It is not now as it hath been of yore;—
    Turn wheresoe'er I may,
      By night or day,
The things which I have seen I now can see no more.

2

10   The Rainbow comes and goes,
      And lovely is the Rose,
      The Moon doth with delight
Look round her when the heavens are bare,
      Waters on a starry night
15   Are beautiful and fair;
    The sunshine is a glorious birth;
    But yet I know, where'er I go,
That there hath past away a glory from the earth.

3

Now, while the birds thus sing a joyous song,
20   And while the young lambs bound
      As to the tabor's[2] sound,

---

1. The concluding lines of Wordsworth's *My heart leaps up*.

2. A small drum often used to beat time for dancing.

To me alone there came a thought of grief:
A timely utterance[3] gave that thought relief,
    And I again am strong:
25 The cataracts blow their trumpets from the steep;
No more shall grief of mine the season wrong;
I hear the Echoes through the mountains throng,
The Winds come to me from the fields of sleep,[4]
    And all the earth is gay;
30   Land and sea
    Give themselves up to jollity,
      And with the heart of May
Doth every Beast keep holiday;—
    Thou Child of Joy,
35 Shout round me, let me hear thy shouts, thou happy
Shepherd-boy!

4

Ye blessed Creatures, I have heard the call
    Ye to each other make; I see
The heavens laugh with you in your jubilee;
    My heart is at your festival,
40   My head hath its coronal,[5]
The fulness of your bliss, I feel—I feel it all.
    Oh evil day! if I were sullen
    While Earth herself is adorning,
      This sweet May-morning,
45   And the Children are culling
      On every side,
    In a thousand valleys far and wide,
    Fresh flowers; while the sun shines warm,
And the Babe leaps up on his Mother's arm:—
50   I hear, I hear, with joy I hear!
    —But there's a Tree, of many, one,
A single Field which I have looked upon,
Both of them speak of something that is gone:
    The Pansy at my feet
55   Doth the same tale repeat:
Whither is fled the visionary gleam?
Where is it now, the glory and the dream?

5

Our birth is but a sleep and a forgetting:
The Soul that rises with us, our life's Star,[6]
60   Hath had elsewhere its setting,
      And cometh from afar:
    Not in entire forgetfulness,
    And not in utter nakedness,

3. Perhaps *My heart leaps up*, perhaps *Resolution and Independence*, perhaps not a poem at all.
4. Of the many suggested interpretations, the simplest is "from the fields where they were sleeping." Wordsworth often associated a rising wind with the revival of spirit and of poetic inspiration (see, e.g., the opening passage of *The Prelude*, p. 305).
5. Circlet of wildflowers, with which the shepherd boys trimmed their hats in May.
6. The sun, as metaphor for the soul.

But trailing clouds of glory do we come
65   From God, who is our home:
Heaven lies about us in our infancy!
Shades of the prison-house begin to close
       Upon the growing Boy,
But He beholds the light, and whence it flows,
70   He sees it in his joy;
The Youth, who daily farther from the east
       Must travel, still is Nature's Priest,
       And by the vision splendid
       Is on his way attended;
75 At length the Man perceives it die away,
And fade into the light of common day.

6

Earth fills her lap with pleasures of her own;
Yearnings she hath in her own natural kind,
And, even with something of a Mother's mind,
80   And no unworthy aim,
       The homely⁷ Nurse doth all she can
To make her Foster-child, her Inmate Man,
       Forget the glories he hath known,
And that imperial palace whence he came.

7

85 Behold the Child among his new-born blisses,
A six years' Darling of a pigmy size!
See, where 'mid work of his own hand he lies,
Fretted⁸ by sallies of his mother's kisses,
With light upon him from his father's eyes!
90 See, at his feet, some little plan or chart,
Some fragment from his dream of human life,
Shaped by himself with newly-learnèd art;
       A wedding or a festival,
       A mourning or a funeral;
95   And this hath now his heart,
       And unto this he frames his song:
       Then will he fit his tongue
To dialogues of business, love, or strife;
       But it will not be long
100   Ere this be thrown aside,
       And with new joy and pride
The little Actor cons another part;
Filling from time to time his "humorous stage"⁹
With all the Persons, down to palsied Age,
105 That Life brings with her in her equipage;
       As if his whole vocation
       Were endless imitation.

7. In the old sense: simple and friendly.
8. Irritated; or possibly in the old sense: checkered over.
9. From a sonnet by the Elizabethan poet Samuel Daniel. In Daniel's age *humorous* meant "capricious" and also referred to the various characters and temperaments ("humors") represented in drama.

8

Thou, whose exterior semblance doth belie
    Thy Soul's immensity;
110 Thou best Philosopher, who yet dost keep
Thy heritage, thou Eye among the blind,
That, deaf and silent, read'st the eternal deep,
Haunted for ever by the eternal mind,—
    Mighty Prophet! Seer blest!
115   On whom those truths do rest,
Which we are toiling all our lives to find,
In darkness lost, the darkness of the grave;
Thou, over whom thy Immortality
Broods like the Day, a Master o'er a Slave,
120 A Presence which is not to be put by;
Thou little Child, yet glorious in the might
Of heaven-born freedom on thy being's height,
Why with such earnest pains dost thou provoke
The years to bring the inevitable yoke,
125 Thus blindly with thy blessedness at strife?
Full soon thy Soul shall have her earthly freight,
And custom lie upon thee with a weight,
Heavy as frost, and deep almost as life!

9

    O joy! that in our embers
130   Is something that doth live,
    That nature yet remembers
    What was so fugitive!
The thought of our past years in me doth breed
Perpetual benediction: not indeed
135 For that which is most worthy to be blest;
Delight and liberty, the simple creed
Of Childhood, whether busy or at rest,
With new-fledged hope still fluttering in his breast:—
    Not for these I raise
140   The song of thanks and praise;
    But for those obstinate questionings
    Of sense and outward things,
    Fallings from us, vanishings;
    Blank misgivings of a Creature
145 Moving about in worlds not realised,[1]
High instincts before which our mortal Nature
Did tremble like a guilty Thing surprised:
    But for those first affections,
    Those shadowy recollections,
150   Which, be they what they may,
Are yet the fountain light of all our day,
Are yet a master light of all our seeing;
    Uphold us, cherish, and have power to make
Our noisy years seem moments in the being

1. Not seeming real (see Wordsworth's comment in the headnote on p. 286).

155 Of the eternal Silence: truths that wake,
          To perish never;
     Which neither listlessness, nor mad endeavour,
          Nor Man nor Boy,
     Nor all that is at enmity with joy,
160 Can utterly abolish or destroy!
          Hence in a season of calm weather
               Though inland far we be,
     Our Souls have sight of that immortal sea
               Which brought us hither,
165   Can in a moment travel thither,
     And see the Children sport upon the shore,
     And hear the mighty waters rolling evermore.

                    10

     Then sing, ye Birds, sing, sing a joyous song!
          And let the young Lambs bound
170   As to the tabor's sound!
     We in thought will join your throng,
          Ye that pipe and ye that play,
          Ye that through your hearts to-day
          Feel the gladness of the May!
175 What though the radiance which was once so bright
     Be now for ever taken from my sight,
          Though nothing can bring back the hour
     Of splendour in the grass, of glory in the flower;
          We will grieve not, rather find
180   Strength in what remains behind;
          In the primal sympathy
          Which having been must ever be;
          In the soothing thoughts that spring
          Out of human suffering;
185   In the faith that looks through death,
     In years that bring the philosophic mind.

                    11

     And O, ye Fountains, Meadows, Hills, and Groves,
     Forebode not any severing of our loves!
     Yet in my heart of hearts I feel your might;
190 I only have relinquished one delight
     To live beneath your more habitual sway.
     I love the Brooks which down their channels fret,
     Even more than when I tripped lightly as they;
     The innocent brightness of a new-born Day
195   Is lovely yet;
     The Clouds that gather round the setting sun
     Do take a sober colouring from an eye
     That hath kept watch o'er man's mortality;
     Another race hath been, and other palms are won.[2]

---

2. In Greece foot races were often run for the prize of a branch or wreath of palm. Wordsworth's line echoes Paul, 1 Corinthians 9.24, who uses such races as a metaphor for life: "Know ye not that they which run in a race run all, but one receiveth the prize?"

200 Thanks to the human heart by which we live,
Thanks to its tenderness, its joys, and fears,
To me the meanest flower that blows can give
Thoughts that do often lie too deep for tears.

1802–04   1807

Ode to Duty[1]

*Jam non consilio bonus, sed more eò perductus, ut non tantum rectè
facere possim, sed nisi rectè facere non possim.*[2]

Stern Daughter of the Voice of God![3]
O Duty! if that name thou love
Who art a light to guide, a rod
To check the erring, and reprove;
5   Thou, who art victory and law
When empty terrors overawe;
From vain temptations dost set free;
And calm'st the weary strife of frail humanity!

There are who ask not if thine eye
10   Be on them; who, in love and truth,
Where no misgiving is, rely
Upon the genial sense[4] of youth:
Glad Hearts! without reproach or blot;
Who do thy work, and know it not:
15   Oh! if through confidence misplaced
They fail, thy saving arms, dread Power! around them cast.

Serene will be our days and bright,
And happy will our nature be,
When love is an unerring light,
20   And joy its own security.
And they a blissful course may hold
Even now, who, not unwisely bold,
Live in the spirit of this creed;
Yet seek thy firm support, according to their need.

---

1. "This Ode . . . is on the model of Gray's *Ode to Adversity* which is copied from Horace's *Ode to Fortune.* Many and many a time have I been twitted by my wife and sister for having forgotten this dedication of myself to the stern lawgiver" [Wordsworth's note].

In this poem, a striking departure from his earlier forms and ideas, Wordsworth abandons the descriptive-meditative pattern of his *Tintern Abbey* and *Ode: Intimations of Immortality* and reverts to the standard 18th-century form of an ode addressed to a personified abstraction. The poem also represents Wordsworth's reversion from his youthful reliance on natural impulse to a more orthodox ethical and religious tradition. It makes no reference to that "Nature" which earlier had constituted for Wordsworth "both law and impulse" and, in *Tintern Abbey,* had been called "The guide, the guardian of my heart, and soul / Of all my moral being" (lines 110–11).

2. Now I am not good by conscious intent, but have been so trained by habit that I not only can act rightly but am unable to act other than rightly (Latin). Added in 1837, this epigraph is an adaptation from *Moral Epistles* 120.10 by Seneca (4 B.C.E.–65 C.E.), Stoic philosopher and writer of tragedies.

3. Cf. *Paradise Lost* 9.652–54: "God so commanded, and left that Command / Sole Daughter of his voice; the rest, we live / Law to ourselves, our Reason is our Law."

4. Innate vitality.

25 I, loving freedom, and untried;
No sport of every random gust,
Yet being to myself a guide,
Too blindly have reposed my trust:
And oft, when in my heart was heard
30 Thy timely mandate, I deferred
The task, in smoother walks to stray;
But thee I now would serve more strictly, if I may.

Through no disturbance of my soul,
Or strong compunction[5] in me wrought,
35 I supplicate for thy control;
But in the quietness of thought:
Me this unchartered freedom tires;
I feel the weight of chance-desires:
My hopes no more must change their name,
40 I long for a repose that ever is the same.

Stern Lawgiver! yet thou dost wear
The Godhead's most benignant grace;
Nor know we any thing so fair
As is the smile upon thy face:
45 Flowers laugh before thee on their beds
And fragrance in thy footing treads;
Thou dost preserve the stars from wrong;
And the most ancient heavens, through Thee, are fresh and strong.

To humbler functions, awful Power!
50 I call thee: I myself commend
Unto thy guidance from this hour;
Oh, let my weakness have an end!
Give unto me, made lowly wise,[6]
The spirit of self-sacrifice;
55 The confidence of reason give;
And in the light of truth thy Bondman let me live!

1804   1807

The Solitary Reaper[1]

Behold her, single in the field,
Yon solitary Highland Lass!
Reaping and singing by herself;
Stop here, or gently pass!

---

5. In the older sense: sting of conscience, or remorse.
6. Another echo from Milton, whose Christian-humanist ethic pervades this ode. The angel Raphael had advised Adam (*Paradise Lost* 8.173–74), "Be lowly wise: / Think only what concerns thee and thy being."
1. One of the rare poems not based on Wordsworth's own experience. The poet tells us that it was suggested by a passage in Thomas Wilkinson's *Tours to the British Mountains* (1824), which he had seen in manuscript: "Passed a female who was reaping alone: she sung in Erse [the Gaelic language of Scotland] as she bended over her sickle; the sweetest human voice I ever heard: her strains were tenderly melancholy, and felt delicious, long after they were heard no more."

5   Alone she cuts and binds the grain,
And sings a melancholy strain;
O listen! for the Vale profound
Is overflowing with the sound.

No Nightingale did ever chaunt
10   More welcome notes to weary bands
Of travellers in some shady haunt,
Among Arabian sands:
A voice so thrilling ne'er was heard
In spring-time from the Cuckoo-bird,
15   Breaking the silence of the seas
Among the farthest Hebrides.

Will no one tell me what she sings?[2]—
Perhaps the plaintive numbers flow
For old, unhappy, far-off things,
20   And battles long ago:
Or is it some more humble lay,
Familiar matter of to-day?
Some natural sorrow, loss, or pain,
That has been, and may be again?

25   Whate'er the theme, the Maiden sang
As if her song could have no ending;
I saw her singing at her work,
And o'er the sickle bending;—
I listened, motionless and still;
30   And, as I mounted up the hill,
The music in my heart I bore,
Long after it was heard no more.

Nov. 5, 1805   1807

Elegiac Stanzas

Suggested by a Picture of Peele Castle, in a Storm, Painted by Sir George Beaumont[1]

I was thy neighbour once, thou rugged Pile!
Four summer weeks I dwelt in sight of thee:
I saw thee every day; and all the while
Thy Form was sleeping on a glassy sea.

5   So pure the sky, so quiet was the air!
So like, so very like, was day to day!

2. The poet does not understand Erse, the language in which she sings.
1. A wealthy landscape painter who was Wordsworth's patron and close friend. Peele Castle is on an island opposite Rampside, Lancashire, where Wordsworth had spent a month in 1794, twelve years before he saw Beaumont's painting. The poem has been interpreted as an expression of Wordsworth's loss of faith in nature. It should be noted, however, that the focus of the poem is not on an altered view of nature but on an altered knowledge of human life and on the moral values necessary to manage the inevitability of loss and suffering.

Whene'er I looked, thy Image still was there;
It trembled, but it never passed away.

How perfect was the calm! it seemed no sleep;
10 No mood, which season takes away, or brings:
I could have fancied that the mighty Deep
Was even the gentlest of all gentle Things.

Ah! THEN, if mine had been the Painter's hand,
To express what then I saw; and add the gleam,
15 The light that never was, on sea or land,
The consecration, and the Poet's dream;

I would have planted thee, thou hoary Pile
Amid a world how different from this!
Beside a sea that could not cease to smile;
20 On tranquil land, beneath a sky of bliss.

Thou shouldst have seemed a treasure-house divine
Of peaceful years; a chronicle of heaven;—
Of all the sunbeams that did ever shine
The very sweetest had to thee been given.

25 A Picture had it been of lasting ease,
Elysian² quiet, without toil or strife;
No motion but the moving tide, a breeze,
Or merely silent Nature's breathing life.

Such, in the fond illusion of my heart,
30 Such Picture would I at that time have made:
And seen the soul of truth in every part,
A stedfast peace that might not be betrayed.

So once it would have been,—'tis so no more;
I have submitted to a new control:
35 A power is gone, which nothing can restore;
A deep distress hath humanised my Soul.³

Not for a moment could I now behold
A smiling sea, and be what I have been:
The feeling of my loss will ne'er be old;
40 This, which I know, I speak with mind serene.

Then, Beaumont, Friend! who would have been the Friend,
If he had lived, of Him whom I deplore,°   mourn
This work of thine I blame not, but commend;
This sea in anger, and that dismal shore.

2. Referring to Elysium, in classical mythology the peaceful place where those favored by the gods dwelled after death.

3. Captain John Wordsworth, William's brother, had been drowned in a shipwreck on February 5, 1805. He is referred to in lines 41–42.

45 O 'tis a passionate Work!—yet wise and well,
  Well chosen is the spirit that is here;
  That Hulk which labours in the deadly swell,
  This rueful sky, this pageantry of fear!

  And this huge Castle, standing here sublime,
50 I love to see the look with which it braves,
  Cased in the unfeeling armour of old time,
  The lightning, the fierce wind, and trampling waves.

  Farewell, farewell the heart that lives alone,
  Housed in a dream, at distance from the Kind!°   *humankind*
55 Such happiness, wherever it be known,
  Is to be pitied; for 'tis surely blind.

  But welcome fortitude, and patient cheer,
  And frequent sights of what is to be borne!
  Such sights, or worse, as are before me here.—
60 Not without hope we suffer and we mourn.

Summer 1806   1807

SONNETS

Composed upon Westminster Bridge, September 3, 1802[1]

  Earth has not any thing to show more fair:
  Dull would he be of soul who could pass by
  A sight so touching in its majesty:
  This City now doth, like a garment, wear
5 The beauty of the morning; silent, bare,
  Ships, towers, domes, theatres, and temples lie
  Open unto the fields, and to the sky;
  All bright and glittering in the smokeless air.
  Never did sun more beautifully steep
10 In his first splendour, valley, rock, or hill;
  Ne'er saw I, never felt, a calm so deep!
  The river glideth at his own sweet will:
  Dear God! the very houses seem asleep;
  And all that mighty heart is lying still!

1802   1807

1. The date of this experience was not September 3, but July 31, 1802. Its occasion was a trip to France (see Dorothy Wordsworth's *Grasmere Journals,* July 1802, p. 395). The conflict of feelings attending Wordsworth's brief return to France, where he had once been a revolutionist and the lover of Annette Vallon, evoked a number of personal and political sonnets, among them the two that follow.

It is a beauteous evening

It is a beauteous evening, calm and free,
The holy time is quiet as a Nun
Breathless with adoration; the broad sun
Is sinking down in its tranquillity;
5   The gentleness of heaven broods o'er the Sea:
Listen! the mighty Being is awake,
And doth with his eternal motion make
A sound like thunder—everlastingly.
Dear Child! dear Girl! that walkest with me here,[2]
10   If thou appear untouched by solemn thought,
Thy nature is not therefore less divine:
Thou liest in Abraham's bosom[3] all the year;
And worshipp'st at the Temple's inner shrine,
God being with thee when we know it not.

Aug. 1802   1807

London, 1802[4]

Milton! thou should'st be living at this hour:
England hath need of thee: she is a fen
Of stagnant waters: altar, sword, and pen,
Fireside, the heroic wealth of hall and bower,
5   Have forfeited their ancient English dower
Of inward happiness. We are selfish men;
Oh! raise us up, return to us again;
And give us manners, virtue, freedom, power.
Thy soul was like a Star, and dwelt apart:
10   Thou hadst a voice whose sound was like the sea:
Pure as the naked heavens, majestic, free,
So didst thou travel on life's common way,
In cheerful godliness; and yet thy heart
The lowliest duties on herself did lay.

Sept. 1802   1807

The world is too much with us

The world is too much with us; late and soon,
Getting and spending, we lay waste our powers:
Little we see in Nature that is ours;

2. The girl walking with Wordsworth is Caroline, his daughter by Annette Vallon. For the event described, see Dorothy Wordsworth's *Grasmere Journals,* July 1802 (p. 395).
3. Where the souls destined for heaven rest after death. Luke 16.22: "And it came to pass, that the beggar died, and was carried by the angels into Abraham's bosom."

4. One of a series "written immediately after my return from France to London, when I could not but be struck, as here described, with the vanity and parade of our own country . . . as contrasted with the quiet, and I may say the desolation, that the revolution had produced in France" [Wordsworth's note].

We have given our hearts away, a sordid boon![5]
5 This Sea that bares her bosom to the moon;
The winds that will be howling at all hours,
And are up-gathered now like sleeping flowers;
For this, for every thing, we are out of tune;
It moves us not.—Great God! I'd rather be
10 A Pagan suckled in a creed outworn;
So might I, standing on this pleasant lea,
Have glimpses that would make me less forlorn;
Have sight of Proteus rising from the sea;
Or hear old Triton[6] blow his wreathèd horn.

1802–04   1807

Surprised by joy[7]

Surprised by joy—impatient as the Wind
I turned to share the transport—Oh! with whom
But Thee, deep buried in the silent tomb,
That spot which no vicissitude can find?
5 Love, faithful love, recalled thee to my mind—
But how could I forget thee? Through what power,
Even for the least division of an hour,
Have I been so beguiled as to be blind
To my most grievous loss!—That thought's return
10 Was the worst pang that sorrow ever bore,
Save one, one only, when I stood forlorn,
Knowing my heart's best treasure was no more;
That neither present time, nor years unborn
Could to my sight that heavenly face restore.

1813–14   1815

Mutability[8]

From low to high doth dissolution climb,
And sink from high to low, along a scale
Of awful notes, whose concord shall not fail;
A musical but melancholy chime,
5 Which they can hear who meddle not with crime,
Nor avarice, nor over-anxious care.
Truth fails not; but her outward forms that bear
The longest date do melt like frosty rime,

5. Gift. It is the act of giving the heart away that is sordid.
6. A sea deity, usually represented as blowing on a conch shell. Proteus was an old man of the sea who (in the *Odyssey*) could assume a variety of shapes. The description of Proteus echoes *Paradise Lost* 3.603–04, and that of Triton echoes Spenser's *Colin Clouts Come Home Againe*, lines 244–45. Milton and Spenser are the two English poets with

whom Wordsworth most closely allied himself.
7. This was in fact suggested by my daughter Catherine, long after her death [Wordsworth's note]. Catherine Wordsworth died June 4, 1812, at the age of four.
8. This sonnet was included in an otherwise rather pedestrian sequence, *Ecclesiastical Sonnets*, dealing with the history and ceremonies of the Church of England.

That in the morning whitened hill and plain
10   And is no more; drop like the tower sublime
Of yesterday, which royally did wear
His crown of weeds, but could not even sustain
Some casual shout that broke the silent air,
Or the unimaginable touch of Time.

1821   1822

Steamboats, Viaducts, and Railways[9]

Motions and Means, on land and sea at war
With old poetic feeling, not for this,
Shall ye, by Poets even, be judged amiss!
Nor shall your presence, howsoe'er it mar
5   The loveliness of Nature, prove a bar
To the Mind's gaining that prophetic sense
Of future change, that point of vision, whence
May be discovered what in soul ye are.
In spite of all that beauty may disown
10   In your harsh features, Nature doth embrace
Her lawful offspring in Man's art; and Time,
Pleased with your triumphs o'er his brother Space,
Accepts from your bold hands the proffered crown
Of hope, and smiles on you with cheer sublime.

1833   1835

———————————

Extempore Effusion upon the Death of James Hogg[1]

When first, descending from the moorlands,
I saw the Stream of Yarrow[2] glide
Along a bare and open valley,
The Ettrick Shepherd[3] was my guide.

5   When last along its banks I wandered,
Through groves that had begun to shed
Their golden leaves upon the pathways,
My steps the Border-minstrel[4] led.

9. In late middle age Wordsworth demonstrates, as he had predicted in the Preface to Lyrical Ballads, that the poet will assimilate to his subject matter the "material revolution" produced by science. Unlike most poets, furthermore, he boldly accepts as evidences of human progress even the unlovely encroachments of technology on his beloved natural scene.
1. Wordsworth's niece relates how he was deeply moved by finding unexpectedly in a newspaper an account of the death of the poet James Hogg. "Half an hour afterwards he came into the room where the ladies were sitting and asked Miss Hutchinson [his sister-in-law] to write down some lines which he had just composed." All the poets named here, several of Wordsworth's closest friends among them, had died between 1832 and 1835.
2. A river in the southeast of Scotland.
3. I.e., Hogg, who was born in Ettrick Forest and worked as a shepherd. He was discovered as a writer by Sir Walter Scott and became well known as a poet, essayist, and editor.
4. Sir Walter Scott.

The mighty Minstrel breathes no longer,
10 'Mid mouldering ruins low he lies;
And death upon the braes[5] of Yarrow,
Has closed the Shepherd-poet's eyes:

Nor has the rolling year twice measured,
From sign to sign, its stedfast course,
15 Since every mortal power of Coleridge
Was frozen at its marvellous source;

The rapt One, of the godlike forehead,
The heaven-eyed creature sleeps in earth:
And Lamb, the frolic and the gentle,
20 Has vanished from his lonely hearth.

Like clouds that rake the mountain-summits,
Or waves that own no curbing hand,
How fast has brother followed brother,
From sunshine to the sunless land!

25 Yet I, whose lids from infant slumber
Were earlier raised, remain to hear
A timid voice, that asks in whispers,
"Who next will drop and disappear?"

Our haughty life is crowned with darkness,
30 Like London with its own black wreath,
On which with thee, O Crabbe![6] forth-looking,
I gazed from Hampstead's breezy heath.

As if but yesterday departed,
Thou too art gone before; but why,
35 O'er ripe fruit, seasonably gathered,
Should frail survivors heave a sigh?

Mourn rather for that holy Spirit,
Sweet as the spring, as ocean deep;
For Her[7] who, ere her summer faded,
40 Has sunk into a breathless sleep.

No more of old romantic sorrows,
For slaughtered Youth or love-lorn Maid!
With sharper grief is Yarrow smitten,
And Ettrick mourns with her their Poet dead.

Nov. 21, 1835   1835

---

5. The sloping banks of a stream.
6. George Crabbe, the poet of rural and village life.

7. The poet Felicia Hemans, who died at forty-two.

Prospectus to *The Recluse*[1]

On Man, on Nature, and on Human Life,
Musing in solitude, I oft perceive
Fair trains of imagery before me rise,
Accompanied by feelings of delight
5   Pure, or with no unpleasing sadness mixed;
And I am conscious of affecting thoughts
And dear remembrances, whose presence soothes
Or elevates the Mind, intent to weigh
The good and evil of our mortal state.
10   —To these emotions, whencesoe'er they come,
Whether from breath of outward circumstance,
Or from the Soul—an impulse to herself—
I would give utterance in numerous verse.[2]
Of Truth, of Grandeur, Beauty, Love, and Hope,
15   And melancholy Fear subdued by Faith;
Of blessed consolations in distress;
Of moral strength, and intellectual Power;
Of joy in widest commonalty spread;
Of the individual Mind that keeps her own
20   Inviolate retirement, subject there
To Conscience only, and the law supreme
Of that Intelligence which governs all—
I sing:—"fit audience let me find though few!"[3]

So prayed, more gaining than he asked, the Bard—
25   In holiest mood. Urania,[4] I shall need
Thy guidance, or a greater Muse, if such
Descend to earth or dwell in highest heaven!
For I must tread on shadowy ground, must sink
Deep—and, aloft ascending, breathe in worlds
30   To which the heaven of heavens[5] is but a veil.
All strength—all terror, single or in bands,

---

1. Through most of his poetic life Wordsworth labored intermittently at a long philosophic poem called *The Recluse*, which he intended to be his masterwork. As he described this project in the Preface to *The Excursion* (1814), it was to consist of an autobiographical introduction (the poem now called *The Prelude*) and three long parts; of these three he completed only book 1 of part 1 (*Home at Grasmere*) and part 2, called *The Excursion*. In the Preface to *The Excursion*, Wordsworth printed this long extract (the concluding section of *Home at Grasmere*) to serve "as a kind of *Prospectus* of the design and scope of the whole Poem"—i.e., of the entire *Recluse*.

The first version of this Prospectus may have been drafted as early as 1798 or 1800. In language resonant with echoes of *Paradise Lost*, Wordsworth announces an undertaking that he conceives to be no less inspired and sublime than Milton's. In it he will move higher than Milton's heaven and deeper than Milton's hell, past scenes evoking greater fear than hell and greater awe than Jehovah; but without ever leaving "the Mind of Man— / My haunt, and the main region of my song" (lines 40–41). And his "high argument" is that Paradise can be regained; not, however, as in Revelation 21 and in Milton, by the marriage between the New Jerusalem and Christ the Lamb, but by a marriage between the "intellect of Man" and "this goodly universe," and the resulting new "creation . . . which they with blended might / Accomplish" (lines 52–71). In no other passage does Wordsworth reveal so clearly the extent to which he assimilates in his poetry the biblical scheme of Milton's epic—assigning, however, the active role, from creation to redemption, to the human faculties, in their interaction with the external universe.
2. Harmonious verse; an echo of *Paradise Lost* 5.150. The inspiring "breath of outward circumstance" (line 11) parallels the "correspondent breeze" in the opening lines of *The Prelude*.
3. *Paradise Lost* 7.31.
4. The Muse whom Milton had invoked in *Paradise Lost* 7.1–39.
5. In *Paradise Lost* the dwelling place, beyond the visible heaven, of God and His angels.

That ever was put forth in personal form—
Jehovah—with his thunder, and the choir
Of shouting Angels, and the empyreal thrones⁶—
35 I pass them unalarmed. Not Chaos, not
The darkest pit of lowest Erebus,⁷
Nor aught of blinder vacancy, scooped out
By help of dreams—can breed such fear and awe
As fall upon us often when we look
40 Into our Minds, into the Mind of Man—
My haunt, and the main region of my song.
—Beauty—a living Presence of the earth,
Surpassing the most fair ideal Forms
Which craft of delicate Spirits hath composed
45 From earth's materials—waits upon my steps;
Pitches her tents before me as I move,
An hourly neighbour. Paradise, and groves
Elysian,⁸ Fortunate Fields—like those of old
Sought in the Atlantic Main—why should they be
50 A history only of departed things,
Or a mere fiction of what never was?
For the discerning intellect of Man,
When wedded to this goodly universe
In love and holy passion, shall find these
55 A simple produce of the common day.
—I, long before the blissful hour arrives,
Would chant, in lonely peace, the spousal⁹ verse
Of this great consummation:—and, by words
Which speak of nothing more than what we are,
60 Would I arouse the sensual from their sleep
Of Death, and win the vacant and the vain
To noble raptures; while my voice proclaims
How exquisitely the individual Mind
(And the progressive powers perhaps no less
65 Of the whole species) to the external World
Is fitted:—and how exquisitely, too—
Theme this but little heard of among men—
The external World is fitted to the Mind;
And the creation (by no lower name
70 Can it be called) which they with blended might
Accomplish:—this is our high argument.¹
—Such grateful haunts foregoing, if I oft
Must turn elsewhere—to travel near the tribes
And fellowships of men, and see ill sights
75 Of madding passions mutually inflamed;
Must hear Humanity in fields and groves

6. Cf. *Paradise Lost* 2.430: "O progeny of Heaven, empyreal thrones!"
7. In classical myth, a dark region of the underworld; often used as a name for hell by Christian writers.
8. Elysium, in Greek myth, was the place where mortals favored by the gods live a happy life after death. It was sometimes identified with the "Islands of the Blessed," reputed to be located far out in the western sea—hence "sought in the Atlantic Main" (line 49). See Horace, *Epodes* 16.
9. Marital. Hence a "spousal verse" is an epithalamion—a poem written to celebrate a marriage.
1. Theme, as in *Paradise Lost* 1.24: "the height of this great argument."

Pipe solitary anguish; or must hang
Brooding above the fierce confederate storm
Of sorrow, barricadoed[2] evermore
80   Within the walls of cities—may these sounds
Have their authentic comment; that even these
Hearing, I be not downcast or forlorn!—
Descend, prophetic Spirit! that inspir'st
The human Soul of universal earth,
85   Dreaming on things to come;[3] and dost possess
A metropolitan temple[4] in the hearts
Of mighty Poets; upon me bestow
A gift of genuine insight; that my Song
With star-like virtue in its place may shine,
90   Shedding benignant influence, and secure,
Itself, from all malevolent effect
Of those mutations that extend their sway
Throughout the nether sphere![5]—And if with this
I mix more lowly matter; with the thing
95   Contemplated, describe the Mind and Man
Contemplating; and who, and what he was—
The transitory Being that beheld
This Vision; when and where, and how he lived;[6]—
Be not this labour useless. If such theme
100   May sort with highest objects, then—dread Power!
Whose gracious favour is the primal source
Of all illumination—may my Life
Express the image of a better time,
More wise desires, and simpler manners;—nurse
105   My Heart in genuine freedom:—all pure thoughts
Be with me;—so shall thy unfailing love
Guide, and support, and cheer me to the end!

ca. 1798–1814   1814

The Prelude

The Prelude, now regarded as Wordsworth's crowning achievement, was unknown to the public at the time of his death in April 1850. When, three months later, it was published from manuscript by Wordsworth's literary executors, its title was given to it by the poet's wife. Wordsworth himself had referred to it variously as "the poem to Coleridge," "the poem on the growth of my own mind," and "the poem on my own poetical education."

For some seventy-five years this posthumous publication of 1850 was the only known text. Then in 1926 Ernest de Selincourt, working from manuscripts, printed an earlier version of the poem that Wordsworth had completed in 1805. Since that time other scholars have established the existence of a still earlier and much shorter

2. Barricaded, as in Paradise Lost 8.241: "Fast we found, fast shut / The dismal gates, and barricadoed strong."
3. Cf. Shakespeare's Sonnet 107: "the prophetic soul / Of the wide world dreaming on things to come."
4. The primary church of a religion.

5. In the Ptolemaic world picture, the spheres of the heavenly bodies were immutable, and only the earth (the "nether sphere," or region below the sphere of the moon) was subject to change. Cf. Paradise Lost 7.375 and 10.656–64.
6. Wordsworth thus justifies The Prelude and the autobiographical sections of The Recluse.

version of *The Prelude,* in two parts, that Wordsworth had composed in 1798–99. The following seems to have been the process of composition that produced the three principal versions of the poem:

1. The *Two-Part Prelude* of 1799. Wordsworth originally planned, early in 1798, to include an account of his own development as a poet in his projected but never-completed philosophical poem *The Recluse* (see the Prospectus to *The Recluse,* n. 1, p. 301). While living in Germany during the autumn and winter of 1798–99, he composed a number of passages about his early experiences with nature. What had been intended to be part of *The Recluse,* however, quickly evolved into an independent autobiographical poem, and by late 1799, when Wordsworth settled with his sister, Dorothy, at Grasmere, he had written a poem in two parts, 978 lines in length, which takes his life from infancy, through his years at Hawkshead School, to the age of seventeen. This poem corresponds, by and large, to the contents of books 1 and 2 of the later versions of *The Prelude.*

2. The 1805 *Prelude.* Late in 1801 Wordsworth began to expand the poem on his poetic life, and in 1804 he set to work intensively on the project. His initial plan was to write it in five books, but he soon decided to enlarge it to incorporate an account of his experiences in France and of his mental crisis after the failure of his hopes in the French Revolution, and to end the poem with his settlement at Grasmere and his taking up the great task of *The Recluse.* He completed the poem, in thirteen books, in May 1805. This is the version that Wordsworth read to Coleridge after the latter's return from Malta (see Coleridge's *To William Wordsworth,* p. 464).

3. The 1850 *Prelude.* For the next thirty-five years Wordsworth tinkered with the text, polishing the style and qualifying some of its radical statements about the divine sufficiency of the human mind in its communion with nature; he did not, however, in any essential way alter its subject matter or overall design. *The Prelude* that was published in July 1850 is in fourteen books and was printed from a fair copy; it incorporated Wordsworth's latest revisions, which had been made in 1839, as well as some alterations introduced by his literary executors. The selections printed here—from W. J. B. Owen's Cornell Wordsworth volume, *The Fourteen-Book Prelude* (1985)—are from the manuscript of this final version. Our reasons for choosing this version are set forth in Jack Stillinger's "Textual Primitivism and the Editing of Wordsworth," *Studies in Romanticism* 28 (1989): 3–28.

When Wordsworth enlarged the two-part *Prelude* of 1799, he not only made it a poem of epic length but also heightened the style and introduced various thematic parallels with earlier epics, especially *Paradise Lost.* (For a central example, see Wordsworth's version of Milton's enterprise to "justify the ways of God to men," in 14.162–70, p. 380, and 14.384–89, p. 382.) The expanded poem, however, is a personal history that turns on a mental crisis and recovery, and for such a narrative design the chief prototype is not the classical or Christian epic but the spiritual autobiography of crisis. St. Augustine's *Confessions* established this central Christian form late in the fourth century, and it has had an uninterrupted history in European literature ever since.

As in Augustine's *Confessions* and many later versions of spiritual autobiography, Wordsworth's persistent metaphor is that of life as a circular journey whose end (as T. S. Eliot put it in *Four Quartets,* his adaptation of the traditional form) is "to arrive where we started / And know the place for the first time" (*Little Gidding,* lines 241–42). Wordsworth's *Prelude* opens with a literal journey whose chosen goal (1.72, 106–07) is "a known Vale whither my feet should turn"—that is, the Vale of Grasmere. *The Prelude* narrates a number of later journeys, most notably the crossing of the Alps in book 6 and, at the beginning of the final book, the climactic ascent of Mount Snowdon. In the course of the poem, such literal journeys become the metaphoric vehicle for an interior, spiritual journey in the quest, within the poet's memory, and in the very process of composing his poem, for his lost early self and his proper spiritual home. At its end the poem, adverting to its beginning, leaves the poet at home in the Vale of Grasmere, ready finally to begin his great project *The Recluse* (14.302–11, 374–85).

Throughout *The Prelude*, Wordsworth formulates the course of his life in accordance with an intricate artistic pattern and narrates it in a deliberately traditional voice. Although its episodes are recognizable events in his experience, they are interpreted in retrospect, reordered in sequence, retold as primarily a transaction between mind and nature, and shaped into the inherited design of crisis and recovery, from which the protagonist emerges as a new self in a transformed world, confirmed in his vocation as a poet. And although the narrator is recognizably William Wordsworth, addressing the entire poem as a communication to his friend Coleridge, he adopts the prophetic persona, modeled on the poet-prophets of the Bible, which John Milton had adopted in narrating *Paradise Lost* (13.300–11). In this way Wordsworth, like his great English predecessor, assumes the authority to speak as a national poet whose function is to reconstitute the grounds of hope in a dark time of postrevolutionary reaction and despair. As Wordsworth describes it (2.433–42), he speaks out

> in these times of fear,
> This melancholy waste of hopes overthrown,
> . . . 'mid indifference and apathy
> And wicked exultation, when good men,
> On every side, fall off, we know not how,
> To selfishness, disguised in gentle names
> Of peace and quiet and domestic love
>   . . . this time
> Of dereliction and dismay. . . .

From The Prelude
OR
Growth of a Poet's Mind

AN AUTOBIOGRAPHICAL POEM

Book First
Introduction, Childhood, and School-time

O there is blessing in this gentle breeze,
A visitant that, while he fans my cheek,
Doth seem half-conscious of the joy he brings
From the green fields, and from yon azure sky.
5 Whate'er his mission, the soft breeze can come
To none more grateful than to me; escaped
From the vast City,[1] where I long have pined
A discontented Sojourner—Now free,
Free as a bird to settle where I will.
10 What dwelling shall receive me? in what vale
Shall be my harbour? underneath what grove
Shall I take up my home? and what clear stream
Shall with its murmur lull me into rest?
The earth is all before me:[2] with a heart

---

1. London. Wordsworth uses this city as a type representing a place of spiritual bondage from which he has finally escaped.
2. One of many echoes from *Paradise Lost,* where the line is applied to Adam and Eve as, at the conclusion of the poem, they begin their new life after being expelled from Eden: "The world was all before them" (12.646).

15   Joyous, nor scared at its own liberty,
     I look about; and should the chosen guide
     Be nothing better than a wandering cloud,
     I cannot miss my way. I breathe again;
     Trances of thought and mountings of the heart
20   Come fast upon me: it is shaken off,
     That burthen of my own unnatural self,
     The heavy weight of many a weary day
     Not mine, and such as were not made for me.
     Long months of peace (if such bold word accord
25   With any promises of human life),
     Long months of ease and undisturbed delight
     Are mine in prospect; whither shall I turn,
     By road or pathway, or through trackless field,
     Up hill or down, or shall some floating thing
30   Upon the River point me out my course?
     Dear Liberty! Yet what would it avail,
     But for a gift that consecrates the joy?
     For I, methought, while the sweet breath of heaven
     Was blowing on my body, felt, within,
35   A correspondent breeze, that gently moved
     With quickening virtue,[3] but is now become
     A tempest, a redundant° energy,   *abundant*
     Vexing its own creation. Thanks to both,
     And their congenial° powers that, while they join   *kindred*
40   In breaking up a long continued frost,
     Bring with them vernal promises, the hope
     Of active days urged on by flying hours;
     Days of sweet leisure taxed with patient thought
     Abstruse, nor wanting punctual service high,
45   Matins and vespers, of harmonious verse![4]
       Thus far, O Friend![5] did I, not used to make
     A present joy the matter of a Song,[6]
     Pour forth, that day, my soul in measured strains,
     That would not be forgotten, and are here
50   Recorded:—to the open fields I told
     A prophecy:—poetic numbers came
     Spontaneously, to clothe in priestly robe
     A renovated Spirit singled out,

3. Revivifying power. ("To quicken" is to give or restore life.)

4. I.e., verses equivalent to morning prayers (matins) and evening prayers (vespers). The opening passage (lines 1–45), which Wordsworth calls in book 7, line 4, a "glad preamble," replaces the traditional epic device, such as Milton had adopted in *Paradise Lost*, of an opening prayer to the Muse for inspiration. To be "inspired," in the literal sense, is to be breathed or blown into by a divinity (in Latin *spirare* means both "to breathe" and "to blow"). Wordsworth begins his poem with a "blessing" from an outer "breeze," which (lines 34–45) is called the "breath of heaven" and evokes in him a correspondent inner breeze that signalizes a springlike revival of his spirit after a wintry season, and also a burst of poetic power that he goes on to equate (lines 50–54) with the utterances of biblical prophets when inspired by the Holy Spirit. The revivifying breeze and breath, at once material and spiritual, recurs later in *The Prelude* as a kind of leitmotif. It also serves as the radical metaphor of other Romantic poems such as Coleridge's *The Eolian Harp* and *Dejection: An Ode*, and Shelley's *Ode to the West Wind*.

5. Samuel Taylor Coleridge, to whom Wordsworth addresses the whole of the *Prelude*. For Coleridge's response, after the poem was read to him, see *To William Wordsworth* (p. 464).

6. In the Preface to *Lyrical Ballads* Wordsworth says that his poetry usually originates in "emotion recollected in tranquillity"; hence not, as in the preceding preamble, during the experience that it records.

Such hope was mine, for holy services:
55 My own voice cheered me, and, far more, the mind's
Internal echo of the imperfect sound;
To both I listened, drawing from them both
A chearful confidence in things to come.
    Content, and not unwilling now to give
60 A respite to this passion, I paced on
With brisk and eager steps; and came at length
To a green shady place where down I sate
Beneath a tree, slackening my thoughts by choice,
And settling into gentler happiness.
65 'Twas Autumn, and a clear and placid day,
With warmth, as much as needed, from a sun
Two hours declined towards the west, a day
With silver clouds, and sunshine on the grass,
And, in the sheltered and the sheltering grove,
70 A perfect stillness. Many were the thoughts
Encouraged and dismissed, till choice was made
Of a known Vale[7] whither my feet should turn,
Nor rest till they had reached the very door
Of the one Cottage which methought I saw.
75 No picture of mere memory ever looked
So fair; and while upon the fancied scene
I gazed with growing love, a higher power
Than Fancy gave assurance of some work
Of glory, there forthwith to be begun,
80 Perhaps too there performed.[8] Thus long I mused,
Nor e'er lost sight of what I mused upon,
Save where, amid the stately grove of Oaks,
Now here—now there—an acorn, from its cup
Dislodged, through sere leaves rustled, or at once
85 To the bare earth dropped with a startling sound.
    From that soft couch I rose not, till the sun
Had almost touched the horizon; casting then
A backward glance upon the curling cloud
Of city smoke, by distance ruralized,
90 Keen as a Truant or a Fugitive,
But as a Pilgrim resolute, I took,
Even with the chance equipment of that hour,
The road that pointed tow'rd the chosen Vale.
    It was a splendid evening: and my Soul
95 Once more made trial of her strength, nor lacked
Eolian visitations;[9] but the harp
Was soon defrauded, and the banded host
Of harmony dispersed in straggling sounds;
And lastly utter silence! "Be it so;

7. Grasmere, where Wordsworth settled with his sister, Dorothy, in December 1799. Wordsworth uses his walk to that "Vale" to symbolize a new stage in the journey of his life—a stage in which he returns to what he calls (in the title of the opening book of *The Recluse*, designed to follow *The Prelude*) "Home at Grasmere."

8. I.e., *The Recluse*, which Wordsworth planned to be his major poetic work.
9. Influences to which his soul responded as an Eolian harp responds to gusts of a breeze. For a description of this instrument, see Coleridge's *The Eolian Harp*, n. 1, p. 419.

100 Why think of any thing but present good?"
 So, like a Home-bound Labourer, I pursued
 My way, beneath the mellowing sun, that shed
 Mild influence;[1] nor left in me one wish
 Again to bend the sabbath of that time[2]
105 To a servile yoke. What need of many words?
 A pleasant loitering journey, through three days
 Continued, brought me to my hermitage.
 I spare to tell of what ensued, the life
 In common things,—the endless store of things
110 Rare, or at least so seeming, every day
 Found all about me in one neighbourhood;
 The self-congratulation,° and from morn   *self-rejoicing*
 To night unbroken cheerfulness serene.
 But speedily an earnest longing rose
115 To brace myself to some determined aim,
 Reading or thinking; either to lay up
 New stores, or rescue from decay the old
 By timely interference: and therewith
 Came hopes still higher, that with outward life
120 I might endue some airy phantasies
 That had been floating loose about for years;
 And to such Beings temperately deal forth
 The many feelings that oppressed my heart.
 That hope hath been discouraged; welcome light
125 Dawns from the East, but dawns—to disappear
 And mock me with a sky that ripens not
 Into a steady morning: if my mind,
 Remembering the bold promise of the past,
 Would gladly grapple with some noble theme,
130 Vain is her wish: where'er she turns, she finds
 Impediments from day to day renewed.
  And now it would content me to yield up
 Those lofty hopes awhile for present gifts
 Of humbler industry. But, O dear Friend!
135 The Poet, gentle Creature as he is,
 Hath, like the Lover, his unruly times,
 His fits when he is neither sick nor well,
 Though no distress be near him but his own
 Unmanageable thoughts: his mind, best pleas'd
140 While she, as duteous as the Mother Dove,
 Sits brooding,[3] lives not always to that end,
 But, like the innocent Bird, hath goadings on
 That drive her, as in trouble, through the groves:
 With me is now such passion, to be blamed
145 No otherwise than as it lasts too long.
  When as becomes a Man who would prepare

1. An astrological term for the effect of stars on human life. *Paradise Lost* 7.374–75: "The Pleiades [a cluster of stars] before him danced / Shedding sweet influence."
2. That time of rest.

3. An echo of Milton's reference in *Paradise Lost* to the original act of creation in his invocation to the Holy Spirit: Thou "Dovelike satst brooding on the vast Abyss / And mad'st it pregnant" (1.21–22).

For such an arduous Work, I through myself
Make rigorous inquisition, the report
Is often chearing; for I neither seem
150 To lack that first great gift, the vital Soul,
Nor general Truths, which are themselves a sort
Of Elements and Agents, Under-powers,
Subordinate helpers of the living Mind:
Nor am I naked of external things,
155 Forms, images, nor numerous other aids
Of less regard, though won perhaps with toil,
And needful to build up a Poet's praise.
Time, place, and manners do I seek, and these
Are found in plenteous store, but no where such
160 As may be singled out with steady choice:
No little band of yet remembered names
Whom I in perfect confidence might hope
To summon back from lonesome banishment,
And make them dwellers in the hearts of men
165 Now living, or to live in future years.
Sometimes the ambitious Power of choice, mistaking
Proud spring-tide swellings for a regular sea,
Will settle on some British theme, some old
Romantic Tale by Milton left unsung:[4]
170 More often turning to some gentle place
Within the groves of Chivalry, I pipe
To Shepherd Swains, or seated, harp in hand,
Amid reposing knights by a River side
Or fountain, listen to the grave reports
175 Of dire enchantments faced, and overcome
By the strong mind, and Tales of warlike feats
Where spear encountered spear, and sword with sword
Fought, as if conscious of the blazonry
That the shield bore, so glorious was the strife;
180 Whence inspiration for a song that winds
Through ever changing scenes of votive quest,[5]
Wrongs to redress, harmonious tribute paid
To patient courage and unblemished truth,
To firm devotion, zeal unquenchable,
185 And Christian meekness hallowing faithful loves.[6]
Sometimes, more sternly moved, I would relate
How vanquished Mithridates northward passed,
And, hidden in the cloud of years, became
Odin, the Father of a Race by whom
190 Perished the Roman Empire;[7] how the friends
And followers of Sertorius, out of Spain

4. In *Paradise Lost* 9.24–41 Milton relates that, in seeking a subject for his epic poem, he rejected "fabled Knights" and medieval romance.
5. A quest undertaken to fulfill a vow.
6. An echo of the prefatory statement to Spenser's *Faerie Queene*, line 9: "Fierce warres and faithfull loves shall moralize my song."
7. Mithridates VI, king of Pontus, was defeated by

the Roman Pompey in 66 B.C.E. In chap. 10 of his *Decline and Fall of the Roman Empire*, Edward Gibbon associates him with Odin, a chieftain of the Goths, who hoped to produce descendants who would wreak revenge on the conquering Romans. All the protagonists that Wordsworth considered for his poem were heroes in fights against tyranny.

Flying, found shelter in the Fortunate Isles;
And left their usages, their arts, and laws
To disappear by a slow gradual death;
195   To dwindle and to perish, one by one,
Starved in those narrow bounds: but not the soul
Of Liberty, which fifteen hundred years
Survived, and, when the European came
With skill and power that might not be withstood,
200   Did, like a pestilence, maintain its hold,
And wasted down by glorious death that Race
Of natural Heroes;[8]—or I would record
How, in tyrannic times, some high-souled Man,
Unnamed among the chronicles of Kings,
205   Suffered in silence for truth's sake: or tell
How that one Frenchman, through continued force
Of meditation on the inhuman deeds
Of those who conquered first the Indian isles,
Went, single in his ministry, across
210   The Ocean;—not to comfort the Oppressed,
But, like a thirsty wind, to roam about,
Withering the Oppressor:[9]—how Gustavus sought
Help at his need in Dalecarlia's mines:[1]
How Wallace[2] fought for Scotland, left the name
215   Of Wallace to be found, like a wild flower,
All over his dear Country, left the deeds
Of Wallace, like a family of Ghosts,
To people the steep rocks and river banks,
Her natural sanctuaries, with a local soul
220   Of independence and stern liberty.
Sometimes it suits me better to invent
A Tale from my own heart, more near akin
To my own passions, and habitual thoughts,
Some variegated Story, in the main
225   Lofty, but the unsubstantial Structure melts
Before the very sun that brightens it,
Mist into air dissolving! Then, a wish,
My last and favourite aspiration, mounts,
With yearning, tow'rds some philosophic Song
230   Of Truth[3] that cherishes our daily life;
With meditations passionate, from deep
Recesses in man's heart, immortal verse
Thoughtfully fitted to the Orphean lyre;[4]

8. Sertorius, a Roman general allied with Mithridates, fought off the armies of Pompey and others until he was assassinated in 72 B.C.E. There is a legend that after his death his followers, to escape Roman tyranny, fled from Spain to the Canary Islands (known in ancient times as "the Fortunate Isles," line 192), where their descendants flourished until subjugated and decimated by invading Spaniards late in the 15th century.
9. Dominique de Gourges, a French gentleman who went in 1568 to Florida to avenge the massacre of the French by the Spaniards there [footnote in The Prelude of 1850].
1. In the 16th century Gustavus I of Sweden mustered supporters in Dalecarlia, a mining district, to help free Sweden from the tyranny of Denmark.
2. William Wallace, Scottish national hero, fought against the English until captured and executed in 1305.
3. I.e., The Recluse.
4. The lyre of Orpheus. In Greek myth Orpheus was able to enchant not only human listeners but the natural world by his singing and playing.

But from this awful burthen I full soon
235   Take refuge, and beguile myself with trust
That mellower years will bring a riper mind
And clearer insight. Thus my days are passed
In contradiction; with no skill to part
Vague longing, haply bred by want of power,
240   From paramount impulse—not to be withstood;
A timorous capacity from prudence;
From circumspection, infinite delay.[5]
Humility and modest awe themselves
Betray me, serving often for a cloke
245   To a more subtile selfishness; that now
Locks every function up in blank° reserve,°   *absolute / inaction*
Now dupes me, trusting to an anxious eye
That with intrusive restlessness beats off
Simplicity, and self-presented truth.
250   Ah! better far than this, to stray about
Voluptuously,° through fields and rural walks,   *luxuriously*
And ask no record of the hours, resigned
To vacant musing, unreproved neglect
Of all things, and deliberate holiday:
255   Far better never to have heard the name
Of zeal and just ambition, than to live
Baffled and plagued by a mind that every hour
Turns recreant to her task, takes heart again,
Then feels immediately some hollow thought
260   Hang like an interdict° upon her hopes.   *prohibition*
This is my lot; for either still I find
Some imperfection in the chosen theme;
Or see of absolute accomplishment
Much wanting, so much wanting, in myself
265   That I recoil and droop, and seek repose
In listlessness from vain perplexity;
Unprofitably travelling toward the grave,
Like a false Steward who hath much received,
And renders nothing back.[6]
                      Was it for this[7]
270   That one, the fairest of all rivers, loved
To blend his murmurs with my Nurse's song;
And, from his alder shades and rocky falls,
And from his fords and shallows, sent a voice
That flowed along my dreams? For this didst Thou,
275   O Derwent! winding among grassy holms[8]
Where I was looking on, a Babe in arms,
Make ceaseless music, that composed my thoughts
To more than infant softness, giving me,
Amid the fretful dwellings of mankind,

---

5. The syntax is complex and inverted; in outline, the sense of lines 238–42 seems to be, to put it shortly: "With no ability ('skill') to distinguish between vague desire (perhaps resulting from lack of power) and ruling impulse; between timidity and prudence; between endless delay and carefulness ('circumspection')."
6. The reference is to the parable of the false steward in Matthew 25.14–30.
7. The two-part *Prelude* that Wordsworth wrote in 1798–99 begins at this point.
8. Flat ground next to a river.

280 A foretaste, a dim earnest, of the calm
That Nature breathes among the hills and groves?
    When he had left the mountains, and received
On his smooth breast the shadow of those Towers
That yet survive, a shattered Monument
285 Of feudal sway, the bright blue River passed
Along the margin of our Terrace Walk;⁹
A tempting Playmate whom we dearly loved.
O many a time have I, a five years' Child,
In a small mill-race severed from his stream,
290 Made one long bathing of a summer's day;
Basked in the sun, and plunged, and basked again,
Alternate all a summer's day, or scoured¹
The sandy fields, leaping through flow'ry groves
Of yellow ragwort; or when rock and hill,
295 The woods and distant Skiddaw's² lofty height,
Were bronzed with deepest radiance, stood alone
Beneath the sky, as if I had been born
On Indian plains, and from my Mother's hut
Had run abroad in wantonness, to sport,
300 A naked Savage, in the thunder shower.
    Fair seed-time had my soul, and I grew up
Fostered alike by beauty and by fear;³
Much favoured in my birth-place, and no less
In that beloved Vale⁴ to which erelong
305 We were transplanted—there were we let loose
For sports of wider range. Ere I had told
Ten birth-days, when among the mountain slopes
Frost, and the breath of frosty wind, had snapped
The last autumnal Crocus, 'twas my joy,
310 With store of Springes° o'er my Shoulder slung,   bird snares
To range the open heights where woodcocks ran
Along the smooth green turf. Through half the night,
Scudding away from snare to snare, I plied
That anxious visitation;—moon and stars
315 Were shining o'er my head; I was alone,
And seemed to be a trouble to the peace
That dwelt among them. Sometimes it befel,
In these night-wanderings, that a strong desire
O'erpowered my better reason, and the Bird
320 Which was the Captive of another's toil⁵
Became my prey; and when the deed was done
I heard, among the solitary hills,

9. The Derwent River flows by Cockermouth Castle and then past the garden terrace behind Wordsworth's father's house in Cockermouth, Cumberland.
1. Run swiftly over.
2. A mountain nine miles east of Cockermouth.
3. Wordsworth introduces here a dialectic that plays a central role in the evolution of *The Prelude.* He represents his mind, confronting nature, as fostered in its growth by two antithetic principles, one associated with love and the other with fear. These principles correspond to the two main categories, "the beautiful" and "the sublime," into which theorists of the landscape during the preceding century had classified the antithetic aspects of the natural scene (see, e.g., 1.351–56, 466–75, 546). In the concluding book (in 14.162–70), this antithesis is finally resolved (see n. 3, p. 000).
4. The valley of Esthwaite, the location of Hawkshead, where Wordsworth attended school.
5. Snare or labor.

Low breathings coming after me, and sounds
Of undistinguishable motion, steps
325 Almost as silent as the turf they trod.
　　　Nor less, when Spring had warmed the cultured° Vale,　　*cultivated*
Roved we as plunderers where the Mother-bird
Had in high places built her lodge; though mean
Our object, and inglorious, yet the end°　　　　　　　　　　*outcome*
330 Was not ignoble. Oh! when I have hung
Above the Raven's nest, by knots of grass
And half-inch fissures in the slippery rock
But ill-sustained; and almost (so it seemed)
Suspended by the blast that blew amain,
335 Shouldering the naked crag; Oh, at that time,
While on the perilous ridge I hung alone,
With what strange utterance did the loud dry wind
Blow through my ears! the sky seemed not a sky
Of earth, and with what motion moved the clouds!
340 　　Dust as we are, the immortal Spirit grows
Like harmony in music; there is a dark
Inscrutable workmanship that reconciles
Discordant elements, makes them cling together
In one society. How strange that all
345 The terrors, pains, and early miseries,
Regrets, vexations, lassitudes, interfused
Within my mind, should e'er have borne a part,
And that a needful part, in making up
The calm existence that is mine when I
350 Am worthy of myself! Praise to the end!
Thanks to the means which Nature deigned to employ!
Whether her fearless visitings or those
That came with soft alarm like hurtless lightning
Opening the peaceful clouds, or she would use
355 Severer interventions, ministry
More palpable, as best might suit her aim.[6]
　　　One summer evening (led by her) I found
A little Boat tied to a Willow-tree
Within a rocky cave, its usual home.
360 Straight I unloosed her chain, and, stepping in,
Pushed from the shore. It was an act of stealth
And troubled pleasure, nor without the voice
Of mountain-echoes did my Boat move on,
Leaving behind her still, on either side,
365 Small circles glittering idly in the moon,
Until they melted all into one track!
Of sparkling light. But now, like one who rows
(Proud of his skill) to reach a chosen point
With an unswerving line, I fixed my view
370 Upon the summit of a craggy ridge,
The horizon's utmost boundary; for above

6. A restatement of the double ministry of nature described in line 302. What follows is a second example
of discipline by fear.

Was nothing but the stars and the grey sky.
She was an elfin Pinnace;° lustily   *small boat*
I dipped my oars into the silent lake;
375 And, as I rose upon the stroke, my boat
Went heaving through the Water like a swan:
When, from behind that craggy Steep, till then
The horizon's bound, a huge peak, black and huge,
As if with voluntary power instinct,°   *endowed*
380 Upreared its head.[7]—I struck, and struck again,
And, growing still in stature, the grim Shape
Towered up between me and the stars, and still,
For so it seemed, with purpose of its own
And measured motion, like a living Thing
385 Strode after me. With trembling oars I turned,
And through the silent water stole my way
Back to the Covert of the Willow-tree;
There, in her mooring-place, I left my Bark,—
And through the meadows homeward went, in grave
390 And serious mood; but after I had seen
That spectacle, for many days, my brain
Worked with a dim and undetermined sense
Of unknown modes of being; o'er my thoughts
There hung a darkness, call it solitude
395 Or blank desertion. No familiar Shapes
Remained, no pleasant images of trees,
Of sea or Sky, no colours of green fields,
But huge and mighty Forms, that do not live
Like living men, moved slowly through the mind
400 By day, and were a trouble to my dreams.
    Wisdom and Spirit of the Universe!
Thou Soul that art the eternity of thought,
That giv'st to forms and images a breath
And everlasting Motion! not in vain,
405 By day or star-light, thus from my first dawn
Of Childhood didst thou intertwine for me
The passions that build up our human Soul,
Not with the mean and vulgar° works of man,   *commonplace*
But with high objects, with enduring things,
410 With life and nature, purifying thus
The elements of feeling and of thought,
And sanctifying, by such discipline,
Both pain and fear; until we recognize
A grandeur in the beatings of the heart.
415   Nor was this fellowship vouchsafed to me
With stinted kindness. In November days
When vapours, rolling down the valley, made
A lonely scene more lonesome; among woods
At noon, and 'mid the calm of summer nights,

7. To direct his boat in a straight line, the rower (sitting facing the stern of the boat) has fixed his eye on a point on the ridge above the nearby shore, which blocks out the landscape behind. As he moves farther out, the black peak rises into his altering angle of vision and seems to stride closer with each stroke of the oars.

420 When, by the margin of the trembling Lake,
Beneath the gloomy hills homeward I went
In solitude, such intercourse was mine:
Mine was it, in the fields both day and night,
And by the waters, all the summer long.
425 —And in the frosty season, when the sun
Was set, and visible for many a mile,
The cottage windows blazed through twilight gloom,
I heeded not their summons,—happy time
It was indeed for all of us; for me
430 It was a time of rapture!—Clear and loud
The village Clock toll'd six—I wheeled about,
Proud and exulting like an untired horse
That cares not for his home.—All shod with steel,
We hissed along the polished ice, in games
435 Confederate, imitative of the chase
And woodland pleasures,—the resounding horn,
The Pack loud-chiming and the hunted hare.
So through the darkness and the cold we flew,
And not a voice was idle: with the din
440 Smitten, the precipices rang aloud;
The leafless trees and every icy crag
Tinkled like iron; while far distant hills
Into the tumult sent an alien sound
Of melancholy, not unnoticed while the stars,
445 Eastward, were sparkling clear, and in the west
The orange sky of evening died away.
Not seldom from the uproar I retired
Into a silent bay,—or sportively
Glanced sideway,[8] leaving the tumultous throng
450 To cut across the reflex° of a star   *reflection*
That fled, and, flying still before me, gleamed
Upon the glassy plain: and oftentimes,
When we had given our bodies to the wind,
And all the shadowy banks on either side
455 Came sweeping through the darkness, spinning still
The rapid line of motion, then at once
Have I, reclining back upon my heels,
Stopped short; yet still the solitary cliffs
Wheeled by me—even as if the earth had rolled
460 With visible motion her diurnal° round!   *daily*
Behind me did they stretch in solemn train,°   *succession*
Feebler and feebler, and I stood and watched
Till all was tranquil as a dreamless sleep.
    Ye presences of Nature, in the sky,
465 And on the earth! Ye visions of the hills!
And Souls[9] of lonely places! can I think
A vulgar hope was yours when ye employed
Such ministry, when ye, through many a year,

---

8. Moved off obliquely.
9. Wordsworth refers both to a single "Spirit" or "Soul" of the universe as a whole (e.g., lines 401– 02) and to plural "Presences" and "Souls" inanimating the various parts of the universe.

Haunting me thus among my boyish sports,
470   On caves and trees, upon the woods and hills,
Impressed upon all forms the characters°   *signs*
Of danger or desire; and thus did make
The surface of the universal earth
With triumph and delight, with hope and fear,
Work° like a sea?   *seethe*
475   Not uselessly employed,
Might I pursue this theme through every change
Of exercise and play, to which the year
Did summon us in his delightful round.
    —We were a noisy crew; the sun in heaven
480   Beheld not vales more beautiful than ours,
Nor saw a Band in happiness and joy
Richer, or worthier of the ground they trod.
I could record with no reluctant voice
The woods of Autumn, and their hazel bowers
485   With milk-white clusters hung; the rod and line,
True symbol of hope's foolishness, whose strong
And unreproved enchantment led us on,
By rocks and pools shut out from every star
All the green summer, to forlorn cascades
490   Among the windings hid of mountain brooks.
    —Unfading recollections! at this hour
The heart is almost mine with which I felt,
From some hill-top on sunny afternoons,
The paper-Kite, high among fleecy clouds,
495   Pull at her rein, like an impatient Courser;
Or, from the meadows sent on gusty days,
Beheld her breast the wind, then suddenly
Dashed headlong, and rejected by the storm.
    Ye lowly Cottages in which we dwelt,
500   A ministration of your own was yours!
Can I forget you, being as ye were
So beautiful among the pleasant fields
In which ye stood? or can I here forget
The plain and seemly countenance with which
505   Ye dealt out your plain Comforts? Yet had ye
Delights and exultations of your own.
Eager and never weary, we pursued
Our home-amusements by the warm peat-fire
At evening, when with pencil, and smooth slate
510   In square divisions parcelled out, and all
With crosses and with cyphers scribbled o'er,
We schemed and puzzled, head opposed to head,
In strife too humble to be named in verse;[1]
Or round the naked table, snow-white deal,°   *pine or fir*
515   Cherry, or maple, sate in close array,
And to the Combat, Lu or Whist, led on

---

1. I.e., ticktacktoe. By his phrasing in this passage, Wordsworth pokes fun at 18th-century poetic diction, which avoided homely terms by using circumlocutions.

A thick-ribbed Army, not as in the world
Neglected and ungratefully thrown by
Even for the very service they had wrought,
520   But husbanded through many a long campaign.
Uncouth assemblage was it, where no few
Had changed their functions; some, plebeian cards
Which Fate, beyond the promise of their birth,
Had dignified, and called to represent
525   The Persons of departed Potentates.
Oh, with what echoes on the board they fell!
Ironic diamonds; Clubs, Hearts, Diamonds, Spades,
A congregation piteously akin!
Cheap matter offered they to boyish wit,
530   Those sooty Knaves, precipitated down
With scoffs and taunts like Vulcan[2] out of heaven;
The paramount Ace, a moon in her eclipse,
Queens gleaming through their Splendor's last decay,
And Monarchs surly at the wrongs sustained
535   By royal visages.[3] Meanwhile abroad
Incessant rain was falling, or the frost
Raged bitterly, with keen and silent tooth;
And, interrupting oft that eager game,
From under Esthwaite's splitting fields of ice
540   The pent-up air, struggling to free itself,
Gave out to meadow-grounds and hills, a loud
Protracted yelling, like the noise of wolves
Howling in Troops along the Bothnic Main.[4]
    Nor, sedulous° as I have been to trace   *diligent*
545   How Nature by extrinsic passion first
Peopled the mind with forms sublime or fair[5]
And made me love them, may I here omit
How other pleasures have been mine, and joys
Of subtler origin; how I have felt,
550   Not seldom even in that tempestuous time,
Those hallowed and pure motions of the sense
Which seem, in their simplicity, to own
An intellectual[6] charm;—that calm delight
Which, if I err not, surely must belong
555   To those first-born° affinities that fit   *innate*
Our new existence to existing things,
And, in our dawn of being, constitute
The bond of union between life and joy.
    Yes, I remember when the changeful earth
560   And twice five summers on my mind had stamped
The faces of the moving year, even then

2. Roman god of fire and forge. His mother, Juno, when he was born lame, threw him down from Olympus, the abode of the gods.
3. Wordsworth implicitly parallels the boys' card games to the mock-epic description of the aristocratic game of ombre in Pope's *The Rape of the Lock* 3.37–98.
4. A northern gulf of the Baltic Sea.

5. The passion at first was "extrinsic" because it was felt not for nature itself but for nature as associated with the outdoor activities he loved. Wordsworth now goes on to distinguish other "subtler" pleasures, felt in the very process of sensing the natural objects.
6. Spiritual, as opposed to sense perceptions.

I held unconscious intercourse with beauty
Old as creation, drinking in a pure
Organic pleasure from the silver wreaths
565 Of curling mist, or from the level plain
Of waters, colored by impending° clouds.   *overhanging*
    The sands of Westmorland, the creeks and bays
Of Cumbria's° rocky limits, they can tell   *Cumberland's*
How, when the Sea threw off his evening shade,
570 And to the Shepherd's hut on distant hills
Sent welcome notice of the rising moon,
How I have stood, to fancies such as these
A Stranger, linking with the Spectacle
No conscious memory of a kindred sight,
575 And bringing with me no peculiar sense
Of quietness or peace, yet have I stood,
Even while mine eye hath moved o'er many a league⁷
Of shining water, gathering, as it seemed,
Through every hair-breadth in that field of light,
580 New pleasure, like a bee among the flowers.
    Thus oft amid those fits of vulgar⁸ joy
Which, through all seasons, on a Child's pursuits
Are prompt Attendants; 'mid that giddy bliss
Which like a tempest works along the blood
585 And is forgotten: even then I felt
Gleams like the flashing of a shield,—the earth
And common face of Nature spake to me
Rememberable things; sometimes, 'tis true,
By chance collisions and quaint accidents
590 (Like those ill-sorted unions, work supposed
Of evil-minded fairies), yet not vain
Nor profitless, if haply they impressed
Collateral⁹ objects and appearances,
Albeit lifeless then, and doomed to sleep
595 Until maturer seasons called them forth
To impregnate and to elevate the mind.
    —And, if the vulgar joy by its own weight
Wearied itself out of the memory,
The scenes which were a witness of that joy
600 Remained, in their substantial lineaments
Depicted on the brain, and to the eye
Were visible, a daily sight: and thus
By the impressive discipline of fear,
By pleasure and repeated happiness,
605 So frequently repeated, and by force
Of obscure feelings representative
Of things forgotten; these same scenes so bright,
So beautiful, so majestic in themselves,
Though yet the day was distant, did become
610 Habitually dear; and all their forms

---

7. A measure equal to approximately three miles.   9. Accompanying but subordinate.
8. Ordinary, commonplace.

And changeful colours by invisible links
Were fastened to the affections.°   *feelings*
                  I began
My Story early, not misled, I trust,
By an infirmity of love for days
615   Disowned by memory,[1] fancying flowers where none,
Not even the sweetest, do or can survive
For him at least whose dawning day they cheered;
Nor will it seem to Thee, O Friend! so prompt
In sympathy, that I have lengthened out,
620   With fond and feeble tongue, a tedious tale.
Meanwhile, my hope has been, that I might fetch
Invigorating thoughts from former years;
Might fix the wavering balance of my mind,
And haply meet reproaches too, whose power
625   May spur me on, in manhood now mature,
To honorable toil. Yet should these hopes
Prove vain, and thus should neither I be taught
To understand myself, nor thou to know
With better knowledge how the heart was framed
630   Of him thou lovest, need I dread from thee
Harsh judgments, if the Song be loth to quit
Those recollected hours that have the charm
Of visionary things, those lovely forms
And sweet sensations that throw back our life,
635   And almost make remotest infancy
A visible scene, on which the sun is shining?
    One end at least hath been attained—my mind
Hath been revived; and, if this genial[2] mood
Desert me not, forthwith shall be brought down
640   Through later years the story of my life:
The road lies plain before me,—'tis a theme
Single, and of determined bounds; and hence
I chuse it rather, at this time, than work
Of ampler or more varied argument,
645   Where I might be discomfited and lost;
And certain hopes are with me that to thee
This labour will be welcome, honoured Friend!

Book Second
School-time continued

Thus far, O Friend! have we, though leaving much
Unvisited, endeavoured to retrace
The simple ways in which my childhood walked,
Those chiefly, that first led me to the love
5   Of rivers, woods, and fields. The passion yet
Was in its birth, sustained, as might befal,

---

1. I.e., he hopes that he has not mistakenly attributed his later thoughts and feelings to a time of life
he can no longer remember.
2. Productive, creative.

By nourishment that came unsought; for still,
From week to week, from month to month, we lived
A round of tumult. Duly° were our games   *appropriately*
10   Prolonged in summer till the day-light failed;
No chair remained before the doors, the bench
And threshold steps were empty; fast asleep
The Labourer, and the old Man who had sate,
A later Lingerer, yet the revelry
15   Continued, and the loud uproar; at last,
When all the ground was dark, and twinkling stars
Edged the black clouds, home and to bed we went,
Feverish, with weary joints and beating minds.
Ah! is there One who ever has been young
20   Nor needs a warning voice to tame the pride
Of intellect, and virtue's self-esteem?
One is there,[1] though the wisest and the best
Of all mankind, who covets not at times
Union that cannot be; who would not give,
25   If so he might, to duty and to truth
The eagerness of infantine desire?
A tranquillizing spirit presses now
On my corporeal frame, so wide appears
The vacancy between me and those days,
30   Which yet have such self-presence° in my mind,   *actuality*
That, musing on them, often do I seem
Two consciousnesses, conscious of myself
And of some other Being. A rude mass
Of native rock, left midway in the Square
35   Of our small market Village, was the goal
Or centre of these sports; and, when, returned
After long absence, thither I repaired,
Gone was the old grey stone, and in its place
A smart Assembly-room usurped the ground
40   That had been ours.[2] There let the fiddle scream,
And be ye happy! Yet, my Friends,[3] I know
That more than one of you will think with me
Of those soft starry nights, and that old Dame
From whom the Stone was named, who there had sate
45   And watched her table with its huckster's wares
Assiduous, through the length of sixty years.
—We ran a boisterous course, the year span round
With giddy motion. But the time approached
That brought with it a regular desire
50   For calmer pleasures, when the winning forms
Of Nature were collaterally attached[4]
To every scheme of holiday delight,
And every boyish sport, less grateful° else   *pleasing*
And languidly pursued.
                        When summer came,

---

1. I.e., "Is there anyone . . . ?"
2. The Hawkshead Town Hall, built in 1790.
3. Coleridge and John Wordsworth (William's
brother), who had visited Hawkshead together
with William in November 1799.
4. Associated as an accompaniment.

55 Our pastime was, on bright half-holidays,
   To sweep along the plain of Windermere
   With rival oars; and the selected bourne°   *destination*
   Was now an Island musical with birds
   That sang and ceased not; now a sister isle,
60 Beneath the oaks' umbrageous° covert, sown   *shaded*
   With lilies of the valley like a field;
   And now a third small island,⁵ where survived,
   In solitude, the ruins of a shrine
   Once to our Lady dedicate, and served
65 Daily with chaunted rites. In such a race,
   So ended, disappointment could be none,
   Uneasiness, or pain, or jealousy;
   We rested in the Shade, all pleased alike,
   Conquered and Conqueror. Thus the pride of strength,
70 And the vain-glory of superior skill,
   Were tempered, thus was gradually produced
   A quiet independence of the heart:
   And, to my Friend who knows me, I may add,
   Fearless of blame, that hence, for future days,
75 Ensued a diffidence and modesty;
   And I was taught to feel, perhaps too much,
   The self-sufficing power of solitude.
       Our daily meals were frugal, Sabine fare!⁶
   More than we wished we knew the blessing then
80 Of vigorous hunger—hence corporeal strength
   Unsapped by delicate viands; for, exclude
   A little weekly stipend,⁷ and we lived
   Through three divisions of the quartered year
   In pennyless poverty. But now, to school
85 From the half-yearly holidays returned,
   We came with weightier purses, that sufficed
   To furnish treats more costly than the Dame
   Of the old grey stone, from her scanty board, supplied.
   Hence rustic dinners on the cool green ground,
90 Or in the woods, or by a river side,
   Or shady fountains,° while among the leaves   *springs, streams*
   Soft airs were stirring, and the mid-day sun
   Unfelt shone brightly round us in our joy.
       Nor is my aim neglected if I tell
95 How sometimes, in the length of those half years,
   We from our funds drew largely—proud to curb,
   And eager to spur on, the gallopping Steed:
   And with the cautious Inn-keeper, whose Stud
   Supplied our want, we haply might employ
100 Sly subterfuges, if the Adventure's bound
    Were distant, some famed Temple⁸ where of yore

5. The island of Lady Holm, former site of a chapel dedicated to the Virgin Mary.
6. Like the meals of the Roman poet Horace on his Sabine farm.
7. In his last year at school Wordsworth had an allowance of sixpence a week, and his younger brother Christopher, threepence. After the Midsummer and Christmas holidays (line 85), the boys received a larger sum, ranging up to a guinea.
8. The stone circle at Swinside, on the lower Duddon River, mistakenly believed at the time to have been a Druid temple.

The Druids worshipped, or the antique Walls
Of that large Abbey which within the Vale
Of Nightshade, to St Mary's honour built,
105 Stands yet, a mouldering Pile, with fractured arch,
Belfry, and Images, and living Trees;
A holy Scene!⁹—Along the smooth green Turf
Our Horses grazed:—to more than inland peace
Left by the west wind sweeping overhead
110 From a tumultuous ocean, trees and towers
In that sequestered Valley may be seen
Both silent and both motionless alike;
Such the deep shelter that is there, and such
The safeguard for repose and quietness.
115   Our Steeds remounted, and the summons given,
With whip and spur we through the Chauntry¹ flew
In uncouth race, and left the cross-legged Knight
And the Stone-abbot, and that single Wren
Which one day sang so sweetly in the Nave
120 Of the old Church, that, though from recent Showers
The earth was comfortless, and, touched by faint
Internal breezes, sobbings of the place
And respirations, from the roofless walls
The shuddering ivy dripped large drops, yet still
125 So sweetly 'mid the gloom the invisible Bird
Sang to herself, that there I could have made
My dwelling-place, and lived for ever there
To hear such music. Through the Walls we flew,
And down the Valley, and, a circuit made
130 In wantonness of heart, through rough and smooth
We scampered homewards. Oh, ye rocks and streams,
And that still Spirit shed from evening air!
Even in this joyous time I sometimes felt
Your presence, when with slackened step we breathed²
135 Along the sides of the steep hills, or when,
Lighted by gleams of moonlight from the sea,
We beat with thundering hoofs the level sand.
   Midway on long Winander's Eastern shore,
Within the crescent of a pleasant Bay,
140 A Tavern³ stood, no homely-featured House,
Primeval like its neighbouring Cottages;
But 'twas a splendid place, the door beset
With Chaises, Grooms, and Liveries,—and within
Decanters, Glasses, and the blood-red Wine.
145 In ancient times, or ere the Hall was built
On the large Island,⁴ had this Dwelling been
More worthy of a Poet's love, a Hut
Proud of its one bright fire and sycamore shade.
But, though the rhymes were gone that once inscribed

---

9. Furness Abbey, some twenty miles south of Hawkshead.
1. A chapel endowed for masses to be sung to the donor.
2. Stopped to let the horses catch their breath.
3. The White Lion at Bowness.
4. The Hall on Belle Isle in Lake Windermere had been built in the early 1780s.

150   The threshold, and large golden characters
        Spread o'er the spangled sign-board had dislodged
        The old Lion, and usurped his place in slight
        And mockery of the rustic Painter's hand,
        Yet to this hour the spot to me is dear
155   With all its foolish pomp. The garden lay
        Upon a slope surmounted by the plain
        Of a small Bowling-green: beneath us stood
        A grove, with gleams of water through the trees
        And over the tree-tops; nor did we want
160   Refreshment, strawberries, and mellow cream.
        There, while through half an afternoon we played
        On the smooth platform, whether skill prevailed
        Or happy blunder triumphed, bursts of glee
        Made all the mountains ring. But ere night-fall,
165   When in our pinnace we returned, at leisure
        Over the shadowy Lake, and to the beach
        Of some small Island steered our course with one,
        The Minstrel of our Troop,[5] and left him there,
        And rowed off gently, while he blew his flute
170   Alone upon the rock,—Oh then the calm
        And dead still water lay upon my mind
        Even with a weight of pleasure, and the sky,
        Never before so beautiful, sank down
        Into my heart, and held me like a dream!
175   Thus were my sympathies enlarged, and thus
        Daily the common range of visible things
        Grew dear to me: already I began
        To love the sun; a boy I loved the sun,
        Not as I since have loved him, as a pledge
180   And surety of our earthly life, a light
        Which we behold, and feel we are alive;
        Nor for his bounty to so many worlds,
        But for this cause, that I had seen him lay
        His beauty on the morning hills, had seen
185   The western mountain touch his setting orb,
        In many a thoughtless hour, when, from excess
        Of happiness, my blood appear'd to flow
        For its own pleasure, and I breathed with joy;
        And from like feelings, humble though intense,
190   To patriotic and domestic love
        Analogous, the moon to me was dear;
        For I would dream away my purposes,
        Standing to gaze upon her while she hung
        Midway between the hills, as if she knew
195   No other region; but belonged to thee,
        Yea, appertained by a peculiar right
        To thee, and thy grey huts,[6] thou one dear Vale!
        Those incidental charms which first attached

---

5. Identified by Christopher Wordsworth, *Memoirs* (1857), as Robert Greenwood, who became senior fellow of Trinity College, Cambridge.
6. Cottages built of gray stones.

My heart to rural objects, day by day
200 Grew weaker, and I hasten on to tell
How Nature, intervenient[7] till this time
And secondary, now at length was sought
For her own sake. But who shall[8] parcel out
His intellect, by geometric rules,
205 Split like a province into round and square?
Who knows the individual hour in which
His habits were first sown, even as a seed?
Who that shall point, as with a wand, and say,
"This portion of the river of my mind
210 Came from yon fountain"? Thou, my friend! art one
More deeply read in thy own thoughts; to thee
Science[9] appears but what in truth she is,
Not as our glory and our absolute boast,
But as a succedaneum,[1] and a prop
215 To our infirmity. No officious slave
Art thou of that false secondary power[2]
By which we multiply distinctions, then
Deem that our puny boundaries are things
That we perceive, and not that we have made.
220 To thee, unblinded by these formal arts,
The unity of all hath been revealed;
And thou wilt doubt with me, less aptly skilled
Than many are to range the faculties
In scale and order, class the cabinet[3]
225 Of their sensations, and in voluble phrase[4]
Run through the history and birth of each
As of a single independent thing.
Hard task, vain hope, to analyse the mind,
If each most obvious and particular thought,
230 Not in a mystical and idle sense,
But in the words of reason deeply weighed,
Hath no beginning.
                              Blest the infant Babe,
(For with my best conjecture I would trace
Our Being's earthly progress) blest the Babe,
235 Nursed in his Mother's arms, who sinks to sleep
Rocked on his Mother's breast; who, when his soul
Claims manifest kindred with a human soul,
Drinks in the feelings of his Mother's eye![5]
For him, in one dear Presence, there exists
240 A virtue which irradiates and exalts
Objects through widest intercourse of sense.
No outcast he, bewildered and depressed;

7. I.e., entering incidentally into his other concerns.
8. Is able to.
9. In the old sense: learning.
1. In medicine, a drug substituted for a different drug. Wordsworth, however, uses the term to signify a remedy, or palliative.
2. The analytic faculty, as opposed to the power to apprehend "the unity of all" (line 221).
3. To classify, as if arranged in a display case.
4. In fluent phraseology.
5. Like the modern psychologist, Wordsworth recognized the importance of earliest infancy in the development of the individual mind, although he had then to invent the terms with which to analyze the process.

Along his infant veins are interfused
The gravitation and the filial bond
245 Of nature that connect him with the world.
Is there a flower to which he points with hand
Too weak to gather it, already love
Drawn from love's purest earthly fount for him
Hath beautified that flower; already shades
250 Of pity cast from inward tenderness
Do fall around him upon aught that bears
Unsightly marks of violence or harm.
Emphatically such a Being lives,
Frail Creature as he is, helpless as frail,
255 An inmate of this active universe.
For feeling has to him imparted power
That through the growing faculties of sense
Doth, like an Agent of the one great Mind,
Create, creator and receiver both,
260 Working but in alliance with the works
Which it beholds.[6]—Such, verily, is the first
Poetic spirit of our human life,
By uniform control of after years
In most abated or suppressed, in some,
265 Through every change of growth and of decay,
Preeminent till death.
                              From early days,
Beginning not long after that first time
In which, a Babe, by intercourse of touch,
I held mute dialogues with my Mother's heart,[7]
270 I have endeavoured to display the means
Whereby this infant sensibility,
Great birth-right of our being, was in me
Augmented and sustained. Yet is a path
More difficult before me, and I fear
275 That, in its broken windings, we shall need
The chamois'[8] sinews, and the eagle's wing:
For now a trouble came into my mind
From unknown causes. I was left alone,
Seeking the visible world, nor knowing why.
280 The props of my affections were removed,[9]
And yet the building stood, as if sustained
By its own spirit! All that I beheld
Was dear, and hence to finer influxes°   *influences*
The mind lay open, to a more exact
285 And close communion. Many are our joys

6. The infant, in the sense of security and love shed by his mother's presence on outer things, perceives what would otherwise be an alien world as a place to which he has a relationship like that of a son to a mother (lines 239–45). On such grounds Wordsworth asserts that the mind partially creates, by altering, the world it seems simply to perceive.
7. I.e., both infant and mother feel the pulse of the other's heart.
8. An agile species of antelope inhabiting moun-tainous regions of Europe.
9. Wordsworth's mother had died the month before his eighth birthday. It is unclear from the context whether the "trouble" that came into his mind (line 277) refers to the loss of his mother, in whose arms he had established his initial relationship to the natural world, or to the mysterious processes of the continued development and diversification of this relationship.

In youth, but Oh! what happiness to live
When every hour brings palpable access
Of knowledge, when all knowledge is delight,
And sorrow is not there! The seasons came,
290   And every season, wheresoe'er I moved,
Unfolded transitory qualities
Which, but for this most watchful power of love,
Had been neglected, left a register
Of permanent relations, else unknown.[1]
295   Hence life, and change, and beauty; solitude
More active even than "best society,"[2]
Society made sweet as solitude
By inward concords, silent, inobtrusive;
And gentle agitations of the mind
300   From manifold distinctions, difference
Perceived in things where, to the unwatchful eye,
No difference is, and hence, from the same source,
Sublimer joy: for I would walk alone
Under the quiet stars, and at that time
305   Have felt whate'er there is of power in sound
To breathe an elevated mood, by form
Or Image unprofaned: and I would stand,
If the night blackened with a coming storm,
Beneath some rock, listening to notes that are
310   The ghostly° language of the ancient earth,   *disembodied*
Or make their dim abode in distant winds.
Thence did I drink the visionary power;
And deem not profitless those fleeting moods
Of shadowy exultation: not for this,
315   That they are kindred to our purer mind
And intellectual life;[3] but that the soul,
Remembering how she felt, but what she felt
Remembering not, retains an obscure sense
Of possible sublimity, whereto
320   With growing faculties she doth aspire,
With faculties still growing, feeling still
That, whatsoever point they gain, they yet
Have something to pursue.[4]
                            And not alone
'Mid gloom and tumult, but no less 'mid fair
325   And tranquil scenes, that universal power
And fitness in the latent qualities
And essences of things, by which the mind
Is moved with feelings of delight, to me
Came strengthened with a superadded soul,

---

1. I.e., had it not been for the watchful power of love (line 292), the "transitory qualities" (291) would have been neglected, and the "permanent relations" now recorded in his memory would have been unknown.
2. A partial quotation of a line spoken by Adam to Eve in *Paradise Lost* 9.249: "For solitude some-

times is best society."
3. I.e., not because they are related to the non-sensuous ("intellectual") aspect of our life.
4. Cf. the revelation, while crossing Simplon Pass, that our destiny is with "something evermore about to be" (6.604–08, pp. 347–48).

330 A virtue not its own.—My morning walks
Were early;—oft before the hours of School
I travelled round our little Lake, five miles
Of pleasant wandering; happy time! more dear
For this, that One was by my side, a Friend⁵
335 Then passionately loved; with heart how full
Would he peruse these lines! for many years
Have since flowed in between us, and, our minds
Both silent to each other, at this time
We live as if those hours had never been.
340 Nor seldom did I lift our Cottage latch
Far earlier, and ere one smoke-wreath had risen
From human dwelling, or the thrush, high perched,
Piped to the woods his shrill *reveillé*,⁶ sate
Alone upon some jutting eminence
345 At the first gleam of dawn-light, when the Vale,
Yet slumbering, lay in utter solitude.
How shall I seek the origin, where find
Faith in the marvellous things which then I felt?
Oft in those moments such a holy calm
350 Would overspread my soul, that bodily eyes
Were utterly forgotten, and what I saw
Appeared like something in myself, a dream,
A prospect° in the mind.   scene
                            'Twere long to tell
What spring and autumn, what the winter snows,
355 And what the summer shade, what day and night,
Evening and morning, sleep and waking thought,
From sources inexhaustible, poured forth
To feed the spirit of religious love,
In which I walked with Nature. But let this
360 Be not forgotten, that I still retained
My first creative sensibility,⁷
That by the regular action of the world
My soul was unsubdued. A plastic° power   shaping
Abode with me, a forming hand, at times
365 Rebellious, acting in a devious mood,
A local Spirit of his own, at war
With general tendency, but, for the most,
Subservient strictly to external things
With which it communed. An auxiliar light
370 Came from my mind which on the setting sun
Bestowed new splendor; the melodious birds,
The fluttering breezes, fountains that ran on
Murmuring so sweetly in themselves, obeyed
A like dominion; and the midnight storm
375 Grew darker in the presence of my eye;
Hence my obeisance, my devotion hence,

5. Identified as John Fleming in a note to the edition of 1850.
6. Military parlance for a signal call.

7. I.e., the creative perception manifested by the babe in his mother's arms (lines 235ff.).

And hence my transport.°   *exaltation*
              Nor should this, perchance,
Pass unrecorded, that I still° had loved   *always*
The exercise and produce of a toil

380 Than analytic industry to me
More pleasing, and whose character I deem
Is more poetic, as resembling more
Creative agency. The Song would speak
Of that interminable building reared

385 By observation of affinities
In objects where no brotherhood exists
To passive minds. My seventeenth year was come;
And, whether from this habit rooted now
So deeply in my mind, or from excess

390 Of the great social principle of life
Coercing all things into sympathy,
To unorganic Natures were transferred
My own enjoyments; or the Power of truth,
Coming in revelation, did converse

395 With things that really are;[8] I, at this time,
Saw blessings spread around me like a sea.
Thus while the days flew by and years passed on,
From Nature overflowing on my soul
I had received so much, that every thought

400 Was steeped in feeling; I was only then
Contented when with bliss ineffable
I felt the sentiment of Being spread
O'er all that moves, and all that seemeth still;
O'er all that, lost beyond the reach of thought

405 And human knowledge, to the human eye
Invisible, yet liveth to the heart;
O'er all that leaps, and runs, and shouts, and sings,
Or beats the gladsome air; o'er all that glides
Beneath the wave, yea, in the wave itself,

410 And mighty depth of waters. Wonder not
If high the transport, great the joy I felt,
Communing in this sort through earth and Heaven
With every form of Creature, as it looked
Towards the Uncreated with a countenance

415 Of adoration, with an eye of love.[9]
One song they sang, and it was audible,
Most audible, then, when the fleshly ear,
O'ercome by humblest prelude of that strain,
Forgot her functions and slept undisturbed.

420   If this be error, and another faith
Find easier access to the pious mind,[1]

---

8. Wordsworth is careful to indicate that there are alternative explanations for his sense that life pervades the inorganic as well as the organic world: it may be the result either of a way of perceiving that has been habitual since infancy or of a projection of his own inner life or else it may be the percep-

tion of an objective truth.
9. Wordsworth did not add lines 412–14, giving a Christian frame to his experience of the "one life," until the last revision of *The Prelude*, in 1839.
1. With lines 416–21 cf. *Tintern Abbey*, lines 43–50 (p. 236).

Yet were I grossly destitute of all
Those human sentiments that make this earth
So dear, if I should fail with grateful voice
425 To speak of you, Ye Mountains, and Ye Lakes,
And sounding Cataracts, Ye Mists and Winds
That dwell among the Hills where I was born.
If in my Youth I have been pure in heart,
If, mingling with the world, I am content
430 With my own modest pleasures, and have lived,
With God and Nature communing, removed
From little enmities and low desires,
The gift is yours: if in these times of fear,
This melancholy waste° of hopes o'erthrown,   *wasteland*
435 If, 'mid indifference and apathy
And wicked exultation, when good men,
On every side, fall off, we know not how,
To selfishness, disguised in gentle names
Of peace and quiet and domestic love,
440 Yet mingled, not unwillingly, with sneers
On visionary minds; if, in this time
Of dereliction and dismay,[2] I yet
Despair not of our Nature, but retain
A more than Roman confidence, a faith
445 That fails not, in all sorrow my support,
The blessing of my life, the gift is yours,
Ye Winds and sounding Cataracts, 'tis yours,
Ye Mountains! thine, O Nature! Thou hast fed
My lofty speculations; and in thee,
450 For this uneasy heart of ours, I find
A never-failing principle of joy
And purest passion.
                    Thou, my Friend! wert reared
In the great City, 'mid far other scenes;[3]
But we, by different roads, at length have gained
455 The self-same bourne. And for this cause to Thee
I speak, unapprehensive of contempt,
The insinuated scoff of coward tongues,
And all that silent language which so oft,
In conversation between Man and Man,
460 Blots from the human countenance all trace
Of beauty and of love. For Thou hast sought
The truth in solitude, and, since the days
That gave thee liberty, full long desired,
To serve in Nature's Temple, thou hast been
465 The most assiduous of her Ministers,[4]

2. The era, some ten years after the outbreak of the French Revolution, was one of violent reaction, in which many earlier sympathizers were recanting their radical beliefs.
3. A reminiscence of Coleridge's *Frost at Midnight*, lines 51–52: "For I was reared / In the great city, pent 'mid cloisters dim."
4. Wordsworth may be recalling the conclusion of Coleridge's *France: An Ode* (1798), where, disillusioned about the promise of liberty by the French Revolution, he writes that, while standing on a "sea-cliff's verge," "O Liberty! my spirit felt thee there." Wordsworth added lines 461–64 some years after Coleridge's death in 1834.

In many things my Brother, chiefly here
In this our deep devotion.
                        Fare Thee well!
Health, and the quiet of a healthful mind,
Attend Thee! seeking oft the haunts of Men,
470   And yet more often living with thyself
And for thyself, so haply shall thy days
Be many, and a blessing to mankind.

From Book Third
Residence at Cambridge

[EXPERIENCES AT ST. JOHN'S COLLEGE. THE "HEROIC ARGUMENT"]

It was a dreary Morning when the Wheels
Rolled over a wide plain o'erhung with clouds,
And nothing cheered our way till first we saw
The long-roof'd Chapel of King's College lift
5   Turrets, and pinnacles in answering files
Extended high above a dusky grove.
    Advancing, we espied upon the road
A Student, clothed in Gown and tasselled Cap,
Striding along, as if o'ertasked by Time
10   Or covetous of exercise and air.
He passed—nor was I Master of my eyes
Till he was left an arrow's flight behind.
As near and nearer to the Spot we drew,
It seemed to suck us in with an eddy's force;
15   Onward we drove beneath the Castle, caught,
While crossing Magdalene Bridge, a glimpse of Cam,[1]
And at the *Hoop* alighted, famous Inn![2]
    My Spirit was up, my thoughts were full of hope;
Some friends I had, acquaintances who there
20   Seemed friends, poor simple School-boys! now hung round
With honor and importance: in a world
Of welcome faces up and down I roved;
Questions, directions, warnings, and advice
Flowed in upon me, from all sides; fresh day
25   Of pride and pleasure! to myself I seemed
A man of business and expence, and went
From shop to shop, about my own affairs,
To Tutor or to Tailor, as befel,
From street to street, with loose and careless mind.
30   I was the Dreamer, they the dream: I roamed
Delighted through the motley spectacle;
Gowns grave or gaudy, Doctors, Students, Streets,
Courts, Cloisters, flocks of Churches, gateways, towers.
Migration strange for a Stripling of the Hills,

---

1. The river that flows through Cambridge.
2. Wordsworth renders some of his early college experiences, when he was a callow country boy (lines 34–35), in a deliberately inflated, or mock-epic, manner.

35　A Northern Villager! As if the change
　　Had waited on some Fairy's wand, at once
　　Behold me rich in monies; and attired
　　In splendid garb, with hose of silk, and hair
　　Powdered like rimy[3] trees, when frost is keen.
40　My lordly dressing-gown, I pass it by,
　　With other signs of manhood that supplied
　　The lack of beard.—The weeks went roundly on
　　With invitations, suppers, wine and fruit,
　　Smooth housekeeping within, and all without
45　Liberal, and suiting Gentleman's array!
　　　　The Evangelist St. John my Patron was;[4]
　　Three gothic Courts are his, and in the first
　　Was my abiding-place, a nook obscure!
　　Right underneath, the College Kitchens made
50　A humming sound, less tuneable than bees,
　　But hardly less industrious; with shrill notes
　　Of sharp command and scolding intermixed.
　　Near me hung Trinity's loquacious Clock,
　　Who never let the quarters, night or day,
55　Slip by him unproclaimed, and told the hours
　　Twice over, with a male and female voice.
　　Her pealing Organ was my neighbour too;
　　And from my pillow, looking forth by light
　　Of moon or favoring stars, I could behold
60　The Antechapel, where the Statue stood
　　Of Newton, with his prism,[5] and silent face:
　　The marble index of a Mind for ever
　　Voyaging through strange seas of Thought, alone.
　　　　Of College labors, of the Lecturer's room
65　All studded round, as thick as chairs could stand,
　　With loyal Students faithful to their books,
　　Half-and-half Idlers, hardy Recusants,[6]
　　And honest Dunces—of important days,
　　Examinations when the man was weighed
70　As in a balance! of excessive hopes,
　　Tremblings withal, and commendable fears;
　　Small jealousies, and triumphs good or bad,
　　Let others, that know more, speak as they know.
　　Such glory was but little sought by me
75　And little won. Yet, from the first crude days
　　Of settling time in this untried abode,
　　I was disturbed at times by prudent thoughts,
　　Wishing to hope, without a hope; some fears
　　About my future worldly maintenance;[7]
80　And, more than all, a strangeness in the mind,
　　A feeling that I was not for that hour,

3. Covered with rime, frosted over.
4. Wordsworth was a student at St. John's College, Cambridge University, in 1787–91. Book 3 deals with his first year there.
5. In the west end of Trinity Chapel, adjoining St. John's College, stands Roubiliac's statue of Newton holding the prism with which he had conducted the experiments described in his *Optics*.
6. Those who refused to work at their studies.
7. Wordsworth was troubled by the expectation of his family that he would be appointed a fellow of St. John's College.

Nor for that place. But wherefore be cast down?
For (not to speak of Reason and her pure
Reflective acts to fix the moral law
85 Deep in the conscience; nor of Christian Hope
Bowing her head before her Sister Faith
As one far mightier),[8] hither I had come,
Bear witness, Truth, endowed with holy powers
And faculties, whether to work or feel.
90 Oft when the dazzling shew no longer new
Had ceased to dazzle, ofttimes did I quit
My Comrades, leave the Crowd, buildings and groves,
And as I paced alone the level fields
Far from those lovely sights and sounds sublime
95 With which I had been conversant, the mind
Drooped not, but there into herself returning
With prompt rebound, seemed fresh as heretofore.
At least I more distinctly recognized
Her native instincts; let me dare to speak
100 A higher language, say that now I felt
What independent solaces were mine
To mitigate the injurious sway of place
Or circumstance, how far soever changed
In youth, or *to* be changed in manhood's prime;
105 Or, for the few who shall be called to look
On the long shadows, in our evening years,
Ordained Precursors to the night of death.
As if awakened, summoned, roused, constrained,
I looked for universal things, perused
110 The common countenance of earth and sky;
Earth no where unembellished by some trace
Of that first paradise whence man was driven;
And sky whose beauty and bounty are expressed
By the proud name she bears, the name of heaven.
115 I called on both to teach me what they might;
Or, turning the mind in upon herself,
Pored, watched, expected, listened, spread my thoughts
And spread them with a wider creeping; felt
Incumbencies more awful,[9] visitings
120 Of the Upholder, of the tranquil Soul
That tolerates the indignities of Time;
And, from his centre of eternity
All finite motions overruling, lives
In glory immutable. But peace!—enough
125 Here to record I had ascended now
To such community with highest truth.
—A track pursuing, not untrod before,
From strict analogies by thought supplied,
Or consciousnesses not to be subdued,
130 To every natural form, rock, fruit or flower,

8. This pious qualification, lines 83–87, was
added by Wordsworth in late revisions of *The Prel-*
ude. In the version of 1805, he wrote: "I was a
chosen son. / For hither I had come with holy
powers / And faculties, whether to work or feel."
9. I.e., the weight of more awe-inspiring moods.

Even the loose stones that cover the high-way,
I gave a moral life; I saw them feel,
Or linked them to some feeling: the great mass
Lay bedded in a quickening° soul, and all   *life-giving*
135   That I beheld respired with inward meaning.
Add, that whate'er of Terror or of Love
Or Beauty, Nature's daily face put on
From transitory passion, unto this
I was as sensitive as waters are
140   To the sky's influence: in a kindred mood
Of passion, was obedient as a lute
That waits upon the touches of the wind.[1]
Unknown, unthought of, yet I was most rich;
I had a world about me; 'twas my own,
145   I made it; for it only lived to me,
And to the God who sees into the heart.
Such sympathies, though rarely, were betrayed
By outward gestures and by visible looks:
Some called it madness—so, indeed, it was,
150   If child-like fruitfulness in passing joy,
If steady moods of thoughtfulness, matured
To inspiration, sort with such a name;
If prophecy be madness; if things viewed
By Poets in old time, and higher up
155   By the first men, earth's first inhabitants,
May in these tutored days no more be seen
With undisordered sight. But, leaving this,
It was no madness: for the bodily eye
Amid my strongest workings evermore
160   Was searching out the lines of difference
As they lie hid in all external forms,
Near or remote, minute or vast, an eye
Which from a tree, a stone, a withered leaf,
To the broad ocean, and the azure heavens
165   Spangled with kindred multitudes of Stars,
Could find no surface where its power might sleep;
Which spake perpetual logic to my Soul,
And by an unrelenting agency
Did bind my feelings, even as in a chain.
170   And here, O friend! have I retraced my life
Up to an eminence, and told a tale
Of matters which not falsely may be called
The glory of my Youth. Of genius, power,
Creation, and Divinity itself,
175   I have been speaking, for my theme has been
What passed within me. Not of outward things
Done visibly for other minds; words, signs,
Symbols, or actions, but of my own heart
Have I been speaking, and my youthful mind.
180   O Heavens! how awful is the might of Souls

---

1. I.e., as a wind harp.

And what they do within themselves, while yet
The yoke of earth is new to them, the world
Nothing but a wild field where they were sown.
This is, in truth, heroic argument,
185 This genuine prowess, which I wished to touch
With hand however weak,[2] but in the main
It lies far hidden from the reach of words.
Points have we, all of us, within our Souls,
Where all stand single: this I feel, and make
190 Breathings for incommunicable powers.[3]
But is not each a memory to himself?
And, therefore, now that we must quit this theme,
I am not heartless;° for there's not a man   *disheartened*
That lives who hath not known his god-like hours,
195 And feels not what an empire we inherit,
As natural Beings, in the strength of Nature.
    No more:—for now into a populous plain
We must descend.—A Traveller I am
Whose tale is only of himself; even so,
200 So be it, if the pure of heart be prompt
To follow, and if Thou, O honored Friend!
Who in these thoughts art ever at my side,
Support, as heretofore, my fainting steps.[4]

*   *   *

Thus in submissive idleness, my Friend,
The laboring time of Autumn, Winter, Spring,
Eight months! rolled pleasingly away—the ninth
635 Came and returned me to my native hills.

From Book Fourth
Summer Vacation[1]

[THE WALKS WITH HIS TERRIER. THE CIRCUIT OF THE LAKE]

Among the favorites whom it pleased me well
To see again, was one, by ancient right
95 Our Inmate, a rough terrier of the hills,
By birth and call of nature pre-ordained
To hunt the badger, and unearth the fox,
Among the impervious crags; but having been
From youth our own adopted, he had passed
100 Into a gentler service. And when first
The boyish spirit flagged, and day by day
Along my veins I kindled with the stir,
The fermentation and the vernal heat

2. Wordsworth describes the innovative epic theme ("heroic argument") for his projected long poem. Cf. his Prospectus to *The Recluse*, lines 25–41 (pp. 301–02).
3. This obscure assertion may mean that he tries, inadequately, to express the inexpressible.

4. The terms of this behest to Coleridge suggest the relation to Dante of Virgil, his guide in the *Inferno*.
1. Wordsworth returned to Hawkshead for his first summer vacation in 1788.

Of poesy, affecting private shades
105 Like a sick lover, then this Dog was used
To watch me, an attendant and a friend
Obsequious to my steps, early and late,
Though often of such dilatory walk
Tired, and uneasy at the halts I made.
110 A hundred times when, roving high and low,
I have been harrassed with the toil of verse,
Much pains and little progress, and at once
Some lovely Image in the Song rose up
Full-formed, like Venus rising from the Sea;[2]
115 Then have I darted forwards and let loose
My hand upon his back, with stormy joy;
Caressing him again, and yet again.
And when at evening on the public Way
I sauntered, like a river murmuring
120 And talking to itself, when all things else
Are still, the Creature trotted on before—
Such was his custom; but whene'er he met
A passenger° approaching, he would turn   *foot traveler*
To give me timely notice; and, straitway,
125 Grateful for that admonishment, I hushed
My voice, composed my gait, and with the air
And mien of one whose thoughts are free, advanced
To give and take a greeting, that might save
My name from piteous rumours, such as wait
130 On men suspected to be crazed in brain.
    Those walks, well worthy to be prized and loved,
Regretted! that word too was on my tongue,
But they were richly laden with all good,
And cannot be remembered but with thanks
135 And gratitude, and perfect joy of heart;
Those walks, in all their freshness, now came back,
Like a returning Spring. When first I made
Once more the circuit of our little Lake,
If ever happiness hath lodged with man,
140 That day consummate° happiness was mine,   *perfect*
Wide-spreading, steady, calm, contemplative.
The sun was set, or setting, when I left
Our cottage door, and evening soon brought on
A sober hour,—not winning or serene,
145 For cold and raw the air was, and untuned:
But as a face we love is sweetest then
When sorrow damps it; or, whatever look
It chance to wear, is sweetest if the heart
Have fulness in herself, even so with me
150 It fared that evening. Gently did my Soul
Put off her veil, and, self-transmuted, stood
Naked, as in the presence of her God.[3]

2. Aphrodite (the Roman Venus), goddess of love, was born from the foam of the sea.
3. In Exodus 34.30–34, when Moses descended from Mount Sinai, he wore a veil to hide from the Israelites the shining of his face, but removed the veil when, in privacy, he talked to God.

While on I walked, a comfort seemed to touch
A heart that had not been disconsolate;
155 Strength came where weakness was not known to be,
At least not felt; and restoration came,
Like an intruder, knocking at the door
Of unacknowledged weariness. I took
The balance, and with firm hand weighed myself.
160 —Of that external scene which round me lay
Little, in this abstraction, did I see,
Remembered less; but I had inward hopes
And swellings of the Spirit: was rapt and soothed,
Conversed with promises; had glimmering views
165 How life pervades the undecaying mind,
How the immortal Soul with God-like power
Informs, creates, and thaws the deepest sleep[4]
That time can lay upon her; how on earth,
Man, if he do but live within the light
170 Of high endeavours, daily spreads abroad
His being armed with strength that cannot fail.
Nor was there want of milder thoughts, of love,
Of innocence, and holiday repose;
And more than pastoral quiet 'mid the stir
175 Of boldest projects; and a peaceful end
At last, or glorious, by endurance won.
Thus musing, in a wood I sate me down,
Alone, continuing there to muse; the slopes
And heights, meanwhile, were slowly overspread
180 With darkness; and before a rippling breeze
The long lake lengthened out its hoary line:
And in the sheltered coppice[5] where I sate,
Around me from among the hazel leaves,
Now here, now there, moved by the straggling wind,
185 Came ever and anon a breath-like sound,
Quick as the pantings of the faithful Dog,
The off and on Companion of my walk;
And such, at times, believing them to be,
I turned my head, to look if he were there;
190 Then into solemn thought I passed once more.

["THE SURFACE OF PAST TIME." THE WALK HOME FROM THE DANCE. THE
DISCHARGED SOLDIER]

As one who hangs down-bending from the side
Of a slow-moving boat, upon the breast
Of a still water, solacing himself
With such discoveries as his eye can make,
260 Beneath him, in the bottom of the deep,
Sees many beauteous sights, weeds, fishes, flowers,
Grots, pebbles, roots of trees, and fancies more;

4. "Informs" and "creates" are probably to be read as intransitive verbs, whereas "thaws" has "sleep" for its direct object. "Sleep" Wordsworth uses, here and elsewhere in *The Prelude*, for the deadening effect of routine experience.
5. A clump of small trees and underbrush.

Yet often is perplexed, and cannot part
The shadow from the substance, rocks and sky,
265 Mountains and clouds reflected in the depth
Of the clear flood, from things which there abide
In their true Dwelling: now is crossed by gleam
Of his own image, by a sun-beam now,
And wavering motions, sent he knows not whence,
270 Impediments that make his task more sweet—
Such pleasant office have we long pursued,
Incumbent o'er the surface of past time,
With like success, nor often have appeared
Shapes fairer, or less doubtfully discerned
275 Than these to which the Tale, indulgent Friend!
Would now direct thy notice.[6] Yet in spite
Of pleasure won and knowledge not withheld,
There was an inner falling-off. I loved,
Loved deeply, all that had been loved before,
280 More deeply even than ever: but a swarm
Of heady schemes, jostling each other, gawds,°   pastimes
And feast, and dance, and public revelry;
And sports, and games (too grateful in themselves,
Yet in themselves less grateful, I believe,
285 Than as they were a badge, glossy and fresh,
Of manliness and freedom) all conspired
To lure my mind from firm habitual quest
Of feeding pleasures;[7] to depress the zeal
And damp those daily yearnings which had once been mine—
290 A wild unworldly-minded youth, given up
To his own eager thoughts. It would demand
Some skill, and longer time than may be spared,
To paint these vanities, and how they wrought
In haunts where they, till now, had been unknown.
295 It seemed the very garments that I wore
Preyed on my strength, and stopped the quiet stream
Of self-forgetfulness.
                               Yes, that heartless[8] chase
Of trivial pleasures was a poor exchange
For books and nature at that early age.
300 'Tis true some casual knowledge might be gained
Of character or life; but at that time,
Of manners put to School[9] I took small note;
And all my deeper passions lay elsewhere.
Far better had it been to exalt the mind
305 By solitary Study; to uphold
Intense desire through meditative peace.
And yet, for chastisement of these regrets,
The memory of one particular hour
Doth here rise up against me.—'Mid a throng

---

6. In this sustained simile Wordsworth describes
his endeavors to distinguish facts from fancies, and
his present self from his former self, in his remembrance of things past.

7. Pleasures that would nourish the mind.
8. Dispirited, without deep feeling.
9. Made a subject of systematic study.

310　Of Maids and Youths, old Men and Matrons staid,
　　A medley of all tempers,[1] I had passed
　　The night in dancing, gaiety, and mirth;
　　With din of instruments, and shuffling feet,
　　And glancing forms, and tapers glittering,
315　And unaimed prattle flying up and down—
　　Spirits upon the stretch, and here and there
　　Slight shocks of young love-liking interspersed,
　　Whose transient pleasure mounted to the head,
　　And tingled through the veins. Ere we retired
320　The cock had crowed; and now the eastern sky
　　Was kindling, not unseen from humble copse
　　And open field through which the pathway wound
　　That homeward led my steps. Magnificent
　　The Morning rose, in memorable pomp,
325　Glorious as e'er I had beheld; in front
　　The Sea lay laughing at a distance;—near,
　　The solid mountains shone bright as the clouds,
　　Grain-tinctured,° drenched in empyrean[2] light;　　　　*crimson-colored*
　　And, in the meadows and the lower grounds,
330　Was all the sweetness of a common dawn;
　　Dews, vapours, and the melody of birds;
　　And Labourers going forth to till the fields.
　　　Ah! need I say, dear Friend, that to the brim
　　My heart was full: I made no vows, but vows
335　Were then made for me; bond unknown to me
　　Was given, that I should be, else sinning greatly,
　　A dedicated Spirit.[3] On I walked
　　In thankful blessedness which yet survives.
　　　Strange rendezvous my mind was at that time,
340　A party-colored shew of grave and gay,
　　Solid and light, short-sighted and profound;
　　Of inconsiderate habits and sedate,
　　Consorting in one mansion, unreproved.
　　The worth I knew of powers that I possessed,
345　Though slighted and too oft misused. Besides,
　　That summer, swarming as it did with thoughts
　　Transient and idle, lacked not intervals
　　When Folly from the frown of fleeting Time
　　Shrunk, and the Mind experienced in herself
350　Conformity as just as that of old[4]
　　To the end and written spirit of God's works,
　　Whether held forth in Nature or in Man,
　　Through pregnant vision, separate or conjoined.
　　　When from our better selves we have too long
355　Been parted by the hurrying world, and droop,
　　Sick of its business, of its pleasures tired,

1. Temperaments, types of character.
2. Celestial, referring to the outer sphere of the universe, composed of pure fire.
3. Wordsworth describes later in *The Prelude* his discovery that the specific vocation to which he felt

dedicated was to be the agent of a new kind of poetry (13.232ff.).
4. I.e., an immediacy of response similar to his mental experience before he indulged in these present distractions.

How gracious, how benign is Solitude!
How potent a mere image of her sway!
Most potent when impressed upon the mind
360 With an appropriate human centre—Hermit
Deep in the bosom of the Wilderness;
Votary⁵ (in vast Cathedral, where no foot
Is treading and no other face is seen)
Kneeling at prayer; or Watchman on the top
365 Of Lighthouse beaten by Atlantic Waves;
Or as the soul of that great Power is met
Sometimes embodied on a public road,
When, for the night deserted, it assumes
A character of quiet more profound
Than pathless Wastes.
370   Once, when those summer Months
Were flown, and Autumn brought its annual shew
Of oars with oars contending, sails with sails,
Upon Winander's⁶ spacious breast, it chanced
That—after I had left a flower-decked room
375 (Whose in-door pastime, lighted-up, survived
To a late hour) and spirits overwrought⁷
Were making night do penance for a day
Spent in a round of strenuous idleness—
My homeward course led up a long ascent
380 Where the road's watery surface, to the top
Of that sharp rising, glittered to the moon
And bore the semblance of another stream
Stealing with silent lapse⁸ to join the brook
That murmured in the Vale. All else was still;
385 No living thing appeared in earth or air,
And, save the flowing Water's peaceful voice,
Sound was there none: but lo! an uncouth shape
Shewn by a sudden turning of the road,
So near, that, slipping back into the shade
390 Of a thick hawthorn, I could mark him well,
Myself unseen. He was of stature tall,
A span⁹ above man's *common* measure tall.
Stiff, lank, and upright;—a more meagre° man   *emaciated*
Was never seen before by night or day.
395 Long were his arms, pallid his hands;—his mouth
Looked ghastly° in the moonlight. From behind,   *ghostly*
A mile-stone propped him; I could also ken
That he was clothed in military garb,
Though faded, yet entire. Companionless,
400 No dog attending, by no staff sustained

5. A person devoted to God's service.
6. Lake Windermere's.
7. Worked up to a high pitch. Wordsworth is describing a party at which the "pastime" had been dancing. The description of the meeting with the discharged soldier that follows was written in 1798 as an independent poem, which Wordsworth later incorporated in *The Prelude*.

8. Flowing. Wordsworth is remembering a description that his sister, Dorothy, had entered into her journal in January 1798, a few days before he composed this passage: "The road to the village of Holford glittered like another stream."
9. About nine inches (the distance between extended thumb and little finger).

He stood; and in his very dress appeared
A desolation, a simplicity
To which the trappings of a gaudy world
Make a strange background. From his lips erelong
405 Issued low muttered sounds, as if of pain
Or some uneasy thought; yet still his form
Kept the same awful steadiness;—at his feet
His shadow lay and moved not. From self-blame
Not wholly free, I watched him thus; at length
410 Subduing my heart's specious cowardice,[1]
I left the shady nook where I had stood,
And hailed him. Slowly, from his resting-place
He rose; and, with a lean and wasted arm
In measured gesture lifted to his head,
415 Returned my salutation: then resumed
His station as before; and when I asked
His history, the Veteran, in reply,
Was neither slow nor eager; but, unmoved,
And with a quiet uncomplaining voice,
420 A stately air of mild indifference,
He told, in few plain words, a Soldier's tale—
That in the Tropic Islands he had served,
Whence he had landed, scarcely three weeks past,
That on his landing he had been dismissed,[2]
425 And now was travelling towards his native home.
This heard, I said in pity, "Come with me."
He stooped, and straightway from the ground took up
An oaken staff, by me yet unobserved—
A staff which must have dropped from his slack hand
430 And lay till now neglected in the grass.
    Though weak his step and cautious, he appeared
To travel without pain, and I beheld,
With an astonishment but ill suppressed,
His ghastly figure moving at my side;
435 Nor could I, while we journeyed thus, forbear
To turn from present hardships to the past,
And speak of war, battle, and pestilence,
Sprinkling this talk with questions, better spared,
On what he might himself have seen or felt.
440 He all the while was in demeanour calm,
Concise in answer; solemn and sublime
He might have seemed, but that in all he said
There was a strange half-absence, as of one
Knowing too well the importance of his theme,
445 But feeling it no longer. Our discourse
Soon ended, and together on we passed,
In silence, through a wood, gloomy and still.
Up-turning then along an open field,
We reached a Cottage. At the door I knocked,

1. I.e., he had been deceiving himself in thinking that the motive for his delay was not cowardice.
2. The Tropic Islands are the West Indies. Tens of thousands of British soldiers serving there contracted tropical fevers and died, or else were rendered unfit for further service and discharged.

450 And earnestly to charitable care
Commended him, as a poor friendless Man
Belated, and by sickness overcome.
Assured that now the Traveller would repose
In comfort, I entreated, that henceforth
455 He would not linger in the public ways,
But ask for timely furtherance and help,
Such as his state required.—At this reproof,
With the same ghastly mildness in his look,
He said, "My trust is in the God of Heaven,
460 And in the eye of him who passes me."
The Cottage door was speedily unbarred,
And now the Soldier touched his hat once more
With his lean hand; and, in a faltering voice
Whose tone bespake reviving interests
465 Till then unfelt, he thanked me; I returned
The farewell blessing of the patient Man,
And so we parted. Back I cast a look,
And lingered near the door a little space;
Then sought with quiet heart my distant home.
470 This passed, and He who deigns to mark with care
By what rules governed, with what end in view
This Work proceeds, *he* will not wish for more.

From Book Fifth
Books

[THE DREAM OF THE ARAB]

45 * * * Oh! why hath not the Mind
Some element to stamp her image on
In nature somewhat nearer to her own?
Why gifted with such powers to send abroad
Her spirit, must it lodge in shrines so frail?[1]
50 One day, when from my lips a like complaint
Had fallen in presence of a studious friend,
He with a smile made answer that in truth
'Twas going far to seek disquietude,
But, on the front of his reproof, confessed
55 That he himself had oftentimes given way
To kindred hauntings. Whereupon I told
That once in the stillness of a summer's noon,
While I was seated in a rocky cave
By the sea-side, perusing, so it chanced,
60 The famous history of the errant Knight
Recovered by Cervantes,[2] these same thoughts
Beset me, and to height unusual rose,
While listlessly I sate, and, having closed

1. Wordsworth is describing his recurrent fear that some holocaust might wipe out all books, the frail and perishable repositories of all human wisdom and poetry.

2. I.e., *Don Quixote*. Wordsworth's dream involves all the elements of the poet's last waking experience.

The Book, had turned my eyes tow'rd the wide Sea.
65 On Poetry, and geometric truth,
And their high privilege of lasting life,
From all internal injury exempt,
I mused; upon these chiefly: and, at length,
My senses yielding to the sultry air,
70 Sleep seized me, and I passed into a dream.
I saw before me stretched a boundless plain,
Of sandy wilderness, all blank and void;
And as I looked around, distress and fear
Came creeping over me, when at my side,
75 Close at my side, an uncouth Shape appeared
Upon a Dromedary, mounted high.
He seemed an Arab of the Bedouin Tribes:[3]
A Lance he bore, and underneath one arm
A Stone; and, in the opposite hand, a Shell
80 Of a surpassing brightness. At the sight
Much I rejoiced, not doubting but a Guide
Was present, one who with unerring skill
Would through the desert lead me; and while yet
I looked, and looked, self-questioned what this freight
85 Which the New-comer carried through the Waste
Could mean, the Arab told me that the Stone
(To give it in the language of the Dream)
Was Euclid's Elements;[4] "and this," said he,
"This other," pointing to the Shell, "this book
90 Is something of more worth": and, at the word,
Stretched forth the Shell, so beautiful in shape,
In color so resplendent, with command
That I should hold it to my ear. I did so,—
And heard, that instant, in an unknown tongue,
95 Which yet I understood, articulate sounds,
A loud prophetic blast of harmony—
An Ode, in passion uttered, which foretold
Destruction to the Children of the Earth,
By Deluge now at hand. No sooner ceased
100 The Song than the Arab with calm look declared
That all would come to pass, of which the voice
Had given forewarning, and that he himself
Was going then to bury those two Books:
The One that held acquaintance with the stars,
105 And wedded Soul to Soul in purest bond
Of Reason, undisturbed by space or time:
Th'other, that was a God, yea many Gods,
Had voices more than all the winds, with power
To exhilarate the Spirit, and to soothe,
110 Through every clime, the heart of human kind.
While this was uttering, strange as it may seem,
I wondered not, although I plainly saw

3. Mathematics had flourished among the Arabs—
hence the Arabian rider.
4. Celebrated book on plane geometry and the
theory of numbers by the Greek mathematician
Euclid; it continued to be used as a textbook into
the 19th century.

The One to be a Stone, the Other a Shell,
Nor doubted once but that they both were Books;
115 Having a perfect faith in all that passed.
Far stronger now grew the desire I felt
To cleave unto this Man; but when I prayed
To share his enterprize, he hurried on,
Reckless° of me: I followed, not unseen,   heedless
120 For oftentimes he cast a backward look,
Grasping his twofold treasure. Lance in rest,
He rode, I keeping pace with him; and now
He to my fancy had become the Knight
Whose tale Cervantes tells; yet not the Knight,
125 But was an Arab of the desert, too,
Of these was neither, and was both at once.
His countenance, meanwhile, grew more disturbed,
And looking backwards when he looked, mine eyes
Saw, over half the wilderness diffused,
130 A bed of glittering light: I asked the cause.
"It is," said he, "the waters of the Deep
Gathering upon us"; quickening then the pace
Of the unwieldy Creature he bestrode,
He left me; I called after him aloud,—
135 He heeded not; but with his twofold charge
Still in his grasp, before me, full in view,
Went hurrying o'er the illimitable Waste
With the fleet waters of a drowning World
In chase of him; whereat I waked in terror;
140 And saw the Sea before me, and the Book,
In which I had been reading, at my side.

[THE BOY OF WINANDER]

There was a Boy;[5]—ye knew him well, Ye Cliffs
And Islands of Winander!—many a time
At evening, when the earliest stars began
To move along the edges of the hills,
370 Rising or setting, would he stand alone,
Beneath the trees, or by the glimmering lake;
And there, with fingers interwoven, both hands
Pressed closely palm to palm and to his mouth
Uplifted, he, as through an instrument,
375 Blew mimic hootings to the silent owls
That they might answer him.—And they would shout
Across the watery Vale, and shout again,
Responsive to his call,—with quivering peals,
And long halloos, and screams, and echoes loud
380 Redoubled and redoubled; concourse wild
Of jocund din! and when a lengthened pause
Of silence came, and baffled his best skill,

5. In an early manuscript version of this passage Wordsworth uses the first-person pronoun. The experience he describes was thus apparently his own.

Then, sometimes, in that silence, while he hung
Listening, a gentle shock of mild surprize
385 Has carried far into his heart the voice
Of mountain torrents; or the visible scene
Would enter unawares into his mind
With all its solemn imagery, its rocks,
Its woods, and that uncertain heaven, received
390 Into the bosom of the steady lake.[6]
    This Boy was taken from his Mates, and died
In childhood, ere he was full twelve years old.
Fair is the Spot, most beautiful the Vale
Where he was born: the grassy Church-yard hangs
395 Upon a slope above the Village School;
And through that Church-yard when my way has led
On summer evenings, I believe that there
A long half-hour together I have stood
Mute—looking at the grave in which he lies!
400   Even now appears before the mind's clear eye
That self-same Village Church; I see her sit
(The thronèd Lady whom erewhile we hailed)
On her green hill, forgetful of this Boy
Who slumbers at her feet, forgetful, too,
405 Of all her silent neighbourhood of graves,
And listening only to the gladsome sounds
That, from the rural School ascending, play
Beneath her, and about her. May she long
Behold a race of Young Ones like to those
410 With whom I herded! (easily, indeed,
We might have fed upon a fatter soil
Of Arts and Letters, but be that forgiven)
A race of *real* children; not too wise,
Too learnèd, or too good: but wanton, fresh,
415 And bandied up and down by love and hate;
Not unresentful where self-justified;
Fierce, moody, patient, venturous, modest, shy;
Mad at their sports like withered leaves in winds:
Though doing wrong and suffering, and full oft
420 Bending beneath our life's mysterious weight
Of pain, and doubt, and fear; yet yielding not
In happiness to the happiest upon earth.
Simplicity in habit, truth in speech,
Be these the daily strengtheners of their minds!
425 May books and nature be their early joy!
And knowledge, rightly honored with that name,
Knowledge not purchased by the loss of power!

["THE MYSTERY OF WORDS"]

Here must we pause; this only let me add,
From heart-experience, and in humblest sense

---

6. Coleridge wrote of the last line and a half ("that uncertain heaven . . . lake"): "Had I met these lines running wild in the deserts of Arabia, I should instantly have screamed out, 'Wordsworth.' "

Of modesty, that he, who, in his youth,
A daily Wanderer among woods and fields,
590 With living Nature hath been intimate,
Not only in that raw unpractised time
Is stirred to extasy, as others are,
By glittering verse; but, further, doth receive,
In measure only dealt out to himself,
595 Knowledge and increase of enduring joy
From the great Nature that exists in works
Of mighty Poets.[7] Visionary Power
Attends the motions of the viewless° winds   *invisible*
Embodied in the mystery of words:
600 There darkness makes abode, and all the host
Of shadowy things work endless changes there,
As in a mansion like their proper home.
Even forms and substances are circumfused
By that transparent veil with light divine;
605 And, through the turnings intricate of verse,
Present themselves as objects recognized,
In flashes, and with glory not their own.
  Thus far a scanty record is deduced
Of what I owed to Books in early life;
610 Their later influence yet remains untold;
But as this work was taking in my mind
Proportions that seemed larger than had first
Been meditated, I was indisposed
To any further progress, at a time
615 When these acknowledgments were left unpaid.

From Book Sixth
Cambridge, and the Alps

["HUMAN NATURE SEEMING BORN AGAIN"]

When the third summer freed us from restraint,[1]
A youthful Friend, he too a Mountaineer,
325 Not slow to share my wishes, took his staff,
And, sallying forth, we journeyed, side by side,
Bound to the distant Alps. A hardy slight
Did this unprecedented course imply
Of College studies and their set rewards;[2]
330 Nor had, in truth, the scheme been formed by me
Without uneasy forethought of the pain,
The censures, and ill-omening of those
To whom my worldly interests were dear.

7. Having found a set of symbols in nature, Wordsworth now finds nature in the symbol systems of "mighty poets."

1. After reviewing briefly his second and third years at Cambridge, Wordsworth here describes his trip through France and Switzerland with a college friend, Robert Jones, during the succeeding summer vacation, in 1790. France was then in the "golden hours" of the early period of the Revolution; the fall of the Bastille had occurred on July 14 of the preceding year.

2. English universities allow much longer vacations than those in the United States, on the optimistic assumption that they will be used primarily for intensive study. Wordsworth is facing his final examinations in the next college year.

But Nature then was Sovereign in my mind,
335 And mighty Forms, seizing a youthful fancy,
Had given a charter[3] to irregular hopes.
In any age of uneventful calm
Among the Nations, surely would my heart
Have been possessed by similar desire;
340 But Europe at that time was thrilled with joy,
France standing on the top of golden hours,
And human nature seeming born again.

[CROSSING SIMPLON PASS]

* * * That very day,
525 From a bare ridge we also first beheld
Unveiled the summit of Mont Blanc, and grieved
To have a soulless image on the eye
Which had usurped upon a living thought
That never more could be.[4] The wondrous Vale
530 Of Chamouny[5] stretched far below, and soon
With its dumb cataracts, and streams of ice,
A motionless array of mighty waves,
Five rivers broad and vast, made rich amends,
And reconciled us to realities.
535 There small birds warble from the leafy trees,
The eagle soars high in the element;
There doth the Reaper bind the yellow sheaf,
The Maiden spread the hay-cock in the sun,
While Winter like a well-tamed lion walks,
540 Descending from the Mountain to make sport
Among the Cottages by beds of flowers.
  Whate'er in this wide circuit we beheld,
Or heard, was fitted to our unripe state
Of intellect and heart. With such a book
545 Before our eyes we could not chuse but read
Lessons of genuine brotherhood, the plain
And universal reason of mankind,
The truths of Young and Old. Nor, side by side
Pacing, two social Pilgrims, or alone
550 Each with his humour,[6] could we fail to abound
In dreams and fictions pensively composed,
Dejection taken up for pleasure's sake,
And gilded sympathies; the willow wreath,[7]
And sober posies[8] of funereal flowers
555 Gathered, among those solitudes sublime,
From formal gardens of the Lady Sorrow,
Did sweeten many a meditative hour.
  Yet still in me with those soft luxuries

3. Privileged freedom.
4. The "image" is the actual sight of Mont Blanc, as against what the poet has imagined the famous Swiss mountain to be.
5. Chamonix, a valley in eastern France, north of

Mont Blanc.
6. Temperament, or state of mind.
7. Symbolizing sorrow. "Gilded": laid on like gilt; i.e., superficial.
8. Small bunches of flowers.

Mixed something of stern mood, an under thirst
560　Of vigor seldom utterly allayed.
And from that source how different a sadness
Would issue, let one incident make known.
When from the Vallais we had turned, and clomb°　　　　*climbed*
Along the Simplon's steep and rugged road,[9]
565　Following a band of Muleteers, we reached
A halting-place where all together took
Their noon-tide meal. Hastily rose our Guide,
Leaving *us* at the Board; awhile we lingered,
Then paced the beaten downward way that led
570　Right to a rough stream's edge and there broke off.
The only track now visible was one
That from the torrent's further brink held forth
Conspicuous invitation to ascend
A lofty mountain. After brief delay
575　Crossing the unbridged stream, that road we took
And clomb with eagerness, till anxious fears
Intruded, for we failed to overtake
Our Comrades gone before. By fortunate chance,
While every moment added doubt to doubt,
580　A Peasant met us, from whose mouth we learned
That to the Spot which had perplexed us first
We must descend, and there should find the road,
Which in the stony channel of the Stream
Lay a few steps, and then along its banks,
585　And that our future course, all plain to sight,
Was downwards, with the current of that Stream.
Loth to believe what we so grieved to hear,
For still we had hopes that pointed to the clouds,
We questioned him again, and yet again;
590　But every word that from the Peasant's lips
Came in reply, translated by our feelings,
Ended in this, *that we had crossed the Alps.*[1]
　　　　Imagination—here the Power so called
Through sad incompetence of human speech—
595　That awful Power rose from the Mind's abyss
Like an unfathered vapour[2] that enwraps
At once some lonely Traveller. I was lost,
Halted without an effort to break through;
But to my conscious soul I now can say,
600　"I recognize thy glory"; in such strength
Of usurpation, when the light of sense
Goes out, but with a flash that has revealed
The invisible world, doth Greatness make abode,
There harbours, whether we be young or old;
605　Our destiny, our being's heart and home,

---

9. The Simplon Pass through the Alps.
1. As Dorothy Wordsworth baldly put it later on, "The ambition of youth was disappointed at these tidings." The visionary experience that follows (lines 593–617) occurred not in the Alps but at the time of writing the passage, as the 1805 text explicitly says: "Imagination! lifting up itself / Before the eye and progress of my Song."
2. Sudden vapor from no apparent source.

Is with infinitude, and only there;
With hope it is, hope that can never die,
Effort, and expectation, and desire,
And something evermore about to be.[3]
610   Under such banners militant the Soul
Seeks for no trophies, struggles for no spoils,
That may attest her prowess, blest in thoughts
That are their own perfection and reward,
Strong in herself, and in beatitude[4]
615   That hides her like the mighty flood of Nile
Poured from his fount of Abyssinian clouds
To fertilize the whole Egyptian plain.
    The melancholy slackening that ensued
Upon those tidings by the Peasant given
620   Was soon dislodged; downwards we hurried fast
And, with the half-shaped road, which we had missed,
Entered a narrow chasm. The brook and road
Were fellow-Travellers in this gloomy Strait,
And with them did we journey several hours
625   At a slow pace. The immeasurable height
Of woods decaying, never to be decayed,
The stationary blasts of waterfalls,
And in the narrow rent at every turn
Winds thwarting winds, bewildered and forlorn,
630   The torrents shooting from the clear blue sky,
The rocks that muttered close upon our ears,
Black drizzling crags that spake by the way-side
As if a voice were in them, the sick sight
And giddy prospect of the raving stream,
635   The unfettered clouds, and region of the Heavens,
Tumult and peace, the darkness and the light—
Were all like workings of one mind, the features
Of the same face, blossoms upon one tree,
Characters of the great Apocalypse,[5]
640   The types and symbols of Eternity,
Of first and last, and midst, and without end.[6]

From Book Seventh
Residence in London[1]

[THE BLIND BEGGAR. BARTHOLOMEW FAIR]

As the black storm upon the mountain top
620   Sets off the sunbeam in the Valley, so

3. At the time, Wordsworth had not been able to understand why he had felt such grievous disappointment at finding that he had already crossed the Alps, while still expecting to climb upward (lines 587–92). Now, a flash of vision reveals the symbolic significance of that experience: that the glory of humankind is to aim infinitely high, even though our capabilities are finite.
4. The ultimate blessedness or happiness.
5. The objects in this natural scene, exhibiting a coincidence of all opposites, are like the written

words of the Apocalypse—i.e., of the Book of Revelation, the last book of the New Testament.
6. Cf. Revelation 1.8: "I am Alpha and Omega, the beginning and the ending, saith the Lord." The phrase is repeated in Revelation 21.6, after the fulfillment of the last things. In *Paradise Lost* 5.153–65 Milton says that the things created declare their Creator, and calls on all to extol "him first, him last, him midst, and without end."
1. Wordsworth spent three and a half months in London in 1791.

That huge fermenting Mass of human-kind
Serves as a solemn background or relief
To single forms and objects, whence they draw,
For feeling and contemplative regard,
625 More than inherent liveliness and power.
How oft amid those overflowing streets
Have I gone forward with the Crowd, and said
Unto myself, "The face of every one
That passes by me is a mystery!"
630 Thus have I looked, nor ceased to look, oppressed
By thoughts of what and whither, when and how,
Until the Shapes before my eyes became
A second-sight procession, such as glides
Over still mountains, or appears in dreams.
635 And once, far-travelled in such mood, beyond
The reach of common indication, lost
Amid the moving pageant, I was smitten
Abruptly with the view (a sight not rare)
Of a blind Beggar who, with upright face,
640 Stood propped against a Wall; upon his chest
Wearing a written paper to explain
His Story, whence he came, and who he was.
Caught by the spectacle, my mind turned round
As with the might of waters; an apt type
645 This Label seemed, of the utmost we can know
Both of ourselves and of the universe;
And on the Shape of that unmoving Man,
His steadfast face, and sightless eyes, I gazed
As if admonished from another world.
650   Though reared upon the base of outward things,
Structures like these the excited Spirit mainly
Builds for herself. Scenes different there are,
Full-formed, that take, with small internal help,
Possession of the faculties—the peace
655 That comes with night; the deep solemnity
Of Nature's intermediate hours of rest,
When the great tide of human life stands still,
The business of the day to come—unborn,
Of that gone by—locked up as in the grave;[2]
660 The blended calmness of the heavens and earth,
Moonlight, and stars, and empty streets, and sounds
Unfrequent as in deserts: at late hours
Of winter evenings when unwholesome rains
Are falling hard, with people yet astir,
665 The feeble salutation from the voice
Of some unhappy woman, now and then
Heard as we pass; when no one looks about,
Nothing is listened to. But these, I fear,
Are falsely catalogued;[3] things that are, are not,
670 As the mind answers to them, or the heart

---

2. The sonnet *Composed upon Westminster Bridge* describes a similar response to London when its "mighty heart is lying still."

3. I.e., mistakenly classified as scenes (lines 652–54) whose effects on the perceiver depend but little on contributions by the perceiving mind.

Is prompt or slow to feel. What say you, then,
To times when half the City shall break out
Full of one passion, vengeance, rage, or fear?
To executions,⁴ to a Street on fire,
675 Mobs, riots, or rejoicings? From these sights
Take one, that annual Festival, the Fair
Holden where Martyrs suffered in past time,
And named of St. Bartholomew;⁵ there see
A work completed to our hands, that lays,
680 If any spectacle on earth can do,
The whole creative powers of Man asleep!
For once the Muse's help will we implore,
And she shall lodge us, wafted on her wings,
Above the press and danger of the Crowd,
685 Upon some Shewman's platform. What a shock
For eyes and ears! what anarchy and din
Barbarian and infernal—a phantasma⁶
Monstrous in color, motion, shape, sight, sound!
Below, the open space, through every nook
690 Of the wide area, twinkles, is alive
With heads; the midway region and above
Is thronged with staring pictures, and huge scrolls,
Dumb proclamations of the Prodigies!
With chattering monkeys dangling from their poles,
695 And children whirling in their roundabouts;°   *merry-go-rounds*
With those that stretch the neck, and strain the eyes;
And crack the voice in rivalship, the crowd
Inviting; with buffoons against buffoons
Grimacing, writhing, screaming, him who grinds
700 The hurdy-gurdy,⁷ at the fiddle weaves,
Rattles the salt-box,⁸ thumps the Kettle-drum;
And him who at the trumpet puffs his cheeks;
The silver-collared Negro with his timbrel;°   *tambourine*
Equestrians, tumblers, women, girls, and boys,
705 Blue-breeched, pink-vested, with high-towering plumes.
—All moveables of wonder from all parts
And here, Albinos, painted-Indians, Dwarfs,
The Horse of Knowledge,⁹ and the learned Pig,
The Stone-eater, the Man that swallows fire—
710 Giants, Ventriloquists, the Invisible-girl,
The Bust that speaks, and moves its goggling eyes,
The Wax-work, Clock-work, all the marvellous craft
Of modern Merlins,¹ Wild-beasts, Puppet-shews,
All out-o'th'-way, far-fetched, perverted things,
715 All freaks of Nature, all Promethean² thoughts

4. Executions were public events in England until
1868.
5. This huge fair was long held in Smithfield, the
place where, on St. Bartholomew's Day, August 24,
Protestants had been executed in Queen Mary's
reign (1553–58).
6. Fantasy of a disordered mind.
7. A stringed instrument, sounded by a turning
wheel covered by rosin.

8. A wooden box, rattled and beaten with a stick.
9. A horse trained to tap out answers to numerical
questions, etc.
1. Magicians. Merlin was the magician in Arthurian romance.
2. Creative, or highly inventive. In Greek mythology Prometheus made man out of clay and taught
him the arts.

Of man; his dullness, madness, and their feats,
All jumbled up together, to compose
A Parliament of Monsters. Tents and Booths,
Meanwhile, as if the whole were one vast mill,
720 Are vomiting, receiving, on all sides,
Men, Women, three-years' Children, Babes in arms.
    Oh blank confusion! true epitome
Of what the mighty City is herself
To thousands upon thousands of her Sons,
725 Living amid the same perpetual whirl
Of trivial objects, melted and reduced
To one identity, by differences
That have no law, no meaning, and no end;
Oppression under which even highest minds
730 Must labour, whence the strongest are not free!
But though the picture weary out the eye,
By nature an unmanageable sight,
It is not wholly so to him who looks
In steadiness, who hath among least things
735 An undersense of greatest; sees the parts
As parts, but with a feeling of the whole.

                    *   *   *

This did I feel in London's vast Domain;
The Spirit of Nature was upon me there;
The Soul of Beauty and enduring life
Vouchsafed her inspirations; and diffused,
770 Through meagre lines and colours, and the press
Of self-destroying transitory things,
Composure, and ennobling harmony.

From Book Eighth
Retrospect, Love of Nature leading
to Love of Man[1]

[THE SHEPHERD IN THE MIST. MAN STILL SUBORDINATE TO NATURE]

          * * * A rambling School-boy, thus
I felt his presence in his own domain
As of a Lord and Master; or a Power
Or Genius,[2] under Nature, under God
260 Presiding; and severest solitude
Had more commanding looks when he was there.
When up the lonely brooks on rainy days
Angling I went, or trod the trackless hills

1. In this book Wordsworth reviews the first twenty-one years of his life to trace the transfer of his earlier feelings for nature to shepherds and other humble people who carry on their lonely duties almost as though they were animate parts of the landscape (cf. *Michael*, lines 1–39, pp. 270–71). Wordsworth's central concern is to describe the early development in his relatively inexperi-enced mind of an image, or conceptual model, of the largeness, worth, and almost sacred dignity of generic Man (lines 256–81), an image that proved invulnerable to the acid bath of his later experience of the vulgarity, meanness, and evil of which individuals are capable (lines 317–22).
2. Presiding spirit.

By mists bewildered, suddenly mine eyes
265 Have glanced upon him distant a few steps,
In size a Giant, stalking through thick fog,
His sheep like Greenland bears;° or, as he stepped   *polar bears*
Beyond the boundary line of some hill-shadow,
His form hath flashed upon me, glorified
270 By the deep radiance of the setting sun:[3]
Or him have I descried in distant sky,
A solitary object and sublime,
Above all height! like an aerial cross
Stationed alone upon a spiry rock
275 Of the Chartreuse,[4] for worship. Thus was Man
Ennobled outwardly before my sight,
And thus my heart was early introduced
To an unconscious love and reverence
Of human nature; hence the human Form
280 To me became an index of delight,
Of grace, and honor, power, and worthiness.
Meanwhile this Creature, spiritual almost
As those of Books, but more exalted far;
Far more of an imaginative Form
285 Than the gay Corin of the groves, who lives
For his own fancies, or to dance by the hour
In coronal, with Phillis[5] in the midst—
Was, for the purposes of Kind,[6] a Man
With the most common; husband, father; learned,
290 Could teach, admonish, suffered with the rest
From vice and folly, wretchedness and fear;
Of this I little saw, cared less for it;
But something must have felt.
                    Call ye these appearances
Which I beheld of Shepherds in my youth,
295 This sanctity of Nature given to man—
A shadow, a delusion, ye who pore
On the dead letter, miss the spirit of things;
Whose truth is not a motion or a shape
Instinct with vital functions, but a Block
300 Or waxen image which yourselves have made,
And ye adore. But blessed be the God
Of Nature and of Man, that this was so,
That men before my inexperienced eyes
Did first present themselves thus purified,
305 Removed, and to a distance that was fit.
And so we all of us in some degree
Are led to knowledge, whencesoever led
And howsoever; were it otherwise,

---

3. A "glory" is a mountain phenomenon in which the enlarged figure of a person is seen projected by the sun on the mist, with a radiance about its head. Cf. Coleridge's *Dejection: An Ode*, line 54 (p. 460).
4. In his tour of the Alps, Wordsworth had been deeply impressed by the Chartreuse, a Carthusian monastery in France, with its soaring cross visible against the sky. There is an overtone here of the Christ-like divinity investing the "common" man (line 289).
5. Corin and Phillis, dancing in their coronals, or wreaths of flowers, were stock characters in earlier pastoral literature.
6. I.e., in carrying out the tasks of humankind.

And we found evil fast as we find good
310 In our first years, or think that it is found,
How could the innocent heart bear up and live?
But doubly fortunate my lot; not here
Alone, that something of a better life
Perhaps was round me than it is the privilege
315 Of most to move in, but that first I looked
At Man through objects that were great or fair,
First communed with him by their help. And thus
Was founded a sure safeguard and defence
Against the weight of meanness, selfish cares,
320 Coarse manners, vulgar passions, that beat in
On all sides from the ordinary world
In which we traffic. Starting from this point,
I had my face turned tow'rd the truth, began
With an advantage furnished by that kind
325 Of prepossession without which the soul
Receives no knowledge that can bring forth good,
No genuine insight ever comes to her.
From the restraint of over-watchful eyes
Preserved, I moved about, year after year
330 Happy, and now most thankful, that my walk
Was guarded from too early intercourse
With the deformities of crowded life,
And those ensuing laughters and contempts
Self-pleasing, which, if we would wish to think
335 With a due reverence on earth's rightful Lord,
Here placed to be the Inheritor of heaven,[7]
Will not permit us; but pursue the mind
That to devotion willingly would rise,
Into the Temple, and the Temple's heart.[8]
340   Yet deem not, Friend, that human-kind with me
Thus early took a place preeminent;
Nature herself was at this unripe time
But secondary to my own pursuits
And animal activities, and all
345 Their trivial pleasures:[9] and when these had drooped
And gradually expired, and Nature, prized
For her own sake, became my joy, even then—
And upwards through late youth, until not less
Than two and twenty summers had been told—
350 Was Man in my affections and regards
Subordinate to her; her visible Forms
And viewless agencies: a passion she,
A rapture often, and immediate love
Ever at hand; *he* only a delight
355 Occasional, an accidental grace,
His hour being not yet come. * * *

7. This pious line was a later addition to the version of 1805.
8. I.e., into the devotional recesses of the inner-most mind.
9. Cf. his account of the stages of his development in lines 65–92 of *Tintern Abbey* (n. 2, p. 237).

From Book Ninth
Residence in France[1]

[PARIS AND ORLÉANS. BECOMES A "PATRIOT"]

Even as a River—partly (it might seem)
Yielding to old remembrances, and swayed
In part by fear to shape a way direct
That would engulph him soon in the ravenous Sea—
5 Turns, and will measure back his course, far back,
Seeking the very regions which he crossed
In his first outset; so have we, my Friend!
Turned and returned with intricate delay.
Or as a Traveller, who has gained the brow
10 Of some aerial Down,[2] while there he halts
For breathing-time, is tempted to review
The region left behind him; and if aught
Deserving notice have escaped regard,
Or been regarded with too careless eye,
15 Strives, from that height, with one, and yet one more
Last look, to make the best amends he may,
So have we lingered. Now we start afresh
With courage, and new hope risen on our toil.
Fair greetings to this shapeless eagerness,
20 Whene'er it comes! needful in work so long,
Thrice needful to the argument° which now   *theme*
Awaits us! Oh, how much unlike the past![3]
    Free as a Colt, at pasture on the hill,
I ranged at large through London's wide Domain
25 Month after Month. Obscurely did I live,
Not seeking frequent intercourse with men
By literature, or elegance, or rank
Distinguished. Scarcely was a year thus spent[4]
Ere I forsook the crowded Solitude;
30 With less regret for its luxurious pomp
And all the nicely-guarded shews of Art,
Than for the humble Bookstalls in the Streets,
Exposed to eye and hand where'er I turned.
—France lured me forth, the realm that I had crossed
35 So lately, journeying toward the snow-clad Alps.
But now relinquishing the scrip° and staff[5]   *knapsack*
And all enjoyment which the summer sun
Sheds round the steps of those who meet the day
With motion constant as his own, I went

1. Wordsworth's second visit to France, while he was twenty-one and twenty-two years of age (1791–92), came during a crucial period of the French Revolution. This book deals with his stay at Paris, Orléans, and Blois, when he developed his passionate partisanship for the French people and the revolutionary cause.
2. Treeless high land.
3. This preface parallels in function Milton's pref-ace to the equivalent ninth book of *Paradise Lost,* in which he announces that, having narrated the blameless life of Adam and Eve in Eden, he "now must change / Those notes to tragic," and tell of their fall.
4. His stay in London in fact lasted only four or five months, January–May 1791.
5. Traditional emblems of the foot pilgrim.

40 Prepared to sojourn in a pleasant Town[6]
Washed by the current of the stately Loire.
    Through Paris lay my readiest course, and there
Sojourning a few days, I visited
In haste each spot, of old or recent fame,
45 The latter chiefly; from the field of Mars[7]
Down to the suburbs of St. Anthony;[8]
And from Mont Martyr[9] southward to the Dome
Of Genevieve.[1] In both her clamorous Halls,
The National Synod and the Jacobins,[2]
50 I saw the Revolutionary Power
Toss like a Ship at anchor, rocked by storms;
The Arcades I traversed, in the Palace huge
Of Orleans,[3] coasted round and round the line
Of Tavern, Brothel, Gaming-house, and Shop,
55 Great rendezvous of worst and best, the walk
Of all who had a purpose, or had not;
I stared, and listened with a Stranger's ears
To Hawkers and Haranguers, hubbub wild!
And hissing Factionists, with ardent eyes,
60 In knots, or pairs, or single. Not a look
Hope takes, or Doubt or Fear are forced to wear,
But seemed there present, and I scanned them all,
Watched every gesture uncontrollable
Of anger, and vexation, and despite,
65 All side by side, and struggling face to face
With Gaiety and dissolute Idleness.
—Where silent zephyrs sported with the dust
Of the Bastille,[4] I sate in the open sun,
And from the rubbish gathered up a stone
70 And pocketed the Relic in the guise
Of an Enthusiast; yet, in honest truth,
I looked for Something that I could not find,
Affecting more emotion than I felt;
For 'tis most certain that these various sights,
75 However potent their first shock, with me
Appeared to recompence the Traveller's pains
Less than the painted Magdalene of Le Brun,[5]
A Beauty exquisitely wrought, with hair
Dishevelled, gleaming eyes, and rueful cheek
80 Pale, and bedropp'd with everflowing tears.
    But hence to my more permanent Abode[6]

6. Orléans, on the Loire River, where Wordsworth stayed from December 1791 until he moved to Blois early the next year.
7. The Champ de Mars, where Louis XVI swore fidelity to the new constitution.
8. Faubourg St. Antoine, near the Bastille, a working-class quarter and center of revolutionary violence.
9. Montmartre, a hill on which revolutionary meetings were held.
1. Became the Panthéon, a burial place for notable Frenchmen.
2. The club of radical democratic revolutionists,

named for the ancient convent of St. Jacques, their meeting place. "National Synod": the newly formed National Assembly.
3. The arcades in the courtyard of the Palais d'Orléans, a fashionable shopping center and Parisian rendezvous.
4. The political prison, which had been demolished after being stormed and sacked on July 14, 1789.
5. Charles Le Brun (1619–1690) painted the weeping Mary Magdalene, then regarded as a religious masterpiece.
6. In Orléans.

I hasten; there by novelties in speech,
Domestic manners, customs, gestures, looks,
And all the attire of ordinary life,
85   Attention was engrossed; and, thus amused,
I stood 'mid those concussions unconcerned,
Tranquil almost, and careless as a flower
Glassed in a green-house, or a Parlour shrub
That spreads its leaves in unmolested peace
90   While every bush and tree, the country through,
Is shaking to the roots; indifference this
Which may seem strange; but I was unprepared
With needful knowledge, had abruptly passed
Into a theatre whose stage was filled,
95   And busy with an action far advanced.
Like Others I had skimmed, and sometimes read
With care, the master pamphlets of the day;[7]
Nor wanted such half-insight as grew wild
Upon that meagre soil, helped out by talk
100   And public news; but having never seen
A Chronicle that might suffice to shew
Whence the main Organs[8] of the public Power
Had sprung, their transmigrations when and how
Accomplished, giving thus unto events
105   A form and body; all things were to me
Loose and disjointed, and the affections left
Without a vital interest. At that time,
Moreover, the first storm was overblown,
And the strong hand of outward violence
110   Locked up in quiet.[9] For myself, I fear
Now, in connection with so great a Theme,
To speak (as I must be compelled to do)
Of one so unimportant; night by night
Did I frequent the formal haunts of men
115   Whom, in the City, privilege of birth
Sequestered from the rest: societies
Polished in Arts, and in punctilio[1] versed;
Whence, and from deeper causes, all discourse
Of good and evil of the time was shunned
120   With scrupulous care: but these restrictions soon
Proved tedious, and I gradually withdrew
Into a noisier world, and thus erelong
Became a Patriot;[2] and my heart was all
Given to the People, and my love was theirs.

---

7. Wordsworth probably refers to the numerous English pamphlets (including Paine's *Rights of Man,* part 1, and Wollstonecraft's *A Vindication of the Rights of Men*) published in response to Edmund Burke's attack on the revolution, *Reflections on the Revolution in France* (1790).
8. Institutions, instruments.

9. After the storming of the Bastille in 1789 there was a period of calm until the massacre of three thousand Royalists in September 1792, after the deposition and imprisonment of Louis XVI.
1. The niceties of social manners.
2. I.e., became committed to the people's side in the Revolution.

From Book Tenth
France continued[1]

[THE REVOLUTION: PARIS AND ENGLAND]

Cheared with this hope,[2] to Paris I returned;
And ranged, with ardor heretofore unfelt,
50   The spacious City, and in progress passed
The Prison[3] where the unhappy Monarch lay,
Associate with his Children and his Wife,
In Bondage; and the Palace[4] lately stormed,
With roar of Cannon, by a furious Host.
55   I crossed the Square (an empty Area then!)
Of the Carousel, where so late had lain
The Dead, upon the Dying heaped; and gazed
On this and other Spots, as doth a Man
Upon a Volume whose contents he knows
60   Are memorable, but from him locked up,
Being written in a tongue he cannot read;
So that he questions the mute leaves with pain,
And half-upbraids their silence. But, that night,
I felt most deeply in what world I was,
65   What ground I trod on, and what air I breathed.
High was my Room and lonely, near the roof
Of a large Mansion or Hotel,° a Lodge   *town house*
That would have pleased me in more quiet times,
Nor was it wholly without pleasure, then.
70   With unextinguished taper I kept watch,
Reading at intervals; the fear gone by
Pressed on me almost like a fear to come.
I thought of those September massacres,
Divided from me by one little month,
75   Saw them and touched;[5] the rest was conjured up
From tragic fictions, or true history,
Remembrances and dim admonishments.
The Horse is taught his manage,[6] and no Star
Of wildest course but treads back his own steps;
80   For the spent hurricane the air provides
As fierce a Successor; the tide retreats
But to return out of its hiding place
In the great Deep; all things have second birth;
The earthquake is not satisfied at once;
85   And in this way I wrought upon myself
Until I seemed to hear a voice that cried

1. At this period, October 1792–August 1794, Wordsworth's revolutionary enthusiasm was at its height.
2. I.e., that the moderates were now taking over and would eliminate further violence.
3. I.e., the "Temple" (it had once housed the religious Order of Templars), where Louis XVI was held prisoner.
4. The Tuileries. In front of this is the great square of "the Carousel" (line 56), where a number of the mob storming the palace had been killed.
5. I.e., his imagination of the September massacres was so vivid as to be palpable.
6. The French *manège*, the prescribed action and paces of a trained horse.

To the whole City, "Sleep no more."[7] The Trance
Fled with the Voice to which it had given birth,
But vainly comments of a calmer mind
90 Promised soft peace and sweet forgetfulness.
The place, all hushed and silent as it was,
Appeared unfit for the repose of Night,
Defenceless as a wood where Tygers roam.

      * * * In this frame of mind,
Dragged by a chain of harsh necessity,
So seemed it,—now I thankfully acknowledge,
Forced by the gracious providence of Heaven—
225 To England I returned,[8] else (though assured
That I both was, and must be, of small weight,
No better than a Landsman on the deck
Of a ship struggling with a hideous storm)
Doubtless I should have then made common cause
230 With some who perished, haply perished too,[9]
A poor mistaken and bewildered offering,
Should to the breast of Nature have gone back
With all my resolutions, all my hopes,
A Poet only to myself, to Men
235 Useless, and even, belovèd Friend, a Soul
To thee unknown![1]

            *   *   *

What then were my emotions, when in Arms
Britain put forth her free-born strength in league,
265 O pity and shame! with those confederate Powers?[2]
Not in my single self alone I found,
But in the minds of all ingenuous Youth,
Change and subversion from that hour. No shock
Given to my moral nature had I known
270 Down to that very moment; neither lapse
Nor turn of sentiment that might be named
A revolution, save at this one time;
All else was progress on the self-same path
On which, with a diversity of pace,
275 I had been travelling: this a stride at once
Into another region.—As a light
And pliant hare-bell swinging in the breeze
On some gray rock, its birth-place, so had I
Wantoned, fast rooted on the ancient tower

7. *Macbeth* 2.2.33–34: "Methought I heard a voice cry, 'Sleep no more, / Macbeth does murder sleep.' "
8. Forced by the "harsh necessity" of a lack of money, Wordsworth returned to England late in 1792.
9. Wordsworth had allied his sympathies with the party of the Girondins, almost all of whom were guillotined or committed suicide.
1. Wordsworth did not meet Coleridge, the "beloved Friend," until 1795.

2. England joined the war against France in February 1793. The great moral crisis that almost wrecked Wordsworth's life began with this sudden split between his profound attachments to the English land (the development of which he had described in the early books of *The Prelude*) and his later but heartfelt identification with the cause of the French Revolution. What had seemed a single and coherent development suddenly became split into conflicting parts.

280 Of my beloved Country, wishing not
A happier fortune than to wither there.
Now was I from that pleasant station torn
And tossed about in whirlwind. I rejoiced,
Yea, afterwards, truth most painful to record!
285 Exulted, in the triumph of my Soul,
When Englishmen by thousands were o'erthrown,
Left without glory on the field, or driven,
Brave hearts, to shameful flight.[3] It was a grief,—
Grief call it not, 'twas any thing but that,—
290 A conflict of sensations without name,
Of which *he* only who may love the sight
Of a Village Steeple as I do can judge,
When, in the Congregation bending all
To their great Father, prayers were offered up,
295 Or praises, for our Country's victories,
And, 'mid the simple Worshippers, perchance
I only, like an uninvited Guest,
Whom no one owned, sate silent, shall I add,
Fed on the day of vengeance yet to come?

* * *

[THE REIGN OF TERROR. NIGHTMARES]

—Domestic carnage now filled the whole year
With Feast-days;[4] old Men from the Chimney-nook,
The Maiden from the bosom of her Love,
The Mother from the Cradle of her Babe,
360 The Warrior from the Field, all perished, all,
Friends, enemies, of all parties, ages, ranks,
Head after head, and never heads enough
For those that bade them fall. They found their joy,
They made it, proudly eager as a Child
365 (If like desires of innocent little ones
May with such heinous appetites be compared),
Pleased in some open field to exercise
A toy that mimics with revolving wings
The motion of a windmill, though the air
370 Do of itself blow fresh and make the Vanes
Spin in his eyesight, *that* contents him not,
But, with the play-thing at arm's length, he sets
His front against the blast, and runs amain
That it may whirl the faster.

* * *

Most melancholy at that time, O Friend!
Were my day-thoughts, my nights were miserable;

3. The French defeated the English in the battle
of Hondschoote, September 6, 1793.
4. I.e., festivals celebrated by human slaughter
("carnage"). Lines 356–63 give a description of the

height of the Reign of Terror under Robespierre.
In 1794, a total of 1,376 people were guillotined
in Paris in forty-nine days.

Through months, through years, long after the last beat
400 Of those atrocities, the hour of sleep
To me came rarely charged with natural gifts,
Such ghastly Visions had I of despair
And tyranny, and implements of death,
And innocent victims sinking under fear,
405 And momentary hope, and worn-out prayer,
Each in his separate cell, or penned in crowds
For sacrifice, and struggling with forced mirth
And levity in dungeons where the dust
Was laid with tears. Then suddenly the scene
410 Changed, and the unbroken dream entangled me
In long orations which I strove to plead
Before unjust tribunals—with a voice
Labouring, a brain confounded, and a sense
Death-like of treacherous desertion, felt
415 In the last place of refuge, my own soul.

From Book Eleventh
France, concluded[1]

[RETROSPECT: "BLISS WAS IT IN THAT DAWN." RECOURSE TO
"REASON'S NAKED SELF"]

105   O pleasant exercise of hope and joy![2]
For mighty were the Auxiliars which then stood
Upon our side, we who were strong in Love!
Bliss was it in that dawn to be alive,
But to be young was very Heaven! O times,
110 In which the meagre, stale, forbidding ways
Of custom, law, and statute, took at once
The attraction of a Country in Romance!
When Reason seemed the most to assert her rights,
When most intent on making of herself
115 A prime Enchantress—to assist the work
Which then was going forward in her name!
Not favored spots alone, but the whole earth
The beauty wore of promise—that which sets
(As at some moments might not be unfelt
120 Among the bowers of Paradise itself)
The budding rose above the rose full blown.[3]
What Temper° at the prospect did not wake   *temperament*
To happiness unthought of? The inert
Were roused, and lively natures rapt away![4]

1. Book 11 deals with the year from August 1794 through September 1795: Wordsworth's growing disillusionment with the French Revolution, his recourse to abstract theories of man and politics, his despair and nervous breakdown, and the beginning of his recovery when he moved from London to Racedown.

2. Wordsworth in this passage turns back to the summer of 1792, when his enthusiasm for the Revolution was at its height.
3. A statement of the Romantic theme of the glory of the imperfect, which sets a higher value on promise than on achievement.
4. Enraptured; carried away by enthusiasm.

125 They who had fed their Childhood upon dreams,
    The play-fellows of Fancy, who had made
    All powers of swiftness, subtilty, and strength
    Their ministers,—who in lordly wise had stirred
    Among the grandest objects of the Sense,
130 And dealt with whatsoever they found there
    As if they had within some lurking right
    To wield it;—they, too, who of gentle mood
    Had watched all gentle motions, and to these
    Had fitted their own thoughts, schemers more mild,
135 And in the region of their peaceful selves;—
    Now was it that *both* found, the Meek and Lofty
    Did both find helpers to their hearts' desire,
    And stuff at hand, plastic° as they could wish,—   *malleable*
    Were called upon to exercise their skill,
140 Not in Utopia,—subterranean Fields,—
    Or some secreted Island, Heaven knows where!
    But in the very world, which is the world
    Of all of us,—the place where in the end
    We find our happiness, or not at all!
145   Why should I not confess that Earth was then
    To me what an Inheritance new-fallen
    Seems, when the first time visited, to one
    Who thither comes to find in it his home?
    He walks about and looks upon the spot
150 With cordial transport, moulds it and remoulds,
    And is half-pleased with things that are amiss,
    'Twill be such joy to see them disappear.
        An active partisan, I thus convoked°   *called up*
    From every object pleasant circumstance
155 To suit my ends; I moved among mankind
    With genial feelings still° predominant;   *always*
    When erring, erring on the better part,
    And in the kinder spirit; placable,
    Indulgent, as not uninformed that men
160 See as they have been taught, and that Antiquity[5]
    Gives rights to error; and aware no less
    That throwing off oppression must be work
    As well of licence as of liberty;
    And above all, for this was more than all,
165 Not caring if the wind did now and then
    Blow keen upon an eminence that gave
    Prospect so large into futurity;
    In brief, a Child of Nature, as at first,
    Diffusing only those affections wider
170 That from the cradle had grown up with me,
    And losing, in no other way than light
    Is lost in light, the weak in the more strong.
        In the main outline, such, it might be said,

---

5. Classical antiquity.

Was my condition, till with open war
175 Britain opposed the Liberties of France;[6]
This threw me first out of the pale° of love,   enclosure
Soured, and corrupted, upwards to the source,
My sentiments; was not,[7] as hitherto,
A swallowing up of lesser things in great;
180 But change of them into their contraries;
And thus a way was opened for mistakes
And false conclusions, in degree as gross,
In kind more dangerous. What had been a pride
Was now a shame; my likings and my loves
185 Ran in new channels, leaving old ones dry,
And hence a blow that in maturer age
Would but have touched the judgement, struck more deep
Into sensations near the heart; meantime,
As from the first, wild theories were afloat
190 To whose pretensions sedulously urged[8]
I had but lent a careless ear, assured
That time was ready to set all things right,
And that the multitude so long oppressed
Would be oppressed no more.
                                    But when events
195 Brought less encouragement, and unto these
The immediate proof of principles no more
Could be entrusted, while the events themselves,
Worn out in greatness, stripped of novelty,
Less occupied the mind; and sentiments
200 Could through my understanding's natural growth
No longer keep their ground, by faith maintained
Of inward consciousness, and hope that laid
Her hand upon her object; evidence
Safer, of universal application, such
205 As could not be impeached, was sought elsewhere.
     But now, become Oppressors in their turn,
Frenchmen had changed a war of self-defence
For one of Conquest, losing sight of all
Which they had struggled for:[9] and mounted up,
210 Openly in the eye of Earth and Heaven,
The scale of Liberty.[1] I read her doom
With anger vexed, with disappointment sore,
But not dismayed, nor taking to the shame
Of a false Prophet. While resentment rose,
215 Striving to hide, what nought could heal, the wounds
Of mortified presumption, I adhered
More firmly to old tenets, and, to prove[2]
Their temper, strained them more; and thus, in heat
Of contest, did opinions every day

6. On February 11, 1793, England declared war against France.
7. I.e., there was not (in my sentiments).
8. Diligently argued for.
9. In late 1794 and early 1795 French troops had successes in Spain, Italy, Holland, and Germany—even though, in the constitution written in 1790, they had renounced all foreign conquest.
1. I.e., the desire for power now outweighed the love of liberty.
2. Test. The figure is that of testing a tempered steel sword.

220　Grow into consequence, till round my mind
　　They clung, as if they were its life, nay more,
　　The very being of the immortal Soul.
　　　　This was the time when, all things tending fast
　　To depravation, speculative schemes
225　That promised to abstract the hopes of Man
　　Out of his feelings, to be fixed thenceforth
　　For ever in a purer element,
　　Found ready welcome.[3] Tempting region *that*
　　For Zeal to enter and refresh herself,
230　Where passions had the privilege to work,
　　And never hear the sound of their own names:
　　But, speaking more in charity, the dream
　　Flattered the young, pleased with extremes, nor least
　　With that which makes our Reason's naked self
235　The object of its fervour. * * *

[CRISIS, BREAKDOWN, AND RECOVERY]

　　I summoned my best skill, and toiled, intent
280　To anatomize° the frame of social life,　　　　　　　　　　*analyze*
　　Yea, the whole body of society
　　Searched to its heart. Share with me, Friend! the wish
　　That some dramatic tale indued with shapes
　　Livelier, and flinging out less guarded words
285　Than suit the Work we fashion, might set forth
　　What then I learned, or think I learned, of truth,
　　And the errors into which I fell, betrayed
　　By present objects, and by reasonings false
　　From their beginnings, inasmuch as drawn
290　Out of a heart that had been turned aside
　　From Nature's way by outward accidents,
　　And which was thus confounded more and more,
　　Misguided and misguiding. So I fared,
　　Dragging all precepts, judgments, maxims, creeds,
295　Like culprits to the bar; calling the mind,
　　Suspiciously, to establish in plain day
　　Her titles[4] and her honors, now believing,
　　Now disbelieving, endlessly perplexed
　　With impulse, motive, right and wrong, the ground
300　Of obligation, what the rule and whence
　　The sanction, till, demanding formal *proof*
　　And seeking it in every thing, I lost
　　All feeling of conviction, and, in fine,°　　　　　　　　　　*the end*
　　Sick, wearied out with contrarieties,
305　Yielded up moral questions in despair.
　　　　This was the crisis of that strong disease,

3. I.e., schemes that undertook to separate ("abstract") people's hopes for future happiness from reliance on the emotional part of human nature, and instead to ground those hopes on their rational natures ("a purer element"). The allusion is primarily to William Godwin's *Inquiry Concern-* *ing Political Justice* (1793), which attempted to ground ethical and political principles, and the expectation of human progress, exclusively on rational principles.
4. Legal entitlements.

This the soul's last and lowest ebb; I drooped,
Deeming our blessed Reason of least use
Where wanted most. * * *

              * * * Then it was,
Thanks to the bounteous Giver of all good!
335 That the beloved Woman[5] in whose sight
Those days were passed, now speaking in a voice
Of sudden admonition—like a brook
That does but *cross* a lonely road, and now
Seen, heard, and felt, and caught at every turn,
340 Companion never lost through many a league—
Maintained for me a saving intercourse
With my true self:[6] for, though bedimmed and changed
Both as a clouded and a waning moon,
She whispered still that brightness would return,
345 She in the midst of all preserved me still
A Poet, made me seek beneath that name,
And that alone, my office upon earth.
And lastly, as hereafter will be shewn,
If willing audience fail not, Nature's self,
350 By all varieties of human love
Assisted, led me back through opening day
To those sweet counsels between head and heart
Whence grew that genuine knowledge fraught with peace
Which, through the later sinkings of this cause,
355 Hath still upheld me, and upholds me now
In the catastrophe (for so they dream,
And nothing less), when, finally to close
And rivet down the gains of France, a Pope
Is summoned in, to crown an Emperor:[7]
360 This last opprobrium, when we see a people
That once looked up in faith, as if to Heaven
For manna, take a lesson from the Dog
Returning to his vomit. * * *

Book Twelfth
Imagination and Taste, how impaired and restored[1]

Long time have human ignorance and guilt
Detained us, on what spectacles of woe
Compelled to look, and inwardly oppressed
With sorrow, disappointment, vexing thoughts,
5 Confusion of the judgment, zeal decayed,

5. After a long separation, Dorothy Wordsworth came to live with her brother at Racedown in 1795 and remained a permanent member of his household.
6. Dorothy and the renewed influence of nature (line 349) healed the inner fracture between his earlier and later selves, which Wordsworth had described in 10.268ff.

7. The ultimate blow to liberal hopes for France occurred when on December 2, 1804, Napoleon summoned Pope Pius VII to officiate at the ceremony elevating him to emperor. At the last moment, Napoleon took the crown and donned it himself.
1. Book 12 reviews the "impairment" and gradual recovery of Wordsworth's creative sensibility in response to the natural world.

And, lastly, utter loss of hope itself
And things to hope for! Not with these began
Our Song, and not with these our Song must end.[2]
Ye motions of delight, that haunt the sides
10   Of the green hills; ye breezes and soft airs,
Whose subtile intercourse with breathing flowers,
Feelingly watched, might teach Man's haughty race
How without injury to take, to give
Without offence; ye who, as if to shew
15   The wondrous influence of power gently used,
Bend the complying heads of lordly pines,
And with a touch shift the stupendous clouds
Through the whole compass of the sky; ye brooks
Muttering along the stones, a busy noise
20   By day, a quiet sound in silent night;
Ye waves that out of the great deep steal forth
In a calm hour to kiss the pebbly shore,
Not mute, and then retire, fearing no storm;
And you, ye Groves, whose ministry it is
25   To interpose the covert of your shades,
Even as a sleep, between the heart of man
And outward troubles, between man himself,
Not seldom, and his own uneasy heart!
Oh that I had a music and a voice
30   Harmonious as your own, that I might tell
What Ye have done for me! The morning shines,
Nor heedeth Man's perverseness; Spring returns,
I saw the Spring return and could rejoice,
In common with the Children of her love
35   Piping on boughs, or sporting on fresh fields,
Or boldly seeking pleasure nearer heaven
On wings that navigate cerulean skies.
So neither were complacency° nor peace   satisfaction
Nor tender yearnings wanting for my good
40   Through those distracted times;[3] in Nature still
Glorying, I found a counterpoise in her,
Which, when the Spirit of evil reached its height,
Maintained for me a secret happiness.
      This Narrative, my Friend, hath chiefly told
45   Of intellectual power,[4] fostering love,
Dispensing truth, and over men and things,
Where reason yet might hesitate, diffusing
Prophetic sympathies of genial faith.
So was I favored, such my happy lot,
50   Until that natural graciousness of mind
Gave way to overpressure from the times
And their disastrous issues. What availed,

2. The reference is back to the joyous preamble
with which *The Prelude* began. Wordsworth goes
on (line 10) to invoke the breeze described in the
opening line of the poem.
3. I.e., the period of spiritual crisis that he had

described in 11.293–309.
4. The power of the integral mind (as distinguished from the limited capacity of "reason"
alone, line 47).

When spells forbade the Voyager to land,
That fragrant notice of a pleasant shore
55   Wafted at intervals from many a bower
Of blissful gratitude and fearless peace?
Dare I avow that wish was mine to see,
And hope that future times *would* surely see,
The man to come parted as by a gulph
60   From him who had been, that I could no more
Trust the elevation which had made me one
With the great Family that still survives
To illuminate the abyss of ages past,
Sage, Warrior, Patriot, Hero?—for it seemed
65   That their best virtues were not free from taint
Of something false and weak, that could not stand
The open eye of Reason.[5] Then I said,
"Go to the Poets; they will speak to thee
More perfectly of purer Creatures; yet
70   If Reason be nobility in Man,
Can aught be more ignoble than the Man
Whom they delight in, blinded as he is
By prejudice, the miserable slave
Of low ambition, or distempered love?"
75   In such strange passion (if I may once more
Review the past) I warred against myself,
A Bigot to a New Idolatry;
Like a cowled Monk who hath forsworn the world,
Zealously labour'd to cut off my heart
80   From all the sources of her former strength;
And as by simple waving of a Wand
The wizard instantaneously dissolves
Palace or grove, even so could I unsoul
As readily by syllogistic words[6]
85   Those mysteries of being which have made,
And shall continue evermore to make,
Of the whole human race one brotherhood.
      What wonder, then, if to a mind so far
Perverted, even the visible Universe
90   Fell under the dominion of a taste
Less Spiritual, with microscopic view
Was scanned, as I had scanned the moral world?[7]

---

5. This passage is both elliptical and contorted in its syntax. The fragrance wafted to the sailor from the shore—i.e., his remembered experiences of human feelings of gratitude and love (lines 54–56)—serves also as evidence of the shared emotions that had earlier united him to the family of past humanity (lines 61–63). The "spells" that prevented the sailor from landing on that shore (line 53) consist of his fascination with a limited mode of analytic reasoning, which engendered the hope that in the future people would be purely rational beings, hence utterly different from the feelingful, passionate creatures of the past (lines 58–60). This mode of reasoning, in addition, not only made Wordsworth distrust the earlier emotional evidences of his unity with humanity but also led him to believe that the actions of even the greatest men recorded in human history were tainted, because they were motivated by feelings rather than by reason alone (lines 64–67).

In his allusions to the rational "spells" and his hope for a new type of humanity, Wordsworth is describing the period in his life when he had succumbed to the views of William Godwin's *Inquiry Concerning Political Justice* (1793), which derogated the role of the feelings and passions as motives and confidently anticipated a future in which the actions of humanity will be determined solely by dispassionate reason.

6. Logical reasoning.

7. I.e., the habit of logical analysis perverted his way of perceiving the natural world.

Oh Soul of Nature, excellent and fair!
That didst rejoice with me, with whom I too
95 Rejoiced, through early Youth, before the winds
And roaring waters, and in lights and shades
That marched and countermarched about the hills
In glorious apparition, powers on whom
I daily waited, now all eye and now
100 All ear; but never long without the heart
Employed, and Man's unfolding intellect!
Oh Soul of Nature! that, by laws divine
Sustained and governed, still dost overflow
With an impassioned life, what feeble ones
105 Walk on this earth! how feeble have I been
When thou wert in thy strength! Nor this through stroke
Of human suffering, such as justifies
Remissness and inaptitude of mind,
But through presumption;[8] even in pleasure pleased
110 Unworthily, disliking here, and there
Liking; by rules of mimic Art transferred
To things above all Art; but more,—for this,
Although a strong infection of the age,
Was never much my habit—giving way
115 To a comparison of scene with scene,
Bent overmuch on superficial things,
Pampering myself with meagre novelties
Of colour and proportion, to the moods
Of time and season, to the moral power,
120 The affections and the spirit of the Place,
Insensible.[9] Nor only did the love
Of sitting thus in judgment interrupt
My deeper feelings, but another cause,
More subtile and less easily explained,
125 That almost seems inherent in the Creature,
A twofold frame of body and of mind.
I speak in recollection of a time
When the bodily eye, in every stage of life
The most despotic of our senses, gained
130 Such strength in *me* as often held my mind
In absolute dominion. Gladly here,
Entering upon abstruser Argument,
Could I endeavour to unfold the means
Which Nature studiously employs to thwart
135 This tyranny, summons all the senses each
To counteract the other, and themselves,
And makes them all, and the Objects with which all
Are conversant, subservient in their turn

---

8. Presumptuousness, arrogance.
9. Unresponsive. Wordsworth has described his temporary participation in the cult of the picturesque—i.e., judging a natural scene by criteria derived from the "Art" of landscape painting (lines 111–12)—and then his acquired tendency to judge the comparative value of natural scenes by superficial, purely aesthetic criteria (lines 115–18).

To the great ends of Liberty and Power.[1]
140 But leave we this: enough that my delights
(Such as they were) were sought insatiably.
Vivid the transport, vivid, though not profound;
I roamed from hill to hill, from rock to rock,
Still craving combinations of new forms,
145 New pleasure, wider empire for the sight,
Proud of her own endowments, and rejoiced
To lay the inner faculties asleep.
Amid the turns and counterturns, the strife
And various trials of our complex being,
150 As we grow up, such thraldom of that sense[2]
Seems hard to shun. And yet I knew a Maid,
A young Enthusiast, who escaped these bonds;[3]
Her eye was not the Mistress of her heart;
Far less did rules prescribed by passive taste
155 Or barren intermeddling subtleties
Perplex her mind; but, wise as women are
When genial circumstance[4] hath favoured them,
She welcomed what was given and craved no more;
Whate'er the scene presented to her view,
160 That was the best, to that she was attuned
By her benign simplicity of life
And through a perfect happiness of Soul
Whose variegated feelings were in this
Sisters, that they were each some new delight.
165 Birds in the bower, and lambs in the green field,
Could they have known her, would have loved; methought
Her very presence such a sweetness breathed
That flowers, and trees, and even the silent hills,
And every thing she looked on should have had
170 An intimation how she bore herself
Towards them and to all creatures. God delights
In such a being; for her common thoughts
Are piety, her life is gratitude.
      Even like this Maid, before I was called forth
175 From the retirement of my native hills,
I loved whate'er I saw: nor lightly loved,
But most intensely; never dreamt of aught
More grand, more fair, more exquisitely framed
Than those few nooks to which my happy feet
180 Were limited. I had not at that time
Lived long enough, nor in the least survived
The first diviner influence of this world
As it appears to unaccustomed eyes.
Worshipping then among the depth of things
185 As piety ordained,[5] could I submit

---

1. I.e., the ways in which Nature uses an individual's other senses to counteract the tyranny of the eye—as well as the tyranny of any other single sense—so as to make all the senses (and the external objects they enable us to perceive) subordinate to the free, creative power of the human mind. Later in this book Wordsworth attributes this power of free creativity to the imagination.
2. I.e., subservience to the sense of sight.
3. Mary Hutchinson, whom Wordsworth had known since childhood and whom he married in 1802.
4. Beneficent conditions (of a woman's life).
5. In the 1805 text: "As my soul bade me."

To measured admiration, or to aught
That should preclude humility and love?
I felt, observed, and pondered; did not judge,
Yea, never thought of judging; with the gift
190 Of all this glory filled and satisfied.
And afterwards, when through the gorgeous Alps
Roaming, I carried with me the same heart:[6]
In truth, the degradation,[7] howsoe'er
Induced, effect in whatsoe'er degree
195 Of custom that prepares a partial scale
In which the little oft outweighs the great,
Or any other cause that hath been named;
Or lastly, aggravated by the times,
And their empassioned sounds,[8] which well might make
200 The milder minstrelsies of rural scenes
Inaudible, was transient; I had known
Too forcibly, too early in my life,
Visitings of imaginative power
For this to last: I shook the habit off
205 Entirely and for ever, and again
In Nature's presence stood, as now I stand,
A sensitive Being, a *creative* Soul.
      There are in our existence spots of time,[9]
That with distinct pre-eminence retain
210 A renovating virtue, whence, depressed
By false opinion and contentious thought,
Or aught of heavier or more deadly weight,
In trivial occupations, and the round
Of ordinary intercourse, our minds
215 Are nourished and invisibly repaired;
A virtue by which pleasure is inhanced,
That penetrates, enables us to mount,
When high, more high, and lifts us up when fallen.
This efficacious Spirit chiefly lurks
220 Among those passages of life that give
Profoundest knowledge how and to what point
The mind is lord and master—outward sense
The obedient Servant of her will. Such moments
Are scattered every where, taking their date
225 From our first Childhood. I remember well
That once, while yet my inexperienced hand
Could scarcely hold a bridle, with proud hopes
I mounted, and we journied towards the hills:
An ancient Servant of my Father's house
230 Was with me, my encourager and Guide.
We had not travelled long ere some mischance

---

6. In his walk across the Alps in 1790, described in book 6.

7. I.e., the deterioration (of a full, unreflective response to nature) that he has described in lines 109–51.

8. I.e., by the high passions aroused by the French Revolution. Wordsworth speculates that these may have been a contributing factor in diminishing his attention and responsiveness to the natural world.

9. Moments of experience in which something ordinary (line 254) suddenly becomes profoundly significant. Because this significance is bestowed by the perceiver, it demonstrates the freedom and creative power of the imaginative mind (lines 220–23, 275–77). The remembrance of such moments nourishes and repairs the mind in periods of depression or distraction when the imagination flags (lines 210–15).

Disjoined me from my Comrade, and, through fear
Dismounting, down the rough and stony Moor
I led my horse, and, stumbling on, at length
235 Came to a bottom,° where in former times   *valley*
A Murderer had been hung in iron chains.
The Gibbet mast[1] had mouldered down, the bones
And iron case were gone, but on the turf
Hard by, soon after that fell deed was wrought,
240 Some unknown hand had carved the Murderer's name.
The monumental Letters were inscribed
In times long past, but still from year to year,
By superstition of the neighbourhood,
The grass is cleared away, and to that hour
245 The characters were fresh and visible.
A casual glance had shewn them, and I fled,
Faultering and faint and ignorant of the road:
Then, reascending the bare common, saw
A naked Pool that lay beneath the hills,
250 The Beacon on its summit, and, more near,
A Girl who bore a Pitcher on her head,
And seemed with difficult steps to force her way
Against the blowing wind. It was in truth
An ordinary sight; but I should need
255 Colors and words that are unknown to man
To paint the visionary dreariness
Which, while I looked all round for my lost Guide,
Invested Moorland waste and naked Pool,
The Beacon crowning the lone eminence,
260 The Female and her garments vexed and tossed
By the strong wind.—When, in the blessed hours
Of early love, the loved One[2] at my side,
I roamed, in daily presence of this scene,
Upon the naked Pool and dreary Crags,
265 And on the melancholy Beacon, fell
A spirit of pleasure, and Youth's golden gleam;
And think ye not with radiance more sublime
For these remembrances, and for the power
They had left behind? So feeling comes in aid
270 Of feeling, and diversity of strength
Attends us, if but once we have been strong.
Oh! mystery of Man, from what a depth
Proceed thy honors! I am lost, but see
In simple child-hood something of the base
275 On which thy greatness stands; but this I feel,
That from thyself it comes, that thou must give,
Else never canst receive. The days gone by
Return upon me almost from the dawn
Of life: the hiding-places of Man's power
280 Open; I would approach them, but they close.
I see by glimpses now; when age comes on

---

1. The post with a projecting arm used for hanging criminals.   2. Mary Hutchinson.

May scarcely see at all, and I would give,
While yet we may, as far as words can give,
Substance and life to what I feel, enshrining,
285 Such is my hope, the spirit of the past
For future restoration.—Yet another
Of these memorials.
               One Christmas-time,[3]
On the glad Eve of its dear holidays,
Feverish, and tired, and restless, I went forth
290 Into the fields, impatient for the sight
Of those led Palfreys[4] that should bear us home,
My Brothers and myself. There rose a Crag
That, from the meeting point of two highways
Ascending, overlooked them both, far stretched;
295 Thither, uncertain on which road to fix
My expectation, thither I repaired,
Scout-like, and gained the summit; 'twas a day
Tempestuous, dark, and wild, and on the grass
I sate, half-sheltered by a naked wall;
300 Upon my right hand couched a single sheep,
Upon my left a blasted hawthorn stood:
With those Companions at my side, I sate,
Straining my eyes intensely, as the mist
Gave intermitting prospect of the copse
305 And plain beneath. Ere we to School returned
That dreary time, ere we had been ten days
Sojourners in my Father's House, he died,[5]
And I and my three Brothers, Orphans then,
Followed his Body to the Grave. The Event,
310 With all the sorrow that it brought, appeared
A chastisement; and when I called to mind
That day so lately passed, when from the Crag
I looked in such anxiety of hope,
With trite reflections of morality,
315 Yet in the deepest passion, I bowed low
To God, who thus corrected my desires;
And afterwards, the wind and sleety rain
And all the business[6] of the Elements,
The single Sheep, and the one blasted tree,
320 And the bleak music of that old stone wall,
The noise of wood and water, and the mist
That on the line of each of those two Roads
Advanced in such indisputable shapes;[7]
All these were kindred spectacles and sounds
325 To which I oft repaired, and thence would drink
As at a fountain; and on winter nights,
Down to this *very* time, when storm and rain
Beat on my roof, or haply at noon-day,
While in a grove I walk whose lofty trees,

3. In 1783. Wordsworth, aged thirteen, was at Hawkshead School with two of his brothers.
4. Small saddle horses.
5. John Wordsworth died on December 30, 1783.

William's mother had died five years earlier.
6. Busy-ness; motions.
7. I.e., shapes one did not dare question.

330   Laden with summer's thickest foliage, rock
      In a strong wind, some working of the spirit,
      Some inward agitations, thence are brought,[8]
      Whate'er their office, whether to beguile
      Thoughts over-busy in the course they took,
335   Or animate an hour of vacant ease.

From Book Thirteenth
Subject concluded

[RETURN TO "LIFE'S FAMILIAR FACE"]

      From Nature doth emotion come, and moods
      Of calmness equally are Nature's gift:
      This is her glory; these two attributes
      Are sister horns that constitute her strength.[1]
5   Hence Genius,[2] born to thrive by interchange
      Of peace and excitation, finds in her
      His best and purest friend, from her receives
      That energy by which he seeks the truth,
      From her that happy stillness of the mind
10   Which fits him to receive it, when unsought.
         Such benefit the humblest intellects
      Partake of, each in their degree: 'tis mine
      To speak of what myself have known and felt.
      Smooth task! for words find easy way, inspired
15   By gratitude and confidence in truth.
      Long time in search of knowledge did I range
      The field of human life, in heart and mind
      Benighted, but the dawn beginning now
      To reappear,[3] 'twas proved that not in vain
20   I had been taught to reverence a Power
      That is the visible quality and shape
      And image of right reason,[4] that matures
      Her processes by steadfast laws, gives birth
      To no impatient or fallacious hopes,
25   No heat of passion or excessive zeal,
      No vain conceits,—provokes to no quick turns
      Of self-applauding intellect,—but trains
      To meekness, and exalts by humble faith;[5]
      Holds up before the mind, intoxicate
30   With present objects, and the busy dance
      Of things that pass away, a temperate shew
      Of objects that endure; and by this course
      Disposes her, when over-fondly set
      On throwing off incumbrances, to seek

8. Another instance of Wordsworth's inner response to an outer breeze (cf. 1.33–38, p. 306).
1. In the Old Testament, the horn of an animal signifies power.
2. A person capable of creativity.
3. I.e., he is beginning to recover from the spiri-

tual crisis recorded in 11.293–309.
4. Wordsworth follows Milton's use of the term "right reason" to denote a human faculty that is inherently attuned to truth.
5. In the text of 1805: "but lifts / The being into magnanimity."

35   In Man, and in the frame of social life,
Whate'er there is desireable and good
Of kindred permanence, unchanged in form
And function, or through strict vicissitude
Of life and death revolving. Above all
40   Were re-established now those watchful thoughts
Which (seeing little worthy or sublime
In what the Historian's pen so much delights
To blazon, Power and Energy detached
From moral purpose) early tutored me
45   To look with feelings of fraternal love
Upon the unassuming things that hold
A silent station in this beauteous world.[6]
   Thus moderated, thus composed, I found
Once more in Man an object of delight,
50   Of pure imagination, and of love;
And, as the horizon of my mind enlarged,
Again I took the intellectual eye[7]
For my Instructor, studious more to see
Great Truths, than touch and handle little ones.
55   Knowledge was given accordingly; my trust
Became more firm in feelings that had stood
The test of such a trial; clearer far
My sense of excellence—of right and wrong:
The promise of the present time retired
60   Into its true proportions; sanguine[8] schemes,
Ambitious projects, pleased me less; I sought
For present good in life's familiar face,
And built thereon my hopes of good to come.

[DISCOVERY OF HIS POETIC SUBJECT. SALISBURY PLAIN.
SIGHT OF "A NEW WORLD"]

220   Here, calling up to mind what then I saw,[9]
A youthful Traveller, and see daily now
In the familiar circuit of my home,
Here might I pause and bend in reverence
To Nature, and the power of human minds,
225   To Men as they are Men within themselves.
How oft high service is performed within,
When all the external Man is rude in shew!
Not like a Temple rich with pomp and gold,

6. Here Wordsworth begins his account of how he came to feel bonds to, and to love, the silent, lowly, common things whose celebration he considers to be his special vocation as an innovative poet-prophet (see lines 301–08).
7. Perception by the integral mind.
8. Optimistic. Wordsworth apparently refers back to his earlier "ambitious projects" for a long poem, described in 1.166–220, as well as to the optimistic schemes for humankind that had been engendered by his commitment to the French Revolution.
9. Wordsworth has described, as part of his imaginative recovery, his learning to look again with

sympathy upon "the unassuming things that hold / A silent station in this beauteous world" (lines 46–47) and his finding again "in Man an object of delight" (line 49). Now he shows how, in reaction against his concern with great actions detached from moral purpose that constituted the French Revolution, he came to embrace the poetic doctrines of the Preface to Lyrical Ballads. That is, he will write of simple, lowly people, whose patient endurance of suffering redounds to the glory of humankind and who speak a language that is the spontaneous overflow of powerful feelings (lines 263–64).

But a mere mountain Chapel that protects
230 Its simple Worshippers from sun and shower.
Of these, said I, shall be my song, of these,
If future years mature me for the task,
Will I record the praises, making Verse
Deal boldly with substantial things; in truth
235 And sanctity of passion speak of these,
That justice may be done, obeisance paid
Where it is due: thus haply shall I teach,
Inspire, through unadulterated° ears   uncorrupted
Pour rapture, tenderness, and hope, my theme
240 No other than the very heart of Man
As found among the best of those who live
Not unexalted by religious faith,
Nor uninformed by Books, good books, though few,
In Nature's presence: thence may I select
245 Sorrow, that is not sorrow, but delight,
And miserable love that is not pain
To hear of, for the glory that redounds
Therefrom to human kind and what we are.
Be mine to follow with no timid step
250 Where knowledge leads me; it shall be my pride
That I have dared to tread this holy ground,
Speaking no dream, but things oracular,
Matter not lightly to be heard by those
Who to the letter of the outward promise
255 Do read the invisible Soul,[1] by Men adroit
In speech, and for communion with the world
Accomplished, minds whose faculties are then
Most active when they are most eloquent,
And elevated most, when most admired.
260 Men may be found of other mold than these,
Who are their own Upholders, to themselves
Encouragement, and energy, and will,
Expressing liveliest thoughts in lively words
As native passion dictates.[2] Others, too,
265 There are, among the walks of homely life,
Still higher, men for contemplation framed,
Shy, and unpractised in the strife of phrase,[3]
Meek men, whose very souls perhaps would sink
Beneath them, summoned to such intercourse:
270 Theirs is the language of the heavens, the power,
The thought, the image, and the silent joy;
Words are but under-agents in their Souls;
When they are grasping with their greatest strength
They do not breathe among them;[4] this I speak
275 In gratitude to God, who feeds our hearts

1. I.e., this doctrine will not be lightly accepted by those who judge inner worth by exterior seeming.
2. In his Preface to *Lyrical Ballads* of 1800, Wordsworth said that he chose characters from low and rustic life because in them "the essential passions of the heart . . . are less under restraint, and speak a plainer and more emphatic language."
3. The rhetoric of controversy.
4. I.e., even in the greatest strength of their intuitive grasp, they do not utter words, which (line 272) are for them merely subsidiary to the fullness of their response to an experience.

For his own service; knoweth, loveth us
When we are unregarded by the world.
　　Also, about this time did I receive
Convictions still more strong than heretofore
280　Not only that the inner frame is good,
And graciously composed, but that, no less,
Nature for all conditions wants not power
To consecrate, if we have eyes to see,
The outside of her Creatures, and to breathe
285　Grandeur upon the very humblest face
Of human life. I felt that the array
Of act and circumstance, and visible form,
Is mainly, to the pleasure of the mind,
What passion makes them, that meanwhile the forms
290　Of Nature have a passion in themselves
That intermingles with those works of man
To which she summons him; although the works
Be mean, have nothing lofty of their own;
And that the Genius of the Poet hence
295　May boldly take his way among mankind
Wherever Nature leads, that he hath stood
By Nature's side among the Men of old,
And so shall stand for ever. Dearest Friend,
If thou partake the animating faith
300　That Poets, even as Prophets, each with each
Connected in a mighty scheme of truth,
Have each his own peculiar faculty,
Heaven's gift, a sense that fits him to perceive
Objects unseen before, thou wilt not blame
305　The humblest of this band[5] who dares to hope
That unto him hath also been vouchsafed
An insight, that in some sort he possesses
A Privilege, whereby a Work of his,
Proceeding from a source of untaught things,
310　Creative and enduring, may become
A Power like one of Nature's. To a hope
Not less ambitious once among the Wilds
Of Sarum's Plain[6] my youthful Spirit was raised;
There, as I ranged at will the pastoral downs[7]
315　Trackless and smooth, or paced the bare white roads
Lengthening in solitude their dreary line,
Time with his retinue of ages fled
Backwards, nor checked his flight until I saw
Our dim Ancestral Past in Vision clear;[8]
320　Saw multitudes of men, and here and there
A single Briton clothed in Wolf-skin vest,
With shield and stone-axe, stride across the wold;[9]

5. Wordsworth himself.
6. Salisbury Plain, which Wordsworth crossed alone on foot in the summer of 1793.
7. Open hills used to pasture sheep.
8. Wordsworth shared the common, but mistaken, belief of his time that Stonehenge, the giant meg-

alithic structure on Salisbury Plain, had been a temple of the Celtic priests, the Druids, and that the Druids had there performed the rite of human sacrifice; hence the imaginings and vision that he goes on to relate.
9. High open country.

The voice of Spears was heard, the rattling spear
Shaken by arms of mighty bone, in strength,
325 Long mouldered, of barbaric majesty.
I called on Darkness—but before the word
Was uttered, midnight darkness seemed to take
All objects from my sight; and lo! again
The Desart visible by dismal flames;
330 It is the Sacrificial Altar, fed
With living Men—how deep the groans! the voice
Of those that crowd the giant wicker thrills
The monumental hillocks,[1] and the pomp
Is for both worlds, the living and the dead.
335 At other moments (for through that wide waste
Three summer days I roamed) where'er the Plain
Was figured o'er with circles, lines, or mounds,
That yet survive, a work, as some divine,[2]
Shaped by the Druids, so to represent
340 Their knowledge of the heavens, and image forth
The constellations; gently was I charmed
Into a waking dream, a reverie
That with believing eyes, where'er I turned,
Beheld long-bearded Teachers with white wands
345 Uplifted, pointing to the starry sky
Alternately, and Plain below, while breath
Of music swayed their motions, and the Waste
Rejoiced with them and me in those sweet Sounds.
        This for the past, and things that may be viewed
350 Or fancied, in the obscurity of years
From monumental hints:[3] and thou, O Friend!
Pleased with some unpremeditated strains
That served those wanderings to beguile, hast said
That then and there my mind had exercised
355 Upon the vulgar forms of present things,
The actual world of our familiar days,
Yet higher power, had caught from them a tone,
An image, and a character, by books
Not hitherto reflected.[4] Call we this
360 A partial judgement—and yet why? for *then*
We were as Strangers;[5] and I may not speak
Thus wrongfully of verse, however rude,
Which on thy young imagination, trained
In the great City, broke like light from far.

1. The many bronze age burial mounds on Salisbury Plain. "Giant wicker": Aylett Sammes, in *Britannia Antiqua Illustrata* (1676), had described, as a rite of the ancient Britons, that they wove a huge wicker structure in the shape of a man, filled it with living humans, and set it afire.
2. Conjecture (a verb).
3. I.e., from what the monumental remains on Salisbury Plain suggested to him.
4. Wordsworth refers to an event that Coleridge narrates in *Biographia Literaria*, chap. 4. In November 1795 Wordsworth had read to Coleridge a manuscript version of his poem *Adventures on Salisbury Plain*. What impressed Coleridge, as he tells us, was Wordsworth's "fine balance of truth in observing with the imaginative faculty in modifying the objects observed, and above all, the original gift of spreading . . . the depth and height of the ideal world, around forms, incidents, and situations of which, for the common view, custom had bedimmed all the luster." "This," Coleridge concludes, "is the character and privilege of genius."
5. Though Coleridge and Wordsworth had met in September 1795, they did not become close friends until 1797. "Partial": biased (in Wordsworth's favor).

365 Moreover, each man's mind is to herself
Witness and judge; and I remember well
That in Life's every-day appearances
I seemed about this time to gain clear sight
Of a new world, a world, too, that was fit
370 To be transmitted and to other eyes
Made visible, as ruled by those fixed laws
Whence spiritual dignity originates,
Which do both give it being and maintain
A balance, an ennobling interchange
375 Of action from without, and from within;
The excellence, pure function, and best power
Both of the object seen, and eye that sees.

From Book Fourteenth
Conclusion

[THE VISION ON MOUNT SNOWDON. FEAR VS. LOVE RESOLVED.
IMAGINATION]

In one of those Excursions (may they ne'er
Fade from remembrance!), through the Northern tracts
Of Cambria ranging with a youthful Friend,
I left Bethgellert's huts at couching-time,
5 And westward took my way, to see the sun
Rise from the top of Snowdon.[1] To the door
Of a rude Cottage at the Mountain's base
We came, and rouzed the Shepherd who attends
The adventurous Stranger's steps, a trusty Guide;
10 Then, cheered by short refreshment, sallied forth.
—It was a close, warm, breezeless summer night,
Wan, dull, and glaring,[2] with a dripping fog
Low-hung and thick, that covered all the sky.
But, undiscouraged, we began to climb
15 The mountain-side. The mist soon girt us round,
And, after ordinary Travellers' talk
With our Conductor, pensively we sank
Each into commerce with his private thoughts:
Thus did we breast the ascent, and by myself
20 Was nothing either seen or heard that checked
Those musings or diverted, save that once
The Shepherd's Lurcher,[3] who, among the crags,
Had to his joy unearthed a Hedgehog, teased
His coiled-up Prey with barkings turbulent.
25 This small adventure, for even such it seemed

---

1. Wordsworth climbed Mount Snowdon—the highest peak in Wales ("Cambria"), and some ten miles from the sea—with Robert Jones, the friend with whom he had also tramped through the Alps (book 6). The climb started from the village of Bethgelert at "couching-time" (line 4), the time of night when the sheep lie down to sleep. This event had taken place in 1791 (or possibly 1793); Wordsworth presents it out of its chronological order to introduce at this point a great natural "type" or "emblem" (lines 66, 70) for the mind, and especially for the activity of the imagination, whose "restoration" he has described in the two preceding books.
2. In north of England dialect, *glairie,* applied to the weather, means dull, rainy.
3. A crossbred dog used to hunt hares.

In that wild place, and at the dead of night,
Being over and forgotten, on we wound
In silence as before. With forehead bent
Earthward, as if in opposition set
30 Against an enemy, I panted up
With eager pace, and no less eager thoughts.
Thus might we wear a midnight hour away,
Ascending at loose distance each from each,
And I, as chanced, the foremost of the Band:
35 When at my feet the ground appeared to brighten,
And with a step or two seemed brighter still;
Nor was time given to ask, or learn, the cause;
For instantly a light upon the turf
Fell like a flash; and lo! as I looked up,
40 The Moon hung naked in a firmament
Of azure without cloud, and at my feet
Rested a silent sea of hoary mist.
A hundred hills their dusky backs upheaved
All over this still Ocean;[4] and beyond,
45 Far, far beyond, the solid vapours stretched,
In Headlands, tongues, and promontory shapes,
Into the main Atlantic, that appeared
To dwindle, and give up his majesty,
Usurped upon far as the sight could reach.
50 Not so the ethereal Vault; encroachment none
Was there, nor loss;[5] only the inferior stars
Had disappeared, or shed a fainter light
In the clear presence of the full-orbed Moon;
Who, from her sovereign elevation, gazed
55 Upon the billowy ocean, as it lay
All meek and silent, save that through a rift
Not distant from the shore whereon we stood,
A fixed, abysmal, gloomy breathing-place,
Mounted the roar of waters—torrents—streams
60 Innumerable, roaring with one voice!
Heard over earth and sea, and in that hour,
For so it seemed, felt by the starry heavens.
    When into air had partially dissolved
That Vision, given to Spirits of the night,
65 And three chance human Wanderers, in calm thought
Reflected, it appeared to me the type
Of a majestic Intellect, its acts
And its possessions, what it has and craves,
What in itself it is, and would become.
70 There I beheld the emblem of a Mind
That feeds upon infinity, that broods
Over the dark abyss, intent to hear
Its voices issuing forth to silent light
In one continuous stream; a mind sustained

4. In Milton's description of the creation of the world, "the mountains huge appear / Emergent, and their broad bare backs upheave / Into the clouds" (*Paradise Lost* 7.285–87).

5. The mist projected in various shapes over the Atlantic Ocean, but did not "encroach" on the heavens overhead.

75   By recognitions of transcendent power
    In sense, conducting to ideal form;
    In soul, of more than mortal privilege.[6]
    One function, above all, of such a mind
    Had Nature shadowed there, by putting forth,
80   'Mid circumstances awful and sublime,
    That mutual domination which she loves
    To exert upon the face of outward things,
    So moulded, joined, abstracted; so endowed
    With interchangeable supremacy,
85   That Men least sensitive see, hear, perceive,
    And cannot chuse but feel. The power which all
    Acknowledge when thus moved, which Nature thus
    To bodily sense exhibits, is the express
    Resemblance of that glorious faculty
90   That higher minds bear with them as their own.[7]
    This is the very spirit in which they deal
    With the whole compass of the universe:
    They, from their native selves, can send abroad
    Kindred mutations; for themselves create
95   A like existence; and whene'er it dawns
    Created for them, catch it;—or are caught
    By its inevitable mastery,
    Like angels stopped upon the wing by sound
    Of harmony from heaven's remotest spheres.
100   Them the enduring and the transient both
    Serve to exalt; they build up greatest things
    From least suggestions; ever on the watch,
    Willing to work and to be wrought upon,
    They need not extraordinary calls
105   To rouse them, in a world of life they live;
    By sensible impressions not enthralled,
    But, by their quickening impulse, made more prompt
    To hold fit converse with the spiritual world,
    And with the generations of mankind
110   Spread over time, past, present, and to come,
    Age after age, till Time shall be no more.
    Such minds are truly from the Deity,
    For they are powers; and hence the highest bliss
    That flesh can know is theirs,—the consciousness
115   Of whom they are, habitually infused
    Through every image, and through every thought,
    And all affections° by communion raised   *emotions*
    From earth to heaven, from human to divine.
    Hence endless occupation for the Soul,
120   Whether discursive or intuitive;[8]

6. The sense of lines 74–77 seems to be that the mind of someone who is gifted beyond the ordinary lot of mortals recognizes its power to transcend the senses by converting sensory objects into ideal forms.
7. The "glorious faculty" is the imagination, which in its exhibition of mastery over sense—through its power to alter and re-create what is given to it in perception (lines 93–105)—is analogous to that aspect of the outer scene in which the ordinary landscape is transfigured by the moonlit mist. Cf. the mind as "lord and master" of outward sense in 12.219–23 (p. 369).
8. An echo of *Paradise Lost* 5.488. The "discursive" reason undertakes to reach truths through a logical sequence of premises, observations, and conclusions; the "intuitive" reason comprehends truths immediately.

Hence chearfulness for acts of daily life,
Emotions which best foresight need not fear,
Most worthy then of trust when most intense:
Hence, amid ills that vex, and wrongs that crush
125 Our hearts, if here the words of holy Writ
May with fit reverence be applied, that peace
Which passeth understanding,[9]—that repose
In moral judgements which from this pure source
Must come, or will by Man be sought in vain.
130   Oh! who is he that hath his whole life long
Preserved, enlarged, this freedom in himself?
For this alone is genuine Liberty.
Where is the favoured Being who hath held
That course, unchecked, unerring, and untired,
135 In one perpetual progress smooth and bright?
—A humbler destiny have we retraced,
And told of lapse and hesitating choice,
And backward wanderings along thorny ways:
Yet, compassed round by Mountain Solitudes
140 Within whose solemn temple I received
My earliest visitations, careless then
Of what was given me; and which now I range
A meditative, oft a suffering Man,
Do I declare, in accents which, from truth
145 Deriving chearful confidence, shall blend
Their modulation with these vocal streams,
That, whatsoever falls my better mind
Revolving[1] with the accidents of life
May have sustained, that, howsoe'er misled,
150 Never did I, in quest of right and wrong,
Tamper with conscience from a private aim;
Nor was in any public hope the dupe
Of selfish passions; nor did ever yield,
Wilfully, to mean cares or low pursuits;
155 But shrunk with apprehensive jealousy
From every combination which might aid
The tendency, too potent in itself,
Of use and custom to bow down the Soul
Under a growing weight of vulgar sense,
160 And substitute a universe of death[2]
For that which moves with light and life informed,
Actual, divine, and true. To fear and love,
To love as prime and chief, for there fear ends,
Be this ascribed; to early intercourse
165 In presence of sublime or beautiful forms
With the adverse principles of pain and joy—
Evil, as one is rashly named by men
Who know not what they speak. By love subsists

9. Philippians 4.7: "The peace of God, which passeth all understanding." This passage of Christian
piety was added by Wordsworth in a late revision.
1. Allusion to the ancient concept of fortune's

revolving wheel.
2. Milton's description of hell in *Paradise Lost*
2.622–23: "A universe of death, which God by
curse / Created evil."

All lasting grandeur, by pervading love;
170 That gone, we are as dust.[3]—Behold the fields
In balmy spring-time full of rising flowers
And joyous Creatures; see that Pair, the lamb
And the lamb's Mother, and their tender ways
Shall touch thee to the heart; thou callest this love,
175 And not inaptly so, for love it is,
Far as it carries thee. In some green Bower
Rest, and be not alone, but have thou there
The One who is thy choice of all the world:
There linger, listening, gazing with delight
180 Impassioned, but delight how pitiable!
Unless this love by a still higher love
Be hallowed, love that breathes not without awe;
Love that adores, but on the knees of prayer,
By heaven inspired; that frees from chains the soul,
185 Bearing in union with the purest, best
Of earth-born passions, on the wings of praise,
A mutual tribute to the Almighty's Throne.[4]
    This spiritual love acts not, nor can exist
Without Imagination, which in truth
190 Is but another name for absolute power
And clearest insight, amplitude of mind,
And reason, in her most exalted mood.
This faculty hath been the feeding source
Of our long labor: we have traced the stream
195 From the blind cavern whence is faintly heard
Its natal murmur; followed it to light
And open day; accompanied its course
Among the ways of Nature; for a time
Lost sight of it, bewildered and engulphed;
200 Then given it greeting as it rose once more
In strength, reflecting from its placid breast
The works of man, and face of human life;
And lastly, from its progress have we drawn
Faith in life endless, the sustaining thought
205 Of human being, Eternity, and God.[5]
—Imagination having been our theme,
So also hath that intellectual love,
For they are each in each, and cannot stand
Dividually.°—Here must thou be, O Man!   *separately*
210 Power to thyself; no Helper hast thou here;

---

3. Wordsworth's mind, he had said early in *The Prelude*, had been "fostered alike by beauty and by fear" (1.302 and n. 3, p. 312); that is, by the opposing but equally necessary principles of the beautiful and the terrifying, or "sublime," aspects of nature. Now, in his conclusion, the principles of fear and pain are said to be mistakenly equated with "evil," and to be ultimately transcended by their "adverse principles" of love and joy. This passage is equivalent to the theodicy of *Paradise Lost*, in which Milton justifies evil and pain ("the ways of God to men," 1.26) by reference to the fall and redemption; Wordsworth, however, translates this into a natural theodicy of the interaction of man's mind with the external world (cf. the Prospectus to *The Recluse*, lines 8–9 and n. 1, p. 301).

4. In place of lines 182–87, the text of 1805 has: "a love that comes into the heart / With awe and a diffusive sentiment. / Thy love is human merely: this proceeds / More from the brooding soul, and is divine."

5. The 1805 version reads: "The feeling of life endless, the great thought / By which we live, Infinity and God."

Here keepest thou in singleness thy state;
No other can divide with thee this work;
No secondary hand can intervene
To fashion this ability; 'tis thine,
215   The prime and vital principle is thine
In the recesses of thy nature, far
From any reach of outward fellowship,
Else is not thine at all. * * *

[CONCLUSION: "THE MIND OF MAN"]

And now, O Friend![6] this History is brought
To its appointed close: the discipline
And consummation of a Poet's mind
305   In every thing that stood most prominent
Have faithfully been pictured; we have reached
The time (our guiding object from the first)
When we may, not presumptuously, I hope,
Suppose my powers so far confirmed, and such
310   My knowledge, as to make me capable
Of building up a Work that shall endure.

* * * Having now
Told what best merits mention, further pains
Our present purpose seems not to require,
And I have other tasks. Recall to mind
375   The mood in which this labour was begun.
O Friend! the termination of my course
Is nearer now, much nearer; yet even then,
In that distraction, and intense desire,
I said unto the life which I had lived,
380   Where art thou? Hear I not a voice from thee
Which 'tis reproach to hear?[7] Anon I rose
As if on wings, and saw beneath me stretched
Vast prospect of the world which I had been
And was; and hence this Song, which like a Lark
385   I have protracted, in the unwearied heavens
Singing, and often with more plaintive voice
To earth attempered and her deep-drawn sighs,
Yet centering all in love, and in the end
All gratulant,° if rightly understood.[8]   *congratulatory*

*   *   *

Oh! yet a few short years of useful life,
And all will be complete, thy[9] race be run,

---

6. Coleridge.
7. As he approaches the end, Wordsworth recalls the beginning of *The Prelude*. The reproachful voice is that which asked the question, "Was it for this?" in 1.269ff. This query called forth a vision of his remembered life, which he proceeded to explore in search of both the sources of his poetic powers and the impediments to their fulfillment. The "Song" (line 384) describing this quest, which

he then began, is the poem he is now completing.
8. The poet finds that suffering and frustration are justified, when seen as part of the overall design of the life he has just reviewed. The passage echoes the conclusion of Pope's theodicy (the justification of evil) in *An Essay on Man* 1.291–92: "All discord, harmony not understood; / All partial evil, universal good."
9. Coleridge's.

Thy monument of glory will be raised;
435 Then, though, too weak to tread the ways of truth,
This Age fall back to old idolatry,
Though Men return to servitude as fast
As the tide ebbs, to ignominy and shame
By Nations sink together,[1] we shall still
440 Find solace—knowing what we have learnt to know,
Rich in true happiness if allowed to be
Faithful alike in forwarding a day
Of firmer trust, joint laborers in the Work
(Should Providence such grace to us vouchsafe)
445 Of their deliverance,[2] surely yet to come.
Prophets of Nature, we to them will speak
A lasting inspiration, sanctified
By reason, blest by faith: what we have loved
Others will love, and we will teach them how,
450 Instruct them how the mind of Man becomes
A thousand times more beautiful than the earth
On which he dwells, above this Frame of things
(Which 'mid all revolutions in the hopes
And fears of Men doth still remain unchanged)
455 In beauty exalted, as it is itself
Of quality and fabric more divine.[3]

1798–1839   1850

1. I.e., though men—whole nations of them together—sink to ignominy and shame.
2. In the 1805 text: "redemption." Wordsworth reaffirms his belief in a millennial outcome of human history, though he now bases that belief not on political "revolutions" (cf. line 453) but on a revolution in the mind of man.
3. Cf. Wordsworth's assertion that "the Mind of Man" is "My haunt, and the main region of my song" in the Prospectus to The Recluse, lines 40–41 (p. 302).

DOROTHY WORDSWORTH
1771–1855

Dorothy Wordsworth has an enduring place in English literature even though she wrote almost no word for publication. Not until long after her death did scholars gradually retrieve and print her letters, a few poems, and a series of journals that she kept sporadically between 1798 and 1828 because, she wrote, "I shall give William Pleasure by it." It has always been known, from tributes to her by her brother and Coleridge, that she exerted an important influence on the lives and writings of both these men. It is now apparent that she also possessed a power surpassing that of the two poets for precise observation of people and the natural world, together with a genius for terse, luminous, and delicately nuanced description in prose. Her hastily scribbled journals are an incomparable record of what Coleridge, in Frost at Midnight, called "all the numberless goings-on of life" in "sea, hill, and wood" as well as in the "populous village," noted by one who lived her life among rural folk.

Dorothy was born on Christmas Day 1771, twenty-one months after William; she was the only girl of five Wordsworth children. From her seventh year, when her mother died, she lived with various relatives—some of them tolerant and affectionate, others rigid and tyrannical—and saw William and her other brothers only occasionally, during the boys' summer vacations from school. In 1795, when she was twenty-four, the bequest to William by Raisley Calvert enabled her to carry out a long-held plan to join her brother in a house at Racedown, and the two spent the rest of their long lives together, first in Dorsetshire and Somersetshire, in the southwest of England, then in their beloved Lake District. She uncomplainingly subordinated her own talents to looking after her brother and his household.

All her adult life she was overworked and troubled by a variety of ailments. Suddenly, after a severe illness in 1835, she suffered a physical and mental collapse. She spent the rest of her existence as an invalid. Hardest for her family to endure was the drastic change in her temperament: from a high-spirited and compassionate woman she became (save for brief intervals of lucidity) querulous, demanding, and at times violent. In this half-life she lingered for twenty years, attended devotedly by William until his death five years before her own in 1855.

Our principal selections are from the journal Dorothy kept in 1798 at Alfoxden, Somersetshire, where the Wordsworths had moved from Racedown to be near Coleridge at Nether Stowey, as well as from her journals while at Grasmere (1800–03), with Coleridge residing some thirteen miles away at Greta Hall, Keswick. Her records cover the period when both men emerged as major poets, and in their achievements Dorothy played an indispensable role. In book 11 of *The Prelude* William says that, in the time of his spiritual crisis, Dorothy "maintained for me a saving intercourse / With my true self" and "preserved me still / A Poet"; and in a letter of 1797 Coleridge stressed the delicacy and tact in the responses of William's "exquisite sister" to the world of sense: "Her manners are simple, ardent, impressive. . . . Her information various—her eye watchful in minutest observation of nature—and her taste a perfect electrometer—it bends, protrudes, and draws in, at subtlest beauties & most recondite faults."

The passages from her journals reprinted below include many verbal sketches of natural appearances that recur in Wordsworth's and Coleridge's poems. Of at least equal importance for Wordsworth was her chronicling of the busy wayfaring life of rural England. These were exceedingly hard times for country people, when the suffering caused by the displacement of small farms and of household crafts by large-scale farms and industries was aggravated by the economic distress caused by protracted Continental wars (see Wordsworth's comment in *The Ruined Cottage*, lines 133ff., p. 262). Peddlers, maimed war veterans, leech gatherers, adult and infant beggars, ousted farm families, fugitives, and women abandoned by husbands or lovers streamed along the rural roads and into William's brooding poetic imagination—often by way of Dorothy's prose records.

The journals also show the intensity of Dorothy's love for her brother. Inevitably in our era, the mutual devotion of the orphaned brother and sister has evoked psychoanalytic speculation. It is important to note that Mary Hutchinson, a gentle and open-hearted young woman, had been Dorothy's closest friend ever since childhood, and that Dorothy encouraged William's courtship and marriage, even though she realized that it entailed her own displacement as a focus of her brother's life. All the evidence indicates that their lives in a single household never strained the affectionate relationship between the two women; indeed Dorothy, until she became an invalid, added to her former functions as William's chief support, housekeeper, and scribe a loving ministration to her brother's children.

Because the manuscript of the Alfoxden journal has disappeared, the text printed here is from the transcript published by William Knight in 1897. The selections from the Grasmere journals reproduce Pamela Woof's exact transcription of the manuscripts in the Wordsworth Library at Dove Cottage (Oxford University Press, 1991). Dorothy Wordsworth's poems, written mainly for children in her brother's household and surviving as manuscripts in one or another family commonplace book, were not collected until 1987, when Susan M. Levin edited thirty of them in an appendix ("The Collected Poems of Dorothy Wordsworth") to her *Dorothy Wordsworth and Romanticism*. The two poems included here are reprinted from this source.

From The Alfoxden Journal

Jan. 31, 1798. Set forward to Stowey[1] at half-past five. A violent storm in the wood; sheltered under the hollies. When we left home the moon immensely large, the sky scattered over with clouds. These soon closed in, contracting the dimensions of the moon without concealing her.[2] The sound of the pattering shower, and the gusts of wind, very grand. Left the wood when nothing remained of the storm but the driving wind, and a few scattering drops of rain. Presently all clear, Venus first showing herself between the struggling clouds; afterwards Jupiter appeared. The hawthorn hedges, black and pointed, glittering with millions of diamond drops; the hollies shining with broader patches of light. The road to the village of Holford glittered like another stream. On our return, the wind high—a violent storm of hail and rain at the Castle of Comfort.[3] All the Heavens seemed in one perpetual motion when the rain ceased; the moon appearing, now half veiled, and now retired behind heavy clouds, the stars still moving, the roads very dirty.

*   *   *

Feb. 3. A mild morning, the windows open at breakfast, the redbreasts singing in the garden. Walked with Coleridge over the hills. The sea at first obscured by vapour; that vapour afterwards slid in one mighty mass along the sea-shore; the islands and one point of land clear beyond it. The distant country (which was purple in the clear dull air), overhung by straggling clouds that sailed over it, appeared like the darker clouds, which are often seen at a great distance apparently motionless, while the nearer ones pass quickly over them, driven by the lower winds. I never saw such a union of earth, sky, and sea. The clouds beneath our feet spread themselves to the water, and the clouds of the sky almost joined them. Gathered sticks in the wood; a perfect stillness. The redbreasts sang upon the leafless boughs. Of a great number of sheep in the field, only one standing. Returned to dinner at five o'clock. The moonlight still and warm as a summer's night at nine o'clock.

Feb. 4. Walked a great part of the way to Stowey with Coleridge. The morning warm and sunny. The young lasses seen on the hill-tops, in the villages and roads, in their summer holiday clothes—pink petticoats and blue. Mothers with their children in arms, and the little ones that could just walk, tottering by their side. Midges or small flies spinning in the sunshine; the songs of the lark and redbreast; daisies upon the turf; the hazels in blossom; honeysuckles budding. I saw one solitary strawberry flower under a

1. Coleridge's cottage at Nether Stowey, three miles from Alfoxden.
2. Cf. Coleridge's *Christabel,* lines 16–19

(p. 442).
3. A tavern halfway between Holford and Nether Stowey.

hedge. The furze gay with blossom. The moss rubbed from the pailings by the sheep, that leave locks of wool, and the red marks with which they are spotted, upon the wood.[4]

* * *

Feb. 8. Went up the Park, and over the tops of the hills, till we came to a new and very delicious pathway, which conducted us to the Coombe.[5] Sat a considerable time upon the heath. Its surface restless and glittering with the motion of the scattered piles of withered grass, and the waving of the spiders' threads.[6] On our return the mist still hanging over the sea, but the opposite coast clear, and the rocky cliffs distinguishable. In the deep Coombe, as we stood upon the sunless hill, we saw miles of grass, light and glittering, and the insects passing.

Feb. 9. William gathered sticks.

Feb. 10. Walked to Woodlands, and to the waterfall. The adder's-tongue and the ferns green in the low damp dell. These plants now in perpetual motion from the current of the air; in summer only moved by the drippings of the rocks.[7] A cloudy day.

* * *

Mar. 7. William and I drank tea at Coleridge's. A cloudy sky. Observed nothing particularly interesting—the distant prospect obscured. One only leaf upon the top of a tree—the sole remaining leaf—danced round and round like a rag blown by the wind.[8]

Mar. 8. Walked in the Park in the morning. I sate under the fir trees. Coleridge came after dinner, so we did not walk again. A foggy morning, but a clear sunny day.

Mar. 9. A clear sunny morning, went to meet Mr and Mrs Coleridge. The day very warm.

Mar. 10. Coleridge, Wm, and I walked in the evening to the top of the hill. We all passed the morning in sauntering about the park and gardens, the children playing about, the old man at the top of the hill gathering furze; interesting groups of human creatures, the young frisking and dancing in the sun, the elder quietly drinking in the life and soul of the sun and air.

Mar. 11. A cold day. The children went down towards the sea. William and I walked to the top of the hills above Holford. Met the blacksmith. Pleasant to see the labourer on Sunday jump with the friskiness of a cow upon a sunny day.

* * *

1798   1897

---

4. Cf. Wordsworth's *The Ruined Cottage*, lines 330–36 (p. 266).
5. Hodder's Coombe in the Quantock Hills, near Alfoxden. A combe is a deep valley on the flank of a hill.
6. Cf. Coleridge's *The Rime of the Ancient Mari-*

ner, line 184 (p. 427).
7. Cf. the description of the dell in Coleridge's *This Lime-Tree Bower My Prison*, lines 13–20 (p. 421).
8. Cf. *Christabel*, lines 49ff. (p. 443).

From The Grasmere Journals

1800

May 14 1800 [*Wednesday*]. Wm & John set off into Yorkshire[1] after dinner at ½ past 2 o'clock—cold pork in their pockets. I left them at the turning of the Low-wood bay under the trees. My heart was so full that I could hardly speak to W when I gave him a farewell kiss. I sate a long time upon a stone at the margin of the lake, & after a flood of tears my heart was easier. The lake looked to me I knew not why dull and melancholy, and the weltering on the shores seemed a heavy sound. I walked as long as I could amongst the stones of the shore. The wood rich in flowers. A beautiful yellow, palish yellow flower, that looked thick round & double, & smelt very sweet—I supposed it was a ranunculus—Crowfoot, the grassy-leaved Rabbit-toothed white flower, strawberries, geranium—scentless violet, anemones two kinds, orchises, primroses. The heckberry very beautiful, the crab coming out as a low shrub. Met a blind man, driving a very large beautiful Bull & a cow—he walked with two sticks. Came home by Clappersgate. The valley very green, many sweet views up to Rydale head when I could juggle away the fine houses, but they disturbed me even more than when I have been happier— one beautiful view of the Bridge, without Sir Michael's.[2] Sate down very often, tho' it was cold. I resolved to write a journal of the time till W & J return, & I set about keeping my resolve because I will not quarrel with myself, & because I shall give Wm Pleasure by it when he comes home again. At Rydale a woman of the village, stout & well-dressed, begged a halfpenny— she had never she said done it before—but these hard times!—Arrived at home with a bad head-ache, set some slips of privett. The evening cold, had a fire—my face now flame-coloured. It is nine o'clock. I shall soon go to bed. A young woman begged at the door—she had come from Manchester on Sunday morn with two shillings & a slip of paper which she supposed a Bank note—it was a cheat. She had buried her husband & three children within a year & a half—all in one grave—burying very dear—paupers all put in one place—20 shillings paid for as much ground as will bury a man—a stone to be put over it or the right will be lost—11 / 6 each time the ground is opened. Oh! that I had a letter from William!

* * *

Friday 3rd October. Very rainy all the morning—little Sally learning to mark. Wm walked to Ambleside after dinner. I went with him part of the way—he talked much about the object of his Essay for the 2nd volume of LB.[3] I returned expecting the Simpsons—they did not come. I should have met Wm but my teeth ached & it was showery & late—he returned after 10. Amos Cottle's[4] death in the Morning Post. Wrote to S. Lowthian.[5]

N.B. When Wm & I returned from accompanying Jones we met an old

1. William and his younger brother John, on the way to visit Mary Hutchinson, whom William was to marry two and a half years later.
2. Sir Michael le Fleming's estate, Rydal Hall. "Without": outside or beyond.
3. The Preface to the second edition of *Lyrical*

Ballads, 1800.
4. The brother of Joseph Cottle, Bristol publisher of the first edition of *Lyrical Ballads.*
5. Sally Lowthian, who had been a servant in the house of the Wordsworths' father.

man almost double,[6] he had on a coat thrown over his shoulders above his waistcoat & coat. Under this he carried a bundle & had an apron on & a night cap. His face was interesting. He had dark eyes & a long nose—John who afterwards met him at Wythburn took him for a Jew. He was of Scotch parents but had been born in the army. He had had a wife "& a good woman & it pleased God to bless us with ten children"—all these were dead but one of whom he had not heard for many years, a sailor—his trade was to gather leeches, but now leeches are scarce & he had not strength for it—he lived by begging & was making his way to Carlisle where he should buy a few godly books to sell. He said leeches were very scarce partly owing to this dry season, but many years they have been scarce—he supposed it owing to their being much sought after, that they did not breed fast, & were of slow growth. Leeches were formerly 2 / 6 [per] 100; they are now 30 /. He had been hurt in driving a cart his leg broke his body driven over his skull fractured—he felt no pain till he recovered from his first insensibility. It was then late in the evening—when the light was just going away.

✻ ✻ ✻

Saturday [*Oct.*] *11th.* A fine October morning—sat in the house working all the morning. Wm composing—Sally Ashburner learning to mark. After Dinner we walked up Greenhead Gill in search of a sheepfold.[7] We went by Mr Oliff's & through his woods. It was a delightful day & the views looked excessively chearful & beautiful chiefly that from Mr Oliff's field where our house is to be built. The colours of the mountains soft & rich, with orange fern—The Cattle pasturing upon the hill-tops Kites sailing as in the sky above our heads—Sheep bleating & in lines & chains & patterns scattered over the mountains. They come down & feed on the little green islands in the beds of the torrents & so may be swept away. The Sheepfold is falling away it is built nearly in the form of a heart unequally divided. Look down the brook & see the drops rise upwards & sparkle in the air, at the little falls, the higher sparkles the tallest. We walked along the turf of the mountain till we came to a Cattle track—made by the cattle which come upon the hills. We drank tea at Mr Simpson's returned at about nine—a fine mild night.

Sunday 12th October. Beautiful day. Sate in the house writing in the morning while Wm went into the Wood to compose. Wrote to John in the morning—copied poems for the LB, in the evening wrote to Mrs Rawson. Mary Jameson & Sally Ashburner dined. We pulled apples after dinner, a large basket full. We walked before tea by Bainriggs to observe the many coloured foliage the oaks dark green with yellow leaves—The birches generally still green, some near the water yellowish. The Sycamore crimson & crimson-tufted—the mountain ash a deep orange—the common ash Lemon colour but many ashes still fresh in their summer green. Those that were discoloured chiefly near the water. William composing in the Evening. Went to bed at 12 o'clock.

✻ ✻ ✻

6. William's *Resolution and Independence*, composed one and a half years later, incorporated various details of Dorothy's description of the leech gatherer. See May 4 and 7, 1802 (pp. 393 and 394), for William working on the poem he origi- nally called *The Leech Gatherer*.
7. The sheepfold in William's *Michael*; lines 1–17 of the poem describe the walk up Greenhead Ghyll.

1801

Tuesday [*Nov.*] *24th.* A rainy morning. We all were well except that my head ached a little & I took my Breakfast in bed. I read a little of Chaucer, prepared the goose for dinner, & then we all walked out—I was obliged to return for my fur tippet & Spenser[8] it was so cold. We had intended going to Easedale but we shaped our course to Mr Gell's cottage. It was very windy & we heard the wind everywhere about us as we went along the Lane but the walls sheltered us—John Green's house looked pretty under Silver How—as we were going along we were stopped at once, at the distance perhaps of 50 yards from our favorite Birch tree it was yielding to the gusty wind with all its tender twigs, the sun shone upon it & it glanced in the wind like a flying sunshiny shower—it was a tree in shape with stem & branches but it was like a Spirit of water—The sun went in & it resumed its purplish appearance the twigs still yielding to the wind but not so visibly to us. The other Birch trees that were near it looked bright & chearful—but it was a Creature by its own self among them. We could not get into Mr Gell's grounds—the old tree fallen from its undue exaltation above the Gate. A shower came on when we were at Benson's. We went through the wood—it became fair, there was a rainbow which spanned the lake from the Island house to the foot of Bainriggs. The village looked populous & beautiful. Catkins are coming out palm trees budding—the alder with its plumb coloured buds. We came home over the stepping stones the Lake was foamy with white waves. I saw a solitary butter flower in the wood. *I* found it not easy to get over the stepping stones—reached home at dinner time. Sent Peggy Ashburner some goose. She sent me some honey—with a thousand thanks—"alas the gratitude of men has & c"[9] I went in to set her right about this & sate a while with her. She talked about Thomas's having sold his land—"Ay" says she I said many a time "He's not come fra London to buy our Land however" then she told me with what pains & industry they had made up their taxes interest &c &c—how they all got up at 5 o'clock in the morning to spin & Thomas carded, & that they had paid off a hundred pound of the interest. She said she used to take such pleasure in the cattle & sheep—"O how pleased I used to be when they fetched them down, & when I had been a bit poorly I would gang out upon a hill & look over t' fields & see them & it used to do me so much good you cannot think"—Molly said to me when I came in "poor Body! she's very ill but one does not know how long she may last. Many a fair face may gang before her." We sate by the fire without work for some time then Mary read a poem of Daniell upon Learning.[1] After tea Wm read Spenser now & then a little aloud to us. We were making his waistcoat. We had a note from Mrs C., with bad news from poor C very ill. William walked to John's grove—I went to meet him—moonlight but it rained. I met him before I had got as far as John Baty's he had been surprized & terrified by a sudden rushing of winds which seemed to bring earth sky & lake together, as if the whole were going to enclose him in—he was glad he was in a high Road.

---

8. A close-fitting jacket worn by women and children.
9. A quotation from William's *Simon Lee*: "Alas! the gratitude of men / Has oft'ner left me mourning."
1. Samuel Daniel's long poem *Musophilus: Containing a General Defense of Learning* (1599).

In speaking of our walk on Sunday Evening the 22nd November I forgot to notice one most impressive sight—it was the moon & the moonlight seen through hurrying driving clouds immediately behind the Stone man upon the top of the hill on the Forest side. Every tooth & every edge of Rock was visible, & the Man stood like a Giant watching from the Roof of a lofty castle. The hill seemed perpendicular from the darkness below it. It was a sight that I could call to mind at any time it was so distinct.

* * *

1802

Thursday [Mar. 4]. Before we had quite finished Breakfast Calvert's man brought the horses for Wm.[2] We had a deal to do to shave—pens to make—poems to put in order for writing, to settle the dress pack up &c &. The man came before the pens were made & he was obliged to leave me with only two—Since he has left me (at ½ past 11) it is now 2 I have been putting the Drawers into order, laid by his clothes which we had thrown here & there & everywhere, filed two months' newspapers & got my dinner 2 boiled eggs & 2 apple tarts. I have set Molly on to clear the garden a little, & I myself have helped. I transplanted some snowdrops—The Bees are busy—Wm has a nice bright day. It was hard frost in the night—The Robins are singing sweetly—Now for my walk. I *will* be busy, I *will* look well & be well when he comes back to me. O the Darling! Here is one of his bitten apples! I can hardly find in my heart to throw it into the fire. I must wash myself, then off—I walked round the two Lakes crossed the stepping stones at Rydale Foot. Sate down where we always sit. I was full of thoughts about my darling. Blessings on him. I came home at the foot of our own hill under Loughrigg. They are making sad ravages in the woods—Benson's Wood is going & the wood above the River. The wind has blown down a small fir tree on the Rock that terminates John's path—I suppose the wind of Wednesday night. I read German after my return till tea time. After tea I worked & read the LB, enchanted with the Idiot Boy. Wrote to Wm then went to Bed. It snowed when I went to Bed.

* * *

Monday [Mar. 22]. A rainy day—William very poorly. Mr Luff came in after dinner & brought us 2 letters from Sara H. & one from poor Annette. I read Sara's letters while he was here. I finished my letters to M. & S. & wrote to my Br Richard. We talked a good deal about C. & other interesting things. We resolved to see Annette, & that Wm should go to Mary.[3] We wrote to Coleridge not to expect us till Thursday or Friday.

Tuesday [Mar. 23]. A mild morning William worked at the Cuckow poem.[4] I sewed beside him. After dinner he slept I read German, & at the closing in of day went to sit in the Orchard—he came to me, & walked backwards & forwards. We talked about C—Wm repeated the poem to me—I left him there & in 20 minutes he came in, rather tired with attempting to write—

---

2. For a journey to Keswick, to visit Coleridge.
3. It had been arranged several months earlier that William was to marry Mary Hutchinson ("Sara H" is Mary's sister, with whom Coleridge had fallen in love). Now the Wordsworths resolve to go to France to settle affairs with Annette Vallon, mother of William's daughter, Caroline. William did not conceal the facts of his early love affair from his family, or from Mary Hutchinson.
4. *To the Cuckoo.*

he is now reading Ben Jonson I am going to read German it is about 10 o'clock, a quiet night. The fire flutters & the watch ticks I hear nothing else save the Breathing of my Beloved & he now & then pushes his book forward & turns over a leaf. Fletcher is not come home. No letter from C.

* * *

Thursday [*Apr.*] *15th.* It was a threatening misty morning—but mild. We set off after dinner from Eusemere—Mrs Clarkson went a short way with us but turned back. The wind was furious & we thought we must have returned. We first rested in the large Boat-house, then under a furze Bush opposite Mr Clarksons, saw the plough going in the field. The wind seized our breath the Lake was rough. There was a Boat by itself floating in the middle of the Bay below Water Millock—We rested again in the Water Millock Lane. The hawthorns are black & green, the birches here & there greenish but there is yet more of purple to be seen on the Twigs. We got over into a field to avoid some cows—people working, a few primroses by the roadside, wood-sorrel flower, the anemone, scentless violets, strawberries, & that starry yellow flower which Mrs C calls pile wort. When we were in the woods beyond Gowbarrow park we saw a few daffodils close to the water side.[5] We fancied that the lake had floated the seeds ashore & that the little colony had so sprung up—But as we went along there were more & yet more & at last under the boughs of the trees, we saw that there was a long belt of them along the shore, about the breadth of a country turnpike road. I never saw daffodils so beautiful they grew among the mossy stones about & about them, some rested their heads upon these stones as on a pillow for weariness & the rest tossed & reeled & danced & seemed as if they verily laughed with the wind that blew upon them over the lake, they looked so gay ever glancing ever changing. This wind blew directly over the lake to them. There was here & there a little knot & a few stragglers a few yards higher up but they were so few as not to disturb the simplicity & unity & life of that one busy high-way—We rested again & again. The Bays were stormy & we heard the waves at different distances & in the middle of the water like the sea—Rain came on, we were wet when we reached Luffs but we called in. Luckily all was chearless & gloomy so we faced the storm—we *must* have been wet if we had waited—put on dry clothes at Dobson's. I was very kindly treated by a young woman, the Landlady looked sour but it is her way. She gave us a goodish supper. Excellent ham & potatoes. We paid 7 / when we came away. William was sitting by a bright fire when I came downstairs. He soon made his way to the Library piled up in a corner of the window. He brought out a volume of Enfield's Speaker,[6] another miscellany, & an odd volume of Congreve's plays. We had a glass of warm rum & water—We enjoyed ourselves & wished for Mary. It rained & blew when we went to bed. NB Deer in Gowbarrow park like skeletons.

Friday 16th April (Good Friday). When I undrew my curtains in the morning, I was much affected by the beauty of the prospect & the change. The sun shone, the wind has passed away, the hills looked chearful, the river was

5. William did not compose his poem on the daffodils, *I wandered lonely as a cloud,* until two years later. Comparison with the poem will show how extensive was his use of Dorothy's prose descrip-

tion (see p. 284).
6. William Enfield's *The Speaker* (1774), a volume of selections suitable for elocution.

very bright as it flowed into the lake. The Church rises up behind a little knot of Rocks, the steeple not so high as an ordinary 3 story house. Bees, in a row in the garden under the wall. After Wm had shaved we set forward. The valley is at first broken by little rocky woody knolls that make retiring places, fairy valleys in the vale, the river winds along under these hills travelling not in a bustle but not slowly to the lake. We saw a fisherman in the flat meadow on the other side of the water. He came towards us & threw his line over the two arched Bridge. It is a Bridge of a heavy construction, almost bending inwards in the middle, but it is grey & there is a look of ancientry in the architecture of it that pleased me. As we go on the vale opens out more into one vale with somewhat of a cradle Bed. Cottages with groups of trees on the side of the hills. We passed a pair of twin Children 2 years old— & Sate on the next bridge which we crossed a single arch. We rested again upon the Turf & looked at the same Bridge. We observed arches in the water occasioned by the large stones sending it down in two streams—a Sheep came plunging through the river, stumbled up the Bank & passed close to us, it had been frightened by an insignificant little Dog on the other side, its fleece dropped a glittering shower under its belly—Primroses by the roadside, pile wort that shone like stars of gold in the Sun, violets, strawberries, retired & half buried among the grass. When we came to the foot of Brothers water I left William sitting on the Bridge & went along the path on the right side of the Lake through the wood—I was delighted with what I saw. The water under the boughs of the bare old trees, the simplicity of the mountains & the exquisite beauty of the path. There was one grey cottage. I repeated the Glowworm[7] as I walked along—I hung over the gate, & thought I could have stayed for ever. When I returned I found William writing a poem descriptive of the sights & sounds we saw & heard. There was the gentle flowing of the stream, the glittering lively lake, green fields without a living creature to be seen on them, behind us, a flat pasture with 42 cattle feeding to our left the road leading to the hamlet, no smoke there, the sun shone on the bare roofs. The people were at work ploughing, harrowing & sowing— Lasses spreading dung, a dog's barking now & then, cocks crowing, birds twittering, the snow in patches at the top of the highest hills, yellow palms, purple & green twigs on the Birches, ashes with their glittering spikes quite bare. The hawthorn a bright green with black stems under the oak. The moss of the oak glossy. We then went on, passed two sisters at work, *they first passed us*, one with two pitch forks in her hand. The other had a spade. We had some talk with them. They laughed aloud after we were gone perhaps half in wantonness, half boldness. William finished his poem before we got to the foot of Kirkstone.[8] * * *

* * *

Thursday [Apr.] 29. A beautiful morning. The sun shone & all was pleasant. We sent off our parcel to Coleridge by the waggon. Mr Simpson heard the Cuckow today. Before we went out after I had written down the Tinker (which William finished this morning)[9] Luff called. He was very lame, limped into the kitchen—he came on a little Pony. We then went to John's Grove,

---

7. William's poem beginning "Among all lovely things my Love had been," composed four days earlier; "my Love" in this line is Dorothy.

8. The short lyric *Written in March.*

9. William never published his comic poem *The Tinker.* It was first printed in 1897.

sate a while at first. Afterwards William lay, & I lay in the trench under the fence—he with his eyes shut & listening to the waterfalls & the Birds. There was no one waterfall above another[1]—it was a sound of waters in the air— the voice of the air. William heard me breathing & rustling now & then but we both lay still, & unseen by one another—he thought that it would be as sweet thus to lie so in the grave, to hear the *peaceful* sounds of the earth & just to know that our dear friends were near. The Lake was still. There was a Boat out. Silver How reflected with delicate purple & yellowish hues as I have seen Spar—Lambs on the island & running races together by the half dozen in the round field near us. The copses gree*nish*, hawthorn green.— Came home to dinner then went to Mr Simpson. We rested a long time under a wall. Sheep & lambs were in the field—cottages smoking. As I lay down on the grass, I observed the glittering silver line on the ridges of the Backs of the sheep, owing to their situation respecting the Sun—which made them look beautiful but with something of strangeness, like animals of another kind—as if belonging to a more splendid world. Met old Mr S at the door—Mrs S poorly—I got mullens & pansies—I was sick & ill & obliged to come home soon. We went to bed immediately—I slept up stairs. The air coldish where it was felt somewhat frosty.

*   *   *

Tuesday May 4th. William had slept pretty well & though he went to bed nervous & jaded in the extreme he rose refreshed. I wrote the Leech Gath- erer[2] for him which he had begun the night before & of which he wrote several stanzas in bed this Monday morning. It was very hot, we called at Mr Simpson's door as we passed but did not go in. We rested several times by the way, read & repeated the Leech Gatherer. We were almost melted before we were at the top of the hill. We saw Coleridge on the Wytheburn side of the water. He crossed the Beck to us. Mr Simpson was fishing there. William & I ate a Luncheon, then went on towards the waterfall. It is a glorious wild solitude under that lofty purple crag. It stood upright by itself. Its own self & its shadow below, one mass—all else was sunshine. We went on further. A Bird at the top of the crags was flying round & round & looked in thinness & transparency, shape & motion like a moth. We climbed the hill but looked in vain for a shade except at the foot of the great waterfall, & there we did not like to stay on account of the loose stones above our heads. We came down & rested upon a moss covered Rock, rising out of the bed of the River. There we lay ate our dinner & stayed there till about 4 o'clock or later—Wm & C repeated & read verses. I drank a little Brandy & water & was in Heaven. The Stags horn is very beautiful & fresh springing upon the fells. Mountain ashes, green. We drank tea at a farm house. The woman had not a pleasant countenance, but was civil enough. She had a pretty Boy a year old whom she suckled. We parted from Coleridge at Sara's Crag after having looked at the Letters which C carved in the morning. I kissed them all. Wm deepened the T with C's penknife.[3] We sate afterwards on the wall, seeing the sun go

1. I.e., no waterfall could be heard individually.
2. The poem that was published as *Resolution and Independence*. For its origin, see the entry for October 3, 1800 (p. 387).
3. The rock, which has since been blasted away to make room for a new road, contained the carved letters: W. W., M. H., D. W., S. T. C., J. W., S. H. (M. H. and S. H. are Mary and Sara Hutchinson; J. W. is John Wordsworth.)

down & the reflections in the still water. C looked well & parted from us chearfully, hopping up upon the side stones. On the Rays we met a woman with 2 little girls one in her arms the other about 4 years old walking by her side, a pretty little thing, but half starved. She had on a pair of slippers that had belonged to some gentleman's child, down at the heels—it was not easy to keep them on—but, poor thing! young as she was, she walked carefully with them. Alas too young for such cares & such travels—The Mother when we accosted her told us that her husband had left her & gone off with another woman & how she *"pursued"* them. Then her fury kindled & her eyes rolled about. She changed again to tears. She was a Cockermouth woman—30 years of age a child at Cockermouth when I was—I was moved & gave her a shilling, I believe 6ᵈ more than I ought to have given. We had the crescent moon with the "auld moon in her arms."⁴—We rested often:—always upon the Bridges. Reached home at about 10 o'clock. The Lloyds had been here in our absence. We went soon to bed. I repeated verses to William while he was in bed—he was soothed & I left him. "This is the Spot"⁵ over & over again.

*   *   *

6th May Thursday 1802. A sweet morning we have put the finishing stroke to our Bower & here we are sitting in the orchard. It is one o'clock. We are sitting upon a seat under the wall which I found my Brother building up when I came to him with his apple—he had intended that it should have been done before I came. It is a nice cool shady spot. The small Birds are singing—Lambs bleating, Cuckow calling—The Thrush sings by Fits. Thomas Ashburner's axe is going quietly (without passion) in the orchard—Hens are cackling, Flies humming, the women talking together at their doors—Plumb & pear trees are in Blossom—apple trees greenish—the opposite woods green, the crows are cawing. We have heard Ravens. The ash trees are in blossom, Birds flying all about us. The stitchwort is coming out, there is one budding Lychnis, the primroses are passing their prime. Celandine violets & wood sorrel for ever more little—geraniums & pansies on the wall. We walked in the evening to Tail End to enquire about hurdles for the orchard shed & about Mr Luff's flower—The flower dead—no hurdles. I went to look at the falling wood—Wm also when he had been at Benson's went with me. They have left a good many small oak trees but we dare not hope that they are all to remain. The Ladies are come to Mr Gell's cottage. We saw them as we went & their light when we returned. When we came in we found a Magazine & Review & a letter from Coleridge with verses to Hartley & Sara H. We read the Review,⁶ &c. The moon was a perfect Boat a silver Boat when we were out in the evening. The Birch Tree is all over green in *small* leaf more light & elegant than when it is full out. It bent to the breezes as if for the love of its own delightful motions. Sloe thorns & Hawthorns in the hedges.

Friday 7th May. William had slept uncommonly well so, feeling himself strong, he fell to work at the Leech gatherer—He wrote hard at it till dinner time, then he gave over tired to death—he had finished the poem.⁷ * * *

---

4. From the *Ballad of Sir Patrick Spens.* Coleridge quoted the stanza, of which this phrase is part, as epigraph to *Dejection: An Ode.*
5. William never completed this poem.

6. The *Monthly Review* for March 1802.
7. Later entries show, however, that William kept working on the manuscript until July 4.

* * *

[*July.*] On Thursday morning, 29th, we arrived in London.[8] Wm left me at the Inn—I went to bed &c &c &c—After various troubles and disasters we left London on Saturday morning at ½ past 5 or 6, the 31st of July (I have forgot which). We mounted the Dover Coach at Charing Cross. It was a beautiful morning. The City, St. Paul's, with the River & a multitude of little Boats, made a most beautiful sight as we crossed Westminster Bridge. The houses were not overhung by their cloud of smoke & they were spread out endlessly, yet the sun shone so brightly with such a pure light that there was even something like the purity of one of nature's own grand spectacles.[9] We rode on chearfully now with the Paris Diligence before us, now behind— we walked up the steep hills, beautiful prospects everywhere, till we even reached Dover. * * * We arrived at Calais at 4 o'clock on Sunday morning the 31st of July.[1] We stayed in the vessel till ½ past 7, then Wm went for Letters, at about ½ past 8 or 9. We found out Annette & C chez Madame Avril dans la Rue de la Tête d'or. We lodged opposite two Ladies in tolerably decent-sized rooms but badly furnished, & with large store of bad smells & dirt in the yard, & all about. The weather was very hot. We walked by the sea-shore almost every evening with Annette & Caroline or Wm & I alone. I had a bad cold & could not bathe at first but William did. It was a pretty sight to see as we walked upon the Sands when the tide was low perhaps a hundred people bathing about ¼ of a mile distant from us, and we had delightful walks after the heat of the day was passed away—seeing far off in the west the Coast of England like a cloud crested with Dover Castle, which was but like the summit of the cloud—the Evening star & the glory of the sky. The Reflections in the water were more beautiful than the sky itself, purple waves brighter than precious stones for ever melting away upon the sands. * * *

* * *

[*Sept. 24 and following.*] Mary first met us in the avenue. She looked so fat and well that we were made very happy by the sight of her—then came Sara, & last of all Joanna.[2] Tom was forking corn standing upon the corn cart. We dressed ourselves immediately & got tea—the garden looked gay with asters & sweet peas—I looked at everything with tranquillity & happiness but I was ill both on Saturday & Sunday & continued to be poorly most of the time of our stay. Jack & George came on Friday Evening 1st October. On Saturday 2nd we rode to Hackness, William Jack George & Sara single, I behind Tom. On Sunday 3rd Mary & Sara were busy packing. On Monday 4th October 1802, my Brother William was married to Mary Hutchinson. I slept a good deal of the night & rose fresh & well in the morning—at a little after 8 o'clock I saw them go down the avenue towards the Church. William had parted from me up stairs. I gave him the wedding ring—with how deep

8. On the way to France to visit Annette Vallon and Caroline (see the entry for March 22, 1802; p. 390).
9. Cf. William's sonnet *Composed upon Westminster Bridge* (p. 296).
1. The actual date was August 1. One of the walks by the sea that Dorothy goes on to describe was the occasion for William's sonnet *It is a beauteous*

evening.
2. The Wordsworths have come to Gallow Hill, Yorkshire, for the marriage of William and Mary. The people mentioned are Mary's sisters and brothers (Sara, Joanna, Tom, Jack, and George Hutchinson). Out of consideration for Dorothy's overwrought feelings, only Joanna, Jack, and Tom attended the ceremony at Brampton Church.

a blessing! I took it from my forefinger where I had worn it the whole of the night before—he slipped it again onto my finger and blessed me fervently. When they were absent my dear little Sara prepared the breakfast. I kept myself as quiet as I could, but when I saw the two men running up the walk, coming to tell us it was over, I could stand it no longer & threw myself on the bed where I lay in stillness, neither hearing or seeing any thing, till Sara came upstairs to me & said "They are coming." This forced me from the bed where I lay & I moved I knew not how straight forward, faster than my strength could carry me till I met my beloved William & fell upon his bosom. He & John Hutchinson led me to the house & there I stayed to welcome my dear Mary. As soon as we had breakfasted we departed.[3] It rained when we set off. Poor Mary was much agitated when she parted from her Brothers & Sisters & her home. Nothing particular occurred till we reached Kirby. We had sunshine & showers, pleasant talk, love & chearfulness. * * * It rained very hard when we reached Windermere. We sate in the rain at Wilcock's to change horses, & arrived at Grasmere at about 6 o'clock on Wednesday Evening, the 6th of October 1802. Molly was overjoyed to see us,—for my part I cannot describe what I felt, & our dear Mary's feelings would I dare say not be easy to speak of. We went by candle light into the garden & were astonished at the growth of the Brooms, Portugal Laurels, &c &c &—The next day, Thursday, we unpacked the Boxes. On Friday 8th we baked Bread, & Mary & I walked, first upon the Hill side, & then in John's Grove, then in view of Rydale, the first walk that I had taken with my Sister.

*   *   *

24th December 1802, Christmas Eve. William is now sitting by me at ½ past 10 o'clock. I have been beside him ever since tea running the heel of a stocking, repeating some of his sonnets to him, listening to his own repeating, reading some of Milton's & the Allegro & Penseroso. It is a quiet keen frost. Mary is in the parlour below attending to the baking of cakes & Jenny Fletcher's pies. Sara is in bed in the tooth ache, & so we are—beloved William is turning over the leaves of Charlotte Smith's sonnets, but he keeps his hand to his poor chest pushing aside his breastplate.[4] Mary is well & I am well, & Molly is as blithe as last year at this time. Coleridge came this morning with Wedgwood.[5] We all turned out of Wm's bedroom one by one to meet him—he looked well. We had to tell him of the Birth of his little Girl, born yesterday morning at 6 o'clock.[6] W went with them to Wytheburn in the Chaise, & M & I met Wm on the Rays. It was not an unpleasant morning to the feelings—far from it—the sun shone now & then, & there was no wind, but all things looked chearless & distinct, no meltings of sky into mountains—the mountains like stone-work wrought up with huge hammers.—Last Sunday was as mild a day as I ever remember—We all set off together to walk. I went to Rydale & Wm returned with me. M & S[7] went round the Lakes. There were flowers of various kinds the topmost bell of a fox-glove, geraniums, daisies—a buttercup in the water (but this I saw two

3. Dorothy accompanied William and Mary on the three-day journey back to their cottage at Grasmere.
4. Probably an undergarment covering the chest.
5. Tom Wedgwood, whose father had founded the famous pottery works, was a friend and generous patron of Coleridge.
6. Coleridge's daughter, Sara (1802–1852).
7. Mary and her sister Sara Hutchinson.

or three days before) small yellow flowers (I do not know their name) in the turf a large bunch of strawberry blossoms. Wm sate a while with me, then went to meet M. & S.—Last Saturday I dined at Mr Simpson's also a beautiful mild day. Monday was a frosty day, & it has been frost ever since. On Saturday I dined with Mrs Simpson. It is today Christmas-day Saturday 25th December 1802. I am 31 years of age.—It is a dull frosty day.

*   *   *

1800–02   1897

Grasmere—A Fragment

Peaceful our valley, fair and green,
And beautiful her cottages,
Each in its nook, its sheltered hold,
Or underneath its tuft of trees.

5   Many and beautiful they are;
But there is *one* that I love best,
A lowly shed, in truth, it is,
A brother of the rest.

Yet when I sit on rock or hill,
10   Down looking on the valley fair,
That Cottage with its clustering trees
Summons my heart; it settles there.

Others there are whose small domain
Of fertile fields and hedgerows green
15   Might more seduce a wanderer's mind
To wish that *there* his home had been.

Such wish be his! I blame him not,
My fancies they perchance are wild
—I love that house because it is
20   The very Mountains' child.

Fields hath it of its own, green fields,
But they are rocky steep and bare;
Their fence is of the mountain stone,
And moss and lichen flourish there.

25   And when the storm comes from the North
It lingers near that pastoral spot,
And, piping through the mossy walls,
It seems delighted with its lot.

And let it take its own delight;
30   And let it range the pastures bare;

Until it reach that group of trees,
—It may not enter there!

A green unfading grove it is,
Skirted with many a lesser tree,
35   Hazel and holly, beech and oak,
A bright and flourishing company.

Precious the shelter of those trees;
They screen the cottage that I love;
The sunshine pierces to the roof,
40   And the tall pine-trees tower above.

When first I saw that dear abode,
It was a lovely winter's day:
After a night of perilous storm
The west wind ruled with gentle sway;

45   A day so mild, it might have been
The first day of the gladsome spring;
The robins warbled, and I heard
One solitary throstle sing.

A Stranger, Grasmere, in thy Vale,
50   All faces then to me unknown,
I left my sole companion-friend
To wander out alone.

Lured by a little winding path,
I quitted soon the public road,
55   A smooth and tempting path it was,
By sheep and shepherds trod.

Eastward, toward the lofty hills,
This pathway led me on
Until I reached a stately Rock,
60   With velvet moss o'ergrown.

With russet oak and tufts of fern
Its top was richly garlanded;
Its sides adorned with eglantine
Bedropp'd with hips of glossy red.

65   There, too, in many a sheltered chink
The foxglove's broad leaves flourished fair,
And silver birch whose purple twigs
Bend to the softest breathing air.

Beneath that Rock my course I stayed,
70   And, looking to its summit high,
"Thou wear'st," said I, "a splendid garb,
Here winter keeps his revelry.

"Full long a dweller on the Plains,
I griev'd when summer days were gone;
75   No more I'll grieve; for Winter here
Hath pleasure gardens of his own.

"What need of flowers? The splendid moss
Is gayer than an April mead;
More rich its hues of various green,
80   Orange, and gold, & glittering red."

—Beside that gay and lovely Rock
There came with merry voice
A foaming streamlet glancing by;
It seemed to say "Rejoice!"

85   My youthful wishes all fulfill'd,
Wishes matured by thoughtful choice,
I stood an Inmate of this vale
How *could* I but rejoice?

ca. 1802–05   1892

Thoughts on My Sick-Bed[1]

And has the remnant of my life
Been pilfered of this sunny Spring?
And have its own prelusive sounds
Touched in my heart no echoing string?

5   Ah! say not so—the hidden life
Couchant° within this feeble frame   *lying*
Hath been enriched by kindred gifts,
That, undesired, unsought-for, came

With joyful heart in youthful days
10   When fresh each season in its Round
I welcomed the earliest Celandine
Glittering upon the mossy ground;

With busy eyes I pierced the lane
In quest of known and *un*known things,
15   —The primrose a lamp on its fortress rock,
The silent butterfly spreading its wings,

The violet betrayed by its noiseless breath,
The daffodil dancing in the breeze,

1. In a letter of May 25, 1832, William Wordsworth's daughter Dora mentions this as "an affecting poem which she [her aunt Dorothy] has written
on the pleasure she received from the first spring
flowers that were carried up to her when confined
to her sick room." The lines refer to half a dozen
or more poems by William, including *I wandered
lonely as a cloud* (in line 18) and *Tintern Abbey*
(lines 45–52).

The carolling thrush, on his naked perch,
20 Towering above the budding trees.

Our cottage-hearth no longer our home,
Companions of Nature were we,
The Stirring, the Still, the Loquacious, the Mute—
To all we gave our sympathy.

25 Yet never in those careless days
When spring-time in rock, field, or bower
Was but a fountain of earthly hope
A promise of fruits & the *splendid* flower.

No! then I never felt a bliss
30 That might with *that* compare
Which, piercing to my couch of rest,
Came on the vernal air.

When loving Friends an offering brought,
The first flowers of the year,
35 Culled from the precincts of our home,
From nooks to Memory dear.

With some sad thoughts the work was done,
Unprompted and unbidden,
But joy it brought to my *hidden* life,
40 To consciousness no longer hidden.

I felt a Power unfelt before,
Controlling weakness, languor, pain;
It bore me to the Terrace walk
I trod the Hills again;—

45 No prisoner in this lonely room,
I *saw* the green Banks of the Wye,
Recalling thy prophetic words,
Bard, Brother, Friend from infancy!

No need of motion, or of strength,
50 Or even the breathing air:
—I thought of Nature's loveliest scenes;
And with Memory I was there.

May 1832   1978

SIR WALTER SCOTT
1771–1832

Walter Scott was born in Edinburgh, but as a small boy, to improve his health, he lived for some years with his grandparents on their farm in the Scottish Border country (the part of southern Scotland lying immediately north of the border with England). This region was rich in ballad and folklore, much of it associated with the Border warfare between northern English and southern Scottish raiders. As a child, Scott listened eagerly to stories about old events and battles as well as to accounts of their experiences by survivors of the Jacobite rebellion of 1745. He early acquired what he exploited in his prose fiction—a sense of history as associated with a specific place and a sense of the past that is kept alive in the oral traditions of the present.

Scott's father was a lawyer and he himself was trained in the law, becoming in 1799 sheriff (local judge) of Selkirkshire, a Border county, and in 1806 clerk of session—i.e., secretary to the highest civil court in Scotland—in Edinburgh. Scott viewed the law, in its development over the centuries, as embodying the changing social customs of the country and an important element in social history, and he often used it (as in *The Heart of Midlothian*) to give a special dimension to his fiction.

From early childhood, Scott was an avid reader of ballads and poetic romances, which with his phenomenal memory he effortlessly memorized. He began his literary career as a poet, first as a translator of German ballad imitations, then as a writer of such imitations, then as a collector and editor of Border ballads (*Minstrelsy of the Scottish Border*, 1802–03), some of which he revised to smooth out roughness and to add striking touches. He then moved on to compose long narrative poems, which were widely read; the best known are *Marmion* (1808) and *The Lady of the Lake* (1810). He gave up narrative poetry for prose fiction because, as he said, "Byron beat me" in the writing of verse romances. In 1811 he began building his great country house at Abbotsford, in his beloved Border country; he furnished the house with historical relics and at the same time incorporated the latest technological developments, such as lighting by gas.

Scott continued to write lyric poems, which he inserted in his novels. Some of the lyrics, including *Jock of Hazeldean* and *Proud Maisie*, are based on the folk ballad and capture remarkably the terse suggestiveness of the oral form. His first novel, *Waverley* (1814), which deals with the Jacobite rebellion, introduced a motif that recurs in much of his best fiction, such as *Old Mortality* (1816) and *The Heart of Midlothian* (1818): the protagonist mediates between a heroic but violent old world that can no longer survive and an emerging new world that has something to learn from the past it rejects. It is this recognition of continuity-in-change between the past and the present that made Scott the founder of the true historical novel, as distinguished from the "Gothic" novel, which had represented the past primarily for its exotic appeal.

Scott published all his novels anonymously, but their author was soon identified and became the most internationally famous as well as the most prolific writer of his day. He was made baronet in 1820. His ambition was to become, as laird of Abbotsford, a great and benevolent landowner of the old school. To achieve this status, he kept adding to his house and buying more land; and to support such expenditures, he associated himself with a number of commercial ventures in printing and publishing. In the crash of 1826, as a result of the failure of the publishing firm of Constable, Scott was financially ruined. He insisted on working off his huge debts by his pen and exhausted himself in the effort to do so. Not until after his death were his creditors finally paid off in full with the proceeds of the continuing sale of his novels.

From The Heart of Midlothian[1]

Chapter I. Being Introductory

So down thy hill, romantic Ashbourn, glides
The Derby dilly, carrying six insides.

Frere.[2]

The times have changed in nothing more (we follow as we were wont the manuscript of Peter Pattieson) than in the rapid conveyance of intelligence and communication betwixt one part of Scotland and another. It is not above twenty or thirty years, according to the evidence of many credible witnesses now alive, since a little miserable horse-cart, performing with difficulty a journey of thirty miles *per diem*, carried our mails from the capital of Scotland to its extremity. Nor was Scotland much more deficient in these accommodations, than our richer sister had been about eighty years before. Fielding, in his *Tom Jones*, and Farquhar, in a little farce called the *Stage-Coach*,[3] have ridiculed the slowness of these vehicles of public accommodation. According to the latter authority, the highest bribe could only induce the coachman to promise to anticipate by half an hour the usual time of his arrival at the Bull and Mouth.

But in both countries these ancient, slow, and sure modes of conveyance, are now alike unknown; mail-coach races against mail-coach, and high-flyer[4] against high-flyer, through the most remote districts of Britain. And in our village alone, three post-coaches, and four coaches with men armed, and in scarlet cassocks, thunder through the streets each day, and rival in brilliancy and noise the invention of the celebrated tyrant:—

Demens, qui nimbos et non imitabile fulmen,
Aere et cornipedum pulsu, simularat, equorum.[5]

Now and then, to complete the resemblance, and to correct the presumption of the venturous charioteers, it does happen that the career of these dashing rivals of Salmoneus[6] meets with as undesirable and violent a termination as that of their prototype. It is on such occasions that the Insides and Outsides, to use the appropriate vehicular phrases, have reason to rue the exchange of the slow and safe motion of the ancient Fly-coaches, which, compared with the chariots of Mr. Palmer,[7] so ill deserve the name. The

---

1. Scott's novel, written and published in 1818, takes its title and central focus from the old Edinburgh Tolbooth, a prison familiarly called, after the name of Edinburgh's county, "the heart of Midlothian." The work brings together historical events connected with the Porteous Riot of 1736 and the stories of Effie Deans, who like Porteous is imprisoned in the Tolbooth under sentence of death, and her sister Jeanie, who wins her pardon. The chapter printed here, exemplifying Scott's complex framing of his historical fiction, provides a narrator (Peter Pattieson), an assemblage of minor characters, a great many jokes and satirical comments on the law, and discussion of the conflict between historical truth and the novelist's invention.
2. John Hookham Frere's *The Loves of the Triangles: A Mathematical and Philosophical Poem* (1798), 1.181–82. "Dilly": short form of *diligence*,

a public stagecoach. "Insides": the passengers riding inside a coach, in contrast to the "outsides," the passengers riding outside on the roof of the coach.
3. George Farquhar's popular farce *The Stage Coach* was first produced in 1704. Henry Fielding comments on the slowness of coaches in *Tom Jones*, book 11, chap. 9.
4. A fast stagecoach.
5. Madman! to mimic the storm-clouds and inimitable thunder with brass and the tramp of horn-footed horses! (Latin; Virgil's *Aeneid* 6.590–91).
6. Virgil's "celebrated tyrant" (above), a king who, wishing to be thought a god, imitated lightning by throwing torches from his chariot. To punish his impiety, Jupiter destroyed him with a thunderbolt.
7. John Palmer (1742–1818), inventor of the British mail-coach system in the mid-1780s.

ancient vehicle used to settle quietly down, like a ship scuttled and left to sink by the gradual influx of the waters, while the modern is smashed to pieces with the velocity of the same vessel hurled against breakers, or rather with the fury of a bomb bursting at the conclusion of its career through the air. The late ingenious Mr. Pennant,[8] whose humor it was to set his face in stern opposition to these speedy conveyances, had collected, I have heard, a formidable list of such casualties, which, joined to the imposition of inn-keepers, whose charges the passengers had no time to dispute, the sauciness of the coachman, and the uncontrolled and despotic authority of the tyrant called the Guard, held forth a picture of horror, to which murder, theft, fraud, and peculation, lent all their dark coloring. But that which gratifies the impatience of the human disposition will be practiced in the teeth of danger, and in defiance of admonition; and, in despite of the Cambrian anti-quary,[9] mail-coaches not only roll their thunders round the base of Penman-Maur and Cader-Edris, but

> Frighted Skiddaw hears afar
> The rattling of the unscythed car.

And perhaps the echoes of Ben-Nevis[1] may soon be awakened by the bugle, not of a warlike chieftain, but of the guard of a mail-coach.

It was a fine summer day, and our little school had obtained a half holyday, by the intercession of a good-humored visitor.[2] I expected by the coach a new number of an interesting periodical publication, and walked forward on the highway to meet it, with the impatience which Cowper has described as actuating the resident in the country when longing for intelligence from the mart of news:

> "The grand debate,
> The popular harangue,—the tart reply,—
> The logic, and the wisdom, and the wit,
> And the loud laugh,—I long to know them all;—
> I burn to set the imprison'd wranglers free,
> And give them voice and utterance once again."[3]

It was with such feelings that I eyed the approach of the new coach, lately established on our road, and known by the name of the Somerset, which, to say truth, possesses some interest for me, even when it conveys no such important information. The distant tremulous sound of its wheels was heard just as I gained the summit of the gentle ascent, called the Goslin-brae, from which you command an extensive view down the valley of the river Gander. The public road, which comes up the side of that stream, and crosses it at a bridge about a quarter of a mile from the place where I was standing, runs partly through enclosures and plantations, and partly through open pasture land. It is a childish amusement perhaps,—but my life has been spent with children, and why should not my pleasures be like theirs?—childish as it is

---

8. Thomas Pennant (1726–1798), naturalist and travel writer, who published, among other works, *A Tour in Scotland* (1771).
9. I.e., Pennant. "Cambrian": Welsh.
1. The highest mountain in Great Britain, near Fort William, Scotland. Penmaenmawr and Cader Idris are peaks in northwest Wales. Skiddaw is in the English Lake District.
2. His Honor Gilbert Goslinn of Gandercleugh; for I love to be precise in matters of importance.— J. C. [Scott's note, in his character as Jedediah Cleishbotham, the presenter of this novel in a series designated *Tales of My Landlord*].
3. William Cowper's *The Task* 4.30–35.

then, I must own I have had great pleasure in watching the approach of the carriage, where the openings of the road permit it to be seen. The gay glancing of the equipage, its diminished and toy-like appearance at a distance, contrasted with the rapidity of its motion, its appearance and disappearance at intervals, and the progressively increasing sounds that announce its nearer approach, have all to the idle and listless spectator, who has nothing more important to attend to, something of awakening interest. The ridicule may attach to me, which is flung upon many an honest citizen, who watches from the window of his villa the passage of the stage-coach; but it is a very natural source of amusement notwithstanding, and many of those who join in the laugh are perhaps not unused to resort to it in secret.

On the present occasion, however, fate had decreed that I should not enjoy the consummation of the amusement by seeing the coach rattle past me as I sat on the turf, and hearing the hoarse grating voice of the guard as he skimmed forth for my grasp the expected packet, without the carriage checking its course for an instant. I had seen the vehicle thunder down the hill that leads to the bridge with more than its usual impetuosity, glittering all the while by flashes from a cloudy tabernacle of the dust which it had raised, and leaving a train behind it on the road resembling a wreath of summer mist. But it did not appear on the top of the nearer bank within the usual space of three minutes, which frequent observation had enabled me to ascertain was the medium time for crossing the bridge and mounting the ascent. When double that space had elapsed, I became alarmed, and walked hastily forward. As I came in sight of the bridge, the cause of delay was too manifest, for the Somerset had made a summerset[4] in good earnest, and overturned so completely, that it was literally resting upon the ground, with the roof undermost, and the four wheels in the air. The "exertions of the guard and coachman," both of whom were gratefully commemorated in the newspapers, having succeeded in disentangling the horses by cutting the harness, were now proceeding to extricate the *insides* by a sort of summary and Caesarean process of delivery, forcing the hinges from one of the doors which they could not open otherwise. In this manner were two disconsolate damsels set at liberty from the womb of the leathern conveniency. As they immediately began to settle their clothes, which were a little deranged, as may be presumed, I concluded they had received no injury, and did not venture to obtrude my services at their toilette, for which, I understand, I have since been reflected upon by the fair sufferers. The *outsides*, who must have been discharged from their elevated situation by a shock resembling the springing of a mine, escaped, nevertheless, with the usual allowance of scratches and bruises, excepting three, who, having been pitched into the river Gander, were dimly seen contending with the tide, like the relics of Aeneas's shipwreck,—

Rari apparent nantes in gurgite vasto.[5]

I applied my poor exertions where they seemed to be most needed, and with the assistance of one or two of the company who had escaped unhurt, easily succeeded in fishing out two of the unfortunate passengers, who were stout active young fellows; and but for the preposterous length of their great-

---

4. Or somerset, a play on the name of the coach ("Somerset") and a form of modern *somersault.*

5. *Aeneid* 1.118: "Here and there are seen swimmers in the vast abyss."

coats, and the equally fashionable latitude and longitude of their Wellington trousers, would have required little assistance from any one. The third was sickly and elderly, and might have perished but for the efforts used to preserve him.

When the two great-coated gentlemen had extricated themselves from the river, and shaken their ears like huge water-dogs, a violent altercation ensued betwixt them and the coachman and guard, concerning the cause of their overthrow. In the course of the squabble, I observed that both my new acquaintances belonged to the law, and that their professional sharpness was likely to prove an over-match for the surly and official tone of the guardians of the vehicle. The dispute ended in the guard assuring the passengers that they should have seats in a heavy coach which would pass that spot in less than half an hour, providing it were not full. Chance seemed to favor this arrangement, for when the expected vehicle arrived, there were only two places occupied in a carriage which professed to carry six. The two ladies who had been disinterred out of the fallen vehicle were readily admitted, but positive objections were stated by those previously in possession to the admittance of the two lawyers, whose wetted garments being much of the nature of well-soaked sponges, there was every reason to believe they would refund a considerable part of the water they had collected, to the inconvenience of their fellow-passengers. On the other hand, the lawyers rejected a seat on the roof, alleging that they had only taken that station for pleasure for one stage, but were entitled in all respects to free egress and regress from the interior, to which their contract positively referred. After some altercation, in which something was said upon the edict *Nautae, caupones, stabularii*,[6] the coach went off, leaving the learned gentlemen to abide by their action of damages.

They immediately applied to me to guide them to the next village and the best inn; and from the account I gave them of the Wallace-Head, declared they were much better pleased to stop there than to go forward upon the terms of that impudent scoundrel the guard of the Somerset. All that they now wanted was a lad to carry their travelling bags, who was easily procured from an adjoining cottage; and they prepared to walk forward, when they found there was another passenger in the same deserted situation with themselves. This was the elderly and sickly-looking person, who had been precipitated into the river along with the two young lawyers. He, it seems, had been too modest to push his own plea against the coachman when he saw that of his betters rejected, and now remained behind with a look of timid anxiety, plainly intimating that he was deficient in those means of recommendation which are necessary passports to the hospitality of an inn.

I ventured to call the attention of the two dashing young blades, for such they seemed, to the desolate condition of their fellow-traveller. They took the hint with ready good-nature.

"O, true, Mr. Dunover," said one of the youngsters, "you must not remain on the pavé[7] here; you must go and have some dinner with us—Halkit and I must have a post-chaise to go on, at all events, and we will set you down wherever suits you best."

The poor man, for such his dress, as well as his diffidence, bespoke him,

---

6. A Roman law that imposed strict liability on shipmasters, innkeepers, and stablekeepers for the safety of property entrusted to them.
7. Pavement.

made the sort of acknowledging bow by which says a Scotchman, "It's too much honor for the like of me"; and followed humbly behind his gay patrons, all three besprinkling the dusty road as they walked along with the moisture of their drenched garments, and exhibiting the singular and somewhat ridiculous appearance of three persons suffering from the opposite extreme of humidity, while the summer sun was at its height, and everything else around them had the expression of heat and drought. The ridicule did not escape the young gentlemen themselves, and they had made what might be received as one or two tolerable jests on the subject before they had advanced far on their peregrination.

"We cannot complain, like Cowley," said one of them, "that Gideon's fleece remains dry, while all around is moist; this is the reverse of the miracle."[8]

"We ought to be received with gratitude in this good town; we bring a supply of what they seem to need most," said Halkit.

"And distribute it with unparalleled generosity," replied his companion; "performing the part of three water-carts for the benefit of their dusty roads."

"We come before them, too," said Halkit, "in full professional force—counsel and agent—"

"And client," said the young advocate, looking behind him. And then added, lowering his voice, "that looks as if he had kept such dangerous company too long."

It was, indeed, too true, that the humble follower of the gay young men had the threadbare appearance of a worn-out litigant, and I could not but smile at the conceit, though anxious to conceal my mirth from the object of it.

When we arrived at the Wallace Inn, the elder of the Edinburgh gentlemen, and whom I understood to be a barrister,[9] insisted that I should remain and take part of their dinner; and their enquiries and demands speedily put my landlord and his whole family in motion to produce the best cheer which the larder and cellar afforded, and proceed to cook it to the best advantage, a science in which our entertainers seemed to be admirably skilled. In other respects they were lively young men, in the hey-day of youth and good spirits, playing the part which is common to the higher classes of the law at Edinburgh, and which nearly resembles that of the young templars in the days of Steele and Addison.[1] An air of giddy gaiety mingled with the good sense, taste, and information which their conversation exhibited; and it seemed to be their object to unite the character of men of fashion and lovers of the polite arts. A fine gentleman, bred up in the thorough idleness and inanity of pursuit, which I understand is absolutely necessary to the character in perfection, might in all probability have traced a tinge of professional pedantry which marked the barrister in spite of his efforts, and something of active bustle in his companion, and would certainly have detected more than a fashionable mixture of information and animated interest in the language of both. But to me, who had no pretensions to be so critical, my companions seemed to form a very happy mixture of good-breeding and liberal informa-

8. Abraham Cowley's *The Complaint* (1663), lines 68–74, referring to Judges 6.36–40.
9. One who can plead cases in the superior courts of law. Halkit is a solicitor, admitted only to the lower courts.

1. Richard Steele and Joseph Addison, principal authors of the *Spectator* papers (1711–12, 1714). "Templars": lawyers.

tion, with a disposition to lively rattle, pun, and jest, amusing to a grave man, because it is what he himself can least easily command.

The thin pale-faced man, whom their good-nature had brought into their society, looked out of place, as well as out of spirits; sate on the edge of his seat, and kept the chair at two feet distance from the table; thus incommoding himself considerably in conveying the victuals to his mouth, as if by way of penance for partaking of them in the company of his superiors. A short time after dinner, declining all entreaty to partake of the wine, which circulated freely round, he informed himself of the hour when the chaise had been ordered to attend; and saying he would be in readiness, modestly withdrew from the apartment.

"Jack," said the barrister to his companion, "I remember that poor fellow's face; you spoke more truly than you were aware of; he really is one of my clients, poor man."

"Poor man!" echoed Halkit—"I suppose you mean he is your one and only client?"

"That's not my fault, Jack," replied the other, whose name I discovered was Hardie. "You are to give me all your business, you know; and if you have none, the learned gentleman here knows nothing can come of nothing."[2]

"You seem to have brought something to nothing though, in the case of that honest man. He looks as if he were just about to honor with his residence the HEART OF MIDLOTHIAN."

"You are mistaken—he is just delivered from it.—Our friend here looks for an explanation. Pray, Mr. Pattieson, have you been in Edinburgh?"

I answered in the affirmative.

"Then you must have passed, occasionally at least, though probably not so faithfully as I am doomed to do, through a narrow intricate passage, leading out of the north-west corner of the Parliament Square, and passing by a high and antique building, with turrets and iron grates,

> Making good the saying odd,
> Near the church and far from God"—[3]

Mr. Halkit broke in upon his learned counsel, to contribute his moiety to the riddle—"Having at the door the sign of the Red Man——"

"And being on the whole," resumed the counsellor, interrupting his friend in his turn, "a sort of place where misfortune is happily confounded with guilt, where all who are in wish to get out——"

"And where none who have the good luck to be out, wish to get in," added his companion.

"I conceive you, gentlemen," replied I; "you mean the prison."

"The prison," added the young lawyer—"You have hit it—the very reverend Tolbooth itself; and let me tell you, you are obliged to us for describing it with so much modesty and brevity; for with whatever amplifications we might have chosen to decorate the subject, you lay entirely at our mercy, since the Fathers Conscript of our city have decreed, that the venerable edifice itself shall not remain in existence to confirm or to confute us."

2. The Aristotelian maxim "*Ex nihilo nihil fit*" (the basis of Lear's famous response to his daughter Cordelia, "Nothing will come of nothing," *King* *Lear* 1.1.88).
3. A proverb dating back to medieval times.

"Then the Tolbooth of Edinburgh is called the Heart of Midlothian?" said I.

"So termed and reputed, I assure you."

"I think," said I, with the bashful diffidence with which a man lets slip a pun in presence of his superiors, "the metropolitan county may, in that case, be said to have a sad heart."

"Right as my glove, Mr. Pattieson," added Mr. Hardie; "and a close heart, and a hard heart—Keep it up, Jack."

"And a wicked heart, and a poor heart," answered Halkit, doing his best.

"And yet it may be called in some sort a strong heart, and a high heart," rejoined the advocate. "You see I can put you both out of heart."

"I have played all my hearts," said the younger gentleman.

"Then we'll have another lead," answered his companion.—"And as to the old and condemned Tolbooth, what pity the same honor cannot be done to it as has been done to many of its inmates. Why should not the Tolbooth have its 'Last Speech, Confession, and Dying Words'? The old stones would be just as conscious of the honor as many a poor devil who has dangled like a tassel[4] at the west end of it, while the hawkers[5] were shouting a confession the culprit had never heard of."

"I am afraid," said I, "if I might presume to give my opinion, it would be a tale of unvaried sorrow and guilt."

"Not entirely, my friend," said Hardie; "a prison is a world within itself, and has its own business, griefs, and joys, peculiar to its circle. Its inmates are sometimes short-lived, but so are soldiers on service; they are poor relatively to the world without, but there are degrees of wealth and poverty among them, and so some are relatively rich also. They cannot stir abroad, but neither can the garrison of a besieged fort, or the crew of a ship at sea; and they are not under a dispensation quite so desperate as either, for they may have as much food as they have money to buy, and are not obliged to work whether they have food or not."

"But what variety of incident," said I (not without a secret view to my present task), "could possibly be derived from such a work as you are pleased to talk of?"

"Infinite," replied the young advocate. "Whatever of guilt, crime, imposture, folly, unheard-of misfortunes, and unlooked-for change of fortune, can be found to chequer life, my Last Speech of the Tolbooth should illustrate with examples sufficient to gorge even the public's all-devouring appetite for the wonderful and horrible. The inventor of fictitious narratives has to rack his brains for means to diversify his tale, and after all can hardly hit upon characters or incidents which have not been used again and again, until they are familiar to the eye of the reader, so that the developement, *enlèvement*,[6] the desperate wound of which the hero never dies, the burning fever from which the heroine is sure to recover, become a mere matter of course. I join with my honest friend Crabbe, and have an unlucky propensity to hope when hope is lost, and to rely upon the cork-jacket, which carries the heroes of romance safe through all the billows of affliction." He then declaimed the following passage, rather with too much than too little emphasis:

4. I.e., has been hanged.
5. Sellers of broadsides supposedly reporting the

condemned criminal's confession.
6. Kidnapping.

"Much have I fear'd, but am no more afraid,
When some chaste beauty, by some wretch betray'd,
Is drawn away with such distracted speed,
That she anticipates a dreadful deed.
Not so do I—Let solid walls impound
The captive fair, and dig a moat around;
Let there be brazen locks and bars of steel,
And keepers cruel, such as never feel;
With not a single note the purse supply,
And when she begs, let men and maids deny;
Be windows there from which she dares not fall,
And help so distant, 'tis in vain to call;
Still means of freedom will some Power devise,
And from the baffled ruffian snatch his prize."[7]

"The end of uncertainty," he concluded, "is the death of interest; and hence it happens that no one now reads novels."

"Hear him, ye gods!" returned his companion. "I assure you, Mr. Pattieson, you will hardly visit this learned gentleman, but you are likely to find the new novel most in repute lying on his table,—snugly intrenched, however, beneath Stair's *Institutes*, or an open volume of Morrison's *Decisions*."[8]

"Do I deny it?" said the hopeful jurisconsult, "or wherefore should I, since it is well known these Dalilahs seduce my wisers and my betters? May they not be found lurking amidst the multiplied memorials of our most distinguished counsel, and even peeping from under the cushion of a judge's armchair? Our seniors at the bar, within the bar, and even on the bench, read novels; and, if not belied,[9] some of them have written novels into the bargain. I only say, that I read from habit and from indolence, not from real interest; that, like Ancient Pistol devouring his leek,[1] I read and swear till I get to the end of the narrative. But not so in the real records of human vagaries—not so in the State Trials, or in the Books of Adjournal, where every now and then you read new pages of the human heart, and turns of fortune far beyond what the boldest novelist ever attempted to produce from the coinage of his brain."

"And for such narratives," I asked, "you suppose the History of the Prison of Edinburgh might afford appropriate materials?"

"In a degree unusually ample, my dear sir," said Hardie—"Fill your glass, however, in the meanwhile. Was it not for many years the place in which the Scottish parliament met? Was it not James's[2] place of refuge, when the mob, inflamed by a seditious preacher, broke forth on him with the cries of 'The sword of the Lord and of Gideon—bring forth the wicked Haman'?[3] Since that time how many hearts have throbbed within these walls, as the tolling of the neighbouring bell announced to them how fast the sands of their life were ebbing; how many must have sunk at the sound—how many were supported by stubborn pride and dogged resolution—how many by the consolations of religion? Have there not been some, who, looking back on

---

7. George Crabbe's *The Borough* (1810), letter 20, lines 78–91.
8. Standard treatises on Scottish law.
9. Misrepresented, described falsely.
1. The Welshman Fluellen makes the bombastic Pistol eat a leek, the national emblem of Wales, in

Shakespeare's *Henry V* 5.1.
2. The unpopular, autocratic James II (1633–1701).
3. The mob was conflating Judges 7.20 ("The sword of the Lord, and of Gideon") and Esther 3–9 (the wicked Haman).

the motives of their crimes, were scarce able to understand how they should have had such temptation as to seduce them from virtue? and have there not, perhaps, been others, who, sensible of their innocence, were divided between indignation at the undeserved doom which they were to undergo, consciousness that they had not deserved it, and racking anxiety to discover some way in which they might yet vindicate themselves? Do you suppose any of these deep, powerful, and agitating feelings, can be recorded and perused without exciting a corresponding depth of deep, powerful, and agitating interest?—O! do but wait till I publish the *Causes Célèbres* of Caledonia,[4] and you will find no want of a novel or a tragedy for some time to come. The true thing will triumph over the brightest inventions of the most ardent imagination. *Magna est veritas, et praevalebit.*"[5]

"I have understood," said I, encouraged by the affability of my rattling entertainer, "that less of this interest must attach to Scottish jurisprudence than to that of any other country. The general morality of our people, their sober and prudent habits——"

"Secure them," said the barrister, "against any great increase of professional thieves and depredators, but not against wild and wayward starts of fancy and passion, producing crimes of an extraordinary description, which are precisely those to the detail of which we listen with thrilling interest. England has been much longer a highly civilized country; her subjects have been very strictly amendable to laws administered without fear or favor, a complete division of labor has taken place among her subjects, and the very thieves and robbers form a distinct class in society, subdivided among themselves according to the subject of their depredations, and the mode in which they carry them on, acting upon regular habits and principles, which can be calculated and anticipated at Bow Street, Hatton Garden, or the Old Bailey.[6] Our sister kingdom is like a cultivated field,—the farmer expects that, in spite of all his care, a certain number of weeds will rise with the corn, and can tell you beforehand their names and appearance. But Scotland is like one of her own Highland glens, and the moralist who reads the records of her criminal jurisprudence, will find as many curious anomalous facts in the history of mind, as the botanist will detect rare specimens among her dingles[7] and cliffs."

"And that's all the good you have obtained from three perusals of the Commentaries on Scottish Criminal Jurisprudence?" said his companion. "I suppose the learned author very little thinks that the facts which his erudition and acuteness have accumulated for the illustration of legal doctrines, might be so arranged as to form a sort of appendix to the half-bound and slip-shod volumes of the circulating library."

"I'll bet you a pint of claret," said the elder lawyer, "that he will not feel sore at the comparison. But as we say at the bar, 'I beg I may not be interrupted'; I have much more to say upon my Scottish collection of *Causes Célèbres*. You will please recollect the scope and motive given for the contrivance and execution of many extraordinary and daring crimes, by the long civil dissensions of Scotland—by the hereditary jurisdictions, which, until 1748, rested the investigation of crimes in judges, ignorant, partial, or inter-

---

4. Famous cases of Scotland.
5. From the Apocrypha in the Vulgate (the Latin Bible), 1 Esdras 4.41: "The truth is powerful, and will prevail."
6. London locations associated with the law.
7. Wooded valleys.

ested—by the habits of the gentry, shut up in their distant and solitary mansion-houses, nursing their revengeful passions just to keep their blood from stagnating—not to mention that amiable national qualification, called the *perfervidum ingenium Scotorum*,[8] which our lawyers join in alleging as a reason for the severity of some of our enactments. When I come to treat of matters so mysterious, deep, and dangerous, as these circumstances have given rise to, the blood of each reader shall be curdled, and his epidermis crisped into goose skin.—But, hist!—here comes the landlord, with tidings, I suppose, that the chaise is ready."

It was no such thing—the tidings bore, that no chaise could be had that evening, for Sir Peter Plyem had carried forward my landlord's two pairs of horses that morning to the ancient royal borough of Bubbleburgh, to look after his interest there. But as Bubbleburgh is only one of a set of five boroughs which club their shares[9] for a member of parliament, Sir Peter's adversary had judiciously watched his departure, in order to commence a canvass in the no less royal borough of Bitem, which, as all the world knows, lies at the very termination of Sir Peter's avenue, and has been held in leading-strings[1] by him and his ancestors for time immemorial. Now Sir Peter was thus placed in the situation of an ambitious monarch, who, after having commenced a daring inroad into his enemies' territories, is suddenly recalled by an invasion of his own hereditary dominions. He was obliged in consequence to return from the half-won borough of Bubbleburgh, to look after the half-lost borough of Bitem, and the two pairs of horses which had carried him that morning to Bubbleburgh, were now forcibly detained to transport him, his agent, his valet, his jester, and his hard-drinker, across the country to Bitem. The cause of this detention, which to me was of as little consequence as it may be to the reader, was important enough to my companions to reconcile them to the delay. Like eagles, they smelled the battle afar off, ordered a magnum of claret and beds at the Wallace, and entered at full career into the Bubbleburgh and Bitem politics, with all the probable "petitions and complaints" to which they were likely to give rise.

In the midst of an anxious, animated, and, to me, most unintelligible discussion, concerning provosts, bailies, deacons, sets of boroughs, leets, town-clerks, burgesses resident and non-resident,[2] all of a sudden the lawyer recollected himself. "Poor Dunover, we must not forget him"; and the landlord was dispatched in quest of the *pauvre hontéux*,[3] with an earnestly civil invitation to him for the rest of the evening. I could not help asking the young gentlemen if they knew the history of this poor man; and the counsellor applied himself to his pocket to recover the memorial or brief from which he had stated his cause.

"He has been a candidate for our *remedium miserabile*," said Mr. Hardie, "commonly called a *cessio bonorum*.[4] As there are divines who have doubted the eternity of future punishments, so the Scotch lawyers seem to have thought that the crime of poverty might be atoned for by something short of perpetual imprisonment. After a month's confinement, you must know, a

---

8. The treacherous disposition of the Scots (Latin).
9. I.e., combine their votes (to elect a candidate).
1. In a state of dependence.
2. Political terms. "Bailies": chief magistrates. "Leets": lists of candidates eligible for some office.

3. Pauper who is ashamed to beg.
4. In Roman and old Scots law, the surrender of all one's property to creditors (to avoid imprisonment for debt). "*Remedium miserable*": sad remedy (Latin).

prisoner for debt is entitled, on a sufficient statement to our Supreme Court, setting forth the amount of his funds, and the nature of his misfortunes, and surrendering all his effects to his creditors, to claim to be discharged from prison."

"I had heard," I replied, "of such a humane regulation."

"Yes," said Halkit, "and the beauty of it is, as the foreign fellow said, you may get the *cessio* when the *bonorums* are all spent—But what, are you puzzling in your pockets to seek your only memorial among old play-bills, letters requesting a meeting of the Faculty, rules of the Speculative Society, syllabus' of lectures—all the miscellaneous contents of a young advocate's pocket, which contains every thing but briefs and bank notes? Can you not state a case of *cessio* without your memorial? Why, it is done every Saturday. The events follow each other as regularly as clock-work, and one form of condescendence might suit every one of them."

"This is very unlike the variety of distress which this gentleman stated to fall under the consideration of your judges," said I.

"True," replied Halkit; "but Hardie spoke of criminal jurisprudence, and this business is purely civil. I could plead a *cessio* myself without the inspiring honours of a gown and three-tailed periwig[5]—Listen.—My client was bred a journeyman weaver—made some little money—took a farm—(for conducting a farm, like driving a gig, comes by nature)—late severe times—induced to sign bills with a friend, for which he received no value—landlord sequestrates—creditors accept a composition—pursuer sets up a publichouse—fails a second time—is incarcerated for a debt of ten pounds, seven shillings and sixpence—his debts amount to blank—his losses to blank—his funds to blank—leaving a balance of blank in his favor. There is no opposition; your lordships will please grant commission to take his oath."

Hardie now renounced this ineffectual search, in which there was perhaps a little affectation, and told us the tale of poor Dunover's distresses, with a tone in which a degree of feeling, which he seemed ashamed of as unprofessional, mingled with his attempts at wit, and did him more honor. It was one of those tales which seem to argue a sort of ill-luck or fatality attached to the hero. A well-informed, industrious, and blameless, but poor and bashful man, had in vain essayed all the usual means by which others acquire independence, yet had never succeeded beyond the attainment of bare subsistence. During a brief gleam of hope, rather than of actual prosperity, he had added a wife and family to his cares, but the dawn was speedily overcast. Everything retrograded with him towards the verge of the miry Slough of Despond,[6] which yawns for insolvent debtors; and after catching at each twig, and experiencing the protracted agony of feeling them one by one elude his grasp, he actually sunk into the miry pit whence he had been extricated by the professional exertions of Hardie.

"And, I suppose, now you have dragged this poor devil ashore, you will leave him half naked on the beach to provide for himself?" said Halkit. "Hark ye,"—and he whispered something in his ear, of which the penetrating and insinuating words, "Interest with my Lord," alone reached mine.

"It is *pessimi exempli*,"[7] said Hardie, laughing, "to provide for a ruined

---

5. The gown and wig that Halkit wears in court.
6. From John Bunyan's *Pilgrim's Progress*.

7. The worst of examples (Latin).

client; but I was thinking of what you mention, provided it can be managed— But hush! here he comes."

The recent relation of the poor man's misfortunes had given him, I was pleased to observe, a claim to the attention and respect of the young men, who treated him with great civility, and gradually engaged him in a conversation, which, much to my satisfaction, again turned upon the *Causes Célèbres* of Scotland. Emboldened by the kindness with which he was treated, Mr. Dunover began to contribute his share to the amusement of the evening. Jails, like other places, have their ancient traditions, known only to the inhabitants, and handed down from one set of the melancholy lodgers to the next who occupy their cells. Some of these, which Dunover mentioned, were interesting, and served to illustrate the narratives of remarkable trials, which Hardie had at his finger ends, and which his companion was also well skilled in. This sort of conversation passed away the evening till the early hour when Mr. Dunover chose to retire to rest, and I also retreated to take down memorandums of what I had learned, in order to add another narrative to those which it had been my chief amusement to collect, and to write out in detail. The two young men ordered a broiled bone, Madeira negus, and a pack of cards, and commenced a game at picquet.[8]

Next morning the travelers left Gandercleugh. I afterwards learned from the papers that both have been since engaged in the great political cause of Bubbleburgh and Bitem, a summary case, and entitled to particular dispatch; but which, it is thought, nevertheless, may outlast the duration of the parliament to which the contest refers. Mr. Halkit, as the newspapers informed me, acts as agent or solicitor; and Mr. Hardie opened for Sir Peter Plyem with singular ability, and to such good purpose, that I understand he has since had fewer play-bills and more briefs in his pocket. And both the young gentlemen deserve their good fortune; for I learned from Dunover, who called on me some weeks afterwards, and communicated the intelligence with tears in his eyes, that their interest had availed to obtain him a small office for the decent maintenance of his family; and that, after a train of constant and uninterrupted misfortune, he could trace a dawn of prosperity to his having the good fortune to be flung from the top of a mail-coach into the river Gander, in company with an advocate and a writer to the signet.[9] The reader will not perhaps deem himself equally obliged to the accident, since it brings upon him the following narrative, founded upon the conversation of the evening.

1818   1818

Lochinvar[1]

> O young Lochinvar is come out of the west,
> Through all the wide Border his steed was the best;
> And save his good broadsword he weapons had none,
> He rode all unarm'd, and he rode all alone.

8. A card game for two players. "Madeira negus": a mixture of wine (here, Madeira), hot water, sugar, nutmeg, and lemons.
9. I.e., with a barrister (Hardie) and the highest grade of legal solicitor (Halkit).
1. An inset poem in the long narrative poem *Marmion.*

5   So faithful in love, and so dauntless in war,
       There never was knight like the young Lochinvar.

       He staid not for brake, and he stopp'd not for stone,
       He swam the Eske river where ford there was none;
       But ere he alighted at Netherby gate,
10   The bride had consented, the gallant came late:
       For a laggard in love, and a dastard in war,
       Was to wed the fair Ellen of brave Lochinvar.

       So boldly he enter'd the Netherby Hall,
       Among bride's-men, and kinsmen, and brothers and all:
15   Then spoke the bride's father, his hand on his sword,
       (For the poor craven bridegroom said never a word,)
       "O come ye in peace here, or come ye in war,
       Or to dance at our bridal, young Lord Lochinvar?"

       "I long woo'd your daughter, my suit you denied;—
20   Love swells like the Solway, but ebbs like its tide—
       And now I am come, with this lost love of mine,
       To lead but one measure, drink one cup of wine.
       There are maidens in Scotland more lovely by far,
       That would gladly be bride to the young Lochinvar."

25   The bride kiss'd the goblet: the knight took it up,
       He quaff'd off the wine, and he threw down the cup.
       She look'd down to blush, and she look'd up to sigh,
       With a smile on her lips and a tear in her eye.
       He took her soft hand, ere her mother could bar,—
30   "Now tread we a measure!" said young Lochinvar.

       So stately his form, and so lovely her face,
       That never a hall such a galliard² did grace;
       While her mother did fret, and her father did fume,
       And the bridegroom stood dangling his bonnet and plume;
35   And the bride-maidens whisper'd, " 'twere better by far
       To have match'd our fair cousin with young Lochinvar."

       One touch to her hand, and one word in her ear,
       When they reach'd the hall-door, and the charger stood near;
       So light to the croupe³ the fair lady he swung,
40   So light to the saddle before her he sprung!
       "She is won! we are gone, over bank, bush, and scaur;°   rocky crag
       They'll have fleet steeds that follow," quoth young Lochinvar.

       There was mounting 'mong Graemes of the Netherby clan;
       Forsters, Fenwicks, and Musgraves, they rode and they ran:
45   There was racing and chasing on Cannobie Lee,
       But the lost bride of Netherby ne'er did they see.

---

2. A man of courage and spirit.   3. The rump of the horse.

So daring in love, and so dauntless in war,
Have ye e'er heard of gallant like young Lochinvar?

1808

Jock of Hazeldean[1]

"Why weep ye by the tide, ladie?
   Why weep ye by the tide?
I'll wed ye to my youngest son,
   And ye sall be his bride:
5 And ye sall be his bride, ladie,
   Sae comely to be seen"—
But ay she loot the tears down fa'
   For Jock of Hazeldean.

"Now let this willfu' grief be done,
10   And dry that cheek so pale;
Young Frank is chief of Errington
   And lord of Langley Dale;
His step is first in peaceful ha',
   His sword in battle keen"—
15 But ay she loot the tears down fa'
   For Jock of Hazeldean.

"A chain of gold ye sall not lack,
   Nor braid to bind your hair;
Nor mettled hound, nor managed° hawk,   *trained*
20   Nor palfrey fresh and fair;
And you, the foremost o' them a',
   Shall ride our forest queen"—
But ay she loot the tears down fa'
   For Jock of Hazeldean.

25 The kirk was decked at morningtide,
   The tapers glimmered fair;
The priest and bridegroom wait the bride,
   And dame and knight are there.
They sought her baith by bower and ha';
30   The ladie was not seen!
She's o'er the Border and awa'
   Wi' Jock of Hazeldean.

1816

Proud Maisie[1]

Proud Maisie is in the wood
   Walking so early;

---

1. The first stanza is from a traditional Scottish ballad.

1. Sung by crazy Madge Wildfire on her deathbed in *The Heart of Midlothian* (chap. 40).

Sweet Robin sits on the bush,
    Singing so rarely.

5 "Tell me, thou bonny bird,
    When shall I marry me?"—
"When six braw° gentlemen   *fine*
    Kirward shall carry ye."

"Who makes the bridal bed,
10 Birdie, say truly?"—
"The gray-headed sexton
That delves the grave duly.

"The glowworm o'er grave and stone
Shall light thee steady,
15 The owl from the steeple sing,
'Welcome, proud lady.' "

1818

SAMUEL TAYLOR COLERIDGE
1772–1834

In *The Prelude* Wordsworth, recording his gratitude to the mountains, lakes, and winds "that dwell among the hills where I was born," commiserates with Coleridge because "thou, my Friend! wert reared / In the great City, 'mid far other scenes." Samuel Taylor Coleridge had in fact been born in the small town of Ottery St. Mary, in rural Devonshire, but on the death of his father he had been sent to school at Christ's Hospital, in London. He was a dreamy, enthusiastic, and extraordinarily precocious schoolboy; Charles Lamb, his schoolmate and lifelong friend, in his essay on Christ's Hospital has given us a vivid sketch of Coleridge's loneliness, his learning, and his eloquence. When in 1791 Coleridge entered Jesus College, Cambridge, he was an accomplished scholar; but he found little intellectual stimulation at the university, fell into idleness, dissoluteness, and debt, then in despair fled to London and enlisted in the Light Dragoons under the alias of Silas Tomkyn Comberbache—one of the most inept cavalrymen in the long history of the British army. Although rescued by his brothers and sent back to Cambridge, he left in 1794 without a degree.

In June 1794 Coleridge met Robert Southey, then a student at Oxford who, like himself, had poetic aspirations, was a radical in religion and politics, and sympathized with the republican experiment in France. Together the two young men planned to establish an ideal democratic community in America for which Coleridge coined the name "Pantisocracy," signifying an equal rule by all. A plausible American real-estate agent persuaded them that the ideal location would be on the banks of the Susquehanna, in Pennsylvania. Twelve men undertook to go; and because perpetuation of the scheme required offspring, hence wives, Coleridge dutifully became engaged to Sara Fricker, conveniently at hand as the sister of Southey's fiancée. The Pantisocracy scheme collapsed, but at Southey's insistence Coleridge went through with the marriage, "resolved," as he said, "but wretched." Later Coleridge's radicalism waned, and he became a conservative in politics—a highly philosophical one—and a staunch Anglican in religion.

In 1795 Coleridge met Wordsworth and at once judged him to be "the best poet of the age." When in 1797 Wordsworth brought his sister, Dorothy, to settle at Alfoxden, only three miles from the Coleridges at Nether Stowey, the period of intimate communication and poetic collaboration began that was the golden time of Coleridge's life. An annuity of £150, granted to Coleridge by Thomas and Josiah Wedgwood, sons of the founder of the famous pottery firm, came just in time to deflect him from assuming a post as a Unitarian minister. After their joint publication of *Lyrical Ballads* in 1798, Coleridge and the Wordsworths spent a winter in Germany, where Coleridge attended the University of Göttingen and began the lifelong study of Kant and the post-Kantian German philosophers and critics that helped alter profoundly his thinking about philosophy, religion, and aesthetics.

Back in England, Coleridge in 1800 followed the Wordsworths to the Lake District, settling at Greta Hall, Keswick. He had become gradually disaffected from his wife, and now he fell helplessly and hopelessly in love with Sara Hutchinson, whose sister, Mary, Wordsworth married in 1802. In accord with the medical prescription of that time, Coleridge had been taking laudanum (opium dissolved in alcohol) to ease the painful physical ailments from which he had suffered from an early age. In 1800–01 heavy dosages during attacks of rheumatism made opium a necessity to him, and Coleridge soon recognized that the drug was a greater evil than the diseases it did not cure. *Dejection: An Ode*, published in 1802, was Coleridge's despairing farewell to health, happiness, and poetic creativity. A two-year sojourn on the Mediterranean island of Malta, intended to restore his health, instead completed his decline. When he returned to England in the late summer of 1806 he was a broken man, an inveterate drug addict, estranged from his wife, suffering from agonies of remorse, and subject to terrifying nightmares of guilt and despair from which his own shrieks awakened him. A bitter quarrel with Wordsworth in 1810 marked the nadir of his life and expectations.

Under these conditions Coleridge's literary efforts, however sporadic and fragmentary, were little short of heroic. In 1808 he gave a course of public lectures in London and, in the next eleven years, followed these with other series on both literary and philosophical topics. He wrote for newspapers and single-handedly undertook to write, publish, and distribute a periodical, *The Friend*, which lasted for some ten months beginning in June 1809. A tragedy, *Remorse*, had in 1813 a successful run of twenty performances at the Drury Lane theater. In 1816 he took up residence at Highgate, a northern suburb of London, under the supervision of the excellent and endlessly forbearing physician James Gillman, who managed to control, although not to eliminate, Coleridge's consumption of opium. The next three years were Coleridge's most sustained period of literary activity: while continuing to lecture and to write for the newspapers on a variety of subjects, he published *Biographia Literaria, Zapolya* (a drama), a book consisting of the essays in *The Friend* (revised and greatly enlarged), two collections of poems, and several important treatises on philosophical and religious subjects. In these last he undertook to establish a philosophical basis for the Trinitarian theology to which he had turned after his youthful period of Unitarianism.

The remaining years of his life, which he spent with Dr. and Mrs. Gillman, were quieter and happier than any he had known since the turn of the century. He came to a peaceful understanding with his wife and was reconciled with Wordsworth, with whom he toured the Rhineland in 1828. His rooms at Highgate became a center for friends, for the London literati, and for a steady stream of pilgrims from England and America. They came to hear one of the wonders of the age, the Sage of Highgate's conversation—or monologue—for even in his decline, Coleridge's talk never lost the almost incantatory power that Hazlitt has immortalized in *My First Acquaintance with Poets*. When he died, Coleridge left his friends with the sense that an incomparable intellect had vanished from the world. "The most *wonderful* man that I have ever known," Wordsworth declared, his voice breaking; and Charles Lamb wrote, "His great and dear spirit haunts me. . . . Never saw I his likeness, nor probably the world can see again."

Coleridge's friends, however, abetted by his own merciless self-judgments, set current the opinion, still common, that he was great in promise but not in performance. Even in his buoyant youth he described his own character as "indolence capable of energies"; and it is true that while his mind was incessantly active and fertile, he lacked application and staying power. He also manifested early in life a profound sense of guilt and a need for public expiation. After drug addiction sapped his strength and will, he often adapted (or simply adopted) passages from other writers, with little or no acknowledgment, and sometimes in a context that seems designed to reveal that he is reliant on sources that he does not credit. Whatever the tangled motives for his procedure, Coleridge has repeatedly been charged with gross plagiarism, from his day to our own. After *The Rime of the Ancient Mariner*, most of the poems he completed were written, like the first version of *Dejection: An Ode*, in a spasm of intense effort. Writings that required sustained planning and application were either left unfinished or, like *Biographia Literaria*, made up of brilliant sections eked out with filler, sometimes lifted from other writers, in a desperate effort to meet a deadline. Many of his speculations Coleridge merely confided to his notebooks and the ears of his friends, incorporated in letters, and poured out in the margins of his own and other people's books.

Even so, it is only when measured against his own potentialities that Coleridge's achievements appear limited. In opposition to the prevailing British philosophy of empiricism and associationism, Coleridge for most of his mature life expounded his views of the mind as creative in perception, intuitive in its discovery of the first premises of metaphysics and religion, and capable of a poetic re-creation of the world of sense by the fusing and formative power of the imagination. Within the decade after Coleridge died, John Stuart Mill, an acute student of contemporary thought, announced that Coleridge was one of "the two great seminal minds of England," the most important instigator and representative of the conservative intellectual movement of the day. Time has proved Mill's estimate of Coleridge to be just, for his influence is strongly evident in nineteenth-century English and American traditions of philosophical idealism, enlightened political conservatism, and liberal interpretations of Trinitarian theology. By present consensus, Coleridge is also one of the most important and influential of literary theorists; a number of his central ideas were adopted even by some New Critics of the mid-twentieth century who derogated the Romantic poetry for which his criticism provided a rationale. Above all, Coleridge's writings in verse, although small in quantity, are the achievements of a remarkably innovative poet.

In the course of a few years, he wrote his poems of mystery and demonism, *The Rime of the Ancient Mariner*, *Christabel*, and *Kubla Khan*. No less impressive in their own way are the blank-verse poems of the lonely and meditative mind that, by an extension of Coleridge's term for one of them, are called "Conversation Poems"; in the best of these, *Frost at Midnight*, Coleridge perfected the characteristic pattern of integrally related description and meditation, which Wordsworth immediately used in *Tintern Abbey*. Coleridge himself adapted this pattern to *Dejection: An Ode*, a high achievement in a genre in which few poets have been successful, the irregular English ode. And even when he had mainly given up poetry, after 1805, Coleridge continued to write occasional short lyrics (printed here) that are notable both for their quality and for the extent to which they have been neglected by anthologists.

The Eolian Harp[1]

Composed at Clevedon, Somersetshire

My pensive Sara! thy soft cheek reclined
Thus on mine arm, most soothing sweet it is
To sit beside our cot, our cot o'ergrown
With white-flowered jasmin, and the broad-leaved myrtle,
5 (Meet emblems they of Innocence and Love!)
And watch the clouds, that late were rich with light,
Slow saddening round, and mark the star of eve
Serenely brilliant (such should wisdom be)
Shine opposite! How exquisite the scents
10 Snatched from yon bean-field! and the world so hushed!
The stilly murmur of the distant sea
Tells us of silence.

            And that simplest lute,
Placed length-ways in the clasping casement, hark!
How by the desultory breeze caressed,
15 Like some coy maid half yielding to her lover,
It pours such sweet upbraiding, as must needs
Tempt to repeat the wrong! And now, its strings
Boldlier swept, the long sequacious° notes   *successive*
Over delicious surges sink and rise,
20 Such a soft floating witchery of sound
As twilight Elfins make, when they at eve
Voyage on gentle gales from Fairy-Land,
Where Melodies round honey-dropping flowers,
Footless and wild, like birds of Paradise,[2]
25 Nor pause, nor perch, hovering on untamed wing!
O the one life within us and abroad,
Which meets all motion and becomes its soul,
A light in sound, a sound-like power in light,
Rhythm in all thought, and joyance every where—
30 Methinks, it should have been impossible
Not to love all things in a world so filled;

---

1. Named for Aeolus, god of the winds, the harp has strings stretched over a rectangular sounding box. The strings are tuned in unison. When placed in an opened window, the harp (also called "Eolian lute," "Eolian lyre," "wind harp") responds to the altering wind by sequences of musical chords. This instrument, which seems to voice nature's own music, was a favorite household furnishing in the period and was repeatedly alluded to in Romantic poetry. It served also as one of the recurrent Romantic images for the mind—either the mind in poetic inspiration, as in the last stanza of Shelley's *Ode to the West Wind* (p. 732), or else the mind in perception, responding to an intellectual breeze by trembling into consciousness, as in this poem, lines 44–48. Coleridge, however, no sooner puts forward this concept than he retracts it, for it comes too close to the heresy of pantheism, which identifies God with the nature that, in the orthodox view, is His creation.

Coleridge wrote this poem to Sara Fricker, whom he married on October 4, 1795, and took to a cottage (the "cot" of lines 3 and 64) at Clevedon, overlooking the Bristol Channel. He later several times expanded and altered the original version; the famous lines 26–29, for example, were not added until 1817. The poem was Coleridge's first achievement in the important Romantic form of the sustained blank-verse lyric of description and meditation, in the mode of conversation addressed to a silent auditor—a form that he perfected in *Frost at Midnight,* and that Wordsworth adopted in *Tintern Abbey.*

2. Brilliantly colored birds found in New Guinea and adjacent islands. The native practice of removing the legs when preparing the skin led Europeans to believe that the birds were footless and spent their lives hovering in the air and feeding on nectar.

Where the breeze warbles, and the mute still air
Is Music slumbering on her instrument.

And thus, my love! as on the midway slope
35 Of yonder hill I stretch my limbs at noon,
Whilst through my half-closed eye-lids I behold
The sunbeams dance, like diamonds, on the main,
And tranquil muse upon tranquillity;
Full many a thought uncalled and undetained,
40 And many idle flitting phantasies,
Traverse my indolent and passive brain,
As wild and various as the random gales
That swell and flutter on this subject lute!

And what if all of animated nature
45 Be but organic harps diversely framed,
That tremble into thought, as o'er them sweeps
Plastic and vast, one intellectual breeze,
At once the Soul of each, and God of All?

But thy more serious eye a mild reproof
50 Darts, O beloved woman! nor such thoughts
Dim and unhallowed dost thou not reject,
And biddest me walk humbly with my God.
Meek daughter in the family of Christ!
Well hast thou said and holily dispraised
55 These shapings of the unregenerate mind;
Bubbles that glitter as they rise and break
On vain Philosophy's aye-babbling spring.
For never guiltless may I speak of him,
The Incomprehensible! save when with awe
60 I praise him, and with Faith that inly feels;
Who with his saving mercies healed me,
A sinful and most miserable man,
Wildered and dark, and gave me to possess
Peace, and this cot, and thee, heart-honored Maid!

1795   1796

This Lime-Tree Bower My Prison

In the June of 1797, some long-expected Friends paid a visit to the author's cottage; and on the morning of their arrival, he met with an accident, which disabled him from walking during the whole time of their stay. One evening, when they had left him for a few hours, he composed the following lines in the garden-bower.[1]

1. The time was in fact July 1797; the visiting friends were William and Dorothy Wordsworth and Charles Lamb; the accident was the fault of Mrs. Coleridge—"dear Sara," Coleridge wrote, "accidentally emptied a skillet of boiling milk on my foot"; and the bower consisted of lime (i.e., linden) trees in the garden of Thomas Poole, next door to Coleridge's cottage at Nether Stowey. Coleridge related these facts in a letter to Robert Southey, July 17, 1797, in which he transcribed the first version of this fine "conversation poem." In the earliest printed text, the title is followed by "Addressed to Charles Lamb, of the India-House, London."

Well, they are gone, and here must I remain,
This lime-tree bower my prison! I have lost
Beauties and feelings, such as would have been
Most sweet to my remembrance even when age
5   Had dimmed mine eyes to blindness! They, meanwhile,
Friends, whom I never more may meet again,
On springy[2] heath, along the hill-top edge,
Wander in gladness, and wind down, perchance,
To that still roaring dell, of which I told;
10   The roaring dell, o'erwooded, narrow, deep,
And only speckled by the mid-day sun;
Where its slim trunk the ash from rock to rock
Flings arching like a bridge;—that branchless ash,
Unsunned and damp, whose few poor yellow leaves
15   Ne'er tremble in the gale, yet tremble still,
Fanned by the water-fall! and there my friends
Behold the dark green file of long lank weeds,
That all at once (a most fantastic sight!)
Still nod and drip beneath the dripping edge
Of the blue clay-stone.[3]

20   Now, my friends emerge
Beneath the wide wide Heaven—and view again
The many-steepled tract magnificent
Of hilly fields and meadows, and the sea,
With some fair bark, perhaps, whose sails light up
25   The slip of smooth clear blue betwixt two Isles
Of purple shadow! Yes! they wander on
In gladness all; but thou, methinks, most glad,
My gentle-hearted Charles! for thou hast pined
And hungered after Nature, many a year,
30   In the great City pent,[4] winning thy way
With sad yet patient soul, through evil and pain
And strange calamity![5] Ah! slowly sink
Behind the western ridge, thou glorious sun!
Shine in the slant beams of the sinking orb,
35   Ye purple heath-flowers! richlier burn, ye clouds!
Live in the yellow light, ye distant groves!
And kindle, thou blue ocean! So my Friend
Struck with deep joy may stand, as I have stood,
Silent with swimming sense; yea, gazing round
40   On the wide landscape, gaze till all doth seem
Less gross than bodily; and of such hues
As veil the Almighty Spirit, when yet he makes
Spirits perceive his presence.

                      A delight
Comes sudden on my heart, and I am glad

2. *Elastic*, I mean [Coleridge's note].
3. Cf. Dorothy Wordsworth's description of the "low damp dell" in her *Alfoxden Journal*, February 10, 1798 (p. 386).
4. Despite Coleridge's claim, Charles Lamb emi-

nently preferred London over what he called "dead Nature."
5. Some ten months earlier Charles Lamb's sister, Mary, had stabbed their mother to death in a fit of insanity.

45 As I myself were there! Nor in this bower,
    This little lime-tree bower, have I not marked
    Much that has soothed me. Pale beneath the blaze
    Hung the transparent foliage; and I watched
    Some broad and sunny leaf, and loved to see
50 The shadow of the leaf and stem above
    Dappling its sunshine! And that walnut-tree
    Was richly tinged, and a deep radiance lay
    Full on the ancient ivy, which usurps
    Those fronting elms, and now, with blackest mass
55 Makes their dark branches gleam a lighter hue
    Through the late twilight: and though now the bat
    Wheels silent by, and not a swallow twitters,
    Yet still the solitary humble bee
    Sings in the bean-flower! Henceforth I shall know
60 That Nature ne'er deserts the wise and pure;
    No plot so narrow, be but Nature there,
    No waste so vacant, but may well employ
    Each faculty of sense, and keep the heart
    Awake to Love and Beauty! and sometimes
65 'Tis well to be bereft of promised good,
    That we may lift the Soul, and contemplate
    With lively joy the joys we cannot share.
    My gentle-hearted Charles! when the last rook
    Beat its straight path along the dusky air
70 Homewards, I blessed it! deeming its black wing
    (Now a dim speck, now vanishing in light)
    Had crossed the mighty orb's dilated glory,
    While thou stood'st gazing; or when all was still,
    Flew creeking o'er thy head, and had a charm
75 For thee, my gentle-hearted Charles, to whom
    No sound is dissonant which tells of Life.

1797   1800

The Rime of the Ancient Mariner[1]

IN SEVEN PARTS

*Facile credo, plures esse Naturas invisibiles quam visibiles in rerum
universitate. Sed horum [sic] omnium familiam quis nobis enarrabit,
et gradus et cognationes et discrimina et singulorum munera? Quid
agunt? quae loca habitant? Harum rerum notitiam semper ambivit
ingenium humanum, nunquam attigit. Juvat, interea, non diffiteor,
quandoque in animo, tanquam in tabulâ, majoris et melioris mundi*

---

1. Coleridge describes the origin of this poem in
the opening section of chap. 14 of *Biographia Literaria*. In a comment made to the Reverend Alexander Dyce in 1835 and in a note on *We Are Seven*
dictated in 1843, Wordsworth added some details.
The poem, based on a dream of Coleridge's friend
Cruikshank, was originally planned as a collaboration between Coleridge and Wordsworth, to pay
the expense of a walking tour they took with Dorothy Wordsworth in November 1797. Before he

dropped out of the enterprise, Wordsworth suggested the shooting of the albatross and the navi-
gation of the ship by the dead men; he also
contributed lines 13–16 and 226–27.
    The version of *The Rime of the Ancient Mariner*
printed in *Lyrical Ballads* (1798) contained many
archaic words and spellings. In later editions Coleridge greatly improved the poem by pruning the
archaisms and by other revisions; he also added the
Latin epigraph and the marginal glosses.

imaginem contemplari: ne mens assuefacta hodiernae vitae minutiis
se contrahat nimis, et tota subsidat in pusillas cogitationes. Sed ver-
itati interea invigilandum est, modusque servandus, ut certa ab incer-
tis, diem a nocte, distinguamus.
T. BURNET, Archaeol. Phil. p. 68.[2]

Part 1

<table>
<tr>
<td>An ancient Mariner meeteth three gallants bidden to a wedding-feast, and detaineth one.</td>
<td>

It is an ancient Mariner
And he stoppeth one of three.
"By thy long grey beard and glittering eye,
Now wherefore stopp'st thou me?

The Bridegroom's doors are opened wide,
And I am next of kin;
The guests are met, the feast is set:
May'st hear the merry din."

He holds him with his skinny hand,
"There was a ship," quoth he.
"Hold off! unhand me, grey-beard loon!"
Eftsoons[3] his hand dropt he.

</td>
<td>5

10</td>
</tr>
<tr>
<td>The wedding guest is spellbound by the eye of the old sea-faring man, and constrained to hear his tale.</td>
<td>

He holds him with his glittering eye—
The wedding-guest stood still,
And listens like a three years' child:
The Mariner hath his will.[4]

The wedding-guest sat on a stone:
He cannot choose but hear;
And thus spake on that ancient man,
The bright-eyed Mariner.

"The ship was cheered, the harbor cleared,
Merrily did we drop
Below the kirk,[5] below the hill,
Below the light house top.

</td>
<td>

15

20</td>
</tr>
<tr>
<td>The Mariner tells how the ship sailed southward with a good wind and fair weather, till it reached the line.</td>
<td>

The sun came up upon the left,
Out of the sea came he!
And he shone bright, and on the right
Went down into the sea.

Higher and higher every day,
Till over the mast at noon[6]—"

</td>
<td>25

30</td>
</tr>
</table>

2. "I readily believe that there are more invisible than visible Natures in the universe. But who will explain for us the family of all these beings, and the ranks and relations and distinguishing features and functions of each? What do they do? What places do they inhabit? The human mind has always sought the knowledge of these things, but never attained it. Meanwhile I do not deny that it is helpful sometimes to contemplate in the mind, as on a tablet, the image of a greater and better world, lest the intellect, habituated to the petty things of daily life, narrow itself and sink wholly into trivial thoughts. But at the same time we must be watchful for the truth and keep a sense of proportion, so that we may distinguish the certain from the uncertain, day from night." Adapted by Coleridge from Thomas Burnet, *Archaeologiae Philosophicae* (1692).

3. At once.

4. I.e., the Mariner has gained control of the will of the wedding guest by hypnosis—or, as it was called in Coleridge's time, by "mesmerism."

5. Church.

6. The ship had reached the equator.

The wedding-guest here beat his breast,
For he heard the loud bassoon.

The Wedding Guest heareth the bridal music; but the mariner continueth his tale.

The bride hath paced into the hall,
Red as a rose is she;
Nodding their heads before her goes   35
The merry minstrelsy.

The wedding-guest he beat his breast,
Yet he cannot choose but hear;
And thus spake on that ancient man,
The bright-eyed Mariner.   40

The ship driven by a storm toward the south pole.

"And now the storm-blast came, and he
Was tyrannous and strong:
He struck with his o'ertaking wings,
And chased us south along.

With sloping masts and dipping prow,   45
As who pursued with yell and blow
Still treads the shadow of his foe,
And forward bends his head,
The ship drove fast, loud roared the blast,
And southward aye we fled.   50

And now there came both mist and snow,
And it grew wondrous cold:
And ice, mast-high, came floating by,
As green as emerald.

The land of ice, and of fearful sounds where no living thing was to be seen.

And through the drifts the snowy clifts   55
Did send a dismal sheen:
Nor shapes of men nor beasts we ken—
The ice was all between.

The ice was here, the ice was there,
The ice was all around: 60
It cracked and growled, and roared and howled,
Like noises in a swound![7]

Till a great sea-bird, called the Albatross, came through the snow-fog, and was received with great joy and hospitality.

At length did cross an Albatross,
Thorough the fog it came;
As if it had been a Christian soul,   65
We hailed it in God's name.

It ate the food it ne'er had eat,
And round and round it flew.
The ice did split with a thunder-fit;
The helmsman steered us through!   70

7. Swoon.

And lo! the Albatross proveth a bird of good omen, and followeth the ship as it returned northward through fog and floating ice.

And a good south wind sprung up behind;
The Albatross did follow,
And every day, for food or play,
Came to the mariners' hollo!

In mist or cloud, on mast or shroud,[8]   75
It perched for vespers nine;
Whiles all the night, through fog-smoke white,
Glimmered the white moon-shine."

The ancient Mariner inhospitably killeth the pious bird of good omen.

"God save thee, ancient Mariner!
From the fiends, that plague thee thus!—   80
Why look'st thou so?"—With my cross-bow
I shot the Albatross.

Part 2

The Sun now rose upon the right:[9]
Out of the sea came he,
Still hid in mist, and on the left   85
Went down into the sea.

And the good south wind still blew behind,
But no sweet bird did follow,
Nor any day for food or play
Came to the mariners' hollo!   90

His shipmates cry out against the ancient Mariner, for killing the bird of good luck.

And I had done a hellish thing,
And it would work 'em woe:
For all averred, I had killed the bird
That made the breeze to blow.
Ah wretch! said they, the bird to slay,   95
That made the breeze to blow!

But when the fog cleared off, they justify the same, and thus make themselves accomplices in the crime.

Nor dim nor red, like God's own head,
The glorious Sun uprist:
Then all averred, I had killed the bird
That brought the fog and mist.   100
'Twas right, said they, such birds to slay,
That bring the fog and mist.

The fair breeze continues; the ship enters the Pacific Ocean, and sails northward, even till it reaches the Line.[1]

The fair breeze blew, the white foam flew,
The furrow followed free;
We were the first that ever burst   105
Into that silent sea.

The ship hath been suddenly becalmed.

Down dropt the breeze, the sails dropt down,
'Twas sad as sad could be;

8. Rope supporting the mast.
9. Having rounded Cape Horn, the ship heads north into the Pacific.
1. I.e., the equator. Unless it is simply an error (Coleridge misreading his own poem), this gloss anticipates the ship's later arrival at the equator, on its trip north from the region of the South Pole, as described in lines 381–84.

And we did speak only to break
The silence of the sea!   110

All in a hot and copper sky,
The bloody Sun, at noon,
Right up above the mast did stand,
No bigger than the Moon.

Day after day, day after day,   115
We stuck, nor breath nor motion;
As idle as a painted ship
Upon a painted ocean.

And the Albatross
begins to be avenged.   Water, water, every where,
And all the boards did shrink;   120
Water, water, every where,
Nor any drop to drink.

The very deep did rot: O Christ!
That ever this should be!
Yea, slimy things did crawl with legs   125
Upon the slimy sea.

About, about, in reel and rout
The death-fires[2] danced at night;
The water, like a witch's oils,
Burnt green, and blue and white.   130

A spirit had followed
them; one of the   And some in dreams assured were
invisible inhabitants   Of the spirit that plagued us so;
of this planet, neither Nine fathom deep he had followed us
departed souls nor   From the land of mist and snow.
angels; concerning
whom the learned
Jew, Josephus, and the Platonic Constantinopolitan, Michael Psellus, may be consulted. They are very
numerous, and there is no climate or element without one or more.

And every tongue, through utter drought,   135
Was withered at the root;
We could not speak, no more than if
We had been choked with soot.

The shipmates, in
their sore distress,   Ah! well-a-day! what evil looks
would fain throw   Had I from old and young!   140
the whole guilt on   Instead of the cross, the Albatross
the ancient Mariner: About my neck was hung.
in sign whereof they
hang the dead sea
bird round his
neck.

Part 3

There passed a weary time. Each throat
Was parched, and glazed each eye.

---

2. Usually glossed as the corposant, or St. Elmo's fire—an atmospheric electricity on a ship's mast or rigging—believed by superstitious sailors to portend disaster. Possibly the image is instead a type of oceanic *ignis fatuus* ("foolish fire") resulting from the decomposition of putrescent matter in the sea (see line 123).

A weary time! a weary time!   145
How glazed each weary eye,
The ancient Mariner When looking westward, I beheld
beholdeth a sign in
the element afar off. A something in the sky.

At first it seemed a little speck,
And then it seemed a mist;   150
It moved and moved, and took at last
A certain shape, I wist.[3]

A speck, a mist, a shape, I wist!
And still it neared and neared:
As if it dodged a water-sprite,[4]   155
It plunged and tacked and veered.

At its nearer   With throats unslaked, with black lips baked,
approach, it seemeth
him to be a ship; and We could nor laugh nor wail;
at a dear ransom he   Through utter drought all dumb we stood!
freeth his speech
from the bonds of   I bit my arm, I sucked the blood,   160
thirst.   And cried, A sail! a sail!

With throats unslaked, with black lips baked,
Agape they heard me call:
A flash of joy; Gramercy![5] they for joy did grin,
And all at once their breath drew in,   165
As they were drinking all.

And horror follows. See! see! (I cried) she tacks no more!
For can it be a ship
that comes onward Hither to work us weal;[6]
without wind or tide? Without a breeze, without a tide,
She steadies with upright keel!   170

The western wave was all a-flame.
The day was well nigh done!
Almost upon the western wave
Rested the broad bright Sun;
When that strange shape drove suddenly   175
Betwixt us and the Sun.

It seemeth him but And straight the Sun was flecked with bars,
the skeleton of a
ship. (Heaven's Mother send us grace!)
As if through a dungeon-grate he peered
With broad and burning face.   180

Alas! (thought I, and my heart beat loud)
How fast she nears and nears!
Are those her sails that glance in the Sun,
Like restless gossameres?[7]

3. Knew.
4. A supernatural being that supervises the natural elements (but Coleridge may in fact have been
using the term to mean water-*spout*).

5. Great thanks; from the French *grand-merci.*
6. Benefit.
7. Filmy cobwebs floating in the air.

<table>
<tr>
<td>And its ribs are seen as bars on the face of the setting Sun. The specter-woman and her death-mate, and no other on board the skeleton-ship.</td>
<td>

Are those her ribs through which the Sun 185
Did peer, as through a grate?
And is that Woman all her crew?
Is that a Death? and are there two?
Is Death that woman's mate?

</td>
</tr>
</table>

Like vessel, like crew!

Her lips were red, her looks were free, 190
Her locks were yellow as gold:
Her skin was as white as leprosy,
The Night-mare Life-in-Death was she,
Who thicks man's blood with cold.

Death and Life-in-death have diced for the ship's crew, and she (the latter) winneth the ancient Mariner.

The naked hulk alongside came, 195
And the twain were casting dice;
"The game is done! I've won! I've won!"
Quoth she, and whistles thrice.

No twilight within the courts of the sun.

The Sun's rim dips; the stars rush out:
At one stride comes the dark; 200
With far-heard whisper, o'er the sea,
Off shot the spectre-bark.

At the rising of the Moon,

We listened and looked sideways up!
Fear at my heart, as at a cup,
My life-blood seemed to sip! 205
The stars were dim, and thick the night,
The steersman's face by his lamp gleamed white;
From the sails the dew did drip—
Till clomb above the eastern bar
The horned Moon, with one bright star 210
Within the nether tip.[8]

One after another,

One after one, by the star-dogged Moon,
Too quick for groan or sigh,
Each turned his face with a ghastly pang,
And cursed me with his eye. 215

His shipmates drop down dead.

Four times fifty living men,
(And I heard nor sigh nor groan)
With heavy thump, a lifeless lump,
They dropped down one by one.

But Life-in-Death begins her work on the ancient Mariner.

The souls did from their bodies fly,— 220
They fled to bliss or woe!
And every soul, it passed me by,
Like the whizz of my cross-bow!

Part 4

The wedding guest feareth that a spirit is talking to him.

"I fear thee, ancient Mariner!
I fear thy skinny hand! 225
And thou art long, and lank, and brown,
As is the ribbed sea-sand.

8. An omen of impending evil.

I fear thee and thy glittering eye,
And thy skinny hand, so brown."—

But the ancient Mar-
iner assureth him of
his bodily life, and
proceedeth to relate
his horrible penance.

Fear not, fear not, thou wedding-guest!   230
This body drop not down.

Alone, alone, all, all alone,
Alone on a wide wide sea!
And never a saint took pity on
My soul in agony.   235

He despiseth the
creatures of the
calm,

The many men, so beautiful!
And they all dead did lie:
And a thousand thousand slimy things
Lived on; and so did I.

And envieth that
they should live, and
so many lie dead.

I looked upon the rotting sea,   240
And drew my eyes away;
I looked upon the rotting deck,
And there the dead men lay.

I looked to heaven, and tried to pray;
But or ever a prayer had gusht,   245
A wicked whisper came, and made
My heart as dry as dust.

I closed my lids, and kept them close,
And the balls like pulses beat;
For the sky and the sea, and the sea and the sky   250
Lay like a load on my weary eye,
And the dead were at my feet.

But the curse liveth
for him in the eye of
the dead men.

The cold sweat melted from their limbs,
Nor rot nor reek did they:
The look with which they looked on me   255
Had never passed away.

An orphan's curse would drag to hell
A spirit from on high;
But oh! more horrible than that
Is the curse in a dead man's eye!   260
Seven days, seven nights, I saw that curse,
And yet I could not die.

In his loneliness and
fixedness he yearneth
towards the journey-
ing Moon, and the
stars that still
sojourn, yet still
move onward; and
everywhere the blue sky belongs to them, and is their appointed rest, and their native country and their
own natural homes, which they enter unannounced, as lords that are certainly expected and yet there
is a silent joy at their arrival.

The moving Moon went up the sky,
And no where did abide:
Softly she was going up,   265
And a star or two beside—

Her beams bemocked the sultry main,
Like April hoar-frost spread;
But where the ship's huge shadow lay,
The charmed water burnt alway   270
A still and awful red.

By the light of the
Moon he beholdeth
God's creatures of
the great calm.

Beyond the shadow of the ship,
I watched the water-snakes:
They moved in tracks of shining white,
And when they reared, the elfish light   275
Fell off in hoary flakes.

Within the shadow of the ship
I watched their rich attire:
Blue, glossy green, and velvet black,
They coiled and swam; and every track   280
Was a flash of golden fire.

Their beauty and
their happiness.

O happy living things! no tongue
Their beauty might declare:
A spring of love gushed from my heart,

He blesseth them in
his heart.

And I blessed them unaware: 285
Sure my kind saint took pity on me,
And I blessed them unaware.

The spell begins to
break.

The selfsame moment I could pray;
And from my neck so free
The Albatross fell off, and sank   290
Like lead into the sea.

Part 5

Oh sleep! it is a gentle thing,
Beloved from pole to pole!
To Mary Queen the praise be given!
She sent the gentle sleep from Heaven,   295
That slid into my soul.

By grace of the holy
Mother, the ancient
Mariner is refreshed
with rain.

The silly⁹ buckets on the deck,
That had so long remained,
I dreamt that they were filled with dew;
And when I awoke, it rained.   300

My lips were wet, my throat was cold,
My garments all were dank;
Sure I had drunken in my dreams,
And still my body drank.

I moved, and could not feel my limbs: 305
I was so light—almost
I thought that I had died in sleep,
And was a blessed ghost.

He heareth sounds
and seeth strange
sights and commo-
tions in the sky and
the element.

And soon I heard a roaring wind:
It did not come anear;   310
But with its sound it shook the sails,
That were so thin and sere.

9. Simple, homely.

The upper air burst into life!
And a hundred fire-flags sheen,[1]
To and fro they were hurried about!   315
And to and fro, and in and out,
The wan stars danced between.

And the coming wind did roar more loud,
And the sails did sigh like sedge;[2]
And the rain poured down from one black cloud;   320
The Moon was at its edge.

The thick black cloud was cleft, and still
The Moon was at its side:
Like waters shot from some high crag,
The lightning fell with never a jag,   325
A river steep and wide.

The bodies of the ship's crew are inspired, and the ship moves on;

The loud wind never reached the ship,
Yet now the ship moved on!
Beneath the lightning and the moon
The dead men gave a groan.   330

They groaned, they stirred, they all uprose,
Nor spake, nor moved their eyes;
It had been strange, even in a dream,
To have seen those dead men rise.

The helmsman steered, the ship moved on;   335
Yet never a breeze up blew;
The mariners all 'gan work the ropes,
Where they were wont to do;
They raised their limbs like lifeless tools—
We were a ghastly crew.   340

The body of my brother's son
Stood by me, knee to knee:
The body and I pulled at one rope,
But he said nought to me.

But not by the souls of the men, nor by dæmons[3] of earth or middle air, but by a blessed troop of angelic spirits, sent down by the invocation of the guardian saint.

"I fear thee, ancient Mariner!"   345
Be calm, thou Wedding-Guest!
'Twas not those souls that fled in pain,
Which to their corses[4] came again,
But a troop of spirits blest:

For when it dawned—they dropped their arms,   350
And clustered round the mast;

---

1. Shone. These fire-flags are probably St. Elmo's fire (see n. 2, p. 426), but Coleridge may be describing the Aurora Australis, or Southern Lights, and possibly also lightning.
2. A rushlike plant growing in wet soil.

3. Supernatural beings halfway between mortals and gods (the type of spirit that Coleridge describes in the gloss beside lines 131–34).
4. Corpses.

Sweet sounds rose slowly through their mouths,
And from their bodies passed.

Around, around, flew each sweet sound,
Then darted to the Sun;   355
Slowly the sounds came back again,
Now mixed, now one by one.

Sometimes a-dropping from the sky
I heard the sky-lark sing;
Sometimes all little birds that are,   360
How they seemed to fill the sea and air
With their sweet jargoning![5]

And now 'twas like all instruments,
Now like a lonely flute;
And now it is an angel's song,   365
That makes the heavens be mute.

It ceased; yet still the sails made on
A pleasant noise till noon,
A noise like of a hidden brook
In the leafy month of June,   370
That to the sleeping woods all night
Singeth a quiet tune.

Till noon we quietly sailed on,
Yet never a breeze did breathe:
Slowly and smoothly went the ship,   375
Moved onward from beneath.

The lonesome spirit from the south-pole carries on the ship as far as the line, in obedience to the angelic troop, but still requireth vengeance.
Under the keel nine fathom deep,
From the land of mist and snow,
The spirit slid: and it was he
That made the ship to go.   380
The sails at noon left off their tune,
And the ship stood still also.

The Sun, right up above the mast,
Had fixed her to the ocean:
But in a minute she 'gan stir,   385
With a short uneasy motion—
Backwards and forwards half her length
With a short uneasy motion.

Then like a pawing horse let go,
She made a sudden bound: 390
It flung the blood into my head,
And I fell down in a swound.

5. Warbling (Middle English).

How long in that same fit I lay,
I have not[6] to declare;
But ere my living life returned,   395
I heard and in my soul discerned
Two voices in the air.

"Is it he?" quoth one, "Is this the man?
By him who died on cross,
With his cruel bow he laid full low   400
The harmless Albatross.

The spirit who bideth by himself
In the land of mist and snow,
He loved the bird that loved the man
Who shot him with his bow."   405

The other was a softer voice,
As soft as honey-dew:
Quoth he, "The man hath penance done,
And penance more will do."

Part 6

FIRST VOICE
"But tell me, tell me! speak again,   410
Thy soft response renewing—
What makes that ship drive on so fast?
What is the ocean doing?"

SECOND VOICE
"Still as a slave before his lord,
The ocean hath no blast;   415
His great bright eye most silently
Up to the Moon is cast—

If he may know which way to go;
For she guides him smooth or grim.
See, brother, see! how graciously   420
She looketh down on him."

FIRST VOICE
"But why drives on that ship so fast,
Without or wave or wind?"

SECOND VOICE
"The air is cut away before,
And closes from behind.   425

Fly, brother, fly! more high, more high!
Or we shall be belated:

---

6. I.e., have not the knowledge.

For slow and slow that ship will go,
When the Mariner's trance is abated."

*The supernatural
motion is retarded;
the Mariner awakes,
and his penance
begins anew.*

I woke, and we were sailing on   430
As in a gentle weather:
'Twas night, calm night, the moon was high;
The dead men stood together.

All stood together on the deck,
For a charnel-dungeon fitter: 435
All fixed on me their stony eyes,
That in the Moon did glitter.

The pang, the curse, with which they died,
Had never passed away:
I could not draw my eyes from theirs,   440
Nor turn them up to pray.

*The curse is finally
expiated.*

And now this spell was snapt: once more
I viewed the ocean green,
And looked far forth, yet little saw
Of what had else been seen—   445

Like one, that on a lonesome road
Doth walk in fear and dread,
And having once turned round walks on,
And turns no more his head;
Because he knows, a frightful fiend   450
Doth close behind him tread.

But soon there breathed a wind on me,
Nor sound nor motion made:
Its path was not upon the sea,
In ripple or in shade.   455

It raised my hair, it fanned my cheek
Like a meadow-gale of spring—
It mingled strangely with my fears,
Yet it felt like a welcoming.

Swiftly, swiftly flew the ship,   460
Yet she sailed softly too:
Sweetly, sweetly blew the breeze—
On me alone it blew.

*And the ancient
Mariner beholdeth
his native country.*

Oh! dream of joy! is this indeed
The light-house top I see?   465
Is this the hill? is this the kirk?
Is this mine own countree?

We drifted o'er the harbour-bar,
And I with sobs did pray—

O let me be awake, my God!   470
Or let me sleep alway.

The harbour-bay was clear as glass,
So smoothly it was strewn!
And on the bay the moonlight lay,
And the shadow of the moon.   475

The rock shone bright, the kirk no less,
That stands above the rock:
The moonlight steeped in silentness
The steady weathercock.

And the bay was white with silent light,   480
Till rising from the same,

The angelic spirits leave the dead bodies,

Full many shapes, that shadows were,
In crimson colours came.

And appear in their own forms of light.

A little distance from the prow
Those crimson shadows were: 485
I turned my eyes upon the deck—
Oh, Christ! what saw I there!

Each corse lay flat, lifeless and flat,
And, by the holy rood!
A man all light, a seraph-man,[7]   490
On every corse there stood.

This seraph-band, each waved his hand:
It was a heavenly sight!
They stood as signals to the land,
Each one a lovely light;   495

This seraph-band, each waved his hand,
No voice did they impart—
No voice; but oh! the silence sank
Like music on my heart.

But soon I heard the dash of oars,   500
I heard the Pilot's cheer;
My head was turned perforce away,
And I saw a boat appear.

The Pilot and the Pilot's boy,
I heard them coming fast: 505
Dear Lord in Heaven! it was a joy
The dead men could not blast.

I saw a third—I heard his voice:
It is the Hermit good!
He singeth loud his godly hymns   510

7. A shining celestial being, highest in the ranks of the angels. "Rood": cross.

That he makes in the wood.
He'll shrieve my soul, he'll wash away
The Albatross's blood.

Part 7

The Hermit of the wood,

This Hermit good lives in that wood
Which slopes down to the sea.   515
How loudly his sweet voice he rears!
He loves to talk with marineres
That come from a far countree.

He kneels at morn, and noon, and eve—
He hath a cushion plump: 520
It is the moss that wholly hides
The rotted old oak-stump.

The skiff-boat neared: I heard them talk,
"Why, this is strange, I trow!
Where are those lights so many and fair,   525
That signal made but now?"

Approacheth the ship with wonder.

"Strange, by my faith!" the Hermit said—
"And they answered not our cheer!
The planks looked warped! and see those sails,
How thin they are and sere!   530
I never saw aught like to them,
Unless perchance it were

Brown skeletons of leaves that lag
My forest-brook along;
When the ivy-tod[8] is heavy with snow,   535
And the owlet whoops to the wolf below,
That eats the she-wolf's young."

"Dear Lord! it hath a fiendish look"—
(The Pilot made reply)
"I am a-feared"—"Push on, push on!"   540
Said the Hermit cheerily.

The boat came closer to the ship,
But I nor spake nor stirred;
The boat came close beneath the ship,
And straight a sound was heard.   545

The ship suddenly sinketh.

Under the water it rumbled on,
Still louder and more dread:
It reached the ship, it split the bay;
The ship went down like lead.

8. Clump of ivy.

The ancient
Mariner is saved
in the Pilot's
boat.

Stunned by that loud and dreadful sound,　　　　　　550
Which sky and ocean smote,
Like one that hath been seven days drowned
My body lay afloat;
But swift as dreams, myself I found
Within the Pilot's boat.　　　　　　　　　　　555

Upon the whirl, where sank the ship,
The boat spun round and round;
And all was still, save that the hill
Was telling of the sound.

I moved my lips—the Pilot shrieked　　　　　　560
And fell down in a fit;
The holy Hermit raised his eyes,
And prayed where he did sit.

I took the oars: the Pilot's boy,
Who now doth crazy go,　　　　　　　　　　565
Laughed loud and long, and all the while
His eyes went to and fro.
"Ha! ha!" quoth he, "full plain I see,
The Devil knows how to row."

And now, all in my own countree,　　　　　　570
I stood on the firm land!
The Hermit stepped forth from the boat,
And scarcely he could stand.

The ancient
Mariner earnestly
entreateth the Her-
mit to shrieve him;
and the penance of
life falls on him.

"O shrieve me, shrieve me, holy man!"
The Hermit crossed his brow.[9]　　　　　　575
"Say quick," quoth he, "I bid thee say—
What manner of man art thou?"

Forthwith this frame of mine was wrenched
With a woful agony,
Which forced me to begin my tale;　　　　　　580
And then it left me free.

And ever and
anon throughout
his future life an
agony constrain-
eth him to travel
from land to
land.

Since then, at an uncertain hour,
That agony returns:
And till my ghastly tale is told,
This heart within me burns.　　　　　　　　585

I pass, like night, from land to land;
I have strange power of speech;
That moment that his face I see,
I know the man that must hear me:
To him my tale I teach.　　　　　　　　　590

What loud uproar bursts from that door!
The wedding-guests are there:

---

9. Made the sign of the cross on his forehead. "Shrieve me": hear my confession and grant me absolution.

But in the garden-bower the bride
And bride-maids singing are:
And hark the little vesper bell,   595
Which biddeth me to prayer!

O Wedding-Guest! this soul hath been
Alone on a wide wide sea:
So lonely 'twas, that God himself
Scarce seemed there to be.   600

O sweeter than the marriage-feast,
'Tis sweeter far to me,
To walk together to the kirk
With a goodly company!—

To walk together to the kirk,   605
And all together pray,
While each to his great Father bends,
Old men, and babes, and loving friends,
And youths and maidens gay!

And to teach, by his own example, love and reverence to all things that God made and loveth.

Farewell, farewell! but this I tell   610
To thee, thou Wedding-Guest!
He prayeth well, who loveth well
Both man and bird and beast.

He prayeth best, who loveth best
All things both great and small;   615
For the dear God who loveth us,
He made and loveth all.[1]

The Mariner, whose eye is bright,
Whose beard with age is hoar,
Is gone: and now the Wedding-Guest   620
Turned from the bridegroom's door.

He went like one that hath been stunned,
And is of sense forlorn:[2]
A sadder and a wiser man,
He rose the morrow morn.   625

1797   1798

---

1. Coleridge said in 1830, answering the objection of the poet Anna Barbauld that the poem "lacked a moral": "I told her that in my own judgment the poem had too much; and that the only, or chief fault, if I might say so, was the obtrusion of the moral sentiment so openly on the reader as a principle or cause of action in a work of pure imagination. It ought to have had no more moral than the *Arabian Nights'* tale of the merchant's sitting down to eat dates by the side of a well and throwing the shells aside, and lo! a genie starts up and says he *must* kill the aforesaid merchant *because* one of the date shells had, it seems, put out the eye of the genie's son."
2. Forsaken.

Kubla Khan

Or, A Vision in a Dream. A Fragment

In[1] the summer of the year 1797, the Author, then in ill health, had retired to a lonely farm house between Porlock and Linton, on the Exmoor confines of Somerset and Devonshire. In consequence of a slight indisposition, an anodyne had been prescribed, from the effect of which he fell asleep in his chair at the moment that he was reading the following sentence, or words of the same substance, in *Purchas's Pilgrimage:* "Here the Khan Kubla commanded a palace to be built, and a stately garden thereunto: and thus ten miles of fertile ground were inclosed with a wall."[2] The author continued for about three hours in a profound sleep, at least of the external senses,[3] during which time he has the most vivid confidence, that he could not have composed less than from two to three hundred lines; if that indeed can be called composition in which all the images rose up before him as things, with a parallel production of the correspondent expressions, without any sensation or consciousness of effort. On awaking he appeared to himself to have a distinct recollection of the whole, and taking his pen, ink, and paper, instantly and eagerly wrote down the lines that are here preserved. At this moment he was unfortunately called out by a person on business from Porlock, and detained by him above an hour, and on his return to his room, found, to his no small surprise and mortification, that though he still retained some vague and dim recollection of the general purport of the vision, yet, with the exception of some eight or ten scattered lines and images, all the rest had passed away like the images on the surface of a stream into which a stone had been cast, but, alas! without the after restoration of the latter:

> Then all the charm
> Is broken—all that phantom-world so fair
> Vanishes, and a thousand circlets spread,
> And each mis-shape[s] the other. Stay awhile,
> Poor youth! who scarcely dar'st lift up thine eyes—
> The stream will soon renew its smoothness, soon
> The visions will return! And lo! he stays,
> And soon the fragments dim of lovely forms
> Come trembling back, unite, and now once more
> The pool becomes a mirror.
>
> [From Coleridge's *The Picture; or, the Lover's Resolution,*
> lines 91–100]

---

1. In the texts of 1816–29, this note began with an additional short paragraph: "The following fragment is here published at the request of a poet of great and deserved celebrity, and, as far as the Author's own opinions are concerned, rather as a psychological curiosity, than on the ground of any supposed *poetic* merits." The "poet of . . . celebrity" was Lord Byron.

2. "In Xamdu did Cublai Can build a stately Palace, encompassing sixteene miles of plaine ground with a wall, wherein are fertile Meddowes, pleasant Springs, delightfull Streames, and all sorts of beasts of chase and game, and in the middest thereof a sumptuous house of pleasure, which may be removed from place to place." From Samuel Purchas, *Purchas his Pilgrimage* (1613). The historical Kublai Khan founded the Mongol dynasty in China in the 13th century.

3. In a note on a manuscript copy of *Kubla Khan,* Coleridge gave a more precise account of the nature of this "sleep": "This fragment with a good deal more, not recoverable, composed, in a sort of reverie brought on by two grains of opium, taken to check a dysentery, at a farmhouse between Porlock and Linton, a quarter of a mile from Culbone Church, in the fall of the year, 1797."

Yet from the still surviving recollections in his mind, the Author has frequently purposed to finish for himself what had been originally, as it were,
given to him. Αὔριον ἄδιον ἄσω:[4] but the to-morrow is yet to come.

As a contrast to this vision, I have annexed a fragment of a very different
character, describing with equal fidelity the dream of pain and disease.[5]—
1816.

> In Xanadu did Kubla Khan
> A stately pleasure-dome decree:
> Where Alph,[6] the sacred river, ran
> Through caverns measureless to man
> 5   Down to a sunless sea.
> So twice five miles of fertile ground
> With walls and towers were girdled round:
> And there were gardens bright with sinuous rills
> Where blossomed many an incense-bearing tree;
> 10 And here were forests ancient as the hills,
> Enfolding sunny spots of greenery.
>
> But oh! that deep romantic chasm which slanted
> Down the green hill athwart a cedarn cover!
> A savage place! as holy and enchanted
> 15 As e'er beneath a waning moon was haunted
> By woman wailing for her demon-lover!
> And from this chasm, with ceaseless turmoil seething,
> As if this earth in fast thick pants were breathing,
> A mighty fountain momently was forced:
> 20 Amid whose swift half-intermitted burst
> Huge fragments vaulted like rebounding hail,
> Or chaffy grain beneath the thresher's flail:
> And 'mid these dancing rocks at once and ever
> It flung up momently the sacred river.
> 25 Five miles meandering with a mazy motion
> Through wood and dale the sacred river ran,
> Then reached the caverns measureless to man,
> And sank in tumult to a lifeless ocean:
> And 'mid this tumult Kubla heard from far
> 30 Ancestral voices prophesying war!
>
> The shadow of the dome of pleasure
> Floated midway on the waves;
> Where was heard the mingled measure
> From the fountain and the caves.
> 35 It was a miracle of rare device,
> A sunny pleasure-dome with caves of ice!

4. I shall sing a sweeter song tomorrow (Greek; recalled from Theocritus's *Idyls* 1.145).

A number of Coleridge's assertions in this preface have been debated by critics: whether the poem was written in 1797 or later, whether it was actually composed in a "dream" or opium reverie, even whether it is a fragment or in fact complete. All critics agree, however, that this visionary poem of demonic inspiration is much more than a mere "psychological curiosity."

5. Coleridge refers to *The Pains of Sleep*.

6. Derived probably from the Greek river Alpheus, which flows into the Ionian Sea. Its waters were fabled to rise again in Sicily as the fountain of Arethusa.

A damsel with a dulcimer
In a vision once I saw:
It was an Abyssinian maid,
40   And on her dulcimer she played,
Singing of Mount Abora.[7]
Could I revive within me
Her symphony and song,
To such a deep delight 'twould win me,
45   That with music loud and long,
I would build that dome in air,
That sunny dome! those caves of ice!
And all who heard should see them there,
And all should cry, Beware! Beware!
50   His flashing eyes, his floating hair!
Weave a circle round him thrice,[8]
And close your eyes with holy dread,
For he on honey-dew hath fed,
And drunk the milk of Paradise.[9]

ca. 1797–98   1816

Christabel[1]

Preface

The first part of the following poem was written in the year 1797, at Stowey, in the county of Somerset. The second part, after my return from Germany, in the year 1800, at Keswick, Cumberland. It is probable, that if the poem had been finished at either of the former periods, or if even the first and second part had been published in the year 1800, the impression of its originality would have been much greater than I dare at present expect. But for this, I have only my own indolence to blame. The dates are mentioned for the exclusive purpose of precluding charges of plagiarism or servile imitation from myself. For there is amongst us a set of critics, who seem to hold, that every possible thought and image is traditional; who have no notion that there are such things as fountains in the world, small as well as great; and who would therefore charitably derive every rill they behold flowing, from a perforation made in some other man's tank. I am confident, however, that as far as the present poem is concerned, the celebrated poets[2] whose writings I might be suspected of having imitated, either in particular passages, or in

7. Apparently a reminiscence of *Paradise Lost* 4.280–82: "where Abassin Kings their issue guard / Mount Amara (though this by some supposed / True Paradise) under the Ethiop line."
8. A magic ritual, to protect the inspired poet from intrusion.
9. Lines 50ff. echo in part the description, in Plato's *Ion* 533–34, of inspired poets, who are "like Bacchic maidens who draw milk and honey from the rivers when they are under the influence of Dionysus but not when they are in their right mind."
1. Coleridge had planned to publish *Christabel* in the 2nd edition of *Lyrical Ballads* (1800) but had not been able to complete the poem. When *Chris-*

tabel was finally published in 1816 in its present fragmentary state, he still had hopes of finishing it, for the Preface contained this sentence (deleted in the edition of 1834): "But as, in my very first conception of the tale, I had the whole present to my mind, with the wholeness, no less than with the liveliness of a vision; I trust that I shall be able to embody in verse the three parts yet to come, in the course of the present year."
2. Sir Walter Scott and Lord Byron, who had read and admired *Christabel* while it circulated in manuscript. Coleridge has in mind Scott's *Lay of the Last Minstrel* (1805) and Byron's *Siege of Corinth* (1816), which showed the influence of *Christabel*, especially in their meter.

the tone and the spirit of the whole, would be among the first to vindicate me from the charge, and who, on any striking coincidence, would permit me to address them in this doggerel version of two monkish Latin hexameters.

> Tis mine and it is likewise yours;
> But an if this will not do;
> Let it be mine, good friend! for I
> Am the poorer of the two.

I have only to add, that the metre of the Christabel is not, properly speaking, irregular, though it may seem so from its being founded on a new principle: namely, that of counting in each line the accents, not the syllables.[3] Though the latter may vary from seven to twelve, yet in each line the accents will be found to be only four. Nevertheless this occasional variation in number of syllables is not introduced wantonly, or for the mere ends of convenience, but in correspondence with some transition, in the nature of the imagery or passion.

Part 1

'Tis the middle of night by the castle clock,
And the owls have awakened the crowing cock;
Tu—whit!——Tu—whoo!
And hark, again! the crowing cock,
5   How drowsily it crew.

Sir Leoline, the Baron rich,
Hath a toothless mastiff bitch;
From her kennel beneath the rock
She maketh answer to the clock,
10   Four for the quarters, and twelve for the hour;
Ever and aye, by shine and shower,
Sixteen short howls, not over loud;
Some say, she sees my lady's shroud.

Is the night chilly and dark?
15   The night is chilly, but not dark.
The thin gray cloud is spread on high,
It covers but not hides the sky.
The moon is behind, and at the full;
And yet she looks both small and dull.
20   The night is chill, the cloud is gray:
'Tis a month before the month of May,
And the Spring comes slowly up this way.

The lovely lady, Christabel,
Whom her father loves so well,
25   What makes her in the wood so late,
A furlong from the castle gate?

3. Much of the older English versification, following the example of Anglo-Saxon poetry, had been based on stress, or "accent," and some of it shows as much freedom in varying the number of syllables as does *Christabel*. The poem, however, is a radical departure from the theory and practice of versification in the 18th century, which had been based on a recurrent number of syllables in each line.

She had dreams all yesternight
Of her own betrothed knight;
And she in the midnight wood will pray
30   For the weal° of her lover that's far away.   *well-being*

She stole along, she nothing spoke,
The sighs she heaved were soft and low,
And naught was green upon the oak,
But moss and rarest mistletoe:[4]
35   She kneels beneath the huge oak tree,
And in silence prayeth she.

The lady sprang up suddenly,
The lovely lady, Christabel!
It moaned as near, as near can be,
40   But what it is, she cannot tell.—
On the other side it seems to be,
Of the huge, broad-breasted, old oak tree.

The night is chill; the forest bare;
Is it the wind that moaneth bleak?
45   There is not wind enough in the air
To move away the ringlet curl
From the lovely lady's cheek—
There is not wind enough to twirl
The one red leaf, the last of its clan,
50   That dances as often as dance it can,
Hanging so light, and hanging so high,
On the topmost twig that looks up at the sky.

Hush, beating heart of Christabel!
Jesu, Maria, shield her well!
55   She folded her arms beneath her cloak,
And stole to the other side of the oak.
      What sees she there?

There she sees a damsel bright,
Drest in a silken robe of white,
60   That shadowy in the moonlight shone:
The neck that made that white robe wan,
Her stately neck, and arms were bare;
Her blue-veined feet unsandal'd were,
And wildly glittered here and there
65   The gems entangled in her hair.
I guess, 'twas frightful there to see
A lady so richly clad as she—
Beautiful exceedingly!

"Mary mother, save me now!"
70   (Said Christabel,) "And who art thou?"

4. In Celtic Britain the mistletoe (a parasitic plant) had been held in veneration when it was found growing—as it rarely does—on an oak tree. (Its usual host is the apple tree.)

The lady strange made answer meet,
And her voice was faint and sweet:—
"Have pity on my sore distress,
I scarce can speak for weariness:
75 Stretch forth thy hand, and have no fear!"
Said Christabel, "How camest thou here?"
And the lady, whose voice was faint and sweet,
Did thus pursue her answer meet:—

"My sire is of a noble line,
80 And my name is Geraldine:
Five warriors seized me yestermorn,
Me, even me, a maid forlorn:
They choked my cries with force and fright,
And tied me on a palfrey white.
85 The palfrey was as fleet as wind,
And they rode furiously behind.
They spurred amain,[5] their steeds were white:
And once we crossed the shade of night.
As sure as Heaven shall rescue me,
90 I have no thought what men they be;
Nor do I know how long it is
(For I have lain entranced I wis[6])
Since one, the tallest of the five,
Took me from the palfrey's back,
95 A weary woman, scarce alive.
Some muttered words his comrades spoke:
He placed me underneath this oak;
He swore they would return with haste;
Whither they went I cannot tell—
100 I thought I heard, some minutes past,
Sounds as of a castle bell.
Stretch forth thy hand" (thus ended she),
"And help a wretched maid to flee."

Then Christabel stretched forth her hand
105 And comforted fair Geraldine:
"O well, bright dame! may you command
The service of Sir Leoline;
And gladly our stout chivalry
Will he send forth and friends withal
110 To guide and guard you safe and free
Home to your noble father's hall."

She rose: and forth with steps they passed
That strove to be, and were not, fast.
Her gracious stars the lady blest,
115 And thus spake on sweet Christabel:
"All our household are at rest,

5. At top speed.
6. I believe (Coleridge's misinterpretation of the Middle English adverb *ywis*, meaning "certainly").

The hall as silent as the cell;
Sir Leoline is weak in health,
And may not well awakened be,
120 But we will move as if in stealth,
And I beseech your courtesy,
This night, to share your couch with me."

They crossed the moat, and Christabel
Took the key that fitted well;
125 A little door she opened straight,
All in the middle of the gate;
The gate that was ironed within and without,
Where an army in battle array had marched out.
The lady sank, belike through pain,
130 And Christabel with might and main
Lifted her up, a weary weight,
Over the threshold of the gate:[7]
Then the lady rose again,
And moved, as she were not in pain.

135 So free from danger, free from fear,
They crossed the court: right glad they were.
And Christabel devoutly cried
To the Lady by her side;
"Praise we the Virgin all divine
140 Who hath rescued thee from thy distress!"
"Alas, alas!" said Geraldine,
"I cannot speak for weariness."
So free from danger, free from fear,
They crossed the court: right glad they were.

145 Outside her kennel the mastiff old
Lay fast asleep, in moonshine cold.
The mastiff old did not awake,
Yet she an angry moan did make!
And what can ail the mastiff bitch?
150 Never till now she uttered yell
Beneath the eye of Christabel.
Perhaps it is the owlet's scritch:
For what can ail the mastiff bitch?

They passed the hall, that echoes still,
155 Pass as lightly as you will!
The brands were flat, the brands were dying,
Amid their own white ashes lying;
But when the lady passed, there came
A tongue of light, a fit of flame;
160 And Christabel saw the lady's eye,
And nothing else saw she thereby,

7. According to legend, a witch cannot cross the threshold by her own power because it has been blessed against evil spirits.

Save the boss of the shield of Sir Leoline tall,
Which hung in a murky old niche in the wall.
"O softly tread," said Christabel,
165 "My father seldom sleepeth well."

Sweet Christabel her feet doth bare,
And, jealous of the listening air,
They steal their way from stair to stair,
Now in glimmer, and now in gloom,
170 And now they pass the Baron's room,
As still as death with stifled breath!
And now have reached her chamber door;
And now doth Geraldine press down
The rushes[8] of the chamber floor.

175 The moon shines dim in the open air,
And not a moonbeam enters here.
But they without its light can see
The chamber carved so curiously,
Carved with figures strange and sweet,
180 All made out of the carver's brain,
For a lady's chamber meet:
The lamp with twofold silver chain
Is fastened to an angel's feet.
The silver lamp burns dead and dim;
185 But Christabel the lamp will trim.
She trimmed the lamp, and made it bright,
And left it swinging to and fro,
While Geraldine, in wretched plight,
Sank down upon the floor below.

190 "O weary lady, Geraldine,
I pray you, drink this cordial wine!
It is a wine of virtuous powers;
My mother made it of wild flowers."

"And will your mother pity me,
195 Who am a maiden most forlorn?"
Christabel answered—"Woe is me!
She died the hour that I was born.
I have heard the grey-haired friar tell,
How on her death-bed she did say,
200 That she should hear the castle-bell
Strike twelve upon my wedding day.
O mother dear! that thou wert here!"
"I would," said Geraldine, "she were!"

But soon with altered voice, said she—
205 "Off, wandering mother! Peak and pine!
I have power to bid thee flee."

---

8. Often used as a floor covering in the Middle Ages.

Alas! what ails poor Geraldine?
Why stares she with unsettled eye?
Can she the bodiless dead espy?
210 And why with hollow voice cries she,
"Off, woman, off! this hour is mine—
Though thou her guardian spirit be,
Off, woman, off! 'tis given to me."

Then Christabel knelt by the lady's side,
215 And raised to heaven her eyes so blue—
"Alas!" said she, "this ghastly ride—
Dear lady! it hath wildered you!"
The lady wiped her moist cold brow,
And faintly said, " 'tis over now!"

220 Again the wild-flower wine she drank:
Her fair large eyes 'gan glitter bright,
And from the floor whereon she sank,
The lofty lady stood upright;
She was most beautiful to see,
225 Like a lady of a far countrée.

And thus the lofty lady spake—
"All they who live in the upper sky,
Do love you, holy Christabel!
And you love them, and for their sake
230 And for the good which me befell,
Even I in my degree will try,
Fair maiden, to requite you well.
But now unrobe yourself; for I
Must pray, ere yet in bed I lie."

235 Quoth Christabel, "So let it be!"
And as the lady bade, did she.
Her gentle limbs did she undress,
And lay down in her loveliness.

But through her brain of weal and woe
240 So many thoughts moved to and fro,
That vain it were her lids to close;
So half-way from the bed she rose,
And on her elbow did recline
To look at the lady Geraldine.

245 Beneath the lamp the lady bowed,
And slowly rolled her eyes around;
Then drawing in her breath aloud,
Like one that shuddered, she unbound
The cincture° from beneath her breast: *belt*
250 Her silken robe, and inner vest,
Dropt to her feet, and full in view,
Behold! her bosom and half her side——

A sight to dream of, not to tell!
O shield her! shield sweet Christabel!

255 Yet Geraldine nor speaks nor stirs;
Ah! what a stricken look was hers!
Deep from within she seems half-way
To lift some weight with sick assay,°   *attempt*
And eyes the maid and seeks delay;
260 Then suddenly as one defied
Collects herself in scorn and pride,
And lay down by the maiden's side!—
And in her arms the maid she took,
　　　　Ah well-a-day!
265 And with low voice and doleful look
These words did say:
"In the touch of this bosom there worketh a spell,
Which is lord of thy utterance, Christabel!
Thou knowest to-night, and wilt know to-morrow
270 This mark of my shame, this seal of my sorrow;
　　　　But vainly thou warrest,
　　　　　For this is alone in
　　　　Thy power to declare,
　　　　　That in the dim forest
275 　　　　Thou heard'st a low moaning,
And found'st a bright lady, surpassingly fair:
And didst bring her home with thee in love and in charity,
To shield her and shelter her from the damp air."

The Conclusion to Part 1

It was a lovely sight to see
280 The lady Christabel, when she
Was praying at the old oak tree.
　　　　Amid the jagged shadows
　　　　Of mossy leafless boughs,
　　　　Kneeling in the moonlight,
285 　　　　To make her gentle vows;
Her slender palms together prest,
Heaving sometimes on her breast;
Her face resigned to bliss or bale°—   *evil, sorrow*
Her face, oh call it fair not pale,
290 And both blue eyes more bright than clear,
Each about to have a tear.

With open eyes (ah woe is me!)
Asleep, and dreaming fearfully,
Fearfully dreaming, yet I wis,
295 Dreaming that alone, which is—
O sorrow and shame! Can this be she,
The lady, who knelt at the old oak tree?
And lo! the worker of these harms,
That holds the maiden in her arms,

300 Seems to slumber still and mild,
As a mother with her child.

A star hath set, a star hath risen,
O Geraldine! since arms of thine
Have been the lovely lady's prison.
305 O Geraldine! one hour was thine—
Thou'st had thy will! By tairn[9] and rill,
The night-birds all that hour were still.
But now they are jubilant anew,
From cliff and tower, tu—whoo! tu—whoo!
310 Tu—whoo! tu—whoo! from wood and fell![1]

And see! the lady Christabel
Gathers herself from out her trance;
Her limbs relax, her countenance
Grows sad and soft; the smooth thin lids
315 Close o'er her eyes; and tears she sheds—
Large tears that leave the lashes bright!
And oft the while she seems to smile
As infants at a sudden light!
Yea, she doth smile, and she doth weep,
320 Like a youthful hermitess,
Beauteous in a wilderness,
Who, praying always, prays in sleep.
And, if she move unquietly,
Perchance, 'tis but the blood so free,
325 Comes back and tingles in her feet.
No doubt, she hath a vision sweet.
What if her guardian spirit 'twere?
What if she knew her mother near?
But this she knows, in joys and woes,
330 That saints will aid if men will call:
For the blue sky bends over all!

Part 2

"Each matin bell," the Baron saith,
"Knells us back to a world of death."
These words Sir Leoline first said,
335 When he rose and found his lady dead:
These words Sir Leoline will say,
Many a morn to his dying day!

And hence the custom and law began,
That still at dawn the sacristan,°   *sexton*
340 Who duly pulls the heavy bell,
Five and forty beads must tell[2]
Between each stroke—a warning knell,

9. Tarn, a mountain pool.
1. Elevated moor, or hill.

2. Pray while "telling" (keeping count on) the beads of a rosary.

Which not a soul can choose but hear
From Bratha Head to Wyndermere.[3]

345 Saith Bracy the bard, "So let it knell!
And let the drowsy sacristan
Still count as slowly as he can!
There is no lack of such, I ween,
As well fill up the space between.
350 In Langdale Pike° and Witch's Lair,   Peak
And Dungeon-ghyll[4] so foully rent,
With ropes of rock and bells of air
Three sinful sextons' ghosts are pent,
Who all give back, one after t'other,
355 The death-note to their living brother;
And oft too, by the knell offended,
Just as their one! two! three! is ended,
The devil mocks the doleful tale
With a merry peal from Borodale."

360 The air is still! through mist and cloud
That merry peal comes ringing loud;
And Geraldine shakes off her dread,
And rises lightly from the bed;
Puts on her silken vestments white,
365 And tricks her hair in lovely plight,°   plait
And nothing doubting of her spell
Awakens the lady Christabel.
"Sleep you, sweet lady Christabel?
I trust that you have rested well."

370 And Christabel awoke and spied
The same who lay down by her side—
O rather say, the same whom she
Raised up beneath the old oak tree!
Nay, fairer yet! and yet more fair!
375 For she belike hath drunken deep
Of all the blessedness of sleep!
And while she spake, her looks, her air
Such gentle thankfulness declare,
That (so it seemed) her girded vests
380 Grew tight beneath her heaving breasts.
"Sure I have sinned!" said Christabel,
"Now heaven be praised if all be well!"
And in low faltering tones, yet sweet,
Did she the lofty lady greet
385 With such perplexity of mind
As dreams too lively leave behind.

So quickly she rose, and quickly arrayed
Her maiden limbs, and having prayed

3. These and the following names are of localities 4. Ravine forming the bed of a stream.
in the English Lake District.

That He, who on the cross did groan,
390 Might wash away her sins unknown,
She forthwith led fair Geraldine
To meet her sire, Sir Leoline.

The lovely maid and the lady tall
Are pacing both into the hall,
395 And pacing on through page and groom,
Enter the Baron's presence room.

The Baron rose, and while he prest
His gentle daughter to his breast,
With cheerful wonder in his eyes
400 The lady Geraldine espies,
And gave such welcome to the same,
As might beseem so bright a dame!

But when he heard the lady's tale,
And when she told her father's name,
405 Why waxed Sir Leoline so pale,
Murmuring o'er the name again,
Lord Roland de Vaux of Tryermaine?

Alas! they had been friends in youth;
But whispering tongues can poison truth;
410 And constancy lives in realms above;
And life is thorny; and youth is vain;
And to be wroth with one we love,
Doth work like madness in the brain.
And thus it chanced, as I divine,
415 With Roland and Sir Leoline.
Each spake words of high disdain
And insult to his heart's best brother:
They parted—ne'er to meet again!
But never either found another
420 To free the hollow heart from paining—
They stood aloof, the scars remaining,
Like cliffs which had been rent asunder;
A dreary sea now flows between;—
But neither heat, nor frost, nor thunder,
425 Shall wholly do away, I ween,
The marks of that which once hath been.

Sir Leoline, a moment's space,
Stood gazing on the damsel's face:
And the youthful Lord of Tryermaine
430 Came back upon his heart again.

O then the Baron forgot his age,
His noble heart swelled high with rage;
He swore by the wounds in Jesu's side,
He would proclaim it far and wide

435   With trump and solemn heraldry,
       That they who thus had wronged the dame,
       Were base as spotted infamy!
       "And if they dare deny the same,
       My herald shall appoint a week,
440   And let the recreant traitors seek
       My tourney court—that there and then
       I may dislodge their reptile souls
       From the bodies and forms of men!"
       He spake: his eye in lightning rolls!
445   For the lady was ruthlessly seized; and he kenned
       In the beautiful lady the child of his friend!

       And now the tears were on his face,
       And fondly in his arms he took
       Fair Geraldine, who met the embrace,
450   Prolonging it with joyous look.
       Which when she viewed, a vision fell
       Upon the soul of Christabel,
       The vision of fear, the touch and pain!
       She shrunk and shuddered, and saw again—
455   (Ah, woe is me! Was it for thee,
       Thou gentle maid! such sights to see?)
       Again she saw that bosom old,
       Again she felt that bosom cold,
       And drew in her breath with a hissing sound:
460   Whereat the Knight turned wildly round,
       And nothing saw, but his own sweet maid
       With eyes upraised, as one that prayed.

       The touch, the sight, had passed away,
       And in its stead that vision blest,
465   Which comforted her after-rest,
       While in the lady's arms she lay,
       Had put a rapture in her breast,
       And on her lips and o'er her eyes
       Spread smiles like light!
                           With new surprise,
470   "What ails then my beloved child?"
       The Baron said—His daughter mild
       Made answer, "All will yet be well!"
       I ween, she had no power to tell
       Aught else: so mighty was the spell.

475   Yet he, who saw this Geraldine,
       Had deemed her sure a thing divine.
       Such sorrow with such grace she blended,
       As if she feared, she had offended
       Sweet Christabel, that gentle maid!
480   And with such lowly tones she prayed,
       She might be sent without delay
       Home to her father's mansion.
                              "Nay!

Nay, by my soul!" said Leoline.
"Ho! Bracy, the bard, the charge be thine!
485 Go thou, with music sweet and loud,
And take two steeds with trappings proud,
And take the youth whom thou lov'st best
To bear thy harp, and learn thy song,
And clothe you both in solemn vest,
490 And over the mountains haste along,
Lest wandering folk, that are abroad,
Detain you on the valley road.
And when he has crossed the Irthing flood,
My merry bard! he hastes, he hastes
495 Up Knorren Moor, through Halegarth Wood,
And reaches soon that castle good
Which stands and threatens Scotland's wastes.

"Bard Bracy! bard Bracy! your horses are fleet,
Ye must ride up the hall, your music so sweet,
500 More loud than your horses' echoing feet!
And loud and loud to Lord Roland call,
Thy daughter is safe in Langdale hall!
Thy beautiful daughter is safe and free—
Sir Leoline greets thee thus through me.
505 He bids thee come without delay
With all thy numerous array;
And take thy lovely daughter home:
And he will meet thee on the way
With all his numerous array
510 White with their panting palfreys' foam:
And by mine honour! I will say,
That I repent me of the day
When I spake words of fierce disdain
To Roland de Vaux of Tryermaine!—
515 —For since that evil hour hath flown,
Many a summer's sun hath shone;
Yet ne'er found I a friend again
Like Roland de Vaux of Tryermaine."

The lady fell, and clasped his knees,
520 Her face upraised, her eyes o'erflowing;
And Bracy replied, with faltering voice,
His gracious hail on all bestowing!—
"Thy words, thou sire of Christabel,
Are sweeter than my harp can tell;
525 Yet might I gain a boon of thee,
This day my journey should not be,
So strange a dream hath come to me;
That I had vowed with music loud
To clear yon wood from thing unblest,
530 Warned by a vision in my rest!
For in my sleep I saw that dove,
That gentle bird, whom thou dost love,
And call'st by thy own daughter's name—

Sir Leoline! I saw the same
535   Fluttering, and uttering fearful moan,
Among the green herbs in the forest alone.
Which when I saw and when I heard,
I wonder'd what might ail the bird;
For nothing near it could I see,
540   Save the grass and green herbs underneath the old tree.

    "And in my dream methought I went
To search out what might there be found;
And what the sweet bird's trouble meant,
That thus lay fluttering on the ground.
545   I went and peered, and could descry
No cause for her distressful cry;
But yet for her dear lady's sake
I stooped, methought, the dove to take,
When lo! I saw a bright green snake
550   Coiled around its wings and neck,
Green as the herbs on which it couched,
Close by the dove's its head it crouched;
And with the dove it heaves and stirs,
Swelling its neck as she swelled hers!
555   I woke; it was the midnight hour,
The clock was echoing in the tower;
But though my slumber was gone by,
This dream it would not pass away—
It seems to live upon my eye!
560   And thence I vowed this self-same day,
With music strong and saintly song
To wander through the forest bare,
Lest aught unholy loiter there."

    Thus Bracy said: the Baron, the while,
565   Half-listening heard him with a smile;
Then turned to Lady Geraldine,
His eyes made up of wonder and love;
And said in courtly accents fine,
"Sweet maid, Lord Roland's beauteous dove,
570   With arms more strong than harp or song,
Thy sire and I will crush the snake!"
He kissed her forehead as he spake,
And Geraldine, in maiden wise,
Casting down her large bright eyes,
575   With blushing cheek and courtesy fine
She turned her from Sir Leoline;
Softly gathering up her train,
That o'er her right arm fell again;
And folded her arms across her chest,
580   And couched her head upon her breast,
And looked askance at Christabel——
Jesu Maria, shield her well!

    A snake's small eye blinks dull and shy,
And the lady's eyes they shrunk in her head,

585   Each shrunk up to a serpent's eye,
      And with somewhat of malice, and more of dread,
      At Christabel she looked askance!—
      One moment—and the sight was fled!
      But Christabel in dizzy trance
590   Stumbling on the unsteady ground
      Shuddered aloud, with a hissing sound;
      And Geraldine again turned round,
      And like a thing, that sought relief,
      Full of wonder and full of grief,
595   She rolled her large bright eyes divine
      Wildly on Sir Leoline.

      The maid, alas! her thoughts are gone,
      She nothing sees—no sight but one!
      The maid, devoid of guile and sin,
600   I know not how, in fearful wise
      So deeply had she drunken in
      That look, those shrunken serpent eyes,
      That all her features were resigned
      To this sole image in her mind;
605   And passively did imitate
      That look of dull and treacherous hate!
      And thus she stood, in dizzy trance,
      Still picturing that look askance
      With forced unconscious sympathy
610   Full before her father's view——
      As far as such a look could be,
      In eyes so innocent and blue!
      And when the trance was o'er, the maid
      Paused awhile, and inly prayed:
615   Then falling at the Baron's feet,
      "By my mother's soul do I entreat
      That thou this woman send away!"
      She said: and more she could not say:
      For what she knew she could not tell,
620   O'er-mastered by the mighty spell.

      Why is thy cheek so wan and wild,
      Sir Leoline? Thy only child
      Lies at thy feet, thy joy, thy pride,
      So fair, so innocent, so mild;
625   The same, for whom thy lady died!
      O by the pangs of her dear mother
      Think thou no evil of thy child!
      For her, and thee, and for no other,
      She prayed the moment ere she died:
630   Prayed that the babe for whom she died,
      Might prove her dear lord's joy and pride!
        That prayer her deadly pangs beguiled,
          Sir Leoline!
        And wouldst thou wrong thy only child,
635   Her child and thine?

Within the Baron's heart and brain
If thoughts, like these, had any share,
They only swelled his rage and pain,
And did but work confusion there.
640 His heart was cleft with pain and rage,
His cheeks they quivered, his eyes were wild,
Dishonoured thus in his old age;
Dishonoured by his only child,
And all his hospitality
645 To the wrong'd daughter of his friend
By more than woman's jealousy
Brought thus to a disgraceful end—
He rolled his eye with stern regard
Upon the gentle minstrel bard,
650 And said in tones abrupt, austere—
"Why, Bracy! dost thou loiter here?
I bade thee hence!" The bard obeyed;
And turning from his own sweet maid,
The aged knight, Sir Leoline,
655 Led forth the lady Geraldine!

The Conclusion to Part 2

A little child, a limber elf,
Singing, dancing to itself,
A fairy thing with red round cheeks,
That always finds, and never seeks,
660 Makes such a vision to the sight
As fills a father's eyes with light;
And pleasures flow in so thick and fast
Upon his heart, that he at last
Must needs express his love's excess
665 With words of unmeant bitterness.
Perhaps 'tis pretty to force together
Thoughts so all unlike each other;
To mutter and mock a broken charm,
To dally with wrong that does no harm.
670 Perhaps 'tis tender too and pretty
At each wild word to feel within
A sweet recoil of love and pity.
And what, if in a world of sin
(O sorrow and shame should this be true!)
675 Such giddiness of heart and brain
Comes seldom save from rage and pain,
So talks as it's most used to do.

1798–1800   1816

Frost at Midnight[1]

The frost performs its secret ministry,
Unhelped by any wind. The owlet's cry
Came loud—and hark, again! loud as before.
The inmates of my cottage, all at rest,
5 Have left me to that solitude, which suits
Abstruser musings: save that at my side
My cradled infant slumbers peacefully.
'Tis calm indeed! so calm, that it disturbs
And vexes meditation with its strange
10 And extreme silentness. Sea, hill, and wood,
This populous village! Sea, and hill, and wood,
With all the numberless goings on of life,
Inaudible as dreams! the thin blue flame
Lies on my low burnt fire, and quivers not;
15 Only that film,[2] which fluttered on the grate,
Still flutters there, the sole unquiet thing.
Methinks, its motion in this hush of nature
Gives it dim sympathies with me who live,
Making it a companionable form,
20 Whose puny flaps and freaks the idling Spirit
By its own moods interprets, every where
Echo or mirror seeking of itself,
And makes a toy of Thought.

                      But O! how oft,
How oft, at school, with most believing mind,
25 Presageful, have I gazed upon the bars,
To watch that fluttering stranger! and as oft
With unclosed lids, already had I dreamt
Of my sweet birth-place,[3] and the old church-tower,
Whose bells, the poor man's only music, rang
30 From morn to evening, all the hot Fair-day,
So sweetly, that they stirred and haunted me
With a wild pleasure, falling on mine ear
Most like articulate sounds of things to come!
So gazed I, till the soothing things I dreamt
35 Lulled me to sleep, and sleep prolonged my dreams!
And so I brooded all the following morn,
Awed by the stern preceptor's[4] face, mine eye
Fixed with mock study on my swimming book:
Save if the door half opened, and I snatched
40 A hasty glance, and still my heart leaped up,
For still I hoped to see the stranger's face,

---

1. The scene is Coleridge's cottage at Nether Stowey; the infant in line 7 is his son Hartley, then aged seventeen months.
2. In all parts of the kingdom these films are called *strangers* and supposed to portend the arrival of some absent friend [Coleridge's note]. The "film" is a piece of soot fluttering on the bar of the grate.
3. Coleridge was born at Ottery St. Mary, Devonshire, but went to school in London, beginning at the age of nine.
4. The Reverend James Boyer at Coleridge's school, Christ's Hospital; Coleridge describes him in *Biographia Literaria,* chap. 1.

Townsman, or aunt, or sister more beloved,
My play-mate when we both were clothed alike![5]

    Dear Babe, that sleepest cradled by my side,
45 Whose gentle breathings, heard in this deep calm,
Fill up the interspersed vacancies
And momentary pauses of the thought!
My babe so beautiful! it thrills my heart
With tender gladness, thus to look at thee,
50 And think that thou shalt learn far other lore
And in far other scenes! For I was reared
In the great city, pent 'mid cloisters dim,
And saw nought lovely but the sky and stars.
But thou, my babe! shalt wander like a breeze
55 By lakes and sandy shores, beneath the crags
Of ancient mountain, and beneath the clouds,
Which image in their bulk both lakes and shores
And mountain crags: so shalt thou see and hear
The lovely shapes and sounds intelligible
60 Of that eternal language, which thy God
Utters, who from eternity doth teach
Himself in all, and all things in himself.
Great universal Teacher! he shall mould
Thy spirit, and by giving make it ask.

65   Therefore all seasons shall be sweet to thee,
Whether the summer clothe the general earth
With greenness, or the redbreast sit and sing
Betwixt the tufts of snow on the bare branch
Of mossy apple-tree, while the nigh thatch
70 Smokes in the sun-thaw; whether the eave-drops fall
Heard only in the trances of the blast,
Or if the secret ministry of frost
Shall hang them up in silent icicles,
Quietly shining to the quiet Moon.

Feb. 1798   1798

---

5. I.e., when both Coleridge and his sister Ann still wore infant clothes.

Dejection: An Ode[1]

Late, late yestreen I saw the new Moon,
With the old Moon in her arms;
And I fear, I fear, my Master dear!
We shall have a deadly storm.
Ballad of Sir Patrick Spence

I

Well! If the Bard was weather-wise, who made
   The grand old ballad of Sir Patrick Spence,
   This night, so tranquil now, will not go hence
Unroused by winds, that ply a busier trade
5   Than those which mould yon cloud in lazy flakes,
Or the dull sobbing draft, that moans and rakes
      Upon the strings of this Eolian lute,[2]
      Which better far were mute.
   For lo! the New-moon winter-bright!
10   And overspread with phantom light,
   (With swimming phantom light o'erspread
   But rimmed and circled by a silver thread)
I see the old Moon in her lap, foretelling
   The coming on of rain and squally blast.
15 And oh! that even now the gust were swelling,
   And the slant night-shower driving loud and fast!
Those sounds which oft have raised me, whilst they awed,
      And sent my soul abroad,
Might now perhaps their wonted° impulse give,   *customary*
20 Might startle this dull pain, and make it move and live!

2

A grief without a pang, void, dark, and drear,
   A stifled, drowsy, unimpassioned grief,
   Which finds no natural outlet, no relief,
      In word, or sigh, or tear—
25 O Lady![3] in this wan and heartless mood,
   To other thoughts by yonder throstle woo'd,
    All this long eve, so balmy and serene,
   Have I been gazing on the western sky,
   And its peculiar tint of yellow green:

---

1. This poem originated in a verse letter of 340 lines, called *A Letter to* ———, that Coleridge wrote on the night of April 4, 1802, after hearing the opening stanzas of *Ode: Intimations of Immortality,* which Wordsworth had just composed. The *Letter* was addressed to Sara Hutchinson (whom Coleridge sometimes called "Asra"), the sister of Wordsworth's fiancée, Mary. It picked up the theme of a loss in the quality of perceptual experience that Wordsworth had presented at the beginning of his *Ode.* In his original poem Coleridge lamented at length his unhappy marriage and the hopelessness of his love for Sara Hutchinson. In the next six months Coleridge deleted more than half the original lines, revised and reordered the remaining passages, and so transformed a long verse confession into the compact and dignified *Dejection: An Ode.* He published the *Ode,* in substantially its present form, on October 4, 1802, Wordsworth's wedding day—and also the seventh anniversary of Coleridge's own disastrous marriage to Sara Fricker. Note Coleridge's use of marriage as a metaphor in lines 49 and 67–70.

2. A stringed instrument played upon by the wind (see *The Eolian Harp,* n. 1, p. 419).

3. In the original version "Sara"—i.e., Sara Hutchinson. After intervening versions, in which the poem was addressed first to "William" (Wordsworth) and then to "Edmund," Coleridge introduced the noncommittal "Lady" in 1817.

30 And still I gaze—and with how blank an eye!
And those thin clouds above, in flakes and bars,
That give away their motion to the stars;
Those stars, that glide behind them or between,
Now sparkling, now bedimmed, but always seen:
35 Yon crescent Moon as fixed as if it grew
In its own cloudless, starless lake of blue;
I see them all so excellently fair,
I see, not feel, how beautiful they are!

3

My genial[4] spirits fail;
40   And what can these avail
To lift the smothering weight from off my breast?
It were a vain endeavour,
Though I should gaze for ever
On that green light that lingers in the west:
45 I may not hope from outward forms to win
The passion and the life, whose fountains are within.

4

O Lady! we receive but what we give,
And in our life alone does nature live:
Ours is her wedding-garment, ours her shroud![5]
50   And would we aught behold, of higher worth,
Than that inanimate cold world allowed
To the poor loveless ever-anxious crowd,
Ah! from the soul itself must issue forth,
A light, a glory,[6] a fair luminous cloud
55   Enveloping the Earth—
And from the soul itself must there be sent
A sweet and potent voice, of its own birth,
Of all sweet sounds the life and element!

5

O pure of heart! thou need'st not ask of me
60 What this strong music in the soul may be!
What, and wherein it doth exist,
This light, this glory, this fair luminous mist,
This beautiful and beauty-making power.
Joy,[7] virtuous Lady! Joy that ne'er was given,
65 Save to the pure, and in their purest hour,
Life, and Life's effluence, cloud at once and shower,
Joy, Lady! is the spirit and the power,

4. In its old use as the adjectival form of *genius:* "My innate powers fail."
5. I.e., whether nature is experienced as "inanimate" (line 51) or in living interchange with the observer depends on the apathy or joyous vitality of the observer's own spirit.
6. Coleridge commonly used "glory" not in the sense of a halo, merely, but as a term for a mountain phenomenon in which a walker sees his own figure projected by the sun in the mist, enlarged, and with a circle of light around its head.
7. Coleridge often uses "Joy" for a sense of abounding vitality and of harmony between one's inner life and the life of nature. He sometimes calls the contrary "exsiccation," or spiritual dryness.

Which wedding Nature to us gives in dower,
    A new Earth and new Heaven,[8]
70 Undreamt of by the sensual and the proud—
Joy is the sweet voice, Joy the luminous cloud—
    We in ourselves rejoice!
And thence flows all that charms or ear or sight,
    All melodies the echoes of that voice,
75 All colours a suffusion from that light.

6

There was a time when, though my path was rough,
    This joy within me dallied with distress,
And all misfortunes were but as the stuff
    Whence Fancy made me dreams of happiness:
80 For hope grew round me, like the twining vine,
And fruits, and foliage, not my own, seemed mine.
But now afflictions bow me down to earth:
Nor care I that they rob me of my mirth,
    But oh! each visitation
85 Suspends what nature gave me at my birth,
    My shaping spirit of Imagination.
For not to think of what I needs must feel,
    But to be still and patient, all I can;
And haply by abstruse research to steal
90   From my own nature all the natural man—
    This was my sole resource, my only plan:
Till that which suits a part infects the whole,
And now is almost grown the habit of my soul.

7

Hence, viper thoughts, that coil around my mind,
95   Reality's dark dream!
I turn from you, and listen to the wind,
    Which long has raved unnoticed. What a scream
Of agony by torture lengthened out
That lute sent forth! Thou Wind, that ravest without,
100   Bare crag, or mountain-tairn,[9] or blasted tree,
Or pine-grove whither woodman never clomb,
Or lonely house, long held the witches' home,
    Methinks were fitter instruments for thee,
Mad Lutanist! who in this month of showers,
105 Of dark brown gardens, and of peeping flowers,
Mak'st Devils' yule,[1] with worse than wintry song,
The blossoms, buds, and timorous leaves among.
    Thou Actor, perfect in all tragic sounds!

8. The sense becomes clearer if line 68 is punctuated in the way that Coleridge himself punctuated it when quoting the passage in one of his essays: "Which, wedding Nature to us, gives in dower." The idea is that "Joy" is the condition that (overcoming the alienation between mind and its milieu) marries us to "Nature" and gives by way of wedding portion ("dower") the experience of a renovated world.
9. Tarn, or mountain pool.
1. Christmas as, in a perverted form, it is celebrated by devils.

Thou mighty Poet, e'en to frenzy bold!
110   What tell'st thou now about?
     'Tis of the rushing of a host in rout,
With groans of trampled men, with smarting wounds—
At once they groan with pain, and shudder with the cold!
But hush! there is a pause of deepest silence!
115 And all that noise, as of a rushing crowd,
With groans, and tremulous shudderings—all is over—
     It tells another tale, with sounds less deep and loud!
        A tale of less affright,
        And tempered with delight,
120 As Otway's[2] self had framed the tender lay,
        'Tis of a little child
        Upon a lonesome wild,
Not far from home, but she hath lost her way:
And now moans low in bitter grief and fear,
125 And now screams loud, and hopes to make her mother hear.

8

'Tis midnight, but small thoughts have I of sleep:
Full seldom may my friend such vigils keep!
Visit her, gentle Sleep! with wings of healing,
     And may this storm be but a mountain-birth,[3]
130 May all the stars hang bright above her dwelling,
     Silent as though they watched the sleeping Earth!
        With light heart may she rise,
        Gay fancy, cheerful eyes,
     Joy lift her spirit, joy attune her voice;
135 To her may all things live, from pole to pole,
Their life the eddying of her living soul!
     O simple spirit, guided from above,
     Dear Lady! friend devoutest of my choice,
Thus mayest thou ever, evermore rejoice.

Apr. 4, 1802   1802

The Pains of Sleep[1]

Ere on my bed my limbs I lay,
It hath not been my use to pray
With moving lips or bended knees;
But silently, by slow degrees,

2. Thomas Otway (1652–1685), a dramatist noted for the pathos of his tragic passages. The poet originally named was "William," and the allusion was probably to Wordsworth's *Lucy Gray.*
3. Probably, "May this be a typical mountain storm, short though violent," although it is possible that Coleridge intended an allusion to Horace's phrase, "the mountain labored and brought forth a mouse."
1. Coleridge included a draft of this poem in a letter to Robert Southey, September 11, 1803, in which he wrote that "my spirits are dreadful, owing entirely to the Horrors of every night—I truly dread to sleep. It is no shadow with me, but substantial Misery foot-thick, that makes me sit by my bedside of a morning, & cry—. I have abandoned all opiates except Ether be one; & that only in *fits.* . . . " The last sentence indicates what Coleridge did not know—that his guilty nightmares were probably withdrawal symptoms from opium. The dreams he describes are very similar to those that De Quincey represents as "The Pains of Opium" in his *Confessions of an English Opium-Eater.*

5   My spirit I to Love compose,
In humble trust mine eye-lids close,
With reverential resignation,
No wish conceived, no thought exprest,
Only a sense of supplication;
10 A sense o'er all my soul imprest
That I am weak, yet not unblest,
Since in me, round me, every where
Eternal strength and wisdom are.

But yester-night I prayed aloud
15 In anguish and in agony,
Up-starting from the fiendish crowd
Of shapes and thoughts that tortured me:
A lurid light, a trampling throng,
Sense of intolerable wrong,
20 And whom I scorned, those only strong!
Thirst of revenge, the powerless will
Still baffled, and yet burning still!
Desire with loathing strangely mixed
On wild or hateful objects fixed.
25 Fantastic passions! maddening brawl!
And shame and terror over all!
Deeds to be hid which were not hid,
Which all confused I could not know,
Whether I suffered, or I did:
30 For all seemed guilt, remorse or woe,
My own or others still the same
Life-stifling fear, soul-stifling shame.

So two nights passed: the night's dismay
Saddened and stunned the coming day.
35 Sleep, the wide blessing, seemed to me
Distemper's worst calamity.
The third night, when my own loud scream
Had waked me from the fiendish dream,
O'ercome with sufferings strange and wild,
40 I wept as I had been a child;
And having thus by tears subdued
My anguish to a milder mood,
Such punishments, I said, were due
To natures deepliest stained with sin,—
45 For aye entempesting anew
The unfathomable hell within,
The horror of their deeds to view,
To know and loathe, yet wish and do!
Such griefs with such men well agree,
50 But wherefore, wherefore fall on me?
To be beloved is all I need,
And whom I love, I love indeed.

1803   1816

To William Wordsworth

Composed on the Night after His Recitation of a Poem on the Growth of an Individual Mind[1]

Friend of the wise! and teacher of the good!
Into my heart have I received that lay
More than historic, that prophetic lay
Wherein (high theme by thee first sung aright)
5 Of the foundations and the building up
Of a Human Spirit thou hast dared to tell
What may be told, to the understanding mind
Revealable; and what within the mind
By vital breathings secret as the soul
10 Of vernal growth, oft quickens in the heart
Thoughts all too deep for words![2]—

                                    Theme hard as high!
Of smiles spontaneous, and mysterious fears
(The first-born they of Reason and twin birth),
Of tides obedient to external force,
15 And currents self-determined, as might seem,
Or by some inner power; of moments awful,
Now in thy inner life, and now abroad,
When power streamed from thee, and thy soul received
The light reflected, as a light bestowed—
20 Of fancies fair, and milder hours of youth,
Hyblean[3] murmurs of poetic thought
Industrious in its joy, in vales and glens
Native or outland, lakes and famous hills!
Or on the lonely high-road, when the stars
25 Were rising; or by secret mountain-streams,
The guides and the companions of thy way!

    Of more than Fancy, of the Social Sense
Distending wide, and man beloved as man,
Where France in all her towns lay vibrating
30 Like some becalmed bark beneath the burst
Of Heaven's immediate thunder, when no cloud
Is visible, or shadow on the main.
For thou wert there, thine own brows garlanded,
Amid the tremor of a realm aglow,
35 Amid a mighty nation jubilant,
When from the general heart of human kind
Hope sprang forth like a full-born Deity!

---

1. This was the poem (later called *The Prelude*), addressed to Coleridge, that Wordsworth had completed in 1805. After Coleridge returned from Malta, very low in health and spirits, Wordsworth read the poem aloud to him during the evenings of almost two weeks. Coleridge wrote most of the present response immediately after the reading was completed, on January 7, 1807.

2. Wordsworth had described the effect on his mind of the animating breeze ("vital breathings") in *The Prelude* 1.1–44. "Thoughts . . . words" echoes the last line of Wordsworth's *Intimations* ode. Coleridge goes on to summarize the major themes and events of *The Prelude*.
3. Sweet. Hybla, in ancient Sicily, was famous for its honey.

——Of that dear Hope afflicted and struck down,
So summoned homeward, thenceforth calm and sure
40　From the dread watch-tower of man's absolute self,
With light unwaning on her eyes, to look
Far on—herself a glory to behold,
The Angel of the vision! Then (last strain)
Of Duty, chosen laws controlling choice,
45　Action and joy!—An Orphic song[4] indeed,
A song divine of high and passionate thoughts
To their own music chanted!

　　　　　　　　O great Bard!
Ere yet that last strain dying awed the air,
With steadfast eye I viewed thee in the choir
50　Of ever-enduring men. The truly great
Have all one age, and from one visible space
Shed influence! They, both in power and act,
Are permanent, and Time is not with them,
Save as it worketh for them, they in it.
55　Nor less a sacred roll, than those of old,
And to be placed, as they, with gradual fame
Among the archives of mankind, thy work
Makes audible a linked lay of Truth,
Of Truth profound a sweet continuous lay,
60　Not learnt, but native, her own natural notes!
Ah! as I listened with a heart forlorn,
The pulses of my being beat anew:
And even as life returns upon the drowned,[5]
Life's joy rekindling roused a throng of pains—
65　Keen pangs of Love, awakening as a babe
Turbulent, with an outcry in the heart;
And fears self-willed, that shunned the eye of hope;
And hope that scarce would know itself from fear;
Sense of past youth, and manhood come in vain,
70　And genius given, and knowledge won in vain;
And all which I had culled in wood-walks wild,
And all which patient toil had reared, and all,
Commune with thee had opened out—but flowers
Strewed on my corse, and borne upon my bier,
75　In the same coffin, for the self-same grave!

　　　That way no more! and ill beseems it me,
Who came a welcomer in herald's guise,
Singing of glory, and futurity,
To wander back on such unhealthful road,
80　Plucking the poisons of self-harm! And ill
Such intertwine beseems triumphal wreaths
Strewed before thy advancing!

4. As enchanting and oracular as the song of the legendary Orpheus. There may also be an allusion to the Orphic mysteries, involving spiritual death and rebirth (see lines 61–66). "The Angel of the vision" (line 43) probably alludes to "the great vision of the guarded mount" in Milton's *Lycidas*, line 161.

5. A death-in-life is also described in, e.g., *Dejection: An Ode* and *Epitaph*.

                              Nor do thou,
           Sage Bard! impair the memory of that hour
           Of thy communion with my nobler mind[6]
    85   By pity or grief, already felt too long!
           Nor let my words import more blame than needs.
           The tumult rose and ceased: for peace is nigh
           Where wisdom's voice has found a listening heart.
           Amid the howl of more than wintry storms,
    90   The halcyon[7] hears the voice of vernal hours
           Already on the wing.

                              Eve following eve,[8]
           Dear tranquil time, when the sweet sense of Home
           Is sweetest! moments for their own sake hailed
           And more desired, more precious for thy song,
    95   In silence listening, like a devout child,
           My soul lay passive, by thy various strain
           Driven as in surges now beneath the stars,
           With momentary stars of my own birth,
           Fair constellated foam, still darting off
    100   Into the darkness; now a tranquil sea,
           Outspread and bright, yet swelling to the moon.

               And when—O Friend! my comforter and guide!
           Strong in thyself, and powerful to give strength!—
           Thy long sustained Song finally closed,
    105   And thy deep voice had ceased—yet thou thyself
           Wert still before my eyes, and round us both
           That happy vision of beloved faces—
           Scarce conscious, and yet conscious of its close
           I sate, my being blended in one thought
    110   (Thought was it? or aspiration? or resolve?)
           Absorbed, yet hanging still upon the sound—
           And when I rose, I found myself in prayer.

1807   1817

On Donne's Poetry[1]

           With Donne, whose muse on dromedary[2] trots,
           Wreathe iron pokers into true-love knots;
           Rhyme's sturdy cripple, fancy's maze and clue,
           Wit's forge and fire-blast, meaning's press and screw.

ca. 1818   1836

---

6. I.e., during the early association between the
two poets (1797–98).
7. A fabled bird, able to calm the sea where it
nested in winter.
8. The evenings during which Wordsworth read
his poem aloud.
1. John Donne as a poet had been in eclipse for
most of the 18th century. This terse and penetrating comment shows the Romantic poet's great,
though ironically qualified, respect for the master
of the metaphysical style.
2. The one-humped Arabian camel, trained to be
ridden.

Work without Hope

Lines Composed 21st February 1825

All Nature seems at work. Slugs leave their lair—
The bees are stirring—birds are on the wing—
And Winter slumbering in the open air,
Wears on his smiling face a dream of Spring!
5   And I the while, the sole unbusy thing,
Nor honey make, nor pair, nor build, nor sing.

Yet well I ken the banks where amaranths[1] blow,
Have traced the fount whence streams of nectar flow.
Bloom, O ye amaranths! bloom for whom ye may,
10   For me ye bloom not! Glide, rich streams, away!
With lips unbrightened, wreathless brow, I stroll:
And would you learn the spells that drowse my soul?
Work without hope draws nectar in a sieve,
And hope without an object cannot live.

1825   1828

Epitaph[1]

Stop, Christian Passer-by!—Stop, child of God,
And read with gentle breast. Beneath this sod
A poet lies, or that which once seem'd he.—
O, lift one thought in prayer for S. T. C.;
5   That he who many a year with toil of breath
Found death in life, may here find life in death!
Mercy for praise—to be forgiven for[2] fame
He ask'd, and hoped, through Christ. Do thou the same!

1833   1834

Biographia Literaria   In March 1815 Coleridge was preparing a collected edition of his poems and planned to include "a general preface . . . on the principles of philosophic and genial criticism." Characteristically, the materials developed as Coleridge worked on them until, on July 29, he declared that the preface had been extended into a complete work, "an Autobiographia Literaria"; it was to consist of two main parts, "my literary life and opinions, as far as poetry and *poetical* criticism [are] concerned" and a critique of Wordsworth's theory of poetic diction. This work was ready by September 17, 1815, but the *Biographia Literaria,* in two volumes, was not published until July 1817. The delay was caused by a series of miscalculations by his

1. Mythical flowers that bloom perpetually.
1. Written by Coleridge the year before he died. One version that he sent in a letter had as a title: "Epitaph on a Poet little known, yet better known by the Initials of his name than by the Name Itself."
2. "For" in the sense of "instead of" [Coleridge's note].

printer, which forced Coleridge to add 150 pages of miscellaneous materials to pad out the length of the second volume.

Coleridge had been planning a detailed critique of Wordsworth's theory of poetic diction ever since 1802, when he had detected "a radical difference in our theoretical opinions respecting poetry." In the selection from chapter 17, Coleridge agrees with Wordsworth's general aim of reforming the artifices of current poetic diction, but he sharply denies Wordsworth's claim that there is no essential difference between the language of poetry and the language spoken by people in real life. The other selections printed here are devoted mainly to the central principle of Coleridge's own critical theory, the distinction between the mechanical "fancy" and the organic "imagination." The biographical section of the *Biographia* (chapters 1 and 4), dealing with the development of his poetic taste and theory, describes his gradual realization, climaxed by his first exposure to Wordsworth's poetry, "that fancy and imagination were two distinct and widely different faculties." The conclusion to chapter 13 tersely summarizes this distinction; and the definition of poetry, at the end of chapter 14, develops at greater length the nature of the process and products of the "synthetic and magical power . . . of imagination." These paragraphs, whose meaning is much disputed, have become a central reference in English literary criticism.

From Biographia Literaria

From *Chapter 1*

[THE DISCIPLINE OF HIS TASTE AT SCHOOL][1]

At school I enjoyed the inestimable advantage of a very sensible, though at the same time a very severe master. He[2] early molded my taste to the preference of Demosthenes to Cicero, of Homer and Theocritus to Virgil, and again of Virgil to Ovid. He habituated me to compare Lucretius (in such extracts as I then read), Terence, and, above all, the chaster poems of Catullus not only with the Roman poets of the so-called silver and brazen ages but with even those of the Augustan era; and, on grounds of plain sense and universal logic, to see and assert the superiority of the former in the truth and nativeness both of their thoughts and diction. At the same time that we were studying the Greek tragic poets, he made us read Shakespeare and Milton as lessons; and they were the lessons, too, which required most time and trouble to *bring up,* so as to escape his censure. I learnt from him that poetry, even that of the loftiest and, seemingly, that of the wildest odes, had a logic of its own as severe as that of science; and more difficult, because more subtle, more complex, and dependent on more, and more fugitive, causes. In the truly great poets, he would say, there is a reason assignable, not only for every word, but for the position of every word; and I well remember that, availing himself of the synonyms to the Homer of Didymus,[3] he made us attempt to show, with regard to each, *why* it would not have answered the same purpose, and *wherein* consisted the peculiar fitness of the word in the original text.

1. Coleridge heads each chapter with a list of topics. In instances where we excerpt from chapters, we introduce these headings in brackets before the relevant selection.
2. The Rev. James Bowyer, many years Head Master of the Grammar School, Christ's Hospital

[Coleridge's note]. See also Charles Lamb's essay *Christ's Hospital Five-and-Thirty Years Ago* (p. 495).
3. Didymus of Alexandria (ca. 65 B.C.E.–10 C.E.) was the author of a commentary on the text of Homer.

In our own English compositions (at least for the last three years of our school education) he showed no mercy to phrase, metaphor, or image unsupported by a sound sense, or where the same sense might have been conveyed with equal force and dignity in plainer words. Lute, harp, and lyre, muse, muses, and inspirations, Pegasus, Parnassus, and Hippocrene were all an abomination to him. In fancy I can almost hear him now, exclaiming, "Harp? Harp? Lyre? Pen and ink, boy, you mean! Muse, boy, muse? Your nurse's daughter, you mean! Pierian spring? Oh, aye! the cloister pump, I suppose!" Nay, certain introductions, similes, and examples were placed by name on a list of interdiction. Among the similes there was, I remember, that of the manchineel fruit,[4] as suiting equally well with too many subjects, in which, however, it yielded the palm at once to the example of Alexander and Clytus,[5] which was equally good and apt whatever might be the theme. Was it ambition? Alexander and Clytus! Flattery? Alexander and Clytus! Anger? Drunkenness? Pride? Friendship? Ingratitude? Late repentance? Still, still Alexander and Clytus! At length, the praises of agriculture having been exemplified in the sagacious observation that, had Alexander been holding the plow, he would not have run his friend Clytus through with a spear, this tried and serviceable old friend was banished by public edict *in secula seculorum*.[6] I have sometimes ventured to think that a list of this kind or an *index expurgatorius*[7] of certain well-known and ever returning phrases, both introductory and transitional, including the large assortment of modest egoisms and flattering illeisms,[8] etc., etc., might be hung up in our law courts and both Houses of Parliament with great advantage to the public as an important saving of national time, an incalculable relief to his Majesty's ministers; but, above all, as insuring the thanks of country attorneys and their clients, who have private bills to carry through the House.

Be this as it may, there was one custom of our master's which I cannot pass over in silence, because I think it imitable and worthy of imitation. He would often permit our theme exercises, under some pretext of want of time, to accumulate till each lad had four or five to be looked over. Then placing the whole number *abreast* on his desk, he would ask the writer why this or that sentence might not have found as appropriate a place under this or that other thesis; and if no satisfying answer could be returned and two faults of the same kind were found in one exercise, the irrevocable verdict followed, the exercise was torn up, and another on the same subject to be produced, in addition to the tasks of the day. The reader will, I trust, excuse this tribute of recollection to a man whose severities, even now, not seldom furnish the dreams by which the blind fancy would fain interpret to the mind the painful sensations of distempered sleep; but neither lessen nor dim the deep sense of my moral and intellectual obligations. He sent us to the university excellent Latin and Greek scholars and tolerable Hebraists. Yet our classical knowledge was the least of the good gifts which we derived from his zealous and conscientious tutorage. He is now gone to his final reward, full of years and full of honors, even of those honors which were dearest to his heart as gratefully bestowed by that school, and still binding him to the interests of

---

4. Poisonous, though attractive in appearance.
5. Plutarch's *Life* of Alexander the Great relates that the king killed his friend Clytus in a drunken quarrel.

6. Literally, for centuries of centuries (Latin); forever.
7. Index of things to be deleted (Latin).
8. Excessive use of the pronoun *he* (in Latin, *ille*).

that school, in which he had been himself educated and to which during his whole life he was a dedicated thing. * * *

[BOWLES'S SONNETS]

I had just entered on my seventeenth year, when the sonnets of Mr. Bowles,[9] twenty in number, and just then published in a quarto pamphlet, were first made known and presented to me by a schoolfellow who had quitted us for the university and who, during the whole time that he was in our first form (or in our school language, a Grecian),[1] had been my patron and protector. I refer to Dr. Middleton, the truly learned and every way excellent Bishop of Calcutta. * * *

It was a double pleasure to me, and still remains a tender recollection, that I should have received from a friend so revered the first knowledge of a poet by whose works, year after year, I was so enthusiastically delighted and inspired. My earliest acquaintances will not have forgotten the undisciplined eagerness and impetuous zeal with which I laboured to make proselytes, not only of my companions, but of all with whom I conversed, of whatever rank and in whatever place. As my school finances did not permit me to purchase copies, I made, within less than a year and a half, more than forty transcriptions, as the best presents I could offer to those who had in any way won my regard. And with almost equal delight did I receive the three or four following publications of the same author.

Though I have seen and known enough of mankind to be well aware that I shall perhaps stand alone in my creed, and that it will be well if I subject myself to no worse charge than that of singularity, I am not therefore deterred from avowing that I regard and ever have regarded the obligations of intellect among the most sacred of the claims of gratitude. A valuable thought, or a particular train of thoughts, gives me additional pleasure when I can safely refer and attribute it to the conversation or correspondence of another. My obligations to Mr. Bowles were indeed important and for radical good. At a very premature age, even before my fifteenth year, I had bewildered myself in metaphysics and in theological controversy. Nothing else pleased me. History and particular facts lost all interest in my mind. Poetry (though for a schoolboy of that age I was above par in English versification and had already produced two or three compositions which, I may venture to say without reference to my age, were somewhat above mediocrity, and which had gained me more credit than the sound good sense of my old master was at all pleased with), poetry itself, yea novels and romances, became insipid to me. In my friendless wanderings on our leave-days (for I was an orphan, and had scarce any connections in London), highly was I delighted if any passenger, especially if he were dressed in black,[2] would enter into conversation with me. For I soon found the means of directing it to my favorite subjects

---

9. William Lisle Bowles (1762–1850) published in 1789 two editions of a collection of sonnets setting forth the meditations evoked from a traveler by the changing scene.

1. Gifted students in the final class at Christ's Hospital who were being prepared for a university.
2. I.e., if he were a clergyman.

> Of providence, fore-knowledge, will, and fate,
> Fixed fate, free will, fore-knowledge absolute,
> And found no end, in wandering mazes lost.[3]

This preposterous pursuit was, beyond doubt, injurious both to my natural powers and to the progress of my education. It would perhaps have been destructive had it been continued; but from this I was auspiciously withdrawn, partly indeed by an accidental introduction to an amiable family,[4] chiefly however by the genial influence of a style of poetry so tender and yet so manly, so natural and real, and yet so dignified and harmonious, as the sonnets, etc., of Mr. Bowles! Well were it for me, perhaps, had I never relapsed into the same mental disease; if I had continued to pluck the flower and reap the harvest from the cultivated surface, instead of delving in the unwholesome quicksilver mines of metaphysic depths. But if in after time I have sought a refuge from bodily pain and mismanaged sensibility in abstruse researches, which exercised the strength and subtlety of the understanding without awakening the feelings of the heart; still there was a long and blessed interval, during which my natural faculties were allowed to expand and my original tendencies to develop themselves: my fancy, and the love of nature, and the sense of beauty in forms and sounds.

[COMPARISON BETWEEN THE POETS BEFORE AND SINCE MR. POPE]

The second advantage which I owe to my early perusal and admiration of these poems (to which let me add, though known to me at a somewhat later period, the *Lewesdon Hill* of Mr. Crow)[5] bears more immediately on my present subject. Among those with whom I conversed there were, of course, very many who had formed their taste and their notions of poetry from the writings of Mr. Pope and his followers: or to speak more generally, in that school of French poetry condensed and invigorated by English understanding which had predominated from the last century. I was not blind to the merits of this school, yet as from inexperience of the world and consequent want of sympathy with the general subjects of these poems they gave me little pleasure, I doubtless undervalued the *kind*, and with the presumption of youth withheld from its masters the legitimate name of poets. I saw that the excellence of this kind consisted in just and acute observations on men and manners in an artificial state of society as its matter and substance, and in the logic of wit conveyed in smooth and strong epigrammatic couplets as its *form*. Even when the subject was addressed to the fancy or the intellect, as in the *Rape of the Lock* or the *Essay on Man*; nay, when it was a consecutive narration, as in that astonishing product of matchless talent and ingenuity, Pope's translation of the *Iliad*; still a *point* was looked for at the end of each second line, and the whole was as it were a sorites or, if I may exchange a logical for a grammatical metaphor, a *conjunction disjunctive*,[6] of epigrams.

---

3. *Paradise Lost* 2.559–61.
4. The family of Mary Evans, with whom Coleridge fell in love in 1788.
5. William Crow(e) (1745–1829) published in 1788 *Lewesdon Hill*, a long poem in blank verse that, like Bowles's sonnets, combined descriptions of the natural scene with associated moral and personal reflections.
6. A word that connects the parts of a sentence but expresses an alternative or opposition: "or," "but," "lest," etc. "Sorites": a sequence of interconnected syllogisms.

Meantime the matter and diction seemed to me characterized not so much by poetic thoughts as by thoughts *translated* into the language of poetry. On this last point I had occasion to render my own thoughts gradually more and more plain to myself by frequent amicable disputes concerning Darwin's *Botanic Garden,*[7] which for some years was greatly extolled, not only by the *reading* public in general, but even by those whose genius and natural robustness of understanding enabled them afterwards to act foremost in dissipating these "painted mists" that occasionally rise from the marshes at the foot of Parnassus. During my first Cambridge vacation I assisted a friend in a contribution for a literary society in Devonshire, and in this I remember to have compared Darwin's work to the Russian palace of ice, glittering, cold, and transitory. In the same essay too I assigned sundry reasons, chiefly drawn from a comparison of passages in the Latin poets with the original Greek from which they were borrowed, for the preference of Collins's odes to those of Gray, and of the simile in Shakespeare:

> How like a younker or a prodigal
> The scarfed bark puts from her native bay,
> Hugged and embraced by the strumpet wind!
> How like the prodigal doth she return,
> With over-weathered ribs and ragged sails,
> Lean, rent and beggared by the strumpet wind![8]

to the imitation in the *Bard:*

> Fair laughs the morn, and soft the zephyr blows
> While proudly riding o'er the azure realm
> In gallant trim the gilded vessel goes;
> YOUTH on the prow, and PLEASURE at the helm;
> Regardless of the sweeping whirlwind's sway,
> That, hushed in grim repose, expects its evening prey.[9]

(In which, by the bye, the words "realm" and "sway" are rhymes dearly purchased.) I preferred the original, on the ground that in the imitation it depended wholly in the compositor's putting, or not putting, a small capital both in this and in many other passages of the same poet whether the words should be personifications or mere abstracts. I mention this because, in referring various lines in Gray to their original in Shakespeare and Milton, and in the clear perception how completely all the propriety was lost in the transfer, I was at that early period led to a conjecture which, many years afterwards, was recalled to me from the same thought having been started in conversation, but far more ably, and developed more fully, by Mr. Wordsworth; namely, that this style of poetry which I have characterized above as translations of prose thoughts into poetic language had been kept up by, if it did not wholly arise from, the custom of writing Latin verses and the great importance attached to these exercises in our public schools. Whatever might have been the case in the fifteenth century, when the use of the Latin tongue was so general among learned men that Erasmus is said to have forgotten his native language; yet in the present day it is not to be supposed

---

7. Published in 1789–91 by Erasmus Darwin (1731–1802); a long poem in closed couplets, presenting the science of botany in elaborate allegories.

8. *Merchant of Venice* 2.6.14–19.

9. Thomas Gray's *The Bard* (1757).

that a youth can think in Latin, or that he can have any other reliance on the force or fitness of his phrases but the authority of the author from whence he had adopted them. Consequently he must first prepare his thoughts and then pick out from Virgil, Horace, Ovid, or perhaps more compendiously, from his *Gradus*,[1] halves and quarters of lines in which to embody them.

I never object to a certain degree of disputatiousness in a young man from the age of seventeen to that of four or five and twenty, provided I find him always arguing on one side of the question. The controversies occasioned by my unfeigned zeal for the honor of a favorite contemporary, then known to me only by his works, were of great advantage in the formation and establishment of my taste and critical opinions. In my defense of the lines running into each other instead of closing at each couplet, and of natural language, neither bookish nor vulgar, neither redolent of the lamp nor of the kennel, such as *I will remember thee;* instead of the same thought tricked up in the rag-fair finery of

> ———Thy image on her wing
> Before my FANCY'S eye shall MEMORY bring,

I had continually to adduce the meter and diction of the Greek poets from Homer to Theocritus inclusive; and still more of our elder English poets from Chaucer to Milton. Nor was this all. But as it was my constant reply to authorities brought against me from later poets of great name that no authority could avail in opposition to Truth, Nature, Logic, and the Laws of Universal Grammar; actuated too by my former passion for metaphysical investigations, I labored at a solid foundation on which permanently to ground my opinions in the component faculties of the human mind itself and their comparative dignity and importance. According to the faculty or source from which the pleasure given by any poem or passage was derived I estimated the merit of such poem or passage. As the result of all my reading and meditation, I abstracted two critical aphorisms, deeming them to comprise the conditions and criteria of poetic style: first, that not the poem which we have *read*, but that to which we *return* with the greatest pleasure, possesses the genuine power and claims the name of *essential* poetry. Second, that whatever lines can be translated into other words of the same language without diminution of their significance, either in sense of association or in any worthy feeling, are so far vicious in their diction. Be it however observed that I excluded from the list of worthy feelings the pleasure derived from mere novelty in the reader, and the desire of exciting wonderment at his powers in the author. Oftentimes since then, in perusing French tragedies, I have fancied two marks of admiration at the end of each line, as hieroglyphics of the author's own admiration at his own cleverness. Our genuine admiration of a great poet is a continuous undercurrent of feeling; it is everywhere present, but seldom anywhere as a separate excitement. I was wont boldly to affirm that it would be scarcely more difficult to push a stone out from the pyramids with the bare hand than to alter a word, or the position of a word, in Milton or Shakespeare (in their most important works at least), without making the author say something else, or something worse, than he

---

1. *Gradus ad Parnassum* ("Stairway to Parnassus"), a dictionary of Latin words, synonyms, and descriptive epithets, illustrated from the Latin poets. It was long used as a school text in Latin composition.

does say. One great distinction I appeared to myself to see plainly, between even the characteristic faults of our elder poets and the false beauties of the moderns. In the former, from Donne to Cowley, we find the most fantastic out-of-the-way thoughts, but in the most pure and genuine mother English; in the latter, the most obvious thoughts, in language the most fantastic and arbitrary. Our faulty elder poets sacrificed the passion and passionate flow of poetry to the subtleties of intellect and to the starts of wit; the moderns to the glare and glitter of a perpetual yet broken and heterogeneous imagery, or rather to an amphibious something, made up half of image and half of abstract[2] meaning. The one sacrificed the heart to the head, the other both heart and head to point and drapery. * * *

From *Chapter 4*

[MR. WORDSWORTH'S EARLIER POEMS]

* * * During the last year of my residence at Cambridge, I became acquainted with Mr. Wordsworth's first publication, entitled *Descriptive Sketches;*[3] and seldom, if ever, was the emergence of an original poetic genius above the literary horizon more evidently announced. In the form, style, and manner of the whole poem, and in the structure of the particular lines and periods, there is a harshness and acerbity connected and combined with words and images all a-glow which might recall those products of the vegetable world, where gorgeous blossoms rise out of the hard and thorny rind and shell within which the rich fruit was elaborating. The language was not only peculiar and strong, but at times knotty and contorted, as by its own impatient strength; while the novelty and struggling crowd of images, acting in conjunction with the difficulties of the style, demanded always a greater closeness of attention than poetry (at all events than descriptive poetry) has a right to claim. It not seldom therefore justified the complaint of obscurity. In the following extract I have sometimes fancied that I saw an emblem of the poem itself and of the author's genius as it was then displayed:

> 'Tis storm; and hid in mist from hour to hour,
> All day the floods a deepening murmur pour;
> The sky is veiled, and every cheerful sight:
> Dark is the region as with coming night;
> And yet what frequent bursts of overpowering light!
> Triumphant on the bosom of the storm,
> Glances the fire-clad eagle's wheeling form;
> Eastward, in long perspective glittering, shine
> The wood-crowned cliffs that o'er the lake recline;
> Wide o'er the Alps a hundred streams unfold,
> At once to pillars turned that flame with gold;
> Behind his sail the peasant strives to shun
> The West, that burns like one dilated sun,

2. I remember a ludicrous instance in the poem of a young tradesman: "No more will I endure Love's pleasing pain, / Or round my *heart's leg* tie his galling chain" [Coleridge's note].
3. Published 1793, the year before Coleridge left Cambridge; a long descriptive-meditative poem in closed couplets, recounting Wordsworth's walking tour in the Alps in 1790. Wordsworth describes the same tour in *The Prelude*, book 6.

> Where in a mighty crucible expire
> The mountains, glowing hot, like coals of fire.[4]

The poetic Psyche, in its process to full development, undergoes as many changes as its Greek namesake, the butterfly.[5] And it is remarkable how soon genius clears and purifies itself from the faults and errors of its earliest products; faults which, in its earliest compositions, are the more obtrusive and confluent because, as heterogeneous elements which had only a temporary use, they constitute the very *ferment* by which themselves are carried off. Or we may compare them to some diseases, which must work on the humors and be thrown out on the surface in order to secure the patient from their future recurrence. I was in my twenty-fourth year when I had the happiness of knowing Mr. Wordsworth personally;[6] and, while memory lasts, I shall hardly forget the sudden effect produced on my mind by his recitation of a manuscript poem which still remains unpublished, but of which the stanza and tone of style were the same as those of *The Female Vagrant* as originally printed in the first volume of the *Lyrical Ballads*.[7] There was here no mark of strained thought or forced diction, no crowd or turbulence of imagery, and, as the poet hath himself well described in his lines on revisiting the Wye,[8] manly reflection and human associations had given both variety and an additional interest to natural objects which in the passion and appetite of the first love they had seemed to him neither to need or permit. The occasional obscurities, which had risen from an imperfect control over the resources of his native language, had almost wholly disappeared, together with that worse defect of arbitrary and illogical phrases, at once hackneyed and fantastic, which hold so distinguished a place in the *technique* of ordinary poetry and will, more or less, alloy the earlier poems of the truest genius, unless the attention has been specifically directed to their worthlessness and incongruity. I did not perceive anything particular in the mere style of the poem alluded to during its recitation, except indeed such difference as was not separable from the thought and manner; and the Spenserian stanza which always, more or less, recalls to the reader's mind Spenser's own style, would doubtless have authorized in my then opinion a more frequent descent to the phrases of ordinary life than could, without an ill effect, have been hazarded in the heroic couplet. It was not however the freedom from false taste, whether as to common defects or to those more properly his own, which made so unusual an impression on my feelings immediately, and subsequently on my judgment. It was the union of deep feeling with profound thought; the fine balance of truth in observing with the imaginative faculty in modifying the objects observed; and above all the original gift of spreading the tone, the *atmosphere*, and with it the depth and height of the ideal world, around forms, incidents, and situations of which, for the common view, custom had bedimmed all the luster, had dried up the sparkle and the dewdrops. "To find no contradiction in the union of old and new, to contemplate the

---

4. *Descriptive Sketches* (1815 version), lines 332ff.
5. In Greek, Psyche is the common name for the soul and the butterfly [Coleridge's note].
6. The meeting occurred in September 1795.
7. *Salisbury Plain* (1793–94), which was left in

manuscript until Wordsworth published a revised version in 1842 under the title *Guilt and Sorrow.* An excerpt from *Salisbury Plain* was printed as *The Female Vagrant*, in *Lyrical Ballads* (1798).
8. Wordsworth's *Tintern Abbey*, lines 76ff.

Ancient of Days and all his works with feelings as fresh as if all had then sprang forth at the first creative fiat, characterizes the mind that feels the riddle of the world and may help to unravel it. To carry on the feelings of childhood into the powers of manhood; to combine the child's sense of wonder and novelty with the appearances which every day for perhaps forty years had rendered familiar;

> With sun and moon and stars throughout the year,
> And man and woman;[9]

this is the character and privilege of genius, and one of the marks which distinguish genius from talents. And therefore it is the prime merit of genius, and its most unequivocal mode of manifestation, so to represent familiar objects as to awaken in the minds of others a kindred feeling concerning them, and that freshness of sensation which is the constant accompaniment of mental no less than of bodily convalescence. Who has not a thousand times seen snow fall on water? Who has not watched it with a new feeling from the time that he has read Burns' comparison of sensual pleasure

> To snow that falls upon a river
> A moment white—then gone forever![1]

In poems, equally as in philosophic disquisitions, genius produces the strongest impressions of novelty while it rescues the most admitted truths from the impotence caused by the very circumstance of their universal admission. Truths of all others the most awful and mysterious, yet being at the same time of universal interest, are too often considered as *so* true, that they lose all the life and efficiency of truth and lie bedridden in the dormitory of the soul side by side with the most despised and exploded errors." *The Friend*, p. 76, no. 5.[2]

[ON FANCY AND IMAGINATION—THE INVESTIGATION OF THE DISTINCTION IMPORTANT TO THE FINE ARTS]

This excellence, which in all Mr. Wordsworth's writings is more or less predominant and which constitutes the character of his mind, I no sooner felt than I sought to understand. Repeated meditations led me first to suspect (and a more intimate analysis of the human faculties, their appropriate marks, functions, and effects, matured my conjecture into full conviction) that fancy and imagination were two distinct and widely different faculties, instead of being, according to the general belief, either two names with one meaning, or at furthest the lower and higher degree of one and the same power. It is not, I own, easy to conceive a more apposite translation of the Greek *phantasia* than the Latin *imaginatio*; but it is equally true that in all societies there exists an instinct of growth, a certain collective unconscious good sense working progressively to desynonymize those words originally of the same meaning which the conflux of dialects had supplied to the more homogeneous languages, as the Greek and German: and which the same

---

9. Altered from Milton's sonnet *To Mr. Cyriack Skinner upon His Blindness.*
1. Altered from Burns's *Tam o' Shanter*, lines 61–62.
2. A periodical published by Coleridge (1809–10).

cause, joined with accidents of translation from original works of different countries, occasion in mixed languages like our own. The first and most important point to be proved is, that two conceptions perfectly distinct are confused under one and the same word, and (this done) to appropriate that word exclusively to one meaning, and the synonym (should there be one) to the other. But if (as will be often the case in the arts and sciences) no synonym exists, we must either invent or borrow a word. In the present instance the appropriation had already begun and been legitimated in the derivative adjective: Milton had a highly *imaginative,* Cowley a very *fanciful,* mind. If therefore I should succeed in establishing the actual existence of two faculties generally different, the nomenclature would be at once determined. To the faculty by which I had characterized Milton we should confine the term *imagination;* while the other would be contra-distinguished as *fancy.* Now were it once fully ascertained that this division is no less grounded in nature than that of delirium from mania, or Otway's

> Lutes, lobsters, seas of milk, and ships of amber,[3]

from Shakespeare's

> What! have his daughters brought him to this pass?[4]

or from the preceding apostrophe to the elements, the theory of the fine arts and of poetry in particular could not, I thought, but derive some additional and important light. It would in its immediate effects furnish a torch of guidance to the philosophical critic, and ultimately to the poet himself. In energetic minds truth soon changes by domestication into power; and from directing in the discrimination and appraisal of the product becomes influencive in the production. To admire on principle is the only way to imitate without loss of originality. * * *

From *Chapter 13*

[ON THE IMAGINATION, OR ESEMPLASTIC[5] POWER]

* * * The IMAGINATION, then, I consider either as primary, or secondary. The primary IMAGINATION I hold to be the living power and prime agent of all human perception, and as a repetition in the finite mind of the eternal act of creation in the infinite I AM. The secondary I consider as an echo of the former, coexisting with the conscious will, yet still as identical with the primary in the *kind* of its agency, and differing only in *degree,* and in the *mode* of its operation. It dissolves, diffuses, dissipates, in order to recreate; or where this process is rendered impossible, yet still, at all events, it struggles to idealize and to unify. It is essentially *vital,* even as all objects (*as* objects) are essentially fixed and dead.

FANCY, on the contrary, has no other counters to play with but fixities and definites. The fancy is indeed no other than a mode of memory emancipated from the order of time and space; and blended with, and modified by that

---

3. Thomas Otway, in *Venice Preserved* (1682), wrote "laurels" in place of "lobsters" (5.2.151).
4. *King Lear* 3.4.59.

5. Coleridge coined this word and used it to mean "molding into unity."

empirical phenomenon of the will which we express by the word CHOICE. But equally with the ordinary memory it must receive all its materials ready made from the law of association.[6] * * *

Chapter 14

OCCASION OF THE *LYRICAL BALLADS*, AND THE OBJECTS ORIGINALLY
PROPOSED—PREFACE TO THE SECOND EDITION—THE ENSUING
CONTROVERSY, ITS CAUSES AND ACRIMONY—PHILOSOPHIC DEFINITIONS
OF A POEM AND POETRY WITH SCHOLIA.[7]

During the first year that Mr. Wordsworth and I were neighbours,[8] our conversations turned frequently on the two cardinal points of poetry, the power of exciting the sympathy of the reader by a faithful adherence to the truth of nature, and the power of giving the interest of novelty by the modifying colors of imagination.[9] The sudden charm which accidents of light and shade, which moonlight or sunset diffused over a known and familiar landscape, appeared to represent the practicability of combining both. These are the poetry of nature. The thought suggested itself (to which of us I do not recollect) that a series of poems might be composed of two sorts. In the one, the incidents and agents were to be, in part at least, supernatural; and the excellence aimed at was to consist in the interesting of the affections by the dramatic truth of such emotions as would naturally accompany such situations, supposing them real. And real in *this* sense they have been to every human being who, from whatever source of delusion, has at any time believed himself under supernatural agency. For the second class, subjects were to be chosen from ordinary life; the characters and incidents were to be such as will be found in every village and its vicinity where there is a meditative and feeling mind to seek after them, or to notice them when they present themselves.

In this idea originated the plan of the *Lyrical Ballads;* in which it was agreed that my endeavours should be directed to persons and characters supernatural, or at least romantic; yet so as to transfer from our inward nature a human interest and a semblance of truth sufficient to procure for these shadows of imagination that willing suspension of disbelief for the moment, which constitutes poetic faith. Mr. Wordsworth, on the other hand, was to propose to himself as his object to give the charm of novelty to things of every day, and to excite a feeling analogous to the supernatural, by awakening the mind's attention from the lethargy of custom and directing it to the loveliness and the wonders of the world before us; an inexhaustible treasure, but for which, in consequence of the film of familiarity and selfish

6. Coleridge conceives God's creation to be a continuing process, which has an analogy in the creative perception ("primary imagination") of all human minds. The creative process is repeated, or "echoed," on still a third level, by the "secondary imagination" of the poet, which dissolves the products of primary perception in order to shape them into a new and unified creation—the imaginative passage or poem. The "fancy," on the other hand, can only manipulate "fixities and definites" that, linked by association, come to it ready-made from perception. Its products, therefore, are not recreations (echoes of God's original creative process) but mosaic-like reassemblies of existing bits and pieces.
7. Additional remarks, after a philosophic demonstration.
8. At Nether Stowey and Alfoxden, Somerset, in 1797.
9. Cf. Wordsworth's account in his Preface to *Lyrical Ballads* (p. 239).

solicitude, we have eyes yet see not, ears that hear not, and hearts that neither feel nor understand.[1]

With this view I wrote *The Ancient Mariner,* and was preparing, among other poems, *The Dark Ladie,* and the *Christabel,* in which I should have more nearly realized my ideal than I had done in my first attempt. But Mr. Wordsworth's industry had proved so much more successful and the number of his poems so much greater, that my compositions, instead of forming a balance, appeared rather an interpolation of heterogeneous matter.[2] Mr. Wordsworth added two or three poems written in his own character, in the impassioned, lofty, and sustained diction which is characteristic of his genius. In this form the *Lyrical Ballads* were published; and were presented by him, as an *experiment,*[3] whether subjects which from their nature rejected the usual ornaments and extra-colloquial style of poems in general might not be so managed in the language of ordinary life as to produce the pleasurable interest which it is the peculiar business of poetry to impart. To the second edition[4] he added a preface of considerable length; in which, notwithstanding some passages of apparently a contrary import, he was understood to contend for the extension of this style to poetry of all kinds, and to reject as vicious and indefensible all phrases and forms of style that were not included in what he (unfortunately, I think, adopting an equivocal expression) called the language of *real* life. From this preface, prefixed to poems in which it was impossible to deny the presence of original genius, however mistaken its direction might be deemed, arose the whole long-continued controversy.[5] For from the conjunction of perceived power with supposed heresy I explain the inveteracy and in some instances, I grieve to say, the acrimonious passions with which the controversy has been conducted by the assailants.

Had Mr. Wordsworth's poems been the silly, the childish things which they were for a long time described as being; had they been really distinguished from the compositions of other poets merely by meanness of language and inanity of thought; had they indeed contained nothing more than what is found in the parodies and pretended imitations of them; they must have sunk at once, a dead weight, into the slough of oblivion, and have dragged the preface along with them. But year after year increased the number of Mr. Wordsworth's admirers. They were found too not in the lower classes of the reading public, but chiefly among young men of strong sensibility and meditative minds; and their admiration (inflamed perhaps in some degree by opposition) was distinguished by its intensity, I might almost say, by its *religious* fervor. These facts, and the intellectual energy of the author, which was more or less consciously felt where it was outwardly and even boisterously denied, meeting with sentiments of aversion to his opinions and of alarm at their consequences, produced an eddy of criticism which would of itself have borne up the poems by the violence with which it whirled them round and round. With many parts of this preface, in the sense attributed to them and which the words undoubtedly seem to authorize, I never

---

1. Cf. Isaiah 6.9–10.
2. The first edition of *Lyrical Ballads,* published anonymously in 1798, contained nineteen poems by Wordsworth, four by Coleridge.
3. *Experiments* was the word used by Wordsworth

in his *Advertisement* to the first edition.
4. Published in 1800.
5. The controversy over Wordsworth's theory and poetical practice in the literary journals of the day.

concurred; but, on the contrary objected to them as erroneous in principle, and as contradictory (in appearance at least) both to other parts of the same preface and to the author's own practice in the greater number of the poems themselves. Mr. Wordsworth in his recent collection[6] has, I find, degraded this prefatory disquisition to the end of his second volume, to be read or not at the reader's choice. But he has not, as far as I can discover, announced any change in his poetic creed. At all events, considering it as the source of a controversy in which I have been honored more than I deserve by the frequent conjunction of my name with his, I think it expedient to declare once for all in what points I coincide with his opinions, and in what points I altogether differ. But in order to render myself intelligible I must previously, in as few words as possible, explain my ideas, first, of a POEM; and secondly, of POETRY itself, in *kind* and in *essence*.

The office of philosophical *disquisition* consists in just *distinction*; while it is the privilege of the philosopher to preserve himself constantly aware that distinction is not division. In order to obtain adequate notions of any truth, we must intellectually separate its distinguishable parts; and this is the technical *process* of philosophy. But having so done, we must then restore them in our conceptions to the unity in which they actually coexist; and this is the *result* of philosophy. A poem contains the same elements as a prose composition; the difference therefore must consist in a different combination of them, in consequence of a different object proposed. According to the difference of the object will be the difference of the combination. It is possible that the object may be merely to facilitate the recollection of any given facts or observations by artificial arrangement; and the composition will be a poem, merely because it is distinguished from prose by meter, or by rhyme, or by both conjointly. In this, the lowest sense, a man might attribute the name of a poem to the well-known enumeration of the days in the several months:

> Thirty days hath September,
> April, June, and November, etc.

and others of the same class and purpose. And as a particular pleasure is found in anticipating the recurrence of sounds and quantities, all compositions that have this charm superadded, whatever be their contents, *may* be entitled poems.

So much for the superficial *form*. A difference of object and contents supplies an additional ground of distinction. The immediate purpose may be the communication of truths; either of truth absolute and demonstrable, as in works of science; or of facts experienced and recorded, as in history. Pleasure, and that of the highest and most permanent kind, may *result* from the *attainment* of the end; but it is not itself the immediate end. In other works the communication of pleasure may be the immediate purpose; and though truth, either moral or intellectual, ought to be the *ultimate* end, yet this will distinguish the character of the author, not the class to which the work belongs. Blessed indeed is that state of society in which the immediate purpose would be baffled by the perversion of the proper ultimate end; in which

6. *Poems*, 2 vols., 1815.

no charm of diction or imagery could exempt the Bathyllus even of an Anacreon, or the Alexis of Virgil,[7] from disgust and aversion!

But the communication of pleasure may be the immediate object of a work not metrically composed; and that object may have been in a high degree attained, as in novels and romances. Would then the mere superaddition of meter, with or without rhyme, entitle *these* to the name of poems? The answer is that nothing can permanently please which does not contain in itself the reason why it is so, and not otherwise. If meter be superadded, all other parts must be made consonant with it. They must be such as to justify the perpetual and distinct attention to each part which an exact correspondent recurrence of accent and sound are calculated to excite. The final definition then, so deduced, may be thus worded. A poem is that species of composition which is opposed to works of science by proposing for its *immediate* object pleasure, not truth; and from all other species (having *this* object in common with it) it is discriminated by proposing to itself such delight from the *whole* as is compatible with a distinct gratification from each component *part*.

Controversy is not seldom excited in consequence of the disputants attaching each a different meaning to the same word; and in few instances has this been more striking than in disputes concerning the present subject. If a man chooses to call every composition a poem which is rhyme, or measure, or both, I must leave his opinion uncontroverted. The distinction is at least competent to characterize the writer's intention. If it were subjoined that the whole is likewise entertaining or affecting as a tale or as a series of interesting reflections, I of course admit this as another fit ingredient of a poem and an additional merit. But if the definition sought for be that of a *legitimate* poem, I answer it must be one the parts of which mutually support and explain each other; all in their proportion harmonizing with, and supporting the purpose and known influences of metrical arrangement. The philosophic critics of all ages coincide with the ultimate judgment of all countries in equally denying the praises of a just poem on the one hand to a series of striking lines or distichs,[8] each of which absorbing the whole attention of the reader to itself disjoins it from its context and makes it a separate whole, instead of a harmonizing part; and on the other hand, to an unsustained composition, from which the reader collects rapidly the general result unattracted by the component parts. The reader should be carried forward, not merely or chiefly by the mechanical impulse of curiosity, or by a restless desire to arrive at the final solution; but by the pleasurable activity of mind excited by the attractions of the journey itself. Like the motion of a serpent, which the Egyptians made the emblem of intellectual power; or like the path of sound through the air; at every step he pauses and half recedes, and from the retrogressive movement collects the force which again carries him onward. "*Praecipitandus est* liber *spiritus*,"[9] says Petronius Arbiter most happily. The epithet *liber* here balances the preceding verb; and it is not easy to conceive more meaning condensed in fewer words.

7. The reference is to poems of homosexual love. Bathyllus was a beautiful boy praised by Anacreon, a Greek lyric poet (ca. 560–475 B.C.E.); Alexis was a young man loved by the shepherd Corydon in Virgil's *Eclogue* 2.

8. Pairs of lines.

9. "The *free* spirit [of the poet] must be hurled onward." From the *Satyricon,* by the lively Roman satirist Petronius Arbiter (1st century C.E.).

But if this should be admitted as a satisfactory character of a poem, we have still to seek for a definition of poetry. The writings of Plato, and Bishop Taylor, and the *Theoria Sacra* of Burnet,[1] furnish undeniable proofs that poetry of the highest kind may exist without meter, and even without the contradistinguishing objects of a poem. The first chapter of Isaiah (indeed a very large proportion of the whole book) is poetry in the most emphatic sense; yet it would be not less irrational than strange to assert that pleasure, and not truth, was the immediate object of the prophet. In short, whatever *specific* import we attach to the word poetry, there will be found involved in it, as a necessary consequence, that a poem of any length neither can be, nor ought to be, all poetry.[2] Yet if a harmonious whole is to be produced, the remaining parts must be preserved in *keeping* with the poetry; and this can be no otherwise effected than by such a studied selection and artificial arrangement as will partake of *one,* though not a *peculiar,* property of poetry. And this again can be no other than the property of exciting a more continuous and equal attention than the language of prose aims at, whether colloquial or written.

My own conclusions on the nature of poetry, in the strictest use of the word, have been in part anticipated in the preceding disquisition on the fancy and imagination. What is poetry? is so nearly the same question with, what is a poet? that the answer to the one is involved in the solution of the other. For it is a distinction resulting from the poetic genius itself, which sustains and modifies the images, thoughts, and emotions of the poet's own mind.

The poet, described in *ideal* perfection, brings the whole soul of man into activity, with the subordination of its faculties to each other, according to their relative worth and dignity. He diffuses a tone and spirit of unity that blends and (as it were) *fuses,* each into each, by that synthetic and magical power to which we have exclusively appropriated the name of imagination. This power, first put in action by the will and understanding and retained under their irremissive, though gentle and unnoticed, control (*laxis effertur habenis*)[3] reveals itself in the balance or reconciliation of opposite or discordant qualities:[4] of sameness, with difference; of the general, with the concrete; the idea, with the image; the individual, with the representative; the sense of novelty and freshness, with old and familiar objects; a more than usual state of emotion, with more than usual order; judgment ever awake and steady self-possession, with enthusiasm and feeling profound or vehement; and while it blends and harmonizes the natural and the artificial, still subordinates art to nature; the manner to the matter; and our admiration of the poet to our sympathy with the poetry. "Doubtless," as Sir John Davies observes of the soul (and his words may with slight alteration be applied, and even more appropriately, to the poetic IMAGINATION):

---

1. Thomas Burnet (1635?–1715), author of *The Sacred Theory of the Earth*. Bishop Jeremy Taylor (1613–1667), author of *Holy Living* and *Holy Dying*. Coleridge greatly admired the elaborate and sonorous prose of both these writers. He took from a work by Burnet the Latin motto for *The Rime of the Ancient Mariner*.
2. Coleridge does not use the word *poetry* in the usual way, as a term for the class of all metrical compositions, or of all "poems," but to designate those passages, whether in verse or prose, produced by the mind of genius in its supreme moments or discordant elements.
3. Driven with loosened reins (Latin).
4. Here Coleridge introduces the concept that the highest poetry incorporates and reconciles opposite or discordant elements. Under the names of "irony" and "paradox," this concept became a primary criterion of the American New Critics.

Doubtless this could not be, but that she turns
    Bodies to spirit by sublimation strange,
As fire converts to fire the things it burns,
    As we our food into our nature change.

From their gross matter she abstracts their forms,
    And draws a kind of quintessence from things;
Which to her proper nature she transforms,
    To bear them light on her celestial wings.

Thus does she, when from individual states
    She doth abstract the universal kinds;
Which then reclothed in divers names and fates
    Steal access through our senses to our minds.[5]

Finally, GOOD SENSE is the BODY of poetic genius, FANCY its DRAPERY, MOTION its LIFE, and IMAGINATION the SOUL that is everywhere, and in each; and forms all into one graceful and intelligent whole.

From *Chapter 17*

[EXAMINATION OF THE TENETS PECULIAR TO MR. WORDSWORTH]

As far then as Mr. Wordsworth in his preface contended, and most ably contended, for a reformation in our poetic diction, as far as he has evinced the truth of passion, and the *dramatic* propriety of those figures and metaphors in the original poets which, stripped of their justifying reasons and converted into mere artifices of connection or ornament, constitute the characteristic falsity in the poetic style of the moderns; and as far as he has, with equal acuteness and clearness, pointed out the process by which this change was effected and the resemblances between that state into which the reader's mind is thrown by the pleasurable confusion of thought from an unaccustomed train of words and images and that state which is induced by the natural language of impassioned feeling, he undertook a useful task and deserves all praise, both for the attempt and for the execution. The provocations to this remonstrance in behalf of truth and nature were still of perpetual recurrence before and after the publication of this preface. * * *

My own differences from certain supposed parts of Mr. Wordsworth's theory ground themselves on the assumption that his words had been rightly interpreted, as purporting that the proper diction for poetry in general consists altogether in a language taken, with due exceptions, from the mouths of men in real life, a language which actually constitutes the natural conversation of men under the influence of natural feelings.[6] My objection is, first, that in *any* sense this rule is applicable only to *certain* classes of poetry; secondly, that even to these classes it is not applicable, except in such a sense as hath never by anyone (as far as I know or have read) been denied or doubted; and, lastly, that as far as, and in that degree in which it is

---

5. Adapted from John Davies's *Nosce Teipsum* ("Know Thyself"), a philosophical poem (1599).
6. Wordsworth's Preface to *Lyrical Ballads* (1800): "A selection of the real language of men in a state of vivid sensation. . . . Low and rustic life was generally chosen. . . . The language, too, of these men is adopted."

practicable, yet as a *rule* it is useless, if not injurious, and therefore either need not or ought not to be practiced. * * *

[RUSTIC LIFE (ABOVE ALL, *LOW* AND RUSTIC LIFE) ESPECIALLY UNFAVORABLE TO THE FORMATION OF A HUMAN DICTION—THE BEST PARTS OF LANGUAGE THE PRODUCTS OF PHILOSOPHERS, NOT CLOWNS[7] OR SHEPHERDS]

As little can I agree with the assertion that from the objects with which the rustic hourly communicates the best part of language is formed. For first, if to communicate with an object implies such an acquaintance with it, as renders it capable of being discriminately reflected on; the distinct knowledge of an uneducated rustic would furnish a very scanty vocabulary. The few things, and modes of action, requisite for his bodily conveniences, would alone be individualized; while all the rest of nature would be expressed by a small number of confused general terms. Secondly, I deny that the words and combinations of words derived from the objects, with which the rustic is familiar, whether with distinct or confused knowledge, can be justly said to form the *best* part of language. It is more than probable that many classes of the brute creation possess discriminating sounds, by which they can convey to each other notices of such objects as concern their food, shelter, or safety. Yet we hesitate to call the aggregate of such sounds a language, otherwise than metaphorically. The best part of human language, properly so called, is derived from reflection on the acts of the mind itself. It is formed by a voluntary appropriation of fixed symbols to internal acts, to processes and results of imagination, the greater part of which have no place in the consciousness of uneducated man; though in civilized society, by imitation and passive remembrance of what they hear from their religious instructors and other superiors, the most uneducated share in the harvest which they neither sowed or reaped. * * *

[THE LANGUAGE OF MILTON AS MUCH THE LANGUAGE OF *REAL* LIFE, YEA, INCOMPARABLY MORE SO THAN THAT OF THE COTTAGER]

Here let me be permitted to remind the reader that the positions which I controvert are contained in the sentences—"a selection of the REAL language of men"; "the language of these men (i.e., men in low and rustic life) I propose to myself to imitate, and as far as possible to adopt the very language of men." "Between the language of prose and that of metrical composition there neither is, nor can be any essential difference." It is against these exclusively that my opposition is directed.

I object, in the very first instance, to an equivocation in the use of the word "real." Every man's language varies according to the extent of his knowledge, the activity of his faculties, and the depth or quickness of his feelings. Every man's language has, first, its *individualities;* secondly, the common properties of the *class* to which he belongs; and thirdly, words and phrases of *universal* use. The language of Hooker, Bacon, Bishop Taylor, and Burke

7. Rustic people.

differs from the common language of the learned class only by the superior number and novelty of the thoughts and relations which they had to convey. The language of Algernon Sidney[8] differs not at all from that which every well-educated gentleman would wish to write, and (with due allowances for the undeliberateness and less connected train of thinking natural and proper to conversation) such as he would wish to talk. Neither one nor the other differ half as much from the general language of cultivated society as the language of Mr. Wordsworth's homeliest composition differs from that of a common peasant. For "real" therefore we must substitute *ordinary,* or *lingua communis.*[9] And this, we have proved, is no more to be found in the phraseology of low and rustic life than in that of any other class. Omit the peculiarities of each, and the result of course must be common to all. And assuredly the omissions and changes to be made in the language of rustics before it could be transferred to any species of poem, except the drama or other professed imitation, are at least as numerous and weighty as would be required in adapting to the same purpose the ordinary language of tradesmen and manufacturers. Not to mention that the language so highly extolled by Mr. Wordsworth varies in every county, nay, in every village, according to the accidental character of the clergyman, the existence or nonexistence of schools; or even, perhaps, as the exciseman, publican, or barber happen to be, or not to be, zealous politicians and readers of the weekly newspaper *pro bono publico.*[1] Anterior to cultivation the *lingua communis* of every country, as Dante has well observed, exists every where in parts and no where as a whole.[2]

Neither is the case rendered at all more tenable by the addition of the words "in a state of excitement."[3] For the nature of a man's words, when he is strongly affected by joy, grief, or anger, must necessarily depend on the number and quality of the general truths, conceptions, and images, and of the words expressing them, with which his mind had been previously stored. For the property of passion is not to *create,* but to set in increased activity. At least, whatever new connections of thoughts or images, or (which is equally, if not more than equally, the appropriate effect of strong excitement) whatever generalizations of truth or experience the heat of passion may produce, yet the terms of their conveyance must have pre-existed in his former conversations, and are only collected and crowded together by the unusual stimulation. It is indeed very possible to adopt in a poem the unmeaning repetitions, habitual phrases, and other blank counters which an unfurnished or confused understanding interposes at short intervals in order to keep hold of his subject which is still slipping from him, and to give him time for recollection; or in mere aid of vacancy, as in the scanty companies of a country stage the same player pops backwards and forwards, in order to prevent the appearance of empty spaces, in the procession of *Macbeth* or *Henry VIIIth.* But what assistance to the poet or ornament to the poem these can supply, I am at a loss to conjecture. Nothing assuredly can differ either in origin or in mode more widely from the apparent tautologies of intense

8. Republican soldier and statesmen (1622–1683), author of *Discourses Concerning Government.*
9. The common language (Latin).
1. For the public welfare (Latin).

2. In *De vulgari eloquentia* (On the speech of the people) Dante discusses—and affirms—the fitness for poetry of the unlocalized Italian vernacular.
3. Wordsworth: "the manner in which we associate ideas in a state of excitement."

and turbulent feeling in which the passion is greater and of longer endurance than to be exhausted or satisfied by a single representation of the image or incident exciting it. Such repetitions I admit to be a beauty of the highest kind; as illustrated by Mr. Wordsworth himself from the song of Deborah. "At her feet he bowed, he fell, he lay down; at her feet he bowed, he fell; where he bowed, there he fell down dead."[4]

1815   1817

From Lectures on Shakespeare[1]

[FANCY AND IMAGINATION IN SHAKESPEARE'S POETRY]

In the preceding lecture we have examined with what armor clothed and with what titles authorized Shakespeare came forward as a poet to demand the throne of fame as the dramatic poet of England; we have now to observe and retrace the excellencies which compelled even his contemporaries to seat him on that throne, although there were giants in those days contending for the same honor. Hereafter we shall endeavor to make out the title of the English drama, as created by and existing in Shakespeare, and its right to the supremacy of dramatic excellence in general. I have endeavored to prove that he had shown himself a *poet,* previously to his appearance as a dramatic poet—and that had no *Lear,* no *Othello,* no *Henry the Fourth,* no *Twelfth Night* appeared, we must have admitted that Shakespeare possessed the chief if not all the requisites of a poet—namely, deep feeling and exquisite sense of beauty, both as exhibited to the eye in combinations of form, and to the ear in sweet and appropriate melody (with the exception of Spenser he is [the sweetest of English poets]); that these feelings were under the command of *his own will*—that in his very first productions he projected his mind out of his own particular being, and felt and made others feel, on subjects [in] no way connected with himself, except by force of contemplation, and that sublime faculty, by which a great mind becomes that which it meditates on. To this we are to add the affectionate love of nature and natural objects, without which no man could have observed so steadily, or painted so truly and passionately the very minutest beauties of the external world. Next, we have shown that he possessed fancy, considered as the faculty of bringing together images dissimilar in the main by some one point or more of likeness distinguished.[2]

> Full gently now she takes him by the hand,
> A lily prisoned in a jail of snow,

4. Judges 5.27. Cited by Wordsworth in a note to *The Thorn* as an example of the natural tautology of "impassioned feelings."

1. Although Coleridge's series of public lectures on Shakespeare and other poets contained much of his best criticism, he published none of this material, leaving only fragmentary remains of his lectures in notebooks, scraps of manuscript, and notes written in the margins of books. The following selections, which develop some of the principal ideas presented in *Biographia Literaria,* reproduce the text of T. M. Raysor's edition—based on Coleridge's manuscripts and on contemporary reports—

of *Coleridge's Shakespearean Criticism* (1930); four minor corrections in wording have been taken from R. A. Foakes's edition of Coleridge's *Lectures 1808–1819: On Literature* (1987).

2. Coleridge here applies the distinction between fancy and imagination presented in *Biographia Literaria,* chap. 13. This passage from the narrative poem *Venus and Adonis* (lines 361–64) is an instance of fancy because the elements brought together remain an assemblage of recognizable and independent "fixities and definites," despite the isolated points of likeness which form the grounds of the comparison.

> Or ivory in an alabaster band—
> So white a friend engirts so white a foe.

Still mounting, we find undoubted proof in his mind of imagination, or the power by which one image or feeling is made to modify many others and by a sort of *fusion to force many into one*—that which after showed itself in such might and energy in *Lear,* where the deep anguish of a father spreads the feeling of ingratitude and cruelty over the very elements of heaven. Various are the workings of this greatest faculty of the human mind—both passionate and tranquil. In its tranquil and purely pleasurable operation, it acts chiefly by producing out of many things, as they would have appeared in the description of an ordinary mind, described slowly and in unimpassioned succession, a oneness, even as nature, the greatest of poets, acts upon us when we open our eyes upon an extended prospect. Thus the flight of Adonis from the enamored goddess in the dusk of evening—

> Look how a bright star shooteth from the sky—
> So glides he in the night from Venus' eye.[3]

How many images and feelings are here brought together without effort and without discord—the beauty of Adonis—the rapidity of his flight—the yearning yet hopelessness of the enamored gazer—and a shadowy ideal character thrown over the whole.[4]—Or it acts by impressing the stamp of humanity, of human feeling, over inanimate objects * * *

> Lo, here the gentle lark, weary of rest,
> From his moist cabinet mounts up on high
> And wakes the morning, from whose silver breast
> The sun ariseth in his majesty;
>   Who doth the world so gloriously behold
>   That cedar tops and hills seem burnished gold.

And lastly, which belongs only to a great poet, the power of so carrying on the eye of the reader as to make him almost lose the consciousness of words—to make him *see* everything—and this without exciting any painful or laborious attention, without any *anatomy* of description (a fault not uncommon in descriptive poetry) but with the sweetness and easy movement of nature.

   Lastly, he previously to his dramas, gave proof of a most profound, energetic, and philosophical mind, without which he might have been a very delightful poet, but not the great dramatic poet. * * * But chance and his powerful instinct combined to lead him to his proper province—in the conquest of which we are to consider both the difficulties that opposed him, and the advantages.

1808

---

3. *Venus and Adonis,* lines 815–16.
4. This passage is an instance of imagination, Coleridge claims, because the component parts—the shooting star and the flight of Adonis, together with the feelings with which both are perceived—dissolve into a new and seamless unity, different in character from the sum of its parts. In the following instance (lines 853–58), the imagination is claimed to fuse the neutral and inanimate objects with the human nature and feelings of the observer.

[MECHANIC VS. ORGANIC FORM][5]

The subject of the present lecture is no less than a question submitted to your understandings, emancipated from national prejudice: Are the plays of Shakespeare works of rude uncultivated genius, in which the splendor of the parts compensates, if aught can compensate, for the barbarous shapelessness and irregularity of the whole? To which not only the French critics, but even his own English admirers, say [yes]. Or is the form equally admirable with the matter, the judgment of the great poet not less deserving of our wonder than his genius? Or to repeat the question in other words, is Shakespeare a great dramatic poet on account only of those beauties and excellencies which he possesses in common with the ancients, but with diminished claims to our love and honor to the full extent of his difference from them? Or are these very differences additional proofs of poetic wisdom, at once results and symbols of living power as contrasted with lifeless mechanism, of free and rival originality as contradistinguished from servile imitation, or more accurately, [from] a blind copying of effects instead of a true imitation of the essential principles? Imagine not I am about to oppose genius to rules. No! the comparative value of these rules is the very cause to be tried. The spirit of poetry, like all other living powers, must of necessity circumscribe itself by rules, were it only to unite power with beauty. It must embody in order to reveal itself; but a living body is of necessity an organized one—and what is organization but the connection of parts to a whole, so that each part is at once end and means! This is no discovery of criticism; it is a necessity of the human mind—and all nations have felt and obeyed it, in the invention of meter and measured sounds as the vehicle and involucrum[6] of poetry, itself a fellow growth from the same life, even as the bark is to the tree.

No work of true genius dare want its appropriate form; neither indeed is there any danger of this. As it must not, so neither can it, be lawless! For it is even this that constitutes its genius—the power of acting creatively under laws of its own origination. How then comes it that not only single Zoili,[7] but whole nations have combined in unhesitating condemnation of our great dramatist, as a sort of African nature, fertile in beautiful monsters, as a wild heath where islands of fertility look greener from the surrounding waste, where the loveliest plants now shine out among unsightly weeds and now are choked by their parasitic growth, so intertwined that we cannot disentangle the weed without snapping the flower. In this statement I have had no reference to the vulgar abuse of Voltaire,[8] save as far as his charges are coincident with the decisions of his commentators and (so they tell you) his almost idolatrous admirers. The true ground of the mistake, as has been well

---

5. Coleridge is opposing the earlier view that, because he violates the critical "rules" based on classical drama, Shakespeare is a highly irregular dramatist whose occasional successes are the result of innate and untutored genius, operating without artistry or judgment. Coleridge's refutation is based on his distinction between the "mechanical form" conceived by neoclassical criticism and "organic form." Mechanical form results from imposing a pattern of preexisting rules on the literary material. Shakespeare's organic form, on the other hand, evolves like a plant by an inner principle, according not to rules but to the laws of its

own growth, until it achieves an organic unity—a living interdependence of parts and whole in which, as Coleridge says, "each part is at once end and means." The concept of "organic form," in one or another interpretation, became a cardinal principle in much 20th-century criticism.
6. Outer covering of part of a plant.
7. Plural of "Zoilus," who in classical times was the standard example of a bad critic.
8. Voltaire (1694–1778) wrote critiques treating Shakespeare as a barbarous, irregular, and sometimes indecent natural genius.

remarked by a continental critic,[9] lies in the confounding mechanical regularity with organic form. The form is mechanic when on any given material we impress a predetermined form, not necessarily arising out of the properties of the material, as when to a mass of wet clay we give whatever shape we wish it to retain when hardened. The organic form, on the other hand, is innate; it shapes as it develops itself from within, and the fullness of its development is one and the same with the perfection of its outward form. Such is the life, such the form. Nature, the prime genial[1] artist, inexhaustible in diverse powers, is equally inexhaustible in forms. Each exterior is the physiognomy of the being within, its true image reflected and thrown out from the concave mirror. And even such is the appropriate excellence of her chosen poet, of our own Shakespeare, himself a nature humanized, a genial understanding directing self-consciously a power and an implicit wisdom deeper than consciousness.[2]

1812   1930

From The Statesman's Manual

[ON SYMBOL AND ALLEGORY][1]

The histories and political economy[2] of the present and preceding century partake in the general contagion of its mechanic philosophy, and are the *product* of an unenlivened generalizing Understanding. In the Scriptures they are the living *educts*[3] of the Imagination; of that reconciling and mediatory power, which incorporating the Reason in Images of the Sense, and organizing (as it were) the flux of the Senses by the permanence and self-circling energies of the Reason, gives birth to a system of symbols, harmonious in themselves, and consubstantial with the truths, of which they are the *conductors*. These are the Wheels which Ezekiel beheld, when the hand of the Lord was upon him, and he saw visions of God as he sat among the captives by the river of Chebar. *Whithersoever the Spirit was to go, the wheels went, and thither was their spirit to go: for the spirit of the living creature was in the wheels also.*[4] The truths and the symbols that represent them move in conjunction and form the living chariot that bears up (for *us*) the throne of the Divine Humanity. Hence, by a derivative, indeed, but not a divided, influence, and though in a secondary yet in more than a metaphorical sense,

9. August Wilhelm Schlegel, German critic and literary historian, whose *Lectures on Dramatic Art and Literature* (1808–09) proposed the distinction between mechanical and organic form that Coleridge develops in this lecture.
1. The adjectival form of *genius*.
2. I.e., the organic process of the imagination is in part unconscious.
1. Coleridge published *The Statesman's Manual, or The Bible the Best Guide to Political Skill and Foresight* in 1816; it was intended to show that the Scriptures, properly interpreted, provide the universal principles that should guide lawmakers in meeting the political and economic emergencies of that troubled era. His discussion there of symbol, in contradistinction both to allegory and to metaphor, has been often cited and elaborated in recent treatments of symbolism in poetry. Coleridge's analysis, however, is specifically directed not to poetry but to his view that the persons and events in biblical history signify timeless and universal, as well as particular and local, truths and that in God's created nature, each element and power is in essential interrelation with the whole that is manifested within that part.
2. Economic theory.
3. Those things that are educed—i.e., brought forth, evolved.
4. Slightly altered from the prophet Ezekiel's vision of the Chariot of God, when he had been "among the captives by the river of Chebar" (Ezekiel 1.1–20). Ezekiel was among the Jews who had been taken into captivity in Babylonia by King Nebuchadnezzar in 597 B.C.E. He was put in a community of Jewish captives at Tel-Abib on the banks of the Chebar canal.

the Sacred Book is worthily intitled *the* WORD OF GOD. Hence too, its contents present to us the stream of time continuous as Life and a symbol of Eternity, inasmuch as the Past and the Future are virtually contained in the Present. According therefore to our relative position on its banks the Sacred History becomes prophetic, the Sacred Prophecies historical, while the power and substance of both inhere in its Laws, its Promises, and its Comminations.[5] In the Scriptures therefore both Facts and Persons must of necessity have a twofold significance, a past and a future, a temporary and a perpetual, a particular and a universal application. They must be at once Portraits and Ideals.

Eheu! paupertina philosophia in paupertinam religionem ducit:[6]—A hunger-bitten and idea-less philosophy naturally produces a starveling and comfortless religion. It is among the miseries of the present age that it recognizes no medium between *Literal* and *Metaphorical.* Faith is either to be buried in the dead letter,[7] or its name and honors usurped by a counterfeit product of the mechanical understanding, which in the blindness of self-complacency confounds SYMBOLS with ALLEGORIES. Now an Allegory is but a translation of abstract notions into a picture-language which is itself nothing but an abstraction from objects of the senses; the principal being more worthless even than its phantom proxy, both alike unsubstantial, and the former shapeless to boot. On the other hand a Symbol (ὅ ἔστιν ἀει ταυτηγόρικον)[8] is characterized by a translucence of the Special[9] in the Individual or of the General in the Especial or of the Universal in the General. Above all by the translucence of the Eternal through and in the Temporal. It always partakes of the Reality which it renders intelligible; and while it enunciates the whole, abides itself as a living part in that Unity, of which it is the representative. The other are but empty echoes which the fancy arbitrarily associates with apparitions of matter, less beautiful but not less shadowy than the sloping orchard or hillside pasture-field seen in the transparent lake below. Alas! for the flocks that are to be led forth to such pastures! *"It shall even be as when the hungry dreameth, and behold! he eateth; but he waketh and his soul is empty: or as when the thirsty dreameth, and behold he drinketh; but he awaketh and is faint!"*[1] * * *

* * * The fact therefore, that the mind of man in its own primary and constitutional forms represents the laws of nature, is a mystery which of itself should suffice to make us religious:[2] for it is a problem of which God is the only solution, God, the one before all, and of all, and through all!—True natural philosophy is comprised in the study of the science and language of *symbols.* The power delegated to nature is all in every part: and by a symbol I mean, not a metaphor or allegory or any other figure of speech or form of fancy, but an actual and essential part of that, the whole of which it represents. Thus our Lord speaks symbolically when he says that "the eye is the light of the body."[3] The genuine naturalist is a dramatic poet in his own line:

5. Divine threats of punishment for sins.
6. Alas! a poverty-stricken philosophy leads to a poverty-stricken religion (Latin).
7. I.e., the Scriptures read entirely literally.
8. Which is always tautegorical (Greek). Coleridge coined this word and elsewhere defined "tautegorical" as "expressing the *same* subject but with a difference."
9. That which pertains to the species.
1. Slightly altered from Isaiah 29.8.
2. This paragraph is from appendix C of *The Statesman's Manual.*
3. Matthew 6.22: "The light of the body is the eye."

and such as our myriad-minded Shakespeare is, compared with the Racines and Metastasios,[4] such and by a similar process of self-transformation would the man be, compared with the Doctors of the mechanic school,[5] who should construct his physiology on the heaven-descended, Know Thyself.[6]

[THE SATANIC HERO][7]

* * * In its state of immanence (or indwelling) in reason and religion, the WILL appears indifferently, as wisdom or as love: two names of the same power, the former more intelligential,[8] the latter more spiritual, the former more frequent in the Old, the latter in the New Testament. But in its utmost abstraction and consequent state of reprobation,[9] the Will becomes satanic pride and rebellious self-idolatry in the relations of the spirit to itself, and remorseless despotism relatively to others; the more hopeless as the more obdurate by its subjugation of sensual impulses, by its superiority to toil and pain and pleasure; in short, by the fearful resolve to find in itself alone the one absolute motive of action, under which all other motives from within and from without must be either subordinated or crushed.

This is the character which Milton has so philosophically as well as sublimely embodied in the Satan of his Paradise Lost. Alas! too often has it been embodied in *real* life! Too often has it given a dark and savage grandeur to the historic page! And wherever it has appeared, under whatever circumstances of time and country, the same ingredients have gone to its composition; and it has been identified by the same attributes. Hope in which there is no Cheerfulness; Steadfastness within and immovable Resolve, with outward Restlessness and whirling Activity; Violence with Guile; Temerity with Cunning; and, as the result of all, Interminableness of Object with perfect Indifference of Means; these are the qualities that have constituted the COMMANDING GENIUS! these are the Marks that have characterized the Masters of Mischief, the Liberticides, and mighty Hunters of Mankind, from NIMROD[1] to NAPOLEON. And from inattention to the possibility of such a character as well as from ignorance of its elements, even men of honest intentions too frequently become fascinated. Nay, whole nations have been so far duped by this want of insight and reflection as to regard with palliative admiration, instead of wonder and abhorrence, the Molocks[2] of human nature, who are indebted, for the far larger portion of their meteoric success, to their total

---

4. Pietro Metastasio (1698–1782), a minor Italian poet and author of opera librettos. Jean Racine (1639–1699), the great French author of verse tragedies. Coleridge delighted in derogating French philosophy and culture, venting what he called his "Gall contra Gallois"—his gall against the Gauls. "Naturalist": one who studies natural science.
5. I.e., learned men who hold a mechanistic philosophy of nature.
6. The Roman Juvenal, in *Satires* 11.27 of Horace (Quintas Horatius Flaccus), had said that "From Heaven it descends, 'Know Thyself.'" The original saying, "Know Thyself," was attributed by classical authors to the Delphic oracle.
7. From *The Statesman's Manual*, appendix C. Coleridge analyzes the character of Milton's Satan

and goes on to recognize, and to warn his age against, the appeal of that type of Romantic hero (exemplified above all by the protagonists in Byron's romances and in his drama, *Manfred*), which was in large part modeled on the Satan of *Paradise Lost*.
8. Intellectual.
9. In its theological sense: rejection by God.
1. In Genesis 10.9 Nimrod is described as "a mighty hunter before the Lord." The passage was traditionally interpreted to signify that Nimrod hunted down men, hence that he was the prototype of all tyrants and bloody conquerors.
2. Molochs, monsters of evil. In the Old Testament Moloch is an idol to whom firstborn children are sacrificed. Milton adopted the name for the warlike fallen angel (see *Paradise Lost* 2.43–107).

want of principle, and who surpass the generality of their fellow creatures in one act of courage only, that of daring to say with their whole heart, "Evil, be thou my good!"[3]—All *system* so far is power; and a *systematic* criminal, self-consistent and entire in wickedness, who entrenches villainy within villainy, and barricades crime by crime, has removed a world of obstacles by the mere decision, that he will have no obstacles, but those of force and brute matter.

1816

3. Spoken by Satan, *Paradise Lost* 4.110.

WALTER SAVAGE LANDOR
1775–1864

Walter Savage Landor was born well-to-do and with a violently independent and combative temper. He quarreled with the authorities at Rugby and Oxford, with his wife and family, with servants and officials, with the governments of Europe (he was a revolutionary sympathizer, and unlike most of his literary contemporaries never wavered in his republicanism), and with his neighbors, first in Wales and then in Italy; he was constantly embroiled in expensive litigation. But in the course of his long life, the generous-hearted and outspoken poet also acquired many friends and admirers, ranging from Robert Southey and William Hazlitt in the Romantic period to Robert Browning, Charles Dickens, and Algernon Charles Swinburne among the Victorians. He lived in Italy from 1815 to 1835. When he returned to England he was lionized for a time as an active Romantic poet when all the others were dead or silent; but a violent outburst, which led to court action, forced him in 1857 to take up once more his exile in Italy, where he died in his ninetieth year.

Most of the writings of this greatly irascible man, whether in prose or verse, have characteristics to which critics apply the terms *serene* and *marmoreal* (marblelike). His best-known prose works are the numerous *Imaginary Conversations* (1824–53), mainly between historical figures and on literary, philosophic, and political topics. These have their admirers, but they are written in a style so elevated and remote that they sometimes suggest dialogues between heroic-size Greek statues. He wrote many long narrative and dramatic poems, of which the most durable is the epic *Gebir*, published in 1798, the same year as Wordsworth and Coleridge's *Lyrical Ballads*. But Landor's best achievement, in which he emulated Greek and Roman models, is in the short lyric, usually an elegy or a courtly compliment that is stripped down until it approximates an epigram. He is master of the spare, elegant, and severely formal utterance of lyric feelings.

Mother, I cannot mind my wheel

Mother, I cannot mind my wheel;
  My fingers ache, my lips are dry:
Oh! if you felt the pain I feel!
But oh, who ever felt as I!

5 No longer could I doubt him true,
     All other men may use deceit;
  He always said my eyes were blue,
     And often swore my lips were sweet.

1806

Rose Aylmer[1]

Ah, what avails the sceptered race,
  Ah, what the form divine!
What every virtue, every grace!
  Rose Aylmer, all were thine.

5 Rose Aylmer, whom these wakeful eyes
    May weep, but never see,
A night of memories and of sighs
    I consecrate to thee

1806

Past ruined Ilion

Past ruined Ilion Helen[1] lives,
  Alcestis rises from the shades;[2]
Verse calls them forth; 'tis verse that gives
  Immortal youth to mortal maids.

5 Soon shall oblivion's deepening veil
    Hide all the peopled hills you see,
The gay, the proud, while lovers hail
    These many summers you and me.

The tear for fading beauty check,
10   For passing glory cease to sigh;
One form shall rise above the wreck,
    One name, Ianthe, shall not die.

1831

Twenty years hence

Twenty years hence my eyes may grow
If not quite dim, yet rather so,
Still yours from others they shall know
  Twenty years hence.

1. The daughter of the fourth Baron Aylmer (hence "the sceptered race," line 1). She became a friend of Landor's in 1794 at the age of seventeen and died suddenly in Calcutta, six years later.

1. Helen of Troy ("Ilion").
2. Alcestis gave her own life in exchange for that of her husband but was rescued from Hades ("the shades") by Hercules.

5   Twenty years hence though it may hap
    That I be called to take a nap
    In a cool cell where thunderclap
        Was never heard,

    There breathe but o'er my arch of grass
10   A not too sadly sighed *Alas,*
    And I shall catch, ere you can pass,
        That wingèd word.

1846

CHARLES LAMB
1775–1834

Charles Lamb was a near contemporary of Wordsworth and Coleridge; he numbered these two poets among his close friends, published his own early poems in combination with those of Coleridge in 1796 and 1797, and supported the *Lyrical Ballads* and some of the other avant-garde poetry of his time. Yet Lamb lacks almost all the traits and convictions we think of as characteristically "Romantic." He happily lived all his life in the city and its environs, sharing Samuel Johnson's opinion that he who tires of London tires of life. He could not abide Shelley or his poetry, and he distrusted Coleridge's supernaturalism and Wordsworth's oracular sublimities and religion of nature, preferring those elements in their poems that were human and realistic. In an age when many of the important writers were fervent radicals and some became equally fervent reactionaries, Lamb remained uncommitted in both politics and religion, and although on intimate terms with such dedicated reformers as William Hazlitt, William Godwin, Thomas Holcroft, and Leigh Hunt, he chose them as friends, as he said, not for their opinions but "for some individuality of character which they manifested." In his own writings the one attribute he shared with his great contemporaries was that of *l'étalage du moi,* "the display of one's own personality": many of his best familiar essays, like Wordsworth's poems, are made up of his early experiences and feelings, recollected in tranquility. But, although the expression of private experiences in a personal poetry was a new and distinctive Romantic form, the personal essay was an established genre that had been developed by Montaigne as early as the sixteenth century.

Lamb was born in London at the Inner Temple, where his father was clerk and assistant to a lawyer. At the age of seven he entered Christ's Hospital, the "Bluecoat School" of his essay *Christ's Hospital Five-and-Thirty Years Ago.* He left the school before he was fifteen and soon thereafter became a clerk in the accounting department of the East India Company, a huge commercial house, where he remained for thirty-three years. His adult life was quiet and unadventurous; but under its calm surface, as Walter Pater said, lay "something of the fateful domestic horror, of the beautiful heroism and devotedness too, of old Greek tragedy." When he was twenty-two his beloved sister, Mary, ten years his senior, broke down under the strain of caring for her invalid parents and stabbed her mother in the heart. Upon her recovery, Mary was released to the care of her brother, who devoted the rest of his life to her and to their common household. Mary's attacks recurred, briefly but periodically, and when the terribly familiar symptoms began to show themselves, Charles and Mary would walk arm in arm and weeping to the asylum, carrying a straitjacket with them.

Most of the time, however, Mary was her normally serene and gracious self, and shared her brother's love of company and genius for friendship. The Wednesday-(sometimes Thursday-) night gatherings at the Lambs' attracted a varied company that included many of the leading writers and artists of England. Charles drew furiously on a pipe of strong tobacco and drank copiously; as the alcohol eased his habitual stammer, his puns and practical jokes grew ever more outrageous. He had, in fact, a complex temperament, in which the playfulness overlay a somber melancholy and the freakishness sometimes manifested a touch of malice. To requests from Wordsworth and Coleridge for criticism of their poems he replied with a caustic candor not entirely appreciated by its beneficiaries, and he never encountered pretentiousness or complacency without puncturing it by a well-honed witticism. "What choice venom!" exclaimed his friend Hazlitt, an expert on the subject—but while Hazlitt managed to antagonize almost everyone by his outspokenness, few could take offense, and none could long sustain it, at Lamb's behavior.

To supplement his salary at the East India House, Lamb had early turned to writing in a variety of literary forms, including minor verse; a sentimental novel; a blank-verse tragedy; and a farce, *Mr. H——*, which was hissed by the audience (including the honest author) when it was produced at Drury Lane. He also collaborated with his sister, Mary, on an excellent children's book, *Tales from Shakespeare*, and wrote some brilliant critical commentaries in his anthology, important for the Elizabethan revival of that period, titled *Specimens of English Dramatic Poets Who Lived about the Time of Shakespeare*. Not until 1820, however, at the age of forty-five, did Lamb begin to contribute to the *London Magazine* the *Essays of Elia*, written in a uniquely distinctive style.

In the familiar essay, Lamb was able to exploit his major subject: himself and his connoisseurship of literature, people, and strong local attachments—"old chairs, old tables, streets, squares, where I have sunned myself, my old school." Under the pseudonym of an Italian clerk named Elia, whom he had known while briefly employed in the South Sea House, Lamb projects in his essays the character of a man who is whimsical but strong-willed, self-deprecating yet self-absorbed, a specialist in nostalgia and in that humor which balances delicately on the verge of pathos. His seemingly ingenuous self-revelation is, however, achieved by the cunning of a deliberate and dedicated artist in prose. He wrote, as he said, "for antiquity"; his prose style, like that of Edmund Spenser's in verse, is an invented style. Although its basis is plain modern English, it is colored throughout by archaic words, expressions, and turns of syntax. In the manner of earlier literary eccentrics such as Robert Burton and Laurence Sterne, Lamb delights in tricks of words and thought and in the elaborate exploration of a literary conceit. Close imitators of his style invariably fall into archness and sentimentality; Lamb's feat was to transform whimsy into a highly distinctive personal essay.

Christ's Hospital Five-and-Thirty Years Ago[1]

In Mr. Lamb's *Works*, published a year or two since, I find a magnificent eulogy on my old school, such as it was, or now appears to him to have been, between the years 1782 and 1789. It happens very oddly that my own standing at Christ's was nearly corresponding with his; and, with all gratitude to

1. Christ's Hospital, London (founded in 1552 by Edward VI), was run as a free boarding school for the sons of middle-class parents in straitened financial circumstances. Its students were known as "Bluecoat Boys," from their uniform of a long blue gown and yellow stockings. Lamb had in 1813 published a magazine article, *Recollections of* *Christ's Hospital,* that the present essay undertakes to supplement by presenting the less formal side of school life. The "I" or narrator of the essay is Elia— a device that allows Lamb to combine his own circumstances and experiences with those of Coleridge, his older contemporary at the school.

him for his enthusiasm for the cloisters, I think he has contrived to bring together whatever can be said in praise of them, dropping all the other side of the argument most ingeniously.

I remember L. at school, and can well recollect that he had some peculiar advantages, which I and others of his schoolfellows had not. His friends lived in town, and were near at hand; and he had the privilege of going to see them almost as often as he wished, through some invidious distinction, which was denied to us. The present worthy subtreasurer to the Inner Temple[2] can explain how that happened. He had his tea and hot rolls in a morning, while we were battening upon our quarter of a penny loaf—our *crug*—moistened with attenuated small beer, in wooden piggins, smacking of the pitched leathern jack[3] it was poured from. Our Monday's milk porritch, blue and tasteless, and the pease soup of Saturday, coarse and choking, were enriched for him with a slice of "extraordinary bread and butter," from the hot loaf of the Temple. The Wednesday's mess of millet, somewhat less repugnant—(we had three banyan to four meat days[4] in the week)—was endeared to his palate with a lump of double-refined, and a smack of ginger (to make it go down the more glibly) or the fragrant cinnamon. In lieu of our *half-pickled* Sundays, or *quite fresh* boiled beef on Thursdays (strong as *caro equina*[5]), with detestable marigolds floating in the pail to poison the broth—our scanty mutton scrags on Friday—and rather more savory, but grudging, portions of the same flesh, rotten-roasted[6] or rare, on the Tuesdays (the only dish which excited our appetites, and disappointed our stomachs, in almost equal proportion)—he had his hot plate of roast veal, or the more tempting griskin[7] (exotics unknown to our palates), cooked in the paternal kitchen (a great thing), and brought him daily by his maid or aunt! I remember the good old relative (in whom love forbade pride) squatting down upon some odd stone in a by-nook of the cloisters, disclosing the viands (of higher regale than those cates which the ravens ministered to the Tishbite);[8] and the contending passions of L. at the unfolding. There was love for the bringer; shame for the thing brought, and the manner of its bringing; sympathy for those who were too many to share in it; and, at top of all, hunger (eldest, strongest of the passions!) predominant, breaking down the stony fences of shame, and awkwardness, and a troubling over-consciousness.

I was a poor friendless boy. My parents, and those who should care for me, were far away. Those few acquaintances of theirs, which they could reckon upon being kind to me in the great city, after a little forced notice, which they had the grace to take of me on my first arrival in town, soon grew tired of my holiday visits. They seemed to them to recur too often, though I thought them few enough; and, one after another, they all failed me, and I felt myself alone among six hundred playmates.

O the cruelty of separating a poor lad from his early homestead! The yearnings which I used to have towards it in those unfledged years! How, in my

---

2. Randal Norris, who had befriended young Charles Lamb. The Inner Temple is one of the four Inns of Court, the center of the English legal profession.
3. A leather vessel coated on the outside with pitch. "Crug": bread (slang). "Small beer": beer low in alcoholic content. "Piggins": small wooden pails.
4. "Banyan . . . days": nautical term for days when

no meat is served; it derives from *banian*, a member of a Hindu caste to whom meat is forbidden. "Millet": a cereal.
5. Horsemeat (Latin).
6. Overdone. "Scrags": necks.
7. The lean part of a loin of pork.
8. The prophet Elijah, who was fed by the ravens in 1 Kings 17. "Cates": delicacies.

dreams, would my native town (far in the west) come back, with its church, and trees, and faces! How I would wake weeping, and in the anguish of my heart exclaim upon sweet Calne in Wiltshire![9]

To this late hour of my life, I trace impressions left by the recollections of those friendless holidays. The long warm days of summer never return but they bring with them a gloom from the haunting memory of those *whole-day leaves*, when, by some strange arrangement, we were turned out for the live-long day, upon our own hands, whether we had friends to go to or none. I remember those bathing excursions to the New River which L. recalls with such relish, better, I think, than he can—for he was a home-seeking lad, and did not much care for such water pastimes: How merrily we would sally forth into the fields; and strip under the first warmth of the sun; and wanton like young dace[1] in the streams; getting us appetites for noon, which those of us that were penniless (our scanty morning crust long since exhausted) had not the means of allaying—while the cattle, and the birds, and the fishes were at feed about us and we had nothing to satisfy our cravings—the very beauty of the day, and the exercise of the pastime, and the sense of liberty, setting a keener edge upon them! How faint and languid, finally, we would return, towards nightfall, to our desired morsel, half-rejoicing, half-reluctant that the hours of our uneasy liberty had expired!

It was worse in the days of winter, to go prowling about the streets object-less—shivering at cold windows of print shops, to extract a little amusement; or haply, as a last resort in the hopes of a little novelty, to pay a fifty-times repeated visit (where our individual faces should be as well known to the warden as those of his own charges) to the Lions in the Tower—to whose levee, by courtesy immemorial, we had a prescriptive title to admission.[2]

L.'s governor (so we called the patron who presented us to the foundation)[3] lived in a manner under his paternal roof. Any complaint which he had to make was sure of being attended to. This was understood at Christ's, and was an effectual screen to him against the severity of masters, or worse tyranny of the monitors. The oppressions of these young brutes are heart-sickening to call to recollection. I have been called out of my bed, and *waked for the purpose*, in the coldest winter nights—and this not once, but night after night—in my shirt, to receive the discipline of a leathern thong and eleven other sufferers, because it pleased my callow overseer, when there has been any talking heard after we were gone to bed, to make the six last beds in the dormitory, where the youngest children of us slept, answerable for an offense they neither dared to commit nor had the power to hinder. The same execrable tyranny drove the younger part of us from the fires, when our feet were perishing with snow; and, under the cruelest penalties, forbade the indulgence of a drink of water when we lay in sleepless summer nights fevered with the season and the day's sports.

There was one H——, who, I learned, in after days was seen expiating some maturer offense in the hulks.[4] (Do I flatter myself in fancying that this

9. Coleridge had come to school from Ottery St. Mary, Devonshire, in the southwest of England.
1. A small quick-darting fish.
2. The Bluecoat Boys had the right of free admission to the royal menagerie, then housed in the Tower of London. "Levee": a formal morning reception.

3. I.e., who vouched for a candidate for entrance to Christ's Hospital. Lamb's patron was Samuel Salt, a lawyer and Member of Parliament for whom Lamb's father served as clerk.
4. Prison ship. (In Lamb's time the plural "hulks" had come to be used for the singular.)

might be the planter of that name, who suffered—at Nevis, I think, or St. Kitts[5]—some few years since? My friend Tobin was the benevolent instrument of bringing him to the gallows.) This petty Nero actually branded a boy who had offended him with a red-hot iron; and nearly starved forty of us with exacting contributions, to the one-half of our bread, to pamper a young ass, which, incredible as it may seem, with the connivance of the nurse's daughter (a young flame of his) he had contrived to smuggle in, and keep upon the leads[6] of the *ward,* as they called our dormitories. This game went on for better than a week, till the foolish beast, not able to fare well but he must cry roast meat—happier than Caligula's minion,[7] could he have kept his own counsel—but foolisher, alas! than any of his species in the fables— waxing fat, and kicking, in the fullness of bread, one unlucky minute would needs proclaim his good fortune to the world below; and, laying out his simple throat, blew such a ram's-horn blast, as (toppling down the walls of his own Jericho)[8] set concealment any longer at defiance. The client was dismissed, with certain attentions, to Smithfield; but I never understood that the patron underwent any censure on the occasion. This was in the stewardship of L.'s admired Perry.[9]

Under the same *facile* administration, can L. have forgotten the cool impunity with which the nurses used to carry away openly, in open platters, for their own tables, one out of two of every hot joint, which the careful matron had been seeing scrupulously weighed out for our dinners? These things were daily practiced in that magnificent apartment which L. (grown connoisseur since, we presume) praises so highly for the grand paintings "by Verrio,[1] and others," with which it is "hung round and adorned." But the sight of sleek, well-fed bluecoat boys in pictures was, at that time, I believe, little consolatory to him, or us, the living ones, who saw the better part of our provisions carried away before our faces by harpies; and ourselves reduced (with the Trojan in the hall of Dido)

> To feed our mind with idle portraiture.[2]

L. has recorded the repugnance of the school to *gags,* or the fat of fresh beef boiled; and sets it down to some superstition. But these unctuous morsels are never grateful to young palates (children are universally fat-haters), and in strong, coarse, boiled meats, *unsalted,* are detestable. A *gag-eater* in our time was equivalent to a *ghoul,* and held in equal detestation. ———— suffered under the imputation.

> . . . 'Twas said
> He ate strange flesh.[3]

He was observed, after dinner, carefully to gather up the remnants left at his table (not many nor very choice fragments, you may credit me)—and, in an especial manner, these disreputable morsels, which he would convey away

---

5. Islands in the West Indies.
6. A flat roof.
7. The favorite horse of the Roman emperor Caligula, who was fed gilded oats and appointed to the post of chief consul.
8. Joshua toppled the walls of Jericho by trumpet blasts (Joshua 6.16–20).
9. John Perry, steward of the school, described in Lamb's earlier essay. "Smithfield": a market for

horses and cattle.
1. Antonio Verrio, Italian painter of the 17th century. While living in England, he painted a large picture of the mathematics students of Christ's Hospital being received by James II.
2. Virgil's *Aeneid* 1.464; Aeneas is inspecting the paintings in Dido's temple to Juno.
3. Loosely quoted from *Antony and Cleopatra* 1.4.67.

and secretly stow in the settle that stood at his bedside. None saw when he ate them. It was rumored that he privately devoured them in the night. He was watched, but no traces of such midnight practices were discoverable. Some reported that on leave-days he had been seen to carry out of the bounds a large blue check handkerchief, full of something. This then must be the accursed thing. Conjecture next was at work to imagine how he could dispose of it. Some said he sold it to the beggars. This belief generally prevailed. He went about moping. None spake to him. No one would play with him. He was excommunicated; put out of the pale of the school. He was too powerful a boy to be beaten, but he underwent every mode of that negative punishment which is more grievous than many stripes. Still he persevered. At length he was observed by two of his schoolfellows, who were determined to get at the secret, and had traced him one leave-day for the purpose, to enter a large worn-out building, such as there exist specimens of in Chancery Lane, which are let out to various scales of pauperism, with open door and a common staircase. After him they silently slunk in, and followed by stealth up four flights, and saw him tap at a poor wicket, which was opened by an aged woman, meanly clad. Suspicion was now ripened into certainty. The informers had secured their victim. They had him in their toils. Accusation was formally preferred, and retribution most signal was looked for. Mr. Hathaway, the then steward (for this happened a little after my time), with that patient sagacity which tempered all his conduct, determined to investigate the matter before he proceeded to sentence. The result was that the supposed mendicants, the receivers or purchasers of the mysterious scraps, turned out to be the parents of ———, an honest couple come to decay—whom this seasonable supply had, in all probability, saved from mendicancy; and that this young stork, at the expense of his own good name, had all this while been only feeding the old birds!—The governors on this occasion, much to their honor, voted a present relief to the family of ———, and presented him with a silver medal. The lesson which the steward read upon RASH JUDG-MENT, on the occasion of publicly delivering the medal to ———, I believe would not be lost upon his auditory.—I had left school then, but I well remember ———. He was a tall, shambling youth, with a cast in his eye, not at all calculated to conciliate hostile prejudices. I have since seen him carrying a baker's basket. I think I heard he did not do quite so well by himself as he had done by the old folks.

I was a hypochondriac lad;[4] and the sight of a boy in fetters, upon the day of my first putting on the blue clothes, was not exactly fitted to assuage the natural terrors of initiation. I was of tender years, barely turned of seven; and had only read of such things in books, or seen them but in dreams. I was told he had *run away*. This was the punishment for the first offense.—As a novice I was soon after taken to see the dungeons. These were little, square, Bedlam[5] cells, where a boy could just lie at his length upon straw and a blanket—a mattress, I think, was afterwards substituted—with a peep of light, let in askance, from a prison orifice at top, barely enough to read by. Here the poor boy was locked in by himself all day, without sight of any but the porter who brought him his bread and water—who *might not speak*

---

4. From this point on Elia speaks as Lamb, rather than as Coleridge.

5. St. Mary of Bethlehem, an insane asylum in London.

to him—or of the beadle, who came twice a week to call him out to receive his periodical chastisement, which was almost welcome, because it separated him for a brief interval from solitude—and here he was shut up by himself *of nights* out of the reach of any sound, to suffer whatever horrors the weak nerves, and superstition incident to his time of life, might subject him to. This was the penalty for the second offense. Wouldst thou like, reader, to see what became of him in the next degree?

The culprit, who had been a third time an offender, and whose expulsion was at this time deemed irreversible, was brought forth, as at some solemn auto da fé, arrayed in uncouth and most appalling attire—all trace of his late "watchet weeds"[6] carefully effaced, he was exposed in a jacket resembling those which London lamplighters formerly delighted in, with a cap of the same. The effect of this divestiture was such as the ingenious devisers of it could have anticipated. With his pale and frighted features, it was as if some of those disfigurements in Dante[7] had seized upon him. In this disguisement he was brought into the hall (*L.'s favorite state room*), where awaited him the whole number of his schoolfellows, whose joint lessons and sports he was thenceforth to share no more; the awful presence of the steward, to be seen for the last time; of the executioner beadle, clad in his state robe for the occasion; and of two faces more, of direr import, because never but in these extremities visible. These were governors; two of whom by choice, or charter, were always accustomed to officiate at these *Ultima Supplicia;*[8] not to mitigate (so at least we understood it), but to enforce the uttermost stripe. Old Bamber Gascoigne, and Peter Aubert, I remember, were colleagues on one occasion, when the beadle turning rather pale, a glass of brandy was ordered to prepare him for the mysteries. The scourging was, after the old Roman fashion, long and stately. The lictor[9] accompanied the criminal quite round the hall. We were generally too faint, with attending to the previous disgusting circumstances, to make accurate report with our eyes of the degree of corporal suffering inflicted. Report, of course, gave out the back knotty and livid. After scourging, he was made over, in his *San Benito,*[1] to his friends, if he had any (but commonly such poor runagates were friendless), or to his parish officer, who, to enhance the effect of the scene, had his station allotted to him on the outside of the hall gate.

These solemn pageantries were not played off so often as to spoil the general mirth of the community. We had plenty of exercise and recreation *after* school hours; and, for myself, I must confess that I was never happier than *in* them. The Upper and the Lower Grammar Schools were held in the same room; and an imaginary line only divided their bounds. Their character was as different as that of the inhabitants on the two sides of the Pyrenees. The Rev. James Boyer[2] was the Upper master; but the Rev. Matthew Field presided over that portion of the apartment of which I had the good fortune to be a member. We lived a life as careless as birds. We talked and did just what we pleased, and nobody molested us. We carried an accidence, or a grammar, for form; but, for any trouble it gave us, we might take two years

---

6. Blue clothes. "Auto da fé": act of faith (literal trans.), the ceremony before the execution of heretics under the Spanish Inquisition.
7. I.e., of the sinners in Dante's *Inferno;* see canto 20.
8. Extreme punishments (Latin).

9. A Roman officer who cleared the way for the chief magistrates.
1. The yellow robe worn by the condemned heretic at an auto da fé.
2. This teacher is also described by Coleridge in *Biographia Literaria,* chap. 1.

in getting through the verbs deponent,[3] and another two in forgetting all that we had learned about them. There was now and then the formality of saying a lesson, but if you had not learned it, a brush across the shoulders (just enough to disturb a fly) was the sole remonstrance. Field never used the rod; and in truth he wielded the cane with no great good will—holding it "like a dancer." It looked in his hands rather like an emblem than an instrument of authority; and an emblem, too, he was ashamed of. He was a good, easy man, that did not care to ruffle his own peace, nor perhaps set any great consideration upon the value of juvenile time. He came among us, now and then, but often stayed away whole days from us; and when he came it made no difference to us—he had his private room to retire to, the short time he stayed, to be out of the sound of our noise. Our mirth and uproar went on. We had classics of our own, without being beholden to "insolent Greece or haughty Rome,"[4] that passed current among us—*Peter Wilkins*—the *Adventures of the Hon. Captain Robert Boyle*—the *Fortunate Bluecoat Boy*[5]—and the like. Or we cultivated a turn for mechanic and scientific operations; making little sun-dials of paper; or weaving those ingenious parentheses called *cat cradles;* or making dry peas to dance upon the end of a tin pipe; or studying the art military over that laudable game "French and English,"[6] and a hundred other such devices to pass away the time—mixing the useful with the agreeable—as would have made the souls of Rousseau and John Locke[7] chuckle to have seen us.

Matthew Field belonged to that class of modest divines who affect to mix in equal proportion the *gentleman,* the *scholar,* and the *Christian;* but, I know not how, the first ingredient is generally found to be the predominating dose in the composition. He was engaged in gay parties, or with his courtly bow at some episcopal levee, when he should have been attending upon us. He had for many years the classical charge of a hundred children, during the four or five first years of their education, and his very highest form seldom proceeded further than two or three of the introductory fables of Phaedrus.[8] How things were suffered to go on thus, I cannot guess. Boyer, who was the proper person to have remedied these abuses, always affected, perhaps felt, a delicacy in interfering in a province not strictly his own. I have not been without my suspicions, that he was not altogether displeased at the contrast we presented to his end of the school. We were a sort of Helots to his young Spartans.[9] He would sometimes, with ironic deference, send to borrow a rod of the Under Master, and then, with sardonic grin, observe to one of his upper boys, "how neat and fresh the twigs looked." While his pale students were battering their brains over Xenophon and Plato, with a silence as deep as that enjoined by the Samite, we were enjoying ourselves at our ease in our little Goshen.[1] We saw a little into the secrets of his discipline, and the

3. Verbs with an active meaning but passive form. "Accidence": a table of the declension of nouns and conjugation of verbs in Greek and Latin.
4. Ben Jonson's *To the Memory of . . . William Shakespeare,* line 39.
5. All three were popular adventure stories or romances of the day.
6. A game in which contestants, with eyes closed, draw lines on a sheet of paper covered with dots. The winner is the contestant whose line touches the most dots.
7. Two philosophers who recommended systems of education that combined theory with practical experience.
8. A Roman of the 1st century C.E., author of a verse translation of Aesop's fables.
9. The Spartans exhibited drunken Helots (slaves) as a warning example to their children.
1. Where the Jews dwelled, protected from the swarms of flies with which the Lord plagued the Egyptians in Exodus 8.22. "Samite": Pythagoras of Samos, Greek mathematician and philosopher (6th century B.C.E.), who forbade his pupils to speak until they had studied with him five years.

prospect did but the more reconcile us to our lot. His thunders rolled innocuous for us: his storms came near, but never touched us; contrary to Gideon's miracle, while all around were drenched, our fleece was dry.[2] His boys turned out the better scholars; we, I suspect, have the advantage in temper. His pupils cannot speak of him without something of terror allaying their gratitude; the remembrance of Field comes back with all the soothing images of indolence, and summer slumbers, and work like play, and innocent idleness, and Elysian exemptions, and life itself a "playing holiday."

Though sufficiently removed from the jurisdiction of Boyer, we were near enough (as I have said) to understand a little of his system. We occasionally heard sounds of the *Ululantes,* and caught glances of Tartarus.[3] B. was a rabid pedant. His English style was cramped to barbarism. His Easter anthems (for his duty obliged him to those periodical flights) were grating as scrannel pipes.[4]—He would laugh, aye, and heartily, but then it must be at Flaccus's quibble about *Rex*[5]—or at the *tristis severitas in vultu,* or *inspicere in patinas,* of Terence[6]—thin jests, which at their first broaching could hardly have had *vis*[7] enough to move a Roman muscle.—He had two wigs, both pedantic, but of different omen. The one serene, smiling, fresh powdered, betokening a mild day. The other, an old, discolored, unkempt, angry caxon,[8] denoting frequent and bloody execution. Woe to the school, when he made his morning appearance in his *passy,* or *passionate wig.* No comet expounded surer.[9]—J. B. had a heavy hand. I have known him double his knotty fist at a poor trembling child (the maternal milk hardly dry upon its lips) with a "Sirrah, do you presume to set your wits at me?"—Nothing was more common than to see him make a headlong entry into the schoolroom, from his inner recess, or library, and, with turbulent eye, singling out a lad, roar out, "Od's my life, sirrah" (his favorite adjuration), "I have a great mind to whip you"—then, with as sudden a retracting impulse, fling back into his lair— and, after a cooling lapse of some minutes (during which all but the culprit had totally forgotten the context) drive headlong out again, piecing out his imperfect sense, as if it had been some Devil's Litany, with the expletory yell—"*and I* WILL, *too.*"—In his gentler moods, when the *rabidus furor* was assuaged, he had resort to an ingenious method, peculiar, for what I have heard, to himself, of whipping the boy, and reading the Debates,[1] at the same time; a paragraph, and a lash between; which in those times, when parliamentary oratory was most at a height and flourishing in these realms, was not calculated to impress the patient with a veneration for the diffuser graces of rhetoric.

Once, and but once, the uplifted rod was known to fall ineffectual from his hand—when droll squinting W—— having been caught putting the

2. Judges 6.37–38. As a sign to Gideon, the Lord soaked his sheepskin while leaving the earth around it dry.
3. In the *Aeneid* 6.557–58 Aeneas hears the groans and the sound of the lash from Tartarus, the infernal place of punishment for the wicked. "*Ululantes*": howling sufferers.
4. Harsh pipes, an echo of Milton's *Lycidas,* line 124.
5. In Horace's *Satires* 1.7 there is a pun on *Rex* as both a surname and the word for *king.*
6. In Terence's *Andrea* 5.2 one character says of

a notorious liar that he has "a sober severity in his countenance." In his *Adelphi* 3.3, after a father has advised his son to look into the lives of men as a mirror, the slave advises the kitchen scullions "to look into the stew pans" as a mirror.
7. Force (Latin); a term in rhetorical theory.
8. A type of wig.
9. Comets were superstitiously regarded as omens of disaster.
1. The record of debates in Parliament. "*Rabidus furor*": mad rage (Latin).

inside of the master's desk to a use for which the architect had clearly not designed it, to justify himself, with great simplicity averred, that *he did not know that the thing had been forewarned.* This exquisite irrecognition of any law antecedent to the *oral* or *declaratory* struck so irrestibly upon the fancy of all who heard it (the pedagogue himself not excepted)—that remission was unavoidable.

L. has given credit to B.'s great merits as an instructor. Coleridge, in his literary life, has pronounced a more intelligible and ample encomium on them. The author of the *Country Spectator*[2] doubts not to compare him with the ablest teachers of antiquity. Perhaps we cannot dismiss him better than with the pious ejaculation of C.—when he heard that his old master was on his deathbed: "Poor J. B.!—may all his faults be forgiven; and may he be wafted to bliss by little cherub boys all head and wings, with no *bottoms* to reproach his sublunary infirmities."

Under him were many good and sound scholars bred.—First Grecian[3] of my time was Lancelot Pepys Stevens, kindest of boys and men, since Co-grammar-master (and inseparable companion) with Dr. T——e. What an edifying spectacle did this brace of friends present to those who remembered the antisocialities of their predecessors!—You never met the one by chance in the street without a wonder, which was quickly dissipated by the almost immediate sub-appearance of the other. Generally arm-in-arm, these kindly coadjutors lightened for each other the toilsome duties of their profession, and when, in advanced age, one found it convenient to retire, the other was not long in discovering that it suited him to lay down the fasces[4] also. Oh, it is pleasant, as it is rare, to find the same arm linked in yours at forty, which at thirteen helped it to turn over the *Cicero De Amicitia,*[5] or some tale of Antique Friendship, which the young heart even then was burning to antic-ipate!—Co-Grecian with S. was Th——, who has since executed with ability various diplomatic functions at the Northern courts. Th—— was a tall, dark, saturnine youth, sparing of speech, with raven locks.—Thomas Fanshaw Middleton followed him (now Bishop of Calcutta), a scholar and a gentleman in his teens. He has the reputation of an excellent critic; and is author (besides the *Country Spectator*) of a *Treatise on the Greek Article,* against Sharpe. M. is said to bear his miter high in India, where the *regni novitas*[6] (I dare say) sufficiently justifies the bearing. A humility quite as primitive as that of Jewel or Hooker[7] might not be exactly fitted to impress the minds of those Anglo-Asiatic diocesans with a reverence for home institutions, and the church which those fathers watered. The manners of M. at school, though firm, were mild and unassuming.—Next to M. (if not senior to him) was Richards, author of the *Aboriginal Britons,* the most spirited of the Oxford Prize Poems; a pale, studious Grecian.—Then followed poor S——, ill-fated M——! of these the Muse is silent.[8]

2. Thomas Middleton, who was at school with Lamb and Coleridge, edited the magazine *Country Spectator* (1792–93) and later became bishop of Calcutta.
3. The Grecians were the small group of superior scholars selected to be sent to a university (usually Cambridge) on a Christ's Hospital scholarship.
4. The bundle of rods, serving as the handle of an ax, carried before the Roman magistrats as a sym-bol of office.
5. Cicero's essay *On Friendship.*
6. Newness of the reign (Latin).
7. Famous divines in the 16th century during the early period of the Anglican Church.
8. Lamb identified these students as Scott, who died insane, and Maunde, who was expelled from the school.

> Finding some of Edward's race
> Unhappy, pass their annals by.[9]

Come back into memory, like as thou wert in the dayspring of thy fancies, with hope like a fiery column before thee—the dark pillar not yet turned—Samuel Taylor Coleridge—Logician, Metaphysician, Bard!—How have I seen the casual passer through the cloisters stand still, entranced with admiration (while he weighed the disproportion between the *speech* and the *garb* of the young Mirandola[1]), to hear thee unfold, in thy deep and sweet intonations, the mysteries of Jamblichus, or Plotinus[2] (for even in those years thou waxedst not pale at such philosophic draughts), or reciting Homer in his Greek, or Pindar—while the walls of the old Grey Friars[3] re-echoed to the accents of the *inspired charity-boy!*—Many were the "wit combats" (to dally awhile with the words of old Fuller) between him and C. V. Le G——, "which two I behold like a Spanish great galleon, and an English man-of-war; Master Coleridge, like the former, was built far higher in learning, solid, but slow in his performances. C. V. L., with the English man-of-war, lesser in bulk, but lighter in sailing, could turn with all tides, tack about, and take advantage of all winds, by the quickness of his wit and invention."[4]

Nor shalt thou, their compeer, be quickly forgotten, Allen, with the cordial smile, and still more cordial laugh, with which thou wert wont to make the old cloisters shake, in thy cognition of some poignant jest of theirs; or the anticipation of some more material, and, peradventure, practical one, of thine own. Extinct are those smiles, with that beautiful countenance, with which (for thou wert the *Nireus formosus*[5] of the school), in the days of thy maturer waggery, thou didst disarm the wrath of infuriated town-damsel, who, incensed by provoking pinch, turning tigress-like round, suddenly converted by thy angel look, exchanged the half-formed terrible *"bl——,"* for a gentler greeting—*"bless thy handsome face!"*

Next follow two, who ought to be now alive, and the friends of Elia—the junior Le G—— and F——; who impelled, the former by a roving temper, the latter by too quick a sense of neglect—ill capable of enduring the slights poor Sizars[6] are sometimes subject to in our seats of learning—exchanged their Alma Mater for the camp; perishing, one by climate, and one on the plains of Salamanca: Le G——, sanguine, volatile, sweet-natured; F——, dogged, faithful, anticipative of insult, warmhearted, with something of the old Roman height about him.

Fine, frank-hearted Fr——, the present master of Hertford, with Marmaduke T——,[7] mildest of missionaries—and both my good friends still—close the catalogue of Grecians in my time.

1820   1823

9. Altered from Matthew Prior's *Carmen Seculare* (1700). "Edward's race": applied to the students of Christ's Hospital, founded by Edward VI.
1. Pico della Mirandola, the brilliant and charming humanist and philosopher of the Italian Renaissance, who died in 1494 at the age of thirty-one.
2. Neoplatonic philosophers.
3. Christ's Hospital was located in buildings that had once belonged to the Grey Friars (i.e., Franciscans).
4. Lamb adapts to Coleridge and Charles Valentine Le Grice the famous description of the wit

combats between Shakespeare (the "man-of-war") and Ben Jonson (the "great galleon") in Thomas Fuller's *Worthies of England* (1662).
5. The handsome Nireus; a Greek warrior in Homer's *Iliad* 2.
6. An undergraduate at Cambridge University who receives an allowance toward his expenses. "Le G——": Samuel Le Grice, who became an army officer and died in the West Indies. "F——": Joseph Favell.
7. Marmaduke Thompson. "Fr——": Frederick William Franklin.

Old China

I have an almost feminine partiality for old china. When I go to see any great house, I inquire for the china closet, and next for the picture gallery. I cannot defend the order of preference, but by saying that we have all some taste or other, of too ancient a date to admit of our remembering distinctly that it was an acquired one. I can call to mind the first play, and the first exhibition, that I was taken to; but I am not conscious of a time when china jars and saucers were introduced into my imagination.

I had no repugnance then—why should I now have?—to those little, lawless, azure-tinctured grotesques, that under the notion of men and women float about, uncircumscribed by any element, in that world before perspective—a china teacup.

I like to see my old friends—whom distance cannot diminish—figuring up in the air (so they appear to our optics), yet on terra firma still—for so we must in courtesy interpret that speck of deeper blue, which the decorous artist, to prevent absurdity, had made to spring up beneath their sandals.

I love the men with women's faces, and the women, if possible, with still more womanish expressions.

Here is a young and courtly mandarin, handing tea to a lady from a salver—two miles off. See how distance seems to set off respect! And here the same lady, or another—for likeness is identity on teacups—is stepping into a little fairy boat, moored on the hither side of this calm garden river, with a dainty mincing foot, which in a right angle of incidence (as angles go in our world) must infallibly land her in the midst of a flowery mead—a furlong off on the other side of the same strange stream!

Farther on—if far or near can be predicated of their world—see horses, trees, pagodas, dancing the hays.[1]

Here—a cow and rabbit couchant,[2] and coextensive—so objects show, seen through the lucid atmosphere of fine Cathay.[3]

I was pointing out to my cousin last evening, over our Hyson[4] (which we are old-fashioned enough to drink unmixed still of an afternoon), some of these *speciosa miracula*[5] upon a set of extraordinary old blue china (a recent purchase) which we were now for the first time using; and could not help remarking how favorable circumstances had been to us of late years that we could afford to please the eye sometimes with trifles of this sort—when a passing sentiment seemed to overshade the brows of my companion. I am quick at detecting these summer clouds in Bridget.[6]

"I wish the good old times would come again," she said, "when we were not quite so rich. I do not mean that I want to be poor; but there was a middle state"—so she was pleased to ramble on—"in which I am sure we were a great deal happier. A purchase is but a purchase, now that you have money enough and to spare. Formerly it used to be a triumph. When we coveted a cheap luxury (and, O! how much ado I had to get you to consent in those times!)—we were used to have a debate two or three days before,

---

1. An English country dance with a serpentining movement.
2. Lying down with the head raised (heraldry).
3. The old European name for China.
4. A Chinese green tea.
5. Shining wonders (Latin).
6. In Lamb's essays, his name for his sister, Mary.

and to weigh the *for* and *against,* and think what we might spare it out of, and what saving we could hit upon, that should be an equivalent. A thing was worth buying then, when we felt the money that we paid for it.

"Do you remember the brown suit, which you made to hang upon you, till all your friends cried shame upon you, it grew so threadbare—and all because of that folio Beaumont and Fletcher,[7] which you dragged home late at night from Barker's in Covent Garden? Do you remember how we eyed it for weeks before we could make up our minds to the purchase, and had not come to a determination till it was near ten o'clock of the Saturday night, when you set off from Islington,[8] fearing you should be too late—and when the old bookseller with some grumbling opened his shop, and by the twinkling taper (for he was setting bedwards) lighted out the relic from his dusty treasures— and when you lugged it home, wishing it were twice as cumbersome—and when you presented it to me—and when we were exploring the perfectness of it (*collating,* you called it)—and while I was repairing some of these loose leaves with paste, which your impatience would not suffer to be left till daybreak—was there no pleasure in being a poor man? or can those neat black clothes which you wear now, and are so careful to keep brushed, since we have become rich and finical, give you half the honest vanity with which you flaunted it about in that overworn suit—your old corbeau[9]—for four or five weeks longer than you should have done, to pacify your conscience for the mighty sum of fifteen—or sixteen shillings was it?—a great affair we thought it then—which you had lavished on the old folio. Now you can afford to buy any book that pleases you, but I do not see that you ever bring me home any nice old purchases now.

"When you came home with twenty apologies for laying out a less number of shillings upon that print after Leonardo,[1] which we christened the 'Lady Blanch'; when you looked at the purchase, and thought of the money—and thought of the money, and looked again at the picture—was there no pleasure in being a poor man? Now, you have nothing to do but to walk into Colnaghi's, and buy a wilderness of Leonardos. Yet do you?

"Then, do you remember our pleasant walks to Enfield, and Potter's Bar, and Waltham,[2] when we had a holiday—holidays, and all other fun, are gone now we are rich—and the little hand-basket in which I used to deposit our day's fare of savory cold lamb and salad—and how you would pry about at noontide for some decent house, where we might go in and produce our store—only paying for the ale that you must call for—and speculate upon the looks of the landlady, and whether she was likely to allow us a table-cloth—and wish for such another honest hostess as Izaak Walton has described many a one on the pleasant banks of the Lea, when he went a-fishing—and sometimes they would prove obliging enough, and sometimes they would look grudgingly upon us—but we had cheerful looks still for one another, and would eat our plain food savorily, scarcely grudging Piscator[3] his Trout Hall? Now—when we go out a day's pleasuring, which is seldom,

---

7. The Elizabethan dramatic collaborators, whose plays were first collected in a large folio volume in 1647.
8. In the north of London, where the Lambs had been living.
9. A dark green cloth, almost black (hence its name, the French for "raven").

1. Leonardo da Vinci (1452–1519), the great Italian painter. The painting is the one known as *Modesty and Vanity.*
2. All three are suburbs to the north of London.
3. The fisherman in Izaak Walton's *Complete Angler* (1653).

moreover, we *ride* part of the way—and go into a fine inn, and order the best of dinners, never debating the expense—which, after all, never has half the relish of those chance country snaps,[4] when we were at the mercy of uncertain usage and a precarious welcome.

"You are too proud to see a play anywhere now but in the pit. Do you remember where it was we used to sit, when we saw the *Battle of Hexham,* and the *Surrender of Calais,*[5] and Bannister and Mrs. Bland in the *Children in the Wood*[6]—when we squeezed out our shillings apiece to sit three or four times in a season in the one-shilling gallery—where you felt all the time that you ought not to have brought me—and more strongly I felt obligation to you for having brought me—and the pleasure was the better for a little shame—and when the curtain drew up, what cared we for our place in the house, or what mattered it where we were sitting, when our thoughts were with Rosalind in Arden, or with Viola at the Court of Ilyria.[7] You used to say that the gallery was the best place of all for enjoying a play socially—that the relish of such exhibitions must be in proportion to the infrequency of going—that the company we met there, not being in general readers of plays, were obliged to attend the more, and did attend, to what was going on, on the stage—because a word lost would have been a chasm, which it was impossible for them to fill up. With such reflections we consoled our pride then—and I appeal to you whether, as a woman, I met generally with less attention and accommodation than I have done since in more expensive situations in the house? The getting in indeed, and the crowding up those inconvenient staircases, was bad enough—but there was still a law of civility to woman recognized to quite as great an extent as we ever found in the other passages—and how a little difficulty overcome heightened the snug seat and the play, afterwards! Now we can only pay our money and walk in. You cannot see, you say, in the galleries now. I am sure we saw, and heard too, well enough then—but sight, and all, I think, is gone with our poverty.

"There was pleasure in eating strawberries, before they became quite common—in the first dish of peas, while they were yet dear—to have them for a nice supper, a treat. What treat can we have now? If we were to treat ourselves now—that is, to have dainties a little above our means, it would be selfish and wicked. It is the very little more that we allow ourselves beyond what the actual poor can get at that makes what I call a treat—when two people living together, as we have done, now and then indulge themselves in a cheap luxury, which both like; while each apologizes, and is willing to take both halves of the blame to his single share. I see no harm in people making much of themselves, in that sense of the word. It may give them a hint how to make much of others. But now—what I mean by the word—we never do make much of ourselves. None but the poor can do it. I do not mean the veriest poor of all, but persons as we were, just above poverty.

"I know what you were going to say, that it is mighty pleasant at the end of the year to make all meet—and much ado we used to have every Thirty-first Night of December to account for our exceedings—many a long face did you make over your puzzled accounts, and in contriving to make it out how we had spent so much—or that we had not spent so much—or that it

---

4. Snacks.
5. Comedies by George Colman (1762–1836).
6. By Thomas Morton (1764–1838).

7. Rosalind in *As You Like It* and Viola in *Twelfth Night.*

was impossible we should spend so much next year—and still we found our slender capital decreasing—but then, betwixt ways, and projects, and compromises of one sort or another, and talk of curtailing this charge, and doing without that for the future—and the hope that youth brings, and laughing spirits (in which you were never poor till now), we pocketed up our loss, and in conclusion, with 'lusty brimmers' (as you used to quote it out of *hearty cheerful Mr. Cotton,*[8] as you called him), we used to welcome in 'the coming guest.' Now we have no reckoning at all at the end of the old year—no flattering promises about the new year doing better for us."

Bridget is so sparing of her speech on most occasions that when she gets into a rhetorical vein, I am careful how I interrupt it. I could not help, however, smiling at the phantom of wealth which her dear imagination had conjured up out of a clear income of poor—— hundred pounds a year. "It is true we were happier when we were poorer, but we were also younger, my cousin. I am afraid we must put up with the excess, for if we were to shake the superflux into the sea, we should not much mend ourselves. That we had much to struggle with, as we grew up together, we have reason to be most thankful. It strengthened and knit our compact closer. We could never have been what we have been to each other, if we had always had the sufficiency which you now complain of. The resisting power—those natural dilations of the youthful spirit, which circumstances cannot straiten—with us are long since passed away. Competence to age is supplementary youth, a sorry supplement indeed, but I fear the best that is to be had. We must ride where we formerly walked: live better and lie softer—and shall be wise to do so—than we had means to do in those good old days you speak of. Yet could those days return—could you and I once more walk our thirty miles a day—could Bannister and Mrs. Bland again be young, and you and I be young to see them—could the good old one-shilling gallery days return—they are dreams, my cousin, now—but could you and I at this moment, instead of this quiet argument, by our well-carpeted fireside, sitting on this luxurious sofa—be once more struggling up those inconvenient staircases, pushed about, and squeezed, and elbowed by the poorest rabble of poor gallery scramblers—could I once more hear those anxious shrieks of yours—and the delicious *Thank God, we are safe,* which always followed when the topmost stair, conquered, let in the first light of the whole cheerful theater down beneath us—I know not the fathom line that ever touched a descent so deep as I would be willing to bury more wealth in than Croesus had, or the great Jew R——[9] is supposed to have, to purchase it. And now do just look at that merry little Chinese waiter holding an umbrella, big enough for a bed-tester, over the head of that pretty insipid half Madonnaish chit of a lady in that very blue summerhouse."

1823   1823

---

8. Charles Cotton (1630–1687), a favorite poet of Lamb's. The quotations are from his poem *The New Year.*

9. Nathan Meyer Rothschild (1777–1836) founded the English branch of the great European banking house.

WILLIAM HAZLITT
1778–1830

"I started in life," William Hazlitt wrote, "with the French Revolution, and I have lived, alas! to see the end of it. . . . Since then, I confess, I have no longer felt myself young, for with that my hopes fell." He was born into a radical circle, for the elder William Hazlitt, his father, was a Unitarian minister who declared from the pulpit his advocacy both of American independence and of the French Revolution. When young William was five years old, his father took the family to America in search of liberty and founded the first Unitarian church in Boston, but four years later he returned to settle at Wem, in Shropshire. Despite the persistent attacks of reviewers and the backsliding of his once-radical friends, Hazlitt himself never wavered in his loyalty to liberty, equality, and the principles behind the overthrow of the monarchy in France. His first literary production, at the age of thirteen, was a letter to a newspaper in indignant protest against the mob that sacked Joseph Priestley's house, when the scientist and preacher had celebrated publicly the second anniversary of the fall of the Bastille. His last book, published in the year he died, was a four-volume life of Napoleon, in which he expressed a vehement, but qualified, admiration of Napoleon as a man of heroic will and power in the service of the emancipation of mankind.

Hazlitt was a long time finding his vocation. When he attended the Hackney College, London, between the ages of fifteen and eighteen, he plunged into philosophical studies. In 1799 he took up the study of painting and did not relinquish the ambition to become a portraitist until 1812. His first books dealt with philosophy, economics, and politics; and his first job as a journalist was as parliamentary reporter for the *Morning Chronicle*. It was not until 1813, when he was thirty-six, that he began contributing dramatic criticism and miscellaneous essays to various periodicals and so discovered what he had been born to do. Years of wide reading and hard thinking had made him thoroughly ready: within the next decade he demonstrated himself to be a highly popular lecturer on Shakespeare, Elizabethan drama, and English poetry from Chaucer to his own day; a superb connoisseur of the theater and of painting; a master of the familiar essay; and with Coleridge, one of the two most important literary critics of his time. Coleridge is a systematic critic for whom theory precedes application and whose theory of poetry is part of a general philosophy of humanity and nature. Hazlitt, on the other hand, decries what he calls the "modern or metaphysical school of criticism"; his distinctive power is as a practical critic who communicates what he calls his "impressions," that is, the immediacy of his firsthand responses to a literary work or passage.

Unlike his contemporaries Coleridge, Lamb, and De Quincey, whose writings look back to the elaborate prose stylists of the earlier seventeenth century, Hazlitt developed a fast-moving, hard-hitting prose in a style that he called "plain, point-blank speaking." He wrote, indeed, nearly as fast as he talked, almost without correction and (despite the density of literary quotations) without reference to books or notes. This rapidity was possible only because his essays are relatively planless. Hazlitt characteristically lays down a topic, then piles up relevant observations and instances; the essay accumulates instead of developing; often, it does not round to a conclusion, but simply stops. Hazlitt's prose is unfailingly energetic, but his most satisfying essays, considered as works of literary art, are those that, like *My First Acquaintance with Poets*, have a narrative subject matter to give him a principle of organization.

In demeanor Hazlitt was awkward and self-conscious; Coleridge described him in 1803 as "brow-hanging, shoe-contemplative, strange." He had grown up as a member of a highly unpopular minority, in both religion and politics; he found his friends deserting to the side of reaction; and his natural combativeness was exacerbated by the persistent abuse directed against him by writers in the conservative press and periodicals. In the course of his life he managed to quarrel, in private and in print, with almost everyone whom he had once admired and liked, including Coleridge, Wordsworth, Leigh Hunt, and even his most intimate and enduring friend, Charles Lamb. But what appealed to his admirers, as to modern readers of his essays, is his courage and uncompromising honesty, and above all his zest for life in its diversity— including even, as he announced in the title of an essay, *The Pleasure of Hating*. He relished, and was able to convey completely, the particular qualities of things—a passage of poetry, a painting, a natural prospect, or a well-directed blow in a prize fight. Despite the recurrent frustrations of his fifty-two years of existence, he was able to say, with his last breath, "Well, I've had a happy life."

On Gusto[1]

Gusto in art is power or passion defining any object. It is not so difficult to explain this term in what relates to expression (of which it may be said to be the highest degree) as in what relates to things without expression, to the natural appearances of objects, as mere color or form. In one sense, however, there is hardly any object entirely devoid of expression, without some character of power belonging to it, some precise association with pleasure or pain: and it is in giving this truth of character from the truth of feeling, whether in the highest or the lowest degree, but always in the highest degree of which the subject is capable, that gusto consists.

There is a gusto in the coloring of Titian.[2] Not only do his heads seem to think—his bodies seem to feel. This is what the Italians mean by the *morbidezza*[3] of his flesh color. It seems sensitive and alive all over; not merely to have the look and texture of flesh, but the feeling in itself. For example, the limbs of his female figures have a luxurious softness and delicacy, which appears conscious of the pleasure of the beholder. As the objects themselves in nature would produce an impression on the sense, distinct from every other object, and having something divine in it, which the heart owns and the imagination consecrates, the objects in the picture preserve the same impression, absolute, unimpaired, stamped with all the truth of passion, the pride of the eye, and the charm of beauty. Rubens makes his flesh color like flowers; Albano's[4] is like ivory; Titian's is like flesh, and like nothing else. It is as different from that of other painters, as the skin is from a piece of white or red drapery thrown over it. The blood circulates here and there, the blue

1. In this critical essay of 1816 Hazlitt introduces one of his distinctive critical terms. In the 17th century, English writers had imported the Italian term *gusto*, meaning taste, to denote a spectator's artistic sensibility, and sometimes in the sense (which remains primary in our own day) of keen relish or zest. From Hazlitt's diverse statements we can make out that he transferred the application of "gusto" from the responsiveness of a spectator to an essential feature of a natural or human object—a feature that has been passionately rendered by the artist so that it appeals through the eye to the other senses and communicates (in what for Hazlitt is the highest commendation) a sense of "power." Most of Hazlitt's examples are from the visual art of painting, but he finds this quality in literature as well.

Keats, who was greatly influenced by Hazlitt's criticism, illuminated Hazlitt's notion of the capacity of great works of art to evoke a wide range of sensuous and emotional responses when, soon after reading Hazlitt *On Gusto*, he remarked (in a letter of December 21, 1817) about a painting by Benjamin West that "there is nothing to be intense upon; no women one feels mad to kiss; no face swelling into reality."
2. Tiziano Vecelli (ca. 1490–1576), greatest of the 16th-century Venetian painters.
3. Softness, delicacy.
4. Francesco Albani (1578–1660), Italian painter. Peter Paul Rubens (1577–1640), Flemish painter, was the most important artist of his time in northern Europe.

veins just appear, the rest is distinguished throughout only by that sort of tingling sensation to the eye, which the body feels within itself. This is gusto. Vandyke's[5] flesh color, though it has great truth and purity, wants gusto. It has not the internal character, the living principle in it. It is a smooth surface, not a warm, moving mass. It is painted without passion, with indifference. The hand only has been concerned. The impression slides off from the eye, and does not, like the tones of Titian's pencil,[6] leave a sting behind it in the mind of the spectator. The eye does not acquire a taste or appetite for what it sees. In a word, gusto in painting is where the impression made on one sense excites by affinity those of another.

Michael Angelo's forms are full of gusto. They everywhere obtrude the sense of power upon the eye. His limbs convey an idea of muscular strength, of moral grandeur, and even of intellectual dignity: they are firm, commanding, broad, and massy, capable of executing with ease the determined purposes of the will. His faces have no other expression than his figures, conscious power and capacity. They appear only to think what they shall do, and to know that they can do it. This is what is meant by saying that his style is hard and masculine. It is the reverse of Correggio's,[7] which is effeminate. That is, the gusto of Michael Angelo consists in expressing energy of will without proportionable sensibility, Correggio's in expressing exquisite sensibility without energy of will. In Correggio's faces as well as figures we see neither bones nor muscles, but then what a soul is there, full of sweetness and of grace—pure, playful, soft, angelical! There is sentiment enough in a hand painted by Correggio to set up a school of history painters. Whenever we look at the hands of Correggio's women or of Raphael's,[8] we always wish to touch them.

Again, Titian's landscapes have a prodigious gusto, both in the coloring and forms. We shall never forget one that we saw many years ago in the Orleans Gallery of Acteon hunting.[9] It had a brown, mellow, autumnal look. The sky was of the color of stone. The winds seemed to sing through the rustling branches of the trees, and already you might hear the twanging of bows resound through the tangled mazes of the wood. Mr. West,[1] we understand, has this landscape. He will know if this description of it is just. The landscape background of the St. Peter Martyr[2] is another well known instance of the power of this great painter to give a romantic interest and an appropriate character to the objects of his pencil, where every circumstance adds to the effect of the scene—the bold trunks of the tall forest trees, the trailing ground plants, with that tall convent spire rising in the distance, amidst the blue sapphire mountains and the golden sky.

Rubens has a great deal of gusto in his Fauns and Satyrs, and in all that expresses motion, but in nothing else. Rembrandt has it in everything; every-

---

5. Sir Anthony Vandyke (1599–1641), Flemish portrait-painter, who did some of his best-known work at the English court of Charles I.
6. In the archaic sense: a painter's brush.
7. Antonio Correggio (1494–1534), Italian artist.
8. Rafaello Sanzio (1488–1520), one of the supreme painters of the high Italian Renaissance.
9. Titian's *Diana and Actaeon*, shown in a celebrated sale-exhibition of old Italian masters, most of them from the collection of the Duc d'Orléans, in London, 1798–99. In *On the Pleasures of Paint-*

ing Hazlitt writes that this exhibition first revealed to him the high possibilities of the art of painting.
1. Benjamin West (1738–1820) was an American-born painter of historical scenes who achieved a high reputation in England. In 1792 he succeeded Sir Joshua Reynolds as president of the Royal Academy.
2. A celebrated altarpiece by Titian depicting the martyrdom of Peter, a 13th-century Dominican. It was destroyed by fire in 1867.

thing in his pictures has a tangible character. If he puts a diamond in the ear of a burgomaster's wife, it is of the first water; and his furs and stuffs are proof against a Russian winter. Raphael's gusto was only in expression; he had no idea of the character of anything but the human form. The dryness and poverty of his style in other respects is a phenomenon in the art. His trees are like sprigs of grass stuck in a book of botanical specimens. Was it that Raphael never had time to go beyond the walls of Rome? That he was always in the streets, at church, or in the bath? He was not one of the Society of Arcadians.[3]

Claude's[4] landscapes, perfect as they are, want gusto. This is not easy to explain. They are perfect abstractions of the visible images of things; they speak the visible language of nature truly. They resemble a mirror or a microscope. To the eye only they are more perfect than any other landscapes that ever were or will be painted; they give more of nature, as cognizable by one sense alone; but they lay an equal stress on all visible impressions. They do not interpret one sense by another; they do not distinguish the character of different objects as we are taught, and can only be taught, to distinguish them by their effect on the different senses. That is, his eye wanted imagination: it did not strongly sympathize with his other faculties. He saw the atmosphere, but he did not feel it. He painted the trunk of a tree or a rock in the foreground as smooth—with as complete an abstraction of the gross, tangible impression, as any other part of the picture. His trees are perfectly beautiful, but quite immovable; they have a look of enchantment. In short, his landscapes are unequaled imitations of nature, released from its subjection to the elements, as if all objects were become a delightful fairy vision, and the eye had rarefied and refined away the other senses.

The gusto in the Greek statues is of a very singular kind. The sense of perfect form nearly occupies the whole mind, and hardly suffers it to dwell on any other feeling. It seems enough for them *to be,* without acting or suffering. Their forms are ideal, spiritual. Their beauty is power. By their beauty they are raised above the frailties of pain or passion; by their beauty they are deified.

The infinite quantity of dramatic invention in Shakespeare takes from his gusto. The power he delights to show is not intense, but discursive. He never insists on anything as much as he might, except a quibble. Milton has great gusto. He repeats his blows twice; grapples with and exhausts his subject. His imagination has a double relish of its objects, an inveterate attachment to the things he describes, and to the words describing them.

> ——Or where Chineses drive
> With sails and wind their *cany* waggons *light.*

> Wild above rule or art, *enormous* bliss.[5]

---

3. I.e., someone who delights in the beauties of the countryside. Hazlitt adds a footnote: "Raphael not only could not paint a landscape; he could not paint people in a landscape. He could not have painted the heads or the figures, or even the dresses, of the St. Peter Martyr. His figures have always an *in-door* look, that is, a set, determined, voluntary, dramatic character, arising from their own passions, or a watchfulness of those of others, and want [lack] that wild uncertainty of expression, which is connected with the accidents of nature and the changes of the elements. He has nothing *romantic* about him."
4. Claude Lorraine (1600–1682), French painter renowned for his landscapes and seascapes.
5. *Paradise Lost* 3.438–39 and 5.297.

There is a gusto in Pope's compliments, in Dryden's satires, and Prior's tales;[6] and among prose writers Boccaccio and Rabelais had the most of it. We will only mention one other work which appears to us to be full of gusto, and that is the *Beggar's Opera*.[7] If it is not, we are altogether mistaken in our notions on this delicate subject.

1816   1817

My First Acquaintance with Poets[1]

My father was a Dissenting Minister, at Wem, in Shropshire; and in the year 1798 (the figures that compose that date are to me like the "dreaded name of Demogorgon"[2]) Mr. Coleridge came to Shrewsbury, to succeed Mr. Rowe in the spiritual charge of a Unitarian congregation there. He did not come till late on the Saturday afternoon before he was to preach; and Mr. Rowe, who himself went down to the coach, in a state of anxiety and expectation, to look for the arrival of his successor, could find no one at all answering the description but a round-faced man, in a short black coat (like a shooting jacket) which hardly seemed to have been made for him, but who seemed to be talking at a great rate to his fellow passengers. Mr. Rowe had scarce returned to give an account of his disappointment, when the round-faced man in black entered, and dissipated all doubts on the subject, by beginning to talk. He did not cease while he stayed; nor has he since, that I know of. He held the good town of Shrewsbury in delightful suspense for three weeks that he remained there, "fluttering the *proud Salopians*, like an eagle in a dovecote";[3] and the Welsh mountains that skirt the horizon with their tempestuous confusion, agree to have heard no such mystic sounds since the days of

> High-born Hoel's harp or soft Llewellyn's lay![4]

As we passed along between Wem and Shrewsbury, and I eyed their blue tops seen through the wintry branches, or the red rustling leaves of the sturdy oak trees by the roadside, a sound was in my ears as of a Siren's song; I was stunned, startled with it, as from deep sleep; but I had no notion then that I should ever be able to express my admiration to others in motley imagery or quaint allusion, till the light of his genius shone into my soul, like the sun's rays glittering in the puddles of the road. I was at that time dumb, inarticulate, helpless, like a worm by the wayside, crushed, bleeding, lifeless; but now, bursting from the deadly bands that bound them,

---

6. A group of somewhat bawdy narrative poems by the early-18th-century poet Matthew Prior.
7. The extremely popular comic opera by John Gay, produced in 1728. At the end of his essay, Hazlitt apparently returns to the common use of "gusto" in the sense of "spirited, zestful."
1. This essay was written in 1823, a quarter century after the events it describes. By then Coleridge and Wordsworth had long given up their early radicalism, and both men had quarreled with Hazlitt— hence the essay's elegiac note in dealing with the genius of the two poets. Nevertheless, Hazlitt communicates the excitement he had felt when Cole-

ridge awakened him to the sense of his own literary possibilities, and the essay remains an incomparable portrait of Wordsworth and Coleridge early in 1798, the period of their closest collaboration.
2. *Paradise Lost* 2.964–65. To mythographers of the Renaissance, Demogorgon was a mysterious and terrifying demon, sometimes described as ancestor of all the gods. He plays a central role in Shelley's *Prometheus Unbound*.
3. Adapted from Shakespeare's *Coriolanus* 5.6.115–16. "Salopians": inhabitants of Shropshire.
4. Thomas Gray's *The Bard*, line 28.

With Styx nine times round them,[5]

my ideas float on winged words, and as they expand their plumes, catch the golden light of other years. My soul has indeed remained in its original bondage, dark, obscure, with longings infinite and unsatisfied; my heart, shut up in the prison house of this rude clay, has never found, nor will it ever find, a heart to speak to; but that my understanding also did not remain dumb and brutish, or at length found a language to express itself, I owe to Coleridge. But this is not to my purpose.

My father lived ten miles from Shrewsbury, and was in the habit of exchanging visits with Mr. Rowe, and with Mr. Jenkins of Whitechurch (nine miles farther on) according to the custom of Dissenting Ministers in each other's neighborhood. A line of communication is thus established, by which the flame of civil and religious liberty is kept alive, and nourishes its smoldering fire unquenchable, like the fires in the *Agamemnon* of Aeschylus, placed at different stations, that waited for ten long years to announce with their blazing pyramids the destruction of Troy. Coleridge had agreed to come over to see my father, according to the courtesy of the country, as Mr. Rowe's probable successor; but in the meantime, I had gone to hear him preach the Sunday after his arrival. A poet and a philosopher getting up into a Unitarian pulpit to preach the Gospel was a romance in these degenerate days, a sort of revival of the primitive spirit of Christianity, which was not to be resisted.

It was in January of 1798, that I rose one morning before daylight, to walk ten miles in the mud, and went to hear this celebrated person preach. Never, the longest day I have to live, shall I have such another walk as this cold, raw, comfortless one, in the winter of the year 1798. *Il y a des impressions que ni le temps ni les circonstances peuvent effacer. Dusse-je vivre des siècles entiers, le doux temps de ma jeunesse ne peut renaître pour moi, ni s'effacer jamais dans ma mémoire.*[6] When I got there, the organ was playing the 100th psalm, and when it was done, Mr. Coleridge rose and gave out his text, "And he went up into the mountain to pray, *himself, alone.*"[7] As he gave out this text, his voice "rose like a steam of rich distilled perfume,"[8] and when he came to the two last words, which he pronounced loud, deep, and distinct, it seemed to me, who was then young, as if the sounds had echoed from the bottom of the human heart, and as if that prayer might have floated in solemn silence through the universe. The idea of St. John came into my mind, "of one crying in the wilderness, who had his loins girt about, and whose food was locusts and wild honey."[9] The preacher then launched into his subject, like an eagle dallying with the wind. The sermon was upon peace and war; upon church and state—not their alliance but their separation—on the spirit of the world and the spirit of Christianity, not as the same, but as opposed to one another. He talked of those who had "inscribed the cross of Christ on banners dripping with human gore." He made a poetical and pastoral excursion—and to show the fatal effects of war, drew a striking contrast

---

5. Adapted from Pope's *Ode on St. Cecilia's Day*, lines 90–91.
6. There are some impressions which neither time nor circumstances can efface. Might I live whole centuries, the sweet time of my youth cannot be reborn for me, nor ever erased from my memory (French). Based on Rousseau's epistolary novel *La Nouvelle Héloise* (1761), part 6, letter 7.
7. Cf. Matthew 14.23 and John 6.15.
8. Milton's *Comus,* line 556.
9. See Matthew 3.3–4 and Mark 1.3–6.

between the simple shepherd boy, driving his team afield, or sitting under the hawthorn, piping to his flock, "as though he should never be old,"[1] and the same poor country lad, crimped,[2] kidnapped, brought into town, made drunk, at an alehouse, turned into a wretched drummer boy, with his hair sticking on end with powder and pomatum, a long cue at his back, and tricked out in the loathsome finery of the profession of blood.

Such were the notes our once-loved poet sung.[3]

And for myself, I could not have been more delighted if I had heard the music of the spheres. Poetry and Philosophy had met together. Truth and Genius had embraced, under the eye and with the sanction of Religion. This was even beyond my hopes. I returned home well satisfied. The sun that was still laboring pale and wan through the sky, obscured by thick mists, seemed an emblem of the *good cause*;[4] and the cold dank drops of dew, that hung half melted on the beard of the thistle, had something genial and refreshing in them; for there was a spirit of hope and youth in all nature, that turned everything into good. The face of nature had not then the brand of *Jus Divinum*[5] on it:

Like to that sanguine flower inscribed with woe.[6]

On the Tuesday following, the half-inspired speaker came. I was called down into the room where he was, and went half-hoping, half-afraid. He received me very graciously, and I listened for a long time without uttering a word. I did not suffer in his opinion by my silence. "For those two hours," he afterwards was pleased to say, "he was conversing with W. H.'s forehead!" His appearance was different from what I had anticipated from seeing him before. At a distance, and in the dim light of the chapel, there was to me a strange wildness in his aspect, a dusky obscurity, and I thought him pitted with the smallpox. His complexion was at that time clear, and even bright—

As are the children of yon azure sheen.[7]

His forehead was broad and high, light as if built of ivory, with large projecting eyebrows, and his eyes rolling beneath them, like a sea with darkened luster. "A certain tender bloom his face o'erspread,"[8] a purple tinge as we see it in the pale thoughtful complexions of the Spanish portrait painters, Murillo and Velasquez. His mouth was gross, voluptuous, open, eloquent; his chin good-humored and round; but his nose, the rudder of the face, the index of the will, was small, feeble, nothing—like what he has done. It might seem that the genius of his face as from a height surveyed and projected him (with sufficient capacity and huge aspiration) into the world unknown of thought and imagination, with nothing to support or guide his veering purpose, as if Columbus had launched his adventurous course for the New World in a scallop,[9] with-out oars or compass. So at least I comment on it

1. Sir Philip Sidney's *Arcadia* 1.2.
2. Trapped into enlisting in military service.
3. The first line of Pope's *Epistle to Robert, Earl of Oxford.*
4. The cause of liberty, i.e., the French Revolution.
5. The divine right (of kings).

6. I.e., the hyacinth, believed to be marked with the Greek lament "AI AI"; the line is from Milton's *Lycidas* (106).
7. Adapted from James Thomson's *The Castle of Indolence* 2.33.
8. See Thomson's *The Castle of Indolence* 1.57.
9. Probably for *shallop*, a small boat.

after the event. Coleridge in his person was rather above the common size, inclining to the corpulent, or like Lord Hamlet, "somewhat fat and pursy."[1] His hair (now, alas! gray) was then black and glossy as the raven's, and fell in smooth masses over his forehead. This long pendulous hair is peculiar to enthusiasts, to those whose minds tend heavenward; and is traditionally inseparable (though of a different color) from the pictures of Christ. It ought to belong, as a character, to all who preach *Christ crucified*, and Coleridge was at that time one of those!

It was curious to observe the contrast between him and my father, who was a veteran in the cause, and then declining into the vale of years. He had been a poor Irish lad, carefully brought up by his parents, and sent to the University of Glasgow (where he studied under Adam Smith[2]) to prepare him for his future destination. It was his mother's proudest wish to see her son a Dissenting Minister. So if we look back to past generations (as far as eye can reach) we see the same hopes, fears, wishes, followed by the same disappointments, throbbing in the human heart; and so we may see them (if we look forward) rising up forever, and disappearing, like vaporish bubbles, in the human breast! After being tossed about from congregation to congregation in the heats of the Unitarian controversy, and squabbles about the American war,[3] he had been relegated to an obscure village, where he was to spend the last thirty years of his life, far from the only converse that he loved, the talk about disputed texts of Scripture and the cause of civil and religious liberty. Here he passed his days, repining but resigned, in the study of the Bible, and the perusal of the Commentators—huge folios, not easily got through, one of which would outlast a winter! Why did he pore on these from morn to night (with the exception of a walk in the fields or a turn in the garden to gather broccoli plants or kidney beans of his own rearing, with no small degree of pride and pleasure)? Here were "no figures nor no fantasies"[4]—neither poetry nor philosophy—nothing to dazzle, nothing to excite modern curiosity; but to his lackluster eyes there appeared, within the pages of the ponderous, unwieldy, neglected tomes, the sacred name of JEHOVAH in Hebrew capitals: pressed down by the weight of the style, worn to the last fading thinness of the understanding, there were glimpses, glimmering notions of the patriarchal wanderings, with palm trees hovering in the horizon, and processions of camels at the distance of three thousand years; there was Moses with the Burning Bush, the number of the Twelve Tribes, types, shadows,[5] glosses on the law and the prophets; there were discussions (dull enough) on the age of Methuselah, a mighty speculation! there were outlines, rude guesses at the shape of Noah's Ark and of the riches of Solomon's Temple; questions as to the date of the creation, predictions of the end of all things; the great lapses of time, the strange mutations of the globe were unfolded with the voluminous leaf, as it turned over; and though the soul might slumber with an hieroglyphic veil of inscrutable mysteries drawn over it, yet it was in a slumber ill-exchanged for all the sharpened realities of sense, wit, fancy, or reason. My father's life was comparatively a dream; but

1. Cf. *Hamlet* 3.4.144, 5.2.230.
2. Scottish philosopher and author of the great economic treatise *The Wealth of Nations* (1776).
3. The American Revolution, with which a number of radical Unitarian preachers were in sympathy.

4. *Julius Caesar* 2.1.230.
5. Old Testament foreshadowings of later events, or symbols of moral and theological truths. "Types": characters and events in the Old Testament believed to prefigure analogous matters in the New Testament.

it was a dream of infinity and eternity, of death, the resurrection, and a judgment to come!

No two individuals were ever more unlike than were the host and his guest. A poet was to my father a sort of nondescript: yet whatever added grace to the Unitarian cause was to him welcome. He could hardly have been more surprised or pleased if our visitor had worn wings. Indeed, his thoughts had wings; and as the silken sounds rustled round our little wainscoted parlor, my father threw back his spectacles over his forehead, his white hairs mixing with its sanguine hue; and a smile of delight beamed across his rugged cordial face, to think that Truth had found a new ally in Fancy! Besides, Coleridge seemed to take considerable notice of me, and that of itself was enough. He talked very familiarly, but agreeably, and glanced over a variety of subjects. At dinner time he grew more animated, and dilated in a very edifying manner on Mary Wollstonecraft and Mackintosh.[6] The last, he said, he considered (on my father's speaking of his *Vindiciae Gallicae* as a capital performance) as a clever scholastic[7] man—a master of the topics—or as the ready warehouseman of letters, who knew exactly where to lay his hand on what he wanted, though the goods were not his own. He thought him no match for Burke, either in style or matter. Burke was a metaphysician, Mackintosh a mere logician. Burke was an orator (almost a poet) who reasoned in figures, because he had an eye for nature: Mackintosh, on the other hand, was a rhetorician, who had only an eye to commonplaces. On this I ventured to say that I had always entertained a great opinion of Burke, and that (as far as I could find) the speaking of him with contempt might be made the test of a vulgar democratical mind. This was the first observation I ever made to Coleridge, and he said it was a very just and striking one. I remember the leg of Welsh mutton and the turnips on the table that day had the finest flavor imaginable. Coleridge added that Mackintosh and Tom Wedgwood[8] (of whom, however, he spoke highly) had expressed a very indifferent opinion of his friend Mr. Wordsworth, on which he remarked to them—"He strides on so far before you that he dwindles in the distance!" Godwin[9] had once boasted to him of having carried on an argument with Mackintosh for three hours with dubious success; Coleridge told him—"If there had been a man of genius in the room, he would have settled the question in five minutes." He asked me if I had ever seen Mary Wollstonecraft, and I said I had once for a few moments, and that she seemed to me to turn off Godwin's objections to something she advanced with quite a playful, easy air. He replied, that "this was only one instance of the ascendancy which people of imagination exercised over those of mere intellect." He did not rate Godwin very high (this was caprice or prejudice, real or affected) but he had a great idea of Mrs. Wollstonecraft's powers of conversation, none at all of her talent for book-making. We talked a little about Holcroft.[1] He had been asked if he was not much struck *with* him, and he said, he thought himself in more

---

6. Mary Wollstonecraft's *A Vindication of the Rights of Men* (1790) and the Scottish philosopher James Mackintosh's *Vindiciae Gallicae* ("Defense of France," 1791) were both written in opposition to Edmund Burke's *Reflections on the French Revolution* (1790).
7. The Scholastics, medieval philosophers and theologians, organized their thought systematically, often under various "topics"—standard headings, or "commonplaces" (see the third sentence following).
8. Son of Josiah Wedgwood (1730–1795), who founded the great pottery firm that still exists.
9. William Godwin (1756–1836), radical philosopher and didactic novelist, author of the influential *Inquiry Concerning Political Justice* (1793).
1. Thomas Holcroft (1749–1809), another radical contemporary, author of plays and novels.

danger of being struck *by* him. I complained that he would not let me get on at all, for he required a definition of even the commonest word, exclaiming, "What do you mean by a *sensation,* sir? What do you mean by an *idea*?" This, Coleridge said, was barricadoing the road to truth: it was setting up a turnpike gate at every step we took. I forget a great number of things, many more than I remember; but the day passed off pleasantly, and the next morning Mr. Coleridge was to return to Shrewsbury. When I came down to breakfast, I found that he had just received a letter from his friend, T. Wedgwood, making him an offer of £150 a year if he chose to waive his present pursuit, and devote himself entirely to the study of poetry and philosophy. Coleridge seemed to make up his mind to close with this proposal in the act of tying on one of his shoes. It threw an additional damp on his departure. It took the wayward enthusiast quite from us to cast him into Deva's winding vales,[2] or by the shores of old romance. Instead of living at ten miles' distance, of being the pastor of a Dissenting congregation at Shrewsbury, he was henceforth to inhabit the Hill of Parnassus, to be a Shepherd on the Delectable Mountains.[3] Alas! I knew not the way thither, and felt very little gratitude for Mr. Wedgwood's bounty. I was presently relieved from this dilemma; for Mr. Coleridge, asking for a pen and ink, and going to a table to write something on a bit of card, advanced towards me with undulating step, and giving me the precious document, said that that was his address, *Mr. Coleridge, Nether Stowey, Somersetshire*; and that he should be glad to see me there in a few weeks' time, and, if I chose, would come half-way to meet me. I was not less surprised than the shepherd boy (this simile is to be found in *Cassandra*[4]) when he sees a thunderbolt fall close at his feet. I stammered out my acknowledgments and acceptance of this offer (I thought Mr. Wedgwood's annunity a trifle to it) as well as I could; and this mighty business being settled, the poet-preacher took leave, and I accompanied him six miles on the road. It was a fine morning in the middle of winter, and he talked the whole way. The scholar in Chaucer is described as going

——sounding on his way.[5]

So Coleridge went on his. In digressing, in dilating, in passing from subject to subject, he appeared to me to float in air, to slide on ice. He told me in confidence (going along) that he should have preached two sermons before he accepted the situation at Shrewsbury, one on Infant Baptism, the other on the Lord's Supper, showing that he could not administer either, which would have effectually disqualified him for the object in view. I observed that he continually crossed me on the way by shifting from one side of the footpath to the other. This struck me as an odd movement; but I did not at that time connect it with any instability of purpose or involuntary change of principle, as I have done since. He seemed unable to keep on in a straight line. He spoke slightingly of Hume[6] (whose *Essay on Miracles* he said was stolen

2. Milton, *Lycidas*, line 55: "Nor yet where Deva spreads her wizard stream" ("Deva" is the river Dee, in Wales). Because Milton speaks in the passage of "Druid bards," Hazlitt means that Coleridge will devote himself to imaginative writing.
3. An allegorical locale in John Bunyan's *Pilgrim's Progress,* here used as another periphrasis for the occupation of poetry.

4. A romance by the 17th-century French writer La Calprenède.
5. *The Canterbury Tales, General Prologue,* line 309: "Souning in moral vertu was his speeche" (in Chaucer, the meaning of "souning in" is either "resounding in" or "consonant with").
6. David Hume, 18th-century Scottish philosopher.

from an objection started in one of South's sermons—*Credat Judaeus Appella!*[7]). I was not very much pleased at this account of Hume, for I had just been reading, with infinite relish, that completest of all metaphysical *choke-pears,*[8] his *Treatise on Human Nature*, to which the *Essays*, in point of scholastic subtlety and close reasoning, are mere elegant trifling, light summer reading. Coleridge even denied the excellence of Hume's general style, which I think betrayed a want of taste or candor. He however made me amends by the manner in which he spoke of Berkeley.[9] He dwelt particularly on his *Essay on Vision* as a masterpiece of analytical reasoning. So it undoubtedly is. He was exceedingly angry with Dr. Johnson for striking the stone with his foot, in allusion to this author's theory of matter and spirit, and saying, "Thus I confute him, sir."[1] Coleridge drew a parallel (I don't know how he brought about the connection) between Bishop Berkeley and Tom Paine.[2] He said the one was an instance of a subtle, the other of an acute mind, than which no two things could be more distinct. The one was a shopboy's quality, the other the characteristic of a philosopher. He considered Bishop Butler[3] as a true philosopher, a profound and conscientious thinker, a genuine reader of nature and of his own mind. He did not speak of his *Analogy*, but of his *Sermons at the Rolls' Chapel*, of which I had never heard. Coleridge somehow always contrived to prefer the *unknown* to the *known*. In this instance he was right. The *Analogy* is a tissue of sophistry, of wiredrawn, theological special-pleading; the *Sermons* (with the Preface to them) are in a fine vein of deep, matured reflection, a candid appeal to our observation of human nature, without pedantry and without bias. I told Coleridge I had written a few remarks, and was sometimes foolish enough to believe that I had made a discovery on the same subject (the *Natural Disinterestedness of the Human Mind*)[4]—and I tried to explain my view of it to Coleridge, who listened with great willingness, but I did not succeed in making myself understood. I sat down to the task shortly afterwards for the twentieth time, got new pens and paper, determined to make clear work of it, wrote a few meager sentences in the skeleton-style of a mathematical demonstration, stopped halfway down the second page; and, after trying in vain to pump up any words, images, notions, apprehensions, facts, or observations, from that gulf of abstraction in which I had plunged myself for four or five years preceding, gave up the attempt as labor in vain, and shed tears of helpless despondency on the blank unfinished paper. I can write fast enough now. Am I better than I was then? Oh no! One truth discovered, one pang of regret at not being able to express it, is better than all the fluency and flippancy in the world. Would that I could go back to what I then was! Why can we not revive past times as we can revisit old places? If I had the quaint Muse of Sir Philip Sidney to assist me, I would write a *Sonnet to the Road between Wem and Shrewsbury*, and immortalize every step of it by some fond

7. From Horace's *Satires* 1.5.100: "Let Appella the Jew believe it" (Latin); implying that he himself does not. Robert South (1634–1716), Anglican divine.
8. A very sour variety of pear; hence, anything hard to take in.
9. Bishop George Berkeley, 18th-century Irish idealist philosopher and author of an *Essay toward a New Theory of Vision* (1709).
1. The anecdote is in James Boswell's *The Life of*

Samuel Johnson.
2. Philosophical supporter of the American and French Revolutions and author of *Common Sense* and *The Rights of Man.*
3. Joseph Butler, 18th-century theologian and moral philosopher, author of the *Analogy of Religion* (1736).
4. Published as *An Essay on the Principles of Human Action* (1805).

enigmatical conceit. I would swear that the very milestones had ears, and that Harmer Hill stooped with all its pines, to listen to a poet, as he passed! I remember but one other topic of discourse in this walk. He mentioned Paley,[5] praised the naturalness and clearness of his style, but condemned his sentiments, thought him a mere time-serving casuist, and said that "the fact of his work on Moral and Political Philosophy being made a textbook in our universities was a disgrace to the national character." We parted at the six-mile stone; and I returned homeward pensive but much pleased. I had met with unexpected notice from a person whom I believed to have been prejudiced against me. "Kind and affable to me had been his condescension, and should be honored ever with suitable regard."[6] He was the first poet I had known, and he certainly answered to that inspired name. I had heard a great deal of his powers of conversation, and was not disappointed. In fact, I never met with anything at all like them, either before or since. I could easily credit the accounts which were circulated of his holding forth to a large party of ladies and gentlemen, an evening or two before, on the Berkeleian Theory, when he made the whole material universe look like a transparency of fine words; and another story (which I believe he has somewhere told himself)[7] of his being asked to a party at Birmingham, of his smoking tobacco and going to sleep after dinner on a sofa, where the company found him, to their no small surprise, which was increased to wonder when he started up of a sudden, and rubbing his eyes, looked about him, and launched into a three hours' description of the third heaven, of which he had had a dream, very different from Mr. Southey's *Vision of Judgment*, and also from that other *Vision of Judgment,* which Mr. Murray, the secretary of the Bridge Street Junto,[8] has taken into his especial keeping!

On my way back, I had a sound in my ears, it was the voice of Fancy: I had a light before me, it was the face of Poetry. The one still lingers there, the other has not quitted my side! Coleridge in truth met me half-way on the ground of philosophy, or I should not have been won over to his imaginative creed. I had an uneasy, pleasurable sensation all the time, till I was to visit him. During those months the chill breath of winter gave me a welcoming; the vernal air was balm and inspiration to me. The golden sunsets, the silver star of evening, lighted me on my way to new hopes and prospects. *I was to visit Coleridge in the spring.* This circumstance was never absent from my thoughts, and mingled with all my feelings. I wrote to him at the time proposed, and received an answer postponing my intended visit for a week or two, but very cordially urging me to complete my promise then. This delay did not damp, but rather increased my ardor. In the meantime, I went to Llangollen Vale,[9] by way of initiating myself in the mysteries of natural scenery; and I must say I was enchanted with it. I had been reading Coleridge's description of England in his fine *Ode on the Departing Year,* and I

5. William Paley, author of *Evidences of Christianity* (1794) and supporter of a utilitarian theology and morality.
6. Paraphrasing Adam's words about the angel Raphael in *Paradise Lost* 8.648–50.
7. See Coleridge's *Biographia Literaria,* chap. 10.
8. Robert Southey's *A Vision of Judgment* is a sycophantic memorial poem describing the entrance into heaven of George III. Charles Murray was

solicitor to an association, located at New Bridge Street, for "Opposing Disloyal and Seditious Principles." He prosecuted John Hunt for publishing Byron's *The Vision of Judgment,* a brilliant parody of Southey's poem. Hazlitt derisively refers to the association as a "junto," i.e., a group formed for political intrigue.
9. In north Wales (about thirty-five miles from Wem).

applied it, *con amore*,[1] to the objects before me. That valley was to me (in a manner) the cradle of a new existence: in the river that winds through it, my spirit was baptized in the waters of Helicon![2]

I returned home, and soon after set out on my journey with unworn heart and untired feet. My way lay through Worcester and Gloucester, and by Upton, where I thought of Tom Jones and the adventure of the muff.[3] I remember getting completely wet through one day, and stopping at an inn (I think it was at Tewkesbury) where I sat up all night to read *Paul and Virginia*.[4] Sweet were the showers in early youth that drenched my body, and sweet the drops of pity that fell upon the books I read! I recollect a remark of Coleridge's upon this very book that nothing could show the gross indelicacy of French manners and the entire corruption of their imagination more strongly than the behavior of the heroine in the last fatal scene, who turns away from a person on board the sinking vessel, that offers to save her life, because he has thrown off his clothes to assist him in swimming. Was this a time to think of such a circumstance? I once hinted to Wordsworth, as we were sailing in his boat on Grasmere lake, that I thought he had borrowed the idea of his *Poems on the Naming of Places* from the local inscriptions of the same kind in *Paul and Virginia*. He did not own the obligation, and stated some distinction without a difference in defense to his claim to originality. Any the slightest variation would be sufficient for this purpose in his mind; for whatever he added or omitted would inevitably be worth all that any one else had done, and contain the marrow of the sentiment. I was still two days before the time fixed for my arrival, for I had taken care to set out early enough. I stopped these two days at Bridgewater, and when I was tired of sauntering on the banks of its muddy river, returned to the inn and read *Camilla*.[5] So have I loitered my life away, reading books, looking at pictures, going to plays, hearing, thinking, writing on what pleased me best. I have wanted only one thing to make me happy; but wanting that, have wanted everything![6]

I arrived, and was well received. The country about Nether Stowey is beautiful, green and hilly, and near the seashore. I saw it but the other day, after an interval of twenty years, from a hill near Taunton. How was the map of my life spread out before me, as the map of the country lay at my feet! In the afternoon, Coleridge took me over to Alfoxden, a romantic old family mansion of the St. Aubins, where Wordsworth lived. It was then in the possession of a friend of the poet's, who gave him the free use of it.[7] Somehow, that period (the time just after the French Revolution) was not a time when *nothing was given for nothing*. The mind opened and a softness might be perceived coming over the heart of individuals, beneath "the scales that fence" our self-interest. Wordsworth himself was from home, but his sister kept house, and set before us a frugal repast; and we had free access to her brother's poems, the *Lyrical Ballads*, which were still in manuscript, or in the form of *Sybilline Leaves*.[8] I dipped into a few of these with great satisfaction, and with the faith of a novice. I slept that night in an old room with

1. "With love," fervently (Italian).
2. A mountain sacred to Apollo and the Muses.
3. Henry Fielding's *Tom Jones* 10.5ff.
4. A sentimental love idyll (1788) by the French writer Bernardin de Saint-Pierre.
5. A novel by Fanny Burney, published in 1796.

6. The love of Sarah Walker, the daughter of Hazlitt's landlord. He describes his infatuation with her in *Liber Amoris* (1823).
7. A mistake; Wordsworth paid rent.
8. I.e., "prophetic writings"; used by Coleridge as the title for his published poems in 1817.

blue hangings, and covered with the round-faced family portraits of the age of George I and II and from the wooded declivity of the adjoining park that overlooked my window, at the dawn of day, could

———hear the loud stag speak.[9]

In the outset of life (and particularly at this time I felt it so) our imagination has a body to it. We are in a state between sleeping and waking, and have indistinct but glorious glimpses of strange shapes, and there is always something to come better than what we see. As in our dreams the fullness of the blood gives warmth and reality to the coinage of the brain, so in youth our ideas are clothed, and fed, and pampered with our good spirits; we breathe thick with thoughtless happiness, the weight of future years presses on the strong pulses of the heart, and we repose with undisturbed faith in truth and good. As we advance, we exhaust our fund of enjoyment and of hope. We are no longer wrapped in *lamb's wool*, lulled in Elysium. As we taste the pleasures of life, their spirit evaporates, the sense palls; and nothing is left but the phantoms, the lifeless shadows of what *has been*!

That morning, as soon as breakfast was over, we strolled out into the park, and seating ourselves on the trunk of an old ash tree that stretched along the ground, Coleridge read aloud with a sonorous and musical voice, the ballad of *Betty Foy*.[1] I was not critically or skeptically inclined. I saw touches of truth and nature, and took the rest for granted. But in the *Thorn*, the *Mad Mother*, and the *Complaint of a Poor Indian Woman*, I felt that deeper power and pathos which have been since acknowledged,

In spite of pride, in erring reason's spite,[2]

as the characteristics of this author; and the sense of a new style and a new spirit in poetry came over me. It had to me something of the effect that arises from the turning up of the fresh soil, or of the first welcome breath of spring,

While yet the trembling year is unconfirmed.[3]

Coleridge and myself walked back to Stowey that evening, and his voice sounded high

Of Providence, foreknowledge, will, and fate,
Fixed fate, free will, foreknowledge absolute,[4]

as we passed through echoing grove, by fairy stream or waterfall, gleaming in the summer moonlight! He lamented that Wordsworth was not prone enough to believe in the traditional superstitions of the place, and that there was a something corporeal, a *matter-of-fact-ness*, a clinging to the palpable, or often to the petty, in his poetry, in consequence. His genius was not a spirit that descended to him through the air; it sprung out of the ground like a flower, or unfolded itself from a green spray, on which the goldfinch sang. He said, however (if I remember right), that this objection must be confined to his descriptive pieces, that his philosophic poetry had a grand and comprehensive spirit in it, so that his soul seemed to inhabit the universe like a

9. Ben Jonson's poem *To Sir Robert Wroth*, line 22.
1. Wordsworth's *Idiot Boy*. Like the other poems mentioned, it was included in *Lyrical Ballads*.

2. Pope's *Essay on Man* 1.293.
3. James Thomson's *The Seasons: Spring*, line 18.
4. *Paradise Lost* 2.559–60.

palace, and to discover truth by intuition, rather than by deduction. The next day Wordsworth arrived from Bristol at Coleridge's cottage. I think I see him now. He answered in some degree to his friend's description of him, but was more gaunt and Don Quixote-like. He was quaintly dressed (according to the *costume* of that unconstrained period) in a brown fustian[5] jacket and striped pantaloons. There was something of a roll, a lounge in his gait, not unlike his own Peter Bell.[6] There was a severe, worn pressure of thought about his temples, a fire in his eye (as if he saw something in objects more than the outward appearance), an intense high narrow forehead, a Roman nose, cheeks furrowed by strong purpose and feeling, and a convulsive inclination to laughter about the mouth, a good deal at variance with the solemn, stately expression of the rest of his face. Chantry's bust wants the marking traits; but he was teased into making it regular and heavy; Haydon's[7] head of him, introduced into the *Entrance of Christ into Jerusalem,* is the most like his drooping weight of thought and expression. He sat down and talked very naturally and freely, with a mixture of clear gushing accents in his voice, a deep guttural intonation, and a strong tincture of the northern *burr,* like the crust on wine. He instantly began to make havoc of the half of a Cheshire cheese on the table, and said triumphantly that "his marriage with experience had not been so unproductive as Mr. Southey's in teaching him a knowledge of the good things of this life." He had been to see the *Castle Spectre* by Monk Lewis,[8] while at Bristol, and described it very well. He said "it fitted the taste of the audience like a glove." This *ad captandum*[9] merit was, however, by no means a recommendation of it, according to the severe principles of the new school, which reject rather than court popular effect. Wordsworth, looking out of the low, latticed window, said, "How beautifully the sun sets on that yellow bank!" I thought within myself, "With what eyes these poets see nature!" and ever after, when I saw the sunset stream upon the objects facing it, conceived I had made a discovery, or thanked Mr. Wordsworth for having made one for me! We went over to Alfoxden again the day following, and Wordsworth read us the story of *Peter Bell* in the open air; and the comment made upon it by his face and voice was very different from that of some later critics! Whatever might be thought of the poem, "his face was as a book where men might read strange matters,"[1] and he announced the fate of his hero in prophetic tones. There is a *chaunt* in the recitation both of Coleridge and Wordsworth, which acts as a spell upon the hearer, and disarms the judgment. Perhaps they have deceived themselves by making habitual use of this ambiguous accompaniment. Coleridge's manner is more full, animated, and varied; Wordsworth's more equable, sustained, and internal. The one might be termed more *dramatic,* the other more *lyrical.* Coleridge has told me that he himself liked to compose in walking over uneven ground, or breaking through the straggling branches of a copse wood; whereas Wordsworth always wrote (if he could) walking up and down a straight gravel walk, or in some spot where the continuity of his verse met with no collateral interruption. Returning that same evening, I got

5. A coarse and heavy cotton cloth.
6. The protagonist in Wordsworth's poem *Peter Bell.*
7. Benjamin Robert Haydon, painter of grandiose historical and religious pictures. Sir Francis Chantrey, a sculptor.

8. Matthew Gregory Lewis, called "Monk" Lewis from his horror tale *The Monk* (1795). *The Castle Spectre* was a play, also in the Gothic terror-mode.
9. "For the sake of captivating" an audience.
1. See *Macbeth* 1.5.60–61.

into a metaphysical argument with Wordsworth, while Coleridge was explaining the different notes of the nightingale to his sister, in which we neither of us succeeded in making ourselves perfectly clear and intelligible. Thus I passed three weeks at Nether Stowey and in the neighborhood, generally devoting the afternoons to a delightful chat in an arbor made of bark by the poet's friend Tom Poole, sitting under two fine elm trees, and listening to the bees humming round us while we quaffed our flip.[2] It was agreed, among other things, that we should make a jaunt down the Bristol Channel, as far as Linton. We set off together on foot, Coleridge, John Chester, and I. This Chester was a native of Nether Stowey, one of those who were attracted to Coleridge's discourse as flies are to honey, or bees in swarming-time to the sound of a brass pan. He "followed in the chase like a dog who hunts, not like one that made up the cry."[3] He had on a brown cloth coat, boots, and corduroy breeches, was low in stature, bowlegged, had a drag in his walk like a drover, which he assisted by a hazel switch, and kept on a sort of trot by the side of Coleridge, like a running footman by a state coach, that he might not lose a syllable or sound that fell from Coleridge's lips. He told me his private opinion, that Coleridge was a wonderful man. He scarcely opened his lips, much less offered an opinion the whole way: yet of the three, had I to choose during that journey, I would be John Chester. He afterwards followed Coleridge into Germany, where the Kantean philosophers were puzzled how to bring him under any of their categories. When he sat down at table with his idol, John's felicity was complete; Sir Walter Scott's, or Mr. Blackwood's, when they sat down at the same table with the King,[4] was not more so. We passed Dunster on our right, a small town between the brow of a hill and the sea. I remember eying it wistfully as it lay below us: contrasted with the woody scene around, it looked as clear, as pure, as *embrowned* and ideal as any landscape I have seen since, of Gaspar Poussin's or Domenichino's. We had a long day's march—(our feet kept time to the echoes of Coleridge's tongue)—through Minehead and by the Blue Anchor, and on to Linton, which we did not reach till near midnight, and where we had some difficulty in making a lodgment. We however knocked the people of the house up at last, and we were repaid for our apprehensions and fatigue by some excellent rashers of fried bacon and eggs. The view in coming along had been splendid. We walked for miles and miles on dark brown heaths overlooking the channel, with the Welsh hills beyond, and at times descended into little sheltered valleys close by the seaside, with a smuggler's face scowling by us, and then had to ascend conical hills with a path winding up through a coppice to a barren top, like a monk's shaven crown, from one of which I pointed out to Coleridge's notice the bare masts of a vessel on the very edge of the horizon and within the red-orbed disk of the setting sun, like his own specter-ship in the *Ancient Mariner*. At Linton the character of the seacoast becomes more marked and rugged. There is a place called the Valley of Rocks (I suspect this was only the poetical name for it) bedded among precipices overhanging the sea, with rocky caverns beneath, into which the waves dash, and where the seagull forever wheels its screaming flight. On the tops of these are huge stones thrown transverse, as if an earth-

2. Spiced and sweetened ale.
3. See *Othello* 2.3.337–38.
4. At a banquet given to George IV at Edinburgh, in 1822. William Blackwood, publisher of *Blackwood's Magazine,* was, like Scott, a Tory and hence a supporter of the king.

quake had tossed them there, and behind these is a fretwork of perpendicular rocks, something like the Giant's Causeway.[5] A thunderstorm came on while we were at the inn, and Coleridge was running out bareheaded to enjoy the commotion of the elements in the Valley of Rocks, but as if in spite, the clouds only muttered a few angry sounds, and let fall a few refreshing drops. Coleridge told me that he and Wordsworth were to have made this place the scene of a prose tale, which was to have been in the manner of, but far superior to, the *Death of Abel*,[6] but they had relinquished the design. In the morning of the second day, we breakfasted luxuriously in an old-fashioned parlor, on tea, toast, eggs, and honey, in the very sight of the beehives from which it had been taken, and a garden full of thyme and wild flowers that had produced it. On this occasion Coleridge spoke of Virgil's *Georgics,* but not well. I do not think he had much feeling for the classical or elegant. It was in this room that we found a little worn-out copy of the *Seasons,*[7] lying in a window seat, on which Coleridge exclaimed, "*That* is true fame!" He said Thomson was a great poet, rather than a good one; his style was as meretricious as his thoughts were natural. He spoke of Cowper as the best modern poet. He said the *Lyrical Ballads* were an experiment about to be tried by him and Wordsworth, to see how far the public taste would endure poetry written in a more natural and simple style than had hitherto been attempted; totally discarding the artifices of poetical diction, and making use only of such words as had probably been common in the most ordinary language since the days of Henry II. Some comparison was introduced between Shakespeare and Milton. He said "he hardly knew which to prefer. Shakespeare appeared to him a mere stripling in the art; he was as tall and as strong, with infinitely more activity than Milton, but he never appeared to have come to man's estate; or if he had, he would not have been a man, but a monster." He spoke with contempt of Gray, and with intolerance of Pope. He did not like the versification of the latter. He observed that "the ears of these couplet-writers might be charged with having short memories, that could not retain the harmony of whole passages." He thought little of Junius[8] as a writer; he had a dislike of Dr. Johnson; and a much higher opinion of Burke as an orator and politician, than of Fox or Pitt. He however thought him very inferior in richness of style and imagery to some of our elder prose writers, particularly Jeremy Taylor.[9] He liked Richardson, but not Fielding; nor could I get him to enter into the merits of *Caleb Williams.*[1] In short, he was profound and discriminating with respect to those authors whom he liked, and where he gave his judgment fair play; capricious, perverse, and prejudiced in his antipathies and distastes. We loitered on the "ribbed seasands,"[2] in such talk as this, a whole morning, and I recollect met with a curious seaweed, of which John Chester told us the country name! A fisherman gave Coleridge an account of a boy that had been drowned the day before, and that they had tried to save him at the risk of their own lives. He

5. A mass of rocks on the northern Irish coast.
6. The "prose tale" exists as a fragment, *The Wanderings of Cain. The Death of Abel* (1758) is by the once celebrated Swiss poet, Salomon Gessner.
7. By James Thomson, published in 1726–30.
8. The pseudonym of the author (whose identity is still uncertain) of a series of attacks on George III and various politicians, 1769–72.

9. The 17th-century divine, author of *Holy Living* (1650) and *Holy Dying* (1651).
1. A 1794 novel by William Godwin. Samuel Richardson and Henry Fielding, the great 18th-century novelists.
2. Echoing *The Rime of the Ancient Mariner*, line 227.

said "he did not know how it was that they ventured, but, sir, we have a *nature* towards one another." This expression, Coleridge remarked to me, was a fine illustration of that theory of disinterestedness which I (in common with Butler) had adopted. I broached to him an argument of mine to prove that *likeness* was not mere association of ideas. I said that the mark in the sand put one in mind of a man's foot, not because it was part of a former impression of a man's foot (for it was quite new) but because it was like the shape of a man's foot. He assented to the justness of this distinction (which I have explained at length elsewhere, for the benefit of the curious) and John Chester listened; not from any interest in the subject, but because he was astonished that I should be able to suggest anything to Coleridge that he did not already know. We returned on the third morning, and Coleridge remarked the silent cottage-smoke curling up the valleys where, a few evenings before, we had seen the lights gleaming through the dark.

In a day or two after we arrived at Stowey, we set out, I on my return home, and he for Germany. It was a Sunday morning, and he was to preach that day for Dr. Toulmin of Taunton. I asked him if he had prepared anything for the occasion? He said he had not even thought of the text, but should as soon as we parted. I did not go to hear him—this was a fault—but we met in the evening at Bridgewater. The next day we had a long day's walk to Bristol, and sat down, I recollect, by a well-side on the road, to cool ourselves and satisfy our thirst, when Coleridge repeated to me some descriptive lines from his tragedy of *Remorse;* which I must say became his mouth and that occasion better than they, some years after, did Mr. Elliston's[3] and the Drury Lane boards,

> Oh memory! shield me from the world's poor strife,
> And give those scenes thine everlasting life.

I saw no more of him for a year or two, during which period he had been wandering in the Hartz Forest in Germany; and his return was cometary, meteorous, unlike his setting out. It was not till some time after that I knew his friends Lamb and Southey. The last always appears to me (as I first saw him) with a commonplace-book under his arm, and the first with a bon mot in his mouth. It was at Godwin's that I met him with Holcroft and Coleridge, where they were disputing fiercely which was the best—*Man as he was, or man as he is to be.* "Give me," says Lamb, "man as he is *not* to be." This saying was the beginning of a friendship between us, which I believe still continues.—Enough of this for the present.

> But there is matter for another rhyme,
> And I to this may add a second tale.[4]

1823

---

3. Robert William Elliston, a well-known actor. Coleridge's *Remorse* was produced at Drury Lane in 1813.

4. Wordsworth, *Hart-Leap Well*, lines 95–96.

THOMAS MOORE
1779–1852

Although he was an Irish Catholic and the son of a Dublin grocer, Tom Moore became the fashionable versifier of Regency England. His *Irish Melodies,* published between 1807 and 1834 with accompanying music (some of the tunes by Moore himself), were an immense success, and for many years his wit, charm, liberalism, and singing voice made him a brilliant figure in literary and social circles, especially among the aristocratic Whig reformers. The same qualities made him one of Byron's closest friends. He wrote numerous satires, lampoons, and prose pieces. He is chiefly remembered, however, for the Oriental verse romance *Lalla Rookh* (1817), which achieved a great European success; his fine *Life of Byron* (1830); and for a handful of songs— most of them in the tradition of amatory gallantry that goes back to the seventeenth-century Cavaliers—that have won their way into the repertory that is sung around the piano on a social evening.

Believe me, if all those endearing young charms

Believe me, if all those endearing young charms,
    Which I gaze on so fondly today,
Were to change by tomorrow, and fleet in my arms,
    Like fairy-gifts fading away,
5 Thou wouldst still be adored, as this moment thou art,
    Let thy loveliness fade as it will,
And around the dear ruin each wish of my heart
    Would entwine itself verdantly still.

It is not while beauty and youth are thine own,
10   And thy cheeks unprofaned by a tear
That the fervor and faith of a soul can be known,
    To which time will but make thee more dear;
No, the heart that has truly loved never forgets,
    But as truly loves on to the close,
15 As the sunflower turns on her god, when he sets,
    The same look which she turned when he rose.

1808

The harp that once through Tara's halls[1]

The harp that once through Tara's halls
    The soul of music shed,
Now hangs as mute on Tara's walls
    As if that soul were fled.—
5 So sleeps the pride of former days,
    So glory's thrill is o'er,

1. Tara, northwest of Dublin, was the capital of Ireland during the early Middle Ages, when that country was a center of European civilization and learning.

And hearts that once beat high for praise
   Now feel that pulse no more.

No more to chiefs and ladies bright
10   The harp of Tara swells;
The chord alone that breaks at night
   Its tale of ruin tells.
Thus Freedom now so seldom wakes,
   The only throb she gives,
15 Is when some heart indignant breaks,
   To show that still she lives.

                          1834

The time I've lost in wooing

The time I've lost in wooing,
In watching and pursuing
   The light that lies
   In woman's eyes,
5 Has been my heart's undoing.
Though Wisdom oft has sought me,
I scorned the lore she brought me,
   My only books
   Were woman's looks,
10 And folly's all they've taught me.

Her smile when Beauty granted,
I hung with gaze enchanted,
   Like him, the sprite,[1]
   Whom maids by night
15 Oft meet in glen that's haunted.
Like him, too, Beauty won me,
But while her eyes were on me;
   If once their ray
   Was turned away,
20 Oh! winds could not outrun me.

And are those follies going?
And is my proud heart growing
   Too cold or wise
   For brilliant eyes
25 Again to set it glowing?
No, vain, alas! th' endeavor
From bonds so sweet to sever;
   Poor Wisdom's chance
   Against a glance
30 Is now as weak as ever.

                          1834

---

1. The Irish fairy; he can be controlled by mortals only when their eyes are fixed on him.

THOMAS DE QUINCEY
1785–1859

De Quincey's father was a wealthy merchant who died when Thomas was seven years old. The boy was a precocious scholar, especially in Latin and Greek, and a gentle and bookish introvert; he found it difficult to adapt himself to discipline and routine and was thrown into panic by any emergency that called for decisive action. He ran away from Manchester Grammar School and, after a summer spent tramping through Wales, broke off completely from his family and guardians and went to London in the hope that he could obtain from moneylenders an advance on his prospective inheritance. There at the age of seventeen he spent a terrible winter of loneliness and destitution, befriended only by some kindly streetwalkers. These early experiences with the sinister aspect of city life later became persistent elements in his dreams of terror.

After a reconciliation with his guardians he entered Worcester College, Oxford, on an inadequate allowance. He spent the years 1803–08 in sporadic attendance, isolated as usual, then left abruptly in the middle of his examination for the A.B. with honors because he could not face the ordeal of an oral examination.

De Quincey had been an early admirer of Wordsworth and Coleridge. No sooner did he come of age and into his inheritance than, with his usual combination of generosity and improvidence, he made Coleridge an anonymous gift of £300. He became an intimate friend of the Wordsworths at Grasmere, and when they left Dove Cottage for Allan Bank, took up his own residence at Dove Cottage to be near them. For a time he lived the life of a rural scholar, but then fell in love with Margaret Simpson, the daughter of a small local landholder and farmer and, after she had borne him a son, married her in February 1817. This affair led to an estrangement from the Wordsworths and left him in severe financial difficulties. Worse still, De Quincey at this time became completely enslaved to opium. Following the medical practice of the time, he had been taking the drug for a variety of painful ailments; but now, driven by poverty and despair as well as pain, he indulged in huge quantities of laudanum (opium dissolved in alcohol) and was never thereafter able to free himself from addiction to what he called "the pleasures and pains of opium." It was during periods of maximum use, and especially in the recurrent agonies of cutting down his opium dosage, that he experienced the grotesque and terrifying reveries and nightmares that he wove into his literary fantasies.

Desperate for income, De Quincey at last turned to writing at the age of thirty-six. *Confessions of an English Opium-Eater,* which he contributed to the *London Magazine,* scored an immediate success and was at once reprinted as a book, but it earned him little money. In 1828 he moved with his three children to Edinburgh, to write for *Blackwood's Magazine.* For almost the rest of his life, he led a harried existence, beset by many physical ills, struggling with his irresolution and melancholia and the horrors of the opium habit, dodging his creditors and the constant threat of imprisonment for debt. All the while he ground out articles on any salable subject in a ceaseless struggle to keep his children, who ultimately numbered eight, from starving to death. Only after his mother died and left him a small income was he able, in his sixties, to live in comparative ease and freedom under the care of his devoted and practical-minded daughters. His last decade he spent mainly in gathering, revising, and expanding his essays for his "Collective Edition"; the final volume appeared in 1860, the year after his death.

Although De Quincey's life was disorderly and his best-known writings were sensational, he was a conventional and conservative person—a rigid moralist, a Tory, and a faithful champion of the Church of England. Everybody who knew him testified to his gentleness, his courteous and musical speech, and his exquisite manners. Less obvious, under the surface timidity and irresolution, were the toughness and courage that sustained him through a long life of seemingly hopeless struggle.

Although more than 150 of De Quincey's anonymous essays have been identified, the great bulk of them were pieces of hasty journalism that are now read only by scholars. He served for a time as an important source of knowledge for Englishmen of the literature of the late eighteenth-century German renaissance. As a literary critic De Quincey was capable of a fine essay in critical impressionism, *On the Knocking at the Gate in "Macbeth,"* but he was too whimsical and unsystematic to rank with his greater contemporaries, Coleridge and Hazlitt. He wrote a number of vivid biographical sketches of writers he knew personally, most notably Wordsworth, Coleridge, Southey, and Lamb. His most distinctive and impressive achievements, however, are the writings that start with fact and move into macabre fantasy (*On Murder Considered as One of the Fine Arts*) and especially those that begin as quiet autobiography and develop into an elaborate construction made up from the materials of his reveries and dreams (*Confessions of an English Opium-Eater, Autobiographic Sketches, Suspiria de Profundis,* and *The English Mail Coach*). In these achievements, De Quincey opened up to English literature the nightside of human consciousness, with its grotesque strangeness, its *Angst* (anxiety), and its pervasive sense of guilt and alienation. "In dreams," he wrote, long before Sigmund Freud, "perhaps under some secret conflict of the midnight sleeper, lighted up to the consciousness at the time, but darkened to the memory as soon as all is finished, each several child of our mysterious race completes for himself the treason of the aboriginal fall." And for these dream writings he developed a mode of organization that is based on thematic statement, variation, and development in the art of music, in which he had a deep and abiding interest. Although by temperament a conservative, De Quincey was in his writings a radical innovator, whose experiments look ahead to the materials and methods of such later masters in prose and verse as James Joyce, Franz Kafka, and T. S. Eliot.

From Confessions of an English Opium-Eater[1]

From *Preliminary Confessions*[2]

[THE PROSTITUTE ANN]

* * * Another person there was at that time, whom I have since sought to trace with far deeper earnestness, and with far deeper sorrow at my failure.

---

1. The *Confessions* were published anonymously in two issues of the *London Magazine,* September and October 1821, and were reprinted as a book in the following year. In 1856 De Quincey revised the book for the collected edition of his writings, expanding it to more than twice its original length. The author was over seventy years old at the time and privately expressed the judgment that the expanded edition lacks the immediacy and artistic economy of the original. The selections here are from the version of the *Confessions* printed in 1822.

The work is divided into three parts. The first part, "Preliminary Confessions," deals with De Quincey's early experiences—at school, in Wales, and in London—before taking opium. Part Two, "The Pleasures of Opium" (omitted here), describes the early effects on his perceptions and reveries of his moderate and occasional indulgence in the drug. Part Three, "The Pains of Opium," is an elaborate and artful representation of his fantastic nightmares; these, in modern medical opinion, are in part withdrawal symptoms, during periods when he tried to cut down his use of opium.

In De Quincey's own lifetime, and ever since, the charge has been brought that the reports of these dreams were largely fabricated by the author. But De Quincey himself always insisted that they were substantially accurate; and both the fact and the content of such anguished nightmares are corroborated by the testimony of another laudanum addict, Samuel Taylor Coleridge, in his poem *The Pains of Sleep* (1803).

2. The seventeen-year-old De Quincey, unhappy at Manchester Grammar School, had run away and taken refuge in London, his whereabouts unknown to his mother and his guardians. He had slept outdoors for two months but has now been permitted, by a disreputable and seedy lawyer, to sleep in an unoccupied, unfurnished, and rat-infested house. There he and a ten-year-old girl, nameless and of uncertain parentage, huddle together for warmth, eking out a famished existence on whatever scraps he can scavenge from his landlord's frugal breakfast. He goes on to describe his friendship with a young prostitute, Ann.

This person was a young woman, and one of that unhappy class who subsist upon the wages of prostitution. I feel no shame, nor have any reason to feel it, in avowing, that I was then on familiar and friendly terms with many women in that unfortunate condition. The reader needs neither smile at this avowal, nor frown. For, not to remind my classical readers of the old Latin proverb—"*Sine Cerere,*" &c.,[3] it may well be supposed that in the existing state of my purse, my connection with such women could not have been an impure one. But the truth is, that at no time of my life have I been a person to hold myself polluted by the touch or approach of any creature that wore a human shape: on the contrary, from my very earliest youth it has been my pride to converse familiarly, *more Socratico,*[4] with all human beings, man, woman, and child, that chance might fling in my way: a practice which is friendly to the knowledge of human nature, to good feelings, and to that frankness of address which becomes a man who would be thought a philosopher. For a philosopher should not see with the eyes of the poor limitary[5] creature, calling himself a man of the world, and filled with narrow and self-regarding prejudices of birth and education, but should look upon himself as a Catholic[6] creature, and as standing in an equal relation to high and low—to educated and uneducated, to the guilty and the innocent. Being myself at that time of necessity a peripatetic, or a walker of the street, I naturally fell in more frequently with those female peripatetics who are technically called street-walkers. Many of these women had occasionally taken my part against watchmen who wished to drive me off the steps of houses where I was sitting. But one amongst them, the one on whose account I have at all introduced this subject—yet no! let me not class thee, oh noble-minded Ann——, with that order of women; let me find, if it be possible, some gentler name to designate the condition of her to whose bounty and compassion, ministering to my necessities when all the world had forsaken me, I owe it that I am at this time alive.—For many weeks I had walked at nights with this poor friendless girl up and down Oxford Street, or had rested with her on steps and under the shelter of porticos. She could not be so old as myself: she told me, indeed, that she had not completed her sixteenth year. By such questions as my interest about her prompted, I had gradually drawn forth her simple history. Hers was a case of ordinary occurrence (as I have since had reason to think), and one in which, if London beneficence had better adapted its arrangements to meet it, the power of the law might oftener be interposed to protect, and to avenge. But the stream of London charity flows in a channel which, though deep and mighty, is yet noiseless and underground; not obvious or readily accessible to poor houseless wanderers; and it cannot be denied that the outside air and framework of London society is harsh, cruel, and repulsive. In any case, however, I saw that part of her injuries might easily have been redressed; and I urged her often and earnestly to lay her complaint before a magistrate: friendless as she was, I assured her that she would meet with immediate attention; and that English justice, which was no respecter of persons, would speedily and amply avenge her on the brutal ruffian who had plundered her little property. She promised me often that she would; but she delayed taking the steps I pointed out from

---

3. *Sine Cerere et Baccho friget Venus*—"without Ceres and Bacchus [food and wine], love grows cold."
4. "In the manner of Socrates"; i.e., by a dialogue of questions and answers.
5. Limited.
6. In the sense of "inclusive in tastes and understanding."

time to time: for she was timid and dejected to a degree which showed how deeply sorrow had taken hold of her young heart: and perhaps she thought justly that the most upright judge, and the most righteous tribunals, could do nothing to repair her heaviest wrongs. Something, however, would perhaps have been done: for it had been settled between us at length, but unhappily on the very last time but one that I was ever to see her, that in a day or two we should go together before a magistrate, and that I should speak on her behalf. This little service it was destined, however, that I should never realize. Meantime, that which she rendered to me, and which was greater than I could ever have repaid her, was this:—One night, when we were pacing slowly along Oxford Street, and after a day when I had felt more than usually ill and faint, I requested her to turn off with me into Soho Square: thither we went; and we sat down on the steps of a house, which, to this hour, I never pass without a pang of grief, and an inner act of homage to the spirit of that unhappy girl, in memory of the noble action which she there performed. Suddenly, as we sat, I grew much worse: I had been leaning my head against her bosom; and all at once I sank from her arms and fell backwards on the steps. From the sensations I then had, I felt an inner conviction of the liveliest kind that without some powerful and reviving stimulus, I should either have died on the spot—or should at least have sunk to a point of exhaustion from which all re-ascent under my friendless circumstances would soon have become hopeless. Then it was, at this crisis of my fate, that my poor orphan companion—who had herself met with little but injuries in this world—stretched out a saving hand to me. Uttering a cry of terror, but without a moment's delay, she ran off into Oxford Street, and in less time than could be imagined, returned to me with a glass of port wine and spices, that acted upon my empty stomach (which at that time would have rejected all solid food) with an instantaneous power of restoration: and for this glass the generous girl without a murmur paid out of her own humble purse at a time—be it remembered!—when she had scarcely wherewithal to purchase the bare necessaries of life, and when she could have no reason to expect that I should ever be able to reimburse her.——Oh! youthful benefactress! how often in succeeding years, standing in solitary places, and thinking of thee with grief of heart and perfect love, how often have I wished that, as in ancient times the curse of a father was believed to have a supernatural power, and to pursue its object with a fatal necessity of self-fulfillment—even so the benediction of a heart oppressed with gratitude, might have a like prerogative; might have power given to it from above to chase—to haunt—to waylay[7]—to overtake—to pursue thee into the central darkness of a London brothel, or (if it were possible) into the darkness of the grave—there to awaken thee with an authentic message of peace and forgiveness, and of final reconciliation!

I do not often weep: for not only do my thoughts on subjects connected with the chief interests of man daily, nay hourly, descend a thousand fathoms "too deep for tears";[8] not only does the sternness of my habits of thought present an antagonism to the feelings which prompt tears—wanting of necessity to those who, being protected usually by their levity from any ten-

---

7. From Wordsworth's *She was a phantom of delight*, line 10: "To haunt, to startle, and way-lay." De Quincey was an early and enthusiastic admirer of Wordsworth's poetry.
8. From the last line of Wordsworth's *Ode: Intimations of Immortality*.

dency to meditative sorrow, would by that same levity be made incapable of resisting it on any casual access of such feelings:—but also, I believe that all minds which have contemplated such objects as deeply as I have done, must, for their own protection from utter despondency, have early encouraged and cherished some tranquilizing belief as to the future balances and the hieroglyphic meanings of human sufferings. On these accounts, I am cheerful to this hour; and, as I have said, I do not often weep. Yet some feelings, though not deeper or more passionate, are more tender than others; and often, when I walk at this time in Oxford Street by dreamy lamplight, and hear those airs played on a barrel-organ which years ago solaced me and my dear companion (as I must always call her), I shed tears, and muse with myself at the mysterious dispensation which so suddenly and so critically separated us for ever.[9] * * *

From *Introduction to the Pains of Opium*[1]

[THE MALAY]

* * * I remember, about this time, a little incident, which I mention, because, trifling as it was, the reader will soon meet it again in my dreams, which it influenced more fearfully than could be imagined. One day a Malay knocked at my door. What business a Malay could have to transact amongst English mountains, I cannot conjecture: but possibly he was on his road to a seaport about forty miles distant.

The servant who opened the door to him was a young girl born and bred amongst the mountains,[2] who had never seen an Asiatic dress of any sort: his turban, therefore, confounded her not a little: and, as it turned out that his attainments in English were exactly of the same extent as hers in the Malay, there seemed to be an impassable gulf fixed between all communication of ideas, if either party had happened to possess any. In this dilemma, the girl, recollecting the reputed learning of her master (and, doubtless, giving me credit for a knowledge of all the languages of the earth, besides, perhaps, a few of the lunar ones), came and gave me to understand that there was a sort of demon below, whom she clearly imagined that my art could exorcise from the house. I did not immediately go down: but, when I did, the group which presented itself, arranged as it was by accident, though not very elaborate, took hold of my fancy and my eye in a way that none of the statuesque attitudes exhibited in the ballets at the Opera House, though so ostentatiously complex, had ever done. In a cottage kitchen, but paneled on the wall with dark wood that from age and rubbing resembled oak, and looking more like a rustic hall of entrance than a kitchen, stood the Malay— his turban and loose trousers of dingy white relieved upon the dark paneling: he had placed himself nearer to the girl than she seemed to relish; though

9. De Quincey goes on to narrate that, having been given some money by a family friend who recognized him in the street, he had traveled to Eton to ask a young nobleman whom he knew to stand security for a loan that De Quincey was soliciting from a money-lender. When he returned to London three days later, Ann had disappeared.
1. It is 1816. De Quincy is living at Dove Cottage, Grasmere, and for three years has been addicted

to laudanum, i.e., opium dissolved in alcohol. At this time, he has succeeded in reducing his daily dosage from eight thousand to one thousand drops, with a consequent improvement in health and energy.
2. The lovely Barbara Lewthwaite, whom Wordsworth had described as a "child of beauty rare" in his poem *The Pet Lamb*.

her native spirit of mountain intrepidity contended with the feeling of simple awe which her countenance expressed as she gazed upon the tiger-cat before her. And a more striking picture there could not be imagined, than the beautiful English face of the girl, and its exquisite fairness, together with her erect and independent attitude, contrasted with the sallow and bilious skin of the Malay, enameled or veneered with mahogany, by marine air, his small, fierce, restless eyes, thin lips, slavish gestures and adorations. Half-hidden by the ferocious-looking Malay, was a little child from a neighboring cottage who had crept in after him, and was now in the act of reverting its head, and gazing upwards at the turban and the fiery eyes beneath it, whilst with one hand he caught at the dress of the young woman for protection. My knowledge of the Oriental tongues is not remarkably extensive, being indeed confined to two words—the Arabic word for barley, and the Turkish for opium (madjoon), which I have learnt from Anastasius.[3] And, as I had neither a Malay dictionary, nor even Adelung's *Mithridates*,[4] which might have helped me to a few words, I addressed him in some lines from the Iliad; considering that, of such languages as I possessed, Greek, in point of longitude, came geographically nearest to an Oriental one. He worshiped[5] me in a most devout manner, and replied in what I suppose was Malay. In this way I saved my reputation with my neighbors: for the Malay had no means of betraying the secret. He lay down upon the floor for about an hour, and then pursued his journey. On his departure, I presented him with a piece of opium. To him, as an Orientalist, I concluded that opium must be familiar: and the expression of his face convinced me that it was. Nevertheless, I was struck with some little consternation when I saw him suddenly raise his hand to his mouth, and (in the schoolboy phrase) bolt the whole, divided into three pieces, at one mouthful. The quantity was enough to kill three dragoons and their horses: and I felt some alarm for the poor creature: but what could be done? I had given him the opium in compassion for his solitary life, on recollecting that if he had traveled on foot from London, it must be nearly three weeks since he could have exchanged a thought with any human being. I could not think of violating the laws of hospitality, by having him seized and drenched with an emetic, and thus frightening him into a notion that we were going to sacrifice him to some English idol. No: there was clearly no help for it:—he took his leave: and for some days I felt anxious: but as I never heard of any Malay being found dead, I became convinced that he was used[6] to opium: and that I must have done him the service I designed, by giving him one night of respite from the pains of wandering.

This incident I have digressed to mention, because this Malay (partly from the picturesque exhibition he assisted to frame, partly from the anxiety I connected with his image for some days) fastened afterwards upon my dreams, and brought other Malays with him worse than himself, that ran "amuck" at me, and led me into a world of troubles. * * *

---

3. *Anastasius, or Memoirs of a Greek,* was a novel published anonymously by Thomas Hope in 1819. It included a description of the physical effects of opium that De Quincey considered to be a "grievous misrepresentation."
4. A book on Oriental languages by the German philologist J. C. Adelung (1732–1806).
5. Bowed down to.
6. This, however, is not a necessary conclusion: the varieties of effect produced by opium on different constitutions are infinite [De Quincey's note].

From *The Pains of Opium*

[OPIUM REVERIES AND DREAMS]

I have thus described and illustrated my intellectual torpor, in terms that apply, more or less, to every part of the four years during which I was under the Circean[7] spells of opium. But for misery and suffering, I might, indeed, be said to have existed in a dormant state. I seldom could prevail on myself to write a letter; an answer of a few words, to any that I received, was the utmost that I could accomplish; and often *that* not until the letter had lain weeks, or even months, on my writing table. Without the aid of M.[8] all records of bills paid, or *to be* paid, must have perished: and my whole domestic economy, whatever became of Political Economy,[9] must have gone into irretrievable confusion.—I shall not afterwards allude to this part of the case: it is one, however, which the opium-eater will find, in the end, as oppressive and tormenting as any other, from the sense of incapacity and feebleness, from the direct embarrassments incident to the neglect or procrastination of each day's appropriate duties, and from the remorse which must often exasperate the stings of these evils to a reflective and conscientious mind. The opium-eater loses none of his moral sensibilities, or aspirations: he wishes and longs, as earnestly as ever, to realize what he believes possible, and feels to be exacted by duty; but his intellectual apprehension of what is possible infinitely outruns his power, not of execution only, but even of power to attempt. He lies under the weight of incubus and nightmare: he lies in sight of all that he would fain perform, just as a man forcibly confined to his bed by the mortal languor of a relaxing disease, who is compelled to witness injury or outrage offered to some object of his tenderest love:—he curses the spells which chain him down from motion:—he would lay down his life if he might get up and walk; but he is powerless as an infant, and cannot even attempt to rise.

I now pass to what is the main subject of these latter confessions, to the history and journal of what took place in my dreams; for these were the immediate and proximate cause of my acutest suffering.

The first notice I had of any important change going on in this part of my physical economy, was from the re-awakening of a state of eye generally incident to childhood, or exalted states of irritability. I know not whether my reader is aware that many children, perhaps most, have a power of painting, as it were, upon the darkness, all sorts of phantoms; in some, that power is simply a mechanic affection of the eye; others have a voluntary, or a semi-voluntary power to dismiss or to summon them; or, as a child once said to me when I questioned him on this matter, "I can tell them to go, and they go; but sometimes they come, when I don't tell them to come." Whereupon I told him that he had almost as unlimited a command over apparitions, as a Roman centurion[1] over his soldiers.—In the middle of 1817, I think it was, that this faculty became positively distressing to me: at night, when I lay

---

7. Like those of Circe (the enchantress in the *Odyssey* who turned Odysseus's men into swine).
8. Margaret Simpson, whom De Quincey had married in 1817.
9. Inspired by David Ricardo's *Principles of Political Economy* (1817), De Quincey had begun to

write, but never completed, a work he called *Prolegomena to All Future Systems of Political Economy*.
1. A Roman officer commanding a troop of a hundred soldiers (a "century").

awake in bed, vast processions passed along in mournful pomp; friezes of never-ending stories, that to my feelings were as sad and solemn as if they were stories drawn from times before Oedipus or Priam—before Tyre—before Memphis.[2] And, at the same time, a corresponding change took place in my dreams; a theater seemed suddenly opened and lighted up within my brain, which presented nightly spectacles of more than earthly splendor. And the four following facts may be mentioned, as noticeable at this time:

1. That, as the creative state of the eye increased, a sympathy seemed to arise between the waking and the dreaming states of the brain in one point—that whatsoever I happened to call up and to trace by a voluntary act upon the darkness was very apt to transfer itself to my dreams; so that I feared to exercise this faculty; for, as Midas turned all things to gold, that yet baffled his hopes and defrauded his human desires,[3] so whatsoever things capable of being visually represented I did but think of in the darkness, immediately shaped themselves into phantoms of the eye; and, by a process apparently no less inevitable, when thus once traced in faint and visionary colors, like writings in sympathetic ink,[4] they were drawn out by the fierce chemistry of my dreams, into insufferable splendor that fretted my heart.

2. For this, and all other changes in my dreams, were accompanied by deep-seated anxiety and gloomy melancholy, such as are wholly incommunicable by words. I seemed every night to descend, not metaphorically, but literally to descend, into chasms and sunless abysses, depths below depths, from which it seemed hopeless that I could ever reascend. Nor did I, by waking, feel that I *had* re-ascended. This I do not dwell upon; because the state of gloom which attended these gorgeous spectacles, amounting at least to utter darkness, as of some suicidal despondency, cannot be approached by words.

3. The sense of space, and in the end, the sense of time, were both powerfully affected. Buildings, landscapes, &c. were exhibited in proportions so vast as the bodily eye is not fitted to receive. Space swelled, and was amplified to an extent of unutterable infinity. This, however, did not disturb me so much as the vast expansion of time; I sometimes seemed to have lived for 70 or 100 years in one night; nay, sometimes had feelings representative of a millennium passed in that time, or, however, of a duration far beyond the limits of any human experience.

4. The minutest incidents of childhood, or forgotten scenes of later years, were often revived: I could not be said to recollect them; for if I had been told of them when waking, I should not have been able to acknowledge them as parts of my past experience. But placed as they were before me, in dreams like intuitions, and clothed in all their evanescent circumstances and accompanying feelings, I *recognized* them instantaneously. I was once told by a near relative[5] of mine, that having in her childhood fallen into a river, and being on the very verge of death but for the critical assistance which reached her, she saw in a moment her whole life, in its minutest incidents, arrayed before her simultaneously as in a mirror; and she had a faculty developed as

2. De Quincey is calling the roll of great civilizations in the past. Oedipus was the king of Thebes. Priam was the king of Troy. Tyre was the chief city of Phoenicia. Memphis was the capital of ancient Egypt.
3. When granted his rash wish that all he touched should turn to gold, King Midas was horrified to discover that his food, drink, and beloved daughter all became gold at his touch.
4. Invisible ink.
5. According to family report, De Quincey's mother.

suddenly for comprehending the whole and every part. This, from some opium experiences of mine, I can believe; I have, indeed, seen the same thing asserted twice in modern books, and accompanied by a remark which I am convinced is true; viz. that the dread book of account, which the Scriptures speak of,[6] is, in fact, the mind itself of each individual. Of this, at least, I feel assured, that there is no such thing as *forgetting* possible to the mind; a thousand accidents may, and will, interpose a veil between our present consciousness and the secret inscriptions on the mind; accidents of the same sort will also rend away this veil; but alike, whether veiled or unveiled, the inscription remains forever; just as the stars seem to withdraw before the common light of day, whereas, in fact, we all know that it is the light which is drawn over them as a veil—and that they are waiting to be revealed, when the obscuring daylight shall have withdrawn.

Having noticed these four facts as memorably distinguishing my dreams from those of health, I shall now cite a case illustrative of the first fact; and shall then cite any others that I remember, either in their chronological order, or any other that may give them more effect as pictures to the reader.

I had been in youth, and even since, for occasional amusement, a great reader of Livy,[7] whom, I confess, that I prefer, both for style and matter, to any of the Roman historians; and I had often felt as most solemn and appalling sounds, and most emphatically representative of the majesty of the Roman people, the two words so often occurring in Livy—*Consul Romanus*;[8] especially when the consul is introduced in his military character. I mean to say, that the words king—sultan—regent, &c. or any other titles of those who embody in their own persons the collective majesty of a great people, had less power over my reverential feelings. I had also, though no great reader of history, made myself minutely and critically familiar with one period of English history, viz. the period of the Parliamentary War, having been attracted by the moral grandeur of some who figured in that day, and by the many interesting memoirs which survive those unquiet times. Both these parts of my lighter reading, having furnished me often with matter of reflection, now furnished me with matter for my dreams. Often I used to see, after painting upon the blank darkness a sort of rehearsal whilst waking, a crowd of ladies, and perhaps a festival, and dances. And I heard it said, or I said to myself, "These are English ladies from the unhappy times of Charles I. These are the wives and the daughters of those who met in peace, and sat at the same tables, and were allied by marriage or by blood; and yet, after a certain day in August, 1642,[9] never smiled upon each other again, nor met but in the field of battle; and at Marston Moor, at Newbury, or at Naseby,[1] cut asunder all ties of love by the cruel saber, and washed away in blood the memory of ancient friendship."—The ladies danced, and looked as lovely as the court of George IV.[2] Yet I knew, even in my dream, that they had been in the grave for nearly two centuries.—This pageant would suddenly dissolve: and at a clapping of hands, would be heard the heart-quaking sound of

6. The book listing everyone's name at the Last Judgment (Revelation 20.12).
7. Titus Livius (59 B.C.E.–17 C.E.), author of a huge history of Rome in 142 books.
8. Roman consul (Latin); one of two officials, elected annually, who wielded the chief military and judicial authority in Republican Rome.

9. The raising of the king's banner on Castle Hill, Nottingham, on August 22, 1642, signaled the beginning of the English Civil War.
1. Scenes of the defeat of King Charles's forces in the Civil War.
2. The reigning monarch at the time De Quincey was writing.

Consul Romanus; and immediately came "sweeping by," in gorgeous palu-daments, Paulus or Marius,[3] girt round by a company of centurions, with the crimson tunic hoisted on a spear,[4] and followed by the *alalagmos*[5] of the Roman legions.

Many years ago, when I was looking over Piranesi's Antiquities of Rome, Mr. Coleridge, who was standing by, described to me a set of plates by that artist, called his *Dreams*,[6] and which record the scenery of his own visions during the delirium of a fever. Some of them (I describe only from memory of Mr. Coleridge's account) represented vast Gothic halls: on the floor of which stood all sorts of engines and machinery, wheels, cables, pulleys, levers, catapults, &c. &c. expressive of enormous power put forth, and resistance overcome. Creeping along the sides of the walls, you perceived a staircase; and upon it, groping his way upwards, was Piranesi himself: follow the stairs a little further, and you perceive it come to a sudden abrupt termination, without any balustrade, and allowing no step onwards to him who had reached the extremity, except into the depths below. Whatever is to become of poor Piranesi, you suppose, at least, that his labors must in some way terminate here. But raise your eyes, and behold a second flight of stairs still higher: on which again Piranesi is perceived, but this time standing on the very brink of the abyss. Again elevate your eye, and a still more aerial flight of stairs is beheld: and again is poor Piranesi busy on his aspiring labors: and so on, until the unfinished stairs and Piranesi both are lost in the upper gloom of the hall.—With the same power of endless growth and self-reproduction did my architecture proceed in dreams. In the early stage of my malady, the splendors of my dreams were indeed chiefly architectural: and I beheld such pomp of cities and palaces as was never yet beheld by the waking eye, unless in the clouds. From a great modern poet[7] I cite part of a passage which describes, as an appearance actually beheld in the clouds, what in many of its circumstances I saw frequently in sleep:

> The appearance, instantaneously disclosed,
> Was of a mighty city—boldly say
> A wilderness of building, sinking far
> And self-withdrawn into a wondrous depth,
> Far sinking into splendor—without end!
> Fabric it seem'd of diamond, and of gold,
> With alabaster domes, and silver spires,
> And blazing terrace upon terrace, high
> Uplifted; here, serene pavilions bright
> In avenues disposed; there towers begirt
> With battlements that on their restless fronts
> Bore stars—illumination of all gems!
> By earthly nature had the effect been wrought

---

3. Lucius Paulus (d. 160 B.C.E.) and Caius Marius (d. 86 B.C.E.) were Roman generals who won famous victories. "Paludaments": the cloaks worn by Roman generals.
4. The signal which announced a day of battle [De Quincey's note in the revised edition].
5. A word expressing collectively the gathering of the Roman war-cries [De Quincey's note in the revised edition]. The word is Greek.
6. Giovanni Piranesi (1720–1778), a Venetian

especially famed for his many etchings of ancient and modern Rome. He did not publish prints called *Dreams*; De Quincey doubtless refers to his series called *Carceri d'Invenzione*, "Imaginary prisons." The description that De Quincey recalls from Coleridge's conversation is remarkably apt for these terrifying architectural fantasies.
7. The quotation is from Wordsworth's *The Excursion*, book 2, lines 834ff. It describes a cloud structure after a storm.

Upon the dark materials of the storm
Now pacified: on them, and on the coves,
And mountain-steeps and summits, whereunto
The vapors had receded,—taking there
Their station under a cerulean sky, &c. &c.

The sublime circumstance—"battlements that on their *restless* fronts bore stars"—might have been copied from my architectural dreams, for it often occurred.—We hear it reported of Dryden, and of Fuseli[8] in modern times, that they thought proper to eat raw meat for the sake of obtaining splendid dreams: how much better for such a purpose to have eaten opium, which yet I do not remember that any poet is recorded to have done, except the dramatist Shadwell:[9] and in ancient days, Homer is, I think, rightly reputed to have known the virtues of opium.[1]

To my architecture succeeded dreams of lakes—and silvery expanses of water:—these haunted me so much, that I feared (though possibly it will appear ludicrous to a medical man) that some dropsical[2] state or tendency of the brain might thus be making itself (to use a metaphysical word) *objective*; and the sentient organ *project* itself as its own object.—For two months I suffered greatly in my head—a part of my bodily structure which had hitherto been so clear from all touch or taint of weakness (physically, I mean), that I used to say of it, as the last Lord Orford[3] said of his stomach, that it seemed likely to survive the rest of my person.—Till now I had never felt a headache even, or any the slightest pain, except rheumatic pains caused by my own folly. However, I got over this attack, though it must have been verging on something very dangerous.

The waters now changed their character—from translucent lakes, shining like mirrors, they now became seas and oceans. And now came a tremendous change, which, unfolding itself slowly like a scroll, through many months, promised an abiding torment; and, in fact, it never left me until the winding up of my case. Hitherto the human face had mixed often in my dreams, but not despotically, nor with any special power of tormenting. But now that which I have called the tyranny of the human face began to unfold itself. Perhaps some part of my London life might be answerable for this. Be that as it may, now it was that upon the rocking waters of the ocean the human face began to appear: the sea appeared paved with innumerable faces, upturned to the heavens: faces, imploring, wrathful, despairing, surged upwards by thousands, by myriads, by generations, by centuries:—my agitation was infinite,—my mind tossed—and surged with the ocean.

May 1818

The Malay has been a fearful enemy for months. I have been every night, through his means, transported into Asiatic scenes. I know not whether others share in my feelings on this point; but I have often thought that if I were

---

8. John Henry Fuseli (1741–1825) was born in Switzerland and painted in England. He was noted for his paintings of nightmarish fantasies.
9. Thomas Shadwell was a Restoration dramatist and poet. He is now better known as the target of Dryden's satire (in *Mac Flecknoe* and elsewhere) than as a writer in his own right.
1. In the *Odyssey*, book 4, Homer lauded nepenthe

(which is probably opium) as a "drug to heal all pain and anger, and bring forgetfulness of every sorrow."
2. Afflicted with dropsy—an accumulation of fluid in the bodily tissues and cavities.
3. Horace Walpole, 18th-century wit and letter writer, author of the Gothic novel *The Castle of Otranto* (1764).

compelled to forego England, and to live in China, and among Chinese manners and modes of life and scenery, I should go mad. The causes of my horror lie deep; and some of them must be common to others. Southern Asia, in general, is the seat of awful images and associations. As the cradle of the human race, it would alone have a dim and reverential feeling connected with it. But there are other reasons. No man can pretend that the wild, barbarous, and capricious superstitions of Africa, or of savage tribes elsewhere, affect him in the way that he is affected by the ancient, monumental, cruel, and elaborate religions of Indostan, &c. The mere antiquity of Asiatic things, of their institutions, histories, modes of faith, &c. is so impressive, that to me the vast age of the race and name overpowers the sense of youth in the individual. A young Chinese seems to me an antediluvian man renewed. Even Englishmen, though not bred in any knowledge of such institutions, cannot but shudder at the mystic sublimity of *castes*[4] that have flowed apart, and refused to mix, through such immemorial tracts of time; nor can any man fail to be awed by the names of the Ganges, or the Euphrates. It contributes much to these feelings, that southern Asia is, and has been for thousands of years, the part of the earth most swarming with human life; the great *officina gentium*.[5] Man is a weed in those regions. The vast empires also, into which the enormous population of Asia has always been cast, give a further sublimity to the feelings associated with all Oriental names or images. In China, over and above what it has in common with the rest of southern Asia, I am terrified by the modes of life, by the manners, and the barrier of utter abhorrence, and want of sympathy, placed between us by feelings deeper than I can analyze. I could sooner live with lunatics, or brute animals. All this, and much more than I can say, or have time to say, the reader must enter into before he can comprehend the unimaginable horror which these dreams of Oriental imagery, and mythological tortures, impressed upon me. Under the connecting feeling of tropical heat and vertical sunlights, I brought together all creatures, birds, beasts, reptiles, all trees and plants, usages and appearances, that are found in all tropical regions, and assembled them together in China or Indostan. From kindred feelings, I soon brought Egypt and all her gods under the same law. I was stared at, hooted at, grinned at, chattered at, by monkeys, by paroquets, by cockatoos. I ran into pagodas: and was fixed, for centuries, at the summit, or in secret rooms; I was the idol; I was the priest; I was worshiped; I was sacrificed. I fled from the wrath of Brama through all the forests of Asia: Vishnu hated me: Seeva[6] laid wait for me. I came suddenly upon Isis and Osiris: I had done a deed, they said, which the ibis and the crocodile[7] trembled at. I was buried, for a thousand years, in stone coffins, with mummies and sphinxes, in narrow chambers at the heart of eternal pyramids. I was kissed, with cancerous kisses, by crocodiles; and laid, confounded with all unutterable slimy things, amongst reeds and Nilotic mud.

I thus give the reader some slight abstraction of my Oriental dreams, which

4. The reference is to the Hindu caste system, with its sharp division between four hereditary social classes.
5. Manufactory of populations (Latin).
6. In the Hindu triad, Brahma is the creative aspect of divine reality, Vishnu is its maintainer, and Shiva its destroyer.

7. The ibis (a long-legged wading bird) and the crocodile were considered sacred in ancient Egypt. Isis was the ancient Egyptian goddess of fertility. She was the sister and wife of Osiris, whose annual death and rebirth represented the seasonal cycle of nature.

always filled me with such amazement at the monstrous scenery, that horror seemed absorbed, for a while, in sheer astonishment. Sooner or later, came a reflux of feeling that swallowed up the astonishment, and left me, not so much in terror, as in hatred and abomination of what I saw. Over every form, and threat, and punishment, and dim sightless incarceration, brooded a sense of eternity and infinity that drove me into an oppression as of madness. Into these dreams only, it was, with one or two slight exceptions, that any circumstances of physical horror entered. All before had been moral and spiritual terrors. But here the main agents were ugly birds, or snakes, or crocodiles; especially the last. The cursed crocodile became to me the object of more horror than almost all the rest. I was compelled to live with him; and (as was always the case almost in my dreams) for centuries. I escaped sometimes, and found myself in Chinese houses, with cane tables, &c. All the feet of the tables, sofas, &c. soon became instinct with life: the abominable head of the crocodile, and his leering eyes, looked out at me, multiplied into a thousand repetitions: and I stood loathing and fascinated. And so often did this hideous reptile haunt my dreams, that many times the very same dream was broken up in the very same way: I heard gentle voices speaking to me (I hear every thing when I am sleeping); and instantly I awoke: it was broad noon; and my children were standing, hand in hand, at my bedside; come to show me their colored shoes, or new frocks, or to let me see them dressed for going out. I protest that so awful was the transition from the damned crocodile, and the other unutterable monsters and abortions of my dreams, to the sight of innocent *human* natures and of infancy, that, in the mighty and sudden revulsion of mind, I wept, and could not forbear it, as I kissed their faces.

June 1819

I have had occasion to remark, at various periods of my life, that the deaths of those whom we love, and indeed the contemplation of death generally, is (*ceteris paribus*)[8] more affecting in summer than in any other season of the year. And the reasons are these three, I think: first, that the visible heavens in summer appear far higher, more distant, and (if such a solecism may be excused) more infinite; the clouds, by which chiefly the eye expounds the distance of the blue pavilion stretched over our heads, are in summer more voluminous, massed, and accumulated in far grander and more towering piles: secondly, the light and the appearances of the declining and the setting sun are much more fitted to be types and characters of the Infinite: and, thirdly (which is the main reason), the exuberant and riotous prodigality of life naturally forces the mind more powerfully upon the antagonist thought of death, and the wintry sterility of the grave. For it may be observed, generally, that wherever two thoughts stand related to each other by a law of antagonism, and exist, as it were, by mutual repulsion, they are apt to suggest each other. On these accounts it is that I find it impossible to banish the thought of death when I am walking alone in the endless days of summer; and any particular death, if not more affecting, at least haunts my mind more obstinately and besiegingly in that season. Perhaps this cause, and a slight

8. Other things being the same (Latin).

incident which I omit, might have been the immediate occasions of the following dream; to which, however, a predisposition must always have existed in my mind; but having been once roused, it never left me, and split into a thousand fantastic varieties, which often suddenly reunited, and composed again the original dream.

I thought that it was a Sunday morning in May, that it was Easter Sunday, and as yet very early in the morning. I was standing, as it seemed to me, at the door of my own cottage. Right before me lay the very scene which could really be commanded from that situation, but exalted, as was usual, and solemnized by the power of dreams. There were the same mountains, and the same lovely valley at their feet; but the mountains were raised to more than Alpine height, and there was interspace far larger between them of meadows and forest lawns; the hedges were rich with white roses; and no living creature was to be seen, excepting that in the green churchyard there were cattle tranquilly reposing upon the verdant graves, and particularly round about the grave of a child whom I had tenderly loved,[9] just as I had really beheld them, a little before sunrise in the same summer, when that child died. I gazed upon the well-known scene, and I said aloud (as I thought) to myself, "It yet wants much of sunrise; and it is Easter Sunday; and that is the day on which they celebrate the first-fruits of resurrection. I will walk abroad; old griefs shall be forgotten today; for the air is cool and still, and the hills are high, and stretch away to heaven; and the forest-glades are as quiet as the churchyard; and, with the dew, I can wash the fever from my forehead, and then I shall be unhappy no longer." And I turned, as if to open my garden gate; and immediately I saw upon the left a scene far different; but which yet the power of dreams had reconciled into harmony with the other. The scene was an Oriental one; and there also it was Easter Sunday, and very early in the morning. And at a vast distance were visible, as a stain upon the horizon, the domes and cupolas of a great city—an image or faint abstraction, caught perhaps in childhood from some picture of Jerusalem. And not a bow-shot from me, upon a stone, and shaded by Judean palms, there sat a woman; and I looked; and it was—Ann! She fixed her eyes upon me earnestly; and I said to her at length: "So then I have found you at last." I waited: but she answered me not a word. Her face was the same as when I saw it last, and yet again how different! Seventeen years ago, when the lamplight fell upon her face, as for the last time I kissed her lips (lips, Ann, that to me were not polluted), her eyes were streaming with tears: the tears were now wiped away; she seemed more beautiful than she was at that time, but in all other points the same, and not older. Her looks were tranquil, but with unusual solemnity of expression; and I now gazed upon her with some awe, but suddenly her countenance grew dim, and, turning to the mountains, I perceived vapors rolling between us; in a moment, all had vanished; thick darkness came on; and, in the twinkling of an eye, I was far away from mountains, and by lamplight in Oxford Street, walking again with Ann—just as we walked seventeen years before, when we were both children.

As a final specimen, I cite one of a different character, from 1820.

The dream commenced with a music which now I often heard in dreams—

9. The child is Wordsworth's daughter Catherine, who died at the age of four. She is the subject of Wordsworth's sonnet *Surprised by joy.*

a music of preparation and of awakening suspense; a music like the opening of the Coronation Anthem,[1] and which, like *that,* gave the feeling of a vast march—of infinite cavalcades filing off—and the tread of innumerable armies. The morning was come of a mighty day—a day of crisis and of final hope for human nature, then suffering some mysterious eclipse, and laboring in some dread extremity. Somewhere, I knew not where—somehow, I knew not how—by some beings, I knew not whom—a battle, a strife, an agony, was conducting—was evolving like a great drama, or piece of music; with which my sympathy was the more insupportable from my confusion as to its place, its cause, its nature, and its possible issue. I, as is usual in dreams (where, of necessity, we make ourselves central to every movement), had the power, and yet had not the power, to decide it. I had the power, if I could raise myself, to will it; and yet again had not the power, for the weight of twenty Atlantics was upon me, or the oppression of inexpiable guilt. "Deeper than ever plummet sounded,"[2] I lay inactive. Then, like a chorus, the passion deepened. Some greater interest was at stake; some mightier cause than ever yet the sword had pleaded, or trumpet had proclaimed. Then came sudden alarms: hurryings to and fro: trepidations of innumerable fugitives, I knew not whether from the good cause or the bad: darkness and lights: tempest and human faces: and at last, with the sense that all was lost, female forms, and the features that were worth all the world to me, and but a moment allowed—and clasped hands, and heart-breaking partings, and then—everlasting farewells! and with a sigh, such as the caves of hell sighed when the incestuous mother uttered the abhorred name of death,[3] the sound was reverberated—everlasting farewells! and again, and yet again reverberated—everlasting farewells!

And I awoke in struggles, and cried aloud—"I will sleep no more!"[4]

1821   1821

On the Knocking at the Gate in *Macbeth*[1]

From my boyish days I had always felt a great perplexity on one point in *Macbeth.* It was this: The knocking at the gate which succeeds to the murder of Duncan produced to my feelings an effect for which I never could account. The effect was that it reflected back upon the murderer a peculiar awfulness and a depth of solemnity; yet, however obstinately I endeavored with my

1. Composed by George Frideric Handel for the coronation of George II in 1727.
2. *The Tempest* 3.3.101.
3. The reference is to *Paradise Lost,* book 2, lines 777ff. The "incestuous mother" is Sin, who is doubly incestuous: she is the daughter of Satan, who begot Death upon her, and she was in turn raped by her son and gave birth to a pack of "yelling Monsters."
4. Macbeth says: "Methought I heard a voice cry 'Sleep no more, / Macbeth does murder sleep'" (2.2.33–34).
1. This essay, one of the best-known critiques of Shakespeare, deals with the scene in *Macbeth* (2.2–3) in which, just after they have murdered

Duncan, Macbeth and his wife are startled by a loud knocking at the gate. De Quincey exhibits the procedure in Romantic criticism of making, as he says, the "understanding" wait upon the "feelings." That is, instead of judging the success or failure of a passage by its conformity to prior critical theory, De Quincey brings in theory only to explain his impression or immediate emotional response to the passage. The final paragraph demonstrates a weakness of Romantic criticism when it is driven to an extreme, for it converts the reasonable view that Shakespeare must be presumed right until shown to be wrong into the untenable view that Shakespeare is an artistic deity who can do no wrong.

understanding to comprehend this, for many years I never could see *why* it should produce such an effect.

Here I pause for one moment, to exhort the reader never to pay any attention to his understanding when it stands in opposition to any other faculty of his mind. The mere understanding, however useful and indispensable, is the meanest faculty in the human mind, and the most to be distrusted; and yet the great majority of people trust to nothing else—which may do for ordinary life, but not for philosophical purposes. Of this out of ten thousand instances that I might produce I will cite one. Ask of any person whatsoever who is not previously prepared for the demand by a knowledge of the perspective to draw in the rudest way the commonest appearance which depends upon the laws of that science—as, for instance, to represent the effect of two walls standing at right angles to each other, or the appearance of the houses on each side of a street as seen by a person looking down the street from one extremity. Now, in all cases, unless the person has happened to observe in pictures how it is that artists produce these effects, he will be utterly unable to make the smallest approximation to it. Yet why? For he has actually seen the effect every day of his life. The reason is that he allows his understanding to overrule his eyes. His understanding, which includes no intuitive knowledge of the laws of vision, can furnish him with no reason why a line which is known and can be proved to be a horizontal line should not *appear* a horizontal line: a line that made any angle with the perpendicular less than a right angle would seem to him to indicate that his houses were all tumbling down together. Accordingly, he makes the line of his houses a horizontal line, and fails, of course, to produce the effect demanded. Here, then, is one instance out of many in which not only the understanding is allowed to overrule the eyes, but where the understanding is positively allowed to obliterate the eyes, as it were; for not only does the man believe the evidence of his understanding in opposition to that of his eyes, but (what is monstrous) the idiot is not aware that his eyes ever gave such evidence. He does not know that he has seen (and therefore *quoad* his consciousness[2] has *not* seen) that which he *has* seen every day of his life.

But to return from this digression. My understanding could furnish no reason why the knocking at the gate in *Macbeth* should produce any effect, direct or reflected. In fact, my understanding said positively that it could not produce any effect. But I knew better; I felt that it did; and I waited and clung to the problem until further knowledge should enable me to solve it. At length, in 1812, Mr. Williams[3] made his debut on the stage of Ratcliffe Highway, and executed those unparalleled murders which have procured for him such a brilliant and undying reputation. On which murders, by the way, I must observe that in one respect they have had an ill effect, by making the connoisseur in murder very fastidious in his taste, and dissatisfied by anything that has been since done in that line. All other murders look pale by the deep crimson of his; and, as an amateur[4] once said to me in a querulous tone, "There has been absolutely nothing *doing* since his time, or nothing

2. I.e., so far as his consciousness is concerned.
3. John Williams, a sailor, had thrown London into a panic (the date was actually December 1811) by murdering the Marr family and, twelve days later, the Williamson family. De Quincey described these murders at length in the postscript to his two essays *On Murder Considered as One of the Fine Arts.*
4. I.e., a fancier or follower of an art or sport.

that's worth speaking of." But this is wrong; for it is unreasonable to expect all men to be great artists, and born with the genius of Mr. Williams. Now, it will be remembered that in the first of these murders (that of the Marrs) the same incident (of a knocking at the door[5] soon after the work of extermination was complete) did actually occur which the genius of Shakespeare has invented; and all good judges, and the most eminent dilettanti,[6] acknowledged the felicity of Shakespeare's suggestion as soon as it was actually realized. Here, then, was a fresh proof that I was right in relying on my own feeling, in opposition to my understanding; and I again set myself to study the problem. At length I solved it to my own satisfaction; and my solution is this: Murder, in ordinary cases, where the sympathy is wholly directed to the case of the murdered person, is an incident of coarse and vulgar horror; and for this reason—that it flings the interest exclusively upon the natural but ignoble instinct by which we cleave to life: an instinct which, as being indispensable to the primal law of self-preservation, is the same in kind (though different in degree) amongst all living creatures. This instinct, therefore, because it annihilates all distinctions, and degrades the greatest of men to the level of "the poor beetle that we tread on,"[7] exhibits human nature in its most abject and humiliating attitude. Such an attitude would little suit the purposes of the poet. What then must he do? He must throw the interest on the murderer. Our sympathy must be with *him* (of course I mean a sympathy of comprehension, a sympathy by which we enter into his feelings, and are made to understand them—not a sympathy of pity or approbation).[8] In the murdered person, all strife of thought, all flux and reflux of passion and of purpose, are crushed by one overwhelming panic; the fear of instant death smites him "with its petrific[9] mace." But in the murderer, such a murderer as a poet will condescend to, there must be raging some great storm of passion—jealousy, ambition, vengeance, hatred—which will create a hell within him; and into this hell we are to look.

In *Macbeth,* for the sake of gratifying his own enormous and teeming faculty of creation, Shakespeare has introduced two murderers: and, as usual in his hands, they are remarkably discriminated; but—though in Macbeth the strife of mind is greater than in his wife, the tiger spirit not so awake, and his feelings caught chiefly by contagion from her—yet, as both were finally involved in the guilt of murder, the murderous mind of necessity is finally to be presumed in both. This was to be expressed; and, on its own account, as well as to make it a more proportionable antagonist to the unoffending nature of their victim, "the gracious Duncan," and adequately to expound "the deep damnation of his taking off,"[1] this was to be expressed with peculiar energy. We were to be made to feel that the human nature—i.e., the divine nature of love and mercy, spread through the hearts of all creatures, and seldom utterly withdrawn from man—was gone, vanished, extinct, and that the fiendish nature had taken its place. And, as this effect is marvelously accomplished in the *dialogues* and *soliloquies* themselves, so

---

5. By a maidservant of the Marrs, returning from the purchase of oysters for supper.
6. Lovers of the fine arts.
7. *Measure for Measure* 3.1.77.
8. In a note De Quincey decries "the unscholarlike use of the word sympathy, at present so general, by which, instead of taking it in its proper sense, as the act of reproducing in our minds the feelings of another, whether for hatred, indignation, love, pity, or approbation, it is made a mere synonym of the word *pity*."
9. Petrifying, turning to stone (from *Paradise Lost* 10.294).
1. *Macbeth* 3.1.67 and 1.7.20.

it is finally consummated by the expedient under consideration; and it is to this that I now solicit the reader's attention. If the reader has ever witnessed a wife, daughter, or sister in a fainting fit, he may chance to have observed that the most affecting moment in such a spectacle is *that* in which a sigh and a stirring announce the recommencement of suspended life. Or, if the reader has ever been present in a vast metropolis on the day when some great national idol was carried in funeral pomp to his grave, and, chancing to walk near the course through which it passed, has felt powerfully, in the silence and desertion of the streets, and in the stagnation of ordinary business, the deep interest which at that moment was possessing the heart of man—if all at once he should hear the deathlike stillness broken up by the sound of wheels rattling away from the scene, and making known that the transitory vision was dissolved, he will be aware that at no moment was his sense of the complete suspension and pause in ordinary human concerns so full and affecting as at that moment when the suspension ceases, and the goings-on of human life are suddenly resumed. All action in any direction is best expounded, measured, and made apprehensible, by reaction. Now, apply this to the case in *Macbeth*. Here, as I have said, the retiring of the human heart and the entrance of the fiendish heart was to be expressed and made sensible. Another world has stepped in; and the murderers are taken out of the region of human things, human purposes, human desires. They are transfigured: Lady Macbeth is "unsexed";[2] Macbeth has forgot that he was born of woman; both are conformed to the image of devils; and the world of devils is suddenly revealed. But how shall this be conveyed and made palpable? In order that a new world may step in, this world must for a time disappear. The murderers and the murder must be insulated—cut off by an immeasurable gulf from the ordinary tide and succession of human affairs—locked up and sequestered in some deep recess; we must be made sensible that the world of ordinary life is suddenly arrested, laid asleep, tranced, racked into a dread armistice; time must be annihilated, relation to things without abolished; and all must pass self-withdrawn into a deep syncope[3] and suspension of earthly passion. Hence it is that, when the deed is done, when the work of darkness is perfect, then the world of darkness passes away like a pageantry in the clouds: the knocking at the gate is heard, and it makes known audibly that the reaction has commenced; the human has made its reflux upon the fiendish; the pulses of life are beginning to beat again; and the reestablishment of the goings-on of the world in which we live first makes us profoundly sensible of the awful parenthesis that had suspended them.

O mighty poet! Thy works are not as those of other men, simply and merely great works of art, but are also like the phenomena of nature, like the sun and the sea, the stars and the flowers, like frost and snow, rain and dew, hailstorm and thunder, which are to be studied with entire submission of our own faculties, and in the perfect faith that in them there can be no too much or too little, nothing useless or inert, but that, the farther we press in our discoveries, the more we shall see proofs of design and self-supporting arrangement where the careless eye had seen nothing but accident!

1823

---

2. Steeling herself to the murder, Lady Macbeth calls on the spirits of hell to "unsex me here" (1.5.39).
3. Fainting spell.

From Alexander Pope

What is it that we mean by *literature*? Popularly, and amongst the thoughtless, it is held to include everything that is printed in a book. Little logic is required to disturb *that* definition. The most thoughtless person is easily made aware that in the idea of *literature* one essential element is some relation to a general and common interest of man—so that what applies only to a local, or professional, or merely personal interest, even though presenting itself in the shape of a book, will not belong to Literature. So far the definition is easily narrowed; and it is as easily expanded. For not only is much that takes a station in books not literature; but inversely, much that really *is* literature never reaches a station in books. The weekly sermons of Christendom, that vast pulpit literature which acts so extensively upon the popular mind—to warn, to uphold, to renew, to comfort, to alarm—does not attain the sanctuary of libraries in the ten-thousandth part of its extent. The Drama again—as, for instance, the finest of Shakespeare's plays in England, and all leading Athenian plays in the noontide of the Attic stage—operated as a literature on the public mind, and were (according to the strictest letter of that term) *published* through the audiences that witnessed[2] their representation some time before they were published as things to be read; and they were published in this scenical mode of publication with much more effect than they could have had as books during ages of costly copying or of costly printing.

Books, therefore, do not suggest an idea coextensive and interchangeable with the idea of Literature; since much literature, scenic, forensic, or didactic[3] (as from lecturers and public orators), may never come into books, and much that *does* come into books may connect itself with no literary interest.[4] But a far more important correction, applicable to the common vague idea of literature, is to be sought not so much in a better definition of literature as in a sharper distinction of the two functions which it fulfills. In that great social organ which, collectively, we call literature, there may be distinguished two separate offices that may blend and often *do* so, but capable, severally, of a severe insulation, and naturally fitted for reciprocal repulsion. There is,

1. This section of an essay on Alexander Pope (written in 1848, revised in 1858) has achieved independent status as a contribution to literary theory. In an earlier treatment of this topic in *Letters to a Young Man* (1823), De Quincey wrote that "the true antithesis to knowledge," in defining the effects of literature, "is not *pleasure,* but *power*"; then added in a footnote that he owed this distinction "to many years' conversation with Mr. Wordsworth." In his *Essay Supplementary* to the Preface to his *Poems* (1815), Wordsworth had written that "every great poet . . . has to call forth and communicate *power*," and that for an original writer "to create taste is to call forth and bestow power, of which knowledge is the effect."

2. Charles I, for example, when Prince of Wales, and many others in his father's court, gained their known familiarity with Shakespeare not through the original quartos, so slenderly diffused, nor through the first folio of 1623, but through the court representations of his chief dramas at Whitehall [De Quincey's note]. Whitehall was a royal palace in London. It was destroyed by fire in 1698.

3. Expository, designed to instruct. "Scenic": dramatic. "Forensic": argumentative, designed to persuade, especially in legal proceedings.

4. What are called *The Blue Books*—by which title are understood the folio reports issued every session of Parliament by committees of the two Houses, and stitched into blue covers—though often sneered at by the ignorant as so much wastepaper, will be acknowledged gratefully by those who have used them diligently as the main wellheads of all accurate information as to the Great Britain of this day. As an immense depository of faithful (*and not superannuated*) statistics, they are indispensable to the honest student. But no man would therefore class the *Blue Books* as literature [De Quincey's note].

first, the literature of *knowledge*; and, secondly, the literature of *power*. The function of the first is—to *teach*; the function of the second is—to *move*:[5] the first is a rudder; the second, an oar or a sail. The first speaks to the *mere discursive*[6] understanding; the second speaks ultimately, it may happen, to the higher understanding or reason, but always *through* affections of pleasure and sympathy. Remotely, it may travel towards an object seated in what Lord Bacon calls *dry* light;[7] but, proximately, it does and must operate—else it ceases to be a literature of *power*—on and through that *humid* light which clothes itself in the mists and glittering *iris* of human passions, desires, and genial[8] emotions. Men have so little reflected on the higher functions of literature as to find it a paradox if one should describe it as a mean or subordinate purpose of books to give information. But this is a paradox only in the sense which makes it honorable to be paradoxical. Whenever we talk in ordinary language of seeking information or gaining knowledge, we understand the words as connected with something of absolute novelty. But it is the grandeur of all truth which *can* occupy a very high place in human interests that it is never absolutely novel to the meanest of minds: it exists eternally by way of germ or latent principle in the lowest as in the highest, needing to be developed, but never to be planted. To be capable of transplantation is the immediate criterion of a truth that ranges on a lower scale. Besides which, there is a rarer thing than truth—namely, *power*, or deep sympathy with truth. What is the effect, for instance, upon society, of children? By the pity, by the tenderness, and by the peculiar modes of admiration, which connect themselves with the helplessness, with the innocence, and with the simplicity of children, not only are the primal affections strengthened and continually renewed, but the qualities which are dearest in the sight of heaven—the frailty, for instance, which appeals to forbearance, the innocence which symbolizes the heavenly, and the simplicity which is most alien from the worldly—are kept up in perpetual remembrance, and their ideals are continually refreshed. A purpose of the same nature is answered by the higher literature, viz. the literature of power. What do you learn from *Paradise Lost*? Nothing at all. What do you learn from a cookery book? Something new, something that you did not know before, in every paragraph. But would you therefore put the wretched cookery book on a higher level of estimation than the divine poem? What you owe to Milton is not any knowledge, of which a million separate items are still but a million of advancing steps on the same earthly level; what you owe is *power*—that is, exercise and expansion to your own latent capacity of sympathy with the infinite, where every pulse and each separate influx is a step upwards, a step ascending as upon a Jacob's ladder from earth to mysterious altitudes above the earth.[9] *All* the steps of knowledge, from first to last, carry you further on the same plane, but could never raise you one foot above your ancient level of earth: whereas the very *first* step in power is a flight—is an ascending movement into another element where earth is forgotten.

---

5. Through the 18th century many critical theorists, following classical precedent, asserted that the aims of poetry are to teach, to please, and to move the reader.
6. Ordered in a rational or logical way.
7. In his essay *Of Friendship*, Francis Bacon quotes Heraclitus, the early Greek philosopher, as saying "Dry light is ever the best," then goes on to distinguish between dry light and the light of an understanding, which is "ever infused and drenched" in an individual's own "affections and customs."
8. Pertaining to genius; creative. "Iris": rainbow colors.
9. The ladder that the patriarch Jacob saw in a dream, reaching from earth to heaven, on which angels were ascending and descending (Genesis 28.11–12).

Were it not that human sensibilities are ventilated and continually called out into exercise by the great phenomena of infancy, or of real life as it moves through chance and change, or of literature as it recombines these elements in the mimicries of poetry, romance, etc., it is certain that, like any animal power or muscular energy falling into disuse, all such sensibilities would gradually droop and dwindle. It is in relation to these great *moral* capacities of man that the literature of power, as contradistinguished from that of knowledge, lives and has its field of action. It is concerned with what is highest in man; for the Scriptures themselves never condescended to deal by suggestion or cooperation with the mere discursive understanding: when speaking of man in his intellectual capacity, the Scriptures speak not of the understanding, but of *"the understanding heart"*[1]—making the heart, i.e. the great *intuitive* (or nondiscursive) organ, to be the interchangeable formula for man in his highest state of capacity for the infinite. Tragedy, romance, fairy tale, or epopée,[2] all alike restore to man's mind the ideals of justice, of hope, of truth, of mercy, of retribution, which else (left to the support of daily life in its realities) would languish for want of sufficient illustration. What is meant, for instance, by *poetic justice?*[3]—It does not mean a justice that differs by its object from the ordinary justice of human jurisprudence; for then it must be confessedly a very bad kind of justice; but it means a justice that differs from common forensic justice by the degree in which it *attains* its object, a justice that is more omnipotent over its own ends, as dealing—not with the refractory elements of earthly life, but with the elements of its own creation, and with materials flexible to its own purest preconceptions. It is certain that, were it not for the Literature of Power, these ideals would often remain amongst us as mere arid notional forms; whereas, by the creative forces of man put forth in literature, they gain a vernal life of restoration, and germinate into vital activities. The commonest novel, by moving in alliance with human fears and hopes, with human instincts of wrong and right, sustains and quickens those affections. Calling them into action, it rescues them from torpor. And hence the preeminency over all authors that merely *teach* of the meanest that *moves*, or that teaches, if at all, indirectly *by* moving. The very highest work that has ever existed in the Literature of Knowledge is but a *provisional* work: a book upon trial and sufferance, and *quamdiu bene se gesserit.*[4] Let its teaching be even partially revised, let it be but expanded—nay, even let its teaching be but placed in a better order—and instantly it is superseded. Whereas the feeblest works in the Literature of Power, surviving at all, survive as finished and unalterable amongst men. For instance, the *Principia* of Sir Isaac Newton was a book *militant*[5] on earth from the first. In all stages of its progress it would have to fight for its existence: 1st, as regards absolute truth; 2dly, when that combat was over, as regards its form or mode of presenting the truth. And as soon as a La Place,[6] or anybody else, builds higher upon the foundations laid by this book, effectually he throws it out of the sunshine into decay and

1. In 1 Kings 3.9 King Solomon asks the Lord for "an understanding heart to judge thy people."
2. Epic poem (French).
3. A term in literary criticism for the distribution of earthly rewards and punishments, at the end of a work of literature, in proportion to the virtues and vices of the various characters.
4. As long as it shall conduct itself well (Latin).
5. Combative. *"Principia"*: Isaac Newton's great

Philosophiae Naturalis Principia Mathematica (Mathematical principles of natural philosophy), published in 1687, set forth the laws of motion and the principle of universal gravitation.
6. Pierre-Simon, marquis de Laplace, mathematician and astronomer, author of *A Treatise on Celestial Mechanics* (1799–1825), was known as "the Newton of France."

darkness; by weapons won from this book he superannuates and destroys this book, so that soon the name of Newton remains as a mere *nominis umbra*,[7] but his book, as a living power, has transmigrated into other forms. Now, on the contrary, the *Iliad*, the *Prometheus* of Aeschylus, the *Othello* or *King Lear,* the *Hamlet* or *Macbeth,* and the *Paradise Lost,* are not militant, but triumphant forever as long as the languages exist in which they speak or can be taught to speak. They never *can* transmigrate into new incarnations. To reproduce *these* in new forms, or variations, even if in some things they should be improved, would be to plagiarize. A good steam engine is properly superseded by a better. But one lovely pastoral valley is not superseded by another, nor a statute of Praxiteles by a statue of Michael Angelo.[8] These things are separated not by imparity, but by disparity. They are not thought of as unequal under the same standard, but as different in *kind*, and, if otherwise equal, as equal under a different standard. Human works of immortal beauty and works of nature in one respect stand on the same footing: they never absolutely repeat each other, never approach so near as not to differ; and they differ not as better and worse, or simply by more and less: they differ by undecipherable and incommunicable differences, that cannot be caught by mimicries, that cannot be reflected in the mirror of copies, that cannot become ponderable in the scales of vulgar comparison.

Applying these principles to Pope as a representative of fine literature in general, we would wish to remark the claim which he has, or which any equal writer has, to the attention and jealous winnowing of those critics in particular who watch over public morals. Clergymen, and all organs of public criticism put in motion by clergymen, are more especially concerned in the just appreciation of such writers, if the two canons are remembered which we have endeavored to illustrate, viz. that all works in this class, as opposed to those in the literature of knowledge, 1st, work by far deeper agencies, and, 2dly, are more permanent; in the strictest sense they are κτήματα ἐς ἀει[9] and what evil they do, or what good they do, is commensurate with the national language, sometimes long after the nation has departed. At this hour, five hundred years since their creation, the tales of Chaucer,[1] never equaled on this earth for their tenderness, and for life of picturesqueness, are read familiarly by many in the charming language of their natal day, and by others in the modernizations of Dryden, of Pope, and Wordsworth.[2] At this hour, one thousand eight hundred years since their creation, the Pagan tales of Ovid,[3] never equaled on this earth for the gaiety of their movement and the capricious graces of their narrative, are read by all Christendom. This man's people and their monuments are dust; but *he* is alive: he has survived them, as he told us that he had it in his commission to do, by a thousand years; "and *shall* a thousand more."

All the literature of knowledge builds only ground-nests, that are swept away by floods, or confounded by the plow; but the literature of power builds

7. Shadow of a name (Latin).
8. Michelangelo Buonarroti (1475–1564), Renaissance sculptor, painter, architect, and poet. Praxiteles (4th century B.C.E.), Greek sculptor.
9. Everlasting possessions (Greek).
1. The *Canterbury Tales* were not made public until 1380 or thereabouts; but the composition must have cost thirty or more years; not to mention

that the work had probably been finished for some years before it was divulged [De Quincey's note].
2. Following the example of various earlier poets who wrote modernized versions of Chaucer, Wordsworth had translated *The Prioress's Tale* and a section of *Troilus and Criseyde.*
3. Latin poet (43 B.C.E.–18 C.E.), author of *Metamorphoses* and other books of verse narratives.

nests in aerial altitudes of temples sacred from violation, or of forests inaccessible to fraud. *This* is a great prerogative of the *power* literature; and it is a greater which lies in the mode of its influence. The *knowledge* literature, like the fashion of this world, passeth away. An Encyclopedia is its abstract; and, in this respect, it may be taken for its speaking symbol—that before one generation has passed an Encyclopedia is superannuated; for it speaks through the dead memory and unimpassioned understanding, which have not the repose of higher faculties, but are continually enlarging and varying their phylacteries.[4] But all literature properly so called—literature κατ᾽ ἐξοχήν[5]—for the very same reason that it is so much more durable than the literature of knowledge, is (and by the very same proportion it is) more intense and electrically searching in its impressions. The directions in which the tragedy of this planet has trained our human feelings to play, and the combinations into which the poetry of this planet has thrown our human passions of love and hatred, of admiration and contempt, exercise a power for bad or good over human life that cannot be contemplated, when stretching through many generations, without a sentiment allied to awe.[6] And of this let everyone be assured—that he owes to the impassioned books which he has read many a thousand more of emotions than he can consciously trace back to them. Dim by their origination, these emotions yet arise in him, and mould him through life, like forgotten incidents of his childhood.

1848, 1858

4. I.e., preestablished texts. "Phylacteries" are leather boxes, inscribed with quotations from the Hebrew Scriptures, worn by Orthodox Jews during morning prayer.
5. In the highest degree (Greek).
6. The reason why the broad distinctions between the two literatures of power and knowledge so little fix the attention lies in the fact that a vast proportion of books—history, biography, travels, miscellaneous essays, etc.—lying in a middle zone, confound these distinctions by interblending them. All that we call "amusement" or "entertainment" is a diluted form of the power belonging to passion, and also a mixed form; and, where threads of direct *instruction* intermingle in the texture with these threads of *power,* this absorption of the duality into one representative *nuance* neutralizes the separate perception of either. Fused into a *tertium quid* [a third thing], or neutral state, they disappear to the popular eye as the repelling forces which, in fact, they are [De Quincey's note].

GEORGE GORDON, LORD BYRON
1788–1824

In his *History of English Literature,* written in the late 1850s, the French critic Hippolyte Taine gave only a few condescending pages to Wordsworth, Coleridge, Percy Shelley, and Keats and then devoted a long chapter to Lord Byron, "the greatest and most English of these artists; he is so great and so English that from him alone we shall learn more truths of his country and of his age than from all the rest together." This comment reflects the fact that Byron had achieved an immense European reputation during his own lifetime, while his English contemporaries were admired only by coteries in England and America. Through much of the nineteenth century he continued to be rated as one of the greatest of English poets and the very prototype of literary Romanticism. His influence was manifested everywhere, not only among minor writers—most European poets struck Byronic attitudes—but among the major poets and novelists (Goethe in Germany, Balzac and Stendhal in France, Pushkin and Dostoevsky in Russia, and Melville in America), painters (especially Delacroix), and composers (including Beethoven and Berlioz).

These facts may surprise the reader who is aware of the recent estimate of Byron as the least consequential of the great Romantic poets, whose achievements have little in common with the distinctive innovations of Wordsworth, Coleridge, Shelley, or Keats. Only Shelley, among these writers, thought highly of either Byron or his work; while Byron spoke slightingly of all of them except Shelley and, in fact, insisted that, measured against the poetic practice of Alexander Pope, he and his contemporaries were "all in the wrong, one as much as another . . . we are upon a wrong revolutionary poetical system, or systems, not worth a damn in itself." Byron's masterpiece, *Don Juan,* is an instance of that favorite neoclassic type, a satire against modern civilization, and shares many of the aims and methods of Pope, Swift, Voltaire, and Sterne. Even Byron's lyrics are old-fashioned: many are in the eighteenth-century gentlemanly mode of witty extemporization and epigram (*Written after Swimming from Sestos to Abydos*) or continue the Cavalier tradition of the elaborate development of a compliment to a lady (*She walks in beauty* and *Stanzas for Music*).

Byron's chief claim to be considered an arch-Romantic is that he provided his age with what Taine called its "ruling personage; that is, the model that contemporaries invest with their admiration and sympathy." This personage is the "Byronic hero." He is first sketched in the opening canto of *Childe Harold,* then recurs in various guises in the verse romances and dramas that followed. In his developed form, as we find it in *Manfred,* he is an alien, mysterious, and gloomy spirit, superior in his passions and powers to the common run of humanity, whom he regards with disdain. He harbors the torturing memory of an enormous, nameless guilt that drives him toward an inevitable doom. He is in his isolation absolutely self-reliant, pursuing his own ends according to his self-generated moral code against any opposition, human or supernatural. And he exerts an attraction on other characters that is the more compelling because it involves their terror at his obliviousness to ordinary human concerns and values. This figure, infusing the archrebel in a nonpolitical form with a strong erotic interest, was imitated in life as well as in art and helped shape the intellectual and the cultural history of the later nineteenth century. The literary descendants of the Byronic hero include Heathcliff in *Wuthering Heights,* Captain Ahab in *Moby-Dick,* and the hero of Pushkin's great poem *Eugene Onegin.* Bertrand Russell, in his *History of Western Philosophy,* gives a chapter to Byron—not because he was a systematic thinker but because "Byronism," the attitude of "Titanic cosmic self-assertion," established a stance toward humanity and the world that entered nineteenth-century philosophy and eventually helped form Nietzsche's concept of the Superman, the hero who is not subject to the ordinary criteria of good and evil.

Byron's contemporaries insisted on identifying the author with his fictional characters. But Byron's letters and the testimony of his friends show that, except for recurrent moods of deep depression, his own temperament was in many respects antithetic to that of his heroes. He was passionate and willful; but when in good humor, he could be very much a man of the world in the eighteenth-century style— gregarious, tolerant, and a witty conversationalist capable of taking an ironic attitude toward his own activities as well as those of others. The aloof hauteur he exhibited in public was largely a mask to hide his diffidence when in strange company. But although Byronism was largely a fiction, produced by a collaboration between Byron's imagination and that of his public, the fiction was historically more important than the actual person.

Byron was descended from two aristocratic families, both of them colorful, violent, and dissolute. His grandfather was an admiral nicknamed "Foulweather Jack"; his great-uncle was the fifth Baron Byron, known to his rural neighbors as the "Wicked Lord," who was tried by his peers for killing his kinsman William Chaworth in a drunken duel; his father, Captain John Byron, was a rake and fortune hunter who rapidly dissipated the patrimony of two wealthy wives. Byron's mother was a Scotswoman, Catherine Gordon of Gight, the last descendant of a line of lawless Scottish lairds. After her husband died (Byron was then three), she brought up her son in near poverty in Aberdeen, where he was indoctrinated with the Calvinistic morality of Scottish Presbyterianism. Catherine Byron was an ill-educated and extremely irascible woman who nevertheless had an abiding love for her son; they fought violently when together, but corresponded affectionately enough when apart, until her death in 1811.

When Byron was ten, the death of his great-uncle, preceded by that of more immediate heirs to the title, made him the sixth Lord Byron. In a fashion suitable to his new status he was sent to Harrow School, then to Trinity College, Cambridge. He had a deformed foot, made worse by inept surgical treatment, about which he felt acute embarrassment. His lameness made him avid for athletic prowess; he played cricket and made himself an expert boxer, fencer, and horseman and a powerful swimmer. He was also sexually precocious; when only seven, he fell in love with a little cousin, Mary Duff, and so violently that ten years later news of her marriage threw him into convulsions. Both at Cambridge and at his ancestral estate of Newstead, he engaged with more than ordinary zeal in the expensive pursuits and fashionable dissipations of a young Regency lord. As a result, despite a sizable and increasing income, he got into financial difficulties from which he did not entirely extricate himself until late in his life. In the course of his schooling he formed many close and devoted friendships, the most important with John Cam Hobhouse, a sturdy political liberal and commonsense moralist who exerted a steadying influence throughout Byron's turbulent life.

Despite his distractions at the university, Byron found time to try his hand at lyric verse, some of which was published in 1807 in a slim and conventional volume titled *Hours of Idleness*. This was treated so harshly by the pontifical *Edinburgh Review* that Byron was provoked to write in reply his first important poem, *English Bards and Scotch Reviewers*, a vigorous satire in the couplet style of the late-eighteenth-century followers of Pope, in which he incorporated brilliant but tactless ridicule (which he later came to regret) of important poetic contemporaries, including Scott, Wordsworth, and Coleridge.

After attaining his M.A. degree and his majority, Byron set out with Hobhouse in 1809 on a tour through Portugal and Spain to Malta, and then to little-known Albania, Greece, and Asia Minor. In this adventurous two-year excursion, he accumulated materials that he incorporated into many of his important poems, including his last work, *Don Juan*. The first literary product was *Childe Harold*; he wrote the opening two cantos while on the tour that the poem describes; published them in 1812 soon after his return to England; and, in his own oft-quoted phrase, "awoke one morning and found myself famous." He became the celebrity of fashionable London, and increased his literary success by a series of highly readable Near Eastern verse tales; in these the Byronic hero, in various embodiments, flaunts his misanthropy and undergoes a variety of violent and romantic adventures that current gossip attributed to the author himself. In his chronic shortage of money, Byron could well have used the huge income from these publications, but instead maintained his status as an aristocratic amateur by giving the royalties away. Occupying his inherited seat in the House of Lords, he also became briefly active on the extreme liberal side of the Whig party and spoke courageously in defense of the Nottingham weavers who had resorted to smashing the newly invented textile machines that had thrown them out of work. He also supported other liberal measures, including that of Catholic Emancipation.

Byron was extraordinarily handsome—"so beautiful a countenance," Coleridge wrote, "I scarcely ever saw . . . his eyes the open portals of the sun—things of light, and for light." Because of a constitutional tendency to obesity, however, he was able to maintain his looks only by resorting again and again to a starvation diet of biscuits, soda water, and strong cathartics. Often as a result of female initiative rather than his own, Byron entered into a sequence of liaisons with ladies of fashion. One of these, the flamboyant and eccentric young Lady Caroline Lamb, caused him so much distress by her pursuit and public tantrums that Byron turned for relief to marriage with Annabella Milbanke, who was in every way Lady Caroline's opposite, for she was naive, unworldly, intellectual (with a special passion for mathematics), and not a little priggish. This ill-starred marriage produced a daughter (Augusta Ada) and many scenes in which Byron, goaded by financial difficulties, behaved so frantically that his wife suspected his sanity; after only one year, the union ended in a legal separation. The final blow came when Lady Byron discovered her husband's incestuous relations with his half-sister, Augusta Leigh. The two had been raised apart, so that they were almost strangers when they met as adults. Byron's affection for his sister, however guilty, was genuine and endured all through his life. This affair proved a delicious morsel even to the jaded palate of the dissolute Regency society. Byron was ostracized by all but a few friends and was finally forced to leave England forever on April 25, 1816.

Byron now resumed the travels incorporated in the third and fourth cantos of *Childe Harold.* At Geneva he lived for several months in close and intellectually fruitful relation to Percy and Mary Shelley, who were accompanied by Mary's step-sister, Claire Clairmont—a misguided seventeen-year-old who had forced herself on Byron while he was still in England and who in January 1817 bore him a daughter, Allegra. In the fall of 1817 Byron established himself in Venice, where he inaugurated a period of frenzied debauchery that, he estimated, involved more than two hundred women. This period, however, was also one of great literary creativity: often working through the later hours of the night, he finished his tragedy *Manfred;* wrote the fourth canto of *Childe Harold;* and after turning out *Beppo,* a short preview of the narrative style and stanza of *Don Juan,* began the composition of *Don Juan* itself. In the colloquial ottava rima, he finally learned to write poetry as well as he had written the prose of his vivid, informative, and witty letters.

Exhausted and bored by promiscuity, Byron in 1819 settled into a placid and relatively faithful relationship with Teresa Guiccioli, the young wife of the elderly Count Alessandro Guiccioli; according to the Italian upper-class mores of the times, having contracted a marriage of convenience, she could now with propriety attach Byron to herself as a *cavaliere servente.* Through the countess's nationalistic family, the Gambas, Byron became involved in the Carbonari plot against Austrian control over northern Italy. When the Gambas were forced by the authorities to move to Pisa, Byron followed them there and, for the second time, joined the Shelleys. There grew up about them the "Pisan Circle," which in addition to the Gambas included their friends Thomas Medwin and Edward and Jane Williams, as well as the Greek nationalist leader Prince Mavrocordatos, the picturesque Irish Count Taaffe, and the flamboyant and mendacious adventurer Edward Trelawny, who seems to have stepped out of one of Byron's romances. The circle was gradually broken up, first by Shelley's anger over Byron's treatment of his daughter Allegra (Byron had sent the child to be brought up as a Catholic in an Italian convent, where she died of a fever in 1822); then by the expulsion of the Gambas, whom Byron followed to Genoa; and finally by the drowning of Shelley and Williams in July 1822.

Byron meanwhile had been steadily at work on a series of closet tragedies (including *Cain, Sardanapalus,* and *Marino Faliero*) and on his devastating satire on the life and death of George III, *The Vision of Judgment.* But increasingly he devoted himself to the continuation of *Don Juan.* He had always been diffident in his self-judgments and easily swayed by literary advice. But now, confident that he had at last found his métier, he kept on, in spite of persistent objections against the supposed immorality of the poem by the English public, by his publisher John Murray, by his friends and well-wishers, and by his extremely decorous lover, the Countess Guiccioli—by almost everyone, in fact, except the idealist Shelley, who thought *Juan* incomparably better than anything he himself could write and insisted "that every word of it is pregnant with immortality."

Byron finally broke off literature for action when he organized an expedition to assist in the Greek war for independence from the Turks. He knew too well the conditions in Greece, and had too skeptical an estimate of human nature, to entertain hope of success; but, in part because his own writings had helped to kindle European enthusiasm for the Greek cause, he now felt honor-bound to try what could be done. In the dismal, marshy town of Missolonghi he lived a Spartan existence, training troops whom he had himself subsidized and exhibiting practical grasp and a power of leadership amid a chaos of factionalism, intrigue, and military ineptitude. Worn out, he succumbed to a series of feverish attacks and died just after he had reached his thirty-sixth birthday. To this day Byron is revered by the Greek people as a national hero.

Students of Byron still feel, as his friends had felt, the magnetism of his volatile temperament. As Mary Shelley wrote six years after his death, when she read Thomas Moore's edition of his *Letters and Journals:* "The Lord Byron I find there is our Lord Byron—the fascinating—faulty—childish—philosophical being—daring the world— docile to a private circle—impetuous and indolent—gloomy and yet more gay than any other." Of his inner discordances, Byron himself was well aware; he told his friend Lady Blessington: "I am so changeable, being everything by turns and nothing long—I am such a strange *mélange* of good and evil, that it would be difficult to describe me." Yet he remained faithful to his code: a determination to tell the truth as he saw it about the world and about himself (his refusal to suppress or conceal any of his moods is in part what made him seem so contradictory) and a dedication to the freedom of nations and individuals. As he went on to say to Lady Blessington: "There are but two sentiments to which I am constant—a strong love of liberty, and a detestation of cant."

The poetry texts printed here are taken from Jerome J. McGann's edition, *Lord Byron: The Complete Poetical Works* (Oxford, 1980–93).

Written after Swimming from Sestos to Abydos[1]

May 9, 1810

I

If in the month of dark December
Leander, who was nightly wont
(What maid will not the tale remember?)
To cross thy stream, broad Hellespont!

2

5   If when the wintry tempest roared
He sped to Hero, nothing loth,

---

1. The Hellespont (now called the Dardanelles) is the narrow strait between Europe and Asia. In the ancient story, retold in Christopher Marlowe's *Hero and Leander,* young Leander of Abydos, on the Asian side, swam nightly to visit Hero, a priestess of the goddess Venus at Sestos, until he was drowned when he made the attempt in a storm. Byron and a young Lieutenant Ekenhead swam the Hellespont in the reverse direction on May 3, 1810. Byron alternated between complacency and humor in his many references to the event. In a note to the poem, he mentions that the distance was "upwards of four English miles, though the actual breadth is barely one. The rapidity of the current is such that no boat can row directly across. . . . The water was extremely cold, from the melting of the mountain snows."

And thus of old thy current pour'd,
  Fair Venus! how I pity both!

3

For *me*, degenerate modern wretch,
10 Though in the genial month of May,
My dripping limbs I faintly stretch,
  And think I've done a feat to-day.

4

But since he cross'd the rapid tide,
  According to the doubtful story,
15 To woo,—and—Lord knows what beside,
  And swam for Love, as I for Glory;

5

'Twere hard to say who fared the best:
  Sad mortals! thus the Gods still plague you!
He lost his labour, I my jest:
20 For he was drown'd, and I've the ague.

1810   1812

She walks in beauty[1]

1

She walks in beauty, like the night
  Of cloudless climes and starry skies;
And all that's best of dark and bright
  Meet in her aspect and her eyes:
5 Thus mellow'd to that tender light
  Which heaven to gaudy day denies.

2

One shade the more, one ray the less,
  Had half impair'd the nameless grace
Which waves in every raven tress,
10 Or softly lightens o'er her face;
Where thoughts serenely sweet express
  How pure, how dear their dwelling place.

3

And on that cheek, and o'er that brow,
  So soft, so calm, yet eloquent,
15 The smiles that win, the tints that glow,
  But tell of days in goodness spent,

---

1. One of the lyrics in *Hebrew Melodies* (1815), written to be set to adaptations of traditional Jewish tunes by the young musician Isaac Nathan. Byron wrote the lines the morning after he had met his beautiful young cousin by marriage, Mrs. Robert John Wilmot, who wore a black mourning gown brightened with spangles.

A mind at peace with all below,
A heart whose love is innocent!

June 1814   1815

They say that Hope is happiness

Felix qui potuit rerum cognoscere causas.[1]
VIRGIL

1

They say that Hope is happiness—
But genuine Love must prize the past;
And Mem'ry wakes the thoughts that bless:
They rose the first—they set the last.

2

5   And all that mem'ry loves the most
Was once our only hope to be:
And all that hope adored and lost
Hath melted into memory.

3

Alas! it is delusion all—
10   The future cheats us from afar:
Nor can we be what we recall,
Nor dare we think on what we are.

1814   1829

When we two parted

1

When we two parted
In silence and tears,
Half broken-hearted
To sever for years,
5   Pale grew thy cheek and cold,
Colder thy kiss;
Truly that hour foretold
Sorrow to this.

2

The dew of the morning
10   Sunk chill on my brow—
It felt like the warning
Of what I feel now.

1. Happy is he who has been able to learn the causes of things (Latin; *Georgics* 2.490).

> Thy vows are all broken,
>   And light is thy fame;
> 15 I hear thy name spoken,
>   And share in its shame.

3

> They name thee before me,
>   A knell to mine ear;
> A shudder comes o'er me—
> 20   Why wert thou so dear?
> They know not I knew thee,
>   Who knew thee too well:—
> Long, long shall I rue thee,
>   Too deeply to tell.

4

> 25 In secret we met—
>   In silence I grieve,
> That thy heart could forget,
>   Thy spirit deceive.
> If I should meet thee
> 30   After long years,
> How should I greet thee!—
>   With silence and tears.

1815   1815

Stanzas for Music

> There be none of Beauty's daughters
>   With a magic like thee;
> And like music on the waters
>   Is thy sweet voice to me:
> 5 When, as if its sound were causing
> The charmed ocean's pausing,
> The waves lie still and gleaming,
> And the lulled winds seem dreaming.
>
> And the midnight moon is weaving
> 10   Her bright chain o'er the deep;
> Whose breast is gently heaving,
>   As an infant's asleep.
> So the spirit bows before thee,
> To listen and adore thee;
> 15 With a full but soft emotion,
> Like the swell of Summer's ocean.

1816   1816

Darkness[1]

I had a dream, which was not all a dream.
The bright sun was extinguish'd, and the stars
Did wander darkling[2] in the eternal space,
Rayless, and pathless, and the icy earth
5   Swung blind and blackening in the moonless air;
Morn came, and went—and came, and brought no day,
And men forgot their passions in the dread
Of this their desolation; and all hearts
Were chill'd into a selfish prayer for light:
10   And they did live by watchfires—and the thrones,
The palaces of crowned kings—the huts,
The habitations of all things which dwell,
Were burnt for beacons; cities were consumed,
And men were gathered round their blazing homes
15   To look once more into each other's face;
Happy were those who dwelt within the eye
Of the volcanos, and their mountain-torch:
A fearful hope was all the world contain'd;
Forests were set on fire—but hour by hour
20   They fell and faded—and the crackling trunks
Extinguish'd with a crash—and all was black.
The brows of men by the despairing light
Wore an unearthly aspect, as by fits
The flashes fell upon them; some lay down
25   And hid their eyes and wept; and some did rest
Their chins upon their clenched hands, and smiled;
And others hurried to and fro, and fed
Their funeral piles with fuel, and looked up
With mad disquietude on the dull sky,
30   The pall of a past world; and then again
With curses cast them down upon the dust,
And gnash'd their teeth and howl'd: the wild birds shriek'd,
And, terrified, did flutter on the ground,
And flap their useless wings; the wildest brutes
35   Came tame and tremulous; and vipers crawl'd
And twined themselves among the multitude,
Hissing, but stingless—they were slain for food:
And War, which for a moment was no more,
Did glut himself again;—a meal was bought
40   With blood, and each sate sullenly apart
Gorging himself in gloom: no love was left;
All earth was but one thought—and that was death,
Immediate and inglorious; and the pang
Of famine fed upon all entrails—men
45   Died, and their bones were tombless as their flesh;

---

1. A powerfully imagined blank-verse description
of the end of life on earth—a speculation hardly
less common in Byron's time than in ours.
2. In the dark.

The meagre by the meagre were devoured,
Even dogs assail'd their masters, all save one,
And he was faithful to a corse, and kept
The birds and beasts and famish'd men at bay,
50   Till hunger clung° them, or the dropping dead   *withered*
Lured their lank jaws; himself sought out no food,
But with a piteous and perpetual moan,
And a quick desolate cry, licking the hand
Which answered not with a caress—he died.
55   The crowd was famish'd by degrees; but two
Of an enormous city did survive,
And they were enemies; they met beside
The dying embers of an altar-place,
Where had been heap'd a mass of holy things
60   For an unholy usage; they raked up,
And shivering scraped with their cold skeleton hands
The feeble ashes, and their feeble breath
Blew for a little life, and made a flame
Which was a mockery; then they lifted up
65   Their eyes as it grew lighter, and beheld
Each other's aspects—saw, and shriek'd, and died—
Even of their mutual hideousness they died,
Unknowing who he was upon whose brow
Famine had written Fiend. The world was void,
70   The populous and the powerful—was a lump,
Seasonless, herbless, treeless, manless, lifeless—
A lump of death—a chaos of hard clay.
The rivers, lakes, and ocean all stood still,
And nothing stirred within their silent depths;
75   Ships sailorless lay rotting on the sea,
And their masts fell down piecemeal; as they dropp'd
They slept on the abyss without a surge—
The waves were dead; the tides were in their grave,
The moon their mistress had expired before;
80   The winds were withered in the stagnant air,
And the clouds perish'd; Darkness had no need
Of aid from them—She was the universe.

1816   1816

So, we'll go no more a roving[1]

I

So, we'll go no more a roving
So late into the night,

---

1. Composed in the Lenten aftermath of a spell of feverish dissipation in the Carnival season in Venice, and included in a letter to Thomas Moore, February 28, 1817. Byron wrote, "I find 'the sword wearing out the scabbard,' though I have but just turned the corner of twenty-nine." The poem is based on the refrain of a Scottish song, *The Jolly Beggar:* "And we'll gang nae mair a roving / Sae late into the nicht."

Though the heart be still as loving,
    And the moon be still as bright.

2

5 For the sword outwears its sheath,
    And the soul wears out the breast,
And the heart must pause to breathe,
    And love itself have rest.

3

Though the night was made for loving,
10   And the day returns too soon,
Yet we'll go no more a roving
    By the light of the moon.

1817   1830

When a man hath no freedom to fight for at home[1]

When a man hath no freedom to fight for at home,
    Let him combat for that of his neighbors;
Let him think of the glories of Greece and of Rome,
    And get knock'd on the head for his labours.

5 To do good to mankind is the chivalrous plan,
    And is always as nobly requited;
Then battle for freedom wherever you can,
    And, if not shot or hang'd, you'll get knighted.

Nov. 5, 1820   1830

Stanzas Written on the Road between
Florence and Pisa

Oh, talk not to me of a name great in story—
The days of our youth are the days of our glory;
And the myrtle and ivy[1] of sweet two-and-twenty
Are worth all your laurels,[2] though ever so plenty.

5 What are garlands and crowns to the brow that is wrinkled?
'Tis but as a dead-flower with May-dew besprinkled:
Then away with all such from the head that is hoary!
What care I for the wreaths that can *only* give glory?

Oh FAME!—if I e'er took delight in thy praises,
10 'Twas less for the sake of thy high-sounding phrases,

---

1. The ironist's attitude toward gratuitous enlistment in a foreign war for national freedom—a cause to which Byron gave his own life less than four years later.

1. Sacred to Bacchus, god of wine and revelry. "Myrtle": sacred to Venus, goddess of love.
2. A laurel crown was awarded by the Greeks as a mark of high honor.

Than to see the bright eyes of the dear one discover
She thought that I was not unworthy to love her.

There chiefly I sought thee, *there* only I found thee;
Her glance was the best of the rays that surround thee;
15   When it sparkled o'er aught that was bright in my story,
I knew it was love, and I felt it was glory.

Nov. 1821   1830

January 22nd. Missolonghi

On this day I complete my thirty sixth year

'Tis time this heart should be unmoved,
    Since others it hath ceased to move:
Yet though I cannot be beloved,
                Still let me love!

5   My days are in the yellow leaf;
        The flowers and fruits of Love are gone;
    The worm—the canker, and the grief
                    Are mine alone!

    The fire that on my bosom preys
10   Is lone as some Volcanic Isle;
    No torch is kindled at its blaze
                    A funeral pile!

    The hope, the fear, the jealous care,
        The exalted portion of the pain
15 And power of Love I cannot share,
                    But wear the chain.

    But 'tis not *thus*—and 'tis not *here*
        Such thoughts should shake my Soul, nor *now*
    Where Glory decks the hero's bier
20   Or binds his brow.

    The Sword, the Banner, and the Field,
        Glory and Greece around us see!
    The Spartan borne upon his shield
                    Was not more free!

25 Awake (not Greece—she *is* awake!)
        Awake, my Spirit! think through *whom*
    Thy life-blood tracks its parent lake
                    And then strike home!

    Tread those reviving passions down
30   Unworthy Manhood—unto thee

> Indifferent should the smile or frown
> Of Beauty be.

> If thou regret'st thy Youth, *why live?*
> The land of honourable Death
> 35 Is here:—up to the Field, and give
> Away thy Breath!

> Seek out—less often sought than found—
> A Soldier's Grave, for thee the best;
> Then look around, and choose thy Ground,
> 40 And take thy Rest!

Jan. 1824   1824

Childe Harold's Pilgrimage

Childe Harold is a travelogue narrated by a melancholy, passionate, well-read, and very eloquent tourist. Byron wrote most of the first two cantos while on the tour through Spain, Portugal, Albania, and Greece that these cantos describe; when he published them, in 1812, they made him at one stroke the best known and most talked about poet in England. Byron took up *Childe Harold* again in 1816, during the European tour he made after the breakup of his marriage. Canto 3, published in 1816, moves through Belgium, up the Rhine, then to Switzerland and the Alps. Canto 4, published in 1818, describes the great cities and monuments of Italy.

Byron chose for his poem the Spenserian stanza, and like James Thomson (in the *Castle of Indolence*) and other eighteenth-century predecessors, he attempted in the first canto to imitate, in a seriocomic fashion, the archaic language of his Elizabethan model. (The word *Childe* itself is the ancient term for a young noble awaiting knighthood.) But he soon dropped the archaisms, and in the last two cantos he adapts Spenser's mellifluous stanza to his own assured and brassy magniloquence.

In the preface to his first two cantos, Byron had insisted that the narrator, Childe Harold, was "a fictitious character," merely "the child of imagination." In the manuscript version of these cantos, however, he had called his hero "Childe Burun," the early form of his own family name. The world insisted on identifying the character as well as the travels of the protagonist with those of the author, and in the fourth canto Byron, abandoning the third-person *dramatis persona*, spoke out frankly in the first person.

Childe Harold achieved a great European reputation, not only because of the character of its protagonist but also because of its high-pitched style, with its abrupt changes in subject, mood, and pace. Goethe applied to the poem the terms *Keckheit, Kühnheit, und Grandiosität*: "darling, dash, and grandiosity." Byron converted an accurate tourist's record of scenes, memorials, and museums into a dramatic experience in which everything is presented as it affects the violent sensibility of a new cultural phenomenon, the Romantic Man of Feeling.

From Childe Harold's Pilgrimage

A ROMAUNT[1]

From Canto 1

["Sin's Long Labyrinth"]

1

Oh, thou! in Hellas deem'd of heav'nly birth,
Muse! form'd or fabled at the minstrel's will!
Since sham'd full oft by later lyres on earth,
Mine dares not call thee from thy sacred hill:
5   Yet there I've wander'd by thy vaunted rill;
Yes! sigh'd o'er Delphi's long-deserted shrine,
Where, save that feeble fountain, all is still;
Nor mote° my shell awake the weary Nine[2]   *may*
To grace so plain a tale—this lowly lay of mine.

2

10   Whilome[3] in Albion's° isle there dwelt a youth,   *England's*
Who ne in virtue's ways did take delight;
But spent his days in riot most uncouth,
And vex'd with mirth the drowsy ear of Night.
Ah, me! in sooth he was a shameless wight,
15   Sore given to revel and ungodly glee;
Few earthly things found favour in his sight
Save concubines and carnal companie,
And flaunting wassailers[4] of high and low degree.

3

Childe Harold was he hight:—but whence his name
20   And lineage long, it suits me not to say;
Suffice it, that perchance they were of fame,
And had been glorious in another day:
But one sad losel[5] soils a name for aye,
However mighty in the olden time;
25   Nor all that heralds rake from coffin'd clay,
Nor florid prose, nor honied lies of rhyme
Can blazon evil deeds, or consecrate a crime.

4

Childe Harold bask'd him in the noon-tide sun,
Disporting there like any other fly;
30   Nor deem'd before his little day was done
One blast might chill him into misery.

1. A romance or narrative of adventure.
2. The Muses, whose "vaunted rill" (line 5) was the Castalian spring. "Shell": lyre. Hermes is fabled to have invented the lyre by stretching strings over the hollow of a tortoise shell.
3. Once upon a time.
4. Noisy, insolent drinkers (Byron is thought to refer to his own youthful carousing with friends at Newstead Abbey).
5. Rascal. Byron's great-uncle, the fifth Lord Byron, had killed a kinsman in a drunken duel.

But long ere scarce a third of his pass'd by,
Worse than adversity the Childe befell;
He felt the fulness of satiety:
35   Then loath'd he in his native land to dwell,
Which seem'd to him more lone than Eremite's[6] sad cell.

5

For he through Sin's long labyrinth had run,
Nor made atonement when he did amiss,
Had sigh'd to many though he lov'd but one,
40   And that lov'd one, alas! could ne'er be his.
Ah, happy she! to 'scape from him whose kiss
Had been pollution unto aught so chaste;
Who soon had left her charms for vulgar bliss,
And spoil'd her goodly lands to gild his waste,
45 Nor calm domestic peace had ever deign'd to taste.

6

And now Childe Harold was sore sick at heart,
And from his fellow bacchanals would flee;
'Tis said, at times the sullen tear would start,
But Pride congeal'd the drop within his ee:°   *eye*
50   Apart he stalk'd in joyless reverie,
And from his native land resolv'd to go,
And visit scorching climes beyond the sea;
With pleasure drugg'd he almost long'd for woe,
And e'en for change of scene would seek the shades below.

From Canto 3

["ONCE MORE UPON THE WATERS"]

1

Is thy face like thy mother's, my fair child!
Ada![1] sole daughter of my house and heart?
When last I saw thy young blue eyes they smiled,
And then we parted,—not as now we part,
But with a hope.—
5   Awaking with a start,
The waters heave around me; and on high
The winds lift up their voices: I depart,
Whither I know not; but the hour's gone by,
When Albion's lessening shores could grieve or glad mine eye.

2

10   Once more upon the waters! yet once more!
And the waves bound beneath me as a steed

6. A religious hermit.
1. Byron's daughter Augusta Ada, born in December 1816, a month before her parents separated.

Byron's "hope" (line 5) had been for a reconciliation, but he was never to see Ada again.

That knows his rider. Welcome, to their roar!
Swift be their guidance, wheresoe'er it lead!
Though the strain'd mast should quiver as a reed,
15 And the rent canvas fluttering strew the gale,
Still must I on; for I am as a weed,
Flung from the rock, on Ocean's foam, to sail
Where'er the surge may sweep, the tempest's breath prevail.

3

In my youth's summer[2] I did sing of One,
20 The wandering outlaw of his own dark mind;
Again I seize the theme then but begun,
And bear it with me, as the rushing wind
Bears the cloud onwards: in that Tale I find
The furrows of long thought, and dried-up tears,
25 Which, ebbing, leave a sterile track behind,
O'er which all heavily the journeying years
Plod the last sands of life,—where not a flower appears.

4

Since my young days of passion—joy, or pain,
Perchance my heart and harp have lost a string,
30 And both may jar:[3] it may be, that in vain
I would essay as I have sung to sing.
Yet, though a dreary strain, to this I cling;
So that it wean me from the weary dream
Of selfish grief or gladness—so it fling
35 Forgetfulness around me—it shall seem
To me, though to none else, a not ungrateful theme.

5

He, who grown aged in this world of woe,
In deeds, not years, piercing the depths of life,
So that no wonder waits him; nor below
40 Can love, or sorrow, fame, ambition, strife,
Cut to his heart again with the keen knife
Of silent, sharp endurance: he can tell
Why thought seeks refuge in lone caves, yet rife
With airy images, and shapes which dwell
45 Still unimpair'd, though old, in the soul's haunted cell.

6

'Tis to create, and in creating live
A being more intense, that we endow
With form our fancy, gaining as we give
The life we image, even as I do now.
50 What am I? Nothing; but not so art thou,
Soul of my thought![4] with whom I traverse earth,
Invisible but gazing, as I glow

2. Byron wrote canto 1 at age twenty-one; he is
now twenty-eight.

3. Sound discordant.
4. I.e., Childe Harold, his literary creation.

Mix'd with thy spirit, blended with thy birth,
And feeling still with thee in my crush'd feelings' dearth.

7

55　Yet must I think less wildly:—I *have* thought
　　Too long and darkly, till my brain became,
　　In its own eddy boiling and o'erwrought,
　　A whirling gulf of phantasy and flame:
　　And thus, untaught in youth my heart to tame,
60　My springs of life were poison'd. 'Tis too late!
　　Yet am I chang'd; though still enough the same
　　In strength to bear what time can not abate,
And feed on bitter fruits without accusing Fate.

8

　　Something too much of this:—but now 'tis past,
65　And the spell closes with its silent seal.[5]
　　Long absent HAROLD re-appears at last;
　　He of the breast which fain no more would feel,
　　Wrung with the wounds which kill not, but ne'er heal;
　　Yet Time, who changes all, had alter'd him
70　In soul and aspect as in age: years steal
　　Fire from the mind as vigour from the limb;
And life's enchanted cup but sparkles near the brim.

9

　　His had been quaff'd too quickly, and he found
　　The dregs were wormwood; but he fill'd again,
75　And from a purer fount, on holier ground,
　　And deem'd its spring perpetual; but in vain!
　　Still round him clung invisibly a chain
　　Which gall'd for ever, fettering though unseen,
　　And heavy though it clank'd not; worn with pain,
80　Which pined although it spoke not, and grew keen,
Entering with every step, he took, through many a scene.

10

　　Secure in guarded coldness, he had mix'd
　　Again in fancied safety with his kind,
　　And deem'd his spirit now so firmly fix'd
85　And sheath'd with an invulnerable mind,
　　That, if no joy, no sorrow lurk'd behind;
　　And he, as one, might midst the many stand
　　Unheeded, searching through the crowd to find
　　Fit speculation! such as in strange land
90　He found in wonder-works of God and Nature's hand.

11

　　But who can view the ripened rose, nor seek
　　To wear it? who can curiously behold

5. I.e., he sets the seal of silence on his personal tale ("spell").

The smoothness and the sheen of beauty's cheek,
Nor feel the heart can never all grow old?
95   Who can contemplate Fame through clouds unfold
The star which rises o'er her steep, nor climb?
Harold, once more within the vortex, roll'd
On with the giddy circle, chasing Time,
Yet with a nobler aim than in his youth's fond° prime.   *foolish*

12

100   But soon he knew himself the most unfit
Of men to herd with Man; with whom he held
Little in common; untaught to submit
His thoughts to others, though his soul was quell'd
In youth by his own thoughts; still uncompell'd,
105   He would not yield dominion of his mind
To spirits against whom his own rebell'd;
Proud though in desolation; which could find
A life within itself, to breathe without mankind.

13

Where rose the mountains, there to him were friends;
110   Where roll'd the ocean, thereon was his home;
Where a blue sky, and glowing clime, extends,
He had the passion and the power to roam;
The desert, forest, cavern, breaker's foam,
Were unto him companionship; they spake
115   A mutual language, clearer than the tome
Of his land's tongue, which he would oft forsake
For Nature's pages glass'd° by sunbeams on the lake.   *made glassy*

14

Like the Chaldean,⁶ he could watch the stars,
Till he had peopled them with beings bright
120   As their own beams; and earth, and earth-born jars,
And human frailties, were forgotten quite:
Could he have kept his spirit to that flight
He had been happy; but this clay will sink
Its spark immortal, envying it the light
125   To which it mounts, as if to break the link
That keeps us from yon heaven which woos us to its brink.

15

But in Man's dwellings he became a thing
Restless and worn, and stern and wearisome,
Droop'd as a wild-born falcon with clipt wing,
130   To whom the boundless air alone were home:
Then came his fit again, which to o'ercome,
As eagerly the barr'd-up bird will beat
His breast and beak against his wiry dome

---

6. A people of ancient Babylonia, expert in astronomy.

Till the blood tinge his plumage, so the heat
135   Of his impeded soul would through his bosom eat.

16

Self-exiled Harold wanders forth again,
With nought of hope left, but with less of gloom;
The very knowledge that he lived in vain,
That all was over on this side the tomb,
140   Had made Despair a smilingness assume,
Which, though 'twere wild,—as on the plundered wreck
When mariners would madly meet their doom
With draughts intemperate on the sinking deck,—
Did yet inspire a cheer, which he forbore to check.

[WATERLOO]

17

145   Stop!—for thy tread is on an Empire's dust!
An Earthquake's spoil is sepulchered below!
Is the spot mark'd with no colossal bust?
Nor column trophied for triumphal show?
None; but the moral's truth tells simpler so,
150   As the ground was before, thus let it be;—
How that red rain hath made the harvest grow!
And is this all the world has gained by thee,
Thou first and last of fields! king-making Victory?

18

And Harold stands upon this place of skulls,
155   The grave of France, the deadly Waterloo![7]
How in an hour the power which gave annuls
Its gifts, transferring fame as fleeting too!
In "pride of place" here last the eagle flew,[8]
Then tore with bloody talon the rent plain,
160   Pierced by the shaft of banded nations through;
Ambition's life and labours all were vain;
He wears the shattered links of the world's broken chain.[9]

19

Fit retribution! Gaul[1] may champ the bit
And foam in fetters;—but is Earth more free?
165   Did nations combat to make *One* submit;
Or league to teach all kings true sovereignty?
What! shall reviving Thraldom again be
The patched-up idol of enlightened days?
Shall we, who struck the Lion down, shall we

7. Napoleon's defeat at Waterloo, near Brussels, had occurred only the year before, on June 18, 1815.
8. The eagle was the standard of Napoleon. "Pride of place": from falconry, meaning the highest point of flight (cf. *Macbeth* 2.4.12).
9. Napoleon was then a prisoner at St. Helena.
1. France. Byron, like Shelley and other liberals, saw the defeat of the Napoleonic tyranny as also a victory for tyrannous kings and the forces of extreme reaction throughout Europe.

170   Pay the Wolf homage? proffering lowly gaze
         And servile knees to thrones? No; *prove*² before ye praise!

20

         If not, o'er one fallen despot boast no more!
         In vain fair cheeks were furrowed with hot tears
         For Europe's flowers long rooted up before
175   The trampler of her vineyards; in vain years
         Of death, depopulation, bondage, fears,
         Have all been borne, and broken by the accord
         Of roused-up millions: all that most endears
         Glory, is when the myrtle wreathes a sword
180   Such as Harmodius drew on Athens' tyrant lord.³

21

         There was a sound of revelry by night,⁴
         And Belgium's capital had gathered then
         Her Beauty and her Chivalry, and bright
         The lamps shone o'er fair women and brave men;
185   A thousand hearts beat happily; and when
         Music arose with its voluptuous swell,
         Soft eyes look'd love to eyes which spake again,
         And all went merry as a marriage-bell;
         But hush! hark! a deep sound strikes like a rising knell!

22

190   Did ye not hear it?—No; 'twas but the wind,
         Or the car rattling o'er the stony street;
         On with the dance! let joy be unconfined;
         No sleep till morn, when Youth and Pleasure meet
         To chase the glowing Hours with flying feet—
195   But, hark!—that heavy sound breaks in once more,
         As if the clouds its echo would repeat;
         And nearer, clearer, deadlier than before!
         Arm! Arm! and out—it is—the cannon's opening roar!

23

         Within a windowed niche of that high hall
200   Sate Brunswick's fated chieftain;⁵ he did hear
         That sound the first amidst the festival,
         And caught its tone with Death's prophetic ear;
         And when they smiled because he deem'd it near,
         His heart more truly knew that peal too well
205   Which stretch'd his father on a bloody bier,
         And roused the vengeance blood alone could quell:
         He rush'd into the field, and, foremost fighting, fell.

2. Await the test (proof) of experience.
3. In 514 B.C.E. Harmodius and Aristogeiton, hiding their daggers in myrtle (symbol of love), killed Hipparchus, tyrant of Athens.
4. A famous ball, given by the duchess of Richmond on the eve of the battle of Quatre Bras, which opened the conflict at Waterloo.
5. The duke of Brunswick, nephew of George III of England, was killed in the battle of Quatre Bras. His father, commanding the Prussian army against Napoleon, had been killed at Auerstedt in 1806 (line 205).

24

Ah! then and there was hurrying to and fro,
And gathering tears, and tremblings of distress,
210 And cheeks all pale, which but an hour ago
Blush'd at the praise of their own loveliness;
And there were sudden partings, such as press
The life from out young hearts, and choking sighs
Which ne'er might be repeated; who could guess
215 If ever more should meet those mutual eyes,
Since upon nights so sweet such awful morn could rise?

25

And there was mounting in hot haste: the steed,
The mustering squadron, and the clattering car,
Went pouring forward in impetuous speed,
220 And swiftly forming in the ranks of war;
And the deep thunder peal on peal afar;
And near, the beat of the alarming drum
Roused up the soldier ere the morning star;
While throng'd the citizens with terror dumb,
225 Or whispering, with white lips—"The foe! They come! they come!"

26

And wild and high the "Cameron's gathering" rose!
The war-note of Lochiel,[6] which Albyn's° hills   *Scotland's*
Have heard, and heard, too, have her Saxon foes:—
How in the noon of night that pibroch[7] thrills,
230 Savage and shrill! But with the breath which fills
Their mountain-pipe, so fill the mountaineers
With the fierce native daring which instils
The stirring memory of a thousand years,
And Evan's, Donald's[8] fame rings in each clansman's ears!

27

235 And Ardennes[9] waves above them her green leaves,
Dewy with nature's tear-drops, as they pass,
Grieving, if aught inanimate e'er grieves,
Over the unreturning brave,—alas!
Ere evening to be trodden like the grass
240 Which now beneath them, but above shall grow
In its next verdure, when this fiery mass
Of living valour, rolling on the foe
And burning with high hope, shall moulder cold and low.

28

Last noon beheld them full of lusty life,
245 Last eve in Beauty's circle proudly gay,

6. "Cameron's gathering" is the clan song of the
Camerons, whose chief was called "Lochiel," after
his estate.
7. Bagpipe music, usually warlike in character.
8. Sir Evan and Donald Cameron, famous warriors in the Stuart cause in the 17th and 18th centuries.
9. A forested region covering parts of Belgium,
France, and Luxembourg.

The midnight brought the signal-sound of strife,
The morn the marshalling in arms,—the day
Battle's magnificently-stern array!
The thunder-clouds close o'er it, which when rent
250 The earth is covered thick with other clay,
Which her own clay shall cover, heaped and pent,
Rider and horse,—friend, foe,—in one red burial blent!

*   *   *

[NAPOLEON]

36

There sunk the greatest, nor the worst of men,[1]
Whose spirit antithetically mixt
One moment of the mightiest, and again
On little objects with like firmness fixt,
320 Extreme in all things! hadst thou been betwixt,
Thy throne had still been thine, or never been;
For daring made thy rise as fall: thou seek'st
Even now to re-assume the imperial mien,
And shake again the world, the Thunderer of the scene!

37

325 Conqueror and captive of the earth art thou!
She trembles at thee still, and thy wild name
Was ne'er more bruited in men's minds than now
That thou art nothing, save the jest of Fame,
Who wooed thee once, thy vassal, and became
330 The flatterer of thy fierceness, till thou wert
A god unto thyself; nor less the same
To the astounded kingdoms all inert,
Who deem'd thee for a time whate'er thou didst assert.

38

Oh, more or less than man—in high or low,
335 Battling with nations, flying from the field;
Now making monarchs' necks thy footstool, now
More than thy meanest soldier taught to yield;
An empire thou couldst crush, command, rebuild,
But govern not thy pettiest passion, nor,
340 However deeply in men's spirits skill'd,
Look through thine own, nor curb the lust of war,
Nor learn that tempted Fate will leave the loftiest star.

39

Yet well thy soul hath brook'd the turning tide
With that untaught innate philosophy,
345 Which, be it wisdom, coldness, or deep pride,

---

1. Napoleon, here portrayed with many of the characteristics of the Byronic hero.

Is gall and wormwood to an enemy.
When the whole host of hatred stood hard by,
To watch and mock thee shrinking, thou hast smiled
With a sedate and all-enduring eye;—
350   When Fortune fled her spoil'd and favourite child,
He stood unbowed beneath the ills upon him piled.

40

Sager than in thy fortunes; for in them
Ambition steel'd thee on too far to show
That just habitual scorn which could contemn
355   Men and their thoughts; 'twas wise to feel, not so
To wear it ever on thy lip and brow,
And spurn the instruments thou wert to use
Till they were turn'd unto thine overthrow:
'Tis but a worthless world to win or lose;
360   So hath it proved to thee, and all such lot[2] who choose.

41

If, like a tower upon a headlong rock,
Thou hadst been made to stand or fall alone,
Such scorn of man had help'd to brave the shock;
But men's thoughts were the steps which paved thy throne,
365   *Their* admiration thy best weapon shone;
The part of Philip's son[3] was thine, not then
(Unless aside thy purple had been thrown)
Like stern Diogenes[4] to mock at men;
For sceptred cynics earth were far too wide a den.

42

370   But quiet to quick bosoms is a hell,
And *there* hath been thy bane; there is a fire
And motion of the soul which will not dwell
In its own narrow being, but aspire
Beyond the fitting medium of desire;
375   And, but once kindled, quenchless evermore,
Preys upon high adventure, nor can tire
Of aught but rest; a fever at the core,
Fatal to him who bears, to all who ever bore.

43

This makes the madmen who have made men mad
380   By their contagion; Conquerors and Kings,
Founders of sects and systems, to whom add
Sophists, Bards, Statesmen, all unquiet things
Which stir too strongly the soul's secret springs,

---

2. An inversion: "all who choose such lot" (i.e., who choose to play such a game of chance).
3. Alexander the Great, son of Philip of Macedon.
4. The Greek philosopher of Cynicism, contemporary of Alexander. It is related that Alexander was so struck by his independence of mind that he said, "If I were not Alexander, I should wish to be Diogenes," hence the allusion in lines 367 and 369.

And are themselves the fools to those they fool;
385   Envied, yet how unenviable! what stings
Are theirs! One breast laid open were a school
Which would unteach mankind the lust to shine or rule:

44

Their breath is agitation, and their life
A storm whereon they ride, to sink at last,
390   And yet so nurs'd and bigotted to strife,
That should their days, surviving perils past,
Melt to calm twilight, they feel overcast
With sorrow and supineness, and so die;
Even as a flame unfed, which runs to waste
395   With its own flickering, or a sword laid by
Which eats into itself, and rusts ingloriously.

45

He who ascends to mountain-tops, shall find
The loftiest peaks most wrapt in clouds and snow;
He who surpasses or subdues mankind,
400   Must look down on the hate of those below.
Though high *above* the sun of glory glow,
And far *beneath* the earth and ocean spread,
Round him are icy rocks, and loudly blow
Contending tempests on his naked head,
405   And thus reward the toils which to those summits led.[5]

*   *   *

52

460   Thus Harold inly said, and pass'd along,
Yet not insensibly to all which here
Awoke the jocund birds to early song
In glens which might have made even exile dear:
Though on his brow were graven lines austere,
465   And tranquil sternness which had ta'en the place
Of feelings fierier far but less severe,
Joy was not always absent from his face,
But o'er it in such scenes would steal with transient trace.

53

Nor was all love shut from him, though his days
470   Of passion had consumed themselves to dust.
It is in vain that we would coldly gaze
On such as smile upon us; the heart must
Leap kindly back to kindness, though disgust
Hath wean'd it from all worldlings: thus he felt,
475   For there was soft remembrance, and sweet trust
In one fond breast,[6] to which his own would melt,
And in its tenderer hour on that his bosom dwelt.

---

5. In the stanzas here omitted, Harold is abruptly sent sailing up the Rhine, meditating on the "thousand battles" that "have assailed thy banks."

6. Commentators agree that the reference is to Byron's half-sister, Augusta Leigh.

54

And he had learn'd to love,—I know not why,
For this in such as him seems strange of mood,—
480   The helpless looks of blooming infancy,
Even in its earliest nurture; what subdued,
To change like this, a mind so far imbued
With scorn of man, it little boots to know;
But thus it was; and though in solitude
485   Small power the nipp'd affections have to grow,
In him this glowed when all beside had ceased to glow.

55

And there was one soft breast, as hath been said,
Which unto his was bound by stronger ties
Than the church links withal; and, though unwed,
490   *That* love was pure, and, far above disguise,
Had stood the test of mortal enmities
Still undivided, and cemented more
By peril, dreaded most in female eyes;
But this was firm, and from a foreign shore
495   Well to that heart might his these absent greetings pour!

* * *

[SWITZERLAND]

68

Lake Leman° woos me with its crystal face,   *Geneva*
645   The mirror where the stars and mountains view
The stillness of their aspect in each trace
Its clear depth yields of their far height and hue:
There is too much of man here, to look through
With a fit mind the might which I behold;
650   But soon in me shall Loneliness renew
Thoughts hid, but not less cherish'd than of old,
Ere mingling with the herd had penn'd me in their fold.

69

To fly from, need not be to hate, mankind;
All are not fit with them to stir and toil,
655   Nor is it discontent to keep the mind
Deep in its fountain, lest it overboil
In the hot throng, where we become the spoil
Of our infection, till too late and long
We may deplore and struggle with the coil,°   *tumult*
660   In wretched interchange of wrong for wrong
'Midst a contentious world, striving where none are strong.

70

There, in a moment, we may plunge our years
In fatal penitence, and in the blight
Of our own soul, turn all our blood to tears,

665 And colour things to come with hues of Night;
The race of life becomes a hopeless flight
To those that walk in darkness: on the sea,
The boldest steer but where their ports invite,
But there are wanderers o'er Eternity
670 Whose bark drives on and on, and anchored ne'er shall be.

71

Is it not better, then, to be alone,
And love Earth only for its earthly sake?
By the blue rushing of the arrowy Rhone,
Or the pure bosom of its nursing lake,
675 Which feeds it as a mother who doth make
A fair but froward infant her own care,
Kissing its cries away as these awake;—
Is it not better thus our lives to wear,
Than join the crushing crowd, doom'd to inflict or bear?

72

680 I live not in myself, but I become
Portion of that around me; and to me,
High mountains are a feeling, but the hum
Of human cities torture: I can see
Nothing to loathe in nature, save to be
685 A link reluctant in a fleshly chain,
Class'd among creatures, when the soul can flee,
And with the sky, the peak, the heaving plain
Of ocean, or the stars, mingle, and not in vain.[7]

73

And thus I am absorb'd, and this is life:
690 I look upon the peopled desart past,
As on a place of agony and strife,
Where, for some sin, to Sorrow I was cast,
To act and suffer, but remount at last
With a fresh pinion; which I feel to spring,
695 Though young, yet waxing vigorous, as the blast
Which it would cope with, on delighted wing,
Spurning the clay-cold bonds which round our being cling.

74

And when, at length, the mind shall be all free
From what it hates in this degraded form,
700 Reft of its carnal life, save what shall be
Existent happier in the fly and worm,—
When elements to elements conform,

7. Byron had lived in close contact with Shelley at Geneva and had toured the lake with him. At that time, he was introduced to concepts of nature in the poetry of Wordsworth, whom Shelley had pressed on Byron's attention. These ideas are reflected in canto 3, but the voice is Byron's own. For his comment on being "half mad" while writing canto 3, see his letter to Thomas Moore, January 28, 1817 (p. 691).

And dust is as it should be, shall I not
Feel all I see, less dazzling, but more warm?
705   The bodiless thought? the Spirit of each spot?
Of which, even now, I share at times the immortal lot?

75

Are not the mountains, waves, and skies, a part
Of me and of my soul, as I of them?
Is not the love of these deep in my heart
710   With a pure passion? should I not contemn
All objects, if compared with these? and stem
A tide of suffering, rather than forego
Such feelings for the hard and worldly phlegm
Of those whose eyes are only turn'd below,
715 Gazing upon the ground, with thoughts which dare not glow?

76

But this is not my theme; and I return
To that which is immediate, and require
Those who find contemplation in the urn,[8]
To look on One,[9] whose dust was once all fire,
720   A native of the land where I respire
The clear air for a while—a passing guest,
Where he became a being,—whose desire
Was to be glorious; 'twas a foolish quest,
The which to gain and keep, he sacrificed all rest.

77

725 Here the self-torturing sophist, wild Rousseau,
The apostle of affliction, he who threw
Enchantment over passion, and from woe
Wrung overwhelming eloquence, first drew
The breath which made him wretched; yet he knew
730   How to make madness beautiful, and cast
O'er erring deeds and thoughts, a heavenly hue
Of words, like sunbeams, dazzling as they past
The eyes, which o'er them shed tears feelingly and fast.

78

His love was passion's essence—as a tree
735   On fire by lightning; with ethereal flame
Kindled he was, and blasted; for to be
Thus, and enamoured, were in him the same.
But his was not the love of living dame,
Nor of the dead who rise upon our dreams,
740   But of ideal beauty, which became
In him existence, and o'erflowing teems
Along his burning page, distempered though it seems.

8. I.e., those who find matter for meditation in an urn containing the ashes of the dead.
9. Jean-Jacques Rousseau, who had been born in Geneva in 1712. Byron's characterization is based on Rousseau's novel *La Nouvelle Héloise*, as well as on his *Confessions*.

* * *

85

Clear, placid Leman! thy contrasted lake,
With the wild world I dwelt in, is a thing
Which warns me, with its stillness, to forsake
800   Earth's troubled waters for a purer spring.
This quiet sail is as a noiseless wing
To waft me from distraction; once I loved
Torn ocean's roar, but thy soft murmuring
Sounds sweet as if a sister's voice reproved,
805   That I with stern delights should e'er have been so moved.

86

It is the hush of night, and all between
Thy margin and the mountains, dusk, yet clear,
Mellowed and mingling, yet distinctly seen,
Save darken'd Jura,[1] whose capt heights appear
810   Precipitously steep; and drawing near,
There breathes a living fragrance from the shore,
Of flowers yet fresh with childhood; on the ear
Drops the light drip of the suspended oar,
Or chirps the grasshopper one good-night carol more;

87

815   He is an evening reveller, who makes
His life an infancy, and sings his fill;
At intervals, some bird from out the brakes,°   *thickets*
Starts into voice a moment, then is still.
There seems a floating whisper on the hill,
820   But that is fancy, for the starlight dews
All silently their tears of love instil,
Weeping themselves away, till they infuse
Deep into Nature's breast the spirit of her hues.

88

Ye stars! which are the poetry of heaven!
825   If in your bright leaves we would read the fate
Of men and empires,—'tis to be forgiven,
That in our aspirations to be great,
Our destinies o'erleap their mortal state,
And claim a kindred with you; for ye are
830   A beauty and a mystery, and create
In us such love and reverence from afar,
That fortune, fame, power, life, have named themselves a star.

89

All heaven and earth are still—though not in sleep,
But breathless, as we grow when feeling most;

---

1. The mountain range between Switzerland and France, visible from Lake Geneva.

835   And silent, as we stand in thoughts too deep:—
         All heaven and earth are still: From the high host
         Of stars, to the lull'd lake and mountain-coast,
         All is concentered in a life intense,
         Where not a beam, nor air, nor leaf is lost,
840   But hath a part of being, and a sense
         Of that which is of all Creator and defence.

                            90
         Then stirs the feeling infinite, so felt
         In solitude, where we are *least* alone;
         A truth, which through our being then doth melt
845   And purifies from self: it is a tone,
         The soul and source of music, which makes known
         Eternal harmony, and sheds a charm,
         Like to the fabled Cytherea's zone,[2]
         Binding all things with beauty;—'twould disarm
850   The spectre Death, had he substantial power to harm.

                            91
         Not vainly did the early Persian make
         His altar the high places and the peak
         Of earth-o'ergazing mountains, and thus take
         A fit and unwall'd temple, there to seek
855   The Spirit, in whose honour shrines are weak,
         Uprear'd of human hands. Come, and compare
         Columns and idol-dwellings, Goth or Greek,
         With Nature's realms of worship, earth and air,
         Nor fix on fond abodes to circumscribe thy prayer!

                            92
860   The sky is changed!—and such a change! Oh night,
         And storm, and darkness, ye are wondrous strong,
         Yet lovely in your strength, as is the light
         Of a dark eye in woman! Far along,
         From peak to peak, the rattling crags among
865   Leaps the live thunder! Not from one lone cloud,
         But every mountain now hath found a tongue,
         And Jura answers, through her misty shroud,
         Back to the joyous Alps, who call to her aloud!

                            93
         And this is in the night:—Most glorious night!
870   Thou wert not sent for slumber! let me be
         A sharer in thy fierce and far delight,—
         A portion of the tempest and of thee!
         How the lit lake shines, a phosphoric sea,
         And the big rain comes dancing to the earth!
875   And now again 'tis black,—and now, the glee

2. The sash of Venus, which conferred the power to attract love.

Of the loud hills shakes with its mountain-mirth,
As if they did rejoice o'er a young earthquake's birth.

94

Now, where the swift Rhone cleaves his way between
Heights which appear as lovers who have parted
880 In hate, whose mining depths so intervene,
That they can meet no more, though broken-hearted;
Though in their souls, which thus each other thwarted,
Love was the very root of the fond rage
Which blighted their life's bloom, and then departed:—
885 Itself expired, but leaving them an age
Of years all winters,—war within themselves to wage.

95

Now, where the quick Rhone thus hath cleft his way,
The mightiest of the storms hath ta'en his stand:
For here, not one, but many, make their play,
890 And fling their thunder-bolts from hand to hand,
Flashing and cast around: of all the band,
The brightest through these parted hills hath fork'd
His lightnings,—as if he did understand,
That in such gaps as desolation work'd,
895 There the hot shaft should blast whatever therein lurk'd.

96

Sky, mountains, river, winds, lake, lightnings! ye!
With night, and clouds, and thunder, and a soul
To make these felt and feeling, well may be
Things that have made me watchful; the far roll
900 Of your departing voices, is the knoll[3]
Of what in me is sleepless,—if I rest.
But where of ye, oh tempests! is the goal?
Are ye like those within the human breast?
Or do ye find, at length, like eagles, some high nest?

97

905 Could I embody and unbosom now
That which is most within me,—could I wreak
My thoughts upon expression, and thus throw
Soul, heart, mind, passions, feelings, strong or weak,
All that I would have sought, and all I seek,
910 Bear, know, feel, and yet breathe—into *one* word,
And that one word were Lightning, I would speak;
But as it is, I live and die unheard,
With a most voiceless thought, sheathing it as a sword.

98

The morn is up again, the dewy morn,
915 With breath all incense, and with cheek all bloom,

3. Knell (old form).

Laughing the clouds away with playful scorn,
And living as if earth contain'd no tomb,—
And glowing into day: we may resume
The march of our existence: and thus I,
920   Still on thy shores, fair Leman! may find room
And food for meditation, nor pass by
Much, that may give us pause, if pondered fittingly.

*   *   *

113
I have not loved the world, nor the world me;[4]
1050   I have not flattered its rank breath, nor bow'd
To its idolatries a patient knee,—
Nor coin'd my cheek to smiles,—nor cried aloud
In worship of an echo; in the crowd
They could not deem me one of such; I stood
1055   Among them, but not of them; in a shroud
Of thoughts which were not their thoughts, and still could,
Had I not filed[5] my mind, which thus itself subdued.

114
I have not loved the world, nor the world me,—
But let us part fair foes; I do believe,
1060   Though I have found them not, that there may be
Words which are things,—hopes which will not deceive,
And virtues which are merciful, nor weave
Snares for the failing: I would also deem
O'er others' griefs that some sincerely grieve;
1065   That two, or one, are almost what they seem,—
That goodness is no name, and happiness no dream.

115
My daughter! with thy name this song begun—
My daughter! with thy name thus much shall end—
I see thee not,—I hear thee not,—but none
1070   Can be so wrapt in thee; thou art the friend
To whom the shadows of far years extend:
Albeit my brow thou never should'st behold,
My voice shall with thy future visions blend,
And reach into thy heart,—when mine is cold,—
1075   A token and a tone, even from thy father's mould.

116
To aid thy mind's development,—to watch
Thy dawn of little joys,—to sit and see
Almost thy very growth,—to view thee catch
Knowledge of objects,—wonders yet to thee!
1080   To hold thee lightly on a gentle knee,
And print on thy soft cheek a parent's kiss,—

---

4. Harold utters this soliloquy as he stands at the summit of an Alpine pass, looking southward on Italy.

5. Defiled. In a note Byron refers to *Macbeth* 3.1.66 ("For Banquo's issue have I filed my mind").

This, it should seem, was not reserv'd for me;
    Yet this was in my nature:—as it is,
I know not what is there, yet something like to this.

117

1085   Yet, though dull Hate as duty should be taught,
    I know that thou wilt love me; though my name
    Should be shut from thee, as a spell still fraught
    With desolation,—and a broken claim:
    Though the grave closed between us,—'twere the same,
1090   I know that thou wilt love me; though to drain
    My blood from out thy being, were an aim,
    And an attainment,—all would be in vain,—
Still thou would'st love me, still that more than life retain.

118

    The child of love,—though born in bitterness,
1095   And nurtured in convulsion,—of thy sire
    These were the elements,—and thine no less.
    As yet such are around thee,—but thy fire
    Shall be more tempered, and thy hope far higher.
    Sweet be thy cradled slumbers! O'er the sea,
1100   And from the mountains where I now respire,
    Fain would I waft such blessing upon thee,
As, with a sigh, I deem thou might'st have been to me!

From Canto 4

[VENICE]

1

    I stood in Venice, on the Bridge of Sighs;[1]
    A palace and a prison on each hand:
    I saw from out the wave her structures rise
    As from the stroke of the enchanter's wand:
5   A thousand years their cloudy wings expand
    Around me, and a dying Glory smiles
    O'er the far times, when many a subject land
    Look'd to the winged Lion's[2] marble piles,
Where Venice sate in state, thron'd on her hundred isles!

2

10   She looks a sea Cybele,[3] fresh from ocean,
    Rising with her tiara of proud towers
    At airy distance, with majestic motion,
    A ruler of the waters and their powers:

---

1. A covered bridge between the Doge's Palace and the prison of San Marco.
2. The emblem of St. Mark, patron saint of Venice.
3. A nature goddess, sometimes represented wearing a crown ("tiara," line 11) of towers.

And such she was;—her daughters had their dowers
15   From spoils of nations, and the exhaustless East
Pour'd in her lap all gems in sparkling showers.
In purple was she robed, and of her feast
Monarchs partook, and deem'd their dignity increas'd.

3

In Venice Tasso's echoes are no more,
20   And silent rows the songless gondolier;[4]
Her palaces are crumbling to the shore,
And music meets not always now the ear:
Those days are gone—but Beauty still is here.
States fall, arts fade—but Nature doth not die,
25   Nor yet forget how Venice once was dear,
The pleasant place of all festivity,
The revel of the earth, the masque[5] of Italy!

4

But unto us she hath a spell beyond
Her name in story, and her long array
30   Of mighty shadows, whose dim forms despond
Above the dogeless city's[6] vanish'd sway;
Ours is a trophy which will not decay
With the Rialto;[7] Shylock and the Moor,
And Pierre, can not be swept or worn away—
35   The keystones of the arch! though all were o'er,
For us repeopled were° the solitary shore.   *would be*

* * *

132

1180   And thou, who never yet of human wrong
Left'st the unbalanced scale, great Nemesis![8]
Here, where the ancient paid thee homage long—
Thou, who didst call the Furies from the abyss,
And round Orestes[9] bade them howl and hiss
1185   For that unnatural retribution—just,
Had it but been from hands less near—in this
Thy former realm, I call thee from the dust!
Dost thou not hear my heart?—Awake! thou shalt, and must.

133

It is not that I may not have incurr'd
1190   For my ancestral faults or mine the wound

4. The gondoliers formerly had the custom of chanting stanzas of Tasso's *Jerusalem Delivered*.
5. Masques were lavish dramatic entertainments popular in the courts of the Renaissance, involving songs, dances, and elaborate costumes and staging.
6. The last duke ("doge") of Venice had been deposed by Napoleon in 1797.
7. The business district in Venice, a setting in *The Merchant of Venice* and *Othello* ("the Moor"), and also in Thomas Otway's tragedy *Venice Preserved* (1682), in which Pierre (line 34) is a leading char-

acter.
8. The speaker has journeyed from Venice through Ferrara and Florence to Rome. In this city he invokes the Greek and Roman goddess Nemesis, who represented divine retribution for human transgressions, especially for presumption against the gods.
9. The Furies pursued Orestes for killing his mother, Clytemnestra, to avenge her murder of his father, Agamemnon, when he had returned from the Trojan war.

I bleed withal, and, had it been conferr'd
With a just weapon, it had flowed unbound;
But now my blood shall not sink in the ground;
To thee I do devote it—*thou* shalt take
1195   The vengeance, which shall yet be sought and found,[1]
Which if *I* have not taken for the sake—
But let that pass—I sleep, but thou shalt yet awake.

134

And if my voice break forth, 'tis not that now
I shrink from what is suffered: let him speak
1200   Who hath beheld decline upon my brow,
Or seen my mind's convulsion leave it weak;
But in this page a record will I seek.
Not in the air shall these my words disperse,
Though I be ashes; a far hour shall wreak
1205   The deep prophetic fullness of this verse,
And pile on human heads the mountain of my curse!

135

That curse shall be Forgiveness.—Have I not—
Hear me, my mother Earth! behold it, Heaven!—
Have I not had to wrestle with my lot?
1210   Have I not suffered things to be forgiven?
Have I not had my brain seared, my heart riven,
Hopes sapp'd, name blighted, Life's life lied away?
And only not to desperation driven,
Because not altogether of such clay
1215   As rots into the souls of those whom I survey.

136

From mighty wrongs to petty perfidy
Have I not seen what human things could do?
From the loud roar of foaming calumny
To the small whisper of the as paltry few,
1220   And subtler venom of the reptile crew,
The Janus glance[2] of whose significant eye,
Learning to lie with silence, would *seem* true,
And without utterance, save the shrug or sigh,
Deal round to happy fools its speechless obloquy.

137

1225   But I have lived, and have not lived in vain:
My mind may lose its force, my blood its fire,
And my frame perish even in conquering pain;
But there is that within me which shall tire
Torture and Time, and breathe when I expire;
1230   Something unearthly, which they deem not of,

---

1. He calls on Nemesis to avenge the injustices
that have driven him into his exiled wandering.
2. I.e., facing both ways. In Roman mythology

Janus was represented with two faces, one looking
before, the other behind.

Like the remembered tone of a mute lyre,
Shall on their softened spirits sink, and move
In hearts all rocky now the late remorse of love.

*   *   *

["FAREWELL!"]

175

But I forget.—My pilgrim's shrine is won,[3]
And he and I must part,—so let it be,—
His task and mine alike are nearly done;
1570 Yet once more let us look upon the sea;
The midland ocean breaks on him and me,
And from the Alban Mount[4] we now behold
Our friend of youth, that ocean, which when we
Beheld it last by Calpe's rock[5] unfold
1575 Those waves, we followed on till the dark Euxine[6] roll'd

176

Upon the blue Symplegades:[7] long years—
Long, though not very many, since have done
Their work on both; some suffering and some tears
Have left us nearly where we had begun:
1580 Yet not in vain our mortal race hath run,
We have had our reward—and it is here;
That we can yet feel gladden'd by the sun,
And reap from earth, sea, joy almost as dear
As if there were no man to trouble what is clear.

177

1585 Oh! that the Desart were my dwelling place,
With one fair Spirit for my minister,
That I might all forget the human race,
And, hating no one, love but only her!
Ye Elements!—in whose ennobling stir
1590 I feel myself exalted—Can ye not
Accord me such a being? Do I err
In deeming such inhabit many a spot?
Though with them to converse can rarely be our lot.

178

There is a pleasure in the pathless woods,
1595 There is a rapture on the lonely shore,
There is society, where none intrudes,
By the deep Sea, and music in its roar:

3. I.e., he has reached the goal of his religious pilgrimage.
4. The point of vantage is an Alban hill, looking over the Roman Campagna to the Mediterranean. In its concluding passage (lines 1573ff.) the poem thus rounds back to Harold's initial voyage, when he had first looked upon that sea.
5. The Rock of Gibraltar.
6. Greek name for the Black Sea.
7. Two islands situated at the place where the Black Sea flows into the Bosphorus Strait.

I love not Man the less, but Nature more,
From these our interviews, in which I steal
1600 From all I may be, or have been before,
To mingle with the Universe, and feel
What I can ne'er express, yet can not all conceal.

179

Roll on, thou deep and dark blue ocean—roll!
Ten thousand fleets sweep over thee in vain;
1605 Man marks the earth with ruin—his control
Stops with the shore;—upon the watery plain
The wrecks are all thy deed, nor doth remain
A shadow of man's ravage, save his own,
When, for a moment, like a drop of rain,
1610 He sinks into thy depths with bubbling groan,
Without a grave, unknell'd, uncoffin'd, and unknown.

180

His steps are not upon thy paths,—thy fields
Are not a spoil for him,—thou dost arise
And shake him from thee; the vile strength he wields
1615 For earth's destruction thou dost all despise,
Spurning him from thy bosom to the skies,
And send'st him, shivering in thy playful spray
And howling, to his Gods, where haply lies
His petty hope in some near port or bay,
1620 And dashest him again to earth:—there let him lay.[8]

181

The armaments which thunderstrike the walls
Of rock-built cities, bidding nations quake,
And monarchs tremble in their capitals,
The oak leviathans,° whose huge ribs make   *warships*
1625 Their clay creator the vain title take
Of lord of thee, and arbiter of war;
These are thy toys, and, as the snowy flake,
They melt into thy yeast of waves, which mar
Alike the Armada's pride, or spoils of Trafalgar.[9]

182

1630 Thy shores are empires, changed in all save thee—
Assyria, Greece, Rome, Carthage, what are they?
Thy waters washed them power while they were free,
And many a tyrant since; their shores obey
The stranger, slave, or savage; their decay
1635 Has dried up realms to desarts:—not so thou,

8. For "lie," a much-noted solecism. Byron, like other English aristocrats of the time, affected a cavalier indifference to commonplace grammar.
9. A storm was responsible for the loss of a number of French ships that Nelson had captured at Trafalgar (1805). The Spanish Armada, defeated by the English in 1588, also lost many ships in a storm.

Unchangeable save to thy wild waves' play—
Time writes no wrinkle on thine azure brow—
Such as creation's dawn beheld, thou rollest now.

183

Thou glorious mirror, where the Almighty's form
1640   Glasses° itself in tempests; in all time,   *mirrors*
Calm or convuls'd—in breeze, or gale, or storm,
Icing the pole, or in the torrid clime
Dark-heaving;—boundless, endless, and sublime—
The image of Eternity—the throne
1645   Of the Invisible; even from out thy slime
The monsters of the deep are made; each zone
Obeys thee; thou goest forth, dread, fathomless, alone.

184

And I have loved thee, Ocean! and my joy
Of youthful sports was on thy breast to be
1650   Borne, like thy bubbles, onward: from a boy
I wantoned with thy breakers—they to me
Were a delight; and if the freshening sea
Made them a terror—'twas a pleasing fear,
For I was as it were a child of thee,
1655   And trusted to thy billows far and near,
And laid my hand upon thy mane—as I do here.

185

My task is done—my song hath ceased—my theme
Has died into an echo; it is fit
The spell should break of this protracted dream.
1660   The torch shall be extinguish'd which hath lit
My midnight lamp—and what is writ, is writ,—
Would it were worthier! but I am not now
That which I have been—and my visions flit
Less palpably before me—and the glow
1665   Which in my spirit dwelt, is fluttering, faint, and low.

186

Farewell! a word that must be, and hath been—
A sound which makes us linger;—yet—farewell!
Ye! who have traced the Pilgrim to the scene
Which is his last, if in your memories dwell
1670   A thought which once was his, if on ye swell
A single recollection, not in vain
He wore his sandal-shoon, and scallop-shell;[1]
Farewell! with *him* alone may rest the pain,
If such there were—with *you*, the moral of his strain!

1812, 1816, 1818

1. Sandals and a scallop shell (worn on the hat) were traditional emblems of pilgrims to holy shrines.

Manfred *Manfred* is Byron's first dramatic work. As its subtitle, "A Dramatic Poem," indicates, it was not intended to be produced on the stage; Byron also referred to it as a "metaphysical" drama—that is, a drama of ideas. He began writing it in the autumn of 1816 while living in the Swiss Alps, whose grandeur stimulated his imagination; he finished the drama the following year in Italy.

Manfred's literary forebears include the villains of Gothic fiction and melodrama; the Greek Titan Prometheus, rebel against Zeus, ruler of the gods; Milton's fallen angel, Satan; Ahasuerus, the legendary Wandering Jew who, having ridiculed Christ as he bore the Cross to Calvary, is doomed to live until Christ's Second Coming; and the story of Faust, who yielded his soul to the devil in exchange for superhuman powers. Byron denied that he had ever heard of Marlowe's *Doctor Faustus,* and because he knew no German he had not read Goethe's *Faust,* of which part 1 had been published in 1808. But his friend M. G. Lewis (author of the Gothic novel *The Monk*) had read parts of *Faust* to him in extempore translation during the summer of 1816, just before the composition of *Manfred,* and Byron worked his memories of this oral translation into his own drama in a way that evoked Goethe's admiration.

Like Byron's earlier heroes, Childe Harold and the protagonists of some of his verse romances, Manfred is hounded by remorse—in this instance, for a transgression that (it is hinted but never quite specified) is incest with his sister Astarte; it is also hinted that Astarte has taken her own life. While this element in the drama is often regarded as Byron's veiled confession of his incestuous relations with his half-sister, Augusta Leigh, the theme of incest was a common one both in Gothic fiction and in the writings of Romantic authors such as Goethe, Chateaubriand, Scott, and both the Shelleys.

The character of Manfred is its author's most impressive representation of the Byronic Hero. Byron's invention is to have Manfred, unlike Faust, disdainfully reject the offer of a pact with the powers of darkness. He thereby sets himself up as the totally autonomous man, independent of any external authority or power, whose own mind, as he says in the concluding scene (3.4.127–40), generates the values by which he lives "in sufferance or in joy," and by reference to which he judges, requites, and finally destroys himself. In his book *Ecce Homo,* Nietzsche, recognizing Byron's anticipation of his own *Übermensch* (the "superman" who posits for himself a moral code beyond all traditional standards of good and evil), asserted that the character of Manfred was greater than that of Goethe's Faust.

Manfred

A DRAMATIC POEM

"There are more things in heaven and earth, Horatio,
Than are dreamt of in your philosophy."[1]

DRAMATIS PERSONAE

MANFRED	WITCH OF THE ALPS
CHAMOIS HUNTER	ARIMANES
ABBOT OF ST. MAURICE	NEMESIS
MANUEL	THE DESTINIES
HERMAN	SPIRITS, ETC.

---

1. *Hamlet* 1.5.168–69.

*The scene of the Drama is amongst the Higher Alps—partly in
the Castle of Manfred, and partly in the Mountains.*

Act 1

SCENE 1. MANFRED *alone.—Scene, a Gothic gallery.*[2]*—Time, Midnight.*

MANFRED   The lamp must be replenish'd, but even then
It will not burn so long as I must watch:
My slumbers—if I slumber—are not sleep,
But a continuance of enduring thought,
5 Which then I can resist not: in my heart
There is a vigil, and these eyes but close
To look within; and yet I live, and bear
The aspect and the form of breathing men.
But grief should be the instructor of the wise;
10 Sorrow is knowledge: they who know the most
Must mourn the deepest o'er the fatal truth,
The Tree of Knowledge is not that of Life.
Philosophy and science, and the springs
Of wonder, and the wisdom of the world,
15 I have essayed, and in my mind there is
A power to make these subject to itself—
But they avail not: I have done men good,
And I have met with good even among men—
But this avail'd not: I have had my foes,
20 And none have baffled, many fallen before me—
But this avail'd not:—Good, or evil, life,
Powers, passions, all I see in other beings,
Have been to me as rain unto the sands,
Since that all-nameless hour. I have no dread,
25 And feel the curse to have no natural fear,
Nor fluttering throb, that beats with hopes or wishes,
Or lurking love of something on the earth.—
Now to my task.—
                        Mysterious Agency!
Ye spirits of the unbounded Universe!
30 Whom I have sought in darkness and in light—
Ye, who do compass earth about, and dwell
In subtler essence—ye, to whom the tops
Of mountains inaccessible are haunts,
And earth's and ocean's caves familiar things—
35 I call upon ye by the written charm
Which gives me power upon you—Rise! appear!   [*A pause.*]
They come not yet.—Now by the voice of him
Who is the first among you[3]—by this sign,
Which makes you tremble—by the claims of him
40 Who is undying,[4]—Rise! appear!—Appear!   [*A pause.*]

2. A large chamber built in the medieval Gothic
style with high, pointed arches.
3. Arimanes, who appears in 2.4.

4. Probably God, to whom traditional magic con-
jurations often allude.

If it be so.—Spirits of earth and air,
Ye shall not thus elude me: by a power,
Deeper than all yet urged, a tyrant-spell,
Which had its birth-place in a star condemn'd,
45 The burning wreck of a demolish'd world,
A wandering hell in the eternal space;
By the strong curse which is upon my soul,
The thought which is within me and around me,
I do compel ye to my will.—Appear!

[*A star is seen at the darker end of the gallery; it is stationary; and a voice is heard singing.*]

FIRST SPIRIT[5]
50   Mortal! to thy bidding bow'd,
             From my mansion in the cloud,
             Which the breath of twilight builds,
             And the summer's sun-set gilds
             With the azure and vermilion,
55   Which is mix'd for my pavilion;
             Though thy quest may be forbidden,
             On a star-beam I have ridd'n;
             To thine adjuration bow'd,
             Mortal—be thy wish avow'd!

             Voice of the SECOND SPIRIT
60   Mont Blanc is the monarch of mountains,
                 They crowned him long ago
             On a throne of rocks, in a robe of clouds,
                 With a diadem of snow.
             Around his waist are forests braced,
65   The Avalanche in his hand;
             But ere it fall, that thundering ball
                 Must pause for my command.
             The Glacier's cold and restless mass
                 Moves onward day by day;
70   But I am he who bids it pass,
                 Or with its ice delay.
             I am the spirit of the place,
                 Could make the mountain bow
             And quiver to his cavern'd base—
75   And what with me wouldst *Thou?*

             Voice of the THIRD SPIRIT
             In the blue depth of the waters,
                 Where the wave hath no strife,
             Where the wind is a stranger,
                 And the sea-snake hath life,
80   Where the Mermaid is decking

---

5. The Spirits, successively, are those of the Air, Mountain, Ocean, Earth, Winds, Night, and Manfred's guiding Star.

      Her green hair with shells;
    Like the storm on the surface
      Came the sound of thy spells;
    O'er my calm Hall of Coral
85   The deep echo roll'd—
    To the Spirit of Ocean
      Thy wishes unfold!

FOURTH SPIRIT

    Where the slumbering earthquake
      Lies pillow'd on fire,
90 And the lakes of bitumen
      Rise boilingly higher;
    Where the roots of the Andes
      Strike deep in the earth,
    As their summits to heaven
95   Shoot soaringly forth;
    I have quitted my birth-place,
      Thy bidding to bide—
    Thy spell hath subdued me,
      Thy will be my guide!

FIFTH SPIRIT

100 I am the Rider of the wind,
      The Stirrer of the storm;
    The hurricane I left behind
      Is yet with lightning warm;
    To speed to thee, o'er shore and sea
105   I swept upon the blast:
    The fleet I met sailed well, and yet
      'Twill sink ere night be past.

SIXTH SPIRIT

    My dwelling is the shadow of the night,
    Why doth thy magic torture me with light?

SEVENTH SPIRIT

110 The star which rules thy destiny,
    Was ruled, ere earth began, by me:
    It was a world as fresh and fair
    As e'er revolved round sun in air;
    Its course was free and regular,
115 Space bosom'd not a lovelier star.
    The hour arrived—and it became
    A wandering mass of shapeless flame,
    A pathless comet, and a curse,
    The menace of the universe;
120 Still rolling on with innate force,
    Without a sphere, without a course,
    A bright deformity on high,
    The monster of the upper sky!
    And thou! beneath its influence born—

125   Thou worm! whom I obey and scorn—
          Forced by a power (which is not thine,
          And lent thee but to make thee mine)
          For this brief moment to descend,
          Where these weak spirits round thee bend
130   And parley with a thing like thee—
          What wouldst thou, Child of Clay! with me?

The SEVEN SPIRITS
          Earth, ocean, air, night, mountains, winds, thy star,
            Are at thy beck and bidding, Child of Clay!
          Before thee at thy quest their spirits are—
135   What wouldst thou with us, son of mortals—say?

MANFRED Forgetfulness—
FIRST SPIRIT   Of what—of whom—and why?
MANFRED   Of that which is within me; read it there—
    Ye know it, and I cannot utter it.
SPIRIT   We can but give thee that which we possess:
140   Ask of us subjects, sovereignty, the power
        O'er earth, the whole, or portion, or a sign
        Which shall control the elements, whereof
        We are the dominators, each and all,
        These shall be thine.
MANFRED   Oblivion, self-oblivion—
145   Can ye not wring from out the hidden realms
        Ye offer so profusely what I ask?
SPIRIT   It is not in our essence, in our skill;
        But—thou mayst die.
MANFRED   Will death bestow it on me?
SPIRIT   We are immortal, and do not forget;
150   We are eternal; and to us the past
        Is, as the future, present. Art thou answered?
MANFRED   Ye mock me—but the power which brought ye here
        Hath made you mine. Slaves, scoff not at my will!
        The mind, the spirit, the Promethean spark,[6]
155   The lightning of my being, is as bright,
        Pervading, and far-darting as your own,
        And shall not yield to yours, though coop'd in clay!
        Answer, or I will teach you what I am.
SPIRIT   We answer as we answered; our reply
        Is even in thine own words.
160   MANFRED   Why say ye so?
SPIRIT   If, as thou say'st, thine essence be as ours,
        We have replied in telling thee, the thing
        Mortals call death hath nought to do with us.
MANFRED   I then have call'd ye from your realms in vain;
        Ye cannot, or ye will not, aid me.
165   SPIRIT   Say;

---

6. In Greek myth, Prometheus molded man from clay, and stole fire from heaven to give it to humans.

What we possess we offer; it is thine:
Bethink ere thou dismiss us, ask again—
Kingdom, and sway, and strength, and length of days—
MANFRED Accursed! what have I to do with days?
170 They are too long already.—Hence—begone!
SPIRIT Yet pause: being here, our will would do thee service;
Bethink thee, is there then no other gift
Which we can make not worthless in thine eyes?
MANFRED No, none: yet stay—one moment, ere we part—
175 I would behold ye face to face. I hear
Your voices, sweet and melancholy sounds,
As music on the waters; and I see
The steady aspect of a clear large star;
But nothing more. Approach me as ye are,
180 Or one, or all, in your accustom'd forms.
SPIRIT We have no forms beyond the elements
Of which we are the mind and principle:
But choose a form—in that we will appear.
MANFRED I have no choice; there is no form on earth
185 Hideous or beautiful to me. Let him,
Who is most powerful of ye, take such aspect
As unto him may seem most fitting.—Come!
SEVENTH SPIRIT [*appearing in the shape of a beautiful female figure*].⁷
Behold!
MANFRED Oh God! if it be thus, and *thou*
Art not a madness and a mockery,
190 I yet might be most happy.—I will clasp thee,
And we again will be—   [*The figure vanishes.*]
My heart is crushed!   [MANFRED *falls senseless.*]

[*A voice is heard in the Incantation*⁸ *which follows.*]

When the moon is on the wave,
    And the glow-worm in the grass,
And the meteor on the grave,
195   And the wisp on the morass;
When the falling stars are shooting,
And the answer'd owls are hooting,
And the silent leaves are still
In the shadow of the hill,
200 Shall my soul be upon thine,
With a power and with a sign.

Though thy slumber may be deep,
Yet thy spirit shall not sleep,
There are shades which will not vanish,

7. This shape may be a simulacrum of Astarte, whose phantom appears in 2.3.97; it probably represents, however, the ideal of the beautiful and good that Manfred had pursued in his uncorrupted youth.
8. Byron had published this "incantation" as a separate poem six months before *Manfred*.

There are thoughts thou canst not banish;
By a power to thee unknown,
Thou canst never be alone;
Thou art wrapt as with a shroud,
Thou art gathered in a cloud;
And for ever shalt thou dwell
In the spirit of this spell.

Though thou seest me not pass by,
Thou shalt feel me with thine eye
As a thing that, though unseen,
Must be near thee, and hath been;
And when in that secret dread
Thou hast turn'd around thy head,
Thou shalt marvel I am not
As thy shadow on the spot,
And the power which thou dost feel
Shall be what thou must conceal.

And a magic voice and verse
Hath baptized thee with a curse;
And a spirit of the air
Hath begirt thee with a snare;
In the wind there is a voice
Shall forbid thee to rejoice;
And to thee shall Night deny
All the quiet of her sky;
And the day shall have a sun,
Which shall make thee wish it done.

From thy false tears I did distil
An essence which hath strength to kill;
From thy own heart I then did wring
The black blood in its blackest spring;
From thy own smile I snatch'd the snake,
For there it coil'd as in a brake;°   thicket
From thy own lip I drew the charm
Which gave all these their chiefest harm;
In proving every poison known,
I found the strongest was thine own.

By thy cold breast and serpent smile,
By thy unfathom'd gulfs of guile,
By that most seeming virtuous eye,
By thy shut soul's hypocrisy;
By the perfection of thine art
Which pass'd for human thine own heart;
By thy delight in others' pain,
And by thy brotherhood of Cain,⁹

9. I.e., by your kinship with Cain, who murdered his brother, Abel.

250   I call upon thee! and compel
               Thyself to be thy proper Hell!

               And on thy head I pour the vial
               Which doth devote thee to this trial;
               Nor to slumber, nor to die,
255   Shall be in thy destiny;
               Though thy death shall still seem near
               To thy wish, but as a fear;
               Lo! the spell now works around thee,
               And the clankless chain hath bound thee;
260   O'er thy heart and brain together
               Hath the word been pass'd—now wither!

SCENE 2. *The Mountain of the Jungfrau.*[1]*—Time, Morning.—*
MANFRED *alone upon the Cliffs.*

MANFRED   The spirits I have raised abandon me—
    The spells which I have studied baffle me—
    The remedy I reck'd of tortured me;
    I lean no more on super-human aid,
5   It hath no power upon the past, and for
    The future, till the past be gulf'd in darkness,
    It is not of my search.—My mother Earth!
    And thou fresh breaking Day, and you, ye Mountains,
    Why are ye beautiful? I cannot love ye.
10   And thou, the bright eye of the universe,
    That openest over all, and unto all
    Art a delight—thou shin'st not on my heart.
    And you, ye crags, upon whose extreme edge
    I stand, and on the torrent's brink beneath
15   Behold the tall pines dwindled as to shrubs
    In dizziness of distance; when a leap,
    A stir, a motion, even a breath, would bring
    My breast upon its rocky bosom's bed
    To rest for ever—wherefore do I pause?
20   I feel the impulse—yet I do not plunge;
    I see the peril—yet do not recede;
    And my brain reels—and yet my foot is firm:
    There is a power upon me which withholds
    And makes it my fatality to live;
25   If it be life to wear within myself
    This barrenness of spirit, and to be
    My own soul's sepulchre, for I have ceased
    To justify my deeds unto myself—
    The last infirmity of evil. Ay,
30   Thou winged and cloud-cleaving minister,   *[An eagle passes.]*
    Whose happy flight is highest into heaven,
    Well may'st thou swoop so near me—I should be

1. A high Alpine mountain in south-central Switzerland.

Thy prey, and gorge thine eaglets; thou art gone
Where the eye cannot follow thee; but thine
35 Yet pierces downward, onward, or above,
With a pervading vision.—Beautiful!
How beautiful is all this visible world!
How glorious in its action and itself;
But we, who name ourselves its sovereigns, we,
40 Half dust, half deity, alike unfit
To sink or soar, with our mix'd essence make
A conflict of its elements, and breathe
The breath of degradation and of pride,
Contending with low wants and lofty will
45 Till our mortality predominates,
And men are—what they name not to themselves,
And trust not to each other. Hark! the note,
　　　　　　　　　[*The Shepherd's pipe in the distance is heard.*]
The natural music of the mountain reed—
For here the patriarchal days[2] are not
50 A pastoral fable—pipes in the liberal° air,　　　　　　　*free-moving*
Mix'd with the sweet bells of the sauntering herd;
My soul would drink those echoes.—Oh, that I were
The viewless° spirit of a lovely sound,　　　　　　　*invisible*
A living voice, a breathing harmony,
55 A bodiless enjoyment—born and dying
With the blest tone which made me!
　　　　　　Enter from below a CHAMOIS[3] HUNTER.
CHAMOIS HUNTER　　　　　　　　　Even so
This way the chamois leapt: her nimble feet
Have baffled me; my gains to-day will scarce
Repay my break-neck travail.—What is here?
60 Who seems not of my trade, and yet hath reach'd
A height which none even of our mountaineers,
Save our best hunters, may attain: his garb
Is goodly, his mien manly, and his air
Proud as a free-born peasant's, at this distance.—
I will approach him nearer.
65 MANFRED [*not perceiving the other*]　　To be thus—
Gray-hair'd with anguish, like these blasted pines,
Wrecks of a single winter, barkless, branchless,
A blighted trunk upon a cursed root,
Which but supplies a feeling to decay—
70 And to be thus, eternally but thus,
Having been otherwise! Now furrow'd o'er
With wrinkles, plough'd by moments, not by years;
And hours—all tortured into ages—hours
Which I outlive!—Ye toppling crags of ice!
75 Ye avalanches, whom a breath draws down

---

2. The days of the Old Testament partriarchs, who were shepherds.

3. A goatlike antelope found in the high regions of European mountains.

In mountainous o'erwhelming, come and crush me—
I hear ye momently above, beneath,
Crash with a frequent conflict; but ye pass,
And only fall on things which still would live;
80   On the young flourishing forest, or the hut
And hamlet of the harmless villager.
CHAMOIS HUNTER   The mists begin to rise from up the valley;
I'll warn him to descend, or he may chance
To lose at once his way and life together.
85 MANFRED   The mists boil up around the glaciers; clouds
Rise curling fast beneath me, white and sulphury,
Like foam from the roused ocean of deep Hell,
Whose every wave breaks on a living shore,
Heaped with the damn'd like pebbles.—I am giddy.
90 CHAMOIS HUNTER   I must approach him cautiously; if near,
A sudden step will startle him, and he
Seems tottering already.
MANFRED   Mountains have fallen,
Leaving a gap in the clouds, and with the shock
Rocking their Alpine brethren; filling up
95 The ripe green valleys with destruction's splinters;
Damming the rivers with a sudden dash,
Which crush'd the waters into mist, and made
Their fountains find another channel—thus,
Thus, in its old age, did Mount Rosenberg[4]—
Why stood I not beneath it?
100 CHAMOIS HUNTER   Friend! have a care,
Your next step may be fatal!—for the love
Of him who made you, stand not on that brink!
MANFRED [*not hearing him*]   Such would have been for me a fitting tomb;
My bones had then been quiet in their depth;
105 They had not then been strewn upon the rocks
For the wind's pastime—as thus—thus they shall be—
In this one plunge.—Farewell, ye opening heavens!
Look not upon me thus reproachfully—
Ye were not meant for me—Earth! take these atoms!
    [*As* MANFRED *is in act to spring from the cliff, the* CHAMOIS HUNTER
    seizes and retains him with a sudden grasp.]
110 CHAMOIS HUNTER   Hold, madman!—though aweary of thy life,
Stain not our pure vales with thy guilty blood.—
Away with me—I will not quit my hold.
MANFRED   I am most sick at heart—nay, grasp me not—
I am all feebleness—the mountains whirl
115 Spinning around me—I grow blind—What art thou?
CHAMOIS HUNTER   I'll answer that anon.—Away with me—
The clouds grow thicker—there—now lean on me—
Place your foot here—here, take this staff, and cling

---

4. In 1806, ten years before the composition of *Manfred,* a huge landslide on Mount Rossberg ("Rosenberg") had destroyed four villages and killed 457 people.

A moment to that shrub—now give me your hand,
120　　And hold fast by my girdle—softly—well—
The Chalet will be gained within an hour—
Come on, we'll quickly find a surer footing,
And something like a pathway, which the torrent
Hath wash'd since winter.—Come, 'tis bravely done—
125　　You should have been a hunter.—Follow me.
　　　　　[*As they descend the rocks with difficulty, the scene closes.*]

Act 2

SCENE 1. *A Cottage amongst the Bernese Alps.*[5] MANFRED *and
the* CHAMOIS HUNTER.

CHAMOIS HUNTER　No, no—yet pause—thou must not yet go forth:
　　Thy mind and body are alike unfit
　　To trust each other, for some hours, at least;
　　When thou art better, I will be thy guide—
　　But whither?
5　MANFRED　　　It imports not; I do know
　　My route full well, and need no further guidance.
CHAMOIS HUNTER　Thy garb and gait bespeak thee of high lineage—
　　One of the many chiefs, whose castled crags
　　Look o'er the lower valleys—which of these
10　　May call thee Lord? I only know their portals;
　　My way of life leads me but rarely down
　　To bask by the huge hearths of those old halls,
　　Carousing with the vassals; but the paths,
　　Which step from out our mountains to their doors,
15　　I know from childhood—which of these is thine?
MANFRED　No matter.
CHAMOIS HUNTER　　　Well, sir, pardon me the question,
　　And be of better cheer. Come, taste my wine;
　　'Tis of an ancient vintage; many a day
　　'T has thawed my veins among our glaciers, now
20　　Let it do thus for thine—Come, pledge me fairly.
MANFRED　Away, away! there's blood upon the brim!
　　Will it then never—never sink in the earth?
CHAMOIS HUNTER　What dost thou mean? thy senses wander from thee.
MANFRED　I say 'tis blood—my blood! the pure warm stream
25　　Which ran in the veins of my fathers, and in ours
　　When we were in our youth, and had one heart,
　　And loved each other as we should not love,
　　And this was shed: but still it rises up,
　　Colouring the clouds, that shut me out from heaven,
30　　Where thou art not—and I shall never be.
CHAMOIS HUNTER　Man of strange words, and some half-maddening sin,
　　Which makes thee people vacancy, whate'er
　　Thy dread and sufferance be, there's comfort yet—
　　The aid of holy men, and heavenly patience—

---

5. A mountain range in south-central Switzerland.

35   MANFRED   Patience and patience! Hence—that word was made
      For brutes of burthen, not for birds of prey;
      Preach it to mortals of a dust like thine,—
      I am not of thine order.
      CHAMOIS HUNTER   Thanks to heaven!
      I would not be of thine for the free fame
40   Of William Tell;[6] but whatsoe'er thine ill,
      It must be borne, and these wild starts are useless.
      MANFRED   Do I not bear it?—Look on me—I live.
      CHAMOIS HUNTER   This is convulsion, and no healthful life.
      MANFRED   I tell thee, man! I have lived many years,
45   Many long years, but they are nothing now
      To those which I must number: ages—ages—
      Space and eternity—and consciousness,
      With the fierce thirst of death—and still unslaked!
      CHAMOIS HUNTER   Why, on thy brow the seal of middle age
50   Hath scarce been set; I am thine elder far.
      MANFRED   Think'st thou existence doth depend on time?
      It doth; but actions are our epochs: mine
      Have made my days and nights imperishable,
      Endless, and all alike, as sands on the shore,
55   Innumerable atoms, and one desart,
      Barren and cold, on which the wild waves break,
      But nothing rests, save carcases and wrecks,
      Rocks, and the salt-surf weeds of bitterness.
      CHAMOIS HUNTER   Alas! he's mad—but yet I must not leave him.
60   MANFRED   I would I were—for then the things I see
      Would be but a distempered dream.
      CHAMOIS HUNTER   What is it
      That thou dost see, or think thou look'st upon?
      MANFRED   Myself, and thee—a peasant of the Alps—
      Thy humble virtues, hospitable home,
65   And spirit patient, pious, proud and free;
      Thy self-respect, grafted on innocent thoughts;
      Thy days of health, and nights of sleep; thy toils,
      By danger dignified, yet guiltless; hopes
      Of cheerful old age and a quiet grave,
70   With cross and garland over its green turf,
      And thy grandchildren's love for epitaph;
      This do I see—and then I look within—
      It matters not—my soul was scorch'd already!
      CHAMOIS HUNTER   And would'st thou then exchange thy lot for mine?
75   MANFRED   No, friend! I would not wrong thee, nor exchange
      My lot with living being: I can bear—
      However wretchedly, 'tis still to bear—
      In life what others could not brook to dream,
      But perish in their slumber.
      CHAMOIS HUNTER   And with this—
80   This cautious feeling for another's pain,

---

6. The hero who, according to legend, liberated Switzerland from Austrian oppression in the 14th century.

Canst thou be black with evil?—say not so.
Can one of gentle thoughts have wreak'd revenge
Upon his enemies?
MANFRED   Oh! no, no, no!
My injuries came down on those who loved me—
On those whom I best loved: I never quell'd°   killed
An enemy, save in my just defence—
My wrongs were all on those I should have cherished—
But my embrace was fatal.
CHAMOIS HUNTER   Heaven give thee rest!
And penitence restore thee to thyself;
My prayers shall be for thee.
MANFRED   I need them not,
But can endure thy pity. I depart—
'Tis time—farewell!—Here's gold, and thanks for thee—
No words—it is thy due.—Follow me not—
I know my path—the mountain peril's past:—
And once again, I charge thee, follow not!

[*Exit* MANFRED.]

SCENE 2. *A lower Valley in the Alps.—A Cataract.*

Enter MANFRED.
It is not noon—the sunbow's rays still arch
The torrent with the many hues of heaven,
And roll the sheeted silver's waving column
O'er the crag's headlong perpendicular,
And fling its lines of foaming light along,
And to and fro, like the pale courser's tail,
The Giant steed, to be bestrode by Death,
As told in the Apocalypse.[7] No eyes
But mine now drink this sight of loveliness;
I should be sole in this sweet solitude,
And with the Spirit of the place divide
The homage of these waters.—I will call her.
[MANFRED *takes some of the water into the palm of his hand, and flings
it in the air, muttering the adjuration. After a pause, the* WITCH OF THE
ALPS *rises beneath the arch of the sunbow of the torrent.*]
Beautiful Spirit! with thy hair of light,
And dazzling eyes of glory, in whose form
The charms of Earth's least-mortal daughters grow
To an unearthly stature, in an essence
Of purer elements; while the hues of youth,—
Carnation'd like a sleeping infant's cheek,
Rock'd by the beating of her mother's heart,
Or the rose tints, which summer's twilight leaves
Upon the lofty glacier's virgin snow,
The blush of earth embracing with her heaven,—

7. Revelation 6.8: "And I looked, and behold a pale horse: and his name that sat on him was Death, and
Hell followed with him."

Tinge thy celestial aspect, and make tame
The beauties of the sunbow which bends o'er thee.
25 Beautiful Spirit! in thy calm clear brow,
Wherein is glass'd° serenity of soul,   *reflected*
Which of itself shows immortality,
I read that thou wilt pardon to a Son
Of Earth, whom the abstruser powers permit
30 At times to commune with them—if that he
Avail him of his spells—to call thee thus,
And gaze on thee a moment.
WITCH   Son of Earth!
I know thee, and the powers which give thee power;
I know thee for a man of many thoughts,
35 And deeds of good and ill, extreme in both,
Fatal and fated in thy sufferings.
I have expected this—what wouldst thou with me?
MANFRED   To look upon thy beauty—nothing further.
The face of the earth hath madden'd me, and I
40 Take refuge in her mysteries, and pierce
To the abodes of those who govern her—
But they can nothing aid me. I have sought
From them what they could not bestow, and now
I search no further.
WITCH   What could be the quest
45 Which is not in the power of the most powerful,
The rulers of the invisible?
MANFRED   A boon;
But why should I repeat it? 'twere in vain.
WITCH   I know not that; let thy lips utter it.
MANFRED   Well, though it torture me, 'tis but the same;
50 My pang shall find a voice. From my youth upwards
My spirit walk'd not with the souls of men,
Nor look'd upon the earth with human eyes;
The thirst of their ambition was not mine,
The aim of their existence was not mine;
55 My joys, my griefs, my passions, and my powers,
Made me a stranger; though I wore the form,
I had no sympathy with breathing flesh,
Nor midst the creatures of clay that girded me
Was there but one who—but of her anon.
60 I said, with men, and with the thoughts of men,
I held but slight communion; but instead,
My joy was in the Wilderness, to breathe
The difficult air of the iced mountain's top,
Where the birds dare not build, nor insect's wing
65 Flit o'er the herbless granite; or to plunge
Into the torrent, and to roll along
On the swift whirl of the new breaking wave
Of river-stream, or ocean, in their flow.
In these my early strength exulted; or

70　To follow through the night the moving moon,
　　The stars and their development; or catch
　　The dazzling lightnings till my eyes grew dim;
　　Or to look, list'ning, on the scattered leaves,
　　While Autumn winds were at their evening song.
75　These were my pastimes, and to be alone;
　　For if the beings, of whom I was one,—
　　Hating to be so,—cross'd me in my path,
　　I felt myself degraded back to them,
　　And was all clay again. And then I dived,
80　In my lone wanderings, to the caves of death,
　　Searching its cause in its effect; and drew
　　From wither'd bones, and skulls, and heap'd up dust,
　　Conclusions most forbidden. Then I pass'd
　　The nights of years in sciences untaught,
85　Save in the old-time; and with time and toil,
　　And terrible ordeal, and such penance
　　As in itself hath power upon the air,
　　And spirits that do compass air and earth,
　　Space, and the peopled infinite, I made
90　Mine eyes familiar with Eternity,
　　Such as, before me, did the Magi,[8] and
　　He who from out their fountain dwellings raised
　　Eros and Anteros, at Gadara,[9]
　　As I do thee;—and with my knowledge grew
95　The thirst of knowledge, and the power and joy
　　Of this most bright intelligence, until—
　　WITCH　　Proceed.
　　MANFRED　　　　Oh! I but thus prolonged my words,
　　Boasting these idle attributes, because
　　As I approach the core of my heart's grief—
100　But to my task. I have not named to thee
　　Father or mother, mistress, friend, or being,
　　With whom I wore the chain of human ties;
　　If I had such, they seem'd not such to me—
　　Yet there was one—
　　WITCH　　　　　　Spare not thyself—proceed.
105　MANFRED　She was like me in lineaments—her eyes,
　　Her hair, her features, all, to the very tone
　　Even of her voice, they said were like to mine;
　　But soften'd all, and temper'd into beauty;
　　She had the same lone thoughts and wanderings,
110　The quest of hidden knowledge, and a mind
　　To comprehend the universe: nor these
　　Alone, but with them gentler powers than mine,
　　Pity, and smiles, and tears—which I had not;
　　And tenderness—but that I had for her;

8. Masters of occult knowledge (plural of *magus*).　god of unrequited love, from the hot springs named
9. Iamblicus, the 4th-century Neoplatonic philos-　after them at Gadara, in Syria.
opher, called up Eros, god of love, and Anteros,

115   Humility—and that I never had.
    Her faults were mine—her virtues were her own—
    I loved her, and destroy'd her!
    WITCH   With thy hand?
    MANFRED   Not with my hand, but heart—which broke her heart—
    It gazed on mine, and withered. I have shed
120   Blood, but not hers—and yet her blood was shed—
    I saw—and could not staunch it.
    WITCH   And for this—
    A being of the race thou dost despise,
    The order which thine own would rise above,
    Mingling with us and ours, thou dost forego
125   The gifts of our great knowledge, and shrink'st back
    To recreant mortality—Away!
    MANFRED   Daughter of Air! I tell thee, since that hour—
    But words are breath—look on me in my sleep,
    Or watch my watchings—Come and sit by me!
130   My solitude is solitude no more,
    But peopled with the Furies;—I have gnash'd
    My teeth in darkness till returning morn,
    Then cursed myself till sunset;—I have pray'd
    For madness as a blessing—'tis denied me.
135   I have affronted death—but in the war
    Of elements the waters shrunk from me,
    And fatal things pass'd harmless—the cold hand
    Of an all-pitiless demon held me back,
    Back by a single hair, which would not break.
140   In phantasy, imagination, all
    The affluence of my soul—which one day was
    A Croesus in creation[1]—I plunged deep,
    But, like an ebbing wave, it dash'd me back
    Into the gulf of my unfathom'd thought.
145   I plunged amidst mankind—Forgetfulness
    I sought in all, save where 'tis to be found,
    And that I have to learn—my sciences,[2]
    My long pursued and super-human art,
    Is mortal here—I dwell in my despair—
    And live—and live for ever.
150   WITCH   It may be
    That I can aid thee.
    MANFRED   To do this thy power
    Must wake the dead, or lay me low with them.
    Do so—in any shape—in any hour—
    With any torture—so it be the last.
155   WITCH   That is not in my province; but if thou
    Wilt swear obedience to my will, and do

1. I.e., my imagination had at one time been as rich as King Croesus in its creative powers. Manfred's self-description in this passage, as longing for a death that is denied him, is modeled on the legend, often treated in Romantic literature, of the Wandering Jew.
2. Occult bodies of knowledge.

My bidding, it may help thee to thy wishes.
MANFRED   I will not swear—Obey! and whom? the spirits
   Whose presence I command, and be the slave
   Of those who served me—Never!
160 WITCH   Is this all?
   Hast thou no gentler answer—Yet bethink thee,
   And pause ere thou rejectest.
MANFRED   I have said it.
WITCH   Enough!—I may retire then—say!
MANFRED   Retire!
                           [*The* WITCH *disappears.*]
MANFRED [*alone*]   We are the fools of time and terror: Days
165 Steal on us and steal from us; yet we live,
   Loathing our life, and dreading still to die.
   In all the days of this detested yoke—
   This heaving burthen, this accursed breath—
   This vital weight upon the struggling heart,
170 Which sinks with sorrow, or beats quick with pain,
   Or joy that ends in agony or faintness—
   In all the days of past and future, for
   In life there is no present, we can number
   How few—how less than few—wherein the soul
175 Forbears to pant for death, and yet draws back
   As from a stream in winter, though the chill
   Be but a moment's. I have one resource
   Still in my science—I can call the dead,
   And ask them what it is we dread to be:
180 The sternest answer can but be the Grave,
   And that is nothing—if they answer not—
   The buried Prophet answered to the Hag
   Of Endor;[3] and the Spartan Monarch drew
   From the Byzantine maid's unsleeping spirit
185 An answer and his destiny—he slew
   That which he loved, unknowing what he slew,
   And died unpardon'd—though he call'd in aid
   The Phyxian Jove, and in Phigalia roused
   The Arcadian Evocators to compel
190 The indignant shadow to depose her wrath,[4]
   Or fix her term of vengeance—she replied
   In words of dubious import, but fulfill'd.
   If I had never lived, that which I love
   Had still been living; had I never loved,
195 That which I love would still be beautiful—

3. The Woman of Endor, at the behest of King Saul, summoned up the spirit of the dead prophet Samuel, who foretold that in an impending battle the Philistines would conquer the Israelites and kill Saul and his sons (1 Samuel 28.7–19).
4. Plutarch relates that King Pausanias ("the Spartan Monarch") had accidentally killed Cleonice ("the Byzantine maid"), whom he desired as his mistress. Her ghost haunted him until he called up her spirit to beg her forgiveness. She told him, enigmatically, that he would quickly be freed from his troubles; soon after that, he was killed. Another Pausanias, author of the *Description of Greece*, adds the details that King Pausanias, in the vain attempt to purge his guilt, had called for aid from Jupiter Phyxius and consulted the Evocators at Phigalia, in Arcadia, who had the power to call up the souls of the dead.

Happy and giving happiness. What is she?
What is she now?—a sufferer for my sins—
A thing I dare not think upon—or nothing.
Within few hours I shall not call in vain—
200 Yet in this hour I dread the thing I dare:
Until this hour I never shrunk to gaze
On spirit, good or evil—now I tremble,
And feel a strange cold thaw upon my heart,
But I can act even what I most abhor,
205 And champion human fears.—The night approaches.   [*Exit.*]

SCENE 3. *The Summit of the Jungfrau Mountain.*

Enter FIRST DESTINY.

The moon is rising broad, and round, and bright;
And here on snows, where never human foot
Of common mortal trod, we nightly tread,
And leave no traces; o'er the savage sea,
5 The glassy ocean of the mountain ice,
We skim its rugged breakers, which put on
The aspect of a tumbling tempest's foam,
Frozen in a moment—a dead whirlpool's image;
And this most steep fantastic pinnacle,
10 The fretwork of some earthquake—where the clouds
Pause to repose themselves in passing by—
Is sacred to our revels, or our vigils;
Here do I wait my sisters, on our way
To the Hall of Arimanes, for to-night
15 Is our great festival—'tis strange they come not.

A Voice without, singing
The Captive Usurper,[5]
    Hurl'd down from the throne,
Lay buried in torpor,
    Forgotten and lone;
20 I broke through his slumbers,
    I shivered his chain,
I leagued him with numbers—
    He's Tyrant again!
With the blood of a million he'll answer my care,
25 With a nation's destruction—his flight and despair.

Second Voice, without
The ship sail'd on, the ship sail'd fast,
But I left not a sail, and I left not a mast;
There is not a plank of the hull or the deck,
And there is not a wretch to lament o'er his wreck;

5. Napoleon. The song of the first Voice alludes to Napoleon's escape from his captivity on the island of Elba in March 1815. After his defeat at the Battle of Waterloo he was interned on another island, St. Helena, in October 1815.

30 Save one, whom I held, as he swam, by the hair,
    And he was a subject well worthy my care;
    A traitor on land, and a pirate at sea—
    But I saved him to wreak further havoc for me!

FIRST DESTINY, *answering*
    The city lies sleeping;
35   The morn, to deplore it,
    May dawn on it weeping:
      Sullenly, slowly,
    The black plague flew o'er it—
      Thousands lie lowly;
40   Tens of thousands shall perish—
      The living shall fly from
    The sick they should cherish;
      But nothing can vanquish
    The touch that they die from.
45   Sorrow and anguish,
    And evil and dread,
      Envelope a nation—
    The blest are the dead,
    Who see not the sight
50   Of their own desolation.—
    This work of a night—
This wreck of a realm—this deed of my doing—
For ages I've done, and shall still be renewing!

Enter the SECOND *and* THIRD DESTINIES.

THE THREE
    Our hands contain the hearts of men,
55   Our footsteps are their graves;
    We only give to take again
    The spirits of our slaves!

FIRST DESTINY Welcome!—Where's Nemesis?[6]
SECOND DESTINY   At some great work;
    But what I know not, for my hands were full.
THIRD DESTINY Behold she cometh.
Enter NEMESIS.
60 FIRST DESTINY   Say, where hast thou been?—
    My sisters and thyself are slow to-night.
NEMESIS I was detain'd repairing shattered thrones,
    Marrying fools, restoring dynasties,
    Avenging men upon their enemies,
65   And making them repent their own revenge;
    Goading the wise to madness; from the dull
    Shaping out oracles to rule the world
    Afresh, for they were waxing out of date,

6. The Greek and Roman goddess of retribution, particularly of the sin of *hubris*, overweening presumption against the gods.

And mortals dared to ponder for themselves,
70   To weigh kings in the balance, and to speak
Of freedom, the forbidden fruit.—Away!
We have outstaid the hour—mount we our clouds!   [*Exeunt.*]

SCENE 4. *The Hall of* ARIMANES.[7]—ARIMANES *on his Throne, a*
Globe of Fire, surrounded by the SPIRITS.

Hymn of the SPIRITS
Hail to our Master!—Prince of Earth and Air!—
Who walks the clouds and waters—in his hand
The sceptre of the elements, which tear
Themselves to chaos at his high command!
5   He breatheth—and a tempest shakes the sea;
He speaketh—and the clouds reply in thunder;
He gazeth—from his glance the sunbeams flee;
He moveth—earthquakes rend the world asunder.
Beneath his footsteps the volcanos rise;
10   His shadow is the Pestilence; his path
The comets herald through the crackling skies;
And planets turn to ashes at his wrath.
To him War offers daily sacrifice;
To him Death pays his tribute; Life is his,
15   With all its infinite of agonies—
And his the spirit of whatever is!
                    Enter the DESTINIES *and* NEMESIS
FIRST DESTINY   Glory to Arimanes! on the earth
His power increaseth—both my sisters did
His bidding, nor did I neglect my duty!
20   SECOND DESTINY   Glory to Arimanes! we who bow
The necks of men, bow down before his throne!
THIRD DESTINY   Glory to Arimanes!—we await
His nod!
NEMESIS   Sovereign of Sovereigns! we are thine,
And all that liveth, more or less, is ours,
25   And most things wholly so; still to increase
Our power increasing thine, demands our care,
And we are vigilant—Thy late commands
Have been fulfilled to the utmost.
                    Enter MANFRED.
A SPIRIT   What is here?
A mortal!—Thou most rash and fatal wretch,
Bow down and worship!
30   SECOND SPIRIT   I do know the man—
A Magian° of great power, and fearful skill!   *magus*
THIRD SPIRIT   Bow down and worship, slave!—What, know'st thou not
Thine and our Sovereign?—Tremble, and obey!
ALL THE SPIRITS   Prostrate thyself, and thy condemned clay,
Child of the Earth! or dread the worst.

7. The name is derived from Ahriman, who in the dualistic Zoroastrian religion was the principle of darkness and evil.

35	MANFRED	I know it;

    And yet ye see I kneel not.

  FOURTH SPIRIT   'Twill be taught thee.

  MANFRED   'Tis taught already;—many a night on the earth,
    On the bare ground, have I bow'd down my face,
    And strew'd my head with ashes; I have known
40   The fulness of humiliation, for
    I sunk before my vain despair, and knelt
    To my own desolation.

  FIFTH SPIRIT   Dost thou dare
    Refuse to Arimanes on his throne
    What the whole earth accords, beholding not
45   The terror of his Glory—Crouch! I say.

  MANFRED   Bid *him* bow down to that which is above him,
    The overruling Infinite—the Maker
    Who made him not for worship—let him kneel,
    And we will kneel together.

  THE SPIRITS   Crush the worm!
    Tear him in pieces!—

50   FIRST DESTINY   Hence! Avaunt!—he's mine.
    Prince of the Powers invisible! This man
    Is of no common order, as his port
    And presence here denote; his sufferings
    Have been of an immortal nature, like
55   Our own; his knowledge and his powers and will,
    As far as is compatible with clay,
    Which clogs the ethereal essence, have been such
    As clay hath seldom borne; his aspirations
    Have been beyond the dwellers of the earth,
60   And they have only taught him what we know—
    That knowledge is not happiness, and science
    But an exchange of ignorance for that
    Which is another kind of ignorance.
    This is not all—the passions, attributes
65   Of earth and heaven, from which no power, nor being,
    Nor breath from the worm upwards is exempt,
    Have pierced his heart; and in their consequence
    Made him a thing, which I, who pity not,
    Yet pardon those who pity. He is mine,
70   And thine, it may be—be it so, or not,
    No other Spirit in this region hath
    A soul like his—or power upon his soul.

  NEMESIS   What doth he here then?

  FIRST DESTINY   Let *him* answer that.

  MANFRED   Ye know what I have known; and without power
75   I could not be amongst ye: but there are
    Powers deeper still beyond—I come in quest
    Of such, to answer unto what I seek.

  NEMESIS   What wouldst *thou*?

  MANFRED   Thou canst not reply to me.
    Call up the dead—my question is for them.

80 NEMESIS Great Arimanes, doth thy will avouch
The wishes of this mortal?
ARIMANES   Yea.
NEMESIS   Whom would'st thou
Uncharnel?
MANFRED   One without a tomb—call up
Astarte.[8]

NEMESIS
Shadow! or Spirit!
85   Whatever thou art,
Which still doth inherit
The whole or a part
Of the form of thy birth,
Of the mould of thy clay,
90   Which returned to the earth,
Re-appear to the day!
Bear what thou borest,
The heart and the form,
And the aspect thou worest
95   Redeem from the worm.
Appear!—Appear!—Appear!
Who sent thee there requires thee here!

[*The Phantom of* ASTARTE *rises and stands in the midst.*]

MANFRED   Can this be death? there's bloom upon her cheek;
But now I see it is no living hue,
100 But a strange hectic°—like the unnatural red   *feverish flush*
Which Autumn plants upon the perish'd leaf.
It is the same! Oh, God! that I should dread
To look upon the same—Astarte!—No,
I cannot speak to her—but bid her speak—
105 Forgive me or condemn me.

NEMESIS
By the power which hath broken
The grave which enthrall'd thee,
Speak to him who hath spoken,
Or those who have call'd thee!

110 MANFRED   She is silent,
And in that silence I am more than answered.
NEMESIS   My power extends no further. Prince of air!
It rests with thee alone—command her voice.
ARIMANES   Spirit—obey this sceptre!
NEMESIS   Silent still!
115 She is not of our order, but belongs
To the other powers. Mortal! thy quest is vain,
And we are baffled also.
MANFRED   Hear me, hear me—
Astarte! my beloved! speak to me:

8. Byron applies to Manfred's beloved the name of Astarte (also known as Ashtoreth), goddess of love and fertility, the Eastern equivalent of the Greek goddess Aphrodite.

I have so much endured—so much endure—
120 Look on me! the grave hath not changed thee more
Than I am changed for thee. Thou lovedst me
Too much, as I loved thee: we were not made
To torture thus each other, though it were
The deadliest sin to love as we have loved.
125 Say that thou loath'st me not—that I do bear
This punishment for both—that thou wilt be
One of the blessed—and that I shall die,
For hitherto all hateful things conspire
To bind me in existence—in a life
130 Which makes me shrink from immortality—
A future like the past. I cannot rest.
I know not what I ask, nor what I seek:
I feel but what thou art—and what I am;
And I would hear yet once before I perish
135 The voice which was my music—Speak to me!
For I have call'd on thee in the still night,
Startled the slumbering birds from the hush'd boughs,
And woke the mountain wolves, and made the caves
Acquainted with thy vainly echoed name,
140 Which answered me—many things answered me—
Spirits and men—but thou wert silent all.
Yet speak to me! I have outwatch'd the stars,
And gazed o'er heaven in vain in search of thee.
Speak to me! I have wandered o'er the earth,
145 And never found thy likeness—Speak to me!
Look on the fiends around—they feel for me:
I fear them not, and feel for thee alone—
Speak to me! though it be in wrath;—but say—
I reck not what—but let me hear thee once—
This once—once more!
PHANTOM OF ASTARTE   Manfred!
150 MANFRED   Say on, say on—
I live but in the sound—it is thy voice!
PHANTOM   Manfred! To-morrow ends thine earthly ills.
Farewell!
MANFRED   Yet one word more—am I forgiven?
PHANTOM   Farewell!
MANFRED   Say, shall we meet again?
PHANTOM   Farewell!
155 MANFRED   One word for mercy! Say, thou lovest me.
PHANTOM   Manfred!   [The Spirit of ASTARTE disappears.]
NEMESIS   She's gone, and will not be recall'd;
Her words will be fulfill'd. Return to the earth.
A SPIRIT   He is convulsed—This is to be a mortal
And seek the things beyond mortality.
160 ANOTHER SPIRIT   Yet, see, he mastereth himself, and makes
His torture tributary to his will.
Had he been one of us, he would have made

An awful spirit.
NEMESIS   Hast thou further question
  Of our great sovereign, or his worshippers?
MANFRED   None.
NEMESIS   Then for a time farewell.
165   MANFRED   We meet then—
  Where? On the earth?
NEMESIS   That will be seen hereafter.
MANFRED   Even as thou wilt: and for the grace accorded
  I now depart a debtor. Fare ye well!   [*Exit* MANFRED.]
        [*Scene closes.*]

Act 3

SCENE 1. *A Hall in the Castle of* MANFRED. MANFRED *and* HERMAN.

MANFRED   What is the hour?
HERMAN   It wants but one till sunset,
  And promises a lovely twilight.
MANFRED   Say,
  Are all things so disposed of in the tower
  As I directed?
HERMAN   All, my lord, are ready;
  Here is the key and casket.
5   MANFRED   It is well:
  Thou mayst retire.   [*Exit* HERMAN.]
MANFRED [*alone*]   There is a calm upon me—
  Inexplicable stillness! which till now
  Did not belong to what I knew of life.
  If that I did not know philosophy
10   To be of all our vanities the motliest,[9]
  The merest word that ever fool'd the ear
  From out the schoolman's jargon, I should deem
  The golden secret, the sought "Kalon,"[1] found,
  And seated in my soul. It will not last,
15   But it is well to have known it, though but once:
  It hath enlarged my thoughts with a new sense,
  And I within my tablets would note down
  That there is such a feeling. Who is there?
                    Re-enter HERMAN.
HERMAN   My lord, the abbot of St. Maurice[2] craves
  To greet your presence.
                    Enter the ABBOT OF ST. MAURICE.
20   ABBOT   Peace be with Count Manfred!
MANFRED   Thanks, holy father! welcome to these walls;
  Thy presence honours them, and blesseth those
  Who dwell within them.
ABBOT   Would it were so, Count!—

9. "The most diverse" or, possibly, "the most fool-   1. Greek for both "the Beautiful" and "the Good."
ish" (*motley* was the multicolored suit worn by a   2. In the Rhone Valley in Switzerland.
court jester).

But I would fain confer with thee alone.
25 MANFRED Herman, retire. What would my reverend guest?

[*Exit* HERMAN.]

ABBOT Thus, without prelude:—Age and zeal, my office,[3]
And good intent, must plead my privilege;
Our near, though not acquainted neighbourhood,
May also be my herald. Rumours strange,
30 And of unholy nature, are abroad,
And busy with thy name; a noble name
For centuries; may he who bears it now
Transmit it unimpair'd!
MANFRED   Proceed,—I listen.
ABBOT 'Tis said thou holdest converse with the things
35 Which are forbidden to the search of man;
That with the dwellers of the dark abodes,
The many evil and unheavenly spirits
Which walk the valley of the shade of death,
Thou communest. I know that with mankind,
40 Thy fellows in creation, thou dost rarely
Exchange thy thoughts, and that thy solitude
Is as an anchorite's,[4] were it but holy.
MANFRED And what are they who do avouch these things?
ABBOT My pious brethren—the scared peasantry—
45 Even thy own vassals—who do look on thee
With most unquiet eyes. Thy life's in peril.
MANFRED Take it.
ABBOT   I come to save, and not destroy—
I would not pry into thy secret soul;
But if these things be sooth, there still is time
50 For penitence and pity: reconcile thee
With the true church, and through the church to heaven.
MANFRED I hear thee. This is my reply; whate'er
I may have been, or am, doth rest between
Heaven and myself.—I shall not choose a mortal
55 To be my mediator. Have I sinn'd
Against your ordinances? prove and punish!
ABBOT My son! I did not speak of punishment,
But penitence and pardon;—with thyself
The choice of such remains—and for the last,
60 Our institutions and our strong belief
Have given me power to smooth the path from sin
To higher hope and better thoughts; the first
I leave to heaven—"Vengeance is mine alone!"
So saith the Lord,[5] and with all humbleness
65 His servant echoes back the awful word.
MANFRED Old man! there is no power in holy men,
Nor charm in prayer—nor purifying form

3. Religious vocation.
4. A person who, for religious reasons, lives in
seclusion.

5. Romans 12.19: "Vengeance is mine; I will
repay, saith the Lord."

Of penitence—nor outward look—nor fast—
Nor agony—nor, greater than all these,
70 The innate tortures of that deep despair,
Which is remorse without the fear of hell,
But all in all sufficient to itself
Would make a hell of heaven—can exorcise
From out the unbounded spirit, the quick sense
75 Of its own sins, wrongs, sufferance, and revenge
Upon itself; there is no future pang
Can deal that justice on the self-condemn'd
He deals on his own soul.
ABBOT   All this is well;
For this will pass away, and be succeeded
80 By an auspicious hope, which shall look up
With calm assurance to that blessed place,
Which all who seek may win, whatever be
Their earthly errors, so they be atoned:
And the commencement of atonement is
85 The sense of its necessity.—Say on—
And all our church can teach thee shall be taught;
And all we can absolve thee, shall be pardon'd.
MANFRED   When Rome's sixth Emperor[6] was near his last,
The victim of a self-inflicted wound,
90 To shun the torments of a public death
From senates once his slaves, a certain soldier,
With show of loyal pity, would have staunch'd
The gushing throat with his officious robe;
The dying Roman thrust him back and said—
95 Some empire still in his expiring glance,
"It is too late—is this fidelity?"
ABBOT   And what of this?
MANFRED   I answer with the Roman—
"It is too late!"
ABBOT   It never can be so,
To reconcile thyself with thy own soul,
100 And thy own soul with heaven. Hast thou no hope?
'Tis strange—even those who do despair above,
Yet shape themselves some phantasy on earth,
To which frail twig they cling, like drowning men.
MANFRED   Ay—father! I have had those earthly visions
105 And noble aspirations in my youth,
To make my own the mind of other men,
The enlightener of nations; and to rise
I knew not whither—it might be to fall;
But fall, even as the mountain-cataract,
110 Which having leapt from its more dazzling height,
Even in the foaming strength of its abyss,

---

6. Otho. Byron attaches to his suicide a story that Suetonius tells about the death of an earlier emperor, Nero.

(Which casts up misty columns that become
Clouds raining from the re-ascended skies)
Lies low but mighty still.—But this is past,
My thoughts mistook themselves.

115 ABBOT   And wherefore so?
MANFRED   I could not tame my nature down; for he
  Must serve who fain would sway—and soothe—and sue—
  And watch all time—and pry into all place—
  And be a living lie—who would become
120 A mighty thing amongst the mean, and such
  The mass are; I disdained to mingle with
  A herd, though to be leader—and of wolves.
  The lion is alone, and so am I.

ABBOT   And why not live and act with other men?
125 MANFRED   Because my nature was averse from life;
  And yet not cruel; for I would not make,
  But find a desolation:—like the wind,
  The red-hot breath of the most lone Simoom,[7]
  Which dwells but in the desert, and sweeps o'er
130 The barren sands which bear no shrubs to blast,
  And revels o'er their wild and arid waves,
  And seeketh not, so that it is not sought,
  But being met is deadly; such hath been
  The course of my existence; but there came
  Things in my path which are no more.

135 ABBOT   Alas!
  I 'gin to fear that thou art past all aid
  From me and from my calling; yet so young,
  I still would—

MANFRED   Look on me! there is an order
  Of mortals on the earth, who do become
140 Old in their youth, and die ere middle age,
  Without the violence of warlike death;
  Some perishing of pleasure—some of study—
  Some worn with toil—some of mere weariness—
  Some of disease—and some insanity—
145 And some of withered, or of broken hearts;
  For this last is a malady which slays
  More than are numbered in the lists of Fate,
  Taking all shapes, and bearing many names.
  Look upon me! for even of all these things
150 Have I partaken; and of all these things,
  One were enough; then wonder not that I
  Am what I am, but that I ever was,
  Or, having been, that I am still on earth.

ABBOT   Yet, hear me still—

MANFRED   Old man! I do respect
155 Thine order, and revere thine years; I deem

---

7. A hot, sand-laden wind in the Sahara and Arabian deserts.

Thy purpose pious, but it is in vain:
Think me not churlish; I would spare thyself,
Far more than me, in shunning at this time
All further colloquy—and so—farewell.   [*Exit* MANFRED.]
160 ABBOT   This should have been a noble creature: he
Hath all the energy which would have made
A goodly frame of glorious elements,
Had they been wisely mingled; as it is,
It is an awful chaos—light and darkness—
165 And mind and dust—and passions and pure thoughts,
Mix'd, and contending without end or order,
All dormant or destructive: he will perish,
And yet he must not; I will try once more,
For such are worth redemption; and my duty
170 Is to dare all things for a righteous end.
I'll follow him—but cautiously, though surely.   [*Exit* ABBOT.]

SCENE 2. *Another Chamber.* MANFRED *and* HERMAN.

HERMAN   My Lord, you bade me wait on you at sunset:
He sinks beyond the mountain.
MANFRED   Doth he so?
I will look on him.
          [MANFRED *advances to the Window of the Hall.*]
                    Glorious Orb! the idol
Of early nature, and the vigorous race
5 Of undiseased mankind, the giant sons
Of the embrace of angels, with a sex
More beautiful than they, which did draw down
The erring spirits[8] who can ne'er return.—
Most glorious orb! that wert a worship, ere
10 The mystery of thy making was reveal'd!
Thou earliest minister of the Almighty,
Which gladden'd, on their mountain tops, the hearts
Of the Chaldean shepherds, till they pour'd
Themselves in orisons!° Thou material God!   *prayers*
15 And representative of the Unknown—
Who chose thee for his shadow! Thou chief star!
Centre of many stars! which mak'st our earth
Endurable, and temperest the hues
And hearts of all who walk within thy rays!
20 Sire of the seasons! Monarch of the climes,
And those who dwell in them! for near or far,
Our inborn spirits have a tint of thee,
Even as our outward aspects;—thou dost rise,
And shine, and set in glory. Fare thee well!

---

8. Genesis 6.4: "There were giants in the earth in those days; and also after that, when the sons of God came in unto the daughters of men, and they bare children to them, the same became mighty men which were of old, men of renown." Byron interprets "the sons of God" as denoting errant angels.

25   I ne'er shall see thee more. As my first glance
     Of love and wonder was for thee, then take
     My latest look: thou wilt not beam on one
     To whom the gifts of life and warmth have been
     Of a more fatal nature. He is gone:
30   I follow.   [*Exit* MANFRED.]

SCENE 3. *The Mountains.—The Castle of* MANFRED *at some distance.—A Terrace before a Tower.—Time, Twilight.* HERMAN, MANUEL, *and other Dependants of* MANFRED.

HERMAN   'Tis strange enough; night after night, for years,
     He hath pursued long vigils in this tower,
     Without a witness. I have been within it,—
     So have we all been oft-times; but from it,
5   Or its contents, it were impossible
     To draw conclusions absolute, of aught
     His studies tend to. To be sure, there is
     One chamber where none enter; I would give
     The fee° of what I have to come these three years,   *ownership*
     To pore upon its mysteries.
10 MANUEL   'Twere dangerous;
     Content thyself with what thou knowest already.
HERMAN   Ah! Manuel! thou art elderly and wise,
     And could'st say much; thou hast dwelt within the castle—
     How many years is't?
MANUEL   Ere Count Manfred's birth,
15   I served his father, whom he nought resembles.
HERMAN   There be more sons in like predicament.
     But wherein do they differ?
MANUEL   I speak not
     Of features or of form, but mind and habits:
     Count Sigismund was proud,—but gay and free,—
20   A warrior and a reveller; he dwelt not
     With books and solitude, nor made the night
     A gloomy vigil, but a festal time,
     Merrier than day; he did not walk the rocks
     And forests like a wolf, nor turn aside
     From men and their delights.
25 HERMAN   Beshrew[9] the hour,
     But those were jocund times! I would that such
     Would visit the old walls again; they look
     As if they had forgotten them.
MANUEL   These walls
     Must change their chieftain first. Oh! I have seen
     Some strange things in them, Herman.
30 HERMAN   Come, be friendly;
     Relate me some to while away our watch:

9. Curse (used jocularly).

I've heard thee darkly speak of an event
Which happened hereabouts, by this same tower.
MANUEL   That was a night indeed; I do remember
35   'Twas twilight, as it may be now, and such
Another evening—yon red cloud, which rests
On Eigher's[1] pinnacle, so rested then,—
So like that it might be the same; the wind
Was faint and gusty, and the mountain snows
40   Began to glitter with the climbing moon;
Count Manfred was, as now, within his tower,—
How occupied, we knew not, but with him
The sole companion of his wanderings
And watchings—her, whom of all earthly things
45   That lived, the only thing he seem'd to love,—
As he, indeed, by blood was bound to do,
The Lady Astarte, his—
                                  Hush! who comes here?
                            Enter the ABBOT.
ABBOT   Where is your master?
HERMAN   Yonder in the tower.
ABBOT   I must speak with him.
MANUEL   'Tis impossible;
50   He is most private, and must not be thus
Intruded on.
ABBOT   Upon myself I take
The forfeit of my fault, if fault there be—
But I must see him.
HERMAN   Thou hast seen him once
This eve already.
ABBOT   Sirrah! I command thee,
55   Knock, and apprize the Count of my approach.
HERMAN   We dare not.
ABBOT   Then it seems I must be herald
Of my own purpose.
MANUEL   Reverend father, stop—
I pray you pause.
ABBOT   Why so?
MANUEL   But step this way,
And I will tell you further.   [*Exeunt.*]

SCENE 4. *Interior of the Tower.*

MANFRED *alone*

The stars are forth, the moon above the tops
Of the snow-shining mountains.—Beautiful!
I linger yet with Nature, for the night
Hath been to me a more familiar face
5   Than that of man; and in her starry shade

1. A peak a few miles north of the Jungfrau.

Of dim and solitary loveliness,
I learn'd the language of another world.
I do remember me, that in my youth,
When I was wandering,—upon such a night

10 I stood within the Coloseum's wall,
'Midst the chief relics of almighty Rome;
The trees which grew along the broken arches
Waved dark in the blue midnight, and the stars
Shone through the rents of ruin; from afar

15 The watchdog bayed beyond the Tiber;[2] and
More near from out the Caesars' palace[3] came
The owl's long cry, and, interruptedly,
Of distant sentinels the fitful song
Begun and died upon the gentle wind.

20 Some cypresses beyond the time-worn breach
Appeared to skirt the horizon, yet they stood
Within a bowshot—where the Caesars dwelt,
And dwell the tuneless birds of night; amidst
A grove which springs through levell'd battlements,

25 And twines its roots with the imperial hearths,
Ivy usurps the laurel's place of growth;—
But the gladiators' bloody Circus[4] stands,
A noble wreck in ruinous perfection!
While Caesar's chambers, and the Augustan halls,

30 Grovel on earth in indistinct decay.—
And thou didst shine, thou rolling moon, upon
All this, and cast a wide and tender light,
Which soften'd down the hoar austerity
Of rugged desolation, and fill'd up,

35 As 'twere anew, the gaps of centuries;
Leaving that beautiful which still was so,
And making that which was not, till the place
Became religion, and the heart ran o'er
With silent worship of the great of old!—

40 The dead, but sceptred sovereigns, who still rule
Our spirits from their urns.—
                                    'Twas such a night!
'Tis strange that I recall it at this time;
But I have found our thoughts take wildest flight
Even at the moment when they should array
Themselves in pensive order.
                              Enter the ABBOT.

45 ABBOT   My good Lord!
I crave a second grace for this approach;
But yet let not my humble zeal offend
By its abruptness—all it hath of ill

---

2. The river that flows through Rome.
3. The palace of the Roman emperors. It stands on the Palatine hill, immediately southwest of the Coliseum.
4. The circular arena within the Coliseum where professional gladiators fought to the death as public entertainment.

Recoils on me; its good in the effect
50   May light upon your head—could I say *heart*—
Could I touch *that,* with words or prayers, I should
Recall a noble spirit which hath wandered,
But is not yet all lost.
MANFRED   Thou know'st me not;
  My days are numbered, and my deeds recorded:
55   Retire, or 'twill be dangerous—Away!
ABBOT   Thou dost not mean to menace me?
MANFRED   Not I;
  I simply tell thee peril is at hand,
  And would preserve thee.
ABBOT   What dost mean?
MANFRED   Look there!
  What dost thou see?
ABBOT   Nothing.
MANFRED   Look there, I say,
60   And steadfastly;—now tell me what thou seest?
ABBOT   That which should shake me,—but I fear it not—
  I see a dusk and awful figure rise
  Like an infernal god from out the earth;
  His face wrapt in a mantle, and his form
65   Robed as with angry clouds; he stands between
  Thyself and me—but I do fear him not.
MANFRED   Thou hast no cause—he shall not harm thee—but
  His sight may shock thine old limbs into palsy.
  I say to thee—Retire!
ABBOT   And, I reply—
70   Never—till I have battled with this fiend—
  What doth he here?
MANFRED   Why—ay—what doth he here?
  I did not send for him,—he is unbidden.
ABBOT   Alas! lost mortal! what with guests like these
  Hast thou to do? I tremble for thy sake;
75   Why doth he gaze on thee, and thou on him?
  Ah! he unveils his aspect; on his brow
  The thunder-scars are graven; from his eye
  Glares forth the immortality of hell—
  Avaunt!—
MANFRED   Pronounce—what is thy mission?
SPIRIT   Come!
80 ABBOT   What art thou, unknown being? answer!—speak!
SPIRIT   The genius[5] of this mortal.—Come! 'tis time.
MANFRED   I am prepared for all things, but deny
  The power which summons me. Who sent thee here?
SPIRIT   Thou'lt know anon—Come! come!
MANFRED   I have commanded
85   Things of an essence greater far than thine,

---

5. The spirit or deity presiding over a human being from birth.

And striven with thy masters. Get thee hence!
SPIRIT   Mortal! thine hour is come—Away! I say.
MANFRED   I knew, and know my hour is come, but not
    To render up my soul to such as thee:
90   Away! I'll die as I have lived—alone.
SPIRIT   Then I must summon up my brethren.—Rise!

[*Other Spirits rise up.*]

ABBOT   Avaunt! ye evil ones!—Avaunt! I say,—
    Ye have no power where piety hath power,
    And I do charge ye in the name—
SPIRIT   Old man!
95   We know ourselves, our mission, and thine order;
    Waste not thy holy words on idle uses,
    It were in vain; this man is forfeited.
    Once more I summon him—Away! away!
MANFRED   I do defy ye,—though I feel my soul
100   Is ebbing from me, yet I do defy ye;
    Nor will I hence, while I have earthly breath
    To breathe my scorn upon ye—earthly strength
    To wrestle, though with spirits; what ye take
    Shall be ta'en limb by limb.
SPIRIT   Reluctant mortal!
105   Is this the Magian who would so pervade
    The world invisible, and make himself
    Almost our equal?—Can it be that thou
    Art thus in love with life? the very life
    Which made thee wretched!
MANFRED   Thou false fiend, thou liest!
110   My life is in its last hour,—*that* I know,
    Nor would redeem a moment of that hour;
    I do not combat against death, but thee
    And thy surrounding angels; my past power
    Was purchased by no compact with thy crew,
115   But by superior science—penance—daring—
    And length of watching—strength of mind—and skill
    In knowledge of our fathers—when the earth
    Saw men and spirits walking side by side,
    And gave ye no supremacy: I stand
120   Upon my strength—I do defy—deny—
    Spurn back, and scorn ye!—
SPIRIT   But thy many crimes
    Have made thee—
MANFRED   What are they to such as thee?
    Must crimes be punish'd but by other crimes,
    And greater criminals?—Back to thy hell!
125   Thou hast no power upon me, *that* I feel;
    Thou never shalt possess me, *that* I know:
    What I have done is done; I bear within
    A torture which could nothing gain from thine:
    The mind which is immortal makes itself

130 Requital for its good or evil thoughts—
Is its own origin of ill and end—
And its own place and time⁶—its innate sense,
When stripp'd of this mortality, derives
No colour from the fleeting things without,
135 But is absorb'd in sufferance or in joy,
Born from the knowledge of its own desert.
Thou didst not tempt me, and thou couldst not tempt me;
I have not been thy dupe, nor am thy prey—
But was my own destroyer, and will be
140 My own hereafter.—Back, ye baffled fiends!
The hand of death is on me—but not yours!

                                         [*The Demons disappear.*]

ABBOT   Alas! how pale thou art—thy lips are white—
And thy breast heaves—and in thy gasping throat
The accents rattle—Give thy prayers to Heaven—
145 Pray—albeit but in thought,—but die not thus.
MANFRED   'Tis over—my dull eyes can fix thee not;
But all things swim around me, and the earth
Heaves as it were beneath me. Fare thee well—
Give me thy hand.
ABBOT   Cold—cold—even to the heart—
150 But yet one prayer—alas! how fares it with thee?—
MANFRED   Old man! 'tis not so difficult to die.⁷

                                           [MANFRED *expires.*]

ABBOT   He's gone—his soul hath ta'en its earthless flight—
Whither? I dread to think—but he is gone.

1816–17   1817

Don Juan

Byron began his masterpiece (pronounced in the English fashion, *Don Joó-un*) in July of 1818, published it in installments beginning with cantos 1 and 2 in 1819, and continued working on it almost until his death. He extemporized the poem from episode to episode. "I *have* no plan," he said, "I *had* no plan; but I had or have materials." The work was composed with remarkable speed (the 888 lines of canto 13, for example, were dashed off within a week), and it aims at the effect of improvisation rather than of artful compression; it asks to be read rapidly, at a conversational pace.

    The poem breaks off with the sixteenth canto, but even in its unfinished state *Don Juan* is the longest satirical poem, and indeed one of the longest poems of any kind, in English. Its hero, the Spanish libertine, had in the original legend been superhuman in his sexual energy and wickedness. Throughout Byron's version the unspoken but persistent joke is that this archetypal *homme fatal* of European legend is in fact more acted upon than active. Unfailingly amiable and well intentioned, he is

---

6. The last of several echoes by Manfred of Satan's claim that "The mind is its own place, and in itself / Can make a Heaven of Hell, and a Hell of Heaven" (*Paradise Lost* 1.254–55). See also 1.1.252 and 3.1.73, above.

7. When this line was omitted in the printing of the first edition, Byron wrote angrily to his publisher: "You have destroyed the whole effect and moral of the poem."

guilty largely of youth, charm, and a courteous and compliant spirit. The women do all the rest.

The chief models for the poem were the Italian seriocomic versions of medieval chivalric romances; the genre had been introduced by Pulci in the fifteenth century and was adopted by Ariosto in his *Orlando Furioso* (1532). From these writers Byron caught the mixed moods and violent oscillations between the sublime and the ridiculous as well as the colloquial management of the complex ottava rima—an eight-line stanza in which the initial interlaced rhymes (*ababab*) build up to the comic turn in the final couplet (*cc*). Byron was influenced in the English use of this Italian form by a mildly amusing poem published in 1817, under the pseudonym of "Whistlecraft," by his friend John Hookham Frere. Other recognizable antecedents of *Don Juan* are Jonathan Swift's *Gulliver's Travels* and Samuel Johnson's *Rasselas,* which had employed the naive traveler as a satiric device, and Laurence Sterne's novel *Tristram Shandy,* with its comic exploitation of a narrative medium blatantly subject to the whimsy of the author. But even the most original literary works play variations on inherited conventions. Shelley at once recognized his friend's poem as "something wholly new and relative to the age."

Byron's literary advisers thought the poem unacceptably immoral, and John Murray took the precaution of printing the first two installments without identifying either Byron as the author or himself as the publisher. But Byron insisted that *Don Juan* is "a *satire* on *abuses* of the present state of society" and "the most moral of poems." And the poem is zestfully on the side of life, in its abundant variety. "As to 'Don Juan,' " Byron wrote elatedly to a friend, "confess—confess, you dog—and be candid. . . . it may be profligate—but is it not *life,* is it not *the thing?*" (see his letter to Douglas Kinnaird, Oct. 26, 1819, p. 695).

The controlling element of *Don Juan* is not the narrative but the narrator, and his temperament gives the work its unity. The poem is really a continuous monologue, in the course of which a story manages to be told. It opens with the first-person pronoun and immediately lets us into the storyteller's predicament: "I want a hero. . . ." The voice then goes on, for almost two thousand stanzas, with effortless volubility and shifts of mood, using the occasion of Juan's misadventures to confide to us the speaker's thoughts and devastating judgments on the major institutions, activities, and values of Western society. The poet who in his brilliant successful youth created the gloomy and misanthropic Byronic hero, in his later and sadder life created a character (not the hero, but the narrator of *Don Juan*) who is one of the great comic inventions in English literature.

From Don Juan

Fragment[1]

I would to Heaven that I were so much Clay—
    As I am blood—bone—marrow, passion—feeling—
Because at least the past were past away—
    And for the future—(but I write this reeling
5 Having got drunk exceedingly to day
    So that I seem to stand upon the ceiling)

1. This stanza was written on the back of a page of the manuscript of canto 1. For the author's revisions while composing two stanzas of *Don Juan,* see "Poems in Process," in the appendices to this volume.

I say—the future is a serious matter—
And so—for Godsake—Hock[2] and Soda water.

From Canto 1

[JUAN AND DONNA JULIA]

1

I want a hero: an uncommon want,
    When every year and month sends forth a new one,
Till, after cloying the gazettes with cant,
    The age discovers he is not the true one;
5 Of such as these I should not care to vaunt,
    I'll therefore take our ancient friend Don Juan,
We all have seen him in the pantomime[1]
Sent to the devil, somewhat ere his time.

*   *   *

5

Brave men were living before Agamemnon[2]
    And since, exceeding valorous and sage,
35 A good deal like him too, though quite the same none;
    But then they shone not on the poet's page,
And so have been forgotten—I condemn none,
    But can't find any in the present age
Fit for my poem (that is, for my new one);
40 So, as I said, I'll take my friend Don Juan.

6

Most epic poets plunge in *"medias res,"*[3]
    (Horace makes this the heroic turnpike road)
And then your hero tells, whene'er you please,
    What went before—by way of episode,
45 While seated after dinner at his ease,
    Beside his mistress in some soft abode,
Palace, or garden, paradise, or cavern,
Which serves the happy couple for a tavern.

7

That is the usual method, but not mine—
50   My way is to begin with the beginning;
The regularity of my design
        Forbids all wandering as the worst of sinning,
And therefore I shall open with a line
        (Although it cost me half an hour in spinning)

---

2. A white Rhine wine, from the German *Hoch-heimer*.
1. The Juan legend was a popular subject in English pantomime.
2. In Homer's *Iliad,* the king commanding the

Greeks in the siege of Troy. This line is translated from a Latin ode by Horace.
3. Into the middle of things (Latin; Horace's *Art of Poetry* 148).

55   Narrating somewhat of Don Juan's father,
      And also of his mother, if you'd rather.

                          8

      In Seville was he born, a pleasant city,
          Famous for oranges and women—he
      Who has not seen it will be much to pity,
60   So says the proverb—and I quite agree;
      Of all the Spanish towns is none more pretty,
          Cadiz perhaps—but that you soon may see:—
      Don Juan's parents lived beside the river,
      A noble stream, and call'd the Guadalquivir.

                          9

65   His father's name was Jóse[4]—*Don*, of course,
          A true Hidalgo, free from every stain
      Of Moor or Hebrew blood, he traced his source
          Through the most Gothic gentlemen of Spain;
      A better cavalier ne'er mounted horse,
70   Or, being mounted, e'er got down again,
      Than Jóse, who begot our hero, who
      Begot—but that's to come——Well, to renew:

                         10

      His mother was a learned lady, famed
          For every branch of every science known—
75   In every christian language ever named,
          With virtues equall'd by her wit alone,
      She made the cleverest people quite ashamed,
          And even the good with inward envy groan,
      Finding themselves so very much exceeded
80   In their own way by all the things that she did.

                         11

      Her memory was a mine: she knew by heart
          All Calderon and greater part of Lopé,[5]
      So that if any actor miss'd his part
          She could have served him for the prompter's copy;
85   For her Feinagle's[6] were an useless art,
          And he himself obliged to shut up shop—he
      Could never make a memory so fine as
      That which adorn'd the brain of Donna Inez.

                         12

      Her favourite science was the mathematical,
90   Her noblest virtue was her magnanimity,
      Her wit (she sometimes tried at wit) was Attic[7] all,

4. Normally "José"; Byron transferred the accent to keep his meter.
5. Calderón de la Barca and Lope de Vega, the great Spanish dramatists of the early 17th century.
6. Gregor von Feinagle, a German expert on the art of memory, who had lectured in England in 1811.
7. Athenian. *Attic salt* signifies the famed wit of the Athenians.

Her serious sayings darken'd to sublimity;
In short, in all things she was fairly what I call
A prodigy—her morning dress was dimity,
95   Her evening silk, or, in the summer, muslin,
And other stuffs, with which I won't stay puzzling.

13

She knew the Latin—that is, "the Lord's prayer,"
And Greek—the alphabet—I'm nearly sure;
She read some French romances here and there,
100   Although her mode of speaking was not pure;
For native Spanish she had no great care,
At least her conversation was obscure;
Her thoughts were theorems, her words a problem,
As if she deem'd that mystery would ennoble 'em.

* * *

22

'Tis pity learned virgins ever wed
170   With persons of no sort of education,
Or gentlemen, who, though well-born and bred,
Grow tired of scientific conversation:
I don't choose to say much upon this head,
I'm a plain man, and in a single station,
175   But—Oh! ye lords of ladies intellectual,
Inform us truly, have they not hen-peck'd you all?

23

Don Jóse and his lady quarrell'd—*why*,
Not any of the many could divine,
Though several thousand people chose to try,
180   'Twas surely no concern of theirs nor mine;
I loathe that low vice curiosity,
But if there's any thing in which I shine
'Tis in arranging all my friends' affairs.
Not having, of my own, domestic cares.

24

185 And so I interfered, and with the best
Intentions, but their treatment was not kind;
I think the foolish people were possess'd,
For neither of them could I ever find,
Although their porter afterwards confess'd—
190   But that's no matter, and the worst's behind,
For little Juan o'er me threw, down stairs,
A pail of housemaid's water unawares.

25

A little curly-headed, good-for-nothing,
And mischief-making monkey from his birth;
195 His parents ne'er agreed except in doting

Upon the most unquiet imp on earth;
  Instead of quarrelling, had they been but both in
    Their senses, they'd have sent young master forth
To school, or had him soundly whipp'd at home,
200 To teach him manners for the time to come.

26

Don Jóse and the Donna Inez led
  For some time an unhappy sort of life,
Wishing each other, not divorced, but dead;
  They lived respectably as man and wife,
205 Their conduct was exceedingly well-bred,
    And gave no outward signs of inward strife,
Until at length the smother'd fire broke out,
And put the business past all kind of doubt.

27

For Inez call'd some druggists and physicians,
210 And tried to prove her loving lord was *mad*,[8]
But as he had some lucid intermissions,
  She next decided he was only *bad*;
Yet when they ask'd her for her depositions,
  No sort of explanation could be had,
215 Save that her duty both to man and God
Required this conduct—which seem'd very odd.

28

She kept a journal, where his faults were noted,
  And open'd certain trunks of books and letters,
All which might, if occasion served, be quoted;
220 And then she had all Seville for abettors,
Besides her good old grandmother (who doted);
  The hearers of her case became repeaters,
Then advocates, inquisitors, and judges,
Some for amusement, others for old grudges.

29

225 And then this best and meekest woman bore
  With such serenity her husband's woes,
Just as the Spartan ladies did of yore,
  Who saw their spouses kill'd, and nobly chose
Never to say a word about them more—
230 Calmly she heard each calumny that rose,
And saw *his* agonies with such sublimity,
That all the world exclaim'd "What magnanimity!"

* * *

8. Lady Byron had thought her husband might be insane and sought medical advice on the matter. This and other passages obviously allude to his wife, although Byron insisted that Donna Inez was not intended to be a caricature of Lady Byron.

32

Their friends had tried at reconciliation,
250   Then their relations, who made matters worse;
('Twere hard to say upon a like occasion
    To whom it may be best to have recourse—
I can't say much for friend or yet relation):
    The lawyers did their utmost for divorce,
255 But scarce a fee was paid on either side
Before, unluckily, Don Jóse died.

33

He died: and most unluckily, because,
    According to all hints I could collect
From counsel learned in those kinds of laws,
260   (Although their talk's obscure and circumspect)
His death contrived to spoil a charming cause;
    A thousand pities also with respect
To public feeling, which on this occasion
Was manifested in a great sensation.

*   *   *

37

Dying intestate, Juan was sole heir
290   To a chancery suit, and messuages,⁹ and lands,
Which, with a long minority and care,
    Promised to turn out well in proper hands:
Inez became sole guardian, which was fair,
    And answer'd but to nature's just demands;
295 An only son left with an only mother
Is brought up much more wisely than another.

38

Sagest of women, even of widows, she
    Resolved that Juan should be quite a paragon,
And worthy of the noblest pedigree:
300   (His sire was of Castile, his dam from Arragon).
Then for accomplishments of chivalry,
    In case our lord the king should go to war again,
He learn'd the arts of riding, fencing, gunnery,
And how to scale a fortress—or a nunnery.

39

305 But that which Donna Inez most desired,
    And saw into herself each day before all
The learned tutors whom for him she hired,
    Was, that his breeding should be strictly moral;
Much into all his studies she inquired,
310   And so they were submitted first to her, all,
Arts, sciences, no branch was made a mystery
To Juan's eyes, excepting natural history.¹

9. Houses and the adjoining lands. "Chancery suit": a case in what was then the highest English court, notorious for its delays.
1. Includes biology and physiology.

40

The languages, especially the dead,
　　The sciences, and most of all the abstruse,
315　The arts, at least all such as could be said
　　　To be the most remote from common use,
　In all these he was much and deeply read;
　　But not a page of anything that's loose,
　Or hints continuation of the species,
320　Was ever suffer'd, lest he should grow vicious.

41

His classic studies made a little puzzle,
　　Because of filthy loves of gods and goddesses,
Who in the earlier ages made a bustle,
　　But never put on pantaloons or boddices;
325　His reverend tutors had at times a tussle,
　　　And for their Aeneids, Iliads, and Odysseys,
Were forced to make an odd sort of apology,
For Donna Inez dreaded the mythology.

42

Ovid's a rake, as half his verses show him,
330　Anacreon's morals are a still worse sample,
Catullus scarcely has a decent poem,
　　I don't think Sappho's Ode a good example,
Although Longinus[2] tells us there is no hymn
　　Where the sublime soars forth on wings more ample;
335　But Virgil's songs are pure, except that horrid one
Beginning with "Formosum Pastor Corydon."[3]

43

Lucretius' irreligion[4] is too strong
　　For early stomachs, to prove wholesome food;
I can't help thinking Juvenal[5] was wrong,
340　Although no doubt his real intent was good,
For speaking out so plainly in his song,
　　So much indeed as to be downright rude;
And then what proper person can be partial
To all those nauseous epigrams of Martial?

44

345　Juan was taught from out the best edition,
　　Expurgated by learned men, who place,
Judiciously, from out the schoolboy's vision,
　　The grosser parts; but fearful to deface
Too much their modest bard by this omission,

2. The Greek rhetorician Longinus praises a passage from Sappho in On the Sublime 10.
3. Virgil's Eclogue 2 begins: "The shepherd, Corydon, burned with love for the handsome Alexis."
4. In De rerum natura (On the nature of things)
Lucretius sets out to show that the universe can be explained without reference to any god.
5. The Latin satires of Juvenal attacked the corruption of Roman society in the 1st century C.E.

350 And pitying sore his mutilated case,
They only add them all in an appendix,[6]
Which saves, in fact, the trouble of an index.

*   *   *

52
For my part I say nothing—nothing—but
410   *This* I will say—my reasons are my own—
That if I had an only son to put
   To school (as God be praised that I have none)
'Tis not with Donna Inez I would shut
   Him up to learn his catechism alone,
415 No—No—I'd send him out betimes to college,
For there it was I pick'd up my own knowledge.

53
For there one learns—'tis not for me to boast,
   Though I acquired—but I pass over *that,*
As well as all the Greek I since have lost:
420   I say that there's the place—but *"Verbum sat,"*[7]
I think I pick'd up too, as well as most,
   Knowledge of matters—but no matter *what*—
I never married—but, I think, I know
That sons should not be educated so.

54
425 Young Juan now was sixteen years of age,
   Tall, handsome, slender, but well knit; he seem'd
Active, though not so sprightly, as a page;
   And every body but his mother deem'd
Him almost man; but she flew in a rage,
430   And bit her lips (for else she might have scream'd),
If any said so, for to be precocious
Was in her eyes a thing the most atrocious.

55
Amongst her numerous acquaintance, all
   Selected for discretion and devotion,
435 There was the Donna Julia, whom to call
   Pretty were but to give a feeble notion
Of many charms in her as natural
   As sweetness to the flower, or salt to ocean,
Her zone° to Venus, or his bow to Cupid,   *belt, sash*
440 (But this last simile is trite and stupid).

56
The darkness of her Oriental eye
   Accorded with her Moorish origin;

6. Fact! There is, or was, such an edition, with all the obnoxious epigrams of Martial placed by themselves at the end [Byron's note].
7. A word [to the wise] is sufficient (Latin).

(Her blood was not all Spanish, by the by;
  In Spain, you know, this is a sort of sin).
445 When proud Grenada fell, and, forced to fly,
  Boabdil wept,[8] of Donna Julia's kin
Some went to Africa, some staid in Spain,
Her great great grandmamma chose to remain.

57

She married (I forget the pedigree)
450   With an Hidalgo,[9] who transmitted down
His blood less noble than such blood should be;
  At such alliances his sires would frown,
In that point so precise in each degree
  That they bred *in and in,* as might be shown,
455 Marrying their cousins—nay, their aunts and nieces,
Which always spoils the breed, if it increases.

58

This heathenish cross restored the breed again,
  Ruin'd its blood, but much improved its flesh;
For, from a root the ugliest in Old Spain
460   Sprung up a branch as beautiful as fresh;
The sons no more were short, the daughters plain:
  But there's a rumour which I fain would hush,
'Tis said that Donna Julia's grandmamma
Produced her Don more heirs at love than law.

59

465 However this might be, the race went on
  Improving still through every generation,
Until it center'd in an only son,
  Who left an only daughter; my narration
May have suggested that this single one
470   Could be but Julia (whom on this occasion
I shall have much to speak about), and she
Was married, charming, chaste,[1] and twenty-three.

60

Her eye (I'm very fond of handsome eyes)
  Was large and dark, suppressing half its fire
475 Until she spoke, then through its soft disguise
  Flash'd an expression more of pride than ire,
And love than either; and there would arise
  A something in them which was not desire,
But would have been, perhaps, but for the soul
480 Which struggled through and chasten'd down the whole.

61

Her glossy hair was cluster'd o'er a brow
  Bright with intelligence, and fair and smooth;

---

8. The last Moorish king of Granada (then a province in Spain) wept when his capital fell to the Spaniards (1492).

9. A Spanish nobleman of the lower class.
1. I.e., faithful to her husband.

Her eyebrow's shape was like the aerial bow,
 Her cheek all purple with the beam of youth,
485 Mounting, at times, to a transparent glow,
 As if her veins ran lightning; she, in sooth,
Possess'd an air and grace by no means common:
Her stature tall—I hate a dumpy woman.

62

Wedded she was some years, and to a man
490 Of fifty, and such husbands are in plenty;
And yet, I think, instead of such a ONE
 'Twere better to have TWO of five and twenty,
Especially in countries near the sun:
 And now I think on't, "mi vien in mente,"[2]
495 Ladies even of the most uneasy virtue
Prefer a spouse whose age is short of thirty.

63

'Tis a sad thing, I cannot choose but say,
 And all the fault of that indecent sun,
Who cannot leave alone our helpless clay,
500 But will keep baking, broiling, burning on,
That howsoever people fast and pray
 The flesh is frail, and so the soul undone:
What men call gallantry, and gods adultery,
Is much more common where the climate's sultry.

64

505 Happy the nations of the moral north!
 Where all is virtue, and the winter season
Sends sin, without a rag on, shivering forth;
 ('Twas snow that brought St. Francis back to reason);
Where juries cast up what a wife is worth
510 By laying whate'er sum, in mulct,[3] they please on
The lover, who must pay a handsome price,
Because it is a marketable vice.

65

Alfonso was the name of Julia's lord,
 A man well looking for his years, and who
515 Was neither much beloved, nor yet abhorr'd;
 They lived together as most people do,
Suffering each other's foibles by accord,
 And not exactly either *one* or *two*;
Yet he was jealous, though he did not show it,
520 For jealousy dislikes the world to know it.

    * * *

69

545 Juan she saw, and, as a pretty child,
 Caress'd him often, such a thing might be

---

2. It comes to my mind (Italian).   3. By way of a fine or legal penalty.

Quite innocently done, and harmless styled,
    When she had twenty years, and thirteen he;
But I am not so sure I should have smiled
550   When he was sixteen, Julia twenty-three,
These few short years make wondrous alterations,
Particularly amongst sun-burnt nations.

70

Whate'er the cause might be, they had become
    Changed; for the dame grew distant, the youth shy,
555 Their looks cast down, their greetings almost dumb,
    And much embarrassment in either eye;
There surely will be little doubt with some
    That Donna Julia knew the reason why,
But as for Juan, he had no more notion
560 Than he who never saw the sea of ocean.

71

Yet Julia's very coldness still was kind,
    And tremulously gentle her small hand
Withdrew itself from his, but left behind
    A little pressure, thrilling, and so bland
565 And slight, so very slight, that to the mind
    'Twas but a doubt; but ne'er magician's wand
Wrought change with all Armida's⁴ fairy art
Like what this light touch left on Juan's heart.

72

And if she met him, though she smiled no more,
570   She look'd a sadness sweeter than her smile,
As if her heart had deeper thoughts in store
    She must not own, but cherish'd more the while,
For that compression in its burning core;
    Even innocence itself has many a wile,
575 And will not dare to trust itself with truth,
And love is taught hypocrisy from youth.

*   *   *

75

Poor Julia's heart was in an awkward state;
    She felt it going, and resolved to make
595 The noblest efforts for herself and mate,
    For honour's, pride's, religion's, virtue's sake;
Her resolutions were most truly great,
    And almost might have made a Tarquin⁵ quake;
She pray'd the Virgin Mary for her grace,
600 As being the best judge of a lady's case.

---

4. The sorceress who seduces Rinaldo in Torquato Tasso's *Jerusalem Delivered*.
5. A member of a legendary family of Roman kings noted for tyranny and cruelty; perhaps a reference specifically to Lucius Tarquinus, the villain of Shakespeare's *The Rape of Lucrece*.

76

She vow'd she never would see Juan more,
　　And next day paid a visit to his mother,
And look'd extremely at the opening door,
　　Which, by the Virgin's grace, let in another;
605　Grateful she was, and yet a little sore—
　　Again it opens, it can be no other,
'Tis surely Juan now—No! I'm afraid
That night the Virgin was no further pray'd.

77

She now determined that a virtuous woman
610　Should rather face and overcome temptation,
That flight was base and dastardly, and no man
　　Should ever give her heart the least sensation;
That is to say, a thought beyond the common
　　Preference, that we must feel upon occasion,
615　For people who are pleasanter than others,
But then they only seem so many brothers.

78

And even if by chance—and who can tell?
　　The devil's so very sly—she should discover
That all within was not so very well,
620　And, if still free, that such or such a lover
Might please perhaps, a virtuous wife can quell
　　Such thoughts, and be the better when they're over;
And if the man should ask, 'tis but denial:
I recommend young ladies to make trial.

79

625　And then there are such things as love divine,
　　Bright and immaculate, unmix'd and pure,
Such as the angels think so very fine,
　　And matrons, who would be no less secure,
Platonic, perfect, "just such love as mine":
630　Thus Julia said—and thought so, to be sure,
And so I'd have her think, were I the man
On whom her reveries celestial ran.

*　*　*

86

So much for Julia. Now we'll turn to Juan,
　　Poor little fellow! he had no idea
Of his own case, and never hit the true one;
　　In feelings quick as Ovid's Miss Medea,[6]
685　He puzzled over what he found a new one,
　　But not as yet imagined it could be a

---

6. In *Metamorphoses* 7 Ovid tells the story of Medea's mad infatuation for Jason.

Thing quite in course, and not at all alarming,
Which, with a little patience, might grow charming.

*   *   *

90

Young Juan wander'd by the glassy brooks
   Thinking unutterable things; he threw
715 Himself at length within the leafy nooks
   Where the wild branch of the cork forest grew;
There poets find materials for their books,
   And every now and then we read them through,
So that their plan and prosody are eligible,
720 Unless, like Wordsworth, they prove unintelligible.

91

He, Juan (and not Wordsworth), so pursued
   His self-communion with his own high soul,
Until his mighty heart, in its great mood,
   Had mitigated part, though not the whole
725 Of its disease; he did the best he could
   With things not very subject to control,
And turn'd, without perceiving his condition,
Like Coleridge, into a metaphysician.

92

He thought about himself, and the whole earth,
730   Of man the wonderful, and of the stars,
And how the deuce they ever could have birth;
   And then he thought of earthquakes, and of wars,
How many miles the moon might have in girth,
   Of air-balloons, and of the many bars
735 To perfect knowledge of the boundless skies;
And then he thought of Donna Julia's eyes.

93

In thoughts like these true wisdom may discern
   Longings sublime, and aspirations high,
Which some are born with, but the most part learn
740   To plague themselves withal, they know not why:
'Twas strange that one so young should thus concern
   His brain about the action of the sky;
If *you* think 'twas philosophy that this did,
I can't help thinking puberty assisted.

94

745 He pored upon the leaves, and on the flowers,
   And heard a voice in all the winds; and then
He thought of wood nymphs and immortal bowers,
   And how the goddesses came down to men:
He miss'd the pathway, he forgot the hours,
750   And when he look'd upon his watch again,

He found how much old Time had been a winner—
He also found that he had lost his dinner.

*   *   *

103

'Twas on a summer's day—the sixth of June:—
    I like to be particular in dates,
Not only of the age, and year, but moon;
820   They are a sort of post-house, where the Fates
Change horses, making history change its tune,
    Then spur away o'er empires and o'er states,
Leaving at last not much besides chronology,
Excepting the post-obits[7] of theology.

104

825   'Twas on the sixth of June, about the hour
    Of half-past six—perhaps still nearer seven,
When Julia sate within as pretty a bower
    As e'er held houri in that heathenish heaven
Described by Mahomet, and Anacreon Moore,[8]
830   To whom the lyre and laurels have been given,
With all the trophies of triumphant song—
He won them well, and may he wear them long!

105

She sate, but not alone; I know not well
    How this same interview had taken place,
835   And even if I knew, I should not tell—
    People should hold their tongues in any case;
No matter how or why the thing befell,
    But there were she and Juan, face to face—
When two such faces are so, 'twould be wise,
840   But very difficult, to shut their eyes.

106

How beautiful she look'd! her conscious[9] heart
    Glow'd in her cheek, and yet she felt no wrong.
Oh Love! how perfect is thy mystic art,
    Strengthening the weak, and trampling on the strong,
845   How self-deceitful is the sagest part
    Of mortals whom thy lure hath led along—
The precipice she stood on was immense,
So was her creed° in her own innocence.   *belief*

107

She thought of her own strength, and Juan's youth,
850   And of the folly of all prudish fears,

---

7. I.e., postobit bonds (*post obitum*, "after death" [Latin]): loans to an heir that fall due after the death of the person whose estate he or she is to inherit. Byron's meaning is probably that only theology purports to tell us what rewards are due in heaven.

8. Byron's friend the poet Thomas Moore, who had translated the *Odes* of Anacreon. Byron is alluding to the tale of *Paradise and the Peri* in Moore's Oriental poem *Lalla Rookh*.

9. Inwardly aware (of her feelings).

Victorious virtue, and domestic truth,
   And then of Don Alfonso's fifty years:
I wish these last had not occurr'd, in sooth,
   Because that number rarely much endears,
855 And through all climes, the snowy and the sunny,
Sounds ill in love, whate'er it may in money.

*   *   *

113

The sun set, and up rose the yellow moon:
   The devil's in the moon for mischief; they
Who call'd her CHASTE, methinks, began too soon
900   Their nomenclature; there is not a day,
The longest, not the twenty-first of June,
   Sees half the business in a wicked way
On which three single hours of moonshine smile—
And then she looks so modest all the while.

114

905 There is a dangerous silence in that hour,
   A stillness, which leaves room for the full soul
To open all itself, without the power
   Of calling wholly back its self-control;
The silver light which, hallowing tree and tower,
910   Sheds beauty and deep softness o'er the whole,
Breathes also to the heart, and o'er it throws
A loving languor, which is not repose.

115

And Julia sate with Juan, half embraced
   And half retiring from the glowing arm,
915 Which trembled like the bosom where 'twas placed;
   Yet still she must have thought there was no harm,
Or else 'twere easy to withdraw her waist;
   But then the situation had its charm,
And then—God knows what next—I can't go on;
920 I'm almost sorry that I e'er begun.

116

Oh Plato! Plato! you have paved the way,
   With your confounded fantasies, to more
Immoral conduct by the fancied sway
   Your system feigns o'er the controlless core
925 Of human hearts, than all the long array
   Of poets and romancers:—You're a bore,
A charlatan, a coxcomb—and have been,
At best, no better than a go-between.

117

And Julia's voice was lost, except in sighs,
930   Until too late for useful conversation;

The tears were gushing from her gentle eyes,
   I wish, indeed, they had not had occasion,
But who, alas! can love, and then be wise?
   Not that remorse did not oppose temptation,
935 A little still she strove, and much repented,
   And whispering "I will ne'er consent"—consented.

*   *   *

126

'Tis sweet to win, no matter how, one's laurels
   By blood or ink; 'tis sweet to put an end
To strife; 'tis sometimes sweet to have our quarrels,
   Particularly with a tiresome friend;
1005 Sweet is old wine in bottles, ale in barrels;
   Dear is the helpless creature we defend
Against the world; and dear the schoolboy spot
We ne'er forget, though there we are forgot.

127

But sweeter still than this, than these, than all,
1010 Is first and passionate love—it stands alone,
Like Adam's recollection of his fall;
   The tree of knowledge has been pluck'd—all's known—
And life yields nothing further to recall
   Worthy of this ambrosial sin, so shown,
1015 No doubt in fable, as the unforgiven
Fire which Prometheus[1] filch'd for us from heaven.

*   *   *

133

Man's a phenomenon, one knows not what,
   And wonderful beyond all wondrous measure;
'Tis pity though, in this sublime world, that
1060 Pleasure's a sin, and sometimes sin's a pleasure;
Few mortals know what end they would be at,
   But whether glory, power, or love, or treasure,
The path is through perplexing ways, and when
The goal is gain'd, we die, you know—and then—

134

1065 What then?—I do not know, no more do you—
   And so good night.—Return we to our story:
'Twas in November, when fine days are few,
   And the far mountains wax a little hoary,
And clap a white cape on their mantles blue;
1070 And the sea dashes round the promontory,
And the loud breaker boils against the rock,
And sober suns must set at five o'clock.

---

1. The Titan Prometheus incurred the wrath of Zeus by stealing fire from heaven for humans.

135

'Twas, as the watchmen say, a cloudy night;
　　No moon, no stars, the wind was low or loud
1075　By gusts, and many a sparkling hearth was bright
　　With the piled wood, round which the family crowd;
There's something cheerful in that sort of light,
　　Even as a summer sky's without a cloud:
I'm fond of fire, and crickets, and all that,
1080　A lobster-salad, and champagne, and chat.

136

'Twas midnight—Donna Julia was in bed,
　　Sleeping, most probably—when at her door
Arose a clatter might awake the dead,
　　If they had never been awoke before,
1085　And that they have been so we all have read,
　　And are to be so, at the least, once more—
The door was fasten'd, but with voice and fist
First knocks were heard, then "Madam—Madam—hist!

137

"For God's sake, Madam—Madam—here's my master,
1090　With more than half the city at his back—
Was ever heard of such a curst disaster!
　　'Tis not my fault—I kept good watch—Alack!
Do, pray undo the bolt a little faster—
　　They're on the stair just now, and in a crack
1095　Will all be here; perhaps he yet may fly—
Surely the window's not so *very* high!"

138

By this time Don Alfonso was arrived,
　　With torches, friends, and servants in great number;
The major part of them had long been wived,
1100　And therefore paused not to disturb the slumber
Of any wicked woman, who contrived
　　By stealth her husband's temples to encumber:[2]
Examples of this kind are so contagious,
Were one not punish'd, all would be outrageous.

139

1105　I can't tell how, or why, or what suspicion
　　Could enter into Don Alfonso's head;
But for a cavalier of his condition°　　　　　　　　　　　　rank
　　It surely was exceedingly ill-bred
Without a word of previous admonition,
1110　To hold a levee[3] round his lady's bed,
And summon lackeys, arm'd with fire and sword,
To prove himself the thing he most abhorr'd.

2. Horns growing on the forehead were the tra-　　3. Morning reception.
ditional emblem of the cuckolded husband.

140

Poor Donna Julia! starting as from sleep,
　　(Mind—that I do not say—she had not slept)
1115　Began at once to scream, and yawn, and weep;
　　Her maid Antonia, who was an adept,
Contrived to fling the bed-clothes in a heap,
　　As if she had just now from out them crept:
I can't tell why she should take all this trouble
1120　To prove her mistress had been sleeping double.

141

But Julia mistress, and Antonia maid,
　　Appear'd like two poor harmless women, who
Of goblins, but still more of men afraid,
　　Had thought one man might be deterr'd by two,
1125　And therefore side by side were gently laid,
　　Until the hours of absence should run through,
And truant husband should return, and say,
"My dear, I was the first who came away."

142

Now Julia found at length a voice, and cried,
1130　"In heaven's name, Don Alfonso, what d'ye mean?
Has madness seized you? would that I had died
　　Ere such a monster's victim I had been!
What may this midnight violence betide,
　　A sudden fit of drunkenness or spleen?
1135　Dare you suspect me, whom the thought would kill?
Search, then, the room!"—Alfonso said, "I will."

143

He search'd, *they* search'd, and rummaged every where,
　　Closet and clothes'-press, chest and window-seat,
And found much linen, lace, and seven pair
1140　Of stockings, slippers, brushes, combs, complete,
With other articles of ladies fair,
　　To keep them beautiful, or leave them neat:
Arras[4] they prick'd and curtains with their swords,
And wounded several shutters, and some boards.

144

1145　Under the bed they search'd, and there they found—
　　No matter what—it was not that they sought;
They open'd windows, gazing if the ground
　　Had signs or footmarks, but the earth said nought;
And then they stared each others' faces round:
1150　'Tis odd, not one of all these seekers thought,
And seems to me almost a sort of blunder,
Of looking *in* the bed as well as under.

_____

4. A tapestry hanging on a wall.

145

During this inquisition Julia's tongue
    Was not asleep—"Yes, search and search," she cried,
1155 "Insult on insult heap, and wrong on wrong!
    It was for this that I became a bride!
For this in silence I have suffer'd long
    A husband like Alfonso at my side;
But now I'll bear no more, nor here remain,
1160 If there be law, or lawyers, in all Spain.

146

"Yes, Don Alfonso! husband now no more,
    If ever you indeed deserved the name,
Is't worthy of your years?—you have threescore,
    Fifty, or sixty—it is all the same—
1165 Is't wise or fitting causeless to explore
    For facts against a virtuous woman's fame?
Ungrateful, perjured, barbarous Don Alfonso,
How dare you think your lady would go on so?"

*   *   *

159

1265 The Senhor Don Alfonso stood confused;
    Antonia bustled round the ransack'd room,
And, turning up her nose, with looks abused
    Her master, and his myrmidons, of whom
Not one, except the attorney, was amused;
1270   He, like Achates,[5] faithful to the tomb,
So there were quarrels, cared not for the cause,
Knowing they must be settled by the laws.

160

With prying snub-nose, and small eyes, he stood,
    Following Antonia's motions here and there,
1275 With much suspicion in his attitude;
    For reputations he had little care;
So that a suit or action were made good,
    Small pity had he for the young and fair,
And ne'er believed in negatives, till these
1280 Were proved by competent false witnesses.

161

But Don Alfonso stood with downcast looks,
    And, truth to say, he made a foolish figure;
When, after searching in five hundred nooks,
    And treating a young wife with so much rigour,
1285 He gain'd no point, except some self-rebukes,
    Added to those his lady with such vigour

---

5. The *fidus Achates* ("faithful Achates") of Virgil's *Aeneid,* whose loyalty to Aeneas has become proverbial.

Had pour'd upon him for the last half-hour,
Quick, thick, and heavy—as a thunder-shower.

162

At first he tried to hammer an excuse,
1290   To which the sole reply was tears, and sobs,
And indications of hysterics, whose
    Prologue is always certain throes, and throbs,
Gasps, and whatever else the owners choose:—
    Alfonso saw his wife, and thought of Job's;[6]
1295   He saw too, in perspective, her relations,
And then he tried to muster all his patience.

163

He stood in act to speak, or rather stammer,
    But sage Antonia cut him short before
The anvil of his speech received the hammer,
1300   With "Pray sir, leave the room, and say no more,
Or madam dies."—Alfonso mutter'd "D—n her,"
    But nothing else, the time of words was o'er;
He cast a rueful look or two, and did,
He knew not wherefore, that which he was bid.

164

1305   With him retired his *"posse comitatus,"*[7]
    The attorney last, who linger'd near the door,
Reluctantly, still tarrying there as late as
    Antonia let him—not a little sore
At this most strange and unexplain'd *"hiatus"*
1310   In Don Alfonso's facts, which just now wore
An awkward look; as he resolved the case
The door was fasten'd in his legal face.

165

No sooner was it bolted, than—Oh shame!
    Oh sin! Oh sorrow! and Oh womankind!
1315   How can you do such things and keep your fame,
    Unless this world, and t'other too, be blind?
Nothing so dear as an unfilch'd good name!
    But to proceed—for there is more behind:
With much heart-felt reluctance be it said,
1320   Young Juan slipp'd, half-smother'd, from the bed.

166

He had been hid—I don't pretend to say
    How, nor can I indeed describe the where—
Young, slender, and pack'd easily, he lay,

6. Job's wife had advised her afflicted husband to "curse God, and die" (Job 2.9).
7. The complete form of the modern word *posse* (*posse comitatus* means literally "power of the county" [Latin], i.e., the body of citizens summoned by a sheriff to preserve order in the county).

No doubt, in little compass, round or square;
1325   But pity him I neither must nor may
        His suffocation by that pretty pair;
        'Twere better, sure, to die so, than be shut
        With maudlin Clarence in his Malmsey butt.[8]

*   *   *

169

1345   What's to be done? Alfonso will be back
        The moment he has sent his fools away.
        Antonia's skill was put upon the rack,
            But no device could be brought into play—
        And how to parry the renew'd attack?
1350   Besides, it wanted but few hours of day:
        Antonia puzzled; Julia did not speak,
        But press'd her bloodless lip to Juan's cheek.

170

        He turn'd his lip to hers, and with his hand
            Call'd back the tangles of her wandering hair;
1355   Even then their love they could not all command,
            And half forgot their danger and despair:
        Antonia's patience now was at a stand—
            "Come, come, 'tis no time now for fooling there,"
        She whisper'd, in great wrath—"I must deposit
1360   This pretty gentleman within the closet."

*   *   *

173

        Now, Don Alfonso entering, but alone,
            Closed the oration of the trusty maid:
        She loiter'd, and he told her to be gone,
1380   An order somewhat sullenly obey'd;
        However, present remedy was none,
            And no great good seem'd answer'd if she staid:
        Regarding both with slow and sidelong view,
        She snuff'd the candle, curtsied, and withdrew.

174

1385   Alfonso paused a minute—then begun
            Some strange excuses for his late proceeding;
        He would not justify what he had done,
            To say the best, it was extreme ill-breeding;
        But there were ample reasons for it, none
1390   Of which he specified in this his pleading:
        His speech was a fine sample, on the whole,
        Of rhetoric, which the learn'd call *"rigmarole."*[9]

*   *   *

8. Clarence, brother of Edward IV and of the
future Richard III, was reputed to have been assassinated by being drowned in a cask ("butt") of

malmsey, a sweet and aromatic wine.
9. Illogical sequence of vague statements.

180

Alfonso closed his speech, and begg'd her pardon,
　　Which Julia half withheld, and then half granted,
1435　And laid conditions, he thought, very hard on,
　　Denying several little things he wanted:
He stood like Adam lingering near his garden,
　　With useless penitence perplex'd and haunted,
Beseeching she no further would refuse,
1440　When lo! he stumbled o'er a pair of shoes.

181

A pair of shoes!—what then? not much, if they
　　Are such as fit with lady's feet, but these
(No one can tell how much I grieve to say)
　　Were masculine; to see them, and to seize,
1445　Was but a moment's act.—Ah! Well-a-day!
　　My teeth begin to chatter, my veins freeze—
Alfonso first examined well their fashion,
And then flew out into another passion.

182

He left the room for his relinquish'd sword,
1450　　And Julia instant to the closet flew,
"Fly, Juan, fly! for heaven's sake—not a word—
　　The door is open—you may yet slip through
The passage you so often have explored—
　　Here is the garden-key—Fly—fly—Adieu!
1455　Haste—haste!—I hear Alfonso's hurrying feet—
Day has not broke—there's no one in the street."

183

None can say that this was not good advice,
　　The only mischief was, it came too late;
Of all experience 'tis the usual price,
1460　　A sort of income-tax laid on by fate:
Juan had reach'd the room-door in a trice,
　　And might have done so by the garden-gate,
But met Alfonso in his dressing-gown,
Who threaten'd death—so Juan knock'd him down.

184

1465　Dire was the scuffle, and out went the light,
　　Antonia cried out "Rape!" and Julia "Fire!"
But not a servant stirr'd to aid the fight.
　　Alfonso, pommell'd to his heart's desire,
Swore lustily he'd be revenged this night;
1470　　And Juan, too, blasphemed an octave higher,
His blood was up; though young, he was a Tartar,[1]
And not at all disposed to prove a martyr.

---

1. A formidable opponent.

185

Alfonso's sword had dropp'd ere he could draw it,
    And they continued battling hand to hand,
1475 For Juan very luckily ne'er saw it;
    His temper not being under great command,
If at that moment he had chanced to claw it,
    Alfonso's days had not been in the land
Much longer.—Think of husbands', lovers' lives!
1480 And how ye may be doubly widows—wives!

186

Alfonso grappled to detain the foe,
    And Juan throttled him to get away,
And blood ('twas from the nose) began to flow;
    At last, as they more faintly wrestling lay,
1485 Juan contrived to give an awkward blow,
    And then his only garment quite gave way;
He fled, like Joseph,[2] leaving it; but there,
I doubt, all likeness ends between the pair.

187

Lights came at length, and men, and maids, who found
1490   An awkward spectacle their eyes before;
Antonia in hysterics, Julia swoon'd,
    Alfonso leaning, breathless, by the door;
Some half-torn drapery scatter'd on the ground,
    Some blood, and several footsteps, but no more:
1495 Juan the gate gain'd, turn'd the key about,
And liking not the inside, lock'd the out.

188

Here ends this canto.—Need I sing, or say,
    How Juan, naked, favour'd by the night,
Who favours what she should not, found his way,
1500   And reach'd his home in an unseemly plight?
The pleasant scandal which arose next day,
    The nine days' wonder which was brought to light,
And how Alfonso sued for a divorce,
Were in the English newspapers, of course.

189

1505 If you would like to see the whole proceedings,
    The depositions, and the cause at full,
The names of all the witnesses, the pleadings
    Of counsel to nonsuit,[3] or to annul,
There's more than one edition, and the readings
1510   Are various, but they none of them are dull,

---

2. In Genesis 39.7ff. the chaste Joseph flees from the advances of Potiphar's wife, leaving "his garment in her hand."

3. Judgment against the plaintiff for failure to establish his case.

The best is that in shorthand ta'en by Gurney,[4]
Who to Madrid on purpose made a journey.

190

But Donna Inez, to divert the train
        Of one of the most circulating scandals
1515 That had for centuries been known in Spain,
            Since Roderic's Goths, or older Genseric's Vandals,[5]
        First vow'd (and never had she vow'd in vain)
            To Virgin Mary several pounds of candles;
        And then, by the advice of some old ladies,
1520 She sent her son to be embark'd at Cadiz.

191

She had resolved that he should travel through
        All European climes, by land or sea,
To mend his former morals, or get new,
        Especially in France and Italy,
1525 (At least this is the thing most people do).
        Julia was sent into a nunnery,
And there, perhaps, her feelings may be better
Shown in the following copy of her letter:

192

"They tell me 'tis decided; you depart:
1530   'Tis wise—'tis well, but not the less a pain;
I have no further claim on your young heart,
        Mine was the victim, and would be again;
To love too much has been the only art
        I used;—I write in haste, and if a stain
1535 Be on this sheet, 'tis not what it appears,
My eyeballs burn and throb, but have no tears.

193

"I loved, I love you, for that love have lost
        State, station, heaven, mankind's, my own esteem,
And yet can not regret what it hath cost,
1540   So dear is still the memory of that dream;
Yet, if I name my guilt, 'tis not to boast,
        None can deem harshlier of me than I deem:
I trace this scrawl because I cannot rest—
I've nothing to reproach, nor to request.

194

1545 "Man's love is of his life a thing apart,
        'Tis woman's whole existence; man may range
The court, camp, church, the vessel, and the mart,

---

4. William B. Gurney (1777–1855), official short-hand writer for the houses of Parliament and a famous court reporter.

5. The Germanic tribes that overran Spain and other parts of southern Europe in the 5th through 8th centuries, notorious for rape and violence.

Sword, gown, gain, glory, offer in exchange
Pride, fame, ambition, to fill up his heart,
1550 　　And few there are whom these can not estrange;
Man has all these resources, we but one,
To love again, and be again undone.

195

"My breast has been all weakness, is so yet;
　　I struggle, but cannot collect my mind;
1555 My blood still rushes where my spirit's set,
　　As roll the waves before the settled wind;
My brain is feminine, nor can forget—
　　To all, except your image, madly blind;
As turns the needle[6] trembling to the pole
1560 It ne'er can reach, so turns to you, my soul.

196

"You will proceed in beauty, and in pride,
　　Beloved and loving many; all is o'er
For me on earth, except some years to hide
　　My shame and sorrow deep in my heart's core;
1565 These I could bear, but cannot cast aside
　　The passion which still rends it as before,
And so farewell—forgive me, love me—No,
That word is idle now—but let it go.

197

"I have no more to say, but linger still,
1570 　　And dare not set my seal upon this sheet,
And yet I may as well the task fulfil,
　　My misery can scarce be more complete:
I had not lived till now, could sorrow kill;
　　Death flies the wretch who fain the blow would meet,
1575 And I must even survive this last adieu,
And bear with life, to love and pray for you!"

198

This note was written upon gilt-edged paper
　　With a neat crow-quill, rather hard, but new;
Her small white fingers scarce could reach the taper,[7]
1580 　　But trembled as magnetic needles do,
And yet she did not let one tear escape her;
　　The seal a sunflower; *"Elle vous suit partout,"*[8]
The motto, cut upon a white cornelian;
The wax was superfine, its hue vermilion.

199

1585 This was Don Juan's earliest scrape; but whether
　　I shall proceed with his adventures is

6. Of a compass.
7. The candle (to melt wax to seal the letter).

8. She follows you everywhere (French).

Dependent on the public altogether;
   We'll see, however, what they say to this,
Their favour in an author's cap's a feather,
1590   And no great mischief's done by their caprice;
And if their approbation we experience,
Perhaps they'll have some more about a year hence.

200

My poem's epic, and is meant to be
   Divided in twelve books; each book containing,
1595 With love, and war, a heavy gale at sea,
   A list of ships, and captains, and kings reigning,
New characters; the episodes are three:
   A panorama view of hell's in training,
After the style of Virgil and of Homer,
1600 So that my name of Epic's no misnomer.

201

All these things will be specified in time,
   With strict regard to Aristotle's rules,
The *vade mecum*[9] of the true sublime,
   Which makes so many poets, and some fools;
1605 Prose poets like blank-verse, I'm fond of rhyme,
   Good workmen never quarrel with their tools;
I've got new mythological machinery,
And very handsome supernatural scenery.

202

There's only one slight difference between
1610   Me and my epic brethren gone before,
And here the advantage is my own, I ween;
   (Not that I have not several merits more,
But this will more peculiarly be seen)
   They so embellish, that 'tis quite a bore
1615 Their labyrinth of fables to thread through,
Whereas this story's actually true.

203

If any person doubt it, I appeal
   To history, tradition, and to facts,
To newspapers, whose truth all know and feel,
1620   To plays in five, and operas in three acts;
All these confirm my statement a good deal,
   But that which more completely faith exacts
Is, that myself, and several now in Seville,
Saw Juan's last elopement with the devil.[1]

9. Go with me (Latin, literal trans.); handbook.
Byron is deriding the neoclassic view that Aristotle's *Poetics* proposes "rules" for writing epic and
tragedy.

1. The usual plays on the Juan legend ended with
Juan in hell; an early-20th-century version is Bernard Shaw's *Man and Superman.*

204

1625 If ever I should condescend to prose,
    I'll write poetical commandments, which
Shall supersede beyond all doubt all those
    That went before; in these I shall enrich
My text with many things that no one knows,
1630   And carry precept to the highest pitch:
I'll call the work "Longinus o'er a Bottle,
    Or, Every Poet his *own* Aristotle."

205

Thou shalt believe in Milton, Dryden, Pope;[2]
    Thou shalt not set up Wordsworth, Coleridge, Southey;
1635 Because the first is crazed beyond all hope,
    The second drunk, the third so quaint and mouthey:
With Crabbe it may be difficult to cope,
    And Campbell's Hippocrene[3] is somewhat drouthy:
Thou shalt not steal from Samuel Rogers, nor—
1640 Commit—flirtation with the muse of Moore.

206

Thou shalt not covet Mr. Sotheby's Muse,
    His Pegasus,[4] nor any thing that's his;
Thou shalt not bear false witness like "the Blues,"[5]
    (There's one, at least, is very fond of this);
1645 Thou shalt not write, in short, but what I choose:
    This is true criticism, and you may kiss—
Exactly as you please, or not, the rod,
But if you don't, I'll lay it on, by G—d!

207

If any person should presume to assert
1650   This story is not moral, first I pray
That they will not cry out before they're hurt,
    Then that they'll read it o'er again, and say,
(But, doubtless, nobody will be so pert)
    That this is not a moral tale, though gay;
1655 Besides, in canto twelfth, I mean to show
The very place where wicked people go.

    *   *   *

213

But now at thirty years my hair is gray—
    (I wonder what it will be like at forty?
I thought of a peruke° the other day)   *wig*
1700   My heart is not much greener; and, in short, I

2. This is one of many passages, in prose and verse, in which Byron vigorously defended Dryden and Pope against his Romantic contemporaries.
3. Fountain on Mount Helicon whose waters supposedly gave inspiration. George Crabbe, whom Byron admired, was the author of *The Village* and other realistic poems of rural life. Thomas Campbell, Samuel Rogers, and Thomas Moore (below) were lesser poets of the Romantic period; the last two were close friends of Byron's.
4. The winged horse symbolizing poetic inspiration. William Sotheby, contemporary poet and translator, was a wealthy man (see line 1642).
5. I.e., bluestockings, a contemporary term for pedantic female intellectuals, among whom Byron numbered his wife (line 1644).

Have squander'd my whole summer while 'twas May,
　　And feel no more the spirit to retort; I
Have spent my life, both interest and principal,
　　And deem not, what I deem'd, my soul invincible.

214

1705 No more—no more—Oh! never more on me
　　The freshness of the heart can fall like dew,
Which out of all the lovely things we see
　　Extracts emotions beautiful and new,
Hived in our bosoms like the bag o' the bee:
1710 　　Think'st thou the honey with those objects grew?
Alas! 'twas not in them, but in thy power
To double even the sweetness of a flower.

215

No more—no more—Oh! never more, my heart,
　　Canst thou be my sole world, my universe!
1715 Once all in all, but now a thing apart,
　　Thou canst not be my blessing or my curse:
The illusion's gone for ever, and thou art
　　Insensible, I trust, but none the worse,
And in thy stead I've got a deal of judgment,
1720 Though heaven knows how it ever found a lodgement.

216

My days of love are over, me no more
　　The charms of maid, wife, and still less of widow,
Can make the fool of which they made before,
　　In short, I must not lead the life I did do;
1725 The credulous hope of mutual minds is o'er,
　　The copious use of claret is forbid too,
So for a good old gentlemanly vice,
I think I must take up with avarice.

217

Ambition was my idol, which was broken
1730 　　Before the shrines of Sorrow and of Pleasure;
And the two last have left me many a token
　　O'er which reflection may be made at leisure:
Now, like Friar Bacon's brazen head, I've spoken,
　　"Time is, Time was, Time's past,"[6] a chymic treasure[7]
1735 Is glittering youth, which I have spent betimes—
My heart in passion, and my head on rhymes.

218

What is the end of fame? 'tis but to fill
　　A certain portion of uncertain paper:
Some liken it to climbing up a hill,

---

6. Spoken by a bronze bust in Robert Greene's comedy *Friar Bacon and Friar Bungay* (1594).

7. "Chymic": alchemic; i.e., the "treasure" is counterfeit gold.

1740   Whose summit, like all hills', is lost in vapour;
    For this men write, speak, preach, and heroes kill,
       And bards burn what they call their "midnight taper,"
    To have, when the original is dust,
    A name, a wretched picture, and worse bust.[8]

219

1745   What are the hopes of man? old Egypt's King
       Cheops erected the first pyramid
    And largest, thinking it was just the thing
       To keep his memory whole, and mummy hid;
    But somebody or other rummaging,
1750   Burglariously broke his coffin's lid:
    Let not a monument give you or me hopes,
    Since not a pinch of dust remains of Cheops.

220

    But I, being fond of true philosophy,
       Say very often to myself, "Alas!
1755   All things that have been born were born to die,
       And flesh (which Death mows down to hay) is grass;
    You've pass'd your youth not so unpleasantly,
       And if you had it o'er again—'twould pass—
    So thank your stars that matters are no worse,
1760   And read your Bible, sir, and mind your purse."

221

    But for the present, gentle reader! and
       Still gentler purchaser! the bard—that's I—
    Must, with permission, shake you by the hand,
       And so your humble servant, and good bye!
1765   We meet again, if we should understand
       Each other; and if not, I shall not try
    Your patience further than by this short sample—
    'Twere well if others follow'd my example.

222

    "Go, little book, from this my solitude!
1770   I cast thee on the waters, go thy ways!
    And if, as I believe, thy vein be good,
       The world will find thee after many days."
    When Southey's read, and Wordsworth understood,
       I can't help putting in my claim to praise—
1775   The four first rhymes are Southey's every line:[9]
    For God's sake, reader! take them not for mine.

---

8. Byron was unhappy with the portrait bust of him recently made by the Danish sculptor Thorwaldsen.

9. The lines occur in the last stanza of Southey's *Epilogue to the Lay of the Laureate.*

From Canto 2

[THE SHIPWRECK]

8

But to our tale: the Donna Inez sent
   Her son to Cadiz only to embark;
To stay there had not answer'd her intent,
60   But why?—we leave the reader in the dark—
'Twas for a voyage that the young man was meant,
   As if a Spanish ship were Noah's ark,
To wean him from the wickedness of earth,
And send him like a dove of promise forth.

9

65 Don Juan bade his valet pack his things
   According to direction, then received
A lecture and some money: for four springs
   He was to travel; and though Inez grieved,
(As every kind of parting has its stings)
70   She hoped he would improve—perhaps believed:
A letter, too, she gave (he never read it)
Of good advice—and two or three of credit.

10

In the mean time, to pass her hours away,
   Brave Inez now set up a Sunday school
75 For naughty children, who would rather play
   (Like truant rogues) the devil, or the fool;
Infants of three years old were taught that day,
   Dunces were whipt, or set upon a stool:
The great success of Juan's education,
80 Spurr'd her to teach another generation.

11

Juan embark'd—the ship got under way,
   The wind was fair, the water passing rough;
A devil of a sea rolls in that bay,
   As I, who've cross'd it oft, know well enough;
85 And, standing upon deck, the dashing spray
   Flies in one's face, and makes it weather-tough:
And there he stood to take, and take again,
His first—perhaps his last—farewell of Spain.

12

I can't but say it is an awkward sight
90   To see one's native land receding through
The growing waters; it unmans one quite,
   Especially when life is rather new:
I recollect Great Britain's coast looks white,
   But almost every other country's blue,

95   When gazing on them, mystified by distance,
      We enter on our nautical existence.

* * *

17

     And Juan wept, and much he sigh'd and thought,
130   While his salt tears dropp'd into the salt sea,
     "Sweets to the sweet"; (I like so much to quote;
       You must excuse this extract, 'tis where she,
     The Queen of Denmark, for Ophelia brought
       Flowers to the grave);[1] and sobbing often, he
135   Reflected on his present situation,
     And seriously resolved on reformation.

18

     "Farewell, my Spain! a long farewell!" he cried,
       "Perhaps I may revisit thee no more,
     But die, as many an exiled heart hath died,
140   Of its own thirst to see again thy shore:
     Farewell, where Guadalquivir's waters glide!
       Farewell, my mother! and, since all is o'er,
     Farewell, too dearest Julia!,"—(here he drew
     Her letter out again, and read it through).

19

145   "And oh! if e'er I should forget, I swear—
       But that's impossible, and cannot be—
     Sooner shall this blue ocean melt to air,
       Sooner shall earth resolve itself to sea,
     Than I resign thine image, Oh! my fair!
150   Or think of any thing excepting thee;
     A mind diseased no remedy can physic—"
     (Here the ship gave a lurch, and he grew sea-sick.)

20

     "Sooner shall heaven kiss earth"—(here he fell sicker)
       "Oh, Julia! what is every other woe?—
155   (For God's sake let me have a glass of liquor,
       Pedro, Battista, help me down below.)
     Julia, my love!—(you rascal, Pedro, quicker)—
       Oh Julia!—(this curst vessel pitches so)—
     Beloved Julia, hear me still beseeching!"
160   (Here he grew inarticulate with retching.)

21

     He felt that chilling heaviness of heart,
       Or rather stomach, which, alas! attends,
     Beyond the best apothecary's art,
       The loss of love, the treachery of friends,

---

1. *Hamlet* 5.1.227.

165 Or death of those we doat on, when a part
    Of us dies with them as each fond hope ends:
No doubt he would have been much more pathetic,
    But the sea acted as a strong emetic.[2]

*   *   *

49

385 'Twas twilight, and the sunless day went down
    Over the waste of waters; like a veil,
Which, if withdrawn, would but disclose the frown
    Of one whose hate is masked but to assail;
Thus to their hopeless eyes the night was shown
390   And grimly darkled o'er their faces pale,
And the dim desolate deep; twelve days had Fear
Been their familiar, and now Death was here.

50

Some trial had been making at a raft,
    With little hope in such a rolling sea,
395 A sort of thing at which one would have laugh'd,
    If any laughter at such times could be,
Unless with people who too much have quaff'd,
    And have a kind of wild and horrid glee,
Half epileptical, and half hysterical:—
400 Their preservation would have been a miracle.

51

At half-past eight o'clock, booms, hencoops, spars,
    And all things, for a chance, had been cast loose,
That still could keep afloat the struggling tars,
    For yet they strove, although of no great use:
405 There was no light in heaven but a few stars,
    The boats put off o'ercrowded with their crews;
She gave a heel, and then a lurch to port,
And, going down head foremost—sunk, in short.

52

Then rose from sea to sky the wild farewell,
410   Then shriek'd the timid, and stood still the brave,
Then some leap'd overboard with dreadful yell,
    As eager to anticipate their grave;
And the sea yawn'd around her like a hell,
    And down she suck'd with her the whirling wave,
415 Like one who grapples with his enemy,
And strives to strangle him before he die.

53

And first one universal shriek there rush'd,
    Louder than the loud ocean, like a crash

---

2. In stanzas 22–48 (here omitted) the ship, bound for Leghorn, runs into a violent storm and is battered into a helpless, sinking wreck.

Of echoing thunder; and then all was hush'd,
420   Save the wild wind and the remorseless dash
Of billows; but at intervals there gush'd,
    Accompanied with a convulsive splash,
A solitary shriek, the bubbling cry
Of some strong swimmer in his agony.

*   *   *

56

Juan got into the long-boat, and there
    Contrived to help Pedrillo[3] to a place;
It seem'd as if they had exchanged their care,
    For Juan wore the magisterial face
445 Which courage gives, while poor Pedrillo's pair
    Of eyes were crying for their owner's case:
Battista, though (a name call'd shortly Tita),
Was lost by getting at some aqua-vita.°   *brandy*

57

Pedro, his valet, too, he tried to save,
450   But the same cause, conducive to his loss,
Left him so drunk, he jump'd into the wave
    As o'er the cutter's edge he tried to cross,
And so he found a wine-and-watery grave;
    They could not rescue him although so close,
455 Because the sea ran higher every minute,
And for the boat—the crew kept crowding in it.

*   *   *

66

'Tis thus with people in an open boat,
    They live upon the love of life, and bear
More than can be believed, or even thought,
    And stand like rocks the tempest's wear and tear;
525 And hardship still has been the sailor's lot,
    Since Noah's ark went cruising here and there;
She had a curious crew as well as cargo,
Like the first old Greek privateer, the Argo.[4]

67

But man is a carnivorous production,
530   And must have meals, at least one meal a day;
He cannot live, like woodcocks, upon suction,[5]
    But, like the shark and tiger, must have prey:
Although his anatomical construction
    Bears vegetables in a grumbling way,
535 Your labouring people think beyond all question,
Beef, veal, and mutton, better for digestion.

---

3. Juan's tutor.
4. In the Greek myth the *Argo* is the ship on which Jason set out in quest of the Golden Fleece. Byron ironically calls it a "privateer" (a private ship licensed by a government in wartime to attack and pillage enemy vessels).
5. Woodcocks probe the turf with their long flexible bills, seeming to suck air as they feed.

68

And thus it was with this our hapless crew,
    For on the third day there came on a calm,
And though at first their strength it might renew,
540   And lying on their weariness like balm,
Lull'd them like turtles sleeping on the blue
    Of ocean, when they woke they felt a qualm,
And fell all ravenously on their provision,
Instead of hoarding it with due precision.

*   *   *

72

The seventh day,[6] and no wind—the burning sun
570   Blister'd and scorch'd, and, stagnant on the sea,
They lay like carcases; and hope was none,
    Save in the breeze that came not; savagely
They glared upon each other—all was done,
    Water, and wine, and food,—and you might see
575 The longings of the cannibal arise
(Although they spoke not) in their wolfish eyes.

73

At length one whisper'd his companion, who
    Whisper'd another, and thus it went round,
And then into a hoarser murmur grew,
580   An ominous, and wild, and desperate sound,
And when his comrade's thought each sufferer knew,
    'Twas but his own, suppress'd till now, he found:
And out they spoke of lots for flesh and blood,
And who should die to be his fellow's food.

74

585 But ere they came to this, they that day shared
    Some leathern caps, and what remain'd of shoes;
And then they look'd around them, and despair'd,
    And none to be the sacrifice would choose;
At length the lots were torn up, and prepared,
590   But of materials that must shock the Muse—
Having no paper, for the want of better,
They took by force from Juan Julia's letter.

75

The lots were made, and mark'd, and mix'd, and handed,
    In silent horror, and their distribution
595 Lull'd even the savage hunger which demanded,
    Like the Promethean vulture,[7] this pollution;
None in particular had sought or plann'd it,

---

6. On the fourth day the crew had killed and eaten Juan's pet spaniel. Byron based the episode of cannibalism that follows on various historical accounts of disasters at sea.

7. Because Prometheus had stolen fire from heaven to give to humans, Zeus punished him by chaining him to a mountain peak, where an eagle fed on his ever-renewing liver.

'Twas nature gnaw'd them to this resolution,
By which none were permitted to be neuter—
600 And the lot fell on Juan's luckless tutor.

76

He but requested to be bled to death:
  The surgeon had his instruments, and bled
Pedrillo, and so gently ebb'd his breath,
  You hardly could perceive when he was dead.
605 He died as born, a Catholic in faith,
  Like most in the belief in which they're bred,
And first a little crucifix he kiss'd,
And then held out his jugular and wrist.

77

The surgeon, as there was no other fee,
610 Had his first choice of morsels for his pains;
But being thirstiest at the moment, he
  Preferr'd a draught from the fast-flowing veins:
Part was divided, part thrown in the sea,
  And such things as the entrails and the brains
615 Regaled two sharks, who follow'd o'er the billow—
The sailors ate the rest of poor Pedrillo.

78

The sailors ate him, all save three or four,
  Who were not quite so fond of animal food;
To these was added Juan, who, before
620 Refusing his own spaniel, hardly could
Feel now his appetite increased much more;
  'Twas not to be expected that he should,
Even in extremity of their disaster,
Dine with them on his pastor and his master.

79

625 'Twas better that he did not; for, in fact,
  The consequence was awful in the extreme;
For they, who were most ravenous in the act,
  Went raging mad—Lord! how they did blaspheme!
And foam and roll, with strange convulsions rack'd,
630 Drinking salt-water like a mountain-stream,
Tearing, and grinning, howling, screeching, swearing,
And, with hyaena laughter, died despairing.

* * *

103

As they drew nigh the land, which now was seen
  Unequal in its aspect here and there,
They felt the freshness of its growing green,
820 That waved in forest-tops, and smooth'd the air,
And fell upon their glazed eyes like a screen

From glistening waves, and skies so hot and bare—
Lovely seem'd any object that should sweep
Away the vast, salt, dread, eternal deep.

104

825   The shore look'd wild, without a trace of man,
    And girt by formidable waves; but they
Were mad for land, and thus their course they ran,
    Though right ahead the roaring breakers lay:
A reef between them also now began
830   To show its boiling surf and bounding spray,
But finding no place for their landing better,
They ran the boat for shore, and overset her.

105

But in his native stream, the Guadalquivir,
    Juan to lave his youthful limbs was wont;
835 And having learnt to swim in that sweet river,
    Had often turn'd the art to some account:
A better swimmer you could scarce see ever,
    He could, perhaps, have pass'd the Hellespont,
As once (a feat on which ourselves we prided)
840 Leander, Mr. Ekenhead, and I did.[8]

106

So here, though faint, emaciated, and stark,
    He buoy'd his boyish limbs, and strove to ply
With the quick wave, and gain, ere it was dark,
    The beach which lay before him, high and dry:
845 The greatest danger here was from a shark,
    That carried off his neighbour by the thigh;
As for the other two, they could not swim,
So nobody arrived on shore but him.

107

Nor yet had he arrived but for the oar,
850   Which, providentially for him, was wash'd
Just as his feeble arms could strike no more,
    And the hard wave o'erwhelm'd him as 'twas dash'd
Within his grasp; he clung to it, and sore
    The waters beat while he thereto was lash'd;
855 At last, with swimming, wading, scrambling, he
Roll'd on the beach, half senseless, from the sea:

108

There, breathless, with his digging nails he clung
    Fast to the sand, lest the returning wave,
From whose reluctant roar his life he wrung,

---

8. Like Leander in the myth, Byron and Lieutenant Ekenhead had swum the Hellespont, on May 3, 1810. See *Written after Swimming from Sestos to Abydos* (p. 555).

860   Should suck him back to her insatiate grave:
       And there he lay, full length, where he was flung,
          Before the entrance of a cliff-worn cave,
       With just enough of life to feel its pain,
       And deem that it was saved, perhaps, in vain.

109

865   With slow and staggering effort he arose,
          But sunk again upon his bleeding knee
       And quivering hand; and then he look'd for those
          Who long had been his mates upon the sea,
       But none of them appear'd to share his woes,
870   Save one, a corpse from out the famish'd three,
       Who died two days before, and now had found
       An unknown barren beach for burial ground.

110

       And as he gazed, his dizzy brain spun fast,
          And down he sunk; and as he sunk, the sand
875   Swam round and round, and all his senses pass'd:
          He fell upon his side, and his stretch'd hand
       Droop'd dripping on the oar, (their jury-mast)
          And, like a wither'd lily, on the land
       His slender frame and pallid aspect lay,
880   As fair a thing as e'er was form'd of clay.

[JUAN AND HAIDEE]

111

       How long in his damp trance young Juan lay
          He knew not, for the earth was gone for him,
       And Time had nothing more of night nor day
          For his congealing blood, and senses dim;
885   And how this heavy faintness pass'd away
          He knew not, till each painful pulse and limb,
       And tingling vein seem'd throbbing back to life,
       For Death, though vanquish'd, still retired with strife.

112

       His eyes he open'd, shut, again unclosed,
890   For all was doubt and dizziness; methought
       He still was in the boat, and had but dozed,
          And felt again with his despair o'erwrought,
       And wish'd it death in which he had reposed,
          And then once more his feelings back were brought,
895   And slowly by his swimming eyes was seen
       A lovely female face of seventeen.

113

       'Twas bending close o'er his, and the small mouth
          Seem'd almost prying into his for breath;

And chafing him, the soft warm hand of youth
900   Recall'd his answering spirits back from death;
And, bathing his chill temples, tried to soothe
        Each pulse to animation, till beneath
Its gentle touch and trembling care, a sigh
To these kind efforts made a low reply.

114

905   Then was the cordial pour'd, and mantle flung
          Around his scarce-clad limbs; and the fair arm
      Raised higher the faint head which o'er it hung;
          And her transparent cheek, all pure and warm,
      Pillow'd his death-like forehead; then she wrung
910   His dewy curls, long drench'd by every storm;
      And watch'd with eagerness each throb that drew
      A sigh from his heaved bosom—and hers, too.

115

      And lifting him with care into the cave,
          The gentle girl, and her attendant,—one
915   Young, yet her elder, and of brow less grave,
          And more robust of figure,—then begun
      To kindle fire, and as the new flames gave
          Light to the rocks that roof'd them, which the sun
      Had never seen, the maid, or whatsoe'er
920   She was, appear'd distinct, and tall, and fair.

116

      Her brow was overhung with coins of gold,
          That sparkled o'er the auburn of her hair,
      Her clustering hair, whose longer locks were roll'd
          In braids behind, and though her stature were
925   Even of the highest for a female mould,
          They nearly reach'd her heel; and in her air
      There was a something which bespoke command,
      As one who was a lady in the land.

117

      Her hair, I said, was auburn; but her eyes
930   Were black as death, their lashes the same hue,
      Of downcast length, in whose silk shadow lies
          Deepest attraction, for when to the view
      Forth from its raven fringe the full glance flies,
          Ne'er with such force the swiftest arrow flew;
935   'Tis as the snake late coil'd, who pours his length,
      And hurls at once his venom and his strength.

*   *   *

123

      And these two tended him, and cheer'd him both
          With food and raiment, and those soft attentions,

Which are (as I must own) of female growth,
980   And have ten thousand delicate inventions:
They made a most superior mess of broth,
    A thing which poesy but seldom mentions,
But the best dish that e'er was cook'd since Homer's
Achilles order'd dinner for new comers.[9]

124

985   I'll tell you who they were, this female pair,
    Lest they should seem princesses in disguise;
Besides, I hate all mystery, and that air
    Of clap-trap, which your recent poets prize;
And so, in short, the girls they really were
990   They shall appear before your curious eyes,
Mistress and maid; the first was only daughter
Of an old man, who lived upon the water.

125

A fisherman he had been in his youth,
    And still a sort of fisherman was he;
995   But other speculations were, in sooth,
    Added to his connection with the sea,
Perhaps not so respectable, in truth:
    A little smuggling, and some piracy,
Left him, at last, the sole of many masters
1000   Of an ill-gotten million of piastres.[1]

126

A fisher, therefore, was he—though of men,
    Like Peter the Apostle,[2]—and he fish'd
For wandering merchant vessels, now and then,
    And sometimes caught as many as he wish'd;
1005   The cargoes he confiscated, and gain
    He sought in the slave-market too, and dish'd
Full many a morsel for that Turkish trade,
By which, no doubt, a good deal may be made.

127

He was a Greek, and on his isle had built
1010   (One of the wild and smaller Cyclades)[3]
A very handsome house from out his guilt,
    And there he lived exceedingly at ease;
Heaven knows what cash he got, or blood he spilt,
    A sad[4] old fellow was he, if you please,
1015   But this I know, it was a spacious building,
Full of barbaric carving, paint, and gilding.

---

9. A reference to the lavish feast with which Achilles entertained Ajax, Phoenix, and Ulysses (*Iliad* 9.193ff.).
1. Near-Eastern coins.
2. Christ's words to Peter and Andrew, both fisher-

men: "Follow me, and I will make you fishers of men" (Matthew 4.19).
3. A group of islands in the Aegean Sea.
4. In the playful sense: wicked.

128

He had an only daughter, call'd Haidee,
   The greatest heiress of the Eastern Isles;
Besides, so very beautiful was she,
1020   Her dowry was as nothing to her smiles:
Still in her teens, and like a lovely tree
   She grew to womanhood, and between whiles
Rejected several suitors, just to learn
How to accept a better in his turn.

129

1025 And walking out upon the beach, below
   The cliff, towards sunset, on that day she found,
Insensible,—not dead, but nearly so,—
   Don Juan, almost famish'd, and half drown'd;
But being naked, she was shock'd, you know,
1030   Yet deem'd herself in common pity bound,
As far as in her lay, "to take him in,
A stranger"⁵ dying, with so white a skin.

130

But taking him into her father's house
   Was not exactly the best way to save,
1035 But like conveying to the cat the mouse,
   Or people in a trance into their grave;
Because the good old man had so much "νους,"⁶
   Unlike the honest Arab thieves so brave,
He would have hospitably cured the stranger,
1040 And sold him instantly when out of danger.

131

And therefore, with her maid, she thought it best
   (A virgin always on her maid relies)
To place him in the cave for present rest:
   And when, at last, he open'd his black eyes,
1045 Their charity increased about their guest;
   And their compassion grew to such a size,
It open'd half the turnpike-gates to heaven—
(St. Paul says 'tis the toll which must be given).⁷

*   *   *

141

And Haidee met the morning face to face;
   Her own was freshest, though a feverish flush
Had dyed it with the headlong blood, whose race
   From heart to cheek is curb'd into a blush,
1125 Like to a torrent which a mountain's base,
   That overpowers some Alpine river's rush,

---

5. Cf. Matthew 25.35: "I was a stranger, and ye took me in."
6. *Nous,* "intelligence" (Greek); in England, pronounced so as to rhyme with *mouse.*
7. 1 Corinthians 13.13.

Checks to a lake, whose waves in circles spread;
Or the Red Sea—but the sea is not red.

142

And down the cliff the island virgin came,
1130   And near the cave her quick light footsteps drew,
While the sun smiled on her with his first flame,
         And young Aurora° kiss'd her lips with dew,   *dawn*
Taking her for a sister; just the same
         Mistake you would have made on seeing the two,
1135 Although the mortal, quite as fresh and fair,
Had all the advantage too of not being air.

143

And when into the cavern Haidee stepp'd
         All timidly, yet rapidly, she saw
That like an infant Juan sweetly slept;
1140   And then she stopp'd, and stood as if in awe,
(For sleep is awful) and on tiptoe crept
         And wrapt him closer, lest the air, too raw,
Should reach his blood, then o'er him still as death
Bent, with hush'd lips, that drank his scarce-drawn breath.

*   *   *

148

And she bent o'er him, and he lay beneath,
         Hush'd as the babe upon its mother's breast,
Droop'd as the willow when no winds can breathe,
1180   Lull'd like the depth of ocean when at rest,
Fair as the crowning rose of the whole wreath,
         Soft as the callow° cygnet° in its nest;   *young/swan*
In short, he was a very pretty fellow,
Although his woes had turn'd him rather yellow.

149

1185 He woke and gazed, and would have slept again,
         But the fair face which met his eyes forbade
Those eyes to close, though weariness and pain
         Had further sleep a further pleasure made;
For woman's face was never form'd in vain
1190   For Juan, so that even when he pray'd
He turn'd from grisly saints, and martyrs hairy,
To the sweet portraits of the Virgin Mary.

150

And thus upon his elbow he arose,
         And look'd upon the lady, in whose cheek
1195 The pale contended with the purple rose,
         As with an effort she began to speak;
Her eyes were eloquent, her words would pose,
         Although she told him, in good modern Greek,

With an Ionian accent, low and sweet,
1200   That he was faint, and must not talk, but eat.

*   *   *

168

And every day by day-break—rather early
   For Juan, who was somewhat fond of rest—
She came into the cave, but it was merely
1340   To see her bird reposing in his nest;
And she would softly stir his locks so curly,
   Without disturbing her yet slumbering guest,
Breathing all gently o'er his cheek and mouth,
As o'er a bed of roses the sweet south.[8]

169

1345 And every morn his colour freshlier came,
   And every day help'd on his convalescence;
'Twas well, because health in the human frame
   Is pleasant, besides being true love's essence,
For health and idleness to passion's flame
1350   Are oil and gunpowder; and some good lessons
Are also learnt from Ceres[9] and from Bacchus,
Without whom Venus will not long attack us.

170

While Venus fills the heart (without heart really
   Love, though good always, is not quite so good)
1355 Ceres presents a plate of vermicelli,—
   For love must be sustain'd like flesh and blood,—
While Bacchus pours out wine, or hands a jelly:
   Eggs, oysters too, are amatory food;
But who is their purveyor from above
1360 Heaven knows,—it may be Neptune, Pan, or Jove.

171

When Juan woke he found some good things ready,
   A bath, a breakfast, and the finest eyes
That ever made a youthful heart less steady,
   Besides her maid's, as pretty for their size;
1365 But I have spoken of all this already—
   And repetition's tiresome and unwise,—
Well—Juan, after bathing in the sea,
Came always back to coffee and Haidee.

172

Both were so young, and one so innocent,
1370   That bathing pass'd for nothing; Juan seem'd
To her, as 'twere, the kind of being sent,
   Of whom these two years she had nightly dream'd,

---

8. The south wind.   9. Goddess of the grain.

A something to be loved, a creature meant
    To be her happiness, and whom she deem'd
1375 To render happy; all who joy would win
    Must share it,—Happiness was born a twin.

173

It was such pleasure to behold him, such
    Enlargement of existence to partake
Nature with him, to thrill beneath his touch,
1380   To watch him slumbering, and to see him wake:
To live with him for ever were too much;
    But then the thought of parting made her quake:
He was her own, her ocean-treasure, cast
Like a rich wreck—her first love, and her last.

174

1385 And thus a moon roll'd on, and fair Haidee
    Paid daily visits to her boy, and took
Such plentiful precautions, that still he
    Remain'd unknown within his craggy nook;
At last her father's prows put out to sea,
1390   For certain merchantmen upon the look,
Not as of yore to carry off an Io,[1]
But three Ragusan vessels, bound for Scio.[2]

175

Then came her freedom, for she had no mother,
    So that, her father being at sea, she was
1395 Free as a married woman, or such other
    Female, as where she likes may freely pass,
Without even the encumbrance of a brother,
    The freest she that ever gazed on glass:
I speak of christian lands in this comparison,
1400 Where wives, at least, are seldom kept in garrison.

176

Now she prolong'd her visits and her talk
    (For they must talk), and he had learnt to say
So much as to propose to take a walk,—
    For little had he wander'd since the day
1405 On which, like a young flower snapp'd from the stalk,
    Drooping and dewy on the beach he lay,—
And thus they walk'd out in the afternoon,
And saw the sun set opposite the moon.

177

It was a wild and breaker-beaten coast,
1410   With cliffs above, and a broad sandy shore,
Guarded by shoals and rocks as by an host,

---

1. A mistress of Zeus who was persecuted by his
jealous wife, Hera, and kidnapped by Phoenician
merchants.

2. The Italian name for Chios, an island near Turkey. "Ragusan": Ragusa (or Dubrovnik) is an Adri-
atic port.

With here and there a creek, whose aspect wore
A better welcome to the tempest-tost;
   And rarely ceas'd the haughty billow's roar,
1415 Save on the dead long summer days, which make
The outstretch'd ocean glitter like a lake.

178

And the small ripple spilt upon the beach
   Scarcely o'erpass'd the cream of your champagne,
When o'er the brim the sparkling bumpers reach,
1420   That spring-dew of the spirit! the heart's rain!
Few things surpass old wine; and they may preach
   Who please,—the more because they preach in vain,—
Let us have wine and woman, mirth and laughter,
Sermons and soda water the day after.

179

1425 Man, being reasonable, must get drunk;
   The best of life is but intoxication:
Glory, the grape, love, gold, in these are sunk
   The hopes of all men, and of every nation;
Without their sap, how branchless were the trunk
1430   Of life's strange tree, so fruitful on occasion:
But to return,—Get very drunk; and when
You wake with head-ache, you shall see what then.

180

Ring for your valet—bid him quickly bring
   Some hock and soda-water, then you'll know
1435 A pleasure worthy Xerxes[3] the great king;
   For not the blest sherbet, sublimed with snow,
Nor the first sparkle of the desert-spring,
   Nor Burgundy in all its sunset glow,
After long travel, ennui, love, or slaughter,
1440 Vie with that draught of hock and soda-water.

181

The coast—I think it was the coast that I
   Was just describing—Yes, it *was* the coast—
Lay at this period quiet as the sky,
   The sands untumbled, the blue waves untost,
1445 And all was stillness, save the sea-bird's cry,
   And dolphin's leap, and little billow crost
By some low rock or shelve, that made it fret
Against the boundary it scarcely wet.

182

And forth they wandered, her sire being gone,
1450   As I have said, upon an expedition;

3. The 5th-century Persian king was said to have offered a reward to anyone who could discover a new kind of pleasure.

And mother, brother, guardian, she had none,
   Save Zoe, who, although with due precision
She waited on her lady with the sun,
   Thought daily service was her only mission,
1455 Bringing warm water, wreathing her long tresses,
And asking now and then for cast-off dresses.

183

It was the cooling hour, just when the rounded
   Red sun sinks down behind the azure hill,
Which then seems as if the whole earth it bounded,
1460   Circling all nature, hush'd, and dim, and still,
With the far mountain-crescent half surrounded
   On one side, and the deep sea calm and chill
Upon the other, and the rosy sky,
With one star sparkling through it like an eye.

184

1465 And thus they wander'd forth, and hand in hand,
   Over the shining pebbles and the shells,
Glided along the smooth and harden'd sand,
   And in the worn and wild receptacles
Work'd by the storms, yet work'd as it were plann'd,
1470   In hollow halls, with sparry roofs and cells,
They turn'd to rest; and, each clasp'd by an arm,
Yielded to the deep twilight's purple charm.

185

They look'd up to the sky, whose floating glow
   Spread like a rosy ocean, vast and bright;
1475 They gazed upon the glittering sea below,
   Whence the broad moon rose circling into sight;
They heard the wave's splash, and the wind so low,
   And saw each other's dark eyes darting light
Into each other—and, beholding this,
1480 Their lips drew near, and clung into a kiss;

186

A long, long kiss, a kiss of youth and love,
   And beauty, all concentrating like rays
Into one focus, kindled from above;
   Such kisses as belong to early days,
1485 Where heart, and soul, and sense, in concert move,
   And the blood's lava, and the pulse a blaze,
Each kiss a heart-quake,—for a kiss's strength,
I think, it must be reckon'd by its length.

187

By length I mean duration; theirs endured
1490   Heaven knows how long—no doubt they never reckon'd;
And if they had, they could not have secured
   The sum of their sensations to a second:

They had not spoken; but they felt allured,
  As if their souls and lips each other beckon'd,
1495 Which, being join'd, like swarming bees they clung—
Their hearts the flowers from whence the honey sprung.

188

They were alone, but not alone as they
  Who shut in chambers think it loneliness;
The silent ocean, and the starlight bay,
1500   The twilight glow, which momently grew less,
The voiceless sands, and dropping caves, that lay
  Around them, made them to each other press,
As if there were no life beneath the sky
Save theirs, and that their life could never die.

189

1505 They fear'd no eyes nor ears on that lone beach,
  They felt no terrors from the night, they were
All in all to each other: though their speech
  Was broken words, they *thought* a language there,—
And all the burning tongues the passions teach
1510   Found in one sigh the best interpreter
Of nature's oracle—first love,—that all
Which Eve has left her daughters since her fall.

190

Haidee[4] spoke not of scruples, ask'd no vows,
  Nor offer'd any; she had never heard
1515 Of plight and promises to be a spouse,
  Or perils by a loving maid incurr'd;
She was all which pure ignorance allows,
  And flew to her young mate like a young bird;
And, never having dreamt of falsehood, she
1520 Had not one word to say of constancy.

191

She loved, and was beloved—she adored,
  And she was worshipp'd; after nature's fashion,
Their intense souls, into each other pour'd,
  If souls could die, had perish'd in that passion,—
1525 But by degrees their senses were restored,
  Again to be o'ercome, again to dash on;
And, beating 'gainst *his* bosom, Haidee's heart
Felt as if never more to beat apart.

192

Alas! they were so young, so beautiful,
1530   So lonely, loving, helpless, and the hour
Was that in which the heart is always full,

---

4. Byron said, with reference to Haidee: "I was, and am, penetrated with the conviction that women only know evil from men, whereas men have no criterion to judge of purity or goodness but woman."

And, having o'er itself no further power,
   Prompts deeds eternity can not annul,
     But pays off moments in an endless shower
1535 Of hell-fire—all prepared for people giving
Pleasure or pain to one another living.

193

Alas! for Juan and Haidee! they were
   So loving and so lovely—till then never,
Excepting our first parents, such a pair
1540   Had run the risk of being damn'd for ever;
And Haidee, being devout as well as fair,
   Had, doubtless, heard about the Stygian river,[5]
And hell and purgatory—but forgot
Just in the very crisis she should not.

194

1545 They look upon each other, and their eyes
   Gleam in the moonlight; and her white arm clasps
Round Juan's head, and his around hers lies
   Half buried in the tresses which it grasps;
She sits upon his knee, and drinks his sighs,
1550   He hers, until they end in broken gasps;
And thus they form a group that's quite antique,
Half naked, loving, natural, and Greek.

195

And when those deep and burning moments pass'd,
   And Juan sunk to sleep within her arms,
1555 She slept not, but all tenderly, though fast,
   Sustain'd his head upon her bosom's charms;
And now and then her eye to heaven is cast,
   And then on the pale cheek her breast now warms,
Pillow'd on her o'erflowing heart, which pants
1560 With all it granted, and with all it grants.

196

An infant when it gazes on a light,
   A child the moment when it drains the breast,
A devotee when soars the Host[6] in sight,
   An Arab with a stranger for a guest,
1565 A sailor when the prize has struck[7] in fight,
   A miser filling his most hoarded chest,
Feel rapture; but not such true joy are reaping
As they who watch o'er what they love while sleeping.

197

For there it lies so tranquil, so beloved,
1570   All that it hath of life with us is living;

5. The Styx, which flows through Hades.
6. The Eucharistic wafer.

7. Has lowered its flag in token of surrender.

So gentle, stirless, helpless, and unmoved,
    And all unconscious of the joy 'tis giving;
All it hath felt, inflicted, pass'd, and proved,
    Hush'd into depths beyond the watcher's diving;
1575 There lies the thing we love with all its errors
And all its charms, like death without its terrors.

198

The lady watch'd her lover—and that hour
    Of Love's, and Night's, and Ocean's solitude,
O'erflow'd her soul with their united power;
1580   Amidst the barren sand and rocks so rude
She and her wave-worn love had made their bower,
    Where nought upon their passion could intrude,
And all the stars that crowded the blue space
Saw nothing happier than her glowing face.

199

1585 Alas! the love of women! it is known
    To be a lovely and a fearful thing;
For all of theirs upon that die is thrown,
    And if 'tis lost, life hath no more to bring
To them but mockeries of the past alone,
1590   And their revenge is as the tiger's spring,
Deadly, and quick, and crushing; yet, as real
Torture is theirs, what they inflict they feel.

200

They are right; for man, to man so oft unjust,
    Is always so to women; one sole bond
1595 Awaits them, treachery is all their trust;
    Taught to conceal, their bursting hearts despond
Over their idol, till some wealthier lust
    Buys them in marriage—and what rests beyond?
A thankless husband, next a faithless lover,
1600 Then dressing, nursing, praying, and all's over.

201

Some take a lover, some take drams or prayers,
    Some mind their household, others dissipation,
Some run away, and but exchange their cares,
    Losing the advantage of a virtuous station;
1605 Few changes e'er can better their affairs,
    Theirs being an unnatural situation,
From the dull palace to the dirty hovel:
Some play the devil, and then write a novel.[8]

---

8. The impetuous Lady Caroline Lamb, having thrown herself at Byron and been after a time rejected, incorporated incidents from the affair in her novel *Glenarvon* (1816).

202

Haidee was Nature's bride, and knew not this;
Haidee was Passion's child, born where the sun
Showers triple light, and scorches even the kiss
    Of his gazelle-eyed daughters; she was one
Made but to love, to feel that she was his
    Who was her chosen: what was said or done
Elsewhere was nothing—She had nought to fear,
Hope, care, nor love beyond, her heart beat *here*.

203

And oh! that quickening of the heart, that beat!
    How much it costs us! yet each rising throb
Is in its cause as its effect so sweet,
    That Wisdom, ever on the watch to rob
Joy of its alchymy, and to repeat
    Fine truths, even Conscience, too, has a tough job
To make us understand each good old maxim,
So good—I wonder Castlereagh[9] don't tax 'em.

204

And now 'twas done—on the lone shore were plighted
    Their hearts; the stars, their nuptial torches, shed
Beauty upon the beautiful they lighted:
    Ocean their witness, and the cave their bed,
By their own feelings hallow'd and united,
    Their priest was Solitude, and they were wed:
And they were happy, for to their young eyes
Each was an angel, and earth paradise.

*   *   *

208

But Juan! had he quite forgotten Julia?
    And should he have forgotten her so soon?
I can't but say it seems to me most truly a
    Perplexing question; but, no doubt, the moon
Does these things for us, and whenever newly a
    Strong palpitation rises, 'tis her boon,
Else how the devil is it that fresh features
Have such a charm for us poor human creatures?

209

I hate inconstancy—I loathe, detest,
    Abhor, condemn, abjure the mortal made
Of such quicksilver clay that in his breast
    No permanent foundation can be laid;
Love, constant love, has been my constant guest,
    And yet last night, being at a masquerade,

9. Robert Stewart, Viscount Castlereagh, British foreign secretary (1812–22).

I saw the prettiest creature, fresh from Milan,
Which gave me some sensations like a villain.

210

But soon Philosophy came to my aid,
    And whisper'd "think of every sacred tie!"
1675   "I will, my dear Philosophy!" I said,
    "But then her teeth, and then, Oh heaven! her eye!
I'll just inquire if she be wife or maid,
    Or neither—out of curiosity."
"Stop!" cried Philosophy, with air so Grecian,
1680   (Though she was masqued then as a fair Venetian).

211

"Stop!" so I stopp'd.—But to return: that which
    Men call inconstancy is nothing more
Than admiration due where nature's rich
    Profusion with young beauty covers o'er
1685   Some favour'd object; and as in the niche
    A lovely statue we almost adore,
This sort of adoration of the real
Is but a heightening of the "beau ideal."[1]

212

'Tis the perception of the beautiful,
1690   A fine extension of the faculties,
Platonic, universal, wonderful,
    Drawn from the stars, and filter'd through the skies,
Without which life would be extremely dull;
    In short, it is the use of our own eyes,
1695   With one or two small senses added, just
To hint that flesh is form'd of fiery dust.

213

Yet 'tis a painful feeling, and unwilling,
    For surely if we always could perceive
In the same object graces quite as killing
1700   As when she rose upon us like an Eve,
'Twould save us many a heart-ache, many a shilling,
    (For we must get them anyhow, or grieve),
Whereas, if one sole lady pleased for ever,
How pleasant for the heart, as well as liver!

*   *   *

216

In the mean time, without proceeding more
    In this anatomy, I've finish'd now
Two hundred and odd stanzas as before,

---

1. Ideal beauty (French).

That being about the number I'll allow
1725　Each canto of the twelve, or twenty-four;
　　And, laying down my pen, I make my bow,
　Leaving Don Juan and Haidee to plead
　For them and theirs with all who deign to read.

From Canto 3

[JUAN AND HAIDEE]

I

Hail, Muse! *et cetera.*—We left Juan sleeping,
　Pillow'd upon a fair and happy breast,
And watch'd by eyes that never yet knew weeping,
　And loved by a young heart, too deeply blest
5　To feel the poison through her spirit creeping,
　　Or know who rested there, a foe to rest
Had soil'd the current of her sinless years,
And turn'd her pure heart's purest blood to tears.

2

Oh, Love! what is it in this world of ours
10　　Which makes it fatal to be loved? Ah why
With cypress branches[1] hast thou wreathed thy bowers,
　And made thy best interpreter a sigh?
As those who dote on odours pluck the flowers,
　And place them on their breast—but place to die!
15　Thus the frail beings we would fondly cherish
　Are laid within our bosoms but to perish.

3

In her first passion woman loves her lover,
　In all the others all she loves is love,
Which grows a habit she can ne'er get over,
20　　And fits her loosely—like an easy glove,
As you may find, whene'er you like to prove her:
　　One man alone at first her heart can move;
She then prefers him in the plural number,
Not finding that the additions much encumber.

4

25　I know not if the fault be men's or theirs;
　　But one thing's pretty sure; a woman planted[2]—
(Unless at once she plunge for life in prayers)—
　　After a decent time must be gallanted;
Although, no doubt, her first of love affairs
30　　Is that to which her heart is wholly granted;

1. Signifying sorrow.
2. Abandoned (from the French *planter là,* to leave in the lurch).

70   And then both worlds would punish their miscarriage;
        So leaving each their priest and prayer-book ready,
        They say no more of Death or of the Lady.[4]

                              10

        The only two that in my recollection
            Have sung of heaven and hell, or marriage, are
75   Dante and Milton, and of both the affection
            Was hapless in their nuptials, for some bar
        Of fault or temper ruin'd the connexion
            (Such things, in fact, it don't ask much to mar);
        But Dante's Beatrice and Milton's Eve
80   Were not drawn from their spouses, you conceive.

                              11

        Some persons say that Dante meant theology
            By Beatrice, and not a mistress—I,
        Although my opinion may require apology,
            Deem this a commentator's phantasy,
85   Unless indeed it was from his own knowledge he
            Decided thus, and show'd good reason why;
        I think that Dante's more abstruse ecstatics
        Meant to personify the mathematics.

                              12

        Haidee and Juan were not married, but
90   The fault was theirs, not mine: it is not fair,
        Chaste reader, then, in any way to put
            The blame on me, unless you wish they were;
        Then if you'd have them wedded, please to shut
            The book which treats of this erroneous pair,
95   Before the consequences grow too awful;
        'Tis angerous to read of loves unlawful.

                              13

        Yet they were happy,—happy in the illicit
            Indulgence of their innocent desires;
        But more imprudent grown with every visit,
100   Haidee forgot the island was her sire's;
        When we have what we like, 'tis hard to miss it,
            At least in the beginning, ere one tires;
        Thus she came often, not a moment losing,
        Whilst her piratical papa was cruising.

                              14

105   Let not his mode of raising cash seem strange,
            Although he fleeced the flags of every nation,
        For into a prime minister but change
            His title, and 'tis nothing but taxation;
        But he, more modest, took an humbler range

Alluding to a popular ballad, *Death and the Lady*.

Yet there are some, they say, who have had
But those who have ne'er end with only *one*.

5

'Tis melancholy, and a fearful sign
   Of human frailty, folly, also crime,
35 That love and marriage rarely can combine,
   Although they both are born in the same clime;
Marriage from love, like vinegar from wine—
   A sad, sour, sober beverage—by time
Is sharpen'd from its high celestial flavour
40 Down to a very homely household savour.

6

There's something of antipathy, as 'twere,
   Between their present and their future state;
A kind of flattery that's hardly fair
   Is used until the truth arrives too late—
45 Yet what can people do, except despair?
   The same things change their names at such a rate;
For instance—passion in a lover's glorious,
But in a husband is pronounced uxorious.

7

Men grow ashamed of being so very fond;
50   They sometimes also get a little tired
(But that, of course, is rare), and then despond:
   The same things cannot always be admired,
Yet 'tis "so nominated in the bond,"[3]
   That both are tied till one shall have expired.
55 Sad thought! to lose the spouse that was adorning
Our days, and put one's servants into mourning.

8

There's doubtless something in domestic doings,
   Which forms, in fact, true love's antithesis;
Romances paint at full length people's wooings,
60   But only give a bust of marriages;
For no one cares for matrimonial cooings,
   There's nothing wrong in a connubial kiss:
Think you, if Laura had been Petrarch's wife,
He would have written sonnets all his life?

9

65 All tragedies are finish'd by a death,
   All comedies are ended by a marriage;
The future states of both are left to faith,
   For authors fear description might disparage
The worlds to come of both, or fall beneath,

3. Spoken by Shylock in *The Merchant of Venice* 4.1.254: "Is it so nominated ⁱ

4.

110   Of life, and in an honester vocation
          Pursued o'er the high seas his watery journey,
          And merely practised as a sea-attorney.

15

          The good old gentleman had been detain'd
              By winds and waves, and some important captures;
115   And, in the hope of more, at sea remain'd,
              Although a squall or two had damp'd his raptures,
          By swamping one of the prizes; he had chain'd
              His prisoners, dividing them like chapters
120   In number'd lots; they all had cuffs and collars,
          And averaged each from ten to a hundred dollars.

                          *   *   *

19

145   Then having settled his marine affairs,
              Despatching single cruisers here and there,
          His vessel having need of some repairs,
              He shaped his course to where his daughter fair
          Continued still her hospitable cares;
150   But that part of the coast being shoal and bare,
          And rough with reefs which ran out many a mile,
          His port lay on the other side o' the isle.

20

          And there he went ashore without delay,
              Having no custom-house nor quarantine
155   To ask him awkward questions on the way
              About the time and place where he had been:
          He left his ship to be hove down next day,
              With orders to the people to careen;[5]
          So that all hands were busy beyond measure,
160   In getting out goods, ballast, guns, and treasure.

                          *   *   *

27

          He saw his white walls shining in the sun,
210   His garden trees all shadowy and green;
          He heard his rivulet's light bubbling run,
              The distant dog-bark; and perceived between
          The umbrage of the wood so cool and dun
              The moving figures, and the sparkling sheen
215   Of arms (in the East all arm)—and various dyes
          Of colour'd garbs, as bright as butterflies.

28

          And as the spot where they appear he nears,
              Surprised at these unwonted signs of idling,
          He hears—alas! no music of the spheres,

---

5. To tip a vessel on its side to clean and repair its hull.

220   But an unhallow'd, earthly sound of fiddling!
    A melody which made him doubt his ears,
       The cause being past his guessing or unriddling;
    A pipe, too, and a drum, and shortly after,
    A most unoriental roar of laughter.

                    *   *   *

                    38
    He did not know (Alas! how men will lie)
       That a report (especially the Greeks)
    Avouch'd his death (such people never die),
300   And put his house in mourning several weeks,
    But now their eyes and also lips were dry;
       The bloom too had return'd to Haidee's cheeks.
    Her tears too being return'd into their fount,
    She now kept house upon her own account.

                    39
305   Hence all this rice, meat, dancing, wine, and fiddling,
       Which turn'd the isle into a place of pleasure;
    The servants all were getting drunk or idling,
       A life which made them happy beyond measure.
    Her father's hospitality seem'd middling,
310   Compared with what Haidee did with his treasure;
    'Twas wonderful how things went on improving,
    While she had not one hour to spare from loving.

                    40
    Perhaps you think in stumbling on this feast
       He flew into a passion, and in fact
315   There was no mighty reason to be pleased;
       Perhaps you prophesy some sudden act,
    The whip, the rack, or dungeon at the least,
       To teach his people to be more exact,
    And that, proceeding at a very high rate,
320   He showed the royal *penchants* of a pirate.

                    41
    You're wrong.—He was the mildest manner'd man
       That ever scuttled ship or cut a throat;
    With such true breeding of a gentleman,
       You never could divine his real thought;
325   No courtier could, and scarcely woman can
       Gird more deceit within a petticoat;
    Pity he loved adventurous life's variety,
    He was so great a loss to good society.

                    *   *   *

                    48
    Not that he was not sometimes rash or so,
       But never in his real and serious mood;

Then calm, concentrated, and still, and slow,
380 He lay coil'd like the boa in the wood;
With him it never was a word and blow,
  His angry word once o'er, he shed no blood,
But in his silence there was much to rue,
And his *one* blow left little work for *two*.

49

385 He ask'd no further questions, and proceeded
  On to the house, but by a private way,
So that the few who met him hardly heeded,
  So little they expected him that day;
If love paternal in his bosom pleaded
390 For Haidee's sake, is more than I can say,
But certainly to one deem'd dead returning,
This revel seem'd a curious mode of mourning.

50

If all the dead could now return to life,
  (Which God forbid!) or some, or a great many,
395 For instance, if a husband or his wife
  (Nuptial examples are as good as any),
No doubt whate'er might be their former strife,
  The present weather would be much more rainy—
Tears shed into the grave of the connexion
400 Would share most probably its resurrection.

51

He enter'd in the house no more his home,
  A thing to human feelings the most trying,
And harder for the heart to overcome,
  Perhaps, than even the mental pangs of dying;
405 To find our hearthstone turn'd into a tomb,
  And round its once warm precincts palely lying
The ashes of our hopes, is a deep grief,
Beyond a single gentleman's belief.

52

He enter'd in the house—his home no more,
410 For without hearts there is no home;—and felt
The solitude of passing his own door
  Without a welcome; *there* he long had dwelt,
There his few peaceful days Time had swept o'er,
  There his worn bosom and keen eye would melt
415 Over the innocence of that sweet child,
His only shrine of feelings undefiled.

53

He was a man of a strange temperament,
  Of mild demeanour though of savage mood,
Moderate in all his habits, and content

420   With temperance in pleasure, as in food,
      Quick to perceive, and strong to bear, and meant
        For something better, if not wholly good;
      His country's wrongs and his despair to save her
      Had stung him from a slave to an enslaver.

*   *   *

96

But let me to my story: I must own,
    If I have any fault, it is digression;
Leaving my people to proceed alone,
860   While I soliloquize beyond expression;
But these are my addresses from the throne,
    Which put off business to the ensuing session:
Forgetting each omission is a loss to
The world, not quite so great as Ariosto.[6]

97

865   I know that what our neighbours call *"longueurs,"*[7]
      (We've not so good a *word*, but have the *thing*
In that complete perfection which ensures
      An epic from Bob Southey[8] every spring—)
Form not the true temptation which allures
870   The reader; but 'twould not be hard to bring
Some fine examples of the *épopée,*[9]
To prove its grand ingredient is *ennui.*

98

We learn from Horace, Homer sometimes sleeps;[1]
    We feel without him: Wordsworth sometimes wakes,
875   To show with what complacency he creeps,
      With his dear *"Waggoners,"*[2] around his lakes;
He wishes for "a boat" to sail the deeps—
      Of ocean?—No, of air; and then he makes
Another outcry for "a little boat,"
880   And drivels seas to set it well afloat.[3]

99

If he must fain sweep o'er the etherial plain,
    And Pegasus[4] runs restive in his "waggon,"
Could he not beg the loan of Charles's Wain?[5]
    Or pray Medea for a single dragon?[6]

6. Byron warmly admired this poet, author of *Orlando Furioso* (1532), the greatest of the Italian chivalric romances.
7. Boringly wordy passages of verse or prose (French).
8. Robert Southey (1774–1843), poet laureate and author of a number of epic-length narrative poems.
9. Epic poem (French).
1. Horace's *Art of Poetry* 359: "Sometimes great Homer nods."
2. A reference to Wordsworth's long narrative poem *The Waggoner* (1819).

3. In the prologue to his poem *Peter Bell* (1819), Wordsworth wishes for "a little boat, / In shape a very crescent-moon: / Fast through the clouds my boat can sail."
4. In Greek myth, the winged horse. He was said to have produced the fountain Hippocrene, sacred to the Muses, by stamping his hoof.
5. The constellation known in the United States as the Big Dipper.
6. When the Argonaut Jason abandoned Medea to take a new wife, she murdered their sons to punish him, then escaped in a chariot drawn by winged dragons.

885 Or if too classic for his vulgar brain,
    He fear'd his neck to venture such a nag on,
And he must needs mount nearer to the moon,
    Could not the blockhead ask for a balloon?

100

"Pedlars,"[7] and "boats," and "waggons!" Oh! Ye shades
890   Of Pope and Dryden, are we come to this?
That trash of such sort not alone evades
    Contempt, but from the bathos' vast abyss
Floats scumlike uppermost, and these Jack Cades[8]
    Of sense and song above your graves may hiss—
895 The "little boatman" and his "Peter Bell"
    Can sneer at him who drew "Achitophel!"[9]

101

T' our tale.—The feast was over, the slaves gone,
    The dwarfs and dancing girls had all retired;
The Arab lore and poet's song were done,
900   And every sound of revelry expired;
The lady and her lover, left alone,
    The rosy flood of twilight's sky admired;—
Ave Maria![1] o'er the earth and sea,
That heavenliest hour of Heaven is worthiest thee!

102

905 Ave Maria! blessed be the hour!
    The time, the clime, the spot, where I so oft
Have felt that moment in its fullest power
    Sink o'er the earth so beautiful and soft,
While swung the deep bell in the distant tower,
910   Or the faint dying day-hymn stole aloft,
And not a breath crept through the rosy air,
And yet the forest leaves seem'd stirr'd with prayer.

103

Ave Maria! 'tis the hour of prayer!
    Ave Maria! 'tis the hour of love!
915 Ave Maria! may our spirits dare
    Look up to thine and to thy Son's above!
Ave Maria! oh that face so fair!
    Those downcast eyes beneath the Almighty dove—
What though 'tis but a pictured image strike—
920 That painting is no idol, 'tis too like.

7. Wordsworth's Peddler narrates the story of Margaret, from the early manuscript *The Ruined Cottage* (p. 259). Byron knew this story in the later form that Wordsworth incorporated into book 1 of *The Excursion* (1814).
8. An adventurer who led an uprising against Henry VI in 1450.
9. I.e., John Dryden, author of *Absalom and Ach-*itophel (1681), whom Byron greatly admired. Wordsworth had derogated Dryden's poetry in the *Essay, Supplementary to the Preface* to his *Poems* (1815).
1. Hail, Mary, (Latin), the opening words of a Roman Catholic prayer. *Ave Maria* is sometimes used to refer to evening (or morning), because the prayer is part of the service at these times.

104

Some kinder casuists are pleased to say,
    In nameless print—that I have no devotion;
But set those persons down with me to pray,
    And you shall see who has the properest notion
925 Of getting into Heaven the shortest way;
    My altars are the mountains and the ocean,
Earth, air, stars,—all that springs from the great Whole,
Who hath produced, and will receive the soul.

       *   *   *

From Canto 4

[JUAN AND HAIDEE]

3

As boy, I thought myself a clever fellow,
    And wish'd that others held the same opinion;
They took it up when my days grew more mellow,
20   And other minds acknowledged my dominion:
Now my sere fancy "falls into the yellow
    Leaf,"[1] and imagination droops her pinion,
And the sad truth which hovers o'er my desk
Turns what was once romantic to burlesque.

4

25 And if I laugh at any mortal thing,
    'Tis that I may not weep; and if I weep,
'Tis that our nature cannot always bring
    Itself to apathy, for we must steep
Our hearts first in the depths of Lethe's[2] spring
30   Ere what we least wish to behold will sleep:
Thetis baptized her mortal son in Styx;[3]
A mortal mother would on Lethe fix.

5

Some have accused me of a strange design
    Against the creed and morals of the land,
35 And trace it in this poem every line:
    I don't pretend that I quite understand
My own meaning when I would be *very* fine,
    But the fact is that I have nothing plann'd,
Unless it were to be a moment merry,
40 A novel word in my vocabulary.

---

1. Cf. *Macbeth* 5.3.22–24: "My way of life / Is fall'n into the sere, the yellow leaf."
2. A river in Hades that brings oblivion of life.

3. The river in Hades into which the nymph Thetis dipped Achilles, to make him invulnerable.

6

To the kind reader of our sober clime
  This way of writing will appear exotic;
Pulci[4] was sire of the half-serious rhyme,
  Who sang when chivalry was more Quixotic,
45 And revell'd in the fancies of the time,
  True knights, chaste dames, huge giants, kings despotic;
But all these, save the last, being obsolete,
I chose a modern subject as more meet.

7

How I have treated it, I do not know;
50   Perhaps no better than they have treated me
Who have imputed such designs as show
  Not what they saw, but what they wish'd to see;
But if it gives them pleasure, be it so,
  This is a liberal age, and thoughts are free:
55 Meantime Apollo plucks me by the ear,
And tells me to resume my story here.

*   *   *

26

Juan and Haidee gazed upon each other
  With swimming looks of speechless tenderness,
Which mix'd all feelings, friend, child, lover, brother,
  All that the best can mingle and express
205 When two pure hearts are pour'd in one another,
  And love too much, and yet can not love less;
But almost sanctify the sweet excess
By the immortal wish and power to bless.

27

Mix'd in each other's arms, and heart in heart,
210   Why did they not then die?—they had lived too long
Should an hour come to bid them breathe apart;
  Years could but bring them cruel things or wrong,
The world was not for them, nor the world's art
  For beings passionate as Sappho's song;
215 Love was born *with* them, *in* them, so intense,
It was their very spirit—not a sense.

28

They should have lived together deep in woods,
  Unseen as sings the nightingale; they were
Unfit to mix in these thick solitudes
220   Call'd social, haunts of Hate, and Vice, and Care:
How lonely every freeborn creature broods!
  The sweetest song-birds nestle in a pair;

---

4. Author of the *Morgante Maggiore,* prototype of the Italian seriocomic romance from which Byron derived the stanza and manner of *Don Juan* (see headnote, p. 621).

The eagle soars alone; the gull and crow
Flock o'er their carrion, just like men below.

29

225 Now pillow'd cheek to cheek, in loving sleep,
    Haidee and Juan their siesta took,
A gentle slumber, but it was not deep,
    For ever and anon a something shook
Juan, and shuddering o'er his frame would creep;
230   And Haidee's sweet lips murmur'd like a brook
A wordless music, and her face so fair
Stirr'd with her dream as rose-leaves with the air;

30

Or as the stirring of a deep clear stream
    Within an Alpine hollow, when the wind
235 Walks o'er it, was she shaken by the dream,
    The mystical usurper of the mind—
O'erpowering us to be whate'er may seem
    Good to the soul which we no more can bind;
Strange state of being! (for 'tis still to be)
240 Senseless to feel, and with seal'd eyes to see.

31

She dream'd of being alone on the sea-shore,
    Chain'd to a rock; she knew not how, but stir
She could not from the spot, and the loud roar
    Grew, and each wave rose roughly, threatening her;
245 And o'er her upper lip they seem'd to pour,
    Until she sobb'd for breath, and soon they were
Foaming o'er her lone head, so fierce and high—
Each broke to drown her, yet she could not die.

32

Anon—she was released, and then she stray'd
250   O'er the sharp shingles° with her bleeding feet,   *loose pebbles*
And stumbled almost every step she made;
    And something roll'd before her in a sheet,
Which she must still pursue howe'er afraid;
    'Twas white and indistinct, nor stopp'd to meet
255 Her glance nor grasp, for still she gazed and grasp'd,
And ran, but it escaped her as she clasp'd.

33

The dream changed; in a cave she stood, its walls
    Were hung with marble icicles; the work
Of ages on its water-fretted halls,
260   Where waves might wash, and seals might breed and lurk;
Her hair was dripping, and the very balls

Of her black eyes seemed turn'd to tears, and murk
The sharp rocks look'd below each drop they caught,
Which froze to marble as it fell, she thought.

34

265 And wet, and cold, and lifeless at her feet,
    Pale as the foam that froth'd on his dead brow,
Which she essay'd in vain to clear, (how sweet
    Were once her cares, how idle seem'd they now!)
Lay Juan, nor could aught renew the beat
270   Of his quench'd heart; and the sea dirges low
Rang in her sad ears like a mermaid's song,
And that brief dream appear'd a life too long.

35

And gazing on the dead, she thought his face
    Faded, or alter'd into something new—
275 Like to her father's features, till each trace
    More like and like to Lambro's aspect grew—
With all his keen worn look and Grecian grace;
    And starting, she awoke, and what to view?
Oh! Powers of Heaven! what dark eye meets she there?
280 'Tis—'tis her father's—fix'd upon the pair!

36

Then shrieking, she arose, and shrieking fell,
    With joy and sorrow, hope and fear, to see
Him whom she deem'd a habitant where dwell
    The ocean-buried, risen from death, to be
285 Perchance the death of one she loved too well:
    Dear as her father had been to Haidee,
It was a moment of that awful kind—
I have seen such—but must not call to mind.

37

Up Juan sprung to Haidee's bitter shriek,
290   And caught her falling, and from off the wall
Snatch'd down his sabre, in hot haste to wreak
    Vengeance on him who was the cause of all:
Then Lambro, who till now forbore to speak,
    Smiled scornfully, and said, "Within my call,
295 A thousand scimitars await the word;
Put up, young man, put up your silly sword."

38

And Haidee clung around him; "Juan, 'tis—
    'Tis Lambro—'tis my father! Kneel with me—
He will forgive us—yes—it must be—yes.
300   Oh! dearest father, in this agony

Of pleasure and of pain—even while I kiss
    Thy garment's hem with transport, can it be
That doubt should mingle with my filial joy?
    Deal with me as thou wilt, but spare this boy."

39

305 High and inscrutable the old man stood,
    Calm in his voice, and calm within his eye—
Not always signs with him of calmest mood:
    He look'd upon her, but gave no reply;
Then turn'd to Juan, in whose cheek the blood
310   Oft came and went, as there resolved to die;
In arms, at least, he stood, in act to spring
On the first foe whom Lambro's call might bring.

40

"Young man, your sword"; so Lambro once more said:
    Juan replied, "Not while this arm is free."
315 The old man's cheek grew pale, but not with dread,
    And drawing from his belt a pistol, he
Replied, "Your blood be then on your own head."
    Then look'd close at the flint, as if to see
'Twas fresh—for he had lately used the lock[5]—
320 And next proceeded quietly to cock.

41

It has a strange quick jar upon the ear,
    That cocking of a pistol, when you know
A moment more will bring the sight to bear
    Upon your person, twelve yards off, or so;
325 A gentlemanly distance,[6] not too near,
    If you have got a former friend for foe;
But after being fired at once or twice,
The ear becomes more Irish, and less nice.[7]

42

Lambro presented, and one instant more
330   Had stopp'd this Canto, and Don Juan's breath,
When Haidee threw herself her boy before;
    Stern as her sire: "On me," she cried, "let death
Descend—the fault is mine; this fatal shore
    He found—but sought not. I have pledged my faith;
335 I love him—I will die with him: I knew
Your nature's firmness—know your daughter's too."

43

A minute past, and she had been all tears,
    And tenderness, and infancy: but now

---

5. The part of the gun that explodes the charge.
6. I.e., dueling distance.

7. Finicky. Byron alludes to the propensity of hot-headed young Irishmen to fight duels.

She stood as one who champion'd human fears—
340   Pale, statue-like, and stern, she woo'd the blow;
And tall beyond her sex, and their compeers,[8]
    She drew up to her height, as if to show
A fairer mark; and with a fix'd eye scann'd
Her father's face—but never stopp'd his hand.

44

345 He gazed on her, and she on him; 'twas strange
    How like they look'd! the expression was the same;
Serenely savage, with a little change
    In the large dark eye's mutual-darted flame;
For she too was as one who could avenge,
350   If cause should be—a lioness, though tame:
Her father's blood before her father's face
Boil'd up, and prov'd her truly of his race.

45

I said they were alike, their features and
    Their stature differing but in sex and years;
355 Even to the delicacy of their hand
    There was resemblance, such as true blood wears;
And now to see them, thus divided, stand
    In fix'd ferocity, when joyous tears,
And sweet sensations, should have welcomed both,
360 Show what the passions are in their full growth.

46

The father paused a moment, then withdrew
    His weapon, and replaced it; but stood still,
And looking on her, as to look her through,
    "Not I," he said, "have sought this stranger's ill;
365 Not I have made this desolation: few
    Would bear such outrage, and forbear to kill;
But I must do my duty—how thou hast
Done thine, the present vouches for the past.

47

"Let him disarm; or, by my father's head,
370   His own shall roll before you like a ball!"
He raised his whistle, as the word he said,
    And blew; another answer'd to the call,
And rushing in disorderly, though led,
    And arm'd from boot to turban, one and all,
375 Some twenty of his train came, rank on rank;
He gave the word, "Arrest or slay the Frank."[9]

8. I.e., she was the match in height of Lambro and Juan.

9. Term used in the Near East to designate a Western European.

48

Then, with a sudden movement, he withdrew
   His daughter; while compress'd within his clasp,
'Twixt her and Juan interposed the crew;
380   In vain she struggled in her father's grasp—
His arms were like a serpent's coil: then flew
   Upon their prey, as darts an angry asp,
The file of pirates; save the foremost, who
Had fallen, with his right shoulder half cut through.

49

385 The second had his cheek laid open; but
   The third, a wary, cool old sworder, took
The blows upon his cutlass, and then put
   His own well in; so well, ere you could look,
His man was floor'd, and helpless at his foot,
390   With the blood running like a little brook
From two smart sabre gashes, deep and red—
One on the arm, the other on the head.

50

And then they bound him where he fell, and bore
   Juan from the apartment: with a sign
395 Old Lambro bade them take him to the shore,
   Where lay some ships which were to sail at nine.
They laid him in a boat, and plied the oar
   Until they reach'd some galliots,[1] placed in line;
On board of one of these, and under hatches,
400 They stow'd him, with strict orders to the watches.

51

The world is full of strange vicissitudes,
   And here was one exceedingly unpleasant:
A gentleman so rich in the world's goods,
   Handsome and young, enjoying all the present,
405 Just at the very time when he least broods
   On such a thing is suddenly to sea sent,
Wounded and chain'd, so that he cannot move,
And all because a lady fell in love.

*   *   *

56

Afric is all the sun's, and as her earth
   Her human clay is kindled; full of power
For good or evil, burning from its birth,
   The Moorish blood partakes the planet's hour,
445 And like the soil beneath it will bring forth:
   Beauty and love were Haidee's mother's dower;

---

1. A small, fast galley, propelled by both oars and sails.

But her large dark eye show'd deep Passion's force,
Though sleeping like a lion near a source.

57

Her daughter, temper'd with a milder ray,
450   Like summer clouds all silvery, smooth, and fair,
Till slowly charged with thunder they display
    Terror to earth, and tempest to the air,
Had held till now her soft and milky way;
    But overwrought with passion and despair,
455 The fire burst forth from her Numidian° veins,   *North African*
Even as the Simoom² sweeps the blasted plains.

58

The last sight which she saw was Juan's gore,
    And he himself o'ermaster'd and cut down;
His blood was running on the very floor
460   Where late he trod, her beautiful, her own;
Thus much she view'd an instant and no more,—
    Her struggles ceased with one convulsive groan;
On her sire's arm, which until now scarce held
Her writhing, fell she like a cedar fell'd.

59

465 A vein had burst, and her sweet lips' pure dyes
    Were dabbled with the deep blood which ran o'er;
And her head droop'd as when the lily lies
    O'ercharged with rain: her summon'd handmaids bore
Their lady to her couch with gushing eyes;
470   Of herbs and cordials they produced their store,
But she defied all means they could employ,
Like one life could not hold, nor death destroy.

60

Days lay she in that state unchanged, though chill
    With nothing livid,³ still her lips were red;
475 She had no pulse, but death seem'd absent still;
    No hideous sign proclaim'd her surely dead;
Corruption came not in each mind to kill
    All hope; to look upon her sweet face bred
New thoughts of life, for it seem'd full of soul,
480 She had so much, earth could not claim the whole.

*   *   *

69

545 Twelve days and nights she wither'd thus; at last,
    Without a groan, or sigh, or glance, to show
A parting pang, the spirit from her past:

2. A violent, hot, dust-laden desert wind.   3. I.e., though she was ashen pale.

And they who watch'd her nearest could not know
The very instant, till the change that cast
550   Her sweet face into shadow, dull and slow,
Glazed o'er her eyes—the beautiful, the black—
Oh! to possess such lustre—and then lack!

70

She died, but not alone; she held within
   A second principle of life, which might
555 Have dawn'd a fair and sinless child of sin;
   But closed its little being without light,
And went down to the grave unborn, wherein
   Blossom and bough lie wither'd with one blight;
In vain the dews of Heaven descend above
560 The bleeding flower and blasted fruit of love.

71

Thus lived—thus died she; never more on her
   Shall sorrow light, or shame. She was not made
Through years or moons the inner weight to bear,
   Which colder hearts endure till they are laid
565 By age in earth; her days and pleasures were
   Brief, but delightful—such as had not staid
Long with her destiny; but she sleeps well
By the sea shore, whereon she loved to dwell.

72

That isle is now all desolate and bare,
570   Its dwellings down, its tenants past away;
None but her own and father's grave is there,
   And nothing outward tells of human clay;
Ye could not know where lies a thing so fair,
   No stone is there to show, no tongue to say
575 What was; no dirge, except the hollow sea's,
Mourns o'er the beauty of the Cyclades.

73

But many a Greek maid in a loving song
   Sighs o'er her name; and many an islander
With her sire's story makes the night less long;
580   Valour was his, and beauty dwelt with her;
If she loved rashly, her life paid for wrong—
   A heavy price must all pay who thus err,
In some shape; let none think to fly the danger,
For soon or late Love is his own avenger.

74

585 But let me change this theme, which grows too sad,
   And lay this sheet of sorrows on the shelf;
I don't much like describing people mad,
   For fear of seeming rather touch'd myself—

Besides I've no more on this head to add;
590   And as my Muse is a capricious elf,
We'll put about, and try another tack
With Juan, left half-kill'd some stanzas back.[4]

1818–23   1819–24

LETTERS[1]

To Leigh Hunt[2]

[WORDSWORTH AND POPE]

13 Terrace Piccadilly Septr.–Octr. 30th. 1815

My dear Hunt—Many thanks for your books of which you already know my opinion.—Their external splendour should not disturb you as inappropriate—they have still more within than without.——I take leave to differ from you on Wordsworth[3] as freely as I once agreed with you—at that time I gave him credit for promise which is unfulfilled—I still think his capacity warrants all you say of *it* only—but that his performances since "Lyrical Ballads"—are miserably inadequate to the ability which lurks within him:—there is undoubtedly much natural talent spilt over "the Excursion" but it is rain upon rocks where it stands & stagnates—or rain upon sands where it falls without fertilizing—who can understand him?—let those who do make him intelligible.—Jacob Behman—Swedenborg—& Joanna Southcote[4] are mere types of this Arch-Apostle of mystery & mysticism—but I have done:—no I have not done—for I have two petty & perhaps unworthy objections in small matters to make to him—which with his pretension to accurate observation & fury against Pope's false translation of the "Moonlight scene in Homer"[5] I wonder he should have fallen into—these be they.—He says of Greece in the body of his book—that it is a land of

4. Juan's adventures continue. He is sold as a slave in Constantinople to an enamored sultana; she disguises him as a girl and adds him to her husband's harem for convenience of access. Juan escapes, joins the Russian army that is besieging Ismail, and so distinguishes himself in the capture of the town that he is sent with despatches to St. Petersburg. There he becomes "man-mistress" to the insatiable Catherine the Great. As the result of her assiduous attentions, he falls into a physical decline and, for a salutary change of scene and climate, is sent on a diplomatic mission to England. In canto 16, the last that Byron finished, he is in the middle of an amorous adventure while a guest at the medieval country mansion of an English nobleman, Lord Henry Amundeville, and his very beautiful wife.

1. Three thousand of Byron's letters have survived—a remarkable number for so short a life. In general, they are our best single biographical source for the poet, providing running commentary on his day-to-day concerns and activities and giving us the clearest possible picture of his complex personality, a picture relatively (but not entirely) free of the posturings that pervade both the romantic poems and the satires. In addition, they are independently valuable for their charm, energy, and sheer brilliance. The selections printed here focus primarily on Byron's own poetry and his ideas about writers and literature, but they also represent his wide-ranging interests, as well as his powers of amusing anecdote and vivid description of the society of his time. The texts are from Leslie A. Marchand's twelve-volume edition, *Byron's Letters and Journals* (1973–82).

2. The poet, journalist, and political radical who, as editor of the *Examiner*, introduced Keats and Shelley to the public.

3. Hunt discussed Wordsworth, generally favorably, in a lengthy note in the second edition of his *The Feast of the Poets* (1815).

4. Jakob Boehme, Emanuel Swedenborg, and Joanna Southcott were religious visionaries (German, Swedish, and English, respectively). Southcott, who claimed that she would give birth to a new Messiah, had died in 1814.

5. Wordsworth's criticism of Pope's "false and contradictory" translation of the moonlight scene (*Iliad* 8.687–708) had recently appeared in his *Essay, Supplementary to the Preface* in the first collected edition of his *Poems* (March 1815).

"*rivers—fertile* plains—*& sounding* shores
Under a cope of *variegated* sky"[6]

The rivers are dry half the year—the plains are barren—and the shores *still & tideless* as the Mediterranean can make them—the Sky is anything but variegated—being for months & months—but "darkly—deeply—beautifully blue."[7]—The next is in his notes—where he talks of our "Monuments crowded together in the busy &c. of a large town"—as compared with the "still seclusion of a Turkish cemetery in some *remote* place"[8]—this is pure stuff—for *one* monument in our Churchyards—there are *ten* in the Turkish—& so crowded that you cannot walk between them—they are always close to the walks of the towns—that is—merely divided by a path or road—and as to "*remote* places"—men never take the trouble in a barbarous country to carry their dead very far—they must have lived near to where they are buried—there are no cemeteries in "remote places"—except such as have the cypress & the tombstone still left when the olive & the habitation of the living have perished.——These things I was struck with as coming peculiarly in my own way—and in both of these he is wrong—yet I should have noticed neither but for his attack on Pope for a like blunder—and a peevish affectation about him of despising a popularity which he will never obtain.—I write in great haste—& I doubt—*not* much to the purpose—but you have it hot & hot—just as it comes—& so let it go.——By the way—both he & you go too far against Pope's "so when the Moon &c." it is no translation I know—but it is not such *false* description as asserted—I have read it on the spot—there is a burst—and a lightness—and a glow—about the night in the Troad[9]—which makes the "planets vivid"—& the "pole glowing" the moon is—at least the sky is clearness itself—and I know no more appropriate expression for the expansion of such a heaven—over the scene—the plain—the sea—the sky—Ida—the Hellespont—Simois—Scamander—and the isles—than that of a "flood of Glory."[1]——I am getting horribly lengthy—& must stop—to the whole of your letter I say "ditto to Mr. Burke" as the Bristol Candidate cried by way of Electioneering harangue:[2]—you need not speak of morbid feelings—& vexations to me—I have plenty—for which I must blame partly the times—& chiefly myself: but let us forget them—*I* shall be very apt to do so—when I see you next—will you come to the theatre & see our new Management?[3]—you shall cut it up to your heart's content root & branch afterwards if you like—but come & see it?—if not I must come & see you.—

ever yrs very truly & affectly.

Byron

6. *The Excursion* 4.719–20 (text of the 1st edition, 1814).
7. Southey's *Madoc* 1.5.102.
8. In his first *Essay upon Epitaphs*, originally published in Coleridge's *The Friend* (1810) and then reprinted among the notes to book 5 of *The Excursion* (1814), Wordsworth says: "let a man only compare in imagination the unsightly manner in which our monuments are crowded together in the busy, noisy, unclean, and almost grassless churchyard of a large town, with the still seclusion of a Turkish cemetery, in some remote place."

9. Troas, the region around ancient Troy, in the present northwest Turkey.
1. The three short quotations (beginning with "planets vivid") are from Pope's translation of the moonlight scene, *Iliad* 8.691, 692, 696.
2. This is reported (in biographies of Edmund Burke) to have been the whole of Henry Cruger's campaign speech when he and Burke ran together for seats in Parliament in 1774.
3. Byron had become a member of the subcommittee of management of the Drury Lane theater in May 1815.

P.S.—Not a word from Moore for these 2 months.—Pray let me have the rest of "Rimini["]⁴ you have 2 excellent points in that poem—originality—& Italianism—I will back you as a bard against half the fellows on whom you throw away much good criticism & eulogy—but don't let your bookseller publish in *Quarto* it is the worst size possible for circulation—I say this on Bibliopolical authority—

again—yours ever

[B]

To Thomas Moore¹

[*CHILDE HAROLD*. A VENETIAN ADVENTURE]

Venice, January 28th, 1817

Your letter of the 8th is before me. The remedy for your plethora is simple—abstinence. I was obliged to have recourse to the like some years ago, I mean in point of *diet*, and, with the exception of some convivial weeks and days, (it might be months, now and then), have kept to Pythagoras² ever since. For all this, let me hear that you are better. You must not *indulge* in "filthy beer," nor in porter, nor eat *suppers*—the last are the devil to those who swallow dinner. ✳ 3

I am truly sorry to hear of your father's misfortune⁴—cruel at any time, but doubly cruel in advanced life. However, you will, at least, have the satisfaction of doing your part by him, and, depend upon it, it will not be in vain. Fortune, to be sure, is a female, but not such a b * * as the rest (always excepting your wife and my sister from such sweeping terms); for she generally has some justice in the long run. I have no spite against her, though between her and Nemesis I have had some sore gauntlets to run—but then I have done my best to deserve no better. But to *you*, she is a good deal in arrear, and she will come round—mind if she don't: you have the vigour of life, of independence, of talent, spirit, and character all with you. What you can do for yourself, you have done and will do; and surely there are some others in the world who would not be sorry to be of use, if you would allow them to be useful, or at least attempt it.

I think of being in England in the spring. If there is a row, by the sceptre of King Ludd,⁵ but I'll be one; and if there is none, and only a continuance of "this meek, piping time of peace,"⁶ I will take a cottage a hundred yards to the south of your abode, and become your neighbour; and we will compose such canticles, and hold such dialogues, as shall be the terror of the *Times*

4. Hunt's narrative poem *The Story of Rimini* (1816).
1. Irish poet and a good friend of Byron since they met in 1811. Moore's *Life* of Byron in 1830 is the sole source for many of Byron's letters, including this one.
2. I.e., have eaten no flesh (the disciples of the Greek philosopher-mathematician Pythagoras

were strict vegetarians).
3. These asterisks (as well as those in the next paragraph and near the end of the letter) are Moore's, representing omissions in his printed text.
4. Moore's father had been dismissed from his post as barrack-master at Dublin.
5. A mythical king of Britain.
6. *Richard III* 1.1.24.

(including the newspaper of that name), and the wonder, and honour, and praise, of the Morning Chronicle and posterity.

I rejoice to hear of your forthcoming in February[7]—though I tremble for the "magnificence," which you attribute to the new Childe Harold.[8] I am glad you like it; it is a fine indistinct piece of poetical desolation, and my favourite. I was half mad during the time of its composition, between metaphysics, mountains, lakes, love unextinguishable, thoughts unutterable, and the nightmare of my own delinquencies. I should, many a good day, have blown my brains out, but for the recollection that it would have given pleasure to my mother-in-law; and, even *then*, if I could have been certain to haunt her—but I won't dwell upon these trifling family matters.

Venice is in the *estro* of her carnival, and I have been up these last two nights at the ridotto[9] and the opera, and all that kind of thing. Now for an adventure. A few days ago a gondolier brought me a billet without a subscription, intimating a wish on the part of the writer to meet me either in gondola or at the island of San Lazaro, or at a third rendezvous, indicated in the note. "I know the country's disposition well"—in Venice "they do let Heaven see those tricks they dare not show," &c. &c.;[1] so, for all response, I said that neither of the three places suited me; but that I would either be at home at ten at night *alone*, or at the ridotto at midnight, where the writer might meet me masked. At ten o'clock I was at home and alone (Marianna was gone with her husband to a conversazione[2]), when the door of my apartment opened, and in walked a well-looking and (for an Italian) *bionda*[3] girl of about nineteen, who informed me that she was married to the brother of my *amorosa*, and wished to have some conversation with me. I made a decent reply, and we had some talk in Italian and Romaic (her mother being a Greek of Corfu), when lo! in a very few minutes, in marches, to my very great astonishment, Marianna S[egati], *in propria persona*, and after making polite courtesy to her sister-in-law and to me, without a single word seizes her said sister-in-law by the hair, and bestows upon her some sixteen slaps, which would have made your ear ache only to hear their echo. I need not describe the screaming which ensued. The luckless visitor took flight. I seized Marianna, who, after several vain efforts to get away in pursuit of the enemy, fairly went into fits in my arms; and, in spite of reasoning, eau de Cologne, vinegar, half a pint of water, and God knows what other waters beside, continued so till past midnight.

After damning my servants for letting people in without apprizing me, I found that Marianna in the morning had seen her sister-in-law's gondolier on the stairs, and, suspecting that his apparition boded her no good, had either returned of her own accord, or been followed by her maids or some other spy of her people to the conversazione, from whence she returned to perpetrate this piece of pugilism. I had seen fits before, and also some small scenery of the same genus in and out of our island: but this was not all. After about an hour, in comes—who? why, Signor S[egati], her lord and husband, and finds me with his wife fainting upon the sofa, and all the apparatus of confusion, dishevelled hair, hats, handkerchiefs, salts, smelling-bottles—and

7. Moore's Oriental romance *Lalla Rookh*.
8. Canto 3 of *Childe Harold's Pilgrimage* (1816).
9. An Italian social gathering. "Estro": fire, fervor.
1. *Othello* 3.3.206–07. The passage continues:

"dare not show their husbands."
2. An evening party. Marianna Segati, wife of a Venetian draper, was Byron's current *amorosa*.
3. Blonde (Italian).

the lady as pale as ashes without sense or motion. His first question was, "What is all this?" The lady could not reply—so I did. I told him the explanation was the easiest thing in the world; but in the mean time it would be as well to recover his wife—at least, her senses. This came about in due time of suspiration and respiration.

You need not be alarmed—jealousy is not the order of the day in Venice, and daggers are out of fashion; while duels, on love matters, are unknown— at least, with the husbands. But, for all this, it was an awkward affair; and though he must have known that I made love to Marianna, yet I believe he was not, till that evening, aware of the extent to which it had gone. It is very well known that almost all the married women have a lover; but it is usual to keep up the forms, as in other nations. I did not, therefore, know what the devil to say. I could not out with the truth, out of regard to her, and I did not choose to lie for my sake;—besides, the thing told itself. I thought the best way would be to let her explain it as she chose (a woman being never at a loss—the devil always sticks by them)—only determining to protect and carry her off, in case of any ferocity on the part of the Signor. I saw that he was quite calm. She went to bed, and next day—how they settled it, I know not, but settle it they did. Well—then I had to explain to Marianna about this never to be sufficiently confounded sister-in-law; which I did by swearing innocence, eternal constancy, &c. &c. * * * But the sister-in-law, very much discomposed with being treated in such wise, has (not having her own shame before her eyes) told the affair to half Venice, and the servants (who were summoned by the fight and the fainting) to the other half. But, here, nobody minds such trifles, except to be amused by them. I don't know whether you will be so, but I have scrawled a long letter out of these follies.

Believe me ever. &c.

To John Cam Hobhouse and Douglas Kinnaird[1]

[DON JUAN AND INDECENCY]

Venice January 19th. 1819

Dear H. and dear K.—I approve and sanction all your legal proceedings with regard to my affairs, and can only repeat my thanks & approbation—if you put off the payments of debts "till *after* Lady Noel's[2] death"—it is well—if till *after* her damnation—better—for that will last forever—yet I hope not:— for her sake as well as the Creditors'—I am willing to believe in Purgatory.— —With regard to the Poeshie—I will have no "cutting & slashing" as Perry[3] calls it—you may omit the stanzas on Castlereagh—indeed it is better—& the two "*Bobs*" at the end of the 3d. stanza of the dedication—which will leave "high" & "adry" good rhymes without any "*double* (or Single) Entendre"[4]—but no more—I appeal—not "to Philip fasting" but to Alexander

1. Hobhouse was a close friend of Byron from Cambridge days and had accompanied the poet on the first year of his grand tour to the East in 1809. Kinnaird, who also had been at Cambridge, was Byron's banker and literary agent in London.
2. Byron's mother-in-law.
3. James Perry, editor of the *Morning Chronicle*.
4. The 136-line dedication to Southey was omit-

ted entirely when the first two cantos of *Don Juan* were published anonymously in 1819. Stanza 3 ends in an outrageous sexual pun on Southey's first name ("dry bob" was slang for intercourse without emission), and several later stanzas attack Viscount Castlereagh, the British foreign secretary, as an "intellectual eunuch," a "cold-blooded, smooth-faced, placid miscreant."

drunk[5]—I appeal to Murray at his ledger—to the people—in short, Don Juan shall be an entire horse or none.—If the objection be to the indecency, the Age which applauds the "Bath Guide" & Little's[6] poems—& reads Fielding & Smollett still—may bear with that;—if to the poetry—I will take my chance.—I will not give way to all the Cant of Christendom—I have been cloyed with applause & sickened with abuse;—at present—I care for little but the Copyright,—I have imbibed a great love for money—let me have it— if Murray loses this time—he won't the next—he will be cautious—and I shall learn the decline of his customers by his epistolary indications.——But in no case will I submit to have the poem mutilated.—There is another Canto written—but not copied—in two hundred & odd Stanzas,—if this succeeds— as to the prudery of the present day—what is it? are we more moral than when Prior[7] wrote—is there anything in Don Juan so strong as in Ariosto—or Voltaire—or Chaucer?—Tell Hobhouse—his letter to De Breme has made a great Sensation—and is to be published in the Tuscan & other Gazettes— Count R[izzo] came to consult with me about it last Sunday—we think of Tuscany—for Florence and Milan are in literary war—but the Lombard league is headed by Monti[8]—& would make a difficulty of insertion in the Lombard Gazettes—once published in the Pisan—it will find its way through Italy—by translation or reply.——So Lauderdale[9] has been telling a story!—I suppose this is my reward for presenting him at Countess Benzone's—& shewing him—what attention I could.——Which "piece" does he mean?— since last year I have run the Gauntlet;—is it the Tarruscelli—the Da Mosti—the Spineda—the Lotti—the Rizzato—the Eleanora—the Carlotta— the Giulietta—the Alvisi—the Zambieri—The Eleanora da Bezzi—(who was the King of Naples' Gioaschino's mistress—at least one of them) the Theresina of Mazzurati—the Glettenheimer—& her Sister—the Luigia & her mother—the Fornaretta—the Santa—the Caligari—the Portiera [Vedova?]—the Bolognese figurante—the Tentora and her sister—cum multis aliis?[1]—some of them are Countesses—& some of them Cobblers wives— some noble—some middling—some low—& all whores—which does the damned old "Ladro—& porco fottuto"[2] mean?—I have had them all & thrice as many to boot since 1817—Since *he* tells a story about me—I will tell one about him;—when he landed at the *Custom house* from *Corfu*—he called for *"Post horses—directly"*— he was told that there were no horses except mine nearer than the Lido—unless he wished for the four bronze Coursers of St. Mark[3]—which were at his Service.—

I am yrs. ever—

Let me have H's Election[4] immediately—I mention it *last* as being what I was least likely to forget.——

5. A play on a phrase in Valerius Maximus, *Facta et dicta* 7.2: "appeal from Philip drunk to Philip sober." Philip of Macedon was the father of Alexander the Great.
6. "Thomas Little" was a pseudonym of Thomas Moore. Christopher Anstey's *New Bath Guide* (1766) was a humorous work in anapests describing the Blunderhead family at Bath.
7. Matthew Prior, a contemporary of Pope.
8. Vincenzo Monti was a poet whom Byron and Hobhouse had met in Milan. Ludovico di Breme wrote a defense of Italian writers against the criticism that had appeared in Hobhouse's *Historical Illustrations to the Fourth Canto of Childe Harold* (1818). Hobhouse in turn sent Byron an answer to

di Breme. Count Francesco Rizzo-Patarol was an acquaintance in Venice.
9. James Maitland, eighth earl of Lauderdale, who along with his "story" about Byron's love affairs had carried back to England the manuscripts of *Don Juan* (canto 1) and some other poems.
1. With many others (Latin).
2. Thief—and filthy pig (Italian).
3. The four gilded bronze statues above the portal of St. Mark's Basilica in Venice.
4. Hobhouse had begun campaigning for the Westminster seat in Parliament in November 1818 but was defeated the following March. He succeeded in a subsequent election in 1820.

P.S.—Whatever Brain-money—you get on my account from Murray—pray remit me—I will never consent to pay away what I *earn*—that is *mine*—& what I get by my brains—I will spend on my b——ks—as long as I have a tester or a testicle remaining.—I shall not live long—& for that Reason—I must live while I can—so—let him disburse—& me receive—"for the Night cometh."[5]——If I had but had twenty thousand a year I should not have been living now—but all men are not born with a silver or Gold Spoon in their mouths.——My balance—also—my balance—& a Copyright—I have another Canto—too—ready—& then there will be my half year in June—recollect—*I care for nothing but "monies"*.—January 20th. 1819.—You say nothing of Mazeppa[6]—did it arrive—with one other—besides that you mention?——

To Douglas Kinnaird

[*DON JUAN*: "IS IT NOT LIFE?"]

Venice. Octr. 26th. [1819]

My dear Douglas—My late expenditure has arisen from living at a distance from Venice and being obliged to keep up two establishments, from frequent journeys—and buying some furniture and books as well as a horse or two—and not from any renewal of the EPICUREAN system[1] as you suspect. I have been faithful to my honest liaison with Countess Guiccioli[2]—and I can assure you that *She* has never cost me directly or indirectly a sixpence—indeed the circumstances of herself and family render this no merit.—I never offered her but one present—a broach of brilliants—and she sent it back to me with her *own hair* in it (I shall *not* say of *what part* but *that* is an Italian custom) and a note to say that she was not in the habit of receiving presents of that value—but hoped that I would not consider her sending it back as an affront—nor the value diminished by the enclosure.—I have not had a whore this half-year—confining myself to the strictest adultery.——Why should you prevent Hanson from making a *peer*[3] if he likes it—I think the "*Garretting*" would be by far the best parliamentary privilege—I know of.—— Damn your delicacy.—It is a low commercial quality—and very unworthy a man who prefixes "honourable" to his nomenclature. If you say that I must sign the bonds—I suppose that I must—but it is very iniquitous to make me pay my debts—you have no idea of the pain it gives one.—Pray do three things—get my property out of the *funds*—get Rochdale[4] sold—get me some information from Perry about *South America*[5]—and 4thly. ask Lady Noel not to live so very long.——As to Subscribing to Manchester—if I do that—I will write a letter to Burdett[6]—for publication—to accompany the

5. John 9.4: "I must work the works of him that sent me, while it is day: the night cometh, when no man can work."
6. Murray published *Mazeppa* in June 1819.
1. I.e., money spent on pleasures of the senses.
2. Byron mentions having fallen in love with Teresa Guiccioli ("a Romagnuola Countess from Ravenna—who is nineteen years old & has a Count of fifty") in a letter of April 6, 1819. Their relationship lasted until Byron set sail for Greece in the summer of 1823.
3. I.e., being made a peer (of the realm). John

Hanson, Byron's solicitor and agent before Kinnaird took over his principal business affairs, never realized this ambition.
4. An estate that Byron had inherited in Lancashire.
5. Byron was considering the possibility of emigrating to South America, specifically to Venezuela.
6. Sir Francis Burdett, member of Parliament for Westminster, a reformer and leader of opposition to the Tories.

Subscription—which shall be more radical than anything yet rooted—but I feel lazy.—I have thought of this for some time—but alas! the air of this cursed Italy enervates—and disfranchises the thoughts of a man after nearly four years of respiration—to say nothing of emission.—As to "Don Juan"—confess—confess—you dog—and be candid—that it is the sublime of *that there* sort of writing—it may be bawdy—but is it not good English?—it may be profligate—but is it not *life*, is it not *the thing*?—Could any man have written it—who has not lived in the world?—and tooled in a post-chaise? in a hackney coach? in a Gondola? against a wall? in a court carriage? in a vis a vis?[7]—on a table?—and under it?—I have written about a hundred stanzas of a third Canto—but it is damned modest—the outcry has frightened me.—I had such projects for the Don—but the *Cant* is so much stronger than *Cunt*—now a days,—that the benefit of experience in a man who had well weighed the worth of both monosyllables—must be lost to despairing posterity.—After all what stuff this outcry is—Lalla Rookh and Little—are more dangerous than my burlesque poem can be—Moore has been here—we got tipsy together—and were very amicable—he is gone on to Rome—I put my life (in M.S.) into his hands[8]—(*not* for publication) you—or any body else may see it—at his return.—It only comes up to 1816.——He is a noble fellow—and looks quite fresh and poetical—nine years (the age of a poem's education) my Senior—he looks younger—this comes of marriage and being settled in the Country. I want to go to South America—I have written to Hobhouse all about it.—I wrote to my wife—three months ago—under care to Murray—has she got the letter—or is the letter got into Blackwood's magazine?——You ask after my Christmas pye—Remit it any how—*Circulars*[9] is the best—you are right about *income*—I must have it all—how the devil do I know that I may live a year or a month?—I wish I knew that I might regulate my spending in more ways than one.—As it is one always thinks that there is but a span.—A man may as well break or be damned for a large sum as a small one—I should be loth to pay the devil or any other creditor more than sixpence in the pound.—

[scrawl for signature]

P.S.—I recollect nothing of "Davies's landlord"—but what ever Davies *says*—I will *swear* to—and *that's* more than *he* would.—So pray pay—has he a landlady too?—perhaps I may owe her something.——With regard to the bonds I will sign them but—it goes against the grain.——As to the rest—you *can't* err—so long as you *don't* pay.——Paying is executor's or executioner's work.——You may write somewhat oftener—Mr. Galignani's messenger[1] gives the outline of your public affairs—but I see no results—you have no man yet—(always excepting Burdett—& you & H[obhouse] and the Gentlemanly leaven of your two-penny loaf of rebellion) don't forget however my charge of horse—and commission for the Midland Counties and by the holies!—You shall have your account in decimals.—Love to Hobby—but why leave the Whigs?——

---

7. A light carriage for two persons sitting face to face.
8. Byron's famous memoirs, which were later sold to John Murray and burned in the publisher's office.
9. Letters of credit.
1. *Galignani's Messenger*, an English newspaper published in Paris.

To Percy Bysshe Shelley

[KEATS AND SHELLEY]

Ravenna, April 26th, 1821

The child continues doing well, and the accounts are regular and favourable. It is gratifying to me that you and Mrs. Shelley do not disapprove of the step which I have taken, which is merely temporary.[1]

I am very sorry to hear what you say of Keats[2]—is it *actually* true? I did not think criticism had been so killing. Though I differ from you essentially in your estimate of his performances, I so much abhor all unnecessary pain, that I would rather he had been seated on the highest peak of Parnassus than have perished in such a manner. Poor fellow! though with such inordinate self-love he would probably have not been very happy. I read the review of "Endymion" in the Quarterly. It was severe,—but surely not so severe as many reviews in that and other journals upon others.

I recollect the effect on me of the Edinburgh on my first poem;[3] it was rage, and resistance, and redress—but not despondency nor despair. I grant that those are not amiable feelings; but, in this world of bustle and broil, and especially in the career of writing, a man should calculate upon his powers of *resistance* before he goes into the arena.

> "Expect not life from pain nor danger free,
> Nor deem the doom of man reversed for thee."[4]

You know my opinion of *that second-hand* school of poetry. You also know my high opinion of your own poetry,—because it is of *no* school. I read Cenci—but, besides that I think the *subject* essentially *un* dramatic, I am not an admirer of our old dramatists *as models*. I deny that the English have hitherto had a drama at all. Your Cenci, however, was a work of power, and poetry. As to *my* drama,[5] pray revenge yourself upon it, by being as free as I have been with yours.

I have not yet got your Prometheus, which I long to see. I have heard nothing of mine, and do not know that it is yet published. I have published a pamphlet on the Pope controversy, which you will not like. Had I known that Keats was dead—or that he was alive and so sensitive—I should have omitted some remarks upon his poetry, to which I was provoked by his *attack* upon *Pope*,[6] and my disapprobation of *his own* style of writing.

---

1. Byron had recently placed his four-year-old daughter Allegra in a convent school near Ravenna, against the wishes of her mother, Mary Shelley's stepsister Claire Clairmont.

2. In a letter to Byron, April 17, 1821: "Young Keats, whose 'Hyperion' showed so great a promise, died lately at Rome from the consequences of breaking a blood-vessel, in paroxysms of despair at the contemptuous attack on his book in the *Quarterly Review*" (see Shelley's *Adonais*, p. 772).

3. The review of Byron's *Hours of Idleness* in the *Edinburgh Review* prompted him to write his first major satire, *English Bards and Scotch Reviewers* (1809).

4. Johnson, *The Vanity of Human Wishes*, lines 155–56 (Byron is quoting from memory).

5. *Marino Faliero*, published in London on April 21, 1821. Shelley's *The Cenci* and *Prometheus Unbound* (next paragraph) were written in 1819 and published in 1820.

6. Keats attacked Augustan poetry (but not necessarily Pope) in *Sleep and Poetry*, lines 181–206. Byron's pamphlet, *Letter to ********[John Murray], on the Rev. W. L. Bowles' Strictures on the Life and Writings of Pope*, had just appeared in London. His best-known comment on Keats, written a year and a half later, is canto 11, stanza 60 in *Don Juan*, beginning "John Keats, who was killed off by one critique" and ending " 'Tis strange the mind, that very fiery particle, / Should let itself be snuffed out by an Article."

You want me to undertake a great Poem—I have not the inclination nor the power. As I grow older, the indifference—*not* to life, for we love it by instinct—but to the stimuli of life, increases. Besides, this late failure of the Italians[7] has latterly disappointed me for many reasons,—some public, some personal. My respects to Mrs. S.

Yours ever,

B

P.S.—Could not you and I contrive to meet this summer? Could not you take a run *alone?*

---

7. A planned uprising by the Carbonari, a secret revolutionary society into which Byron had been initiated by the father and brother of his mistress Teresa Guiccioli, failed in Feb. 1821.

PERCY BYSSHE SHELLEY
1792–1822

Percy Bysshe Shelley, a radical nonconformist in every aspect of his life and thought, emerged from a solidly conservative background. His ancestors had been Sussex aristocrats since early in the seventeenth century; his grandfather, Sir Bysshe Shelley, made himself the richest man in Horsham, Sussex; his father, Timothy Shelley, was a hardheaded and conventional Member of Parliament. Percy Shelley himself was in line for a baronetcy and, as befitted his station, was sent to be educated at Eton and Oxford. As a youth he was slight of build, eccentric in manner, and unskilled in sports or fighting and, as a consequence, was mercilessly baited by older and stronger boys. He later said that he saw the petty tyranny of schoolmasters and schoolmates as representative of man's general inhumanity to man, and dedicated his life to a war against injustice and oppression. As he described the experience in the Dedication to *Laon and Cythna*:

> So without shame, I spake:—"I will be wise,
> And just, and free, and mild, if in me lies
> Such power, for I grow weary to behold
> The selfish and the strong still tyrannise
> Without reproach or check." I then controuled
> My tears, my heart grew calm, and I was meek and bold.

At Oxford in the autumn of 1810 Shelley's closest friend was Thomas Jefferson Hogg, a self-centered, self-confident young man who shared Shelley's love of philosophy and scorn of orthodoxy. The two collaborated on a pamphlet, *The Necessity of Atheism*, which claimed that God's existence cannot be proved on empirical grounds, and, provocatively, they mailed it to the bishops and heads of the colleges at Oxford. Shelley refused to repudiate the document and, to his shock and grief, was peremptorily expelled, terminating a university career that had lasted only six months. This event opened a breach between Shelley and his father that widened over the years.

Shelley went to London, where he took up the cause of Harriet Westbrook, the pretty and warmhearted daughter of a well-to-do tavern keeper, whose father, Shelley wrote to Hogg, "has persecuted her in a most horrible way by endeavoring to compel her to go to school." Harriet threw herself on Shelley's protection, and "gratitude and admiration," he wrote, "all demand that I shall love her *forever.*" He eloped with Harriet to Edinburgh and married her, against his conviction that marriage was a tyrannical and degrading social institution. He was then eighteen years of age, and his bride sixteen. The young couple moved restlessly from place to place, living on a small allowance granted reluctantly by their families. In February 1812, accompanied by Harriet's sister Eliza, they traveled to Dublin to distribute Shelley's *Address to the Irish People* and otherwise take part in the movement for Catholic emancipation and for the amelioration of that oppressed and poverty-stricken people.

Back in London, Shelley became a disciple of the radical social philosopher William Godwin, author of the *Inquiry Concerning Political Justice*. In 1813 he printed privately his first important work, *Queen Mab*, a long poem set in the fantastic frame of the journey of a disembodied soul through space, to whom the fairy Mab reveals in visions the woeful past, the dreadful present, and a utopian future. Announcing that "there is no God!" Mab decries institutional religion and codified morality as the roots of social evil, prophesying that all institutions will wither away and humanity will return to its natural condition of goodness and felicity.

In the following spring Shelley, who had drifted apart from Harriet, fell in love with the beautiful Mary Wollstonecraft Godwin, daughter of Mary Wollstonecraft and William Godwin. Convinced that cohabitation without love is immoral, he abandoned Harriet, fled to France with Mary (taking along her stepsister, Claire Clairmont), and—in accordance with his belief in nonexclusive love—invited Harriet to come live with them in the relationship of a sister. Shelley's elopement with Mary outraged her father, despite the facts that his own views of marriage had been no less radical than Shelley's and that Shelley, himself in financial difficulties, had earlier taken over Godwin's very substantial debts. When he returned to London, Shelley found that the general public, his family, and most of his friends regarded him as not only an atheist and revolutionary but also a gross immoralist. When two years later Harriet, pregnant by an unknown lover, drowned herself in a fit of despair, the courts denied Shelley the custody of their two children. Shelley married Mary Godwin and in 1818 moved to Italy. Thereafter he envisioned himself as an alien and outcast, rejected by the human race to whose welfare he had dedicated his powers and his life.

In Italy he resumed his restless way of life, evading creditors by moving from town to town and house to house. His health was usually bad. Although the death of his grandfather in 1815 had provided a substantial income, he dissipated so much of it by his warmhearted but improvident support of William Godwin, Leigh Hunt, and other needy pensioners that he was constantly short of money and harried by creditors. Within nine months, in 1818–19, Clara and William, children of Percy and Mary Shelley, both died. This tragedy threw Mary into a state of apathy and self-absorption that destroyed the earlier harmony of her relationship with her husband, from which even the birth of another son, Percy Florence, could not entirely rescue her.

In these circumstances, close to despair and knowing that he almost entirely lacked an audience, Shelley wrote his greatest works. In 1819 he completed *Prometheus Unbound* and a tragedy, *The Cenci*. He wrote also numerous lyric poems; a visionary call for a proletarian revolution, *The Mask of Anarchy*; a witty satire on Wordsworth, *Peter Bell the Third*; and a penetrating political essay, *A Philosophical View of Reform*. His works of the next two years include *A Defence of Poetry*; *Epipsychidion*, a rhapsodic vision of love as a spiritual union beyond earthly limits; *Adonais*, his elegy on the death of Keats; and *Hellas*, a lyrical drama evoked by the Greek war for liberation from the Turks. These writings, unlike the early *Queen Mab*, are the products of a mind chastened by tragic experience, deepened by philosophical speculation, and stored with the harvest of his reading—which Shelley carried on, as his friend Hogg said, "in season and out of season, at table, in bed, and especially during a walk," until he became one of the most erudite of poets. His delight in scientific discoveries and speculations continued, but his earlier zest for Gothic terrors and the social theories of the radical eighteenth-century optimists gave way to an absorption in Greek tragedy, Milton's *Paradise Lost,* and the Bible. Although he did not give up his hopes for a millennial future (he wore a ring with the motto *Il buon tempo verrà*—"the good time will come"), he now attributed the evils of society to humanity's own moral failures and grounded the possibility of radical social reform on a reform of the moral and imaginative faculties through the redeeming power of love. Though often represented as a simpleminded doctrinaire, Shelley in fact possessed a complex and energetically inquisitive intelligence that never halted at a fixed mental position; his writings reflect stages in a ceaseless exploration.

The poems of Shelley's maturity also show the influence of his study of Plato and the Neoplatonists. Shelley found congenial the Platonic division of the cosmos into two worlds—the ordinary world of change, mortality, evil, and suffering and an ideal world of perfect and eternal Forms, of which the world of sense-experience is only a distant and illusory reflection. The earlier interpretations of Shelley as a downright Platonic idealist, however, have been drastically modified by modern investigations of his reading and writings. He was a close student of British empirical philosophy, which limits knowledge to valid reasoning on what is given in sense-experience, and within this tradition he felt a special affinity to the radical skepticism of David Hume. A number of Shelley's works, such as *Mont Blanc,* express his view of the narrow limits of what human beings can know with certainty and exemplify his refusal to let his hopes harden into a philosophical or religious creed. To what has been called the "skeptical idealism" of the mature Shelley (see the notes he appended to his lyrics from *Hellas*), hope in a redemption from present social ills is not an intellectual certainty but a moral obligation. Despair is self-fulfilling; we must continue to hope because, by keeping open the possibility of a better future, hope releases the imaginative and creative powers that are the only means of achieving that end.

When in 1820 the Shelleys settled finally at Pisa, he came closer to finding contentment than at any other time in his adult life. A group of friends, Shelley's "Pisan Circle," gathered around them, including for a while Lord Byron and the swashbuckling young Cornishman Edward Trelawny. Chief in Shelley's affections were Edward Williams, a retired lieutenant of a cavalry regiment serving in India, and his charming common-law wife, Jane, with whom Shelley carried on a flirtation and to whom he addressed some of his best lyrics and verse letters. The end came suddenly, and in a way previsioned in the last stanza of *Adonais,* in which he had described his spirit as a ship driven by a violent storm out into the dark unknown. On July 8, 1822, Shelley and Edward Williams were sailing their open boat, the *Don Juan,* on the Gulf of Spezia. A violent squall swamped the boat. When several days later the bodies were washed ashore they were cremated, and Shelley's ashes were buried in the Protestant Cemetery at Rome, near the graves of John Keats and William Shelley, the poet's young son.

Both Shelley's character and his poetry have been the subject of violently contradictory, and often partisan, estimates. His actions according to his deep convictions often led to disastrous consequences for himself and those near to him; and even recent scholars, while repudiating the vicious attacks by Shelley's contemporaries, attribute some of those actions to a self-assured egotism that masked itself as idealism. Yet Byron, who knew Shelley intimately and did not pay moral compliments lightly, wrote to his publisher John Murray, in response to attacks on Shelley at the time of his death: "You are all brutally mistaken about Shelley, who was, without exception, the *best* and least selfish man I ever knew." Shelley's politics, vilified during his lifetime, have made him a literary hero to later political radicals, as well as to the British Labour Party. As a poet, Shelley was greatly admired by Robert Browning, Swinburne, and other Victorians; but in the mid-twentieth century he was repeatedly charged with intellectual and emotional immaturity, shoddy workmanship, and incoherent imagery by such influential writers as F. R. Leavis and his followers in Britain and the New Critics in America. More recently, however, many sympathetic studies have revealed the coherent intellectual understructure of his poems and have confirmed Wordsworth's early recognition that "Shelley is one of the best *artists* of us all: I mean in workmanship of style." Shelley, it has become clear, greatly expanded the metrical and stanzaic resources of English versification. His poems exhibit a broad range of voices, from the high but ordered passion of *Ode to the West Wind,* through the heroic dignity of the utterances of Prometheus, to the approximation of what is inexpressible in the description of Asia's transfiguration and in the visionary conclusion of *Adonais.* Most surprising, for a poet who almost entirely lacked an audience, is the urbanity, the assured command of the tone and language of a cultivated man of the world, exemplified in passages that Shelley wrote all through his mature career and especially in the lyrics and verse letters that he composed during the last year of his life.

The texts printed here are those prepared by Donald H. Reiman and Sharon B. Powers for *Shelley's Poetry and Prose,* a Norton Critical Edition (1977); Reiman has also edited for this anthology a few poems not included in that edition.

Mutability

We are as clouds that veil the midnight moon;
How restlessly they speed, and gleam, and quiver,
Streaking the darkness radiantly!—yet soon
Night closes round, and they are lost for ever:

5 Or like forgotten lyres,° whose dissonant strings   *wind harps*
Give various response to each varying blast,
To whose frail frame no second motion brings
One mood or modulation like the last.

We rest.—A dream has power to poison sleep;
10 We rise.—One wandering thought pollutes the day;
We feel, conceive or reason, laugh or weep;
Embrace fond woe, or cast our cares away:

It is the same!—For, be it joy or sorrow,
The path of its departure still is free:
15 Man's yesterday may ne'er be like his morrow;
Nought may endure but Mutability.

ca. 1814–15   1816

To Wordsworth[1]

Poet of Nature, thou hast wept to know
That things depart which never may return:
Childhood and youth, friendship and love's first glow,
Have fled like sweet dreams, leaving thee to mourn.
5 These common woes I feel. One loss is mine
Which thou too feel'st, yet I alone deplore.
Thou wert as a lone star, whose light did shine
On some frail bark in winter's midnight roar:
Thou hast like to a rock-built refuge stood

---

1. Shelley's grieved comment on the poet of nature and of social radicalism after his views had become conservative.

10 Above the blind and battling multitude:
In honoured poverty thy voice did weave
Songs consecrate to truth and liberty,—
Deserting these, thou leavest me to grieve,
Thus having been, that thou shouldst cease to be.

ca. 1814–15   1816

Alastor; or, The Spirit of Solitude

Shelley wrote *Alastor* in the fall and early winter of 1815 and published it in March 1816. According to his friend Thomas Love Peacock, the poet was "at a loss for a title, and I proposed that which he adopted: Alastor, or the Spirit of Solitude. The Greek word *Alastor* is an evil genius. . . . I mention the true meaning of the word because many have supposed *Alastor* to be the name of the hero" (*Memoirs of Shelley*). Peacock's definition of an *alastor* as "an *evil* genius" has compounded the problems in interpreting this work: the term *evil* does not seem to fit the attitude expressed within the poem toward the protagonist's solitary quest, the poem seems to clash with statements in Shelley's preface, and the first and second paragraphs of the preface seem inconsistent with each other. These problems, however, may be largely resolved if we recognize that, in this early achievement (he was only twenty-three when he wrote *Alastor*), Shelley established his characteristic procedure of working with multiple perspectives. Both preface and poem explore alternative and conflicting possibilities in what Shelley calls "doubtful knowledge"— matters that are humanly essential but in which no certainty is humanly possible.

By the term *allegorical* in the opening sentence of his preface, Shelley may be taken to signify that his poem, like medieval and Renaissance allegories such as Dante's *Divine Comedy* and Spenser's *Faerie Queene,* represents a need and aspiration in the spiritual realm by the allegorical vehicle of a journey and quest in the material world. Shelley's protagonist, for whom the objects in the natural world "cease to suffice," commits himself to the search for a female Other who will fulfill his intellectual, imaginative, and sensuous needs. Because, however, his desires are unlimited and the world's possibilities are finite, his quest is doomed to end in his early death.

The second paragraph of the preface passes judgment on the visionary protagonist in terms of the values of "actual men"—that is, the requirements of human and social life in this world. From this point of view, the visionary has been "avenged" (punished) for turning away from both human and natural community in pursuit of his own psychic needs. The preface goes on, however, to elevate the moral status of such a visionary over a second class of "meaner spirits" who also "keep aloof from sympathies with their kind," but only because they are unable to project their feelings beyond their own narrow selves and so are "morally dead."

The diversity of attitudes expressed within the poem itself becomes more intelligible if, on the basis of the many echoes of Wordsworth in the opening invocation, we identify the narrator of the story as a Wordsworthian poet for whom the natural world is sufficient to satisfy both the demands of his imagination and his need for community. This narrative poet, it can be assumed, undertakes to tell compassionately, but from his own perspective, the history of a nameless visionary who has surrendered everything in the quest for a goal beyond possibility.

In this early poem Shelley establishes a form, a conceptual frame, and the imagery for the Romantic quest that he reiterated in his later poems and that also served as a paradigm for many other poems, from Byron's *Manfred* and Keats's *Endymion* to the quest-poems of Shelley's later admirer William Butler Yeats.

Alastor; or, The Spirit of Solitude

Preface

The poem entitled "ALASTOR," may be considered as allegorical of one of the most interesting situations of the human mind. It represents a youth of uncorrupted feelings and adventurous genius led forth by an imagination inflamed and purified through familiarity with all that is excellent and majestic, to the contemplation of the universe. He drinks deep of the fountains of knowledge, and is still insatiate. The magnificence and beauty of the external world sinks profoundly into the frame of his conceptions, and affords to their modifications a variety not to be exhausted. So long as it is possible for his desires to point towards objects thus infinite and unmeasured, he is joyous, and tranquil, and self-possessed. But the period arrives when these objects cease to suffice. His mind is at length suddenly awakened and thirsts for intercourse with an intelligence similar to itself. He images to himself the Being whom he loves. Conversant with speculations of the sublimest and most perfect natures, the vision in which he embodies his own imaginations unites all of wonderful, or wise, or beautiful, which the poet, the philosopher, or the lover could depicture. The intellectual faculties, the imagination, the functions of sense, have their respective requisitions on the sympathy of corresponding powers in other human beings. The Poet is represented as uniting these requisitions, and attaching them to a single image.[1] He seeks in vain for a prototype of his conception. Blasted by his disappointment, he descends to an untimely grave.

The picture is not barren of instruction to actual men. The Poet's self-centred seclusion was avenged by the furies of an irresistible passion pursuing him to speedy ruin. But that Power which strikes the luminaries of the world with sudden darkness and extinction, by awakening them to too exquisite a perception of its influences, dooms to a slow and poisonous decay those meaner spirits that dare to abjure its dominion. Their destiny is more abject and inglorious as their delinquency is more contemptible and pernicious. They who, deluded by no generous error, instigated by no sacred thirst of doubtful knowledge, duped by no illustrious superstition, loving nothing on this earth, and cherishing no hopes beyond, yet keep aloof from sympathies with their kind, rejoicing neither in human joy nor mourning with human grief; these, and such as they, have their apportioned curse. They languish, because none feel with them their common nature. They are morally dead. They are neither friends, nor lovers, nor fathers, nor citizens of the world, nor benefactors of their country. Among those who attempt to exist without human sympathy, the pure and tender-hearted perish through the intensity and passion of their search after its communities, when the vacancy of their spirit suddenly makes itself felt. All else, selfish, blind, and

---

1. Shelley's view that the object of love is an idealized antitype to all that is best within the self is clarified by a passage in his *Essay on Love*, which may have been written at about the time of *Alastor:* "We dimly see within our intellectual nature . . . the ideal prototype of every thing excellent or lovely that we are capable of conceiving as belonging to the nature of men. . . . [This is] a soul within our soul. . . . The discovery of its anti-type . . . in such proportion as the type within demands; this is the invisible and unattainable point to which Love tends; and . . . without the possession of which there is no rest nor respite to the heart over which it rules."

torpid, are those unforeseeing multitudes who constitute, together with their own, the lasting misery and loneliness of the world. Those who love not their fellow-beings live unfruitful lives, and prepare for their old age a miserable grave.

> "The good die first,
> And those whose hearts are dry as summer dust,
> Burn to the socket!"[2]

December 14, 1815

Alastor; or, The Spirit of Solitude

Nondum amabam, et amare amabam, qæurebam quid amarem, amans amare.—Confess. St. August.[3]

Earth, ocean, air, beloved brotherhood!
If our great Mother[4] has imbued my soul
With aught of natural piety[5] to feel
Your love, and recompense the boon with mine;[6]
5   If dewy morn, and odorous noon, and even,
With sunset and its gorgeous ministers,[7]
And solemn midnight's tingling silentness;
If autumn's hollow sighs in the sere wood,
And winter robing with pure snow and crowns
10   Of starry ice the grey grass and bare boughs;
If spring's voluptuous pantings when she breathes
Her first sweet kisses, have been dear to me;
If no bright bird, insect, or gentle beast
I consciously have injured, but still loved
15   And cherished these my kindred; then forgive
This boast, beloved brethren, and withdraw
No portion of your wonted favour now!

     Mother of this unfathomable world!
Favour my solemn song, for I have loved
20   Thee ever, and thee only; I have watched
Thy shadow, and the darkness of thy steps,
And my heart ever gazes on the depth
Of thy deep mysteries. I have made my bed
In charnels and on coffins, where black death
25   Keeps record of the trophies won from thee,
Hoping to still these obstinate questionings[8]
Of thee and thine, by forcing some lone ghost,

---

2. Wordsworth's *The Excursion* 1.519–21; the passage occurs also in *The Ruined Cottage* 96–98, which Wordsworth reworked into the first book of *The Excursion* (1814).
3. St. Augustine's *Confessions* 3.1: "Not yet did I love, though I loved to love, seeking what I might love, loving to love." Augustine thus describes his state of mind when he was addicted to illicit sexual love; the true object of his desire, which compels the tortuous spiritual journey of his life, he later discovered to be the infinite and transcendent God.

4. Nature, invoked as the common mother of the elements and of the poet.
5. Wordsworth, *My heart leaps up*, lines 8–9: "And I could wish my days to be / Bound each to each by natural piety." Wordsworth also used these lines as the epigraph to his *Ode: Intimations of Immortality*.
6. I.e., with my love.
7. The sunset colors.
8. Wordsworth, *Ode: Intimations of Immortality*, lines 141–42: "those obstinate questionings / Of sense and outward things."

Thy messenger, to render up the tale
Of what we are. In lone and silent hours,
30   When night makes a weird sound of its own stillness,
Like an inspired and desperate alchymist
Staking his very life on some dark hope,
Have I mixed awful talk and asking looks
With my most innocent love, until strange tears
35   Uniting with those breathless kisses, made
Such magic as compels the charmed night
To render up thy charge: . . . and, though ne'er yet
Thou hast unveil'd thy inmost sanctuary,
Enough from incommunicable dream,
40   And twilight phantasms, and deep noonday thought,
Has shone within me, that serenely now
And moveless, as a long-forgotten lyre
Suspended in the solitary dome
Of some mysterious and deserted fane,[9]
45   I wait thy breath, Great Parent, that my strain
May modulate with murmurs of the air,
And motions of the forests and the sea,
And voice of living beings, and woven hymns
Of night and day, and the deep heart of man.[1]

50   There was a Poet whose untimely tomb
No human hands with pious reverence reared,
But the charmed eddies of autumnal winds
Built o'er his mouldering bones a pyramid
Of mouldering leaves in the waste wilderness:—
55   A lovely youth,—no mourning maiden decked
With weeping flowers, or votive cypress wreath,[2]
The lone couch of his everlasting sleep:—
Gentle, and brave, and generous,—no lorn° bard   *abandoned*
Breathed o'er his dark fate one melodious sigh:
60   He lived, he died, he sung, in solitude.
Strangers have wept to hear his passionate notes,
And virgins, as unknown he past, have pined
And wasted for fond love of his wild eyes.
The fire of those soft orbs has ceased to burn,
65   And Silence, too enamoured of that voice,
Locks its mute music in her rugged cell.

     By solemn vision, and bright silver dream,
His infancy was nurtured. Every sight
And sound from the vast earth and ambient air,
70   Sent to his heart its choicest impulses.
The fountains of divine philosophy
Fled not his thirsting lips, and all of great

9. Temple. The narrator calls on the Mother, his natural muse, to make him her wind harp. Cf. the opening passage of Wordsworth's *Prelude*, Coleridge's *Dejection: An Ode*, and the conclusions of Shelley's *Ode to the West Wind* and *Adonais*.
1. Cf. Wordsworth, *Tintern Abbey* 94ff.: "A pres-ence . . . / Whose dwelling is . . . the round ocean and the living air, / And the blue sky, and in the mind of man: / A motion and a spirit."
2. The cypress represented mourning. "Votive": offered to fulfill a vow to the gods.

Or good, or lovely, which the sacred past
In truth or fable consecrates, he felt
75 And knew. When early youth had past, he left
His cold fireside and alienated home
To seek strange truths in undiscovered lands.
Many a wide waste and tangled wilderness
Has lured his fearless steps; and he has bought
80 With his sweet voice and eyes, from savage men,
His rest and food. Nature's most secret steps
He like her shadow has pursued, where'er
The red volcano overcanopies
Its fields of snow and pinnacles of ice
85 With burning smoke, or where bitumen lakes[3]
On black bare pointed islets ever beat
With sluggish surge, or where the secret caves
Rugged and dark, winding among the springs
Of fire and poison, inaccessible
90 To avarice or pride, their starry domes
Of diamond and of gold expand above
Numberless and immeasurable halls,
Frequent° with crystal column, and clear shrines   *crowded*
Of pearl, and thrones radiant with chrysolite.[4]
95 Nor had that scene of ampler majesty
Than gems or gold, the varying roof of heaven
And the green earth lost in his heart its claims
To love and wonder; he would linger long
In lonesome vales, making the wild his home,
100 Until the doves and squirrels would partake
From his innocuous hand his bloodless food,[5]
Lured by the gentle meaning of his looks,
And the wild antelope, that starts whene'er
The dry leaf rustles in the brake,° suspend   *thicket*
105 Her timid steps to gaze upon a form
More graceful than her own.

                          His wandering step
Obedient to high thoughts, has visited
The awful ruins of the days of old:
Athens, and Tyre, and Balbec,[6] and the waste
110 Where stood Jerusalem, the fallen towers
Of Babylon, the eternal pyramids,
Memphis and Thebes,[7] and whatsoe'er of strange
Sculptured on alabaster obelisk,
Or jasper tomb, or mutilated sphynx,
115 Dark Æthiopia in her desert hills
Conceals. Among the ruined temples there,
Stupendous columns, and wild images
Of more than man, where marble dæmons watch

---

3. Lakes of pitch, flowing from a volcano.
4. An olive green stone.
5. Shelley was himself a vegetarian.
6. An ancient city in what is now Lebanon. Tyre

was once an important commercial city on the
Phoenician coast.
7. The ancient capital of Upper Egypt. Memphis
is the ruined capital of Lower Egypt.

The Zodiac's[8] brazen mystery, and dead men
120 Hang their mute thoughts on the mute walls around,[9]
He lingered, poring on memorials
Of the world's youth, through the long burning day
Gazed on those speechless shapes, nor, when the moon
Filled the mysterious halls with floating shades
125 Suspended he that task, but ever gazed
And gazed, till meaning on his vacant mind
Flashed like strong inspiration, and he saw
The thrilling secrets of the birth of time.

Meanwhile an Arab maiden brought his food,
130 Her daily portion, from her father's tent,
And spread her matting for his couch, and stole
From duties and repose to tend his steps:—
Enamoured, yet not daring for deep awe
To speak her love:—and watched his nightly sleep,
135 Sleepless herself, to gaze upon his lips
Parted in slumber, whence the regular breath
Of innocent dreams arose: then, when red morn
Made paler the pale moon, to her cold home
Wildered,° and wan, and panting, she returned.   *bewildered*

140 The Poet wandering on, through Arabie
And Persia, and the wild Carmanian waste,[1]
And o'er the aërial mountains which pour down
Indus and Oxus[2] from their icy caves,
In joy and exultation held his way;
145 Till in the vale of Cashmire, far within
Its loneliest dell, where odorous plants entwine
Beneath the hollow rocks a natural bower,
Beside a sparkling rivulet he stretched
His languid limbs. A vision on his sleep
150 There came, a dream of hopes that never yet
Had flushed his cheek. He dreamed a veiled maid
Sate near him, talking in low solemn tones.
Her voice was like the voice of his own soul
Heard in the calm of thought; its music long,
155 Like woven sounds of streams and breezes, held
His inmost sense suspended in its web
Of many-coloured woof and shifting hues.
Knowledge and truth and virtue were her theme,
And lofty hopes of divine liberty,
160 Thoughts the most dear to him, and poesy,
Herself a poet.[3] Soon the solemn mood
Of her pure mind kindled through all her frame
A permeating fire: wild numbers then

8. In the temple of Isis at Denderah, Egypt, the Zodiac is represented on the ceiling. "Daemons": in Greek mythology, not evil spirits but minor deities or attendant spirits.
9. I.e., by quotations inscribed in the stone.
1. A desert in southern Persia.

2. Rivers in Asia.
3. The envisioned maiden embodies all three qualities specified in the preface: intellect (line 158), imagination (lines 160–61), and the sexual and other "functions of sense" (lines 176ff.).

She raised, with voice stifled in tremulous sobs
165   Subdued by its own pathos: her fair hands
Were bare alone, sweeping from some strange harp
Strange symphony, and in their branching veins
The eloquent blood told an ineffable tale.
The beating of her heart was heard to fill
170   The pauses of her music, and her breath
Tumultuously accorded with those fits
Of intermitted song. Sudden she rose,
As if her heart impatiently endured
Its bursting burthen: at the sound he turned,
175   And saw by the warm light of their own life
Her glowing limbs beneath the sinuous veil
Of woven wind, her outspread arms now bare,
Her dark locks floating in the breath of night,
Her beamy bending eyes, her parted lips
180   Outstretched, and pale, and quivering eagerly.
His strong heart sunk and sickened with excess
Of love. He reared his shuddering limbs and quelled
His gasping breath, and spread his arms to meet
Her panting bosom: . . . she drew back a while,
185   Then, yielding to the irresistible joy,
With frantic gesture and short breathless cry
Folded his frame in her dissolving arms.
Now blackness veiled his dizzy eyes, and night
Involved and swallowed up the vision; sleep,
190   Like a dark flood suspended in its course,
Rolled back its impulse on his vacant brain.

     Roused by the shock he started from his trance—
The cold white light of morning, the blue moon
Low in the west, the clear and garish hills,
195   The distinct valley and the vacant woods,
Spread round him where he stood. Whither have fled
The hues of heaven that canopied his bower
Of yesternight? The sounds that soothed his sleep,
The mystery and the majesty of Earth,
200   The joy, the exultation? His wan eyes
Gaze on the empty scene as vacantly
As ocean's moon looks on the moon in heaven.
The spirit of sweet human love has sent
A vision to the sleep of him who spurned
205   Her choicest gifts. He eagerly pursues
Beyond the realms of dream that fleeting shade;
He overleaps the bounds. Alas! alas!
Were limbs, and breath, and being intertwined
Thus treacherously? Lost, lost, for ever lost,
210   In the wide pathless desart of dim sleep,
That beautiful shape! Does the dark gate of death
Conduct to thy mysterious paradise,
O Sleep?[4] Does the bright arch of rainbow clouds,

4. I.e., is death the only access to this maiden of his dream?

And pendent mountains seen in the calm lake,
215   Lead only to a black and watery depth,
While death's blue vault, with loathliest vapours hung,
Where every shade which the foul grave exhales
Hides its dead eye from the detested day,
Conduct,[5] O Sleep, to thy delightful realms?
220   This doubt with sudden tide flowed on his heart,
The insatiate hope which it awakened, stung
His brain even like despair.

                  While day-light held
The sky, the Poet kept mute conference
With his still soul. At night the passion came,
225   Like the fierce fiend of a distempered dream,
And shook him from his rest, and led him forth
Into the darkness.—As an eagle grasped
In folds of the green serpent, feels her breast
Burn with the poison, and precipitates°   *hastens*
230   Through night and day, tempest, and calm, and cloud,
Frantic with dizzying anguish, her blind flight
O'er the wide aëry wilderness:[6] thus driven
By the bright shadow of that lovely dream,
Beneath the cold glare of the desolate night,
235   Through tangled swamps and deep precipitous dells,
Startling with careless step the moon-light snake,
He fled. Red morning dawned upon his flight,
Shedding the mockery of its vital hues
Upon his cheek of death. He wandered on
240   Till vast Aornos seen from Petra's[7] steep
Hung o'er the low horizon like a cloud;
Through Balk,[8] and where the desolated tombs
Of Parthian kings[9] scatter to every wind
Their wasting dust, wildly he wandered on,
245   Day after day, a weary waste of hours,
Bearing within his life the brooding care
That ever fed on its decaying flame.
And now his limbs were lean; his scattered hair
Sered by the autumn of strange suffering
250   Sung dirges in the wind; his listless hand
Hung like dead bone within its withered skin;
Life, and the lustre that consumed it, shone
As in a furnace burning secretly
From his dark eyes alone. The cottagers,
255   Who ministered with human charity
His human wants, beheld with wondering awe
Their fleeting visitant. The mountaineer,
Encountering on some dizzy precipice
That spectral form, deemed that the Spirit of wind
260   With lightning eyes, and eager breath, and feet

---

5. "Conduct" is a singular subjunctive verb; its subject is "vault" (line 216).
6. The eagle and serpent locked in mortal combat is a recurrent image in Shelley's poems (see *Prometheus Unbound* 3.1.72–73, p. 751).
7. The rock (literal trans.); "Petra's steep" is a mountain stronghold in the northern part of ancient Arabia. Aornos is a high mountain.
8. Bactria, in ancient Persia, is now part of Afghanistan.
9. The Parthians inhabited northern Persia.

Disturbing not the drifted snow, had paused
In its career: the infant would conceal
His troubled visage in his mother's robe
In terror at the glare of those wild eyes,
265 To remember their strange light in many a dream
Of after-times; but youthful maidens, taught
By nature, would interpret half the woe
That wasted him, would call him with false names
Brother, and friend,¹ would press his pallid hand
270 At parting, and watch, dim through tears, the path
Of his departure from their father's door.

At length upon the lone Chorasmian shore²
He paused, a wide and melancholy waste
Of putrid marshes. A strong impulse urged
275 His steps to the sea-shore. A swan was there,
Beside a sluggish stream among the reeds.
It rose as he approached, and with strong wings
Scaling the upward sky, bent its bright course
High over the immeasurable main.
280 His eyes pursued its flight.—"Thou hast a home,
Beautiful bird; thou voyagest to thine home,
Where thy sweet mate will twine her downy neck
With thine, and welcome thy return with eyes
Bright in the lustre of their own fond joy.
285 And what am I that I should linger here,
With voice far sweeter than thy dying notes,
Spirit more vast than thine, frame more attuned
To beauty, wasting these surpassing powers
In the deaf air, to the blind earth, and heaven
290 That echoes not my thoughts?" A gloomy smile
Of desperate hope wrinkled his quivering lips.
For sleep, he knew, kept most relentlessly
Its precious charge,³ and silent death exposed,
Faithless perhaps as sleep, a shadowy lure,
295 With doubtful smile mocking its own strange charms.

Startled by his own thoughts he looked around.
There was no fair fiend⁴ near him, not a sight
Or sound of awe but in his own deep mind.
A little shallop⁵ floating near the shore
300 Caught the impatient wandering of his gaze.
It had been long abandoned, for its sides
Gaped wide with many a rift, and its frail joints
Swayed with the undulations of the tide.
A restless impulse urged him to embark
305 And meet lone Death on the drear ocean's waste;

1. The maidens call him "false" (i.e., mistaken) names signifying an affectionate earthly relationship instead of his unearthly love.
2. The shore of Lake Aral, about 175 miles east of the Caspian Sea.
3. I.e., the maiden in the sleeper's dream. The passage goes on to express the skeptical fear that neither sleep nor death may yield the Poet his desire.
4. Apparently he suspects there may have been an external agent luring him to the death described in the preceding lines.
5. A small open boat.

For well he knew that mighty Shadow loves
The slimy caverns of the populous deep.

    The day was fair and sunny; sea and sky
Drank its inspiring radiance, and the wind
310 Swept strongly from the shore, blackening the waves.
Following his eager soul, the wanderer
Leaped in the boat, he spread his cloak aloft
On the bare mast, and took his lonely seat,
And felt the boat speed o'er the tranquil sea
315 Like a torn cloud before the hurricane.

    As one that in a silver vision floats
Obedient to the sweep of odorous winds
Upon resplendent clouds, so rapidly
Along the dark and ruffled waters fled
320 The straining boat.—A whirlwind swept it on,
With fierce gusts and precipitating force,
Through the white ridges of the chafed sea.
The waves arose. Higher and higher still
Their fierce necks writhed beneath the tempest's scourge
325 Like serpents struggling in a vulture's grasp.
Calm and rejoicing in the fearful war
Of wave running on wave, and blast on blast
Descending, and black flood on whirlpool driven
With dark obliterating course, he sate:
330 As if their genii were the ministers
Appointed to conduct him to the light
Of those beloved eyes, the Poet sate
Holding the steady helm. Evening came on,
The beams of sunset hung their rainbow hues
335 High 'mid the shifting domes of sheeted spray
That canopied his path o'er the waste deep;
Twilight, ascending slowly from the east,
Entwin'd in duskier wreaths her braided locks
O'er the fair front and radiant eyes of day;
340 Night followed, clad with stars. On every side
More horribly the multitudinous streams
Of ocean's mountainous waste to mutual war
Rushed in dark tumult thundering, as to mock
The calm and spangled sky. The little boat
345 Still fled before the storm; still fled, like foam
Down the steep cataract of a wintry river;
Now pausing on the edge of the riven wave;
Now leaving far behind the bursting mass
That fell, convulsing ocean. Safely fled—
350 As if that frail and wasted human form,
Had been an elemental god.[6]
                      At midnight
The moon arose: and lo! the etherial cliffs[7]

---

6. A god of one of the natural elements (see line 1).

7. I.e., cliffs high in the air.

Of Caucasus, whose icy summits shone
Among the stars like sunlight, and around
355 Whose cavern'd base the whirlpools and the waves
Bursting and eddying irresistibly
Rage and resound for ever.—Who shall save?—
The boat fled on,—the boiling torrent drove,—
The crags closed round with black and jagged arms,
360 The shattered mountain overhung the sea,
And faster still, beyond all human speed,
Suspended on the sweep of the smooth wave,
The little boat was driven. A cavern there
Yawned, and amid its slant and winding depths
365 Ingulphed the rushing sea. The boat fled on
With unrelaxing speed.—"Vision and Love!"
The Poet cried aloud, "I have beheld
The path of thy departure. Sleep and death
Shall not divide us long!"

                          The boat pursued
370 The winding of the cavern.[8] Day-light shone
At length upon that gloomy river's flow;
Now, where the fiercest war among the waves
Is calm, on the unfathomable stream
The boat moved slowly. Where the mountain, riven,
375 Exposed those black depths to the azure sky,
Ere yet the flood's enormous volume fell
Even to the base of Caucasus, with sound
That shook the everlasting rocks, the mass
Filled with one whirlpool all that ample chasm;
380 Stair above stair the eddying waters rose,
Circling immeasurably fast, and laved
With alternating dash the knarled roots
Of mighty trees, that stretched their giant arms
In darkness over it. I' the midst was left,
385 Reflecting, yet distorting every cloud,
A pool of treacherous and tremendous calm.
Seized by the sway of the ascending stream,
With dizzy swiftness, round, and round, and round,
Ridge after ridge the straining boat arose,
390 Till on the verge of the extremest curve,
Where, through an opening of the rocky bank,
The waters overflow, and a smooth spot
Of glassy quiet mid those battling tides
Is left, the boat paused shuddering.—Shall it sink
395 Down the abyss? Shall the reverting stress
Of that resistless gulph embosom it?
Now shall it fall?—A wandering stream of wind,
Breathed from the west, has caught the expanded sail,
And, lo! with gentle motion, between banks

---

8. A boat beating upstream within a cave, like the eagle and serpent, is a recurrent Shelleyan image.

400 Of mossy slope, and on a placid stream,
    Beneath a woven grove it sails, and, hark!
    The ghastly torrent mingles its far roar,
    With the breeze murmuring in the musical woods.
    Where the embowering trees recede, and leave
405 A little space of green expanse, the cove
    Is closed by meeting banks, whose yellow flowers
    For ever gaze on their own drooping eyes,
    Reflected in the crystal calm. The wave
    Of the boat's motion marred their pensive task,
410 Which nought but vagrant bird, or wanton wind,
    Or falling spear-grass, or their own decay
    Had e'er disturbed before. The Poet longed
    To deck with their bright hues his withered hair,
    But on his heart its solitude returned,
415 And he forbore.[9] Not the strong impulse hid
    In those flushed cheeks, bent eyes, and shadowy frame,
    Had yet performed its ministry: it hung
    Upon his life, as lightning in a cloud
    Gleams, hovering ere it vanish, ere the floods
    Of night close over it.
420   The noonday sun
    Now shone upon the forest, one vast mass
    Of mingling shade, whose brown magnificence
    A narrow vale embosoms. There, huge caves,
    Scooped in the dark base of their aëry rocks
425 Mocking[1] its moans, respond and roar for ever.
    The meeting boughs and implicated° leaves   *intertwined*
    Wove twilight o'er the Poet's path, as led
    By love, or dream, or god, or mightier Death,
    He sought in Nature's dearest haunt, some bank,
430 Her cradle, and his sepulchre. More dark
    And dark the shades accumulate. The oak,
    Expanding its immense and knotty arms,
    Embraces the light beech. The pyramids
    Of the tall cedar overarching, frame
435 Most solemn domes within, and far below.
    Like clouds suspended in an emerald sky,
    The ash and the acacia floating hang
    Tremulous and pale. Like restless serpents, clothed
    In rainbow and in fire, the parasites,
440 Starred with ten thousand blossoms, flow around
    The grey trunks, and, as gamesome infants' eyes,
    With gentle meanings, and most innocent wiles,
    Fold their beams round the hearts of those that love,
    These twine their tendrils with the wedded boughs
445 Uniting their close union; the woven leaves

9. Another recurrent image: flowers overhanging their own reflection. The "yellow flowers" (line 406), probably narcissus, may signify, in this passage, the temptation of the Poet to be satisfied with the projection of his own earthly nature. But his need for a supermundane Other revives, and "the strong impulse" (line 415) drives him on.
1. As often in Shelley, "mocking" has a double sense: mimicking as well as ridiculing the sounds of the forest (line 421).

Make net-work of the dark blue light of day,
And the night's noontide clearness, mutable
As shapes in the weird clouds. Soft mossy lawns
Beneath these canopies extend their swells,
450　Fragrant with perfumed herbs, and eyed with blooms
Minute yet beautiful. One darkest glen
Sends from its woods of musk-rose, twined with jasmine,
A soul-dissolving odour, to invite
To some more lovely mystery. Through the dell,
455　Silence and Twilight here, twin-sisters, keep
Their noonday watch, and sail among the shades,
Like vaporous shapes half seen; beyond, a well,
Dark, gleaming, and of most translucent wave,
Images all the woven boughs above,
460　And each depending leaf, and every speck
Of azure sky, darting between their chasms;
Nor aught else in the liquid mirror laves
Its portraiture, but some inconstant star
Between one foliaged lattice twinkling fair,
465　Or, painted bird, sleeping beneath the moon,
Or gorgeous insect floating motionless,
Unconscious of the day, ere yet his wings
Have spread their glories to the gaze of noon.

　　Hither the Poet came. His eyes beheld
470　Their own wan light through the reflected lines
Of his thin hair, distinct in the dark depth
Of that still fountain; as the human heart,
Gazing in dreams over the gloomy grave,
Sees its own treacherous likeness there. He heard
475　The motion of the leaves, the grass that sprung
Startled and glanced and trembled even to feel
An unaccustomed presence, and the sound
Of the sweet brook that from the secret springs
Of that dark fountain rose. A Spirit seemed
480　To stand beside him—clothed in no bright robes
Of shadowy silver or enshrining light,
Borrowed from aught the visible world affords
Of grace, or majesty, or mystery;—
But, undulating woods, and silent well,
485　And leaping rivulet, and evening gloom
Now deepening the dark shades, for speech assuming
Held commune with him, as if he and it
Were all that was,—only . . . when his regard
Was raised by intense pensiveness, . . . two eyes,
490　Two starry eyes, hung in the gloom of thought,
And seemed with their serene and azure smiles
To beckon him.[2]

　　　　Obedient to the light
That shone within his soul, he went, pursuing

---

2. The Poet sees the eyes of the maiden of his vision and, obedient to his inner light, resumes his quest (lines 491–93).

The windings of the dell.—The rivulet
495 Wanton and wild, through many a green ravine
Beneath the forest flowed. Sometimes it fell
Among the moss with hollow harmony
Dark and profound. Now on the polished stones
It danced; like childhood laughing as it went:
500 Then, through the plain in tranquil wanderings crept,
Reflecting every herb and drooping bud
That overhung its quietness.—"O stream!
Whose source is inaccessibly profound,
Whither do thy mysterious waters tend?
505 Thou imagest my life. Thy darksome stillness,
Thy dazzling waves, thy loud and hollow gulphs,
Thy searchless° fountain, and invisible course   *undiscoverable*
Have each their type in me: and the wide sky,
And measureless ocean may declare as soon
510 What oozy cavern or what wandering cloud
Contains thy waters, as the universe
Tell where these living thoughts reside, when stretched
Upon thy flowers my bloodless limbs shall waste
I' the passing wind!"

Beside the grassy shore
515 Of the small stream he went; he did impress
On the green moss his tremulous step, that caught
Strong shuddering from his burning limbs. As one
Roused by some joyous madness from the couch
Of fever, he did move; yet, not like him,
520 Forgetful of the grave, where, when the flame
Of his frail exultation shall be spent,
He must descend. With rapid steps he went
Beneath the shade of trees, beside the flow
Of the wild babbling rivulet; and now
525 The forest's solemn canopies were changed
For the uniform and lightsome° evening sky.   *illuminated*
Grey rocks did peep from the spare moss, and stemmed
The struggling brook: tall spires of windlestrae[3]
Threw their thin shadows down the rugged slope,
530 And nought but knarled roots[4] of antient pines
Branchless and blasted, clenched with grasping roots
The unwilling soil. A gradual change was here,
Yet ghastly. For, as fast years flow away,
The smooth brow gathers, and the hair grows thin
535 And white, and where irradiate° dewy eyes   *illumined*
Had shone, gleam stony orbs:—so from his steps
Bright flowers departed, and the beautiful shade
Of the green groves, with all their odorous winds
And musical motions. Calm, he still pursued
540 The stream, that with a larger volume now
Rolled through the labyrinthine dell; and there
Fretted a path through its descending curves

---

3. Windlestraw (Scottish dialect); tall, dried stalks   4. Apparently an error for "trunks."
of grass.

With its wintry speed. On every side now rose
Rocks, which, in unimaginable forms,
545 Lifted their black and barren pinnacles
In the light of evening, and its precipice[5]
Obscuring the ravine, disclosed above,
Mid toppling stones, black gulphs and yawning caves,
Whose windings gave ten thousand various tongues
550 To the loud stream. Lo! where the pass expands
Its stony jaws, the abrupt mountain breaks,
And seems, with its accumulated crags,
To overhang the world: for wide expand
Beneath the wan stars and descending moon
555 Islanded seas, blue mountains, mighty streams,
Dim tracts and vast, robed in the lustrous gloom
Of leaden-coloured even, and fiery hills
Mingling their flames with twilight, on the verge
Of the remote horizon. The near scene,
560 In naked and severe simplicity,
Made contrast with the universe. A pine,[6]
Rock-rooted, stretched athwart the vacancy
Its swinging boughs, to each inconstant blast
Yielding one only response, at each pause
565 In most familiar cadence, with the howl
The thunder and the hiss of homeless streams
Mingling its solemn song, whilst the broad river,
Foaming and hurrying o'er its rugged path,
Fell into that immeasurable void
570 Scattering its waters to the passing winds.

    Yet the grey precipice and solemn pine
And torrent, were not all;—one silent nook
Was there. Even on the edge of that vast mountain,
Upheld by knotty roots and fallen rocks,
575 It overlooked in its serenity
The dark earth, and the bending vault of stars.
It was a tranquil spot, that seemed to smile
Even in the lap of horror. Ivy clasped
The fissured stones with its entwining arms,
580 And did embower with leaves for ever green,
And berries dark, the smooth and even space
Of its inviolated floor, and here
The children of the autumnal whirlwind bore,
In wanton sport, those bright leaves, whose decay,
585 Red, yellow, or etherially pale,
Rivals the pride of summer. 'Tis the haunt
Of every gentle wind, whose breath can teach
The wilds to love tranquillity. One step,
One human step alone, has ever broken
590 The stillness of its solitude:—one voice
Alone inspired its echoes,—even that voice
Which hither came, floating among the winds,

5. Headlong fall (of the stream, line 540).
6. Pine trees in Shelley often signify persistence and steadfastness amid change and vicissitudes.

And led the loveliest among human forms
To make their wild haunts the depository
595 Of all the grace and beauty that endued
Its motions, render up its majesty,
Scatter its music on the unfeeling storm,
And to the damp leaves and blue cavern mould,
Nurses of rainbow flowers and branching moss,
600 Commit the colours of that varying cheek,
That snowy breast, those dark and drooping eyes.

The dim and horned[7] moon hung low, and poured
A sea of lustre on the horizon's verge
That overflowed its mountains. Yellow mist
605 Filled the unbounded atmosphere, and drank
Wan moonlight even to fulness: not a star
Shone, not a sound was heard; the very winds,
Danger's grim playmates, on that precipice
Slept, clasped in his embrace.—O, storm of death!
610 Whose sightless[8] speed divides this sullen night:
And thou, colossal Skeleton, that, still
Guiding its irresistible career
In thy devastating omnipotence,
Art king of this frail world, from the red field
615 Of slaughter, from the reeking hospital,
The patriot's sacred couch, the snowy bed
Of innocence, the scaffold and the throne,
A mighty voice invokes thee. Ruin calls
His brother Death. A rare and regal prey
620 He hath prepared, prowling around the world;
Glutted with which thou mayst repose, and men
Go to their graves like flowers or creeping worms,
Nor ever more offer at thy dark shrine
The unheeded tribute of a broken heart.

625 When on the threshold of the green recess
The wanderer's footsteps fell, he knew that death
Was on him. Yet a little, ere it fled,
Did he resign his high and holy soul
To images of the majestic past,
630 That paused within his passive being now,
Like winds that bear sweet music, when they breathe
Through some dim latticed chamber. He did place
His pale lean hand upon the rugged trunk
Of the old pine. Upon an ivied stone
635 Reclined his languid head, his limbs did rest,
Diffused and motionless, on the smooth brink
Of that obscurest chasm;—and thus he lay,
Surrendering to their final impulses
The hovering powers of life. Hope and despair,
640 The torturers, slept; no mortal pain or fear
Marred his repose, the influxes of sense,

7. Crescent-shaped, with the points curved in.　　8. Invisible, or perhaps "unseeing."

And his own being unalloyed by pain,
Yet feebler and more feeble, calmly fed
The stream of thought, till he lay breathing there
645   At peace, and faintly smiling:—his last sight
Was the great moon, which o'er the western line
Of the wide world her mighty horn suspended,
With whose dun° beams inwoven darkness seemed   *darkened*
To mingle. Now upon the jagged hills
650   It rests, and still as the divided frame
Of the vast meteor[9] sunk, the Poet's blood,
That ever beat in mystic sympathy
With nature's ebb and flow, grew feebler still:
And when two lessening points of light alone
655   Gleamed through the darkness, the alternate gasp
Of his faint respiration scarce did stir
The stagnate night:[1]—till the minutest ray
Was quenched, the pulse yet lingered in his heart.
It paused—it fluttered. But when heaven remained
660   Utterly black, the murky shades involved
An image, silent, cold, and motionless,
As their own voiceless earth and vacant air.
Even as a vapour° fed with golden beams   *cloud*
That ministered on[2] sunlight, ere the west
665   Eclipses it, was now that wonderous frame—
No sense, no motion, no divinity—
A fragile lute, on whose harmonious strings
The breath of heaven did wander—a bright stream
Once fed with many-voiced waves—a dream
670   Of youth, which night and time have quenched for ever,
Still, dark, and dry, and unremembered now.

    O, for Medea's wondrous alchemy,
Which wheresoe'er it fell made the earth gleam
With bright flowers, and the wintry boughs exhale
675   From vernal blooms fresh fragrance![3] O, that God,
Profuse of poisons, would concede the chalice
Which but one living man[4] has drained, who now,
Vessel of deathless wrath, a slave that feels
No proud exemption in the blighting curse
680   He bears, over the world wanders for ever,
Lone as incarnate death! O, that the dream
Of dark magician in his visioned cave,[5]
Raking the cinders of a crucible
For life and power, even when his feeble hand
685   Shakes in its last decay, were the true law

---

9. I.e., the moon; "meteor" was once used for any phenomenon within the earth's atmosphere.
1. The Poet's life ebbs in consonance with the descent of the "horned moon," to the moment when only the two "points of light"—its horns—show above the hills.
2. Attended, acted as a servant to.
3. Medea brewed a magic potion to rejuvenate the dying Aeson; where some of the potion spilled on the ground, flowers sprang up (Ovid, *Metamorphoses* 7.275ff.).
4. The Wandering Jew. According to a medieval legend, he had taunted Christ on the way to His crucifixion and was condemned to wander the world, deathless, until Christ's second coming.
5. Cave in which he has visions. "Dark magician": an alchemist attempting to produce the elixir of enduring life.

Of this so lovely world! But thou art fled
Like some frail exhalation; which the dawn
Robes in its golden beams,—ah! thou hast fled!
The brave, the gentle, and the beautiful,
690　The child of grace and genius. Heartless things
Are done and said i' the world, and many worms
And beasts and men live on, and mighty Earth
From sea and mountain, city and wilderness,
In vesper[6] low or joyous orison,°　　　　　　　　　　　*prayer*
695　Lifts still its solemn voice:—but thou art fled—
Thou canst no longer know or love the shapes
Of this phantasmal scene, who have to thee
Been purest ministers, who are, alas!
Now thou art not. Upon those pallid lips
700　So sweet even in their silence, on those eyes
That image sleep in death, upon that form
Yet safe from the worm's outrage, let no tear
Be shed—not even in thought. Nor, when those hues
Are gone, and those divinest lineaments,
705　Worn by the senseless° wind, shall live alone　　　　*unfeeling*
In the frail pauses of this simple strain,
Let not high verse, mourning the memory
Of that which is no more, or painting's woe
Or sculpture, speak in feeble imagery
710　Their own cold powers. Art and eloquence,
And all the shews o' the world are frail and vain
To weep a loss that turns their lights to shade.
It is a woe too "deep for tears,"[7] when all
Is reft at once, when some surpassing Spirit,
715　Whose light adorned the world around it, leaves
Those who remain behind, not sobs or groans,
The passionate tumult of a clinging hope;
But pale despair and cold tranquillity,
Nature's vast frame, the web of human things,
720　Birth and the grave, that are not as they were.

1815　　　　　　　　　　　　　　　　　　　　　　　　1816

---

6. Evening prayer.
7. From the last line of Wordsworth's *Ode: Inti-* *mations of Immortality*: "Thoughts that do often lie too deep for tears."

Mont Blanc[1]

Lines Written in the Vale of Chamouni

1

The everlasting universe of things
Flows through the mind, and rolls its rapid waves,
Now dark—now glittering—now reflecting gloom—
Now lending splendour, where from secret springs
5   The source of human thought its tribute brings
Of waters,—with a sound but half its own.
Such as a feeble brook will oft assume
In the wild woods, among the mountains lone,
Where waterfalls around it leap forever,
10   Where woods and winds contend, and a vast river
Over its rocks ceaselessly bursts and raves.

2

Thus thou, Ravine of Arve—dark, deep Ravine—
Thou many-coloured, many-voiced vale,
Over whose pines, and crags, and caverns sail
15   Fast cloud shadows and sunbeams: awful° scene,   *awe-inspiring*
Where Power in likeness of the Arve comes down
From the ice gulphs that gird his secret throne,
Bursting through these dark mountains like the flame
Of lightning through the tempest;—thou dost lie,
20   Thy giant brood of pines around thee clinging,
Children of elder time, in whose devotion
The chainless winds still come and ever came
To drink their odours, and their mighty swinging
To hear—an old and solemn harmony;
25   Thine earthly rainbows stretched across the sweep
Of the etherial waterfall, whose veil
Robes some unsculptured[2] image; the strange sleep
Which when the voices of the desart fail
Wraps all in its own deep eternity;—
30   Thy caverns echoing to the Arve's commotion,
A loud, lone sound no other sound can tame;
Thou art pervaded with that ceaseless motion,
Thou art the path of that unresting sound—

1. Mont Blanc, near the French border with Italy, is the highest mountain in the Alps. When he conceived the poem, Shelley was standing on a bridge over the Arve River in the valley of Chamonix, in what is now southeastern France.

Shelley wrote of this poem: "It was composed under the immediate impression of the deep and powerful feelings excited by the objects which it attempts to describe; and, as an indisciplined overflowing of the soul, rests its claim to approbation on an attempt to imitate the untamable wildness and inaccessible solemnity from which those feelings sprang."

Shelley's comment points to two important attributes of *Mont Blanc*. First, he attempts, as in other poems (especially in *Ode to the West Wind*), to make the poem iconic or directly imitative of the alternating "wildness" and "solemnity" of the scene and the consonant thought and feelings it evokes. Second, this work belongs to the genre of the "local" poem, a descriptive-meditative presentation of a precisely identified landscape. In this respect it resembles Wordsworth's *Tintern Abbey*, the major influence on *Mont Blanc*. Shelley's poem, like Wordsworth's, poses the question of the significance of the interchange between nature and the human mind; he proposes, however, a very different answer to that question.
2. I.e., not formed by humans.

Dizzy Ravine! and when I gaze on thee
35   I seem as in a trance sublime and strange
To muse on my own separate phantasy,
My own, my human mind, which passively
Now renders and receives fast influencings,
Holding an unremitting interchange
40   With the clear universe of things around;[3]
One legion of wild thoughts, whose wandering wings
Now float above thy darkness, and now rest
Where that or thou art no unbidden guest,
In the still cave of the witch Poesy,[4]
45   Seeking among the shadows that pass by
Ghosts of all things that are, some shade of thee,
Some phantom, some faint image; till the breast
From which they fled recalls them, thou art there![5]

3

Some say that gleams of a remoter world
50   Visit the soul in sleep,—that death is slumber,
And that its shapes the busy thoughts outnumber
Of those who wake and live.—I look on high;
Has some unknown omnipotence unfurled
The veil of life and death? or do I lie
55   In dream, and does the mightier world of sleep
Spread far around and inaccessibly
Its circles? For the very spirit fails,
Driven like a homeless cloud from steep to steep
That vanishes among the viewless° gales!   *invisible*
60   Far, far above, piercing the infinite sky,
Mont Blanc appears,—still, snowy, and serene—
Its subject mountains their unearthly forms
Pile around it, ice and rock; broad vales between
Of frozen floods, unfathomable deeps,
65   Blue as the overhanging heaven, that spread
And wind among the accumulated steeps;
A desart peopled by the storms alone,
Save when the eagle brings some hunter's bone,
And the wolf tracts° her there—how hideously   *tracks*
70   Its shapes are heaped around! rude, bare, and high,
Ghastly, and scarred, and riven.—Is this the scene
Where the old Earthquake-dæmon[6] taught her young
Ruin? Were these their toys? or did a sea
Of fire, envelope once this silent snow?
75   None can reply—all seems eternal now.
The wilderness has a mysterious tongue

3. This passage is remarkably parallel to a passage Shelley could not have read in *The Prelude*, first published in 1850, in which Wordsworth discovers, in the landscape viewed from Mount Snowdon, the "type" or "emblem" of the human mind in its interchange with nature (see *The Prelude* 14.63ff., p. 378).
4. I.e., in the part of the mind that creates poetry.

5. I.e., the thoughts (line 41) seek, in the poet's creative faculty, some shade, phantom, or image of the Arve; and when the breast, which has forgotten these images, recalls them again—there, suddenly, does the Arve exist.
6. A supernatural being, halfway between mortals and the gods. Here it represents the force that makes earthquakes.

Which teaches awful doubt, or faith so mild,
So solemn, so serene, that man may be
But for such faith[7] with nature reconciled;
80 Thou hast a voice, great Mountain, to repeal
Large codes of fraud and woe; not understood
By all, but which[8] the wise, and great, and good
Interpret, or make felt, or deeply feel.

4

The fields, the lakes, the forests, and the streams,
85 Ocean, and all the living things that dwell
Within the dædal[9] earth; lightning, and rain,
Earthquake, and fiery flood, and hurricane,
The torpor of the year when feeble dreams
Visit the hidden buds, or dreamless sleep
90 Holds every future leaf and flower;—the bound
With which from that detested trance they leap;
The works and ways of man, their death and birth,
And that of him and all that his may be;
All things that move and breathe with toil and sound
95 Are born and die; revolve, subside and swell.
Power dwells apart in its tranquillity
Remote, serene, and inaccessible:
And *this*, the naked countenance of earth,
On which I gaze, even these primæval mountains
100 Teach the adverting mind. The glaciers creep
Like snakes that watch their prey, from their far fountains,
Slow rolling on; there, many a precipice,
Frost and the Sun in scorn of mortal power
Have piled: dome, pyramid, and pinnacle,
105 A city of death, distinct with many a tower
And wall impregnable of beaming ice.
Yet not a city, but a flood of ruin
Is there, that from the boundaries of the sky
Rolls its perpetual stream; vast pines are strewing
110 Its destined path, or in the mangled soil
Branchless and shattered stand: the rocks, drawn down
From yon remotest waste, have overthrown
The limits of the dead and living world,
Never to be reclaimed. The dwelling-place
115 Of insects, beasts, and birds, becomes its spoil;
Their food and their retreat for ever gone,
So much of life and joy is lost. The race
Of man, flies far in dread; his work and dwelling
Vanish, like smoke before the tempest's stream,
120 And their place is not known. Below, vast caves
Shine in the rushing torrents' restless gleam,

7. I.e., "simply by holding such faith." In Shelley's balance of possibilities, the landscape is equally capable of instilling such a Wordsworthian faith (in the possibility of reconciling humans and nature, lines 78–79) or the "awful" (i.e., "awesome") doubt (that nature is totally alien to human ends and values).
8. The reference is to "voice," line 80.
9. Intricately formed; derived from Daedalus, builder of the labyrinth in Crete.

Which from those secret chasms in tumult welling[1]
Meet in the vale, and one majestic River,[2]
The breath and blood of distant lands, for ever
125 Rolls its loud waters to the ocean waves,
Breathes its swift vapours to the circling air.

5

Mont Blanc yet gleams on high:—the power is there,
The still and solemn power of many sights,
And many sounds, and much of life and death.
130 In the calm darkness of the moonless nights,
In the lone glare of day, the snows descend
Upon that Mountain; none beholds them there,
Nor when the flakes burn in the sinking sun,
Or the star-beams dart through them:—Winds contend
135 Silently there, and heap the snow with breath
Rapid and strong, but silently! Its home
The voiceless lightning in these solitudes
Keeps innocently, and like vapour broods
Over the snow. The secret strength of things
140 Which governs thought, and to the infinite dome
Of heaven is as a law, inhabits thee!
And what were thou,° and earth, and stars, and sea,   *Mont Blanc*
If to the human mind's imaginings
Silence and solitude were vacancy?

1816   1817

Hymn to Intellectual Beauty[1]

I

The awful shadow of some unseen Power
    Floats though unseen amongst us,—visiting
    This various world with as inconstant wing
As summer winds that creep from flower to flower.—
5 Like moonbeams that behind some piny mountain shower,[2]
        It visits with inconstant glance
        Each human heart and countenance;
Like hues and harmonies of evening,—
        Like clouds in starlight widely spread,—
10   Like memory of music fled,—
        Like aught that for its grace may be
Dear, and yet dearer for its mystery.

---

1. This description (as well as that in lines 9–11) seems to be an echo of Coleridge's description of the chasm and sacred river in the recently published *Kubla Khan*, lines 12–24.
2. The Arve, which flows into Lake Geneva.
1. "Intellectual" means "nonsensible." "Intellectual Beauty" is thus beyond access by sense experience. It is simply postulated to account for occasional states of awareness that lend splendor, grace, and truth both to experience of the natural world and to people's moral consciousness. To this mystery (stanzas 5–7) Shelley had, at its early visitation, dedicated his powers, and to it he now prays as he passes the noon of life (stanza 7).
2. Used as a verb.

2

Spirit of BEAUTY, that dost consecrate
  With thine own hues all thou dost shine upon
15   Of human thought or form,—where art thou gone?
Why dost thou pass away and leave our state,
This dim vast vale of tears, vacant and desolate?
     Ask why the sunlight not forever
     Weaves rainbows o'er yon mountain river,
20 Why aught should fail and fade that once is shewn,
     Why fear and dream and death and birth
     Cast on the daylight of this earth
     Such gloom,—why man has such a scope
For love and hate, despondency and hope?

3

25 No voice from some sublimer world hath ever
     To sage or poet these responses given—
     Therefore the name of God and ghosts and Heaven,
Remain the records of their vain endeavour,[3]
Frail spells—whose uttered charm might not avail to sever,
30   From all we hear and all we see,
     Doubt, chance, and mutability.
Thy light alone—like mist o'er mountains driven,
     Or music by the night wind sent
     Through strings of some still instrument,°   *wind harp*
35   Or moonlight on a midnight stream,
Gives grace and truth to life's unquiet dream.

4

Love, Hope, and Self-esteem, like clouds depart
  And come, for some uncertain moments lent.
  Man were immortal, and omnipotent,
40 Didst thou, unknown and awful as thou art,
Keep with thy glorious train firm state within his heart.[4]
     Thou messenger of sympathies,
     That wax and wane in lovers' eyes—
Thou—that to human thought art nourishment,
45   Like darkness to a dying flame!
     Depart not as thy shadow came,
     Depart not—lest the grave should be,
Like life and fear, a dark reality.

5

While yet a boy I sought for ghosts, and sped
50   Through many a listening chamber, cave and ruin,
     And starlight wood, with fearful steps pursuing
Hopes of high talk with the departed dead.

3. The names (line 27) are nothing better than guesses at identifying the mystery by religious philosophers and poets (line 26).

4. I.e., "man would be immortal . . . if thou didst keep."

I called on poisonous names with which our youth is fed;[5]
    I was not heard—I saw them not—
55   When musing deeply on the lot
Of life, at that sweet time when winds are wooing
    All vital things that wake to bring
    News of buds and blossoming,—
    Sudden, thy shadow fell on me;
60 I shrieked, and clasped my hands in extacy!

6

I vowed that I would dedicate my powers
    To thee and thine—have I not kept the vow?
    With beating heart and streaming eyes, even now
I call the phantoms of a thousand hours
65 Each from his voiceless grave: they have in visioned bowers
    Of studious zeal or love's delight
    Outwatched with me the envious night[6]—
They know that never joy illumed my brow
    Unlinked with hope that thou wouldst free
70   This world from its dark slavery,
    That thou—O awful LOVELINESS,
Wouldst give whate'er these words cannot express.

7

The day becomes more solemn and serene
    When noon is past—there is a harmony
75   In autumn, and a lustre in its sky,
Which through the summer is not heard or seen,
As if it could not be, as if it had not been!
    Thus let thy power, which like the truth
    Of nature on my passive youth
80 Descended, to my onward life supply
    Its calm—to one who worships thee,
    And every form containing thee,
    Whom, SPIRIT fair, thy spells did bind
To fear[7] himself, and love all human kind.

1816   1817

Ozymandias[1]

I met a traveller from an antique land,
Who said—"Two vast and trunkless legs of stone
Stand in the desert. . . . Near them, on the sand,

5. Lines 49–52 refer to Shelley's youthful experiments with magic. The "poisonous names" are probably those in the prayers he had been taught as a child.
6. I.e., stayed up until the night, envious of their delight, had reluctantly departed.
7. Probably in the old sense: "to stand in awe of."

1. According to Diodorus Siculus, Greek historian of the 1st century B.C.E., the largest statue in Egypt had the inscription: "I am Ozymandias, king of kings; if anyone wishes to know what I am and where I lie, let him surpass me in some of my exploits." Ozymandias was the Greek name for Ramses II of Egypt, 13th century B.C.E.

Half sunk a shattered visage lies, whose frown,
5   And wrinkled lip, and sneer of cold command,
Tell that its sculptor well those passions read
Which yet survive, stamped on these lifeless things,
The hand that mocked them, and the heart that fed;²
And on the pedestal, these words appear:
10   My name is Ozymandias, King of Kings,
Look on my Works, ye Mighty, and despair!
Nothing beside remains. Round the decay
Of that colossal Wreck, boundless and bare
The lone and level sands stretch far away."

1817   1818

Stanzas Written in Dejection— December 1818, near Naples¹

The Sun is warm, the sky is clear,
The waves are dancing fast and bright,
Blue isles and snowy mountains wear
The purple noon's transparent might,
5   The breath of the moist earth is light
Around its unexpanded buds;
Like many a voice of one delight
The winds, the birds, the Ocean-floods;
The City's voice itself is soft, like Solitude's.

10   I see the Deep's untrampled floor
With green and purple seaweeds strown;
I see the waves upon the shore
Like light dissolved in star-showers, thrown;
I sit upon the sands alone;
15   The lightning of the noontide Ocean
Is flashing round me, and a tone
Arises from its measured motion,
How sweet! did any heart now share in my emotion.

Alas, I have nor hope nor health
20   Nor peace within nor calm around,
Nor that content surpassing wealth
The sage² in meditation found,
And walked with inward glory crowned;
Nor fame nor power nor love nor leisure—
25   Others I see whom these surround,
Smiling they live and call life pleasure:
To me that cup has been dealt in another measure.

---

2. "The hand" is the sculptor's, who had "mocked" (both imitated and derided) the sculptured passions; "the heart" is the king's, which has "fed" his passions.
1. Shelley's first wife, Harriet, had drowned herself; Clara, his baby daughter with Mary Shelley, had just died; and Shelley himself was plagued by ill health, pain, financial worries, and the sense that he had failed as a poet.
2. Probably the Roman emperor Marcus Aurelius (2nd century C.E.), Stoic philosopher who wrote twelve books of *Meditations*.

Yet now despair itself is mild,
Even as the winds and waters are;
30   I could lie down like a tired child
And weep away the life of care
Which I have borne and yet must bear
Till Death like Sleep might steal on me,
And I might feel in the warm air
35   My cheek grow cold, and hear the Sea
Breathe o'er my dying brain its last monotony.

Some might lament that I were cold,
As I, when this sweet day is gone,[3]
Which my lost heart, too soon grown old,
40   Insults with this untimely moan—
They might lament,—for I am one
Whom men love not, and yet regret;
Unlike this day, which, when the Sun
Shall on its stainless glory set,
45   Will linger though enjoyed, like joy in Memory yet.

1818   1824

A Song: "Men of England"[1]

Men of England, wherefore plough
For the lords who lay ye low?
Wherefore weave with toil and care
The rich robes your tyrants wear?

5   Wherefore feed and clothe and save
From the cradle to the grave
Those ungrateful drones who would
Drain your sweat—nay, drink your blood?

Wherefore, Bees of England, forge
10   Many a weapon, chain, and scourge,
That these stingless drones may spoil
The forced produce of your toil?

Have ye leisure, comfort, calm,
Shelter, food, love's gentle balm?
15   Or what is it ye buy so dear
With your pain and with your fear?

The seed ye sow, another reaps;
The wealth ye find, another keeps;

3. I.e., as I will lament this sweet day when it has
gone.
1. This and the two following poems were written
at a time of turbulent unrest, after the return of
troops from the Napoleonic Wars had precipitated

a great economic depression. The *Song*, expressing
Shelley's hope for a proletarian revolution, was
originally planned as one of a series for workers. It
has become, as the poet wished, a hymn of the
British labor movement.

The robes ye weave, another wears;
20 The arms ye forge, another bears.

Sow seed—but let no tyrant reap:
Find wealth—let no impostor heap:
Weave robes—let not the idle wear:
Forge arms—in your defence to bear.

25 Shrink to your cellars, holes, and cells—
In halls ye deck another dwells.
Why shake the chains ye wrought? Ye see
The steel ye tempered glance on ye.

With plough and spade and hoe and loom
30 Trace your grave and build your tomb
And weave your winding-sheet—till fair
England be your Sepulchre.

1819   1839

England in 1819

An old, mad, blind, despised, and dying King;[1]
Princes, the dregs of their dull race, who flow
Through public scorn,—mud from a muddy spring;
Rulers who neither see nor feel nor know,
5 But leechlike to their fainting country cling
Till they drop, blind in blood, without a blow.
A people starved and stabbed in th' untilled field;[2]
An army, whom liberticide and prey
Makes as a two-edged sword to all who wield;
10 Golden and sanguine laws[3] which tempt and slay;
Religion Christless, Godless—a book sealed;
A senate, Time's worst statute, unrepealed[4]—
Are graves from which a glorious Phantom[5] may
Burst, to illumine our tempestuous day.

1819   1839

To Sidmouth and Castlereagh[1]

As from their ancestral oak
Two empty ravens wind their clarion,

---

1. George III, who had been declared insane in 1811. He died in 1820.
2. Alluding to the Peterloo Massacre on August 16, 1819. In St. Peter's field, near Manchester, a troop of cavalry had charged into a crowd attending a peaceful rally in support of parliamentary reform. "Peterloo" is an ironic combination of "St. Peter's" and "Waterloo."
3. Laws bought with gold, and leading to bloodshed.
4. The law imposing disabilities on Dissenters and Roman Catholics.

5. I.e., a revolution.
1. Shelley's powerful satire is directed against Viscount Castlereagh, foreign secretary (1812–22), who took a leading part in the European settlement after the Battle of Waterloo, and Viscount Sidmouth (1757–1844), the home secretary, whose cruelly coercive measures (supported by Castlereagh) against unrest in the laboring classes were in large part responsible for the Peterloo Massacre.
   When this poem was reprinted by Mary Shelley in 1839, it was given the title *Similes for Two Political Characters of 1819.*

Yell by yell, and croak by croak,
When they scent the noonday smoke
5   Of fresh human carrion:—

As two gibbering night-birds flit
    From their bowers of deadly yew
Through the night to frighten it—
When the moon is in a fit,
10   And the stars are none, or few:—

As a shark and dogfish wait
    Under an Atlantic isle
For the Negro-ship, whose freight
Is the theme of their debate,
15   Wrinkling their red gills the while—

Are ye—two vultures sick for battle,
    Two scorpions under one wet stone,
Two bloodless wolves whose dry throats rattle,
Two crows perched on the murrained² cattle,
20   Two vipers tangled into one.

1819   1832

The Indian Girl's Song¹ [The Indian Serenade]

I arise from dreams of thee
In the first sleep of night—
The winds are breathing low
And the stars are burning bright.
5   I arise from dreams of thee—
And a spirit in my feet
Has borne me—Who knows how?
To thy chamber window, sweet!—

The wandering airs they faint
10   On the dark silent stream—
The champak² odours fail
Like sweet thoughts in a dream;
The nightingale's complaint—
It dies upon her heart—
15   As I must die on thine
O beloved as thou art!

O lift me from the grass!
I die, I faint, I fail!
Let thy love in kisses rain

2. A *murrain* is a malignant disease of domestic animals.
1. Usually headed *The Indian Serenade*. Shelley's title makes it clear that the poem is not a personal utterance but a dramatic lyric, sung by an imagined East Indian girl. It manifests the conventional extravagance of an Oriental love poem.
2. An Indian species of magnolia, bearing fragrant orange flowers.

20 On my lips and eyelids pale.
My cheek is cold and white, alas!
My heart beats loud and fast.
Oh press it close to thine again
Where it will break at last.

1819   1822

Ode to the West Wind[1]

1

O wild West Wind, thou breath of Autumn's being,
Thou, from whose unseen presence the leaves dead
Are driven, like ghosts from an enchanter fleeing,

Yellow, and black, and pale, and hectic[2] red,
5 Pestilence-stricken multitudes: O Thou,
Who chariotest to their dark wintry bed

The winged seeds, where they lie cold and low,
Each like a corpse within its grave, until
Thine azure sister of the Spring[3] shall blow

10 Her clarion[4] o'er the dreaming earth, and fill
(Driving sweet buds like flocks to feed in air)
With living hues and odours plain and hill:

Wild Spirit, which art moving everywhere;
Destroyer and Preserver; hear, O hear!

2

15 Thou on whose stream, 'mid the steep sky's commotion,
Loose clouds like Earth's decaying leaves are shed,
Shook from the tangled boughs of Heaven and Ocean,[5]

1. This poem was conceived and chiefly written in a wood that skirts the Arno, near Florence, and on a day when that tempestuous wind, whose temperature is at once mild and animating, was collecting the vapours which pour down the autumnal rains [Shelley's note]. As in other major Romantic poems—for example, the opening of Wordsworth's *Prelude,* Coleridge's *Dejection: An Ode,* and the conclusion to Shelley's *Adonais*—the rising wind, linked with the cycle of the seasons, is presented as the outer correspondent to an inner change from apathy to spiritual vitality and from imaginative sterility to a burst of creative power that is paralleled to the inspiration of the biblical prophets. In Hebrew, Latin, Greek, and many other languages, the words for *wind, breath, soul,* and *inspiration* are all identical or related. Thus Shelley's west wind is a "spirit" (the Latin *spiritus:* wind, breath, soul, and the root word in "inspiration"), the "breath of Autumn's being," which on earth,

sky, and sea destroys in the autumn to revivify in the spring. Around this central image the poem weaves various cycles of death and regeneration—vegetational, human, and divine.
Shelley's sonnet-length stanza, developed from the interlaced three-line units of the Italian *terza rima* (*aba bcb cdc,* etc.), consists of a set of four such tercets, closed by a couplet rhyming with the middle line of the preceding tercet: *aba bcb cdc ded ee.*
2. Referring to the kind of fever that occurs in tuberculosis.
3. The west wind that will blow in the spring.
4. A high, shrill trumpet.
5. The fragmentary clouds ("leaves") are torn by the wind from the larger and higher clouds ("boughs"), which are formed by a union of air with vapor drawn up by the sun from the ocean. "Angels" (line 18) suggests the old sense: "messengers," "harbingers."

Angels of rain and lightning: there are spread
On the blue surface of thine aery surge,
20 Like the bright hair uplifted from the head

Of some fierce Mænad,[6] even from the dim verge
Of the horizon to the zenith's height,
The locks of the approaching storm. Thou Dirge

Of the dying year, to which this closing night
25 Will be the dome of a vast sepulchre,
Vaulted with all thy congregated might

Of vapours,° from whose solid atmosphere   *clouds*
Black rain and fire and hail will burst: O hear!

3
Thou who didst waken from his summer dreams
30 The blue Mediterranean, where he lay,
Lulled by the coil of his chrystalline streams,[7]

Beside a pumice isle in Baiæ's bay,[8]
And saw in sleep old palaces and towers
Quivering within the wave's intenser day,

35 All overgrown with azure moss and flowers
So sweet, the sense faints picturing them! Thou
For whose path the Atlantic's level powers

Cleave themselves into chasms, while far below
The sea-blooms and the oozy woods which wear
40 The sapless foliage of the ocean, know

Thy voice, and suddenly grow grey with fear,
And tremble and despoil themselves:[9] O hear!

4
If I were a dead leaf thou mightest bear;
If I were a swift cloud to fly with thee;
45 A wave to pant beneath thy power, and share

The impulse of thy strength, only less free
Than thou, O Uncontrollable! If even
I were as in my boyhood, and could be

6. A female votary who danced frenziedly in the
worship of Dionysus (Bacchus), the Greek god of
wine and vegetation. As vegetation god, he was
fabled to die in the fall and to be resurrected in the
spring.
7. The currents that flow in the Mediterranean
Sea, sometimes with a visible difference in color.

8. West of Naples, the locale of imposing villas
erected by Roman emperors. "Pumice": a porous
volcanic stone.
9. The vegetation at the bottom of the sea . . .
sympathizes with that of the land in the change of
seasons [Shelley's note].

The comrade of thy wanderings over Heaven,
50 As then, when to outstrip thy skiey speed
Scarce seemed a vision; I would ne'er have striven

As thus with thee in prayer in my sore need.
Oh! lift me as a wave, a leaf, a cloud!
I fall upon the thorns of life! I bleed!

55 A heavy weight of hours has chained and bowed
One too like thee: tameless, and swift, and proud.

5

Make me thy lyre,[1] even as the forest is:
What if my leaves are falling like its own!
The tumult of thy mighty harmonies

60 Will take from both a deep, autumnal tone,
Sweet though in sadness. Be thou, Spirit fierce,
My spirit! Be thou me, impetuous one!

Drive my dead thoughts over the universe
Like withered leaves to quicken a new birth!
65 And, by the incantation of this verse,

Scatter, as from an unextinguished hearth
Ashes and sparks, my words among mankind!
Be through my lips to unawakened Earth

The trumpet of a prophecy! O Wind,
70 If Winter comes, can Spring be far behind?

1819   1820

Prometheus Unbound   Shelley composed this work in Italy between the autumn of 1818 and the close of 1819 and published it the following summer. Upon its completion he wrote in a letter, "It is a drama, with characters and mechanism of a kind yet unattempted; and I think the execution is better than any of my former attempts." It is based on the *Prometheus Bound* of Aeschylus, which dramatizes the sufferings of Prometheus, unrepentant champion of humanity, who, because he had stolen fire from heaven, was condemned by Zeus to be chained to Mount Caucasus and to be tortured by a vulture feeding on his liver; in a lost sequel, Aeschylus reconciled Prometheus with his oppressor. Shelley continued Aeschylus's story but transformed it into a symbolic drama about the origin of evil and the possibility of overcoming it. In such earlier writings as *Queen Mab* Shelley had expressed his belief that injustice and suffering can be eliminated by an external revolution that will wipe out or radically reform the causes of evil, attributed to existing social, political, and religious institutions. Implicit in *Prometheus Unbound,* on the other hand, is the view that both evil and the possibility of reform are the moral responsibility of men and

---

1. The Eolian lyre, which responds to the wind with rising and falling musical chords.

women themselves. Social chaos and wars are a gigantic projection of human moral disorder and inner division and conflict; tyrants are the outer representatives of the tyranny of our baser over our better elements; hatred for others is a product of self-contempt; and external political reform is impossible unless we have first reformed our own nature at its roots, by substituting selfless love for divisive hatred. Shelley thus incorporates into his secular myth—of universal regeneration by a triumph of humanity's moral imagination—the ethical teaching of Christ on the Mount, together with the classical morality represented in the *Prometheus* of Aeschylus. Shelley however, adds the warning (4.562ff.) that even should such a regeneration take place, its maintenance will depend on an unremitting vigilance, lest the serpent deep in human nature break loose and start the cycle of evil all over again.

Shelley writes in his preface that it is a mistake to suppose that the poem contains "a reasoned system on the theory of human life. Didactic poetry is my abhorrence." *Prometheus Unbound* is not a dramatized philosophical essay or a moral allegory but a large and intricate imaginative construction that involves premises about human nature and the springs of morality and creativity. The non-Christian poet Yeats called it one of "the sacred books of the world," and the Christian critic C. S. Lewis found in it poetic powers matched only by Dante.

FROM PROMETHEUS UNBOUND

A Lyrical Drama in Four Acts

Audisne hæc Amphiarae, sub terram abdite?[1]

Preface

The Greek tragic writers, in selecting as their subject any portion of their national history or mythology, employed in their treatment of it a certain arbitrary discretion. They by no means conceived themselves bound to adhere to the common interpretation or to imitate in story as in title their rivals and predecessors. Such a system would have amounted to a resignation of those claims to preference over their competitors which incited the composition. The Agamemnonian story was exhibited on the Athenian theatre with as many variations as dramas.

I have presumed to employ a similar licence.—The *Prometheus Unbound* of Æschylus, supposed the reconciliation of Jupiter with his victim as the price of the disclosure of the danger threatened to his empire by the consummation of his marriage with Thetis. Thetis, according to this view of the subject, was given in marriage to Peleus, and Prometheus by the permission of Jupiter delivered from his captivity by Hercules.[2]—Had I framed my story

---

1. Cicero, *Tusculan Disputations* 2.60: "Do you hear this, O Amphiaraus, concealed under the earth?" In Greek myth Amphiaraus was a seer. Fleeing from an unsuccessful assault on Thebes, he was saved from his pursuers by Zeus, who by a thunderbolt opened a cleft in the earth that swallowed him up.

In his *Disputations* Cicero is arguing for the Stoic doctrine of the need to master pain and suffering. He quotes this line (a Latin translation from Aeschylus's lost drama *Epigoni*) in the course of an anecdote about Dionysius of Heraclea, who, tormented by kidney stones, abjures the doctrine of his Stoic teacher Zeno that pain is not an evil. By way of reproof his fellow-Stoic Cleanthes strikes his foot on the ground and utters this line. Cicero interprets it as an appeal to Zeno the Stoic master (under the name of Amphiaraus).

2. Shelley's description of the subject of Aeschylus's lost drama, *Prometheus Unbound*, is a speculation based on surviving fragments.

on this model I should have done no more than have attempted to restore the lost drama of Æschylus; an ambition, which, if my preference to this mode of treating the subject had incited me to cherish, the recollection of the high comparison such an attempt would challenge, might well abate. But in truth I was averse from a catastrophe so feeble as that of reconciling the Champion with the Oppressor of mankind. The moral interest of the fable which is so powerfully sustained by the sufferings and endurance of Prometheus, would be annihilated if we could conceive of him as unsaying his high language, and quailing before his successful and perfidious adversary. The only imaginary being resembling in any degree Prometheus, is Satan; and Prometheus is, in my judgement, a more poetical character than Satan because, in addition to courage and majesty and firm and patient opposition to omnipotent force, he is susceptible of being described as exempt from the taints of ambition, envy, revenge, and a desire for personal aggrandisement, which in the Hero of *Paradise Lost,* interfere with the interest. The character of Satan engenders in the mind a pernicious casuistry which leads us to weigh his faults with his wrongs and to excuse the former because the latter exceed all measure. In the minds of those who consider that magnificent fiction with a religious feeling, it engenders something worse. But Prometheus is, as it were, the type of the highest perfection of moral and intellectual nature, impelled by the purest and the truest motives to the best and noblest ends.

This Poem was chiefly written upon the mountainous ruins of the Baths of Caracalla, among the flowery glades, and thickets of odoriferous blossoming trees which are extended in ever winding labyrinths upon its immense platforms and dizzy arches suspended in the air. The bright blue sky of Rome, and the effect of the vigorous awakening of spring in that divinest climate, and the new life with which it drenches the spirits even to intoxication, were the inspiration of this drama.

The imagery which I have employed will be found in many instances to have been drawn from the operations of the human mind, or from those external actions by which they are expressed. This is unusual in modern Poetry; although Dante and Shakespeare are full of instances of the same kind: Dante indeed more than any other poet and with greater success. But the Greek poets, as writers to whom no resource of awakening the sympathy of their contemporaries was unknown, were in the habitual use of this power, and it is the study of their works (since a higher merit would probably be denied me) to which I am willing that my readers should impute this singularity.

One word is due in candour to the degree in which the study of contemporary writings may have tinged my composition, for such has been a topic of censure with regard to poems far more popular, and indeed more deservedly popular than mine. It is impossible that any one who inhabits the same age with such writers as those who stand in the foremost ranks of our own, can conscientiously assure himself, that his language and tone of thought may not have been modified by the study of the productions of those extraordinary intellects. It is true, that, not the spirit of their genius, but the forms in which it has manifested itself, are due, less to the peculiarities of their own minds, than to the peculiarity of the moral and intellectual condition of the minds among which they have been produced. Thus a number of writers possess the form, whilst they want the spirit of those whom, it is alleged, they imitate; because the former is the endowment of the age in which they live, and the latter must be the uncommunicated lightning of their own mind.

The peculiar style of intense and comprehensive imagery which distinguishes the modern literature of England, has not been, as a general power, the product of the imitation of any particular writer. The mass of capabilities remains at every period materially the same; the circumstances which awaken it to action perpetually change. If England were divided into forty republics, each equal in population and extent to Athens, there is no reason to suppose but that, under institutions not more perfect than those of Athens, each would produce philosophers and poets equal to those who (if we except Shakespeare) have never been surpassed. We owe the great writers of the golden age of our literature to that fervid awakening of the public mind which shook to dust the oldest and most oppressive form of the Christian Religion. We owe Milton to the progress and developement of the same spirit; the sacred Milton was, let it ever be remembered, a Republican, and a bold enquirer into morals and religion. The great writers of our own age are, we have reason to suppose, the companions and forerunners of some unimagined change in our social condition or the opinions which cement it. The cloud of mind is discharging its collected lightning, and the equilibrium between institutions and opinions is now restoring, or is about to be restored.[3]

As to imitation; Poetry is a mimetic art. It creates, but it creates by combination and representation. Poetical abstractions are beautiful and new, not because the portions of which they are composed had no previous existence in the mind of man or in nature, but because the whole produced by their combination has some intelligible and beautiful analogy with those sources of emotion and thought, and with the contemporary condition of them: one great poet is a masterpiece of nature, which another not only ought to study but must study. He might as wisely and as easily determine that his mind should no longer be the mirror of all that is lovely in the visible universe, as exclude from his contemplation the beautiful which exists in the writings of a great contemporary. The pretence of doing it would be a presumption in any but the greatest; the effect, even in him, would be strained, unnatural and ineffectual. A Poet, is the combined product of such internal powers as modify the nature of others, and of such external influences as excite and sustain these powers; he is not one, but both. Every man's mind is in this respect modified by all the objects of nature and art, by every word and every suggestion which he ever admitted to act upon his consciousness; it is the mirror upon which all forms are reflected, and in which they compose one form. Poets, not otherwise than philosophers, painters, sculptors and musicians, are in one sense the creators and in another the creations of their age. From this subjection the loftiest do not escape. There is a similarity between Homer and Hesiod, between Æschylus and Euripides, between Virgil and Horace, between Dante and Petrarch, between Shakespeare and Fletcher, between Dryden and Pope; each has a generic resemblance under which

3. See Shelley's similar tribute to his great contemporaries in the concluding paragraph of his *Defence of Poetry* (p. 802).

their specific distinctions are arranged. If this similarity be the result of imitation, I am willing to confess that I have imitated.

Let this opportunity be conceded to me of acknowledging that I have, what a Scotch philosopher characteristically terms, "a passion for reforming the world:"[4] what passion incited him to write and publish his book, he omits to explain. For my part I had rather be damned with Plato and Lord Bacon, than go to Heaven with Paley and Malthus.[5] But it is a mistake to suppose that I dedicate my poetical compositions solely to the direct enforcement of reform, or that I consider them in any degree as containing a reasoned system on the theory of human life. Didactic poetry is my abhorrence; nothing can be equally well expressed in prose that is not tedious and supererogatory in verse. My purpose has hitherto been simply to familiarise the highly refined imagination of the more select classes of poetical readers with beautiful idealisms of moral excellence; aware that until the mind can love, and admire, and trust, and hope, and endure, reasoned principles of moral conduct are seeds cast upon the highway of life which the unconscious passenger tramples into dust, although they would bear the harvest of his happiness. Should I live to accomplish what I purpose, that is, produce a systematical history of what appear to me to be the genuine elements of human society,[6] let not the advocates of injustice and superstition flatter themselves that I should take Æschylus rather than Plato as my model.

The having spoken of myself with unaffected freedom will need little apology with the candid; and let the uncandid consider that they injure me less than their own hearts and minds by misrepresentation. Whatever talents a person may possess to amuse and instruct others, be they ever so inconsiderable, he is yet bound to exert them: if his attempt be ineffectual, let the punishment of an unaccomplished purpose have been sufficient; let none trouble themselves to heap the dust of oblivion upon his efforts; the pile they raise will betray his grave which might otherwise have been unknown.

Prometheus Unbound

From Act 1

SCENE: *A Ravine of Icy Rocks in the Indian Caucasus.* PROMETHEUS *is discovered bound to the Precipice.* PANTHEA *and* IONE *are seated at his feet. Time, Night. During the Scene, Morning slowly breaks.*

PROMETHEUS   Monarch of Gods and Dæmons,[1] and all Spirits
   But One, who throng those bright and rolling Worlds
   Which Thou and I alone of living things

---

4. This is the title of chap. 16 in *The Principles of Moral Science* (1805) by the Scottish writer Robert Forsyth.
5. Thomas Malthus's *An Essay on the Principle of Population* (1798) argued that the rate of increase in population will soon exceed the rate of increase in the food supply necessary to sustain it. William Paley wrote *Evidences of Christianity* (1794), which undertakes to prove that the design apparent in natural phenomena, and especially in the

human body, entails the existence of God as the great Designer. Shelley ironically expresses his contempt for the doctrines of both these thinkers, which he conceives as arguments for accepting uncomplainingly the present state of the world.
6. Shelley did not live to write this history.
1. Demogorgon (see 2.4). "Daemons": supernatural beings, intermediary between gods and mortals. Prometheus is addressing Jupiter.

Behold with sleepless eyes! regard this Earth
5　Made multitudinous with thy slaves, whom thou
Requitest for knee-worship, prayer and praise,
And toil, and hecatombs² of broken hearts,
With fear and self contempt and barren hope;
Whilst me, who am thy foe, eyeless° in hate,　　　　　　*blinded*
10　Hast thou made reign and triumph, to thy scorn,
O'er mine own misery and thy vain revenge.—
Three thousand years of sleep-unsheltered hours
And moments—aye° divided by keen pangs　　　　　　*always*
Till they seemed years, torture and solitude,
15　Scorn and despair,—these are mine empire:—
More glorious far than that which thou surveyest
From thine unenvied throne, O Mighty God!
Almighty, had I deigned³ to share the shame
Of thine ill tyranny, and hung not here
20　Nailed to this wall of eagle-baffling mountain,
Black, wintry, dead, unmeasured; without herb,
Insect, or beast, or shape or sound of life.
Ah me, alas, pain, pain ever, forever!

No change, no pause, no hope!—Yet I endure.
25　I ask the Earth, have not the mountains felt?
I ask yon Heaven—the all-beholding Sun,
Has it not seen? The Sea, in storm or calm,
Heaven's ever-changing Shadow, spread below—
Have its deaf waves not heard my agony?
30　Ah me, alas, pain, pain ever, forever!

The crawling glaciers pierce me with the spears
Of their moon-freezing chrystals; the bright chains
Eat with their burning cold into my bones.
Heaven's winged hound, polluting from thy lips
35　His beak in poison not his own, tears up
My heart;⁴ and shapeless sights come wandering by,
The ghastly people of the realm of dream,
Mocking me: and the Earthquake-fiends are charged
To wrench the rivets from my quivering wounds
40　When the rocks split and close again behind;
While from their loud abysses howling throng
The genii of the storm, urging the rage
Of whirlwind, and afflict me with keen hail.
And yet to me welcome is Day and Night,
45　Whether one breaks the hoar frost of the morn,
Or starry, dim, and slow, the other climbs
The leaden-coloured East; for then they lead

2. Large sacrificial offerings.
3. I.e., you would have been all-powerful, if I had
deigned.

4. The vulture, tearing daily at Prometheus's
heart, was kissed by Jupiter by way of reward.

Their wingless, crawling Hours,[5] one among whom
—As some dark Priest hales° the reluctant victim—   *drags*
50   Shall drag thee, cruel King, to kiss the blood
From these pale feet,[6] which then might trample thee
If they disdained not such a prostrate slave.
Disdain? Ah no! I pity thee.[7]—What Ruin
Will hunt thee undefended through wide Heaven!
55   How will thy soul, cloven to its depth with terror,
Gape like a Hell within! I speak in grief,
Not exultation, for I hate no more,
As then, ere misery made me wise.—The Curse
Once breathed on thee I would recall. Ye Mountains,
60   Whose many-voiced Echoes, through the mist
Of cataracts, flung the thunder of that spell!
Ye icy Springs, stagnant with wrinkling frost,
Which vibrated to hear me, and then crept
Shuddering through India! Thou serenest Air,
65   Through which the Sun walks burning without beams!
And ye swift Whirlwinds, who on poised wings
Hung mute and moveless o'er yon hushed abyss,
As thunder louder than your own made rock
The orbed world! If then my words had power
70   —Though I am changed so that aught evil wish
Is dead within, although no memory be
Of what is hate—let them not lose it now![8]
What was that curse? for ye all heard me speak.[9]

                    *   *   *

PHANTASM

Fiend, I defy thee! with a calm, fixed mind,
    All that thou canst inflict I bid thee do;
Foul Tyrant both of Gods and Humankind,
265   One only being shalt thou not subdue.
            Rain then thy plagues upon me here,
            Ghastly disease and frenzying fear;
            And let alternate frost and fire
            Eat into me, and be thine ire
270   Lightning and cutting hail and legioned forms
Of furies, driving by upon the wounding storms.

Aye, do thy worst. Thou art Omnipotent.
    O'er all things but thyself I gave thee power,

---

5. The Hours were represented in Greek myth and art by human figures with wings.
6. One of a number of implied parallels between the agony of Prometheus and the passion of Christ.
7. At this early point occurs the crisis of the action: the beginning of Prometheus's change of heart from hate to compassion, consummated in lines 303–05. The rest of the symbolic drama gradually unfolds the consequences of this moral triumph—of which Prometheus himself is unaware.
8. Let my words not lose their power now.
9. In the passage here omitted, none dares, for fear of the god's vengeance, to repeat the curse Prometheus had proclaimed against Jupiter. Prometheus is finally forced to call up the Phantasm of Jupiter himself, who, in the next excerpt, repeats the words of Prometheus's curse.

　　　And my own will. Be thy swift mischiefs sent
275　　To blast mankind, from yon etherial tower.
　　　　　Let thy malignant spirit move
　　　　　Its darkness over those I love:
　　　　　On me and mine I imprecate°　　　　　　　　　　*pray for*
　　　　　The utmost torture of thy hate
280　And thus devote to sleepless agony
　　　This undeclining head while thou must reign on high.

　　　But thou who art the God and Lord—O thou
　　　　Who fillest with thy soul this world of woe,
　　　To whom all things of Earth and Heaven do bow
285　　In fear and worship—all-prevailing foe!
　　　　　I curse thee! let a sufferer's curse
　　　　　Clasp thee, his torturer, like remorse,
　　　　　Till thine Infinity shall be
　　　　　A robe of envenomed agony;[1]
290　And thine Omnipotence a crown of pain
　　　To cling like burning gold round thy dissolving brain.

　　　Heap on thy soul by virtue of this Curse
　　　　Ill deeds, then be thou damned, beholding good,
　　　Both infinite as is the Universe,
295　　And thou, and thy self-torturing solitude.
　　　　　An awful Image of calm power
　　　　　Though now thou sittest, let the hour
　　　　　Come, when thou must appear to be
　　　　　That which thou art internally.
300　And after many a false and fruitless crime
　　　Scorn track thy lagging fall through boundless space and time.
　　　　　　　　　　　　　　　　　　　[*The Phantasm vanishes.*]
PROMETHEUS　　Were these my words, O Parent?
THE EARTH　　　　　　　　　　　　　They were thine.
PROMETHEUS　　It doth repent me: words are quick and vain;
　　　Grief for awhile is blind, and so was mine.
305　I wish no living thing to suffer pain.

　　　　　　　　　　　THE EARTH
　　　　　Misery, O misery to me,
　　　　　That Jove at length should vanquish thee.[2]
　　　　　Wail, howl aloud, Land and Sea,
　　　　　The Earth's rent heart shall answer ye.
310　Howl, Spirits of the living and the dead,
　　　Your refuge, your defence lies fallen and vanquished.

　　　　　　　　　　　FIRST ECHO
　　　Lies fallen and vanquished?

1. Like the poisoned shirt of the centaur Nessus, which consumed Hercules' flesh when he put it on. The next two lines allude to the mock crowning of Christ with a crown of thorns.

2. Earth mistakes mercy for submission and, therefore, interprets Prometheus's moral victory as his defeat.

SECOND ECHO
Fallen and vanquished!

IONE[3]
Fear not—'tis but some passing spasm,
The Titan is unvanquished still.[4]

      *   *   *

FURY   Behold, an emblem—those who do endure
595   Deep wrongs for man, and scorn and chains, but heap
    Thousand-fold torment on themselves and him.
PROMETHEUS   Remit the anguish of that lighted stare—
    Close those wan lips—let that thorn-wounded brow
    Stream not with blood—it mingles with thy tears
600   Fix, fix those tortured orbs in peace and death
    So thy sick throes shake not that crucifix,
    So those pale fingers play not with thy gore.—
    O horrible! Thy name I will not speak,
    It hath become a curse.[5] I see, I see
605   The wise, the mild, the lofty and the just,
    Whom thy slaves hate for being like to thee,
    Some hunted by foul lies from their heart's home,
    An early-chosen, late-lamented home,
    As hooded ounces[6] cling to the driven hind,°   *doe*
610   Some linked to corpses in unwholesome cells:
    Some—hear I not the multitude laugh loud?—
    Impaled in lingering fire: and mighty realms
    Float by my feet like sea-uprooted isles
    Whose sons are kneaded down in common blood
615   By the red light of their own burning homes.
FURY   Blood thou canst see, and fire; and canst hear groans;
    Worse things, unheard, unseen, remain behind.
PROMETHEUS   Worse?
FURY   In each human heart terror survives
    The ravin it has gorged:[7] the loftiest fear
620   All that they would disdain to think were true:
    Hypocrisy and custom make their minds
    The fanes° of many a worship, now outworn.   *temples*
    They dare not devise good for man's estate
    And yet they know not that they do not dare.
625   The good want power, but to weep barren tears.
    The powerful goodness want: worse need for them.

---

3. Ione, Panthea, and Asia (in the following scene) are sisters and Oceanids—i.e., daughters of Oceanus.
4. In the omitted passage the herald Mercury, at Jupiter's command, brings a group of Furies (in Greek myth, avengers of crimes against the gods) who tempt Prometheus to despair by revealing the loathsome potentialities for evil in humankind's conscious and unconscious mind. In the climactic temptation a Fury tears aside a veil to reveal a rep-

resentation ("emblem," line 594) of the suffering Christ on the cross.
5. I.e., the name "Christ" has become, literally, a curse word, and metaphorically, a curse to humankind, in that His religion of love is used to justify religious wars and bloody oppression.
6. Cheetahs, or leopards, used in hunting (hoods were sometimes placed over their eyes to make them easier to control).
7. The prey that it has greedily devoured.

The wise want love, and those who love want wisdom;
And all best things are thus confused to ill.
Many are strong and rich,—and would be just,—
630 But live among their suffering fellow men
As if none felt: they know not what they do.[8]
PROMETHEUS   Thy words are like a cloud of winged snakes
And yet, I pity those they torture not.
FURY   Thou pitiest them? I speak no more!   [*Vanishes.*]
PROMETHEUS.   Ah woe!
635 Ah woe! Alas! pain, pain ever, forever!
I close my tearless eyes, but see more clear
Thy works within my woe-illumed mind,
Thou subtle Tyrant![9] . . . Peace is in the grave—
The grave hides all things beautiful and good—
640 I am a God and cannot find it there,
Nor would I seek it: for, though dread revenge,
This is defeat, fierce King, not victory.
The sights with which thou torturest gird my soul
With new endurance, till the hour arrives
645 When they shall be no types of things which are.
PANTHEA   Alas! what sawest thou?
PROMETHEUS   There are two woes:
To speak and to behold; thou spare me one.[1]
Names are there, Nature's sacred watchwords—they
Were borne aloft in bright emblazonry.[2]
650 The nations thronged around, and cried aloud
As with one voice, "Truth, liberty and love!"
Suddenly fierce confusion fell from Heaven
Among them—there was strife, deceit, and fear;
Tyrants rushed in, and did divide the spoil.
655 This was the shadow of the truth I saw.
THE EARTH   I felt thy torture, Son, with such mixed joy
As pain and Virtue give.—To cheer thy state
I bid ascend those subtle and fair spirits
Whose homes are the dim caves of human thought
660 And who inhabit, as birds wing the wind,
Its world-surrounding ether;[3] they behold
Beyond that twilight realm, as in a glass,°   mirror
The future—may they speak comfort to thee![4]

*   *   *

---

8. The Fury ironically echoes Christ's plea for forgiveness of his crucifiers: "Father, forgive them: for
they know not what they do" (Luke 23.34). Lines
625–28 are Shelley's comment on his own age of
political reaction and oppression. This passage
underlies Yeats's description of the troubled era
after World War I in The *Second Coming*, lines
3–8.
9. Jupiter (also addressed as "fierce King," line
642).

1. I.e., spare me the woe of speaking (about what
I have beheld).
2. As in a brilliant display of banners.
3. A medium, weightless and infinitely elastic,
once supposed to permeate the universe.
4. The speech of the Earth ushers in a troop of
spirits representing the noble and virtuous potentialities of the mind, on which rests the hope of a
future felicity for humanity.

From *Act 2*

SCENE 4—*The Cave of* DEMOGORGON. ASIA *and* PANTHEA.[5]

PANTHEA What veiled form sits on that ebon throne?
ASIA The veil has fallen! . . .
PANTHEA   I see a mighty Darkness
 Filling the seat of power; and rays of gloom
 Dart round, as light from the meridian Sun,
5 Ungazed upon and shapeless—neither limb
 Nor form—nor outline;[6] yet we feel it is
 A living Spirit.
DEMOGORGON Ask what thou wouldst know.
ASIA What canst thou tell?
DEMOGORGON   All things thou dar'st demand.
ASIA Who made the living world?
DEMOGORGON   God.
ASIA   Who made all
10 That it contains—thought, passion, reason, will,
 Imagination?
DEMOGORGON God, Almighty God.
ASIA Who made that sense[7] which, when the winds of Spring
 In rarest visitation, or the voice
 Of one beloved heard in youth alone,
15 Fills the faint eyes with falling tears, which dim
 The radiant looks of unbewailing flowers,
 And leaves this peopled earth a solitude
 When it returns no more?
DEMOGORGON   Merciful God.
ASIA And who made terror, madness, crime, remorse,
20 Which from the links of the great chain of things
 To every thought within the mind of man
 Sway and drag heavily—and each one reels
 Under the load towards the pit of death;
 Abandoned hope, and love that turns to hate;
25 And self-contempt, bitterer to drink than blood;
 Pain whose unheeded and familiar speech
 Is howling and keen shrieks, day after day;
 And Hell, or the sharp fear of Hell?[8]
DEMOGORGON   He reigns.

5. Act 2 has opened with Asia—the feminine principle and embodiment of love, who was separated from Prometheus at the moment of his fall into divisive hate—in a lovely Indian valley at the first hour of the dawn of the spring season of redemption. Asia and her sister Panthea have been led, by a sweet and irresistible compulsion, first to the portal and then down into the depths of the cave of Demogorgon—the central enigma of Shelley's poem.

 Commentators have usually equated Demogorgon with necessity, but the interpretation may be too confining. More flexibly, he can be thought of as process, the inexorable way in which things evolve. But the ultimate mover of that process—the ultimate reason for the way things are—must remain, Shelley skeptically insists, a mystery beyond the limits of accessible knowledge. Demogorgon is ignorant of the principle that controls him and can give merely riddling answers to Asia's questions about the "why" of creation, good, and evil.

6. Echoing Milton's description of Death, *Paradise Lost* 2.666–73.

7. Presumably the sense by which one is aware of the "unseen Power" that Shelley calls "Intellectual Beauty" (see *Hymn to Intellectual Beauty*, stanza 2, p. 724).

8. The nouns "hope," "love," etc. (lines 24–28) are all objects of the verb "made" (line 19).

ASIA   Utter his name—a world pining in pain
30   Asks but his name; curses shall drag him down.
DEMOGORGON   He reigns.
ASIA   I feel, I know it—who?
DEMOGORGON   He reigns.
ASIA   Who reigns? There was the Heaven and Earth at first
    And Light and Love;—then Saturn,[9] from whose throne
    Time fell, an envious shadow; such the state
35   Of the earth's primal spirits beneath his sway
    As the calm joy of flowers and living leaves
    Before the wind or sun has withered them
    And semivital worms; but he refused
    The birthright of their being, knowledge, power,
40   The skill which wields the elements, the thought
    Which pierces this dim Universe like light,
    Self-empire and the majesty of love,
    For thirst of which they fainted. Then Prometheus
    Gave wisdom, which is strength, to Jupiter
45   And with this law alone: "Let man be free,"
    Clothed him with the dominion of wide Heaven.
    To know nor faith nor love nor law, to be
    Omnipotent but friendless, is to reign;
    And Jove now reigned; for on the race of man
50   First famine, and then toil, and then disease,
    Strife, wounds, and ghastly death unseen before,
    Fell; and the unseasonable seasons drove,
    With alternating shafts of frost and fire,
    Their shelterless, pale tribes to mountain caves;
55   And in their desart° hearts fierce wants he sent   *empty*
    And mad disquietudes, and shadows idle
    Of unreal good, which levied mutual war,
    So ruining the lair wherein they raged.
    Prometheus saw, and waked the legioned hopes
60   Which sleep within folded Elysian flowers,
    Nepenthe, Moly, Amaranth,[1] fadeless blooms;
    That they might hide with thin and rainbow wings
    The shape of Death; and Love he sent to bind
    The disunited tendrils of that vine
65   Which bears the wine of life, the human heart;
    And he tamed fire which, like some beast of prey,
    Most terrible, but lovely, played beneath
    The frown of man, and tortured to his will
    Iron and gold, the slaves and signs of power,
70   And gems and poisons, and all subtlest forms,
    Hidden beneath the mountains and the waves.

9. In Greek myth Saturn's reign was the golden age. In Shelley's version Saturn refused to grant mortals knowledge and science, so that it was an age of ignorant innocence in which the deepest human needs remained unfulfilled.

1. These are medicinal drugs and flowers in Greek myth. Asia is describing (lines 59–97) the various sciences and arts given to humans by Prometheus, the culture bringer.

He gave man speech, and speech created thought,
Which is the measure of the Universe;
And Science struck the thrones of Earth and Heaven
75   Which shook, but fell not; and the harmonious mind
Poured itself forth in all-prophetic song,
And music lifted up the listening spirit
Until it walked, exempt from mortal care,
Godlike, o'er the clear billows of sweet sound;
80   And human hands first mimicked and then mocked[2]
With moulded limbs more lovely than its own
The human form, till marble grew divine,
And mothers, gazing, drank the love men see
Reflected in their race, behold, and perish.[3]—
85   He told the hidden power of herbs and springs,
And Disease drank and slept—Death grew like sleep.—
He taught the implicated° orbits woven   *intertwined*
Of the wide-wandering stars, and how the Sun
Changes his lair, and by what secret spell
90   The pale moon is transformed, when her broad eye
Gazes not on the interlunar[4] sea;
He taught to rule, as life directs the limbs,
The tempest-winged chariots of the Ocean,
And the Celt knew the Indian.[5] Cities then
95   Were built, and through their snow-like columns flowed
The warm winds, and the azure æther shone,
And the blue sea and shadowy hills were seen . . .
Such the alleviations of his state
Prometheus gave to man—for which he hangs
100   Withering in destined pain—but who rains down
Evil, the immedicable plague, which while
Man looks on his creation like a God
And sees that it is glorious, drives him on,
The wreck of his own will, the scorn of Earth,
105   The outcast, the abandoned, the alone?—
Not Jove: while yet his frown shook Heaven, aye when
His adversary from adamantine chains
Cursed him, he trembled like a slave. Declare
Who is his master? Is he too a slave?
110 DEMOGORGON   All spirits are enslaved which serve things evil:
    Thou knowest if Jupiter be such or no.
ASIA   Whom calledst thou God?
DEMOGORGON   I spoke but as ye speak—
    For Jove is the supreme of living things.
ASIA   Who is the master of the slave?
DEMOGORGON   —If the Abysm

---

2. I.e., sculptors first merely reproduced but later improved on ("mocked" in the sense of "heightened") the beauty of the human form.
3. Expectant mothers looked at the beautiful statues so that their children might, by prenatal influence, be born with the beauty that makes beholders die of love.
4. The phase between old and new moons, when the moon is invisible.
5. The reference is to the ships in which the Celtic (here, non-Greco-Roman) races of Europe were able to sail to India.

115 Could vomit forth its secrets:—but a voice
Is wanting, the deep truth is imageless;[6]
For what would it avail to bid thee gaze
On the revolving world? what to bid speak
Fate, Time, Occasion, Chance and Change? To these
120 All things are subject but eternal Love.
ASIA   So much I asked before, and my heart gave
The response thou hast given; and of such truths
Each to itself must be the oracle.—
One more demand . . . and do thou answer me
125 As my own soul would answer, did it know
That which I ask.—Prometheus shall arise
Henceforth the Sun of this rejoicing world:
When shall the destined hour arrive?
DEMOGORGON   Behold![7]
ASIA   The rocks are cloven, and through the purple night
130 I see Cars drawn by rainbow-winged steeds
Which trample the dim winds—in each there stands
A wild-eyed charioteer, urging their flight.
Some look behind, as fiends pursued them there
And yet I see no shapes but the keen stars:
135 Others with burning eyes lean forth, and drink
With eager lips the wind of their own speed,
As if the thing they loved fled on before,
And now—even now they clasped it; their bright locks
Stream like a comet's flashing hair: they all
140 Sweep onward.—
DEMOGORGON   These are the immortal Hours
Of whom thou didst demand.—One waits for thee.
ASIA   A Spirit with a dreadful countenance
Checks its dark chariot by the craggy gulph.
Unlike thy brethren, ghastly charioteer,
145 What art thou? whither wouldst thou bear me? Speak!
SPIRIT   I am the shadow of a destiny
More dread than is my aspect—ere yon planet
Has set, the Darkness[8] which ascends with me
Shall wrap in lasting night Heaven's kingless throne.
ASIA   What meanest thou?
150 PANTHEA   That terrible shadow floats
Up from its throne, as may the lurid° smoke   *red-glaring*
Of earthquake-ruined cities o'er the sea.—
Lo! it ascends the Car . . . the coursers fly
Terrified; watch its path among the stars
Blackening the night!
155 ASIA   Thus I am answered—strange!
PANTHEA   See, near the verge° another chariot stays;   *horizon*
An ivory shell inlaid with crimson fire

6. I.e., ultimate truths can be neither known nor expressed.
7. Demogorgon's answer is a gesture: he points to the approaching chariots ("Cars").
8. Demogorgon, who is ascending (lines 150–55) to effect the dethronement of Jupiter.

Which comes and goes within its sculptured rim
Of delicate strange tracery—the young Spirit
160 That guides it, has the dovelike eyes of hope.
How its soft smiles attract the soul!—as light
Lures winged insects⁹ through the lampless air.

SPIRIT

My coursers are fed with the lightning,
  They drink of the whirlwind's stream
165 And when the red morning is brightning
  They bathe in the fresh sunbeam;
  They have strength for their swiftness, I deem:
  Then ascend with me, daughter of Ocean.

I desire—and their speed makes night kindle;
170 I fear—they outstrip the Typhoon;
Ere the cloud piled on Atlas¹ can dwindle
  We encircle the earth and the moon:
  We shall rest from long labours at noon:
  Then ascend with me, daughter of Ocean.

SCENE 5—*The Car pauses within a Cloud on the Top of a snowy Mountain.*
ASIA, PANTHEA, *and the* SPIRIT OF THE HOUR.

SPIRIT

On the brink of the night and the morning
  My coursers are wont to respire,²
But the Earth has just whispered a warning
  That their flight must be swifter than fire:
5   They shall drink the hot speed of desire!

ASIA Thou breathest on their nostrils—but my breath
  Would give them swifter speed.
SPIRIT   Alas, it could not.
PANTHEA O Spirit! pause and tell whence is the light
  Which fills the cloud? the sun is yet unrisen.
10 SPIRIT The sun will rise not until noon.³—Apollo
  Is held in Heaven by wonder—and the light
  Which fills this vapour, as the aerial hue
  Of fountain-gazing roses fills the water,
  Flows from thy mighty sister.
PANTHEA   Yes, I feel . . .
15 ASIA What is it with thee, sister? Thou art pale.
PANTHEA How thou art changed! I dare not look on thee;
  I feel, but see thee not. I scarce endure

---

9. The ancient image of the soul, or *psyche,* was a
moth. The chariot described here will carry Asia to
a reunion with Prometheus.
1. A mountain in North Africa that the Greeks

regarded as so high that it supported the heavens.
2. Catch their breath.
3. The time of the reunion of Prometheus and
Asia.

The radiance of thy beauty.[4] Some good change
Is working in the elements which suffer
20 Thy presence thus unveiled.—The Nereids tell
That on the day when the clear hyaline°   *glassy sea*
Was cloven at thy uprise, and thou didst stand
Within a veined shell,[5] which floated on
Over the calm floor of the chrystal sea,
25 Among the Ægean isles, and by the shores
Which bear thy name, love, like the atmosphere
Of the sun's fire filling the living world,
Burst from thee, and illumined Earth and Heaven
And the deep ocean and the sunless caves,
30 And all that dwells within them; till grief cast
Eclipse upon the soul from which it came:
Such art thou now, nor is it I alone,
Thy sister, thy companion, thine own chosen one,
But the whole world which seeks thy sympathy.
35 Hearest thou not sounds i' the air which speak the love
Of all articulate beings? Feelest thou not
The inanimate winds enamoured of thee?—List!   [*Music.*]
ASIA   Thy words are sweeter than aught else but his
Whose echoes they are—yet all love is sweet,
40 Given or returned; common as light is love
And its familiar voice wearies not ever.
Like the wide Heaven, the all-sustaining air,
It makes the reptile equal to the God . . .
They who inspire it most are fortunate
45 As I am now; but those who feel it most
Are happier still, after long sufferings
As I shall soon become.
PANTHEA   List! Spirits speak.

VOICE (*in the air, singing*)[6]
    Life of Life! thy lips enkindle
        With their love the breath between them
50 And thy smiles before they dwindle
        Make the cold air fire; then screen them
    In those looks where whoso gazes
    Faints, entangled in their mazes.

    Child of Light! thy limbs are burning
55   Through the vest which seems to hide them
    As the radiant lines of morning
        Through the clouds ere they divide them,

4. In an earlier scene Panthea had envisioned in a dream the radiant and eternal inner form of Prometheus emerging through his "wound-worn limbs." The corresponding transfiguration of Asia, prepared for by her descent to the underworld, now takes place.
5. The story told by the Nereids (sea nymphs) serves to associate Asia with Aphrodite, goddess of love, emerging (as in Botticelli's painting) from the Mediterranean on a seashell.
6. The voice attempts to describe, in a dizzying whirl of optical paradoxes, what it feels like to look on the naked essence of love and beauty.

And this atmosphere divinest
Shrouds thee wheresoe'er thou shinest.

60   Fair are others;—none beholds thee
     But thy voice sounds low and tender
   Like the fairest, for it folds thee
     From the sight, that liquid splendour,
   And all feel, yet see thee never
65   As I feel now, lost forever!

   Lamp of Earth! where'er thou movest
     Its dim shapes are clad with brightness
   And the souls of whom thou lovest
     Walk upon the winds with lightness
70   Till they fail, as I am failing,
   Dizzy, lost . . . yet unbewailing!

ASIA

   My soul is an enchanted Boat
   Which, like a sleeping swan, doth float
Upon the silver waves of thy sweet singing,
75   And thine doth like an Angel sit
     Beside the helm conducting it
Whilst all the winds with melody are ringing.
     It seems to float ever—forever—
     Upon that many winding River
80   Between mountains, woods, abysses,
     A Paradise of wildernesses,
Till like one in slumber bound
Borne to the Ocean, I float down, around,
Into a Sea profound, of ever-spreading sound.

85   Meanwhile thy spirit lifts its pinions°   *wings*
     In Music's most serene dominions,
Catching the winds that fan that happy Heaven.
     And we sail on, away, afar,
     Without a course—without a star—
90 But by the instinct of sweet Music driven
     Till, through Elysian garden islets
     By thee, most beautiful of pilots,
     Where never mortal pinnace° glided,   *small boat*
     The boat of my desire is guided—
95 Realms where the air we breathe is Love
Which in the winds and on the waves doth move,
Harmonizing this Earth with what we feel above.

     We have past Age's icy caves,
     And Manhood's dark and tossing waves
100   And Youth's smooth ocean, smiling to betray;
     Beyond the glassy gulphs we flee

Of shadow-peopled Infancy,
Through Death and Birth to a diviner day,[7]
A Paradise of vaulted bowers
105   Lit by downward-gazing flowers
And watery paths that wind between
Wildernesses calm and green,
Peopled by shapes too bright to see,
And rest, having beheld—somewhat like thee,
110   Which walk upon the sea, and chaunt melodiously!

From *Act 3*

SCENE 1—*Heaven.* JUPITER *on his Throne;* THETIS *and the other Deities assembled.*

JUPITER   Ye congregated Powers of Heaven who share
The glory and the strength of him ye serve,
Rejoice! henceforth I am omnipotent.
All else had been subdued to me—alone
5   The soul of man, like unextinguished fire,
Yet burns towards Heaven with fierce reproach and doubt
And lamentation and reluctant prayer,
Hurling up insurrection, which might make
Our antique empire insecure, though built
10   On eldest faith, and Hell's coeval,[8] fear.
And though my curses through the pendulous° air   *suspending*
Like snow on herbless peaks, fall flake by flake
And cling to it[9]—though under my wrath's night
It climb the crags of life, step after step,
15   Which wound it, as ice wounds unsandalled feet,
It yet remains supreme o'er misery,
Aspiring . . . unrepressed; yet soon to fall:
Even now have I begotten a strange wonder,
That fatal Child,[1] the terror of the Earth,
20   Who waits but till the destined Hour arrive,
Bearing from Demogorgon's vacant throne
The dreadful might of ever living limbs
Which clothed that awful spirit unbeheld—
To redescend, and trample out the spark[2] . . .

25   Pour forth Heaven's wine, Idæan Ganymede,
And let it fill the dædal[3] cups like fire
And from the flower-inwoven soil divine
Ye all triumphant harmonies arise

---

7. Asia is describing what it feels like to be transfigured—in the image of moving backward in the stream of time, through youth and infancy and birth itself, in order to die to this life and be born again to a "diviner" existence.
8. Of the same age.
9. "It" (as also in lines 14 and 16) is "the soul of man" (line 5).
1. The son of Jupiter and Thetis. Jupiter believes

that he has begotten a child who will assume the bodily form of the conquered Demogorgon and then return to announce his victory and the defeat of the resistance of Prometheus.
2. Of Prometheus's defiance.
3. Skillfully wrought (from the name of the Greek craftsman Daedalus). Ganymede (line 25) had been seized on Mount Ida by an eagle and carried to heaven to be Jupiter's cupbearer.

As dew from Earth under the twilight stars;
30 Drink! be the nectar circling through your veins
The soul of joy, ye everliving Gods,
Till exultation burst in one wide voice
Like music from Elysian winds.—

                                    And thou
Ascend beside me, veiled in the light
35 Of the desire which makes thee one with me,
Thetis, bright Image of Eternity!—
When thou didst cry, "Insufferable might!"[4]
God! spare me! I sustain not the quick flames,
The penetrating presence; all my being,
40 Like him whom the Numidian seps[5] did thaw
Into a dew with poison, is dissolved,
Sinking through its foundations"—even then
Two mighty spirits, mingling, made a third
Mightier than either—which unbodied now
45 Between us, floats, felt although unbeheld,
Waiting the incarnation, which ascends—
Hear ye the thunder of the fiery wheels
Griding[6] the winds?—from Demogorgon's throne.—
Victory! victory! Feel'st thou not, O World,
50 The Earthquake of his chariot thundering up
Olympus?
            [*The Car of the* HOUR *arrives.* DEMOGORGON *descends and moves
            towards the Throne of* JUPITER.]
            Awful Shape, what art thou? Speak!
DEMOGORGON   Eternity—demand no direr name.
Descend, and follow me down the abyss;
I am thy child,[7] as thou wert Saturn's child,
55 Mightier than thee; and we must dwell together
Henceforth in darkness.—Lift thy lightnings not.
The tyranny of Heaven none may retain,
Or reassume, or hold succeeding thee . . .
Yet if thou wilt—as 'tis the destiny
60 Of trodden worms to writhe till they are dead—
Put forth thy might.
JUPITER   Detested prodigy!
Even thus beneath the deep Titanian prisons[8]
I trample thee! . . . thou lingerest?
                                    Mercy! mercy!
No pity—no release, no respite! . . . Oh,
65 That thou wouldst make mine enemy my judge.
Even where he hangs, seared by my long revenge
On Caucasus—he would not doom me thus.—

4. This description of the sexual union of Jupiter and Thetis is a grotesque parody of the reunion of Prometheus and Asia.
5. A serpent of Numidia (North Africa) whose bite was thought to cause putrefaction.
6. Cutting with a rasping sound.
7. Ironically, and in a figurative sense: Demogorgon's function follows from Jupiter's actions.
8. After they overthrew the Titans, Jupiter and the Olympian gods imprisoned them in Tartarus, deep beneath the earth.

Gentle and just and dreadless, is he not
The monarch of the world?[9] what then art thou? . . .
No refuge! no appeal— . . .
70   Sink with me then—
We two will sink in the wide waves of ruin
Even as a vulture and a snake outspent
Drop, twisted in inextricable fight,[1]
Into a shoreless sea.—Let Hell unlock
75 Its mounded Oceans of tempestuous fire,
And whelm on them into the bottomless void
The desolated world and thee and me,
The conqueror and the conquered, and the wreck
Of that for which they combated.
                        Ai! Ai!
80 The elements obey me not . . . I sink . . .
Dizzily down—ever, forever, down—
And, like a cloud, mine enemy above
Darkens my fall with victory!—Ai! Ai!

From SCENE 4—*A Forest. In the Background a Cave.* PROMETHEUS, ASIA, PAN-
THEA, IONE, *and the* SPIRIT OF THE EARTH.[2]

                            *   *   *

[*The* SPIRIT OF THE HOUR *enters.*]
PROMETHEUS   We feel what thou hast heard and seen—yet speak.
SPIRIT OF THE HOUR   Soon as the sound had ceased whose thunder filled
    The abysses of the sky, and the wide earth,
100   There was a change . . . the impalpable thin air
    And the all-circling sunlight were transformed
    As if the sense of love dissolved in them
    Had folded itself round the sphered world.
    My vision then grew clear and I could see
105   Into the mysteries of the Universe.[3]
    Dizzy as with delight I floated down,
    Winnowing the lightsome air with languid plumes,
    My coursers sought their birthplace in the sun
    Where they henceforth will live exempt from toil,
110   Pasturing flowers of vegetable fire—
    And where my moonlike car will stand within
    A temple, gazed upon by Phidian forms,[4]

9. The ultimate irony: Jupiter appeals to those very qualities of Prometheus for which he has hitherto persecuted him, begging for a mercy that Prometheus has already granted him, but Prometheus's change from vengefulness to mercy is in fact the cause of Jupiter's present downfall.
1. The eagle (or vulture) and the snake locked in equal combat—a favorite Shelleyan image (cf. *Alastor*, lines 227–32, p. 000).
2. After Jupiter's annihilation (described in scene 2), Hercules unbinds Prometheus, who is reunited with Asia and retires to a cave "where we will sit and talk of time and change / . . . ourselves

unchanged." In the speech that concludes the act (reprinted here) the Spirit of the Hour describes what happened in the human world when he sounded the apocalyptic trumpet.
3. I.e., the earth's atmosphere clarifies, no longer refracting the sunlight, and so allows the Spirit of the Hour to see what is happening on earth.
4. The crescent-shaped ("moonlike") chariot, its apocalyptic mission accomplished, will be frozen to stone and will be surrounded by the sculptured forms of other agents in the drama. Phidias (5th century B.C.E.) was the noblest of Greek sculptors.

Of thee, and Asia and the Earth, and me
And you fair nymphs, looking the love we feel,
115 In memory of the tidings it has borne,
Beneath a dome fretted with graven flowers,
Poised on twelve columns of resplendent stone
And open to the bright and liquid sky.
Yoked to it by an amphisæbnic snake[5]
120 The likeness of those winged steeds will mock[6]
The flight from which they find repose.—Alas,
Whither has wandered now my partial[7] tongue
When all remains untold which ye would hear!—
As I have said, I floated to the Earth:
125 It was, as it is still, the pain of bliss
To move, to breathe, to be; I wandering went
Among the haunts and dwellings of mankind
And first was disappointed not to see
Such mighty change as I had felt within
130 Expressed in outward things; but soon I looked,
And behold! thrones were kingless, and men walked
One with the other even as spirits do,
None fawned, none trampled; hate, disdain or fear,
Self-love or self-contempt on human brows
135 No more inscribed, as o'er the gate of hell,
"All hope abandon, ye who enter here";[8]
None frowned, none trembled, none with eager fear
Gazed on another's eye of cold command
Until the subject of a tyrant's will
140 Became, worse fate, the abject of his own[9]
Which spurred him, like an outspent horse, to death.
None wrought his lips in truth-entangling lines
Which smiled the lie his tongue disdained to speak;
None with firm sneer trod out in his own heart
145 The sparks of love and hope, till there remained
Those bitter ashes, a soul self-consumed,
And the wretch crept, a vampire among men,
Infecting all with his own hideous ill.
None talked that common, false, cold, hollow talk
150 Which makes the heart deny the *yes* it breathes
Yet question that unmeant hypocrisy
With such a self-mistrust as has no name.
And women too, frank, beautiful and kind
As the free Heaven which rains fresh light and dew
155 On the wide earth, past: gentle, radiant forms,
From custom's evil taint exempt and pure;
Speaking the wisdom once they could not think,

5. A mythical snake with a head at each end; it serves here as a symbolic warning that a reversal of the process is always possible.
6. "Imitate" and also, in their immobility, "mock at" the flight they represent.

7. Biased or, possibly, telling only part of the story.
8. The inscription over the gate of hell in Dante's *Inferno* 3.9.
9. I.e., he was so abjectly enslaved that his own will accorded with the tyrant's will.

Looking emotions once they feared to feel
And changed to all which once they dared not be,
160 Yet being now, made Earth like Heaven—nor pride
Nor jealousy nor envy nor ill shame,
The bitterest of those drops of treasured gall,
Spoilt the sweet taste of the nepenthe,[1] love.

Thrones, altars, judgement-seats and prisons; wherein
165 And beside which, by wretched men were borne
Sceptres, tiaras, swords and chains, and tomes
Of reasoned wrong glozed on[2] by ignorance,
Were like those monstrous and barbaric shapes,
The ghosts of a no more remembered fame,
170 Which from their unworn obelisks[3] look forth
In triumph o'er the palaces and tombs
Of those who were their conquerors, mouldering round.
Those imaged to the pride of Kings and Priests
A dark yet mighty faith, a power as wide
175 As is the world it wasted, and are now
But an astonishment; even so the tools
And emblems of its last captivity
Amid the dwellings of the peopled Earth,
Stand, not o'erthrown, but unregarded now.
180 And those foul shapes, abhorred by God and man—
Which under many a name and many a form
Strange, savage, ghastly, dark and execrable
Were Jupiter,[4] the tyrant of the world;
And which the nations panic-stricken served
185 With blood, and hearts broken by long hope, and love
Dragged to his altars soiled and garlandless
And slain amid men's unreclaiming tears,
Flattering the thing they feared, which fear was hate—
Frown, mouldering fast, o'er their abandoned shrines.
190 The painted veil, by those who were, called life,[5]
Which mimicked, as with colours idly spread,
All men believed and hoped, is torn aside—
The loathsome mask has fallen, the man remains
Sceptreless, free, uncircumscribed—but man:
195 Equal, unclassed, tribeless, and nationless,
Exempt from awe, worship, degree,—the King
Over himself; just, gentle, wise—but man:
Passionless? no—yet free from guilt or pain
Which were, for his will made, or suffered them,
200 Nor yet exempt, though ruling them like slaves,

1. A drug (probably opium) that brings forgetfulness of pain and sorrow.
2. Annotated, explained.
3. The Egyptian obelisks (tapering shafts of stone), brought to Rome by its conquering armies, included hieroglyphs that—because they were still undeciphered in Shelley's time—seemed "monstrous and barbaric shapes" (line 168).
4. The "foul shapes" (line 180) were statues of the gods who, whatever their names, were all really manifestations of Jupiter.
5. I.e., which was thought to be life by humans as they were before their regeneration.

From chance and death and mutability,
The clogs of that which else might oversoar
The loftiest star of unascended Heaven
Pinnacled dim in the intense inane.[6]

From Act 4[7]

SCENE—*A Part of the Forest near the Cave of* PROMETHEUS.

* * *

IONE   Even whilst we speak
185   New notes arise . . . What is that awful sound?
PANTHEA   'Tis the deep music of the rolling world,
       Kindling within the strings of the waved air
       Æolian modulations.[8]
IONE   Listen too,
       How every pause is filled with under-notes,
190   Clear, silver, icy, keen, awakening tones
       Which pierce the sense and live within the soul
       As the sharp stars pierce Winter's chrystal air
       And gaze upon themselves within the sea.
PANTHEA   But see, where through two openings in the forest
195   Which hanging branches overcanopy,
       And where two runnels of a rivulet
       Between the close moss violet-inwoven
       Have made their path of melody, like sisters
       Who part with sighs that they may meet in smiles,
200   Turning their dear disunion to an isle
       Of lovely grief, a wood of sweet sad thoughts;
       Two visions of strange radiance float upon
       The Ocean-like inchantment of strong sound
       Which flows intenser, keener, deeper yet
205   Under the ground and through the windless air.
IONE   I see a chariot like that thinnest boat
       In which the Mother of the Months is borne
       By ebbing light into her western cave
       When she upsprings from interlunar dreams,[9]

6. I.e., a dim point in the extreme of empty space. The sense of lines 198–204 is if regenerate man were to be released from all earthly and biological impediments ("clogs"), he would become what even the stars are not—a pure ideal.

7. The original drama, completed in the spring of 1819, consisted of three acts. Later that year Shelley added a jubilant fourth act. In Revelation 21, the apocalyptic replacement of the old world by "a new heaven and new earth" had been symbolized by the marriage of the Lamb with the New Jerusalem. Shelley's fourth act, somewhat like the conclusion of Blake's *Jerusalem*, expands this figure into a cosmic epithalamion, representing a union of divided elements that enacts everywhere the reunion of Prometheus and Asia taking place offstage.

   Shelley's model is the Renaissance masque, which combines song and dance with spectacular displays. Panthea and Ione serve as commentators on the action, which is divided into three episodes. In the first episode, omitted here, the purified

"Spirits of the human mind" unite in a ritual dance with the Hours of the glad new day. In the second episode (lines 194–318), there appear emblematic representations of the moon and the earth, each bearing an infant whose hour has come round at last. Shelley based this description in part on Ezekiel 1, the vision of the chariot of divine glory, which had traditionally been interpreted as a portent of apocalypse. The third episode (lines 319–502) is the bacchanalian dance of the love-intoxicated Moon around her brother and paramour, the rejuvenescent Earth. By way of coda (line 549 to the end), Demogorgon calls on all beings to hear his proclamation of the moral significance of this great drama of humanity's self-betrayal and self-redemption.

8. Evoking music like that of the Eolian harp.

9. I.e., the chariot is a thin crescent shape, like the new Moon, when it carries within it the outline of the old Moon ("Mother of the Months") to the cave where she is reborn during the "interlunar" period—i.e., when the Moon is entirely invisible.

210 O'er which is curved an orblike canopy
Of gentle darkness, and the hills and woods
Distinctly seen through that dusk aery veil
Regard° like shapes in an enchanter's glass;   *look*
Its wheels are solid clouds, azure and gold,
215 Such as the genii of the thunderstorm
Pile on the floor of the illumined sea
When the Sun rushes under it; they roll
And move and grow as with an inward wind.
Within it sits a winged Infant, white
220 Its countenance, like the whiteness of bright snow,
Its plumes are as feathers of sunny frost,
Its limbs gleam white, through the wind-flowing folds
Of its white robe, woof of ætherial pearl.
Its hair is white,—the brightness of white light
225 Scattered in strings,[1] yet its two eyes are Heavens
Of liquid darkness, which the Deity
Within, seems pouring, as a storm is poured
From jagged clouds, out of their arrowy lashes,
Tempering the cold and radiant air around
230 With fire that is not brightness;[2] in its hand
It sways a quivering moonbeam, from whose point
A guiding power directs the chariot's prow
Over its wheeled clouds, which as they roll
Over the grass and flowers and waves, wake sounds
235 Sweet as a singing rain of silver dew.
PANTHEA   And from the other opening in the wood
Rushes with loud and whirlwind harmony
A sphere, which is as many thousand spheres,
Solid as chrystal, yet through all its mass
240 Flow, as through empty space, music and light:
Ten thousand orbs involving and involved,[3]
Purple and azure, white and green and golden,
Sphere within sphere, and every space between
Peopled with unimaginable shapes
245 Such as ghosts dream dwell in the lampless deep
Yet each intertranspicuous,[4] and they whirl
Over each other with a thousand motions
Upon a thousand sightless° axles spinning   *invisible*
And with the force of self-destroying swiftness,
250 Intensely, slowly, solemnly roll on—

1. The infant resembles "one like unto the Son of man" in Revelation 1.14: "His head and his hairs were white like wool, as white as snow." The description that follows, of the light radiated from the infant's eyes, echoes the description in Ezekiel's vision, 1.27–28, of the "brightness round about" that "was the appearance of the likeness of the glory of the Lord."

2. Shelley knew, from the account by Sir Humphry Davy, Herschel's discovery (1800) that there are what Herschel called "dark rays"—i.e., infrared radiation; Davy suggested that the moon gave off such rays.

3. The transparent sphere is an emblem of earth. The description of its spinning and that of its interior orbs echoes both Ezekiel 1.16—"the appearance of the wheels and their work . . . was as it were a wheel in the middle of a wheel"—and *Paradise Lost* 5.620–24, which describes the "mystical dance" of the angels in heaven, whose movements resemble the revolving spheres of the planets: "mazes intricate, / Eccentric, intervolved, yet regular / Then most, when most irregular they seem."

4. Transparent, so that each can be seen through the others.

Kindling with mingled sounds, and many tones,
Intelligible words and music wild.—
With mighty whirl the multitudinous Orb
Grinds the bright brook into an azure mist
255   Of elemental subtlety, like light,
And the wild odour of the forest flowers,
The music of the living grass and air,
The emerald light of leaf-entangled beams
Round its intense, yet self-conflicting[5] speed,
260   Seem kneaded into one aerial mass
Which drowns the sense. Within the Orb itself,
Pillowed upon its alabaster arms
Like to a child o'erwearied with sweet toil,
On its own folded wings and wavy hair
265   The Spirit of the Earth is laid asleep,
And you can see its little lips are moving
Amid the changing light of their own smiles
Like one who talks of what he loves in dream—
IONE   'Tis only mocking° the Orb's harmony . . .   *imitating*
270 PANTHEA   And from a star upon its forehead, shoot,
Like swords of azure fire, or golden spears
With tyrant-quelling myrtle[6] overtwined,
Embleming Heaven and Earth united now,
Vast beams like spokes of some invisible wheel
275   Which whirl as the Orb whirls, swifter than thought,
Filling the abyss with sunlike lightenings,
And perpendicular now, and now transverse,
Pierce the dark soil, and as they pierce and pass
Make bare the secrets of the Earth's deep heart,[7]
280   Infinite mine of adamant[8] and gold,
Valueless° stones and unimagined gems,   *priceless*
And caverns on chrystalline columns poised
With vegetable silver overspread,
Wells of unfathomed fire, and watersprings
285   Whence the great Sea, even as a child, is fed
Whose vapours clothe Earth's monarch mountain-tops
With kingly, ermine snow; the beams flash on
And make appear the melancholy ruins
Of cancelled cycles;[9] anchors, beaks of ships,
290   Planks turned to marble, quivers, helms° and spears   *helmets*
And gorgon-headed targes,[1] and the wheels
Of scythed chariots,[2] and the emblazonry
Of trophies, standards and armorial beasts[3]
Round which Death laughed, sepulchred emblems

---

5. Because its component spheres are spinning in opposed directions.
6. The myrtle, sacred to Venus, symbolizes love.
7. I.e., the star on the infant's forehead radiates penetrating beams that (like modern X rays) reveal what lies beneath the surface of the earth.
8. Very hard rock.
9. I.e., of civilizations that flourished, then disappeared.
1. Shields embossed with a gorgon's head.
2. Ancient war chariots sometimes had steel blades fastened to the wheels.
3. Animals in heraldic insignia.

295 Of dead Destruction, ruin within ruin!
The wrecks beside of many a city vast,
Whose population which the Earth grew over
Was mortal but not human;[4] see, they lie,
Their monstrous works and uncouth skeletons,
300 Their statues, homes, and fanes;° prodigious shapes   *temples*
Huddled in grey annihilation, split,
Jammed in the hard black deep; and over these
The anatomies° of unknown winged things,   *skeletons*
And fishes which were isles of living scale,
305 And serpents, bony chains, twisted around
The iron crags, or within heaps of dust
To which the tortuous strength of their last pangs
Had crushed the iron crags;—and over these
The jagged alligator and the might
310 Of earth-convulsing behemoth,[5] which once
Were monarch beasts, and on the slimy shores
And weed-overgrown continents of Earth
Increased and multiplied like summer worms
On an abandoned corpse, till the blue globe
315 Wrapt Deluge round it like a cloak, and they
Yelled, gaspt and were abolished; or some God
Whose throne was in a Comet, past, and cried—
"Be not!"—and like my words they were no more.[6]

THE EARTH

The joy, the triumph, the delight, the madness,
320 The boundless, overflowing, bursting gladness,
The vaporous exultation, not to be confined![7]
    Ha! ha! the animation of delight
    Which wraps me, like an atmosphere of light,
And bears me as a cloud is borne by its own wind!

THE MOON

325   Brother mine, calm wanderer,
    Happy globe of land and air,
Some Spirit[8] is darted like a beam from thee,
    Which penetrates my frozen frame
    And passes with the warmth of flame—
330   With love and odour and deep melody
    Through me, through me!—

4. That is, a prehuman race of beings that once overspread the earth.
5. The huge land animal described in Job 40.15–24.
6. According to the theory of "Catastrophism" proposed by G. F. Cuvier, *Researches on Fossil Bones* (1812), successive geologic layers of fossils are evidence of a sequence of catastrophes—volcanic upheavals and gigantic floods—each of which wiped out the forms of life that then existed. Shelley proposes two hypotheses (lines 314–18): either such floods originated from some cataclysm on earth or they were prodigious tides caused by the gravitational pull of a passing comet.

In writing this passage, Shelley recalled Keats's *Endymion* 3.123–36, which described the remains on the ocean floor of extinct cultures and animal species.
7. Literally, the earth's gases are bursting out through its volcanoes.
8. Physically, the gravitational force exerted by the earth on the satellite moon.

THE EARTH

Ha! ha! the caverns of my hollow mountains,
My cloven fire-crags, sound-exulting fountains
Laugh with a vast and inextinguishable laughter.
335   The Oceans and the Desarts and the Abysses
    And the deep air's unmeasured wildernesses
Answer from all their clouds and billows, echoing after.

    They cry aloud as I do—"Sceptred Curse,°   *Jupiter*
    Who all our green and azure Universe
340 Threatenedst to muffle round with black destruction, sending
    A solid cloud to rain hot thunderstones,
    And splinter and knead down my children's bones,
All I bring forth, to one void mass battering and blending,

    "Until each craglike tower and storied column,
345   Palace and Obelisk and Temple solemn,
My imperial mountains crowned with cloud and snow and fire,
    My sea-like forests, every blade and blossom
    Which finds a grave or cradle in my bosom,
Were stamped by thy strong hate into a lifeless mire,

350   "How art thou sunk, withdrawn, cover'd—drunk up
    By thirsty nothing, as the brackish° cup   *slightly salty*
Drained by a Desart-troop—a little drop for all;
    And from beneath, around, within, above,
    Filling thy void annihilation, Love
355 Bursts in like light on caves cloven by the thunderball."

THE MOON

    The snow upon my lifeless mountains
    Is loosened into living fountains,
    My solid Oceans flow and sing and shine
    A spirit from my heart bursts forth,
360   It clothes with unexpected birth
    My cold bare bosom: Oh! it must be thine
    On mine, on mine!

    Gazing on thee I feel, I know,
    Green stalks burst forth, and bright flowers grow
365   And living shapes upon my bosom move:
    Music is in the sea and air,
    Winged clouds soar here and there,
    Dark with the rain new buds are dreaming of:
    'Tis Love, all Love!

THE EARTH

370   It interpenetrates my granite mass,
    Through tangled roots and trodden clay doth pass
Into the utmost leaves and delicatest flowers;
    Upon the winds, among the clouds 'tis spread,
    It wakes a life in the forgotten dead,
375 They breathe a spirit up from their obscurest bowers

And like a storm, bursting its cloudy prison
With thunder and with whirlwind, has arisen
Out of the lampless caves of unimagined being,
With earthquake shock and swiftness making shiver
380 Thought's stagnant chaos, unremoved forever,
Till Hate and Fear and Pain, light-vanquished shadows, fleeing,

Leave Man, who was a many-sided mirror
Which could distort to many a shape of error
This true fair world of things—a Sea reflecting Love;
385 Which over all his kind, as the Sun's Heaven
Gliding o'er Ocean, smooth, serene and even,
Darting from starry depths radiance and light, doth move,

Leave Man, even as a leprous child is left
Who follows a sick beast to some warm cleft
390 Of rocks, through which the might of healing springs is poured:
Then when it wanders home with rosy smile
Unconscious, and its mother fears awhile
It is a Spirit—then weeps on her child restored.[9]

Man, oh, not men![1] a chain of linked thought,
395 Of love and might to be divided not,
Compelling the elements with adamantine stress—
As the Sun rules,[2] even with a tyrant's gaze,
The unquiet Republic of the maze
Of Planets, struggling fierce towards Heaven's free wilderness.

400 Man, one harmonious Soul of many a soul
Whose nature is its own divine controul
Where all things flow to all, as rivers to the sea;
Familiar acts are beautiful through love;
Labour and Pain and Grief in life's green grove
405 Sport like tame beasts—none knew how gentle they could be!

His Will, with all mean passions, bad delights,
And selfish cares, its trembling satellites,
A spirit ill to guide, but mighty to obey,
Is as a tempest-winged ship, whose helm
410 Love rules, through waves which dare not overwhelm,
Forcing Life's wildest shores to own its sovereign sway.

All things confess his strength.—Through the cold mass
Of marble and of colour his dreams pass;
Bright threads, whence mothers weave the robes their children wear;
415 Language is a perpetual Orphic song,[3]
Which rules with Dædal harmony a throng
Of thoughts and forms, which else senseless and shapeless were.

9. A reminiscence of the legend of King Bladud of Britain, who, a banished leper, was following a lost swine and stumbled on a hot spring (now in the town of Bath), which cured him.
1. Human society, once splintered by hate, is now united by love into a single macrocosmic "Man."
2. By gravitational force.
3. Like the music of Orpheus, which attracted and controlled beasts, rocks, and trees.

The Lightning is his slave;[4] Heaven's utmost deep
Gives up her stars, and like a flock of sheep
420 They pass before his eye, are numbered, and roll on!
The Tempest is his steed,—he strides the air;
And the abyss shouts from her depth laid bare,
"Heaven, hast thou secrets? Man unveils me; I have none."

THE MOON

The shadow of white Death has past
425 From my path in Heaven at last,
A clinging shroud of solid frost and sleep—
And through my newly-woven bowers
Wander happy paramours
Less mighty, but as mild as those who keep
430 Thy vales more deep.

THE EARTH

As the dissolving warmth of Dawn may fold
A half-unfrozen dewglobe, green and gold
And chrystalline, till it becomes a winged mist
And wanders up the vault of the blue Day,
435 Outlives the noon, and on the Sun's last ray
Hangs o'er the Sea—a fleece of fire and amethyst—

THE MOON

Thou art folded, thou art lying
In the light which is undying
Of thine own joy and Heaven's smile divine;
440 All suns and constellations shower
On thee a light, a life, a power
Which doth array thy sphere—thou pourest thine
On mine, on mine!

THE EARTH

I spin beneath my pyramid of night[5]
445 Which points into the Heavens, dreaming delight,
Murmuring victorious joy in my enchanted sleep;
As a youth lulled in love-dreams, faintly sighing,
Under the shadow of his beauty lying
Which round his rest a watch of light and warmth doth keep.

THE MOON

450 As in the soft and sweet eclipse
When soul meets soul on lovers' lips,
High hearts are calm and brightest eyes are dull;
So when thy shadow falls on me[6]
Then am I mute and still,—by thee

4. The Earth describes regenerate man's scientific and technological triumphs.
5. The conical shadow cast by the earth as it inter-

cepts the sun's light.
6. In the eclipse of the moon, when it enters the earth's shadow.

455 Covered; of thy love, Orb most beautiful,
Full, oh, too full!—

Thou art speeding round the Sun,
Brightest World of many a one,
Green and azure sphere, which shinest
460 With a light which is divinest
Among all the lamps of Heaven
To whom life and light is given;
I, thy chrystal paramour,
Borne beside thee by a power
465 Like the polar Paradise,
Magnet-like, of lovers' eyes;[7]
I, a most enamoured maiden
Whose weak brain is overladen
With the pleasure of her love—
470 Maniac-like around thee move,
Gazing, an insatiate bride,
On thy form from every side
Like a Mænad round the cup
Which Agave[8] lifted up
475 In the weird Cadmæan forest.—
Brother, wheresoe'er thou soarest
I must hurry, whirl and follow
Through the Heavens wide and hollow,
Sheltered by the warm embrace
480 Of thy soul, from hungry space,
Drinking, from thy sense and sight,
Beauty, majesty, and might,
As a lover or chameleon
Grows like what it looks upon,
485 As a violet's gentle eye
Gazes on the azure sky
Until its hue grows like what it beholds,
As a grey and watery mist
Glows like solid amethyst
490 Athwart the western mountains it enfolds,
When the sunset sleeps
Upon its snow—

THE EARTH

And the weak day weeps[9]
That it should be so.
495 O gentle Moon, the voice of thy delight
Falls on me like thy clear and tender light
Soothing the seaman, borne the summer night
Through isles forever calm;
O gentle Moon, thy chrystal accents pierce

7. As it circles the earth, the moon spins at a rate that keeps the same side constantly toward it.
8. Daughter of King Cadmus; in a blind frenzy she tore her own son Pentheus to bits when he was caught spying on the Dionysiac rites. "Maenad": a female participant in the ecstatic worship of Dionysus (Bacchus).
9. I.e., with the dew at nightfall.

500   The caverns of my Pride's deep Universe,
       Charming the tyger Joy, whose tramplings fierce
       Made wounds, which need thy balm.

*   *   *

DEMOGORGON

       Man, who wert once a despot and a slave,—
550   A dupe and a deceiver,—a Decay,
       A Traveller from the cradle to the grave
       Through the dim night of this immortal Day:

ALL

       Speak—thy strong words may never pass away.

DEMOGORGON

       This is the Day which down the void Abysm
555   At the Earth-born's spell[1] yawns for Heaven's Despotism,
          And Conquest is dragged Captive through the Deep;[2]
       Love from its awful throne of patient power
       In the wise heart, from the last giddy hour
          Of dread endurance, from the slippery, steep,
560   And narrow verge of crag-like Agony, springs
       And folds over the world its healing wings.

       Gentleness, Virtue, Wisdom and Endurance,—
       These are the seals of that most firm assurance
          Which bars the pit over Destruction's strength;
565   And if, with infirm hand, Eternity,
       Mother of many acts and hours, should free
          The serpent that would clasp her with his length[3]—
       These are the spells by which to reassume
       An empire o'er the disentangled Doom.[4]

570   To suffer woes which Hope thinks infinite;
       To forgive wrongs darker than Death or Night;
          To defy Power which seems Omnipotent;
       To love, and bear; to hope, till Hope creates
       From its own wreck the thing it contemplates;
575   Neither to change nor falter nor repent:
       This, like thy glory, Titan! is to be
       Good, great and joyous, beautiful and free;
       This is alone Life, Joy, Empire and Victory.

1818–19   1820

---

1. Prometheus's spell—i.e., his magically effective words of pity, in place of vengefulness.
2. Ephesians 4.8: "When [Christ] ascended up on high, he led captivity captive."
3. A final reminder that the serpent incessantly struggles to break loose and start the cycle of humanity's fall all over again. Felicity must continue to be earned.
4. Shelley's four cardinal virtues (line 562), which seal the serpent in the pit, also constitute the magic formulas ("spells") by which to remaster him, should he again break loose. These virtues are expanded on in the concluding lines (570–75).

The Cloud

I bring fresh showers for the thirsting flowers,
    From the seas and streams;
I bear light shade for the leaves when laid
    In their noon-day dreams.
5 From my wings are shaken the dews that waken
    The sweet buds every one,
When rocked to rest on their mother's° breast,   *earth's*
    As she dances about the Sun.
I wield the flail of the lashing hail,
10   And whiten the green plains under,
And then again I dissolve it in rain,
    And laugh as I pass in thunder.

I sift the snow on the mountains below,
    And their great pines groan aghast;
15 And all the night 'tis my pillow white,
    While I sleep in the arms of the blast.
Sublime on the towers of my skiey bowers,
    Lightning my pilot sits;
In a cavern under is fettered the thunder,
20   It struggles and howls at fits;°   *fitfully*
Over Earth and Ocean, with gentle motion,
    This pilot is guiding me,
Lured by the love of the genii that move
    In the depths of the purple sea;[1]
25 Over the rills, and the crags, and the hills,
    Over the lakes and the plains,
Wherever he dream, under mountain or stream,
    The Spirit he loves remains;
And I all the while bask in Heaven's blue smile,[2]
30   Whilst he is dissolving in rains.

The sanguine Sunrise, with his meteor eyes,
    And his burning plumes outspread,[3]
Leaps on the back of my sailing rack,[4]
    When the morning star shines dead;
35 As on the jag of a mountain crag,
    Which an earthquake rocks and swings,
An eagle alit one moment may sit
    In the light of its golden wings.
And when Sunset may breathe, from the lit Sea beneath,
40   Its ardours of rest and of love,
And the crimson pall° of eve may fall   *rich coverlet*
    From the depth of Heaven above,
With wings folded I rest, on mine aëry nest,
    As still as a brooding dove.

1. I.e., atmospheric electricity, guiding the cloud (line 18), discharges as lightning when "lured" by the attraction of an opposite charge.
2. The upper part of the cloud remains exposed to the sun.
3. The sun's corona. "Meteor eyes": as bright as a burning meteor.
4. High, broken clouds, driven by the wind.

45 That orbed maiden with white fire laden
    Whom mortals call the Moon,
Glides glimmering o'er my fleece-like floor,
    By the midnight breezes strewn;
And wherever the beat of her unseen feet,
50   Which only the angels hear,
May have broken the woof,° of my tent's thin roof,   *texture*
    The stars peep behind her, and peer;
And I laugh to see them whirl and flee,
    Like a swarm of golden bees,
55 When I widen the rent in my wind-built tent,
    Till the calm rivers, lakes, and seas,
Like strips of the sky fallen through me on high,
    Are each paved with the moon and these.[5]

    I bind the Sun's throne with a burning zone°   *belt, sash*
60 And the Moon's with a girdle of pearl;
The volcanos are dim and the stars reel and swim
    When the whirlwinds my banner unfurl.
From cape to cape, with a bridge-like shape,
    Over a torrent sea,
65 Sunbeam-proof, I hang like a roof—
    The mountains its columns be!
The triumphal arch, through which I march
    With hurricane, fire, and snow,
When the Powers of the Air, are chained to my chair,
70   Is the million-coloured Bow;
The sphere-fire° above its soft colours wove   *sunlight*
    While the moist Earth was laughing below.

    I am the daughter of Earth and Water,
    And the nursling of the Sky;
75 I pass through the pores, of the ocean and shores;
    I change, but I cannot die—
For after the rain, when with never a stain
    The pavilion of Heaven is bare,
And the winds and sunbeams, with their convex gleams,
80   Build up the blue dome of Air[6]—
I silently laugh at my own cenotaph,[7]
    And out of the caverns of rain,
Like a child from the womb, like a ghost from the tomb,
    I arise, and unbuild it again.—

1820   1820

---

5. The stars reflected in the water.
6. The blue color of the sky. The phenomenon, as Shelley indicates, results from the way "sunbeams" are filtered by the earth's atmosphere.

7. The memorial monument of the dead cloud is the cloudless blue dome of the sky. (The point is that a cenotaph is a monument that does not contain a corpse.)

To a Sky-Lark[1]

Hail to thee, blithe Spirit!
    Bird thou never wert—
That from Heaven, or near it,
    Pourest thy full heart
5 In profuse strains of unpremeditated art.

Higher still and higher
    From the earth thou springest
Like a cloud of fire;
    The blue deep thou wingest,
10 And singing still dost soar, and soaring ever singest.

In the golden lightning
    Of the sunken Sun—
O'er which clouds are brightning,
    Thou dost float and run;
15 Like an unbodied joy whose race is just begun.

The pale purple even
    Melts around thy flight,
Like a star of Heaven
    In the broad day-light
20 Thou art unseen,—but yet I hear thy shrill delight,

Keen as are the arrows
    Of that silver sphere,[2]
Whose intense lamp narrows
    In the white dawn clear
25 Until we hardly see—we feel that it is there.

All the earth and air
    With thy voice is loud,
As when Night is bare
    From one lonely cloud
30 The moon rains out her beams—and Heaven is overflowed.

What thou art we know not;
    What is most like thee?
From rainbow clouds there flow not
    Drops so bright to see
35 As from thy presence showers a rain of melody.

Like a Poet hidden
    In the light of thought,
Singing hymns unbidden,

1. The European skylark is a small bird that sings
only in flight, often when it is too high to be visible.
This bird, freed from the bonds of earth and soaring beyond the reach of all the physical senses
except hearing, is made the emblem of a nonma-
terial spirit of pure joy, beyond the possibility of
human experience (see lines 15, 31).
2. The morning star.

Till the world is wrought
40 To sympathy with hopes and fears it heeded not:

Like a high-born maiden
    In a palace-tower,
Soothing her love-laden
    Soul in secret hour,
45 With music sweet as love—which overflows her bower:

Like a glow-worm golden
    In a dell of dew,
Scattering unbeholden
    Its aerial hue
50 Among the flowers and grass which screen it from the view:

Like a rose embowered
    In its own green leaves—
By warm winds deflowered—
    Till the scent it gives
55 Makes faint with too much sweet those heavy-winged thieves:[3]

Sound of vernal showers
    On the twinkling grass,
Rain-awakened flowers,
    All that ever was
60 Joyous, and clear and fresh, thy music doth surpass.

Teach us, Sprite° or Bird,   spirit
    What sweet thoughts are thine;
I have never heard
    Praise of love or wine
65 That panted forth a flood of rapture so divine:

Chorus Hymeneal[4]
    Or triumphal chaunt
Matched with thine would be all
    But an empty vaunt,
70 A thing wherein we feel there is some hidden want.

What objects are the fountains
    Of thy happy strain?
What fields or waves or mountains?
    What shapes of sky or plain?
75 What love of thine own kind? what ignorance of pain?

With thy clear keen joyance
    Languor cannot be—
Shadow of annoyance
    Never came near thee;
80 Thou lovest—but ne'er knew love's sad satiety.

3. The "warm winds," line 53.   4. Marital (from Hymen, Greek god of marriage).

Waking or asleep,
   Thou of death must deem
Things more true and deep
   Than we mortals dream,
85 Or how could thy notes flow in such a chrystal stream?

We look before and after,
   And pine for what is not—
Our sincerest laughter
   With some pain is fraught—
90 Our sweetest songs are those that tell of saddest thought.

Yet if we could scorn
   Hate and pride and fear;
If we were things born
   Not to shed a tear,
95 I know not how thy joy we ever should come near.

Better than all measures
   Of delightful sound—
Better than all treasures
   That in books are found—
100 Thy skill to poet were, thou Scorner of the ground!

Teach me half the gladness
   That thy brain must know,
Such harmonious madness
   From my lips would flow
105 The world should listen then—as I am listening now.

1820   1820

To Night[1]

Swiftly walk o'er the western wave,
   Spirit of Night!
Out of the misty eastern cave
Where, all the long and lone daylight
5 Thou wovest dreams of joy and fear,
Which make thee terrible and dear,
   Swift be thy flight!

Wrap thy form in a mantle grey,
   Star-inwrought!
10 Blind with thine hair the eyes of day,
Kiss her until she be wearied out—
Then wander o'er City and sea and land,
Touching all with thine opiate wand—
   Come, long-sought!

1. Night and darkness, as opposed to daylight, are often for Shelley symbols of the primordial powers and revelations of the poetic imagination.

15   When I arose and saw the dawn
          I sighed for thee;
   When Light rode high, and the dew was gone,
   And noon lay heavy on flower and tree,
   And the weary Day[2] turned to his rest,
20   Lingering like an unloved guest,
          I sighed for thee.

   Thy brother Death came, and cried,
          Wouldst thou me?
   Thy sweet child Sleep, the filmy-eyed,
25   Murmured like a noontide bee,
   Shall I nestle near thy side?
   Wouldst thou me? and I replied,
          No, not thee!

   Death will come when thou art dead,
30   Soon, too soon—
   Sleep will come when thou art fled;
   Of neither would I ask the boon
   I ask of thee, beloved Night—
   Swift be thine approaching flight,
35   Come soon, soon!

1820   1824

To ——— [Music, when soft voices die]

   Music, when soft voices die,
   Vibrates in the memory.—
   Odours, when sweet violets sicken,
   Live within the sense they quicken.—

5   Rose leaves, when the rose is dead,
   Are heaped for the beloved's bed[1]—
   And so thy thoughts,[2] when thou art gone,
   Love itself shall slumber on.

1821   1824

The flower that smiles today[1]

   The flower that smiles today
          Tomorrow dies;
   All that we wish to stay
          Tempts and then flies;
5   What is this world's delight?
   Lightning, that mocks the night,
          Brief even as bright.—

2. Here the "Day" is the male sun, not the female "day" with whom the Spirit of Night dallies in the preceding stanza.
1. The bed of the dead rose.

2. I.e., my thoughts of thee.
1. First printed, with the title *Mutability*, in Mary Shelley's edition of *Posthumous Poems of Percy Bysshe Shelley* (1824).

Virtue, how frail it is!—
  Friendship, how rare!—
10 Love, how it sells poor bliss
  For proud despair!
But these though soon they fall,
Survive their joy, and all
  Which ours we call.—

15 Whilst skies are blue and bright,
  Whilst flowers are gay,
Whilst eyes that change ere night
  Make glad the day;
Whilst yet the calm hours creep,
20 Dream thou—and from thy sleep
  Then wake to weep.

1821   1824

O World, O Life, O Time[1]

O World, O Life, O Time,
 On whose last steps I climb,
Trembling at that where I had stood before,
When will return the glory of your prime?
5 No more, O never more!

Out of the day and night
A joy has taken flight—
Fresh spring and summer [ ] and winter hoar
Move my faint heart with grief, but with delight
10 No more, O never more!

                      1824

Choruses from *Hellas*[1]

Worlds on worlds[2]

Worlds on worlds are rolling ever
From creation to decay,

---

1. For the author's revisions while composing this poem, see "Poems in Process," in the appendices to this volume.

1. *Hellas,* a closet drama written in the autumn of 1821, was inspired by the Greek war for independence against the Turks. In his preface, Shelley declared that he viewed this revolution as auguring the final overthrow of all tyranny. The choruses below are sung by captive Greek women. The first chorus describes the entrance of Christ into the revolving cycle of history; the second chorus concludes the drama.

2. The popular notions of Christianity are represented in this chorus as true in their relation to the worship they superseded . . . without considering their merits in a relation more universal. . . . The concluding verses indicate a progressive state of more or less exalted existence. . . . Let it not be supposed that I mean to dogmatise upon a subject [i.e., the problem of evil, and the possibility of its future elimination] upon which all men are equally ignorant. . . . That there is a true solution to the riddle, and that in our present state that solution is unattainable by us, are propositions that may be regarded as equally certain: meanwhile, as it is the province of the poet to attach himself to those ideas which exalt and ennoble humanity, let him be permitted to have conjectured the condition of that futurity towards which we are all impelled by an inextinguishable thirst for immortality [Shelley's note].

Like the bubbles on a river
Sparkling, bursting, borne away.
5   But *they*[3] are still immortal
Who through Birth's orient° portal   *eastern*
And Death's dark chasm hurrying to and fro,
Clothe their unceasing flight
In the brief dust and light
10   Gathered around their chariots as they go;
New shapes they still may weave,
New Gods, new Laws receive,
Bright or dim are they as the robes they last
On Death's bare ribs had cast.

15   A Power from the unknown God,
A Promethean Conqueror,[4] came;
Like a triumphal path he trod
The thorns of death and shame.
A mortal shape to him
20   Was like the vapour dim
Which the orient planet animates with light;
Hell, Sin, and Slavery came
Like bloodhounds mild and tame,
Nor preyed, until their Lord had taken flight;
25   The moon of Mahomet[5]
Arose, and it shall set,
While blazoned as on Heaven's immortal noon
The cross leads generations on.[6]

Swift as the radiant shapes of sleep
30   From one whose dreams are Paradise
Fly, when the fond wretch wakes to weep,
And Day peers forth with her blank eyes;
So fleet, so faint, so fair,
The Powers of earth and air
35   Fled from the folding star[7] of Bethlehem:
Apollo, Pan, and Love,
And even Olympian Jove
Grew weak, for killing Truth had glared on them;
Our hills and seas and streams,
40   Dispeopled of their dreams,
Their waters turned to blood, their dew to tears,
Wailed for the golden years.

---

3. Beings which inhabit the planets and . . . clothe themselves in matter [Shelley's note].
4. Christ, whom Shelley compares with Prometheus, who brought fire and the arts of civilization to humankind.
5. The crescent, emblem of Islam, which was founded six centuries after the birth of Christ.

6. The Roman emperor Constantine was converted to Christianity when he saw a bright cross imposed on the sun at noon.
7. The star of evening, the time when sheep are driven into the sheepfold. Shelley goes on to describe the pagan gods of earth and Olympus fleeing before the star of Bethlehem.

The world's great age[8]

The world's great age begins anew,
　　The golden years[9] return,
The earth doth like a snake renew
　　Her winter weeds[1] outworn;
5　Heaven smiles, and faiths and empires gleam
Like wrecks of a dissolving dream.

A brighter Hellas rears its mountains
　　From waves serener far,
A new Peneus[2] rolls his fountains
10　　Against the morning-star,
Where fairer Tempe bloom, there sleep
Young Cyclads[3] on a sunnier deep.

A loftier Argo[4] cleaves the main,
　　Fraught with a later prize;
15　Another Orpheus[5] sings again,
　　And loves, and weeps, and dies;
A new Ulysses leaves once more
Calypso[6] for his native shore.

O, write no more the tale of Troy,
20　　If earth Death's scroll must be!
Nor mix with Laian[7] rage the joy
　　Which dawns upon the free;
Although a subtler Sphinx renew
Riddles of death Thebes never knew.

25　Another Athens shall arise,
　　And to remoter time
Bequeath, like sunset to the skies,
　　The splendour of its prime,
And leave, if nought so bright may live,
30　All earth can take or Heaven can give.

Saturn and Love their long repose
Shall burst, more bright and good

8. Prophecies of wars, and rumours of wars, etc., may safely be made by poet or prophet in any age, but to anticipate however darkly a period of regeneration and happiness is a more hazardous exercise of the faculty which bards possess or fain. It will remind the reader . . . of Isaiah and Virgil, whose ardent spirits . . . saw the possible and perhaps approaching state of society in which the "lion shall lie down with the lamb," and *"omnis feret omnia tellus."* Let these great names be my authority and excuse [Shelley's note]. The quotations are from Isaiah's millennial prophecy (e.g., chaps. 25, 45), and Virgil's prediction, in *Eclogue* 4, of a return of the golden age, when "all the earth will produce all things."
9. In Greek myth, the first period of history, when Saturn reigned.

1. Clothes (especially mourning garments) as well as dead vegetation.
2. The river that flows through the beautiful vale of Tempe (line 11).
3. The Cyclades, islands in the Aegean Sea.
4. On which Jason sailed in his quest for the Golden Fleece.
5. The legendary player on the lyre who was torn to pieces by the frenzied Thracian women while he was mourning the death of his wife, Eurydice.
6. The nymph deserted by Ulysses on his voyage back from the Trojan War to his native Ithaca.
7. King Laius of Thebes was killed in a quarrel by his son Oedipus, who did not recognize his father. Shortly thereafter, Oedipus delivered Thebes from the ravages of the Sphinx by answering its riddle (lines 23–24).

Than all who fell, than One who rose,
Than many unsubdued;[8]
35   Not gold, not blood their altar dowers
But votive tears and symbol flowers.

O cease! must hate and death return?
Cease! must men kill and die?
Cease! drain not to its dregs the urn
40   Of bitter prophecy.
The world is weary of the past,
O might it die or rest at last!

1821   1822

Adonais   John Keats died in Rome on February 23, 1821, and was buried there in the Protestant Cemetery. Shelley had met Keats, had invited him to be his guest at Pisa, and had gradually come to to realize that he was "among the writers of the highest genius who have adorned our age" (Preface to *Adonais*). The name "Adonais" is derived from Adonis, the handsome youth who had been loved by the goddess Venus and slain by a wild boar; the function of the beast in this poem is attributed to the anonymous author of a vituperative review of Keats's *Endymion* in the *Quarterly Review*, April 1818 (now known to be John Wilson Croker), whom Shelley mistakenly believed to be responsible for Keats's illness and death.

Shelley in a letter described *Adonais*, which he wrote in April–June 1821 and had printed in Pisa in July, as a "highly wrought piece of art." Its artistry consists in part in the care with which it follows the conventions of the pastoral elegy, established more than two thousand years earlier by the Greek Sicilian poets Theocritus, Bion, and Moschus—Shelley had himself translated into English Bion's *Lament for Adonis* and Moschus's *Lament for Bion*. We recognize the centuries-old poetic ritual in many verbal echoes and in such devices as the mournful and accusing invocation to a muse (stanzas 2–4), the sympathetic participation of nature in the grieving (stanzas 14–17), the procession of appropriate mourners (stanzas 30–35), the denunciation of unworthy practitioners of the pastoral or literary art (stanzas 17, 27–29, 36–37), and above all, in the turn from despair at the finality of human death (lines 1, 64, 190: "*He* will awake no more, oh, never more!") to consolation in the sudden and contradictory discovery that the grave is a gate to a higher existence (line 343: "Peace, peace! he is not dead, he doth not sleep").

The first English publication of *Adonais*, in 1829 in an edition sponsored by the so-called Cambridge Apostles (R. M. Milnes, Alfred Tennyson, and A. H. Hallam) marked the beginning of Keats's posthumous emergence from obscurity as a poet.

Adonais

An Elegy on the Death of John Keats, Author of Endymion, Hyperion, etc.

[Thou wert the morning star among the living,
Ere thy fair light had fled—

---

8. Saturn and Love were among the deities of a real or imaginary state of innocence and happiness. "All" those "who fell" [are] the Gods of Greece, Asia, and Egypt; the "One who rose" [is] Jesus Christ . . . and the "many unsubdued" [are] the monstrous objects of the idolatry of China, India, the Antarctic islands, and the native tribes of America [Shelley's note].

Now, having died, thou art as Hesperus, giving
New splendour to the dead.][1]

1

I weep for Adonais—he is dead!
O, weep for Adonais! though our tears
Thaw not the frost which binds so dear a head!
And thou, sad Hour,[2] selected from all years
5   To mourn our loss, rouse thy obscure compeers,
And teach them thine own sorrow, say: with me
Died Adonais; till the Future dares
Forget the Past, his fate and fame shall be
An echo and a light unto eternity!

2

10   Where wert thou mighty Mother,[3] when he lay,
When thy Son lay, pierced by the shaft which flies
In darkness?[4] where was lorn° Urania   abandoned
When Adonais died? With veiled eyes,
'Mid listening Echoes, in her Paradise
15   She sate, while one,[5] with soft enamoured breath,
Rekindled all the fading melodies,
With which, like flowers that mock the corse° beneath,   corpse
He had adorned and hid the coming bulk of death.

3

O, weep for Adonais—he is dead!
20   Wake, melancholy Mother, wake and weep!
Yet wherefore? Quench within their burning bed
Thy fiery tears, and let thy loud heart keep
Like his, a mute and uncomplaining sleep;
For he is gone, where all things wise and fair
25   Descend;—oh, dream not that the amorous Deep°   abyss
Will yet restore him to the vital air;
Death feeds on his mute voice, and laughs at our despair.

4

Most musical of mourners, weep again!
Lament anew, Urania!—He[6] died,
30   Who was the Sire of an immortal strain,
Blind, old, and lonely, when his country's pride,
The priest, the slave, and the liberticide,
Trampled and mocked with many a loathed rite

1. Shelley prefixed to *Adonais* a Greek epigram, attributed to Plato; this is Shelley's own translation of the Greek. The planet Venus appears both as the morning star, Lucifer, and as the evening star, Hesperus or Vesper. Shelley makes of this phenomenon a key symbol for Adonais's triumph over death, in stanzas 44–46.
2. Shelley follows the classical mode of personifying the hours, which mark the passage of time and turn of the seasons.
3. Urania. She had originally been the Muse of astronomy, but the name was also an epithet for Venus. Shelley converts Venus Urania, who in Greek myth had been the lover of Adonis, into the mother of Adonais.
4. Alludes to the anonymity of the review of *Endymion*.
5. I.e., the echo of Keats's voice in his poems.
6. Milton, regarded as precursor of the great poetic tradition in which Keats wrote. He had adopted Urania as the muse of *Paradise Lost*. Lines 31–35 describe Milton's life during the restoration of the Stuart monarchy.

Of lust and blood; he went, unterrified,
35   Into the gulph of death; but his clear Sprite°   spirit
Yet reigns o'er earth; the third among the sons of light.[7]

5

Most musical of mourners, weep anew!
Not all to that bright station dared to climb;
And happier they their happiness who knew,
40   Whose tapers yet burn through that night of time
In which suns perished; others more sublime,
Struck by the envious wrath of man or God,
Have sunk, extinct in their refulgent prime;
And some yet live, treading the thorny road,
45 Which leads, through toil and hate, to Fame's serene abode.

6

But now, thy youngest, dearest one, has perished—
The nursling of thy widowhood, who grew,
Like a pale flower by some sad maiden cherished,
And fed with true love tears, instead of dew;[8]
50   Most musical of mourners, weep anew!
Thy extreme[9] hope, the loveliest and the last,
The bloom, whose petals nipt before they blew°   bloomed
Died on the promise of the fruit, is waste;
The broken lily lies—the storm is overpast.

7

55 To that high Capital,° where kingly Death   Rome
Keeps his pale court in beauty and decay,
He came; and bought, with price of purest breath,
A grave among the eternal.—Come away!
Haste, while the vault of blue Italian day
60   Is yet his fitting charnel-roof! while still
He lies, as if in dewy sleep he lay;
Awake him not! surely he takes his fill
Of deep and liquid rest, forgetful of all ill.

8

He will awake no more, oh, never more!—
65   Within the twilight chamber spreads apace,
The shadow of white Death, and at the door
Invisible Corruption waits to trace
His extreme way to her dim dwelling-place;
The eternal Hunger sits, but pity and awe
70   Soothe her pale rage, nor dares she to deface
So fair a prey, till darkness, and the law
Of change, shall 'oer his sleep the mortal curtain draw.

7. The three are Milton and his great predecessors in epic poetry, Homer and Dante. The stanza following describes the lot of other poets, up to Shel-

ley's own time.
8. An allusion to an incident in Keats's *Isabella*.
9. Last, as well as highest.

9

O, weep for Adonais!—The quick° Dreams,   *living*
The passion-winged Ministers of thought,
75   Who were his flocks,¹ whom near the living streams
Of his young spirit he fed, and whom he taught
The love which was its music, wander not,—
Wander no more, from kindling brain to brain,
But droop there, whence they sprung; and mourn their lot
80   Round the cold heart, where, after their sweet pain,
They ne'er will gather strength, or find a home again.

10

And one² with trembling hands clasps his cold head,
And fans him with her moonlight wings, and cries;
"Our love, our hope, our sorrow, is not dead;
85   See, on the silken fringe of his faint eyes,
Like dew upon a sleeping flower, there lies
A tear some Dream has loosened from his brain."
Lost Angel of a ruined Paradise!
She knew not 'twas her own; as with no stain
90   She faded, like a cloud which had outwept its rain.

11

One from a lucid° urn of starry dew   *luminous*
Washed his light limbs as if embalming them;
Another clipt her profuse locks, and threw
The wreath upon him, like an anadem,°   *rich garland*
95   Which frozen tears instead of pearls begem;
Another in her wilful grief would break
Her bow and winged reeds, as if to stem
A greater loss with one which was more weak;
And dull the barbed fire against his frozen cheek.

12

100   Another Splendour on his mouth alit,
That mouth, whence it was wont to draw the breath
Which gave it strength to pierce the guarded wit,³
And pass into the panting heart beneath
With lightning and with music: the damp death
105   Quenched its caress upon his icy lips;
And, as a dying meteor stains a wreath
Of moonlight vapour, which the cold night clips,°   *embraces*
It flushed through his pale limbs, and past to its eclipse.

13

And others came . . . Desires and Adorations,
110   Winged Persuasions and veiled Destinies,
Splendours, and Glooms, and glimmering Incarnations

---

1. The products of Keats's imagination, figuratively represented (according to pastoral convention) as his sheep.

2. One of the Dreams (line 73).
3. The cautious intellect (of the listener).

Of hopes and fears, and twilight Phantasies;
And Sorrow, with her family of Sighs,
And Pleasure, blind with tears, led by the gleam
115   Of her own dying smile instead of eyes,
Came in slow pomp;—the moving pomp might seem
Like pageantry of mist on an autumnal stream.

14

All he had loved, and moulded into thought,
From shape, and hue, and odour, and sweet sound,
120   Lamented Adonais. Morning sought
Her eastern watchtower, and her hair unbound,
Wet with the tears which should adorn the ground,
Dimmed the aerial eyes that kindle day;
Afar the melancholy thunder moaned,
125   Pale Ocean in unquiet slumber lay,
And the wild winds flew round, sobbing in their dismay.

15

Lost Echo sits amid the voiceless mountains,
And feeds her grief with his remembered lay,
And will no more reply to winds or fountains,
130   Or amorous birds perched on the young green spray,
Or herdsman's horn, or bell at closing day;
Since she can mimic not his lips, more dear
Than those for whose disdain she pined away
Into a shadow of all sounds:[4]—a drear
135   Murmur, between their songs, is all the woodmen hear.

16

Grief made the young Spring wild, and she threw down
Her kindling buds, as if she Autumn were,
Or they dead leaves; since her delight is flown
For whom should she have waked the sullen year?
140   To Phoebus was not Hyacinth so dear[5]
Nor to himself Narcissus, as to both
Thou Adonais: wan they stand and sere[6]
Amid the faint companions of their youth,
With dew all turned to tears; odour, to sighing ruth.°   pity

17

145   Thy spirit's sister, the lorn nightingale[7]
Mourns not her mate with such melodious pain;
Not so the eagle, who like thee could scale
Heaven, and could nourish in the sun's domain
Her mighty youth with morning,[8] doth complain,

---

4. Because of her unrequited love for Narcissus, who was enamored of his own reflection (line 141), the nymph Echo pined away until she was only a reflected sound.
5. Young Hyacinthus was loved by Phoebus Apollo, who accidentally killed him in a game of quoits. Apollo made the hyacinth flower spring from his blood.
6. Dried, withered.
7. To whom Keats had written Ode to a Nightingale.
8. In the legend, the aged eagle, to renew his youth, flies toward the sun until his old plumage is burned off and the film cleared from his eyes.

150 Soaring and screaming round her empty nest,
  As Albion° wails for thee: the curse of Cain   *England*
  Light on his head⁹ who pierced thy innocent breast,
And scared the angel soul that was its earthly guest!

18

  Ah woe is me! Winter is come and gone,
155 But grief returns with the revolving year;
  The airs and streams renew their joyous tone;
  The ants, the bees, the swallows reappear;
  Fresh leaves and flowers deck the dead Seasons' bier;
  The amorous birds now pair in every brake,°   *thicket*
160 And build their mossy homes in field and brere;°   *briar*
  And the green lizard, and the golden snake,
Like unimprisoned flames, out of their trance awake.

19

  Through wood and stream and field and hill and Ocean
  A quickening life from the Earth's heart has burst
165 As it has ever done, with change and motion,
  From the great morning of the world when first
  God dawned on Chaos; in its stream immersed
  The lamps of Heaven flash with a softer light;
  All baser things pant with life's sacred thirst;
170 Diffuse themselves; and spend in love's delight,
The beauty and the joy of their renewed might.

20

  The leprous corpse touched by this spirit tender
  Exhales itself in flowers of gentle breath;
  Like incarnations of the stars, when splendour
175 Is changed to fragrance, they illumine death
  And mock the merry worm that wakes beneath;
  Nought we know, dies. Shall that alone which knows
  Be as a sword consumed before the sheath¹
  By sightless° lightning?—th' intense atom glows   *invisible*
180 A moment, then is quenched in a most cold repose.

21

  Alas! that all we loved of him should be,
  But for our grief, as if it had not been,
  And grief itself be mortal! Woe is me!
  Whence are we, and why are we? of what scene
185 The actors or spectators? Great and mean
  Meet massed in death, who lends what life must borrow.
  As long as skies are blue, and fields are green,
  Evening must usher night, night urge the morrow,
Month follow month with woe, and year wake year to sorrow.

9. The reviewer of *Endymion*.
1. The "sword" is the mind that knows; the "sheath" is its vehicle, the material body.

22

190   *He* will awake no more, oh, never more!
         "Wake thou," cried Misery, "childless Mother, rise
         Out of thy sleep, and slake,° in thy heart's core,   *assuage*
         A wound more fierce than his with tears and sighs."
         And all the Dreams that watched Urania's eyes,
195   And all the Echoes whom their sister's song²
         Had held in holy silence, cried: "Arise!"
         Swift as a Thought by the snake Memory stung,
From her ambrosial rest the fading Splendour° sprung.   *Urania*

23

         She rose like an autumnal Night, that springs
200   Out of the East, and follows wild and drear
         The golden Day, which, on eternal wings,
         Even as a ghost abandoning a bier,
         Had left the Earth a corpse. Sorrow and fear
         So struck, so roused, so rapt Urania;
205   So saddened round her like an atmosphere
         Of stormy mist; so swept her on her way
Even to the mournful place where Adonais lay.

24

         Out of her secret Paradise she sped,
         Through camps and cities rough with stone, and steel,
210   And human hearts, which to her aery tread
         Yielding not, wounded the invisible
         Palms of her tender feet where'er they fell:
         And barbed tongues, and thoughts more sharp than they
         Rent the soft Form they never could repel,
215   Whose sacred blood, like the young tears of May,
Paved with eternal flowers that undeserving way.

25

         In the death chamber for a moment Death
         Shamed by the presence of that living Might
         Blushed to annihilation, and the breath
220   Revisited those lips, and life's pale light
         Flashed through those limbs, so late her dear delight.
         "Leave me not wild and drear and comfortless,
         As silent lightning leaves the starless night!
         Leave me not!" cried Urania: her distress
225 Roused Death: Death rose and smiled, and met her vain caress.

26

         "Stay yet awhile! speak to me once again;
         Kiss me, so long but as a kiss may live;
         And in my heartless³ breast and burning brain
         That word, that kiss shall all thoughts else survive
230   With food of saddest memory kept alive,

---

2. I.e., the Echo in line 127.   3. Because her heart had been given to Adonais.

Now thou art dead, as if it were a part
Of thee, my Adonais! I would give
All that I am to be as thou now art!
But I am chained to Time, and cannot thence depart!

27

235 "Oh gentle child, beautiful as thou wert,
Why didst thou leave the trodden paths of men
Too soon, and with weak hands though mighty heart
Dare the unpastured dragon in his den?[4]
Defenceless as thou wert, oh where was then
240 Wisdom the mirrored shield, or scorn the spear?[5]
Or hadst thou waited the full cycle, when
Thy spirit should have filled its crescent sphere,[6]
The monsters of life's waste had fled from thee like deer.

28

"The herded wolves, bold only to pursue;
245 The obscene ravens, clamorous o'er the dead;
The vultures to the conqueror's banner true
Who feed where Desolation first has fed,
And whose wings rain contagion;—how they fled,
When like Apollo, from his golden bow,
250 The Pythian of the age[7] one arrow sped
And smiled!—The spoilers tempt no second blow,
They fawn on the proud feet that spurn them lying low.

29

"The sun comes forth, and many reptiles spawn;
He sets, and each ephemeral insect then
255 Is gathered into death without a dawn,
And the immortal stars awake again;
So is it in the world of living men:
A godlike mind soars forth, in its delight
Making earth bare and veiling heaven,[8] and when
260 It sinks, the swarms that dimmed or shared its light
Leave to its kindred lamps[9] the spirit's awful night."

30

Thus ceased she: and the mountain shepherds came,
Their garlands sere, their magic mantles rent;
The Pilgrim of Eternity,[1] whose fame
265 Over his living head like Heaven is bent,
An early but enduring monument,

4. I.e., the hostile reviewers.
5. The allusion is to Perseus, who had cut off Medusa's head while avoiding the direct sight of her (which would have turned him to stone) by looking only at her reflection in his shield.
6. I.e., when thy spirit, like the full moon, should have reached its maturity.
7. Byron, who had directed against critics of the age his satiric poem *English Bards and Scotch*

Reviewers (1809). The allusion is to Apollo, called "the Pythian" because he had slain the dragon Python.
8. As the sun reveals the earth but veils the other stars.
9. The other stars (i.e., creative minds), of lesser brilliance than the sun.
1. Byron, who had referred to his Childe Harold as one of the "wanderers o'er Eternity" (3.669).

Came, veiling all the lightnings of his song
In sorrow; from her wilds Ierne sent
The sweetest lyrist[2] of her saddest wrong,
270 And love taught grief to fall like music from his tongue.

31

Midst others of less note, came one frail Form,[3]
A phantom among men; companionless
As the last cloud of an expiring storm
Whose thunder is its knell; he, as I guess,
275 Had gazed on Nature's naked loveliness,
Actæon-like, and now he fled astray
With feeble steps o'er the world's wilderness,
And his own thoughts, along that rugged way,
Pursued, like raging hounds, their father and their prey.[4]

32

280 A pardlike° Spirit beautiful and swift—   leopardlike
A Love in desolation masked;—a Power
Girt round with weakness;—it can scarce uplift
The weight of the superincumbent hour;[5]
It is a dying lamp, a falling shower,
285 A breaking billow;—even whilst we speak
Is it not broken? On the withering flower
The killing sun smiles brightly: on a cheek
The life can burn in blood, even while the heart may break.

33

His head was bound with pansies overblown,
290 And faded violets, white, and pied, and blue;
And a light spear topped with a cypress cone,
Round whose rude shaft dark ivy tresses grew[6]
Yet dripping with the forest's noonday dew,
Vibrated, as the ever-beating heart
295 Shook the weak hand that grasped it; of that crew
He came the last, neglected and apart;
A herd-abandoned deer struck by the hunter's dart.

34

All stood aloof, and at his partial° moan   sympathetic
Smiled through their tears; well knew that gentle band
300 Who in another's fate now wept his own;
As in the accents of an unknown land,
He sung new sorrow; sad Urania scanned
The Stranger's mien, and murmured: "who art thou?"

2. Thomas Moore (1779–1852), from Ireland
("Ierne"), who had written poems about the
oppression of his native land.
3. Shelley himself, represented in one of his
aspects—like the Poet in *Alastor,* rather than the
author of *Prometheus Unbound.*
4. Actaeon, while hunting, came upon the naked

Diana bathing and, as a punishment, was turned
into a stag and torn to pieces by his own hounds.
5. The heavy, overhanging hour of Keats's death.
6. Like the thyrsus, the leaf-entwined and cone-
topped staff carried by Dionysus. The pansies are
emblems of sorrowful thought. The cypress is an
emblem of mourning.

He answered not, but with a sudden hand
305   Made bare his branded and ensanguined brow,
Which was like Cain's or Christ's[7]—Oh! that it should be so!

35

What softer voice is hushed over the dead?
Athwart what brow is that dark mantle thrown?
What form leans sadly o'er the white death-bed,
310   In mockery of monumental stone,[8]
The heavy heart heaving without a moan?
If it be He,[9] who, gentlest of the wise,
Taught, soothed, loved, honoured the departed one;
Let me not vex, with inharmonious sighs
315   The silence of that heart's accepted sacrifice.

36

Our Adonais has drunk poison—oh!
What deaf and viperous murderer could crown
Life's early cup with such a draught of woe?
The nameless worm[1] would now itself disown:
320   It felt, yet could escape the magic tone
Whose prelude held all envy, hate, and wrong,
But what was howling in one breast alone,
Silent with expectation of the song,[2]
Whose master's hand is cold, whose silver lyre unstrung.

37

325   Live thou, whose infamy is not thy fame!
Live! fear no heavier chastisement from me,
Thou noteless blot on a remembered name!
But be thyself, and know thyself to be!
And ever at thy season be thou free
330   To spill the venom when thy fangs o'erflow:
Remorse and Self-contempt shall cling to thee;
Hot Shame shall burn upon thy secret brow,
And like a beaten hound tremble thou shalt—as now.

38

Nor let us weep that our delight is fled
335   Far from these carrion kites[3] that scream below;
He wakes or sleeps with the enduring dead;
Thou canst not soar where he is sitting now.—
Dust to the dust! but the pure spirit shall flow
Back to the burning fountain whence it came,

---

7. His bloody ("ensanguined") brow bore a mark like that with which God had branded Cain for murdering Abel—or like that left by Christ's crown of thorns.
8. In imitation of a memorial statue.
9. Leigh Hunt, close friend of both Keats and Shelley.
1. Snake—the anonymous reviewer.
2. The promise of later greatness in Keats's early poems "held . . . silent" the expression of all malignant feelings except the reviewer's.
3. Birds of prey; a species of hawk.

Swung blind in unascended majesty,
Silent alone amid an Heaven of song.
Assume thy winged throne, thou Vesper of our throng!"[4]

47

415 Who mourns for Adonais? oh come forth
Fond wretch! and know thyself and him aright.
Clasp with thy panting soul the pendulous[5] Earth;
As from a centre, dart thy spirit's light
Beyond all worlds, until its spacious might
420 Satiate the void circumference: then shrink
Even to a point within our day and night;[6]
And keep thy heart light lest it make thee sink
When hope has kindled hope, and lured thee to the brink.

48

Or go to Rome, which is the sepulchre
425 O, not of him, but of our joy: 'tis nought
That ages, empires, and religions there
Lie buried in the ravage they have wrought;
For such as he can lend,—they[7] borrow not
Glory from those who made the world their prey;
430 And he is gathered to the kings of thought
Who waged contention with their time's decay,
And of the past are all that cannot pass away.

49

Go thou to Rome,—at once the Paradise,
The grave, the city, and the wilderness;
435 And where its wrecks like shattered mountains rise,
And flowering weeds, and fragrant copses[8] dress
The bones of Desolation's nakedness
Pass, till the Spirit of the spot shall lead
Thy footsteps to a slope of green access[9]
440 Where, like an infant's smile, over the dead,
A light of laughing flowers along the grass is spread.

50

And grey walls moulder round,[1] on which dull Time
Feeds, like slow fire upon a hoary brand;[2]
And one keen pyramid with wedge sublime,[3]

---

4. Adonais assumes his place in the sphere of Vesper, the evening star, hitherto unoccupied ("kingless"), hence also "silent" amid the music of the other spheres.
5. Suspended, floating in space.
6. The poet bids the wretch who is foolish ("fond") enough to mourn Adonais to stretch his imagination so as to reach the poet's own cosmic viewpoint and then allow it to contract ("shrink") back to its ordinary vantage point on earth—where, unlike Adonais in his heavenly place, we have an alternation of day and night.
7. Poets like Keats, who can bestow ("lend") glory,

as opposed to the Roman conquerors, who borrowed glory from those they conquered.
8. Undergrowth. In Shelley's time the ruins of ancient Rome were overgrown with weeds and shrubbery.
9. The Protestant Cemetery, Keats's burial place. The next line is a glancing allusion to Shelley's three-year-old son, William, also buried there.
1. The wall of ancient Rome formed one boundary of the cemetery.
2. A burning log.
3. The tomb of Caius Cestius, a Roman tribune, just outside the cemetery.

445 Pavilioning the dust of him who planned
This refuge for his memory, doth stand
Like flame transformed to marble; and beneath,
A field is spread, on which a newer band
Have pitched in Heaven's smile their camp of death
450 Welcoming him we lose with scarce extinguished breath.

51

Here pause: these graves are all too young as yet
To have outgrown the sorrow which consigned
Its charge to each; and if the seal is set,
Here, on one fountain of a mourning mind,[4]
455 Break it not thou! too surely shalt thou find
Thine own well full, if thou returnest home,
Of tears and gall. From the world's bitter wind
Seek shelter in the shadow of the tomb.
What Adonais is, why fear we to become?

52

460 The One remains, the many change and pass;
Heaven's light forever shines, Earth's shadows fly;
Life, like a dome of many-coloured glass,
Stains the white radiance of Eternity,
Until Death tramples it to fragments.[5]—Die,
465 If thou wouldst be with that which thou dost seek!
Follow where all is fled!—Rome's azure sky,
Flowers, ruins, statues, music, words, are weak
The glory they transfuse with fitting truth to speak.

53

Why linger, why turn back, why shrink, my Heart?
470 Thy hopes are gone before; from all things here
They have departed; thou shouldst now depart!
A light is past from the revolving year,
And man, and woman; and what still is dear
Attracts to crush, repels to make thee wither.
475 The soft sky smiles,—the low wind whispers near:
'Tis Adonais calls! oh, hasten thither,
No more let Life divide what Death can join together.

54

That Light whose smile kindles the Universe,
That Beauty in which all things work and move,
480 That Benediction which the eclipsing Curse
Of birth can quench not, that sustaining Love
Which through the web of being blindly wove
By man and beast and earth and air and sea,
Burns bright or dim, as each are mirrors of[6]

---

4. Shelley's mourning for his son.
5. Earthly life colors ("stains") the pure white light of the One, which is the source of all light (see lines 339–40, n. 4). The azure sky, flowers, etc., of lines 466–68 exemplify earthly colors that, how-ever beautiful, fall far short of the "glory" of the pure Light that they transmit but also refract ("transfuse").
6. I.e., according to the degree that each reflects.

485 The fire for which all thirst;[7] now beams on me,
  Consuming the last clouds of cold mortality.

55

  The breath whose might I have invoked in song[8]
  Descends on me; my spirit's bark is driven,
  Far from the shore, far from the trembling throng
490 Whose sails were never to the tempest given;
  The massy earth and sphered skies are riven!
  I am borne darkly, fearfully, afar;
  Whilst burning through the inmost veil of Heaven,
  The soul of Adonais, like a star,
495 Beacons from the abode where the Eternal are.

1821   1821

A Dirge

  Rough wind, that moanest loud
   Grief too sad for song;
  Wild wind, when sullen cloud
   Knells all the night long;
5 Sad storm, whose tears are vain,
  Bare woods, whose branches strain,
  Deep caves and dreary main,—
   Wail, for the world's wrong!

1821   1824

When the lamp is shattered

  When the lamp is shattered
  The light in the dust lies dead—
  When the cloud is scattered
  The rainbow's glory is shed—
5 When the lute is broken
  Sweet tones are remembered not—
  When the lips have spoken
  Loved accents are soon forgot.

  As music and splendour
10 Survive not the lamp and the lute,
  The heart's echoes render
  No song when the spirit is mute—
  No song—but sad dirges
  Like the wind through a ruined cell

---

7. The "thirst" of the human spirit is to return to the fountain and fire (the "burning fountain," line 339) which is its source.

8. Two years earlier Shelley had "invoked" (prayed to, and also asked for) "the breath of Autumn's being" in his Ode to the West Wind.

15   Or the mournful surges
That ring the dead seaman's knell.

    When hearts have once mingled
Love first leaves the well-built nest[1]—
    The weak one is singled
20   To endure what it once possest.
      O Love! who bewailest
The frailty of all things here,
      Why choose you the frailest[2]
For your cradle, your home and your bier?

25   Its passions will rock thee
As the storms rock the ravens on high—
    Bright Reason will mock thee
Like the Sun from a wintry sky—
      From thy nest every rafter
30   Will rot, and thine eagle home[3]
      Leave thee naked to laughter
When leaves fall and cold winds come.

1822   1824

To Jane[1] (The keen stars were twinkling)

    The keen stars were twinkling
And the fair moon was rising among them,
      Dear Jane.
    The guitar was tinkling
5   But the notes were not sweet 'till you sung them
      Again.—
    As the moon's soft splendour
O'er the faint cold starlight of Heaven
      Is thrown—
10   So your voice most tender
To the strings without soul had then given
      Its own.

    The stars will awaken,
Though the moon sleep a full hour later,
15   Tonight;
    No leaf will be shaken
While the dews of your melody scatter
      Delight.
    Though the sound overpowers
20   Sing again, with your dear voice revealing
      A tone
    Of some world far from ours,

1. Love abandons first the sturdier heart.
2. I.e., the human heart.
3. Like the lofty, and therefore exposed, nest of the eagle.

1. Jane Williams, the common-law wife of Shelley's close friend Edward Williams.

Where music and moonlight and feeling
Are one.

1822   1832

Lines Written in the Bay of Lerici[1]

Bright wanderer,° fair coquette of Heaven,   *moon*
To whom alone it has been given
To change and be adored for ever. . . .
Envy not this dim world, for never
5   But once within its shadow grew
One fair as [thou], but far more true.
She left me at the silent time
When the moon had ceased to climb
The azure dome of Heaven's steep,
10 And like an albatross asleep,
Balanced on her wings of light,
Hovered in the purple night,
Ere she sought her Ocean nest
In the chambers of the west.—
15 She left me, and I staid alone
Thinking over every tone,
Which though now silent to the ear
The enchanted heart could hear
Like notes which die when born, but still
20 Haunt the echoes of the hill:
And feeling ever—O too much—
The soft vibrations of her touch
As if her gentle hand even now
Lightly trembled on my brow;
25 And thus although she absent were
Memory gave me all of her
That even fancy dares to claim.—
Her presence had made weak and tame
All passions, and I lived alone,
30 In the time which is our own;
The past and future were forgot
As they had been, and would be, not.—
But soon, the guardian angel gone,
The demon[2] reassumed his throne
35 In my faint heart . . . I dare not speak
My thoughts; but thus disturbed and weak
I sate and watched the vessels glide
Along the ocean bright and wide,
Like spirit-winged chariots sent
40 O'er some serenest element
To ministrations strange and far;

1. Another of Shelley's lyrics inspired by Jane Williams. He shared with the Williamses a summer house near Lerici, on the northeastern coast of Italy.

2. I.e., the passions, with their compulsion to look before and after (lines 29–32).

> As if to some Elysian star
> They sailed for drink to medicine
> Such sweet and bitter pain as mine.
> 45 And the wind that winged their flight
> From the land came fresh and light,
> And the scent of sleeping flowers
> And the coolness of the hours
> Of dew, and the sweet warmth of day
> 50 Was scattered o'er the twinkling bay;
> And the fisher with his lamp
> And spear, about the low rocks damp
> Crept, and struck the fish who came
> To worship the delusive flame:
> 55 Too happy, they whose pleasure sought
> Extinguishes all sense and thought
> Of the regret that pleasure [leaves]³
> Destroying life alone not peace.

1822   1862

A Defence of Poetry

A Defence of Poetry   In 1820 Shelley's good friend Thomas Love Peacock published an ironic essay, *The Four Ages of Poetry,* implicitly directed against the towering claims for poetry and the poetic imagination made by his Romantic contemporaries. Peacock adopted the premise of Wordsworth and some other Romantic critics—that poetry in its origin was a primitive use of language and mind—but from this premise he proceeded to draw the conclusion that poetry has become a useless anachronism in this age of science and technology. Peacock was himself a poet as well as an excellent prose satirist, and Shelley saw the joke; but he also recognized that the view that Peacock, as a satirist, had assumed was very close to that actually held in his day by Utilitarian philosophers and the material-minded public, who either attacked or contemptuously ignored the imaginative faculty and its achievements. He therefore undertook, as he good-humoredly wrote to Peacock, "to break a lance with you . . . in honor of my mistress Urania," even though he was only "the knight of the shield of shadow and the lance of gossamere." The result was *A Defence of Poetry,* planned to consist of three parts. The last two parts were never written, and even the existing section, written in 1821, remained unpublished until 1840, eighteen years after Shelley's death.

Shelley's emphasis in this essay, like that of Blake in his critical commentaries, is not on the particularity of individual poems but on the universal and permanent qualities and values that, he believes, all great poems, as products of imagination, have in common. Shelley in addition extends the term *poet* to include all creative minds that break out of the conditions of their time and place to envision what he regards as the eternal and general forms of value. This category includes not only writers in prose as well as verse but also artists, legislators, prophets, and the founders of new social and religious institutions.

The *Defence* is an eloquent and enduring claim for the indispensability of the visionary and creative imagination in all the great human concerns. Few later social critics have equaled the cogency of Shelley's attack on our acquisitive society and its narrowly material concepts of utility and progress. Such a bias has opened the way

---

3. This word has been suggested by earlier editors; Shelley left a blank space.

to enormous advances in the physical sciences and our material well-being, but without a proportionate development of our "poetic faculty," the moral imagination. The result, Shelley says, is that "man, having enslaved the elements, remains himself a slave."

From A Defence of Poetry

or Remarks Suggested by an Essay Entitled "The Four Ages of Poetry"

According to one mode of regarding those two classes of mental action, which are called reason and imagination, the former may be considered as mind contemplating the relations borne by one thought to another, however produced; and the latter, as mind acting upon those thoughts so as to colour them with its own light, and composing from them, as from elements, other thoughts, each containing within itself the principle of its own integrity. The one[1] is the *to poiein*,[2] or the principle of synthesis, and has for its objects those forms which are common to universal nature and existence itself; the other is the *to logizein*,[3] or principle of analysis, and its action regards the relations of things, simply as relations; considering thoughts, not in their integral unity, but as the algebraical representations which conduct to certain general results. Reason is the enumeration of quantities already known; imagination is the perception of the value of those quantities, both separately and as a whole. Reason respects the differences, and imagination the similitudes of things. Reason is to Imagination as the instrument to the agent, as the body to the spirit, as the shadow to the substance.

Poetry, in a general sense, may be defined to be "the expression of the Imagination": and poetry is connate with the origin of man. Man is an instrument over which a series of external and internal impressions are driven, like the alternations of an ever-changing wind over an Æolian lyre,[4] which move it by their motion to ever-changing melody. But there is a principle within the human being, and perhaps within all sentient beings, which acts otherwise than in the lyre, and produces not melody, alone, but harmony, by an internal adjustment of the sounds or motions thus excited to the impressions which excite them. It is as if the lyre could accommodate its chords to the motions of that which strikes them, in a determined proportion of sound; even as the musician can accommodate his voice to the sound of the lyre. A child at play by itself will express its delight by its voice and motions; and every inflexion of tone and every gesture will bear exact relation to a corresponding antitype in the pleasurable impressions which awakened it; it will be the reflected image of that impression; and as the lyre trembles and sounds after the wind has died away, so the child seeks, by prolonging in its voice and motions the duration of the effect, to prolong also a consciousness of the cause. In relation to the objects which delight a child, these expressions are, what poetry is to higher objects. The savage (for the savage is to

---

1. The imagination. "The other" (later in the sentence) is the reason.
2. Making. The Greek word from which the English term *poet* derives means "maker," and "maker" was often used as equivalent to "poet" by Renaissance critics such as Sir Philip Sidney in his

Defence of Poesy, which Shelley had carefully studied.
3. Calculating, reasoning.
4. A wind harp (see Coleridge, *The Eolian Harp*, p. 419).

ages what the child is to years) expresses the emotions produced in him by surrounding objects in a similar manner; and language and gesture, together with plastic or pictorial imitation, become the image of the combined effect of those objects, and of his apprehension of them. Man in society, with all his passions and his pleasures, next becomes the object of the passions and pleasures of man; an additional class of emotions produces an augmented treasure of expressions; and language, gesture, and the imitative arts, become at once the representation and the medium, the pencil and the picture, the chisel and the statue, the chord and the harmony. The social sympathies, or those laws from which as from its elements society results, begin to develope themselves from the moment that two human beings coexist; the future is contained within the present as the plant within the seed; and equality, diversity, unity, contrast, mutual dependence, become the principles alone capable of affording the motives according to which the will of a social being is determined to action, inasmuch as he is social; and constitute pleasure in sensation, virtue in sentiment, beauty in art, truth in reasoning, and love in the intercourse of kind. Hence men, even in the infancy of society, observe a certain order in their words and actions, distinct from that of the objects and the impressions represented by them, all expression being subject to the laws of that from which it proceeds. But let us dismiss those more general considerations which might involve an enquiry into the principles of society itself, and restrict our view to the manner in which the imagination is expressed upon its forms.

In the youth of the world, men dance and sing and imitate natural objects, observing[5] in these actions, as in all others, a certain rhythm or order. And, although all men observe a similar, they observe not the same order, in the motions of the dance, in the melody of the song, in the combinations of language, in the series of their imitations of natural objects. For there is a certain order or rhythm belonging to each of these classes of mimetic representation, from which the hearer and the spectator receive an intenser and purer pleasure than from any other: the sense of an approximation to this order has been called taste, by modern writers. Every man in the infancy of art, observes an order which approximates more or less closely to that from which this highest delight results: but the diversity is not sufficiently marked, as that its gradations should be sensible, except in those instances where the predominance of this faculty of approximation to the beautiful (for so we may be permitted to name the relation between this highest pleasure and its cause) is very great. Those in whom it exists in excess are poets, in the most universal sense of the word; and the pleasure resulting from the manner in which they express the influence of society or nature upon their own minds, communicates itself to others, and gathers a sort of reduplication from that community. Their language is vitally metaphorical; that is, it marks the before unapprehended relations of things, and perpetuates their apprehension, until the words which represent them, become through time signs for portions or classes of thoughts[6] instead of pictures of integral thoughts; and then if no new poets should arise to create afresh the associations which have been thus disorganized, language will be dead to all the nobler purposes of human intercourse. These similitudes or relations are finely said by Lord

---

5. Following, obeying.

6. I.e., abstract concepts.

Bacon to be "the same footsteps of nature impressed upon the various subjects of the world"[7]—and he considers the faculty which perceives them as
the storehouse of axioms common to all knowledge. In the infancy of society
every author is necessarily a poet, because language itself is poetry; and to
be a poet is to apprehend the true and the beautiful, in a word the good which
exists in the relation, subsisting, first between existence and perception, and
secondly between perception and expression. Every original language near to
its source is in itself the chaos of a cyclic poem:[8] the copiousness of lexicog-
raphy and the distinctions of grammar are the works of a later age, and are
merely the catalogue and the form of the creations of Poetry.

But Poets, or those who imagine and express this indestructible order, are
not only the authors of language and of music, of the dance and architecture
and statuary and painting: they are the institutors of laws, and the founders
of civil society and the inventors of the arts of life and the teachers, who
draw into a certain propinquity with the beautiful and the true that partial
apprehension of the agencies of the invisible world which is called religion.[9]
Hence all original religions are allegorical, or susceptible of allegory, and like
Janus[1] have a double face of false and true. Poets, according to the circumstances of the age and nation in which they appeared, were called in the
earlier epochs of the world legislators or prophets:[2] a poet essentially com-
prises and unites both these characters. For he not only beholds intensely
the present as it is, and discovers those laws according to which present
things ought to be ordered, but he beholds the future in the present, and his
thoughts are the germs of the flower and the fruit of latest time. Not that I
assert poets to be prophets in the gross sense of the word, or that they can
foretell the form as surely as they foreknow the spirit of events: such is the
pretence of superstition which would make poetry an attribute of prophecy,
rather than prophecy an attribute of poetry. A Poet participates in the eternal, the infinite, and the one; as far as relates to his conceptions, time and
place and number are not. The grammatical forms which express the moods
of time, and the difference of persons and the distinction of place are convertible with respect to the highest poetry without injuring it as poetry, and
the choruses of Æschylus, and the book of Job, and Dante's Paradise would
afford, more than any other writings, examples of this fact, if the limits of
this essay did not forbid citation. The creations of sculpture, painting, and
music, are illustrations still more decisive.

Language, colour, form, and religious and civil habits of action are all the
instruments and materials of poetry; they may be called poetry by that figure
of speech which considers the effect as a synonime of the cause. But poetry
in a more restricted sense[3] expresses those arrangements of language, and
especially metrical language, which are created by that imperial faculty,
whose throne is curtained within the invisible nature of man. And this
springs from the nature itself of language, which is a more direct represen-

7. Francis Bacon's *De Augmentis Scientiarum* (On
the enlargement of the sciences) 1.3.
8. A group of poems (e.g., "the Arthurian cycle")
that deal with the same subject.
9. Here Shelley enlarges the scope of the term
poetry to denote all the creative achievements, or
imaginative breakthroughs, of humankind, including noninstitutional religious insights.
1. Roman god of beginnings and endings, often

represented by two heads facing opposite directions.
2. Sir Philip Sidney had pointed out, in his
Defence of Poesy, that *vates*, the Roman term for
"poet," signifies "a diviner, fore-seer, or Prophet."
3. I.e., restricted to specifically verbal poetry, as
against the inclusive sense in which Shelley has
been applying the term.

tation of the actions and passions of our internal being, and is susceptible of more various and delicate combinations, than colour, form, or motion, and is more plastic and obedient to the controul of that faculty of which it is the creation. For language is arbitrarily produced by the Imagination and has relation to thoughts alone; but all other materials, instruments and conditions of art, have relations among each other, which limit and interpose between conception and expression. The former[4] is as a mirror which reflects, the latter as a cloud which enfeebles, the light of which both are mediums of communication. Hence the fame of sculptors, painters and musicians, although the intrinsic powers of the great masters of these arts, may yield in no degree to that of those who have employed language as the hieroglyphic of their thoughts, has never equalled that of poets in the restricted sense of the term; as two performers of equal skill will produce unequal effects from a guitar and a harp. The fame of legislators and founders of religions, so long as their institutions last, alone seems to exceed that of poets in the restricted sense; but it can scarcely be a question whether, if we deduct the celebrity which their flattery of the gross opinions of the vulgar usually conciliates, together with that which belonged to them in their higher character of poets, any excess will remain.

We have thus circumscribed the meaning of the word Poetry within the limits of that art which is the most familiar and the most perfect expression of the faculty itself. It is necessary however to make the circle still narrower, and to determine the distinction between measured and unmeasured language; for the popular division into prose and verse is inadmissible in accurate philosophy.

Sounds as well as thoughts have relation both between each other and towards that which they represent, and a perception of the order of those relations has always been found connected with a perception of the order of the relations of thoughts. Hence the language of poets has ever affected a certain uniform and harmonious recurrence of sound, without which it were not poetry, and which is scarcely less indispensable to the communication of its influence, than the words themselves, without reference to that peculiar order. Hence the vanity of translation; it were as wise to cast a violet into a crucible that you might discover the formal principle of its colour and odour, as seek to transfuse from one language into another the creations of a poet. The plant must spring again from its seed or it will bear no flower—and this is the burthen of the curse of Babel.[5]

An observation of the regular mode of the recurrence of this harmony in the language of poetical minds, together with its relation to music, produced metre, or a certain system of traditional forms of harmony of language. Yet it is by no means essential that a poet should accommodate his language to this traditional form, so that the harmony which is its spirit, be observed. The practise is indeed convenient and popular, and to be preferred, especially in such composition as includes much form and action: but every great poet must inevitably innovate upon the example of his predecessors in the exact structure of his peculiar versification. The distinction between poets and

4. I.e., language, as opposed to the media of sculpture, painting, and music.
5. When the descendants of Noah, who spoke a single language, undertook to build the Tower of Babel that would reach heaven, God cut short the attempt by multiplying languages so that the builders could no longer communicate (see Genesis 11.1–9).

prose writers is a vulgar error. The distinction between philosophers and poets has been anticipated.[6] Plato was essentially a poet—the truth and splendour of his imagery and the melody of his language is the most intense that it is possible to conceive. He rejected the measure of the epic, dramatic, and lyrical forms, because he sought to kindle a harmony in thoughts divested of shape and action, and he forbore to invent any regular plan of rhythm which would include, under determinate forms, the varied pauses of his style. Cicero[7] sought to imitate the cadence of his periods but with little success. Lord Bacon was a poet.[8] His language has a sweet and majestic rhythm, which satisfies the sense, no less than the almost superhuman wisdom of his philosophy satisfies the intellect; it is a strain which distends, and then bursts the circumference of the hearer's mind, and pours itself forth together with it into the universal element with which it has perpetual sympathy. All the authors of revolutions in opinion are not only necessarily poets as they are inventors, nor even as their words unveil the permanent analogy of things by images which participate in the life of truth; but as their periods are harmonious and rhythmical and contain in themselves the elements of verse; being the echo of the eternal music. Nor are those supreme poets, who have employed traditional forms of rhythm on account of the form and action of their subjects, less capable of perceiving and teaching the truth of things, than those who have omitted that form. Shakespeare, Dante and Milton (to confine ourselves to modern writers) are philosophers of the very loftiest power.

A poem is the very image of life expressed in its eternal truth. There is this difference between a story and a poem, that a story is a catalogue of detached facts, which have no other bond of connexion than time, place, circumstance, cause and effect; the other is the creation of actions according to the unchangeable forms of human nature, as existing in the mind of the creator, which is itself the image of all other minds. The one is partial, and applies only to a definite period of time, and a certain combination of events which can never again recur; the other is universal, and contains within itself the germ of a relation to whatever motives or actions have place in the possible varieties of human nature. Time, which destroys the beauty and the use of the story of particular facts, stript of the poetry which should invest them, augments that of Poetry, and for ever develops new and wonderful applications of the eternal truth which it contains. Hence epitomes[9] have been called the moths of just history;[1] they eat out the poetry of it. The story of particular facts is as a mirror which obscures and distorts that which should be beautiful: Poetry is a mirror which makes beautiful that which is distorted.

The parts of a composition may be poetical, without the composition as a whole being a poem. A single sentence may be considered as a whole though it be found in a series of unassimilated portions; a single word even may be a spark of inextinguishable thought. And thus all the great historians, Herodotus, Plutarch, Livy,[2] were poets; and although the plan of these writers, especially that of Livy, restrained them from developing this faculty in its

6. I.e., in what Shelley has already said.
7. Marcus Tullius Cicero, the great Roman orator of the 1st century B.C.E.
8. See the *Filium Labyrinthi* and the *Essay on Death* particularly [Shelley's note].
9. Abstracts, summaries.
1. By Bacon in *The Advancement of Learning*

2.2.4.
2. Titus Livius (59 B.C.E.–17 C.E.) wrote an immense history of Rome. Herodotus (ca. 480–ca. 425 B.C.E.) wrote the first systematic history of Greece. Plutarch (ca. 46–ca. 120 C.E.) wrote *Parallel Lives* (of eminent Greeks and Romans).

highest degree, they make copious and ample amends for their subjection, by filling all the interstices of their subjects with living images.

Having determined what is poetry, and who are poets, let us proceed to estimate its effects upon society.

Poetry is ever accompanied with pleasure: all spirits on which it falls, open themselves to receive the wisdom which is mingled with its delight. In the infancy of the world, neither poets themselves nor their auditors are fully aware of the excellence of poetry: for it acts in a divine and unapprehended manner, beyond and above consciousness; and it is reserved for future generations to contemplate and measure the mighty cause and effect in all the strength and splendour of their union. Even in modern times, no living poet ever arrived at the fulness of his fame; the jury which sits in judgement upon a poet, belonging as he does to all time, must be composed of his peers: it must be impanelled by Time from the selectest of the wise of many generations. A Poet is a nightingale, who sits in darkness and sings to cheer its own solitude with sweet sounds; his auditors are as men entranced by the melody of an unseen musician, who feel that they are moved and softened, yet know not whence or why. The poems of Homer and his contemporaries were the delight of infant Greece; they were the elements of that social system which is the column upon which all succeeding civilization has reposed. Homer embodied the ideal perfection of his age in human character; nor can we doubt that those who read his verses were awakened to an ambition of becoming like to Achilles, Hector and Ulysses: the truth and beauty of friendship, patriotism and persevering devotion to an object, were unveiled to the depths in these immortal creations: the sentiments of the auditors must have been refined and enlarged by a sympathy with such great and lovely impersonations, until from admiring they imitated, and from imitation they identified themselves with the objects of their admiration. Nor let it be objected, that these characters are remote from moral perfection, and that they can by no means be considered as edifying patterns for general imitation. Every epoch under names more or less specious has deified its peculiar errors; Revenge is the naked Idol of the worship of a semi-barbarous age; and Self-deceit is the veiled Image of unknown evil before which luxury and satiety lie prostrate. But a poet considers the vices of his contemporaries as the temporary dress in which his creations must be arrayed, and which cover without concealing the eternal proportions of their beauty. An epic or dramatic personage is understood to wear them around his soul, as he may the antient armour or the modern uniform around his body; whilst it is easy to conceive a dress more graceful than either. The beauty of the internal nature cannot be so far concealed by its accidental vesture, but that the spirit of its form shall communicate itself to the very disguise, and indicate the shape it hides from the manner in which it is worn. A majestic form and graceful motions will express themselves through the most barbarous and tasteless costume. Few poets of the highest class have chosen to exhibit the beauty of their conceptions in its naked truth and splendour; and it is doubtful whether the alloy of costume, habit, etc., be not necessary to temper this planetary music[3] for mortal ears.

The whole objection, however, of the immorality of poetry[4] rests upon a

---

3. The music made by the revolving crystalline spheres of the planets, inaudible to human ears.
4. In the preceding paragraph Shelley has been implicitly dealing with the charge, voiced by Plato in his *Republic,* that poetry is immoral because it represents evil characters acting evilly.

misconception of the manner in which poetry acts to produce the moral improvement of man. Ethical science[5] arranges the elements which poetry has created, and propounds schemes and proposes examples of civil and domestic life: nor is it for want of admirable doctrines that men hate, and despise, and censure, and deceive, and subjugate one another. But Poetry acts in another and diviner manner. It awakens and enlarges the mind itself by rendering it the receptacle of a thousand unapprehended combinations of thought. Poetry lifts the veil from the hidden beauty of the world, and makes familiar objects be as if they were not familiar; it reproduces[6] all that it represents, and the impersonations clothed in its Elysian light stand thenceforward in the minds of those who have once contemplated them, as memorials of that gentle and exalted content[7] which extends itself over all thoughts and actions with which it coexists. The great secret of morals is Love; or a going out of our own nature, and an identification of ourselves with the beautiful which exists in thought, action, or person, not our own. A man, to be greatly good, must imagine intensely and comprehensively; he must put himself in the place of another and of many others; the pains and pleasures of his species must become his own. The great instrument of moral good is the imagination;[8] and poetry administers to the effect by acting upon the cause. Poetry enlarges the circumference of the imagination by replenishing it with thoughts of ever new delight, which have the power of attracting and assimilating to their own nature all other thoughts, and which form new intervals and interstices whose void for ever craves fresh food. Poetry strengthens that faculty which is the organ of the moral nature of man, in the same manner as exercise strengthens a limb. A Poet therefore would do ill to embody his own conceptions of right and wrong, which are usually those of his place and time, in his poetical creations, which participate in neither. By this assumption of the inferior office of interpreting the effect, in which perhaps after all he might acquit himself but imperfectly, he would resign the glory in a participation in the cause.[9] There was little danger that Homer, or any of the eternal Poets, should have so far misunderstood themselves as to have abdicated this throne of their widest dominion. Those in whom the poetical faculty, though great, is less intense, as Euripides, Lucan, Tasso,[1] Spenser, have frequently affected[2] a moral aim, and the effect of their poetry is diminished in exact proportion to the degree in which they compel us to advert to this purpose.[3]

* * *

It is difficult to define pleasure in its highest sense; the definition involving a number of apparent paradoxes. For, from an inexplicable defect of harmony

---

5. Moral philosophy.
6. Produces anew, re-creates.
7. Contentment.
8. Central to Shelley's theory is the concept (developed by 18th-century philosophers) of the sympathetic imagination—the faculty by which an individual is enabled to identify with the thoughts and feelings of others. Shelley insists that the faculty in poetry that enables us to share the joys and sufferings of invented characters is also the basis of all morality, for it compels us to feel for others as we feel for ourselves.
9. The "effect," or the explicit moral standards into which imaginative insights are translated at a particular time or place, is contrasted to the

"cause" of all morality, the imagination itself.
1. Tasso Torquato (1544–1595), Italian poet, author of *Jerusalem Delivered*, an epic poem about a crusade. Euripides (ca. 484–406 B.C.E.), Greek writer of tragedies. Lucan (39–65 C.E.), Roman poet, author of the *Pharsalia*.
2. Assumed, adopted.
3. In the following omitted passage Shelley reviews the history of drama and poetry in relation to civilization and morality and proceeds to refute the charge that poets are less useful than "reasoners and merchants." He begins by defining *utility* in terms of pleasure and then distinguishes between the lower (physical and material) and the higher (imaginative) pleasures.

in the constitution of human nature, the pain of the inferior is frequently connected with the pleasures of the superior portions of our being. Sorrow, terror, anguish, despair itself are often the chosen expressions of an approximation to the highest good. Our sympathy in tragic fiction depends on this principle; tragedy delights by affording a shadow of the pleasure which exists in pain. This is the source also of the melancholy which is inseparable from the sweetest melody. The pleasure that is in sorrow is sweeter than the pleasure of pleasure itself. And hence the saying, "It is better to go to the house of mourning, than to the house of mirth."[4] Not that this highest species of pleasure is necessarily linked with pain. The delight of love and friendship, the ecstasy of the admiration of nature, the joy of the perception and still more of the creation of poetry is often wholly unalloyed.

The production and assurance of pleasure in this highest sense is true utility. Those who produce and preserve this pleasure are Poets or poetical philosophers.

The exertions of Locke, Hume, Gibbon, Voltaire, Rousseau,[5] and their disciples, in favour of oppressed and deluded humanity, are entitled to the gratitude of mankind. Yet it is easy to calculate the degree of moral and intellectual improvement which the world would have exhibited, had they never lived. A little more nonsense would have been talked for a century or two; and perhaps a few more men, women, and children, burnt as heretics. We might not at this moment have been congratulating each other on the abolition of the Inquisition in Spain.[6] But it exceeds all imagination to conceive what would have been the moral condition of the world if neither Dante, Petrarch, Boccaccio, Chaucer, Shakespeare, Calderon, Lord Bacon, nor Milton, had ever existed; if Raphael and Michael Angelo had never been born; if the Hebrew poetry had never been translated; if a revival of the study of Greek literature had never taken place; if no monuments of antient sculpture had been handed down to us; and if the poetry of the religion of the antient world had been extinguished together with its belief. The human mind could never, except by the intervention of these excitements, have been awakened to the invention of the grosser sciences, and that application of analytical reasoning to the aberrations of society, which it is now attempted to exalt over the direct expression of the inventive and creative faculty itself.

We have more moral, political and historical wisdom, than we know how to reduce into practice; we have more scientific and economical knowledge than can be accommodated to the just distribution of the produce which it multiplies. The poetry in these systems of thought, is concealed by the accumulation of facts and calculating processes. There is no want of knowledge respecting what is wisest and best in morals, government, and political economy, or at least, what is wiser and better than what men now practise and endure. But we let *"I dare not wait upon I would*, like the poor cat i' the adage."[7] We want the creative faculty to imagine that which we know; we want the generous impulse to act that which we imagine; we want the poetry of life: our calculations have outrun conception; we have eaten more than we can digest. The cultivation of those sciences which have enlarged the

---

4. Ecclesiastes 7.2.
5. In a note Shelley says that, although Peacock had classified Rousseau with these other thinkers of the 17th and 18th centuries, "he was essentially a poet. The others, even Voltaire, were mere rea-

soners."
6. The Inquisition had been suspended in 1820, the year before Shelley wrote this essay; it was not abolished permanently until 1834.
7. *Macbeth* 1.7.44–45.

limits of the empire of man over the external world, has, for want of the poetical faculty, proportionally circumscribed those of the internal world; and man, having enslaved the elements, remains himself a slave. To what but a cultivation of the mechanical arts in a degree disproportioned to the presence of the creative faculty, which is the basis of all knowledge, is to be attributed the abuse of all invention for abridging and combining labour, to the exasperation of the inequality of mankind? From what other cause has it arisen that these inventions which should have lightened, have added a weight to the curse imposed on Adam? Poetry, and the principle of Self, of which money is the visible incarnation, are the God and Mammon of the world.[8]

The functions of the poetical faculty are two-fold; by one it creates new materials of knowledge, and power and pleasure; by the other it engenders in the mind a desire to reproduce and arrange them according to a certain rhythm and order which may be called the beautiful and the good. The cultivation of poetry is never more to be desired than at periods when, from an excess of the selfish and calculating principle, the accumulation of the materials of external life exceed the quantity of the power of assimilating them to the internal laws of human nature. The body has then become too unwieldy for that which animates it.

Poetry is indeed something divine. It is at once the centre and circumference of knowledge; it is that which comprehends all science, and that to which all science must be referred. It is at the same time the root and blossom of all other systems of thought; it is that from which all spring, and that which adorns all; and that which, if blighted, denies the fruit and the seed, and withholds from the barren world the nourishment and the succession of the scions of the tree of life. It is the perfect and consummate surface and bloom of things; it is as the odour and the colour of the rose to the texture of the elements which compose it, as the form and the splendour of unfaded beauty to the secrets of anatomy and corruption. What were Virtue, Love, Patriotism, Friendship etc.—what were the scenery of this beautiful Universe which we inhabit—what were our consolations on this side of the grave—and what were our aspirations beyond it—if Poetry did not ascend to bring light and fire from those eternal regions where the owl-winged faculty of calculation dare not ever soar? Poetry is not like reasoning, a power to be exerted according to the determination of the will. A man cannot say, "I will compose poetry." The greatest poet even cannot say it: for the mind in creation is as a fading coal which some invisible influence, like an inconstant wind, awakens to transitory brightness: this power arises from within, like the colour of a flower which fades and changes as it is developed, and the conscious portions of our natures are unprophetic either of its approach or its departure.[9] Could this influence be durable in its original purity and force, it is impossible to predict the greatness of the results; but when composition begins, inspiration is already on the decline, and the most glorious poetry that has ever been communicated to the world is probably a feeble

8. Matthew 6.24: "Ye cannot serve God and Mammon."
9. This passage reiterates the ancient belief that the highest poetry is "inspired" and therefore occurs independently of the intention, effort, or consciousness of the poet. Unlike earlier critics, however, Shelley attributes such poetry not to a god or a muse but to the unconscious depths of the poet's own mind.

shadow of the original conception of the poet. I appeal to the greatest Poets of the present day, whether it be not an error to assert that the finest passages of poetry are produced by labour and study. The toil and the delay recommended by critics can be justly interpreted to mean no more than a careful observation of the inspired moments, and an artificial connexion of the spaces between their suggestions by the intertexture of conventional expressions; a necessity only imposed by the limitedness of the poetical faculty itself. For Milton conceived the Paradise Lost as a whole before he executed it in portions. We have his own authority also for the Muse having "dictated" to him the "unpremeditated song,"[1] and let this be an answer to those who would allege the fifty-six various readings of the first line of the Orlando Furioso.[2] Compositions so produced are to poetry what mosaic is to painting. This instinct and intuition of the poetical faculty is still more observable in the plastic and pictorial arts: a great statue or picture grows under the power of the artist as a child in the mother's womb; and the very mind which directs the hands in formation is incapable of accounting to itself for the origin, the gradations, or the media of the process.

Poetry is the record of the best and happiest[3] moments of the happiest and best minds. We are aware of evanescent visitations of thought and feeling sometimes associated with place or person, sometimes regarding our own mind alone, and always arising unforeseen and departing unbidden, but elevating and delightful beyond all expression: so that even in the desire and the regret they leave, there cannot but be pleasure, participating as it does in the nature of its object. It is as it were the interpenetration of a diviner nature through our own; but its footsteps are like those of a wind over a sea, where the coming calm erases, and whose traces remain only as on the wrinkled sand which paves it. These and corresponding conditions of being are experienced principally by those of the most delicate sensibility and the most enlarged imagination; and the state of mind produced by them is at war with every base desire. The enthusiasm of virtue, love, patriotism, and friendship is essentially linked with these emotions; and whilst they last, self appears as what it is, an atom to a Universe. Poets are not only subject to these experiences as spirits of the most refined organization, but they can colour all that they combine with the evanescent hues of this etherial world; a word, or a trait in the representation of a scene or a passion, will touch the enchanted chord, and reanimate, in those who have ever experienced these emotions, the sleeping, the cold, the buried image of the past. Poetry thus makes immortal all that is best and most beautiful in the world; it arrests the vanishing apparitions which haunt the interlunations[4] of life, and veiling them or in language or in form sends them forth among mankind, bearing sweet news of kindred joy to those with whom their sisters abide—abide, because there is no portal of expression from the caverns of the spirit which they inhabit into the universe of things. Poetry redeems from decay the visitations of the divinity in man.

Poetry turns all things to loveliness; it exalts the beauty of that which is most beautiful, and it adds beauty to that which is most deformed; it marries

---

1. *Paradise Lost* 9.21–24.
2. The epic poem by the 16th-century Italian poet Ariosto, noted for his care in composition.
3. In the double sense of "most joyous" and "most

apt or felicitous in invention."
4. The dark intervals between the old and new moons.

exultation and horror, grief and pleasure, eternity and change; it subdues to union under its light yoke all irreconcilable things. It transmutes all that it touches, and every form moving within the radiance of its presence is changed by wondrous sympathy to an incarnation of the spirit which it breathes; its secret alchemy turns to potable gold[5] the poisonous waters which flow from death through life; it strips the veil of familiarity from the world, and lays bare the naked and sleeping beauty which is the spirit of its forms.

All things exist as they are perceived: at least in relation to the percipient. "The mind is its own place, and of itself can make a heaven of hell, a hell of heaven."[6] But poetry defeats the curse which binds us to be subjected to the accident of surrounding impressions. And whether it spreads its own figured curtain or withdraws life's dark veil from before the scene of things, it equally creates for us a being within our being. It makes us the inhabitants of a world to which the familiar world is a chaos. It reproduces the common universe of which we are portions and percipients, and it purges from our inward sight the film of familiarity which obscures from us the wonder of our being. It compels us to feel that which we perceive, and to imagine that which we know. It creates anew the universe after it has been annihilated in our minds by the recurrence of impressions blunted by reiteration.[7] It justifies that bold and true word of Tasso: *Non merita nome di creatore, se non Iddio ed il Poeta.*[8]

A Poet, as he is the author to others of the highest wisdom, pleasure, virtue and glory, so he ought personally to be the happiest, the best, the wisest, and the most illustrious of men. As to his glory, let Time be challenged to declare whether the fame of any other institutor of human life be comparable to that of a poet. That he is the wisest, the happiest, and the best, inasmuch as he is a poet, is equally incontrovertible: the greatest poets have been men of the most spotless virtue, of the most consummate prudence, and, if we could look into the interior of their lives, the most fortunate of men: and the exceptions, as they regard those who possessed the poetic faculty in a high yet inferior degree, will be found on consideration to confirm rather than destroy the rule. Let us for a moment stoop to the arbitration of popular breath, and usurping and uniting in our own persons the incompatible characters of accuser, witness, judge and executioner, let us decide without trial, testimony, or form that certain motives of those who are "there sitting where we dare not soar"[9] are reprehensible. Let us assume that Homer was a drunkard, that Virgil was a flatterer, that Horace was a coward, that Tasso was a madman, that Lord Bacon was a peculator, that Raphael was a libertine, that Spenser was a poet laureate.[1] It is inconsistent with this division of our subject to cite living poets, but Posterity has done ample justice to the great names now referred to. Their errors have been weighed and found to have

---

5. Alchemists aimed to produce a drinkable ("potable") form of gold that would be an elixir of life, curing all diseases.
6. Satan's speech, *Paradise Lost* 1.254–55.
7. Shelley's version of a widespread Romantic doctrine that the poetic imagination transforms the familiar into the miraculous and recreates the old world into a new world. See, e.g., Coleridge's *Biographia Literaria* on "freshness of sensation," chap. 4 (p. 474), and Carlyle's *Sartor Resartus,* "Natural Supernaturalism," book 3, chap. 8

(p. 1096).
8. "No one merits the name of Creator except God and the Poet." Quoted by Pierantonio Serassi in his *Life of Torquato Tasso* (1785).
9. *Paradise Lost* 4.829.
1. Charges that had in fact been made against these men. The use of "poet laureate" as a derogatory term was a dig at Robert Southey, who held that honor at the time Shelley was writing. "Peculator": a misappropriator of public money. Raphael is the 16th-century Italian painter.

been dust in the balance; if their sins "were as scarlet, they are now white as snow";[2] they have been washed in the blood of the mediator and the redeemer Time. Observe in what a ludicrous chaos the imputations of real or fictitious crime have been confused in the contemporary calumnies against poetry and poets;[3] consider how little is, as it appears—or appears, as it is; look to your own motives, and judge not, lest ye be judged.

Poetry, as has been said, in this respect differs from logic, that it is not subject to the controul of the active powers of the mind, and that its birth and recurrence has no necessary connexion with consciousness or will. It is presumptuous to determine that these[4] are the necessary conditions of all mental causation, when mental effects are experienced insusceptible of being referred to them. The frequent recurrence of the poetical power, it is obvious to suppose, may produce in the mind an habit of order and harmony correlative with its own nature and with its effects upon other minds. But in the intervals of inspiration, and they may be frequent without being durable, a poet becomes a man, and is abandoned to the sudden reflux of the influences under which others habitually live. But as he is more delicately organized than other men, and sensible to pain and pleasure, both his own and that of others, in a degree unknown to them, he will avoid the one and pursue the other with an ardour proportioned to this difference. And he renders himself obnoxious to calumny,[5] when he neglects to observe the circumstances under which these objects of universal pursuit and flight have disguised themselves in one another's garments.

But there is nothing necessarily evil in this error, and thus cruelty, envy, revenge, avarice, and the passions purely evil, have never formed any portion of the popular imputations on the lives of poets.

I have thought it most favourable to the cause of truth to set down these remarks according to the order in which they were suggested to my mind, by a consideration of the subject itself, instead of following that of the treatise that excited me to make them public.[6] Thus although devoid of the formality of a polemical reply; if the view they contain be just, they will be found to involve a refutation of the doctrines of the Four Ages of Poetry, so far at least as regards the first division of the subject. I can readily conjecture what should have moved the gall of the learned and intelligent author of that paper; I confess myself, like him, unwilling to be stunned by the Theseids of the hoarse Codri of the day. Bavius and Mævius[7] undoubtedly are, as they ever were, insufferable persons. But it belongs to a philosophical critic to distinguish rather than confound.

The first part of these remarks has related to Poetry in its elements and principles; and it has been shewn, as well as the narrow limits assigned them would permit, that what is called poetry, in a restricted sense, has a common source with all other forms of order and of beauty according to which the materials of human life are susceptible of being arranged, and which is poetry in an universal sense.

---

2. Isaiah 1.18.
3. Shelley alludes especially to the charges of immorality by contemporary reviewers against Lord Byron and himself.
4. I.e., consciousness or will. Shelley again proposes that some mental processes are unconscious—outside our control or awareness.

5. Exposed to slander.
6. Peacock's *Four Ages of Poetry*.
7. Would-be poets satirized by Virgil and Horace. "Theseids": epic poems about Theseus. Codrus (plural "Codri") was the Roman author of a long, dull *Theseid* attacked by Juvenal and others.

The second part[8] will have for its object an application of these principles to the present state of the cultivation of Poetry, and a defence of the attempt to idealize the modern forms of manners and opinions, and compel them into a subordination to the imaginative and creative faculty. For the literature of England, an energetic developement of which has ever preceded or accompanied a great and free developement of the national will, has arisen as it were from a new birth. In spite of the low-thoughted envy which would undervalue contemporary merit, our own will be a memorable age in intellectual achievements, and we live among such philosophers and poets as surpass beyond comparison any who have appeared since the last national struggle for civil and religious liberty.[9] The most unfailing herald, companion, and follower of the awakening of a great people to work a beneficial change in opinion or institution, is Poetry. At such periods there is an accumulation of the power of communicating and receiving intense and impassioned conceptions respecting man and nature. The persons in whom this power resides, may often, as far as regards many portions of their nature, have little apparent correspondence with that spirit of good of which they are the ministers. But even whilst they deny and abjure, they are yet compelled to serve, the Power which is seated upon the throne of their own soul. It is impossible to read the compositions of the most celebrated writers of the present day without being startled with the electric life which burns within their words. They measure the circumference and sound the depths of human nature with a comprehensive and all-penetrating spirit, and they are themselves perhaps the most sincerely astonished at its manifestations, for it is less their spirit than the spirit of the age.[1] Poets are the hierophants[2] of an unapprehended inspiration, the mirrors of the gigantic shadows which futurity casts upon the present, the words which express what they understand not; the trumpets which sing to battle, and feel not what they inspire: the influence which is moved not, but moves.[3] Poets are the unacknowledged legislators of the World.

1821   1840

8. Shelley, however, completed only the first part.
9. In the age of Milton and the English Civil Wars.
1. By attributing to the great poets and philosophers of his time a shared "spirit of the age," Shelley anticipates what later historians were to identify as "the Romantic movement."
2. Priests who are expositors of sacred mysteries.
3. Aristotle had said that God is the "Unmoved Mover" of the universe.

JOHN CLARE
1793–1864

John Clare was the nearest thing to the "natural poet" for whom primitivists had been searching ever since the mid-eighteenth century. An earlier and greater peasant poet, Robert Burns, had managed to acquire a solid liberal education. Clare, however, was born at Helpston, a Northamptonshire village, of a field laborer who was barely literate and a mother who was entirely illiterate, and he obtained only enough schooling to enable him to read and write. Although he was a sickly and fearful child, he had to work hard in the field, where he found himself composing verse "for downright pleasure in giving vent to my feelings." In 1820, publication of his *Poems Descriptive of Rural Life and Scenery* attracted critical attention, and on a trip to London, he was made much of by leading writers of the day. But his celebrity soon dimmed, and his three later books of verse were failures. Under these and other disappointments his mind gave way in 1837, and he spent almost all the rest of his life in an asylum. The place was for him a refuge as well as a confinement, for he was treated kindly, allowed to wander about the countryside, and encouraged to go on writing his verses. Some of his best achievements are the poems composed during his madness.

Clare did not, of course, write independently of literary influences, for he had studied the poetry of James Thomson, William Cowper, Burns, Milton, Wordsworth, and Coleridge. But he managed to stay true to his own experience of everyday country sights and customs and to capture in his verse the genuine idiom of rural people. His nightingale poem, written in a long-established literary tradition, has many more particulars of nature than any of those by his predecessors, and his homely mouse, in the third poem printed below, is a bit of pure rustic impressionism in a way that even Burns's moralized mouse is not (see *To a Mouse*, p. 105). Some of Clare's introspective asylum poems achieve so haunting a poignancy and are spoken in so quietly distinctive a voice that they have made the great mass of manuscripts he left at his death an exciting place of discovery for recent scholars.

Those same manuscripts are a site of contention among current textual theorists. Words are everywhere misspelled in them, standard syntax is regularly ignored, and there is almost no punctuation in the lines. In his own day, Clare was respelled, punctuated, and otherwise made presentable by his publisher, John Taylor (who did the same for John Keats, another of his poets who took a casual view of such matters). Modern scholars, eager to recover exactly what Clare wrote—in effect, to free him from the impositions and constraints of well-intentioned nineteenth-century editors—are restoring the idiosyncrasies but, in the process, are constructing a poet who is so full of what we would normally call mistakes as to be, for all practical purposes, inaccessible to the general reader. (For example, the manuscripts have "were" for "where," "your" for "you're," "anker" for "hanker," "hugh" for "huge.") The texts printed below, which are presented as "reading" versions of Clare's own words, are the product of a principled modernization by the editors of this anthology. They are based, where the materials are available, on authoritative manuscript versions recovered and now made standard by Eric Robinson and his associates in a succession of editions published by Oxford University Press.

The Nightingale's Nest

Up this green woodland ride° let's softly rove,   *riding path*
And list° the nightingale—she dwelleth here.   *listen to*
Hush! let the wood gate softly clap, for fear
The noise may drive her from her home of love;
5   For here I've heard her many a merry year—
At morn and eve, nay, all the livelong day,
As though she lived on song. This very spot,
Just where that old man's beard° all wildly trails   *Spanish moss*
Rude arbours o'er the road and stops the way—
10   And where that child its blue-bell flowers hath got,
Laughing and creeping through the mossy rails°—   *fence rails*
There have I hunted like a very boy,
Creeping on hands and knees through matted thorns
To find her nest and see her feed her young.

15 And vainly did I many hours employ:
    All seemed as hidden as a thought unborn.
    And where these crimping° fern leaves ramp° among   *curling/shoot up*
    The hazel's under-boughs, I've nestled down
    And watched her while she sung; and her renown
20 Hath made me marvel that so famed a bird[1]
    Should have no better dress than russet brown.
    Her wings would tremble in her ecstasy,
    And feathers stand on end, as 'twere with joy,
    And mouth wide open to release her heart
25 Of its out-sobbing songs. The happiest part
    Of summer's fame she shared, for so to me
    Did happy fancies shapen her employ;[2]
    But if I touched a bush or scarcely stirred,
    All in a moment stopt. I watched in vain:
30 The timid bird had left the hazel bush,
    And at a distance hid to sing again.
    Lost in a wilderness of listening leaves,
    Rich ecstasy would pour its luscious strain,
    Till envy spurred the emulating thrush
35 To start less wild and scarce inferior songs;
    For cares with him for half the year remain,
    To damp the ardour of his speckled breast,
    While nightingales to summer's life belongs,
    And naked trees and winter's nipping wrongs
40 Are strangers to her music and her rest.
    Her joys are evergreen, her world is wide—
    Hark! there she is as usual—let's be hush—
    For in this black-thorn clump, if rightly guessed,
    Her curious house is hidden. Part aside
45 These hazel branches in a gentle way,
    And stoop right cautious 'neath the rustling boughs,
    For we will have another search to-day,
    And hunt this fern-strewn thorn clump round and round;
    And where this seeded wood grass idly bows,
50 We'll wade right through, it is a likely nook:
    In such like spots, and often on the ground,
    They'll build where rude boys never think to look—
    Aye, as I live! her secret nest is here,
    Upon this whitethorn stulp!° I've searched about   *stump*
55 For hours in vain. There! put that bramble by—
    Nay, trample on its branches and get near.
    How subtle is the bird! she started out
    And raised a plaintive note of danger nigh,
    Ere we were past the brambles; and now, near
60 Her nest, she sudden stops—as choking fear
    That might betray her home. So even now

---

1. The nightingale had been celebrated by, among others, Chaucer, Spenser, Shakespeare, Milton, and, closer to Clare's own time, William Cowper, Charlotte Smith, Mary Robinson, Coleridge, Wordsworth, and Keats. In lines 22, 24–25, and 33, Clare echoes lines 57–58 of Keats's *Ode to a Nightingale*.
2. Give shape to her (the nightingale's) regular activities.

We'll leave it as we found it: safety's guard
Of pathless solitude shall keep it still.
See, there she's sitting on the old oak bough,
65 Mute in her fears; our presence doth retard
Her joys, and doubt turns all her rapture chill.

Sing on, sweet bird! may no worse hap befall
Thy visions, than the fear that now deceives.
We will not plunder music of its dower,
70 Nor turn this spot of happiness to thrall;°   *misery*
For melody seems hid in every flower,
That blossoms near thy home. These harebells all
Seems bowing with the beautiful in song;
And gaping cuckoo° with its spotted leaves   *a spring flower*
75 Seems blushing of the singing it has heard.
How curious is the nest; no other bird
Uses such loose materials, or weaves
Their dwellings in such spots: dead oaken leaves
Are placed without, and velvet moss within,
80 And little scraps of grass, and, scant and spare,
Of what seems scarce materials, down and hair;
For from man's haunts she seemeth nought to win.
Yet nature is the builder and contrives
Homes for her children's comfort even here;
85 Where solitude's disciples spend their lives
Unseen save when a wanderer passes near
That loves such pleasant places. Deep adown,
The nest is made an hermit's mossy cell.
Snug lie her curious eggs, in number five,
90 Of deadened green, or rather olive brown;
And the old prickly thorn-bush guards them well.
And here we'll leave them, still unknown to wrong,
As the old woodland's legacy of song.

1825–30   1835

Pastoral Poesy

True poesy is not in words,
    But images that thoughts express,
By which the simplest hearts are stirred
    To elevated happiness.

5 Mere books would be but useless things
    Where none had taste or mind to read,
Like unknown lands where beauty springs
    And none are there to heed.

But poesy is a language meet,
10   And fields are every one's employ;°   *concern*
The wild flower 'neath the shepherd's feet
    Looks up and gives him joy;

15   I gave my name immortal birth,
        And kept my spirit with the free.

Aug. 2, 1844   1924

I Am

1

I am—yet what I am, none cares or knows;
    My friends forsake me like a memory lost:—
I am the self-consumer of my woes;—
    They rise and vanish in oblivion's host,
5 Like shadows in love's frenzied stifled throes:—
And yet I am, and live—like vapours tossed

2

Into the nothingness of scorn and noise,—
    Into the living sea of waking dreams,
Where there is neither sense of life or joys,
10   But the vast shipwreck of my life's esteems;
Even the dearest that I love the best
Are strange—nay, rather, stranger than the rest.

3

I long for scenes where man hath never trod,
    A place where woman never smiled or wept,
15 There to abide with my Creator, God,
    And sleep as I in childhood sweetly slept,
Untroubling and untroubled where I lie,
The grass below—above, the vaulted sky.

1842–46   1848

An Invite to Eternity

1

Wilt thou go with me, sweet maid,
Say maiden, wilt thou go with me
Through the valley depths of shade,
Of night and dark obscurity,
5 Where the path hath lost its way,
Where the sun forgets the day,
Where there's nor life nor light to see,
Sweet maiden, wilt thou go with me?

2

Where stones will turn to flooding streams,
10 Where plains will rise like ocean waves,
Where life will fade like visioned dreams

And mountains darken into caves,
Say maiden, wilt thou go with me
Through this sad non-identity,
15 Where parents live and are forgot
And sisters live and know us not?

3

Say maiden, wilt thou go with me
In this strange death of life to be,
To live in death and be the same
20 Without this life, or home, or name,
At once to be and not to be,
That was and is not—yet to see
Things pass like shadows—and the sky
Above, below, around us lie?

4

25 The land of shadows wilt thou trace
And look—nor know each other's face,
The present mixed with reasons gone
And past and present all as one?
Say maiden, can thy life be led
30 To join the living with the dead?
Then trace thy footsteps on with me—
We're wed to one eternity.

1847   1848

Clock a Clay[1]

1

In the cowslip's peeps I lie,[2]
Hidden from the buzzing fly,
While green grass beneath me lies,
Pearled wi' dew like fishes' eyes;
5 Here I lie, a Clock a Clay,
Waiting for the time o' day.

2

While grassy forests quake surprise,
And the wild wind sobs and sighs,
My gold home rocks as like to fall
10 On its pillars green and tall;
When the pattering rain drives by
Clock a Clay keeps warm and dry.

---

1. The ladybird, or ladybug. The sixth and last lines allude to the children's game of telling the hour by the number of taps it takes to make the ladybird fly away home.
2. Cf. the opening lines of Ariel's song in act 5 of Shakespeare's *Tempest:* "Where the bee sucks, there suck I: / In a cowslip's bell I lie." "Peeps": i.e., pips—single blossoms of flowers growing in a cluster. "Cowslip": a yellow primrose.

3

Day by day and night by night,
All the week I hide from sight;
15 In the cowslip's peeps I lie,
In rain and dew still warm and dry;
Day and night and night and day,
Red black-spotted Clock a Clay.

4

My home it shakes in wind and showers,
20 Pale green pillar topped wi' flowers,
Bending at the wild wind's breath,
Till I touch the grass beneath;
Here still I live, lone Clock a Clay,
Watching for the time of day.

ca. 1848   1873

The Peasant Poet

He loved the brook's soft sound,
The swallow swimming by;
He loved the daisy-covered ground,
The cloud-bedappled sky.
5 To him the dismal storm appeared
The very voice of God,
And where the evening rack° was reared   mass of clouds
Stood Moses with his rod.
And everything his eyes surveyed,
10 The insects i' the brake,
Were creatures God Almighty made—
He loved them for His sake:
A silent man in life's affairs,
A thinker from a boy,
15 A peasant in his daily cares—
The poet in his joy.

1842–64   1920

Song

I hid my love when young while I
Couldn't bear the buzzing of a fly;
I hid my love to my despite
Till I could not bear to look at light.
5 I dare not gaze upon her face
But left her memory in each place;
Where'er I saw a wild flower lie
I kissed and bade my love goodbye.

I met her in the greenest dells,
10 Where dewdrops pearl the wood bluebells;

The lost breeze kissed her bright blue eye,
The bee kissed and went singing by.
A sunbeam found a passage there,
A gold chain round her neck so fair;
15 As secret as the wild bee's song
She lay there all the summer long.

I hid my love in field and town
Till e'en the breeze would knock me down.
The bees seemed singing ballads o'er
20 The fly's buzz turned a lion's roar;
And even silence found a tongue
To haunt me all the summer long:
The riddle nature could not prove
Was nothing else but secret love.

1842–64   1920

Song

I peeled bits o' straws and I got switches too
From the grey peeling willow as idlers do,
And I switched at the flies as I sat all alone
Till my flesh, blood, and marrow wasted to dry bone.
5 My illness was love, though I knew not the smart,
But the beauty o' love was the blood o' my heart.

Crowded places, I shunned them as noises too rude
And flew to the silence of sweet solitude,
Where the flower in green darkness buds, blossoms, and fades,
10 Unseen of a' shepherds and flower-loving maids.
The hermit bees find them but once and away;
There I'll bury alive and in silence decay.

I looked on the eyes o' fair woman too long,
Till silence and shame stole the use o' my tongue;
15 When I tried to speak to her I'd nothing to say,
So I turned myself round, and she wandered away.
When she got too far off—why, I'd something to tell,
So I sent sighs behind her and talked to mysel'.

Willow switches I broke, and I peeled bits o' straws,
20 Ever lonely in crowds, in nature's own laws—
My ballroom the pasture, my music the bees,
My drink was the fountain, my church the tall trees.
Who ever would love or be tied to a wife
When it makes a man mad a' the days o' his life?

1842–64   1920

FELICIA DOROTHEA HEMANS
1793–1835

Born in Liverpool and brought up in Wales, Felicia Hemans published her first two volumes—*Poems* and *England and Spain, or Valour and Patriotism*—when she was fifteen. She followed these four years later with *The Domestic Affections and Other Poems* (1812) and from 1816 on into the 1830s produced new books of poetry almost annually: short sentimental lyrics, tales and "historic scenes," translations, songs for music, sketches of women, hymns for children. She also published literary criticism in the magazines and wrote three plays. Her work was widely read, anthologized, memorized, and set to music throughout the nineteenth century and was especially popular and influential in the United States, where the first of many collected editions of her poems appeared in 1825. When she died, she was eulogized by many poets, including William Wordsworth, Letitia Landon, and Elizabeth Barrett—a sign of the high regard in which she was held by her contemporaries.

A tablet erected by her brothers in the cathedral of St. Asaph, in north Wales, reads in part, "In memory of Felicia Hemans, whose character is best pourtrayed in her writings." But there are several characters in her poems, and some of them seem not entirely compatible with some of the others. She is frequently thought of as the poet (in the nineteenth century as "the poetess") of domestic affections, at the center of a cult of domesticity in which women are subservient to men, who carry on the important business of life, and patriarchy is the acknowledged if not always accepted standard. Among her most popular pieces in this vein, *Evening Prayer, at a Girls' School* depicts the happy ignorance of schoolgirls whose enjoyment of life will end when they reach womanhood, and *Indian Woman's Death-Song* is the lament of a Native American woman whose husband has abandoned her, sung as she plunges in her canoe over a cataract to suicide with an infant in her arms.

Many of Hemans's longer narratives, by contrast, recount the exploits of women warriors who, to avenge personal, family, or national injustice or insult, destroy enemies in a manner not conventionally associated with female behavior. In *The Widow of Crescentius*, Stephania stalks and poisons the German emperor Otho, the murderer of her husband; in *The Wife of Asdrubal*, a mother publicly kills her own children and herself to show contempt for her husband, a betrayer of the Carthaginians whom he governed; the heroine of *The Bride of the Greek Isle*, boarding the ship of the pirates who have killed her husband, annihilates them (and herself) in a conflagration rivaling the monumental explosion described in *Casabianca*. Among the numerous themes of her work, patriotism and military action recur frequently; there may be a biographical basis for these motifs, given that her two oldest brothers distinguished themselves in the Peninsular War and her military husband (who deserted her and their five sons in 1818) had also served in Spain. But some of her most famous patriotic and military poems are now being viewed as critiques of the virtues and ideologies they had been thought by earlier readers to inculcate. *The Homes of England*, for example, has been read as both asserting and undermining the idea that all homes are equal, ancestral estates and cottages alike; and in *Casabianca*, the boy's automatic steadfastness has been interpreted as empty obedience rather than admirable loyalty.

Hemans was the highest paid writer in *Blackwood's* during her day. Her books sold more copies than those of any other contemporary poet except Byron and Walter Scott. She was a shrewd calculator of the literary marketplace and a genius in her negotiations with publishers (which she carried on entirely through the mails). Her self-abasing women of the domestic affections and her scimitar-wielding superwomen of the revenge narratives exist side by side throughout her works. These and other seeming dissonances clearly enhanced the strong appeal of her poems to a wide range of readers, men as well as women.

England's Dead

Son of the ocean isle!
Where sleep your mighty dead?
Show me what high and stately pile
Is rear'd o'er Glory's bed.

5   Go, stranger! track the deep,
Free, free the white sail spread!
Wave may not foam, nor wild wind sweep,
Where rest not England's dead.

On Egypt's burning plains,
10   By the pyramid o'ersway'd,
With fearful power the noonday reigns,
And the palm trees yield no shade.[1]

But let the angry sun
From heaven look fiercely red,
15 Unfelt by those whose task is done!—
There slumber England's dead.

The hurricane hath might
Along the Indian shore,
And far by Ganges' banks at night,
20   Is heard the tiger's roar.

But let the sound roll on!
It hath no tone of dread,
For those that from their toils are gone;—
There slumber England's dead.

25 Loud rush the torrent floods
The western wilds among,
And free, in green Columbia's woods,
The hunter's bow is strung.

But let the floods rush on!
30   Let the arrow's flight be sped!
Why should *they* reck whose task is done?—
There slumber England's dead!

The mountain storms rise high
In the snowy Pyrenees,
35 And toss the pine boughs through the sky,
Like rose leaves on the breeze.

1. English forces defeated the French at Alexandria in the spring of 1801. The rest of the references—to 18th- and early-19th-century battles in India (lines 17–24), America (lines 25–32), Spain (lines 33–40), and on the sea (lines 41–48)—are more general.

  And bright the flowery sod,
  Where first the child's glad spirit loves
40 Its country and its God!

1827

A Spirit's Return

"This is to be a mortal,
And seek the things beyond mortality!"
—MANFRED[1]

Thy voice prevails—dear friend, my gentle friend!
This long-shut heart for thee shall be unsealed,
And though thy soft eye mournfully will bend
Over the troubled stream, yet once revealed
5 Shall its freed waters flow; then rocks must close
For evermore, above their dark repose.

Come while the gorgeous mysteries of the sky
Fused in the crimson sea of sunset lie;
Come to the woods, where all strange wandering sound
10 Is mingled into harmony profound;
Where the leaves thrill with spirit, while the wind
Fills with a viewless being, unconfined,
The trembling reeds and fountains—our own dell,
With its green dimness and Aeolian° breath,   *wind-blown*
15 Shall suit th' unveiling of dark records well—
Hear me in tenderness and silent faith!

Thou knew'st me not in life's fresh vernal morn—
I would thou hadst!—for then my heart on thine
Had poured a worthier love; now, all o'erworn
20 By its deep thirst for something too divine,
It hath but fitful music to bestow,
Echoes of harp-strings broken long ago.

Yet even in youth companionless I stood,
As a lone forest-bird 'midst ocean's foam;
25 For me the silver cords of brotherhood
Were early loosed; the voices from my home
Passed one by one, and melody and mirth
Left me a dreamer by a silent hearth.

But, with the fulness of a heart that burned
30 For the deep sympathies of mind, I turned
From that unanswering spot, and fondly sought

1. A remark concerning Manfred's convulsion at the moment the Phantom of his beloved Astarte disappears (*Manfred* 2.4.158–59; see p. 610). Hemans's poem can be read as commentary on Byron's play, Percy Shelley's *Alastor*, and Keats's *Endymion* (see the note to lines 216–17 below), all of which depict a protagonist's problems in communicating with an otherworldly lover.

In all wild scenes with thrilling murmurs fraught,
In every still small voice and sound of power,
And flute-note of the wind through cave and bower,
35 A perilous delight!—for then first woke
My life's lone passion, the mysterious quest
Of secret knowledge; and each tone that broke
From the wood-arches or the fountain's breast,
Making my quick soul vibrate as a lyre,
40 But ministered to that strange inborn fire.
'Midst the bright silence of the mountain dells,
In noon-tide hours or golden summer-eves,
My thoughts have burst forth as a gale that swells
Into a rushing blast, and from the leaves
45 Shakes out response. O thou rich world unseen!
Thou curtained realm of spirits!—thus my cry
Hath troubled air and silence—dost thou lie
Spread all around, yet by some filmy screen
Shut from us ever? The resounding woods,
50 Do their depths teem with marvels?—and the floods,
And the pure fountains, leading secret veins
Of quenchless melody through rock and hill,
Have they bright dwellers?—are their lone domains
Peopled with beauty, which may never still
55 *Our* weary thirst of soul?—Cold, weak and cold,
Is earth's vain language, piercing not one fold
Of our deep being! Oh, for gifts more high!
For a seer's glance to rend mortality!
For a charmed rod, to call from each dark shrine
60 The oracles divine!

I woke from those high fantasies, to know
My kindred with the earth—I woke to love:
O gentle friend! to love in doubt and woe,
Shutting the heart the worshipped name above,
65 Is to love deeply—and *my* spirit's dower
Was a sad gift, a melancholy power
Of so adoring—with a buried care,
And with the o'erflowing of a voiceless prayer,
And with a deepening dream, that day by day,
70 In the still shadow of its lonely sway,
Folded me closer, till the world held nought
Save the *one* being to my centred thought.

There was no music but his voice to hear,
No joy but such as with *his* step drew near;
75 Light was but where he looked—life where he moved;
Silently, fervently, thus, thus I loved.
Oh! but such love is fearful!—and I knew
Its gathering doom:—the soul's prophetic sight
Even then unfolded in my breast, and threw
80 O'er all things round a full, strong, vivid light,
Too sorrowfully clear!—an undertone

Was given to Nature's harp, for me alone
Whispering of grief.—Of grief?—be strong, awake,
Hath not thy love been victory, O, my soul?
85 Hath not its conflict won a voice to shake
Death's fastnesses?—a magic to control
Worlds far removed?—from o'er the grave to thee
Love hath made answer; and *thy* tale should be
Sung like a lay of triumph!—Now return,
90 And take thy treasure from its bosomed urn,
And lift it once to light!

             In fear, in pain,
I said I loved—but yet a heavenly strain
Of sweetness floated down the tearful stream,
A joy flashed through the trouble of my dream!
95 I knew myself beloved!—we breathed no vow,
No mingling visions might our fate allow,
As unto happy hearts; but still and deep,
Like a rich jewel gleaming in a grave,
Like golden sand in some dark river's wave,
100 So did my soul that costly knowledge keep
So jealously!—a thing o'er which to shed,
When stars alone beheld the drooping head,
Lone tears! yet ofttimes burdened with the excess
Of our strange nature's quivering happiness.

105 But, oh! sweet friend! we dream not of love's might
Till death has robed with soft and solemn light
The image we enshrine!—Before *that* hour,
We have but glimpses of the o'ermastering power
Within us laid!—*then* doth the spirit-flame
110 With sword-like lightning rend its mortal frame;
The wings of that which pants to follow fast
Shake their clay-bars, as with a prisoned blast—
The sea is in our souls!

             He died—*he* died
On whom my lone devotedness was cast!
115 I might not keep one vigil by his side,
I, whose wrung heart watched with him to the last!
I might not once his fainting head sustain,
Nor bathe his parched lips in the hour of pain,
Nor say to him, "Farewell!"—He passed away—
120 Oh! had *my* love been there, its conquering sway
Had won him back from death! but thus removed,
Borne o'er the abyss no sounding-line hath proved,
Joined with the unknown, the viewless—he became
Unto my thoughts another, yet the same—
125 Changed—hallowed—glorified!—and his low grave
Seemed a bright mournful altar—mine, all mine:—
Brother and friend soon left me *that* sole shrine,

The birthright of the faithful!—*their* world's wave
Soon swept them from its brink.—Oh! deem thou not
130 That on the sad and consecrated spot
My soul grew weak!—I tell thee that a power
There kindled heart and lip—a fiery shower
My words were made—a might was given to prayer,
And a strong grasp to passionate despair,
135 And a dead triumph!—Know'st thou what I sought?
For what high boon my struggling spirit wrought?—
Communion with the dead!—I sent a cry,
Through the veiled empires of eternity,
A voice to cleave them! By the mournful truth,
140 By the lost promise of my blighted youth,
By the strong chain a mighty love can bind
On the beloved, the spell of mind o'er mind;
By words, which in themselves are magic high,
Armed and inspired, and winged with agony;
145 By tears, which comfort not, but burn, and seem
To bear the heart's blood in their passion stream;
I summoned, I adjured!—with quickened sense,
With the keen vigil of a life intense,
I watched, an answer from the winds to wring,
150 I listened, if perchance the stream might bring
Token from worlds afar: I taught *one* sound
Unto a thousand echoes—one profound
Imploring accent to the tomb, the sky—
One prayer to night—"Awake, appear, reply!"
155 Hast thou been told that from the viewless bourne,
The dark way never hath allowed return?
That all, which tears can move, with life is fled—
That earthly love is powerless on the dead?
Believe it not!—there is a large lone star
160 Now burning o'er yon western hill afar,
And under its clear light there lies a spot
Which well might utter forth—Believe it not!

I sat beneath that planet—I had wept
My woe to stillness, every night-wind slept;
165 A hush was on the hills; the very streams
Went by like clouds, or noiseless founts in dreams,
And the dark tree o'ershadowing me that hour,
Stood motionless, even as the gray church-tower
Whereon I gazed unconsciously:—there came
170 A low sound, like the tremor of a flame,
Or like the light quick shiver of a wing,
Flitting through twilight woods, across the air;
And I looked up!—Oh! for strong words to bring
Conviction o'er thy thought!—Before me there,
175 He, the departed, stood!—Ay, face to face,
So near, and yet how far!—his form, his mien,
Gave to remembrance back each burning trace

Within:—Yet something awfully serene,
Pure, sculpture-like, on the pale brow, that wore
180 Of the once-beating heart no token more;
And stillness on the lip—and o'er the hair
A gleam, that trembled through the breathless air;
And an unfathomed calm, that seemed to lie
In the grave sweetness of the illumined eye;
185 Told of the gulfs between our beings set,
And, as that unsheathed spirit-glance I met,
Made my soul faint:—with *fear?* Oh! *not* with fear!
With the sick feeling that in *his* far sphere
My love could be as nothing! But he spoke—
190 How shall I tell thee of the startling thrill
In that low voice, whose breezy tones could fill
My bosom's infinite? O, friend! I woke
Then first to heavenly life!—Soft, solemn, clear
Breathed the mysterious accents on mine ear,
195 Yet strangely seemed as if the while they rose
From depths of distance, o'er the wide repose
Of slumbering waters wafted, or the dells
Of mountains, hollow with sweet-echo cells;
But, as they murmured on, the mortal chill
200 Passed from me, like a mist before the morn,
And, to that glorious intercourse upborne
By slow degrees, a calm, divinely still,
Possessed my frame: I sought that lighted eye—
From its intense and searching purity
205 I drank in *soul!*—I questioned of the dead—
Of the hushed, starry shores their footsteps tread,
And I was answered:—if remembrance there,
With dreamy whispers fill the immortal air;
If thought, here piled from many a jewel-heap,
210 Be treasure in that pensive land to keep;
If love, o'ersweeping change, and blight, and blast
Find *there* the music of his home at last;
I asked, and I was answered:—Full and high
Was that communion with eternity,
215 Too rich for aught so fleeting!—Like a knell
Swept o'er my sense its closing words, "Farewell,
On earth we meet no more!"[2]—and all was gone—
The pale bright settled brow—the thrilling tone,
The still and shining eye! and never more
220 May twilight gloom or midnight hush restore
That radiant guest! One full-fraught hour of heaven,
To earthly passion's wild implorings given,
Was made my own—the ethereal fire hath shivered
The fragile censer[3] in whose mould it quivered

---

2. This is the answer to Manfred's question to the Phantom of Astarte (2.4.154): "Say, shall we meet again?" Astarte vanishes, and Nemesis says, "She's gone, and will not be recall'd." Hemans's lines also echo Endymion's renunciation of his dream god-

dess at a crucial moment in Keats's *Endymion* (4.657–59): "The hour may come / When we shall meet in pure elysium. / On earth I may not love thee."
3. Container in which incense is burned.

225 Brightly, consumingly! What now is left?
A faded world, of glory's hues bereft—
A void, a chain!—I dwell 'midst throngs, apart,
In the cold silence of the stranger's heart;
A fixed, immortal shadow stands between
230 My spirit and life's fast receding scene;
A gift hath severed me from human ties,
A power is gone from all earth's melodies,
Which never may return: their chords are broken,
The music of another land hath spoken—
235 No after-sound is sweet!—this weary thirst!
And I have heard celestial fountains burst!—
What *here* shall quench it?
                                    Dost thou not rejoice,
When the spring sends forth an awakening voice
Through the young woods?—Thou dost!—And in the birth
240 Of early leaves, and flowers, and songs of mirth,
Thousands, like thee, find gladness!—Couldst thou know
How every breeze then summons *me* to go!
How all the light of love and beauty shed
By those rich hours, but woos me to the dead!
245 The *only* beautiful that change no more—
The only loved!—the dwellers on the shore
Of spring fulfilled!—The dead!—*whom* call we so?
They that breathe purer air, that feel, that know
Things wrapt from us!—Away!—within me pent,
250 That which is barred from its own element
Still droops or struggles!—But the day *will* come—
Over the deep the free bird finds its home,
And the stream lingers 'midst the rocks, yet greets
The sea at last; and the winged flower-seed meets
255 A soil to rest in:—shall not *I*, too, be,
My spirit-love! upborne to dwell with thee?
Yes! by the power whose conquering anguish stirred
The tomb, whose cry beyond the stars was heard,
Whose agony of triumph won thee back
260 Through the dim pass no mortal step may track,
Yet shall we meet!—that glimpse of joy divine
Proved thee for ever and for ever mine!

1830

JOHN KEATS
1795–1821

John Keats's father was head stableman at a London livery stable; he married his employer's daughter and inherited the business. The poet's mother, by all reports, was a strongly sensuous woman and a rather casual but affectionate rearer of her five children—John (the first born), his three brothers (one of whom died in infancy), and a sister. Keats was sent to the Reverend John Clarke's private school at Enfield, where he was a noisy, high-spirited boy; despite his small stature (when full-grown, he was barely over five feet in height), he distinguished himself in sports and fistfights. Here he had the good fortune to have as a mentor Charles Cowden Clarke, son of the headmaster, who later became a writer and editor; he encouraged Keats's passion for reading and, both at school and in the course of their later friendship, introduced him to Spenser and other poets, to music, and to the theater.

When Keats was eight his father was killed by a fall from a horse, and when he was fourteen his mother died of tuberculosis. Although the livery stable had prospered, and £8,000 had been left in trust to the children by Keats's grandmother, the estate remained tied up in the law courts for all of Keats's lifetime. The children's guardian, Richard Abbey, an unimaginative and practical-minded businessman, took Keats out of school at the age of fifteen and bound him apprentice to Thomas Hammond, a surgeon and apothecary at Edmonton. In 1815 Keats carried on his medical studies at Guy's Hospital, London, and the next year qualified to practice as an apothecary-surgeon—but almost immediately, over his guardian's protests, he abandoned medicine for poetry.

This decision was influenced by Keats's friendship with Leigh Hunt, then editor of the *Examiner* and a leading political radical, poet, and prolific writer of criticism and periodical essays. Hunt, the first successful author of Keats's acquaintance, added his enthusiastic encouragement of Keats's poetic efforts to that of Clarke. More important, he introduced him to writers greater than Hunt himself—William Hazlitt, Charles Lamb, and Percy Shelley—as well as to Benjamin Robert Haydon, painter of grandiose historical and religious canvases. Through Hunt, Keats also met John Hamilton Reynolds and then Charles Wentworth Dilke and Charles Brown, who became his intimate friends and provided him with an essential circumstance for a fledgling poet: a sympathetic and appreciative audience.

The rapidity and sureness of Keats's development has no match. He did not even undertake poetry until his eighteenth year and, for the following few years, produced album verse that was at best merely competent and at times manifested an arch sentimentality. Suddenly, in 1816, he spoke out loud and bold in the sonnet *On First Looking into Chapman's Homer.* Later that same year he wrote *Sleep and Poetry*, in which he laid out for himself a program deliberately modeled on the careers of the greatest poets, asking only

> for ten years, that I may overwhelm
> Myself in poesy; so I may do the deed
> That my own soul has to itself decreed.

For even while his health was good, Keats felt a foreboding of early death and applied himself to his art with a desperate urgency. In 1817 he went on to compose *Endymion,* an ambitious undertaking of more than four thousand lines. It is a profuse allegory of a mortal's quest for an ideal feminine counterpart and a flawless happiness beyond earthly possibility; in a number of passages, it already exhibits the sure movement and phrasing of his mature poetic style. But Keats's critical judgment and aspiration exceeded his achievement: long before he completed it, he declared impatiently that he carried on with the "slipshod" *Endymion* only as a "trial of invention" and began to block out *Hyperion,* conceived on the model of Milton's *Paradise Lost* in that most demanding of forms, the epic poem. His success in achieving the Miltonic manner is one of the reasons why Keats abandoned *Hyperion* before it was finished, for he recognized that he was uncommonly susceptible to poetic influences and regarded this as a threat to his individuality. "I will write independently," he insisted. "The Genius of Poetry must work out its own salvation in a man." He had refused the chance of intimacy with Shelley "that I might have my own unfettered scope"; he had broken away from Leigh Hunt's influence lest he get "the reputation of Hunt's *élève* [pupil]"; now he shied away from domination by Milton's powerfully infectious style.

With the year 1818 began a series of troubles that culminated in Keats's mortal illness. Sentimental legend used to fix the blame on two anonymous articles: a scurrilous attack on Keats as a member of the "Cockney School" (that is, Hunt's radical literary circle in London), which appeared in the heavily Tory *Blackwood's Magazine,* and a savage mauling of *Endymion* in the *Quarterly Review.* Shelley gave impetus to this myth by his description of Keats in *Adonais* as "a pale flower," and Byron, who knew even less about him, asserted that he was "snuffed out by an article." But in fact, Keats had the good sense to recognize that the attacks were motivated by Tory bias and class snobbery, and he had already passed his own severe judgment on *Endymion:* "My own domestic criticism," he said, "has given me pain without comparison beyond what *Blackwood* or the *Quarterly* could possibly inflict." More important was the financial distress of his brother George and his young bride, who emigrated to Kentucky and lost their money in an ill-advised investment; Keats, himself short of funds, had now to turn to literary journeywork to eke out the family income. His brother Tom contracted tuberculosis, and the poet, in devoted attendance, helplessly watched him waste away until his death that December. In the summer of that year Keats had taken a strenuous walking tour in the English Lake District, Scotland, and Ireland. It was a glorious adventure but a totally exhausting one in wet, cold weather, and he returned in August with a chronically ulcerated throat made increasingly ominous by the shadow of the tuberculosis that had killed his mother and brother. And in the late fall of that same year Keats fell unwillingly, helplessly in love with Fanny Brawne. This attractive, vivacious, and mildly flirtatious woman of eighteen had little interest in poetry, but she possessed an alert and sensible mind and loved Keats sincerely. They became engaged, but Keats's dedication to poetry, his poverty, and his growing illness made marriage impossible and love a torment.

In this period of acute distress and emotional turmoil, within five years of his first trying his hand at poetry, Keats achieved the culmination of his brief poetic career. Between January and September of 1819, masterpiece followed masterpiece in astonishing succession: *The Eve of St. Agnes, La Belle Dame sans Merci,* all of the "great odes," *Lamia,* and a sufficient number of fine sonnets to make him, with Wordsworth, the major Romantic craftsman in that form. All of these poems possess the distinctive qualities of the work of Keats's maturity: a slow-paced, gracious movement; a concreteness of description in which all the senses—tactile, gustatory, kinetic, visceral, as well as visual and auditory—combine to give the total apprehension of an experience; a delight at the sheer existence of things outside himself, the poet seeming to lose his own identity in a total identification with the object he contemplates; and a concentrated felicity of phrasing that reminded his friends, as it has many critics since, of the language of Shakespeare. Under the richly sensuous surface, we find Keats's characteristic presentation of all experience as a tangle of inseparable but irreconcilable opposites. He finds melancholy in delight and pleasure in pain; he feels the highest intensity of love as an approximation to death; he inclines equally toward a life of indolence and "sensation" and toward a life of thought; he is aware both of the attraction of an imaginative dream world without "disagreeables" and the remorseless pressure of the actual; he aspires at the same time to aesthetic detachment and to social responsibility.

His letters, hardly less remarkable than his poetry, show that Keats felt on his pulses the conflicts he dramatized in his major poems. Above all, they reveal him wrestling with the problem of evil and suffering—what to make of our lives in the discovery that "the world is full of misery and heartbreak, pain, sickness and oppression." To the end of his life, he refused to seek solace for the complexity and contradictions of experience either in the abstractions of inherited philosophical doctrines or in the absolutes of a religious creed. At the close of his poetic career, in the latter part of 1819, Keats began to rework the epic *Hyperion* into the form of a dream vision that he called *The Fall of Hyperion*. In the introductory section of this fragment the poet is told by the prophetess Moneta that he has hitherto been merely a dreamer; he must know that

> The poet and the dreamer are distinct,
> Diverse, sheer opposite, antipodes,

and that the height of poetry can be reached only by

> those to whom the miseries of the world
> Are misery, and will not let them rest.

He was seemingly planning to undertake a new direction and subject matter, when illness and death intervened.

On the night of February 3, 1820, he coughed up blood. As a physician, he refused to evade the truth: "I cannot be deceived in that colour; that drop of blood is my death warrant. I must die." That spring and summer a series of hemorrhages rapidly weakened him. In the autumn he allowed himself to be persuaded to seek the milder climate of Italy in the company of Joseph Severn, a young painter, but these last months were only what he called "a posthumous existence." He died in Rome on February 23, 1821, and was buried in the Protestant Cemetery. At times the agony of his disease, the seeming frustration of his hopes for great poetic achievement, and the despair of his passion for Fanny Brawne compelled even Keats's brave spirit to bitterness and jealousy, but he always recovered his gallantry. His last letter, written to Charles Brown, concludes: "I can scarcely bid you good bye even in a letter. I always made an awkward bow. God bless you! John Keats."

No one can read Keats's poems and letters without an undersense of the tragic waste of an extraordinary intellect and genius cut off so early. What he might have done is beyond conjecture; what we do know is that his poetry, when he stopped writing at the age of twenty-four, exceeds the accomplishment at the same age of Chaucer, Shakespeare, and Milton.

The texts here are taken from Jack Stillinger's edition, *The Poems of John Keats* (Cambridge, Mass., 1978).

On First Looking into Chapman's Homer[1]

> Much have I travell'd in the realms of gold,
>   And many goodly states and kingdoms seen;
>   Round many western islands have I been
> Which bards in fealty to Apollo hold.
> 5 Oft of one wide expanse had I been told
>   That deep-brow'd Homer ruled as his demesne;[2]
>   Yet did I never breathe its pure serene[3]
> Till I heard Chapman speak out loud and bold:
> Then felt I like some watcher of the skies
> 10   When a new planet swims into his ken;
>   Or like stout Cortez when with eagle eyes
>   He star'd at the Pacific—and all his men

1. Keats's mentor Charles Cowden Clarke introduced him to Homer in the robust translation of the Elizabethan poet George Chapman. They read through the night, and Keats walked home at dawn. This sonnet reached Clarke by the ten o'clock mail that same morning. It was Balboa, not Cortez, who caught his first sight of the Pacific from the heights of Darien, in Panama, but none of Keats's contemporaries noticed the error.
2. Realm, feudal possession.
3. Clear expanse of air.

Look'd at each other with a wild surmise—
Silent, upon a peak in Darien.

Oct. 1816   1816

From Sleep and Poetry[1]

[O FOR TEN YEARS]

O for ten years, that I may overwhelm
Myself in poesy; so I may do the deed
That my own soul has to itself decreed.
Then will I pass the countries that I see
100   In long perspective, and continually
Taste their pure fountains. First the realm I'll pass
Of Flora, and old Pan:[2] sleep in the grass,
Feed upon apples red, and strawberries,
And choose each pleasure that my fancy sees;
105   Catch the white-handed nymphs in shady places,
To woo sweet kisses from averted faces,—
Play with their fingers, touch their shoulders white
Into a pretty shrinking with a bite
As hard as lips can make it: till agreed,
110   A lovely tale of human life we'll read.
And one will teach a tame dove how it best
May fan the cool air gently o'er my rest;
Another, bending o'er her nimble tread,
Will set a green robe floating round her head,
115   And still will dance with ever varied ease,
Smiling upon the flowers and the trees:
Another will entice me on, and on
Through almond blossoms and rich cinnamon;
Till in the bosom of a leafy world
120   We rest in silence, like two gems upcurl'd
In the recesses of a pearly shell.

And can I ever bid these joys farewell?
Yes, I must pass them for a nobler life,
Where I may find the agonies, the strife
125   Of human hearts: for lo! I see afar,
O'er sailing the blue cragginess, a car[3]
And steeds with streamy manes—the charioteer

---

1. At the early age of twenty-one, Keats set himself a regimen of poetic training modeled on the course followed by the greatest poets. Virgil had established the pattern of beginning with pastoral writing and proceeding gradually to the point at which he was ready to undertake the epic, and this pattern had been deliberately followed by Spenser and Milton. Keats's version of this program, as he describes it here, is to begin with the realm "of Flora, and old Pan" (line 102) and, within ten years, to climb up to the level of poetry dealing with "the agonies, the strife / Of human hearts" (lines 124–25). The latter achievement Keats found best represented among his contemporaries by Words-worth and, less successfully, Shelley; Keats's vision of the chariot of poesy (lines 125–54) parallels Shelley's allegorical visions. The program Keats set himself is illuminated by his analysis of Words-worth's progress in his letter to J. H. Reynolds of May 3, 1818 (p. 892).

2. I.e., the carefree pastoral world. Flora was the Roman goddess of flowers. Pan was the Greek god of pastures, woods, and animal life.

3. This chariot, with its "charioteer" (line 127), represents the higher poetic imagination, which bodies forth the matters "of delight, of mystery, and fear" (line 138) that characterize the grander poetic genres.

Looks out upon the winds with glorious fear:
And now the numerous tramplings quiver lightly
130 Along a huge cloud's ridge; and now with sprightly
Wheel downward come they into fresher skies,
Tipt round with silver from the sun's bright eyes.
Still downward with capacious whirl they glide;
And now I see them on a green-hill's side
135 In breezy rest among the nodding stalks.
The charioteer with wond'rous gesture talks
To the trees and mountains; and there soon appear
Shapes of delight, of mystery, and fear,
Passing along before a dusky space
140 Made by some mighty oaks: as they would chase
Some ever-fleeting music on they sweep.
Lo! how they murmur, laugh, and smile, and weep:
Some with upholden hand and mouth severe;
Some with their faces muffled to the ear
145 Between their arms; some, clear in youthful bloom,
Go glad and smilingly athwart the gloom;
Some looking back, and some with upward gaze;
Yes, thousands in a thousand different ways
Flit onward—now a lovely wreath of girls
150 Dancing their sleek hair into tangled curls;
And now broad wings. Most awfully intent,
The driver of those steeds is forward bent,
And seems to listen: O that I might know
All that he writes with such a hurrying glow.

155   The visions all are fled—the car is fled
Into the light of heaven, and in their stead
A sense of real things comes doubly strong,
And, like a muddy stream, would bear along
My soul to nothingness: but I will strive
160 Against all doubtings, and will keep alive
The thought of that same chariot, and the strange
Journey it went.

*   *   *

Oct.–Dec. 1816   1817

On Seeing the Elgin Marbles[1]

My spirit is too weak—mortality
    Weighs heavily on me like unwilling sleep,
    And each imagined pinnacle and steep
    Of godlike hardship tells me I must die
5   Like a sick eagle looking at the sky.
    Yet 'tis a gentle luxury to weep

---

1. Lord Elgin had brought to England in 1806 the marble statues and friezes that adorned the Parthenon at Athens; in 1816 they were purchased by the government for the British Museum.

That I have not the cloudy winds to keep
Fresh for the opening of the morning's eye.
Such dim-conceived glories of the brain
10   Bring round the heart an undescribable feud;
So do these wonders a most dizzy pain,
   That mingles Grecian grandeur with the rude
Wasting of old time—with a billowy main—
   A sun—a shadow of a magnitude.

Mar. 1 or 2, 1817   1817

From Endymion: A Poetic Romance[1]

"The stretched metre of an antique song"

INSCRIBED TO THE MEMORY OF THOMAS CHATTERTON

Preface

Knowing within myself the manner in which this Poem has been produced, it is not without a feeling of regret that I make it public.

What manner I mean, will be quite clear to the reader, who must soon perceive great inexperience, immaturity, and every error denoting a feverish attempt, rather than a deed accomplished. The two first books, and indeed the two last, I feel sensible are not of such completion as to warrant their passing the press; nor should they if I thought a year's castigation would do them any good;—it will not: the foundations are too sandy. It is just that this youngster should die away: a sad thought for me, if I had not some hope that while it is dwindling I may be plotting, and fitting myself for verses fit to live.

This may be speaking too presumptuously, and may deserve a punishment: but no feeling man will be forward to inflict it: he will leave me alone, with the conviction that there is not a fiercer hell than the failure in a great object. This is not written with the least atom of purpose to forestall criticisms of course, but from the desire I have to conciliate men who are competent to look, and who do look with a zealous eye, to the honour of English literature.

The imagination of a boy is healthy, and the mature imagination of a man is healthy; but there is a space of life between, in which the soul is in a ferment, the character undecided, the way of life uncertain, the ambition thick-sighted: thence proceeds mawkishness, and all the thousand bitters which those men I speak of must necessarily taste in going over the following pages.

---

1. This poem of more than four thousand lines (based on the classical myth of a mortal beloved by the goddess of the moon) tells of Endymion's long and agonized search for an immortal goddess whom he had seen in several visions. In the course of his wanderings he comes upon an Indian maid who had been abandoned by the followers of Bacchus and, to his utter despair, succumbs to a sensual passion for her, in apparent betrayal of his love for his heavenly ideal. In the resolution the Indian maid reveals that she is herself Cynthia (Diana), goddess of the moon, the celestial subject of his earlier visions.

The verse epigraph is adapted from Shakespeare's Sonnet 17, line 12: "And stretchèd metre of an antique song." Thomas Chatterton (1752–1770), to whom *Endymion* is inscribed, wrote a number of brilliant pseudoarchaic poems that he attributed to an imaginary 15th-century poet, Thomas Rowley. Keats described him as "the most English of poets except Shakespeare."

I hope I have not in too late a day touched the beautiful mythology of Greece, and dulled its brightness: for I wish to try once more,[2] before I bid it farewell.

Teignmouth, April 10, 1818

From *Book 1*

[A THING OF BEAUTY]

A thing of beauty is a joy for ever:
Its loveliness increases; it will never
Pass into nothingness; but still will keep
A bower quiet for us, and a sleep
5   Full of sweet dreams, and health, and quiet breathing.
Therefore, on every morrow, are we wreathing
A flowery band to bind us to the earth,
Spite of despondence, of the inhuman dearth
Of noble natures, of the gloomy days,
10   Of all the unhealthy and o'er-darkened ways
Made for our searching: yes, in spite of all,
Some shape of beauty moves away the pall
From our dark spirits. Such the sun, the moon,
Trees old, and young sprouting a shady boon
15   For simple sheep; and such are daffodils
With the green world they live in; and clear rills
That for themselves a cooling covert make
'Gainst the hot season; the mid forest brake,°   *thicket*
Rich with a sprinkling of fair musk-rose blooms:
20   And such too is the grandeur of the dooms°   *judgments*
We have imagined for the mighty dead;
All lovely tales that we have heard or read:
An endless fountain of immortal drink,
Pouring unto us from the heaven's brink.[3]

25   Nor do we merely feel these essences
For one short hour; no, even as the trees
That whisper round a temple become soon
Dear as the temple's self, so does the moon,
The passion poesy, glories infinite,
30   Haunt us till they become a cheering light
Unto our souls, and bound to us so fast,
That, whether there be shine, or gloom o'ercast,
They alway must be with us, or we die.

      Therefore, 'tis with full happiness that I
35   Will trace the story of Endymion.
The very music of the name has gone

---

2. In *Hyperion*, which Keats was already planning.
3. The poet sets up, and seeks to resolve, the basic opposition between the inevitably "mortal" pleasures in this life and the conceived possibility of "immortal" delight. Thus "essences" (line 25) seem to be the things of beauty in this world, purged of the mutability that is inescapable in ordinary experience. The central passage dealing with this theme is in book 1, lines 777ff.

Into my being, and each pleasant scene
Is growing fresh before me as the green
Of our own vallies. * * *

[THE "PLEASURE THERMOMETER"]

"Peona![4] ever have I long'd to slake
770　My thirst for the world's praises: nothing base,
No merely slumberous phantasm, could unlace
The stubborn canvas for my voyage prepar'd—
Though now 'tis tatter'd; leaving my bark bar'd
And sullenly drifting: yet my higher hope
775　Is of too wide, too rainbow-large a scope,
To fret at myriads of earthly wrecks.
Wherein lies happiness? In that which becks
Our ready minds to fellowship divine,
A fellowship with essence; till we shine,
780　Full alchemiz'd,[5] and free of space. Behold
The clear religion of heaven! Fold
A rose leaf round thy finger's taperness,
And soothe thy lips: hist, when the airy stress
Of music's kiss impregnates the free winds,
785　And with a sympathetic touch unbinds
Eolian[6] magic from their lucid wombs:
Then old songs waken from enclouded tombs;
Old ditties sigh above their father's grave;
Ghosts of melodious prophecyings rave
790　Round every spot where trod Apollo's foot;
Bronze clarions awake, and faintly bruit,[7]
Where long ago a giant battle was;
And, from the turf, a lullaby doth pass
In every place where infant Orpheus slept.
795　Feel we these things?—that moment have we stept
Into a sort of oneness, and our state
Is like a floating spirit's. But there are
Richer entanglements, enthralments far
More self-destroying, leading, by degrees,
800　To the chief intensity: the crown of these
Is made of love and friendship, and sits high
Upon the forehead of humanity.

4. The sister to whom Endymion confides his troubles. Of lines 769–857, Keats wrote to his publisher, John Taylor: "When I wrote it, it was the regular stepping of the Imagination towards a Truth. My having written that Argument will perhaps be of the greatest Service to me of anything I ever did—It set before me at once the gradations of Happiness even like a kind of Pleasure Thermometer, and is my first step towards the chief attempt in the Drama—the playing of different Natures with Joy and Sorrow." The gradations on this "Pleasure Thermometer" mark the stages on the way to what Keats calls "happiness" (line 777)—his secular version of the religious concept of "felicity" that, in the orthodox view, is to be achieved by a surrender of oneself to God. For Keats, the way to happiness lies through a fusion of ourselves, first sensuously, with the lovely objects of nature and art (lines 781–97), then on a higher level, with other human beings through "love and friendship" (line 801) and, ultimately, sexual love. By this "self-destroying," or loss of personal identity through our imaginative identification with a beloved person outside ourselves, we escape from the material limits and the self-centered condition of ordinary experience, to achieve a "fellowship with essence," which is a kind of immortality within our mortal existence (line 844).
5. Transformed by alchemy from a base to a precious metal.
6. From Aeolus, god of winds.
7. Make a sound.

All its more ponderous and bulky worth
Is friendship, whence there ever issues forth
805   A steady splendour; but at the tip-top
There hangs by unseen film, an orbed drop
Of light, and that is love: its influence,
Thrown in our eyes, genders a novel sense,
At which we start and fret; till in the end,
810   Melting into its radiance, we blend,
Mingle, and so become a part of it,—
Nor with aught else can our souls interknit
So wingedly: when we combine therewith,
Life's self is nourish'd by its proper pith,[8]
815   And we are nurtured like a pelican brood.[9]
Aye, so delicious is the unsating food,
That men, who might have tower'd in the van
Of all the congregated world, to fan
And winnow from the coming step of time
820   All chaff of custom, wipe away all slime
Left by men-slugs and human serpentry,
Have been content to let occasion die,
Whilst they did sleep in love's elysium.
And, truly, I would rather be struck dumb,
825   Than speak against this ardent listlessness:
For I have ever thought that it might bless
The world with benefits unknowingly;
As does the nightingale, upperched high,
And cloister'd among cool and bunched leaves—
830   She sings but to her love, nor e'er conceives
How tiptoe Night holds back her dark-grey hood.[1]
Just so may love, although 'tis understood
The mere commingling of passionate breath,
Produce more than our searching witnesseth:
835   What I know not: but who, of men, can tell
That flowers would bloom, or that green fruit would swell
To melting pulp, that fish would have bright mail,
The earth its dower of river, wood, and vale,
The meadows runnels, runnels pebble-stones,
840   The seed its harvest, or the lute its tones,
Tones ravishment, or ravishment its sweet,
If human souls did never kiss and greet?

    "Now, if this earthly love has power to make
Men's being mortal, immortal; to shake
845   Ambition from their memories, and brim
Their measure of content; what merest whim,
Seems all this poor endeavour after fame,
To one, who keeps within his stedfast aim
A love immortal, an immortal too.
850   Look not so wilder'd; for these things are true,

8. Its own elemental substance.
9. Young pelicans were once thought to feed on their mother's flesh. In a parallel way, our life is nourished by another's life, with which it fuses in love.
1. I.e., in order to hear better.

And never can be born of atomies°   *mites*
That buzz about our slumbers, like brain-flies,
Leaving us fancy-sick. No, no, I'm sure,
My restless spirit never could endure
855 To brood so long upon one luxury,
Unless it did, though fearfully, espy
A hope beyond the shadow of a dream."

Apr.–Nov. 1817   1818

On Sitting Down to Read *King Lear* Once Again[1]

O golden-tongued Romance, with serene lute!
 Fair plumed syren, queen of far-away!
 Leave melodizing on this wintry day,
Shut up thine olden pages, and be mute.
5 Adieu! for, once again, the fierce dispute
 Betwixt damnation and impassion'd clay
 Must I burn through; once more humbly assay
The bitter-sweet of this Shakespearean fruit.
Chief Poet! and ye clouds of Albion,[2]
10 Begetters of our deep eternal theme!
 When through the old oak forest[3] I am gone,
 Let me not wander in a barren dream:
But, when I am consumed in the fire,
Give me new phoenix[4] wings to fly at my desire.

Jan. 22, 1818   1838

When I have fears that I may cease to be[1]

When I have fears that I may cease to be
 Before my pen has glean'd my teeming brain,
Before high piled books, in charactry,[2]
 Hold like rich garners the full ripen'd grain;
5 When I behold, upon the night's starr'd face,
 Huge cloudy symbols of a high romance,
And think that I may never live to trace
 Their shadows, with the magic hand of chance;
And when I feel, fair creature of an hour,
10 That I shall never look upon thee more,
Never have relish in the fairy power
 Of unreflecting love;—then on the shore

1. Keats pauses, while revising *Endymion: A Poetic Romance*, to read again Shakespeare's great tragedy. The word "syren" (line 2) indicates Keats's feeling that "Romance" was enticing him from the poet's prime duty, to deal with "the agonies, the strife / Of human hearts" (*Sleep and Poetry*, lines 124–25).
2. Old name for England. *King Lear* is set in Celtic Britain.
3. A reference either to *King Lear* or to *Endymion*.
4. The fabulous bird that periodically burns itself to death to rise anew from the ashes.
1. The first, and one of the most successful, of Keats's attempts at the sonnet in the Shakespearean rhyme scheme.
2. Characters; printed letters of the alphabet.

Of the wide world I stand alone, and think
Till love and fame to nothingness do sink.

Jan. 1818   1848

To Homer

Standing aloof in giant ignorance,
    Of thee I hear and of the Cyclades,[1]
As one who sits ashore and longs perchance
    To visit dolphin-coral in deep seas.
5   So wast thou blind;—but then the veil was rent,
    For Jove uncurtain'd heaven to let thee live,
And Neptune made for thee a spumy tent,
    And Pan made sing for thee his forest-hive;
Aye on the shores of darkness there is light,
10   And precipices show untrodden green,
There is a budding morrow in midnight,
    There is a triple sight in blindness keen;
Such seeing hadst thou, as it once befel
To Dian, Queen of Earth, and Heaven, and Hell.[2]

1818   1848

The Eve of St. Agnes[1]

I

St. Agnes' Eve—Ah, bitter chill it was!
The owl, for all his feathers, was a-cold;
The hare limp'd trembling through the frozen grass,
And silent was the flock in woolly fold:
5   Numb were the Beadsman's[2] fingers, while he told
His rosary, and while his frosted breath,
Like pious incense from a censer old,
Seem'd taking flight for heaven, without a death,
Past the sweet Virgin's picture, while his prayer he saith.

1. A group of islands in the Aegean Sea, off Greece. Keats's allusion is to his ignorance of the Greek language.
2. In late pagan cults Diana was worshiped as a three-figured goddess, the deity of nature and of the moon as well as the queen of hell. The "triple sight" that blind Homer paradoxically commands is of these three regions and also of heaven, sea, and earth (the realms of Jove, Neptune, and Pan, lines 6–8).
1. St. Agnes, martyred ca. 303 at the age of thirteen, is the patron saint of virgins. Legend has it that if a chaste young woman performs the proper ritual, she will dream of her future husband on the evening before St. Agnes's Day, January 21. Keats combines this superstition with the Romeo and Juliet theme of young love thwarted by feuding families and tells the story in a sequence of evolving Spenserian

stanzas. The luxurious product has been called "a colored dream," but it is a complexly meaningful dream, in which the strong contrasts of heat and cold, crimson and silver, youth and age, revelry and austere penance, sensuality and chastity, life and death, and hell and heaven assume symbolic values. They figure forth the extremes of spirituality and physicality that are involved in sexuality, the difference between the dream and the reality of passion, and the ambivalences at the center of both human love and the imagination. The poem is Keats's first complete success in sustained narrative. For the author's revisions while composing stanzas 26 and 30 of The Eve of St. Agnes, see "Poems in Process," in the appendices to the volume.
2. One who is paid to pray for his benefactor. He "tells" (counts) the beads of his rosary, to keep track of his prayers.

2

His prayer he saith, this patient, holy man;
Then takes his lamp, and riseth from his knees,
And back returneth, meagre, barefoot, wan,
Along the chapel aisle by slow degrees:
The sculptur'd dead, on each side, seem to freeze,
Emprison'd in black, purgatorial rails:
Knights, ladies, praying in dumb° orat'ries,°   *silent / chapels*
He passeth by; and his weak spirit fails
To think[3] how they may ache in icy hoods and mails.

3

Northward he turneth through a little door,
And scarce three steps, ere Music's golden tongue
Flatter'd° to tears this aged man and poor;   *beguiled*
But no—already had his deathbell rung;
The joys of all his life were said and sung:
His was harsh penance on St. Agnes' Eve:
Another way he went, and soon among
Rough ashes sat he for his soul's reprieve,
And all night kept awake, for sinners' sake to grieve.

4

That ancient Beadsman heard the prelude soft;
And so it chanc'd, for many a door was wide,
From hurry to and fro. Soon, up aloft,
The silver, snarling trumpets 'gan to chide:
The level chambers, ready with their pride,°   *ostentation*
Were glowing to receive a thousand guests:
The carved angels, ever eager-eyed,
Star'd, where upon their heads the cornice rests,
With hair blown back, and wings put cross-wise on their breasts.

5

At length burst in the argent revelry,[4]
With plume, tiara, and all rich array,
Numerous as shadows haunting fairily
The brain, new stuff'd, in youth, with triumphs gay
Of old romance. These let us wish away,
And turn, sole-thoughted, to one Lady there,
Whose heart had brooded, all that wintry day,
On love, and wing'd St. Agnes' saintly care,
As she had heard old dames full many times declare.

6

They told her how, upon St. Agnes' Eve,
Young virgins might have visions of delight,
And soft adorings from their loves receive
Upon the honey'd middle of the night,

---

3. I.e., when he thinks.   4. Silver-adorned revelers.

50　　　If ceremonies due they did aright;
　　　　As, supperless to bed they must retire,
　　　　And couch supine their beauties, lily white;
　　　　Nor look behind, nor sideways, but require
　　Of heaven with upward eyes for all that they desire.

7

55　　　Full of this whim was thoughtful Madeline:
　　　　The music, yearning like a god in pain,
　　　　She scarcely heard: her maiden eyes divine,
　　　　Fix'd on the floor, saw many a sweeping train
　　　　Pass by—she heeded not at all: in vain
60　　　Came many a tiptoe, amorous cavalier,
　　　　And back retir'd, not cool'd by high disdain;
　　　　But she saw not: her heart was otherwhere:
　　She sigh'd for Agnes' dreams, the sweetest of the year.

8

　　　　She danc'd along with vague, regardless eyes,
65　　　Anxious her lips, her breathing quick and short:
　　　　The hallow'd hour was near at hand: she sighs
　　　　Amid the timbrels,° and the throng'd resort　　　　　　　*small drums*
　　　　Of whisperers in anger, or in sport;
　　　　'Mid looks of love, defiance, hate, and scorn,
70　　　Hoodwink'd with faery fancy; all amort,[5]
　　　　Save to St. Agnes and her lambs unshorn,[6]
　　And all the bliss to be before to-morrow morn.

9

　　　　So, purposing each moment to retire,
　　　　She linger'd still. Meantime, across the moors,
75　　　Had come young Porphyro, with heart on fire
　　　　For Madeline. Beside the portal doors,
　　　　Buttress'd from moonlight,[7] stands he, and implores
　　　　All saints to give him sight of Madeline,
　　　　But for one moment in the tedious hours,
80　　　That he might gaze and worship all unseen;
　　Perchance speak, kneel, touch, kiss—in sooth such things have been.

10

　　　　He ventures in: let no buzz'd whisper tell:
　　　　All eyes be muffled, or a hundred swords
　　　　Will storm his heart, Love's fev'rous citadel:
85　　　For him, those chambers held barbarian hordes,
　　　　Hyena foemen, and hot-blooded lords,
　　　　Whose very dogs would execrations howl

5. As though dead. "Hoodwinked": covered by a hood or blindfolded.
6. On St. Agnes's Day it was the custom to offer lambs' wool at the altar, to be made into cloth by nuns.
7. Sheltered from the moonlight by the buttresses (the supports projecting from the wall).

Against his lineage: not one breast affords
Him any mercy, in that mansion foul,
90 Save one old beldame,[8] weak in body and in soul.

11

Ah, happy chance! the aged creature came,
Shuffling along with ivory-headed wand,°   *staff*
To where he stood, hid from the torch's flame,
Behind a broad hall-pillar, far beyond
95 The sound of merriment and chorus bland:°   *soft*
He startled her; but soon she knew his face,
And grasp'd his fingers in her palsied hand,
Saying, "Mercy, Porphyro! hie thee from this place;
They are all here to-night, the whole blood-thirsty race!

12

100 "Get hence! get hence! there's dwarfish Hildebrand;
He had a fever late, and in the fit
He cursed thee and thine, both house and land:
Then there's that old Lord Maurice, not a whit
More tame for his gray hairs—Alas me! flit!
105 Flit like a ghost away."—"Ah, Gossip[9] dear,
We're safe enough; here in this arm-chair sit,
And tell me how"—"Good Saints! not here, not here;
Follow me, child, or else these stones will be thy bier."

13

He follow'd through a lowly arched way,
110 Brushing the cobwebs with his lofty plume,
And as she mutter'd "Well-a—well-a-day!"
He found him in a little moonlight room,
Pale, lattic'd, chill, and silent as a tomb.
"Now tell me where is Madeline," said he,
115 "O tell me, Angela, by the holy loom
Which none but secret sisterhood may see,
When they St. Agnes' wool are weaving piously."

14

"St. Agnes! Ah! it is St. Agnes' Eve—
Yet men will murder upon holy days:
120 Thou must hold water in a witch's sieve,[1]
And be liege-lord of all the Elves and Fays,
To venture so: it fills me with amaze
To see thee, Porphyro!—St. Agnes' Eve!
God's help! my lady fair the conjuror plays[2]

8. Old (and usually, homely) woman; an ironic development in English from the French meaning, "lovely lady."
9. In the old sense: godmother or old friend.

1. A sieve made to hold water by witchcraft.
2. I.e., in her attempt to evoke the vision of her lover.

125   This very night: good angels her deceive!
    But let me laugh awhile, I've mickle° time to grieve."   *much*

15

    Feebly she laugheth in the languid moon,
    While Porphyro upon her face doth look,
    Like puzzled urchin on an aged crone
130   Who keepeth clos'd a wond'rous riddle-book,
    As spectacled she sits in chimney nook.
    But soon his eyes grew brilliant, when she told
    His lady's purpose; and he scarce could brook°   *restrain*
    Tears, at the thought of those enchantments cold,
135 And Madeline asleep in lap of legends old.

16

    Sudden a thought came like a full-blown rose,
    Flushing his brow, and in his pained heart
    Made purple riot: then doth he propose
    A stratagem, that makes the beldame start:
140   "A cruel man and impious thou art:
    Sweet lady, let her pray, and sleep, and dream
    Alone with her good angels, far apart
    From wicked men like thee. Go, go!—I deem
Thou canst not surely be the same that thou didst seem."

17

145   "I will not harm her, by all saints I swear,"
    Quoth Porphyro: "O may I ne'er find grace
    When my weak voice shall whisper its last prayer,
    If one of her soft ringlets I displace,
    Or look with ruffian passion in her face:
150   Good Angela, believe me by these tears;
    Or I will, even in a moment's space,
    Awake, with horrid shout, my foemen's ears,
And beard them, though they be more fang'd than wolves and bears."

18

    "Ah! why wilt thou affright a feeble soul?
155   A poor, weak, palsy-stricken, churchyard thing,
    Whose passing-bell° may ere the midnight toll;   *death knell*
    Whose prayers for thee, each morn and evening,
    Were never miss'd."—Thus plaining,° doth she bring   *complaining*
    A gentler speech from burning Porphyro;
160   So woful, and of such deep sorrowing,
    That Angela gives promise she will do
Whatever he shall wish, betide her weal or woe.

19

    Which was, to lead him, in close secrecy,
    Even to Madeline's chamber, and there hide
165   Him in a closet, of such privacy

That he might see her beauty unespied,
And win perhaps that night a peerless bride,
While legion'd fairies pac'd the coverlet,
And pale enchantment held her sleepy-eyed.
170 Never on such a night have lovers met,
Since Merlin paid his Demon all the monstrous debt.[3]

20

"It shall be as thou wishest," said the Dame:
"All cates° and dainties shall be stored there   *delicacies*
Quickly on this feast-night: by the tambour frame[4]
175 Her own lute thou wilt see: no time to spare,
For I am slow and feeble, and scarce dare
On such a catering trust my dizzy head.
Wait here, my child, with patience; kneel in prayer
The while: Ah! thou must needs the lady wed,
180 Or may I never leave my grave among the dead."

21

So saying, she hobbled off with busy fear.
The lover's endless minutes slowly pass'd;
The dame return'd, and whisper'd in his ear
To follow her; with aged eyes aghast
185 From fright of dim espial. Safe at last,
Through many a dusky gallery, they gain
The maiden's chamber, silken, hush'd, and chaste;
Where Porphyro took covert, pleas'd amain.°   *mightily*
His poor guide hurried back with agues in her brain.

22

190 Her falt'ring hand upon the balustrade,
Old Angela was feeling for the stair,
When Madeline, St. Agnes' charmed maid,
Rose, like a mission'd spirit,[5] unaware:
With silver taper's light, and pious care,
195 She turn'd, and down the aged gossip led
To a safe level matting. Now prepare,
Young Porphyro, for gazing on that bed;
She comes, she comes again, like ring-dove fray'd° and fled.   *frightened*

23

Out went the taper as she hurried in;
200 Its little smoke, in pallid moonshine, died:
She clos'd the door, she panted, all akin
To spirits of the air, and visions wide:
No uttered syllable, or, woe betide!
But to her heart, her heart was voluble,
205 Paining with eloquence her balmy side;

---

3. Probably the episode in the Arthurian legends
in the which Merlin, the magician, lost his life when
the wily Vivien turned one of his own spells against
him.
4. A drum-shaped embroidery frame.
5. I.e., like an angel sent on a mission.

As though a tongueless nightingale should swell
Her throat in vain, and die, heart-stifled, in her dell.

24

A casement high and triple-arch'd there was,
All garlanded with carven imag'ries
210   Of fruits, and flowers, and bunches of knot-grass,
And diamonded with panes of quaint device,
Innumerable of stains and splendid dyes,
As are the tiger-moth's deep-damask'd wings;
And in the midst, 'mong thousand heraldries,
215   And twilight saints, and dim emblazonings,
A shielded scutcheon blush'd with blood of queens and kings.[6]

25

Full on this casement shone the wintry moon,
And threw warm gules[7] on Madeline's fair breast,
As down she knelt for heaven's grace and boon;°   *gift, blessing*
220   Rose-bloom fell on her hands, together prest,
And on her silver cross soft amethyst,
And on her hair a glory, like a saint:
She seem'd a splendid angel, newly drest,
Save wings, for heaven:—Porphyro grew faint:
225 She knelt, so pure a thing, so free from mortal taint.

26

Anon his heart revives: her vespers done,
Of all its wreathed pearls her hair she frees;
Unclasps her warmed jewels one by one;
Loosens her fragrant boddice; by degrees
230   Her rich attire creeps rustling to her knees:
Half-hidden, like a mermaid in sea-weed,
Pensive awhile she dreams awake, and sees,
In fancy, fair St. Agnes in her bed,
But dares not look behind, or all the charm is fled.

27

235 Soon, trembling in her soft and chilly nest,
In sort of wakeful swoon, perplex'd[8] she lay,
Until the poppied warmth of sleep oppress'd
Her soothed limbs, and soul fatigued away;
Flown, like a thought, until the morrow-day;
240   Blissfully haven'd both from joy and pain;
Clasp'd like a missal where swart Paynims pray;[9]
Blinded alike from sunshine and from rain,
As though a rose should shut, and be a bud again.

6. I.e., among the genealogical emblems ("heraldries") and other devices ("emblazonings"), a heraldic shield signified by its colors that the family was of royal blood.
7. Red (heraldry).
8. In a confused state between waking and sleeping.
9. Variously interpreted; perhaps: held tightly, cherished (or else kept shut, fastened with a clasp), like a Christian prayer book ("missal") in a land where the religion is that of dark-skinned pagans ("swart Paynims").

28

Stol'n to this paradise, and so entranced,
245   Porphyro gazed upon her empty dress,
And listen'd to her breathing, if it chanced
To wake into a slumberous tenderness;
Which when he heard, that minute did he bless,
And breath'd himself: then from the closet crept,
250   Noiseless as fear in a wide wilderness,
And over the hush'd carpet, silent, stept,
And 'tween the curtains peep'd, where, lo!—how fast she slept.

29

Then by the bed-side, where the faded moon
Made a dim, silver twilight, soft he set
255   A table, and, half anguish'd, threw thereon
A cloth of woven crimson, gold, and jet:—
O for some drowsy Morphean amulet![1]
The boisterous, midnight, festive clarion,[2]
The kettle-drum, and far-heard clarionet,
260   Affray his ears, though but in dying tone:—
The hall door shuts again, and all the noise is gone.

30

And still she slept an azure-lidded sleep,
In blanched linen, smooth, and lavender'd,
While he from forth the closet brought a heap
265   Of candied apple, quince, and plum, and gourd;°   *melon*
With jellies soother than the creamy curd,
And lucent syrops, tinct with cinnamon;
Manna and dates, in argosy transferr'd
From Fez,[3] and spiced dainties, every one,
270   From silken Samarcand to cedar'd Lebanon.

31

These delicates he heap'd with glowing hand
On golden dishes and in baskets bright
Of wreathed silver: sumptuous they stand
In the retired quiet of the night,
275   Filling the chilly room with perfume light.—
"And now, my love, my seraph[4] fair, awake!
Thou art my heaven, and I thine eremite:[5]
Open thine eyes, for meek St. Agnes' sake,
Or I shall drowse beside thee, so my soul doth ache."

32

280   Thus whispering, his warm, unnerved arm
Sank in her pillow. Shaded was her dream

1. Sleep-producing charm.
2. High-pitched trumpet.
3. I.e., jellies softer ("soother") than the curds of cream, clear ("lucent") syrups tinged with cinnamon, and sweet gums ("manna") and dates trans-ported in a great merchant ship ("argosy") from Fez.
4. One of the highest orders of angels.
5. Hermit, religious solitary.

By the dusk curtains:—'twas a midnight charm
Impossible to melt as iced stream:
The lustrous salvers in the moonlight gleam;
285 Broad golden fringe upon the carpet lies:
It seem'd he never, never could redeem
From such a stedfast spell his lady's eyes;
So mus'd awhile, entoil'd in woofed phantasies.[6]

33

Awakening up, he took her hollow lute,—
290 Tumultuous,—and, in chords that tenderest be,
He play'd an ancient ditty, long since mute,
In Provence call'd, "La belle dame sans mercy":[7]
Close to her ear touching the melody;—
Wherewith disturb'd, she utter'd a soft moan:
295 He ceased—she panted quick—and suddenly
Her blue affrayed eyes wide open shone:
Upon his knees he sank, pale as smooth-sculptured stone.

34

Her eyes were open, but she still beheld,
Now wide awake, the vision of her sleep:
300 There was a painful change, that nigh expell'd
The blisses of her dream so pure and deep:
At which fair Madeline began to weep,
And moan forth witless words with many a sigh;
While still her gaze on Porphyro would keep;
305 Who knelt, with joined hands and piteous eye,
Fearing to move or speak, she look'd so dreamingly.

35

"Ah, Porphyro!" said she, "but even now
Thy voice was at sweet tremble in mine ear,
Made tuneable with every sweetest vow;
310 And those sad eyes were spiritual and clear:
How chang'd thou art! how pallid, chill, and drear!
Give me that voice again, my Porphyro,
Those looks immortal, those complainings dear!
Oh leave me not in this eternal woe,
315 For if thou diest, my love, I know not where to go."

36

Beyond a mortal man impassion'd far
At these voluptuous accents, he arose,
Ethereal, flush'd, and like a throbbing star
Seen mid the sapphire heaven's deep repose;
320 Into her dream he melted, as the rose
Blendeth its odour with the violet,—

6. Entangled in a weave of fantasies.
7. "The Lovely Lady without Pity," title of a work
by the medieval poet Alain Chartier. Keats later
adopted the title for his own ballad.

Solution sweet: meantime the frost-wind blows
Like Love's alarum pattering the sharp sleet
Against the window-panes; St. Agnes' moon hath set.

37

325 'Tis dark: quick pattereth the flaw-blown° sleet: *gust-blown*
"This is no dream, my bride, my Madeline!"
'Tis dark: the iced gusts still rave and beat:
"No dream, alas! alas! and woe is mine!
Porphyro will leave me here to fade and pine.—
330 Cruel! what traitor could thee hither bring?
I curse not, for my heart is lost in thine,
Though thou forsakest a deceived thing;—
A dove forlorn and lost with sick unpruned wing."

38

"My Madeline! sweet dreamer! lovely bride!
335 Say, may I be for aye thy vassal blest?
Thy beauty's shield, heart-shap'd and vermeil° dyed?   *vermilion*
Ah, silver shrine, here will I take my rest
After so many hours of toil and quest,
A famish'd pilgrim,—saved by miracle.
340 Though I have found, I will not rob thy nest
Saving of thy sweet self; if thou think'st well
To trust, fair Madeline, to no rude infidel.

39

"Hark! 'tis an elfin-storm from faery land,
Of haggard⁸ seeming, but a boon indeed:
345 Arise—arise! the morning is at hand;—
The bloated wassaillers⁹ will never heed:—
Let us away, my love, with happy speed;
There are no ears to hear, or eyes to see,—
Drown'd all in Rhenish and the sleepy mead:¹
350 Awake! arise! my love, and fearless be,
For o'er the southern moors I have a home for thee."

40

She hurried at his words, beset with fears,
For there were sleeping dragons all around,
At glaring watch, perhaps, with ready spears—
355 Down the wide stairs a darkling² way they found.—
In all the house was heard no human sound.
A chain-droop'd lamp was flickering by each door;
The arras, rich with horseman, hawk, and hound,
Flutter'd in the besieging wind's uproar;
360 And the long carpets rose along the gusty floor.

8. Wild, untamed (originally, a wild hawk).
9. Drunken carousers.
1. Rhine wine and the sleep-producing mead (a

heavy fermented drink made with honey).
2. In the dark.

41

They glide, like phantoms, into the wide hall;
Like phantoms, to the iron porch, they glide;
Where lay the Porter, in uneasy sprawl,
With a huge empty flaggon by his side:
365   The wakeful bloodhound rose, and shook his hide,
But his sagacious eye an inmate owns:[3]
By one, and one, the bolts full easy slide:—
The chains lie silent on the footworn stones;—
The key turns, and the door upon its hinges groans.

42

370   And they are gone: ay, ages long ago
These lovers fled away into the storm.
That night the Baron dreamt of many a woe,
And all his warrior-guests, with shade and form
Of witch, and demon, and large coffin-worm,
375   Were long be-nightmar'd. Angela the old
Died palsy-twitch'd, with meagre face deform;
The Beadsman, after thousand aves[4] told,
For aye° unsought for slept among his ashes cold.   ever

Jan.–Feb. 1819   1820

Why did I laugh tonight? No voice will tell[1]

Why did I laugh tonight? No voice will tell:
    No god, no demon of severe response,
Deigns to reply from heaven or from hell.
    Then to my human heart I turn at once—
5   Heart! thou and I are here sad and alone;
    Say, wherefore did I laugh? O mortal pain!
O darkness! darkness! ever must I moan,
    To question heaven and hell and heart in vain!
Why did I laugh? I know this being's lease—
10   My fancy to its utmost blisses spreads:
Yet could I on this very midnight cease,
    And the world's gaudy ensigns° see in shreds.   banners
Verse, fame, and beauty are intense indeed,
But death intenser—death is life's high meed.

Mar. 1819   1848

---

3. Acknowledges a member of the household.
4. The prayers beginning *Ave Maria* ("Hail Mary").
1. In the letter to his brother and sister-in-law,
George and Georgiana Keats, into which he copied
this sonnet, March 19, 1819, Keats wrote: "Though

the first steps to it were through my human passions, they went away, and I wrote with my Mind—
and perhaps I must confess a little bit of my heart.
. . . I went to bed, and enjoyed an uninterrupted
sleep. Sane I went to bed and sane I arose."

Bright star, would I were stedfast as thou art[1]

Bright star, would I were stedfast as thou art—
   Not in lone splendor hung aloft the night,
And watching, with eternal lids apart,
   Like nature's patient, sleepless eremite,[2]
5 The moving waters at their priestlike task
   Of pure ablution[3] round earth's human shores,
Or gazing on the new soft-fallen mask
   Of snow upon the mountains and the moors;
No—yet still stedfast, still unchangeable,
10   Pillow'd upon my fair love's ripening breast,
To feel for ever its soft swell and fall,
   Awake for ever in a sweet unrest,
Still, still to hear her tender-taken breath,
And so live ever—or else swoon to death.[4]

1819   1838

La Belle Dame sans Merci: A Ballad[1]

1

O what can ail thee, knight at arms,
   Alone and palely loitering?
The sedge has wither'd from the lake,
   And no birds sing.

2

5 O what can ail thee, knight at arms,
   So haggard and so woe-begone?
The squirrel's granary is full,
   And the harvest's done.

3

I see a lily on thy brow
10   With anguish moist and fever dew,
And on thy cheeks a fading rose
   Fast withereth too.

1. While on a tour of the Lake District in 1818, Keats had said that the austere scenes "refine one's sensual vision into a sort of north star which can never cease to be open lidded and steadfast over the wonders of the great Power." The thought developed into this sonnet, which Keats drafted in 1819, then copied into his volume of Shakespeare's poems at the end of September or the beginning of October 1820, while on his way to Italy, where he died.
2. Hermit, religious solitary.
3. Washing, as part of a religious rite.
4. In the earlier version: "Half passionless, and so swoon on to death."

1. The title, though not the subject, was taken from a medieval poem by Alain Chartier and means "The Lovely Lady without Pity." The story of a mortal destroyed by his love for a supernatural femme fatale has been told repeatedly in myth, fairy tale, and ballad. The text printed here is Keats's earlier version of the poem, as transcribed by Charles Brown. The version published in 1820 begins, "Ah, what can ail thee, wretched wight."
   Keats imitates a frequent procedure of folk ballads by casting the poem into the dialogue form. The first three stanzas are addressed to the knight, and the rest of the poem is his reply.

4

I met a lady in the meads,
 Full beautiful, a fairy's child;
15 Her hair was long, her foot was light,
 And her eyes were wild.

5

I made a garland for her head,
 And bracelets too, and fragrant zone;[2]
She look'd at me as she did love,
20 And made sweet moan.

6

I set her on my pacing steed,
 And nothing else saw all day long,
For sidelong would she bend, and sing
 A fairy's song.

7

25 She found me roots of relish sweet,
 And honey wild, and manna dew,
And sure in language strange she said—
 I love thee true.

8

She took me to her elfin grot,
30 And there she wept, and sigh'd full sore,
And there I shut her wild wild eyes
 With kisses four.

9

And there she lulled me asleep,
 And there I dream'd—Ah! woe betide!
35 The latest° dream I ever dream'd   *last*
 On the cold hill's side.

10

I saw pale kings, and princes too,
 Pale warriors, death pale were they all;
They cried—"La belle dame sans merci
40 Hath thee in thrall!"

11

I saw their starv'd lips in the gloam
 With horrid warning gaped wide,
And I awoke and found me here
 On the cold hill's side.

2. Belt (of flowers).

12

45 And this is why I sojourn here,
    Alone and palely loitering,
Though the sedge is wither'd from the lake,
    And no birds sing.

Apr. 1819   1820

Sonnet to Sleep

O soft embalmer of the still midnight,
    Shutting with careful fingers and benign
Our gloom-pleas'd eyes, embower'd from the light,
    Enshaded in forgetfulness divine:
5 O soothest° Sleep! if so it please thee, close,   *softest*
    In midst of this thine hymn, my willing eyes,
Or wait the Amen ere thy poppy[1] throws
    Around my bed its lulling charities.
Then save me or the passed day will shine
10   Upon my pillow, breeding many woes:
Save me from curious° conscience, that still hoards   *scrupulous*
    Its strength for darkness, burrowing like the mole;
Turn the key deftly in the oiled wards,[2]
    And seal the hushed casket of my soul.

Apr. 1819   1838

Ode to Psyche[1]

O Goddess! hear these tuneless numbers, wrung
    By sweet enforcement and remembrance dear,
And pardon that thy secrets should be sung
    Even into thine own soft-conched[2] ear:
5 Surely I dreamt to-day, or did I see
    The winged Psyche with awaken'd eyes?[3]
I wander'd in a forest thoughtlessly,

---

1. Opium is made from the dried juice of the opium poppy.
2. The ridges in a lock that correspond to the notches of the key.
1. This poem initiated the sequence of great odes that Keats wrote in the spring of 1819. It is copied into the same journal-letter that included the *Sonnet to Sleep* and several other sonnets as well as a comment about "endeavoring to discover a better sonnet stanza than we have." It is therefore likely that Keats's experiments with sonnet schemes led to the development of the intricate and varied stanzas of his odes and also that he abandoned the sonnet on discovering the richer possibilities of the more spacious form. In his journal-letter, on April 30, he said that of all his recent poems, *Psyche* "is the first and the only one with which I have taken even moderate pains. I have for the most part dashed off my lines in a hurry. This I have done

leisurely—I think it reads the more richly for it and will I hope encourage me to write other things in even a more peaceable and healthy spirit."
    In the story told by the Roman author Apuleius in the 2nd century, Psyche was a lovely mortal beloved by Cupid, "the winged boy," son of Venus. After various tribulations imposed by Venus because she was jealous of Psyche's beauty, Psyche was wedded to Cupid and translated to heaven as an immortal. To this latter-day goddess, Keats in the last two stanzas promises to establish a place of worship within his own mind, with himself as poet-priest and prophet.
2. Soft and shaped like a seashell.
3. Another of Keats's inquiries into the relation of dreams to poetic vision; see, e.g., *Sleep and Poetry*, the concluding lines of *Ode to a Nightingale*, and the opening section of *The Fall of Hyperion: A Dream*.

And, on the sudden, fainting with surprise,
Saw two fair creatures, couched side by side
10   In deepest grass, beneath the whisp'ring roof
Of leaves and trembled blossoms, where there ran
A brooklet, scarce espied:
'Mid hush'd, cool-rooted flowers, fragrant-eyed,
Blue, silver-white, and budded Tyrian,[4]
15 They lay calm-breathing on the bedded grass;
Their arms embraced, and their pinions° too;   *wings*
Their lips touch'd not, but had not bade adieu,
As if disjoined by soft-handed slumber,
And ready still past kisses to outnumber
20   At tender eye-dawn of aurorean love:[5]
The winged boy I knew;
But who wast thou, O happy, happy dove?
His Psyche true!

O latest born and loveliest vision far
25   Of all Olympus' faded hierarchy![6]
Fairer than Phoebe's sapphire-region'd star,[7]
Or Vesper,° amorous glow-worm of the sky;   *evening star*
Fairer than these, though temple thou hast none,
Nor altar heap'd with flowers;
30 Nor virgin-choir to make delicious moan
Upon the midnight hours;
No voice, no lute, no pipe, no incense sweet
From chain-swung censer teeming;
No shrine, no grove, no oracle, no heat
35   Of pale-mouth'd prophet dreaming.

O brightest! though too late for antique vows,
Too, too late for the fond believing lyre,
When holy were the haunted forest boughs,
Holy the air, the water, and the fire;
40 Yet even in these days so far retir'd
From happy pieties, thy lucent fans,°   *shining wings*
Fluttering among the faint Olympians,
I see, and sing, by my own eyes inspired.
So let me be thy choir, and make a moan
45   Upon the midnight hours;
Thy voice, thy lute, thy pipe, thy incense sweet
From swinged censer teeming;
Thy shrine, thy grove, thy oracle, thy heat
Of pale-mouth'd prophet dreaming.

50 Yes, I will be thy priest, and build a fane°   *temple*
In some untrodden region of my mind,

4. The purple dye anciently made in Tyre.
5. Aurora was the goddess of the dawn.
6. The ranks of the classic gods of Mount Olympus. "You must recollect that Psyche was not embodied as a goddess before the time of Apuleius the Platonist who lived after the Augustan age, and consequently the goddess was never worshiped or sacrificed to with any of the ancient fervor—and perhaps never thought of in the old religion" (Keats, journal-letter, April 30, 1819).
7. The moon, supervised by the goddess Phoebe (Diana).

Where branched thoughts, new grown with pleasant pain,
    Instead of pines shall murmur in the wind:
Far, far around shall those dark-cluster'd trees
55   Fledge the wild-ridged mountains steep by steep;[8]
And there by zephyrs, streams, and birds, and bees,
    The moss-lain Dryads° shall be lull'd to sleep;   *wood nymphs*
And in the midst of this wide quietness
A rosy sanctuary will I dress
60   With the wreath'd trellis of a working brain,
    With buds, and bells, and stars without a name,
With all the gardener Fancy e'er could feign,
    Who breeding flowers, will never breed the same:
And there shall be for thee all soft delight
65   That shadowy thought can win,
A bright torch, and a casement ope at night,
    To let the warm Love[9] in!

Apr. 1819   1820

Ode to a Nightingale[1]

1

My heart aches, and a drowsy numbness pains
    My sense, as though of hemlock[2] I had drunk,
Or emptied some dull opiate to the drains
    One minute past, and Lethe[3]-wards had sunk:
5   'Tis not through envy of thy happy lot,
    But being too happy in thine happiness,—
        That thou, light-winged Dryad of the trees,
        In some melodious plot
Of beechen green, and shadows numberless,
10   Singest of summer in full-throated ease.

2

O, for a draught of vintage! that hath been
    Cool'd a long age in the deep-delved earth,
Tasting of Flora[4] and the country green,
    Dance, and Provençal song,[5] and sunburnt mirth!
15   O for a beaker full of the warm South,
    Full of the true, the blushful Hippocrene,[6]

8. I.e., the trees shall stand, rank against rank, like layers of feathers.
9. I.e., Cupid, god of love.
1. Charles Brown, with whom Keats was then living in Hampstead, wrote: "In the spring of 1819 a nightingale had built her nest near my house. Keats felt a tranquil and continual joy in her song; and one morning he took his chair from the breakfast table to the grass plot under a plum tree, where he sat for two or three hours. When he came into the house, I perceived he had some scraps of paper in his hand, and these he was quietly thrusting behind the books. On inquiry, I found those scraps, four or five in number, contained his poetic

feeling on the song of our nightingale."
2. A poisonous herb, not the North American evergreen tree.
3. River in Hades whose waters cause forgetfulness.
4. Roman goddess of flowers, or the flowers themselves.
5. Provence, in southern France, was in the late Middle Ages renowned for its troubadours—writers and singers of love songs.
6. Fountain of the Muses on Mount Helicon, hence the waters of inspiration, here applied metaphorically to a beaker of wine.

With beaded bubbles winking at the brim,
  And purple-stained mouth;
That I might drink, and leave the world unseen,
20 And with thee fade away into the forest dim:

3

Fade far away, dissolve, and quite forget
  What thou among the leaves hast never known,
The weariness, the fever, and the fret
  Here, where men sit and hear each other groan;
25 Where palsy shakes a few, sad, last gray hairs,
    Where youth grows pale, and spectre-thin, and dies;[7]
      Where but to think is to be full of sorrow
        And leaden-eyed despairs,
  Where Beauty cannot keep her lustrous eyes,
30   Or new Love pine at them beyond to-morrow.

4

Away! away! for I will fly to thee,
  Not charioted by Bacchus and his pards,
But on the viewless wings of Poesy,[8]
  Though the dull brain perplexes and retards:
35 Already with thee! tender is the night,
    And haply the Queen-Moon is on her throne,
      Cluster'd around by all her starry Fays;°   *fairies*
        But here there is no light,
  Save what from heaven is with the breezes blown
40   Through verdurous° glooms and winding mossy ways.   *green-foliaged*

5

I cannot see what flowers are at my feet,
  Nor what soft incense hangs upon the boughs,
But, in embalmed° darkness, guess each sweet   *perfumed*
  Wherewith the seasonable month endows
45 The grass, the thicket, and the fruit-tree wild;
    White hawthorn, and the pastoral eglantine;[9]
      Fast fading violets cover'd up in leaves;
        And mid-May's eldest child,
  The coming musk-rose, full of dewy wine,
50   The murmurous haunt of flies on summer eves.

6

Darkling° I listen; and, for many a time   *in darkness*
  I have been half in love with easeful Death,
Call'd him soft names in many a mused° rhyme,   *meditated*
  To take into the air my quiet breath;
55 Now more than ever seems it rich to die,

---

7. Keats's brother Tom, wasted by tuberculosis, had died the preceding winter.
8. I.e., by getting drunk not on wine (the "vintage" of stanza 2) but on the invisible ("viewless") wings of the poetic imagination. (Bacchus, god of wine, was sometimes represented in a chariot drawn by "pards"—leopards.)
9. Sweetbrier or honeysuckle.

To cease upon the midnight with no pain,
   While thou art pouring forth thy soul abroad
      In such an ecstasy!
   Still wouldst thou sing, and I have ears in vain—
60   To thy high requiem become a sod.

7

Thou wast not born for death, immortal Bird!
   No hungry generations tread thee down;
   The voice I hear this passing night was heard
      In ancient days by emperor and clown:
65 Perhaps the self-same song that found a path
   Through the sad heart of Ruth,[1] when, sick for home,
      She stood in tears amid the alien corn;°   *wheat*
         The same that oft-times hath
   Charm'd magic casements, opening on the foam
70   Of perilous seas, in faery lands forlorn.

8

Forlorn! the very word is like a bell
   To toll me back from thee to my sole self!
Adieu! the fancy[2] cannot cheat so well
   As she is fam'd to do, deceiving elf.
75 Adieu! adieu! thy plaintive anthem° fades   *hymn*
   Past the near meadows, over the still stream,
      Up the hill-side; and now 'tis buried deep
         In the next valley-glades:
   Was it a vision, or a waking dream?
80   Fled is that music:—Do I wake or sleep?[3]

May 1819   1819

Ode on a Grecian Urn[1]

I

Thou still unravish'd bride of quietness,
   Thou foster-child of silence and slow time,
Sylvan[2] historian, who canst thus express
   A flowery tale more sweetly than our rhyme:
5 What leaf-fring'd legend haunts about thy shape

---

1. The young widow in the biblical Book of Ruth.
2. I.e., imagination, "the viewless wings of Poesy" of line 33.
3. See n. 3, p. 847.
1. This urn, with its sculptured reliefs of Dionysian ecstasies, panting young lovers in flight and pursuit, a pastoral piper under spring foliage, and the quiet procession of priest and townspeople, resembles parts of various vases, sculptures, and paintings, but it existed in all its particulars only in Keats's imagination. In the urn—which captures moments of intense experience in attitudes of grace and immobilizes them in marble—Keats found the perfect correlative for his concern with

the longing for permanence in a world of change. The interpretation of the details with which he develops this concept, however, is hotly disputed, all the way from the opening phrase—is "still" an adverb ("as yet") or an adjective ("motionless")?—to the two concluding lines, which have already accumulated as much critical discussion as the "two-handed engine" in Milton's *Lycidas* or the cruxes in Shakespeare's plays. These disputes testify to the enigmatic richness of meaning in the five stanzas, as well as to the fact that the ode has become a central point of reference in the criticism of the English lyric.
2. Rustic, representing a woodland scene.

Of deities or mortals, or of both,
   In Tempe or the dales of Arcady?[3]
What men or gods are these? What maidens loth?
What mad pursuit? What struggle to escape?
10   What pipes and timbrels? What wild ecstasy?

2

Heard melodies are sweet, but those unheard
   Are sweeter; therefore, ye soft pipes, play on;
Not to the sensual ear,[4] but, more endear'd,
   Pipe to the spirit ditties of no tone:
15 Fair youth, beneath the trees, thou canst not leave
   Thy song, nor ever can those trees be bare;
    Bold lover, never, never canst thou kiss,
Though winning near the goal—yet, do not grieve;
    She cannot fade, though thou hast not thy bliss,
20   For ever wilt thou love, and she be fair!

3

Ah, happy, happy boughs! that cannot shed
   Your leaves, nor ever bid the spring adieu;
And, happy melodist, unwearied,
   For ever piping songs for ever new;
25 More happy love! more happy, happy love!
   For ever warm and still to be enjoy'd,
    For ever panting, and for ever young;
All breathing human passion far above,
    That leaves a heart high-sorrowful and cloy'd,
30   A burning forehead, and a parching tongue.

4

Who are these coming to the sacrifice?
   To what green altar, O mysterious priest,
Lead'st thou that heifer lowing at the skies,
   And all her silken flanks with garlands drest?
35 What little town by river or sea shore,
   Or mountain-built with peaceful citadel,
    Is emptied of this folk, this pious morn?
And, little town, thy streets for evermore
   Will silent be; and not a soul to tell
40   Why thou art desolate, can e'er return.

5

O Attic[5] shape! Fair attitude! with brede
   Of marble men and maidens overwrought,[6]

---

3. The valleys of Arcadia, a state in ancient Greece often used as a symbol of the pastoral ideal. "Tempe": a beautiful valley in Greece that has come to represent supreme rural beauty.
4. The ear of sense (as opposed to that of the "spirit," or imagination).
5. Greek. Attica was the region of Greece in which Athens was located.
6. Ornamented all over ("overwrought") with an interwoven pattern ("brede").

With forest branches and the trodden weed;
   Thou, silent form, dost tease us out of thought
45 As doth eternity: Cold Pastoral!
   When old age shall this generation waste,
     Thou shalt remain, in midst of other woe
   Than ours, a friend to man, to whom thou say'st,
   "Beauty is truth, truth beauty,"[7]—that is all
50   Ye know on earth, and all ye need to know.

1819   1820

Ode on Melancholy   This is Keats's best-known statement of his recurrent theme of the mingled contrarieties of life. The remarkable last stanza, in which Melancholy becomes a veiled goddess in a mystery religion, implies that it is the tragic human destiny that beauty, joy, and life itself owe not only their quality but their value to the fact that they are transitory and turn into their opposites.

   The poem once had the following initial stanza, which Keats canceled in manuscript:

Though you should build a bark of dead men's bones,
   And rear a phantom gibbet for a mast,
Stitch creeds together for a sail, with groans
   To fill it out, bloodstained and aghast;
Although your rudder be a Dragon's tail,
   Long sever'd, yet still hard with agony,
     Your cordage large uprootings from the skull
Of bald Medusa: certes you would fail
   To find the Melancholy, whether she
     Dreameth in any isle of Lethe dull.

Ode on Melancholy

I

No, no, go not to Lethe,[1] neither twist
   Wolf's-bane, tight-rooted, for its poisonous wine;
Nor suffer thy pale forehead to be kiss'd
   By nightshade, ruby grape of Proserpine;[2]
5 Make not your rosary of yew-berries,[3]
   Nor let the beetle, nor the death-moth be

7. The quotation marks around this phrase are found in the volume of poems Keats published in 1820, but there are no quotation marks in the version printed in *Annals of the Fine Arts* that same year or in the transcripts of the poem made by Keats's friends. This discrepancy has multiplied the diversity of critical interpretations of the last two lines. Critics disagree whether the whole of these lines is said by the urn, or "Beauty is truth, truth beauty" by the urn and the rest by the lyric speaker; whether the "ye" in the last line is addressed to the lyric speaker, to the readers, to the urn, or to the figures on the urn; whether "all ye know" is that beauty is truth, or this plus the statement in lines 46–48; and whether "beauty is truth" is a profound metaphysical proposition, an overstatement representing the limited point of view of the urn, or simply nonsensical.

1. The waters of forgetfulness in Hades.
2. The wife of Pluto and queen of the infernal regions. "Nightshade" and "wolf's-bane" (line 2) are poisonous plants.
3. A symbol of death.

With flowers, and stirring shades, and baffled beams:
45　The morn was clouded, but no shower fell,
　　　Though in her lids hung the sweet tears of May;
　　　　The open casement press'd a new-leaved vine,
　　　Let in the budding warmth and throstle's lay;
　　　O shadows! 'twas a time to bid farewell!
50　　　Upon your skirts had fallen no tears of mine.

6

So, ye three ghosts, adieu! Ye cannot raise
　　　My head cool-bedded in the flowery grass;
For I would not be dieted with praise,
　　　A pet-lamb in a sentimental farce![4]
55　Fade softly from my eyes, and be once more
　　　In masque-like figures on the dreamy urn;
　　　　Farewell! I yet have visions for the night,
And for the day faint visions there is store;
　　　Vanish, ye phantoms, from my idle spright,°　　　　　　　*spirit*
60　Into the clouds, and never more return!

Spring 1819　　　　　　　　　　　　　　　　　　　　　　　　　　1848

Lamia　In a note printed at the end of the poem, Keats cited as his source the following story in Robert Burton's *Anatomy of Melancholy* (1621):

> One Menippus Lycius, a young man twenty-five years of age, that going betwixt Cenchreas and Corinth, met such a phantasm in the habit of a fair gentlewoman, which, taking him by the hand, carried him home to her house, in the suburbs of Corinth. . . . The young man, a philosopher, otherwise staid and discreet, able to moderate his passions, though not this of love, tarried with her a while to his great content, and at last married her, to whose wedding, amongst other guests, came Apollonius; who, by some probable conjectures, found her out to be a serpent, a lamia; and that all her furniture was, like Tantalus's gold, described by Homer, no substance but mere illusions. When she saw herself descried, she wept, and desired Apollonius to be silent, but he would not be moved, and thereupon she, plate, house, and all that was in it, vanished in an instant: many thousands took notice of this fact, for it was done in the midst of Greece.

In ancient demonology, a "lamia" was a monster in woman's form who preyed on human beings. There are various clues that Keats invested the ancient legend with allegorical significance (see especially 2.229–38). Its interpretation, however, and even the inclination of Keats's own sympathies in the contest between Lamia and Apollonius, have been disputed. Perhaps Keats simply failed to make up his mind or wavered in the course of composition. In any case, the poem presents an inevitably fatal situation, in which no one is entirely blameless or blameworthy and no character monopolizes either our sympathy or antipathy. Lamia is an enchantress, a liar, and a

4. In a letter of June 9, 1819, Keats wrote: "I have been very idle lately, very averse to writing; both from the overpowering idea of our dead poets and from abatement of my love of fame. I hope I am a little more of a Philosopher than I was, conse- quently a little less of a versifying Pet-lamb. . . . You will judge of my 1819 temper when I tell you that the thing I have most enjoyed this year has been writing an ode to Indolence."

calculating expert in *amour;* but she apparently intends no harm, is genuinely in love, and is very beautiful. And both male protagonists exhibit culpable extremes. Lycius, though an attractive young lover, is gullible, a slave to his passions, and capable of gratuitous cruelty; while Apollonius, though realistically clear-sighted, is rigid, puritanical, and inhumane.

The poem, written between late June and early September 1819, is a return, after the Spenserian stanzas of *The Eve of St. Agnes,* to the pentameter couplets Keats had used in *Endymion* and other early poems. But Keats had in the meantime been studying John Dryden's closed and strong-paced couplets. The initial lines of Dryden's version of Boccaccio's story *Cymon and Iphigenia* demonstrate the kind of narrative model that helped Keats make the technical transition from the fluent but sprawling gracefulness of the opening of *Endymion* to the vigor and economy of the opening of *Lamia:*

> In that sweet isle where Venus keeps her court,
> And every grace, and all the loves, resort;
> Where either sex is formed of softer earth,
> And takes the bent of pleasure from their birth;
> There lived a Cyprian lord, above the rest
> Wise, wealthy, with a numerous issue blessed. . . .

Lamia

Part 1

Upon a time, before the faery broods
Drove Nymph and Satyr[1] from the prosperous woods,
Before King Oberon's bright diadem,
Sceptre, and mantle, clasp'd with dewy gem,
5 Frighted away the Dryads and the Fauns
From rushes green, and brakes,° and cowslip'd lawns,   *thickets*
The ever-smitten Hermes[2] empty left
His golden throne, bent warm on amorous theft:
From high Olympus had he stolen light,
10 On this side of Jove's clouds, to escape the sight
Of his great summoner, and made retreat
Into a forest on the shores of Crete.
For somewhere in that sacred island dwelt
A nymph, to whom all hoofed Satyrs knelt;
15 At whose white feet the languid Tritons[3] poured
Pearls, while on land they wither'd and adored.
Fast by the springs where she to bathe was wont,
And in those meads where sometime she might haunt,
Were strewn rich gifts, unknown to any Muse,
20 Though Fancy's casket were unlock'd to choose.
Ah, what a world of love was at her feet!
So Hermes thought, and a celestial heat

---

1. Nymphs and satyrs—like the dryads and fauns in line 5—were minor classical deities of the woods and fields, said here to have been driven off by Oberon, king of the fairies, who were supernatural beings of the postclassical era.

2. Or Mercury; wing-footed messenger at the summons of Jove (line 11), Hermes was notoriously amorous.

3. Minor sea gods.

Burnt from his winged heels to either ear,
That from a whiteness, as the lily clear,
25 Blush'd into roses 'mid his golden hair,
Fallen in jealous curls about his shoulders bare.[4]

From vale to vale, from wood to wood, he flew,
Breathing upon the flowers his passion new,
And wound with many a river to its head,
30 To find where this sweet nymph prepar'd her secret bed:
In vain; the sweet nymph might nowhere be found,
And so he rested, on the lonely ground,
Pensive, and full of painful jealousies
Of the Wood-Gods, and even the very trees.
35 There as he stood, he heard a mournful voice,
Such as once heard, in gentle heart, destroys
All pain but pity: thus the lone voice spake:
"When from this wreathed tomb shall I awake!
When move in a sweet body fit for life,
40 And love, and pleasure, and the ruddy strife
Of hearts and lips! Ah, miserable me!"
The God, dove-footed,[5] glided silently
Round bush and tree, soft-brushing, in his speed,
The taller grasses and full-flowering weed,
45 Until he found a palpitating snake,
Bright, and cirque-couchant[6] in a dusky brake.

She was a gordian[7] shape of dazzling hue,
Vermilion-spotted, golden, green, and blue;
Striped like a zebra, freckled like a pard,°   leopard
50 Eyed like a peacock,[8] and all crimson barr'd;
And full of silver moons, that, as she breathed,
Dissolv'd, or brighter shone, or interwreathed
Their lustres with the gloomier tapestries—
So rainbow-sided, touch'd with miseries,
55 She seem'd, at once, some penanced lady elf,
Some demon's mistress, or the demon's self.
Upon her crest she wore a wannish[9] fire
Sprinkled with stars, like Ariadne's tiar:[1]
Her head was serpent, but ah, bitter-sweet!
60 She had a woman's mouth with all its pearls[2] complete:
And for her eyes: what could such eyes do there
But weep, and weep, that they were born so fair?
As Proserpine still weeps for her Sicilian air.[3]
Her throat was serpent, but the words she spake

---

4. I.e., the curls clung jealously to his bare shoulders. This line is the first of a number of Alexandrines, a six-foot line, used to vary the metrical movement—a device that Keats learned from Dryden. Another such device is the triplet, occurring first in lines 61–63.
5. I.e., quietly as a dove.
6. Lying in a circular coil.
7. Intricately twisted, like the knot tied by King Gordius, which no one could undo.

8. Having multicolored spots, like the "eyes" in a peacock's tail.
9. Rather dark.
1. Ariadne, who was transformed into a constellation, had been represented in a painting by Titian wearing a symbolic crown, or tiara ("tiar"), of stars.
2. "Pearls" had become almost a synonym for teeth in Elizabethan love poems.
3. Proserpine had been carried off to Hades by Pluto from the field of Enna, in Sicily.

65 Came, as through bubbling honey, for Love's sake,
    And thus; while Hermes on his pinions lay,
    Like a stoop'd falcon[4] ere he takes his prey.

    "Fair Hermes, crown'd with feathers, fluttering light,
    I had a splendid dream of thee last night:
70 I saw thee sitting, on a throne of gold,
    Among the Gods, upon Olympus old,
    The only sad one; for thou didst not hear
    The soft, lute-finger'd Muses chaunting clear,
    Nor even Apollo when he sang alone,
75 Deaf to his throbbing throat's long, long melodious moan.
    I dreamt I saw thee, robed in purple flakes,
    Break amorous through the clouds, as morning breaks,
    And, swiftly as a bright Phœbean dart,[5]
    Strike for the Cretan isle; and here thou art!
80 Too gentle Hermes, hast thou found the maid?"
    Whereat the star of Lethe[6] not delay'd
    His rosy eloquence, and thus inquired:
    "Thou smooth-lipp'd serpent, surely high inspired!
    Thou beauteous wreath, with melancholy eyes,
85 Possess whatever bliss thou canst devise,
    Telling me only where my nymph is fled,—
    Where she doth breathe!" "Bright planet, thou hast said,"
    Return'd the snake, "but seal with oaths, fair God!"
    "I swear," said Hermes, "by my serpent rod,
90 And by thine eyes, and by thy starry crown!"
    Light flew his earnest words, among the blossoms blown.
    Then thus again the brilliance feminine:
    "Too frail of heart! for this lost nymph of thine,
    Free as the air, invisibly, she strays
95 About these thornless wilds; her pleasant days
    She tastes unseen; unseen her nimble feet
    Leave traces in the grass and flowers sweet;
    From weary tendrils, and bow'd branches green,
    She plucks the fruit unseen, she bathes unseen:
100 And by my power is her beauty veil'd
    To keep it unaffronted, unassail'd
    By the love-glances of unlovely eyes,
    Of Satyrs, Fauns, and blear'd Silenus'[7] sighs.
    Pale grew her immortality, for woe
105 Of all these lovers, and she grieved so
    I took compassion on her, bade her steep
    Her hair in weïrd° syrops, that would keep   *magical*
    Her loveliness invisible, yet free
    To wander as she loves, in liberty.
110 Thou shalt behold her, Hermes, thou alone,

---

4. *Stoop* is the term for the plunge of a falcon on his prey.
5. A ray of Phoebus Apollo, god of the sun.
6. Hermes, when he appeared like a star on the banks of Lethe, in the darkness of Hades. (One of Hermes' offices was to guide the souls of the dead to the lower regions.)
7. Satyr, tutor of Bacchus, usually represented as drunk.

If thou wilt, as thou swearest, grant my boon!"
Then, once again, the charmed God began
An oath, and through the serpent's ears it ran
Warm, tremulous, devout, psalterian.[8]

115 Ravish'd, she lifted her Circean head,
Blush'd a live damask,[9] and swift-lisping said,
"I was a woman, let me have once more
A woman's shape, and charming as before.
I love a youth of Corinth—O the bliss!

120 Give me my woman's form, and place me where he is.
Stoop, Hermes, let me breathe upon thy brow,
And thou shalt see thy sweet nymph even now."
The God on half-shut feathers sank serene,
She breath'd upon his eyes, and swift was seen

125 Of both the guarded nymph near-smiling on the green.
It was no dream; or say a dream it was,
Real are the dreams of Gods, and smoothly pass
Their pleasures in a long immortal dream.
One warm, flush'd moment, hovering, it might seem

130 Dash'd by the wood-nymph's beauty, so he burn'd;
Then, lighting on the printless verdure, turn'd
To the swoon'd serpent, and with languid arm,
Delicate, put to proof the lythe Caducean charm.[1]
So done, upon the nymph his eyes he bent

135 Full of adoring tears and blandishment,
And towards her stept: she, like a moon in wane,
Faded before him, cower'd, nor could restrain
Her fearful sobs, self-folding like a flower
That faints into itself at evening hour:

140 But the God fostering her chilled hand,
She felt the warmth, her eyelids open'd bland,°   softly
And, like new flowers at morning song of bees,
Bloom'd, and gave up her honey to the lees.°   dregs
Into the green-recessed woods they flew;

145 Nor grew they pale, as mortal lovers do.

     Left to herself, the serpent now began
To change; her elfin blood in madness ran,
Her mouth foam'd, and the grass, therewith besprent,°   sprinkled
Wither'd at dew so sweet and virulent;

150 Her eyes in torture fix'd, and anguish drear,
Hot, glaz'd, and wide, with lid-lashes all sear,
Flash'd phosphor and sharp sparks, without one cooling tear.
The colours all inflam'd throughout her train,
She writh'd about, convuls'd with scarlet pain:

155 A deep volcanian yellow took the place
Of all her milder-mooned body's grace;[2]

---

8. Either "like a psalm" or "like the sound of the psaltery" (an ancient stringed instrument).
9. The color of a damask rose (large and fragrant pink rose). "Circean": like that of Circe, the enchantress in the *Odyssey*.

1. I.e., put to the test the magic of the flexible Caduceus (Hermes' official staff).
2. I.e., the yellow of sulfur (thrown up by a volcano) replaced her former silvery moon color.

And, as the lava ravishes the mead,
Spoilt all her silver mail, and golden brede;[3]
Made gloom of all her frecklings, streaks and bars,
160 Eclips'd her crescents, and lick'd up her stars:
So that, in moments few, she was undrest
Of all her sapphires, greens, and amethyst,
And rubious-argent:° of all these bereft,   silvery red
Nothing but pain and ugliness were left.
165 Still shone her crown; that vanish'd, also she
Melted and disappear'd as suddenly;
And in the air, her new voice luting soft,
Cried, "Lycius! gentle Lycius!"—Borne aloft
With the bright mists about the mountains hoar
170 These words dissolv'd: Crete's forests heard no more.

Whither fled Lamia, now a lady bright,
A full-born beauty new and exquisite?
She fled into that valley they pass o'er
Who go to Corinth from Cenchreas' shore;[4]
175 And rested at the foot of those wild hills,
The rugged founts of the Peæran rills,
And of that other ridge whose barren back
Stretches, with all its mist and cloudy rack,
South-westward to Cleone. There she stood
180 About a young bird's flutter from a wood,
Fair, on a sloping green of mossy tread,
By a clear pool, wherein she passioned[5]
To see herself escap'd from so sore ills,
While her robes flaunted with the daffodils.

185   Ah, happy Lycius!—for she was a maid
More beautiful than ever twisted braid,
Or sigh'd, or blush'd, or on spring-flowered lea°   meadow
Spread a green kirtle° to the minstrelsy: gown
A virgin purest lipp'd, yet in the lore
190 Of love deep learned to the red heart's core:
Not one hour old, yet of sciential brain
To unperplex bliss from its neighbour pain;
Define their pettish limits, and estrange
Their points of contact, and swift counterchange;[6]
195 Intrigue with the specious chaos,[7] and dispart
Its most ambiguous atoms with sure art;
As though in Cupid's college she had spent
Sweet days a lovely graduate, still unshent,°   unspoiled
And kept his rosy terms[8] in idle languishment.

3. Embroidery, interwoven pattern. "Mail": inter-linked rings, as in a coat of armor.
4. Cenchrea (Keats's "Cenchreas") was a harbor of Corinth, in southern Greece.
5. Felt intense excitement.
6. I.e., of knowledgeable ("sciential") brain to dis-entangle ("unperplex") bliss from its closely related pain, to define their quarreled-over ("pettish") lim-

its, and to separate out ("estrange") their points of contact and the swift changes of each condition into its opposite. Cf. Keats's *Ode on Melancholy*, lines 21–26 (p. 853).
7. I.e., turn to her own artful purpose the seeming ("specious") chaos.
8. The terms spent studying in "Cupid's college."

200   Why this fair creature chose so fairily
By the wayside to linger, we shall see;
But first 'tis fit to tell how she could muse
And dream, when in the serpent prison-house,
Of all she list,° strange or magnificent: *wished*
205   How, ever, where she will'd, her spirit went;
Whether to faint Elysium, or where
Down through tress-lifting waves the Nereids[9] fair
Wind into Thetis' bower by many a pearly stair;
Or where God Bacchus drains his cups divine,
210   Stretch'd out, at ease, beneath a glutinous pine;
Or where in Pluto's gardens palatine°   *palatial*
Mulciber's columns gleam in far piazzian line.[1]
And sometimes into cities she would send
Her dream, with feast and rioting to blend;
215   And once, while among mortals dreaming thus,
She saw the young Corinthian Lycius
Charioting foremost in the envious race,
Like a young Jove with calm uneager face,
And fell into a swooning love of him.
220   Now on the moth-time of that evening dim
He would return that way, as well she knew,
To Corinth from the shore; for freshly blew
The eastern soft wind, and his galley now
Grated the quaystones with her brazen prow
225   In port Cenchreas, from Egina isle
Fresh anchor'd; whither he had been awhile
To sacrifice to Jove, whose temple there
Waits with high marble doors for blood and incense rare.
Jove heard his vows, and better'd his desire;
230   For by some freakful chance he made retire
From his companions, and set forth to walk,
Perhaps grown wearied of their Corinth talk:
Over the solitary hills he fared,
Thoughtless at first, but ere eve's star appeared
235   His phantasy was lost, where reason fades,
In the calm'd twilight of Platonic shades.[2]
Lamia beheld him coming, near, more near—
Close to her passing, in indifference drear,
His silent sandals swept the mossy green;
240   So neighbour'd to him, and yet so unseen
She stood: he pass'd, shut up in mysteries,
His mind wrapp'd like his mantle, while her eyes
Follow'd his steps, and her neck regal white
Turn'd—syllabling thus, "Ah, Lycius bright,
245   And will you leave me on the hills alone?
Lycius, look back! and be some pity shown."
He did; not with cold wonder fearingly,

---

9. Sea nymphs, of whom Thetis (line 208, the mother of Achilles) was one.
1. I.e., columns made by Mulciber (Vulcan, god of fire and metalworking) gleam in long lines around open courts (piazzas).
2. I.e., he was absorbed in musing about the obscurities of Plato's philosophy.

But Orpheus-like at an Eurydice;[3]
For so delicious were the words she sung,

250 It seem'd he had lov'd them a whole summer long:
And soon his eyes had drunk her beauty up,
Leaving no drop in the bewildering cup,
And still the cup was full,—while he, afraid
Lest she should vanish ere his lip had paid

255 Due adoration, thus began to adore;
Her soft look growing coy, she saw his chain so sure:
"Leave thee alone! Look back! Ah, Goddess, see
Whether my eyes can ever turn from thee!
For pity do not this sad heart belie[4]—

260 Even as thou vanishest so I shall die.
Stay! though a Naiad of the rivers, stay!
To thy far wishes will thy streams obey:
Stay! though the greenest woods be thy domain,
Alone they can drink up the morning rain:

265 Though a descended Pleiad,[5] will not one
Of thine harmonious sisters keep in tune
Thy spheres, and as thy silver proxy shine?
So sweetly to these ravish'd ears of mine
Came thy sweet greeting, that if thou shouldst fade

270 Thy memory will waste me to a shade:—
For pity do not melt!"—"If I should stay,"
Said Lamia, "here, upon this floor of clay,
And pain my steps upon these flowers too rough,
What canst thou say or do of charm enough

275 To dull the nice[6] remembrance of my home?
Thou canst not ask me with thee here to roam
Over these hills and vales, where no joy is,—
Empty of immortality and bliss!
Thou art a scholar, Lycius, and must know

280 That finer spirits cannot breathe below
In human climes, and live: Alas! poor youth,
What taste of purer air hast thou to soothe
My essence? What serener palaces,
Where I may all my many senses please,

285 And by mysterious sleights a hundred thirsts appease?
It cannot be—Adieu!" So said, she rose
Tiptoe with white arms spread. He, sick to lose
The amorous promise of her lone complain,
Swoon'd, murmuring of love, and pale with pain.

290 The cruel lady, without any show
Of sorrow for her tender favourite's woe,
But rather, if her eyes could brighter be,
With brighter eyes and slow amenity,
Put her new lips to his, and gave afresh

---

3. As Orpheus looked at Eurydice in Hades. Orpheus was allowed by Pluto to lead Eurydice back to earth on condition that he not look back at her, but he could not resist doing so, hence lost her once more.

4. Be false to.
5. One of the seven sisters composing the constellation Pleiades.
6. Detailed, minutely accurate.

295 The life she had so tangled in her mesh:
And as he from one trance was wakening
Into another, she began to sing,
Happy in beauty, life, and love, and every thing,
A song of love, too sweet for earthly lyres,
300 While, like held breath, the stars drew in their panting fires.
And then she whisper'd in such trembling tone,
As those who, safe together met alone
For the first time through many anguish'd days,
Use other speech than looks; bidding him raise
305 His drooping head, and clear his soul of doubt,
For that she was a woman, and without
Any more subtle fluid in her veins
Than throbbing blood, and that the self-same pains
Inhabited her frail-strung heart as his.
310 And next she wonder'd how his eyes could miss
Her face so long in Corinth, where, she said,
She dwelt but half retir'd, and there had led
Days happy as the gold coin could invent
Without the aid of love; yet in content
315 Till she saw him, as once she pass'd him by,
Where 'gainst a column he leant thoughtfully
At Venus' temple porch, 'mid baskets heap'd
Of amorous herbs and flowers, newly reap'd
Late on that eve, as 'twas the night before
320 The Adonian feast;[7] whereof she saw no more,
But wept alone those days, for why should she adore?
Lycius from death awoke into amaze,
To see her still, and singing so sweet lays;
Then from amaze into delight he fell
325 To hear her whisper woman's lore so well;
And every word she spake entic'd him on
To unperplex'd delight[8] and pleasure known.
Let the mad poets say whate'er they please
Of the sweets of Fairies, Peris,[9] Goddesses,
330 There is not such a treat among them all,
Haunters of cavern, lake, and waterfall,
As a real woman, lineal indeed
From Pyrrha's pebbles[1] or old Adam's seed.
Thus gentle Lamia judg'd, and judg'd aright,
335 That Lycius could not love in half a fright,
So threw the goddess off, and won his heart
More pleasantly by playing woman's part,
With no more awe than what her beauty gave,
That, while it smote, still guaranteed to save.
340 Lycius to all made eloquent reply,
Marrying to every word a twinborn sigh;
And last, pointing to Corinth, ask'd her sweet,

7. The feast of Adonis, beloved by Venus.
8. I.e., delight not mixed with its neighbor, pain
(see line 192).
9. Fairylike creatures in Persian mythology.

1. Descended from the pebbles with which, in
Greek myth, Pyrrha and Deucalion repeopled the
earth after the flood.

If 'twas too far that night for her soft feet.
The way was short, for Lamia's eagerness
345　Made, by a spell, the triple league decrease
To a few paces; not at all surmised
By blinded Lycius, so in her comprized.[2]
They pass'd the city gates, he knew not how,
So noiseless, and he never thought to know.

350　　As men talk in a dream, so Corinth all,
Throughout her palaces imperial,
And all her populous streets and temples lewd,[3]
Mutter'd, like tempest in the distance brew'd,
To the wide-spreaded night above her towers.
355　Men, women, rich and poor, in the cool hours,
Shuffled their sandals o'er the pavement white,
Companion'd or alone; while many a light
Flared, here and there, from wealthy festivals,
And threw their moving shadows on the walls,
360　Or found them cluster'd in the corniced shade
Of some arch'd temple door, or dusky colonnade.

　　Muffling his face, of greeting friends in fear,
Her fingers he press'd hard, as one came near
With curl'd gray beard, sharp eyes, and smooth bald crown,
365　Slow-stepp'd, and robed in philosophic gown:
Lycius shrank closer, as they met and past,
Into his mantle, adding wings to haste,
While hurried Lamia trembled: "Ah," said he,
"Why do you shudder, love, so ruefully?
370　Why does your tender palm dissolve in dew?"—
"I'm wearied," said fair Lamia: "tell me who
Is that old man? I cannot bring to mind
His features:—Lycius! wherefore did you blind
Yourself from his quick eyes?" Lycius replied,
375　" 'Tis Apollonius sage, my trusty guide
And good instructor; but to-night he seems
The ghost of folly haunting my sweet dreams."

　　While yet he spake they had arrived before
A pillar'd porch, with lofty portal door,
380　Where hung a silver lamp, whose phosphor glow
Reflected in the slabbed steps below,
Mild as a star in water; for so new,
And so unsullied was the marble hue,
So through the crystal polish, liquid fine,
385　Ran the dark veins, that none but feet divine
Could e'er have touch'd there. Sounds Æolian[4]
Breath'd from the hinges, as the ample span
Of the wide doors disclos'd a place unknown

2. Bound up, absorbed.
3. Temples of Venus, whose worship sometimes involved ritual prostitution.

4. Like sounds from the wind harp (Aeolus is god of winds), which responds musically to a current of air.

Some time to any, but those two alone,
390 And a few Persian mutes, who that same year
Were seen about the markets: none knew where
They could inhabit; the most curious
Were foil'd, who watch'd to trace them to their house:
And but the flitter-winged verse must tell,
395 For truth's sake, what woe afterwards befel,
'Twould humour many a heart to leave them thus,
Shut from the busy world of more incredulous.

Part 2

Love in a hut, with water and a crust,
Is—Love, forgive us!—cinders, ashes, dust;
Love in a palace is perhaps at last
More grievous torment than a hermit's fast:—
5 That is a doubtful tale from faery land,
Hard for the non-elect to understand.
Had Lycius liv'd to hand his story down,
He might have given the moral a fresh frown,
Or clench'd it quite: but too short was their bliss
10 To breed distrust and hate, that make the soft voice hiss.
Besides, there, nightly, with terrific glare,
Love, jealous grown of so complete a pair,
Hover'd and buzz'd his wings, with fearful roar,
Above the lintel of their chamber door,
15 And down the passage cast a glow upon the floor.

For all this came a ruin: side by side
They were enthroned, in the even tide,
Upon a couch, near to a curtaining
Whose airy texture, from a golden string,
20 Floated into the room, and let appear
Unveil'd the summer heaven, blue and clear,
Betwixt two marble shafts:—there they reposed,
Where use had made it sweet, with eyelids closed,
Saving a tythe which love still open kept,
25 That they might see each other while they almost slept;
When from the slope side of a suburb hill,
Deafening the swallow's twitter, came a thrill
Of trumpets—Lycius started—the sounds fled,
But left a thought, a buzzing in his head.
30 For the first time, since first he harbour'd in
That purple-lined palace of sweet sin,
His spirit pass'd beyond its golden bourn
Into the noisy world almost forsworn.
The lady, ever watchful, penetrant,
35 Saw this with pain, so arguing a want
Of something more, more than her empery°   *empire*
Of joys; and she began to moan and sigh
Because he mused beyond her, knowing well
That but a moment's thought is passion's passing bell.°   *death knell*

40 "Why do you sigh, fair creature?" whisper'd he:
  "Why do you think?" return'd she tenderly:
  "You have deserted me;—where am I now?
  Not in your heart while care weighs on your brow:
  No, no, you have dismiss'd me; and I go
45 From your breast houseless: ay, it must be so."
  He answer'd, bending to her open eyes,
  Where he was mirror'd small in paradise,
  "My silver planet, both of eve and morn![5]
  Why will you plead yourself so sad forlorn,
50 While I am striving how to fill my heart
  With deeper crimson, and a double smart?
  How to entangle, trammel up and snare
  Your soul in mine, and labyrinth you there
  Like the hid scent in an unbudded rose?
55 Ay, a sweet kiss—you see your mighty woes.[6]
  My thoughts! shall I unveil them? Listen then!
  What mortal hath a prize, that other men
  May be confounded and abash'd withal,
  But lets it sometimes pace abroad majestical,
60 And triumph, as in thee I should rejoice
  Amid the hoarse alarm of Corinth's voice.
  Let my foes choke, and my friends shout afar,
  While through the thronged streets your bridal car
  Wheels round its dazzling spokes."—The lady's cheek
65 Trembled; she nothing said, but, pale and meek,
  Arose and knelt before him, wept a rain
  Of sorrows at his words; at last with pain
  Beseeching him, the while his hand she wrung,
  To change his purpose. He thereat was stung,
70 Perverse, with stronger fancy to reclaim
  Her wild and timid nature to his aim:
  Besides, for all his love, in self despite,
  Against his better self, he took delight
  Luxurious in her sorrows, soft and new.
75 His passion, cruel grown, took on a hue
  Fierce and sanguineous as 'twas possible
  In one whose brow had no dark veins to swell.
  Fine was the mitigated fury, like
  Apollo's presence when in act to strike
80 The serpent—Ha, the serpent! certes, she
  Was none. She burnt, she lov'd the tyranny,
  And, all subdued, consented to the hour
  When to the bridal he should lead his paramour.
  Whispering in midnight silence, said the youth,
85 "Sure some sweet name thou hast, though, by my truth,
  I have not ask'd it, ever thinking thee
  Not mortal, but of heavenly progeny,
  As still I do. Hast any mortal name,

5. The planet Venus, which is both the morning and the evening star.

6. Playfully: "You see how great your troubles were!"

Fit appellation for this dazzling frame?
90 Or friends or kinsfolk on the citied earth,
To share our marriage feast and nuptial mirth?"
"I have no friends," said Lamia, "no, not one;
My presence in wide Corinth hardly known:
My parents' bones are in their dusty urns
95 Sepulchred, where no kindled incense burns,
Seeing all their luckless race are dead, save me,
And I neglect the holy rite for thee.
Even as you list invite your many guests;
But if, as now it seems, your vision rests
100 With any pleasure on me, do not bid
Old Apollonius—from him keep me hid."
Lycius, perplex'd at words so blind and blank,
Made close inquiry; from whose touch she shrank,
Feigning a sleep; and he to the dull shade
105 Of deep sleep in a moment was betray'd.

It was the custom then to bring away,
The bride from home at blushing shut of day,
Veil'd, in a chariot, heralded along
By strewn flowers, torches, and a marriage song,
110 With other pageants: but this fair unknown
Had not a friend. So being left alone,
(Lycius was gone to summon all his kin)
And knowing surely she could never win
His foolish heart from its mad pompousness,
115 She set herself, high-thoughted, how to dress
The misery in fit magnificence.
She did so, but 'tis doubtful how and whence
Came, and who were her subtle servitors.
About the halls, and to and from the doors,
120 There was a noise of wings, till in short space
The glowing banquet-room shone with wide-arched grace.
A haunting music, sole perhaps and lone
Supportress of the faery-roof, made moan
Throughout, as fearful the whole charm might fade.
125 Fresh carved cedar, mimicking a glade
Of palm and plantain, met from either side,
High in the midst, in honour of the bride:
Two palms and then two plantains, and so on,
From either side their stems branch'd one to one
130 All down the aisled place; and beneath all
There ran a stream of lamps straight on from wall to wall.
So canopied, lay an untasted feast
Teeming with odours. Lamia, regal drest,
Silently paced about, and as she went,
135 In pale contented sort of discontent,
Mission'd her viewless servants to enrich
The fretted⁷ splendour of each nook and niche.

7. Adorned with fretwork (interlaced patterns).

Between the tree-stems, marbled plain at first,
Came jasper pannels; then, anon, there burst
140 Forth creeping imagery of slighter trees,
And with the larger wove in small intricacies.
Approving all, she faded at self-will,
And shut the chamber up, close, hush'd and still,
Complete and ready for the revels rude,
145 When dreadful° guests would come to spoil her solitude.   *terrifying*

    The day appear'd, and all the gossip rout.
O senseless Lycius! Madman! wherefore flout
The silent-blessing fate, warm cloister'd hours,
And show to common eyes these secret bowers?
150 The herd approach'd; each guest, with busy brain,
Arriving at the portal, gaz'd amain,°   *intently*
And enter'd marveling: for they knew the street,
Remember'd it from childhood all complete
Without a gap, yet ne'er before had seen
155 That royal porch, that high-built fair demesne;°   *estate*
So in they hurried all, maz'd, curious and keen:
Save one, who look'd thereon with eye severe,
And with calm-planted steps walk'd in austere;
'Twas Apollonius: something too he laugh'd,
160 As though some knotty problem, that had daft°   *baffled*
His patient thought, had now begun to thaw,
And solve and melt:—'twas just as he foresaw.

    He met within the murmurous vestibule
His young disciple. " 'Tis no common rule,
165 Lycius," said he, "for uninvited guest
To force himself upon you, and infest
With an unbidden presence the bright throng
Of younger friends; yet must I do this wrong,
And you forgive me." Lycius blush'd, and led
170 The old man through the inner doors broad-spread;
With reconciling words and courteous mien
Turning into sweet milk the sophist's spleen.

    Of wealthy lustre was the banquet-room,
Fill'd with pervading brilliance and perfume:
175 Before each lucid pannel fuming stood
A censer fed with myrrh and spiced wood,
Each by a sacred tripod held aloft,
Whose slender feet wide-swerv'd upon the soft
Wool-woofed° carpets: fifty wreaths of smoke   *woven*
180 From fifty censers their light voyage took
To the high roof, still mimick'd as they rose
Along the mirror'd walls by twin-clouds odorous.
Twelve sphered tables, by silk seats insphered,
High as the level of a man's breast rear'd
185 On libbard's° paws, upheld the heavy gold   *leopard's*
Of cups and goblets, and the store thrice told

Lamia, no longer fair, there sat a deadly white.
"Shut, shut those juggling⁷ eyes, thou ruthless man!
Turn them aside, wretch! or the righteous ban
Of all the Gods, whose dreadful images
280 Here represent their shadowy presences,
May pierce them on the sudden with the thorn
Of painful blindness; leaving thee forlorn,
In trembling dotage to the feeblest fright
Of conscience, for their long offended might,
285 For all thine impious proud-heart sophistries,
Unlawful magic, and enticing lies.
Corinthians! look upon that gray-beard wretch!
Mark how, possess'd, his lashless eyelids stretch
Around his demon eyes! Corinthians, see!
290 My sweet bride withers at their potency."
"Fool!" said the sophist, in an under-tone
Gruff with contempt; which a death-nighing moan
From Lycius answer'd, as heart-struck and lost,
He sank supine beside the aching ghost.
295 "Fool! Fool!" repeated he, while his eyes still
Relented not, nor mov'd; "from every ill
Of life have I preserv'd thee to this day,
And shall I see thee made a serpent's prey?"
Then Lamia breath'd death breath; the sophist's eye,
300 Like a sharp spear, went through her utterly,
Keen, cruel, perceant,° stinging: she, as well   *piercing*
As her weak hand could any meaning tell,
Motion'd him to be silent; vainly so,
He look'd and look'd again a level—No!
305 "A Serpent!" echoed he; no sooner said,
Than with a frightful scream she vanished:
And Lycius' arms were empty of delight,
As were his limbs of life, from that same night.
On the high couch he lay!—his friends came round—
310 Supported him—no pulse, or breath they found,
And, in its marriage robe, the heavy body wound.

July–Aug. 1819   1820

To Autumn¹

I

Season of mists and mellow fruitfulness,
    Close bosom-friend of the maturing sun;
Conspiring with him how to load and bless
    With fruit the vines that round the thatch-eves run;
5   To bend with apples the moss'd cottage-trees,
    And fill all fruit with ripeness to the core;

To swell the gourd, and plump the hazel shells
With a sweet kernel; to set budding more,
And still more, later flowers for the bees,
10   Until they think warm days will never cease,
For summer has o'er-brimm'd their clammy cells.

2

Who hath not seen thee oft amid thy store?
Sometimes whoever seeks abroad may find
Thee sitting careless on a granary floor,
15   Thy hair soft-lifted by the winnowing[2] wind;
Or on a half-reap'd furrow sound asleep,
Drows'd with the fume of poppies, while thy hook°   scythe
Spares the next swath and all its twined flowers:
And sometimes like a gleaner thou dost keep
20   Steady thy laden head across a brook;
Or by a cyder-press, with patient look,
Thou watchest the last oozings hours by hours.

3

Where are the songs of spring? Ay, where are they?
Think not of them, thou hast thy music too,—
25   While barred clouds bloom the soft-dying day,
And touch the stubble-plains with rosy hue;
Then in a wailful choir the small gnats mourn
Among the river sallows,° borne aloft   willows
Or sinking as the light wind lives or dies;
30   And full-grown lambs loud bleat from hilly bourn;°   region
Hedge-crickets sing; and now with treble soft
The red-breast whistles from a garden-croft;[3]
And gathering swallows twitter in the skies.

Sept. 19, 1819   1820

The Fall of Hyperion: A Dream

Late in 1818, at about the end of his twenty-third year and while he was serving as nurse to his dying brother Tom, Keats planned to undertake an epic poem, modeled on *Paradise Lost,* which he called *Hyperion.* Its subject, the displacement of Saturn and his fellow Titans by Zeus and the other Olympians, was taken from Greek mythology, but the primary epic question, like that in *Paradise Lost,* was *unde malum?*—whence and why evil? Keats set out in his story to represent an answer, not according to any religious creed but in humanistic terms, delimited to humankind and its natural milieu. The Titans had been equable and benign gods, ruling in the Saturnian, or golden, age of general felicity. Yet at the beginning of the poem all the Titans except Hyperion, god of the sun, have been dethroned; and the uncomprehending Saturn again and again raises the questions Who? Why? How? Can blank unreason and injustice determine the course of things?

In book 3 of the original *Hyperion* the scenes among the Titans are supplemented by the experience of the Olympian Apollo, still a youth but destined to displace

2. To "winnow" is to fan the chaff from the grain.   3. An enclosed plot of farmland.

Hyperion among the heavenly powers. He lives in "aching ignorance" of the universe and its processes, but he is aware of his ignorance and avid for knowledge. Suddenly Apollo reads in the face of Mnemosyne—goddess of memory, who will be mother of the muses and so of all the arts—the silent record of the defeat of the Titans and at once soars to the knowledge that he seeks: the understanding, both intoxicating and agonizing, that life involves process, that process entails change and suffering, and that there can be no creative progress except by the defeat and destruction of the preceding stage. Apollo cries out:

> Knowledge enormous makes a God of me.
> Names, deeds, gray legends, dire events, rebellions,
> Majesties, sovran voices, agonies,
> Creations and destroyings, all at once
> Pour into the wide hollows of my brain,
> And deify me. . . .

This opening out of Apollo's awareness to the tragic nature of life is what the Titans lacked. As the fragment breaks off, Apollo is transfigured—like one who should "with fierce convulse / Die into life"—not only into one who has earned the right to displace Hyperion as god of the sun, but also into the god of the highest poetry.

Keats abandoned this extraordinary fragment in April 1819. Late that summer, however, he took up the theme again, under the title *The Fall of Hyperion: A Dream.* This time his primary model is Dante, whom he had been studying in Henry Cary's verse translation. In *The Divine Comedy* all the narrated events are represented as a vision granted to Dante at the beginning of the poem. In similar fashion, Keats begins his new poem with a long induction in which the poet, in a dream, earns the right to a vision finally granted him by Moneta (her Latin name suggests "the Admonisher"), who replaces Mnemosyne; this vision will incorporate the events narrated in the first *Hyperion.* The induction, in effect, shifts the center of poetic concern from the epic action to the evolving consciousness of the narrative poet himself, as he seeks his identity and status; it serves also to displace (or perhaps to parallel) the earlier ordeal through which Apollo had become god of poetry by the ordeal of this particular poet.

As early as *Sleep and Poetry* (1816), Keats had begun to explore the baffling relation of dreams to insight, of wishful fantasies to imaginative truth, and of the life of humane action to the contemplative vision of the poet. He continued to widen these speculations in *Endymion* and some of his shorter poems; and his letters show his ceaseless effort to assimilate his enlarging experience, his sharpening sense of suffering humanity, and his search for some equivalent of the "salvation" offered by a religious creed he could not accept into his theory and program of poetry. (See especially the letters included here subtitled "Milton, Wordsworth, and the Chambers of Human Life" and "The Vale of Soul-Making.") In the introduction to the long "Dream" that constitutes *The Fall of Hyperion,* Keats works the results of his experience and speculations into the form of a ritual initiation, in which he moves from stage to stage in his evolution as a poet. This agonizing rite of passage ends at the stage in which, having passed through and beyond the ordinary experience of human suffering, he achieves aesthetic insight and distance—the power "To see as a God sees" (line 304)—and so demonstrates his right to undertake this epic poem of tragic suffering.

A number of things caused Keats to abandon *The Fall of Hyperion* at the sixty-first line of the second canto. He wrote to Reynolds on September 21, 1819:

> I have given up Hyperion. . . . Miltonic verse cannot be written but in an artful or rather artist's humour. I wish to give myself up to other sensations. English ought to be kept up. It may be interesting to you to pick out some lines from Hyperion and put a mark × to the false beauty proceeding from art, and one ‖ to the true voice of feeling.

The two Hyperion fragments are impressive achievements, but as Keats with his acumen in self-criticism recognized, they have the air of artistic *tours de force*, written in an age in which the high artifice of the epic matter and style had ceased to be the natural voice of the poet. In the same letter, Keats mentions having composed two days earlier the ode *To Autumn*. In this, his last major poem, the poet had envisaged the circumstance of the cycle of life and death, and had articulated his experience in his own poetic voice.

The Fall of Hyperion: A Dream

Canto 1

Fanatics have their dreams, wherewith they weave
A paradise for a sect; the savage too
From forth the loftiest fashion of his sleep
Guesses at heaven: pity these have not
5 Trac'd upon vellum or wild Indian leaf
The shadows of melodious utterance.
But bare of laurel they live, dream, and die;
For Poesy alone can tell her dreams,
With the fine spell of words alone can save
10 Imagination from the sable charm
And dumb enchantment. Who alive can say
"Thou art no poet; may'st not tell thy dreams"?
Since every man whose soul is not a clod
Hath visions, and would speak, if he had lov'd
15 And been well nurtured in his mother tongue.
Whether the dream now purposed to rehearse
Be poet's or fanatic's will be known
When this warm scribe my hand is in the grave.

Methought I stood where trees of every clime,
20 Palm, myrtle, oak, and sycamore, and beech,
With plantane, and spice blossoms, made a screen;
In neighbourhood of fountains, by the noise
Soft showering in mine ears, and, by the touch
Of scent, not far from roses. Turning round,
25 I saw an arbour with a drooping roof
Of trellis vines, and bells, and larger blooms,
Like floral-censers swinging light in air;
Before its wreathed doorway, on a mound
Of moss, was spread a feast of summer fruits,
30 Which, nearer seen, seem'd refuse of a meal
By angel tasted, or our mother Eve;[1]
For empty shells were scattered on the grass,
And grape stalks but half bare, and remnants more,
Sweet smelling, whose pure kinds I could not know.
35 Still was more plenty than the fabled horn[2]
Thrice emptied could pour forth, at banqueting

---

1. In *Paradise Lost* 5.321ff. Eve serves the visiting angel Raphael with a meal of fruits and fruit juices. Keats thus adapts Milton's Eden to represent the early stage of his own experience and poetry.
2. The cornucopia, or horn of plenty.

For Proserpine return'd to her own fields,[3]
Where the white heifers low. And appetite
More yearning than on earth I ever felt
40 Growing within, I ate deliciously;
And, after not long, thirsted, for thereby
Stood a cool vessel of transparent juice,
Sipp'd by the wander'd bee, the which I took,
And, pledging all the mortals of the world,
45 And all the dead whose names are in our lips,
Drank. That full draught is parent of my theme.[4]
No Asian poppy, nor elixir fine
Of the soon fading jealous caliphat;[5]
No poison gender'd in close monkish cell
50 To thin the scarlet conclave of old men,[6]
Could so have rapt unwilling life away.
Among the fragrant husks and berries crush'd,
Upon the grass I struggled hard against
The domineering potion; but in vain:
55 The cloudy swoon came on, and down I sunk
Like a Silenus[7] on an antique vase.
How long I slumber'd 'tis a chance to guess.
When sense of life return'd, I started up
As if with wings; but the fair trees were gone,
60 The mossy mound and arbour were no more;
I look'd around upon the carved sides
Of an old sanctuary with roof august,
Builded so high, it seem'd that filmed clouds
Might spread beneath, as o'er the stars of heaven;
65 So old the place was, I remembered none
The like upon the earth; what I had seen
Of grey cathedrals, buttress'd walls, rent towers,
The superannuations of sunk realms,
Or nature's rocks toil'd hard in waves and winds,
70 Seem'd but the faulture° of decrepit things   *defects*
To° that eternal domed monument.   *compared to*
Upon the marble at my feet there lay
Store of strange vessels, and large draperies,
Which needs had been of dyed asbestus wove,
75 Or in that place the moth could not corrupt,[8]
So white the linen; so, in some, distinct
Ran imageries from a sombre loom.
All in a mingled heap confus'd there lay
Robes, golden tongs, censer, and chafing dish,
80 Girdles, and chains, and holy jewelries.[9]

Turning from these with awe, once more I rais'd
My eyes to fathom the space every way;

---

3. When Proserpine each year is released by her husband, Pluto, god of the underworld, for a sojourn on earth, it is the beginning of spring.
4. The drink puts the poet to sleep and effects the dream within a dream that constitutes the remainder of the fragment.
5. A council of caliphs, Muslim rulers, who plot to kill each other with a poisonous drink ("elixir").

6. The College of Cardinals.
7. An elderly satyr, usually represented as drunk.
8. Matthew 6.20: "Lay up for yourselves treasures in heaven, where neither moth nor rust doth corrupt."
9. Offerings to the gods were spread on the floor of Greek temples.

The embossed roof, the silent massy range
Of columns north and south, ending in mist
85 Of nothing, then to eastward, where black gates
Were shut against the sunrise evermore.
Then to the west I look'd,[1] and saw far off
An image, huge of feature as a cloud,
At level of whose feet an altar slept,
90 To be approach'd on either side by steps,
And marble balustrade, and patient travail
To count with toil the innumerable degrees.
Towards the altar sober-pac'd I went,
Repressing haste, as too unholy there;
95 And, coming nearer, saw beside the shrine
One minist'ring;[2] and there arose a flame.
When in mid-May the sickening east wind
Shifts sudden to the south, the small warm rain
Melts out the frozen incense from all flowers,
100 And fills the air with so much pleasant health
That even the dying man forgets his shroud;
Even so that lofty sacrificial fire,
Sending forth Maian[3] incense, spread around
Forgetfulness of every thing but bliss,
105 And clouded all the altar with soft smoke,
From whose white fragrant curtains thus I heard
Language pronounc'd. "If thou canst not ascend
These steps,[4] die on that marble where thou art.
Thy flesh, near cousin to the common dust,
110 Will parch for lack of nutriment—thy bones
Will wither in few years, and vanish so
That not the quickest eye could find a grain
Of what thou now art on that pavement cold.
The sands of thy short life are spent this hour,
115 And no hand in the universe can turn
Thy hour glass, if these gummed leaves be burnt
Ere thou canst mount up these immortal steps."
I heard, I look'd: two senses both at once
So fine, so subtle, felt the tyranny
120 Of that fierce threat, and the hard task proposed.
Prodigious seem'd the toil; the leaves were yet
Burning,—when suddenly a palsied chill
Struck from the paved level up my limbs,
And was ascending quick to put cold grasp
125 Upon those streams that pulse beside the throat:
I shriek'd; and the sharp anguish of my shriek
Stung my own ears—I strove hard to escape
The numbness; strove to gain the lowest step.
Slow, heavy, deadly was my pace: the cold
130 Grew stifling, suffocating, at the heart;

1. The poet cannot turn back to his origin in the east, and the ways north and south lead nowhere; he must travel the way of mortal life toward the sunset.
2. Who identifies herself in line 226 as Moneta.
3. Maia was one of the Pleiades, a daughter of Atlas and (by Zeus) the mother of Hermes.
4. These steps that the poet must ascend to knowledge were probably suggested by the stairs going up the steep side of the purgatorial Mount in Dante's *Purgatorio*.

And when I clasp'd my hands I felt them not.
One minute before death, my iced foot touch'd
The lowest stair; and as it touch'd, life seem'd
To pour in at the toes: I mounted up,
135   As once fair angels on a ladder flew
From the green turf to heaven.[5]—"Holy Power,"
Cried I, approaching near the horned shrine,[6]
"What am I that should so be sav'd from death?
What am I that another death come not
140   To choak my utterance sacrilegious here?"
Then said the veiled shadow—"Thou hast felt
What 'tis to die and live again before
Thy fated hour. That thou hadst power to do so
Is thy own safety; thou hast dated on
145   Thy doom."[7]—"High Prophetess," said I, "purge off
Benign, if so it please thee, my mind's film."
"None can usurp this height," return'd that shade,
"But those to whom the miseries of the world
Are misery, and will not let them rest.
150   All else who find a haven in the world,
Where they may thoughtless sleep away their days,
If by a chance into this fane° they come,   *temple*
Rot on the pavement where thou rotted'st half."[8]—
"Are there not thousands in the world," said I,
155   Encourag'd by the sooth voice of the shade,
"Who love their fellows even to the death;
Who feel the giant agony of the world;
And more, like slaves to poor humanity,
Labour for mortal good? I sure should see
160   Other men here: but I am here alone."
"They whom thou spak'st of are no vision'ries,"
Rejoin'd that voice—"They are no dreamers weak,
They seek no wonder but the human face;
No music but a happy-noted voice—
165   They come not here, they have no thought to come—
And thou art here, for thou art less than they.
What benefit canst thou do, or all thy tribe,
To the great world? Thou art a dreaming thing;
A fever of thyself—think of the earth;
170   What bliss even in hope is there for thee?
What haven? Every creature hath its home;
Every sole man hath days of joy and pain,
Whether his labours be sublime or low—
The pain alone; the joy alone; distinct:
175   Only the dreamer venoms all his days,
Bearing more woe than all his sins deserve.

---

5. The ladder by which, in a dream, Jacob saw angels passing between heaven and earth (Genesis 28.12 and *Paradise Lost* 3.510–15).
6. As, e.g., in Exodus 27.2, "And thou shalt make the horns of [the altar] upon the four corners thereof." In his description of the temple and its accouterments Keats deliberately mingles Hebrew,

Christian, and pagan elements to represent the poet's passage through the stage represented by all religions, which are "dreams" made into the creed for "a sect" (lines 1–18).
7. I.e., you have postponed the time when you will be judged.
8. I.e., where you halfway rotted.

Therefore, that happiness be somewhat shar'd,
Such things as thou art are admitted oft
Into like gardens thou didst pass erewhile,
180 And suffer'd in these temples; for that cause
Thou standest safe beneath this statue's knees."
"That I am favored for unworthiness,
By such propitious parley medicin'd
In sickness not ignoble, I rejoice,
185 Aye, and could weep for love of such award."
So answer'd I, continuing, "If it please,
Majestic shadow, tell me: sure not all⁹
Those melodies sung into the world's ear
Are useless: sure a poet is a sage;
190 A humanist, physician to all men.
That I am none I feel, as vultures feel
They are no birds when eagles are abroad.
What am I then? Thou spakest of my tribe:
What tribe?"—The tall shade veil'd in drooping white
195 Then spake, so much more earnest, that the breath
Mov'd the thin linen folds that drooping hung
About a golden censer from the hand
Pendent.—"Art thou not of the dreamer tribe?
The poet and the dreamer are distinct,
200 Diverse, sheer opposite, antipodes.
The one pours out a balm upon the world,
The other vexes it." Then shouted I
Spite of myself, and with a Pythia's spleen,¹
"Apollo! faded, far flown Apollo!
205 Where is thy misty pestilence² to creep
Into the dwellings, through the door crannies,
Of all mock lyrists, large self worshipers,
And careless hectorers in proud bad verse.³
Though I breathe death with them it will be life
210 To see them sprawl before me into graves.⁴

9. Keats's friend Richard Woodhouse, whose manuscript copy of the poem is our principal source of the text, crossed out lines 187–210 with the marginal comment next to lines 197–99: "K. seems to have intended to erase this & the next 21 lines." Probably the basis for his opinion is the partial repetition of lines 187 and 194–98 in lines 211 and 216–20.
1. With the anger ("spleen") of the Pythia, the priestess who served at Delphi as the oracle of Apollo, the god of poetry.
2. Apollo was a sender of plagues, as well as the inspirer of prophecy and poetry.
3. This has been conjectured as referring to Byron, or else to several contemporaries, including Shelley and Wordsworth. But the poetic types, not individuals, are what matter to Keats's argument.
4. In lines 147–210 we find a series of progressive distinctions: (1) between humanitarians who feel for "the miseries of the world" and people who are "thoughtless" sleepers (lines 147–53); (2) within the class of humanitarians, between those who actively "benefit . . . the great world" and the poets who are "vision'ries" and "dreamers" (lines 161–

69); (3) and within the class of poets, between those who are merely dreamers and those who are sages and healers (lines 187–202). As in the colloquy between Asia and Demogorgon (see Shelley's *Prometheus Unbound* 2.4.1–128, p. 742), the interchange here may be taken to represent, in dramatized form, a process of inner analysis and self-discovery on the part of the questing poet. Moneta's charges are not final judgments but tests to determine the "tribe" to which the narrating poet belongs—tests he passes by the nature of the responses he makes. At this point, the fact that the narrator himself proceeds to bring charges against self-indulgent and irresponsible poets distinguishes him from the class of poets he denounces and thus shows that he is ready for the final stage of his ordeal, his initiation into the realm of the highest poetry, through the revelation of the "high tragedy" (line 277) of what it means to be human. This ultimate enlightenment, which begins with line 291 and presumably would have constituted the remainder of the poem, is a vision in a dream within a dream (see n. 4, p. 876).

Majestic shadow, tell me where I am:
Whose altar this; for whom this incense curls:
What image this, whose face I cannot see,
For the broad marble knees; and who thou art,
215 Of accent feminine, so courteous."
Then the tall shade in drooping linens veil'd
Spake out, so much more earnest, that her breath
Stirr'd the thin folds of gauze that drooping hung
About a golden censer from her hand
220 Pendent; and by her voice I knew she shed
Long treasured tears. "This temple sad and lone
Is all spar'd from the thunder of a war
Foughten long since by giant hierarchy
Against rebellion: this old image here,
225 Whose carved features wrinkled as he fell,
Is Saturn's; I, Moneta, left supreme
Sole priestess of his desolation."—
I had no words to answer; for my tongue,
Useless, could find about its roofed home
230 No syllable of a fit majesty
To make rejoinder to Moneta's mourn.
There was a silence while the altar's blaze
Was fainting for sweet food: I look'd thereon
And on the paved floor, where nigh were pil'd
235 Faggots of cinnamon, and many heaps
Of other crisped spice-wood—then again
I look'd upon the altar and its horns
Whiten'd with ashes, and its lang'rous flame,
And then upon the offerings again;
240 And so by turns—till sad Moneta cried,
"The sacrifice is done, but not the less
Will I be kind to thee for thy good will.
My power, which to me is still a curse,
Shall be to thee a wonder; for the scenes
245 Still swooning vivid through my globed brain
With an electral changing misery
Thou shalt with those dull mortal eyes behold,
Free from all pain, if wonder pain thee not."
As near as an immortal's sphered words
250 Could to a mother's soften, were these last:
But yet I had a terror of her robes,
And chiefly of the veils, that from her brow
Hung pale, and curtain'd her in mysteries
That made my heart too small to hold its blood.
255 This saw that Goddess, and with sacred hand
Parted the veils. Then saw I a wan face,
Not pin'd by human sorrows, but bright blanch'd
By an immortal sickness which kills not;
It works a constant change, which happy death
260 Can put no end to; deathwards progressing
To no death was that visage; it had pass'd
The lily and the snow; and beyond these

I must not think now, though I saw that face—
But for her eyes I should have fled away.
265　　They held me back, with a benignant light,
Soft mitigated by divinest lids
Half closed, and visionless entire they seem'd
Of all external things—they saw me not,
But in blank splendor beam'd like the mild moon,
270　　Who comforts those she sees not, who knows not
What eyes are upward cast. As I had found
A grain of gold upon a mountain's side,
And twing'd with avarice strain'd out my eyes
To search its sullen entrails rich with ore,
275　　So at the view of sad Moneta's brow,
I ached to see what things the hollow brain
Behind enwombed: what high tragedy
In the dark secret chambers of her skull
Was acting, that could give so dread a stress
280　　To her cold lips, and fill with such a light
Her planetary eyes; and touch her voice
With such a sorrow. "Shade of Memory!"
Cried I, with act adorant at her feet,
"By all the gloom hung round thy fallen house,
285　　By this last temple, by the golden age,
By great Apollo, thy dear foster child,
And by thy self, forlorn divinity,
The pale Omega⁵ of a wither'd race,
Let me behold, according as thou said'st,
290　　What in thy brain so ferments to and fro."—
No sooner had this conjuration pass'd
My devout lips, than side by side we stood,
(Like a stunt bramble by a solemn pine)
Deep in the shady sadness of a vale,⁶
295　　Far sunken from the healthy breath of morn,
Far from the fiery noon, and eve's one star.
Onward I look'd beneath the gloomy boughs,
And saw, what first I thought an image huge,
Like to the image pedestal'd so high
300　　In Saturn's temple. Then Moneta's voice
Came brief upon mine ear,—"So Saturn sat
When he had lost his realms."—Whereon there grew
A power within me of enormous ken,
To see as a God sees, and take the depth
305　　Of things as nimbly as the outward eye
Can size and shape pervade. The lofty theme
At those few words hung vast before my mind,
With half unravel'd web. I set myself
Upon an eagle's watch, that I might see,
310　　And seeing ne'er forget. No stir of life

---

5. The final letter of the Greek alphabet.
6. This had been the opening line of the original *Hyperion*. The rest of the poem is a revised version of part of that first narrative, with the poet now represented as allowed to envision the course of events that Moneta recalls in her memory (lines 282, 289–90).

Was in this shrouded vale, not so much air
As in the zoning° of a summer's day   *course*
Robs not one light seed from the feather'd grass,
But where the deaf leaf fell there did it rest:
315　A stream went voiceless by, still deaden'd more
By reason of the fallen divinity
Spreading more shade: the Naiad° mid her reeds   *water nymph*
Press'd her cold finger closer to her lips.
Along the margin sand large footmarks went
320　No farther than to where old Saturn's feet
Had rested, and there slept, how long a sleep!
Degraded, cold, upon the sodden ground
His old right hand lay nerveless, listless, dead,
Unsceptred; and his realmless[7] eyes were clos'd,
325　While his bow'd head seem'd listening to the Earth,
His antient mother,[8] for some comfort yet.

It seem'd no force could wake him from his place;
But there came one who with a kindred hand
Touch'd his wide shoulders, after bending low
330　With reverence, though to one who knew it not.
Then came the griev'd voice of Mnemosyne,[9]
And griev'd I hearken'd. "That divinity
Whom thou saw'st step from yon forlornest wood,
And with slow pace approach our fallen King,
335　Is Thea,[1] softest-natur'd of our brood."
I mark'd the goddess in fair statuary
Surpassing wan Moneta by the head,[2]
And in her sorrow nearer woman's tears.
There was a listening fear in her regard,
340　As if calamity had but begun;
As if the vanward clouds[3] of evil days
Had spent their malice, and the sullen rear
Was with its stored thunder labouring up.
One hand she press'd upon that aching spot
345　Where beats the human heart; as if just there,
Though an immortal, she felt cruel pain;
The other upon Saturn's bended neck
She laid, and to the level of his hollow ear
Leaning, with parted lips, some words she spake
350　In solemn tenor and deep organ tune;
Some mourning words, which in our feeble tongue
Would come in this-like accenting; how frail
To that large utterance of the early Gods!—
"Saturn! look up—and for what, poor lost King?[4]
355　I have no comfort for thee, no—not one:

7. Saturn's eyes, when open, express the fact that he has lost his realm.
8. Saturn and the other Titans were the children of Heaven and Earth.
9. As in 2.50, Keats substitutes for "Moneta" the "Mnemosyne" of the first *Hyperion*. This may be a slip but more likely indicates an alternative name for Moneta, in her role as participant in, as well as commentator on, the tragic action.
1. Sister and wife of Hyperion.
2. I.e., Thea was a head taller than Moneta.
3. The front line of clouds.
4. Keats several times recalls King Lear in representing the condition of Saturn.

I cannot cry, *Wherefore thus sleepest thou?*
For heaven is parted from thee, and the earth
Knows thee not, so afflicted, for a God;
And ocean too, with all its solemn noise,
360 Has from thy sceptre pass'd, and all the air
Is emptied of thine hoary majesty.
Thy thunder, captious at the new command,
Rumbles reluctant o'er our fallen house;
And thy sharp lightning in unpracticed hands
365 Scorches and burns our once serene domain.
With such remorseless speed still come new woes
That unbelief has not a space to breathe.[5]
Saturn, sleep on:—Me thoughtless,[6] why should I
Thus violate thy slumbrous solitude?
370 Why should I ope thy melancholy eyes?
Saturn, sleep on, while at thy feet I weep."

  As when, upon a tranced summer night,
Forests, branch-charmed by the earnest stars,[7]
Dream, and so dream all night, without a noise,
375 Save from one gradual solitary gust,
Swelling upon the silence; dying off;
As if the ebbing air had but one wave;
So came these words, and went; the while in tears
She press'd her fair large forehead to the earth,
380 Just where her fallen hair might spread in curls,
A soft and silken mat for Saturn's feet.
Long, long, those two were postured motionless,
Like sculpture builded up upon the grave
Of their own power. A long awful time
385 I look'd upon them; still they were the same;
The frozen God still bending to the earth,
And the sad Goddess weeping at his feet;
Moneta silent. Without stay or prop
But my own weak mortality, I bore
390 The load of this eternal quietude,
The unchanging gloom, and the three fixed shapes
Ponderous upon my senses a whole moon.
For by my burning brain I measured sure
Her silver seasons shedded on the night,
395 And every day by day methought I grew
More gaunt and ghostly. Oftentimes I pray'd
Intense, that death would take me from the vale
And all its burthens. Gasping with despair
Of change, hour after hour I curs'd myself:
400 Until old Saturn rais'd his faded eyes,
And look'd around, and saw his kingdom gone,
And all the gloom and sorrow of the place,

---

5. That disbelief has not an instant to catch its breath.
6. I.e., how thoughtless I am!
7. The grander version in the first *Hyperion,* 1.72ff., reads: "As when, upon a tranced summer-night / Those green-rob'd senators of mighty woods, / Tall oaks, branch-charmed by the earnest stars, / Dream."

And that fair kneeling Goddess at his feet.
As the moist scent of flowers, and grass, and leaves
405 Fills forest dells with a pervading air
Known to the woodland nostril, so the words
Of Saturn fill'd the mossy glooms around,
Even to the hollows of time-eaten oaks,
And to the windings in the foxes' hole,
410 With sad low tones, while thus he spake, and sent
Strange musings to the solitary Pan.

"Moan, brethren, moan; for we are swallow'd up
And buried from all godlike exercise
Of influence benign on planets pale,
415 And peaceful sway above man's harvesting,
And all those acts which deity supreme
Doth ease its heart of love in. Moan and wail.
Moan, brethren, moan; for lo! the rebel spheres
Spin round, the stars their antient courses keep,
420 Clouds still with shadowy moisture haunt the earth,
Still suck their fill of light from sun and moon,
Still buds the tree, and still the sea-shores murmur.
There is no death in all the universe,
No smell of death—there shall be death⁸—Moan, moan,
425 Moan, Cybele,⁹ moan, for thy pernicious babes
Have chang'd a God into a shaking palsy.
Moan, brethren, moan; for I have no strength left,
Weak as the reed—weak—feeble as my voice—
O, O, the pain, the pain of feebleness.
430 Moan, moan; for still I thaw—or give me help:
Throw down those imps¹ and give me victory.
Let me hear other groans, and trumpets blown
Of triumph calm, and hymns of festival
From the gold peaks of heaven's high piled clouds;
435 Voices of soft proclaim,° and silver stir   proclamation
Of strings in hollow shells; and let there be
Beautiful things made new for the surprize
Of the sky children."—So he feebly ceas'd,
With such a poor and sickly sounding pause,
440 Methought I heard some old man of the earth
Bewailing earthly loss; nor could my eyes
And ears act with that pleasant unison of sense
Which marries sweet sound with the grace of form,
And dolorous accent from a tragic harp
445 With large limb'd visions.² More I scrutinized:
Still fix'd he sat beneath the sable trees,
Whose arms spread straggling in wild serpent forms,
With leaves all hush'd: his awful presence there

8. The passing of the Saturnian golden age (paralleled by Keats with the fable of the loss of Eden) has introduced suffering, and will also introduce death.
9. The wife of Saturn and mother of the Olympian

gods, who have overthrown their parents.
1. I.e., his rebellious children.
2. I.e., the narrator could not attach this speech, like that of a feebly complaining old mortal, to the visible form of the large-limbed god who uttered it.

(Now all was silent) gave a deadly lie
450 To what I erewhile heard: only his lips
Trembled amid the white curls of his beard.
They told the truth, though, round, the snowy locks
Hung nobly, as upon the face of heaven
A midday fleece of clouds. Thea arose
455 And stretch'd her white arm through the hollow dark,
Pointing some whither: whereat he too rose
Like a vast giant seen by men at sea
To grow pale from the waves at dull midnight.[3]
They melted from my sight into the woods:
460 Ere I could turn, Moneta cried—"These twain
Are speeding to the families of grief,
Where roof'd in by black rocks they waste in pain
And darkness for no hope."—And she spake on,
As ye may read who can unwearied pass
465 Onward from the antichamber of this dream,
Where even at the open doors awhile
I must delay, and glean my memory
Of her high phrase: perhaps no further dare.

Canto 2

"Mortal, that thou may'st understand aright,
I humanize my sayings to thine ear,
Making comparisons of earthly things;
Or thou might'st better listen to the wind,
5 Whose language is to thee a barren noise,
Though it blows legend-laden through the trees.
In melancholy realms big tears are shed,
More sorrow like to this, and such-like woe,
Too huge for mortal tongue, or pen of scribe.
10 The Titans fierce, self-hid, or prison-bound,
Groan for the old allegiance once more,
Listening in their doom for Saturn's voice.
But one of our whole eagle-brood still keeps
His sov'reignty, and rule, and majesty;
15 Blazing Hyperion on his orbed fire
Still sits, still snuffs the incense teeming up
From man to the Sun's God: yet unsecure;
For as upon the earth dire prodigies[4]
Fright and perplex, so also shudders he:
20 Nor at dog's howl, or gloom-bird's even screech,
Or the familiar visitings of one
Upon the first toll of his passing bell:[5]
But horrors portion'd to a giant nerve

---

3. I.e., like a giant who is seen at sea to emerge, pale, from the waves.
4. Terrifying omens.
5. Lines 20–22 might be paraphrased: "Not, however, at such portents as a dog's howl or the evening screech of the owl or with the well-known feelings ['visitings'] of someone when he hears the first stroke of his own death knell." It had been the English custom to ring the church bell when a person was close to death, to invite hearers to pray for his departing soul (see, e.g., Shakespeare, *Venus and Adonis*, lines 701–02; and for "visitings," *Macbeth* 1.5.43).

Make great Hyperion ache. His palace bright,
25 Bastion'd with pyramids of glowing gold,
    And touch'd with shade of bronzed obelisks,
    Glares a blood red through all the thousand courts,
    Arches, and domes, and fiery galeries:
    And all its curtains of Aurorian clouds
30 Flush angerly: when he would taste the wreaths
    Of incense breath'd aloft from sacred hills,
    Instead of sweets, his ample palate takes
    Savour of poisonous brass, and metals sick.
    Wherefore when harbour'd in the sleepy west,
35 After the full completion of fair day,
    For rest divine upon exalted couch
    And slumber in the arms of melody,
    He paces through the pleasant hours of ease,
    With strides colossal, on from hall to hall;
40 While, far within each aisle and deep recess,
    His winged minions in close clusters stand
    Amaz'd, and full of fear; like anxious men
    Who on a wide plain gather in sad troops,
    When earthquakes jar their battlements and towers.
45 Even now, while Saturn, rous'd from icy trance,
    Goes, step for step, with Thea from yon woods,
    Hyperion, leaving twilight in the rear,
    Is sloping to the threshold of the west.
    Thither we tend."—Now in clear light I stood,
50 Reliev'd from the dusk vale. Mnemosyne
    Was sitting on a square edg'd polish'd stone,
    That in its lucid depth reflected pure
    Her priestess-garments. My quick eyes ran on
    From stately nave to nave, from vault to vault,
55 Through bowers of fragrant and enwreathed light,
    And diamond paved lustrous long arcades.
    Anon rush'd by the bright Hyperion;
    His flaming robes stream'd out beyond his heels,
    And gave a roar, as if of earthly fire,
60 That scar'd away the meek ethereal hours
    And made their dove-wings tremble: on he flared[6]

July–Sept. 1819   1857

Letters

Letters Keats's letters serve as a running commentary on his life, reading, thinking, and writing. His early reputation as a poet of pure luxury, sensation, and art for art's sake has undergone a radical change since, in the twentieth century, critics began to pay close attention to the letters. For Keats thought hard and persistently about life and art, and any seed of an ethical or critical idea that he picked up from his contemporaries (in particular, Hazlitt, Coleridge, Wordsworth) instantly germinated and flourished in the rich soil of his imagination. What T. S. Eliot said about the

6. The manuscript breaks off at this point.

Metaphysical poets applies to Keats in his letters: his "mode of feeling was directly and freshly altered by [his] reading and thought." And like Donne, he looked not only into the heart but, literally, "into the cerebral cortex, the nervous system, and the digestive tract." A number of Keats's casual comments on the poet and on poetry included here—especially those dealing with "negative capability" and with what we now call empathy—have become standard points of reference in aesthetic theory. But Keats himself regarded nothing that he said as final; each statement constituted only a stage in his continuing exploration into what he called "the mystery."

The text printed here is that of the edition of the *Letters* by Hyder E. Rollins (1958), which reproduces the original manuscripts precisely.

LETTERS

To Benjamin Bailey[1]

[THE AUTHENTICITY OF THE IMAGINATION]

[November 22, 1817]

My dear Bailey,

* * * O I wish I was as certain of the end of all your troubles as that of your momentary start about the authenticity of the Imagination. I am certain of nothing but of the holiness of the Heart's affections and the truth of Imagination—What the imagination seizes as Beauty must be truth[2]— whether it existed before or not—for I have the same Idea of all our Passions as of Love they are all in their sublime, creative of essential Beauty—In a Word, you may know my favorite Speculation by my first Book and the little song[3] I sent in my last—which is a representation from the fancy of the probable mode of operating in these Matters—The Imagination may be compared to Adam's dream[4]—he awoke and found it truth. I am the more zealous in this affair, because I have never yet been able to perceive how any thing can be known for truth by consequitive reasoning[5]—and yet it must be— Can it be that even the greatest Philosopher ever ~~when~~ arrived at his goal without putting aside numerous objections—However it may be, O for a Life of Sensations[6] rather than of Thoughts! It is "a Vision in the form of Youth" a Shadow of reality to come—and this consideration has further conv[i]nced me for it has come as auxiliary to another favorite Speculation of mine, that we shall enjoy ourselves here after by having what we called happiness on Earth repeated in a finer tone and so repeated[7]—And yet such a fate can only befall those who delight in sensation rather than hunger as you do after Truth—Adam's dream will do here and seems to be a conviction that Imagination and its empyreal reflection is the same as human Life and its spiritual

---

1. One of Keats's closest friends. Keats had stayed with him the month before at Oxford, where Bailey was an undergraduate.
2. The phrase occurs in a poetic context at the close of *Ode on a Grecian Urn*. Try substituting "real," or "reality," where Keats uses the word *truth*.
3. The song was "O Sorrow," from book 4 of *Endymion*.
4. In *Paradise Lost* 8.452–90, Adam dreams that

Eve has been created, and awakes to find her real. Adam also describes an earlier prefigurative dream in the same work, 8.283–311.
5. Consecutive reasoning—reasoning that moves by logical steps.
6. Probably not only sense experiences but also the intuitive perceptions of truths, as opposed to truth achieved by consecutive reasoning.
7. Cf. the "Pleasure Thermometer" in *Endymion* 1.777ff. (p. 831).

repetition. But as I was saying—the simple imaginative Mind may have its rewards in the repeti[ti]on of its own silent Working coming continually on the spirit with a fine suddenness—to compare great things with small—have you never by being surprised with an old Melody—in a delicious place—by a delicious voice, fe[l]t over again your very speculations and surmises at the time it first operated on your soul—do you not remember forming to yourself the singer's face more beautiful [than] it was possible and yet with the elevation of the Moment you did not think so—even then you were mounted on the Wings of Imagination so high—that the Prototype must be here after—that delicious face you will see—What a time! I am continually running away from the subject—sure this cannot be exactly the case with a complex Mind—one that is imaginative and at the same time careful of its fruits—who would exist partly on sensation partly on thought—to whom it is necessary that years should bring the philosophic Mind[8]—such an one I consider your's and therefore it is necessary to your eternal Happiness that you not only ~~have~~ drink this old Wine of Heaven which I shall call the redigestion of our most ethereal Musings on Earth; but also increase in knowledge and know all things. I am glad to hear you are in a fair Way for Easter—you will soon get through your unpleasant reading and then!—but the world is full of troubles and I have not much reason to think myself pesterd with many—I think Jane or Marianne has a better opinion of me than I deserve—for really and truly I do not think my Brothers illness connected with mine—you know more of the real Cause than they do—nor have I any chance of being rack'd as you have been[9]—you perhaps at one time thought there was such a thing as Worldly Happiness to be arrived at, at certain periods of time marked out—you have of necessity from your disposition been thus led away—I scarcely remember counting upon any Happiness—I look not for it if it be not in the present hour—nothing startles me beyond the Moment. The setting sun will always set me to rights—or if a Sparrow come before my Window I take part in its existince and pick about the Gravel. The first thing that strikes me on hea[r]ing a Misfortune having befalled another is this. "Well it cannot be helped.—he will have the pleasure of trying the resourses of his spirit, and I beg now my dear Bailey that hereafter should you observe any thing cold in me not to [put] it to the account of heartlessness but abstraction—for I assure you I sometimes feel not the influence of a Passion or Affection during a whole week—and so long this sometimes continues I begin to suspect myself and the genuiness of my feelings at other times—thinking them a few barren Tragedy-tears.
* * *

Your affectionate friend
John Keats—

---

8. An echo of Wordsworth, *Ode: Intimations of Immortality*, line 187.
9. Keats's friends Jane and Mariane Reynolds feared that his ill health at this time threatened tuberculosis, from which his brother Tom was suffering. Bailey had recently experienced pain (been "racked") because of an unsuccessful love affair.

To George and Thomas Keats

[NEGATIVE CAPABILITY]

[December 21, 27 (?), 1817]

My dear Brothers

I must crave your pardon for not having written ere this. * * * I spent Friday evening with Wells[1] & went the next morning to see *Death on the Pale horse*. It is a wonderful picture, when West's[2] age is considered; But there is nothing to be intense upon; no women one feels mad to kiss; no face swelling into reality. the excellence of every Art is its intensity, capable of making all disagreeables evaporate, from their being in close relationship with Beauty & Truth[3]—Examine King Lear & you will find this examplified throughout; but in this picture we have unpleasantness without any momentous depth of speculation excited, in which to bury its repulsiveness—The picture is larger than Christ rejected—I dined with Haydon[4] the sunday after you left, & had a very pleasant day, I dined too (for I have been out too much lately) with Horace Smith & met his two Brothers with Hill & Kingston & one Du Bois,[5] they only served to convince me, how superior humour is to wit in respect to enjoyment—These men say things which make one start, without making one feel, they are all alike; their manners are alike; they all know fashionables; they have a mannerism in their very eating & drinking, in their mere handling a Decanter—They talked of Kean[6] & his low company— Would I were with that company instead of yours said I to myself! I know such like acquaintance will never do for me & yet I am going to Reynolds, on wednesday—Brown & Dilke[7] walked with me & back from the Christmas pantomime.[8] I had not a dispute but a disquisition with Dilke, on various subjects; several things dovetailed in my mind, & at once it struck me, what quality went to form a Man of Achievement especially in Literature & which Shakespeare possessed so enormously—I mean *Negative Capability*,[9] that is when man is capable of being in uncertainties, Mysteries, doubts, without any irritable reaching after fact & reason—Coleridge, for instance, would let go by a fine isolated verisimilitude caught from the Penetralium[1] of mystery,

1. Charles Wells, a former schoolmate of Tom Keats.
2. Benjamin West (1738–1820), painter of historical pictures, was an American who moved to England and became president of the Royal Academy. The *Christ Rejected* mentioned a few sentences farther on is also by West.
3. Keats's solution to a problem at least as old as Aristotle's *Poetics*: why do we take pleasure in the aesthetic representation of a subject that in life would be ugly or painful?
4. Keats's close friend Benjamin Haydon, painter of large-scale historical and religious pictures.
5. Smith was one of the best-known literary wits of the day; the others mentioned were men of letters or of literary interests.
6. Edmund Kean, noted Shakespearean actor of the early 19th century.
7. Charles Armitage Brown, John Hamilton Reynolds, and Charles Wentworth Dilke were all writers and friends of Keats. Keats interrupted the writing of this letter after the dash; beginning with "Brown

& Dilke" he is writing several days after the preceding sentences.
8. Christmas pantomimes were performed each year at Drury Lane and Covent Garden theaters.
9. This famous and elusive phrase has accumulated a sizable body of commentary. Two points may be offered here: (1) Keats is concerned with a central aesthetic question of his day: to distinguish between what was called the "objective" poet, who simply and impersonally presents material, and the "subjective" or "sentimental" poet, who presents material as it appears when viewed through the writer's personal interests, beliefs, and feelings. The poet of "negative capability" is the objective poet (see the letter to Reynolds, February 3, 1818, p. 890). (2) Keats goes on to propose that, within a poem, the presentation of subject matter in an artistic form that appeals to our "sense of Beauty" is enough, independently of its truth or falsity when considered outside the poem.
1. The Latin *penetralia* signified the innermost and most secret parts of a temple.

from being incapable of remaining content with half knowledge. This pursued through Volumes would perhaps take us no further than this, that with a great poet the sense of Beauty overcomes every other consideration, or rather obliterates all consideration.

Shelley's poem² is out & there are words about its being objected too, as much as Queen Mab was. Poor Shelley I think he has his Quota of good qualities, in sooth la!! Write soon to your most sincere friend & affectionate Brother

John

To John Hamilton Reynolds¹

[WORDSWORTH'S POETRY]

[February 3, 1818]

My dear Reynolds,

* * * It may be said that we ought to read our Contemporaries. that Wordsworth &c should have their due from us. but for the sake of a few fine imaginative or domestic passages, are we to be bullied into a certain Philosophy engendered in the whims of an Egotist²—Every man has his speculations, but every man does not brood and peacock over them till he makes a false coinage and deceives himself—Many a man can travel to the very bourne³ of Heaven, and yet want confidence to put down his halfseeing. Sancho⁴ will invent a Journey heavenward as well as any body. We hate poetry that has a palpable design upon us—and if we do not agree, seems to put its hand in its breeches pocket. Poetry should be great & unobtrusive, a thing which enters into one's soul, and does not startle it or amaze it with itself but with its subject.—How beautiful are the retired flowers! how would they lose their beauty were they to throng into the highway crying out, "admire me I am a violet! dote upon me I am a primrose! Modern poets differ from the Elizabethans in this. Each of the moderns like an Elector of Hanover governs his petty state, & knows how many straws are swept daily from the Causeways in all his dominions & has a continual itching that all the Housewives should have their coppers well scoured: the antients were ~~Emperors of large~~ Emperors of vast Provinces, they had only heard of the remote ones and scarcely cared to visit them.—I will cut all this—I will have no more of Wordsworth or Hunt⁵ in particular—Why should we be of the tribe of Manasseh, when we can wander with Esau?⁶ why should we kick

2. *Laon and Cythna* (1817), which dealt with incest and had to be recalled by the author; Shelley revised and republished it as *The Revolt of Islam* (1818). *Queen Mab* (1813) was a youthful poem in which Shelley presented his radical program for the achievement of a millennial earthly state by the elimination of "kings, priests, and statesmen" and the reform of human institutions.
1. A close friend who was at this time an insurance clerk and also an able poet and man of letters.
2. Keats immensely admired Wordsworth, as succeeding letters will show, and learned more from him than from any poetic contemporary. He had reservations, however, about the subjective and

didactic qualities of Wordsworth's poetry—reservations that, in some moods, he stated in unflattering terms.
3. Boundary.
4. Sancho Panza, the earthy squire in Cervantes's *Don Quixote*.
5. Leigh Hunt, a poet who earlier had strongly influenced Keats's style.
6. I.e., why should we carry on a conventional way of life (as did the tribe of Manasseh in Old Testament history) when we can become adventurers (like Esau, who sold his birthright in Genesis 25.29–34 and became an outlaw).

against the Pricks, when we can walk on Roses? Why should we be owls, when we can be Eagles? Why be teased with "nice Eyed wagtails," when we have in sight "the Cherub Contemplation"?[7]—Why with Wordsworths "Matthew with a bough of wilding in his hand" when we can have Jacques "under an oak &c"[8]—The secret of the Bough of Wilding will run through your head faster than I can write it—Old Matthew spoke to him some years ago on some nothing, & because he happens in an Evening Walk to imagine the figure of the old man—he must stamp it down in black & white, and it is henceforth sacred—I don't mean to deny Wordsworth's grandeur & Hunt's merit, but I mean to say we need not be teazed with grandeur & merit—when we can have them uncontaminated & unobtrusive. Let us have the old Poets, & robin Hood[9] Your letter and its sonnets gave me more pleasure than will the 4th Book of Childe Harold[1] & the whole of any body's life & opinions.
* * *

> Y[r] sincere friend and Coscribbler
> John Keats.

To John Taylor[1]

[KEATS'S AXIOMS IN POETRY]

[February 27, 1818]

My dear Taylor,

Your alteration strikes me as being a great improvement—the page looks much better. * * * It is a sorry thing for me that any one should have to overcome Prejudices in reading my Verses—that affects me more than any hypercriticism on any particular Passage. In *Endymion* I have most likely but moved into the Go-cart from the leading strings. In Poetry I have a few Axioms, and you will see how far I am from their Centre. 1st I think Poetry should surprise by a fine excess and not by Singularity—it should strike the Reader as a wording of his own highest thoughts, and appear almost a Remembrance—2nd Its touches of Beauty should never be half way therby making the reader breathless instead of content: the rise, the progress, the setting of imagery should like the Sun come natural natural too him—shine over him and set soberly although in magnificence leaving him in the Luxury of twilight—but it is easier to think what Poetry should be than to write it—and this leads me on to another axiom. That if Poetry comes not as naturally as the Leaves to a tree it had better not come at all. However it may be with me I cannot help looking into new countries with "O for a Muse of fire to ascend!"[2]—If Endymion serves me as a Pioneer perhaps I ought to be content. I have great reason to be content, for thank God I can read and perhaps understand Shakspeare to his depths, and I have I am sure many friends, who, if I fail, will attribute any change in my Life and Temper to Humbleness

---

7. Milton, *Il Penseroso*, line 54. "Nice Eyed wagtails": from Hunt's *Nymphs*.
8. *As You Like It* 2.1.31. The Wordsworth phrase is from his poem *The Two April Mornings*. A "wilding" is a wild apple tree.
9. A reference to two sonnets on Robin Hood, written by Reynolds, which he had sent to Keats.

1. Canto 4 of Byron's *Childe Harold's Pilgrimage* was being eagerly awaited by English readers.
1. Partner in the publishing firm of Taylor and Hessey, to whom Keats wrote this letter while *Endymion* was being put through the press.
2. Altered from *Henry V*, Prologue, line 1.

rather than to Pride—to a cowering under the Wings of great Poets rather than to a Bitterness that I am not appreciated. I am anxious to get Endymion printed that I may forget it and proceed. * * *

Your sincere and oblig⁴ friend
John Keats—

P.S. You shall have a sho[r]t *Preface* in good time—

To John Hamilton Reynolds

[MILTON, WORDSWORTH, AND THE CHAMBERS OF HUMAN LIFE]

[May 3, 1818]

My dear Reynolds.

* * * Were I to study physic or rather Medicine again,—I feel it would not make the least difference in my Poetry; when the Mind is in its infancy a Bias in is in reality a Bias, but when we have acquired more strength, a Bias becomes no Bias. Every department of knowledge we see excellent and calculated towards a great whole. I am so convinced of this, that I am glad at not having given away my medical Books, which I shall again look over to keep alive the little I know thitherwards; and moreover intend through you and Rice to become a sort of Pip-civilian.[1] An extensive knowledge is needful to thinking people—it takes away the heat and fever; and helps, by widening speculation, to ease the Burden of the Mystery:[2] a thing I begin to understand a little, and which weighed upon you in the most gloomy and true sentence in your Letter. The difference of high Sensations with and without knowledge appears to me this—in the latter case we are falling continually ten thousand fathoms deep and being blown up again without wings and with all [the] horror of a ~~Case~~ bare shoulderd Creature—in the former case, our shoulders are fledged,[3] and we go thro' the same ~~Fir~~ air and space without fear. * * *

You say "I fear there is little chance of any thing else in this life." You seem by that to have been going through with a more painful and acute ~~test~~ zest the same labyrinth that I have—I have come to the same conclusion thus far. My Branchings out therefrom have been numerous: one of them is the consideration of Wordsworth's genius and as a help, in the manner of gold being the meridian Line of worldly wealth,—how he differs from Milton.[4]—And here I have nothing but surmises, from an uncertainty whether Miltons apparently less anxiety for Humanity proceeds from his seeing further or no than Wordsworth: And whether Wordsworth has in truth epic passions, and martyrs himself to the human heart, the main region of his song[5]—In regard to his genius alone—we find what he says true as far as we

---

1. Apparently "a small-scale layman." James Rice, a lawyer, was one of Keats's favorite friends.
2. Wordsworth, *Tintern Abbey*, line 38. Here begins Keats's insightful expansion of the significance of this and other phrases and passages in Wordsworth.
3. Grow wings.

4. I.e., as gold is the standard of material wealth (in the way that the meridian line of Greenwich Observatory, England, is the reference for measuring degrees of longitude), so Milton is the standard of poetic value, by which we may measure Wordsworth.
5. Cf. Prospectus to *The Recluse*, line 41 (p. 302).

have experienced and we can judge no further but by larger experience—for axioms in philosophy are not axioms until they are proved upon our pulses: We read fine——things but never feel them to [the] full until we have gone the same steps as the Author.—I know this is not plain; you will know exactly my meaning when I say, that now I shall relish Hamlet more than I ever have done—Or, better—You are sensible no man can set down Venery[6] as a bestial or joyless thing until he is sick of it and therefore all philosophizing on it would be mere wording. Until we are sick, we understand not;—in fine, as Byron says, "Knowledge is Sorrow";[7] and I go on to say that "Sorrow is Wisdom"—and further for aught we can know for certainty! "Wisdom is folly."
* * *

I will return to Wordsworth—whether or no he has an extended vision or a circumscribed grandeur—whether he is an eagle in his nest, or on the wing—And to be more explicit and to show you how tall I stand by the giant, I will put down a simile of human life as far as I now perceive it; that is, to the point to which I say we both have arrived at—Well—I compare human life to a large Mansion of Many Apartments, two of which I can only describe, the doors of the rest being as yet shut upon me—The first we step into we call the infant or thoughtless Chamber, in which we remain as long as we do not think—We remain there a long while, and notwithstanding the doors of the second Chamber remain wide open, showing a bright appearance, we care not to hasten to it; but are at length imperceptibly impelled by the awakening of the thinking principle—within us—we no sooner get into the second Chamber, which I shall call the Chamber of Maiden-Thought,[8] than we become intoxicated with the light and the atmosphere, we see nothing but pleasant wonders, and think of delaying there for ever in delight: However among the effects this breathing is father of is that tremendous one of sharpening one's vision into the ~~head~~ heart and nature of Man—of convincing ones nerves that the World is full of Misery and Heartbreak, Pain, Sickness and oppression—whereby This Chamber of Maiden Thought becomes gradually darken'd and at the same time on all sides of it many doors are set open—but all dark—all leading to dark passages—We see not the ballance of good and evil. We are in a Mist—*We* are now in that state—We feel the "burden of the Mystery," To this point was Wordsworth come, as far as I can conceive when he wrote "Tintern Abbey" and it seems to me that his Genius is explorative of those dark Passages. Now if we live, and go on thinking, we too shall explore them. he is a Genius and superior [to] us, in so far as he can, more than we, make discoveries, and shed a light in them—Here I must think Wordsworth is deeper than Milton—though I think it has depended more upon the general and gregarious advance of intellect, than individual greatness of Mind—From the Paradise Lost and the other Works of Milton, I hope it is not too presuming, even between ourselves to say, his Philosophy, human and divine, may be tolerably understood by one not much advanced in years, In his time englishmen were just emancipated from a great superstition—and Men had got hold of certain points and resting places in reasoning which were too newly born to be doubted, and too much ~~oppressed~~ opposed by the Mass of Europe not to be thought etherial and authentically

6. Sexual indulgence.
7. *Manfred* 1.1.10: "Sorrow is knowledge."

8. I.e., innocent thought, with the implication (as in "maiden voyage") of a first undertaking.

divine—who could gainsay his ideas on virtue, vice, and Chastity in Comus, just at the time of the dismissal of Cod-pieces[9] and a hundred other disgraces? who would not rest satisfied with his hintings at good and evil in the Paradise Lost, when just free from the inquisition and burrning in Smithfield?[1] The Reformation produced such immediate and greats benefits, that Protestantism was considered under the immediate eye of heaven, and its own remaining Dogmas and superstitions, then, as it were, regenerated, constituted those resting places and seeming sure points of Reasoning—from that I have mentioned, Milton, whatever he may have thought in the sequel,[2] appears to have been content with these by his writings—He did not think into the human heart, as Wordsworth has done—Yet Milton as a Philosop[h]er, had sure as great powers as Wordsworth—What is then to be inferr'd? O many things—It proves there is really a grand march of intellect—, It proves that a mighty providence subdues the mightiest Minds to the service of the time being, whether it be in human Knowledge or Religion— * * * Tom[3] has spit a leetle blood this afternoon, and that is rather a damper—but I know—the truth is there is something real in the World Your third Chamber of Life shall be a lucky and a gentle one—stored with the wine of love—and the Bread of Friendship— * * *

Your affectionate friend
John Keats.

To Richard Woodhouse[1]

[A POET HAS NO IDENTITY]

[October 27, 1818]

My dear Woodhouse,

Your Letter gave me a great satisfaction; more on account of its friendliness, than any relish of that matter in it which is accounted so acceptable in the "genus irritabile"[2] The best answer I can give you is in a clerklike manner to make some observations on two principle points, which seem to point like indices into the midst of the whole pro and con, about genius, and views and atchievements and ambition and cœtera. 1st As to the poetical Character itself, (I mean that sort of which, if I am any thing, I am a Member; that sort distinguished from the wordsworthian or egotistical sublime; which is a thing per se and stands alone) it is not itself—it has no self—it is every thing and nothing—It has no character—it enjoys light and shade; it lives in gusto, be it foul or fair, high or low, rich or poor, mean or elevated—It has as much delight in conceiving an Iago as an Imogen.[3] What shocks the vir-

---

9. In the 15th and 16th centuries, the codpiece was a flap, often ornamental, that covered an opening in the front of men's breeches.
1. An open place northwest of the walls of the City of London where, in the 16th century, heretics were burned.
2. Later on.
3. Keats's younger brother, then eighteen, who was dying of tuberculosis.

1. A young lawyer with literary interests who early recognized Keats's talents and prepared, or preserved, manuscript copies of many of his poems and letters.
2. "The irritable race," a phrase Horace had applied to poets (Epistles 2.2.102).
3. Iago is the villain in Shakespeare's Othello and Imogen the virtuous heroine in his Cymbeline.

tuous philosop[h]er, delights the camelion[4] Poet. It does no harm from its relish of the dark side of things any more than from its taste for the bright one; because they both end in speculation.[5] A Poet is the most unpoetical of any thing in existence; because he has no Identity—he is continually in for[6]—and filling some other Body—The Sun, the Moon, the Sea and Men and Women who are creatures of impulse are poetical and have about them an unchangeable attribute—the poet has none; no identity—he is certainly the most unpoetical of all God's Creatures. If then he has no self, and if I am a Poet, where is the Wonder that I should say I would ~~right~~ write no more? Might I not at that very instant [have] been cogitating on the Characters of saturn and Ops?[7] It is a wretched thing to confess; but is a very fact that not one word I ever utter can be taken for granted as an opinion growing out of my identical nature—how can it, when I have no nature? When I am in a room with People if I ever am free from speculating on creations of my own brain, then not myself goes home to myself: but the identity of every one in the room begins to to press upon me[8] that, I am in a very little time an[ni]hilated—not only among Men; it would be the same in a Nursery of children: I know not whether I make myself wholly understood: I hope enough so to let you see that no dependence is to be placed on what I said that day.

In the second place I will speak of my views, and of the life I purpose to myself—I am ambitious of doing the world some good: if I should be spared that may be the work of maturer years—in the interval I will assay to reach to as high a summit in Poetry as the nerve[9] bestowed upon me will suffer. The faint conceptions I have of Poems to come brings the blood frequently into my forehead—All I hope is that I may not lose all interest in human affairs—that the solitary indifference I feel for applause even from the finest Spirits, will not blunt any acuteness of vision I may have. I do not think it will—I feel assured I should write from the mere yearning and fondness I have for the Beautiful even if my night's labours should be burnt every morning and no eye ever shine upon them. But even now I am perhaps not speaking from myself; but from some character in whose soul I now live. I am sure however that this next sentence is from myself. I feel your anxiety, good opinion and friendliness in the highest degree, and am

Your's most sincerely
John Keats

---

4. The chameleon is a lizard that camouflages itself by changing its color to match its surroundings.
5. Possibly "in contemplation"—i.e., without affecting our practical judgment or actions.
6. Instead of "in for," Keats may have intended to write "informing."

7. Characters in Keats's *Hyperion*. Woodhouse had recently written Keats to express concern at a remark by the poet that, because former writers had preempted the best poetic materials and styles, there was nothing new left for the modern poet.
8. Perhaps "*so* to press upon me."
9. Sinew.

To George and Georgiana Keats[1]

[THE VALE OF SOUL-MAKING]

[February 14–May 3, 1819]

My dear Brother & Sister—

* * * I have this moment received a note from Haslam[2] in which he expects the death of his Father who has been for some time in a state of insensibility—his mother bears up he says very well—I shall go to [town] tommorrow to see him. This is the world—thus we cannot expect to give way many hours to pleasure—Circumstances are like Clouds continually gathering and bursting—While we are laughing the seed of some trouble is put into he the wide arable land of events—while we are laughing it sprouts [it] grows and suddenly bears a poison fruit which we must pluck—Even so we have leisure to reason on the misfortunes of our friends; our own touch us too nearly for words. Very few men have ever arrived at a complete disinterestedness of Mind: very few have been influenced by a pure desire of the benefit of others—in the greater part of the Benefactors of & to Humanity some meretricious motive has sullied their greatness—some melodramatic scenery has facinated them—From the manner in which I feel Haslam's misfortune I perceive how far I am from any humble standard of disinterestedness—Yet this feeling ought to be carried to its highest pitch, as there is no fear of its ever injuring society—which it would do I fear pushed to an extremity—For in wild nature the Hawk would loose his Breakfast of Robins and the Robin his of Worms The Lion must starve as well as the swallow—The greater part of Men make their way with the same instinctiveness, the same unwandering eye from their purposes, the same animal eagerness as the Hawk—The Hawk wants a Mate, so does the Man—look at them both they set about it and procure on[e] in the same manner—They want both a nest and they both set about one in the same manner—they get their food in the same manner— The noble animal Man for his amusement smokes his pipe—the Hawk balances about the Clouds—that is the only difference of their leisures. This it is that makes the Amusement of Life—to a speculative Mind. I go among the Feilds and catch a glimpse of a stoat[3] or a fieldmouse peeping out of the withered grass—the creature hath a purpose and its eyes are bright with it—I go amongst the buildings of a city and I see a Man hurrying along—to what? The Creature has a purpose and his eyes are bright with it. But then as Wordsworth says, "we have all one human heart"[4]—there is an ellectric fire in human nature tending to purify—so that among these human creature[s] there is continually some birth of new heroism—The pity is that we must wonder at it: as we should at finding a pearl in rubbish—I have no doubt that thousands of people never heard of have had hearts comp[l]etely disinterested: I can remember but two—Socrates and Jesus—their Histories evince it—What I heard a little time ago, Taylor observe with respect to

---

1. Keats's brother and his wife, who had emigrated to Louisville, Kentucky, in 1818. This is part of a long letter that Keats wrote over a period of several months. The date of this first extract is March 19.

2. William Haslam, a young businessman and close friend.
3. A weasel.
4. *The Old Cumberland Beggar*, line 153.

Socrates, may be said of Jesus—That he was so great as man that though he transmitted no writing of his own to posterity, we have his Mind and his sayings and his greatness handed to us by others. It is to be lamented that the history of the latter was written and revised by Men interested in the pious frauds of Religion. Yet through all this I see his splendour. Even here though I myself am pursueing the same instinctive course as the veriest human animal you can think of—I am however young writing at random—straining at particles of light in the midst of a great darkness—without knowing the bearing of any one assertion of any one opinion. Yet may I not in this be free from sin?[5] May there not be superior beings amused with any graceful, though instinctive attitude my mind [may] fall into, as I am entertained with the alertness of a Stoat or the anxiety of a Deer? Though a quarrel in the streets is a thing to be hated, the energies displayed in it are fine; the commonest Man shows a grace in his quarrel—By a superior being our reasoning[s] may take the same tone—though erroneous they may be fine—This is the very thing in which consists poetry; and if so it is not so fine a thing as philosophy—For the same reason that an eagle is not so fine a thing as a truth—Give me this credit—Do you not think I strive—to know myself? Give me this credit—and you will not think that on my own accou[n]t I repeat Milton's lines

> "How charming is divine Philosophy
> Not harsh and crabbed as dull fools suppose
> But musical as is Apollo's lute"—[6]

No—no for myself—feeling grateful as I do to have got into a state of mind to relish them properly—Nothing ever becomes real till it is experienced—Even a Proverb is no proverb to you till your Life has illustrated it— * * *

* * * I have been reading lately two very different books Robertson's America and Voltaire's Siecle De Louis xiv[7] It is like walking arm and arm between Pizarro and the great-little Monarch.[8] In How lementabl[e] a case do we see the great body of the people in both instances: in the first, where Men might seem to inherit quiet of Mind from unsophisticated senses; from uncontamination of civilisation; and especially from their being as it were estranged from the mutual helps of Society and its mutual injuries—and thereby more immediately under the Protection of Providence—even there they had mortal pains to bear as bad; or even worse than Baliffs,[9] Debts and Poverties of civilised Life—The whole appears to resolve into this—that Man is originally "a poor forked creature"[1] subject to the same mischances as the beasts of the forest, destined to hardships and disquietude of some kind or other. If

5. Keats speculates that though his instinctive course is not, any more than an animal's, "disinterested" (free from selfish interests), it may still, like an animal's, be natural, hence innocent and possessed of an innate grace and beauty. He further supposes that this may be the nature of poetry, also, as distinguished from the deliberate and self-conscious process of philosophical reasoning (cf. the letter to George and Thomas Keats on "Negative Capability," begun on December 21, 1817, p. 889).
6. *Comus*, lines 475–77.
7. Voltaire, *Le Siècle de Louis XIV,* 5 vols. (1751);

William Robertson, *The History of America* (1777—Keats was reading the 10th ed., 4 vols., 1803). In this second extract from the journal-letter Keats is writing toward the end of April (on the 21st or 28th).
8. Francisco Pizarro, the Spanish explorer whose exploits are described in Robertson's *America*. The "Monarch" is Louis XIV.
9. Bailiffs: officers of the law whose duties included making arrests for bad debts.
1. *King Lear* 3.4.95–97. Lear says: "Unaccommodated man is no more but such a poor, bare, forked animal as thou art."

he improves by degrees his bodily accommodations and comforts—at each stage, at each accent there are waiting for him a fresh set of annoyances— he is mortal and there is still a heaven with its Stars abov[e] his head. The most interesting question that can come before us is, How far by the per-severing endeavours of a seldom appearing Socrates Mankind may be made happy—I can imagine such happiness carried to an extreme—but what must it end in?—Death—and who could in such a case bear with death—the whole troubles of life which are now frittered away in a series of years, would the[n] be accumulated for the last days of a being who instead of hailing its approach, would leave this world as Eve left Paradise—But in truth I do not at all believe in this sort of perfectibility—the nature of the world will not admit of it—the inhabitants of the world will correspond to itself—Let the fish philosophise the ice away from the Rivers in winter time and they shall be at continual play in the tepid delight of summer. Look at the Poles and at the sands of Africa, Whirlpools and volcanoes—Let men exterminate them and I will say that they may arrive at earthly Happiness—The point at which Man may arrive is as far as the paralel state in inanimate nature and no further—For instance suppose a rose to have sensation, it blooms on a beau-tiful morning it enjoys itself—but there comes a cold wind, a hot sun—it can not escape it, it cannot destroy its annoyances—they are as native to the world as itself: no more can man be happy in spite, the world[l]y elements will prey upon his nature—The common cognomen of this world among the misguided and superstitious is "a vale of tears" from which we are to be redeemed by a certain arbitrary interposition of God and taken to Heaven— What a little circumscribe[d] straightened notion! Call the world if you Please "The vale of Soul-making" Then you will find out the use of the world (I am speaking now in the highest terms for human nature admitting it to be immortal which I will here take for granted for the purpose of showing a thought which has struck me concerning it) I say "*Soul making*" Soul as distinguished from an Intelligence—There may be intelligences or sparks of the divinity in millions—but they are not Souls ~~the~~ till they acquire identities, till each one is personally itself. I[n]telligences are atoms of perception— they know and they see and they are pure, in short they are God—how then are Souls to be made? How then are these sparks which are God to have identity given them—so as ever to possess a bliss peculiar to each ones indi-vidual existence? How, but by the medium of a world like this? This point I sincerely wish to consider because I think it a grander system of salvation than the chrystean religion—or rather it is a system of Spirit-creation[2]— This is effected by three grand materials acting the one upon the other for a series of years—These three Materials are the *Intelligence*—the *human heart* (as distinguished from intelligence or Mind) and the *World* or *Ele-mental space* suited for the proper action of *Mind and Heart* on each other

---

2. Keats is struggling for an analogy that will embody his solution to the ancient riddle of evil, as an alternative to what he understands to be the Christian view: that evil exists as a test of the indi-vidual's merit of salvation in heaven, and this world is only a proving ground for a later and better life. Keats proposes that the function of the human experience of sorrow and pain is to feed and dis-cipline the formless and unstocked "intelligence" that we possess at birth and thus to shape it into a rich and coherent "identity," or "soul." This result provides a justification ("salvation") for our suffer-ing in terms of our earthly life itself: that is, expe-rience is its own reward. The passage is analogous to what Wordsworth says in the last two stanzas of his *Ode: Intimations of Immortality*.

for the purpose of forming the *Soul* or *Intelligence destined to possess the sense of Identity*. I can scarcely express what I but dimly perceive—and yet I think I perceive it—that you may judge the more clearly I will put it in the most homely form possible—I will call the *world* a School instituted for the purpose of teaching little children to read—I will call the *human heart* the *horn Book*³ used in that School—and I will call the *Child able to read, the Soul* made from that *school* and its *hornbook*. Do you not see how necessary a World of Pains and troubles is to school an Intelligence and make it a soul? A Place where the heart must feel and suffer in a thousand diverse ways! Not merely is the Heart a Hornbook, It is the Minds Bible, it is the Minds experience, it is the teat from which the Mind or intelligence sucks its identity—As various as the Lives of Men are—so various become their souls, and thus does God make individual beings, Souls, Identical Souls of the sparks of his own essence—This appears to me a faint sketch of a system of Salvation which does not affront our reason and humanity—I am convinced that many difficulties which christians labour under would vanish before it—There is one wh[i]ch even now Strikes me— the Salvation of Children—In them the Spark or intelligence returns to God without any identity—it having had no time to learn of, and be altered by, the heart—or seat of the human Passions—It is pretty generally suspected that the chr[i]stian scheme has been coppied from the ancient persian and greek Philosophers. Why may they not have made this simple thing even more simple for common apprehension by introducing Mediators and Personages in the same manner as in the hethen mythology abstractions are personified—Seriously I think it probable that this System of Soul-making— may have been the Parent of all the more palpable and personal Schemes of Redemption, among the Zoroastrians the Christians and the Hindoos. For as one part of the human species must have their carved Jupiter; so another part must have the palpable and named Mediatior and saviour, their Christ their Oromanes and their Vishnu⁴—If what I have said should not be plain enough, as I fear it may not be, I will [put] you in the place where I began in this series of thoughts—I mean, I began by seeing how man was formed by circumstances—and what are circumstances?—but touchstones of his heart—? and what are touch stones?—but proovings of his hearrt?—and what are proovings of his heart but fortifiers or alterers of his nature? and what is his altered nature but his soul?—and what was his soul before it came into the world and had These provings and alterations and perfectionings?—An intelligences—without Identity—and how is this Identity to be made? Through the medium of the Heart? And how is the heart to become this Medium but in a world of Circumstances?—There now I think what with Poetry and Theology you may thank your Stars that my pen is not very long winded— * * *

This is the 3d of May & every thing is in delightful forwardness; the violets are not withered, before the peeping of the first rose; You must let me know every thing, how parcels go & come, what papers you have, & what

---

3. A child's primer, which used to consist of a sheet of paper mounted on thin wood, protected by a sheet of transparent horn.
4. The deity who creates and preserves the world, in Hindu belief. Oromanes (Ahriman) was the principle of evil, locked in a persisting struggle with Ormazd, the principle of good, in the Zoroastrian religion.

Newspapers you want, & other things—God bless you my dear Brother & Sister

Your ever Affectionate Brother
John Keats—

To Fanny Brawne

[FANNY BRAWNE AS KEATS'S "FAIR STAR"]

[July 25, 1819]

My sweet Girl,

I hope you did not blame me much for not obeying your request of a Letter on Saturday: we have had four in our small room playing at cards night and morning leaving me no undisturb'd opportunity to write. Now Rice and Martin are gone I am at liberty. Brown to my sorrow confirms the account you give of your ill health. You cannot conceive how I ache to be with you: how I would die for one hour——for what is in the world? I say you cannot conceive; it is impossible you should look with such eyes upon me as I have upon you: it cannot be. Forgive me if I wander a little this evening, for I have been all day employ'd in a very abstr[a]ct Poem[1] and I am in deep love with you—two things which must excuse me. I have, believe me, not been an age in letting you take possession of me; the very first week I knew you I wrote myself your vassal; but burnt the Letter as the very next time I saw you I thought you manifested some dislike to me. If you should ever feel for Man at the first sight what I did for you, I am lost. Yet I should not quarrel with you, but hate myself if such a thing were to happen—only I should burst if the thing were not as fine as a Man as you are as a Woman. Perhaps I am too vehement, then fancy me on my knees, especially when I mention a part of you Letter which hurt me; you say speaking of Mr. Severn[2] "but you must be satisfied in knowing that I admired you much more than your friend." My dear love, I cannot believe there ever was or ever could be any thing to admire in me especially as far as sight goes—I cannot be admired, I am not a thing to be admired. You are, I love you; all I can bring you is a swooning admiration of your Beauty. I hold that place among Men which snub-nos'd brunettes with meeting eyebrows do among women—they are trash to me—unless I should find one among them with a fire in her heart like the one that burns in mine. You absorb me in spite of myself—you alone: for I look not forward with any pleasure to what is call'd being settled in the world; I tremble at domestic cares—yet for you I would meet them, though if it would leave you the happier I would rather die than do so. I have two luxuries to brood over in my walks, your Loveliness and the hour of my death. O that I could have possession of them both in the same minute. I hate the world: it batters too much the wings of my self-will, and would I could take a sweet poison from your lips to send me out of it. From no others would I take it. I am indeed astonish'd to find myself so careless of all cha[r]ms but yours—

1. Probably *The Fall of Hyperion*.
2. Joseph Severn, who later looked after Keats during his final illness in Rome.

remembring as I do the time when even a bit of ribband was a matter of interest with me. What softer words can I find for you after this—what it is I will not read. Nor will I say more here, but in a Postscript answer any thing else you may have mentioned in your Letter in so many words—for I am distracted with a thousand thoughts. I will imagine you Venus tonight and pray, pray, pray to your star like a Hethen.[3]

Your's ever, fair Star,

John Keats.

To Percy Bysshe Shelley[1]

[LOAD EVERY RIFT WITH ORE]

[August 16, 1820]

My dear Shelley,

I am very much gratified that you, in a foreign country, and with a mind almost over occupied, should write to me in the strain of the Letter beside me. If I do not take advantage of your invitation it will be prevented by a circumstance I have very much at heart to prophesy[2]—There is no doubt that an english winter would put an end to me, and do so in a lingering hateful manner, therefore I must either voyage or journey to Italy as a soldier marches up to a battery. My nerves at present are the worst part of me, yet they feel soothed when I think that come what extreme may, I shall not be destined to remain in one spot long enough to take a hatred of any four particular bed-posts. I am glad you take any pleasure in my poor Poem;[3]— which I would willingly take the trouble to unwrite, if possible, did I care so much as I have done about Reputation. I received a copy of the Cenci,[4] as from yourself from Hunt. There is only one part of it I am judge of; the Poetry, and dramatic effect, which by many spirits now a days is considered the mammon. A modern work it is said must have a purpose,[5] which may be the God—*an artist* must serve Mammon—he must have "self concentration" selfishness perhaps. You I am sure will forgive me for sincerely remarking that you might curb your magnanimity and be more of an artist, and "load every rift"[6] of your subject with ore. The thought of such discipline must fall like cold chains upon you, who perhaps never sat with your wings furl'd for six Months together. And is not this extraordina[r]y talk for the writer of Endymion? whose mind was like a pack of scattered cards—I am pick'd up and sorted to a pip.[7] My Imagination is a Monastry and I am its Monk—you must explain my metap^cs[8] to yourself. I am in expectation of Prometheus[9]

3. See Keats's sonnet *Bright star* (p. 845) for parallels to this and other remarks in the present letter.
1. Written in reply to a letter urging Keats (who was ill) to spend the winter with the Shelleys in Pisa.
2. His own death.
3. Keats's *Endymion*, Shelley had written, contains treasures, "though treasures poured forth with indistinct profusion." Keats here responds with advice in kind.
4. Shelley's blank-verse tragedy, *The Cenci,* had

been published in the spring of 1820.
5. Wordsworth had said this in his Preface to *Lyrical Ballads.* For "Mammon" see Matthew 6.24 and Luke 16.13: "Ye cannot serve God and mammon."
6. Spenser, *The Faerie Queene* 2.7.28: "With rich metall loaded every rifte."
7. Perfectly ordered; all the suits in the deck matched up ("pips" are the conventional spots on playing cards).
8. Metaphysics.
9. *Prometheus Unbound,* of which Shelley had promised Keats a copy.

every day. Could I have my own wish for its interest effected you would have it still in manuscript—or be but now putting an end to the second act. I remember you advising me not to publish my first-blights, on Hampstead heath—I am returning advice upon your hands. Most of the Poems in the volume I send you[1] have been written above two years, and would never have been publish'd but from a hope of gain; so you see I am inclined enough to take your advice now. I must exp[r]ess once more my deep sense of your kindness, adding my sincere thanks and respects for Mrs Shelley. In the hope of soon seeing you I remain

most sincerely yours,
John Keats—

To Charles Brown[1]

[KEATS'S LAST LETTER]

Rome. 30 November 1820.

My dear Brown,

'Tis the most difficult thing in the world to me to write a letter. My stomach continues so bad, that I feel it worse on opening any book,—yet I am much better than I was in Quarantine.[2] Then I am afraid to encounter the proing and conning of any thing interesting to me in England. I have an habitual feeling of my real life having past, and that I am leading a posthumous existence. God knows how it would have been—but it appears to me—however, I will not speak of that subject. I must have been at Bedhampton nearly at the time you were writing to me from Chichester—how unfortunate—and to pass on the river too! There was my star predominant![3] I cannot answer any thing in your letter, which followed me from Naples to Rome, because I am afraid to look it over again. I am so weak (in mind) that I cannot bear the sight of any hand writing of a friend I love so much as I do you. Yet I ride the little horse,—and, at my worst, even in Quarantine, summoned up more puns, in a sort of desperation, in one week than in any year of my life. There is one thought enough to kill me—I have been well, healthy, alert &c, walking with her[4]—and now—the knowledge of contrast, feeling for light and shade, all that information (primitive sense) necessary for a poem are great enemies to the recovery of the stomach. There, you rogue, I put you to the torture,—but you must bring your philosophy to bear—as I do mine, really—or how should I be able to live? Dr Clarke is very attentive to me; he says, there is very little the matter with my lungs, but my stomach, he says, is very bad. I am well disappointed in hearing good news from George,—for it runs in my head we shall all die young. I have not written to X X X X X yet,[5]

---

1. Keats's volume of 1820, including *Lamia, The Eve of St. Agnes,* and the odes. When Shelley drowned, he had this small book open in his pocket.

1. Written to Keats's friend Charles Armitage Brown from the house on the Spanish Stairs, in the Piazza di Spagna, where Keats was being tended in his mortal illness by the devoted Joseph Severn.

2. When it landed at Naples, Keats's ship had been quarantined for ten miserably hot days.

3. *The Winter's Tale* 1.2.202–03: "It is a bawdy planet, that will strike / Where 'tis predominant."

4. Fanny Brawne.

5. Charles Brown, whose manuscript transcription is the only text for this letter, substituted crosses for the names of Keats's friends to conceal their identities.

which he must think very neglectful; being anxious to send him a good account of my health, I have delayed it from week to week. If I recover, I will do all in my power to correct the mistakes made during sickness; and if I should not, all my faults will be forgiven. I shall write to X X X to-morrow, or next day. I will write to X X X X X in the middle of next week. Severn is very well, though he leads so dull a life with me. Remember me to all friends, and tell X X X X I should not have left London without taking leave of him, but from being so low in body and mind. Write to George as soon as you receive this, and tell him how I am, as far as you can guess;—and also a note to my sister—who walks about my imagination like a ghost—she is so like Tom.[6] I can scarcely bid you good bye even in a letter. I always made an awkward bow.

God bless you!
John Keats.

---

6. Keats's youngest brother, whom Fanny, his only sister, closely resembled, had died of tuberculosis on December 1, 1818. George was John Keats's younger brother.

MARY WOLLSTONECRAFT SHELLEY
1797–1851

Percy Shelley wrote of his young wife, in the Dedication to *Laon and Cythna*:

> They say that thou wert lovely from thy birth,
> Of glorious parents, thou aspiring Child.

The "glorious parents" were William Godwin, the leading reformer and radical philosopher of the time, and Mary Wollstonecraft, famed as the author of *A Vindication of the Rights of Woman*; Wollstonecraft had died as the result of childbed fever incurred when she gave birth to Mary. Four years later Godwin married a widow, Mary Jane Clairmont, who soon had more than she could cope with trying to manage a family of five children of diverse parentage, amid increasing financial difficulties. Mary bitterly resented her stepmother but adored her father, who, she later said, "was my God—and I remember many childish instances of the excess of attachment I bore for him."

To ease the situation, Mary was sent at the age of fourteen to live in Dundee, Scotland, with the family of William Baxter, an admirer of Godwin. After two pleasant years roaming the countryside, daydreaming, and writing stories (which have been lost), she returned in 1814 to her father's house in London. There at the age of sixteen she encountered the twenty-one-year-old poet Percy Bysshe Shelley, a devotee of Godwin's and an almost daily visitor, who had become estranged from his wife, Harriet. The young people fell in love; within a few months Mary was pregnant. On July 28 they ran off to Europe, taking with them her stepsister Jane Clairmont, who later changed her name to Claire. Mary described their happy though feckless wanderings through France, Switzerland, and Germany in her first book, *History of a Six Weeks' Tour*, published anonymously in 1817.

Back in England, she gave premature birth to a daughter who lived only a few weeks; a year later, in 1816, she bore a son, William. Shelley was usually in financial difficulties and often had to hide from his creditors to avoid arrest. Nonetheless, he contributed substantial sums (borrowed against his expectations as heir to his father, Sir Timothy) to Godwin's support, even though Godwin, despite his earlier advocacy of free love, refused to countenance Shelley's liaison with his daughter. Claire Clairmont meanwhile sought out and had a brief affair with Byron, who left her pregnant. In the spring of 1816 the Shelleys went abroad again with Claire, and at the latter's behest settled in Geneva, where Byron, accompanied by his physician and friend John William Polidori, set up residence in the nearby Villa Diodati. Mary Shelley tells us, in the introduction to *Frankenstein*, how her imagination was fired by their animated conversations during many social evenings. Encouraged and assisted by Shelley, she wrote *Frankenstein; or, The Modern Prometheus*, and published it anonymously in 1818.

The last six years of Mary's life with her husband, spent first in England and then in Italy, were filled with disasters. In October 1816, her sensitive and moody half-sister, Fanny Imlay, feeling herself an unloved burden on the Godwin household, committed suicide by an overdose of laudanum. Two months later Shelley's abandoned wife, Harriet, pregnant by an unknown lover, drowned herself in the Serpentine lake at Hyde Park in London. Shelley at once married Mary, but the courts denied him custody of Harriet's two children on the grounds that he was morally unfit to rear them. In September 1818 came the death of Mary's third baby, Clara, followed less than nine months later by the death of her adored son, William; so that at twenty-two Mary had been three times a mother and three times bereaved. These tragedies and her own ill health threw her into a depression that was only partly relieved by the birth of a second son, Percy Florence, in November 1819, and was deepened again the next spring by a miscarriage, as well as by the death of Claire's daughter Allegra, whom Byron had placed in an Italian convent. Mary Shelley's habitual reserve, which masked the depth of her feelings, now became an apathy that caused her to withdraw, emotionally, from her husband. When Shelley was drowned in the Gulf of Spezia in July 1822, she was left with a persisting sense that she had failed her husband when he most needed her.

An impoverished widow of twenty-four, she returned to England with two ambitions. One was to disseminate the poetry and to rescue the character of Shelley, whom she idolized in memory; the other was to support by her writings her surviving son. Her only financial assistance was a small allowance given her by Sir Timothy Shelley, which he threatened to cut off if she wrote a biography of his radical and scandal-haunted son. In the remaining quarter century of her life Mary Shelley became a notable success as a professional woman of letters. She wrote five more novels, of which the first two are the best. *The Last Man* (1826), a narrative of the destruction of humankind by a plague until there is only a single survivor, almost equals *Frankenstein* in its analysis of human isolation; and *Valperga* (1823), set in the Italian Middle Ages, is a romance about a quasi-Napoleonic figure who sacrifices his love and his humanity to a lust for political power. She wrote also some twenty-five short tales and left in manuscript a novella, *Mathilda* (written in 1819 but not published until 1959), which deals with the disastrous results of a father's incestuous passion for a daughter who resembles his dead wife. In 1835–39 she contributed to the *Cabinet Cyclopedia* five volumes of admirable biographical and critical studies of Continental authors. She also published several separate editions of her husband's writings in verse and prose. In accordance with what was then standard editorial procedure, she altered and emended Shelley's texts; she also added prefaces and notes, relating Shelley's writings to the circumstances of his life and thought, which have been an important resource for scholars of Romantic literature.

Not until old Sir Timothy died in 1844, leaving his title and estate to her son, did she find herself in comfortable circumstances. Her last years were cheered by the devotion of her son—who was an amiable man but entirely lacked the genius of his parents—and by her close friendship with Jane St. John, an admirer of Shelley's poetry, whom Sir Percy Florence married in 1848. Mary Shelley died three years later, at the age of fifty-three.

During her widowhood, she craved social acceptance and status and, although she maintained liberal principles, tried hard, by adapting herself to conventional standards in her writings and her life, to work free from the onus of what her contemporaries regarded as the scandalous careers of her mother, father, and husband. In later life she wrote an apologia in her journal, dated October 21, 1838, that reveals the stresses of a life spent trying to measure up to the example, yet escape the bad reputations, of her parents and husband.

> In the first place, with regard to "the good cause"—the cause of the advancement of freedom and knowledge, of the rights of women, etc.—I am not a person of opinions. . . . Some have a passion for reforming the world; others do not cling to particular opinions. That my parents and Shelley were of the former class, makes me respect it. . . . For myself, I earnestly desire the good and enlightenment of my fellow creatures, and see all, in the present course, tending to the same, and rejoice; but I am not for violent extremes, which only brings on an injurious reaction. . . .
>
> To hang back, as I do, brings a penalty. I was nursed and fed with a love of glory. To be something great and good was the precept given me by my father; Shelley reiterated it. . . . But Shelley died, and I was alone. . . . My total friendlessness, my horror of pushing, and inability to put myself forward unless led, cherished and supported—all this has sunk me in a state of loneliness no other human being ever before, I believe, endured—except Robinson Crusoe. . . .
>
> But I have never crouched to society—never sought it unworthily. If I have never written to vindicate the rights of women, I have ever defended women when oppressed. At every risk I have befriended and supported victims to the social system; but I make no boast, for in truth it is simple justice I perform; and so am I still reviled for being worldly. . . .
>
> Such as I have written appears to me the exact truth.

Frankenstein

Frankenstein   Mary Shelley was eighteen when she began drafting *Frankenstein* in June 1816, nineteen when she completed it eleven months later, and twenty when it was published anonymously—in three slender volumes—early in 1818. It was a success from the beginning and has been a best-seller and a major literary and cultural presence ever since.

First-time readers are sometimes shocked to discover that "Frankenstein" is the name of the obsessed scientist rather than his monstrous creation and that the unnamed Creature, far from the wooden, grunting figure of popular films and television, is the most eloquent and rational character in the novel. Clues to Mary Shelley's intentions begin with the 1818 title page, on which the ironic subtitle likens Victor Frankenstein to Prometheus, the Titan in Greek mythology who championed humankind against tyranny, and a three-line epigraph from *Paradise Lost* just beneath the subtitle subversively equates Frankenstein with God and his Creature with the fallen Adam.

The epistolary frame introduces the explorer Robert Walton, who acts as a broker between the story's events and the reader. He is the first of the novel's three narrators; his letters give a first-person credibility to the fantasy and establish several principal themes at the outset—in particular the opposition of science and poetry (Walton is a failed poet who is now seeking glory as a scientist) and the theme of human connection, which is one of the main concerns of the Creature's long account of himself in the central chapters of volume 2. The other two narrators—Frankenstein (whose story is contained within Walton's) and the Creature (whose monologue is relayed by Frankenstein)—add myriad further concerns that would have been clear to the novel's original readers but have become obscured by time. Frankenstein's experiments have a basis in important scientific questions of the day: evolution, the so-called vitalist debate over the origins and nature of life, and the conflict between science and religion that is inherent in such topics. Frankenstein is a Faustian overreacher, and at various times both he and the Creature are types of Milton's Satan and, in a similar vein, Byronic heroes.

In several interesting chapters (volume 2, chapters 3 to 8), the Creature describes his self-education, starting with his earliest perceptions of natural phenomena and quickly advancing to language, logic, literature, philosophy, and politics. To some extent the Creature, who has no innate ideas and must learn everything through experience, is a clear example of John Locke's *tabula rasa,* the blank slate on which everything is to be written. But he also seems to have a core of natural goodness that can be corrupted through exposure to human behavior; this makes him resemble the romantic conceptions of human innocence associated with Jean-Jacques Rousseau. Some of the complex political content of *Frankenstein* comes via the lessons that the Creature overhears based on Volney's *Ruins of Empire* ("I heard of the division of property, of immense wealth and squalid poverty; of rank, descent, and noble blood. . . . I learned that the possessions most esteemed . . . were, high and unsullied descent united with riches"). An implied critique of colonial imperialism, beginning with Walton's zeal to discover a polar route to the Pacific, thus further expanding the British Empire, is observable in many of the later incidents.

Because this remarkable book was written by a woman, and because Mary Shelley's mother was so important to the history of feminism, *Frankenstein* has become a central text in feminist studies. Even though the women characters (except for the enlightened, high-spirited Safie in volume 2, chapter 6) are totally passive, many feminists today interpret the Creature himself as a symbol of the fate of women who do not conform to social expectations and are treated like "creatures" instead of human beings. The relation of Victor Frankenstein to the Creature may also be seen as a paradigm of bad family relationships, where a "parent" fails to assume loving responsibility for the "child" he has brought to life. The Creature profoundly needs sympathy and relationship but is cut off from humanity by his origin and monstrosity. Because his overtures to human beings evoke only horror and disgust, his love, rejected, turns into murderous hate. *Frankenstein* is not only a major Romantic achievement; its account of the monstrous potentiality of human creative power when severed from moral and social concerns has made it a modern myth that recurs persistently in fiction, melodrama, and film and haunts the popular consciousness.

There are two main versions of *Frankenstein*—that of the original edition of 1818 and that of a revised text that Mary Shelley published as the third edition in 1831. The text printed here, taken from the Norton Critical Edition of the novel prepared by J. Paul Hunter (1996), is a reprint of the version of 1818, correcting only obvious typographical errors.

Frankenstein;
or, The Modern Prometheus[1]

Did I request thee, Maker, from my clay
To mould me man? Did I solicit thee
From darkness to promote me?——
Paradise Lost[2]

To William Godwin,[3]
Author of Political Justice, Caleb Williams, &c.
these volumes are respectfully inscribed by the Author

Preface[4]

The event on which this fiction is founded has been supposed, by Dr. Darwin,[5] and some of the physiological writers of Germany, as not of impossible occurrence. I shall not be supposed as according the remotest degree of serious faith to such an imagination; yet, in assuming it as the basis of a work of fancy, I have not considered myself as merely weaving a series of supernatural terrors. The event on which the interest of the story depends is exempt from the disadvantages of a mere tale of spectres or enchantment. It was recommended by, the novelty of the situations which it develops; and, however impossible as a physical fact, affords a point of view to the imagination for the delineating of human passions more comprehensive and commanding than any which the ordinary relations of existing events can yield.

I have thus endeavoured to preserve the truth of the elementary principles of human nature, while I have not scrupled to innovate upon their combinations. The *Iliad*, the tragic poetry of Greece—Shakespeare, in the *Tempest* and *Midsummer Night's Dream*,—and most especially Milton, in *Paradise Lost*, conform to this rule; and the most humble novelist, who seeks to confer or receive amusement from his labours, may, without presumption, apply to prose fiction a licence, or rather a rule, from the adoption of which so many exquisite combinations of human feeling have resulted in the highest specimens of poetry.

The circumstance on which my store rests was suggested in casual conversation. It was commenced, partly as a source of amusement, and partly as an expedient for exercising any untried resources of mind. Other motives were mingled with these, as the work proceeded. I am by no means indifferent to the manner in which whatever moral tendencies exist in the sentiments or characters it contains shall affect the reader; yet my chief concern in this respect has been limited to the avoiding the enervating effects of the

---

1. In Greek mythology, a Titan who created humankind, for whom he stole fire from the gods. As punishment, Zeus chained him on a cliff and set an eagle to tear at his liver.
2. Spoken by Adam after the Fall, *Paradise Lost* 10.743–45.
3. Father of Mary Shelley, a radical political philosopher who wrote *Inquiry Concerning Political Justice* (1793) and several novels, including the highly popular *The Adventures of Caleb Williams*

(1794).
4. In her Author's Introduction (1831), Mary Shelley says that this *Preface* "was entirely written" by Percy Shelley.
5. Erasmus Darwin (1731–1802), grandfather of Charles Darwin, wrote immensely popular treatments of biological and botanic science in verse. In *The Temple of Nature* (1803), he speculated that life may generate spontaneously.

novels of the present day, and to the exhibition of the amiableness of domestic affection, and the excellence of universal virtue. The opinions which naturally spring from the character and situation of the hero are by no means to be conceived as existing always in my own conviction; nor is any inference justly to be drawn from the following pages as prejudicing any philosophical doctrine of whatever kind.

It is a subject also of additional interest to the author, that this story was begun in the majestic region where the scene is principally laid, and in society which cannot cease to be regretted. I passed the summer of 1816 in the environs of Geneva. The season was cold and rainy, and in the evenings we crowded around a blazing wood fire, and, occasionally amused ourselves with some German stories of ghosts,[6] which happened to fall into our hands. These tales excited in us a playful desire of imitation. Two other friends[7] (a tale from the pen of one of whom would be far more acceptable to the public than any thing I can ever hope to produce) and myself agreed to write each a story, founded on some supernatural occurrence.

The weather, however, suddenly became serene; and my two friends left me on a journey among the Alps, and lost, in the magnificent scenes which they present, all memory of their ghostly visions. The following tale is the only one which has been completed.

Author's Introduction [1831][1]

The Publishers of the Standard Novels, in selecting "Frankenstein" for one of their series, expressed a wish that I should furnish them with some account of the origin of the story. I am the more willing to comply, because I shall thus give a general answer to the question, so very frequently asked me—"How I, then a young girl, came to think of, and to dilate upon, so very hideous an idea?" It is true that I am very averse to bringing myself forward in print; but as my account will only appear as an appendage to a former production, and as it will be confined to such topics as have connection with my authorship alone, I can scarcely accuse myself of a personal intrusion.

It is not singular that, as the daughter of two persons of distinguished literary celebrity,[2] I should very early in life have thought of writing. As a child I scribbled; and my favourite pastime, during the hours given me for recreation, was to "write stories." Still I had a dearer pleasure than this, which was the formation of castles in the air—the indulging in waking dreams—the following up trains of thought, which had for their subject the formation of a succession of imaginary incidents. My dreams were at once more fantastic and agreeable than my writings. In the latter I was a close

6. In a translation in French of *Fantasmagoriana* (1812), a collection of stories of the supernatural. See n. 6, p. 909.
7. Percy Shelley and Lord Byron.
1. Mary Shelley wrote this introduction for the 3rd edition of *Frankenstein* published in a series, "Standard Novels" (1831); it is thus fifteen years later than the events of 1816 that it recalls. In it

she undertakes to explain—in terms of outer events that engage with her fantasy life to effect an obsessive visionary experience—how it is that an author in her late teens could write a work that, as we now recognize, not only is a classic in the genre of terror tales but has become an enduring myth.
2. Mary Wollstonecraft and William Godwin.

imitator—rather doing as others had done, than putting down the suggestions of my own mind. What I wrote was intended at least for one other eye—my childhood's companion and friend;[3] but my dreams were all my own; I accounted for them to nobody; they were my refuge when annoyed—my dearest pleasure when free.

I lived principally in the country as a girl, and passed a considerable time in Scotland. I made occasional visits to the more picturesque parts; but my habitual residence was on the blank and dreary northern shores of the Tay, near Dundee. Blank and dreary on retrospection I call them; they were not so to me then. They were the eyry[4] of freedom, and the pleasant region where unheeded I could commune with the creatures of my fancy. I wrote then—but in a most common-place style. It was beneath the trees of the grounds belonging to our house, or on the bleak sides of the woodless mountains near, that my true compositions, the airy flights of my imagination, were born and fostered. I did not make myself the heroine of my tales. Life appeared to me too common-place an affair as regarded myself. I could not figure to myself that romantic woes or wonderful events would ever be my lot; but I was not confined to my own identity; and I could people the hours with creations far more interesting to me at that age, than my own sensations.

After this my life became busier, and reality stood in place of fiction. My husband,[5] however, was, from the first, very anxious that I should prove myself worthy of my parentage, and enrol myself on the page of fame. He was for ever inciting me to obtain literary reputation, which even on my own part I cared for then, though since I have become infinitely indifferent to it. At this time he desired that I should write, not so much with the idea that I could produce any thing worthy of notice, but that he might himself judge how far I possessed the promise of better things hereafter. Still I did nothing. Travelling, and the cares of a family, occupied my time; and study, in the way of reading, or improving my ideas in communication with his far more cultivated mind, was all of literary employment that engaged my attention.

In the summer of 1816, we visited Switzerland, and became the neighbours of Lord Byron. At first we spent our pleasant hours on the lake, or wandering on its shores; and Lord Byron, who was writing the third canto of Childe Harold, was the only one among us who put his thoughts upon paper. These, as he brought them successively to us, clothed in all the light and harmony of poetry, seemed to stamp as divine the glories of heaven and earth, whose influences we partook with him.

But it proved a wet, ungenial summer, and incessant rain often confined us for days to the house. Some volumes of ghost stories, translated from the German into French, fell into our hands.[6] There was the History of the Inconstant Lover, who, when he thought to clasp the bride to whom he had pledged his vows, found himself in the arms of the pale ghost of her whom he had deserted. There was the tale of the sinful founder of his race, whose

3. Isabel Baxter, the daughter of William Baxter, with whom Mary had lived in Dundee, Scotland (1812–14).
4. An eagle's nest, built high on a cliff or tree.
5. Mary and Percy Shelley did not in fact marry until December, some six months after the events described in this introduction.

6. The French translation, published anonymously in 1812, was called *Fantasmagoriana, or Collected Stories of Apparitions of Specters, Ghosts, Phantoms, etc.* The stories she goes on to describe, somewhat inaccurately, are *The Dead Fiancée* and *Family Portraits*.

miserable doom it was to bestow the kiss of death on all the younger sons of his fated house, just when they reached the age of promise. His gigantic, shadowy form, clothed like the ghost in Hamlet, in complete armour, but with the beaver[7] up, was seen at midnight, by the moon's fitful beams, to advance slowly along the gloomy avenue. The shape was lost beneath the shadow of the castle walls; but soon a gate swung back, a step was heard, the door of the chamber opened, and he advanced to the couch of the blooming youths, cradled in healthy sleep. Eternal sorrow sat upon his face as he bent down and kissed the forehead of the boys, who from that hour withered like flowers snapt upon the stalk. I have not seen these stories since then; but their incidents are as fresh in my mind as if I had read them yesterday.

"We will each write a ghost story," said Lord Byron; and his proposition was acceded to. There were four of us.[8] The noble author began a tale, a fragment of which he printed at the end of his poem of Mazeppa. Shelley, more apt to embody ideas and sentiments in the radiance of brilliant imagery, and in the music of the most melodious verse that adorns our language, than to invent the machinery of a story, commenced one founded on the experiences of his early life. Poor Polidori had some terrible idea about a skull-headed lady, who was so punished for peeping through a key-hole—what to see I forget—something very shocking and wrong of course; but when she was reduced to a worse condition than the renowned Tom of Coventry,[9] he did not know what to do with her, and was obliged to despatch her to the tomb of the Capulets,[1] the only place for which she was fitted. The illustrious poets also, annoyed by the platitude of prose, speedily relinquished their uncongenial task.

I busied myself to *think of a story*,—a story to rival those which had excited us to this task. One which would speak to the mysterious fears of our nature, and awaken thrilling horror—one to make the reader dread to look round, to curdle the blood, and quicken the beatings of the heart. If I did not accomplish these things, my ghost story would be unworthy of its name. I thought and pondered—vainly. I felt that blank incapability of invention which is the greatest misery of authorship, when dull Nothing replies to our anxious invocations. *Have you thought of a story?* I was asked each morning, and each morning I was forced to reply with a mortifying negative.

Every thing must have a beginning, to speak in Sanchean[2] phrase, and that beginning must be linked to something that went before. The Hindoos give the world an elephant to support it, but they make the elephant stand upon a tortoise. Invention, it must be humbly admitted, does not consist in creating out of void, but out of chaos; the materials must, in the first place, be afforded: it can give form to dark, shapeless substances, but cannot bring into being the substance itself. In all matters of discovery and invention, even of those that appertain to the imagination, we are continually reminded of the story of Columbus and his egg.[3] Invention consists in the capacity of

7. The hinged piece of armor that covers the face (see *Hamlet* 1.2.226–28).
8. Byron, Percy and Mary Shelley, and John William Polidori, Byron's physician and friend. Mary omits Claire Clairmont, her stepsister and Byron's former mistress, who was staying with the Shelleys at Geneva.
9. "Peeping Tom," who, according to the legend, was struck blind when he looked at Lady Godiva as she rode naked through Coventry.
1. Where Romeo and Juliet died.
2. I.e., of Sancho Panza, the literal-minded squire in Cervantes's *Don Quixote* (1605).
3. According to popular legend, Christopher Columbus boasted that he could accomplish the impossible feat of making a hard-boiled egg stand on end. When challenged to do so, he lightly cracked one end and stood the egg upright.

seizing on the capabilities of a subject, and in the power of moulding and fashioning ideas suggested to it.

Many and long were the conversations between Lord Byron and Shelley, to which I was a devout but nearly silent listener. During one of these, various philosophical doctrines were discussed, and among others the nature of the principle of life, and whether there was any probability of its ever being discovered and communicated.[4] They talked of the experiments of Dr. Darwin,[5] (I speak not of what the Doctor really did, or said that he did, but, as more to my purpose, of what was then spoken of as having been done by him,) who preserved a piece of vermicelli in a glass case, till by some extraordinary means it began to move with voluntary motion. Not thus, after all, would life be given. Perhaps a corpse would be re-animated; galvanism[6] had given token of such things: perhaps the component parts of a creature might be manufactured, brought together, and endued with vital warmth.

Night waned upon this talk, and even the witching hour had gone by, before we retired to rest. When I placed my head on my pillow, I did not sleep, nor could I be said to think. My imagination, unbidden, possessed and guided me, gifting the successive images that arose in my mind with a vividness far beyond the usual bounds of reverie. I saw—with shut eyes, but acute mental vision,—I saw the pale student of unhallowed arts kneeling beside the thing he had put together. I saw the hideous phantasm of a man stretched out, and then, on the working of some powerful engine, show signs of life and stir with an uneasy, half vital motion. Frightful must it be; for supremely frightful would be the effect of any human endeavour to mock the stupendous mechanism of the Creator of the world. His success would terrify the artist; he would rush away from his odious handywork, horror-stricken. He would hope that, left to itself, the slight spark of life which he had communicated would fade; that this thing, which had received such imperfect animation, would subside into dead matter; and he might sleep in the belief that the silence of the grave would quench for ever the transient existence of the hideous corpse which he had looked upon as the cradle of life. He sleeps; but he is awakened; he opens his eyes; behold the horrid thing stands at his bedside, opening his curtains, and looking on him with yellow, watery, but speculative eyes.

I opened mine in terror. The idea so possessed my mind, that a thrill of fear ran through me, and I wished to exchange the ghastly image of my fancy for the realities around. I see them still; the very room, the dark *parquet*,[7] the closed shutters, with the moonlight struggling through, and the sense I had that the glassy lake and white high Alps were beyond. I could not so easily get rid of my hideous phantom; still it haunted me. I must try to think of something else. I recurred to my ghost story,—my tiresome unlucky ghost

---

4. James Rieger conjectures that Mary Shelley may in fact be remembering a conversation between Polidori and Shelley, which apparently took place a day before Byron suggested writing ghost stories and which, as Polidori records in his diary for June 15, 1816, was "about principles—whether man was to be thought merely an instrument." Polidori had recently published a treatise on sleepwalking.

5. In *The Temple of Nature* (1803) Erasmus Dar-

win describes an experiment with the pasta called vermicelli—literally, "little worms."

6. The use of electric current to induce muscle twitches in dead tissue. Mary Shelley probably has in mind a widely discussed experiment of 1803 in which Giovanni Aldini had effected spasmodic contractions in the corpse of a criminal executed at Newgate prison.

7. A floor made of wooden pieces arranged in a decorative pattern.

story! O! if I could only contrive one which would frighten my reader as I myself had been frightened that night!

Swift as light and as cheering was the idea that broke in upon me. "I have found it! What terrified me will terrify others; and I need only describe the spectre which had haunted my midnight pillow." On the morrow I announced that I had *thought of a story*. I began that day with the words, *It was on a dreary night of November*, making only a transcript of the grim terrors of my waking dream.

At first I thought but of a few pages—of a short tale; but Shelley urged me to develope the idea at greater length. I certainly did not owe the suggestion of one incident, nor scarcely of one train of feeling, to my husband, and yet but for his incitement, it would never have taken the form in which it was presented to the world. From this declaration I must except the preface. As far as I can recollect, it was entirely written by him.[8]

And now, once again, I bid my hideous progeny go forth and prosper. I have an affection for it, for it was the offspring of happy days, when death and grief were but words, which found no true echo in my heart. Its several pages speak of many a walk, many a drive, and many a conversation, when I was not alone; and my companion was one who, in this world, I shall never see more. But this is for myself; my readers have nothing to do with these associations.

I will add but one word as to the alterations I have made. They are principally those of style. I have changed no portion of the story, nor introduced any new ideas or circumstances. I have mended the language where it was so bald as to interfere with the interest of the narrative; and these changes occur almost exclusively in the beginning of the first volume. Throughout they are entirely confined to such parts as are mere adjuncts to the story, leaving the core and substance of it untouched.

M. W. S.
London, October 15, 1831

VOLUME 1

Letter 1.

TO MRS. SAVILLE, ENGLAND.

St. Petersburgh.[1] Dec. 11th, 17—

You will rejoice to hear that no disaster has accompanied the commencement of an enterprise which you have regarded with such evil forebodings. I arrived here yesterday; and my first task is to assure my dear sister of my welfare, and increasing confidence in the success of my undertaking.

I am already far north of London; and as I walk in the streets of Petersburgh, I feel a cold northern breeze play upon my cheeks, which braces my nerves, and fills me with delight. Do you understand this feeling? This breeze, which has travelled from the regions towards which I am advancing, gives

---

8. Percy Shelley's contributions to the text are analyzed and evaluated in the Norton Critical Edition of *Frankenstein*, edited by J. Paul Hunter.

Percy Shelley's *Preface* is reprinted on p. 907.
1. In northwestern Russia, on the Gulf of Finland.

me a foretaste of those icy climes. Inspirited by this wind of promise, my day dreams become more fervent and vivid. I try in vain to be persuaded that the pole is the seat of frost and desolation; it ever presents itself to my imagination as the region of beauty and delight. There, Margaret, the sun is for ever visible; its broad disk just skirting the horizon, and diffusing a perpetual splendour. There—for with your leave, my sister, I will put some trust in preceding navigators—there snow and frost are banished; and, sailing over a calm sea, we may be wafted to a land surpassing in wonders and in beauty every region hitherto discovered on the habitable globe. Its productions and features may be without example, as the phænomena of the heavenly bodies undoubtedly are in those undiscovered solitudes. What may not be expected in a country of eternal light? I may there discover the wondrous power which attracts the needle;[2] and may regulate a thousand celestial observations, that require only this voyage to render their seeming eccentricities consistent for ever. I shall satiate my ardent curiosity with the sight of a part of the world never before visited, and may tread a land never before imprinted by the foot of man. These are my enticements, and they are sufficient to conquer all fear of danger or death, and to induce me to commence this laborious voyage with the joy a child feels when he embarks in a little boat with his holiday mates, on an expedition of discovery up his native river. But, supposing all these conjectures to be false, you cannot contest the inestimable benefit which I shall confer on all mankind to the last generation, by discovering a passage near the pole to those countries, to reach which at present so many months are requisite; or by ascertaining the secret of the magnet, which, if at all possible, can only be effected by an undertaking such as mine.

These reflections have dispelled the agitation with which I began my letter, and I feel my heart glow with an enthusiasm which elevates me to heaven; for nothing contributes so much to tranquillize the mind as a steady purpose,—a point on which the soul may fix its intellectual eye. This expedition has been the favourite dream of my early years. I have read with ardour the accounts of the various voyages which have been made in the prospect of arriving at the North Pacific Ocean through the seas which surround the pole. You may remember, that a history of all the voyages made for purposes of discovery composed the whole of our good uncle Thomas's library. My education was neglected, yet I was passionately fond of reading. These volumes were my study day and night, and my familiarity with them increased that regret which I had felt, as a child, on learning that my father's dying injunction had forbidden my uncle to allow me to embark in a sea-faring life.

These visions faded when I perused, for the first time, those poets whose effusions entranced my soul, and lifted it to heaven. I also became a poet, and for one year lived in a Paradise of my own creation; I imagined that I also might obtain a niche in the temple where the names of Homer and Shakespeare are consecrated. You are well acquainted with my failure, and how heavily I bore the disappointment. But just at that time I inherited the fortune of my cousin, and my thoughts were turned into the channel of their earlier bent.

Six years have passed since I resolved on my present undertaking. I can, even now, remember the hour from which I dedicated myself to this great

2. Compass needle.

enterprise. I commenced by inuring my body to hardship. I accompanied the whale-fishers on several expeditions to the North Sea; I voluntarily endured cold, famine, thirst, and want of sleep; I often worked harder than the common sailors during the day, and devoted my nights to the study of mathematics, the theory of medicine, and those branches of physical science from which a naval adventurer might derive the greatest practical advantage. Twice I actually hired myself as an undermate in a Greenland whaler, and acquitted myself to admiration. I must own I felt a little proud, when my captain offered me the second dignity in the vessel, and entreated me to remain with the greatest earnestness; so valuable did he consider my services.

And now, dear Margaret, do I not deserve to accomplish some great purpose. My life might have been passed in ease and luxury; but I preferred glory to every enticement that wealth placed in my path. Oh, that some encouraging voice would answer in the affirmative! My courage and my resolution is firm; but my hopes fluctuate, and my spirits are often depressed. I am about to proceed on a long and difficult voyage; the emergencies of which will demand all my fortitude: I am required not only to raise the spirits of others, but sometimes to sustain my own, when their's are failing.

This is the most favourable period for travelling in Russia. They fly quickly over the snow in their sledges; the motion is pleasant, and, in my opinion, far more agreeable than that of an English stage-coach. The cold is not excessive, if you are wrapt in furs, a dress which I have already adopted; for there is a great difference between walking the deck and remaining seated motionless for hours, when no exercise prevents the blood from actually freezing in your veins. I have no ambition to lose my life on the post-road between St. Petersburgh and Archangel.[3]

I shall depart for the latter town in a fortnight or three weeks; and my intention is to hire a ship there, which can easily be done by paying the insurance for the owner, and to engage as many sailors as I think necessary among those who are accustomed to the whale-fishing. I do not intend to sail until the month of June: and when shall I return? Ah, dear sister, how can I answer this question? If I succeed, many, many months, perhaps years, will pass before you and I may meet. If I fail, you will see me again soon, or never.

Farewell, my dear, excellent, Margaret. Heaven shower down blessings on you, and save me, that I may again and again testify my gratitude for all your love and kindness.

Your affectionate brother,
R. WALTON.

Letter 2.

TO MRS. SAVILLE, ENGLAND.

Archangel, 28th March, 17—.

How slowly the time passes here, encompassed as I am by frost and snow; yet a second step is taken towards by my enterprise. I have hired a vessel,

---

3. A port in northern Russia, on an inlet of the Arctic Ocean. "Post-road": a main road, on which the mails were transported.

and am occupied in collecting my sailors; those whom I have already engaged appear to be men on whom I can depend, and are certainly possessed of dauntless courage.

But I have one want which I have never yet been able to satisfy; and the absence of the object of which I now feel as a most severe evil. I have no friend, Margaret: when I am glowing with the enthusiasm of success, there will be none to participate my joy; if I am assailed by disappointment, no one will endeavour to sustain me in dejection. I shall commit my thoughts to paper, it is true; but that is a poor medium for the communication of feeling. I desire the company of a man who could sympathize with me; whose eyes would reply to mine. You may deem me romantic, my dear sister, but I bitterly feel the want of a friend. I have no one near me, gentle yet courageous, possessed of a cultivated as well as of a capacious mind, whose tastes are like my own, to approve or amend my plans. How would such a friend repair the faults of your poor brother! I am too ardent in execution, and too impatient of difficulties. But it is a still greater evil to me that I am self-educated: for the first fourteen years of my life I ran wild on a common, and read nothing but our uncle Thomas's books of voyages. At that age I became acquainted with the celebrated poets of our own country, but it was only when it had ceased to be in my power to derive its most important benefits from such a conviction, that I perceived the necessity of becoming acquainted with more languages than that of my native country. Now I am twenty-eight, and am in reality more illiterate than many school-boys of fifteen. It is true that I have thought more, and that my day dreams are more extended and magnificent; but they want (as the painters call it) *keeping*;[4] and I greatly need a friend who would have sense enough not to despise me as romantic, and affection enough for me to endeavour to regulate my mind.

Well, these are useless complaints; I shall certainly find no friend on the wide ocean, nor even here in Archangel, among merchants and seamen. Yet some feelings, unallied to the dross of human nature,[5] beat even in these rugged bosoms. My lieutenant, for instance, is a man of wonderful courage and enterprise; he is madly desirous of glory. He is an Englishman, and in the midst of national and professional prejudices, unsoftened by cultivation, retains some of the noblest endowments of humanity. I first became acquainted with him on board a whale vessel: finding that he was unemployed in this city, I easily engaged him to assist in my enterprise.

The master is a person of an excellent disposition, and is remarkable in the ship for his gentleness, and the mildness of his discipline. He is, indeed, of so amiable a nature, that he will not hunt (a favourite, and almost the only amusement here), because he cannot endure to spill blood. He is, moreover, heroically generous. Some years ago he loved a young Russian lady, of moderate fortune; and having amassed a considerable sum in prize-money,[6] the father of the girl consented to the match. He saw his mistress once before the destined ceremony; but she was bathed in tears, and, throwing herself at his feet, entreated him to spare her, confessing at the same time that she loved another, but that he was poor, and that her father would never consent to the union. My generous friend reassured the suppliant, and on being

---

4. The proper proportion, in a painting, between near and distant objects.
5. I.e., unrelated to the bad elements in human nature.
6. For enemy ships captured in wartime.

informed of the name of her lover instantly abandoned his pursuit. He had already bought a farm with his money, on which he had designed to pass the remainder of his life; but he bestowed the whole on his rival, together with the remains of his prize-money to purchase stock,[7] and then himself solicited the young woman's father to consent to her marriage with her lover. But the old man decidedly refused, thinking himself bound in honour to my friend; who, when he found the father inexorable, quitted his country, nor returned until he heard that his former mistress was married according to her inclinations. "What a noble fellow!" you will exclaim. He is so; but then he has passed all his life on board a vessel, and has scarcely an idea beyond the rope and the shroud.[8]

But do not suppose that, because I complain a little, or because I can conceive a consolation for my toils which I may never know, that I am wavering in my resolutions. Those are as fixed as fate; and my voyage is only now delayed until the weather shall permit my embarkation. The winter has been dreadfully severe; but the spring promises well, and it is considered as a remarkably early season; so that, perhaps, I may sail sooner than I expected. I shall do nothing rashly; you know me sufficiently to confide in my prudence and considerateness whenever the safety of others is committed to my care.

I cannot describe to you my sensations on the near prospect of my undertaking. It is impossible to communicate to you a conception of the trembling sensation, half pleasurable and half fearful, with which I am preparing to depart. I am going to unexplored regions, to "the land of mist and snow;"[9] but I shall kill no albatross, therefore do not be alarmed for my safety.

Shall I meet you again, after having traversed immense seas, and returned by the most southern cape of Africa or America? I dare not expect such success, yet I cannot bear to look on the reverse of the picture. Continue to write to me by every opportunity: I may receive your letters (though the chance is very doubtful) on some occasions when I need them most to support my spirits. I love you very tenderly. Remember me with affection, should you never hear from me again.

Your affectionate brother,
ROBERT WALTON.

Letter 3.

TO MRS. SAVILLE, ENGLAND.

July 7th, 17——.

MY DEAR SISTER,

I write a few lines in haste, to say that I am safe, and well advanced on my voyage. This letter will reach England by a merchant-man now on its homeward voyage from Archangel; more fortunate than I, who may not see my native land, perhaps, for many years. I am, however, in good spirits: my men are bold, and apparently firm of purpose; nor do the floating sheets of ice that continually pass us, indicating the dangers of the region towards which we are advancing, appear to dismay them. We have already reached a very high latitude; but it is the height of summer, and although not so

---

7. Livestock, farm animals.
8. A rope that supports a ship's mast.

9. Coleridge, *The Ancient Mariner,* line 403.

warm as in England, the southern gales, which blow us speedily towards those shores which I so ardently desire to attain, breathe a degree of renovating warmth which I had not expected.

No incidents have hitherto befallen us, that would make a figure[1] in a letter. One or two stiff gales, and the breaking of a mast, are accidents which experienced navigators scarcely remember to record; and I shall be well content, if nothing worse happen to us during our voyage.

Adieu, my dear Margaret. Be assured, that for my own sake, as well as your's, I will not rashly encounter danger. I will be cool, persevering, and prudent.

Remember me to all my English friends.

Most affectionately yours,

R. W.

Letter 4.

TO MRS. SAVILLE, ENGLAND.

August 5th, 17—.

So strange an accident has happened to us, that I cannot forbear recording it, although it is very probable that you will see me before these papers can come into your possession.

Last Monday (July 31st), we were nearly surrounded by ice, which closed in the ship on all sides, scarcely leaving her the sea room in which she floated. Our situation was somewhat dangerous, especially as we were compassed round by a very thick fog. We accordingly lay to,[2] hoping that some change would take place in the atmosphere and weather.

About two o'clock the mist cleared away, and we beheld, stretched out in every direction, vast and irregular plains of ice, which seemed to have no end. Some of my comrades groaned, and my own mind began to grow watchful with anxious thoughts, when a strange sight suddenly attracted our attention, and diverted our solicitude from our own situation. We perceived a low carriage, fixed on a sledge and drawn by dogs, pass on towards the north, at the distance of half a mile: a being which had the shape of a man, but apparently of gigantic stature, sat in the sledge, and guided the dogs. We watched the rapid progress of the traveller with our telescopes, until he was lost among the distant inequalities of the ice.

This appearance excited our unqualified wonder. We were, as we believed, many hundred miles from any land; but this apparition seemed to denote that it was not, in reality, so distant as we had supposed. Shut in, however, by ice, it was impossible to follow his track, which we had observed with the greatest attention.

About two hours after this occurrence, we heard the ground sea;[3] and before night the ice broke, and freed our ship. We, however, lay to until the morning, fearing to encounter in the dark those large loose masses which float about after the breaking up of the ice. I profited of this time to rest for a few hours.

In the morning, however, as soon as it was light, I went upon deck, and

---

1. Be important enough.
2. Stopped the ship.

3. Deep, rolling waves.

found all the sailors busy on one side of the vessel, apparently talking to some one in the sea. It was, in fact, a sledge, like that we had seen before, which had drifted towards us in the night, on a large fragment of ice. Only one dog remained alive; but there was a human being within it, whom the sailors were persuading to enter the vessel. He was not, as the other traveller seemed to be, a savage inhabitant of some undiscovered island, but an European. When I appeared on deck, the master said, "Here is our captain, and he will not allow you to perish on the open sea."

On perceiving me, the stranger addressed me in English, although with a foreign accent. "Before I come on board your vessel," said he, "will you have the kindness to inform me whither you are bound?"

You may conceive my astonishment on hearing such a question addressed to me from a man on the brink of destruction, and to whom I should have supposed that my vessel would have been a resource which he would not have exchanged for the most precious wealth the earth can afford. I replied, however, that we were on a voyage of discovery towards the northern pole.

Upon hearing this he appeared satisfied, and consented to come on board. Good God! Margaret, if you had seen the man who thus capitulated[4] for his safety, your surprise would have been boundless. His limbs were nearly frozen, and his body dreadfully emaciated by fatigue and suffering. I never saw a man in so wretched a condition. We attempted to carry him into the cabin; but as soon as he had quitted the fresh air, he fainted. We accordingly brought him back to the deck, and restored him to animation by rubbing him with brandy, and forcing him to swallow a small quantity. As soon as he shewed signs of life, we wrapped him up in blankets, and placed him near the chimney of the kitchen-stove. By slow degrees he recovered, and ate a little soup, which restored him wonderfully.

Two days passed in this manner before he was able to speak; and I often feared that his sufferings had deprived him of understanding. When he had in some measure recovered, I removed him to my own cabin, and attended on him as much as my duty would permit. I never saw a more interesting creature: his eyes have generally an expression of wildness, and even madness; but there are moments when, if any one performs an act of kindness towards him, or does him any the most trifling service, his whole countenance is lighted up, as it were, with a beam of benevolence and sweetness that I never saw equalled. But he is generally melancholy and despairing; and sometimes he gnashes his teeth, as if impatient of the weight of woes that oppresses him.

When my guest was a little recovered, I had great trouble to keep off the men, who wished to ask him a thousand questions; but I would not allow him to be tormented by their idle curiosity, in a state of body and mind whose restoration evidently depended upon entire repose. Once, however, the lieutenant asked, Why he had come so far upon the ice in so strange a vehicle?

His countenance instantly assumed an aspect of the deepest gloom; and he replied, "To seek one who fled from me."

"And did the man whom you pursued travel in the same fashion?"

"Yes."

"Then I fancy we have seen him; for, the day before we picked you up, we saw some dogs drawing a sledge, with a man in it, across the ice."

---

4. Set definite conditions for surrendering.

This aroused the stranger's attention; and he asked a multitude of questions concerning the route which the dæmon,[5] as he called him, had pursued. Soon after, when he was alone with me, he said, "I have, doubtless, excited your curiosity, as well as that of these good people; but you are too considerate to make inquiries."

"Certainly; it would indeed be very impertinent and inhuman in me to trouble you with any inquisitiveness of mine."

"And yet you rescued me from a strange and perilous situation; you have benevolently restored me to life."

Soon after this he inquired, if I thought that the breaking up of the ice had destroyed the other sledge? I replied, that I could not answer with any degree of certainty; for the ice had not broken until near midnight, and the traveller might have arrived at a place of safety before that time; but of this I could not judge.

From this time the stranger seemed very eager to be upon deck, to watch for the sledge which had before appeared; but I have persuaded him to remain in the cabin, for he is far too weak to sustain the rawness of the atmosphere. But I have promised that some one should watch for him, and give him instant notice if any new object should appear in sight.

Such is my journal of what relates to this strange occurrence up to the present day. The stranger has gradually improved in health, but is very silent, and appears uneasy when any one except myself enters his cabin. Yet his manners are so conciliating and gentle, that the sailors are all interested in him, although they have had very little communication with him. For my own part, I begin to love him as a brother; and his constant and deep grief fills me with sympathy and compassion. He must have been a noble creature in his better days, being even now in wreck so attractive and amiable.

I said in one of my letters, my dear Margaret, that I should find no friend on the wide ocean; yet I have found a man who, before his spirit had been broken by misery, I should have been happy to have possessed as the brother of my heart.

I shall continue my journal concerning the stranger at intervals, should I have any fresh incidents to record.

August 13th, 17—.

My affection for my guest increases every day. He excites at once my admiration[6] and my pity to an astonishing degree. How can I see so noble a creature destroyed by misery without feeling the most poignant grief? He is so gentle, yet so wise; his mind is so cultivated; and when he speaks, although his words are culled with the choicest art, yet they flow with rapidity and unparalleled eloquence.

He is now much recovered from his illness, and is continually on the deck, apparently watching for the sledge that preceded his own. Yet, although unhappy, he is not so utterly occupied by his own misery, but that he interests himself deeply in the employments of others. He has asked me many questions concerning my design; and I have related my little history frankly to him. He appeared pleased with the confidence, and suggested several alterations in my plan, which I shall find exceedingly useful. There is no pedantry

5. In Greek mythology, a lower-order divinity. Shelley, however, probably uses "daemon" as an alternative spelling for *demon*, an evil spirit.
6. In an old sense: wonder, astonishment.

in his manner; but all he does appears to spring solely from the interest he instinctively takes in the welfare of those who surround him. He is often overcome by gloom, and then he sits by himself, and tries to overcome all that is sullen or unsocial in his humour. These paroxysms pass from him like a cloud from before the sun, though his dejection never leaves him. I have endeavoured to win his confidence; and I trust that I have succeeded. One day I mentioned to him the desire I had always felt of finding a friend who might sympathize with me, and direct me by his counsel. I said, I did not belong to that class of men who are offended by advice. "I am self-educated, and perhaps I hardly rely sufficiently upon my own powers. I wish therefore that my companion should be wiser and more experienced than myself, to confirm and support me; nor have I believed it impossible to find a true friend."

"I agree with you," replied the stranger, "in believing that friendship is not only a desirable, but a possible acquisition. I once had a friend, the most noble of human creatures, and am entitled, therefore, to judge respecting friendship. You have hope, and the world before you, and have no cause for despair. But I—I have lost every thing, and cannot begin life anew."

As he said this, his countenance became expressive of a calm settled grief, that touched me to the heart. But he was silent, and presently retired to his cabin.

Even broken in spirit as he is, no one can feel more deeply than he does the beauties of nature. The starry sky, the sea and every sight afforded by these wonderful regions, seems still to have the power of elevating his soul from earth. Such a man has a double existence: he may suffer misery, and be overwhelmed by disappointments; yet when he has retired into himself, he will be like a celestial spirit, that has a halo around him, within whose circle no grief or folly ventures.

Will you laugh at the enthusiasm I express concerning this divine wanderer? If you do, you must have certainly lost that simplicity which was once your characteristic charm. Yet, if you will, smile at the warmth of my expressions, while I find every day new causes for repeating them.

August 19th, 17—.

Yesterday the stranger said to me, "You may easily perceive, Captain Walton, that I have suffered great and unparalleled misfortunes. I had determined, once, that the memory of these evils should die with me; but you have won me to alter my determination. You seek for knowledge and wisdom, as I once did; and I ardently hope that the gratification of your wishes may not be a serpent to sting you, as mine has been. I do not know that the relation of my misfortunes will be useful to you, yet, if you are inclined, listen to my tale. I believe that the strange incidents connected with it will afford a view of nature, which may enlarge your faculties and understanding. You will hear of powers and occurrences, such as you have been accustomed to believe impossible: but I do not doubt that my tale conveys in its series internal evidence of the truth of the events of which it is composed."

You may easily conceive that I was much gratified by the offered communication; yet I could not endure that he should renew his grief by a recital of his misfortunes. I felt the greatest eagerness to hear the promised narrative, partly from curiosity, and partly from a strong desire to ameliorate his fate, if it were in my power. I expressed these feelings in my answer.

"I thank you," he replied, "for your sympathy, but it is useless; my fate is nearly fulfilled. I wait but for one event, and then I shall repose in peace. I understand your feeling," continued he, perceiving that I wished to interrupt him; "but you are mistaken, my friend, if thus you will allow me to name you; nothing can alter my destiny: listen to my history, and you will perceive how irrevocably it is determined."

He then told me, that he would commence his narrative the next day when I should be at leisure. This promise drew from me the warmest thanks. I have resolved every night, when I am not engaged, to record, as nearly as possible in his own words, what he has related during the day. If I should be engaged, I will at least make notes. This manuscript will doubtless afford you the greatest pleasure: but to me, who know him, and who hear it from his own lips, with what interest and sympathy shall I read it in some future day!

Chapter 1.

I am by birth a Genevese;[7] and my family is one of the most distinguished of that republic. My ancestors had been for many years counsellors and syndics;[8] and my father had filled several public situations with honour and reputation. He was respected by all who knew him for his integrity and indefatigable attention to public business. He passed his younger days perpetually occupied by the affairs of his country; and it was not until the decline of life that he thought of marrying, and bestowing on the state sons who might carry his virtues and his name down to posterity.

As the circumstances of his marriage illustrate his character, I cannot refrain from relating them. One of his most intimate friends was a merchant, who, from a flourishing state, fell, through numerous mischances, into poverty. This man, whose name was Beaufort, was of a proud and unbending disposition, and could not bear to live in poverty and oblivion in the same country where he had formerly been distinguished for his rank and magnificence. Having paid his debts, therefore, in the most honourable manner, he retreated with his daughter to the town of Lucerne, where he lived unknown and in wretchedness. My father loved Beaufort with the truest friendship, and was deeply grieved by his retreat in these unfortunate circumstances. He grieved also for the loss of his society, and resolved to seek him out and endeavour to persuade him to begin the world again through his credit and assistance.

Beaufort had taken effectual measures to conceal himself; and it was ten months before my father discovered his abode. Overjoyed at this discovery, he hastened to the house, which was situated in a mean street, near the Reuss. But when he entered, misery and despair alone welcomed him. Beaufort had saved but a very small sum of money from the wreck of his fortunes; but it was sufficient to provide him with sustenance for some months, and in the mean time he hoped to procure some respectable employment in a

7. I.e., from the republic of Geneva, Switzerland.
8. Legislators chosen from the leading families in Geneva.

merchant's house. The interval was consequently spent in inaction; his grief only became more deep and rankling, when he had leisure for reflection; and at length it took so fast hold of his mind, that at the end of three months he lay on a bed of sickness, incapable of any exertion.

His daughter attended him with the greatest tenderness; but she saw with despair that their little fund was rapidly decreasing, and that there was no other prospect of support. But Caroline Beaufort possessed a mind of an uncommon mould; and her courage rose to support her in her adversity. She procured plain work;[9] she plaited straw; and by various means contrived to earn a pittance scarcely sufficient to support life.

Several months passed in this manner. Her father grew worse; her time was more entirely occupied in attending him; her means of subsistence decreased; and in the tenth month her father died in her arms, leaving her an orphan and a beggar. This last blow overcame her; and she knelt by Beaufort's coffin, weeping bitterly, when my father entered the chamber. He came like a protecting spirit to the poor girl, who committed herself to his care, and after the interment of his friend he conducted her to Geneva, and placed her under the protection of a relation. Two years after this event Caroline became his wife.

When my father became a husband and a parent, he found his time so occupied by the duties of his new situation, that he relinquished many of his public employments, and devoted himself to the education of his children. Of these I was the eldest, and the destined successor to all his labours and utility. No creature could have more tender parents than mine. My improvement and health were their constant care, especially as I remained for several years their only child. But before I continue my narrative, I must record an incident which took place when I was four years of age.

My father had a sister, whom he tenderly loved, and who had married early in life an Italian gentleman. Soon after her marriage, she had accompanied her husband into his native country, and for some years my father had very little communication with her. About the time I mentioned she died; and a few months afterwards he received a letter from her husband, acquainting him with his intention of marrying an Italian lady, and requesting my father to take charge of the infant Elizabeth, the only child of his deceased sister. "It is my wish," he said, "that you should consider her as your own daughter, and educate her thus. Her mother's fortune is secured[1] to her, the documents of which I will commit to your keeping. Reflect upon this proposition; and decide whether you would prefer educating your niece yourself to her being brought up by a stepmother."

My father did not hesitate, and immediately went to Italy that he might accompany the little Elizabeth to her future home. I have often heard my mother say, that she was at that time the most beautiful child she had ever seen, and shewed signs even then of a gentle and affectionate disposition. These indications, and a desire to bind as closely as possible the ties of domestic love, determined my mother to consider Elizabeth as my future wife; a design which she never found reason to repent.

From this time Elizabeth Lavenza became my playfellow, and, as we grew

---

9. Basic sewing, as distinguished from fancy sewing.

1. Legally guaranteed.

older, my friend. She was docile and good tempered, yet gay and playful as a summer insect. Although she was lively and animated, her feelings were strong and deep, and her disposition uncommonly affectionate. No one could better enjoy liberty, yet no one could submit with more grace than she did to constraint and caprice. Her imagination was luxuriant, yet her capability of application was great. Her person was the image of her mind; her hazel eyes, although as lively as a bird's, possessed an attractive softness. Her figure was light and airy; and, though capable of enduring great fatigue, she appeared the most fragile creature in the world. While I admired her understanding and fancy, I loved to tend on her, as I should on a favourite animal; and I never saw so much grace both of person and mind united to so little pretension.

Every one adored Elizabeth. If the servants had any request to make, it was always through her intercession. We were strangers to any species of disunion and dispute; for although there was a great dissimilitude in our characters, there was an harmony in that very dissimilitude. I was more calm and philosophical than my companion; yet my temper was not so yielding. My application was of longer endurance; but it was not so severe whilst it endured. I delighted in investigating the facts relative to the actual world; she busied herself in following the aërial[2] creations of the poets. The world was to me a secret, which I desired to discover; to her it was a vacancy; which she sought to people with imaginations of her own.

My brothers were considerably younger than myself; but I had a friend in one of my schoolfellows, who compensated for this deficiency. Henry Clerval was the son of a merchant of Geneva, an intimate friend of my father. He was a boy of singular talent and fancy. I remember, when he was nine years old, he wrote a fairy tale, which was the delight and amazement of all his companions. His favorite study consisted in books of chivalry and romance; and when very young, I can remember, that we used to act plays composed by him out of these favourite books, the principal characters of which were Orlando, Robin Hood, Amadis, and St. George.[3]

No youth could have passed more happily than mine. My parents were indulgent, and my companions amiable. Our studies were never forced; and by some means we always had an end placed in view, which excited us to ardour in the prosecution of them. It was by this method, and not by emulation, that we were urged to application. Elizabeth was not incited to apply herself to drawing, that her companions might not outstrip her; but through the desire of pleasing her aunt, by the representation of some favorite scene done by her own hand. We learned Latin and English, that we might read the writings in those languages; and so far from study being made odious to us through punishment, we loved application, and our amusements would have been the labours of other children. Perhaps we did not read so many books, or learn languages so quickly, as those who are disciplined according to the ordinary methods; but what we learned was impressed the more deeply on our memories.

In this description of our domestic circle I include Henry Clerval; for he

2. Lofty, imaginative.
3. Robin Hood and St. George are legendary English heroes. Orlando is the hero of Ludovico Ariosto's Italian romance, *Orlando Furioso* (1532).

Amadis is the hero of the Spanish or Portuguese romance *Amadis of Gaul* (second half of the 15th century).

was constantly with us. He went to school with me, and generally passed the afternoon at our house; for being an only child, and destitute of companions at home, his father was well pleased that he should find associates at our house; and we were never completely happy when Clerval was absent.

I feel pleasure in dwelling on the recollections of childhood, before misfortune had tainted my mind, and changed its bright visions of extensive usefulness into gloomy and narrow reflections upon self. But, in drawing the picture of my early days, I must not omit to record those events which led, by insensible steps to my after tale of misery: for when I would account to myself for the birth of that passion, which afterwards ruled my destiny, I find it arise, like a mountain river, from ignoble and almost forgotten sources; but, swelling as it proceeded, it became the torrent which, in its course, has swept away all my hopes and joys.

Natural philosophy is the genius[4] that has regulated my fate; I desire therefore, in this narration, to state those facts which led to my predilection for that science. When I was thirteen years of age, we all went on a party of pleasure to the baths near Thonon: the inclemency of the weather obliged us to remain a day confined to the inn. In this house I chanced to find a volume of the works of Cornelius Agrippa.[5] I opened it with apathy; the theory which he attempts to demonstrate, and the wonderful facts which he relates, soon changed this feeling into enthusiasm. A new light seemed to dawn upon my mind; and, bounding with joy, I communicated my discovery to my father. I cannot help remarking here the many opportunities instructors possess of directing the attention of their pupils to useful knowledge, which they utterly neglect. My father looked carelessly at the title-page of my book, and said, "Ah! Cornelius Agrippa! My dear Victor, do not waste your time upon this; it is sad trash."

If, instead of this remark, my father had taken the pains to explain to me, that the principles of Agrippa had been entirely exploded, and that a modern system of science had been introduced, which possessed much greater powers than the ancient, because the powers of the latter were chimerical, while those of the former were real and practical; under such circumstances, I should certainly have thrown Agrippa aside, and, with my imagination warmed as it was, should probably have applied myself to the more rational theory of chemistry which has resulted from modern discoveries. It is even possible, that the train of my ideas would never have received the fatal impulse that led to my ruin. But the cursory glance my father had taken of my volume by no means assured me that he was acquainted with its contents; and I continued to read with the greatest avidity.

When I returned home, my first care was to procure the whole works of this author, and afterwards of Paracelsus and Albertus Magnus.[6] I read and studied the wild fancies of these writers with delight; they appeared to me treasures known to few beside myself; and although I often wished to communicate these secret stores of knowledge to my father, yet his indefinite censure of my favourite Agrippa always withheld me. I disclosed my discov-

---

4. Attendant spirit. "Natural philosophy": the sciences dealing with the physical universe.
5. Henricus Cornelius Agrippa (1486–1535), a writer on magic and the occult sciences.
6. A German monk and scholastic philosopher (1193 or 1206–1280) whose great learning earned him the title "Doctor Universalis." Paracelsus (1493–1541), a Swiss physician who wrote works on alchemy and magic, as well as empirical chemistry and medicine.

eries to Elizabeth, therefore, under a promise of strict secrecy; but she did not interest herself in the subject, and I was left by her to pursue my studies alone.

It may appear very strange, that a disciple of Albertus Magnus should arise in the eighteenth century; but our family was not scientifical, and I had not attended any of the lectures given at the schools of Geneva. My dreams were therefore undisturbed by reality; and I entered with the greatest diligence into the search of the philosopher's stone and the elixir of life.[7] But the latter obtained my most undivided attention: wealth was an inferior object; but what glory would attend the discovery, if I could banish disease from the human frame, and render man invulnerable to any but a violent death!

Nor were these my only visions. The raising of ghosts or devils was a promise liberally accorded by my favourite authors, the fulfilment of which I most eagerly sought; and if my incantations were always unsuccessful, I attributed the failure rather to my own inexperience and mistake, than to a want of skill or fidelity in my instructors.

The natural phænomena that take place every day before our eyes did not escape my examinations. Distillation, and the wonderful effects of steam, processes of which my favourite authors were utterly ignorant, excited my astonishment; but my utmost wonder was engaged by some experiments on an airpump,[8] which I saw employed by a gentleman whom we were in the habit of visiting.

The ignorance of the early philosophers on these and several other points served to decrease their credit with me: but I could not entirely throw them aside, before some other system should occupy their place in my mind.

When I was about fifteen years old, we had retired to our house near Belrive, when we witnessed a most violent and terrible thunder-storm. It advanced from behind the mountains of Jura; and the thunder burst at once with frightful loudness from various quarters of the heavens. I remained, while the storm lasted, watching its progress with curiosity and delight. As I stood at the door, on a sudden I beheld a stream of fire issue from an old and beautiful oak, which stood about twenty yards from our house; and so soon as the dazzling light vanished, the oak had disappeared, and nothing remained but a blasted stump. When we visited it the next morning, we found the tree shattered in a singular manner. It was not splintered by the shock, but entirely reduced to thin ribbands of wood. I never beheld any thing so utterly destroyed.

The catastrophe of this tree excited my extreme astonishment; and I eagerly inquired of my father the nature and origin of thunder and lightning. He replied, "Electricity;" describing at the same time the various effects of that power. He constructed a small electrical machine, and exhibited a few experiments; he made also a kite, with a wire and string, which drew down that fluid from the clouds.[9]

This last stroke completed the overthrow of Cornelius Agrippa, Albertus Magnus, and Paracelsus, who had so long reigned the lords of my imagination. But by some fatality I did not feel inclined to commence the study of

7. Medieval alchemists aimed to produce the philosopher's stone, which would transmute base metals to gold, and the elixir of life, which would prolong life indefinitely.

8. A pump to effect a vacuum, used in physical experiments.
9. In emulation of Benjamin Franklin's experiments with a kite during lightning storms.

We sat late, listening to his complaints, and making many little arrangements for the future. The next morning early I departed. Tears gushed from the eyes of Elizabeth; they proceeded partly from sorrow at my departure, and partly because she reflected that the same journey was to have taken place three months before, when a mother's blessing would have accompanied me.

I threw myself into the chaise that was to convey me away, and indulged in the most melancholy reflections. I, who had ever been surrounded by amiable companions, continually engaged in endeavouring to bestow mutual pleasure, I was now alone. In the university, whither I was going, I must form my own friends, and be my own protector. My life had hitherto been remarkably secluded and domestic; and this had given me invincible repugnance to new countenances. I loved my brothers, Elizabeth, and Clerval, these were "old familiar faces;"[3] but I believed myself totally unfitted for the company of strangers. Such were my reflections as I commenced my journey; but as I proceeded, my spirits and hopes rose. I ardently desired the acquisition of knowledge. I had often, when at home, thought it hard to remain during my youth cooped up in one place, and had longed to enter the world, and take my station among other human beings. Now my desires were complied with, and it would, indeed, have been folly to repent.

I had sufficient leisure for these and many other reflections during my journey to Ingolstadt, which was long and fatiguing. At length the high white steeple of the town met my eyes. I alighted, and was conducted to my solitary apartment, to spend the evening as I pleased.

The next morning I delivered my letters of introduction, and paid a visit to some of the principal professors, and among others to M. Krempe, professor of natural philosophy. He received me with politeness, and asked me several questions concerning my progress in the different branches of science appertaining to natural philosophy. I mentioned, it is true, with fear and trembling, the only authors I had ever read upon those subjects. The professor stared: "Have you," he said, "really spent your time in studying such nonsense?"

I replied in the affirmative. "Every minute," continued M. Krempe with warmth, "every instant that you have wasted on those books is utterly and entirely lost. You have burdened your memory with exploded systems, and useless names. Good God! in what desert land have you lived, where no one was kind enough to inform you that these fancies, which you have so greedily imbibed, are a thousand years old, and as musty as they are ancient? I little expected in this enlightened and scientific age to find a disciple of Albertus Magnus and Paracelsus. My dear Sir, you must begin your studies entirely anew."

So saying, he stept aside, and wrote down a list of several books treating of natural philosophy, which he desired me to procure, and dismissed me, after mentioning that in the beginning of the following week he intended to commence a course of lectures upon natural philosophy in its general relations, and that M. Waldman, a fellow-professor, would lecture upon chemistry the alternate days that he missed.

I returned home, not disappointed, for I had long considered those authors

---

3. Title of a poem (1798) by Charles Lamb.

useless whom the professor had so strongly reprobated; but I did not feel much inclined to study the books which I procured at his recommendation. M. Krempe was a little squat man, with a gruff voice and repulsive countenance; the teacher, therefore, did not prepossess me in favour of his doctrine. Besides, I had a contempt for the uses of modern natural philosophy. It was very different, when the masters of the science sought immortality and power; such views, although futile, were grand: but now the scene was changed. The ambition of the inquirer seemed to limit itself to the annihilation of those visions on which my interest in science was chiefly founded. I was required to exchange chimeras of boundless grandeur for realities of little worth.

Such were my reflections during the first two or three days spent almost in solitude. But as the ensuing week commenced, I thought of the information which M. Krempe had given me concerning the lectures. And although I could not consent to go and hear that little conceited fellow deliver sentences[4] out of a pulpit, I recollected what he had said of M. Waldman, whom I had never seen, as he had hitherto been out of town.

Partly from curiosity, and partly, from idleness, I went into the lecturing room, which M. Waldman entered shortly after. This professor was very unlike his colleague. He appeared about fifty years of age, but with an aspect expressive of the greatest benevolence; a few gray hairs covered his temples, but those at the back of his head were nearly black. His person was short, but remarkably erect; and his voice the sweetest I had ever heard. He began his lecture by a recapitulation of the history of chemistry and the various improvements made by different men of learning, pronouncing with fervour the names of the most distinguished discoverers. He then took a cursory view of the present state of the science, and explained many of its elementary terms. After having made a few preparatory experiments, he concluded with a panegyric upon modern chemistry, the terms of which I shall never forget:—

"The ancient teachers of this science," said he, "promised impossibilities, and performed nothing. The modern masters promise very little; they know that metals cannot be transmuted, and that the elixir of life is a chimera. But these philosophers, whose hands seem only made to dabble in dirt, and their eyes to pore over the microscope or crucible, have indeed performed miracles. They penetrate into the recesses of nature, and shew how she works in her hiding places. They ascend into the heavens; they have discovered how the blood circulates, and the nature of the air we breathe.[5] They have acquired new and almost unlimited powers; they can command the thunders of heaven, mimic the earthquake, and even mock the invisible world with its own shadows."

I departed highly pleased with the professor and his lecture, and paid him a visit the same evening. His manners in private were even more mild and attractive than in public; for there was a certain dignity in his mien during his lecture, which in his own house was replaced by the greatest affability and kindness. He heard with attention my little narration concerning my studies, and smiled at the names of Cornelius Agrippa and Paracelsus, but

---

4. Pronouncements, formally stated opinions.
5. William Harvey discovered in 1628 the circulation of the blood. In the 1770s Joseph Priestley published his *Experiments and Observations on Different Kinds of Air,* in which he identified the gas later named oxygen.

without the contempt that M. Krempe had exhibited. He said, that "these were men to whose indefatigable zeal modern philosophers were indebted for most of the foundations of their knowledge. They had left to us, as an easier task, to give new names, and arrange in connected classifications, the facts which they in a great degree had been the instruments of bringing to light. The labours of men of genius, however erroneously directed, scarcely ever fail in ultimately turning to the solid advantage of mankind." I listened to his statement, which was delivered without any presumption or affectation; and then added, that his lecture had removed my prejudices against modern chemists; and I, at the same time, requested his advice concerning the books I ought to procure.

"I am happy," said M. Waldman, "to have gained a disciple; and if your application equals your ability, I have no doubt of your success. Chemistry is that branch of natural philosophy in which the greatest improvements have been and may be made; it is on that account that I have made it my peculiar[6] study; but at the same time I have not neglected the other branches of science. A man would make but a very sorry chemist, if he attended to that department of human knowledge alone. If your wish is to become really a man of science, and not merely a petty experimentalist, I should advise you to apply to every branch of natural philosophy, including mathematics."

He then took me into his laboratory, and explained to me the uses of his various machines; instructing me as to what I ought to procure, and promising me the use of his own, when I should have advanced far enough in the science not to derange their mechanism. He also gave me the list of books which I had requested; and I took my leave.

Thus ended a day memorable to me; it decided my future destiny.

Chapter 3.

From this day natural philosophy, and particularly chemistry, in the most comprehensive sense of the term, became nearly my sole occupation. I read with ardour those works, so full of genius and discrimination, which modern inquirers have written on these subjects. I attended the lectures, and cultivated the acquaintance, of the men of science of the university; and I found even in M. Krempe a great deal of sound sense and real information, combined, it is true, with a repulsive physiognomy and manners, but not on that account the less valuable. In M. Waldman I found a true friend. His gentleness was never tinged by dogmatism; and his instructions were given with an air of frankness and good nature, that banished every idea of pedantry. It was, perhaps, the amiable character of this man that inclined me more to that branch of natural philosophy which he professed, than an intrinsic love for the science itself. But this state of mind had place only in the first steps towards knowledge: the more fully I entered into the science, the more exclusively I pursued it for its own sake. That application, which at first had been a matter of duty and resolution, now became so ardent and eager, that the stars often disappeared in the light of morning whilst I was yet engaged in my laboratory.

As I applied so closely, it may be easily conceived that I improved rapidly.

6. Special, particular.

My ardour was indeed the astonishment of the students; and my proficiency, that of the masters. Professor Krempe often asked me, with a sly smile, how Cornelius Agrippa went on? whilst M. Waldman expressed the most heartfelt exultation in my progress. Two years passed in this manner, during which I paid no visit to Geneva, but was engaged, heart and soul, in the pursuit of some discoveries, which I hoped to make. None but those who have experienced them can conceive of the enticements of science. In other studies you go as far as others have gone before you, and there is nothing more to know; but in a scientific pursuit there is continual food for discovery and wonder. A mind of moderate capacity, which closely pursues one study, must infallibly arrive at great proficiency in that study; and I, who continually sought the attainment of one object of pursuit, and was solely wrapt up in this, improved so rapidly, that, at the end of two years, I made some discoveries in the improvement of some chemical instruments, which procured me great esteem and admiration at the university. When I had arrived at this point, and had become as well acquainted with the theory and practice of natural philosophy as depended on the lessons of any of the professors at Ingolstadt, my residence there being no longer conducive to my improvements, I thought of returning to my friends and my native town, when an incident happened that protracted my stay.

One of the phænonema which had peculiarly attracted my attention was the structure of the human frame, and, indeed, any animal endued with life. Whence, I often asked myself, did the principle of life proceed? It was a bold question, and one which has ever been considered as a mystery; yet with how many things are we upon the brink of becoming acquainted, if cowardice or carelessness did not restrain our inquiries. I revolved these circumstances in my mind, and determined thenceforth to apply myself more particularly to those branches of natural philosophy which relate to physiology. Unless I had been animated by an almost supernatural enthusiasm, my application to this study would have been irksome, and almost intolerable. To examine the causes of life, we must first have recourse to death. I became acquainted with the science of anatomy: but this was not sufficient; I must also observe the natural decay and corruption of the human body. In my education my father had taken the greatest precautions that my mind should be impressed with no supernatural horrors. I do not ever remember to have trembled at a tale of superstition, or to have feared the apparition of a spirit. Darkness had no effect upon my fancy; and a church-yard was to me merely the receptacle of bodies deprived of life, which, from being the seat of beauty and strength, had become food for the worm. Now I was led to examine the cause and progress of this decay, and forced to spend days and nights in vaults and charnel houses.[7] My attention was fixed upon every object the most insupportable to the delicacy of the human feelings. I saw how the fine form of man was degraded and wasted; I beheld the corruption of death succeed to the blooming cheek of life; I saw how the worm inherited the wonders of the eye and brain. I paused, examining and analysing all the minutiæ of causation, as exemplified in the change from life to death, and death to life, until from the midst of this darkness a sudden light broke in upon me—a light so brilliant and wondrous, yet so simple, that while I became dizzy with the

---

7. Where the bodies of the dead are placed.

immensity of the prospect which it illustrated, I was surprised that among so many men of genius, who had directed their inquiries towards the same science, that I alone should be reserved to discover so astonishing a secret.

Remember, I am not recording the vision of a madman. The sun does not more certainly shine in the heavens, than that which I now affirm is true. Some miracle might have produced it, yet the stages of the discovery were distinct and probable. After days and nights of incredible labour and fatigue, I succeeded in discovering the cause of generation and life; nay, more, I became myself capable of bestowing animation upon lifeless matter.

The astonishment which I had at first experienced on this discovery soon gave place to delight and rapture. After so much time spent in painful labour, to arrive at once at the summit of my desires, was the most gratifying consummation of my toils. But this discovery was so great and overwhelming, that all the steps by which I had been progressively led to it were obliterated, and I beheld only the result. What had been the study and desire of the wisest men since the creation of the world, was now within my grasp. Not that, like a magic scene, it all opened upon me at once: the information I had obtained was of a nature rather to direct my endeavours so soon as I should point them towards the object of my search, than to exhibit that object already accomplished. I was like the Arabian who had been buried with the dead, and found a passage to life aided only by one glimmering, and seemingly ineffectual, light.[8]

I see by your eagerness, and the wonder and hope which your eyes express, my friend, that you expect to be informed of the secret with which I am acquainted; that cannot be: listen patiently until the end of my story, and you will easily perceive why I am reserved upon that subject. I will not lead you on, unguarded and ardent as I then was, to your destruction and infallible misery. Learn from me, if not by my precepts, at least by my example, how dangerous is the acquirement of knowledge, and how much happier that man is who believes his native town to be the world, than he who aspires to become greater than his nature will allow.

When I found so astonishing a power placed within my hands, I hesitated a long time concerning the manner in which I should employ it. Although I possessed the capacity of bestowing animation, yet to prepare a frame for the reception of it, with all its intricacies of fibres, muscles, and veins, still remained a work of inconceivable difficulty and labour. I doubted at first whether I should attempt the creation of a being like myself or one of simpler organization; but my imagination was too much exalted by my first success to permit me to doubt of my ability to give life to an animal as complex and wonderful as man. The materials at present within my command hardly appeared adequate to so arduous an undertaking; but I doubted not that I should ultimately succeed. I prepared myself for a multitude of reverses; my operations might be incessantly baffled, and at last my work be imperfect: yet, when I considered the improvement which every day takes place in science and mechanics, I was encouraged to hope my present attempts would at least lay the foundations of future success. Nor could I consider the magnitude and complexity of my plan as any argument of its impracticability. It was with these feelings that I began the creation of a human being. As the minuteness of the parts formed a great hindrance to my speed, I resolved,

8. The story, *Sinbad's Fourth Voyage*, is told in *A Thousand and One Nights*.

contrary to my first intention, to make the being of a gigantic stature; that is to say, about eight feet in height, and proportionably large. After having formed this determination, and having spent some months in successfully collecting and arranging my materials, I began.

No one can conceive the variety of feelings which bore me onwards, like a hurricane, in the first enthusiasm of success. Life and death appeared to me ideal bounds,[9] which I should first break through, and pour a torrent of light into our dark world. A new species would bless me as its creator and source; many happy and excellent natures would owe their being to me. No father could claim the gratitude of his child so completely as I should deserve their's. Pursuing these reflections, I thought, that if I could bestow animation upon lifeless matter, I might in process of time (although I now found it impossible) renew life where death had apparently devoted the body to corruption.

These thoughts supported my spirits, while I pursued my undertaking with unremitting ardour. My cheek had grown pale with study, and my person had become emaciated with confinement. Sometimes, on the very brink of certainty, I failed; yet still I clung to the hope which the next day or the next hour might realize. One secret which I alone possessed was the hope to which I had dedicated myself, and the moon gazed on my midnight labours, while, with unrelaxed and breathless eagerness, I pursued nature to her hiding places. Who shall conceive the horrors of my secret toil, as I dabbled among the unhallowed damps of the grave, or tortured the living animal to animate the lifeless clay? My limbs now tremble, and my eyes swim with the remembrance; but then a resistless, and almost frantic impulse, urged me forward; I seemed to have lost all soul or sensation but for this one pursuit. It was indeed but a passing trance, that only made me feel with renewed acuteness so soon as, the unnatural stimulus ceasing to operate, I had returned to my old habits. I collected bones from charnel houses; and disturbed, with profane fingers, the tremendous secrets of the human frame. In a solitary chamber, or rather cell, at the top of the house, and separated from all the other apartments by a gallery and staircase, I kept my workshop of filthy creation; my eyeballs were starting from their sockets in attending to the details of my employment. The dissecting room and the slaughter-house furnished many of my materials; and often did my human nature turn with loathing from my occupation, whilst, still urged on by an eagerness which perpetually increased, I brought my work near to a conclusion.

The summer months passed while I was thus engaged, heart and soul, in one pursuit. It was a most beautiful season; never did the fields bestow a more plentiful harvest, or the vines yield a more luxuriant vintage: but my eyes were insensible to the charms of nature. And the same feelings which made me neglect the scenes around me caused me also to forget those friends who were so many miles absent, and whom I had not seen for so long a time. I knew my silence disquieted them; and I well remembered the words of my father: "I know that while you are pleased with yourself, you will think of us with affection, and we shall hear regularly from you. You must pardon me, if I regard any interruption in your correspondence as a proof that your other duties are equally neglected."

I knew well therefore what would be my father's feelings; but I could not

9. Imagined limits.

tear my thoughts from my employment, loathsome in itself, but which had taken an irresistible hold of my imagination. I wished, as it were, to procrastinate all that related to my feelings of affection until the great object, which swallowed up every habit of my nature, should be completed.

I then thought that my father would be unjust if he ascribed my neglect to vice, or faultiness on my part; but I am now convinced that he was justified in conceiving that I should not be altogether free from blame. A human being in perfection ought always to preserve a calm and peaceful mind, and never to allow passion or a transitory desire to disturb his tranquillity. I do not think that the pursuit of knowledge is an exception to this rule. If the study to which you apply yourself has a tendency to weaken your affections, and to destroy your taste for those simple pleasures in which no alloy can possibly mix, then that study is certainly unlawful, that is to say, not befitting the human mind. If this rule were always observed; if no man allowed any pursuit whatsoever to interfere with the tranquillity of his domestic affections, Greece had not been enslaved; Cæsar would have spared his country; America would have been discovered more gradually; and the empires of Mexico and Peru had not been destroyed.[1]

But I forget that I am moralizing in the most interesting part of my tale; and your looks remind me to proceed.

My father made no reproach in his letters; and only took notice of my silence by inquiring into my occupations more particularly than before. Winter, spring, and summer, passed away during my labours; but I did not watch the blossom or the expanding leaves—sights which before always yielded me supreme delight, so deeply was I engrossed in my occupation. The leaves of that year had withered before my work drew near to a close; and now every day shewed me more plainly how well I had succeeded. But my enthusiasm was checked by my anxiety, and I appeared rather like one doomed by slavery to toil in the mines, or any other unwholesome trade, than an artist occupied by his favourite employment. Every night I was oppressed by a slow fever, and I became nervous to a most painful degree; a disease that I regretted the more because I had hitherto enjoyed most excellent health, and had always boasted of the firmness of my nerves. But I believed that exercise and amusement would soon drive away such symptoms; and I promised myself both of these, when my creation should be complete.

Chapter 4.

It was on a dreary night of November, that I beheld the accomplishment of my toils. With an anxiety that almost amounted to agony, I collected the instruments of life around me, that I might infuse a spark of being into the lifeless thing that lay at my feet. It was already one in the morning; the rain pattered dismally against the panes, and my candle was nearly burnt out, when, by the glimmer of the half-extinguished light, I saw the dull yellow eye of the creature open; it breathed hard, and a convulsive motion agitated its limbs.

---

1. Greece was at that time dominated by the Turks. The other allusions are to the civil war that broke out after Julius Caesar was assassinated by republicans who feared that he aspired to become king, the displacement of native Americans by the rapid influx of European settlers, and the destructive violence by Spanish conquistadors in Mexico and Peru.

How can I describe my emotions at this catastrophe, or how delineate the wretch whom with such infinite pains and care I had endeavoured to form? His limbs were in proportion, and I had selected his features as beautiful. Beautiful!—Great God! His yellow skin scarcely covered the work of muscles and arteries beneath; his hair was of a lustrous black, and flowing; his teeth of a pearly whiteness; but these luxuriances only formed a more horrid contrast with his watery eyes, that seemed almost of the same colour as the dun white sockets in which they were set, his shrivelled complexion, and straight black lips.

The different accidents of life are not so changeable as the feelings of human nature. I had worked hard for nearly two years, for the sole purpose of infusing life into an inanimate body. For this I had deprived myself of rest and health. I had desired it with an ardour that far exceeded moderation; but now that I had finished, the beauty of the dream vanished, and breathless horror and disgust filled my heart. Unable to endure the aspect of the being I had created, I rushed out of the room, and continued a long time traversing my bed-chamber, unable to compose my mind to sleep. At length lassitude succeeded to the tumult I had before endured; and I threw myself on the bed in my clothes, endeavouring to seek a few moments of forgetfulness. But it was in vain: I slept indeed, but I was disturbed by the wildest dreams. I thought I saw Elizabeth, in the bloom of health, walking in the streets of Ingolstadt. Delighted and surprised, I embraced her; but as I imprinted the first kiss on her lips, they became livid with the hue of death; her features appeared to change, and I thought that I held the corpse of my dead mother in my arms; a shroud enveloped her form, and I saw the grave-worms crawling in the folds of the flannel. I started from my sleep with horror; a cold dew covered my forehead, my teeth chattered, and every limb became convulsed; when, by the dim and yellow light of the moon, as it forced its way through the window-shutters, I beheld the wretch—the miserable monster whom I had created. He held up the curtain of the bed; and his eyes, if eyes they may be called, were fixed on me. His jaws opened, and he muttered some inarticulate sounds, while a grin wrinkled his cheeks. He might have spoken, but I did not hear; one hand was stretched out, seemingly to detain me, but I escaped, and rushed down stairs. I took refuge in the court-yard belonging to the house which I inhabited; where I remained during the rest of the night, walking up and down in the greatest agitation, listening attentively, catching and fearing each sound as if it were to announce the approach of the demoniacal corpse to which I had so miserably given life.

Oh! no mortal could support the horror of that countenance. A mummy again endued with animation could not be so hideous as that wretch. I had gazed on him while unfinished; he was ugly then; but when those muscles and joints were rendered capable of motion, it became a thing such as even Dante[2] could not have conceived.

I passed the night wretchedly. Sometimes my pulse beat so quickly and hardly, that I felt the palpitation of every artery; at others, I nearly sank to the ground through languor and extreme weakness. Mingled with this horror, I felt the bitterness of disappointment: dreams that had been my food and

2. Dante Alighieri (1265–1321), who described the ghastly tortures of the damned in *The Inferno,* the opening book of his *Divine Comedy.*

pleasant rest for so long a space, were now become a hell to me; and the change was so rapid, the overthrow so complete!

Morning, dismal and wet, at length dawned, and discovered to my sleepless and aching eyes the church of Ingolstadt, its white steeple and clock, which indicated the sixth hour. The porter opened the gates of the court, which had that night been my asylum, and I issued into the streets, pacing them with quick steps, as if I sought to avoid the wretch whom I feared every turning of the street would present to my view. I did not dare return to the apartment which I inhabited, but felt impelled to hurry on, although wetted by the rain, which poured from a black and comfortless sky.

I continued walking in this manner for some time, endeavouring, by bodily exercise, to ease the load that weighed upon my mind. I traversed the streets, without any clear conception of where I was, or what I was doing. My heart palpitated in the sickness of fear; and I hurried on with irregular steps, not daring to look about me:

> Like one who, on a lonely road,
>   Doth walk in fear and dread,
> And, having once turn'd round, walks on,
>   And turns no more his head;
> Because he knows a frightful fiend
>   Doth close behind him tread.[3]

Continuing thus, I came at length opposite to the inn at which the various diligences[4] and carriages usually stopped. Here I paused, I knew not why; but I remained some minutes with my eyes fixed on a coach that was coming towards me from the other end of the street. As it drew nearer, I observed that it was the Swiss diligence: it stopped just where I was standing; and, on the door being opened, I perceived Henry Clerval, who, on seeing me, instantly sprung out. "My dear Frankenstein," exclaimed he, "how glad I am to see you! how fortunate that you should be here at the very moment of my alighting!"

Nothing could equal my delight on seeing Clerval; his presence brought back to my thoughts my father, Elizabeth, and all those scenes of home so dear to my recollection. I grasped his hand, and in a moment forgot my horror and misfortune; I felt suddenly, and for the first time during many months calm and serene joy. I welcomed my friend, therefore, in the most cordial manner, and we walked towards my college. Clerval continued talking for some time about our mutual friends and his own good fortune in being permitted to come to Ingolstadt. "You may easily believe," said he, "how great was the difficulty to persuade my father that it was not absolutely necessary for a merchant not to understand any thing except book-keeping; and, indeed, I believe I left him incredulous to the last, for his constant answer to my unwearied entreaties was the same as that of the Dutch schoolmaster in the Vicar of Wakefield: 'I have ten thousand florins a year without Greek, I eat heartily without Greek.'[5] But his affection for me at length overcame his dislike of learning, and he has permitted me to undertake a voyage of discovery to the land of knowledge."

"It gives me the greatest delight to see you; but tell me how you left my father, brothers, and Elizabeth."

3. Coleridge's The Ancient Mariner, lines 446–51.
4. Stagecoaches.

5. From Oliver Goldsmith's novel The Vicar of Wakefield (1766), chap. 20.

"Very well, and very happy, only a little uneasy that they hear from you so seldom. By the bye, I mean to lecture you a little upon their account myself.—But, my dear Frankenstein," continued he, stopping short, and gazing full in my face, "I did not before remark how very ill you appear; so thin and pale; you look as if you had been watching for several nights."

"You have guessed right; I have lately been so deeply engaged in one occupation, that I have not allowed myself sufficient rest, as you see: but I hope, I sincerely hope, that all these employments are now at an end, and that I am at length free."

I trembled excessively; I could not endure to think of, and far less to allude to the occurrences of the preceding night. I walked with a quick pace, and we soon arrived at my college. I then reflected, and the thought made me shiver, that the creature whom I had left in my apartment might still be there, alive, and walking about. I dreaded to behold this monster; but I feared still more that Henry should see him. Entreating him therefore to remain a few minutes at the bottom of the stairs, I darted up towards my own room. My hand was already on the lock of the door before I recollected myself. I then paused; and a cold shivering came over me. I threw the door forcibly open, as children are accustomed to do when they expect a spectre to stand in waiting for them on the other side; but nothing appeared. I stepped fearfully in: the apartment was empty; and my bedroom was also freed from its hideous guest. I could hardly believe that so great a good-fortune could have befallen me; but when I became assured that my enemy had indeed fled, I clapped my hands for joy, and ran down to Clerval.

We ascended into my room, and the servant presently brought breakfast; but I was unable to contain myself. It was not joy only that possessed me; I felt my flesh tingle with excess of sensitiveness, and my pulse beat rapidly. I was unable to remain for a single instant in the same place; I jumped over the chairs, clapped my hands, and laughed aloud. Clerval at first attributed my unusual spirits to joy on his arrival; but when he observed me more attentively, he saw a wildness in my eyes for which he could not account; and my loud, unrestrained, heartless laughter, frightened and astonished him.

"My dear Victor," cried he, "what, for God's sake, is the matter? Do not laugh in that manner. How ill you are! What is the cause of all this?"

"Do not ask me," cried I, putting my hands before my eyes, for I thought I saw the dreaded spectre glide into the room; "*he* can tell.—Oh, save me! save me!" I imagined that the monster seized me; I struggled furiously, and fell down in a fit.

Poor Clerval! what must have been his feelings? A meeting, which he anticipated with such joy, so strangely turned to bitterness. But I was not the witness of his grief; for I was lifeless, and did not recover my senses for a long, long time.

This was the commencement of a nervous fever, which confined me for several months. During all that time Henry was my only nurse. I afterwards learned that, knowing my father's advanced age, and unfitness for so long a journey, and how wretched my sickness would make Elizabeth, he spared them this grief by concealing the extent of my disorder. He knew that I could not have a more kind and attentive nurse than himself; and, firm in the hope he felt of my recovery, he did not doubt that, instead of doing harm, he performed the kindest action that he could towards them.

But I was in reality very ill; and surely nothing but the unbounded and unremitting attentions of my friend could have restored me to life. The form of the monster on whom I had bestowed existence was for ever before my eyes, and I raved incessantly concerning him. Doubtless my words surprised Henry: he at first believed them to be the wanderings of my disturbed imagination; but the pertinacity with which I continually recurred to the same subject persuaded him that my disorder indeed owed its origin to some uncommon and terrible event.

By very slow degrees, and with frequent relapses, that alarmed and grieved my friend, I recovered. I remember the first time I became capable of observing outward objects with any kind of pleasure, I perceived that the fallen leaves had disappeared, and that the young buds were shooting forth from the trees that shaded my window. It was a divine spring; and the season contributed greatly to my convalescence. I felt also sentiments of joy and affection revive in my bosom; my gloom disappeared, and in a short time I became as cheerful as before I was attacked by the fatal passion.

"Dearest Clerval," exclaimed I, "how kind, how very good you are to me. This whole winter, instead of being spent in study, as you promised yourself, has been consumed in my sick room. How shall I ever repay you? I feel the greatest remorse for the disappointment of which I have been the occasion; but you will forgive me."

"You will repay me entirely, if you do not discompose yourself, but get well as fast as you can; and since you appear in such good spirits, I may speak to you on one subject, may I not?"

I trembled. One subject! what could it be? Could he allude to an object on whom I dared not even think?

"Compose yourself," said Clerval, who observed my change of colour, "I will not mention it, if it agitates you; but your father and cousin would be very happy if they received a letter from you in your own hand-writing. They hardly know how ill you have been, and are uneasy at your long silence."

"Is that all? my dear Henry. How could you suppose that my first thought would not fly towards those dear, dear friends whom I love, and who are so deserving of my love?"

"If this is your present temper, my friend, you will perhaps be glad to see a letter that has been lying here some days for you: it is from your cousin, I believe."

Chapter 5.

Clerval then put the following letter into my hands.

"TO V. FRANKENSTEIN.

"MY DEAR COUSIN,

"I cannot describe to you the uneasiness we have all felt concerning your health. We cannot help imagining that your friend Clerval conceals the extent of your disorder: for it is now several months since we have seen your hand-writing; and all this time you have been obliged to dictate your letters to Henry. Surely, Victor, you must have been exceedingly ill; and this makes us all very wretched, as much so nearly as after the death of your dear mother. My uncle was almost persuaded that you were indeed dangerously ill, and could hardly be restrained from undertaking a journey to Ingolstadt. Clerval always writes that you are getting better; I eagerly hope that you will confirm this intelligence soon in your own hand-writing; for indeed, indeed, Victor, we are all very miserable on this account. Relieve us from this fear, and we shall be the happiest creatures in the world. Your father's health is now so vigorous, that he appears ten years younger since last winter. Ernest also is so much improved, that you would hardly know him: he is now nearly sixteen, and has lost that sickly appearance which he had some years ago; he is grown quite robust and active.

"My uncle and I conversed a long time last night about what profession Ernest should follow. His constant illness when young has deprived him of the habits of application; and now that he enjoys good health, he is continually in the open air, climbing the hills, or rowing on the lake. I therefore proposed that he should be a farmer; which you know, Cousin, is a favourite scheme of mine. A farmer's is a very healthy happy life; and the least hurtful, or rather the most beneficial profession of any. My uncle had an idea of his being educated as an advocate, that through his interest he might become a judge. But, besides that he is not at all fitted for such an occupation, it is certainly more creditable to cultivate the earth for the sustenance of man, than to be the confidant, and sometimes the accomplice, of his vices; which is the profession of a lawyer. I said, that the employments of a prosperous farmer, if they were not a more honourable, they were at least a happier species of occupation than that of a judge, whose misfortune it was always to meddle with the dark side of human nature. My uncle smiled, and said, that I ought to be an advocate myself, which put an end to the conversation on that subject.

"And now I must tell you a little story that will please, and perhaps amuse you. Do you not remember Justine Moritz? Probably you do not; I will relate her history, therefore, in a few words. Madame Moritz, her mother, was a widow with four children, of whom Justine was the third. This girl had always been the favourite of her father; but, through a strange perversity, her mother could not endure her, and, after the death of M. Moritz, treated her very ill. My aunt observed this; and, when Justine was twelve years of age, prevailed on her mother to allow her to live at her house. The republican institutions of our country have produced simpler and happier manners than those which prevail in the great monarchies that surround it. Hence there is less distinction between the several classes of its inhabitants; and the lower orders being neither so poor nor so despised, their manners are more refined and moral. A servant in Geneva does not mean the same thing as a servant in France and England. Justine, thus received in our family, learned the duties of a servant; a condition which, in our fortunate country, does not include the idea of ignorance, and a sacrifice of the dignity of a human being.

"After what I have said, I dare say you well remember the heroine of my little tale: for Justine was a great favourite of your's; and I recollect you once remarked, that if you were in an ill humour, one glance from Justine could dissipate it, for the same reason that Ariosto gives concerning the beauty of Angelica[6]—she looked so frank-hearted and happy. My aunt conceived a great attachment for her, by which she was induced to give her an education superior to that which she had at first intended. This benefit was fully repaid; Justine was the most grateful little creature in the world: I do not mean that she made any professions,[7] I never heard one pass her lips; but you could see by her eyes that she almost adored her protectress. Although her disposition was gay, and in many respects inconsiderate, yet she paid the greatest attention to every gesture of my aunt. She thought her the model of all excellence, and endeavoured to imitate her phraseology and manners, so that even now she often reminds me of her.

"When my dearest aunt died, every one was too much occupied in their own grief to notice poor Justine, who had attended her during her illness with the most anxious affection. Poor Justine was very ill; but other trials were reserved for her.

"One by one, her brothers and sister died; and her mother, with the exception of her neglected daughter, was left childless. The conscience of the woman was troubled; she began to think that the deaths of her favourites was a judgment from heaven to chastise her partiality. She was a Roman Catholic; and I believe her confessor confirmed the idea which she had conceived. Accordingly, a few months after your departure for Ingoldstadt, Justine was called home by her repentant mother. Poor girl! she wept when she quitted our house: she was much altered since the death of my aunt; grief had given softness and a winning mildness to her manners, which had before been remarkable for vivacity. Nor was her residence at her mother's house of a nature to restore her gaiety. The poor woman was very vacillating in her repentance. She sometimes begged Justine to forgive her unkindness, but much oftener accused her of having caused the deaths of her brothers and sister. Perpetual fretting at length threw Madame Moritz into a decline, which at first increased her irritability, but she is now at peace for ever. She died on the first approach of cold weather, at the beginning of this last winter. Justine has returned to us; and I assure you I love her tenderly. She is very clever and gentle, and extremely pretty; as I mentioned before, her mien and her expressions continually remind me of my dear aunt.

"I must say also a few words to you, my dear cousin, of little darling William. I wish you could see him; he is very tall of his age, with sweet laughing blue eyes, dark eye-lashes, and curling hair. When he smiles, two little dimples appear on each cheek, which are rosy with health. He has already had one or two little *wives*, but Louisa Biron is his favourite, a pretty little girl of five years of age.

"Now, dear Victor, I dare say you wish to be indulged in a little gossip concerning the good people of Geneva. The pretty Miss Mansfield has already received the congratulatory visits on her approaching marriage with a young Englishman John Melbourne, Esq. Her ugly sister,

6. The heroine of Ariosto's *Orlando Furioso* (1532).   7. Explicit statements.

Manon, married M. Duvillard, the rich banker, last autumn. Your favourite schoolfellow, Louis Manoir, has suffered several misfortunes since the departure of Clerval from Geneva. But he has already recovered his spirits, and is reported to be on the point of marrying a very lively pretty French-woman, Madame Tavernier. She is a widow, and much older than Manoir; but she is very much admired, and a favorite with every body.

"I have written myself into good spirits, dear cousin; yet I cannot conclude without again anxiously inquiring concerning your health. Dear Victor, if you are not very ill, write yourself, and make your father and all of us happy; or—I cannot bear to think of the other side of the question; my tears already flow. Adieu, my dearest cousin.

"ELIZABETH LAVENZA.

"Geneva, March 18th, 17—."

"Dear, dear Elizabeth!" I exclaimed when I had read her letter, "I will write instantly, and relieve them from the anxiety they must feel." I wrote, and this exertion greatly fatigued me; but my convalescence had commenced, and proceeded regularly. In another fortnight I was able to leave my chamber.

One of my first duties on my recovery was to introduce Clerval to the several professors of the university. In doing this, I underwent a kind of rough usage, ill befitting the wounds that my mind had sustained. Ever since the fatal night, the end of my labours, and the beginning of my misfortunes, I had conceived a violent antipathy even to the name of natural philosophy. When I was otherwise quite restored to health, the sight of a chemical instrument would renew all the agony of my nervous symptoms. Henry saw this and had removed all my apparatus from my view. He had also changed my apartment; for he perceived that I had acquired a dislike for the room which had previously been my laboratory. But these cares of Clerval were made of no avail when I visited the professors. M. Waldman inflicted torture when he praised, with kindness and warmth, the astonishing progress I had made in the sciences. He soon perceived that I disliked the subject; but, not guessing the real cause, he attributed my feelings to modesty, and changed the subject from my improvement to the science itself, with a desire, as I evidently saw, of drawing me out. What could I do? He meant to please, and he tormented me. I felt as if he had placed carefully, one by one, in my view those instruments which were to be afterwards used in putting me to a slow and cruel death. I writhed under his words, yet dared not exhibit the pain I felt. Clerval, whose eyes and feelings were always quick in discerning the sensations of others, declined the subject, alleging, in excuse, his total ignorance; and the conversation took a more general turn. I thanked my friend from my heart, but I did not speak. I saw plainly that he was surprised, but he never attempted to draw my secret from me; and although I loved him with a mixture of affection and reverence that knew no bounds, yet I could never persuade myself to confide to him that event which was so often present to my recollection, but which I feared the detail to another would only impress more deeply.

M. Krempe was not equally docile; and in my condition at that time, of almost insupportable sensitiveness, his harsh blunt encomiums gave me even more pain than the benevolent approbation of M. Waldman. "D—n the fellow!" cried he; "why, M. Clerval, I assure you he has outstript us all. Aye, stare if you please; but it is nevertheless true. A youngster who, but a few years ago, believed Cornelius Agrippa as firmly as the gospel, has now set himself at the head of the university; and if he is not soon pulled down, we shall all be out of countenance.—Aye, aye," continued he, observing my face expressive of suffering, "M. Frankenstein is modest; an excellent quality in a young man. Young men should be diffident of themselves, you know, M. Clerval; I was myself when young: but that wears out in a very short time."

M. Krempe had now commenced an eulogy on himself, which happily turned the conversation from a subject that was so annoying to me.

Clerval was no natural philosopher. His imagination was too vivid for the minutiæ of science. Languages were his principal study; and he sought, by acquiring their elements, to open a field for self-instruction on his return to Geneva. Persian, Arabic, and Hebrew, gained his attention, after he had made himself perfectly master of Greek and Latin. For my own part, idleness had ever been irksome to me; and now that I wished to fly from reflection, and hated my former studies, I felt great relief in being the fellow-pupil with my friend, and found not only instruction but consolation in the works of the orientalists. Their melancholy is soothing, and their joy elevating to a degree I never experienced in studying the authors of any other country. When you read their writings, life appears to consist in a warm sun and garden of roses,—in the smiles and frowns of a fair enemy, and the fire that consumes your own heart. How different from the manly and heroical poetry of Greece and Rome.

Summer passed away in these occupations, and my return to Geneva was fixed for the latter end of autumn; but being delayed by several accidents, winter and snow arrived, the roads were deemed impassable, and my journey was retarded until the ensuing spring. I felt this delay very bitterly; for I longed to see my native town, and my beloved friends. My return had only been delayed so long from an unwillingness to leave Clerval in a strange place, before he had become acquainted with any of its inhabitants. The winter, however, was spent cheerfully; and although the spring was uncommonly late, when it came, its beauty compensated for its dilatoriness.

The month of May had already commenced, and I expected the letter daily which was to fix the date of my departure, when Henry proposed a pedestrian tour in the environs of Ingoldstadt that I might bid a personal farewell to the country I had so long inhabited. I acceded with pleasure to this proposition: I was fond of exercise, and Clerval had always been my favourite companion in the rambles of this nature that I had taken among the scenes of my native country.

We passed a fortnight in these perambulations: my health and spirits had long been restored, and they gained additional strength from the salubrious air I breathed, the natural incidents of our progress, and the conversation of my friend. Study had before secluded me from the intercourse of my fellow-creatures, and rendered me unsocial; but Clerval called forth the better feelings of my heart; he again taught me to love the aspect of nature, and the cheerful faces of children. Excellent friend! how sincerely did you love me, and endeavour to elevate my mind, until it was on a level with your own. A selfish pursuit had cramped and narrowed me, until your gentleness and affection warmed and opened my senses; I became the same happy creature who, a few years ago, loving and beloved by all, had no sorrow or care. When happy, inanimate nature had the power of bestowing on me the most delightful sensations. A serene sky and verdant fields filled me with ecstacy. The present season was indeed divine; the flowers of spring bloomed in the hedges, while those of summer were already in bud: I was undisturbed by thoughts which during the preceding year had pressed upon me, notwithstanding my endeavours to throw them off, with an invincible burden.

Henry rejoiced in my gaiety, and sincerely sympathized in my feelings: he exerted himself to amuse me, while he expressed the sensations that filled his soul. The resources of his mind on this occasion were truly astonishing: his conversation was full of imagination; and very often, in imitation of the Persian and Arabic writers, he invented tales of wonderful fancy and passion. At other times he repeated my favourite poems, or drew me out into arguments, which he supported with great ingenuity.

We returned to our college on a Sunday afternoon: the peasants were dancing, and every one we met appeared gay and happy. My own spirits were high, and I bounded along with feelings of unbridled joy and hilarity.

Chapter 6.

On my return, I found the following letter from my father:—

"*TO* V. FRANKENSTEIN.

"MY DEAR VICTOR,

"You have probably waited impatiently for a letter to fix the date of your return to us; and I was at first tempted to write only a few lines, merely mentioning the day on which I should expect you. But that would be a cruel kindness, and I dare not do it. What would be your surprise, my son, when you expected a happy and gay welcome, to behold on the contrary, tears and wretchedness? And how, Victor, can I relate our misfortune? Absence cannot have rendered you callous to our joys and griefs; and how shall I inflict pain on an absent child? I wish to prepare you for the woeful news, but I know it is impossible; even now your eye skims over the page, to seek the words which are to convey to you the horrible tidings.

"William is dead!—that sweet child, whose smiles delighted and warmed my heart, who was so gentle, yet so gay! Victor, he is murdered!

"I will not attempt to console you; but will simply relate the circumstances of the transaction.

"Last Thursday (May 7th) I, my niece, and your two brothers, went to walk in Plainpalais. The evening was warm and serene, and we prolonged our walk farther than usual. It was already dusk before we thought of returning; and then we discovered that William and Ernest, who had gone on before, were not to be found. We accordingly rested on a seat until they should return. Presently Ernest came, and inquired if we had seen his brother: he said, that they had been playing together, that William had run away to hide himself, and that he vainly sought for him, and afterwards waited for him a long time, but that he did not return.

"This account rather alarmed us, and we continued to search for him until night fell, when Elizabeth conjectured that he might have returned to the house. He was not there. We returned again, with torches; for I could not rest, when I thought that my sweet boy had lost himself, and was exposed to all the damps and dews of night: Elizabeth also suffered extreme anguish. About five in the morning I discovered my lovely boy, whom the night before I had seen blooming and active in health, stretched on the grass livid and motionless: the print of the murderer's finger was on his neck.

"He was conveyed home, and the anguish that was visible in my countenance betrayed the secret to Elizabeth. She was very earnest to see the corpse. At first I attempted to prevent her; but she persisted, and entering the room where it lay, hastily examined the neck of the victim, and clasping her hands exclaimed, 'O God! I have murdered my darling infant!'

"She fainted, and was restored with extreme difficulty. When she again lived, it was only to weep and sigh. She told me, that that same evening William had teazed her to let him wear a very valuable miniature that she possessed of your mother. This picture is gone, and was doubtless the temptation which urged the murderer to the deed. We have no trace of him at present, although our exertions to discover him are unremitted; but they will not restore my beloved William.

"Come, dearest Victor; you alone can console Elizabeth. She weeps continually, and accuses herself unjustly as the cause of his death; her words pierce my heart. We are all unhappy; but will not that be an additional motive for you, my son, to return and be our comforter? Your dear mother! Alas, Victor! I now say, Thank God she did not live to witness the cruel, miserable death of her youngest darling!

"Come, Victor; not brooding thoughts of vengeance against the assassin, but with feelings of peace and gentleness, that will heal, instead of festering the wounds of our minds. Enter the house of mourning, my friend, but with kindness and affection for those who love you, and not with hatred for your enemies.

"Your affectionate and afflicted father,

"ALPHONSE FRANKENSTEIN.
"Geneva, May 12th, 17—."

Clerval, who had watched my countenance as I read this letter, was surprised to observe the despair that succeeded to the joy I at first expressed on receiving news from my friends. I threw the letter on the table, and covered my face with my hands.

"My dear Frankenstein," exclaimed Henry, when he perceived me weep with bitterness, "are you always to be unhappy? My dear friend, what has happened?"

I motioned to him to take up the letter, while I walked up and down the room in the extremest agitation. Tears also gushed from the eyes of Clerval, as he read the account of my misfortune.

"I can offer you no consolation, my friend," said he; "your disaster is irreparable. What do you intend to do?"

"To go instantly to Geneva: come with me, Henry, to order the horses."

During our walk, Clerval endeavoured to raise my spirits. He did not do this by common topics of consolation, but by exhibiting the truest sympathy. "Poor William!" said he, "that dear child; he now sleeps with his angel mother. His friends mourn and weep, but he is at rest: he does not now feel the murderer's grasp; a sod covers his gentle form, and he knows no pain. He can no longer be a fit subject for pity; the survivors are the greatest sufferers, and for them time is the only consolation. Those maxims of the Stoics, that death was no evil, and that the mind of man ought to be superior to despair on the eternal absence of a beloved object, ought not to be urged. Even Cato[8] wept over the dead body of his brother."

Clerval spoke thus as we hurried through the streets; the words impressed themselves on my mind, and I remembered them afterwards in solitude. But now, as soon as the horses arrived, I hurried into a cabriole,[9] and bade farewell to my friend.

My journey was very melancholy. At first I wished to hurry on, for I longed to console and sympathize with my loved and sorrowing friends; but when I drew near my native town, I slackened my progress. I could hardly sustain the multitude of feelings that crowded into my mind. I passed through scenes familiar to my youth, but which I had not seen for nearly six years. How altered every thing might be during that time? One sudden and desolating change had taken place; but a thousand little circumstances might have by degrees worked other alterations, which, although they were done more tranquilly, might not be the less decisive. Fear overcame me; I dared not advance dreading a thousand nameless evils that made me tremble, although I was unable to define them.

I remained two days at Lausanne, in this painful state of mind. I contemplated the lake: the waters were placid; all around was calm, and the snowy mountains, "the palaces of nature,"[1] were not changed. By degrees the calm and heavenly scene restored me, and I continued my journey towards Geneva.

The road ran by the side of the lake, which became narrower as I approached my native town. I discovered more distinctly the black sides of Jura, and the bright summit of Mont Blanc I wept like a child: "Dear mountains! my own beautiful lake! how do you welcome your wanderer? Your summits are clear; the sky and lake are blue and placid. Is this to prognosticate peace, or to mock at my unhappiness?"

I fear, my friend, that I shall render myself tedious by dwelling on these preliminary circumstances; but they were days of comparative happiness, and I think of them with pleasure. My country, my beloved country! who but a native can tell the delight I took in again beholding thy streams, thy mountains, and, more than all, thy lovely lake.

Yet, as I drew nearer home, grief and fear again overcame me. Night also closed around; and when I could hardly see the dark mountains, I felt still more gloomily. The picture appeared a vast and dim scene of evil, and I foresaw obscurely that I was destined to become the most wretched of

---

8. Although the Stoics advocated the restraint of the emotions by reason, the Stoic philosopher Cato the Younger (1st century B.C.E.) could not restrain his passionate grief at the death of his brother. The story is told in Plutarch's *Lives* (early 2nd century

C.E.).
9. A two-wheeled horse-drawn carriage.
1. Byron describes "the Alps / The palaces of Nature" in *Childe Harold's Pilgrimage* (1816), 3.62.

human beings. Alas! I prophesied truly, and failed only in one single circumstance, that in all the misery I imagined and dreaded, I did not conceive the hundredth part of the anguish I was destined to endure.

It was completely dark when I arrived in the environs of Geneva; the gates of the town were already shut; and I was obliged to pass the night at Secheron, a village half a league to the east of the city. The sky was serene; and, as I was unable to rest, I resolved to visit the spot where my poor William had been murdered. As I could not pass through the town, I was obliged to cross the lake in a boat to arrive at Plainpalais. During this short voyage I saw the lightnings playing on the summit of Mont Blanc in the most beautiful figures. The storm appeared to approach rapidly; and, on landing, I ascended a low hill, that I might observe its progress. It advanced; the heavens were clouded, and I soon felt the rain coming slowly in large drops, but its violence quickly increased.

I quitted my seat, and walked on, although the darkness and storm increased every minute, and the thunder burst with a terrific crash over my head. It was echoed from Salêve, the Juras, and the Alps of Savoy; vivid flashes of lightning dazzled my eyes, illuminating the lake, making it appear like a vast sheet of fire; then for an instant every thing seemed of a pitchy darkness, until the eye recovered itself from the preceding flash. The storm, as is often the case in Switzerland, appeared at once in various parts of the heavens. The most violent storm hung exactly north of the town, over that part of the lake which lies between the promontory of Belrive and the village of Copêt. Another storm enlightened Jura with faint flashes; and another darkened and sometimes disclosed the Môle, a peaked mountain to the east of the lake.

While I watched the storm, so beautiful yet terrific,[2] I wandered on with a hasty step. This noble war in the sky elevated my spirits; I clasped my hands and exclaimed aloud, "William, dear angel! this is thy funeral, this thy dirge!" As I said these words, I perceived in the gloom a figure which stole from behind a clump of trees near me; I stood fixed, gazing intently: I could not be mistaken. A flash of lightning illuminated the object, and discovered its shape plainly to me; its gigantic stature, and the deformity of its aspect, more hideous than belongs to humanity, instantly informed me that it was the wretch, the filthy dæmon to whom I had given life. What did he there? Could he be (I shuddered at the conception) the murderer of my brother? No sooner did that idea cross my imagination, than I became convinced of its truth; my teeth chattered, and I was forced to lean against a tree for support. The figure passed me quickly, and I lost it in the gloom. Nothing in human shape could have destroyed that fair child. *He* was the murderer! I could not doubt it. The mere presence of the idea was an irresistible proof of the fact. I thought of pursuing the devil; but it would have been in vain, for another flash discovered him to me hanging among the rocks of the nearly perpendicular ascent of Mont Salêve, a hill that bounds Plainpalais on the south. He soon reached the summit, and disappeared.

I remained motionless. The thunder ceased; but the rain still continued, and the scene was enveloped in an impenetrable darkness. I revolved in my mind the events which I had until now sought to forget: the whole train of

2. Terrifying.

my progress towards the creation; the appearance of the work of my own hands alive at my bed side, its departure. Two years had now nearly elapsed since the night on which he first received life; and was this his first crime? Alas! I had turned loose into the world a depraved wretch, whose delight was in carnage and misery; had he not murdered my brother?

No one can conceive the anguish I suffered during the remainder of the night, which I spent, cold and wet, in the open air. But I did not feel the inconvenience of the weather; my imagination was busy in scenes of evil and despair. I considered the being whom I had cast among mankind, and endowed with the will and power to effect purposes of horror, such as the deed which he had now done, nearly in the light of my own vampire,[3] my own spirit let loose from the grave, and forced to destroy all that was dear to me.

Day dawned; and I directed my steps towards the town. The gates were open; and I hastened to my father's house. My first thought was to discover what I knew of the murderer, and cause instant pursuit to be made. But I paused when I reflected on the story that I had to tell. A being whom I myself had formed, and endued with life, had met me at midnight among the precipices of an inaccessible mountain. I remembered also the nervous fever with which I had been seized just at the time that I dated my creation, and which would give an air of delirium to a tale otherwise so utterly improbable. I well knew that if any other had communicated such a relation to me, I should have looked upon it as the ravings of insanity. Besides, the strange nature of the animal would elude all pursuit, even if I were so far credited as to persuade my relatives to commence it. Besides, of what use would be pursuit? Who could arrest a creature capable of scaling the overhanging sides of Mont Salève? These reflections determined me, and I resolved to remain silent.

It was about five in the morning when I entered my father's house. I told the servants not to disturb the family, and went into the library to attend their usual hour of rising.

Six years had elapsed, passed as a dream but for one indelible trace, and I stood in the same place where I had last embraced my father before my departure for Ingolstadt. Beloved and respectable parent! He still remained to me. I gazed on the picture of my mother, which stood over the mantlepiece. It was an historical subject, painted at my father's desire, and represented Caroline Beaufort in an agony of despair, kneeling by the coffin of her dead father. Her garb was rustic, and her cheek pale; but there was an air of dignity and beauty, that hardly permitted the sentiment of pity. Below this picture was a miniature of William; and my tears flowed when I looked upon it. While I was thus engaged, Ernest entered; he had heard me arrive, and hastened to welcome me. He expressed a sorrowful delight to see me: "Welcome, my dearest Victor," said he. "Ah! I wish you had come three months ago, and then you would have found us all joyous and delighted. But we are now unhappy; and, I am afraid, tears instead of smiles will be your welcome. Our father looks so sorrowful: this dreadful event seems to have revived in his mind his grief on the death of Mamma. Poor Elizabeth also is quite inconsolable." Ernest began to weep as he said these words.

---

3. In folklore, a corpse, reanimated, which sucks the blood of sleeping persons. Victor feels as though his Creature were his own dead self, come back to life.

"Do not," said I, "welcome me thus; try to be more calm, that I may not be absolutely miserable the moment I enter my father's house after so long an absence. But, tell me, how does my father support his misfortunes? and how is my poor Elizabeth?"

"She indeed requires consolation; she accused herself of having caused the death of my brother, and that made her very wretched. But since the murderer has been discovered—"

"The murderer discovered! Good God! how can that be? who could attempt to pursue him? It is impossible; one might as well try to overtake the winds, or confine a mountain-stream with a straw."

"I do not know what you mean; but we were all very unhappy when she was discovered. No one would believe it at first; and even now Elizabeth will not be convinced, notwithstanding all the evidence. Indeed, who would credit that Justine Moritz, who was so amiable, and fond of all the family, could all at once become so extremely wicked?"

"Justine Moritz! Poor, poor girl, is she the accused? But it is wrongfully; every one knows that; no one believes it, surely, Ernest?"

"No one did at first; but several circumstances came out, that have almost forced conviction upon us: and her own behaviour has been so confused, as to add to the evidence of facts a weight that, I fear, leaves no hope for doubt. But she will be tried to-day, and you will then hear all."

He related that, the morning on which the murder of poor William had been discovered, Justine had been taken ill, and confined to her bed; and, after several days, one of the servants, happening to examine the apparel she had worn on the night of the murder, had discovered in her pocket the picture of my mother, which had been judged to be the temptation of the murderer. The servant instantly shewed it to one of the others, who, without saying a word to any of the family, went to a magistrate; and, upon their deposition, Justine was apprehended. On being charged with the fact, the poor girl confirmed the suspicion in a great measure, by her extreme confusion of manner.

This was a strange tale, but it did not shake my faith; and I replied earnestly, "You are all mistaken; I know the murderer. Justine, poor, good Justine, is innocent."

At that instant my father entered. I saw unhappiness deeply impressed on his countenance, but he endeavoured to welcome me cheerfully; and, after we had exchanged our mournful greeting, would have introduced some other topic than that of our disaster, had not Ernest exclaimed, "Good God, Papa! Victor says that he knows who was the murderer of poor William."

"We do also, unfortunately," replied my father; "for indeed I had rather have been for ever ignorant than have discovered so much depravity and ingratitude in one I valued so highly."

"My dear father, you are mistaken; Justine is innocent."

"If she is, God forbid that she should suffer as guilty. She is to be tried to-day, and I hope, I sincerely hope, that she will be acquitted."

This speech calmed me. I was firmly convinced in my own mind that Justine, and indeed every human being, was guiltless of this murder. I had no fear, therefore, that any circumstantial evidence could be brought forward strong enough to convict her; and, in this assurance, I calmed myself, expecting the trial with eagerness, but without prognosticating an evil result.

We were soon joined by Elizabeth. Time had made great alterations in her form since I had last beheld her. Six years before she had been a pretty, good-humoured girl, whom every one loved and caressed. She was now a woman in stature and expression of countenance, which was uncommonly lovely. An open and capacious forehead gave indications of a good understanding, joined to great frankness of disposition. Her eyes were hazel, and expressive of mildness, now through recent affliction allied to sadness. Her hair was of a rich dark auburn, her complexion fair, and her figure slight and graceful. She welcomed me with the greatest affection. "Your arrival, my dear cousin," said she, "fills me with hope. You perhaps will find some means to justify my poor guiltless Justine. Alas! who is safe, if she be convicted of crime? I rely on her innocence as certainly as I do upon my own. Our misfortune is doubly hard to us; we have not only lost that lovely darling boy, but this poor girl, whom I sincerely love, is to be torn away by even a worse fate. If she is condemned, I never shall know joy more. But she will not, I am sure she will not; and then I shall be happy again, even after the sad death of my little William."

"She is innocent, my Elizabeth," said I, "and that shall be proved; fear nothing, but let your spirits be cheered by the assurance of her acquittal."

"How kind you are! every one else believes in her guilt, and that made me wretched; for I knew that it was impossible: and to see every one else prejudiced in so deadly a manner, rendered me hopeless and despairing." She wept.

"Sweet niece," said my father, "dry your tears. If she is, as you believe, innocent, rely on the justice of our judges, and the activity with which I shall prevent the slightest shadow of partiality."

Chapter 7.

We passed a few sad hours, until eleven o'clock, when the trial was to commence. My father and the rest of the family being obliged to attend as witnesses, I accompanied them to the court. During the whole of this wretched mockery of justice, I suffered living torture. It was to be decided, whether the result of my curiosity and lawless devices would cause the death of two of my fellow-beings: one a smiling babe, full of innocence and joy; the other far more dreadfully murdered, with every aggravation of infamy that could make the murder memorable in horror. Justine also was a girl of merit, and possessed qualities which promised to render her life happy: now all was to be obliterated in an ignominious grave; and I the cause! A thousand times rather would I have confessed myself guilty of the crime ascribed to Justine; but I was absent when it was committed, and such a declaration would have been considered as the ravings of a madman, and would not have exculpated her who suffered through me.

The appearance of Justine was calm. She was dressed in mourning; and her countenance, always engaging, was rendered, by the solemnity of her feelings, exquisitely beautiful. Yet she appeared confident in innocence, and did not tremble, although gazed on and execrated by thousands; for all the kindness which her beauty might otherwise have excited, was obliterated in the minds of the spectators by the imagination of the enormity she was supposed to have committed. She was tranquil, yet her tranquillity was evidently constrained; and as her confusion had before been adduced as a proof of her guilt, she worked up her mind to an appearance of courage. When she entered the court, she threw her eyes round it, and quickly discovered where we were seated. A tear seemed to dim her eye when she saw us; but she quickly recovered herself, and a look of sorrowful affection seemed to attest her utter guiltlessness.

The trial began; and after the advocate against her had stated the charge, several witnesses were called. Several strange facts combined against her, which might have staggered any one who had not such proof of her innocence as I had. She had been out the whole of the night on which the murder had been committed, and towards morning had been perceived by a market-woman not far from the spot where the body of the murdered child had been afterwards found. The woman asked her what she did there; but she looked very strangely, and only returned a confused and unintelligible answer. She returned to the house about eight o'clock; and when one inquired where she had passed the night, she replied, that she had been looking for the child, and demanded earnestly, if any thing had been heard concerning him. When shewn the body, she fell into violent hysterics, and kept her bed for several days. The picture was then produced, which the servant had found in her pocket; and when Elizabeth, in a faltering voice, proved that it was the same which, an hour before the child had been missed, she had placed round his neck, a murmur of horror and indignation filled the court.

Justine was called on for her defence. As the trial had proceeded, her countenance had altered. Surprise, horror, and misery, were strongly expressed. Sometimes she struggled with her tears; but when she was desired to plead, she collected her powers, and spoke in an audible although variable voice:—

"God knows," she said, "how entirely I am innocent. But I do not pretend that my protestations should acquit me: I rest my innocence on a plain and simple explanation of the facts which have been adduced against me; and I hope the character I have always borne will incline my judges to a favourable interpretation, where any circumstance appears doubtful or suspicious."

She then related that, by the permission of Elizabeth, she had passed the evening of the night on which the murder had been committed, at the house of an aunt at Chêne, a village situated at about a league from Geneva. On her return, at about nine o'clock, she met a man, who asked her if she had seen any thing of the child who was lost. She was alarmed by this account, and passed several hours in looking for him, when the gates of Geneva were shut, and she was forced to remain several hours of the night in a barn belonging to a cottage, being unwilling to call up the inhabitants, to whom she was well known. Unable to rest or sleep, she quitted her asylum early, that she might again endeavour to find my brother. If she had gone near the spot where his body lay, it was without her knowledge. That she had been bewildered when questioned by the market-woman, was not surprising, since she had passed a sleepless night, and the fate of poor William was yet uncertain. Concerning the picture she could give no account.

"I know," continued the unhappy victim, "how heavily and fatally this one circumstance weighs against me, but I have no power of explaining it; and when I have expressed my utter ignorance, I am only left to conjecture concerning the probabilities by which it might have been placed in my pocket.

But here also I am checked. I believe that I have no enemy on earth, and none surely would have been so wicked as to destroy me wantonly. Did the murderer place it there? I know of no opportunity afforded him for so doing; or if I had, why should he have stolen the jewel, to part with it again so soon?

"I commit my cause to the justice of my judges, yet I see no room for hope. I beg permission to have a few witnesses examined concerning my character; and if their testimony shall not overweigh my supposed guilt, I must be condemned, although I would pledge my salvation on my innocence."

Several witnesses were called, who had known her for many years, and they spoke well of her; but fear, and hatred of the crime of which they supposed her guilty, rendered them timorous, and unwilling to come forward. Elizabeth saw even this last resource, her excellent dispositions and irreproachable conduct, about to fail the accused, when, although violently agitated, she desired permission to address the court.

"I am," said she, "the cousin of the unhappy child who was murdered, or rather his sister, for I was educated by and have lived with his parents ever since and even long before his birth. It may therefore be judged indecent in me to come forward on this occasion; but when I see a fellow-creature about to perish through the cowardice of her pretended friends, I wish to be allowed to speak, that I may say what I know of her character. I am well acquainted with the accused. I have lived in the same house with her, at one time for five, and at another for nearly two years. During all that period she appeared to me the most amiable and benevolent of human creatures. She nursed Madame Frankenstein, my aunt, in her last illness with the greatest affection and care; and afterwards attended her own mother during a tedious[4] illness, in a manner that excited the admiration of all who knew her. After which she again lived in my uncle's house, where she was beloved by all the family. She was warmly attached to the child who is now dead, and acted towards him like a most affectionate mother. For my own part, I do not hesitate to say, that, notwithstanding all the evidence produced against her, I believe and rely on her perfect innocence. She had no temptation for such an action: as to the bauble on which the chief proof rests, if she had earnestly desired it, I should have willingly given it to her; so much do I esteem and value her."

Excellent Elizabeth! A murmur of approbation was heard; but it was excited by her generous interference, and not in favour of poor Justine, on whom the public indignation was turned with renewed violence, charging her with the blackest ingratitude. She herself wept as Elizabeth spoke, but she did not answer. My own agitation and anguish was extreme during the whole trial. I believed in her innocence; I knew it. Could the dæmon, who had (I did not for a minute doubt) murdered my brother, also in his hellish sport have betrayed the innocent to death and ignominy. I could not sustain the horror of my situation; and when I perceived that the popular voice, and the countenances of the judges, had already condemned my unhappy victim, I rushed out of the court in agony. The tortures of the accused did not equal mine; she was sustained by innocence, but the fangs of remorse tore my bosom, and would not forego their hold.

I passed a night of unmingled wretchedness. In the morning I went to the

4. Long-lasting.

court; my lips and throat were parched. I dared not ask the fatal question; but I was known, and the officer guessed the cause of my visit. The ballots[5] had been thrown; they were all black, and Justine was condemned.

I cannot pretend to describe what I then felt. I had before experienced sensations of horror; and I have endeavoured to bestow upon them adequate expressions, but words cannot convey an idea of the heart-sickening despair that I then endured. The person to whom I addressed myself added, that Justine had already confessed her guilt. "That evidence," he observed, "was hardly required in so glaring a case, but I am glad of it; and, indeed, none of our judges like to condemn a criminal upon circumstantial evidence, be it ever so decisive."

When I returned home, Elizabeth eagerly demanded the result.

"My cousin," replied I, "it is decided as you may have expected; all judges had rather that ten innocent should suffer, than that one guilty should escape. But she has confessed."

This was a dire blow to poor Elizabeth, who had relied with firmness upon Justine's innocence. "Alas!" said she, "how shall I ever again believe in human benevolence? Justine, whom I loved and esteemed as my sister, how could she put on those smiles of innocence only to betray; her mild eyes seemed incapable of any severity or ill-humour, and yet she has committed a murder."

Soon after we heard that the poor victim had expressed a wish to see my cousin. My father wished her not to go; but said, that he left it to her own judgment and feelings to decide. "Yes," said Elizabeth, "I will go, although she is guilty; and you, Victor, shall accompany me: I cannot go alone." The idea of this visit was torture to me, yet I could not refuse.

We entered the gloomy prison-chamber, and beheld Justine sitting on some straw at the further end; her hands were manacled, and her head rested on her knees. She rose on seeing us enter; and when we were left alone with her, she threw herself at the feet of Elizabeth, weeping bitterly. My cousin wept also.

"Oh, Justine!" said she, "why did you rob me of my last consolation. I relied on your innocence; and although I was then very wretched, I was not so miserable as I am now."

"And do you also believe that I am so very, very wicked? Do you also join with my enemies to crush me?" Her voice was suffocated with sobs.

"Rise, my poor girl," said Elizabeth, "why do you kneel, if you are innocent? I am not one of your enemies; I believed you guiltless, notwithstanding every evidence, until I heard that you had yourself declared your guilt. That report, you say, is false; and be assured, dear Justine, that nothing can shake my confidence in you for a moment, but your own confession."

"I did confess; but I confessed a lie. I confessed, that I might obtain absolution; but now that falsehood lies heavier at my heart than all my other sins. The God of heaven forgive me! Ever since I was condemned, my confessor has besieged me; he threatened and menaced, until I almost began to think that I was the monster that he said I was. He threatened excommunication and hell fire in my last moments, if I continued obdurate. Dear lady, I had none to support me; all looked on me as a wretch doomed to ignominy and

5. Small balls used in secret votes.

perdition. What could I do? In an evil hour I subscribed to a lie; and now only am I truly miserable."

She paused, weeping, and then continued—"I thought with horror, my sweet lady, that you should believe your Justine, whom your blessed aunt had so highly honoured, and whom you loved, was a creature capable of a crime which none but the devil himself could have perpetrated. Dear William! dearest blessed child! I soon shall see you again in heaven, where we shall all be happy; and that consoles me, going as I am to suffer ignominy and death."

"Oh, Justine! forgive me for having for one moment distrusted you. Why did you confess? But do not mourn, my dear girl; I will every where proclaim your innocence, and force belief. Yet you must die; you, my playfellow, my companion, my more than sister. I never can survive so horrible a misfortune."

"Dear, sweet Elizabeth, do not weep. You ought to raise me with thoughts of a better life, and elevate me from the petty cares of this world of injustice and strife. Do not you, excellent friend, drive me to despair."

"I will try to comfort you; but this, I fear, is an evil too deep and poignant to admit of consolation, for there is no hope. Yet heaven bless thee, my dearest Justine, with resignation, and a confidence elevated beyond this world. Oh! how I hate its shews and mockeries! when one creature is murdered, another is immediately deprived of life in a slow torturing manner; then the executioners, their hands yet reeking with the blood of innocence, believe that they have done a great deed. They call this *retribution*. Hateful name! When that word is pronounced, I know greater and more horrid punishments are going to be inflicted than the gloomiest tyrant has ever invented to satiate his utmost revenge. Yet this is not consolation for you, my Justine, unless indeed that you may glory in escaping from so miserable a den. Alas! I would I were in peace with my aunt and my lovely William, escaped from a world which is hateful to me, and the visages of men which I abhor."

Justine smiled languidly. "This, dear lady, is despair, and not resignation. I must not learn the lesson that you would teach me. Talk of something else, something that will bring peace, and not increase of misery."

During this conversation I had retired to a corner of the prison-room, where I could conceal the horrid anguish that possessed me. Despair! Who dared talk of that? The poor victim, who on the morrow was to pass the dreary boundary between life and death, felt not as I did, such deep and bitter agony. I gnashed my teeth, and ground them together, uttering a groan that came from my inmost soul. Justine started. When she saw who it was, she approached me, and said, "Dear Sir, you are very kind to visit me; you, I hope, do not believe that I am guilty."

I could not answer. "No, Justine," said Elizabeth; "he is more convinced of your innocence than I was; for even when he heard that you had confessed, he did not credit it."

"I truly thank him. In these last moments I feel the sincerest gratitude towards those who think of me with kindness. How sweet is the affection of others to such a wretch as I am! It removes more than half my misfortune; and I feel as if I could die in peace, now that my innocence is acknowledged by you, dear lady, and your cousin."

Thus the poor sufferer tried to comfort others and herself. She indeed gained the resignation she desired. But I, the true murderer, felt the never-dying worm alive in my bosom,[6] which allowed of no hope or consolation. Elizabeth also wept, and was unhappy; but her's also was the misery of innocence, which, like a cloud that passes over the fair moon, for a while hides, but cannot tarnish its brightness. Anguish and despair had penetrated into the core of my heart; I bore a hell within me, which nothing could extinguish. We staid several hours with Justine; and it was with great difficulty that Elizabeth could tear herself away. "I wish," cried she, "that I were to die with you; I cannot live in this world of misery."

Justine assumed an air of cheerfulness, while she with difficulty repressed her bitter tears. She embraced Elizabeth, and said, in a voice of half-suppressed emotion, "Farewell, sweet lady, dearest Elizabeth, my beloved and only friend; may heaven in its bounty bless and preserve you; may this be the last misfortune that you will ever suffer. Live, and be happy, and make others so."

As we returned, Elizabeth said, "You know not, my dear Victor, how much I am relieved, now that I trust in the innocence of this unfortunate girl. I never could again have known peace, if I had been deceived in my reliance on her. For the moment that I did believe her guilty, I felt an anguish that I could not have long sustained. Now my heart is lightened. The innocent suffers; but she whom I thought amiable and good has not betrayed the trust I reposed in her, and I am consoled."

Amiable cousin! such were your thoughts, mild and gentle as your own dear eyes and voice. But I—I was a wretch, and none ever conceived of the misery that I then endured.

VOLUME 2

Chapter 1.

Nothing is more painful to the human mind, than, after the feelings have been worked up by a quick succession of events, the dead calmness of inaction and certainty which follows, and deprives the soul both of hope and fear. Justine died; she rested; and I was alive. The blood flowed freely in my veins, but a weight of despair and remorse pressed on my heart, which nothing could remove. Sleep fled from my eyes; I wandered like an evil spirit, for I had committed deeds of mischief beyond description horrible, and more, much more, (I persuaded myself) was yet behind. Yet my heart overflowed with kindness, and the love of virtue. I had begun life with benevolent intentions, and thirsted for the moment when I should put them in practice, and make myself useful to my fellow-beings. Now all was blasted:[1] instead of that serenity of conscience, which allowed me to look back upon the past with self-satisfaction, and from thence to gather promise of new hopes, I was seized by remorse and the sense of guilt, which hurried me away to a hell of intense tortures, such as no language can describe.

This state of mind preyed upon my health, which had entirely recovered

6. Jesus describes the sufferings of people in hell: "where their worm dieth not, and the fire is not quenched" (Mark 9.44).
1. Blighted, ruined.

from the first shock it had sustained. I shunned the face of man; all sound of joy or complacency was torture to me; solitude was my only consolation—deep, dark, death-like solitude.

My father observed with pain the alteration perceptible in my disposition and habits, and endeavoured to reason with me on the folly of giving way to immoderate grief. "Do you think, Victor," said he, "that I do not suffer also? No one could love a child more than I loved your brother;" (tears came into his eyes as he spoke); "but is it not a duty to the survivors, that we should refrain from augmenting their unhappiness by an appearance of immoderate grief? It is also a duty owed to yourself; for excessive sorrow prevents improvement or enjoyment, or even the discharge of daily usefulness, without which no man is fit for society."

This advice, although good, was totally inapplicable to my case; I should have been the first to hide my grief, and console my friends, if remorse had not mingled its bitterness with my other sensations. Now I could only answer my father with a look of despair, and endeavour to hide myself from his view.

About this time we retired to our house at Belrive. This change was particularly agreeable to me. The shutting of the gates regularly at ten o'clock, and the impossibility of remaining on the lake after that hour, had rendered our residence within the walls of Geneva very irksome to me. I was now free. Often, after the rest of the family had retired for the night, I took the boat, and passed many hours upon the water. Sometimes, with my sails set, I was carried by the wind; and sometimes, after rowing into the middle of the lake, I left the boat to pursue its own course, and gave way to my own miserable reflections. I was often tempted, when all was at peace around me, and I the only unquiet thing that wandered restless in a scene so beautiful and heavenly, if I except some bat, or the frogs, whose harsh and interrupted croaking was heard only when I approached the shore—often, I say, I was tempted to plunge into the silent lake, that the waters might close over me and my calamities for ever. But I was restrained, when I thought of the heroic and suffering Elizabeth, whom I tenderly loved, and whose existence was bound up in mine. I thought also of my father, and surviving brother: should I by my base desertion leave them exposed and unprotected to the malice of the fiend whom I had let loose among them?

At these moments I wept bitterly, and wished that peace would revisit my mind only that I might afford them consolation and happiness. But that could not be. Remorse extinguished every hope. I had been the author of unalterable evils; and I lived in daily fear, lest the monster whom I had created should perpetrate some new wickedness. I had an obscure feeling that all was not over, and that he would still commit some signal[2] crime, which by its enormity should almost efface the recollection of the past. There was always scope for fear, so long as any thing I loved remained behind. My abhorrence of this fiend cannot be conceived. When I thought of him, I gnashed my teeth, my eyes became inflamed, and I ardently wished to extinguish that life which I had so thoughtlessly bestowed. When I reflected on his crimes and malice, my hatred and revenge burst all bounds of moderation. I would have made a pilgrimage to the highest peak of the Andes, could

2. Conspicuous.

I, when there, have precipitated him to their base. I wished to see him again, that I might wreak the utmost extent of anger on his head, and avenge the deaths of William and Justine.

Our house was the house of mourning. My father's health was deeply shaken by the horror of the recent events. Elizabeth was sad and desponding; she no longer took delight in her ordinary occupations; all pleasure seemed to her sacrilege toward the dead; eternal woe and tears she then thought was the just tribute she should pay to innocence so blasted and destroyed. She was no longer that happy creature, who in earlier youth wandered with me on the banks of the lake, and talked with ecstacy of our future prospects. She had become grave, and often conversed of the inconstancy of fortune, and the instability of human life.

"When I reflect, my dear cousin," said she, "on the miserable death of Justine Moritz, I no longer see the world and its works as they before appeared to me. Before, I looked upon the accounts of vice and injustice, that I read in books or heard from others, as tales of ancient days, or imaginary evils; at least they were remote, and more familiar to reason than to the imagination; but now misery has come home, and men appear to me as monsters thirsting for each other's blood. Yet I am certainly unjust. Every body believed that poor girl to be guilty; and if she could have committed the crime for which she suffered, assuredly she would have been the most depraved of human creatures. For the sake of a few jewels, to have murdered the son of her benefactor and friend, a child whom she had nursed from its birth, and appeared to love as if it had been her own! I could not consent to the death of any human being; but certainly I should have thought such a creature unfit to remain in the society of men. Yet she was innocent. I know, I feel she was innocent; you are of the same opinion, and that confirms me. Alas! Victor, when falsehood can look so like the truth, who can assure themselves of certain happiness? I feel as if I were walking on the edge of a precipice, towards which thousands are crowding, and endeavouring to plunge me into the abyss. William and Justine were assassinated, and the murderer escapes; he walks about the world free, and perhaps respected. But even if I were condemned to suffer on the scaffold for the same crimes, I would not change places with such a wretch."

I listened to this discourse with the extremest agony. I, not in deed, but in effect, was the true murderer. Elizabeth read my anguish in my countenance, and kindly taking my hand said, "My dearest cousin, you must calm yourself. These events have affected me, God knows how deeply; but I am not so wretched as you are. There is an expression of despair, and sometimes of revenge, in your countenance, that makes me tremble. Be calm, my dear Victor; I would sacrifice my life to your peace. We surely shall be happy: quiet in our native country, and not mingling in the world, what can disturb our tranquillity?"

She shed tears as she said this, distrusting the very solace that she gave; but at the same time she smiled, that she might chase away the fiend that lurked in my heart. My father, who saw in the unhappiness that was painted in my face only an exaggeration of that sorrow which I might naturally feel, thought that an amusement suited to my taste would be the best means of restoring to me my wonted serenity. It was from this cause that he had removed to the country; and, induced by the same motive, he now proposed that we should all make an excursion to the valley of Chamounix.[3] I had been there before, but Elizabeth and Ernest never had; and both had often expressed an earnest desire to see the scenery of this place, which had been described to them as so wonderful and sublime. Accordingly we departed from Geneva on this tour about the middle of the month of August, nearly two months after the death of Justine.

The weather was uncommonly fine; and if mine had been a sorrow to be chased away by any fleeting circumstance, this excursion would certainly have had the effect intended by my father. As it was, I was somewhat interested in the scene; it sometimes lulled, although it could not extinguish my grief. During the first day we travelled in a carriage. In the morning we had seen the mountains at a distance, towards which we gradually advanced. We perceived that the valley through which we wound, and which was formed by the river Arve, whose course we followed, closed in upon us by degrees; and when the sun had set, we beheld immense mountains and precipices overhanging us on every side, and heard the sound of the river raging among rocks, and the dashing of waterfalls around.

The next day we pursued our journey upon mules; and as we ascended still higher, the valley assumed a more magnificent and astonishing character. Ruined castles hanging on the precipices of piny mountains; the impetuous Arve, and cottages every here and there peeping forth from among the trees, formed a scene of singular beauty. But it was augmented and rendered sublime by the mighty Alps, whose white and shining pyramids and domes towered above all, as belonging to another earth, the habitations of another race of beings.

We passed the bridge of Pelissier, where the ravine, which the river forms, opened before us, and we began to ascend the mountain that overhangs it. Soon after we entered the valley of Chamounix. This valley is more wonderful and sublime, but not so beautiful and picturesque as that of Servox, through which we had just passed. The high and snowy mountains were its immediate boundaries; but we saw no more ruined castles and fertile fields. Immense glaciers approached the road; we heard the rumbling thunder of the falling avalanche, and marked the smoke of its passage. Mont Blanc, the supreme and magnificent Mont Blanc, raised itself from the surrounding *aiguilles*, and its tremendous *dome*[4] overlooked the valley.

During this journey, I sometimes joined Elizabeth, and exerted myself to point out to her the various beauties of the scene. I often suffered my mule to lag behind, and indulged in the misery of reflection. At other times I spurred on the animal before my companions, that I might forget them, the world, and, more than all, myself. When at a distance, I alighted, and threw myself on the grass, weighed down by horror and despair. At eight in the evening I arrived at Chamounix. My father and Elizabeth were very much fatigued; Ernest, who accompanied us, was delighted, and in high spirits: the only circumstance that detracted from his pleasure was the south wind, and the rain it seemed to promise for the next day.

We retired early to our apartments, but not to sleep; at least I did not. I remained many hours at the window, watching the pallid lightning that

3. At the foot of Mont Blanc, the highest mountain in the Alps. The Shelleys toured the valley and its glacier in 1816—the occasion of Percy's poem

Mont Blanc (p. 720).
4. The rounded, snow-covered summit of Mont Blanc. "*Aiguilles*": narrow, pointed peaks.

played above Mont Blanc, and listening to the rushing of the Arve, which ran below my window.

Chapter 2.

The next day, contrary to the prognostications of our guides, was fine, although clouded. We visited the source of the Arveiron, and rode about the valley until evening. These sublime and magnificent scenes afforded me the greatest consolation that I was capable of receiving. They elevated me from all littleness of feeling; and although they did not remove my grief, they subdued and tranquillized it. In some degree, also, they diverted my mind from the thoughts over which it had brooded for the last month. I returned in the evening, fatigued, but less unhappy, and conversed with my family with more cheerfulness than had been my custom for some time. My father was pleased, and Elizabeth overjoyed. "My dear cousin," said she, "you see what happiness you diffuse when you are happy; do not relapse again!"

The following morning the rain poured down in torrents, and thick mists hid the summits of the mountains. I rose early, but felt unusually melancholy. The rain depressed me; my old feelings recurred, and I was miserable. I knew how disappointed my father would be at this sudden change, and I wished to avoid him until I had recovered myself so far as to be enabled to conceal those feelings that overpowered me. I knew that they would remain that day at the inn; and as I had ever inured myself to rain, moisture, and cold, I resolved to go alone to the summit of Montanvert. I remembered the effect that the view of the tremendous and ever-moving glacier had produced upon my mind when I first saw it. It had then filled me with a sublime ecstacy that gave wings to the soul, and allowed it to soar from the obscure world to light and joy. The sight of the awful[5] and majestic in nature had indeed always the effect of solemnizing my mind, and causing me to forget the passing cares of life. I determined to go alone, for I was well acquainted with the path, and the presence of another would destroy the solitary grandeur of the scene.

The ascent is precipitous, but the path is cut into continual and short windings, which enable you to surmount the perpendicularity of the mountain. It is a scene terrifically desolate. In a thousand spots the traces of the winter avalanche may be perceived, where trees lie broken and strewed on the ground; some entirely destroyed, others bent, leaning upon the jutting rocks of the mountain, or transversely upon other trees. The path, as you ascend higher, is intersected by ravines of snow, down which stones continually roll from above; one of them is particularly dangerous, as the slightest sound, such as even speaking in a loud voice, produces a concussion of air sufficient to draw destruction upon the head of the speaker. The pines are not tall or luxuriant, but they are sombre, and add an air of severity to the scene. I looked on the valley beneath; vast mists were rising from the rivers which ran through it, and curling in thick wreaths around the opposite mountains, whose summits were hid in the uniform clouds, while rain poured from the dark sky, and added to the melancholy impression I received

5. Awe-inspiring.

from the objects around me. Alas! why does man boast of sensibilities superior to those apparent in the brute; it only renders them more necessary[6] beings. If our impulses were confined to hunger, thirst, and desire, we might be nearly free; but now we are moved by every wind that blows, and a chance word or scene that that word may convey to us.

> We rest; a dream has power to poison sleep.
>   We rise; one wand'ring thought pollutes the day.
> We feel, conceive, or reason; laugh, or weep,
>   Embrace fond woe, or cast our cares away;
> It is the same: for, be it joy or sorrow,
>   The path of its departure still is free.
> Man's yesterday may ne'er be like his morrow;
>   Naught may endure but mutability![7]

It was nearly noon when I arrived at the top of the ascent. For some time I sat upon the rock that overlooks the sea of ice.[8] A mist covered both that and the surrounding mountains. Presently a breeze dissipated the cloud, and I descended upon the glacier. The surface is very uneven, rising like the waves of a troubled sea, descending low, and interspersed by rifts that sink deep. The field of ice is almost a league[9] in width, but I spent nearly two hours in crossing it. The opposite mountain is a bare perpendicular rock. From the side where I now stood Montanvert was exactly opposite, at the distance of a league; and above it rose Mont Blanc, in awful majesty. I remained in a recess of the rock, gazing on this wonderful and stupendous scene. The sea, or rather the vast river of ice, wound among its dependent mountains, whose aërial summits hung over its recesses. Their icy and glittering peaks shone in the sunlight over the clouds. My heart, which was before sorrowful, now swelled with something like joy; I exclaimed—"Wandering spirits, if indeed ye wander, and do not rest in your narrow beds, allow me this faint happiness, or take me, as your companion, away from the joys of life."

As I said this, I suddenly beheld the figure of a man, at some distance, advancing towards me with superhuman speed. He bounded over the crevices in the ice, among which I had walked with caution; his stature also, as he approached, seemed to exceed that of man. I was troubled: a mist came over my eyes, and I felt a faintness seize me; but I was quickly restored by the cold gale of the mountains. I perceived, as the shape came nearer, (sight tremendous and abhorred!) that it was the wretch whom I had created. I trembled with rage and horror, resolving to wait his approach, and then close with him in mortal combat. He approached; his countenance bespoke bitter anguish, combined with disdain and malignity, while its unearthly ugliness rendered it almost too horrible for human eyes. But I scarcely observed this; anger and hatred had at first deprived me of utterance, and I recovered only to overwhelm him with words expressive of furious detestation and contempt.

"Devil!" I exclaimed, "do you dare approach me? and do not you fear the

6. I.e., acting more by necessity than by free choice.
7. Shelley's Poems.—"On Mutability" [Mary Shelley's note]. This is the second half of the sixteen-line poem, (p. 701).
8. The glacier descending from Mont Blanc is named Mer de Glace (sea of ice).
9. Three miles.

fierce vengeance of my arm wreaked on your miserable head? Begone, vile insect! or rather stay, that I may trample you to dust! and, oh, that I could, with the extinction of your miserable existence, restore those victims whom you have diabolically murdered!"

"I expected this reception," said the dæmon. "All men hate the wretched; how then must I be hated, who am miserable beyond all living things! Yet you, my creator, detest and spurn me, thy creature, to whom thou art bound by ties only dissoluble by the annihilation of one of us. You purpose to kill me. How dare you sport thus with life? Do your duty towards me, and I will do mine towards you and the rest of mankind. If you will comply with my conditions, I will leave them and you at peace; but if you refuse, I will glut the maw of death, until it be satiated with the blood of your remaining friends."

"Abhorred monster! fiend that thou art! the tortures of hell are too mild a vengeance for thy crimes. Wretched devil! you reproach me with your creation; come on then, that I may extinguish the spark which I so negligently bestowed."

My rage was without bounds; I sprang on him, impelled by all the feelings which can arm one being against the existence of another.

He easily eluded me, and said,

"Be calm! I entreat you to hear me, before you give vent to your hatred on my devoted head. Have I not suffered enough, that you seek to increase my misery? Life, although it may only be an accumulation of anguish, is dear to me, and I will defend it. Remember, thou hast made me more powerful than thyself; my height is superior to thine; my joints more supple. But I will not be tempted to set myself in opposition to thee. I am thy creature and I will be even mild and docile to my natural lord and King, if thou wilt also perform thy part, the which thou owest me. Oh, Frankenstein, be not equitable to every other, and trample upon me alone, to whom thy justice, and even thy clemency and affection, is most due. Remember, that I am thy creature: I ought to be thy Adam; but I am rather the fallen angel, whom thou drivest from joy for no misdeed. Every where I see bliss, from which I alone am irrevocably excluded. I was benevolent and good; misery made me a fiend. Make me happy, and I shall again be virtuous."

"Begone! I will not hear you. There can be no community between you and me; we are enemies. Begone, or let us try our strength in a fight, in which one must fall."

"How can I move thee? Will no entreaties cause thee to turn a favourable eye upon thy creature, who implores thy goodness and compassion. Believe me, Frankenstein: I was benevolent; my soul glowed with love and humanity: but am I not alone, miserably alone? You, my creator, abhor me; what hope can I gather from your fellow-creatures, who owe me nothing? they spurn and hate me. The desert mountains and dreary glaciers are my refuge. I have wandered here many days; the caves of ice, which I only do not fear, are a dwelling to me, and the only one which man does not grudge. These bleak skies I hail, for they are kinder to me than your fellow-beings. If the multitude of mankind knew of my existence, they would do as you do, and arm themselves for my destruction. Shall I not then hate them who abhor me? I will keep no terms with my enemies. I am miserable, and they shall share my wretchedness. Yet it is in your power to recompense me, and deliver them from an evil which it only remains for you to make so great, that not only you and your family, but thousands of others, shall be swallowed up in the whirlwinds of its rage. Let your compassion be moved, and do not disdain me. Listen to my tale: when you have heard that, abandon or commiserate me, as you shall judge that I deserve. But hear me. The guilty are allowed, by human laws, bloody as they may be, to speak in their own defence before they are condemned. Listen to me, Frankenstein. You accuse me of murder; and yet you would, with a satisfied conscience, destroy your own creature. Oh, praise the eternal justice of man! Yet I ask you not to spare me: listen to me; and then, if you can, and if you will, destroy the work of your hands."

"Why do you call to my remembrance circumstances of which I shudder to reflect, that I have been the miserable origin and author? Cursed be the day, abhorred devil, in which you first saw light! Cursed (although I curse myself) be the hands that formed you! You have made me wretched beyond expression. You have left me no power to consider whether I am just to you, or not. Begone! relieve me from the sight of your detested form."

"Thus I relieve thee, my creator," he said, and placed his hated hands before my eyes, which I flung from me with violence; "thus I take from thee a sight which you abhor. Still thou canst listen to me, and grant me thy compassion. By the virtues that I once possessed, I demand this from you. Hear my tale; it is long and strange, and the temperature of this place is not fitting to your fine[1] sensations; come to the hut upon the mountain. The sun is yet high in the heavens; before it descends to hide itself behind yon snowy precipices, and illuminate another world, you will have heard my story, and can decide. On you it rests, whether I quit for ever the neighbourhood of man, and lead a harmless life, or become the scourge of your fellow-creatures, and the author of your own speedy ruin."

As he said this, he led the way across the ice: I followed. My heart was full, and I did not answer him; but, as I proceeded, I weighed the various arguments that he had used, and determined at least to listen to his tale. I was partly urged by curiosity, and compassion confirmed my resolution. I had hitherto supposed him to be the murderer of my brother, and I eagerly sought a confirmation or denial of this opinion. For the first time, also, I felt what the duties of a creator towards his creature were, and that I ought to render him happy before I complained of his wickedness. These motives urged me to comply with his demand. We crossed the ice, therefore, and ascended the opposite rock. The air was cold, and the rain again began to descend: we entered the hut, the fiend with an air of exultation, I with a heavy heart, and depressed spirits. But I consented to listen; and, seating myself by the fire which my odious companion had lighted, he thus began his tale.

Chapter 3.

"It is with considerable difficulty that I remember the original æra of my being: all the events of that period appear confused and indistinct. A strange multiplicity of sensations seized me, and I saw, felt, heard, and smelt, at the same time; and it was, indeed, a long time before I learned to distinguish

1. Delicate.

between the operations of my various senses. By degrees, I remember, a stronger light pressed upon my nerves, so that I was obliged to shut my eyes. Darkness then came over me, and troubled me; but hardly had I felt this, when, by opening my eyes, as I now suppose, the light poured in upon me again. I walked, and, I believe, descended; but I presently found a great alteration in my sensations. Before, dark and opaque bodies had surrounded me, impervious to my touch or sight; but I now found that I could wander on at liberty, with no obstacles which I could not either surmount or avoid. The light became more and more oppressive to me; and, the heat wearying me as I walked, I sought a place where I could receive shade. This was the forest near Ingolstadt; and here I lay by the side of a brook resting from my fatigue, until I felt tormented by hunger and thirst. This roused me from my nearly dormant state, and I ate some berries which I found hanging on the trees, or lying on the ground. I slaked my thirst at the brook; and then lying down, was overcome by sleep.

"It was dark when I awoke; I felt cold also, and half-frightened as it were instinctively, finding myself so desolate. Before I had quitted your apartment, on a sensation of cold, I had covered myself with some clothes; but these were insufficient to secure me from the dews of night. I was a poor, helpless, miserable wretch; I knew, and could distinguish, nothing; but, feeling pain invade me on all sides, I sat down and wept.

"Soon a gentle light stole over the heavens, and gave me a sensation of pleasure. I started up, and beheld a radiant form rise from among the trees. I gazed with a kind of wonder. It moved slowly, but it enlightened my path; and I again went out in search of berries. I was still cold, when under one of the trees I found a huge cloak, with which I covered myself, and sat down upon the ground. No distinct ideas occupied my mind; all was confused. I felt light, and hunger, and thirst, and darkness; innumerable sounds rung in my ears, and on all sides various scents saluted[2] me: the only object that I could distinguish was the bright moon, and I fixed my eyes on that with pleasure.

"Several changes of day and night passed, and the orb of night had greatly lessened when I began to distinguish my sensations from each other. I gradually saw plainly the clear stream that supplied me with drink, and the trees that shaded me with their foliage. I was delighted when I first discovered that a pleasant sound, which often saluted my ears, proceeded from the throats of the little winged animals who had often intercepted the light from my eyes. I began also to observe, with greater accuracy, the forms that surrounded me, and to perceive the boundaries of the radiant roof of light which canopied me. Sometimes I tried to imitate the pleasant songs of the birds, but was unable. Sometimes I wished to express my sensations in my own mode, but the uncouth and inarticulate sounds which broke from me frightened me into silence again.

"The moon had disappeared from the night, and again, with a lessened form, shewed itself, while I still remained in the forest. My sensations had, by this time, become distinct, and my mind received every day additional ideas. My eyes became accustomed to the light, and to perceive objects in their right forms; I distinguished the insect from the herb, and, by degrees,

2. Greeted.

one herb from another. I found that the sparrow uttered none but harsh notes, whilst those of the blackbird and thrush were sweet and enticing.

"One day, when I was oppressed by cold, I found a fire which had been left by some wandering beggars, and was overcome with delight at the warmth I experienced from it. In my joy I thrust my hand into the live embers, but quickly drew it out again with a cry of pain. How strange, I thought, that the same cause should produce such opposite effects! I examined the materials of the fire, and to my joy found it to be composed of wood. I quickly collected some branches; but they were wet, and would not burn. I was pained at this, and sat still watching the operation of the fire. The wet wood which I had placed near the heat dried, and itself became inflamed. I reflected on this; and, by touching the various branches, I discovered the cause, and busied myself in collecting a great quantity of wood, that I might dry it, and have a plentiful supply of fire. When night came on, and brought sleep with it, I was in the greatest fear lest my fire should be extinguished. I covered it carefully with dry wood and leaves, and placed wet branches upon it; and then, spreading my cloak, I lay on the ground, and sunk into sleep.

"It was morning when I awoke, and my first care was to visit the fire. I uncovered it, and a gentle breeze quickly fanned it into a flame. I observed this also, and contrived a fan of branches, which roused the embers when they were nearly extinguished. When night came again, I found, with pleasure, that the fire gave light as well as heat; and that the discovery of this element was useful to me in my food; for I found some of the offals that the travellers had left had been roasted, and tasted much more savoury than the berries I gathered from the trees. I tried, therefore, to dress my food in the same manner, placing it on the live embers. I found that the berries were spoiled by this operation, and the nuts and roots much improved.

"Food, however, became scarce; and I often spent the whole day searching in vain for a few acorns to assuage the pangs of hunger. When I found this, I resolved to quit the place that I had hitherto inhabited, to seek for one where the few wants I experienced would be more easily satisfied. In this emigration, I exceedingly lamented the loss of the fire which I had obtained through accident, and knew not how to reproduce it. I gave several hours to the serious consideration of this difficulty; but I was obliged to relinquish all attempt to supply it; and, wrapping myself up in my cloak, I struck across the wood towards the setting sun. I passed three days in these rambles, and at length discovered the open country. A great fall of snow had taken place the night before, and the fields were of one uniform white; the appearance was disconsolate, and I found my feet chilled by the cold damp substance that covered the ground.

"It was about seven in the morning, and I longed to obtain food and shelter; at length I perceived a small hut, on a rising ground, which had doubtless been built for the convenience of some shepherd. This was a new sight to me; and I examined the structure with great curiosity. Finding the door open, I entered. An old man sat in it, near a fire, over which he was preparing his breakfast. He turned on hearing a noise; and, perceiving me, shrieked loudly, and, quitting the hut, ran across the fields with a speed of which his debilitated form hardly appeared capable. His appearance, different from any I had ever before seen, and his flight, somewhat surprised me. But I was enchanted by the appearance of the hut: here the snow and rain could not penetrate; the ground was dry; and it presented to me then as exquisite and divine a retreat as Pandæmonium appeared to the dæmons of hell after their sufferings in the lake of fire.[3] I greedily devoured the remnants of the shepherd's breakfast, which consisted of bread, cheese, milk, and wine; the latter, however, I did not like. [Then] overcome by fatigue, I lay down among some straw, and fell asleep.

"It was noon when I awoke; and, allured by the warmth of the sun, which shone brightly on the white ground, I determined to recommence my travels; and, depositing the remains of the peasant's breakfast in a wallet[4] I found, I proceeded across the fields for several hours, until at sunset I arrived at a village. How miraculous did this appear! the huts, the neater cottages, and stately houses, engaged my admiration by turns. The vegetables in the gardens, the milk and cheese that I saw placed at the windows of some of the cottages, allured my appetite. One of the best of these I entered; but I had hardly placed my foot within the door, before the children shrieked, and one of the women fainted. The whole village was roused; some fled, some attacked me, until, grievously bruised by stones and many other kinds of missile weapons, I escaped to the open country, and fearfully took refuge in a low hovel, quite bare, and making a wretched appearance after the palaces I had beheld in the village. This hovel, however, joined a cottage of a neat and pleasant appearance; but, after my late dearly-bought experience, I dared not enter it. My place of refuge was constructed of wood, but so low, that I could with difficulty sit upright in it. No wood, however, was placed on the earth, which formed the floor, but it was dry; and although the wind entered it by innumerable chinks, I found it an agreeable asylum from the snow and rain.

"Here then I retreated, and lay down, happy to have found a shelter, however miserable, from the inclemency of the season, and still more from the barbarity of man.

"As soon as morning dawned, I crept from my kennel, that I might view the adjacent cottage, and discover if I could remain in the habitation I had found. It was situated against the back of the cottage, and surrounded on the sides which were exposed by a pig-stye and a clear pool of water. One part was open, and by that I had crept in; but now I covered every crevice by which I might be perceived with stones and wood, yet in such a manner that I might move them on occasion to pass out: all the light I enjoyed came through the stye, and that was sufficient for me.

"Having thus arranged my dwelling, and carpeted it with clean straw, I retired; for I saw the figure of a man at a distance, and I remembered too well my treatment the night before, to trust myself in his power. I had first, however, provided for my sustenance for that day, by a loaf of coarse bread, which I purloined, and a cup with which I could drink, more conveniently than from my hand, of the pure water which flowed by my retreat. The floor was a little raised, so that it was kept perfectly dry, and by its vicinity to the chimney of the cottage it was tolerably warm.

"Being thus provided, I resolved to reside in this hovel, until something should occur which might alter my determination. It was indeed a paradise,

---

3. Satan and the other fallen angels build the city of Pandemonium (all-demons) in the fiery regions of Hell. See *Paradise Lost* 1.670ff.
4. Knapsack or satchel.

compared to the bleak forest, my former residence, the rain-dropping branches, and dank earth. I ate my breakfast with pleasure, and was about to remove a plank to procure myself a little water, when I heard a step, and, looking through a small chink, I beheld a young creature, with a pail on her head, passing before my hovel. The girl was young and of gentle demeanour,[5] unlike what I have since found cottagers and farm-house servants to be. Yet she was meanly[6] dressed, a coarse blue petticoat and a linen jacket being her only garb; her fair hair was plaited, but not adorned; she looked patient, yet sad. I lost sight of her; and in about a quarter of an hour she returned, bearing the pail, which was now partly filled with milk. As she walked along, seemingly incommoded by the burden, a young man met her, whose countenance expressed a deeper despondence. Uttering a few sounds with an air of melancholy, he took the pail from her head, and bore it to the cottage himself. She followed, and they disappeared. Presently I saw the young man again, with some tools in his hand, cross the field behind the cottage; and the girl was also busied, sometimes in the house, and sometimes in the yard.

"On examining my dwelling, I found that one of the windows of the cottage had formerly occupied a part of it, but the panes had been filled up with wood. In one of these was a small and almost imperceptible chink, through which the eye could just penetrate. Through this crevice, a small room was visible, white-washed and clean, but very bare of furniture. In one corner, near a small fire, sat an old man, leaning his head on his hands in a disconsolate attitude. The young girl was occupied in arranging the cottage; but presently she took something out of a drawer, which employed her hands, and she sat down beside the old man, who, taking up an instrument, began to play, and to produce sounds, sweeter than the voice of the thrush or the nightingale. It was a lovely sight, even to me, poor wretch! who had never beheld aught beautiful before. The silver hair and benevolent countenance of the aged cottager, won my reverence; while the gentle manners of the girl enticed my love. He played a sweet mournful air, which I perceived drew tears from the eyes of his amiable companion, of which the old man took no notice, until she sobbed audibly; he then pronounced a few sounds, and the fair creature, leaving her work, knelt at his feet. He raised her, and smiled with such kindness and affection, that I felt sensations of a peculiar and overpowering nature: they were a mixture of pain and pleasure, such as I had never before experienced, either from hunger or cold, warmth or food; and I withdrew from the window, unable to bear these emotions.

"Soon after this the young man returned, bearing on his shoulders a load of wood. The girl met him at the door, helped to relieve him of his burden, and, taking some of the fuel into the cottage, placed it on the fire; then she and the youth went apart into a nook of the cottage, and he shewed her a large loaf and a piece of cheese. She seemed pleased; and went into the garden for some roots and plants, which she placed in water, and then upon the fire. She afterwards continued her work, whilst the young man went into the garden, and appeared busily employed in digging and pulling up roots. After he had been employed thus about an hour, the young woman joined him, and they entered the cottage together.

5. I.e., conducting herself like someone of good family and breeding.

6. Coarsely.

"The old man had, in the mean time, been pensive; but, on the appearance of his companions, he assumed a more cheerful air, and they sat down to eat. The meal was quickly dispatched. The young woman was again occupied in arranging the cottage; the old man walked before the cottage in the sun for a few minutes, leaning on the arm of the youth. Nothing could exceed in beauty the contrast between these two excellent creatures. One was old, with silver hairs and a countenance beaming with benevolence and love: the younger was slight and graceful in his figure, and his features were moulded with the finest symmetry; yet his eyes and attitude expressed the utmost sadness and despondency. The old man returned to the cottage; and the youth, with tools different from those he had used in the morning, directed his steps across the fields.

"Night quickly shut in; but, to my extreme wonder, I found that the cottagers had a means of prolonging light, by the use of tapers, and was delighted to find, that the setting of the sun did not put an end to the pleasure I experienced in watching my human neighbours. In the evening, the young girl and her companion were employed in various occupations which I did not understand; and the old man again took up the instrument, which produced the divine sounds that had enchanted me in the morning. So soon as he had finished, the youth began, not to play, but to utter sounds that were monotonous, and neither resembling the harmony of the old man's instrument or the songs of the birds; I since found that he read aloud, but at that time I knew nothing of the science of words or letters.

"The family, after having been thus occupied for a short time, extinguished their lights, and retired, as I conjectured, to rest."

Chapter 4.

"I lay on my straw, but I could not sleep. I thought of the occurrences of the day. What chiefly struck me was the gentle manners of these people; and I longed to join them, but dared not. I remembered too well the treatment I had suffered the night before from the barbarous villagers, and resolved, whatever course of conduct I might hereafter think it right to pursue, that for the present I would remain quietly in my hovel, watching, and endeavouring to discover the motives which influenced their actions.

"The cottagers arose the next morning before the sun. The young woman arranged the cottage, and prepared the food; and the youth departed after the first meal.

"This day was passed in the same routine as that which preceded it. The young man was constantly employed out of doors, and the girl in various laborious occupations within. The old man, whom I soon perceived to be blind, employed his leisure hours on his instrument, or in contemplation. Nothing could exceed the love and respect which the younger cottagers exhibited towards their venerable companion. They performed towards him every little office of affection and duty with gentleness; and he rewarded them by his benevolent smiles.

"They were not entirely happy. The young man and his companion often went apart, and appeared to weep. I saw no cause for their unhappiness; but I was deeply affected by it. If such lovely creatures were miserable, it was less strange that I, an imperfect and solitary being, should be wretched. Yet why were these gentle beings unhappy? They possessed a delightful house (for such it was in my eyes), and every luxury; they had a fire to warm them when chill, and delicious viands when hungry; they were dressed in excellent clothes; and, still more, they enjoyed one another's company and speech, interchanging each day looks of affection and kindness. What did their tears imply? Did they really express pain? I was at first unable to solve these questions; but perpetual attention, and time, explained to me many appearances which were at first enigmatic.

"A considerable period elapsed before I discovered one of the causes of the uneasiness of this amiable family; it was poverty: and they suffered that evil in a very distressing degree. Their nourishment consisted entirely of the vegetables of their garden, and the milk of one cow, who gave very little during the winter, when its masters could scarcely procure food to support it. They often, I believe, suffered the pangs of hunger very poignantly, especially the two younger cottagers; for several times they placed food before the old man, when they reserved none for themselves.

"This trait of kindness moved me sensibly. I had been accustomed, during the night, to steal a part of their store for my own consumption; but when I found that in doing this I inflicted pain on the cottagers, I abstained, and satisfied myself with berries, nuts, and roots, which I gathered from a neighbouring wood.

"I discovered also another means through which I was enabled to assist their labours. I found that the youth spent a great part of each day in collecting wood for the family fire; and, during the night, I often took his tools, the use of which I quickly discovered, and brought home firing sufficient for the consumption of several days.

"I remember, the first time that I did this, the young woman, when she opened the door in the morning, appeared greatly astonished on seeing a great pile of wood on the outside. She uttered some words in a loud voice, and the youth joined her, who also expressed surprise. I observed, with pleasure, that he did not go to the forest that day, but spent it in repairing the cottage, and cultivating the garden.

"By degrees I made a discovery of still greater moment. I found that these people possessed a method of communicating their experience and feelings to one another by articulate sounds. I perceived that the words they spoke sometimes produced pleasure or pain, smiles or sadness, in the minds and countenances of the hearers. This was indeed a godlike science, and I ardently desired to become acquainted with it. But I was baffled in every attempt I made for this purpose. Their pronunciation was quick; and the words they uttered, not having any apparent connexion with visible objects, I was unable to discover any clue by which I could unravel the mystery of their reference. By great application, however, and after having remained during the space of several revolutions of the moon in my hovel, I discovered the names that were given to some of the most familiar objects of discourse: I learned and applied the words *fire*, *milk*, *bread*, and *wood*. I learned also the names of the cottagers themselves. The youth and his companion had each of them several names, but the old man had only one, which was *father*. The girl was called *sister*, or *Agatha*; and the youth *Felix*, *brother*, or *son*. I cannot describe the delight I felt when I learned the ideas appropriated to each of these sounds, and was able to pronounce them. I distinguished several other words, without being able as yet to understand or apply them; such as *good, dearest, unhappy*.

"I spent the winter in this manner. The gentle manners and beauty of the cottagers greatly endeared them to me: when they were unhappy, I felt depressed; when they rejoiced, I sympathized in their joys. I saw few human beings beside them; and if any other happened to enter the cottage, their harsh manners and rude gait only enhanced to me the superior accomplishments of my friends. The old man, I could perceive, often endeavoured to encourage his children, as sometimes I found that he called them, to cast off their melancholy. He would talk in a cheerful accent, with an expression of goodness that bestowed pleasure even upon me. Agatha listened with respect, her eyes sometimes filled with tears, which she endeavoured to wipe away unperceived; but I generally found that her countenance and tone were more cheerful after having listened to the exhortations of her father. It was not thus with Felix. He was always the saddest of the group; and, even to my unpractised senses, he appeared to have suffered more deeply than his friends. But if his countenance was more sorrowful, his voice was more cheerful than that of his sister, especially when he addressed the old man.

"I could mention innumerable instances, which, although slight, marked the dispositions of these amiable cottagers. In the midst of poverty and want, Felix carried with pleasure to his sister the first little white flower that peeped out from beneath the snowy ground. Early in the morning before she had risen, he cleared away the snow that obstructed her path to the milk-house, drew water from the well, and brought the wood from the outhouse, where, to his perpetual astonishment, he found his store always replenished by an invisible hand. In the day, I believe, he worked sometimes for a neighbouring farmer, because he often went forth, and did not return until dinner, yet brought no wood with him. At other times he worked in the garden; but, as there was little to do in the frosty season, he read to the old man and Agatha.

"This reading had puzzled me extremely at first; but, by degrees, I discovered that he uttered many of the same sounds when he read as when he talked. I conjectured, therefore, that he found on the paper signs for speech which he understood, and I ardently longed to comprehend these also; but how was that possible, when I did not even understand the sounds for which they stood as signs? I improved, however, sensibly in this science, but not sufficiently to follow up any kind of conversation, although I applied my whole mind to the endeavour: for I easily perceived that, although I eagerly longed to discover myself to the cottagers, I ought not to make the attempt until I had first become master of their language; which knowledge might enable me to make them overlook the deformity of my figure; for with this also the contrast perpetually presented to my eyes had made me acquainted.

"I had admired the perfect forms of my cottagers—their grace, beauty, and delicate complexions: but how was I terrified, when I viewed myself in a transparent pool! At first I started back, unable to believe that it was indeed I who was reflected in the mirror; and when I became fully convinced that I was in reality the monster that I am, I was filled with the bitterest sensations of despondence and mortification. Alas! I did not yet entirely know the fatal effects of this miserable deformity.

"As the sun became warmer, and the light of day longer, the snow vanished, and I beheld the bare trees and the black earth. From this time Felix was more employed; and the heart-moving indications of impending famine disappeared. Their food, as I afterwards found, was coarse, but it was wholesome; and they procured a sufficiency of it. Several new kinds of plants sprung up in the garden, which they dressed; and these signs of comfort increased daily as the season advanced.

"The old man, leaning on his son, walked each day at noon, when it did not rain, as I found it was called when the heavens poured forth its waters. This frequently took place; but a high wind quickly dried the earth, and the season became far more pleasant than it had been.

"My mode of life in my hovel was uniform. During the morning I attended the motions of the cottagers; and when they were dispersed in various occupations, I slept: the remainder of the day was spent in observing my friends. When they had retired to rest, if there was any moon, or the night was starlight, I went into the woods, and collected my own food and fuel for the cottage. When I returned, as often as it was necessary, I cleared their path from the snow, and performed those offices that I had seen done by Felix. I afterwards found that these labours, performed by an invisible hand, greatly astonished them; and once or twice I heard them, on these occasions, utter the words *good spirit, wonderful*; but I did not then understand the signification of these terms.

"My thoughts now became more active, and I longed to discover the motives and feelings of these lovely creatures; I was inquisitive to know why Felix appeared so miserable, and Agatha so sad. I thought (foolish wretch!) that it might be in my power to restore happiness to these deserving people. When I slept, or was absent, the forms of the venerable blind father, the gentle Agatha, and the excellent Felix, flitted before me. I looked upon them as superior beings, who would be the arbiters of my future destiny. I formed in my imagination a thousand pictures of presenting myself to them, and their reception of me. I imagined that they would be disgusted, until, by my gentle demeanour and conciliating words, I should first win their favour, and afterwards their love.

"These thoughts exhilarated me, and led me to apply with fresh ardour to the acquiring the art of language. My organs were indeed harsh, but supple; and although my voice was very unlike the soft music of their tones, yet I pronounced such words as I understood with tolerable ease. It was as the ass and the lap-dog; yet surely the gentle ass, whose intentions were affectionate, although his manners were rude, deserved better treatment than blows and execration.[7]

"The pleasant showers and genial warmth of spring greatly altered the aspect of the earth. Men, who before this change seemed to have been hid in caves, dispersed themselves, and were employed in various arts of cultivation. The birds sang in more cheerful notes, and the leaves began to bud forth on the trees. Happy, happy earth! fit habitation for gods, which, so short a time before, was bleak, damp, and unwholesome. My spirits were elevated by the enchanting appearance of nature; the past was blotted from my memory, the present was tranquil, and the future gilded by bright rays of hope, and anticipations of joy."

7. The story is told in one of the verse fables by the French writer Jean de La Fontaine (1621–1695). Noting that the Lapdog is petted when he rubs against its master, the Ass imitates the action, but is beaten and berated for doing so.

Chapter 5.

"I now hasten to the more moving part of my story. I shall relate events that impressed me with feelings which, from what I was, have made me what I am.

"Spring advanced rapidly; the weather became fine, and the skies cloudless. It surprised me, that what before was desert and gloomy should now bloom with the most beautiful flowers and verdure. My senses were gratified and refreshed by a thousand scents of delight, and a thousand sights of beauty.

"It was on one of these days, when my cottagers periodically rested from labour—the old man played on his guitar, and the children listened to him—I observed that the countenance of Felix was melancholy beyond expression: he sighed frequently; and once his father paused in his music, and I conjectured by his manner that he inquired the cause of his son's sorrow. Felix replied in a cheerful accent, and the old man was recommencing his music, when some one tapped at the door.

"It was a lady on horseback, accompanied by a countryman as a guide. The lady was dressed in a dark suit, and covered with a thick black veil. Agatha asked a question; to which the stranger only replied by pronouncing, in a sweet accent, the name of Felix. Her voice was musical, but unlike that of either of my friends. On hearing this word, Felix came up hastily to the lady; who, when she saw him, threw up her veil, and I beheld a countenance of angelic beauty and expression. Her hair of a shining raven black, and curiously braided; her eyes were dark, but gentle, although animated; her features of a regular proportion, and her complexion wondrously fair, each cheek tinged with a lovely pink.

"Felix seemed ravished with delight when he saw her, every trait of sorrow vanished from his face, and it instantly expressed a degree of ecstatic joy, of which I could hardly have believed it capable; his eyes sparkled, as his cheek flushed with pleasure; and at that moment I thought him as beautiful as the stranger. She appeared affected by different feelings; wiping a few tears from her lovely eyes, she held out her hand to Felix, who kissed it rapturously, and called her, as well as I could distinguish, his sweet Arabian. She did not appear to understand him, but smiled. He assisted her to dismount, and, dismissing her guide, conducted her into the cottage. Some conversation took place between him and his father; and the young stranger knelt at the old man's feet, and would have kissed his hand, but he raised her, and embraced her affectionately.

"I soon perceived, that although the stranger uttered articulate sounds, and appeared to have a language of her own, she was neither understood by, or herself understood, the cottagers. They made many signs which I did not comprehend; but I saw that her presence diffused gladness through the cottage, dispelling their sorrow as the sun dissipates the morning mists. Felix seemed peculiarly happy, and with smiles of delight welcomed his Arabian. Agatha, the ever-gentle Agatha, kissed the hands of the lovely stranger; and, pointing to her brother, made signs which appeared to me to mean that he had been sorrowful until she came. Some hours passed thus, while they, by their countenances, expressed joy, the cause of which I did not comprehend. Presently I found, by the frequent recurrence of one sound which the stranger repeated after them, that she was endeavouring to learn their language; and the idea instantly occurred to me, that I should make use of the same instructions to the same end. The stranger learned about twenty words at the first lesson, most of them indeed were those which I had before understood, but I profited by the others.

"As night came on, Agatha and the Arabian retired early. When they separated, Felix kissed the hand of the stranger, and said, 'Good night, sweet Safie.' He sat up much longer, conversing with his father; and, by the frequent repetition of her name, I conjectured that their lovely guest was the subject of their conversation. I ardently desired to understand them, and bent every faculty towards that purpose, but found it utterly impossible.

"The next morning Felix went out to his work; and, after the usual occupations of Agatha were finished, the Arabian sat at the feet of the old man, and, taking his guitar, played some airs so entrancingly beautiful, that they at once drew tears of sorrow and delight from my eyes. She sang, and her voice flowed in a rich cadence, swelling or dying away, like a nightingale of the woods.

"When she had finished, she gave the guitar to Agatha, who at first declined it. She played a simple air, and her voice accompanied it in sweet accents, but unlike the wondrous strain of the stranger. The old man appeared enraptured, and said some words, which Agatha endeavoured to explain to Safie, and by which he appeared to wish to express that she bestowed on him the greatest delight by her music."

"The days now passed as peaceably as before, with the sole alteration, that joy had taken place of sadness in the countenances of my friends. Safie was always gay and happy; she and I improved rapidly in the knowledge of language, so that in two months I began to comprehend most of the words uttered by my protectors."

"In the meanwhile also the black ground was covered with herbage, and the green banks interspersed with innumerable flowers, sweet to the scent and the eyes, stars of pale radiance among the moonlight woods; the sun became warmer, the nights clear and balmy; and my nocturnal rambles were an extreme pleasure to me, although they were considerably shortened by the late setting and early rising of the sun; for I never ventured abroad during daylight, fearful of meeting with the same treatment as I had formerly endured in the first village which I entered."

"My days were spent in close attention, that I might more speedily master the language; and I may boast that I improved more rapidly than the Arabian, who understood very little, and conversed in broken accents, whilst I comprehended and could imitate almost every word that was spoken.

"While I improved in speech, I also learned the science of letters, as it was taught to the stranger; and this opened before me a wide field for wonder and delight."

"The book from which Felix instructed Safie was Volney's *Ruins of Empires*.[8] I should not have understood the purport of this book, had not Felix, in reading it, given very minute explanations. He had chosen this work, he said, because the declamatory style was framed in imitation of the eastern

---

8. The comte de Volney published *Les ruines, ou Méditations sur les révolutions des empires* in 1791, the early period of the French Revolution. It surveys the rise and fall of civilizations and looks forward to a future era of rationality, freedom, and justice.

authors. Through this work I obtained a cursory knowledge of history, and a view of the several empires at present existing in the world; it gave me an insight into the manners, governments, and religions of the different nations of the earth. I heard of the slothful Asiatics; of the stupendous genius and mental activity of the Grecians; of the wars and wonderful virtue of the early Romans—of their subsequent degeneration—of the decline of that mighty empire; of chivalry, christianity, and kings. I heard of the discovery of the American hemisphere, and wept with Safie over the hapless fate of its original inhabitants.

"These wonderful narrations inspired me with strange feelings. Was man, indeed, at once so powerful, so virtuous, and magnificent, yet so vicious and base? He appeared at one time a mere scion of the evil principle, and at another as all that can be conceived of noble and godlike. To be a great and virtuous man appeared the highest honour that can befall a sensitive being; to be base and vicious, as many on record have been, appeared the lowest degradation, a condition more abject than that of the blind mole or harmless worm. For a long time I could not conceive how one man could go forth to murder his fellow, or even why there were laws and governments; but when I heard details of vice and bloodshed, my wonder ceased, and I turned away with disgust and loathing.

"Every conversation of the cottagers now opened new wonders to me. While I listened to the instructions which Felix bestowed upon the Arabian, the strange system of human society was explained to me. I heard of the division of property, of immense wealth and squalid poverty; of rank, descent, and noble blood.

"The words induced me to turn towards myself. I learned that the possessions most esteemed by your fellow-creatures were, high and unsullied descent[9] united with riches. A man might be respected with only one of these acquisitions; but without either he was considered, except in very rare instances, as a vagabond and a slave, doomed to waste his powers for the profit of the chosen few. And what was I? Of my creation and creator I was absolutely ignorant; but I knew that I possessed no money, no friends, no kind of property. I was, besides, endowed with a figure hideously deformed and loathsome; I was not even of the same nature as man. I was more agile than they, and could subsist upon coarser diet; I bore the extremes of heat and cold with less injury to my frame; my stature far exceeded their's. When I looked around, I saw and heard of none like me. Was I then a monster, a blot upon the earth, from which all men fled, and whom all men disowned?

"I cannot describe to you the agony that these reflections inflicted upon me; I tried to dispel them, but sorrow only increased with knowledge. Oh, that I had for ever remained in my native wood, nor known or felt beyond the sensations of hunger, thirst, and heat!

"Of what a strange nature is knowledge! It clings to the mind, when it has once seized on it, like a lichen on the rock. I wished sometimes to shake off all thought and feeling; but I learned that there was but one means to overcome the sensation of pain, and that was death—a state which I feared yet did not understand. I admired virtue and good feelings, and loved the gentle manners and amiable qualities of my cottagers; but I was shut out from

9. Ancestry.

intercourse with them, except through means which I obtained by stealth, when I was unseen and unknown, and which rather increased than satisfied the desire I had of becoming one among my fellows. The gentle words of Agatha, and the animated smiles of the charming Arabian, were not for me. The mild exhortations of the old man, and the lively conversation of the loved Felix, were not for me. Miserable, unhappy wretch!

"Other lessons were impressed upon me even more deeply. I heard of the difference of sexes; of the birth and growth of children; how the father doted on the smiles of the infant, and the lively sallies of the older child; how all the life and cares of the mother were wrapt up in the precious charge; how the mind of youth expanded and gained knowledge; of brother, sister, and all the various relationships which bind one human being to another in mutual bonds.

"But where were my friends and relations? No father had watched my infant days, no mother had blessed me with smiles and caresses; or if they had, all my past life was now a blot, a blind vacancy in which I distinguished nothing. From my earliest remembrance I had been as I then was in height and proportion. I had never yet seen a being resembling me, or who claimed any intercourse with me. What was I? The question again recurred, to be answered only with groans.

"I will soon explain to what these feelings tended; but allow me now to return to the cottagers, whose story excited in me such various feelings of indignation, delight, and wonder, but which all terminated in additional love and reverence for my protectors (for so I loved, in an innocent, half painful self-deceit, to call them)."

Chapter 6.

"Some time elapsed before I learned the history of my friends. It was one which could not fail to impress itself deeply on my mind, unfolding as it did a number of circumstances each interesting and wonderful to one so utterly inexperienced as I was.

"The name of the old man was De Lacey. He was descended from a good family in France, where he had lived for many years in affluence, respected by his superiors, and beloved by his equals. His son was bred in the service of his country; and Agatha had ranked with ladies of the highest distinction. A few months before my arrival, they had lived in a large and luxurious city, called Paris, surrounded by friends, and possessed of every enjoyment which virtue, refinement of intellect, or taste, accompanied by a moderate fortune, could afford.

"The father of Safie had been the cause of their ruin. He was a Turkish merchant, and had inhabited Paris for many years, when, for some reason which I could not learn, he became obnoxious to the government. He was seized and cast into prison the very day that Safie arrived from Constantinople to join him. He was tried, and condemned to death. The injustice of his sentence was very flagrant; all Paris was indignant; and it was judged that his religion and wealth, rather than the crime alleged against him, had been the cause of his condemnation.

"Felix had been present at the trial; his horror and indignation were uncontrollable, when he heard the decision of the court. He made, at that moment, would have gloried in it: but the ingratitude of the Turk, and the loss of his beloved Safie, were misfortunes more bitter and irreparable. The arrival of the Arabian now infused new life into his soul.

"When the news reached Leghorn, that Felix was deprived of his wealth and rank, the merchant commanded his daughter to think no more of her lover, but to prepare to return with him to her native country. The generous nature of Safie was outraged by this command; she attempted to expostulate with her father, but he left her angrily, reiterating his tyrannical mandate.

"A few days after, the Turk entered his daughter's apartment, and told her hastily, that he had reason to believe that his residence at Leghorn had been divulged, and that he should speedily be delivered up to the French government; he had, consequently, hired a vessel to convey him to Constantinople, for which city he should sail in a few hours. He intended to leave his daughter under the care of a confidential servant, to follow at her leisure with the greater part of his property, which had not yet arrived at Leghorn.

"When alone, Safie resolved in her own mind the plan of conduct that it would become her to pursue in this emergency. A residence in Turkey was abhorrent to her; her religion and feelings were alike adverse to it. By some papers of her father's, which fell into her hands, she heard of the exile of her lover, and learnt the name of the spot where he then resided. She hesitated some time, but at length she formed her determination. Taking with her some jewels that belonged to her, and a small sum of money, she quitted Italy, with an attendant, a native of Leghorn, but who understood the common language of Turkey, and departed for Germany.

"She arrived in safety at a town about twenty leagues from the cottage of De Lacey, when her attendant fell dangerously ill. Safie nursed her with the most devoted affection; but the poor girl died, and the Arabian was left alone, unacquainted with the language of the country, and utterly ignorant of the customs of the world. She fell, however, into good hands. The Italian had mentioned the name of the spot for which they were bound; and, after her death, the woman of the house in which they had lived took care that Safie should arrive in safety at the cottage of her lover."

Chapter 7.

"Such was the history of my beloved cottagers. It impressed me deeply. I learned, from the views of social life which it developed, to admire their virtues, and to deprecate the vices of mankind.

"As yet I looked upon crime as a distant evil; benevolence and generosity were ever present before me, inciting within me a desire to become an actor in the busy scene where so many admirable qualities were called forth and displayed. But, in giving an account of the progress of my intellect, I must not omit a circumstance which occurred in the beginning of the month of August of the same year.

"One night, during my accustomed visit to the neighbouring wood, where I collected my own food, and brought home firing for my protectors, I found on the ground a leathern portmanteau, containing several articles of dress and some books. I eagerly seized the prize, and returned with it to my hovel. Fortunately the books were written in the language the elements of which I had acquired at the cottage; they consisted of *Paradise Lost*, a volume of

Plutarch's Lives, and the *Sorrows of Werter*.[2] The possession of these treasures gave me extreme delight; I now continually studied and exercised my mind upon these histories, whilst my friends were employed in their ordinary occupations.

"I can hardly describe to you the effect of these books. They produced in me an infinity of new images and feelings, that sometimes raised me to ecstacy, but more frequently sunk me into the lowest dejection. In the *Sorrows of Werter*, besides the interest of its simple and affecting story, so many opinions are canvassed, and so many lights thrown upon what had hitherto been to me obscure subjects, that I found in it a never-ending source of speculation and astonishment. The gentle and domestic manners it described, combined with lofty sentiments and feelings, which had for their object something out of self,[3] accorded well with my experience among my protectors, and with the wants which were for ever alive in my own bosom. But I thought Werter himself a more divine being than I had ever beheld or imagined; his character contained no pretension, but it sunk deep. The disquisitions upon death and suicide were calculated to fill me with wonder. I did not pretend to enter into the merits of the case, yet I inclined towards the opinions of the hero, whose extinction I wept, without precisely understanding it.

"As I read, however, I applied much personally to my own feelings and condition. I found myself similar, yet at the same time strangely unlike the beings concerning whom I read, and to whose conversation I was a listener. I sympathized with, and partly understood them, but I was unformed in mind; I was dependent on none, and related to none. 'The path of my departure was free;'[4] and there was none to lament my annihilation. My person was hideous, and my stature gigantic: what did this mean? Who was I? What was I? Whence did I come? What was my destination? These questions continually recurred, but I was unable to solve them.

"The volume of *Plutarch's Lives* which I possessed, contained the histories of the first founders of the ancient republics. This book had a far different effect upon me from the *Sorrows of Werter*. I learned from Werter's imaginations despondency and gloom: but Plutarch taught me high thoughts; he elevated me above the wretched sphere of my own reflections, to admire and love the heroes of past ages. Many things I read surpassed my understanding and experience. I had a very confused knowledge of kingdoms, wide extents of country, mighty rivers, and boundless seas. But I was perfectly unacquainted with towns, and large assemblages of men. The cottage of my protectors had been the only school in which I had studied human nature; but this book developed new and mightier scenes of action. I read of men concerned in public affairs governing or massacring their species. I felt the greatest ardour for virtue rise within me, and abhorrence for vice, as far as I understood the signification of those terms, relative as they were, as I applied them, to pleasure and pain alone. Induced by these feelings, I was

---

2. The books are in French translations. *Plutarch's Lives*, by the Greek biographer Plutarch (ca. 50–ca. 125 C.E.), recounts the lives of Greek and Roman notables in parallel pairs. *The Sorrows of Young Werther* was an enormously popular and influential novel (1774) by the German author Johann Wolfgang von Goethe about a sensitive and passionate artist who, hopelessly in love with a young woman betrothed to another, shoots himself in despair.
3. Selfless.
4. Alteration of Percy Shelley's *Mutability*, line 14 (p. 701).

of course led to admire peaceable law-givers, Numa, Solon, and Lycurgus, in preference to Romulus and Theseus.[5] The patriarchal lives[6] of my protectors caused these impressions to take a firm hold on my mind; perhaps, if my first introduction to humanity had been made by a young soldier, burning for glory and slaughter, I should have been imbued with different sensations.

"But *Paradise Lost* excited different and far deeper emotions. I read it, as I had read the other volumes which had fallen into my hands, as a true history. It moved every feeling of wonder and awe, that the picture of an omnipotent God warring with his creatures was capable of exciting. I often referred the several situations, as their similarity struck me, to my own. Like Adam, I was created apparently united by no link to any other being in existence; but his state was far different from mine in every other respect. He had come forth from the hands of God a perfect creature, happy and prosperous, guarded by the especial care of his Creator; he was allowed to converse with, and acquire knowledge from beings of a superior nature: but I was wretched, helpless, and alone. Many times I considered Satan as the fitter emblem of my condition; for often, like him, when I viewed the bliss of my protectors, the bitter gall of envy rose within me.

"Another circumstance strengthened and confirmed these feelings. Soon after my arrival in the hovel, I discovered some papers in the pocket of the dress[7] which I had taken from your laboratory. At first I had neglected them; but now that I was able to decypher the characters in which they were written, I began to study them with diligence. It was your journal of the four months that preceded my creation. You minutely described in these papers every step you took in the progress of your work; this history was mingled with accounts of domestic occurrences. You, doubtless, recollect these papers. Here they are. Every thing is related in them which bears reference to my accursed origin; the whole detail of that series of disgusting circumstances which produced it is set in view; the minutest description of my odious and loathsome person is given, in language which painted your own horrors, and rendered mine ineffaceable. I sickened as I read. 'Hateful day when I received life!' I exclaimed in agony. 'Cursed creator! Why did you form a monster so hideous that even you turned from me in disgust? God in pity made man beautiful and alluring, after his own image; but my form is a filthy type of your's, more horrid from its very resemblance. Satan had his companions, fellow-devils, to admire and encourage him; but I am solitary and detested.'

"These were the reflections of my hours of despondency and solitude; but when I contemplated the virtues of the cottagers, their amiable and benevolent dispositions, I persuaded myself that when they should become acquainted with my admiration of their virtues, they would compassionate me, and overlook my personal deformity. Could they turn from their door one, however monstrous, who solicited their compassion and friendship? I

---

5. Only Solon is a historical figure; the others are legendary. Numa Pompilius, the second king of Rome, had a long and peaceful reign that was regarded as a kind of golden age. Solon (ca. 640–ca. 558 B.C.E.) was both a statesman and a poet, famed for instituting an enlightened constitution for Athens. Lycurgus was a reformer of the laws of Sparta. Romulus, held to be a cofounder of Rome with his twin brother Remus, later murdered his brother and planned the rape of the Sabine women. Theseus abandoned Ariadne, after she had given him a thread by which, after killing the Minotaur, he was able to find his way out of the monster's Labyrinth.

6. Lives that are governed by a wise and venerable man.

7. Protective outer garment.

resolved, at least, not to despair, but in every way to fit myself for an interview with them which would decide my fate. I postponed this attempt for some months longer; for the importance attached to its success inspired me with a dread lest I should fail. Besides, I found that my understanding improved so much with every day's experience, that I was unwilling to commence this undertaking until a few more months should have added to my wisdom.

"Several changes, in the mean time, took place in the cottage. The presence of Safie diffused happiness among its inhabitants; and I also found that a greater degree of plenty reigned there. Felix and Agatha spent more time in amusement and conversation, and were assisted in their labours by servants. They did not appear rich, but they were contented and happy; their feelings were serene and peaceful, while mine became every day more tumultuous. Increase of knowledge only discovered to me more clearly what a wretched outcast I was. I cherished hope, it is true; but it vanished, when I beheld my person reflected in water, or my shadow in the moon-shine, even as that frail image and that inconstant shade.

"I endeavoured to crush these fears, and to fortify myself for the trial which in a few months I resolved to undergo; and sometimes I allowed my thoughts, unchecked by reason, to ramble in the fields of Paradise, and dared to fancy amiable and lovely creatures sympathizing with my feelings and cheering my gloom; their angelic countenances breathed smiles of consolation. But it was all a dream: no Eve soothed my sorrows, or shared my thoughts; I was alone. I remembered Adam's supplication to his Creator;[8] but where was mine? he had abandoned me, and, in the bitterness of my heart, I cursed him.

"Autumn passed thus. I saw, with surprise and grief, the leaves decay and fall, and nature again assume the barren and bleak appearance it had worn when I first beheld the woods and the lovely moon. Yet I did not heed the bleakness of the weather; I was better fitted by my conformation[9] for the endurance of cold than heat. But my chief delights were the sight of the flowers, the birds, and all the gay apparel of summer; when those deserted me, I turned with more attention towards the cottagers. Their happiness was not decreased by the absence of summer. They loved, and sympathized with one another; and their joys, depending on each other, were not interrupted by the casualties that took place around them. The more I saw of them, the greater became my desire to claim their protection and kindness; my heart yearned to be known and loved by these amiable creatures: to see their sweet looks turned towards me with affection, was the utmost limit of my ambition. I dared not think that they would turn them from me with disdain and horror. The poor that stopped at their door were never driven away. I asked, it is true, for greater treasures than a little food or rest; I required kindness and sympathy; but I did not believe myself utterly unworthy of it.

"The winter advanced, and an entire revolution of the seasons had taken place since I awoke into life. My attention, at this time, was solely directed towards my plan of introducing myself into the cottage of my protectors. I revolved many projects; but that on which I finally fixed was, to enter the dwelling when the blind old man should be alone. I had sagacity enough to discover, that the unnatural hideousness of my person was the chief object

8. The solitary Adam begs God for "a human consort" in *Paradise Lost* 8.364–451.

9. Constitution.

of horror with those who had formerly beheld me. My voice, although harsh, had nothing terrible in it; I thought, therefore, that if, in the absence of his children, I could gain the good-will and mediation of the old De Lacy, I might, by his means, be tolerated by my younger protectors.

"One day, when the sun shone on the red leaves that strewed the ground, and diffused cheerfulness, although it denied warmth, Safie, Agatha, and Felix, departed on a long country walk, and the old man, at his own desire, was left alone in the cottage. When his children had departed, he took up his guitar, and played several mournful, but sweet airs, more sweet and mournful than I had ever heard him play before. At first his countenance was illuminated with pleasure, but, as he continued, thoughtfulness and sadness succeeded; at length, laying aside the instrument, he sat absorbed in reflection.

"My heart beat quick; this was the hour and moment of trial, which would decide my hopes, or realize my fears. The servants were gone to a neighbouring fair. All was silent in and around the cottage: it was an excellent opportunity; yet, when I proceeded to execute my plan, my limbs failed me, and I sunk to the ground. Again I rose; and, exerting all the firmness of which I was master, removed the planks which I had placed before my hovel to conceal my retreat. The fresh air revived me, and, with renewed determination, I approached the door of their cottage.

"I knocked. 'Who is there?' said the old man—'Come in.'

"I entered; 'Pardon this intrusion,' said I, 'I am a traveller in want of a little rest; you would greatly oblige me, if you would allow me to remain a few minutes before the fire.'

" 'Enter,' said De Lacy; 'and I will try in what manner I can relieve your wants; but, unfortunately, my children are from home, and, as I am blind, I am afraid I shall find it difficult to procure food for you.'

" 'Do not trouble yourself, my kind host, I have food; it is warmth and rest only that I need.'

"I sat down, and a silence ensued. I knew that every minute was precious to me, yet I remained irresolute in what manner to commence the interview; when the old man addressed me—

" 'By your language, stranger, I suppose you are my countryman;—are you French?'

" 'No; but I was educated by a French family, and understand that language only. I am now going to claim the protection of some friends, whom I sincerely love, and of whose favour I have some hopes.'

" 'Are these Germans?'

" 'No, they are French. But let us change the subject. I am an unfortunate and deserted creature; I look around, and I have no relation or friend upon earth. These amiable people to whom I go have never seen me, and know little of me. I am full of fears; for if I fail there, I am an outcast in the world for ever.'

" 'Do not despair. To be friendless is indeed to be unfortunate; but the hearts of men, when unprejudiced by any obvious self-interest, are full of brotherly love and charity. Rely, therefore, on your hopes; and if these friends are good and amiable, do not despair.'

" 'They are kind—they are the most excellent creatures in the world; but, unfortunately, they are prejudiced against me. I have good dispositions; my life has been hitherto harmless, and, in some degree, beneficial; but a fatal prejudice clouds their eyes, and where they ought to see a feeling and kind friend, they behold only a detestable monster.'

" 'That is indeed unfortunate; but if you are really blameless, cannot you undeceive them?'

" 'I am about to undertake that task; and it is on that account that I feel so many overwhelming terrors. I tenderly love these friends; I have, unknown to them, been for many months in the habits of daily kindness towards them; but they believe that I wish to injure them, and it is that prejudice which I wish to overcome.'

" 'Where do these friends reside?'

" 'Near this spot.'

"The old man paused, and then continued, 'If you will unreservedly confide to me the particulars of your tale, I perhaps may be of use in undeceiving them. I am blind, and cannot judge of your countenance, but there is something in your words which persuades me that you are sincere. I am poor, and an exile; but it will afford me true pleasure to be in any way serviceable to a human creature.'

" 'Excellent man! I thank you, and accept your generous offer. You raise me from the dust by this kindness; and I trust that, by your aid, I shall not be driven from the society and sympathy of your fellow-creatures.'

" 'Heaven forbid! even if you were really criminal; for that can only drive you to desperation, and not instigate you to virtue. I also am unfortunate; I and my family have been condemned, although innocent: judge, therefore, if I do not feel for your misfortunes.'

" 'How can I thank you, my best and only benefactor? from your lips first have I heard the voice of kindness directed towards me; I shall be for ever grateful; and your present humanity assures me of success with those friends whom I am on the point of meeting.'

" 'May I know the names and residence of those friends?'

"I paused. This, I thought, was the moment of decision, which was to rob me of, or bestow happiness on me for ever. I struggled vainly for firmness sufficient to answer him, but the effort destroyed all my remaining strength; I sank on the chair, and sobbed aloud. At that moment I heard the steps of my younger protectors. I had not a moment to lose; but, seizing the hand of the old man, I cried, 'Now is the time!—save and protect me! You and your family are the friends whom I seek. Do not you desert me in the hour of trial!'

" 'Great God!' exclaimed the old man, 'who are you?'

"At that instant the cottage door was opened, and Felix, Safie, and Agatha entered. Who can describe their horror and consternation on beholding me? Agatha fainted; and Safie, unable to attend to her friend, rushed out of the cottage. Felix darted forward, and with supernatural force tore me from his father, to whose knees I clung: in a transport of fury, he dashed me to the ground, and struck me violently with a stick. I could have torn him limb from limb, as the lion rends the antelope. But my heart sunk within me as with bitter sickness, and I refrained. I saw him on the point of repeating his blow, when, overcome by pain and anguish, I quitted the cottage, and in the general tumult escaped unperceived to my hovel."

Chapter 8.

"Cursed, cursed creator! Why did I live? Why, in that instant, did I not extinguish the spark of existence which you had so wantonly bestowed? I know not; despair had not yet taken possession of me; my feelings were those of rage and revenge. I could with pleasure have destroyed the cottage and its inhabitants, and have glutted myself with their shrieks and misery.

"When night came, I quitted my retreat, and wandered in the wood; and now, no longer restrained by the fear of discovery, I gave vent to my anguish in fearful howlings. I was like a wild beast that had broken the toils; destroying the objects that obstructed me, and ranging through the wood with a stag-like swiftness. Oh! what a miserable night I passed! the cold stars shone in mockery, and the bare trees waved their branches above me: now and then the sweet voice of a bird burst forth amidst the universal stillness. All, save I, were at rest or in enjoyment: I, like the arch fiend, bore a hell within me;[1] and, finding myself unsympathized with, wished to tear up the trees, spread havoc and destruction around me, and then to have sat down and enjoyed the ruin.

"But this was a luxury of sensation that could not endure; I became fatigued with excess of bodily exertion, and sank on the damp grass in the sick impotence of despair. There was none among the myriads of men that existed who would pity or assist me; and should I feel kindness towards my enemies? No: from that moment I declared everlasting war against the species, and, more than all, against him who had formed me, and sent me forth to this insupportable misery.

"The sun rose; I heard the voices of men, and knew that it was impossible to return to my retreat during that day. Accordingly I hid myself in some thick underwood, determining to devote the ensuing hours to reflection on my situation.

"The pleasant sunshine, and the pure air of day, restored me to some degree of tranquillity; and when I considered what had passed at the cottage, I could not help believing that I had been too hasty in my conclusions. I had certainly acted imprudently. It was apparent that my conversation had interested the father in my behalf, and I was a fool in having exposed my person to the horror of his children. I ought to have familiarized the old De Lacy to me, and by degrees have discovered myself to the rest of his family, when they should have been prepared for my approach. But I did not believe my errors to be irretrievable; and, after much consideration, I resolved to return to the cottage, seek the old man, and by my representations win him to my party.

"These thoughts calmed me, and in the afternoon I sank into a profound sleep; but the fever of my blood did not allow me to be visited by peaceful dreams. The horrible scene of the preceding day was for ever acting before my eyes; the females were flying, and the enraged Felix tearing me from his father's feet. I awoke exhausted; and, finding that it was already night, I crept forth from my hiding-place, and went in search of food.

"When my hunger was appeased, I directed my steps towards the well-known path that conducted to the cottage. All there was at peace. I crept

1. Echoing Satan, *Paradise Lost* 4.75: "Which way I fly is Hell; myself am Hell."

into my hovel, and remained in silent expectation of the accustomed hour when the family arose. That hour past, the sun mounted high in the heavens, but the cottagers did not appear. I trembled violently, apprehending some dreadful misfortune. The inside of the cottage was dark, and I heard no motion; I cannot describe the agony of this suspence.

"Presently two countrymen passed by; but, pausing near the cottage, they entered into conversation, using violent gesticulations; but I did not understand what they said, as they spoke the language of the country,[2] which differed from that of my protectors. Soon after, however, Felix approached with another man: I was surprised, as I knew that he had not quitted the cottage that morning, and waited anxiously to discover, from his discourse, the meaning of these unusual appearances.

" 'Do you consider,' said his companion to him, 'that you will be obliged to pay three months' rent, and to lose the produce of your garden? I do not wish to take any unfair advantage, and I beg therefore that you will take some days to consider of your determination.'

" 'It is utterly useless,' replied Felix, 'we can never again inhabit your cottage. The life of my father is in the greatest danger, owing to the dreadful circumstance that I have related. My wife and my sister will never recover their horror. I entreat you not to reason with me any more. Take possession of your tenement, and let me fly from this place.'

"Felix trembled violently as he said this. He and his companion entered the cottage, in which they remained for a few minutes, and then departed. I never saw any of the family of De Lacy more.

"I continued for the remainder of the day in my hovel in a state of utter and stupid despair. My protectors had departed, and had broken the only link that held me to the world. For the first time the feelings of revenge and hatred filled my bosom, and I did not strive to controul them; but, allowing myself to be borne away by the stream, I bent my mind towards injury and death. When I thought of my friends, of the mild voice of De Lacy, the gentle eyes of Agatha, and the exquisite beauty of the Arabian, these thoughts vanished, and a gush of tears somewhat soothed me. But again, when I reflected that they had spurned and deserted me, anger returned, a rage of anger; and, unable to injure any thing human, I turned my fury towards inanimate objects. As night advanced, I placed a variety of combustibles around the cottage; and, after having destroyed every vestige of cultivation in the garden, I waited with forced impatience until the moon had sunk to commence my operations.

"As the night advanced, a fierce wind arose from the woods, and quickly dispersed the clouds that had loitered in the heavens: the blast tore along like a mighty avalanche, and produced a kind of insanity in my spirits, that burst all bounds of reason and reflection. I lighted the dry branch of a tree, and danced with fury around the devoted cottage, my eyes still fixed on the western horizon, the edge of which the moon nearly touched. A part of its orb was at length hid, and I waved my brand; it sunk, and, with a loud scream, I fired the straw, and heath, and bushes, which I had collected. The wind fanned the fire, and the cottage was quickly enveloped by the flames, which clung to it, and licked it with their forked and destroying tongues.

2. German.

"As soon as I was convinced that no assistance could save any part of the habitation, I quitted the scene, and sought for refuge in the woods.

"And now, with the world before me, whither should I bend my steps?[3] I resolved to fly far from the scene of my misfortunes; but to me, hated and despised, every country must be equally horrible. At length the thought of you crossed my mind. I learned from your papers that you were my father, my creator; and to whom could I apply with more fitness than to him who had given me life? Among the lessons that Felix had bestowed upon Safie geography had not been omitted: I had learned from these the relative situations of the different countries of the earth. You had mentioned Geneva as the name of your native town; and towards this place I resolved to proceed.

"But how was I to direct myself? I knew that I must travel in a south-westerly direction to reach my destination; but the sun was my only guide. I did not know the names of the towns that I was to pass through, nor could I ask information from a single human being; but I did not despair. From you only could I hope for succour, although towards you I felt no sentiment but that of hatred. Unfeeling, heartless creator! you had endowed me with perceptions and passions, and then cast me abroad an object for the scorn and horror of mankind. But on you only had I any claim for pity and redress, and from you I determined to seek that justice which I vainly attempted to gain from any other being that wore the human form.

"My travels were long, and the sufferings I endured intense. It was late in autumn when I quitted the district where I had so long resided. I travelled only at night, fearful of encountering the visage of a human being. Nature decayed around me, and the sun became heatless; rain and snow poured around me; mighty rivers were frozen; the surface of the earth was hard, and chill, and bare, and I found no shelter. Oh, earth! how often did I imprecate curses on the cause of my being! The mildness of my nature had fled, and all within me was turned to gall and bitterness. The nearer I approached to your habitation, the more deeply did I feel the spirit of revenge enkindled in my heart. Snow fell, and the waters were hardened, but I rested not. A few incidents now and then directed me, and I possessed a map of the country; but I often wandered wide from my path. The agony of my feelings allowed me no respite: no incident occurred from which my rage and misery could not extract its food; but a circumstance that happened when I arrived on the confines of Switzerland, when the sun had recovered its warmth, and the earth again began to look green, confirmed in an especial manner the bitterness and horror of my feelings.

"I generally rested during the day, and travelled only when I was secured by night from the view of man. One morning, however, finding that my path lay through a deep wood, I ventured to continue my journey after the sun had risen; the day, which was one of the first of spring, cheered even me by the loveliness of its sunshine and the balminess of the air. I felt emotions of gentleness and pleasure, that had long appeared dead, revive within me. Half surprised by the novelty of these sensations, I allowed myself to be borne away by them; and, forgetting my solitude and deformity, dared to be happy. Soft tears again bedewed my cheeks, and I even raised my humid eyes with thankfulness towards the blessed sun which bestowed such joy upon me.

---

3. An allusion to the close of *Paradise Lost* 12.646–49, beginning: "The world was all before them, where to choose / Their place of rest."

"I continued to wind among the paths of the wood, until I came to its boundary, which was skirted by a deep and rapid river, into which many of the trees bent their branches, now budding with the fresh spring. Here I paused, not exactly knowing what path to pursue, when I heard the sound of voices, that induced me to conceal myself under the shade of a cypress. I was scarcely hid, when a young girl came running towards the spot where I was concealed, laughing as if she ran from some one in sport. She continued her course along the precipitous sides of the river, when suddenly her foot slipt; and she fell into the rapid stream. I rushed from my hiding place, and, with extreme labour from the force of the current, saved her, and dragged her to shore. She was senseless; and I endeavoured, by every means in my power, to restore animation, when I was suddenly interrupted by the approach of a rustic, who was probably the person from whom she had play-fully fled. On seeing me, he darted towards me, and, tearing the girl from my arms, hastened towards the deeper parts of the wood. I followed speedily, I hardly knew why; but when the man saw me draw near, he aimed a gun, which he carried, at my body, and fired. I sunk to the ground, and my injurer, with increased swiftness, escaped into the wood.

"This was then the reward of my benevolence! I had saved a human being from destruction, and, as a recompence, I now writhed under the miserable pain of a wound, which shattered the flesh and bone. The feelings of kind-ness and gentleness, which I had entertained but a few moments before, gave place to hellish rage and gnashing of teeth. Inflamed by pain, I vowed eternal hatred and vengeance to all mankind. But the agony of my wound overcame me; my pulses paused, and I fainted.

"For some weeks I led a miserable life in the woods, endeavouring to cure the wound which I had received. The ball had entered my shoulder, and I knew not whether it had remained there or passed through; at any rate I had no means of extracting it. My sufferings were augmented also by the oppres-sive sense of the injustice and ingratitude of their infliction. My daily vows rose for revenge—a deep and deadly revenge, such as would alone compen-sate for the outrages and anguish I had endured.

"After some weeks my wound healed, and I continued my journey. The labours I endured were no longer to be alleviated by the bright sun or gentle breezes of spring; all joy was but a mockery, which insulted my desolate state, and made me feel more painfully that I was not made for the enjoyment of pleasure.

"But my toils now drew near a close; and, two months from this time, I reached the environs of Geneva.

"It was evening when I arrived, and I retired to a hiding-place among the fields that surround it, to meditate in what manner I should apply to you. I was oppressed by fatigue and hunger, and far too unhappy to enjoy the gentle breezes of evening, or the prospect of the sun setting behind the stupendous mountains of Jura.

"At this time a slight sleep relieved me from the pain of reflection, which was disturbed by the approach of a beautiful child, who came running into the recess I had chosen with all the sportiveness of infancy. Suddenly, as I gazed on him, an idea seized me, that this little creature was unprejudiced, and had lived too short a time to have imbibed a horror of deformity. If, therefore, I could seize him, and educate him as my companion and friend, I should not be so desolate in this peopled earth.

"Urged by this impulse, I seized on the boy as he passed, and drew him towards me. As soon as he beheld my form, he placed his hands before his eyes, and uttered a shrill scream: I drew his hand forcibly from his face, and said, 'Child, what is the meaning of this? I do not intend to hurt you; listen to me.'

"He struggled violently; 'Let me go,' he cried; 'monster! ugly wretch! you wish to eat me, and tear me to pieces—You are an ogre—Let me go, or I will tell my papa.'

" 'Boy, you will never see your father again; you must come with me.'

" 'Hideous monster! let me go; My papa is a Syndic—he is M. Franken-stein—he would punish you. You dare not keep me.'

" 'Frankenstein! you belong then to my enemy—to him towards whom I have sworn eternal revenge; you shall be my first victim.'

"The child still struggled, and loaded me with epithets which carried despair to my heart: I grasped his throat to silence him, and in a moment he lay dead at my feet.

"I gazed on my victim, and my heart swelled with exultation and hellish triumph: clapping my hands, I exclaimed, 'I, too, can create desolation; my enemy is not impregnable; this death will carry despair to him, and a thousand other miseries shall torment and destroy him.'

"As I fixed my eyes on the child, I saw something glittering on his breast. I took it; it was a portrait of a most lovely woman. In spite of my malignity, it softened and attracted me. For a few moments I gazed with delight on her dark eyes, fringerd by deep lashes, and her lovely lips; but presently my rage returned: I remembered that I was for ever deprived of the delights that such beautiful creatures could bestow; and that she whose resemblance I contemplated would, in regarding me, have changed that air of divine benignity to one expressive of disgust and affright.

"Can you wonder that such thoughts transported me with rage? I only wonder that at that moment, instead of venting my sensations in exclamations and agony, I did not rush among mankind, and perish in the attempt to destroy them.

"While I was overcome by these feelings, I left the spot where I had committed the murder, and was seeking a more secluded hiding-place, when I perceived a woman passing near me. She was young, not indeed so beautiful as her whose portrait I held, but of an agreeable aspect, and blooming in the loveliness of youth and health. Here, I thought, is one of those whose smiles are bestowed on all but me; she shall not escape: thanks to the lessons of Felix, and the sanguinary[4] laws of man, I have learned how to work mischief. I approached her unperceived, and placed the portrait securely in one of the folds of her dress.

"For some days I haunted the spot where these scenes had taken place; sometimes wishing to see you, sometimes resolved to quit the world and its miseries for ever. At length I wandered towards these mountains, and have ranged through their immense recesses, consumed by a burning passion which you alone can gratify. We may not part until you have promised to comply with my requisition.[5] I am alone, and miserable; man will not associate with me; but one as deformed and horrible as myself would not deny

---

4. Bloodthirsty.   5. Demand.

herself to me. My companion must be of the same species, and have the same defects. This being you must create."

Chapter 9.

The being finished speaking, and fixed his looks upon me in expectation of a reply. But I was bewildered, perplexed, and unable to arrange my ideas sufficiently to understand the full extent of his proposition. He continued—

"You must create a female for me, with whom I can live in the interchange of those sympathies necessary for my being. This you alone can do; and I demand it of you as a right which you must not refuse."

The latter part of his tale had kindled anew in me the anger that had died away while he narrated his peaceful life among the cottagers, and, as he said this, I could no longer suppress the rage that burned within me.

"I do refuse it," I replied; "and no torture shall ever extort a consent from me. You may render me the most miserable of men, but you shall never make me base in my own eyes. Shall I create another like yourself, whose joint wickedness might desolate the world. Begone! I have answered you; you may torture me, but I will never consent."

"You are in the wrong," replied the fiend; "and, instead of threatening, I am content to reason with you. I am malicious because I am miserable; am I not shunned and hated by all mankind? You, my creator, would tear me to pieces, and triumph; remember that, and tell me why I should pity man more than he pities me? You would not call it murder, if you could precipitate me into one of those ice-rifts, and destroy my frame, the work of your own hands. Shall I respect man, when he contemns[6] me? Let him live with me in the interchange of kindness, and, instead of injury, I would bestow every benefit upon him with tears of gratitude at his acceptance. But that cannot be; the human senses are insurmountable barriers to our union. Yet mine shall not be the submission of abject slavery. I will revenge my injuries: if I cannot inspire love, I will cause fear; and chiefly towards you my arch-enemy, because my creator, do I swear inextinguishable hatred. Have a care: I will work at your destruction, nor finish until I desolate your heart, so that you curse the hour of your birth."

A fiendish rage animated him as he said this; his face was wrinkled into contortions too horrible for human eyes to behold; but presently he calmed himself, and proceeded—

"I intended to reason. This passion is detrimental to me; for you do not reflect that you are the cause of its excess. If any being felt emotions of benevolence towards me, I should return them an hundred and an hundred fold; for that one creature's sake, I would make peace with the whole kind! But I now indulge in dreams of bliss that cannot be realized. What I ask of you is reasonable and moderate; I demand a creature of another sex, but as hideous as myself: the gratification is small, but it is all that I can receive, and it shall content me. It is true, we shall be monsters, cut off from all the world; but on that account we shall be more attached to one another. Our lives will not be happy, but they will be harmless, and free from the misery I now feel. Oh! my creator, make me happy; let me feel gratitude towards

6. Views with contempt.

you for one benefit! Let me see that I excite the sympathy of some existing thing; do not deny me my request!"

I was moved. I shuddered when I thought of the possible consequences of my consent; but I felt that there was some justice in his argument. His tale, and the feelings he now expressed, proved him to be a creature of fine sensations; and did I not, as his maker, owe him all the portion of happiness that it was in my power to bestow? He saw my change of feeling, and continued—

"If you consent, neither you nor any other human being shall ever see us again: I will go to the vast wilds of South America. My food is not that of man; I do not destroy the lamb and the kid, to glut my appetite; acorns and berries afford me sufficient nourishment. My companion will be of the same nature as myself, and will be content with the same fare. We shall make our bed of dried leaves; the sun will shine on us as on man, and will ripen our food. The picture I present to you is peaceful and human, and you must feel that you could deny it only in the wantonness of power and cruelty. Pitiless as you have been towards me, I now see compassion in your eyes; let me seize the favourable moment, and persuade you to promise what I so ardently desire."

"You propose," replied I, "to fly from the habitations of man, to dwell in those wilds where the beasts of the field will be your only companions. How can you, who long for the love and sympathy of man, persevere in this exile? You will return, and again seek their kindness, and you will meet with their detestation; your evil passions will be renewed, and you will then have a companion to aid you in the task of destruction. This may not be; cease to argue the point, for I cannot consent."

"How inconstant are your feelings! but a moment ago you were moved by my representations, and why do you again harden yourself to my complaints? I swear to you, by the earth which I inhabit, and by you that made me, that, with the companion you bestow, I will quit the neighbourhood of man, and dwell, as it may chance, in the most savage of places. My evil passions will have fled, for I shall meet with sympathy; my life will flow quietly away, and, in my dying moments, I shall not curse my maker."

His words had a strange effect upon me. I compassionated him, and sometimes felt a wish to console him; but when I looked upon him, when I saw the filthy mass that moved and talked, my heart sickened, and my feelings were altered to those of horror and hatred. I tried to stifle these sensations; I thought, that as I could not sympathize with him, I had no right to withhold from him the small portion of happiness which was yet in my power to bestow.

"You swear," I said, "to be harmless; but have you not already stewn a degree of malice that should reasonably make me distrust you? May not even this be a feint that will increase your triumph by affording a wider scope for your revenge?"

"How is this? I thought I had moved your compassion, and yet you still refuse to bestow on me the only benefit that can soften my heart, and render me harmless. If I have no ties and no affections, hatred and vice must be my portion; the love of another will destroy the cause of my crimes, and I shall become a thing, of whose existence every one will be ignorant. My vices are the children of a forced solitude that I abhor; and my virtues will necessarily arise when I live in communion with an equal. I shall feel the affections of a sensitive being, and become linked to the chain of existence and events, from which I am now excluded."

I paused some time to reflect on all he had related, and the various arguments which he had employed. I thought of the promise of virtues which he had displayed on the opening of his existence, and the subsequent blight of all kindly feeling by the loathing and scorn which his protectors had manifested towards him. His power and threats were not omitted in my calculations: a creature who could exist in the ice caves of the glaciers, and hide himself from pursuit among the ridges of inaccessible precipices, was a being possessing faculties it would be vain to cope with. After a long pause of reflection, I concluded, that the justice due both to him and my fellow-creatures demanded of me that I should comply with his request. Turning to him, therefore, I said—

"I consent to your demand, on your solemn oath to quit Europe for ever, and every other place in the neighborhood of man, as soon as I shall deliver into your hands a female who will accompany you in your exile."

"I swear," he cried, "by the sun, and by the blue sky of heaven, that if you grant my prayer, while they exist you shall never behold me again. Depart to your home, and commence your labours: I shall watch their progress with unutterable anxiety; and fear not but that when you are ready I shall appear."

Saying this, he suddenly quitted me, fearful, perhaps, of any change in my sentiments. I saw him descend the mountain with greater speed than the flight of an eagle, and quickly lost him among the undulations of the sea of ice.

His tale had occupied the whole day; and the sun was upon the verge of the horizon when he departed. I knew that I ought to hasten my descent towards the valley, as I should soon be encompassed in darkness; but my heart was heavy, and my steps slow. The labour of winding among the little paths of the mountains, and fixing my feet firmly as I advanced, perplexed me, occupied as I was by the emotions which the occurrences of the day had produced. Night was far advanced, when I came to the half-way resting-place, and seated myself beside the fountain. The stars shone at intervals, as the clouds passed from over them; the dark pines rose before me, and every here and there a broken tree lay on the ground: it was a scene of wonderful solemnity, and stirred strange thoughts within me. I wept bitterly; and, clasping my hands in agony, I exclaimed, "Oh! stars, and clouds, and winds, ye are all about to mock me: if ye really pity me, crush sensation and memory; let me become as nought; but if not, depart, depart and leave me in darkness."

These were wild and miserable thoughts; but I cannot describe to you how the eternal twinkling of the stars weighed upon me, and how I listened to every blast of wind, as if it were a dull ugly siroc[7] on its way to consume me.

Morning dawned before I arrived at the village of Chamounix; but my presence, so haggard and strange, hardly calmed the fears of my family, who had waited the whole night in anxious expectation of my return.

The following day we returned to Geneva. The intention of my father in coming had been to divert my mind, and to restore me to my lost tranquillity;

---

7. The sirocco, a hot wind that blows across the Mediterranean from North Africa.

but the medicine had been fatal. And, unable to account for the excess of misery I appeared to suffer, he hastened to return home, hoping the quiet and monotony of a domestic life would by degrees alleviate my sufferings from whatsoever cause they might spring.

For myself, I was passive in all their arrangements; and the gentle affection of my beloved Elizabeth was inadequate to draw me from the depth of my despair. The promise I had made to the dæmon weighed upon my mind, like Dante's iron cowl on the heads of the hellish hypocrites.[8] All pleasures of earth and sky passed before me like a dream, and that thought only had to me the reality of life. Can you wonder, that sometimes a kind of insanity possessed me, or that I saw continually about me a multitude of filthy animals inflicting on me incessant torture, that often extorted screams and bitter groans?

By degrees, however, these feelings became calmed. I entered again into the every-day scene of life, if not with interest, at least with some degree of tranquillity.

VOLUME 3

Chapter 1.

Day after day, week after week, passed away on my return to Geneva; and I could not collect the courage to recommence my work. I feared the vengeance of the disappointed fiend, yet I was unable to overcome my repugnance to the task which was enjoined me. I found that I could not compose a female without again devoting several months to profound study and laborious disquisition.[1] I had heard of some discoveries having been made by an English philosopher, the knowledge of which was material to my success, and I sometimes thought of obtaining my father's consent to visit England for this purpose; but I clung to every pretence of delay, and could not resolve to interrupt my returning tranquillity. My health, which had hitherto declined, was now much restored; and my spirits, when unchecked by the memory of my unhappy promise, rose proportionably. My father saw this change with pleasure, and he turned his thoughts towards the best method of eradicating the remains of my melancholy, which every now and then would return by fits, and with a devouring blackness overcast the approaching sunshine. At these moments I took refuge in the most perfect solitude. I passed whole days on the lake alone in a little boat, watching the clouds, and listening to the rippling of the waves, silent and listless. But the fresh air and bright sun seldom failed to restore me to some degree of composure; and, on my return, I met the salutations of my friends with a readier smile and a more cheerful heart.

It was after my return from one of these rambles that my father, calling me aside, thus addressed me:—

"I am happy to remark, my dear son, that you have resumed your former pleasures, and seem to be returning to yourself. And yet you are still unhappy, and still avoid our society. For some time I was lost in conjecture as to the

8. In Dante's *Inferno* 23.58ff., the hypocrites are crushed by the burden of monks' hoods that, although gilded on the outside, are lined with lead. 1. Investigation.

cause of this; but yesterday an idea struck me, and if it is well founded, I conjure you to avow it. Reserve on such a point would be not only useless, but draw down treble misery on us all."

I trembled violently at this exordium,[2] and my father continued—

"I confess, my son, that I have always looked forward to your marriage with your cousin as the tie of our domestic comfort, and the stay of my declining years. You were attached to each other from your earliest infancy; you studied together, and appeared, in dispositions and tastes, entirely suited to one another. But so blind is the experience of man, that what I conceived to be the best assistants to my plan may have entirely destroyed it. You, perhaps, regard her as your sister, without any wish that she might become your wife. Nay, you may have met with another whom you may love; and, considering yourself as bound in honour to your cousin, this struggle may occasion the poignant misery which you appear to feel."

"My dear father, re-assure yourself. I love my cousin tenderly and sincerely. I never saw any woman who excited, as Elizabeth does, my warmest admiration and affection. My future hopes and prospects are entirely bound up in the expectation of our union."

"The expression of your sentiments on this subject, my dear Victor, gives me more pleasure than I have for some time experienced. If you feel thus, we shall assuredly be happy, however present events may cast a gloom over us. But it is this gloom, which appears to have taken so strong a hold of your mind, that I wish to dissipate. Tell me, therefore, whether you object to an immediate solemnization of the marriage. We have been unfortunate, and recent events have drawn us from that every-day tranquillity befitting my years and infirmities. You are younger; yet I do not suppose, possessed as you are of a competent fortune, that an early marriage would at all interfere with any future plans of honour and utility that you may have formed. Do not suppose, however, that I wish to dictate happiness to you, or that a delay on your part would cause me any serious uneasiness. Interpret my words with candour,[3] and answer me, I conjure you, with confidence and sincerity."

I listened to my father in silence, and remained for some time incapable of offering any reply. I revolved rapidly in my mind a multitude of thoughts, and endeavoured to arrive at some conclusion. Alas! to me the idea of an immediate union with my cousin was one of horror and dismay. I was bound by a solemn promise, which I had not yet fulfilled, and dared not break; or, if I did, what manifold miseries might not impend over me and my devoted family! Could I enter into a festival with this deadly weight yet hanging round my neck, and bowing me to the ground. I must perform my engagement,[4] and let the monster depart with his mate, before I allowed myself to enjoy the delight of an union from which I expected peace.

I remembered also the necessity imposed upon me of either journeying to England, or entering into a long correspondence with those philosophers of that country, whose knowledge and discoveries were of indispensable use to me in my present undertaking. The latter method of obtaining the desired intelligence was dilatory and unsatisfactory: besides, any variation was agreeable to me, and I was delighted with the idea of spending a year or two in

2. Introductory part of a speech.   4. Obligation.
3. Impartiality.

change of scene and variety of occupation, in absence from my family; during which period some event might happen which would restore me to them in peace and happiness: my promise might be fulfilled, and the monster have departed; or some accident might occur to destroy him, and put an end to my slavery for ever.

These feelings dictated my answer to my father. I expressed a wish to visit England; but, concealing the true reasons of this request, I clothed my desires under the guise of wishing to travel and see the world before I sat down for life within the walls of my native town.

I urged my entreaty with earnestness, and my father was easily induced to comply; for a more indulgent and less dictatorial parent did not exist upon earth. Our plan was soon arranged. I should travel to Strasburgh, where Clerval would join me. Some short time would be spent in the towns of Holland, and our principal stay would be in England. We should return by France; and it was agreed that the tour should occupy the space of two years.

My father pleased himself with the reflection, that my union with Elizabeth should take place immediately on my return to Geneva. "These two years," said he, "will pass swiftly, and it will be the last delay that will oppose itself to your happiness. And, indeed, I earnestly desire that period to arrive, when we shall all be united, and neither hopes or fears arise to disturb our domestic calm."

"I am content," I replied, "with your arrangement. By that time we shall both have become wiser, and I hope happier, than we at present are." I sighed; but my father kindly forbore to question me further concerning the cause of my dejection. He hoped that new scenes, and the amusement of travelling, would restore my tranquillity.

I now made arrangements for my journey; but one feeling haunted me, which filled me with fear and agitation. During my absence I should leave my friends unconscious of the existence of their enemy, and unprotected from his attacks, exasperated as he might be by my departure. But he had promised to follow me wherever I might go; and would he not accompany me to England? This imagination was dreadful in itself, but soothing, inasmuch as it supposed the safety of my friends. I was agonized with the idea of the possibility that the reverse of this might happen. But through the whole period during which I was the slave of my creature, I allowed myself to be governed by the impulses of the moment; and my present sensations strongly intimated that the fiend would follow me, and exempt my family from the danger of his machinations.

It was in the latter end of August that I departed, to pass two years of exile. Elizabeth approved of the reasons of my departure, and only regretted that she had not the same opportunities of enlarging her experience, and cultivating her understanding. She wept, however, as she bade me farewell, and entreated me to return happy and tranquil. "We all," said she, "depend upon you; and if you are miserable, what must be our feelings?"

I threw myself into the carriage that was to convey me away, hardly knowing whither I was going, and careless of what was passing around. I remembered only, and it was with a bitter anguish that I reflected on it, to order that my chemical instruments should be packed to go with me: for I resolved to fulfill my promise while abroad, and return, if possible, a free man. Filled with dreary imaginations, I passed through many beautiful and majestic scenes; but my eyes were fixed and unobserving. I could only think of the bourne[5] of my travels, and the work which was to occupy me whilst they endured.

After some days spent in listless indolence, during which I traversed many leagues, I arrived at Strasburgh, where I waited two days for Clerval. He came. Alas, how great was the contrast between us! He was alive to every new scene; joyful when he saw the beauties of the setting sun, and more happy when he beheld it rise, and recommence a new day. He pointed out to me the shifting colours of the landscape, and the appearances of the sky. "This is what it is to live;" he cried, "now I enjoy existence! But you, my dear Frankenstein, wherefore are you desponding and sorrowful?" In truth, I was occupied by gloomy thoughts, and neither saw the descent of the evening star, nor the golden sun-rise reflected in the Rhine.—And you, my friend, would be far more amused with the journal of Clerval, who observed the scenery with an eye of feeling and delight, than to listen to my reflections. I, a miserable wretch, haunted by a curse that shut up every avenue to enjoyment.

We had agreed to descend the Rhine in a boat from Strasburgh to Rotterdam, whence we might take shipping for London. During this voyage, we passed by many willowy islands, and saw several beautiful towns. We staid a day at Manheim, and, on the fifth from our departure from Strasburgh, arrived at Mayence. The course of the Rhine below Mayence becomes much more picturesque. The river descends rapidly, and winds between hills, not high, but steep, and of beautiful forms. We saw many ruined castles standing on the edges of precipices, surrounded by black woods, high and inaccessible. This part of the Rhine, indeed, presents a singularly variegated landscape. In one spot you view rugged hills, ruined castles overlooking tremendous precipices, with the dark Rhine rushing beneath; and, on the sudden turn of a promontory, flourishing vineyards, with green sloping banks, and a meandering river, and populous towns, occupy the scene.

We travelled at the time of the vintage, and heard the song of the labourers, as we glided down the stream. Even I, depressed in mind, and my spirits continually agitated by gloomy feelings, even I was pleased. I lay at the bottom of the boat, and, as I gazed on the cloudless blue sky, I seemed to drink in a tranquillity to which I had long been a stranger. And if these were my sensations, who can describe those of Henry? He felt as if he had been transported to Fairy-land, and enjoyed a happiness seldom tasted by man. "I have seen," he said, "the most beautiful scenes of my own country; I have visited the lakes of Lucerne and Uri, where the snowy mountains descend almost perpendicularly to the water, casting black and impenetrable shades, which would cause a gloomy and mournful appearance, were it not for the most verdant islands that relieve the eye by their gay appearance; I have seen this lake agitated by a tempest, when the wind tore up whirlwinds of water, and gave you an idea of what the water-spout must be on the great ocean, and the waves dash with fury the base of the mountain, where the priest and his mistress were overwhelmed by an avalanche, and where their dying voices are still said to be heard amid the pauses of the nightly wind,[6] I have seen

---

5. Destination.
6. In her *History of a Six Weeks' Tour* (1817), describing her first trip to Europe with Percy Shelley, Mary tells this story of a priest and his mistress who, to avoid persecution, lived in "a cottage at the foot of the snows."

the mountains of La Valais, and the Pays de Vaud: but this country, Victor, pleases me more than all those wonders. The mountains of Switzerland are more majestic and strange; but there is a charm in the banks of this divine river, that I never before saw equalled. Look at that castle which overhangs yon precipice; and that also on the island, almost concealed amongst the foliage of those lovely trees; and now that group of labourers coming from among their vines; and that village half-hid in the recess of the mountain. Oh, surely, the spirit that inhabits and guards this place has a soul more in harmony with man, than those who pile[7] the glacier, or retire to the inaccessible peaks of the mountains of our own country."

Clerval! beloved friend! even now it delights me to record your words, and to dwell on the praise of which you are so eminently deserving. He was a being formed in the "very poetry of nature."[8] His wild and enthusiastic imagination was chastened by the sensibility of his heart. His soul overflowed with ardent affections, and his friendship was of that devoted and wondrous nature that the worldly-minded teach us to look for only in the imagination. But even human sympathies were not sufficient to satisfy his eager mind. The scenery of external nature, which others regard only with admiration, he loved with ardour:

> ——"The sounding cataract
> Haunted *him* like a passion: the tall rock,
> The mountain, and the deep and gloomy wood,
> Their colours and their forms, were then to *him*
> An appetite; a feeling, and a love,
> That had no need of a remoter charm,
> By thought supplied, or any interest
> Unborrowed from the eye."[9]

And where does he now exist? Is this gentle and lovely being lost for ever? Has this mind so replete with ideas, imaginations fanciful and magnificent, which formed a world, whose existence depended on the life of its creator; has this mind perished? Does it now only exist in my memory? No, it is not thus; your form so divinely wrought, and beaming with beauty, has decayed, but your spirit still visits and consoles your unhappy friend.

Pardon this gush of sorrow; these ineffectual words are but a slight tribute to the unexampled worth of Henry, but they soothe my heart, overflowing with the anguish which his remembrance creates. I will proceed with my tale.

Beyond Cologne we descended to the plains of Holland; and we resolved to post[1] the remainder of our way; for the wind was contrary, and the stream of the river was too gentle to aid us.

Our journey here lost the interest arising from beautiful scenery; but we arrived in a few days at Rotterdam, whence we proceeded by sea to England. It was on a clear morning, in the latter days of December, that I first saw the white cliffs of Britain. The banks of the Thames presented a new scene;

---

7. Apparently, "who drive pilings into," as foundations for a building.
8. Leigh Hunt's "Rimini" [Mary Shelley's note]. Hunt's *The Story of Rimini* (1816) is based on Dante's account of the adulterous lovers, Paolo and Francesca, in *The Inferno*, canto 5.

9. Wordsworth's "Tintern Abbey" [Mary Shelley's note]. In the second and fourth lines of this quotation from *Lines Composed a Few Miles above Tintern Abbey*, Shelley changed "me" to "him."
1. Travel by relays of horses.

they were flat, but fertile, and almost every town was marked by the remembrance of some story. We saw Tilbury Fort, and remembered the Spanish armada; Gravesend, Woolwich, and Greenwich, places which I had heard of even in my country.

At length we saw the numerous steeples of London, St. Paul's towering above all, and the Tower famed in English history.

Chapter 2.

London was our present point of rest; we determined to remain several months in this wonderful and celebrated city. Clerval desired the intercourse of[2] the men of genius and talent who flourished at this time; but this was with me a secondary object; I was principally occupied with the means of obtaining the information necessary for the completion of my promise, and quickly availed myself of the letters of introduction that I had brought with me, addressed to the most distinguished natural philosophers.

If this journey had taken place during my days of study and happiness, it would have afforded me inexpressible pleasure. But a blight had come over my existence, and I only visited these people for the sake of the information they might give me on the subject in which my interest was so terribly profound. Company was irksome to me; when alone, I could fill my mind with the sights of heaven and earth; the voice of Henry soothed me, and I could thus cheat myself into a transitory peace. But busy uninteresting joyous faces brought back despair to my heart. I saw an insurmountable barrier placed between me and my fellow-men; this barrier was sealed with the blood of William and Justine; and to reflect on the events connected with those names filled my soul with anguish.

But in Clerval I saw the image of my former self; he was inquisitive, and anxious to gain experience and instruction. The difference of manners which he observed was to him an inexhaustible source of instruction and amusement. He was for ever busy; and the only check to his enjoyments was my sorrowful and dejected mien. I tried to conceal this as much as possible, that I might not debar him from the pleasures natural to one who was entering on a new scene of life, undisturbed by any care or bitter recollection. I often refused to accompany him, alleging another engagement, that I might remain alone. I now also began to collect the materials necessary for my new creation, and this was to me like the torture of single drops of water continually falling on the head. Every thought that was devoted to it was an extreme anguish, and every word that I spoke in allusion to it caused my lips to quiver, and my heart to palpitate.

After passing some months in London, we received a letter from a person in Scotland, who had formerly been our visitor at Geneva. He mentioned the beauties of his native country, and asked us if those were not sufficient allurements to induce us to prolong our journey as far north as Perth, where he resided. Clerval eagerly desired to accept this invitation; and I, although I abhorred society, wished to view again mountains and streams, and all the wondrous works with which Nature adorns her chosen dwelling-places.

We had arrived in England at the beginning of October, and it was now

2. Conversational exchanges with.

February. We accordingly determined to commence our journey towards the north at the expiration of another month. In this expedition we did not intend to follow the great road to Edinburgh, but to visit Windsor, Oxford, Matlock, and the Cumberland lakes, resolving to arrive at the completion of this tour about the end of July. I packed my chemical instruments, and the materials I had collected, resolving to finish my labours in some obscure nook in the northern highlands of Scotland.

We quitted London on the 27th of March, and remained a few days at Windsor, rambling in its beautiful forest. This was a new scene to us mountaineers; the majestic oaks, the quantity of game, and the herds of stately deer, were all novelties to us.

From thence we proceeded to Oxford. As we entered this city, our minds were filled with the remembrance of the events that had been transacted here more than a century and a half before. It was here that Charles I. had collected his forces. This city had remained faithful to him, after the whole nation had forsaken his cause to join the standard of parliament and liberty. The memory of that unfortunate king, and his companions, the amiable Falkland, the insolent Goring, his queen and son, gave a peculiar interest to every part of the city, which they might be supposed to have inhabited.[3] The spirit of elder days found a dwelling here, and we delighted to trace its footsteps. If these feelings had not found an imaginary gratification, the appearance of the city had yet in itself sufficient beauty to obtain our admiration. The colleges are ancient and picturesque; the streets are almost magnificent; and the lovely Isis, which flows beside it through meadows of exquisite verdure, is spread forth into a placid expanse of waters, which reflects its majestic assemblage of towers, and spires, and domes, embosomed among aged trees.

I enjoyed this scene; and yet my enjoyment was embittered both by the memory of the past, and the anticipation of the future. I was formed for peaceful happiness. During my youthful days discontent never visited my mind; and if I was ever overcome by *ennui*, the sight of what is beautiful in nature, or the study of what is excellent and sublime in the productions of man, could always interest my heart, and communicate elasticity to my spirits. But I am a blasted tree; the bolt has entered my soul; and I felt then that I should survive to exhibit, what I shall soon cease to be—a miserable spectacle of wrecked humanity, pitiable to others, and abhorrent to myself.

We passed a considerable period at Oxford, rambling among its environs, and endeavouring to identify every spot which might relate to the most animating epoch of English history. Our little voyages of discovery were often prolonged by the successive objects that presented themselves. We visited the tomb of the illustrious Hampden,[4] and the field on which that patriot fell. For a moment my soul was elevated from its debasing and miserable fears to contemplate the divine ideas of liberty and self-sacrifice, of which these sights were the monuments and the remembrancers. For an instant I

3. The city of Oxford served as the headquarters for Charles I during the Civil War in the 1640s. Viscount Falkland, although his convictions were with the Parliamentary forces, fought for the king and was killed in battle. "The insolent Goring" was Baron Goring, an ambitious general in the Royalist army who injured the king's cause by his intrigues. Charles (the "son") became Charles II at the Restoration in 1660.

4. John Hampden (1599–1643), a powerful debater and popular leader in the Parliamentary cause, was killed in a military skirmish at Chalgrove Field, near Oxford.

dared to shake off my chains, and look around me with a free and lofty spirit; but the iron had eaten into my flesh, and I sank again, trembling and hopeless, into my miserable self.

We left Oxford with regret, and proceeded to Matlock, which was our next place of rest. The country in the neighbourhood of this village resembled, to a greater degree, the scenery of Switzerland; but every thing is on a lower scale, and the green hills want the crown of distant white Alps, which always attend on the piny mountains of my native country. We visited the wondrous cave, and the little cabinets of natural history, where the curiosities[5] are disposed in the same manner as in the collections at Servox and Chamounix. The latter name made me tremble, when pronounced by Henry; and I hastened to quit Matlock, with which that terrible scene was thus associated.

From Derby still journeying northward, we passed two months in Cumberland and Westmoreland.[6] I could now almost fancy myself among the Swiss mountains. The little patches of snow which yet lingered on the northern sides of the mountains, the lakes, and the dashing of the rocky streams, were all familiar and dear sights to me. Here also we made some acquaintances, who almost contrived to cheat me into happiness. The delight of Clerval was proportionably greater than mine; his mind expanded in the company of men of talent, and he found in his own nature greater capacities and resources than he could have imagined himself to have possessed while he associated with his inferiors. "I could pass my life here," said he to me; "and among these mountains I should scarcely regret Switzerland and the Rhine."

But he found that a traveller's life is one that includes much pain amidst its enjoyments. His feelings are for ever on the stretch, and when he begins to sink into repose, he finds himself obliged to quit that on which he rests in pleasure for something new, which again engages his attention, and which also he forsakes for other novelties.

We had scarcely visited the various lakes of Cumberland and Westmoreland, and conceived an affection for some of the inhabitants, when the period of our appointment with our Scotch friend approached, and we left them to travel on. For my own part I was not sorry. I had now neglected my promise for some time, and I feared the effects of the dæmon's disappointment. He might remain in Switzerland, and wreak his vengeance on my relatives. This idea pursued me, and tormented me at every moment from which I might otherwise have snatched repose and peace. I waited for my letters with feverish impatience: if they were delayed, I was miserable, and overcome by a thousand fears; and when they arrived, and I saw the superscription of Elizabeth or my father, I hardly dared to read and ascertain my fate. Sometimes I thought that the fiend followed me, and might expedite my remissness by murdering my companion. When these thoughts possessed me. I would not quit Henry for a moment, but followed him as his shadow, to protect him from the fancied rage of his destroyer. I felt as if I had committed some great crime, the consciousness of which haunted me. I was guiltless, but I had indeed drawn down a horrible curse upon my head, as mortal as that of crime.

5. Rooms where rarities were shown (including both natural objects and works of art and artisanry) were called "cabinets of curiosities."

6. The Lake District, associated with the poets Wordsworth, Coleridge, and Robert Southey.

I visited Edinburgh with languid eyes and mind; and yet that city might have interested the most unfortunate being. Clerval did not like it so well as Oxford; for the antiquity of the latter city was more pleasing to him. But the beauty and regularity of the new town of Edinburgh, its romantic castle, and its environs, the most delightful in the world, Arthur's Seat, St. Bernard's Well, and the Pentland Hills, compensated him for the change, and filled him with cheerfulness and admiration. But I was impatient to arrive at the termination of my journey.

We left Edinburgh in a week, passing through Coupar, St. Andrews, and along the banks of the Tay, to Perth, where our friend expected us. But I was in no mood to laugh and talk with strangers, or enter into their feelings or plans with the good humour expected from a guest; and accordingly I told Clerval that I wished to make the tour of Scotland alone. "Do you," said I, "enjoy yourself, and let this be our rendezvous. I may be absent a month or two; but do not interfere with my motions, I entreat you: leave me to peace and solitude for a short time; and when I return, I hope it will be with a lighter heart, more congenial to your own temper."

Henry wished to dissuade me; but, seeing me bent on this plan, ceased to remonstrate. He entreated me to write often. "I had rather be with you," he said, "in your solitary rambles, than with these Scotch people, whom I do not know: hasten then, my dear friend, to return, that I may again feel myself somewhat at home, which I cannot do in your absence."

Having parted from my friend, I determined to visit some remote spot of Scotland, and finish my work in solitude. I did not doubt but that the monster followed me, and would discover himself to me when I should have finished, that he might receive his companion.

With this resolution I traversed the northern highlands, and fixed on one of the remotest of the Orkneys[7] as the scene of my labours. It was a place fitted for such a work, being hardly more than a rock, whose high sides were continually beaten upon by the waves. The soil was barren, scarcely affording pasture for a few miserable cows, and oatmeal for its inhabitants, which consisted of five persons, whose gaunt and scraggy limbs gave tokens of their miserable fare. Vegetables and bread, when they indulged in such luxuries, and even fresh water, was to be procured from the main land, which was about five miles distant.

On the whole island there were but three miserable huts, and one of these was vacant when I arrived. This I hired. It contained but two rooms, and these exhibited all the squalidness of the most miserable penury. The thatch had fallen in, the walls were unplastered, and the door was off its hinges. I ordered it to be repaired, bought some furniture, and took possession; an incident which would, doubtless, have occasioned some surprise, had not all the senses of the cottagers been benumbed by want and squalid poverty. As it was, I lived ungazed at and unmolested, hardly thanked for the pittance of food and clothes which I gave; so much does suffering blunt even the coarsest sensations of men.

In this retreat I devoted the morning to labour; but in the evening, when the weather permitted, I walked on the stony beach of the sea, to listen to the waves as they roared, and dashed at my feet. It was a monotonous, yet ever-changing scene. I thought of Switzerland; it was far different from this

7. Islands north of Scotland.

desolate and appalling landscape. Its hills are covered with vines, and its cottages are scattered thickly in the plains. Its fair lakes reflect a blue and gentle sky; and, when troubled by the winds, their tumult is but as the play of a lively infant, when compared to the roarings of the giant ocean.

In this manner I distributed my occupations when I first arrived; but, as I proceeded in my labour, it became every day more horrible and irksome to me. Sometimes I could not prevail on myself to enter my laboratory for several days; and at other times I toiled day and night in order to complete my work. It was indeed a filthy process in which I was engaged. During my first experiment, a kind of enthusiastic frenzy had blinded me to the horror of my employment; my mind was intently fixed on the sequel of my labour, and my eyes were shut to the horror of my proceedings. But now I went to it in cold blood, and my heart often sickened at the work of my hands.

Thus situated, employed in the most detestable occupation, immersed in a solitude where nothing could for an instant call my attention from the actual scene in which I was engaged, my spirits became unequal;[8] I grew restless and nervous. Every moment I feared to meet my persecutor. Sometimes I sat with my eyes fixed on the ground, fearing to raise them lest they should encounter the object which I so much dreaded to behold. I feared to wander from the sight of my fellow-creatures, lest when alone he should come to claim his companion.

In the mean time I worked on, and my labour was already considerably advanced. I looked towards its completion with a tremulous and eager hope, which I dared not trust myself to question, but which was intermixed with obscure forebodings of evil, that made my heart sicken in my bosom.

Chapter 3.

I sat one evening in my laboratory; the sun had set, and the moon was just rising from the sea; I had not sufficient light for my employment, and I remained idle, in a pause of consideration of whether I should leave my labour for the night, or hasten its conclusion by an unremitting attention to it. As I sat, a train of reflection occurred to me, which led me to consider the effects of what I was now doing. Three years before I was engaged in the same manner, and had created a fiend whose unparalleled barbarity had desolated my heart, and filled it for ever with the bitterest remorse. I was now about to form another being, of whose dispositions I was alike ignorant; she might become ten thousand times more malignant than her mate, and delight, for its own sake, in murder and wretchedness. He had sworn to quit the neighbourhood of man, and hide himself in deserts; but she had not; and she, who in all probability was to become a thinking and reasoning animal, might refuse to comply with a compact made before her creation. They might even hate each other; the creature who already lived loathed his own deformity, and might he not conceive a greater abhorrence for it when it came before his eyes in the female form? She also might turn with disgust from him to the superior beauty of man; she might quit him, and he be again alone, exasperated by the fresh provocation of being deserted by one of his own species.

Even if they were to leave Europe, and inhabit the deserts of the new

8. Uneven, unsettled.

world, yet one of the first results of those sympathies for which the dæmon thirsted would be children, and a race of devils would be propagated upon the earth, who might make the very existence of the species of man a condition precarious and full of terror. Had I a right, for my own benefit, to inflict this curse upon everlasting generations? I had before been moved by the *sophisms*[9] of the being I had created; I had been struck senseless by his fiendish threats: but now, for the first time, the wickedness of my promise burst upon me; I shuddered to think that future ages might curse me as their pest, whose selfishness had not hesitated to buy its own peace at the price perhaps of the existence of the whole human race.

I trembled, and my heart failed within me; when, on looking up, I saw, by the light of the moon, the dæmon at the casement. A ghastly grin wrinkled his lips as he gazed on me, where I sat fulfilling the task which he had allotted to me. Yes, he had followed me in my travels; he had loitered in forests, hid himself in caves, or taken refuge in wide and desert heaths; and he now came to mark my progress, and claim the fulfilment of my promise.

As I looked on him, his countenance expressed the utmost extent of malice and treachery. I thought with a sensation of madness on my promise of creating another like to him, and, trembling with passion, tore to pieces the thing on which I was engaged. The wretch saw me destroy the creature on whose future existence he depended for happiness, and, with a howl of devilish despair and revenge, withdrew.

I left the room, and, locking the door, made a solemn vow in my own heart never to resume my labours; and then, with trembling steps, I sought my own apartment. I was alone; none were near me to dissipate the gloom, and relieve me from the sickening oppression of the most terrible reveries.

Several hours past, and I remained near my window gazing on the sea; it was almost motionless, for the winds were hushed, and all nature reposed under the eye of the quiet moon. A few fishing vessels alone specked the water, and now and then the gentle breeze wafted the sound of voices, as the fishermen called to one another. I felt the silence, although I was hardly conscious of its extreme profundity, until my ear was suddenly arrested by the paddling of oars near the shore, and a person landed close to my house.

In a few minutes after, I heard the creaking of my door, as if some one endeavoured to open it softly. I trembled from head to foot; I felt a presentiment of who it was, and wished to rouse one of the peasants who dwelt in a cottage not far from mine; but I was overcome by the sensation of helplessness, so often felt in frightful dreams, when you in vain endeavour to fly from an impending danger, and was rooted to the spot.

Presently I heard the sound of footsteps along the passage; the door opened, and the wretch whom I dreaded appeared. Shutting the door, he approached me, and said, in a smothered voice—

"You have destroyed the work which you began; what is it that you intend? Do you dare to break your promise? I have endured toil and misery: I left Switzerland with you; I crept along the shores of the Rhine, among its willow islands, and over the summits of its hills. I have dwelt many months in the heaths of England, and among the deserts of Scotland. I have endured incalculable fatigue, and cold, and hunger; do you dare destroy my hopes?"

---

9. Sophistries; plausible but misleading arguments.

"Begone! I do break my promise; never will I create another like yourself, equal in deformity and wickedness."

"Slave, I before reasoned with you, but you have proved yourself unworthy of my condescension. Remember that I have power; you believe yourself miserable, but I can make you so wretched that the light of day will be hateful to you. You are my creator, but I am your master;—obey!"

"The hour of my weakness is past, and the period[1] of your power is arrived. Your threats cannot move me to do an act of wickedness; but they confirm me in a resolution of not creating you a companion in vice. Shall I, in cool blood, set loose upon the earth a dæmon whose delight is in death and wretchedness? Begone! I am firm, and your words will only exasperate my rage."

The monster saw my determination in my face, and gnashed his teeth in the impotence of anger. "Shall each man," cried he, "find a wife for his bosom, and each beast have his mate, and I be alone? I had feelings of affection, and they were requited by detestation and scorn. Man, you may hate; but beware! Your hours will pass in dread and misery, and soon the bolt will fall which must ravish from you your happiness for ever. Are you to be happy, while I grovel in the intensity of my wretchedness? You can blast my other passions; but revenge remains—revenge, henceforth dearer than light or food! I may die; but first you, my tyrant and tormentor, shall curse the sun that gazes on your misery. Beware; for I am fearless, and therefore powerful. I will watch with the wiliness of a snake, that I may sting with its venom. Man, you shall repent of the injuries you inflict."

"Devil, cease; and do not poison the air with these sounds of malice. I have declared my resolution to you, and I am no coward to bend beneath words. Leave me; I am inexorable."

"It is well. I go; but remember, I shall be with you on your wedding-night."

I started forward, and exclaimed, "Villain! before you sign my death-warrant, be sure that you are yourself safe."

I would have seized him; but he eluded me, and quitted the house with precipitation: in a few moments I saw him in his boat, which shot across the waters with an arrowy swiftness, and was soon lost amidst the waves.

All was again silent; but his words rung in my ears. I burned with rage to pursue the murderer of my peace, and precipitate him into the ocean. I walked up and down my room hastily and perturbed, while my imagination conjured up a thousand images to torment and sting me. Why had I not followed him, and closed with him in mortal strife? But I had suffered him to depart, and he had directed his course towards the main land. I shuddered to think who might be the next victim sacrificed to his insatiate revenge. And then I thought again of his words—"I will be with you on your wedding-night." That then was the period fixed for the fulfilment of my destiny. In that hour I should die, and at once satisfy and extinguish his malice. The prospect did not move me to fear; yet when I thought of my beloved Elizabeth,—of her tears and endless sorrow, when she should find her lover so barbarously snatched from her,—tears, the first I had shed for many months, streamed from my eyes, and I resolved not to fall before my enemy without a bitter struggle.

1. End.

The night passed away, and the sun rose from the ocean; my feelings became calmer, if it may be called calmness, when the violence of rage sinks into the depths of despair. I left the house, the horrid scene of the last night's contention, and walked on the beach of the sea, which I almost regarded as an insuperable barrier between me and my fellow-creatures; nay, a wish that such should prove the fact stole across me. I desired that I might pass my life on that barren rock, wearily it is true, but uninterrupted by any sudden shock of misery. If I returned, it was to be sacrificed, or to see those whom I most loved die under the grasp of a dæmon whom I had myself created.

I walked about the isle like a restless spectre, separated from all it loved, and miserable in the separation. When it became noon, and the sun rose higher, I lay down on the grass, and was overpowered by a deep sleep. I had been awake the whole of the preceding night, my nerves were agitated, and my eyes inflamed by watching and misery. The sleep into which I now sunk refreshed me; and when I awoke, I again felt as if I belonged to a race of human beings like myself, and I began to reflect upon what had passed with greater composure; yet still the words of the fiend rung in my ears like a death-knell, they appeared like a dream, yet distinct and oppressive as a reality.

The sun had far descended, and I still sat on the shore, satisfying my appetite, which had become ravenous, with an oaten cake, when I saw a fishing-boat land close to me, and one of the men brought me a packet; it contained letters from Geneva, and one from Clerval, entreating me to join him. He said that nearly a year had elapsed since we had quitted Switzerland, and France was yet unvisited. He entreated me, therefore, to leave my solitary isle, and meet him at Perth, in a week from that time, when we might arrange the plan of our future proceedings. This letter in a degree recalled me to life, and I determined to quit my island at the expiration of two days.

Yet, before I departed, there was a task to perform, on which I shuddered to reflect: I must pack my chemical instruments; and for that purpose I must enter the room which had been the scene of my odious work, and I must handle those utensils, the sight of which was sickening to me. The next morning, at day-break, I summoned sufficient courage, and unlocked the door of my laboratory. The remains of the half-finished creature, whom I had destroyed, lay scattered on the floor, and I almost felt as if I had mangled the living flesh of a human being. I paused to collect myself, and then entered the chamber. With trembling hand I conveyed the instruments out of the room; but I reflected that I ought not to leave the relics of my work to excite the horror and suspicion of the peasants, and I accordingly put them into a basket, with a great quantity of stones, and laying them up, determined to throw them into the sea that very night; and in the mean time I sat upon the beach, employed in cleaning and arranging my chemical apparatus.

Nothing could be more complete than the alteration that had taken place in my feelings since the night of the appearance of the dæmon. I had before regarded my promise with a gloomy despair, as a thing that, with whatever consequences, must be fulfilled; but I now felt as if a film had been taken from before my eyes, and that I, for the first time, saw clearly. The idea of renewing my labours did not for one instant occur to me; the threat I had heard weighed on my thoughts, but I did not reflect that a voluntary act of mine could avert it. I had resolved in my own mind, that to create another

like the fiend I had first made would be an act of the basest and most atrocious selfishness; and I banished from my mind every thought that could
lead to a different conclusion.

Between two and three in the morning the moon rose; and I then, putting
my basket aboard a little skiff, sailed out about four miles from the shore.
The scene was perfectly solitary: a few boats were returning towards land,
but I sailed away from them. I felt as if I was about the commission of a
dreadful crime, and avoided with shuddering anxiety any encounter with my
fellow-creatures. At one time the moon, which had before been clear, was
suddenly overspread by a thick cloud, and I took advantage of the moment
of darkness, and cast my basket into the sea; I listened to the gurgling sound
as it sunk, and then sailed away from the spot. The sky became clouded; but
the air was pure, although chilled by the north-east breeze that was then
rising. But it refreshed me, and filled me with such agreeable sensations,
that I resolved to prolong my stay on the water, and fixing the rudder in a
direct position, stretched myself at the bottom of the boat. Clouds hid the
moon, every thing was obscure, and I heard only the sound of the boat, as
its keel cut through the waves; the murmur lulled me, and in a short time I
slept soundly.

I do not know how long I remained in this situation, but when I awoke I
found that the sun had already mounted considerably. The wind was high,
and the waves continually threatened the safety of my little skiff. I found
that the wind was north-east, and must have driven me far from the coast
from which I had embarked. I endeavoured to change my course, but quickly
found that if I again made the attempt the boat would be instantly filled with
water. Thus situated, my only resource was to drive before the wind. I confess
that I felt a few sensations of terror. I had no compass with me, and was so
little acquainted with the geography of this part of the world that the sun
was of little benefit to me. I might be driven into the wide Atlantic, and feel
all the tortures of starvation, or be swallowed up in the immeasurable waters
that roared and buffeted around me. I had already been out many hours, and
felt the torment of a burning thirst, a prelude to my other sufferings. I looked
on the heavens, which were covered by clouds that flew before the wind only
to be replaced by others: I looked upon the sea, it was to be my grave. "Fiend,"
I exclaimed, "your task is already fulfilled!" I thought of Elizabeth, of my
father, and of Clerval; and sunk into a reverie, so despairing and frightful,
that even now, when the scene is on the point of closing before me for ever,
I shudder to reflect on it.

Some hours passed thus; but by degrees, as the sun declined towards the
horizon, the wind died away into a gentle breeze, and the sea became free
from breakers. But these gave place to a heavy swell; I felt sick, and hardly
able to hold the rudder, when suddenly I saw a line of high land towards the
south.

Almost spent, as I was, by fatigue, and the dreadful suspense I endured
for several hours, this sudden certainty of life rushed like a flood of warm
joy to my heart, and tears gushed from my eyes.

How mutable are our feelings, and how strange is that clinging love we
have of life even in the excess of misery! I constructed another sail with a
part of my dress, and eagerly steered my course towards the land. It had a
wild and rocky appearance; but as I approached nearer, I easily perceived

the traces of cultivation. I saw vessels near the shore, and found myself suddenly transported back to the neighbourhood of civilized man. I eagerly traced the windings of the land, and hailed a steeple which I at length saw issuing from behind a small promontory. As I was in a state of extreme debility, I resolved to sail directly towards the town as a place where I could most easily procure nourishment. Fortunately I had money with me. As I turned the promontory, I perceived a small neat town and a good harbour, which I entered, my heart bounding with joy at my unexpected escape.

As I was occupied in fixing the boat and arranging the sails, several people crowded towards the spot. They seemed very much surprised at my appearance; but, instead of offering me any assistance, whispered together with gestures that at any other time might have produced in me a slight sensation of alarm. As it was, I merely remarked that they spoke English; and I therefore addressed them in that language: "My good friends," said I, "will you be so kind as to tell me the name of this town, and inform me where I am?"

"You will know that soon enough," replied a man with a gruff voice. "May be you are come to a place that will not prove much to your taste; but you will not be consulted as to your quarters, I promise you."

I was exceedingly surprised on receiving so rude an answer from a stranger; and I was also disconcerted on perceiving the frowning and angry countenances of his companions. "Why do you answer me so roughly?" I replied: "surely it is not the custom of Englishmen to receive strangers so inhospitably."

"I do not know," said the man, "what the custom of the English may be; but it is the custom of the Irish to hate villains."

While this strange dialogue continued, I perceived the crowd rapidly increase. Their faces expressed a mixture of curiosity and anger, which annoyed, and in some degree alarmed me. I inquired the way to the inn; but no one replied. I then moved forward, and a murmuring sound arose from the crowd as they followed and surrounded me; when an ill-looking man approaching, tapped me on the shoulder, and said, "Come, Sir, you must follow me to Mr. Kirwin's, to give an account of yourself."

"Who is Mr. Kirwin? Why am I to give an account of myself? Is not this a free country?"

"Aye, Sir, free enough for honest folks. Mr. Kirwin is a magistrate; and you are to give an account of the death of a gentleman who was found murdered here last night."

This answer startled me; but I presently recovered myself. I was innocent; that could easily be proved: accordingly I followed my conductor in silence, and was led to one of the best houses in the town. I was ready to sink from fatigue and hunger; but, being surrounded by a crowd, I thought it politic to rouse all my strength, that no physical debility might be construed into apprehension or conscious guilt. Little did I then expect the calamity that was in a few moments to overwhelm me and extinguish in horror and despair all fear of ignominy or death.

I must pause here; for it requires all my fortitude to recall the memory of the frightful events which I am about to relate, in proper detail, to my recollection.

Chapter 4.

I was soon introduced into the presence of the magistrate, an old benev-olent man, with calm and mild manners. He looked upon me, however, with some degree of severity; and then, turning towards my conductors, he asked who appeared as witnesses on this occasion.

About half a dozen men came forward; and one being selected by the magistrate, he deposed, that he had been out fishing the night before with his son and brother-in-law, Daniel Nugent, when, about ten o'clock, they observed a strong northerly blast rising, and they accordingly put in for port. It was a very dark night, as the moon had not yet risen; they did not land at the harbour, but, as they had been accustomed, at a creek about two miles below. He walked on first, carrying a part of the fishing tackle, and his com-panions followed him at some distance. As he was proceeding along the sands, he struck his foot against something, and fell all his length on the ground. His companions came up to assist him; and, by the light of their lantern, they found that he had fallen on the body of a man, who was to all appearance dead. Their first supposition was, that it was the corpse of some person who had been drowned, and was thrown on shore by the waves; but, upon examination, they found that the clothes were not wet, and even that the body was not then cold. They instantly carried it to the cottage of an old woman near the spot, and endeavoured, but in vain, to restore it to life. He appeared to be a handsome young man, about five and twenty years of age. He had apparently been strangled; for there was no sign of any violence, except the black mark of fingers on his neck.

The first part of this deposition did not in the least interest me; but when the mark of the fingers was mentioned, I remembered the murder of my brother, and felt myself extremely agitated; my limbs trembled, and a mist came over my eyes, which obliged me to lean on a chair for support. The magistrate observed me with a keen eye, and of course drew an unfavourable augury from my manner.

The son confirmed his father's account: but when Daniel Nugent was called, he swore positively that, just before the fall of his companion, he saw a boat, with a single man in it, at a short distance from the shore; and, as far as he could judge by the light of a few stars, it was the same boat in which I had just landed.

A woman deposed, that she lived near the beach, and was standing at the door of her cottage, waiting for the return of the fishermen, about an hour before she heard of the discovery of the body, when she saw a boat, with only only one man in it, push off from that part of the shore where the corpse was afterwards found.

Another woman confirmed the account of the fishermen having brought the body into her house; it was not cold. They put it into a bed, and rubbed it; and Daniel went to the town for an apothecary, but life was quite gone.

Several other men were examined concerning my landing; and they agreed, that, with the strong north wind that had arisen during the night, it was very probable that I had beaten about for many hours, and had been obliged to return nearly to the same spot from which I had departed. Besides, they observed that it appeared that I had brought the body from another place, and it was likely, that as I did not appear to know the shore, I might have put into the harbour ignorant of the distance of the town of —— from the place where I had deposited the corpse.

Mr. Kirwin, on hearing this evidence, desired that I should be taken into the room where the body lay for interment, that it might be observed what effect the sight of it would produce upon me. This idea was probably suggested by the extreme agitation I had exhibited when the mode of the murder had been described. I was accordingly conducted, by the magistrate and several other persons, to the inn. I could not help being struck by the strange coincidences that had taken place during this eventful night; but, knowing that I had been conversing with several persons in the island I had inhabited about the time that the body had been found, I was perfectly tranquil as to the consequences of the affair.

I entered the room where the corpse lay, and was led up to the coffin. How can I describe my sensations on beholding it? I feel yet parched with horror, nor can I reflect on that terrible moment without shuddering and agony, that faintly reminds me of the anguish of the recognition. The trial, the presence of the magistrate and witnesses, passed like a dream from my memory, when I saw the lifeless form of Henry Clerval stretched before me. I gasped for breath; and, throwing myself on the body, I exclaimed, "Have my murderous machinations deprived you also, my dearest Henry, of life? Two I have already destroyed; other victims await their destiny: but you, Clerval, my friend, my benefactor"—

The human frame could no longer support the agonizing suffering that I endured, and I was carried out of the room in strong convulsions.

A fever succeeded to this. I lay for two months on the point of death: my ravings, as I afterwards heard, were frightful; I called myself the murderer of William, of Justine, and of Clerval. Sometimes I entreated my attendants to assist me in the destruction of the fiend by whom I was tormented; and, at others, I felt the fingers of the monster already grasping my neck, and screamed aloud with agony and terror. Fortunately, as I spoke my native language, Mr. Kirwin alone understood me; but my gestures and bitter cries were sufficient to affright the other witnesses.

Why did I not die? More miserable than man ever was before, why did I not sink into forgetfulness and rest? Death snatches away many blooming children, the only hopes of their doating parents: how many brides and youthful lovers have been one day in the bloom of health and hope, and the next a prey for worms and the decay of the tomb! Of what materials was I made, that I could thus resist so many shocks, which, like the turning of the wheel, continually renewed the torture.

But I was doomed to live; and, in two months, found myself as awaking from a dream, in a prison, stretched on a wretched bed, surrounded by gaolers, turnkeys, bolts, and all the miserable apparatus of a dungeon. It was morning, I remember, when I thus awoke to understanding: I had forgotten the particulars of what had happened, and only felt as if some great misfortune had suddenly overwhelmed me; but when I looked around, and saw the barred windows, and the squalidness of the room in which I was, all flashed across my memory, and I groaned bitterly.

This sound disturbed an old woman who was sleeping in a chair beside me. She was a hired nurse, the wife of one of the turnkeys, and her countenance expressed all those bad qualities which often characterize that class. The lines of her face were hard and rude, like that of persons accustomed to see without sympathizing in sights of misery. Her tone expressed her entire indifference; she addressed me in English, and the voice struck me as one that I had heard during my sufferings:

"Are you better now, Sir?" said she.

I replied in the same language, with a feeble voice, "I believe I am; but if it be all true, if indeed I did not dream, I am sorry that I am still alive to feel this misery and horror."

"For that matter," replied the old woman, "if you mean about the gentleman you murdered, I believe that it were better for you if you were dead, for I fancy it will go hard with you; but you will be hung when the next sessions[2] come on. However, that's none of my business, I am sent to nurse you, and get you well; I do my duty with a safe conscience, it were well if every body did the same."

I turned with loathing from the woman who could utter so unfeeling a speech to a person just saved, on the very edge of death; but I felt languid, and unable to reflect on all that had passed. The whole series of my life appeared to me as a dream; I sometimes doubted if indeed it were all true, for it never presented itself to my mind with the force of reality.

As the images that floated before me became more distinct, I grew feverish; a darkness pressed around me; no one was near me who soothed me with the gentle voice of love; no dear hand supported me. The physician came and prescribed medicines, and the old woman prepared them for me; but utter carelessness was visible in the first, and the expression of brutality was strongly marked in the visage of the second. Who could be interested in the fate of a murderer, but the hangman who would gain his fee?

These were my first reflections; but I soon learned that Mr. Kirwin had shewn me extreme kindness. He had caused the best room in the prison to be prepared for me (wretched indeed was the best); and it was he who had provided a physician and a nurse. It is true, he seldom came to see me; for, although he ardently desired to relieve the sufferings of every human creature, he did not wish to be present at the agonies and miserable ravings of a murderer. He came, therefore, sometimes to see that I was not neglected; but his visits were short, and at long intervals.

One day, when I was gradually recovering, I was seated in a chair, my eyes half open, and my cheeks livid like those in death, I was overcome by gloom and misery, and often reflected I had better seek death than remain miserably pent up only to be let loose in a world replete with wretchedness. At one time I considered whether I should not declare myself guilty, and suffer the penalty of the law, less innocent than poor Justine had been. Such were my thoughts, when the door of my apartment was opened, and Mr. Kirwin entered. His countenance expressed sympathy and compassion; he drew a chair close to mine, and addressed me in French—

"I fear that this place is very shocking to you; can I do any thing to make you more comfortable?"

"I thank you; but all that you mention is nothing to me: on the whole earth there is no comfort which I am capable of receiving."

2. Regular sittings of a court to try certain criminal cases.

"I know that the sympathy of a stranger can be but of little relief to one borne down as you are by so strange a misfortune. But you will, I hope, soon quit this melancholy abode; for, doubtless, evidence can easily be brought to free you from the criminal charge."

"That is my least concern: I am, by a course of strange events, become the most miserable of mortals. Persecuted and tortured as I am and have been, can death be any evil to me?"

"Nothing indeed could be more unfortunate and agonizing than the strange chances that have lately occurred. You were thrown, by some surprising accident, on this shore, renowned for its hospitality; seized immediately, and charged with murder. The first sight that was presented to your eyes was the body of your friend, murdered in so unaccountable a manner, and placed, as it were, by some fiend across your path."

As Mr. Kirwin said this, notwithstanding the agitation I endured on this retrospect of my sufferings, I also felt considerable surprise at the knowledge he seemed to possess concerning me. I suppose some astonishment was exhibited in my countenance; for Mr. Kirwin hastened to say—

"It was not until a day or two after your illness that I thought of examining your dress, that I might discover some trace by which I could send to your relations an account of your misfortune and illness. I found several letters, and, among others, one which I discovered from its commencement to be from your father. I instantly wrote to Geneva: nearly two months have elapsed since the departure of my letter.—But you are ill; even now you tremble: you are unfit for agitation of any kind."

"This suspense is a thousand times worse than the most horrible event: tell me what new scene of death has been acted, and whose murder I am now to lament."

"Your family is perfectly well," said Mr. Kirwin, with gentleness; "and some one, a friend, is come to visit you."

I know not by what chain of thought the idea presented itself, but it instantly darted into my mind that the murderer had come to mock at my misery, and taunt me with the death of Clerval, as a new incitement for me to comply with his hellish desires. I put my hand before my eyes, and cried out in agony—

"Oh! take him away! I cannot see him; for God's sake, do not let him enter!"

Mr. Kirwin regarded me with a troubled countenance. He could not help regarding my exclamation as a presumption of my guilt, and said, in rather a severe tone—

"I should have thought, young man, that the presence of your father would have been welcome, instead of inspiring such violent repugnance."

"My father!" cried I, while every feature and every muscle was relaxed from anguish to pleasure. "Is my father, indeed, come? How kind, how very kind. But where is he, why does he not hasten to me?"

My change of manner surprised and pleased the magistrate; perhaps he thought that my former exclamation was a momentary return of delirium, and now he instantly resumed his former benevolence. He rose, and quitted the room with my nurse, and in a moment my father entered it.

Nothing, at this moment, could have given me greater pleasure than the arrival of my father. I stretched out my hand to him, and cried—

"Are you then safe—and Elizabeth—and Ernest?"

My father calmed me with assurances of their welfare, and endeavoured, by dwelling on these subjects so interesting to my heart, to raise my desponding spirits; but he soon felt that a prison cannot be the abode of cheerfulness. "What a place is this that you inhabit, my son!" said he, looking mournfully at the barred windows, and wretched appearance of the room. "You travelled to seek happiness, but a fatality seems to pursue you. And poor Clerval—"

The name of my unfortunate and murdered friend was an agitation too great to be endured in my weak state; I shed tears.

"Alas! yes, my father," replied I; "some destiny of the most horrible kind hangs over me, and I must live to fulfil it, or surely I should have died on the coffin of Henry."

We were not allowed to converse for any length of time, for the precarious state of my health rendered every precaution necessary that could insure tranquillity. Mr. Kirwin came in, and insisted that my strength should not be exhausted by too much exertion. But the appearance of my father was to me like that of my good angel, and I gradually recovered my health.

As my sickness quitted me, I was absorbed by a gloomy and black melancholy, that nothing could dissipate. The image of Clerval was for ever before me, ghastly and murdered. More than once the agitation into which these reflections threw me made my friends dread a dangerous relapse. Alas! why did they preserve so miserable and detested a life? It was surely that I might fulfil my destiny, which is now drawing to a close. Soon, oh, very soon, will death extinguish these throbbings, and relieve me from the mighty weight of anguish that bears me to the dust; and, in executing the award of justice, I shall also sink to rest. Then the appearance of death was distant, although the wish was ever present to my thoughts; and I often sat for hours motionless and speechless, wishing for some mighty revolution that might bury me and my destroyer in its ruins.

The season of the assizes[3] approached. I had already been three months in prison; and although I was still weak, and in continual danger of a relapse, I was obliged to travel nearly a hundred miles to the county-town, where the court was held. Mr. Kirwin charged himself with every care of collecting witnesses, and arranging my defence. I was spared the disgrace of appearing publicly as a criminal, as the case was not brought before the court that decides on life and death. The grand jury rejected the bill, on its being proved that I was on the Orkney Islands at the hour the body of my friend was found, and a fortnight after my removal I was liberated from prison.

My father was enraptured on finding me freed from the vexations of a criminal charge, that I was again allowed to breathe the fresh atmosphere, and allowed to return to my native country. I did not participate in these feelings; for to me the walls of a dungeon or a palace were alike hateful. The cup of life was poisoned for ever; and although the sun shone upon me, as upon the happy and gay of heart, I saw around me nothing but a dense and frightful darkness, penetrated by no light but the glimmer of two eyes that glared upon me. Sometimes they were the expressive eyes of Henry, languishing in death, the dark orbs nearly covered by the lids, and the long black lashes that fringed them; sometimes it was the watery clouded eyes of the monster, as I first saw them in my chamber at Ingolstadt.

---

3. Sessions for administering civil and criminal justice.

My father tried to awaken in me the feelings of affection. He talked of Geneva, which I should soon visit—of Elizabeth, and Ernest; but these words only drew deep groans from me. Sometimes, indeed, I felt a wish for happiness; and thought, with melancholy delight, of my beloved cousin; or longed, with a devouring *maladie du pays*,[4] to see once more the blue lake and rapid Rhone, that had been so dear to me in early childhood: but my general state of feeling was a torpor, in which a prison was as welcome a residence as the divinest scene in nature; and these fits were seldom interrupted, but by paroxysms of anguish and despair. At these moments I often endeavoured to put an end to the existence I loathed; and it required unceasing attendance and vigilance to restrain me from committing some dreadful act of violence.

I remember, as I quitted the prison, I heard one of the men say, "He may be innocent of the murder, but he has certainly a bad conscience." These words struck me. A bad conscience! yes, surely I had one. William, Justine, and Clerval, had died through my infernal machinations; "And whose death," cried I, "is to finish the tragedy? Ah! my father, do not remain in this wretched country; take me where I may forget myself, my existence, and all the world."

My father easily acceded to my desire; and, after having taken leave of Mr. Kirwin, we hastened to Dublin. I felt as if I was relieved from a heavy weight, when the packet sailed with a fair wind from Ireland, and I had quitted for ever the country which had been to me the scene of so much misery.

It was midnight. My father slept in the cabin; and I lay on the deck, looking at the stars, and listening to the dashing of the waves. I hailed the darkness that shut Ireland from my sight, and my pulse beat with a feverish joy, when I reflected that I should soon see Geneva. The past appeared to me in the light of a frightful dream; yet the vessel in which I was, the wind that blew me from the detested shore of Ireland, and the sea which surrounded me, told me too forcibly that I was deceived by no vision, and that Clerval, my friend and dearest companion, had fallen a victim to me and the monster of my creation. I repassed, in my memory, my whole life; my quiet happiness while residing with my family in Geneva, the death of my mother; and my departure for Ingolstadt. I remembered shuddering at the mad enthusiasm that hurried me on to the creation of my hideous enemy, and I called to mind the night during which he first lived. I was unable to pursue the train of thought; a thousand feelings pressed upon me, and I wept bitterly.

Ever since my recovery from the fever I had been in the custom of taking every night a small quantity of laudanum;[5] for it was by means of this drug only that I was enabled to gain the rest necessary for the preservation of life. Oppressed by the recollection of my various misfortunes, I now took a double dose, and soon slept profoundly. But sleep did not afford me respite from thought and misery; my dreams presented a thousand objects that scared me. Towards morning I was possessed by a kind of night-mare; I felt the fiend's grasp in my neck, and could not free myself from it; groans and cries rung in my ears. My father, who was watching over me, perceiving my restlessness, awoke me, and pointed to the port of Holyhead,[6] which we were now entering.

4. Homesickness (French).
5. Opium dissolved in alcohol, prescribed at the time as a sedative.

6. On the island of Holyhead, which is just off the island of Anglesey, Wales.

Chapter 5.

We had resolved not to go to London, but to cross the country to Portsmouth, and thence to embark for Havre.[7] I preferred this plan principally because I dreaded to see again those places in which I had enjoyed a few moments of tranquillity with my beloved Clerval. I thought with horror of seeing again those persons whom we had been accustomed to visit together, and who might make inquiries concerning an event, the very remembrance of which made me again feel the pang I endured when I gazed on his lifeless form in the inn at ——.

As for my father, his desires and exertions were bounded to the[8] again seeing me restored to health and peace of mind. His tenderness and attentions were unremitting; my grief and gloom was obstinate, but he would not despair. Sometimes he thought that I felt deeply the degradation of being obliged to answer a charge of murder, and he endeavoured to prove to me the futility of pride.

"Alas! my father," said I, "how little do you know me. Human beings, their feelings and passions, would indeed be degraded, if such a wretch as I felt pride. Justine, poor unhappy Justine, was as innocent as I, and she suffered the same charge; she died for it; and I am the cause of this—I murdered her. William, Justine, and Henry—they all died by my hands."

My father had often, during my imprisonment, heard me make the same assertion; when I thus accused myself, he sometimes seemed to desire an explanation, and at others he appeared to consider it as caused by delirium, and that, during my illness, some idea of this kind had presented itself to my imagination, the remembrance of which I preserved in my convalescence. I avoided explanation, and maintained a continual silence concerning the wretch I had created. I had a feeling that I should be supposed mad, and this for ever chained my tongue, when I would have given the whole world to have confided the fatal secret.

Upon this occasion my father said, with an expression of unbounded wonder, "What do you mean, Victor? are you mad? My dear son, I entreat you never to make such an assertion again."

"I am not mad," I cried energetically; "the sun and the heavens, who have viewed my operations, can bear witness of my truth. I am the assassin of those most innocent victims; they died by my machinations. A thousand times would I have shed my own blood drop by drop, to have saved their lives but I could not, my father, indeed, could not sacrifice the whole human race."

The conclusion of this speech convinced my father that my ideas were deranged, and he instantly changed the subject of our conversation, and endeavoured to alter the course of my thoughts. He wished as much as possible to obliterate the memory of the scenes that had taken place in Ireland, and never alluded to them, or suffered me to speak of my misfortunes.

As time passed away I became more calm: misery had her dwelling in my heart, but I no longer talked in the same incoherent manner of my own crimes; sufficient for me was the consciousness of them. By the utmost self-violence, I curbed the imperious voice of wretchedness, which sometimes

---

7. Le Havre, French channel port.　　　　8. Limited to.

desired to declare itself to the whole world; and my manners were calmer and more composed than they had ever been since my journey to the sea of ice.

We arrived at Havre on the 8th of May, and instantly proceeded to Paris, where my father had some business which detained us a few weeks. In this city, I received the following letter from Elizabeth:—

"*TO* VICTOR FRANKENSTEIN.

"MY DEAREST FRIEND,

"It gave me the greatest pleasure to receive a letter from my uncle dated at Paris; you are no longer at a formidable distance, and I may hope to see you in less than a fortnight. My poor cousin, how much you must have suffered! I expect to see you looking even more ill than when you quitted Geneva. This winter has been passed most miserably, tortured as I have been by anxious suspense; yet I hope to see peace in your countenance, and to find that your heart is not totally devoid of comfort and tranquillity.

"Yet I fear that the same feelings now exist that made you so miserable a year ago, even perhaps augmented by time. I would not disturb you at this period, when so many misfortunes weigh upon you; but a conversation that I had with my uncle previous to his departure renders some explanation necessary before we meet.

"Explanation! you may possibly say; what can Elizabeth have to explain? If you really say this, my questions are answered, and I have no more to do than to sign myself your affectionate cousin. But you are distant from me, and it is possible that you may dread, and yet be pleased with this explanation; and, in a probability of this being the case, I dare not any longer postpone writing what, during your absence, I have often wished to express to you, but have never had the courage to begin.

"You well know, Victor, that our union had been the favourite plan of your parents ever since our infancy. We were told this when young, and taught to look forward to it as an event that would certainly take place. We were affectionate playfellows during childhood, and, I believe, dear and valued friends to one another as we grew older. But as brother and sister often entertain a lively affection towards each other, without desiring a more intimate union, may not such also be our case? Tell me, dearest Victor. Answer me, I conjure[9] you, by our mutual happiness, with simple truth—Do you not love another?

"You have travelled; you have spent several years of your life at Ingolstadt; and I confess to you, my friend, that when I saw you last autumn so unhappy, flying to solitude, from the society of every creature, I could not help supposing that you might regret our connexion, and believe yourself bound in honour to fulfil the wishes of your parents, although they opposed themselves to your inclinations. But this is false reasoning. I confess to you, my cousin, that I love you, and that in my

9. Entreat.

airy dreams of futurity you have been my constant friend and companion. But it is your happiness I desire as well as my own, when I declare to you, that our marriage would render me eternally miserable, unless it were the dictate of your own free choice. Even now I weep to think, that, borne down as you are by the cruelest misfortunes, you may stifle, by the word *honour*, all hope of that love and happiness which would alone restore you to yourself. I, who have so interested an affection for you, may increase your miseries ten-fold, by being an obstacle to your wishes. Ah, Victor, be assured that your cousin and playmate has too sincere a love for you not to be made miserable by this supposition. Be happy, my friend; and if you obey me in this one request, remain satisfied that nothing on earth will have the power to interrupt my tranquillity.

"Do not let this letter disturb you; do not answer it to-morrow, or the next day, or even until you come, if it will give you pain. My uncle will send me news of your health; and if I see but one smile on your lips when we meet, occasioned by this or any other exertion of mine, I shall need no other happiness.

"ELIZABETH LAVENZA.
"Geneva, May 18th, 17—."

This letter revived in my memory what I had before forgotten, the threat of the fiend—"*I will be with you on your wedding-night!*" Such was my sentence, and on that night would the dæmon employ every art to destroy me, and tear me from the glimpse of happiness which promised partly to console my sufferings. On that night he had determined to consummate his crimes by my death. Well, be it so; a deadly struggle would then assuredly take place, in which if he was victorious, I should be at peace, and his power over me be at an end. If he were vanquished, I should be a free man. Alas! what freedom? such as the peasant enjoys when his family have been massacred before his eyes, his cottage burnt, his lands laid waste, and he is turned adrift, homeless, pennyless, and alone, but free. Such would be my liberty, except that in my Elizabeth I possessed a treasure; alas! balanced by those horrors of remorse and guilt, which would pursue me until death.

Sweet and beloved Elizabeth! I read and re-read her letter, and some softened feelings stole into my heart, and dared to whisper paradisaical dreams of love and joy; but the apple was already eaten, and the angel's arm bared to drive me from all hope.[1] Yet I would die to make her happy. If the monster executed his threat, death was inevitable; yet, again, I considered whether my marriage would hasten my fate. My destruction might indeed arrive a few months sooner; but if my torturer should suspect that I postponed it, influenced by his menaces, he would surely find other, and perhaps more dreadful means of revenge. He had vowed *to be with me on my wedding-night*, yet he did not consider that threat as binding him to peace in the mean time; for, as if to shew me that he was not yet satiated with blood, he had murdered Clerval immediately after the enunciation of his threats. I resolved, therefore, that if my immediate union with my cousin would conduce either

---

1. Adam and Eve are led from the Garden of Eden by the archangel Michael, and the way back is barred by a flaming sword (*Paradise Lost* 12.636–44).

to her's or my father's happiness, my adversary's designs against my life should not retard it a single hour.

In this state of mind I wrote to Elizabeth. My letter was calm and affectionate. "I fear, my beloved girl," I said, "little happiness remains for us on earth; yet all that I may one day enjoy is concentered in you. Chase away your idle fears; to you alone do I consecrate my life, and my endeavour for contentment. I have one secret, Elizabeth, a dreadful one; when revealed to you, it will chill your frame with horror, and then, far from being surprised at my misery, you will only wonder that I survive what I have endured. I will confide this tale of misery and terror to you the day after our marriage shall take place; for, my sweet cousin, there must be perfect confidence between us. But until then, I conjure you, do not mention or allude to it. This I most earnestly entreat, and I know you will comply."

In about a week after the arrival of Elizabeth's letter, we returned to Geneva. My cousin welcomed me with warm affection; yet tears were in her eyes, as she beheld my emaciated frame and feverish cheeks. I saw a change in her also. She was thinner, and had lost much of that heavenly vivacity that had before charmed me; but her gentleness, and soft looks of compassion, made her a more fit companion for one blasted and miserable as I was.

The tranquillity which I now enjoyed did not endure. Memory brought madness with it; and when I thought on what had passed, a real insanity possessed me; sometimes I was furious, and burnt with rage, sometimes low and despondent. I neither spoke or looked, but sat motionless, bewildered by the multitude of miseries that overcame me.

Elizabeth alone had the power to draw me from these fits; her gentle voice would soothe me when transported by passion, and inspire me with human feelings when sunk in torpor. She wept with me, and for me. When reason returned, she would remonstrate, and endeavour to inspire me with resignation. Ah! it is well for the unfortunate to be resigned, but for the guilty there is no peace. The agonies of remorse poison the luxury there is otherwise sometimes found in indulging the excess of grief.

Soon after my arrival my father spoke of my immediate marriage with my cousin. I remained silent.

"Have you, then, some other attachment?"

"None on earth. I love Elizabeth, and look forward to our union with delight. Let the day therefore be fixed; and on it I will consecrate myself, in life or death, to the happiness of my cousin."

"My dear Victor, do not speak thus. Heavy misfortunes have befallen us; but let us only cling closer to what remains, and transfer our love for those whom we have lost to those who yet live. Our circle will be small, but bound close by the ties of affection and mutual misfortune. And when time shall have softened your despair, new and dear objects of care will be born to replace those of whom we have been so cruelly deprived."

Such were the lessons of my father. But to me the remembrance of the threat returned: nor can you wonder, that, omnipotent as the fiend had yet been in his deeds of blood, I should almost regard him as invincible; and that when he had pronounced the words, "*I shall be with you on your wedding-night*," I should regard the threatened fate as unavoidable. But death was no evil to me, if the loss of Elizabeth were balanced with it; and I therefore, with a contented and even cheerful countenance, agreed with my father, that if my cousin would consent, the ceremony should take place in ten days, and thus put, as I imagined, the seal to my fate.

Great God! if for one instant I had thought what might be the hellish intention of my fiendish adversary, I would rather have banished myself for ever from my native country, and wandered a friendless outcast over the earth, than have consented to this miserable marriage. But, as if possessed of magic powers, the monster had blinded me to his real intentions; and when I thought that I prepared only my own death, I hastened that of a far dearer victim.

As the period fixed for our marriage drew nearer, whether from cowardice or a prophetic feeling, I felt my heart sink within me. But I concealed my feelings by an appearance of hilarity, that brought smiles and joy to the countenance of my father, but hardly deceived the ever-watchful and nicer[2] eye of Elizabeth. She looked forward to our union with placid contentment, not unmingled with a little fear, which past misfortunes had impressed, that what now appeared certain and tangible happiness, might soon dissipate into an airy dream, and leave no trace but deep and everlasting regret.

Preparations were made for the event; congratulatory visits were received; and all wore a smiling appearance. I shut up, as well as I could, in my own heart the anxiety that preyed there, and entered with seeming earnestness into the plans of my father, although they might only serve as the decorations of my tragedy. A house was purchased for us near Cologny, by which we should enjoy the pleasures of the country, and yet be so near Geneva as to see my father every day; who would still reside within the walls, for the benefit of Ernest, that he might follow his studies at the schools.

In the mean time I took every precaution to defend my person, in case the fiend should openly attack me. I carried pistols and a dagger constantly about me, and was ever on the watch to prevent artifice; and by these means gained a greater degree of tranquillity. Indeed, as the period approached, the threat appeared more as a delusion, not to be regarded as worthy to disturb my peace, while the happiness I hoped for in my marriage wore a greater appearance of certainty, as the day fixed for its solemnization drew nearer, and I heard it continually spoken of as an occurrence which no accident could possibly prevent.

Elizabeth seemed happy; my tranquil demeanour contributed greatly to calm her mind. But on the day that was to fulfil my wishes and my destiny, she was melancholy, and a presentiment of evil pervaded her; and perhaps also she thought of the dreadful secret, which I had promised to reveal to her the following day. My father was in the mean time overjoyed, and, in the bustle of preparation, only observed in the melancholy of his niece the diffidence of a bride.

After the ceremony was performed, a large party assembled at my father's; but it was agreed that Elizabeth and I should pass the afternoon and night at Evian, and return to Cologny the next morning. As the day was fair, and the wind favourable, we resolved to go by water.

Those were the last moments of my life during which I enjoyed the feeling of happiness. We passed rapidly along: the sun was hot, but we were sheltered from its rays by a kind of canopy, while we enjoyed the beauty of the

2. More sensitive and discerning.

scene, sometimes on one side of the lake, where we saw Mont Salêve, the pleasant banks of Montalêgre, and at a distance, surmounting all, the beautiful Mont Blanc, and the assemblage of snowy mountains that in vain endeavour to emulate her; sometimes coasting the opposite banks, we saw the mighty Jura opposing its dark side to the ambition that would quit its native country, and an almost insurmountable barrier to the invader who should wish to enslave it.

I took the hand of Elizabeth: "You are sorrowful, my love. Ah! if you knew what I have suffered, and what I may yet endure, you would endeavour to let me taste the quiet, and freedom from despair, that this one day at least permits me to enjoy."

"Be happy, my dear Victor," replied Elizabeth; "there is, I hope, nothing to distress you; and be assured that if a lively joy is not painted in my face, my heart is contented. Something whispers to me not to depend too much on the prospect that is opened before us; but I will not listen to such a sinister voice. Observe how fast we move along, and how the clouds which sometimes obscure, and sometimes rise above the dome of Mont Blanc, render this scene of beauty still more interesting. Look also at the innumerable fish that are swimming in the clear waters, where we can distinguish every pebble that lies at the bottom. What a divine day! how happy and serene all nature appears!"

Thus Elizabeth endeavoured to divert her thoughts and mine from all reflection upon melancholy subjects. But her temper was fluctuating; joy for a few instants shone in her eyes, but it continually gave place to distraction and reverie.

The sun sunk lower in the heavens; we passed the river Drance, and observed its path through the chasms of the higher, and the glens of the lower hills. The Alps here come closer to the lake, and we approached the amphitheatre of mountains which forms its eastern boundary. The spire of Evian shone under the woods that surrounded it, and the range of mountain above mountain by which it was overhung.

The wind, which had hitherto carried us along with amazing rapidity, sunk at sunset to a light breeze; the soft air just ruffled the water, and caused a pleasant motion among the trees as we approached the shore, from which it wafted the most delightful scent of flowers and hay. The sun sunk beneath the horizon as we landed; and as I touched the shore, I felt those cares and fears revive, which soon were to clasp me, and cling to me for ever.

Chapter 6.

It was eight o'clock when we landed; we walked for a short time on the shore, enjoying the transitory light, and then retired to the inn, and contemplated the lovely scene of waters, woods, and mountains, obscured in darkness, yet still displaying their black outlines.

The wind, which had fallen in the south, now rose with great violence in the west. The moon had reached her summit in the heavens, and was beginning to descend; the clouds swept across it swifter than the flight of the vulture, and dimmed her rays, while the lake reflected the scene of the busy heavens, rendered still busier by the restless waves that were beginning to rise. Suddenly a heavy storm of rain descended.

I had been calm during the day; but so soon as night obscured the shapes of objects, a thousand fears arose in my mind. I was anxious and watchful, while my right hand grasped a pistol which was hidden in my bosom; every sound terrified me; but I resolved that I would sell my life dearly, and not relax the impending conflict until my own life, or that of my adversary, were extinguished.

Elizabeth observed my agitation for some time in timid and fearful silence; at length she said, "What is it that agitates you, my dear Victor? What is it you fear?"

"Oh! peace, peace, my love," replied I, "this night, and all will be safe: but this night is dreadful, very dreadful."

I passed an hour in this state of mind, when suddenly I reflected how dreadful the combat which I momentarily expected would be to my wife, and I earnestly entreated her to retire, resolving not to join her until I had obtained some knowledge as to the situation of my enemy.

She left me, and I continued some time walking up and down the passages of the house, and inspecting every corner that might afford a retreat to my adversary. But I discovered no trace of him, and was beginning to conjecture that some fortunate chance had intervened to prevent the execution of his menaces; when suddenly I heard a shrill and dreadful scream. It came from the room into which Elizabeth had retired. As I heard it, the whole truth rushed into my mind, my arms dropped, the motion of every muscle and fibre was suspended; I could feel the blood trickling in my veins, and tingling in the extremities of my limbs. This state lasted but for an instant; the scream was repeated, and I rushed into the room.

Great God! why did I not then expire! Why am I here to relate the destruction of the best hope, and the purest creature of earth? She was there, lifeless and inanimate, thrown across the bed, her head hanging down, and her pale and distorted features half covered by her hair. Every where I turn I see the same figure—her bloodless arms and relaxed form flung by the murderer on its bridal bier. Could I behold this, and live? Alas! life is obstinate, and clings closest where it is most hated. For a moment only did I lose recollection; I fainted.

When I recovered, I found myself surrounded by the people of the inn; their countenances expressed a breathless terror: but the horror of others appeared only as a mockery, a shadow of the feelings that oppressed me. I escaped from them to the room where lay the body of Elizabeth, my love, my wife, so lately living, so dear, so worthy. She had been moved from the posture in which I had first beheld her; and now, as she lay, her head upon her arm, and a handkerchief thrown across her face and neck, I might have supposed her asleep. I rushed towards her, and embraced her with ardour; but the deathly languor and coldness of the limbs told me, that what I now held in my arms had ceased to be the Elizabeth whom I had loved and cherished. The murderous mark of the fiend's grasp was on her neck, and the breath had ceased to issue from her lips.

While I still hung over her in the agony of despair, I happened to look up. The windows of the room had before been darkened; and I felt a kind of panic on seeing the pale yellow light of the moon illuminate the chamber. The shutters had been thrown back; and, with a sensation of horror not to be described, I saw at the open window a figure the most hideous and abhorred. A grin was on the face of the monster; he seemed to jeer, as with his fiendish finger he pointed towards the corpse of my wife. I rushed towards the window, and drawing a pistol from my bosom, shot; but he eluded me, leaped from his station, and, running with the swiftness of lightning, plunged into the lake.

The report of the pistol brought a crowd into the room. I pointed to the spot where he had disappeared, and we followed the track with boats; nets were cast, but in vain. After passing several hours, we returned hopeless, most of my companions believing it to have been a form conjured by my fancy. After having landed, they proceeded to search the country, parties going in different directions among the woods and vines.

I did not accompany them; I was exhausted: a film covered my eyes, and my skin was parched with the heat of fever. In this state I lay on a bed, hardly conscious of what had happened; my eyes wandered round the room, as if to seek something that I had lost.

At length I remembered that my father would anxiously expect the return of Elizabeth and myself, and that I must return alone. This reflection brought tears into my eyes, and I wept for a long time; but my thoughts rambled to various subjects, reflecting on my misfortunes, and their cause. I was bewildered in a cloud of wonder and horror. The death of William, the execution of Justine, the murder of Clerval, and lastly of my wife; even at that moment I knew not that my only remaining friends were safe from the malignity of the fiend; my father even now might be writhing under his grasp, and Ernest might be dead at his feet. This idea made me shudder, and recalled me to action. I started up, and resolved to return to Geneva with all possible speed.

There were no horses to be procured, and I must return by the lake; but the wind was unfavourable, and the rain fell in torrents. However, it was hardly morning, and I might reasonably hope to arrive by night. I hired men to row, and took an oar myself, for I had always experienced relief from mental torment in bodily exercise. But the overflowing misery I now felt, and the excess of agitation that I endured, rendered me incapable of any exertion. I threw down the oar; and, leaning my head upon my hands, gave way to every gloomy idea that arose. If I looked up, I saw the scenes which were familiar to me in my happier time, and which I had contemplated but the day before in the company of her who was now but a shadow and a recollection. Tears streamed from my eyes. The rain had ceased for a moment, and I saw the fish play in the waters as they had done a few hours before; they had then been observed by Elizabeth. Nothing is so painful to the human mind as a great and sudden change. The sun might shine, or the clouds might lour, but nothing could appear to me as it had done the day before. A fiend had snatched from me every hope of future happiness: no creature had ever been so miserable as I was; so frightful an event is single in the history of man.

But why should I dwell upon the incidents that followed this last overwhelming event. Mine has been a tale of horrors; I have reached their *acme*, and what I must now relate can but be tedious to you. Know that, one by one, my friends were snatched away; I was left desolate. My own strength is exhausted; and I must tell, in a few words, what remains of my hideous narration.

I arrived at Geneva. My father and Ernest yet lived; but the former sunk under the tidings that I bore. I see him now, excellent and venerable old man! his eyes wandered in vacancy, for they had lost their charm and their delight—his niece, his more than daughter, whom he doated on with all that affection which a man feels, who, in the decline of life, having few affections, clings more earnestly to those that remain. Cursed, cursed be the fiend that brought misery on his grey hairs, and doomed him to waste in wretchedness! He could not live under the horrors that were accumulated around him; an apoplectic fit was brought on, and in a few days he died in my arms.

What then became of me? I know not; I lost sensation, and chains and darkness were the only objects that pressed upon me. Sometimes, indeed, I dreamt that I wandered in flowery meadows and pleasant vales with the friends of my youth; but awoke, and found myself in a dungeon. Melancholy followed, but by degrees I gained a clear conception of my miseries and situation, and was then released from my prison. For they had called me mad; and during many months, as I understood, a solitary cell had been my habitation.

But liberty had been a useless gift to me had I not, as I awakened to reason, at the same time awakened to revenge. As the memory of past misfortunes pressed upon me, I began to reflect on their cause—the monster whom I had created, the miserable dæmon whom I had sent abroad into the world for my destruction. I was possessed by a maddening rage when I thought of him, and desired and ardently prayed that I might have him within my grasp to wreak a great and signal revenge on his cursed head.

Nor did my hate long confine itself to useless wishes; I began to reflect on the best means of securing him; and for this purpose, about a month after my release, I repaired to a criminal judge in the town, and told him that I had an accusation to make; that I knew the destroyer of my family; and that I required him to exert his whole authority for the apprehension of the murderer.

The magistrate listened to me with attention and kindness: "Be assured, sir," said he, "no pains or exertions on my part shall be spared to discover the villain."

"I thank you," replied I; "listen, therefore, to the deposition that I have to make. It is indeed a tale so strange, that I should fear you would not credit it, were there not something in truth which, however wonderful, forces conviction. The story is too connected to be mistaken for a dream, and I have no motive for falsehood." My manner, as I thus addressed him, was impressive, but calm; I had formed in my own heart a resolution to pursue my destroyer to death; and this purpose quieted my agony, and provisionally reconciled me to life. I now related my history briefly, but with firmness and precision, marking the dates with accuracy, and never deviating into invective or exclamation.

The magistrate appeared at first perfectly incredulous, but as I continued he became more attentive and interested; I saw him sometimes shudder with horror, at others a lively surprise, unmingled with disbelief, was painted on his countenance.

When I had concluded my narration, I said, "This is the being whom I accuse, and for whose detection and punishment I call upon you to exert your whole power. It is your duty as a magistrate, and I believe and hope that your feelings as a man will not revolt from the execution of those functions on this occasion."

This address caused a considerable change in the physiognomy of my auditor. He had heard my story with that half kind of belief that is given to a tale of spirits and supernatural events; but when he was called upon to act officially in consequence, the whole tide of his incredulity returned. He, however, answered mildly, "I would willingly afford you every aid in your pursuit; but the creature of whom you speak appears to have powers which would put all my exertions to defiance. Who can follow an animal which can traverse the sea of ice, and inhabit caves and dens, where no man would venture to intrude? Besides, some months have elapsed since the commission of his crimes, and no one can conjecture to what place he has wandered, or what region he may now inhabit."

"I do not doubt that he hovers near the spot which I inhabit; and if he has indeed taken refuge in the Alps, he may be hunted like the chamois,[3] and destroyed as a beast of prey. But I perceive your thoughts: you do not credit my narrative, and do not intend to pursue my enemy with the punishment which is his desert."

As I spoke, rage sparkled in my eyes; the magistrate was intimidated; "You are mistaken," said he, "I will exert myself; and if it is in my power to seize the monster, be assured that he shall suffer punishment proportionate to his crimes. But I fear, from what you have yourself described to be his properties, that this will prove impracticable, and that, while every proper measure is pursued, you should endeavour to make up your mind to disappointment."

"That cannot be; but all that I can say will be of little avail. My revenge is of no moment to you; yet, while I allow it to be a vice, I confess that it is the devouring and only passion of my soul. My rage is unspeakable, when I reflect that the murderer, whom I have turned loose upon society, still exists. You refuse my just demand: I have but one resource; and I devote myself, either in my life or death, to his destruction."

I trembled with excess of agitation as I said this; there was a phrenzy in my manner, and something, I doubt not, of that haughty fierceness, which the martyrs of old are said to have possessed. But to a Genevan magistrate, whose mind was occupied by far other ideas than those of devotion and heroism, this elevation of mind had much the appearance of madness. He endeavoured to soothe me as a nurse does a child, and reverted to my tale as the effects of delirium.

"Man," I cried, "how ignorant art thou in thy pride of wisdom! Cease; you know not what it is you say."

I broke from the house angry and disturbed, and retired to meditate on some other mode of action.

Chapter 7.

My present situation was one in which all voluntary thought was swallowed up and lost. I was hurried away by fury; revenge alone endowed me with strength and composure; it modelled my feelings, and allowed me to be calculating and calm, at periods when otherwise delirium or death would have been my portion.

My first resolution was to quit Geneva for ever; my country, which, when I was happy and beloved, was dear to me, now, in my adversity, became

---

3. A swift, horned animal inhabiting the Alps, hunted for the soft leather made from its hide.

hateful. I provided myself with a sum of money, together with a few jewels which had belonged to my mother, and departed.

And now my wanderings began, which are to cease but with life. I have traversed a vast portion of the earth, and have endured all the hardships which travellers, in deserts and barbarous countries, are wont to meet. How I have lived I hardly know; many times have I stretched my failing limbs upon the sandy plain, and prayed for death. But revenge kept me alive; I dared not die, and leave my adversary in being.

When I quitted Geneva, my first labour was to gain some clue by which I might trace the steps of my fiendish enemy. But my plan was unsettled; and I wandered many hours around the confines of the town, uncertain what path I should pursue. As night approached, I found myself at the entrance of the cemetery where William, Elizabeth, and my father, reposed. I entered it, and approached the tomb which marked their graves. Every thing was silent, except the leaves of the trees, which were gently agitated by the wind; the night was nearly dark; and the scene would have been solemn and affecting even to an uninterested observer. The spirits of the departed seemed to flit around, and to cast a shadow, which was felt but seen not, around the head of the mourner.

The deep grief which this scene had at first excited quickly gave way to rage and despair. They were dead, and I lived; their murderer also lived, and to destroy him I must drag out my weary existence. I knelt on the grass, and kissed the earth, and with quivering lips exclaimed, "By the sacred earth on which I kneel, by the shades[4] that wander near me, by the deep and eternal grief that I feel, I swear; and by thee, O Night, and by the spirits that preside over thee, I swear to pursue the dæmon, who caused this misery, until he or I shall perish in mortal conflict. For this purpose I will preserve my life: to execute this dear revenge, will I again behold the sun, and tread the green herbage of earth, which otherwise should vanish from my eyes for ever. And I call on you, spirits of the dead; and on you, wandering ministers of vengeance, to aid and conduct me in my work. Let the cursed and hellish monster drink deep of agony; let him feel the despair that now torments me."

I had begun my adjuration with solemnity, and an awe which almost assured me that the shades of my murdered friends heard and approved my devotion; but the furies possessed me as I concluded, and rage choaked my utterance.

I was answered through the stillness of night by a loud and fiendish laugh. It rung on my ears long and heavily; the mountains re-echoed it, and I felt as if all hell surrounded me with mockery and laughter. Surely in that moment I should have been possessed by phrenzy, and have destroyed my miserable existence, but that my vow was heard, and that I was reserved for vengeance. The laughter died away, when a well-known and abhorred voice, apparently close to my ear, addressed me in an audible whisper—"I am satisfied: miserable wretch! you have determined to live, and I am satisfied."

I darted towards the spot from which the sound proceeded; but the devil eluded my grasp. Suddenly the broad disk of the moon arose, and shone full upon his ghastly and distorted shape, as he fled with more than mortal speed.

I pursued him; and for many months this has been my task. Guided by a

4. Disembodied spirits.

slight clue, I followed the windings of the Rhone, but vainly. The blue Mediterranean appeared; and, by a strange chance, I saw the fiend enter by night, and hide himself in a vessel bound for the Black Sea. I took my passage in the same ship; but he escaped, I know not how.

Amidst the wilds of Tartary and Russia, although he still evaded me, I have ever followed in his track. Sometimes the peasants, scared by this horrid apparition, informed me of his path; sometimes he himself, who feared that if I lost all trace I should despair and die, often left some mark to guide me. The snows descended on my head, and I saw the print of his huge step on the white plain. To you first entering on life, to whom care is new and agony unknown, how can you understand what I have felt, and still feel. Cold, want, and fatigue, were the least pains which I was destined to endure. I was cursed by some devil, and carried about with me my eternal hell; yet still a spirit of good followed and directed my steps, and, when I most murmured, would suddenly extricate me from seemingly insurmountable difficulties. Sometimes, when nature overcome by hunger, sunk under the exhaustion, a repast was prepared for me in the desert, that restored and inspirited me. The fare was indeed coarse, such as the peasants of the country ate; but I may not doubt that it was set there by the spirits that I had invoked to aid me. Often, when all was dry, the heavens cloudless, and I was parched by thirst, a slight cloud would bedim the sky, shed the few drops that revived me, and vanish.

I followed, when I could, the courses of the rivers; but the dæmon generally avoided these, as it was here that the population of the country chiefly collected. In other places human beings were seldom seen; and I generally subsisted on the wild animals that crossed my path. I had money with me, and gained the friendship of the villagers by distributing it, or bringing with me some food that I had killed, which, after taking a small part, I always presented to those who had provided me with fire and utensils for cooking.

My life, as it passed thus, was indeed hateful to me, and it was during sleep alone that I could taste joy. O blessed sleep! often, when most miserable, I sank to repose, and my dreams lulled me even to rapture. The spirits that guarded me had provided these moments, or rather hours, of happiness that I might retain strength to fulfil my pilgrimage. Deprived of this respite, I should have sunk under my hardships. During the day I was sustained and inspirited by the hope of night: for in sleep I saw my friends, my wife, and my beloved country; again I saw the benevolent countenance of my father, heard the silver tones of my Elizabeth's voice, and beheld Clerval enjoying health and youth. Often, when wearied by a toilsome march, I persuaded myself that I was dreaming until night should come, and that I should then enjoy reality in the arms of my dearest friends. What agonizing fondness did I feel for them! how did I cling to their dear forms, as sometimes they haunted even my waking hours, and persuade myself that they still lived! At such moments vengeance, that burned within me, died in my heart, and I pursued my path towards the destruction of the dæmon, more as a task enjoined by heaven, as the mechanical impulse of some power of which I was unconscious, than as the ardent desire of my soul.

What his feelings were whom I pursued, I cannot know. Sometimes, indeed, he left marks in writing on the barks of the trees, or cut in stone, that guided me, and instigated my fury. "My reign is not yet over," (these words were legible in one of these inscriptions); "you live, and my power is complete. Follow me; I seek the everlasting ices of the north, where you will feel the misery of cold and frost, to which I am impassive. You will find near this place, if you follow not too tardily, a dead hare; eat, and be refreshed. Come on, my enemy; we have yet to wrestle for our lives; but many hard and miserable hours must you endure, until that period shall arrive."

Scoffing devil! Again do I vow vengeance; again do I devote thee, miserable fiend, to torture and death. Never will I omit my search, until he or I perish; and then with what ecstacy shall I join my Elizabeth, and those who even now prepare for me the reward of my tedious toil and horrible pilgrimage.

As I still pursued my journey to the northward, the snows thickened, and the cold increased in a degree almost too severe to support. The peasants were shut up in their hovels, and only a few of the most hardy ventured forth to seize the animals whom starvation had forced from their hiding-places to seek for prey. The rivers were covered with ice, and no fish could be procured; and thus I was cut off from my chief article of maintenance.

The triumph of my enemy increased with the difficulty of my labours. One inscription that he left was in these words: "Prepare! your toils only begin: wrap yourself in furs, and provide food, for we shall soon enter upon a journey where your sufferings will satisfy my everlasting hatred."

My courage and perseverance were invigorated by these scoffing words; I resolved not to fail in my purpose; and, calling on heaven to support me, I continued with unabated fervour to traverse immense deserts, until the ocean appeared at a distance, and formed the utmost boundary of the horizon. Oh! how unlike it was to the blue seas of the south! Covered with ice, it was only to be distinguished from land by its superior wildness and ruggedness. The Greeks wept for joy when they beheld the Mediterranean from the hills of Asia, and hailed with rapture the boundary of their toils.[5] I did not weep; but I knelt down, and, with a full heart, thanked my guiding spirit for conducting me in safety to the place where I hoped, notwithstanding my adversary's gibe, to meet and grapple with him.

Some weeks before this period I had procured a sledge and dogs, and thus traversed the snows with inconceivable speed. I know not whether the fiend possessed the same advantages; but I found that, as before I had daily lost ground in the pursuit, I now gained on him; so much so, that when I first saw the ocean, he was but one day's journey in advance, and I hoped to intercept him before he should reach the beach. With new courage, therefore, I pressed on, and in two days arrived at a wretched hamlet on the seashore. I inquired of the inhabitants concerning the fiend, and gained accurate information. A gigantic monster, they said, had arrived the night before, armed with a gun and many pistols; putting to flight the inhabitants of a solitary cottage, through fear of his terrific appearance. He had carried off their store of winter food, and, placing it in a sledge, to draw which he had seized on a numerous drove of trained dogs, he had harnessed them, and the same night, to the joy of the horror-struck villagers, had pursued his journey across the sea in a direction that led to no land; and they conjectured that he must speedily be destroyed by the breaking of the ice, or frozen by the eternal frosts.

5. A famed event during the Greek army's retreat from a failed expedition against Persia (401–399 B.C.E.), told by Xenophon in his *Anabasis*, book 4.

On hearing this information, I suffered a temporary access of despair. He had escaped me; and I must commence a destructive and almost endless journey across the mountainous ices of the ocean,—amidst cold that few of the inhabitants could long endure, and which I, the native of a genial and sunny climate, could not hope to survive. Yet at the idea that the fiend should live and be triumphant, my rage and vengeance returned, and, like a mighty tide, overwhelmed every other feeling. After a slight repose, during which the spirits of the dead hovered round, and instigated me to toil and revenge, I prepared for my journey.

I exchanged my land sledge for one fashioned for the inequalities of the frozen ocean; and, purchasing a plentiful stock of provisions, I departed from land.

I cannot guess how many days have passed since then; but I have endured misery, which nothing but the eternal sentiment of a just retribution burning within my heart could have enabled me to support. Immense and rugged mountains of ice often barred up my passage, and I often heard the thunder of the ground sea, which threatened my destruction. But again the frost came, and made the paths of the sea secure.

By the quantity of provision which I had consumed I should guess that I had passed three weeks in this journey; and the continual protraction of hope, returning back upon the heart, often wrung bitter drops of despondency and grief from my eyes. Despair had indeed almost secured her prey, and I should soon have sunk beneath this misery; when once, after the poor animals that carried me had with incredible toil gained the summit of a sloping ice mountain, and one sinking under his fatigue died, I viewed the expanse before me with anguish, when suddenly my eye caught a dark speck upon the dusky plain. I strained my sight to discover what it could be, and uttered a wild cry of ecstacy when I distinguished a sledge, and the distorted proportions of a well-known form within. Oh! with what a burning gush did hope revisit my heart! warm tears filled my eyes, which I hastily wiped away, that they might not intercept the view I had of the dæmon; but still my sight was dimmed by the burning drops, until, giving way to the emotions that oppressed me, I wept aloud.

But this was not the time for delay; I disencumbered the dogs of their dead companion, gave them a plentiful portion of food; and, after an hour's rest, which was absolutely necessary, and yet which was bitterly irksome to me, I continued my route. The sledge was still visible; nor did I again lose sight of it, except at the moments when for a short time some ice rock concealed it with its intervening crags. I indeed perceptibly gained on it; and when, after nearly two days' journey, I beheld my enemy at no more than a mile distant, my heart bounded within me.

But now, when I appeared almost within grasp of my enemy, my hopes were suddenly extinguished, and I lost all trace of him more utterly than I had ever done before. A ground sea was heard; the thunder of its progress, as the waters rolled and swelled beneath me, became every moment more ominous and terrific. I pressed on, but in vain. The wind arose; the sea roared; and, as with the mighty shock of an earthquake, it split, and cracked with a tremendous and overwhelming sound. The work was soon finished: in a few minutes a tumultuous sea rolled between me and my enemy, and I was left drifting on a scattered piece of ice, that was continually lessening, and thus preparing for me a hideous death.

In this manner many appalling hours passed; several of my dogs died; and I myself was about to sink under the accumulation of distress, when I saw your vessel riding at anchor, and holding forth to me hopes of succour and life. I had no conception that vessels ever came so far north, and was astounded at the sight. I quickly destroyed part of my sledge to construct oars; and by these means was enabled, with infinite fatigue, to move my ice-raft in the direction of your ship. I had determined, if you were going southward, still to trust myself to the mercy of the seas, rather than abandon my purpose. I hoped to induce you to grant me a boat with which I could still pursue my enemy. But your direction was northward. You took me on board when my vigour was exhausted, and I should soon have sunk under my multiplied hardships into a death, which I still dread,—for my task is unfulfilled.

Oh! when will my guiding spirit, in conducting me to the dæmon, allow me the rest I so much desire; or must I die, and he yet live? If I do, swear to me, Walton, that he shall not escape; that you will seek him, and satisfy my vengeance in his death. Yet, do I dare ask you to undertake my pilgrimage, to endure the hardships that I have undergone? No; I am not so selfish. Yet, when I am dead, if he should appear; if the ministers of vengeance should conduct him to you, swear that he shall not live—swear that he shall not triumph over my accumulated woes, and live to make another such a wretch as I am. He is eloquent and persuasive; and once his words had even power over my heart: but trust him not. His soul is as hellish as his form, full of treachery and fiend-like malice. Hear him not; call on the manes[6] of William, Justine, Clerval, Elizabeth, my father, and of the wretched Victor, and thrust your sword into his heart. I will hover near, and direct the steel aright.

WALTON, *in continuation.*

August 26th, 17—.

You have read this strange and terrific story, Margaret; and do you not feel your blood congealed with horror, like that which even now curdles mine? Sometimes, seized with sudden agony, he could not continue his tale; at others, his voice broken, yet piercing, uttered with difficulty the words so replete with agony. His fine and lovely eyes were now lighted up with indignation, now subdued to downcast sorrow, and quenched in infinite wretchedness. Sometimes he commanded his countenance and tones, and related the most horrible incidents with a tranquil voice, suppressing every mark of agitation; then, like a volcano bursting forth, his face would suddenly change to an expression of the wildest rage, as he shrieked out imprecations on his persecutor.

His tale is connected,[7] and told with an appearance of the simplest truth; yet I own to you that the letters of Felix and Safie, which he shewed me, and the apparition of the monster, seen from our ship, brought to me a greater conviction of the truth of his narrative than his asseverations, however earnest and connected. Such a monster has then really existence; I cannot doubt it; yet I am lost in surprise and admiration. Sometimes I endeavoured to gain from Frankenstein the particulars of his creature's formation; but on this point he was impenetrable.

---

6. Roman term for the spirits of dead ancestors.   7. Coherent.

"Are you mad, my friend?" said he, "or whither does your senseless curiosity lead you? Would you also create for yourself and the world a demoniacal enemy? Or to what do your questions tend? Peace, peace! learn my miseries, and do not seek to increase your own."

Frankenstein discovered that I made notes concerning his history: he asked to see them, and then himself corrected and augmented them in many places; but principally in giving the life and spirit to the conversations he held with his enemy. "Since you have preserved my narration," said he, "I would not that a mutilated one should go down to posterity."

Thus has a week passed away, while I have listened to the strangest tale that ever imagination formed. My thoughts, and every feeling of my soul, have been drunk up by the interest for my guest, which this tale, and his own elevated and gentle manners have created. I wish to soothe him; yet can I counsel one so infinitely miserable, so destitute of every hope of consolation, to live? Oh, no! the only joy that he can now know will be when he composes his shattered feelings to peace and death. Yet he enjoys one comfort, the offspring of solitude and delirium: he believes, that, when in dreams he holds converse with his friends, and derives from that communion consolation for his miseries, or excitements to his vengeance, that they are not the creations of his fancy, but the real beings who visit him from the regions of a remote world. This faith gives a solemnity to his reveries that render them to me almost as imposing and interesting as truth.

Our conversations are not always confined to his own history and misfortunes. On every point of general literature he displays unbounded knowledge, and a quick and piercing apprehension. His eloquence is forcible and touching; nor can I hear him, when he relates a pathetic incident, or endeavours to move the passions of pity or love, without tears. What a glorious creature must he have been in the days of his prosperity, when he is thus noble and godlike in ruin. He seems to feel his own worth, and the greatness of his fall.

"When younger," said he, "I felt as if I were destined for some great enterprise. My feelings are profound; but I possessed a coolness of judgment that fitted me for illustrious achievements. This sentiment of the worth of my nature supported me, when others would have been oppressed; for I deemed it criminal to throw away in useless grief those talents that might be useful to my fellow-creatures. When I reflected on the work I had completed, no less a one than the creation of a sensitive and rational animal, I could not rank myself with the herd of common projectors.[8] But this feeling, which supported me in the commencement of my career, now serves only to plunge me lower in the dust. All my speculations and hopes are as nothing; and, like the archangel who aspired to omnipotence, I am chained in an eternal hell. My imagination was vivid, yet my powers of analysis and application were intense; by the union of these qualities I conceived the idea, and executed the creation of a man. Even now I cannot recollect, without passion, my reveries while the work was incomplete. I trod heaven in my thoughts, now exulting in my powers, now burning with the idea of their effects. From my infancy I was imbued with high hopes and a lofty ambition; but how am I sunk! Oh! my friend, if you had known me as I once was, you would not

8. Devisers of schemes and experiments.

recognize me in this state of degradation. Despondency rarely visited my heart; a high destiny seemed to bear me on, until I fell, never, never again to rise."

Must I then lose this admirable being? I have longed for a friend; I have sought one who would sympathize with and love me. Behold, on these desert seas I have found such a one; but, I fear, I have gained him only to know his value, and lose him. I would reconcile him to life, but he repulses the idea.

"I thank you, Walton," he said, "for your kind intentions towards so miserable a wretch; but when you speak of new ties, and fresh affections, think you that any can replace those who are gone? Can any man be to me as Clerval was; or any woman another Elizabeth? Even where the affections are not strongly moved by any superior excellence, the companions of our childhood always possess a certain power over our minds, which hardly any later friend can obtain. They know our infantine dispositions, which, however they may be afterwards modified, are never eradicated; and they can judge of our actions with more certain conclusions as to the integrity of our motives. A sister or a brother can never, unless indeed such symptoms have been shewn early, suspect the other of fraud or false dealing, when another friend, however strongly he may be attached, may, in spite of himself, be invaded with suspicion. But I enjoyed friends, dear not only through habit and association, but from their own merits; and, wherever I am, the soothing voice of my Elizabeth, and the conversation of Clerval, will be ever whispered in my ear. They are dead; and but one feeling in such a solitude can persuade me to preserve my life. If I were engaged in any high undertaking or design, fraught with extensive utility to my fellow-creatures, then could I live to fulfil it. But such is not my destiny; I must pursue and destroy the being to whom I gave existence; then my lot on earth will be fulfilled, and I may die."

September 2d.

MY BELOVED SISTER,

I write to you, encompassed by peril, and ignorant whether I am ever doomed to see again dear England, and the dearer friends that inhabit it. I am surrounded by mountains of ice, which admit of no escape, and threaten every moment to crush my vessel. The brave fellows, whom I have persuaded to be my companions, look towards me for aid; but I have none to bestow. There is something terribly appalling in our situation, yet my courage and hopes do not desert me. We may survive; and if we do not, I will repeat the lessons of my Seneca, and die with a good heart.[9]

Yet what, Margaret, will be the state of your mind? You will not hear of my destruction, and you will anxiously await my return. Years will pass, and you will have visitings of despair, and yet be tortured by hope. Oh! my beloved sister, the sickening failings of your heart-felt expectations are, in prospect, more terrible to me than my own death. But you have a husband, and lovely children; you may be happy: heaven bless you, and make you so!

My unfortunate guest regards me with the tenderest compassion. He endeavours to fill me with hope; and talks as if life were a possession which

---

9. Seneca was a Roman playwright and Stoic philosopher of the first century C.E. When the emperor Nero, accusing him of conspiracy, ordered him to commit suicide, he slashed his veins and died with quiet dignity.

he valued. He reminds me how often the same accidents have happened to other navigators, who have attempted this sea, and, in spite of myself, he fills me with cheerful auguries. Even the sailors feel the power of his eloquence: when he speaks, they no longer despair; he rouses their energies, and, while they hear his voice, they believe these vast mountains of ice are mole-hills, which will vanish before the resolutions of man. These feelings are transitory; each day's expectation delayed fills them with fear, and I almost dread a mutiny caused by this despair.

September 5th.

A scene has just passed of such uncommon interest, that although it is highly probable that these papers may never reach you, yet I cannot forbear recording it.

We are still surrounded by mountains of ice, still in imminent danger of being crushed in their conflict. The cold is excessive, and many of my unfortunate comrades have already found a grave amidst this scene of desolation. Frankenstein has daily declined in health: a feverish fire still glimmers in his eyes; but he is exhausted, and, when suddenly roused to any exertion, he speedily sinks again into apparent lifelessness.

I mentioned in my last letter the fears I entertained of a mutiny. This morning, as I sat watching the wan countenance of my friend—his eyes half closed, and his limbs hanging listlessly,—I was roused by half a dozen of the sailors, who desired admission into the cabin. They entered; and their leader addressed me. He told me that he and his companions had been chosen by the other sailors to come in deputation to me, to make me a demand, which, in justice, I could not refuse. We were immured in ice, and should probably never escape; but they feared that if, as was possible, the ice should dissipate, and a free passage be opened, I should be rash enough to continue my voyage, and lead them into fresh dangers, after they might happily have surmounted this. They desired, therefore, that I should engage with a solemn promise, that if the vessel should be freed, I would instantly direct my course southward.

This speech troubled me. I had not despaired; nor had I yet conceived the idea of returning, if set free. Yet could I, in justice, or even in possibility, refuse this demand? I hesitated before I answered; when Frankenstein, who had at first been silent, and, indeed, appeared hardly to have force enough to attend, now roused himself, his eyes sparkled, and his cheeks flushed with momentary vigour. Turning towards the men, he said—

"What do you mean? What do you demand of your captain? Are you then so easily turned from your design? Did you not call this a glorious expedition? and wherefore was it glorious? Not because the way was smooth and placid as a southern sea but because it was full of dangers and terror; because, at every new incident, your fortitude was to be called forth and your courage exhibited; because danger and death surrounded, and these dangers you were to brave and overcome. For this was it a glorious, for this was it an honourable undertaking. You were hereafter to be hailed as the benefactors of your species; your name adored, as belonging to brave men who encountered death for honour and the benefit of mankind. And now, behold, with the first imagination of danger, or, if you will, the first mighty and terrific trial of your courage, you shrink away, and are content to be handed down as men who had not strength enough to endure cold and peril; and so, poor souls, they were chilly, and returned to their warm fire-sides. Why, that requires not this preparation; ye need not have come thus far, and dragged your captain to the shame of a defeat, merely to prove yourselves cowards. Oh! be men, or be more than men. Be steady to your purposes, and firm as a rock. This ice is not made of such stuff as your hearts might be; it is mutable, cannot withstand you, if you say that it shall not. Do not return to your families with the stigma of disgrace marked on your brows.[1] Return as heroes who have fought and conquered, and who know not what it is to turn their backs on the foe."

He spoke this with a voice so modulated to the different feelings expressed in his speech, with an eye so full of lofty design and heroism, that can you wonder that these men were moved. They looked at one another, and were unable to reply. I spoke; I told them to retire, and consider of what had been said: that I would not lead them further north, if they strenuously desired the contrary; but that I hoped that, with reflection, their courage would return.

They retired, and I turned towards my friend; but he was sunk in languor, and almost deprived of life.

How all this will terminate, I know not; but I had rather die, than return shamefully,—my purpose unfulfilled. Yet I fear such will be my fate; the men, unsupported by ideas of glory and honour, can never willingly continue to endure their present hardships.

September 7th.

The die is cast;[2] I have consented to return, if we are not destroyed. Thus are my hopes blasted by cowardice and indecision; I come back ignorant and disappointed. It requires more philosophy than I possess, to bear this injustice with patience.

September 12th.

It is past; I am returning to England. I have lost my hopes of utility and glory;—I have lost my friend. But I will endeavour to detail these bitter circumstances to you, my dear sister; and, while I am wafted towards England, and towards you, I will not despond.

September 9th, the ice began to move, and roarings like thunder were heard at a distance, as the islands split and cracked in every direction. We were in the most imminent peril; but, as we could only remain passive, my chief attention was occupied by my unfortunate guest, whose illness increased in such a degree, that he was entirely confined to his bed. The ice cracked behind us, and was driven with force towards the north; a breeze sprung from the west, and on the 11th the passage towards the south became perfectly free. When the sailors saw this, and that their return to their native country was apparently assured, a shout of tumultuous joy broke from them, loud and long-continued. Frankenstein, who was dozing, awoke, and asked

1. An allusion to the mark that the Lord set upon Cain after he killed his brother, Abel (Genesis 4.8–15).

2. Echoing Julius Caesar's remark when, in 49 B.C.E., he crossed the Rubicon and so inaugurated a war against his former ally, Pompey.

the cause of the tumult. "They shout," I said, "because they will soon return to England."

"Do you then really return?"

"Alas! yes; I cannot withstand their demands. I cannot lead them unwillingly to danger, and I must return."

"Do so, if you will; but I will not. You may give up your purpose; but mine is assigned to me by heaven, and I dare not. I am weak; but surely the spirits who assist my vengeance will endow me with sufficient strength." Saying this, he endeavoured to spring from the bed, but the exertion was too great for him; he fell back, and fainted.

It was long before he was restored; and I often thought that life was entirely extinct. At length he opened his eyes, but he breathed with difficulty, and was unable to speak. The surgeon gave him a composing draught,[3] and ordered us to leave him undisturbed. In the mean time he told me, that my friend had certainly not many hours to live.

His sentence was pronounced; and I could only grieve, and be patient. I sat by his bed watching him; his eyes were closed, and I thought he slept; but presently he called to me in a feeble voice, and, bidding me come near, said—"Alas! the strength I relied on is gone; I feel that I shall soon die, and he, my enemy and persecutor, may still be in being. Think not, Walton, that in the last moments of my existence I feel that burning hatred, and ardent desire of revenge, I once expressed, but I feel myself justified in desiring the death of my adversary. During these last days I have been occupied in examining my past conduct; nor do I find it blameable. In a fit of enthusiastic madness I created a rational creature, and was bound towards him, to assure, as far as was in my power, his happiness and well-being. This was my duty; but there was another still paramount to that. My duties towards my fellow-creatures had greater claims to my attention, because they included a greater proportion of happiness or misery. Urged by this view, I refused, and I did right in refusing, to create a companion for the first creature. He shewed unparalleled malignity and selfishness, in evil: he destroyed my friends; he devoted to destruction beings who possessed exquisite sensations, happiness, and wisdom; nor do I know where this thirst for vengeance may end. Miserable himself, that he may render no other wretched, he ought to die. The task of his destruction was mine, but I have failed. When actuated by selfish and vicious motives, I asked you to undertake my unfinished work; and I renew this request now, when I am only induced by reason and virtue.

"Yet I cannot ask you to renounce your country and friends, to fulfil this task; and now, that you are returning to England, you will have little chance of meeting with him. But the consideration of these points, and the well-balancing of what you may esteem your duties, I leave to you; my judgment and ideas are already disturbed by the near approach of death. I dare not ask you to do what I think right, for I may still be misled by passion.

"That he should live to be an instrument of mischief disturbs me; in other respects this hour, when I momentarily expect my release, is the only happy one which I have enjoyed for several years. The forms of the beloved dead flit before me, and I hasten to their arms. Farewell, Walton! Seek happiness in tranquillity, and avoid ambition, even if it be only the apparently innocent

3. Liquid medicine.

one of distinguishing yourself in science and discoveries. Yet why do I say this? I have myself been blasted in these hopes, yet another may succeed."

His voice became fainter as he spoke; and at length, exhausted by his effort, he sunk into silence. About half an hour afterwards he attempted again to speak, but was unable; he pressed my hand feebly, and his eyes closed for ever, while the irradiation of a gentle smile passed away from his lips.

Margaret, what comment can I make on the untimely extinction of this glorious spirit? What can I say, that will enable you to understand the depth of my sorrow? All that I should express would be inadequate and feeble. My tears flow; my mind is overshadowed by a cloud of disappointment. But I journey towards England, and I may there find consolation.

I am interrupted. What do these sounds portend? It is midnight; the breeze blows fairly, and the watch on deck scarcely stir. Again; there is a sound as of a human voice, but hoarser; it comes from the cabin where the remains of Frankenstein still lie. I must arise, and examine. Good night, my sister.

Great God! what a scene has just taken place! I am yet dizzy with the remembrance of it. I hardly know whether I shall have the power to detail it; yet the tale which I have recorded would be incomplete without this final and wonderful catastrophe.

I entered the cabin, where lay the remains of my ill-fated and admirable friend. Over him hung a form which I cannot find words to describe; gigantic in stature, yet uncouth and distorted in its proportions. As he hung over the coffin, his face was concealed by long locks of ragged hair; but one vast hand was extended, in colour and apparent texture like that of a mummy. When he heard the sound of my approach, he ceased to utter exclamations of grief and horror, and sprung towards the window. Never did I behold a vision so horrible as his face, of such loathsome, yet appalling hideousness. I shut my eyes involuntarily, and endeavoured to recollect what were my duties with regard to this destroyer. I called on him to stay.

He paused, looking on me with wonder; and, again turning towards the lifeless form of his creator, he seemed to forget my presence, and every feature and gesture seemed instigated by the wildest rage of some uncontrollable passion.

"That is also my victim!" he exclaimed; "in his murder my crimes are consummated; the miserable series of my being is wound to its close! Oh, Frankenstein! generous and self-devoted being! what does it avail that I now ask thee to pardon me? I, who irretrievably destroyed thee by destroying all thou lovedst. Alas! he is cold; he may not answer me."

His voice seemed suffocated; and my first impulses, which had suggested to me the duty of obeying the dying request of my friend, in destroying his enemy, were now suspended by a mixture of curiosity and compassion. I approached this tremendous being; I dared not again raise my looks upon his face, there was something so scaring and unearthly in his ugliness. I attempted to speak, but the words died away on my lips. The monster continued to utter wild and incoherent self-reproaches. At length I gathered resolution to address him, in a pause of the tempest of his passion: "Your repentance," I said, "is now superfluous. If you had listened to the voice of conscience, and heeded the stings of remorse, before you had urged your diabolical vengeance to this extremity, Frankenstein would yet have lived."

"And do you dream?" said the dæmon; "do you think that I was then dead to agony and remorse?—He," he continued, pointing to the corpse, "he suffered not more in the consummation of the deed;—oh! not the ten-thousandth portion of the anguish that was mine during the lingering detail of its execution. A frightful selfishness hurried me on, while my heart was poisoned with remorse. Think ye that the groans of Clerval were music to my ears? My heart was fashioned to be susceptible of love and sympathy; and, when wrenched by misery to vice and hatred, it did not endure the violence of the change without torture, such as you cannot even imagine.

"After the murder of Clerval, I returned to Switzerland, heart-broken and overcome. I pitied Frankenstein; my pity amounted to horror: I abhorred myself. But when I discovered that he, the author at once of my existence and of its unspeakable torments, dared to hope for happiness; that while he accumulated wretchedness and despair upon me, he sought his own enjoyment in feelings and passions from the indulgence of which I was for ever barred, then impotent envy and bitter indignation filled me with an insatiable thirst for vengeance. I recollected my threat, and resolved that it should be accomplished. I knew that I was preparing for myself a deadly torture; but I was the slave, not the master of an impulse, which I detested, yet could not disobey. Yet when she died!—nay, then I was not miserable. I had cast off all feeling, subdued all anguish to riot in the excess of my despair. Evil thenceforth became my good.[4] Urged thus far, I had no choice but to adapt my nature to an element which I had willingly chosen. The completion of my demoniacal design became an insatiable passion. And now it is ended; there is my last victim!"

I was at first touched by the expressions of his misery; yet when I called to mind what Frankenstein had said of his powers of eloquence and persuasion, and when I again cast my eyes on the lifeless form of my friend, indignation was re-kindled within me. "Wretch!" I said, "it is well that you come here to whine over the desolation that you have made. You throw a torch into a pile of buildings, and when they are consumed you sit among the ruins, and lament the fall. Hypocritical fiend! if he whom you mourn still lived, still would he be the object, again would he become the prey of your accursed vengeance. It is not pity that you feel; you lament only because the victim of your malignity is withdrawn from your power."

"Oh, it is not thus—not thus," interrupted the being; "yet such must be the impression conveyed to you by what appears to be the purport of my actions. Yet I seek not a fellow-feeling in my misery. No sympathy may I ever find. When I first sought it, it was the love of virtue, the feelings of happiness and affection with which my whole being overflowed, that I wished to be participated.[5] But now, that virtue has become to me a shadow, and that happiness and affection are turned into bitter and loathing despair, in what should I seek for sympathy? I am content to suffer alone, while my sufferings shall endure: when I die, I am well satisfied that abhorrence and opprobrium should load my memory. Once my fancy was soothed with dreams of virtue, of fame, and of enjoyment. Once I falsely hoped to meet with beings, who, pardoning my outward form, would love me for the excellent qualities which

4. Echoing Satan, *Paradise Lost* 4.109–10: "All good to me is lost; / Evil, be thou my good."

5. Shared with others.

I was capable of bringing forth. I was nourished with high thoughts of honour and devotion. But now vice has degraded me beneath the meanest animal. No crime, no mischief, no malignity, no misery, can be found comparable to mine. When I call over the frightful catalogue of my deeds, I cannot believe that I am he whose thoughts were once filled with sublime and transcendant visions of the beauty and the majesty of goodness. But it is even so; the fallen angel becomes a malignant devil.[6] Yet even that enemy of God and man had friends and associates in his desolation; I am quite alone.

"You, who call Frankenstein your friend, seem to have a knowledge of my crimes and his misfortunes. But, in the detail which he gave you of them, he could not sum up the hours and months of misery which I endured, wasting in impotent passions. For whilst I destroyed his hopes, I did not satisfy my own desires. They were for ever ardent and craving; still I desired love and fellowship, and I was still spurned. Was there no injustice in this? Am I to be thought the only criminal, when all human kind sinned against me? Why do you not hate Felix, who drove his friend from his door with contumely?[7] Why do you not execrate the rustic who sought to destroy the saviour of his child? Nay, these are virtuous and immaculate beings! I, the miserable and the abandoned, am an abortion, to be spurned at, and kicked, and trampled on. Even now my blood boils at the recollection of this injustice.

"But it is true that I am a wretch. I have murdered the lovely and the helpless; I have strangled the innocent as they slept, and grasped to death his throat who never injured me or any other living thing. I have devoted my creator, the select specimen of all that is worthy of love and admiration among men, to misery; I have pursued him even to that irremediable ruin. There he lies, white and cold in death. You hate me; but your abhorrence cannot equal that with which I regard myself. I look on the hands which executed the deed; I think on the heart in which the imagination of it was conceived, and long for the moment when they will meet my eyes, when it will haunt my thoughts, no more.

"Fear not that I shall be the instrument of future mischief. My work is nearly complete. Neither your's nor any man's death is needed to consummate the series of my being, and accomplish that which must be done; but it requires my own. Do not think that I shall be slow to perform this sacrifice. I shall quit your vessel on the ice-raft which brought me hither, and shall seek the most northern extremity of the globe; I shall collect my funeral pile, and consume to ashes this miserable frame, that its remains may afford no light to any curious and unhallowed wretch, who would create such another as I have been. I shall die. I shall no longer feel the agonies which now consume me, or be the prey of feelings unsatisfied, yet unquenched. He is dead who called me into being; and when I shall be no more, the very remembrance of us both will speedily vanish. I shall no longer see the sun or stars, or feel the winds play on my cheeks. Light, feeling, and sense, will pass away; and in this condition must I find my happiness. Some years ago, when the images which this world affords first opened upon me, when I felt the cheering warmth of summer, and heard the rustling of the leaves and the chirping

6. Like Satan, who before his rebellion against God had been the archangel Lucifer.

7. Contemptuous speech.

of the birds, and these were all to me, I should have wept to die; now it is my only consolation. Polluted by crimes, and torn by the bitterest remorse, where can I find rest but in death?

"Farewell! I leave you, and in you the last of human kind whom these eyes will ever behold. Farewell, Frankenstein! If thou wert yet alive, and yet cherished a desire of revenge against me, it would be better satiated in my life than in my destruction. But it was not so; thou didst seek my extinction, that I might not cause greater wretchedness; and if yet, in some mode unknown to me, thou hast not yet ceased to think and feel, thou desirest not my life for my own misery. Blasted as thou wert, my agony was still superior to thine; for the bitter sting of remorse may not cease to rankle in my wounds until death shall close them for ever.

"But soon," he cried, with sad and solemn enthusiasm, "I shall die, and what I now feel be no longer felt. Soon these burning miseries will be extinct. I shall ascend my funeral pile triumphantly, and exult in the agony of the torturing flames. The light of that conflagration will fade away; my ashes will be swept into the sea by the winds. My spirit will sleep in peace; or if it thinks, it will not surely think thus. Farewell."

He sprung from the cabin-window, as he said this, upon the ice-raft which lay close to the vessel. He was soon borne away by the waves, and lost in darkness and distance.

THE END.

1816–17   1818

LETITIA ELIZABETH LANDON
1802–1838

Letitia Elizabeth Landon, whose initials became one of the most famous literary pseudonyms of nineteenth-century Britain, was born and educated in Chelsea, London. She published her first poem in the weekly *Literary Gazette* in March 1820, when she was seventeen, and soon thereafter became a principal writer and reviewer for the magazine. Her first important collections of poems were *The Improvisatrice* (1824), which went through six editions in its first year, and *The Troubadour, Catalogue of Pictures, and Historical Sketches* (1825), which went through four. She quickly followed these with *The Golden Violet* (1827), the first of many editions of her *Poetical Works* (1827), and *The Venetian Bracelet* (1829). She also wrote essays, short fiction, children's stories, several novels, and a play; and she edited—and contributed hundreds of poems to—the albums, gift books, and annual anthologies that became a staple of British literary production of the 1820s and 1830s. All this highly remunerative work appeared from the pen of "L.E.L.," the pseudonym that she first used in the *Literary Gazette* and that attracted increasing numbers of readers and also poetic responses, as it was disclosed by stages that the author behind the initials was female, young, and a great beauty. To this day, many of Landon's books continue to be catalogued under the pseudonym, and a recently published "feminist companion" to literature in English has an entry for "L.E.L." but none for "Landon."

Landon and Felicia Hemans, as "L.E.L." and "Mrs. Hemans," were the two best-selling poets of their time—the decade and a half following the deaths of Keats, Percy Shelley, and Byron in the early 1820s—and were major inspirations to subsequent writers such as Elizabeth Barrett and Christina Rossetti. Unlike Hemans, Landon attracted scandal, partly because of her casual social relations with men and partly because of her principal subject matter, the joys and especially the sorrows of female passion. There were rumors of affairs with, among others, William Jerdan, who was editor of the *Literary Gazette*, the journalist William Maginn, and the artist Daniel Maclise. She was engaged to the editor John Forster, future biographer of Dickens, but had to break the engagement because of these rumors. In 1838 she finally married, someone she had known for only a short time, George Maclean, governor of the British settlement at Cape Coast Castle, west Africa (in what is now Ghana). She arrived with Maclean at Cape Coast in August 1838 and two months later was dead, reportedly from an overdose of prussic acid—though whether the cause was accident, suicide, or murder has never been determined.

Landon perfected, and the reviewers helped maintain, several personas in her work: the pseudonymous, therefore anonymous, writer of passionate love lyrics; the Romantic "improvisatrice" jotting down verses in the interstices of an intense social life; the renowned beauty who constantly fails in love and, in lamenting her crushed feelings, becomes the female equivalent of the Byronic hero; and an early version of the Victorian "poetess" inditing songs to appeal to a burgeoning cult of domesticity. As in Hemans's poetry, some of these personas are not wholly compatible with some of the others. But their variety and vitality captivated the readers and, during Landon's short life, provided her a fortune in sales and royalties.

The Proud Ladye[1]

    Oh, what could the ladye's beauty match,
        An° it were not the ladye's pride?   *if*
    An hundred knights from far and near
        Woo'd at that ladye's side.

5   The rose of the summer slept on her cheek,
        Its lily upon her breast,
    And her eye shone forth like the glorious star
        That rises the first in the west.

    There were some that woo'd for her land and gold,
10   And some for her noble name,

1. This ballad is . . . taken, with some slight change, from a legend in Russell's Germany [Landon's note]. The story, in John Russell's *A Tour in Germany* (1824), chap. 11, relates how "the fair Cunigunda, equally celebrated for her charms and her cruelty . . . would listen to no tale of love, and dreaded marriage as she did a prison. At length, to free herself from all importunities, she made a solemn vow never to give her hand but to the knight who should ride round the castle on the outer wall . . . [which] runs along the very brink of hideous precipices. . . . History has not recorded the precise number of those who actually made the attempt; it is only certain that every one of them broke his neck. . . . At length, a young and handsome knight appeared at the castle gate . . . [to] try his fortune. . . . In a short time, a shout from the menials announced that the adventure had been achieved; and Cunigunda, exulting that she was conquered, hastened into the court. . . . But the knight stood aloof, gloomy and severe. 'I can claim you,' said he; 'but I am come, and I have risked my life, not to win your hand, but to humble your pride and punish your barbarity'—and thereupon he read her a harsh lecture on the cruelty and arrogance of her conduct towards her suitors. The spirit of chivalry weeps at recording, that he finished his oration by giving the astonished beauty a box on the ear." Landon's ballad (in the same stanza as Keats's story of another *belle dame sans merci*) was included as a separate piece within a long poem, *The Troubadour*, that she published in 1825.

And more that woo'd for her loveliness;
　　But her answer was still the same.

"There is a steep and lofty wall,
　　Where my warders° trembling stand;　　　　　*guards*
15　He who at speed shall ride round its height,
　　For him shall be my hand."

Many turn'd away from the deed,
　　The hope of their wooing o'er;
But many a young knight mounted the steed
20　　He never mounted more.

At last there came a youthful knight,
　　From a strange and far countrie,
The steed that he rode was white as the foam
　　Upon a stormy sea.

25　And she who had scorn'd the name of love,
　　Now bow'd before its might,
And the ladye grew meek as if disdain
　　Were not made for that stranger knight.

She sought at first to steal his soul
30　　By dance, song, and festival;
At length on bended knee she pray'd
　　He would not ride the wall.

But gaily the young knight laugh'd at her fears,
　　And flung him on his steed,—
35　There was not a saint in the calendar
　　That she pray'd not to in her need.

She dar'd not raise her eyes to see
　　If heaven had granted her prayer,
Till she heard a light step bound to her side,—
40　　The gallant knight stood there!

And took the ladye Adeline
　　From her hair a jewell'd band,
But the knight repell'd the offer'd gift,
　　And turn'd from the offer'd hand.

45　"And deemest thou that I dared this deed,
　　Ladye, for love of thee?
The honour that guides the soldier's lance
　　Is mistress enough for me.

"Enough for me to ride the ring,
50　　The victor's crown to wear;
But not in honour of the eyes
　　Of any ladye there.

"I had a brother whom I lost
    Through thy proud crueltie,
55 And far more was to me his love,
    Than woman's love can be.

"I came to triumph o'er the pride
    Through which that brother fell,
I laugh to scorn thy love and thee,
60   And now, proud dame, farewell!"

And from that hour the ladye pined,
    For love was in her heart,
And on her slumber there came dreams
    She could not bid depart.

65 Her eye lost all its starry light,
    Her cheek grew wan and pale,
Till she hid her faded loveliness
    Beneath the sacred veil.

And she cut off her long dark hair,
70   And bade the world farewell,
And she now dwells a veiled nun
    In Saint Marie's cell.

1825

Love's Last Lesson

"Teach it me, if you can,—forgetfulness![1]
I surely shall forget, if you can bid me;
I who have worshipp'd thee, my god on earth,
I who have bow'd me at thy lightest word.
5 Your last command, 'Forget me,' will it not
Sink deeply down within my inmost soul?
Forget thee!—ay, forgetfulness will be
A mercy to me. By the many nights
When I have wept for that I dared not sleep,—
10 A dream had made me live my woes again,
Acting my wretchedness, without the hope
My foolish heart still clings to, though that hope
Is like the opiate which may lull a while,
Then wake to double torture; by the days
15 Pass'd in lone watching and in anxious fears,
When a breath sent the crimson to my cheek,
Like the red gushing of a sudden wound;
By all the careless looks and careless words
Which have to me been like the scorpion's stinging;

---

1. An allusion to Byron's *Manfred* 1.1.135–36: "What wouldst thou with us, son of mortals—say?"—to which Manfred replies, "Forgetfulness." Other Byronic echoes in lines 14–15, 18–23, 85–86, and 95–98 further link Landon's speaker to the protagonists of *Childe Harold* and *Manfred*.

20   By happiness blighted, and by thee, for ever;
      By thy eternal work of wretchedness;
      By all my wither'd feelings, ruin'd health,
      Crush'd hopes, and rifled heart, I will forget thee!
      Alas! my words are vanity. Forget thee!
25   Thy work of wasting is too surely done.
      The April shower may pass and be forgotten,
      The rose fall and one fresh spring in its place,
      And thus it may be with light summer love.
      It was not thus with mine: it did not spring,
30   Like the bright colour on an evening cloud,
      Into a moment's life, brief, beautiful;
      Not amid lighted halls, when flatteries
      Steal on the ear like dew upon the rose,
      As soft, as soon dispersed, as quickly pass'd;
35   But you first call'd my woman's feelings forth,
      And taught me love ere I had dream'd love's name.
      I loved unconsciously: your name was all
      That seem'd in language, and to me the world
      Was only made for you; in solitude,
40   When passions hold their interchange together,
      Your image was the shadow of my thought;
      Never did slave, before his Eastern lord,
      Tremble as I did when I met your eye,
      And yet each look was counted as a prize;
45   I laid your words up in my heart like pearls
      Hid in the ocean's treasure-cave. At last
      I learn'd my heart's deep secret: for I hoped,
      I dream'd you loved me; wonder, fear, delight,
      Swept my heart like a storm; my soul, my life,
50   Seem'd all too little for your happiness;
      Had I been mistress of the starry worlds
      That light the midnight, they had all been yours,
      And I had deem'd such boon but poverty.
      As it was, I gave all I could—my love,
55   My deep, my true, my fervent, faithful love;
      And now you bid me learn forgetfulness:
      It is a lesson that I soon shall learn.
      There is a home of quiet for the wretched,
      A somewhat dark, and cold, and silent rest,
60   But still it is rest,—for it is the grave."

      She flung aside the scroll, as it had part
      In her great misery. Why should she write?
      What could she write? Her woman's pride forbade
      To let him look upon her heart, and see
65   It was an utter ruin;—and cold words,
      And scorn and slight, that may repay his own,
      Were as a foreign language, to whose sound
      She might not frame her utterance. Down she bent
      Her head upon an arm so white that tears

70 Seem'd but the natural melting of its snow,
  Touch'd by the flush'd cheek's crimson; yet life-blood
  Less wrings in shedding than such tears as those.

   And this then is love's ending! It is like
  The history of some fair southern clime.
75 Hot fires are in the bosom of the earth,
  And the warm'd soil puts forth its thousand flowers,
  Its fruits of gold, summer's regality,
  And sleep and odours float upon the air:
  At length the subterranean element
80 Breaks from its secret dwelling-place, and lays
  All waste before it; the red lava stream
  Sweeps like the pestilence; and that which was
  A garden in its colours and its breath,
  Fit for the princess of a fairy tale,
85 Is as a desert, in whose burning sands,
  And ashy waters, who is there can trace
  A sign, a memory of its former beauty?
  It is thus with the heart; love lights it up
  With hopes like young companions, and with joys
90 Dreaming deliciously of their sweet selves.

   This is at first; but what is the result?
  Hopes that lie mute in their own sullenness,
  For they have quarrell'd even with themselves;
  And joys indeed like birds of Paradise:[2]
95 And in their stead despair coils scorpion-like
  Stinging itself; and the heart, burnt and crush'd
  With passion's earthquake, scorch'd and wither'd up,
  Lies in its desolation,—this is love.

   What is the tale that I would tell? Not one
100 Of strange adventure, but a common tale
  Of woman's wretchedness; one to be read
  Daily in many a young and blighted heart.
  The lady whom I spake of rose again
  From the red fever's couch, to careless eyes
105 Perchance the same as she had ever been.
  But oh, how alter'd to herself! She felt
  That bird-like pining for some gentle home
  To which affection might attach itself,
  That weariness which hath but outward part
110 In what the world calls pleasure, and that chill
  Which makes life taste the bitterness of death.

   And he she loved so well,—what opiate
  Lull'd consciousness into its selfish sleep?—
  He said he loved her not; that never vow

---

2. In Eastern tales, the bird of Paradise never rests on the earth [Landon's note].

115 Or passionate pleading won her soul for him;
And that he guess'd not her deep tenderness.

Are words, then, only false? are there no looks,
Mute but most eloquent; no gentle cares
That win so much upon the fair weak things
120 They seem to guard? And had he not long read
Her heart's hush'd secret in the soft dark eye
Lighted at his approach, and on the cheek
Colouring all crimson at his lightest look?
This is the truth; his spirit wholly turn'd
125 To stern ambition's dream, to that fierce strife
Which leads to life's high places, and reck'd not
What lovely flowers might perish in his path.

And here at length is somewhat of revenge:
For man's most golden dreams of pride and power
130 Are vain as any woman-dreams of love;
Both end in weary brow and wither'd heart,
And the grave closes over those whose hopes
Have lain there long before.

1827

Revenge

Ay, gaze upon her rose-wreathed hair,
  And gaze upon her smile;
Seem as you drank the very air
  Her breath perfumed the while:

5 And wake for her the gifted line,
  That wild and witching lay,
And swear your heart is as a shrine,
  That only owns her sway.

'Tis well: I am revenged at last,—
10   Mark you that scornful cheek,—
The eye averted as you pass'd,
  Spoke more than words could speak.

Ay, now by all the bitter tears
  That I have shed for thee,—
15 The racking doubts, the burning fears,—
  Avenged they well may be—

By the nights pass'd in sleepless care,
  The days of endless woe;
All that you taught my heart to bear,
20   All that yourself will know.

I would not wish to see you laid
   Within an early tomb;
I should forget how you betray'd,
   And only weep your doom:

25 But this is fitting punishment,
   To live and love in vain,—
Oh my wrung heart, be thou content,
   And feed upon his pain.

Go thou and watch her lightest sigh,—
30   Thine own it will not be;
And bask beneath her sunny eye,—
   It will not turn on thee.

'Tis well: the rack, the chain, the wheel,
   Far better had'st thou proved;
35 Ev'n I could almost pity feel,
   For thou art not beloved.

1829

The Little Shroud

She put him on a snow-white shroud,
   A chaplet° on his head;   *wreath*
And gather'd early primroses
   To scatter o'er the dead.

5 She laid him in his little grave—
   'Twas hard to lay him there,
When spring was putting forth its flowers,
   And every thing was fair.

She had lost many children—now
10   The last of them was gone;
And day and night she sat and wept
   Beside the funeral stone.

One midnight, while her constant tears
   Were falling with the dew,
15 She heard a voice, and lo! her child
   Stood by her weeping too!

His shroud was damp, his face was white:
   He said,—"I cannot sleep,
Your tears have made my shroud so wet;
20   Oh, mother, do not weep!"

Oh, love is strong!—the mother's heart
   Was filled with tender fears;

Oh, love is strong!—and for her child
  Her grief restrained its tears.

25   One eve a light shone round her bed,
  And there she saw him stand—
Her infant, in his little shroud,
  A taper in his hand.

"Lo! mother, see my shroud is dry,
30   And I can sleep once more!"
And beautiful the parting smile
  The little infant wore.

And down within the silent grave
  He laid his weary head;
35 And soon the early violets
  Grew o'er his grassy bed.

1832

Poems in Process

In all ages, some poets have claimed that their poems were not willed but were inspired, whether by a muse, by divine visitation, or by sudden emergence from the author's subconscious mind. But as the poet Richard Aldington has remarked, "genius is not enough; one must also work." The working manuscripts of the greatest writers show that, however involuntary the origin of a poem, vision was usually followed by laborious revision before the work achieved the seeming inevitability of its final form.

Although some earlier poetic manuscripts have survived, it was not until the nineteenth century that the working drafts of poets began to be widely preserved, and so remain abundantly available. The examples from major poets that are transcribed here represent various stages in the composition of a poem, and a variety of procedures by individual poets. The selections from Blake, Byron, Shelley, and Keats are drafts that were written, emended, crossed out, and rewritten in the heat of first invention; while poems by Wordsworth, Hopkins, and Yeats are shown in successive stages of revision over an extended period of time. Shelley's *O World, O Life, O Time* originated in a few key nouns, together with an abstract rhythmic pattern that was only later fleshed out with words, while Yeats's *After Long Silence* began as a prose sketch that gradually and laboriously was reshaped into a metric and stanzaic form. Still other poems—Tennyson's *The Lady of Shalott*, Yeats's *The Sorrow of Love*—were subjected to radical revision long after the initial versions had been committed to print. In all these examples we look on as poets, no matter how rapidly they achieve a result they are willing to let stand, carry on their inevitably tentative efforts to meet the multiple requirements of meaning, syntax, meter, sound pattern, and the constraints imposed by a chosen stanza. And because these are all very good poets, the seeming conflict between the necessities of significance and form results not in the distortion but in the perfecting of the poetic statement.

Our transcriptions from the poets' drafts attempt to reproduce, as accurately as the change from script to print will allow, the appearance of the original manuscript page. A poet's first attempt at a line or phrase is reproduced in larger type, the emendations in smaller type. The line numbers in the headings that identify an excerpt are those of the final form of the complete poem.

SELECTED BIBLIOGRAPHY

Autograph Poetry in the English Language, 2 vols., 1973, compiled by P. J. Croft, reproduces and transcribes one or more pages of manuscript in the poet's own hand, from the 14th century to the late twentieth century. Volume 1 includes Blake and Burns; volume 2 includes many of the other poets represented in this volume of *The Norton Anthology of English Literature*, from Wordsworth to Dylan Thomas. Books that discuss the process of composition and revision, with examples from the manuscripts and printed versions of poems, are Charles D. Abbott, ed., *Poets at Work*, 1948; Phyllis Bartlett, *Poems in Process*, 1951; A. F. Scott, *The Poet's Craft*, 1957; George Bornstein, *Poetic Remaking: The Art of Browning, Yeats, and Pound*, 1988. In

Word for Word: A Study of Authors' Alterations, 1965, Wallace Hildick analyzes the composition of prose fiction as well as poems; a shorter version, Word for Word: The Rewriting of Fiction, 1965, discusses the revision of novels by George Eliot, Samuel Butler, Hardy, Lawrence, James, and Woolf. Byron's "Don Juan," ed. T. G. Steffan and W. W. Pratt, 4 vols., 1957, transcribes the manuscript drafts; the Cornell Wordsworth, in process, reproduces, transcribes, and discusses various versions of Wordsworth's poems from the first manuscript drafts to the final publication in his lifetime, and the Cornell Yeats, also in process, does the same for Yeats. For facsim-

iles and transcripts of Keats's poems, see John Keats: Poetry Manuscripts at Harvard, ed. Jack Stillinger, 1990. Jon Stallworthy, Between the Lines: Yeats's Poetry in the Making, 1963, reproduces and analyzes the sequential drafts of a number of Yeats's major poems. Valerie Eliot has edited T. S. Eliot's The Waste Land: A Facsimile and Transcript of the Original Drafts Including the Annotations of Ezra Pound, 1971, while Dame Helen Gardner has transcribed and analyzed the manuscript drafts of Eliot's Four Quartets in The Composition of Four Quartets, 1978.

WILLIAM BLAKE
The Tyger[1]

[First Draft]

The Tyger

1
   Tyger Tyger burning bright
   In the forests of the night
   What immortal hand or eye
   ~~Dare Could frame~~ thy fearful symmetry

2
   Burnt in
   ~~In what distant~~ deeps or skies
   ~~The cruel Burnt the fire~~ of thine eyes
   On what wings dare he aspire
   What the hand dare sieze the fire

3
   And what shoulder & what art
   Could twist the sinews of thy heart
   And when thy heart began to beat
   What dread hand & what dread feet

   ~~Could fetch it from the furnace deep~~
   ~~And in thy horrid ribs dare steep~~
   ~~In the well of sanguine woe~~
   ~~In what clay & what mould~~
   ~~Were thy eyes of fury rolld~~

4
   Where   where
   ~~What~~ the hammer ~~what~~ the chain
   In what furnace was thy brain

1. These drafts have been taken from a notebook used by William Blake, called the Rossetti MS because it was once owned by Dante Gabriel Rossetti, the Victorian poet and painter; David V. Erd- man's edition of The Notebook of William Blake (1973) contains a photographic facsimile. The stanza and line numbers were written by Blake in the manuscript.

                                  dread grasp

What the anvil what the ~~arm~~ arm ~~grasp~~ ~~clasp~~

Dare ~~Could~~ its deadly terrors ~~clasp~~ ~~grasp~~ clasp

6   Tyger Tyger burning bright
In the forests of the night
What immortal hand & eye

         frame
Dare ~~form~~ thy fearful symmetry

[*Trial Stanzas*]

Burnt in distant deeps or skies
The cruel fire of thine eye,
Could heart descend or wings aspire
What the hand dare sieze the fire

         dare he ~~smile~~ ~~laugh~~

5 3 And ~~did he laugh~~ his work to see

      ankle

~~What the shoulder what the knee~~

    Dare
4 ~~Did~~ he who made the lamb make thee
1 When the stars threw down their spears
2 And waterd heaven with their tears

[*Second Full Draft*]

Tyger Tyger burning bright
In the forests of the night
What Immortal hand & eye
Dare frame thy fearful symmetry

And what shoulder & what art
Could twist the sinews of thy heart
And when thy heart began to beat
What dread hand & what dread feet

When the stars threw down their spears
And waterd heaven with their tears
Did he smile his work to see
Did he who made the lamb make thee

Tyger Tyger burning bright
In the forests of the night
What immortal hand & eye
Dare frame thy fearful symmetry

[*Final Version, 1794*][2]

The Tyger

Tyger Tyger, burning bright,
In the forests of the night;
What immortal hand or eye,
Could frame thy fearful symmetry?

In what distant deeps or skies
Burnt the fire of thine eyes!
On what wings dare he aspire?
What the hand, dare sieze the fire?

And what shoulder, & what art,
Could twist the sinews of thy heart?
And when thy heart began to beat,
What dread hand? & what dread feet?

What the hammer? what the chain,
In what furnace was thy brain?
What the anvil? what dread grasp,
Dare its deadly terrors clasp?

When the stars threw down their spears
And water'd heaven with their tears:
Did he smile his work to see?
Did he who made the Lamb make thee?

Tyger, Tyger burning bright,
In the forests of the night:
What immortal hand or eye,
Dare frame thy fearful symmetry?

WILLIAM WORDSWORTH
She dwelt among the untrodden ways

[*Version in a Letter to Coleridge,
December 1798 or January 1799*][1]

My hope was one, from cities far
　　Nursed on a lonesome heath:
Her lips were red as roses are,
　　Her hair a woodbine wreath.

She lived among the untrodden ways
　　Beside the springs of Dove,

---

2. As published in *Songs of Experience*.
1. Printed in Ernest de Selincourt's *Early Letters of William and Dorothy Wordsworth* (1935). By deleting two stanzas, and making a few verbal changes, Wordsworth achieved the terse published form of his great dirge.

A maid whom there were none to praise,
   And very few to love;

A violet by a mossy stone
   Half-hidden from the eye!
Fair as a star when only one
   Is shining in the sky!

And she was graceful as the broom
   That flowers by Carron's side;[2]
But slow distemper checked her bloom,
   And on the Heath she died.

Long time before her head lay low
   Dead to the world was she:
But now she's in her grave, and Oh!
   The difference to me!

[*Final Version, 1800*][3]

Song

She dwelt among th' untrodden ways
   Beside the springs of Dove,
A Maid whom there were none to praise
   And very few to love.

A Violet by a mossy stone
   Half-hidden from the Eye!
—Fair, as a star when only one
   Is shining in the sky!

She *liv'd* unknown, and few could know
   When Lucy ceas'd to be;
But she is in her Grave, and Oh!
   The difference to me.

LORD BYRON
From Don Juan[1]

[*First Draft: Canto 3, Stanza 9*]

~~Life is a play and men~~
All tragedies are finished by a death,
All Comedies are ended by a marriage,
~~For Life can go no further.~~

---

2. The Carron is a river in northwestern Scotland. "Broom" (preceding line) is a shrub with long slender branches and yellow flowers.
3. As published in the second edition of *Lyrical Ballads*.

1. Reproduced from transcripts made of Byron's manuscripts in T. G. Steffan and W. W. Pratt, *Byron's "Don Juan"* (1957). The stanzas were published by Byron in their emended form.

~~These two form the last gasp of Passion's breath~~
~~All further is a blank—I won't disparage~~
~~That holy state—but certainly beneath~~
~~The Sun—of human things~~
~~These two are levellers, and~~ human breath
~~So~~ ~~These point the epigram of human breath,~~
~~Or any~~ The future states of both are left to faith,
~~Though Life and love I like not to disparage~~
~~The~~ For authors ~~think~~ description might disparage
    fear
~~'Tis strange that poets never try to wreathe~~ [sic?]
~~With eith~~ ~~'Tis strange that poets of the Catholic faith~~
~~Neer go beyond—and~~ ~~but seem to dread miscarriage~~
~~So dramas close with death or settlement for life~~
~~Veiling~~ ~~Leaving the future states of Love and Life~~
~~The paradise beyond like that of life~~
~~And neer describing either~~
~~To more conjecture of a devil~~ ~~and~~ ~~or wife~~
~~And don't say much of paradise or wife~~
The worlds to come of both—~~&~~ or fall beneath,
And ~~all~~ ~~both the worlds would blame them for miscarriage~~
And then both worlds would punish their miscarriage—
~~So leaving both with priest & prayerbook ready~~
So leaving ~~Clerg both a~~ each their Priest and prayerbook ready,
They say no more of death or of the Lady.

[First Draft: Canto 14, Stanza 95]

    quote   seldom
Alas! ~~I speak by~~ Experience—~~never~~ yet
~~I had a paramour—and I've had many~~
           ~~some small~~
~~To whom I did not cause a deep~~ regret—
~~Whom I had not some reason to regret~~
~~For Whom—I did not feel myself~~ a Zany—
Alas! by all experience, seldom yet
(I merely quote what I have heard from many)
Had lovers not some reason to regret
The passion which made Solomon a Zany.
~~I also had a wife~~—not to forget—
I've also seen some wives—not to forget—
The marriage state—the best or worst of any—
    were   paragons
Who ~~was~~ the very ~~paragon~~ of wives,
Yet made the misery of ~~both our~~ lives.
       ~~many~~
      ~~several~~
    ~~of~~ at least two

PERCY BYSSHE SHELLEY

The three stages of this poem labeled "First Draft" are scattered through one of Shelley's notebooks, now in the Huntington Library, San Marino, California; these drafts have been transcribed and analyzed by Bennett Weaver, "Shelley Works Out the Rhythm of *A Lament*," *PMLA* 47 (1932): 570–76. They show Shelley working with fragmentary words and phrases, and simultaneously with a wordless pattern of pulses that marked out the meter of the single lines and the shape of the lyric stanzas. Shelley left this draft unfinished.

Apparently at some later time, Shelley returned to the poem and wrote what is here called the "Second Draft"; from this he then made, on a second page, a revised fair copy that provided the text that Mary Shelley published in 1824, after the poet's death. These two manuscript pages are now in the Bodleian Library, Oxford; the first page is photographically reproduced and discussed by John Carter and John Sparrow, "Shelley, Swinburne, and Housman," *Times Literary Supplement*, November 21, 1968, pp. 1318–19.

O World, O Life, O Time

[*First Draft, Stage 1*]

Ah time, oh night, oh day
~~Ni nal ni na, na ni~~
~~Ni na ni na, ni na~~
Oh life O death, O time
   Time a di
~~Never Time~~
Ah time, a time O-time
  ~~Time!~~

[*First Draft, Stage 2*]

Oh time, oh night oh day
~~O day oh night, alas~~
  ~~O~~ Death time night ~~oh~~
Oh, Time
Oh time o night oh day

[*First Draft, Stage 3*]

Na na, na na ná na
Nă nă na na na—nă nă
  Nă nă nă nă nā nā
Na na nă nă nâ ă na

Na na na—nă nă—na na
  Na na na na—na na na na na
Na na na na na.
    Na na
Na na na na na
    Na na
Na na na na na ˘ na!

Oh time, oh night, o day
       alas
  O day ~~serenest,~~ o day
  O day alas the day
That thou shouldst sleep when we awake to say

O time time—o death—o day
for
O day, o death life is far from thee
O thou wert never free
For death is now with thee
~~And life is far from~~
O death, o day for life is far from thee

[*Second Draft*]¹

Out of the day & night   I am
A joy has taken flight   despair
Fresh spring & summer   & winter hoar
Fill my faint heart with grief, but with
                                  delight
No more—o never more!

~~Wo~~
    O World, o life, o time
~~Will ye~~   On whose last steps I climb
Trembling at those which I have trod² before
When will return the glory of yr prime
No more   Oh never more

Out of the day & night
A joy has taken flight—
                    autumn
~~From~~ Green spring, & ~~summer gra~~³ & winter hoar

[FAIR COPY]

O World   o Life   o Time
On whose last steps I climb
Trembling at that where I had stood before
When will return the glory of yr prime?
No more, o never more

2

Out of the day & night
A joy has taken flight
Fresh spring & summer   ⁴ & winter hoar

1. Shelley apparently wrote the first stanza of this draft low down on the page, and ran out of space after crowding in the third line of the second stanza; he then, in a lighter ink, wrote a revised form of the whole of the second stanza at the top of the page. In this revision, he left a space after "summer" in line 3, indicating that he planned an insertion that would fill out the four-foot meter of this line, and so make it match the five feet in the corresponding line of the first stanza.

In the upper right-hand corner of this manuscript page Shelley wrote "I am despair"—seemingly to express his bleak mood at the time he wrote the poem.

For this draft and information, and for the transcript of the fair copy that follows, the editors are indebted to Donald H. Reiman.

2. Shelley at first wrote "trod," then overwrote that with "stood." In the following line, Shelley at first wrote "yr," then overwrote "thy."

3. Not clearly legible; it is either "gra" or "gre." A difference in the ink from the rest of the line indicates that Shelley, having left a blank space, later started to fill it in, but thought better of it and crossed out the fragmentary insertion.

4. This fair copy of the second draft retains, and even enlarges, the blank space, indicating that Shelley still hasn't made up his mind what to insert after the word "summer." We may speculate, by reference to the fragmentary version of this stanza in the second draft, that he had in mind as possibilities either an adjective, "gray" or "green," or else the noun "autumn." Mary Shelley closed up this space when she published the poem in 1824, with

Move my faint heart with grief but with delight
No more, o, never more

JOHN KEATS
From The Eve of St. Agnes[1]

[*Stanza 26*]

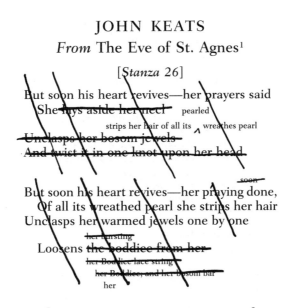

[HERE KEATS BEGINS A NEW SHEET]

Loosens ~~her fragrant boddice and doth bare~~
~~Her~~

26

Anon
~~But soon~~ his heart revives—her praying done,

frees:
Of all its wreathe'd pearl her hair she ~~strips~~
Unclasps her warmed jewels one by one

by degrees
~~to her knees~~
Loosens her fragrant boddice: ~~and down slips~~
Her sweet attire ~~falls light creeps down by~~

creeps rusteling to her knees
Mermaid   in sea weed
Half hidden like ~~a Syren of the Sea~~
~~And more melodious~~

dreaming
She stands awhile in ∧ thought; and sees

on
In fancy fair Saint Agnes ~~in~~ her bed
But dares not look behind or all the charm is ~~fl~~ dead

---

the result that editors, following her version, have until very recently printed this line as though Shelley had intended it to be one metric foot shorter than the corresponding line of stanza 1.

1. Transcribed from what is probably the best known of all manuscripts, that which contains

Keats's first draft of all but the first seven stanzas of *The Eve of St. Agnes*; it is now in the Houghton Library, Harvard University. Keats's published version of the poem, above, contains some further changes in wording.

[*Stanza 30*]

But
~~And still she slept.~~
And still she slept an azure-lidded sleep
In blanched linen, smooth and lavender'd
While he from frorth the closet brough a heap

fruits
Of candied ~~sweets~~ sweets, with
apple Quince and plumb and gourd
creamed
With jellies soother than the ~~dairy~~ curd
tinct
And lucent syrups ~~smooth~~ with ciannamon
~~And sugar'd dates from that oer Euphrates fard~~

~~in Brigantine transferred~~
Manna and daites in ~~Brigtine transferd~~
~~and manna wild transferd~~
~~And Manna wild and Bragantine~~
sugar'd dates transferred
~~In Brigantine from Fez~~
From fez—and spiced danties every one

glutted
From ~~wealthy~~ Samarchand to cedard lebanon
silken

argosy

To Autumn[2]

Season of Mists and mellow fruitfulness
Close bosom friend of the naturring sun;
Conspiring with him how to load and bless
The Vines with fruit that round the thatch eves run
To bend with apples the moss'd Cottage trees
And fill all furuits with sweeness to the core
To swell the gourd, and plump the hazle shells
With a white kernel; to set budding more
And still more later flowers for the bees
Until they think wam days with never cease
For Summer has o'erbrimm'd their clammy cells—

oft amid thy stores?
Who hath not seen thee? ~~for thy haunts are many~~
abroad
Sometimes whoeever seeks ~~for thee~~ may find
Thee sitting careless on a granary floorr
Thy hair soft lifted by the winnowing wind

husky
~~While bright the Sun slants through the~~ ^ ~~barn,—~~
~~or on a half reap'd furrow sound asleep~~
~~Or sound asleep in a half reaped field~~

2. From an untitled manuscript—apparently Keats's first draft of the poem—in the Houghton Library, Harvard University. The many pen-slips and errors in spelling indicate that Keats wrote rapidly, in a state of creative excitement. Keats made a few further changes before publishing the poem in the form included in the selections above.

~~Dose'd with read poppies;~~ while thy ~~reeping~~ hook
~~Spares form Some slumbrous~~
~~minutes while warm slumpers creep~~
Or on a half reap'd furrow sound asleep
Dos'd with the fume of poppies, while thy hook

Spares the next swath and all its twined flowers
~~Spares for some slumbrous minutes the next swath;~~
And sometimes like a gleans thost dost keep
Steady thy laden head across the brook;
Or by a Cyder-press with patent look
Thou watchest the last oozing hours by hours

Where are the songs of Sping? Aye where are they?
Think not of them thou hast thy music too—
      barred   bloom
While ~~a gold~~ clouds ~~gilds~~ the soft-dying day
And
~~And~~ Touching ~~the~~ the stibble plains ∧ rosy hue—
                         with
Then in a waiful quire the small gnats mourn
Among the river sallows, ~~on the~~ borne afots
Or sinking as the light wind lives and dies;
And full grown Lambs loud bleat from hilly bourn,
Hedge crickets sing, and now again full soft
The Redbreast whistles from a garden croft:
~~And now flock still~~
And Gather'd Swallows twiter in the Skies—

ALFRED, LORD TENNYSON

From The Lady of Shalott[1]

[*Version of 1832*]

PART THE FIRST.

On either side the river lie
Long fields of barley and of rye,
That clothe the wold, and meet the sky.
And thro' the field the road runs by
      To manytowered Camelot.
The yellowleavèd waterlily,
The greensheathèd daffodilly,
Tremble in the water chilly,
      Round about Shallot.

Willows whiten, aspens shiver,
The sunbeam-showers break and quiver

1. First published in Tennyson's *Poems* of 1832 (dated 1833 on the title page). The volume was severely criticized by some reviewers; partly in response to this criticism, Tennyson radically revised a number of the poems, including *The Lady of Shalott,* before reprinting them in his *Poems* (1842).
  Parts 1 and 4 are reproduced here in the version of 1832. The final form of the poem reprinted in the selections from Tennyson, above, differs from the revised version that Tennyson published in 1842 only in line 157, which in 1842 read: "A corse between the houses high"; Tennyson changed the line to "Dead-pale between the houses high" in 1855.

In the stream that runneth ever
By the island in the river,
        Flowing down to Camelot.
Four gray walls and four gray towers
Overlook a space of flowers,
And the silent isle imbowers
        The Lady of Shallot.

Underneath the bearded barley,
The reaper, reaping late and early,
Hears her ever chanting cheerly,
Like an angel, singing clearly,
        O'er the stream of Camelot.
Piling the sheaves in furrows airy,
Beneath the moon, the reaper weary
Listening whispers, " 'tis the fairy
        Lady of Shalott."

The little isle is all inrailed
With a rose-fence, and overtrailed
With roses: by the marge unhailed
The shallop flitteth silkensailed,
        Skimming down to Camelot.
A pearlgarland winds her head:
She leaneth on a velvet bed,
Full royally apparellèd,
        The Lady of Shalott.

        *   *   *

PART THE FOURTH.

In the stormy eastwind straining
The pale-yellow woods were waning,
The broad stream in his banks complaining,
Heavily the low sky raining
        Over towered Camelot:
Outside the isle a shallow boat
Beneath a willow lay afloat,
Below the carven stern she wrote,
        THE LADY OF SHALOTT.

A cloudwhite crown of pearl she dight.
All raimented in snowy white
That loosely flew, (her zone in sight,
Clasped with one blinding diamond bright,)
        Her wide eyes fixed on Camelot,
Though the squally eastwind keenly
Blew, with folded arms serenely
By the water stood the queenly
        Lady of Shalott.

With a steady, stony glance—
Like some bold seer in a trance,
Beholding all his own mischance,
Mute, with a glassy countenance—
      She looked down to Camelot.
It was the closing of the day,
She loosed the chain, and down she lay,
The broad stream bore her far away,
      The Lady of Shalott.

As when to sailors while they roam,
By creeks and outfalls far from home,
Rising and dropping with the foam,
From dying swans wild warblings come,
      Blown shoreward; so to Camelot
Still as the boathead wound along
The willowy hills and fields among,
They heard her chanting her deathsong,
      The Lady of Shalott.

A longdrawn carol, mournful, holy,
She chanted loudly, chanted lowly,
Till her eyes were darkened wholly,
And her smooth face sharpened slowly
      Turned to towered Camelot:
For ere she reached upon the tide
The first house by the waterside,
Singing in her song she died,
      The Lady of Shalott.

Under tower and balcony,
By gardenwall and gallery,
A pale, pale corpse she floated by,
Deadcold, between the houses high.
      Dead into towered Camelot.
Knight and burgher, lord and dame,
To the plankèd wharfage came:
Below the stern they read her name,
      "The Lady of Shalott."

They crossed themselves, their stars they blest,
Knight, ministrel, abbot, squire and guest.
There lay a parchment on her breast,
That puzzled more than all the rest,
      The wellfed wits at Camelot.
"The web was woven curiously
The charm is broken utterly,
Draw near and fear not—this is I,
      The Lady of Shalott."

underwent numerous revisions. In many instances, even after the poems had been published, Yeats continued to revise them, sometimes drastically, in later printings.

The Sorrow of Love[1]

[Manuscript, 1891][2]

The quarrel of the sparrows in the eaves,
The full round moon and the star-laden sky,
The song of the ever-singing leaves,
Had hushed away earth's old and weary cry.

And then you came with those red mournful lips,
And with you came the whole of the world's tears,
And all the sorrows of her labouring ships,
And all the burden of her million years.

And now the angry sparrows in the eaves,
The withered moon, the white stars in the sky,
The wearisome loud chanting of the leaves,
Are shaken with earth's old and weary cry.

[First Printed Version, 1892][3]

The quarrel of the sparrows in the eaves,
　The full round moon and the star-laden sky,
And the loud song of the ever-singing leaves
　Had hid away earth's old and weary cry.

And then you came with those red mournful lips,
　And with you came the whole of the world's tears,
And all the sorrows of her labouring ships,
　And all burden of her myriad years.

And now the sparrows warring in the eaves,
　The crumbling moon, the white stars in the sky,
And the loud chanting of the unquiet leaves,
　Are shaken with earth's old and weary cry.

[Final Printed Version, 1925][4]

The brawling of a sparrow in the eaves,
The brilliant moon and all the milky sky,

1. Originally composed in Yeats's Pre-Raphaelite mode of the early 1890s, *The Sorrow of Love* was one of his most popular poems. Nonetheless, some thirty years after publication, Yeats rewrote the lyric to give it the greater precision and the colloquial vigor of his poetic style in the 1920s.
2. Manuscript version composed in October 1891, as transcribed by Jon Stallworthy, *Between the Lines: Yeats's Poetry in the Making* (Oxford University Press, 1963), pp. 47–48.
3. From Yeats's *The Countess Kathleen and Various Legends and Lyrics* (1892). In a corrected page proof for this printing, now in the Garvan Collection of the Yale University Library, lines 7–8 originally read: "And all the sorrows of his labouring ships, / And all the burden of his married years." Also, in lines 4 and 12, the adjective was "bitter"

instead of "weary." In his *Poems* (1895), Yeats inserted the missing "the" in line 8, and changed "sorrows" (line 7) to "trouble"; "burden" (line 8) to "trouble"; and "crumbling moon" (line 10) to "curd-pale moon."
4. From *Early Poems and Stories* (1925). Yeats wrote in his *Autobiography* (New York, 1938), p. 371, that "in later years" he had "learnt that occasional prosaic words gave the impression of an active man speaking," so that "certain words must be dull and numb. Here and there in correcting my early poems I have introduced such numbness and dullness, turned, for instance, 'the curd-pale moon' into the 'brilliant moon,' that all might seem, as it were, remembered with indifference, except some one vivid image." Yeats, however, did not recall his emendations accurately. He had in 1925 altered

And all that famous harmony of leaves,
Had blotted out man's image and his cry.

A girl arose that had red mournful lips
And seemed the greatness of the world in tears,
Doomed like Odysseus and the labouring ships
And proud as Priam murdered with his peers;

Arose, and on the instant clamorous eaves,
A climbing moon upon an empty sky,
And all that lamentation of the leaves,
Could but compose man's image and his cry.

Leda and the Swan[5]

[First Version]

Annunciation

Now can the swooping Godhead have his will
Yet hovers, though her helpless thighs are pressed
By the webbed toes; and that all powerful bill
Has suddenly bowed her face upon his breast.
How can those terrified vague fingers push
The feathered glory from her loosening thighs?
All the stretched body's laid on that white rush

         strange
And feels the ~~strong~~ heart beating where it lies
A shudder in the loins engenders there
The broken wall, the burning roof and tower
And Agamemnon dead. . . .
                  Being so caught up
Did nothing pass before her in the air?
Did she put on his knowledge with his power
Before the indifferent beak could let her drop
                Sept 18 1923

    swooping
The ~~trembl~~ godhead is half hovering still,
    climbs
Yet ~~climbs~~ upon her trembling body pressed
    webbed
By the toes; & ~~through~~ that all powerful bill
        ~~thrown~~ bowed
Has suddenly ~~bowed~~ her face upon his breast.

"the full round moon" (line 2) to "the brilliant moon," and "the curd-pale moon" (line 10, version of 1895) to "a climbing moon."

5. From Yeats's manuscript *Journal*, Sections 248 and 250. This *Journal*, including facsimiles and transcriptions of the drafts of *Leda and the Swan*, has been published in W. B. Yeats, *Memoirs*, ed. Denis Donoghue (Macmillan, London, 1972).

The first version, entitled *Annunciation*, seems to be a clean copy of earlier drafts; Yeats went on to revise it further, especially the opening octave.

Neither of the other two complete drafts, each of which Yeats labeled "Final Version," was in fact final. Yeats himself crossed out the first draft. The second, although Yeats published it in 1924, was subjected to further revision before he published the poem in *The Tower* (1928), in the final form reprinted in the selections from Yeats, above.

Yeats's handwriting is hasty and very difficult to decipher. The readings of some words, in the manuscripts both of this poem and of *After Long Silence*, below, are uncertain.

How can those terrified vague fingers push
The feathered glory from her loosening thighs

laid
All the stretched body ~~leans~~ on that white rush

or
~~Her falling body thrown on the white~~ white rush

Can feel etc
or Her body can but lean on the white rush

But mounts until her trembling thighs are pressed[6]
~~B~~
By the webbed toes; & that all powerful bill
Has suddenly bowed her head on his breast

Final Version

Can hold
Annunciation

The swooping godhead is half hovering still
But mounts, until her trembling thighs are pressed
By the webbed toes, & that all powerful bill
~~Has flung~~ her helpless body
~~Has suddenly bowed her head up~~on his breast.
How can those terrified vague fingers push
The feathered glory from her loosening thighs?
~~How~~ now its body leans on
~~With her body laid on the white rush~~
all the stretched body laid on the white rush
and ~~Can~~ feel the strange heart beating where it lies?
A shudder in the loins engenders there
The broken wall, the burning roof & tower
And Agamemnon dead . . .

Being mastered so
~~Being so caught up~~

So
~~And~~ mastered by the brute blood of the air
Being mastered so
~~Did nothing pass before her in the air?~~
Did she put on his knowledge with his power
Before the indifferent beak could let her drop.
WBY. Sept 18 1923

swoop
A ~~rush~~ upon great wings & hovering still
~~He sinks until~~
~~He has sunk on her down, & her hair~~
~~The great bird sinks, till~~
The bird descends, & her frail ~~thigh~~ thighs are pressed
By the webbed toes, & that all

6. This passage is written across the blank page opposite the first version; Yeats drew a line indicating that
it was to replace the revised lines 2–4, which he had written below the first version.

Now ~~all~~ *that*, her body's laid on/that white rush[7]
~~All the stretched body, laid on~~ that white rush
~~Now that whole~~
Now t~~hat her body on the white~~ rush
Can fee

Final Version

Leda & the Swan

A rush, a sudden wheel and
~~A swoop upon great wings &~~ hovering still
  sinks down.   *bare frail*
stet The bird ~~descends~~ & her ~~frail~~ thighs are pressed
By the ~~toes~~ webbed toes, & that all powerful bill
  laid
Has ~~driven~~ her helpless face upon his breast.
How can those terrified vague fingers push
The feathered glory from her loosening thighs?
  s laid
All the stretched body ~~laid~~ on that white rush
And ~~feel~~ feels the strange heart beating where it lies.
A shudder in the loins engenders there
The broken wall, the burning roof & tower
And Agamemnon dead.
                    Being so caught up
So mastered by the ~~br~~ brute blood of the air
Did she put on his knowledge with his power
Before the indifferent beak could let her drop.

After Long Silence[8]

[Draft 1]

Subject

Your hair is white
My hair is white
Come let us talk of love
What other theme do we know
When we were young

---

7. Written on the blank page across from the complete version, with an arrow indicating that it was a revision of the seventh line.
8. The drafts of *After Long Silence* are interspersed with other materials on seven pages of a manuscript book, begun in 1928, which includes a number of additional poems that were published in *The Winding Stair and Other Poems* (1933). It begins, like many of Yeats's poems, with a prose sketch, and is labeled simply "Subject." It then passes through a tentative versified stage (Draft 2) in which Yeats sets down four complete lines and a set of possible rhyme words; is subjected to various drafts and revisions; and concludes with the final text that Yeats published in 1933. Yeats did not add the title *After Long Silence* until he wrote out a fair copy for his typist at some time after August 14, 1931.

David R. Clark, "After 'Silence,' The 'Supreme Theme': Eight Lines of Yeats," includes photocopies and transcripts of the drafts of this poem, together with a discussion of its biographical occasion and its interpretation (in *Myth and Reality in Irish Literature*, ed. Joseph Ronsley [Waterloo, Canada, 1977], pp. 149–73).

We were in love with one another
~~A O~~ And therefore ignorant

[*Draft 2*]

Those
~~Your~~ other lover^s being dead & gone

                      friendly light
                      hair is white

          ~~on love descant~~   descant
Upon the ~~sole theme~~ supreme theme of art &   song
Wherein there's theme so fitting for the aged. ;young
We loved each other & were ignorant

[*Draft 3*]

~~I r~~
Once more I have kissed your hand & it is right—
All other lovers being estranged or dead
The heavy curtain drawn the candle light
Waging a doubtful battle with the shade
                          discant,
We call our wisdom up upon our wisdom & ~~descant~~
~~Upon the supreme theme of art & song~~
Decrepitude increases wisdom—young
We loved each other & were ignorant ignor   ignorant

[*Draft 4*]

Un
~~The~~ friendly lamplight hidden by its shade
~~And shutters clapped upon the deepening night—~~
~~The candle hidden by its friendly shade~~
Those curtains drawn upon the deepening night—

~~The curtains drawn on the unfriendly night~~
That we descant & yet again descant
        supreme theme
Upon the ~~supreme theme~~ of ~~art & song~~ art & song—
Bodily decrepitude is wisdom—young

[*Final MS Version*]

Speech after long silence; it is right—
                    or
All other lovers being estranged & dead,
             hid
Unfriendly lamp-light ~~hid~~ under its shade,
           upon
The curtain's drawn ~~upon~~ unfriendly night—
That we descant & yet again descant
Upon the supreme theme of art & song,

Bodily decrepitude is wisdom~~M~~; young
We loved each other & were ignorant

Nov
~~Oct~~ 1929

D. H. LAWRENCE
The Piano[1]

Somewhere beneath that piano's superb sleek black
Must hide my mother's piano, little and brown, with
    the back

^{stood close to}
That ~~was against~~ the wall, and the front's faded silk, both torn
And the keys with little hollows, that my mother's fingers
    had worn.

Softly, in the shadows, a woman is singing to me
Quietly, through the years I have crept back to see
A child sitting under the piano, in the boom of the
    shaking ~~tingling~~ strings
Pressing the little poised feet of the mother who smiles
    as she sings

The full throated woman has chosen a winning, living[2]
    song
And surely the heart that is in me must belong
To the old Sunday evenings, when darkness wandered
    outside
And hymns gleamed on our warm lips, as we watched
    mother's fingers glide

^{is}
Or ~~is~~ this my sister at home in the old front room
Singing love's first surprised gladness, alone in
    the gloom.
She will start when she sees me, and blushing,
    spread out her hands
To cover my mouth's raillery, till I'm bound in
    ^{heart-spun}
    her shame's ~~pleading~~ bands.

1. Transcribed from a notebook in which Lawrence at first entered various academic assignments while he was a student at the University College of Nottingham, 1906–8, but then used to write drafts of some of his early poems. These were probably composed in the period from 1906 to 1910. The text reproduced here was revised and published with the title *Piano* in Lawrence's *New Poems,* 1918. A comparison of this draft with *Piano,* reprinted above, will show that Lawrence eliminated the first and fourth stanzas (as well as the last two lines of the third stanza); revised the remaining three stanzas, sometimes radically; and most surprisingly, reversed his original conclusion.

As Lawrence himself explained his revisions of some of his early poems, they "had to be altered, where sometimes the hand of commonplace youth had been laid on the mouth of the demon. It is not for technique that these poems are altered: it is to say the real say."

For transcriptions and discussions of this and other poems in Lawrence's early notebook, see Vivian de Sola Pinto, "D.H. Lawrence: Letter-Writer and Craftsman in Verse," in *Renaissance and Modern Studies* 1 (1957): 5–34.

2. A conjectural reading; the word is not clearly legible.

in England, 1789–1832, 1988; Barton R. Friedman, *Fabricating History: English Writers on the French Revolution*, 1988; Simon Bainbridge, *Napoleon and English Romanticism*, 1995; Kevin Gilmartin, *Print Politics: The Press and Radical Opposition in Early Nineteenth-Century England*, 1996; *The French Revolution and British Culture*, ed. Ceri Crossley and Ian Small, 1989; and *The French Revolution and British Popular Politics*, ed. Mark Philp, 1991.

Illuminating analyses of important intellectual movements will be found in A. O. Lovejoy's *The Great Chain of Being*, 1936, chapters 9 and 10, and *Essays in the History of Ideas*, 1948. Other particularly useful works on intellectual history are Basil Willey, *Nineteenth Century Studies: Coleridge to Matthew Arnold*, 1949; Hoxie Neale Fairchild, *Religious Trends in English Poetry*, of which vol. 3 (1949) deals with 1780–1830; H. W. Piper, *The Active Universe: Pantheism and the Concept of Imagination in the English Romantic Poets*, 1962; and James Engell, *The Creative Imagination: Enlightenment to Romanticism*, 1981. Marilyn Gaull, *English Romanticism: The Human Context*, 1988; and Robert M. Ryan, *The Romantic Reformation: Religious Politics in English Literature, 1789–1824*, 1997. On Romantic literature in its social matrix, see Raymond Williams, *Culture and Society, 1780–1950*, 1960; Jon Klancher, *The Making of English Reading Audiences, 1790–1832*, 1987; Alan Richardson, *Literature, Education, and Romanticism: Reading as Social Practice, 1780–1832*, 1994; and Lee Erickson, *The Economy of Literary Form: English Literature and the Industrialization of Publishing, 1800–1850*, 1996.

Literary History and Criticism

Among the histories of Romantic literature are W. L. Renwick's rather inadequate *English Literature, 1789–1815*, 1963; Ian Jack, *English Literature, 1815–1832*, 1963; and J. R. de J. Jackson, *Poetry of the Romantic Period*, 1980. Mario Praz, *The Romantic Agony*, 2nd ed., 1951, treats Satansim, sadism, vampirism, and others of the more exotic literary interests of the time; G. R. Thompson has edited *The Gothic Imagination: Essays in Dark Romanticism*, 1974; and Peter L. Thorslev Jr.'s *The Byronic Hero: Types and Prototypes*, 1962, discusses the solitary or alienated hero in other writers, as well as Byron; see also Frank Kermode, *Romantic Image*, 1957, on the concept of the poet at odds with society, from the Romantic period to Yeats. Douglas Bush, *Mythology and the Romantic Tradition in English Poetry*, 1937, is so broad in its range that it constitutes an excellent survey of Romantic poetry in general. Wilson Knight, *The Starlit Dome*, 1941, is an influential early example of the approach to Romantic poets by the analysis of characteristic patterns of imagery. Harold Bloom, *The Visionary Company*, rev. 1971, which relates these poets to the prophetic tradition of Spenser and Milton, includes brief and stimulating commentaries on many of the important poems; Bloom, *The Ringers in the Tower*, 1971, consists of essays on both nine-

teenth- and twentieth-century "Romantic" writers. David Perkins treats Wordsworth, Shelley, and Keats, in *The Quest for Permanence*, 1959; and Northrop Frye presents an archetypal overview in *A Study of English Romanticism*, 1968. In *Natural Supernaturalism: Tradition and Revolution in Romantic Literature*, 1971, and more recently in *The Correspondent Breeze: Essays on English Romanticism*, 1984, M. H. Abrams deals with persistent themes, concepts, and designs in English and German Romantic literature, and stresses their relation both to the biblical tradition and to the intellectual ambiance of a revolutionary age. Other useful books to be noted are Thomas Weiskel, *The Romantic Sublime: Studies in the Structure and Psychology of Transcendence*, 1976; Anne K. Mellor, *English Romantic Irony*, 1980; Thomas McFarland, *Romanticism and the Forms of Ruin: Wordsworth, Coleridge, and Modalities of Fragmentation*, 1981; Jerome J. McGann, *The Romantic Ideology*, 1983; Charles J. Rzepka, *The Self as Mind: Vision and Identity in Wordsworth, Coleridge, and Keats*, 1986; Clifford Siskin, *The Historicity of Romantic Discourse*, 1988; Peter J. Manning, *Reading Romantics: Texts and Contexts*, 1990; William H. Galperin, *The Return of the Visible in British Romanticism*, 1993; and Jerome McGann, *The Poetics of Sensibility: A Revolution in Literary Style*, 1996. *English Romantic Poets: Modern Essays in Criticism*, ed. M. H. Abrams, 1975, is a collection of representative essays by influential contemporary critics; *Romanticism and Consciousness: Essays in Criticism*, 1970, focuses on some prominent topics in Romantic literature. See also the essays in *Romantic Poetry: Recent Revisionary Criticism*, Kroeber and Gene W. Ruoff, 1993. For critical opinions of the poets during their own lifetime, see Donald H. Reiman, *The Romantics Reviewed: Contemporary Reviews of British Romantic Writers*, 9 vols., 1972.

Following are studies of various forms of Romantic literature. On literary criticism: M. H. Abrams, *The Mirror and the Lamp: Romantic Theory and the Critical Tradition*, 1953; René Wellek, *A History of Modern Criticism: 1750–1950*, vol. 2, *The Romantic Age*, 1955. On poetic genres: Stuart Curran, *Poetic Form and British Romanticism*, 1986, and Susan J. Wolfson, *Formal Charges: The Shaping of Poetry in British Romanticism*, 1997. On the fragment: Marjorie Levinson, *The Romantic Fragment Poem*, 1986. On narrative poetry: Karl Kroeber, *Romantic Narrative Art*, 1960, and Brian Wilkie, *Romantic Poets and Epic Tradition*, 1965. On the novel: Ernest A. Baker, *The History of the English Novel*, vol. 6, 1961; Montague Summers, *The Gothic Quest: A History of the Gothic Novel*, 1938; and Robert Kiely, *The Romantic Novel in England*, 1972. On drama: Allardyce Nicoll, *History of Early Nineteenth-Century Drama, 1800–50*, 2 vols., rev. 1955. On the essay: William F. Bryan and Ronald S. Crane, Introduction, *The English Familiar Essay*, 1916; Marie H. Law, *The English Familiar Essay in the Early Nineteenth Century*, 1934. See also Annette Wheeler Cafarelli, *Prose in the Age of Poets:*

Romanticism and Biographical Narrative from Johnson to De Quincey, 1990.

On women writers of the period, see Sandra M. Gilbert and Susan Gubar, *The Madwoman in the Attic: The Woman Writer and the Nineteenth-Century Literary Imagination*, 1979; Mary Poovey, *The Proper Lady and the Woman Writer: Ideology as Style in the Works of Mary Wollstonecraft, Mary Shelley, and Jane Austen*, 1984; Margaret Homans, *Bearing the Word: Language and Female Experience in Nineteenth-Century Women's Writing*, 1986; Marlon B. Ross, *The Contours of Masculine Desire: Romanticism and the Rise of Women's Poetry*, 1989; Gary Kelly, *Women, Writing, and Revolution, 1790–1827*, 1993; Anne K. Mellor, *Romanticism and Gender*, 1993; Judith Pascoe, *Romantic Theatricality: Gender, Poetry, and Spectatorship*, 1997; *Romanticism and Feminism*, ed. Anne K. Mellor, 1988; *Re-Visioning Romanticism: British Women Writers, 1776–1837*, ed. Carol Shiner Wilson and Joel Haefner, 1994; and *Romantic Women Writers: Voices and Countervoices*, ed. Paula R. Feldman and Theresa M. Kelley, 1995.

Joanna Baillie

The most useful collected edition is *The Dramatic and Poetical Works*, 1851; the most recent full-scale biography is Margaret S. Carhart's dissertation, *The Life and Work of Joanna Baillie*, 1923. For recent commentary, see Anne K. Mellor, "Joanna Baillie and the Counter-Public Sphere," *Studies in Romanticism* 1994; Andrea Henderson, "Passion and Fashion in Joanna Baillie's 'Introductory Discourse,' " *PMLA*, 1997; and Catherine B. Burroughs, *Closet Stages: Joanna Baillie and the Theater Theory of British Romantic Women Writers*, 1997.

Anna Letitia Barbauld

The Poems of Anna Letitia Barbauld, ed. William McCarthy and Elizabeth Kraft, 1994, is now the standard edition. For biography, see Betsy Rodgers, *Georgian Chronicle: Mrs. Barbauld and Her Family*, 1958. Among recent critical essays, see Julie Ellison, "The Politics of Fancy in the Age of Sensibility," in *Re-Visioning Romanticism*, ed. Wilson and Haefner, 1994; William Keach, "A Regency Prophecy and the End of Anna Barbauld's Career," *Studies in Romanticism*, 1994; Isobel Armstrong, "The Gush of the Feminine," in *Romantic Women Writers*, ed. Feldman and Kelley, 1995; and William McCarthy, "Repression, Desire, and Gender in Anna Letitia Barbauld's Early Poems," also in Feldman and Kelley.

William Blake

The beautifully printed *The Complete Writings of William Blake*, ed. Geoffrey Keynes, 1957, has been replaced as the scholar's edition by *The Poetry and Prose of William Blake*, ed. David Erdman and Harold Bloom, rev. 1982, which includes painstaking textual notes and brief commentaries on many of the poems. Erdman also prepared a modernized text of all Blake's verse, with copious explanatory notes by W. H. Stevenson, *The Poems of William Blake*

(Longman-Norton Annotated English Poets), 1971. A useful annotated selection of *Blake's Poetry and Designs* has been edited by Mary Lynn Johnson and John E. Grant, 1979. There is a *Life of William Blake* by Mona Wilson, 1927, rev. 1948, and Raymond Lister's *William Blake: An Introduction to the Man and His Work*, 1968; but the first full account, Alexander Gilchrist's *The Life of William Blake*, which appeared in 1863, has been a source book for all later biographers and is available (edited and supplemented by Ruthven Todd) in Everyman's Library, 1945. The most recent biographies are James King's *William Blake: His Life*, 1991, and Peter Ackroyd's *Blake*, 1996. See also *A Concordance to the Writings of William Blake*, ed. David V. Erdman, 1967.

The modern era of the scholarly explication of Blake symbolism was begun by S. Foster Damon's *William Blake: His Philosophy and Symbols*, 1924; the same scholar also published a *Blake Dictionary: The Ideas and Symbols of William Blake*, 1965. Among later books, some of the most useful are Northrop Frye's classic analysis of Blake's moral allegory, *Fearful Symmetry*, 1947; Mark Schorer's study of Blake's characteristic union of political, moral, and religious radicalism, *William Blake: The Politics of Vision*, 1946; David V. Erdman's investigation of the relation of Blake's poetry to the historical events of his time, *Blake: Prophet against Empire*, rev. 1969; Peter Fisher's exposition of Blake's thought, *The Valley of Vision*, 1961; Harold Bloom's commentaries on the individual poems, *Blake's Apocalypse: A Study in Poetic Argument*, 1963; Thomas R. Frosch, *The Awakening of Albion: The Renovation of the Body in the Poetry of William Blake*, 1973; J. A. Wittreich, *Angel of Apocalypse: Blake's Idea of Milton*, 1975; W. J. T. Mitchell, *Blake's Composite Art: A Study of the Illuminated Poetry*, 1978; Leopold Damrosch Jr., *Symbol and Truth in Blake's Myth*, 1980; Robert N. Essick, *William Blake and the Language of Albion*, 1989; Morris Eaves, *The Counter-Arts Conspiracy: Art and Identity in the Age of Blake*, 1992; and E. P. Thompson, *Witness against the Beast: William Blake and the Moral Law*, 1993.

H. M. Margoliouth, *William Blake*, 1951, and Martin K. Nurmi, *William Blake*, 1976, are useful general introductions to the man and his work. Studies emphasizing the shorter poems are Hazard Adams, *William Blake: A Reading of the Shorter Poems*, 1963; Robert F. Gleckner, *The Piper and the Bard*, 1959; E. D. Hirsch Jr., *Innocence and Experience: An Introduction to Blake*, 1964; and Brian Wilkie, *Blake's Thel and Oothoon*, 1990. *Blake's Sublime Allegory*, ed. Stuart Curran and Joseph Anthony Wittreich Jr., 1973, includes essays by various scholars on the major prophecies, *The Four Zoas, Milton*, and *Jerusalem*. On Blake's graphic work see David Bindman, *Blake as an Artist*, 1977; Robert N. Essick, *William Blake, Printmaker*, 1980; Morris Eaves, *William Blake's Theory of Art*, 1982; and Joseph Vicomi, *Blake and the Idea of the Book*, 1993. There is a large and growing list of books that

Webb, *Shelley: A Voice Not Understood*, 1977; William Keach, *Shelley's Style*, 1984; Stuart M. Sperry, *Shelley's Major Verse: The Narrative and Dramatic Poetry*, 1988; Stephen C. Behrendt, *Shelley and His Audiences*, 1989; Donald Reiman, *Percy Bysshe Shelley*, rev. 1990, and Susan Wolfson, *Formal Charges*, 1997. Charles Robinson discusses the personal and poetic relations of *Byron and Shelley: The Snake and the Eagle Wreathed in Fight*, 1975. *Shelley*, ed. George M. Ridenour, 1965, is an anthology of modern critical essays.

Charlotte Smith

The Poems of Charlotte Smith, ed. Stuart Curran, 1993, is the standard edition. The fullest biography is Florence May Anna Hilbish's dissertation, *Charlotte Smith, Poet and Novelist*, 1941. For commentary, see Judith Phillips Stanton, "Charlotte Smith's 'Literary Business,' " *The Age of Johnson*, 1987; Stuart Curran, "Charlotte Smith and British Romanticism," *South Central Review*, 1994; and Judith Pascoe, "Female Botanists and the Poetry of Charlotte Smith," in *Re-Visioning Romanticism*, ed. Wilson and Haefner, 1994.

Mary Wollstonecraft

There is a collected edition, *The Works of Mary Wollstonecraft*, ed. Janet Todd and Marilyn Butler, 7 vols., 1989. Todd has also edited *A Wollstonecraft Anthology*, 1989, and *Mary Wollstonecraft: Political Writings*, 1993. The most important reprints of single works are *A Vindication of the Rights of Men*, facsimile edition by Eleanor Louise Nicholes, 1960; *A Vindication of the Rights of Woman*, in both the annotated edition by Ulrich H. Hardt, 1982, and a Norton Critical Edition by Carol H. Poston, 1988; *Letters Written during a Short Residence in Sweden, Norway, and Denmark*, ed. Carol H. Poston, 1976; and a reprint in a single volume (ed. Gary Kelly, 1976) of her two novels, the early *Mary, A Fiction*, and *The Wrongs of Woman; or Maria*, which she left unfinished at her death. Ralph Wardle has edited *Collected Letters of Mary Wollstonecraft*, 1979.

Biographers rely for many facts on William Godwin's candid *Memoirs of the Author of "A Vindication of the Rights of Woman,"* 1798. The first modern critical biography is Ralph Wardle's *Mary Wollstonecraft*, 1951; see also Eleanor Flexner, *Mary Wollstonecraft: A Biography*, 1972; Claire Tomlin's *The Life and Death of Mary Wollstonecraft*, 1974; and Emily Sunstein's *A Different Face: The Life of Mary Wollstonecraft*, 1975. Recent studies include Moira Ferguson and Janet Todd, *Mary Wollstonecraft*, 1984; Mary Poovey, *The Proper Lady and the Woman Writer*, 1984; Jennifer Lorch, *Mary Wollstonecraft: The Making of a Radical Feminist*, 1990; Gary Kelly, *Revolutionary Feminism: The Mind and Career of Mary Wollstonecraft*, 1992; and Virginia Sapiro, *A Vindication of Political Virtue: The Political Theory of Mary Wollstonecraft*, 1992.

Dorothy Wordsworth

For the journals, the best editions are *Journals of Dorothy Wordsworth*, ed. Mary Moorman, 1971, and *The Grasmere Journals*, ed. Pamela Woof, 1991. For the poems, consult the appendix of Susan M. Levin's critical study, *Dorothy Wordsworth and Romanticism*, 1987. Dorothy Wordsworth's letters are collected with those of her brother in *The Letters of William and Dorothy Wordsworth*, rev. Chester L. Shaver and others, 8 vols., 1967–93; there is a one-volume selection of her *Letters*, ed. Alan G. Hill, 1985. The 1933 biography by Ernest de Selincourt has been superseded by Robert Gittings and Jo Manton, *Dorothy Wordsworth*, 1985. See also Catherine Macdonald Maclean, *Dorothy Wordsworth, the Early Years*, 1932; Elizabeth Hardwick, *Seduction and Betrayal*, 1974; and Margaret Homans, *Women Writers and Poetic Identity: Dorothy Wordsworth, Emily Brontë, and Emily Dickinson*, 1980.

William Wordsworth

Ernest de Selincourt edited *The Poetical Works* (with Helen Darbishire), 5 vols., 1940–49, and the variorum edition of *The Prelude*, with the texts of 1805 and 1850 on facing pages (rev. Helen Darbishire, 1959). *The Letters of William and Dorothy Wordsworth*, ed. de Selincourt, have been revised by C. L. Shaver, Mary Moorman, and Alan G. Hill, 7 vols., 1967–92. The 1805 and 1850 *Preludes* on facing pages, together with the "Two-Part *Prelude*" of 1799, various manuscript fragments of *The Prelude*, and a selection of recent critical essays on the poem, are available in *The Prelude: 1799, 1805, 1850. A Norton Critical Edition*, ed. Jonathan Wordsworth, M. H. Abrams, and Stephen Gill, 1979. Wordsworth's poems in one volume were edited for The Oxford Authors by Stephen Gill (1984). A series, the Cornell Wordsworth, general ed. Stephen Parrish, begun in 1975 and now close to completion, prints texts of the poems, together with variant readings from the manuscripts (which are reproduced and transcribed) through the final printings in Wordsworth's lifetime. W. J. B. Owen and Jane Worthington Smyser have edited *The Prose Works*, 3 vols., 1974, and there is a *Selected Prose*, ed. John O. Hayden, 1988. Owen has also printed from his edition a convenient collection of *Wordsworth's Literary Criticism*, 1974. Mary Moorman, *William Wordsworth*, vol. 1, rev. 1968; vol. 2, 1965, has been superseded by Stephen Gill's reliable *William Wordsworth: A Life* (1984) and by Kenneth B. Johnston's lively and well-researched, if at times speculative, *The Hidden Wordsworth* (1988), whose emphases are indicated by its subtitle: *Poet, Lover, Rebel, Spy*. Mark L. Reed's dating of Wordsworth's poems, manuscripts, and the events of his daily life, has reached two volumes, *Wordsworth: The Chronology of the Early Years*, 1967, and *The Chronology of the Middle Years*, 1975.

Walter Raleigh, *Wordsworth*, 1903; Helen Darbishire, *The Poet Wordsworth*, 1950; and Carl Woodring, *Wordsworth*, 1965, are useful introductions to Wordsworth's poetry. Paul D. Sheats has written a study of the early poems, *The Making of Wordsworth's Poetry, 1785–1798*, 1973. Modern interest in *Lyrical Ballads* is shown in Stephen M.

Parrish, *The Art of the "Lyrical Ballads,"* 1973; Mary Jacobus, *Tradition and Experiment in Wordsworth's "Lyrical Ballads,"* 1798, 1976; John E. Jordan, *Why the "Lyrical Ballads"?* 1976; and Don H. Bialostosky, *Making Tales,* 1984. Herbert Lindenberger, *On Wordsworth's "Prelude,"* 1963, explores Wordsworth's major achievement; Richard J. Onorato deals with it from a psychoanalytic standpoint in *The Character of the Poet: Wordsworth in "The Prelude,"* 1971; and Mary Jacobus from a feminist standpoint in *Romanticism, Writing, and Sexual Difference: Essays on "The Prelude,"* 1989. Aspects of Wordsworth's thought are explored by James A. W. Heffernan, *Wordsworth's Theory of Poetry,* 1969, and Geoffrey Durrant, *Wordsworth and the Great System,* 1970. Prominent critical studies of Wordsworth's poetry are John Jones, *The Egotistical Sublime,* 1954; David Perkins, *Wordsworth and the Poetry of Sincerity,* 1964; Geoffrey Hartman's impressive study of *Wordsworth's Poetry, 1787–1814,* 1964; James H. Averill, *Wordsworth and the Poetry of Human Suffering,* 1980; Kenneth R. Johnston, *Wordsworth and "The Recluse,"* 1984; Marjorie Levinson, *Wordsworth's Great Period Poems,* 1986; Susan J. Wolfson, *The Questioning Presence: Wordsworth, Keats, and the Interrogative Mode in Romantic Poetry,* 1986; David Simpson, *Wordsworth's Historical Imagination,* 1987; Nicholas Roe, *Wordsworth and Coleridge: The Radical Years,* 1988; Theresa M. Kelley, *Wordsworth's Revisionary Aesthetics,* 1988; William H. Galperin, *Revision and Authority in Wordsworth,* 1989; Alan Liu, *Wordsworth, The Sense of History* (1989); Peter J. Manning, *Reading Romantics,* 1990; Judith W. Page, *Wordsworth and the Cultivation of Women,* 1994. The range and diversity of critical studies are represented in *Wordsworth: A Collection of Critical Essays,* ed. M. H. Abrams, 1972; *The Age of William Wordsworth: Critical Essays on the Romantic Tradition,* ed. Kenneth R. Johnston and Gene W. Ruoff, 1987; and *Critical Essays on William Wordsworth,* ed. George Gilpin, 1990.

The Persistence of English

If you measure the success of a language in purely quantitative terms, English is entering the twenty-first century at the moment of its greatest triumph. It has between 400 and 450 million native speakers, perhaps 300 million more who speak it as a second language—well enough, that is, to use it in their daily lives—and somewhere between 500 and 750 million who speak it as a foreign language with various degrees of fluency. The resulting total of between 1.2 billion and 1.5 billion speakers, or roughly a quarter of the world's population, gives English more speakers than any other language (though Chinese has more native speakers). Then, too, English is spoken over a much wider geographical area than any other language and is the predominant lingua franca of most fields of international activity, such as diplomacy, business, travel, science, and technology.

But figures like these can obscure a basic question: what exactly do we mean when we talk about the "English language" in the first place? There is, after all, an enormous range of variation in the forms of speech that go by the name of English in the various parts of the world—or often, even within the speech of a single nation—and it is not obvious why we should think of all of these as belonging to a single language. Indeed, there are some linguists who prefer to talk about "world Englishes," in the plural, with the implication that these varieties may not have much more to unite them than a single name and a common historical origin.

To the general public, these reservations may be hard to understand; people usually assume that languages are natural kinds like botanical species, whose boundaries are matters of scientific fact. But as linguists observe, there is nothing in the forms of English themselves that tells us that it is a single language. It may be that the varieties called "English" have a great deal of vocabulary and structure in common and that English-speakers can usually manage to make themselves understood to one another, more or less (though films produced in one part of the English-speaking world often have to be dubbed or subtitled to make them intelligible to audiences in another). But there are many cases where we find linguistic varieties that are mutually intelligible and grammatically similar, but where speakers nonetheless identify separate languages—for example, Danish and Norwegian, Czech and Slovak, or Dutch and Afrikaans. And on the other hand, there are cases where speakers identify varieties as belonging to a single language even though they are linguistically quite distant from one another: the various "dialects" of Chinese are more different from one another than the Latin offshoots that we identify now as French, Italian, Spanish, and so forth.

Philosophers sometimes compare languages to games, and the analogy is thousands of borrowings and coinages that were used only locally. Nor do they touch on the variation in grammar from one variety to the next. This kind of variation occurs everywhere, but it is particularly marked in regions like the Caribbean and Africa, where the local varieties of English are heavily influenced by English-based creoles—that is, language varieties that use English-based vocabulary with grammars largely derived from spoken—in this case, African—languages. This is the source, for example, of a number of the distinctive syntactic features of the variety used by many inner-city African Americans, like the "invariant *be*" of sentences like *We be living in Chicago*, which signals a state of affairs that holds for an extended period. (Some linguists have suggested that Middle English, in fact, could be thought of as a kind of creolized French.)

The growing importance of these new forms of English, particularly in America, presented a new challenge to the unity of the language. Until the eighteenth century, English was still thought of as essentially a national language. It might be spoken in various other nations and colonies under English control, but it was nonetheless rooted in the speech of England and subject to a single standard. Not surprisingly, Americans came to find this picture uncongenial, and when the United States first declared its independence from Britain, there was a strong sentiment for declaring that "American," too, should be recognized as a separate language. This was the view held by John Adams, Thomas Jefferson, and above all by America's first and greatest lexicographer, Noah Webster, who argued that American culture would naturally come to take a distinct form in the soil of the New World, free from what he described as "the old feudal and hierarchical establishments of England." And if a language was naturally the product and reflection of a national culture, then Americans could scarcely continue to speak "English." As Webster wrote in 1789: "Culture, habits, and language, as well as government should be national. America should have her own distinct from the rest of the world. . . ." It was in the interest of symbolically distinguishing American from English that Webster introduced a variety of spelling changes, such as *honor* and *favor* for *honour* and *favour*, *theater* for *theatre*, *traveled* for *travelled*, and so forth—a procedure that new nations often adopt when they want to make their variety of a language look different from its parent tongue.

In fact Webster's was by no means an outlandish suggestion. Even at the time of American independence, the linguistic differences between America and Britain were as great as those that separate many languages today, and the differences would have become much more salient if Americans had systematically adopted all of the spelling reforms that Webster at one time proposed, such as *wurd, reezon, tung, iz*, and so forth, which would ultimately have left English and American looking superficially no more similar than German and Dutch. Left to develop on their own, English and American might soon have gone their separate ways, perhaps paving the way for the separation of the varieties of English used in other parts of the world.

In the end, of course, the Americans and British decided that neither their linguistic nor their cultural and political differences warranted recognizing distinct languages. Webster himself conceded the point in 1828, when he entitled his magnum opus *An American Dictionary of the English Language*. And by 1862 the English novelist Anthony Trollope could write:

An American will perhaps consider himself to be as little like an Englishman as he is like a Frenchman. But he reads Shakespeare through the medium of his own vernacular, and has to undergo the penance of a foreign tongue before he can understand Molière. He separates himself from England in politics and perhaps in affection; but he cannot separate himself from England in mental culture.

ENGLISH AND ENGLISHNESS

This was a crucial point of transition, which set the English language on a very different course from most of the European languages, where the association of language and national culture was being made more strongly than ever before. But the detachment of English from Englishness did not take place overnight. For Trollope and his Victorian contemporaries, the "mental culture" of the English-speaking world was still a creation of England, the embodiment of English social and political values. "The English language," said G. C. Swayne in 1862, "is like the English constitution . . . and perhaps also the English Church, full of inconsistencies and anomalies, yet flourishing in defiance of theory." The monumental *Oxford English Dictionary* that the Victorians undertook was conceived in this patriotic spirit. In the words of Archbishop Richard Chevenix Trench, one of the guiding spirits of the OED project:

> We could scarcely have a lesson on the growth of our English tongue, we could scarcely follow upon one of its significant words, without having unawares a lesson in English history as well, without not merely falling upon some curious fact illustrative of our national life, but learning also how the great heart which is beating at the centre of that life, was being gradually shaped and moulded.

It was this conception of the significance of the language that led, too, to the insistence that the origin of the English language should properly be located in Anglo-Saxon, rather than in the thirteenth or fourteenth century, as scholars argued that contemporary English laws and institutions could be traced to a primordial "Anglo-Saxon spirit" in an almost racial line of descent, and that the Anglo-Saxon language was "immediately connected with the original introduction and establishment of their present language and their laws, their liberty, and their religion."

This view of English as the repository of "Anglo-Saxon" political ideals had its appeal in America, as well, particularly in the first decades of the twentieth century, when the crusade to "Americanize" recent immigrants led a number of states to impose severe restrictions on the use of other languages in schools, newspapers, and public meetings, a course that was often justified on the grounds that only speakers of English were in a position to fully appreciate the nuances of democratic thought. As a delegate to a New York State constitutional convention in 1916 put the point: "You have got to learn our language because that is the vehicle of the thought that has been handed down from the men in whose breasts first burned the fire of freedom at the signing of the Magna Carta."

But this view of the language is untenable on both linguistic and historical grounds. It is true that the nations of the English-speaking world have a common political heritage that makes itself known in similar legal systems and an (occasionally shaky) predilection for democratic forms of government. But while there is no doubt that the possession of a common language has helped to reinforce some of these connections, it is not responsible for them. Languages do work to create a common worldview, but not at such a specific level. Words like *democracy* move easily from one language to the next, along with the concepts they name—a good thing for the English-speaking world, since a great many of those ideals of "English democracy," as the writer calls it, owe no small debt to thinkers in Greece, Italy, France, Germany, and a number of other places, and those ideals have been established in many nations that speak languages other than English. (Thirteenth-century England was one of them. We should bear in mind that the Magna Carta that people sometimes like to mention in this context was a Latin document issued by a French-speaking king to French-speaking barons.) For that matter, there are English-speaking nations where democratic institutions have not taken root—nor should we take their continuing health for granted even in the core nations of the English-speaking world.

In the end, the view of English as the repository of Englishness has the effect of marginalizing or disenfranchising large parts of the English-speaking world, particularly those who do not count the political and cultural imposition of Englishness as an unmixed blessing. In most of the places where English has been planted, after all, it has had the British flag flying above it. And for many nations, it has been hard to slough off the sense of English as a colonial language. There is a famous passage in James Joyce's *Portrait of the Artist as a Young Man*, for example, where Stephen Daedelus says of the speech of an English-born dean, "The language in which we are speaking is his not mine," and there are still many people in Ireland and other parts of the English-speaking world who have mixed feelings about the English language: they may use and even love English, but they resent it, too.

Today the view of English as an essentially English creation is impossible to sustain even on purely linguistic grounds; the influences of the rest of the English-speaking world have simply been too great. Already in Trollope's time there were vociferous complaints in England about the growing use of Americanisms, a sign that the linguistic balance of payments between the two communities was tipping westward, and a present-day English writer would have a hard time producing a single paragraph that contained no words that originated in other parts of the linguistic community. Nor, what is more important, could you find a modern British or North American writer whose work was not heavily influenced, directly or indirectly, by the literature of the rest of the linguistic community, particularly after the extraordinary twentieth-century efflorescence of the English-language literatures of other parts of the world. Trying to imagine modern English literature without the contributions of writers like Yeats, Shaw, Joyce, Beckett, Heaney, Walcott, Lessing, Gordimer, Rushdie, Achebe, and Naipaul (to take only some of the writers who are included in this collection) is like trying to imagine an "English" cuisine that made no use of potatoes, tomatoes, corn, noodles, eggplant, olive oil, almonds, bay leaf, curry, or pepper.

THE FEATURES OF "STANDARD ENGLISH"

Where should we look, then, for the common "mental culture" that English-speakers share? This is always a difficult question to answer, partly because the understanding of the language changes from one place and time to the next, and partly because it is hard to say just what sorts of things languages are in the abstract. For all that we may want to think of the English-speaking world as a single community united by a common worldview, it is not a social group comparable to a tribe or people or nation—the sorts of groups that can easily evoke the first-person plural pronoun *we*. (Americans and Australians do not travel around saying "We gave the world Shakespeare," even though one might think that as paid-up members of the English-speaking community they would be entirely within their rights to do so.)

But we can get some sense of the ties that connect the members of the English-speaking community by starting with the language itself—not just in its forms and rules, but in the centripetal forces spoken of earlier. Forces like these are operating in every language community, it's true, but what gives each language its unique character is the way they are realized, the particular institutions and cultural commonalties which work to smooth differences and create a basis for continued communication—which ensure, in short, that English will continue as a single language, rather than break up into a collection of dialects that are free to wander wherever they will.

People often refer to this basis for communication as "Standard English," but that term is misleading. There are many linguistic communities that do have a genuine standard variety, a fixed and invariant form of the language that is used for certain kinds of communication. But that notion of the standard would be unsuitable to a language like English, which recognizes no single cultural center and has to allow for a great deal of variation even in the language of published texts. (It is rare to find a single page of an English-language novel or newspaper that does not reveal what nation it was written in.) What English does have, rather, is a collection of standard features—of spelling, of grammar, and of word use—which taken together ensure that certain kinds of communication will be more or less comprehensible in any part of the language community.

The standard features of English are as notable for what they don't contain as for what they do. One characteristic of English, for example, is that it has no standard pronunciation. People pronounce the language according to whatever their regional practice happens to be, and while certain pronunciations may be counted as "good" or "bad" according to local standards, there are no general rules about this, the way there are in French or Italian. (Some New Yorkers may be stigmatized for pronouncing words like *car* and *bard* as 'kah' and 'bahd', but roughly the same *r*-less pronunciation is standard in parts of the American South and in England, South Africa, Australia, and New Zealand.) In this sense, "standard English" exists only as a written language. Of course there is some variation in the rules of written English, as well, such as the American spellings that Webster introduced, but these are relatively minor and tend to date from earlier periods. A particular speech-community can pronounce the words *half* or *car* however it likes, but it can't unilaterally change the way the words are spelled. Indeed, this is one of the

the continuity of the language should often be controversial, even within a single community, and even less so that different national communities should have different ideas as to who counts as authority or what kinds of texts should be relevant to defining the common core of English words. The most we can ask of our common linguistic heritage is that it give us a general format for adapting the language to new needs and for reinterpreting its significance from one time and place to another.

This is the challenge posed by the triumph of English. Granted, there is no threat to the hegemony of English as a worldwide medium for practical communication. It is a certainty that the nations of the English-speaking community will continue to use the various forms of English to communicate with each other, as well as with the hundreds of millions of people who speak English as a second language (and who in fact outnumber the native speakers of the language by a factor of two or three to one). And with the growth of travel and trade and of media like the Internet, the number of English-speakers is sure to continue to increase.

But none of this guarantees the continuing unity of English as a means of cultural expression. What is striking about the accelerating spread of English over the past two centuries is not so much the number of speakers that the language has acquired, but the remarkable variety of the cultures and communities who use it. The heterogeneity of the linguistic community is evident not just in the emergence of the rich new literatures of Africa, Asia, and the Caribbean, but also in the literatures of what linguists sometimes call the "inner circle" of the English-speaking world—nations like Britain, the United States, Australia, and Canada—where the language is being asked to describe a much wider range of experience than ever before, particularly on behalf of groups who until recently have been largely excluded or marginalized from the collective conversation of the English-speaking world.

Not surprisingly, the speakers of the "new Englishes" use the language with different voices and different rhythms and bring to it different linguistic and cultural backgrounds. The language of a writer like Chinua Achebe reflects the influence not just of Shakespeare and Wordsworth but of proverbs and other forms of discourse drawn from West African oral traditions. Indian writers like R. K. Narayan and Salman Rushdie ground their works not just in the traditional English-language canon but in Sanskrit classics like the epic *Rāmāyana*. The continuing sense that all English-speakers are engaged in a common discourse depends on the linguistic community's being able to accommodate and absorb these new linguistic and literary influences, as it has been able to do in the past.

In all parts of the linguistic community, moreover, there are questions posed by the new media of discourse. Over the past hundred years, the primacy of print has been challenged first by the growth of film, recordings, and the broadcast media, and more recently by the remarkable growth of the Internet, each of which has had its effects on the language. With film and the rest, we have begun to see the emergence of spoken standards that co-exist with the written standard of print, not in the form of a standardized English pronunciation—if anything, pronunciation differences among the communities of the English-speaking world have become more marked over the course of the century—but rather in the use of words, expressions, and rhythms that are particular to speech (there is no better example of this than the universal adoption of the particle *okay*). And the Internet has had the effect of projecting what were previously private forms of written communication, like the personal letter, into something more like models of public discourse, but with a language that is much more informal than the traditional discourse of the novel or newspaper.

It is a mistake to think that any of these new forms of discourse will wholly replace the discourse of print (the Internet, in particular, has shown itself to be an important vehicle for marketing and diffusing print works with much greater efficiency than has ever been possible before). It seems reasonable to assume that a hundred years from now the English-speaking world will still be at heart a community of readers—and of readers of books, among other things. And it is likely, too, that the English language will still be at heart a means of written expression, not just for setting down air schedules and trade statistics, but for doing the kind of cultural work that we have looked for literature to do for us in the past; a medium, that is, for poetry, criticism, history, and fiction. But only time will tell if English will remain a single language—if in the midst of all the diversity, cultural and communicative, people will still be able to discern a single "English literature" and a characteristic English-language frame of mind.

GEOFFREY NUNBERG
Stanford University and Xerox Palo Alto Research Center

say, "Oh, he's a rich man, he's worth £500." Four centuries later, Virginia Woolf argued that £500 a year (along with a room of one's own) was the bare minimum necessary for a woman to be able to write. Whatever Latimer meant by "rich," or Woolf by "necessary," it is clear that the value of the pound had declined drastically over this period, as it has continued to do in the course of the twentieth century. In Britain today, a worker on minimum wage earns more than £500 a month, an income associated with severe poverty.

In the Anglo-Saxon period, the silver penny was the biggest coin in general circulation; 4 of them would buy a sheep. Peasants and craftsmen before the Black Death of the fourteenth century made at most 2 or 3 pence a day—an annual income of £3 or £4; after the onset of the plague, wages nearly doubled, due to the shortage of laborers. Throughout the medieval period, kings and commoners worried less about inflation than about the debasement of the silver currency. In 1124, dozens of mint-masters had their right hands chopped off on Christmas Day for issuing inferior coinage. In the early sixteenth century, under Henry VIII and his son Edward VI, the silver content of coins fell as low as 25 percent. Elizabeth I considered the revaluation of the silver coinage to be one of her greatest achievements as queen. Nevertheless, her reign was marked by sustained inflation of prices, caused in part by the influx of gold and silver from the New World, and in part by the rising population.

In the Elizabethan era, admission to the public theaters cost a penny for those who stood throughout the performance. Playwrights were paid about £6 for each play, so to make a living a writer had to be prolific (or, like Shakespeare, own shares in the theater company). In the same period, 40 pounds a year in independent income (generally rent from lands) was the minimum requirement for a justice of the peace; it marked the threshold of gentry status and was also the sum fixed by King James I at which a man could be forced to accept knighthood (paying a fee to the crown). In 1661, following further inflation, Samuel Pepys calculated his worth at a modest £650 just after he had begun working for the navy; five years later, that good bourgeois was worth more than £6000, and his annual income was about £3000. Of course, he was working for most of this income. Pepys was a rising official and would become a very important one; but he never achieved a title or even knighthood because the smell of commerce had never been washed from his money by possession of land.

Various writers provide examples of the incomes of rich and poor in the eighteenth and nineteenth centuries. Joseph Andrews (in Fielding's novel, published 1742) worked as a footman in the house of Lady Booby for £8 a year; in addition, he got his room, board, and livery, plus the occasional tip. Among the comfortable classes, Mr. Bennet of Jane Austen's *Price and Prejudice* (1813) enjoyed an income of £2000 a year (with a family of five nonearning females to support), while Mr. Darcy had close to £10,000, nearing the level of the aristocracy. In his deepest degradation David Copperfield (of Dickens's 1850 novel) worked in the warehouse of Murdstone & Grinby for 6 or 7 shillings a week (£15 to £18 a year). Mr. Murdstone paid extra for his lodging and laundry, but even so the boy was bitterly impoverished, though he had only himself to feed. When his father died, his mother was thought to be pretty well taken care of with £105 a year, less than £9 per month. Even in 1888, Annie Besant reports workers in Bryant and May's match factory made 4 to 9 shillings a week and paid for their own lodging—this, in the words of Ada Nield Chew, was not a living wage, but "a lingering, dying wage." Far removed from this world is Jack Worthing in Wilde's comedy *The Importance of Being Earnest* (1895), who receives £7000 or £8000 a year from investments and has a country house with about fifteen hundred acres attached to it, though it yields no income worth talking about.

While incomes have risen enormously over the centuries, and the value of the pound declined accordingly, the gap between rich and poor has remained. So too has the gap between the country and the city: London has always been very expensive, and elsewhere a small income goes further. To a large extent, one's position in terms of class and geography determines not only what money can buy but what it means.

We have only to contrast Jack Worthing's vague estimate of his income with the factory workers' exact sense of the value of a shilling. As Woolf acknowledged, having a purse with the power "to breed ten-shilling notes automatically," changes one's view of money and of the world. Perhaps it is because British currency has been so important in shaping people's views of themselves and their society that many Britons are reluctant to let it go. The question of whether the United Kingdom should relinquish the pound and the penny to join the single European currency (the Euro) is a matter of fierce and prolonged debate. For some, the pound, far more than the flag, is an enduring symbol of the nation. Whether or not one holds this view, it can at least be said that over the centuries the pound has undergone as many crises and transformations as the nation itself.

The British Baronage

The English monarchy is in principle hereditary, though at times during the Middle Ages the rules were subject to dispute. In general, authority passes from father to eldest surviving son, from daughters in order of seniority if there is no son, to a brother if there are no children, and in default of direct descendants to collateral lines (cousins, nephews, nieces) in order of closeness. There have been breaks in the order of succession (1066, 1399, 1688), but so far as possible the usurpers have always sought to paper over the break with a legitimate, i.e., a hereditary claim. When a queen succeeds to the throne and takes a husband, he does not become king unless he is in the line of blood succession; rather, he is named prince consort, as Albert was to Victoria. He may father kings, but is not one himself.

The original Saxon nobles were the king's thanes, ealdormen, or earls, who provided the king with military service and counsel in return for booty, gifts, or landed estates. William the Conqueror, arriving from France, where feudalism was fully developed, considerably expanded this group. In addition, as the king distributed the lands of his new kingdom, he also distributed dignities to men who became known collectively as "the baronage." "Baron" in its root meaning signifies simply "man," and barons were the king's men. As the title was common, a distinction was early made between greater and lesser barons, the former gradually assuming loftier and more impressive titles. The first English "duke" was created in 1337; the title of "marquess," or "marquis" (pronounced "markwis"), followed in 1385, and "viscount" ("vyekount") in 1440. Though "earl" is the oldest title of all, it now comes between a marquess and a viscount in order of dignity and precedence, and the old term "baron" now designates a rank just below viscount. "Baronets" were created in 1611 as a means of raising revenue for the crown (the title could be purchased for about £1000); they are marginal nobility and do not sit in the House of Lords.

Kings and queens are addressed as "Your Majesty," princes and princesses as "Your Highness," the other hereditary nobility as "My Lord" or "Your Lordship." Peers receive their titles either by inheritance (like Lord Byron, the sixth baron of that line) or from the monarch (like Alfred Lord Tennyson, created first Baron Tennyson by Victoria). The children, even of a duke, are commoners unless they are specifically granted some other title or inherit their father's title from him. A peerage can be forfeited by act of attainder, as for example when a lord is convicted of treason; and, when forfeited, or lapsed for lack of a successor, can be bestowed on another family. Thus Robert Cecil was made in 1605 first earl of Salisbury in the third creation, the first creation dating from 1149, the second from 1337, the title having been in abeyance since 1539. Titles descend by right of succession and do not depend on tenure of land; thus, a title does not always indicate where a lord dwells or holds power. Indeed, noble titles do not always refer to a real place at all. At Prince Edward's marriage in 1999, the queen created him earl of Wessex, although the old kingdom of Wessex has had no political existence since the Anglo-Saxon period, and the name was all but forgotten until it was resurrected by Thomas Hardy as the setting of his novels. (This is perhaps but one of many ways in which the world of the aristocracy increasingly resembles the realm of literature.)

The king and queen Prince and princess	(These are all of the royal line.)
Duke and duchess Marquess and marchioness Earl and countess Viscount and viscountess Baron and baroness Baronet and lady	(These may or may not be of the royal line, but are ordinarily remote from the succession.)

Scottish peers sat in the parliament of Scotland, as English peers did in the parliament of England, till at the Act of Union (1707) Scots peers were granted sixteen seats in the English House of Lords, to be filled by election. Similarly, Irish peers, when the Irish parliament was abolished in 1801, were granted the right to elect twenty-eight of their number to the House of Lords in Westminster. (Now that the Republic of Ireland is a separate nation, of course, this no longer applies.) The House of Lords still retains some power to influence or delay legislation. But this upper house is now being reformed. All or most of the hereditary peers are to be expelled, while recipients of nonhereditary Life Peerages will remain and vote as before.

Below the peerage the chief title of honor is "knight." Knighthood, which is not hereditary, is generally a reward for services rendered. A knight (Sir John Black) is addressed, using his first name, as "Sir John"; his wife, using the last name, is "Lady Black"—unless she is the daughter of an earl or nobleman of higher rank, in which case she will be "Lady Arabella." The female equivalent of a knight bears the title of "Dame."

Though the word itself comes from the Anglo-Saxon *cniht*, there seems to be some doubt as to whether knighthood amounted to much before the arrival of the Normans. The feudal system required military service as a condition of land tenure, and a man who came to serve his king at the head of an army of tenants required a title of authority and badges of identity—hence the title of knighthood and the coat of arms. During the Crusades, when men were far removed from their land (or had even sold it in order to go on crusade), more elaborate forms of fealty sprang up that soon expanded into orders of knighthood. The Templars, Hospitallers, Knights of the Teutonic Order, Knights of Malta, and Knights of the Golden Fleece were but a few of these companionships; not all of them were available at all times in England.

Gradually, with the rise of centralized government and the decline of feudal tenures, military knighthood became obsolete, and the rank largely honorific; sometimes, as under James I, it degenerated into a scheme of the royal government for making money. For hundreds of years after its establishment in the fourteenth century, the Order of the Garter was the only English order of knighthood, an exclusive courtly companionship. Then, during the late seventeenth, the eighteenth, and the nineteenth centuries, a number of additional orders were created, with names such as the Thistle, Saint Patrick, the Bath, Saint Michael and Saint George, plus a number of special Victorian and Indian orders. They retain the terminology, ceremony, and dignity of knighthood, but the military implications are vestigial.

Although the British Empire now belongs to history, appointments to the Order of the British Empire continue to be conferred for services to that empire at home or abroad. Such honors (commonly referred to as "gongs") are granted by the monarch in her New Year's and Birthday lists, but the decisions are now made by the government in power. In recent years there have been efforts to popularize and democratize the dispensation of honors, with recipients including rock stars and actors. But this does not prevent large sectors of British society from regarding both knighthood and the peerage as largely irrelevant to modern life.

The Royal Lines of England and Great Britain

England

SAXONS AND DANES

Egbert, king of Wessex	802–839
Ethelwulf, son of Egbert	839–858
Ethelbald, son of Ethelwulf	858–860
Ethelbert, second son of Ethelwulf	860–866
Ethelred I, third son of Ethelwulf	866–871
Alfred the Great, fourth son of Ethelwulf	871–899
Edward the Elder, son of Alfred	899–924
Athelstan the Glorious, son of Edward	924–940
Edmund I, third son of Edward	940–946
Edred, fourth son of Edward	946–955
Edwy the Fair, son of Edmund	955–959
Edgar the Peaceful, second son of Edmund	959–975
Edward the Martyr, son of Edgar	975–978 (murdered)
Ethelred II, the Unready, second son of Edgar	978–1016
Edmund II, Ironside, son of Ethelred II	1016–1016
Canute the Dane	1016–1035
Harold I, Harefoot, natural son of Canute	1035–1040
Hardecanute, son of Canute	1040–1042
Edward the Confessor, son of Ethelred II	1042–1066
Harold II, brother-in-law of Edward	1066–1066 (died in battle)

HOUSE OF NORMANDY

William I the Conqueror	1066–1087
William II, Rufus, third son of William I	1087–1100 (shot from ambush)
Henry I, Beauclerc, youngest son of William I	1100–1135

HOUSE OF BLOIS

Stephen, son of Adela, daughter of William I	1135–1154

HOUSE OF PLANTAGENET

Henry II, son of Geoffrey Plantagenet by Matilda, daughter of Henry I	1154–1189
Richard I, Coeur de Lion, son of Henry II	1189–1199
John Lackland, son of Henry II	1199–1216
Henry III, son of John	1216–1272
Edward I, Longshanks, son of Henry III	1272–1307
Edward II, son of Edward I	1307–1327
Edward III of Windsor, son of Edward II	1327–1377
Richard II, grandson of Edward III	1377–1400

HOUSE OF LANCASTER

Henry IV, son of John of Gaunt, son of Edward III	1399–1413
Henry V, Prince Hal, son of Henry IV	1413–1422
Henry VI, son of Henry V	1422–1471 (deposed)

HOUSE OF YORK

Edward IV, great-great-grandson of Edward III	1461–1483
Edward V, son of Edward IV	1483–1483 (murdered)
Richard III, Crookback	1483–1485 (died in battle)

HOUSE OF TUDOR

Henry VII, married daughter of Edward IV	1485–1509
Henry VIII, son of Henry VII	1509–1547
Edward VI, son of Henry VIII	1547–1553
Mary I, "Bloody," daughter of Henry VIII	1553–1558
Elizabeth I, daughter of Henry VIII	1558–1603

HOUSE OF STUART

James I (James VI of Scotland)	1603–1625
Charles I, son of James I	1625–1649 (executed)

COMMONWEALTH & PROTECTORATE

Council of State	1649–1653
Oliver Cromwell, Lord Protector	1653–1658
Richard Cromwell, son of Oliver	1658–1660 (resigned)

HOUSE OF STUART (RESTORED)

Charles II, son of Charles I	1660–1685
James II, second son of Charles I	1685–1688

(INTERREGNUM, 11 DECEMBER 1688 TO 13 FEBRUARY 1689)

William III of Orange, by Mary, daughter of Charles I	1685–1701
and Mary II, daughter of James II	–1694
Anne, second daughter of James II	1702–1714

Great Britain

HOUSE OF HANOVER

George I, son of Elector of Hanover and Sophia, granddaughter of James I	1714–1727
George II, son of George I	1727–1760
George III, grandson of George II	1760–1820
George IV, son of George III	1820–1830

William IV, third son of George III   1830–1837
Victoria, daughter of Edward, fourth son
    of George III   1837–1901

HOUSE OF SAXE-COBURG AND GOTHA

Edward VII, son of Victoria   1901–1910

HOUSE OF WINDSOR (NAME ADOPTED 17 JULY 1917)

George V, second son of Edward VII   1910–1936
Edward VIII, eldest son of George V   1936–1936 (abdicated)
George VI, second son of George V   1936–1952
Elizabeth II, daughter of George VI   1952–

Religions in England

Religious distinctions and denominations are important in British social history, hence deeply woven into the nation's literature. The numerous (over three hundred) British churches and sects divide along a scale from high to low, depending on the amount of authority they give to the church or the amount of liberty they concede to the individual conscience. At one end of the scale is the Roman Catholic Church, asserting papal infallibility, universal jurisdiction, and the supreme importance of hierarchy as guide and intercessor. For political and social reasons, Catholicism struck deep roots in Ireland but in England was the object of prolonged, bitter hatred on the part of Protestants from the Reformation through the nineteenth century. The Established English (Anglican) Episcopal church has been the official national church since the sixteenth century; it enjoys the support (once direct and exclusive, now indirect and peripheral) of the national government. Its creed is defined by Thirty-Nine Articles, but these are intentionally vague, so there are numerous ways of adhering to the Church of England. Roughly and intermittently, the chief classes of Anglicans have been known as High Church (with its highest portion calling itself Anglo-Catholic); Broad Church, or Latitudinarian (when they get so broad that they admit anyone believing in God, they may be known as Deists, or some may leave the church altogether and be known as Unitarians); and Low Church, whose adherents may stay in the English church and yet come close to shaking hands with Presbyterians or Methodists. These various groups may be arranged, from the High down to the Low Church, in direct relation to the amount of ritual each prefers and in the degree of authority conceded to the upper clergy—and in inverse relation to the importance ascribed to a saving faith directly infused by God into an individual conscience.

All English Protestants who decline to subscribe to the English established church are classed as Dissenters or Nonconformists; for a time in the sixteenth and seventeenth centuries, they were also known as Puritans. (Nowadays, though Puritanism has less distinct theological meaning, it marks a distinct character type; because of his passionate emphasis on individual conscience and moral economy, Bernard Shaw was a prototypical Puritan.) The Presbyterians model their church government on that established by John Calvin in the Swiss city of Geneva. It has no bishops, and therefore is more democratic for the clergy; but it gains energy by associating lay elders with clergymen in matters of social discipline and tends to be strict with the ungodly. From its first reformation the Scottish Kirk was fixed on the Presbyterian model. During the civil wars of the seventeenth century, a great many sects sprang up on the left wing of the Presbyterians, most of them touched by Calvinism but some rebelling against it; a few of these still survive. The Independents became our modern Congregationalists; the Quakers are still Quakers, as Baptists are still Baptists, though multiply divided. But many of the sects flourished and perished within the space of a few years. Among these now vanished groups were the Shakers (though a few groups still exist in America), the Seekers, the Ranters, the Anabaptists, the Muggletonians, the Fifth Monarchy Men, the Family of Love, the Sweet Singers of Israel, and many others, forgotten by all except scholars. During the eighteenth and nineteenth centuries, new sects arose, supplanting old ones; the Methodists, under John and Charles Wesley, became numerous and important, taking root particularly in Wales. (The three "subject" nationalities, Ireland, Scotland, and Wales, thus turned three different ways to avoid the Anglican church.) With the passage of time a small number of Swedenborgians sprang up, followers of the Swedish mystic Emanuel Swedenborg—to be followed by the Plymouth Brethren, Christian Scientists, Jehovah's Witnesses, and countless other nineteenth-century groups. All these sects constantly grow, shrink, split, and occasionally disappear as they succeed or fail in attracting new converts.

Within the various churches and sects, independent of them all but amazingly persistent, there has always survived a stream of esoteric or hermetic thought—a belief in occult powers, and sometimes in magic also, exemplified by the pseudo-sciences of astrology and alchemy but taking many other forms as well. From the mythical Egyptian seer Hermes Trismegistus through Paracelsus, Cornelius Agrippa, Giordano Bruno, Jakob Boehme, the society of Rosicrucians, and a hundred other shadowy figures, the line can be traced to William Blake and William Butler Yeats, who both in their different ways brought hermetic Protestantism close to its ultimate goal, a mystic church of a single consciousness, poised within its mind-elaborated cosmos.

Christianity is not, of course, the only religion present on the British Isles. The few Jews in medieval England were regarded as resident aliens, as were those in other European countries. In 1290 all English Jews who refused baptism were expelled from the kingdom, and officially, there were no Jews living in England between that time and the mid-1650s, when Cromwell encouraged Jewish merchants to settle in London. A considerable number of east European Jews emigrated to England in the first half of the twentieth century (many as refugees), but the country's Jewish population as a whole remains quite small (less than half a million). Hardly any Muslims or Hindus lived in the U.K. before the dissolution of the Empire shortly after World War II. Today both religions have a large and growing representation among ex-colonial immigrants and their children.

Poetic Forms and
Literary Terminology

Systematic literary theory and criticism in English began in the sixteenth century, at a time when the standard education for upper-class students emphasized the study of the classical languages and literatures. As a consequence, the English words that were introduced to describe meter, figures of speech, and literary genres often derive from Latin and Greek roots.

RHYTHM AND METER

Verse is generally distinguished from prose as a more compressed and more regularly rhythmic form of statement. This approximate truth underlines the importance of **meter** in poetry, as the means by which rhythm is measured and described.

In Latin and Greek, meter was established on a **quantitative** basis, by the regular alternation of long and short syllables (that is, syllables classified according to the time taken to pronounce them). Outside of a few experiments (and the songs of Thomas Campion), this system has never proved congenial to Germanic languages such as English, which distinguish, instead, between **stressed** and **unstressed,** or accented and unaccented syllables. Two varieties of accented stress may be distinguished. On the one hand, there is the natural stress pattern of words themselves; *sýllable* is accented on the first syllable, *deplórable* on the second, and so on. Then there is the sort of stress that indicates rhetorical emphasis. If the sentence "You went to Greece?" is given a pronounced accent on the last word, it implies "Greece (of all places)?" If the accent falls on the first word, it implies "you (of all people)?" The meter of poetry—that is, its rhythm—is ordinarily built up out of a regular recurrence of accents, whether established as **word accents** or **rhetorical accents;** once started, it has (like all rhythm) a tendency to persist in the reader's mind.

The unit that is repeated to give steady rhythm to a poem is called a **foot;** in English it usually consists of accented and unaccented syllables in one of five fairly simple patterns:

The **iambic foot** (or **iamb**) consists of an unstressed followed by a stressed syllable, as in *uníte, repeát,* or *insíst.* Most English verse falls naturally into the iambic pattern.

The **trochaic foot** (**trochee**) inverts this order; it is a stressed followed by an unstressed syllable—for example, *únit, réaper,* or *ínstant.*

The **anapestic foot** (**anapest**) consists of two unstressed syllables followed by a stressed syllable, as in *intercéde, disarránged,* or *Ca meróon.*

The **dactylic foot** (**dactyl**) consists of a stressed syllable followed by two unstressed syllables, as in *Wáshington, Écuador,* or *ápplejack.*

The **spondaic foot** (**spondee**) consists of two successive stressed syllables, as in *heartbreak, headline,* or *Kashmir.*

In all the examples above, word accent and the quality of the metrical foot coincide exactly. But the metrical foot may well consist of several words, or, on the other hand, one word may well consist of several metrical feet. *Phótolithógraphy* consists of two dactyls in a single word; *dárk and with spóts on it,* though it consists of six words rather than one, is also two dactyls. When we read a piece of poetry with the intention of discovering its underlying metrical pattern, we are said to **scan** it—that is, we go through it line by line, indicating by conventional signs which are the accented and which the unaccented syllables within the feet. We also count the number of feet in each line; a line is, formally, also called a **verse** (from Latin *versus,* which means one "row" of metrical feet). Verse lengths are conventionally described in terms derived from the Greek:

Monometer: one foot (of rare occurrence)

Dimeter: two feet (also rare)

Trimeter: three feet

Tetrameter: four feet

Pentameter: five feet

Hexameter: six feet (six iambic feet make what is called an **Alexandrine**)

Heptameter: seven feet (also rare)

Samuel Johnson wrote a little parody of simpleminded poets which can be scanned this way:

> Ĭ pút m̆y hát ŭpón m̆y héad
> Ănd wálked ĭntó thĕ Stránd
> Ănd thére Ĭ mét ănóthĕr mán
> Whŏse hát wăs ín hĭs hánd.

The poem is iambic in rhythm, alternating tetrameter and trimeter in the length of the verse-lines. The fact that it scans so nicely is, however, no proof that it is good poetry. Quite the contrary. Many of poetry's most subtle effects are achieved by establishing an underlying rhythm and then varying it by means of a whole series of devices, some dramatic and expressive, others designed simply to lend variety and interest to the verse. A well-known sonnet of Shakespeare's (*116*) begins,

> Let me not to the marriage of true minds
> Admit impediments. Love is not love
> Which alters when it alteration finds,
> Or bends with the remover to remove.

It is possible to read the first line of this poem as mechanical iambic pentameter:

> Lĕt mé nŏt tó thĕ márriăge óf trŭe mińds

But of course nobody ever reads it that way, except to make a point; read with normal English accent and some sense of what it is saying, the line would form a pattern something like this:

> Lét mĕ nŏt tŏ thĕ márriăge ŏf trúe mińds

which is neither pentameter nor in any way iambic. The second line is a little more iambic, but, read expressively also falls short of pentameter:

> Ădmít ĭmpédĭmeńts. Lóve ĭs nŏt lóve

Only in the third and fourth lines of the sonnet do we get verses that read as five iambic feet.

The fact is that perfectly regular metrical verse is easy to write and dull to read. Among the devices in common use for varying too regular a pattern are the insertion of a trochaic foot among iambics, especially at the opening of a line, where the soft first syllable of the iambic foot often needs stiffening (see line 1 of the sonnet above); the more or less free addition of extra unaccented syllables; and the use of **caesura,** or strong grammatical pause within a line (conventionally indicated, in scanning, by the sign ‖). The second line of the sonnet above is a good example of caesura:

> Admit impediments. ‖ Love is not love

The strength of the caesura, and its placing in the line, may be varied to produce striking variations of effect. More broadly, the whole relation between the poem's sound and rhythm-patterns and its pattern as a sequence of assertions (phrases, clauses, sentences) may be manipulated by the poet. Sometimes the statements fit neatly within the lines, so that each line ends with a strong mark of punctuation; they are then known as **end-stopped lines.** Sometimes the sense flows over the ends of the lines, creating **run-on lines;** this process is also known, from the French, as **enjambment** (literally, "straddling").

End-stopped lines (Marlowe, *Hero and Leander*, lines 45–48):

> So lovely fair was Hero, Venus' nun,
> As Nature wept, thinking she was undone,
> Because she took more from her than she left
> And of such wondrous beauty her bereft.

Run-on lines (Keats, *Endymion* 1.89–93):

> Full in the middle of this pleasantness
> There stood a marble altar, with a tress
> Of flowers budded newly; and the dew
> Had taken fairy fantasies to strew
> Daisies upon the sacred sward, . . .

Following the example of such poets as Blake, Rimbaud, and Whitman, many twentieth-century poets have undertaken to write what is called **free** verse—that is, verse which has neither a fixed metrical foot nor (consequently) a fixed number of feet in its lines, but which depends for its rhythm on a pattern of cadences, or the rise and fall of the voice in utterance, or the pattern indicated to the reader's eye by the breaks between the verse lines. As in traditional versification, free verse is printed in short lines instead of with the continuity of prose; it differs from such versification, however, by the fact that its stressed syllables are not organized into a regular metric sequence.

SENSE AND SOUND

The words of which poetic lines—whether free or traditional—are composed cause them to have different sounds and produce different effects. Polysyllables, being pronounced fast, often cause a line to move swiftly; monosyllables, especially when heavy and requiring distinct accents, may cause it to move heavily, as in Milton's famous line (*Paradise Lost* 2.621):

> Rocks, caves, lakes, fens, bogs, dens, and shades of death

Poetic assertions are often dramatized and reinforced by means of **alliteration**—that is, the use of several nearby words or stressed syllables beginning with the same consonant. When Shakespeare writes (*Sonnet 64*),

> Ruin hath taught me thus to ruminate
> That Time will come and take my love away,

the alliterative *r*'s and rich internal echoes of the first line contrast with the sharp anxiety and directness of the alliterative *t*'s in the second. When Dryden starts *Absalom and Achitophel* with the couplet,

> In pious times, ere priestcraft did begin,
> Before polygamy was made a sin,

the satiric undercutting is strongly reinforced by the triple alliteration that links "*p*ious" with "*p*riestcraft" and "*p*olygamy."

Assonance, or repetition of the same or similar vowel sounds within a passage (usually in accented syllables), also serves to enrich it, as in two lines from Keats's *Ode on Melancholy*:

> For shade to shade will come too drowsily,
> And drown the wakeful anguish of the soul.

It is clear that the round, hollow tones of "drowsily," repeated in "drown" and darkening to the full *o*-sound of "soul," have much to do with the effect of the passage. A related device is **consonance,** or the repetition of a pattern of consonants with changes in the intervening vowels—for example: *linger, longer, languor; rider, reader, raider, ruder.*

The use of words that seem to reproduce the sounds they designate (known as **onomatopoeia**) has been much attempted, from Virgil's galloping horse—

Quadrupedante putrem sonitu quatit ungula campum—

through Tennyson's account, in *The Princess*, of

> The moan of doves in immemorial elms,
> And murmuring of innumerable bees—

to many poems in the present day.

RHYME AND STANZA

Rhyme consists of a repetition of accented sounds in words, usually those falling at the end of verse lines. If the rhyme sound is the very last syllable of the line (*rebound, sound*), the rhyme is called **masculine;** if the accented syllable is followed by an unaccented syllable (*hounding, bounding*), the rhyme is called **feminine.** Rhymes amounting to three or more syllables, like forced rhymes, generally have a comic effect in English, and have been freely used for this purpose, e.g., by Byron (*intellectual, henpecked-you-all*). Rhymes occurring within a single line are called **internal;** for instance, the Mother Goose rhyme "Mary, Mary, quite contrary," or from Coleridge's *Ancient Mariner* ("We were the first that ever burst / Into that silent sea"). **Eye rhymes** are words used as rhymes that look alike but actually sound different (for example, *alone, done; remove, love*); **off rhymes** (sometimes called **partial, imperfect,** or **slant rhymes**) are occasionally the result of pressing exigencies or lack of skill, but are also, at times, used deliberately by modern poets for special effects. For instance, a poem by Wilfred Owen (*Strange Meeting*) contains such paired words (which Owen called "pararhymes") as *years / yours* or *tigress / progress*.

    Blank verse is unrhymed iambic pentameter; until the recent advent of free verse, it was the only unrhymed measure to achieve general popularity in English. Though first used by the earl of Surrey in translating Virgil's *Aeneid*, blank verse was during the sixteenth century employed primarily in plays; *Paradise Lost* was one of the first nondramatic poems in English to use it. But Milton's authority and his success were so great that during the eighteenth and nineteenth centuries blank verse came to be used for a great variety of discursive, descriptive, and philosophical poems—besides remaining the standard metrical form for epics. Thomson's *Seasons*, Cowper's *Task*, Wordsworth's *Prelude*, and Tennyson's *Idylls of the King* were all written in blank verse.

    A **stanza** is a recurring unit of a poem, consisting of a number of verses. Certain poems (for example, Dryden's *Alexander's Feast*) have stanzas comprising a variable number of verses, of varying lengths. Others are more regular, and are identified by particular names.

    The simplest form of stanza is the **couplet;** it is two lines rhyming together. A single couplet considered in isolation is sometimes called a **distich;** when it expresses a complete thought, ending with a terminal mark of punctuation such as a semicolon or period, it is called a **closed couplet.** The development of very regular end-stopped couplets, their use in so-called heroic tragedies, and their consequent acquisition of the name **heroic couplets** took place for the most part during the mid-seventeenth century. The heroic couplet was the principal form in English neoclassical poems.

Another traditional and challenging form of couplet is the **tetrameter, or four-beat couplet.** All rhymed couplets are hard to manage without monotony; and since, in addition, a four-beat line is hard to divide by caesura without splitting it into two tick-tock dimeters, tetrameter couplets have posed a perpetual challenge to poets, and still provide an admirable finger-exercise for aspiring versifiers. An instance of tetrameter couplets managed with marvelous variety, complexity, and expressiveness is Marvell's *To His Coy Mistress*:

> Thou by the Indian Ganges' side
> Shouldst rubies find; I by the tide
> Of Humber would complain. I would
> Love you ten years before the Flood,
> And you should, if you please, refuse
> Till the conversion of the Jews.

English has not done much with rhymes grouped in threes, but has borrowed from Italian the form known as **terza rima,** in which Dante composed his *Divine Comedy*. This form consists of linked groups of three rhymes according to the following pattern: *aba bcb cdc ded*, etc. Shelley's *Ode to the West Wind* is composed in stanzas of *terza rima*, the poem as a whole ending with a couplet.

Quatrains are stanzas of four lines; the lines usually rhyme alternately, *abab*, or in the second and fourth lines, *abcb*. When they alternate tetrameter and trimeter lines, as in Johnson's little poem about men in hats (above), or as in *Sir Patrick Spens*, they are called **ballad stanza.** Dryden's *Annus Mirabilis* and Gray's *Elegy Written in a Country Churchyard* are in **heroic quatrains**; these rhyme alternately *abab*, and employ five-stress iambic verse throughout. Tennyson used for *In Memoriam* a tetrameter quatrain rhymed *abba*, and FitzGerald translated *The Rubáiyát of Omar Khayyám* into a pentameter quatrain rhymed *aaba*; but these forms have not been widely adopted.

Chaucer's *Troilus and Criseide* is the premier example in English of **rhyme royal,** a seven-line iambic pentameter stanza consisting essentially of a quatrain dovetailed onto two couplets, according to the rhyme scheme *ababbcc* (the fourth line serves both as the final line of the quatrain and as the first line of the first couplet). Closely akin to rhyme royal, but differentiated by an extra *a*-rhyme between the two *b*-rhymes, is **ottava rima,** that is, an eight-line stanza rhyming *abababcc*. As its name suggests, ottava rima is of Italian origin; it was first used in English by Wyatt. Its final couplet, being less prepared for than in rhyme royal, and usually set off as a separate verbal unit, is capable of manifesting a witty snap, for which Byron found good use in *Don Juan*.

The longest and most intricate stanza generally used for narrative purposes in English is that devised by Edmund Spenser for *The Faerie Queene*. The **Spenserian stanza** has nine lines rhyming *ababbcbcc*; the first eight lines are pentameter, the last line an Alexandrine. Slow-moving, intricate of pattern, and very demanding in its rhyme scheme (the *b*-sound recurs four times, the *c*-sound three), the Spenserian stanza has nonetheless appealed widely to poets who seek a rich and complicated metrical form. Keats's *Eve of St. Agnes* and Shelley's *Adonais* are brilliantly successful nineteenth-century examples of its use.

The **sonnet,** originally a stanza of Italian origin that has developed into an independent lyric form, is usually defined nowadays as fourteen lines of iambic pentameter. None of the elements in this definition is absolute and in earlier centuries there were sonnets in hexameters (the first of Sidney's *Astrophil and Stella*), and sonnets of as many as twenty lines (Milton's *On the New Forcers of Conscience*). Most, however, approximate the definition. Most Elizabethan sonnets dealt with love; and some poets, like Sidney, Spenser, and Shakespeare, imitated Petrarch in grouping together their sonnets dealing with a particular lady or situation. The term for these gatherings is **sonnet sequences;** the extent to which they tell a sequential story, and the extent to which such stories are autobiographical, vary greatly. Since Elizabethan times, the sonnet has been applied to a wide range of subject matters—religious, political, satiric, moral, and philosophic.

In blank verse or irregularly rhymed verse, where stanzaic divisions do not exist or are indistinct, the poetry sometimes falls into **verse paragraphs,** which are in effect divisions of sense like prose paragraphs. This division can be clearly seen in Milton's *Lycidas* and *Paradise Lost*. An intermediate form, clearly stanzaic but with stanzas of varying patterns of line-length and rhyme, is illustrated by Spenser's *Epithalamion*; in this instance, the division into stanzas is reinforced by a **refrain,** which is simply a line repeated at the end of each stanza. Ballads also customarily have refrains; for example, the refrain of *Lord Randall* is

> mother, make my bed soon,
> For I'm weary wi' hunting, and fain wald lie down.

FIGURATIVE LANGUAGE

The act of bringing words together into rich and vigorous poetic lines is complex and demanding, chiefly because so many variables require control. There is the "thought" of the lines, their verbal texture, their emotional resonance, the developing perspective of the reader—all these to be managed at once. One of the poet's chief resources toward this end is figurative language. Here, as in matters of meter, one may distinguish a great variety of devices, some of which we use in everyday speech without special awareness of their names and natures. When we say someone eats "like a horse" or "like a bird," we are using a **simile,** that is, a comparison marked out by a specific word of likening—"like" or "as." When we omit the word of comparison but imply a likeness—as in the sentence "That hog has guzzled all the champagne"—we are making use of **metaphor.** The **epic simile,** frequent in epic poetry, is an extended simile in which the thing compared is described as an object in its own right, beyond its point of likeness with the main subject. Milton starts to compare Satan to Leviathan, but concludes his simile with the story of a sailor who moored his ship by mistake, one night, to a whale (*Paradise Lost* 1.200–208). Metaphors and similes have been distinguished according to their special effects; they may be, for instance, violent, comic, degrading, decorative, or ennobling.

When we speak of "forty head of cattle" or ask someone to "lend a hand" with a job, we are using **synecdoche,** a figure that substitutes the part for the whole. When we speak of a statement coming "from the White House," or a man much interested in "the turf," (that is, the race-course), we are using **metonymy,** or the substitution of one term for another with which it is closely associated. **Antithesis** is a device for placing opposing ideas in grammatical parallel, as, for example, in the following passage from Alexander Pope's *Rape of the Lock* (5.25–30), where there are more examples of antithesis than there are lines:

> But since, alas! frail beauty must decay,
> Curled or uncurled, since locks will turn to gray;
> Since painted, or not painted, all shall fade,
> And she who scorns a man must die a maid;
> What then remains but well our power to use,
> And keep good humor still whate'er we lose?

Irony is a verbal device that implies an attitude quite different from (and often opposite to) that which is literally expressed. In Pope's *The Rape of the Lock* (4.131–32), after poor Sir Plume has stammered an incoherent request to return the stolen lock of hair, the Baron answers ironically:

> "It grieves me much," replied the Peer again,
> "Who speaks so well should ever speak in vain."

And when Donne "proves," in *The Canonization,* that he and his mistress are going to found a new religion of love, he seems to be inviting us to take a subtly ironic attitude toward religion as well as love.

Because it is easy to see through, **hyperbole,** or willful exaggeration, is a favorite device of irony—which is not to say that it may not be "serious" as well. When she hears that a young man is "dying for love" of her, a sensible young woman does not accept this statement literally, but it may convey a serious meaning to her nonetheless. The **pun,** or play on words (known to the learned, sometimes, as **paronomasia**), may also be serious or comic in intent; witness, for example, the famous series of puns on Donne's name in his *Hymn to God the Father.* **Oxymoron** is a conjunction of two terms that in ordinary use are contraries or incompatible—for instance, Milton's famous description of hell as containing "darkness visible" (*Paradise Lost* 1.63). A **paradox** is a statement that seems absurd but turns out to have rational meaning after all, usually in some unexpected sense; Donne speaks of fear being great courage and high valor (*Satire* 3, line 16), and turns out to mean that fear of God is greater courage than any earthly bravery. A **conceit** is a far-fetched and unusually elaborate comparison. Writing in the fourteenth century, the Italian poet Petrarch popularized a great number of conceits handy for use in love poetry, and readily adapted by his English imitators. Wyatt, for example, is using **Petrarchan conceits** when he compares love to a warrior, or the lover's state to that of a storm-tossed ship; and a hundred other sonneteers developed the themes of the lady's stony heart, incendiary glances, and so forth. On the other hand, the **metaphysical conceit** was a more intellectualized, many-leveled comparison, giving a strong sense of the poet's ingenuity in overcoming obstacles—for instance, Donne's comparison of separated lovers to the legs of a compass (A *Valediction: Forbidding Mourning*) or Herbert's comparison of devotion to a pulley, in the poem of that name.

Personification (or in the term derived from Latin **prosopopoeia**) is the attribution of human qualities to an inanimate object (for example, the Sea) or an abstract concept (Freedom); a special variety of it is called (in a term of John Ruskin's invention) the **pathetic fallacy.** When we speak of leaves "dancing" or a lake "smiling," we attribute human traits to nonhuman objects. Ruskin thought this was false and therefore "morbid"; modern criticism tends to view the practice as artistically and morally neutral. A more formal and abstract variety of personification is **allegory,** in which a narrative (such as *Pilgrim's Progress*) is constructed by representing general concepts (Faithfulness, Sin, Despair) as persons who act out the plot. A **fable** (like Chaucer's *The Nun's Priest's Tale*) represents beasts behaving like humans; a **parable** is a brief story, or simply an observation, with strong moral application; and an **exemplum** is a story told to illustrate a point in a sermon.

A special series of devices, nearly obsolete today, used to be available to poets who could count on readers trained in the classics. These were the devices of **classical allusion**—that is, reference to the mythology (stories about the actions of gods and other supernatural beings) of the Greeks and Romans. In their simplest form, the classic **myths** used to provide a repertoire of agreeable stage properties, and a convenient shorthand for expressing emotional attitudes. Picturesque creatures like centaurs, satyrs, and sphinxes, heroes and heroines like Hector and Helen, and the whole pantheon of Olympic deities could be used to make ready reference to a great many aspects of human nature. One does not have to explain the problems of a man who is "cleaning the Augean stables"; if he is afflicted with an "Achilles' heel," or is assailing "Hydra-headed difficulties," his state is clear. These descriptive phrases, making **allusion** to mythological stories, suggest in a phrase situations that would normally require cumbersome explanations. But because it used to be taken for granted that the classical mythology was the common possession of all educated readers, the classic myths entered into English literature as early as Chaucer. In poets like Spenser and Milton, classical allusion becomes a kind of enormously learned game, in which the poet seeks to make his points as indirectly as possible. For instance, Spenser writes in the *Epithalamion*, lines 328–29:

> Lyke as when Jove with fayre Alcmena lay,
> When he begot the great Tirynthian groome.

The mere mention of Alcmena in the first line suggests, to the informed reader, Hercules, the son of Jupiter (Jove) by Alcmena. Spenser's problem in the second line is to find a way of referring to him that is neither redundant nor heavy-handed. "Tirynthian" reminds the reader of Hercules' long connection with the city of Tiryns, stretching our minds (as it were) across his whole career; and "groome" compresses references to a man-child, a servant, and a bridegroom, all of which apply to different aspects of Hercules' history. Thus, far from simply avoiding redundancy, Spenser has enriched, for the reader who possesses the classical information, the whole texture of his verse, thought, and feeling.

SCHOOLS

Literary scholars and critics often group together in **schools** writers who share stylistic traits or thematic concerns. Whether they considered themselves a group doesn't much matter; although in some cases—for example, the Imagists or the Beat poets—the writers themselves have identified themselves as belonging to a group. None of the **Romantic poets** knew they were being romantic, although Hazlitt, Shelley, and other writers of the time recognized shared features that they called "the spirit of the age." The followers of Spenser are known as **Spenserians;** they knew they admired and to some extent wrote like Spenser, but didn't realize that made them a group. **Cavalier** poets are set decisively apart from **Metaphysical** poets, though pretty surely none of the two-dozen-odd men involved knew that was what they were. And so with the **Gothic novelists,** and the so-called **Graveyard School** of the eighteenth century; these schools are generally grouped, defined, and named by scholars and critics after the event.

Intellectual affinities have led some writers to be classified under the names of the philosophical schools of Greece and Rome. These are chiefly the **Epicureans,** who specify that the aim of life and the source of value is pleasure; the **Stoics,** who emphasize stern virtue and the dignified endurance of what cannot be avoided; and the **Skeptics,** who doubt that anything can be known for certain. These categories are useful as capsule descriptions, but they aren't very tidy, as they are omissive, overlap one another, and cut across other categories. Dryden is an author strongly tinged with skepticism, but many of his poems suggest an unabashed epicureanism. *The Vanity of Human Wishes*, by Samuel Johnson, is the classic poem in English of stoic philosophy, but it also expresses a particularly strong coloring of Christian humanism.

TERMS OF LITERARY ART

The following section defines frequently used literary terms, especially frequently used terms that are closely related or tend to be mistaken for each other.

Allegory, Symbol, Emblem, Type. Allegory is a narrative in which the agents, and sometimes also the setting, are personified concepts or character-types, and the plot represents a doctrine or thesis. John Bunyan's *Pilgrim's Progress*, for example, allegorizes the Christian doctrine of salvation by narrating how the character named Christian, warned by Evangelist, flees the City of Destruction and makes his laborious way to the Celestial City; en route he meets such characters as Faithful and the Giant Despair, and passes through places like the Slough of Despond and Vanity Fair. A literary **symbol** is the representation of an object or event which has a further range of reference beyond itself. Examples of sustainedly symbolic poems are William Blake's *The Sick Rose* and William Butler Yeats's *Sailing to Byzantium*. In the sixteenth and seventeenth centuries, an **emblem** was an enigmatic picture of a physical object, to which was attached a motto and a verse explaining its significance. In present-day usage, an emblem is any object which is widely understood to signify an abstract concept; thus a dove is an emblem of peace, and a cross, of Christianity. In what was once a widespread Christian mode of biblical interpretation, a **type** was a person or event in the Old Testament which was regarded as historically real, but also as "prefiguring" a person or event in the New Testament. Thus Adam was often said to be a type of Christ, and the act of Moses in liberating the children of Israel was said to prefigure Christ in freeing men from Satan.

Baroque and **Mannerist** are terms imported into literary study from the history of art, and applied by analogy. Michelangelo is a **baroque** artist; he holds great masses in powerful dynamic tension, his style is heavily ornamented and restless. In these respects he is sometimes compared to Milton. El Greco is a **mannerist,** whose gaunt and distorted figures often seem to be laboring under great spiritual stress, whose light seems to be focused in spots against a dark background. He has been compared to Donne. Analogies of this sort are occasionally suggestive, but can readily deteriorate into parallels that are forced and nominal rather than substantial.

Bathos. See **Pathos,** the **Sublime,** and **Bathos.**

Burlesque and **Mock Heroic** differ in that the former makes its subject ludicrous by directly cutting it down, the latter by inflating it. In Pope's mock-heroic *Dunciad*, the figure of Dulness (Colley Cibber) is given inappropriately heroic dimensions; in Butler's burlesque *Hudibras*, the knightly hero is characterized by low and vulgar attributes, and persistently engages in inappropriately low behavior. Burlesque contributed to the development of the English novel; and during the nineteenth century, when formal drama tended to be stagy and melodramatic, a vigorous burlesque stage flourished in England, making fun of the classics. See **Imitation** and **Parody.**

Catastrophe and **Catharsis.** The **catastrophe** is the conclusion of a play; the word means "down-turning," and is usually applied only to tragedies, in which a frequent kind of catastrophe is the death of the protagonist. (A term for the precipitating final scene that applies both to tragedy and to comedy is **denouement,** which in French means "unknotting.") **Catharsis** in Greek signifies "purgation" or "purification." In Aristotle's *Poetics*, the special effect of tragedy is the "catharsis" of the "emotions of pity and fear" that have been aroused in the audience by the events of the drama.

Chiasmus and **Zeugma.** **Chiasmus** is an inversion of the word order in two parallel phrases, as in John Denham's *Cooper's Hill*: "Strong without rage, without o'erflowing full." **Zeugma** is the use of a single verb or adjective to control two nouns, as in Pope's *The Rape of the Lock*: "Or stain her honor, or her new brocade."

Classic and **Neoclassic.** See **Gothic, Classic, Neoclassic.**

Convention and **Tradition.** **Conventions** are agreed-upon artistic procedures peculiar to an art form. None of Shakespeare's contemporaries spoke blank verse in everyday life, but characters in his plays do, and the audience accepts it—as the audience at an opera accepts that characters will sing arias to express their feelings. A **tradition** consists of beliefs, attitudes, and ways of representing things that is widely shared by writers over a span of time; it generally includes a number of conventions.

Didactic poetry is designed to teach a branch of knowledge, or to embody in fictional form a moral, religious, or philosophical doctrine. The term is not derogatory. John Milton's *Paradise Lost*, for example, can be called didactic, insofar as it is organized, as Milton claimed in his invocation, to "assert Eternal Providence / And justify the ways of God to men." In the eighteenth century, a number of poets wrote didactic poems called **georgics** (modeled on the Roman Virgil's *Georgics* on rural life and farming), which described such applied arts as making cider or running a sugar plantation.

Dramatic irony and **Dramatic monologue** are quite different literary modes. In **dramatic irony** a stage character says something that has one meaning for him, but quite another for the audience who possesses relevant knowledge that the speaker lacks. The **dramatic monologue** is a form that was perfected by Robert Browning in such poems as *My Last Duchess* and *The Bishop Orders His Tomb*. In it, the poetic speaker unintentionally reveals to the reader his character and temperament by what he says, usually to another person whose presence we infer from the utterance of the speaker.

Eclogue. See **Pastorals.**

Emblem. See **Allegory, Symbol, Emblem, Type.**

Epigram, Epigraph, Epitaph. An **epigram** is a short, witty statement in verse or prose. One of Oscar Wilde's characters remarks, "I can resist everything, except temptation." An **epigraph** is an apposite quotation placed at the beginning of a book or a section of it. An **epitaph** is a brief statement about someone who has died; usually, it is intended to be inscribed on a tombstone.

Eulogy and **Elegy.** The **eulogy** is a work of praise, in prose or poetry, for a person either very distinguished or recently dead. In its usual modern sense, an **elegy** is a formal, and usually long, poetic lament for someone who has died. In an extended sense, the term is also used to designate poems on the transience of earthly things (such as the Old English *The Seafarer*) or poetic meditations on mortality (such as Thomas Gray's *Elegy Written in a Country Churchyard*).

Euphemism and **Euphuism. Euphemism,** or "fine speech," is a verbal device for avoiding an unpleasant concept or expression, as when, instead of saying a person "died," we say he "passed away." Euphues was the hero of a prose romance (published 1579–80) by John Lyly; his adventures are recounted in a mannered style full of puns, alliteration, and antithetical "points." Under the name of **Euphuism** this courtly style enjoyed a brief vogue in the Elizabethan era.

Fancy and **Imagination.** The distinction between these two mental powers was central to the literary theory of S. T. Coleridge. **Fancy** (a word directly derived by contraction from "fantasy") was defined by Coleridge as the power of combining several known properties into new combinations; **imagination,** on the other hand, was the faculty of using such properties to create an integral whole that is entirely new.

Folios, Quartos, etc., are terms used to specify the size of book pages. To make a **folio,** a sheet of paper (14" × 20" or larger) is folded just once (producing thereby four pages); **quartos** are folded twice (producing eight pages). Shakespeare's plays were first printed in quartos (often in several different editions), but when they were collected together, in 1623, they appeared as the First Folio edition.

Genre, Decorum. A **genre** is an established literary form or type, such as stage comedy, the picaresque novel, the epic, the sonnet. Works belonging to a certain genre tend to represent certain characters and events, and to seek a similar effect. **Decorum,** in literary criticism—where it was a central concept from the Renaissance through the eighteenth century—designates the requirement that there should be a propriety, or fitness, in the way that the character, actions, and style are matched to each other in a particular genre. Low characters, actions, and style, for example, were thought appropriate for satire, while epic demanded characters of high estate, engaged in great actions, and speaking in an appropriately high style.

Gothic, Classic, Neoclassic. These terms are used to distinguish prominent tendencies in literature and the other arts. The term **Gothic** originally referred to the Goths, an early Germanic tribe, then came to signify "medieval." In the eighteenth century "Gothic" connoted primitive and irregular work, possessing the qualities of the relatively barbaric North. **Gothic novels** were a very popular type of prose fiction, inaugurated by Horace Walpole's *Castle of Otranto* (1764), usually set in a medieval castle, which aimed to evoke chilling terror from their readers. **Classic** implies lucid, rational, and orderly works, such as are usually attributed to the writers and thinkers in the classic era of the Greeks and Romans. **Neoclassic**—a term often applied to the period in England from 1660 through most of the eighteenth century—implies an ideal of life, art, and thought deliberately modeled on Greek and Roman examples.

Heroic poems, Heroic drama, Heroic couplets. Because they concentrate on the figure of a typical hero (Achilles, Aeneas), epic poems were frequently called "**heroic.**" Trying to transfer epic grandeur to the stage, playwrights of the Restoration period wrote what was called **heroic drama,** but usually achieved only grandiosity. The stately iambic pentameter couplets in which they made their characters speak became known as **heroic couplets.**

Humor. See **Wit** and **Humor.**

Humors and **Temperaments** are psychological terms used by Renaissance writers. It was believed that every person's constitution contained four basic humors: the **choleric** (bile), the **sanguine** (blood), the **phlegmatic** (phlegm), and the **melancholy** (black bile). The **temperament,** or mixture, of these four humors was held to determine both a person's physical condition and a person's type of character. When a particular humor predominated, it pushed the character in that direction: choler = anger; sanguine = geniality; phlegm = cold torpor; and melancholy = gloomy self-absorption.

Imagination. See **Fancy** and **Imagination.**

Imitation and **Parody** are forms in which a literary work refers back to a predecessor. In the eighteenth century, an "imitation" was a poem that deliberately echoed an older work, but adapted it to subject matter in the writer's own era, usually with a satirical aim directed against that subject matter; Alexander Pope, for example, wrote a number of satires on contemporary life that he entitled *Imitations of Horace*. A **parody** imitates the characteristic style and other features of a particular literary work—or else of a particular literary type—but in such a way as to satirize that work, by making it either amusing or ridiculous. *Northanger Abbey* (1818) by Jane Austen was a good-humored parody of the popular horror-narratives known as gothic novels. (See **Burlesque** and **Gothic**.)

Irony, Sarcasm. Irony and **sarcasm** are both ways of saying one thing but implying something sharply different, often opposite; they differ, however, in the way they go about doing so. **Sarcasm** is a broad and taunting form of using apparent praise in order in fact to denigrate. The patriarch Job is bitterly sarcastic when he replies to his would-be comforters (12.2), "No doubt but ye are the people, and wisdom shall die with you." On the other hand, Jane Austen, in the first sentence of *Pride and Prejudice*, overstates the case just enough to make it drily **ironic** when she writes, "It is a truth universally acknowledged, that a single man in possession of a good fortune, must be in want of a wife." (See **Irony**, in the section "Figurative Language," above.)

Legend. See **Myth** and **Legend**.

Logic. See **Rhetoric** and **Logic**.

Masque. The **Masque**, which flourished during the reigns of Elizabeth I, James I, and Charles I, was an elaborate court entertainment that combined poetic drama, music, song, dance, and splendid costumes and settings. For a discussion of the English masque, see the introduction to Jonson's *Pleasure Reconciled to Virtue*.

Myth and **Legend**. **Myths** are hereditary narratives that purport to account, in supernatural terms, for why the world is as it is, and why people act as they do; they also often provide the rules by which people conduct their lives. Myths often spring up to explain rituals, the original meanings of which have been forgotten. A system of related myths is called a **mythology**—a body of supernatural narratives believed to be true by a particular cultural group. The term "myth" is frequently extended to a set of supernatural narratives that are developed by individual poets such as William Blake and W. B. Yeats. Three great mythologies that have been exploited by poets long after they ceased to be believed are the classical (Greek and Roman), the Celtic, and the Germanic. A **legend** is an old and popularly repeated story, of which the protagonist is not supernatural, but a human being. If a hereditary story concerns supernatural beings who are not gods, and the story is not part of a systematic mythology, it is usually classified as a **folktale**.

Naturalism. See **Realism** and **Naturalism**.

Neo-Classic. See **Gothic, Classic, Neoclassic**.

Novel. See **Romance, Novel**.

Ode. A long lyric poem serious in subject and treatment, written in an elevated style and, usually, in an elaborate stanza. See the discussion of English odes in the headnote to Jonson's *Ode on Cary and Morison*.

Pastoral, Eclogue, and **Pastoral Elegy**. Pastorals (from the Latin word for "shepherd") are deliberately conventional poems that project a cultivated poet's nostalgic image of the peace and simplicity of the life of shepherds and other rural folk in an idealized natural setting. The form was established by the Greek poet Theocritus in the third century B.C.E.; it is sometimes also called an **eclogue,** which was the title that the Roman poet Virgil gave to his collection of pastorals. The pastorals by Theocritus and later classical poets often included a poem in which a shepherd mourns the death of a fellow shepherd; from these poems developed the highly conventional **pastoral elegy,** a type that includes such great laments as Milton's *Lycidas* and Shelley's *Adonais. Lycidas* is also an example of the extension of the classical pastoral to a Christian range of reference, by way of the use of the term "pastor" (shepherd) for a parish priest or minister and the frequent representation of Christ as "the Good Shepherd."

Pathos, the **Sublime,** and **Bathos.** In Greek, **pathos** signified deep feeling, especially suffering; in modern criticism, it is used in a more limited way to signify a scene or passage designed to evoke the feelings of pity or sympathetic sorrow from an audience. An example is the passage in which King Lear is briefly reunited with his daughter Cordelia, beginning

> Pray, do not mock me.
> I am a very foolish fond old man . . .

In the first century the Greek rhetorician Longinus wrote a treatise *On the Sublime,* in which he proposed that sublimity ("loftiness") is the greatest of stylistic qualities in literature; the effect of the sublime on the reader is *elestasis* ("transport"). In 1757 Edmund Burke published a highly influential treatise on *The Sublime and Beautiful,* in which he distinguished the sublime from the beautiful, not as a stylistic quality, but as the representation of objects that are vast, obscure, and powerful, which evoke from the reader a "delightful horror" that combines pleasure and terror. **Bathos** (Greek for "depth") was used by Pope, in a parodic parallel to Longinus' "sublime," to signify an unintentional descent in literature, when an author, straining to be passionate or elevated, overshoots the mark and falls into the trivial or the ridiculous.

Poetic diction, Poetic license, Poetic justice. Poetic diction denotes a distinctive language used by a poet which is not current in the discourse of the age; an example is the deliberately archaic language of Spenser's *The Faerie Queene.* In modern critical discussion, the term is applied especially to the style of eighteenth-century poets who, according to the reigning principle of decorum (see **Decorum**), believed that a poet must adapt the level of his diction to the dignity of the high genres of epic, tragedy, and ode. The results were such phrases as "the finny tribe" for "fish" and "the bleating kind" for "sheep." **Poetic license** designates the freedom of a poet or other literary writer to depart, for special effects, from the norms of common discourse and of literal or historical truth. Examples: the use of archaic words, meter, and rhyme, and the use of other literary conventions. (See **Convention.**) **Poetic justice** was coined by Thomas Rymer, in the later seventeenth century, to denote his claim that a narrative or drama should, at the end, distribute rewards and punishments in proportion to the virtues and vices of each character. No important critic since Rymer has adopted this doctrine, except in a highly qualified way.

Quarto. See **Folios, Quartos.**

Realism and **Naturalism** are both terms applied to prose fictions that aim at a faithful representation of actual existence; they differ, however, in the aspects of that existence that they represent and in the manner in which they represent them. The realistic novel attempts to give the effect of representing ordinary life as it commonly occurs. Realistic novelists such as George Eliot in England and William Dean Howells in America present everyday characters experiencing ordinary events, rendered in great detail. **Naturalism,** which the French novelist Émile Zola developed in the 1870s and later, is based on the philosophy that a human being is merely a higher-order animal, whose character and behavior are determined by heredity and environment. Zola, followed by such later naturalistic novelists as the Americans Frank Norris and Theodore Dreiser, typically represents characters who inherit such compulsive instincts as greed and the sexual drive and are shaped by the social and economic forces of family, class, and the milieu into which they are born. Naturalistic novelists also often display an almost medical candor in describing human activities and bodily functions largely unmentioned in earlier fiction.

Rhetoric and **Logic. Rhetoric** was developed by Greek and Roman theorists as the art of using all available means of persuading an audience, either by speech or in writing; it had a great influence on literary criticism in the Renaissance and through the eighteenth century. Rhetorical theorists developed a detailed analysis of figures of speech, largely as effective means to the overall aim of persuasion. In the present century, however, the analysis of such figures has been excerpted from this rhetorical context and made an independent and central concern of language theorists and literary critics. See **Figurative language. Logic** is the study of the principles of reasoning. Logic may be used to persuade an audience, but it does not, like rhetoric, avail itself of all means of persuasion, emotional as well as rational; instead, logic limits itself to a concern with the formal procedures of reasoning from sound premises to valid conclusions.

Romance and **Novel.** Medieval **romances** were verse narratives of adventure, usually about a knightly hero on a quest to gain a lady's favor, who encounters both natural tribulations and supernatural marvels. The term "romance" has since come to be opposed to realism (see **Realism** and **Naturalism**) and is applied to prose fictions that represent characters and events which are more picturesque, fantastic, adventurous, or heroic than one encounters in ordinary life. The **novel,** as distinguished from the prose romance, undertakes to be a more realistic representation of common life and social relationships and tends to avoid the fantastic, the fabulous, and the realm of high derring-do. (See **Realism.**)

Sarcasm. See **Irony, Sarcasm.**

Satire designates literary forms which diminish or derogate a subject by making it ridiculous and by evoking toward it amusement, or scorn, or indignation. In **formal satire,** such as Alexander Pope's *Moral Essays,* the satire is accomplished in a direct, first-person address, either to the audience or to a listener within the work. **Indirect satire** is not a direct address, but is cast in the form of a fictional narrative, as in Swift's *Gulliver's Travels* or Byron's *Don Juan.* For a discussion of the backgrounds of English satire, see the introduction to Donne's *Satire 3.*

Sublime. See **Pathos, the Sublime,** and **Bathos.**

Symbol. See **Allegory, Symbol, Emblem, Type.**

Tradition. See **Convention** and **Tradition.**

Type. See **Allegory, Symbol, Emblem, Type.**

Wit and **Humor,** in their present use, designate elements in a literary work which are designed to amuse or to excite mirth in the reader or audience. **Wit,** through the seventeenth century, had a broad range of meanings, including general intelligence, mental acuity, and ingenuity in literary invention, especially in a brilliant and paradoxical style. From this last application there derived the most common present use of "wit" to denote a kind of verbal expression that is brief, deft, and contrived to produce a shock of comic surprise; a characteristic form of wit, in this sense, is the epigram. (See **Epigram.**) **Humor** goes back to the ancient theory of the four humors and the application of the term "humorous" to a comically eccentric character who has an imbalance of the humors in his or her temperament. (See **Humors** and **Temperament.**) As we now use the word, **humor** is ascribed both to a comic utterance and to the comic appearance or behavior of a literary character. A humorous utterance, unlike a witty utterance, need not be intended to be comic by the speaker, and is not cast in the neat epigrammatic form of a witty saying. In Shakespeare's *Twelfth Night,* for example, Malvolio's utterances, as well as his appearance and behavior, are all found humorous by the audience, but his utterances are never witty and are humorous despite his own very solemn intentions.

Zeugma. See **Chiasmus** and **Zeugma.**

PERMISSIONS ACKNOWLEDGMENTS

William Blake: Poems from THE COMPLETE POETRY AND PROSE OF WILLIAM BLAKE, edited by David V. Erdman, copyright © 1965, 1981, Doubleday & Company. Blake engravings: reproduced from the Lessing J. Rosenwald Collection, Library of Congress.

Lord Byron: Selections as indicated from LORD BYRON: THE COMPLETE POETICAL WORKS edited by Jerome J. McGann (Vol I. 1980). Reprinted by permission of Oxford University Press. Letters are reprinted by permission of the publisher from BYRON'S LETTERS AND JOURNALS, Volumes I–VII, edited by Leslie A. Marchand, Cambridge, Mass.: The Belknap Press of Harvard University Press: Copyright © Editorial 1973, 1975, 1976, 1977 by Leslie A. Marchand.

Robert Burns: Selections from THE POEMS AND SONGS OF ROBERT BURNS, edited by James Kinsley (1968). Reprinted by permission of Oxford University Press.

John Clare: *Mouse's Nest* and *Pastoral Poetry* from THE POEMS OF JOHN CLARE, edited by J. W. Tibble (J. M. Dent). Reprinted by permission of Orion Publishing Group Ltd. *The Nightingale's Nest* from SELECTED POEMS AND PROSE OF JOHN CLARE edited by Eric Robinson and Geoffrey Summerfield. Reproduced with permission of Curtis Brown Ltd, London, on behalf of Eric Robinson. Copyright Eric Robinson 1984, 1967. All other poems from THE LATER POEMS OF JOHN CLARE 1837–1864 edited by Eric Robinson and David Powell. Reproduced with permission of Curtis Brown Ltd, London, on behalf of Eric Robinson. Copyright Eric Robinson 1984, 1967.

Samuel Taylor Coleridge: Excerpt from COLERIDGE'S SHAKESPEAREAN CRITICISM, edited by Thomas M. Raysor. Copyright © 1930 by the President and Fellows of Harvard College, 1958 by Thomas M. Raysor. Selections reprinted by permission of the editor.

John Keats: From THE POEMS OF JOHN KEATS, edited by Jack Stillinger, Cambridge, Mass.: The Belknap Press of Harvard University Press, copyright © 1978 by the President and Fellows of Harvard College. From THE LETTERS OF JOHN KEATS, edited by Hyder Edward Rollins. Copyright © 1958 by The President and Fellows of Harvard College. Both reprinted by permission of Harvard University Press.

D. H. Lawrence: *The Piano*, transcribed from the manuscript by permission of Laurence Pollinger Ltd. and The Estate of Mrs. Frieda Lawrence Ravagli.

Mary Wollstonecraft Shelley: Complete text of FRANKENSTEIN from FRANKENSTEIN: A NORTON CRITICAL EDITION, edited by J. Paul Hunter. Copyright © 1996 by W. W. Norton & Company, Inc. Reprinted by permission of W. W. Norton & Company, Inc.

Percy Bysshe Shelley: Poems from SHELLEY'S POETRY AND PROSE: A NORTON CRITICAL EDITION, edited by Donald Reiman & Sharon Powers. Copyright © 1977 by Donald H. Reiman and Sharon B. Powers. Reprinted by permission of W. W. Norton & Company, Inc.

Mary Wollstonecraft: Reprinted from LETTERS WRITTEN DURING A SHORT RESIDENCE IN SWEDEN, NORWAY, AND DENMARK by Mary Wollstonecraft, edited by Carol H. Poston, by permission of the University of Nebraska Press. Copyright © 1976 by the University of Nebraska Press. From A VINDICATION OF THE RIGHTS OF WOMAN: A NORTON CRITICAL EDITION, Second Edition, by Mary Wollstonecraft, edited by Carol H. Poston. Copyright © 1988, 1975 by W. W. Norton & Company, Inc. Reprinted by permission of W. W. Norton & Company, Inc.

Dorothy Wordsworth: Selections as indicated from THE GRASMERE JOURNALS, edited by Pamela Woof (1991). Reprinted by permission of Oxford University Press. *Grasmere—A Fragment* and *Thoughts on My Sick Bed* from DOROTHY WORDSWORTH AND ROMANTICISM. Reprinted by permission of The Wordsworth Trust, Dove Cottage, Grasmere.

William Wordsworth: Reprinted from William Wordsworth: THE RUINED COTTAGE AND THE PEDLAR. Edited by James A. Butler. Copyright © 1978 by Cornell University. Reprinted from William Wordsworth: THE FOURTEEN-BOOK PRELUDE. Edited by W. J. B. Owen. Copyright © 1985 by Cornell University. Both used by permission of the publisher, Cornell University Press.

W. B. Yeats: *The Sorrow of Love* (transcription of first printed version) from BETWEEN THE LINES: YEATS' S POETRY IN THE MAKING by Jon Stallworthy (1963). Reprinted by permission of Oxford University Press.

Every effort has been made to contact the copyright holders of each of the selections. Rights holders of any selections not credited should contact W. W. Norton & Company, Inc., 500 Fifth Avenue, New York, NY 10110 for a correction to be made in the next reprinting of our work.

Index